W9-ABY-683

THE WAR OF THE REVOLUTION

·The M Co·

THE MACMILLAN COMPANY
NEW YORK · CHICAGO
DALLAS · ATLANTA · SAN FRANCISCO
LONDON · MANILA

THE MACMILLAN COMPANY
OF CANADA, LIMITED
TORONTO

THE WAR OF
THE REVOLUTION

By *CHRISTOPHER WARD*

Edited by *JOHN RICHARD ALDEN*

IN TWO VOLUMES

VOLUME ONE

THE MACMILLAN COMPANY : NEW YORK

1952

PRINTED IN THE UNITED STATES OF AMERICA

BY THE HADDON CRAFTSMEN, SCRANTON, PA.

The maps on pages 217, 299, 345, 367, 583, 601, 607, 727, 759, 789, 805, 819, and 829 also appear in *The Delaware Continentals, 1776–1783*, by Christopher L. Ward, copyright, 1941, by the Historical Society of Delaware.

Editor's Preface

The origins of *The War of the Revolution* are to be found in part in the late Mr. Ward's studies of the history of the Delaware Line. His volume on *The Delaware Continentals, 1776–1783*, published in 1941, contains much more than the story of one of the best units in the Continental army. Approximately one half of Mr. Ward's last work is to be found in his earlier monograph, which was put forth in a limited edition and which deserved a much wider circulation. This material, which deals with land operations in the middle and southern states after 1776, was revised by the author. To it Mr. Ward added about forty new chapters on the campaign of 1775; operations in New England, northern New York, and Canada; border conflicts; and the Yorktown campaign.

The author intended to write a history of the campaigns on land rather than a complete history of the war. He largely accomplished his purpose, although his manuscript, as submitted to the editor, contained no account of the war beyond the Alleghenies. The editor has supplied a brief description of that portion of the conflict in one chapter, emphasizing the role of George Rogers Clark.

A few words about the labors of the editor. *The War of the Revolution,* with the exception of the chapter mentioned in the preceding paragraph, has been little altered by the editor. Additions to the citations and bibliography have been inserted in order to present a few of the more important scholarly contributions concerning the War of Independence not available to the author. Some obvious errors in the text which Mr. Ward would surely have removed had they been brought to his attention have been corrected.

In so large a work, other mistakes undoubtedly remain, despite the efforts of both author and editor. The editor has also tried to perform the last minute tasks of completing citations and bibliographical entries, and similar duties. *The War of the Revolution* remains, however, the work of Mr. Ward in point of view, interpretation, emphasis, and all fundamental matters.

Relying largely upon more or less standard secondary authorities and printed source material, the author has written a detailed and accurate account of the military operations on land of the War of Independence. He has contributed a most useful work of reference. He has also added to the great store of splendid writing upon the Revolutionary period. His account of the day of Lexington and Concord thrilled even an editor who was not unfamiliar with the events of April 19, 1775.

It is not possible for the editor to express the gratitude of the author to all the persons who assisted him. Mr. Kenneth Roberts and Mr. Carl Van Doren gave him helpful advice. The editor must declare his appreciation of services performed by three assistant instructors attached to the Department of History of the University of Nebraska, Miss Lois Christensen, Mr. Carl Bader, Jr., and Mr. Philip Holmgren. Dr. John Powell, Professor G. W. Gray, and Mr. Rodman Ward gave him advice, encouragement, and help in various ways.

JOHN RICHARD ALDEN

Preface

This book is not a history of the American Revolution. It is a history of the war that was caused by the Revolution. As John Adams well said: "A history of the first war of the United States is a very different thing from a history of the American Revolution. . . . The revolution was in the minds of the people and in the union of the colonies, both of which were accomplished before hostilities commenced. This revolution and union were gradually forming from the years 1760 to 1776."

With the Revolution as thus properly described, this book is not concerned, except in the brief résumé of the causes of the war in the first chapter. Its aim is to tell the story of the war on land, the campaigns, battles, sieges, marches, encampments, bivouacs, the strategy and tactics, the hardships, and the endurance of hardship. It is purely military in its intention and scope.

The war, from the first shot at Lexington in 1775 to the cessation of hostilities in 1782, lasted nearly eight years. It was fought in a territory extending from Quebec southward to Georgia and from the Atlantic seaboard westward to the frontier settlements. Many of its campaigns, in the various regions in which they were fought, were simultaneous.

In the spring of 1776, while the American army under Arnold was still struggling to keep a foothold in Canada, a British army under Henry Clinton was on its way south to attack Charleston in South Carolina. On September 11, 1777, while Washington was fighting the Battle of the Brandywine, Burgoyne was on his way down the Hudson to Saratoga.

It will be seen, then, that an attempt to tell the tale of the various campaigns and battles in strict chronological order would involve leaping, chapter by chapter, from one campaign to another, from the North to the South and from the East to the West, and would result in hopeless confusion. Fortunately for the sake of clarity in this chronicle, the whole territory involved was fought over, by different armies, in well defined sections, in the North from Canada down to the Mason and Dixon line, in the South from Virginia down to Georgia, with practically no overlapping. It has therefore been thought best to treat the campaigns separately in the two sections, thus enabling the reader to follow the movements of the armies and the progress of the various campaigns with a minimum of confusion.

While making no pretensions to the role of a military expert, the author has ventured to express opinions as to the strategy and tactics employed in some of the operations herein recorded. In doing so, he relies upon the dictum of Baron Jomini in that eminently authoritative military treatise, *Précis de l'art de la guerre*, "The theory of the great speculative combinations of war is simple enough in itself; it only requires intelligence and attentive reflection," and upon von Moltke's statement that "strategy is the application of common sense to the conduct of war."

CHRISTOPHER WARD

Contents

VOLUME ONE

The War in the North

VOLUME TWO

The War in the South

Maps

VOLUME ONE

VOLUME TWO

The War in the North

CHAPTER 1

The Causes of the War

Tuesday, the 17th of May, 1774, was an unpleasant day in Boston. A pelting rain, driven by a strong east wind, poured upon the town. Gutters ran full; hollows in the cobbled streets became puddles. The few of its citizens who owned umbrellas found some shelter under those newfangled, cumbrous contrivances of oiled silk or linen spread on clumsy ribs of whalebone.[1] The thousands of others who were abroad that day could only turn the brims of their hats down, the collars of their coats up, wrap their cloaks around them, and take the storm as it came, with a philosophical endurance born of habit.

But the provincial troop of horse, the Ancient and Honourable Artillery Company, the Boston Grenadier Corps, fine, tall fellows in notably handsome uniforms, and more companies of militia, drawn up in line along King Street, could not even flap their hats or turn up their collars. They had to stand stiffly at attention in their ordered ranks, while the rain beat upon their faces and dripped from their noses and chins.

The Boston Cadets, the "Governor's Own," were equally defenseless as they marched against the blast down King Street. So were "a number of His Majesty's Council, several Members of the Commons House of Assembly [and] many principal Gentlemen of the town" who followed the soldiers, in dripping discomfort.

At the Long Wharf the procession halted. The military formed its ranks, and the gentlemen following grouped themselves in proper disposition as a reception committee. All eyes, not only those of the official party but those also of the thronging multitude of common people gathered around and behind them, were turned upon one of His Britannic Majesty's ships of war lying at the wharf.

There was a ruffle of drums aboard the ship; the guns on the other war vessels in the harbor and in the batteries in the town began a thunderous salute and the bells in all the steeples rang out as the expected guests, brave in scarlet coats and white breeches that glittered with gold braid, descended the gangplank and were welcomed with all due form and ceremony and with more or less sincerity according to the political principles of the individual greeters. Whether Boston liked it or not, it was indeed an occasion of moment, for these impressively arrayed military personages were none other than Lieutenant General the Honorable Thomas Gage, commander in chief of all His Majesty's forces in the American colonies and Governor of the Province of Massachusetts Bay, and his staff—his "family," in the language of the period.

The official greetings over, a procession was formed. Led by the guard of honor, the great man with his entourage and the official civilians, followed by thousands of unofficial sight-seers, proceeded up King Street. The rain, on their backs now, was no doubt less discomforting.

The troop of horse, the artillerymen, the grenadiers, and the embodied militia, all amateur soldier boys, stood stiffly at attention while their officers gave these awe-inspiring professionals their very best in the way of a military salute, which the general politely returned. They then fell in behind the procession in its march up King Street to the Town House.

In the Council Chamber, His Excellency presented his commission and was sworn in by the President of the Council. From the balcony of the State House, the High Sheriff read the new Governor's proclamation "continuing all Officers &c in their places till further orders." It was answered by "three huzzas from the concourse of the people," three volleys of musketry from the soldiers of Boston, and the discharge of the Ancient and Honourables' three three-pounder brass fieldpieces.[2]

After the Governor had "received the compliments of civil and military officers and other gentry" and reviewed the militia he was escorted to Faneuil Hall, "where an elegant entertainment was provided at the expence of the province. . . . Many loyal toasts were drank, and the strictest harmony and decorum observed." He then rode in a carriage to the Province House, his official residence.[3]

From all these sights and sounds one might have supposed that it was a day of rejoicing in Boston, that the coming of the new governor was hailed by the people as a fortunate event. But no, the flapping flags, the pealing bells, the saluting guns, all the parade and circumstance of welcome were mere matters of form; the huzzas of the populace were no more than throat-deep. The people of Boston knew what his coming meant and what his orders were; they dreaded what he had come to do. Against him and what he represented, Boston harbored strong feelings of antagonism.

Gage was no stranger in America. After about seventeen years of military service in Britain and on the continent of Europe, he had come to America in 1755 and had taken part in Braddock's disastrous expedition against the French and Indians. He had fought bravely under Braddock, and also under Abercromby in the ill-fated British attack upon Ticonderoga in 1758. Serving as governor of Montreal after the conquest of Canada, he had become commander in chief of the British army in America late in 1763, succeeding his good friend Sir Jeffrey Amherst. His wife, born Margaret Kemble, was an American and a member of a prominent New Jersey family, a cousin of Philip Schuyler and a relative of colonial Van Cortlandts and Bayards. He was a good soldier and was devoted to his duty. He was handsome and dignified, his manners were pleasing; and he was described by the historian William Smith as "a good-natured, peaceable, sociable man." With these qualities, and replacing at least temporarily the hated Governor Thomas Hutchinson, he might have been received with pleasure—would have been so received ten years earlier.

On the other hand, Bostonians had known of him as the commander of the British forces in America who had directed the activities of the four regiments sent to town in 1768, and they had not forgotten the consequent bloody affair in their streets in 1770. To be sure, the regulars had been ordered to Boston by the British cabinet, and Gage had merely executed its orders; but the memory of the "Boston Massacre" would have diminished his welcome now, even if he had come with the most amicable intentions. But he had, in fact, come under orders from his government to deprive the town and the whole province of much of their liberty, and also to close the port of Boston to commerce, which could paralyze the town's chief industries, impoverish its substantial citizens, beggar its working people, and bring them near to starvation. The whole affair of his reception, although many Bostonians sincerely welcomed him, was a triumph of good manners over deep-seated, implacable, and not unjustified resentment.[4]

To appreciate the situation, to understand the causes that gradually developed from mere muttered discontent an animosity that led to violent resistance and finally to the War which it is the purpose of this book to chronicle, one must go back a matter of a decade, to the year 1763.

For a much longer time than that the American colonies had been subject to certain restrictions imposed by the government of Great Britain. The

Navigation Acts, which restrained or rather canalized their sea-borne commerce for the benefit of the shipping interests of the mother country, the Molasses Act, which penalized the importation of molasses and sugar from other than British sources, the various acts which forbade the development of manufactures in the colonies, might seem to have been sufficient to arouse rebellious sentiments in the minds of the colonists long before the year 1763. But in fact there were certain advantages to the Americans in their operation. There were also certain extralegal methods of evasion, which served to lighten their burdensome features. So that, on the whole, there was little opposition to them on the part of the inhabitants of the colonies, and their relations with the home government were not strained. Indeed, the era preceding 1763 came in after days to be regarded by them as a golden age to which they would fain return.

In that year the Peace of Paris ended the Seven Years' War in Europe, a part of which was the French and Indian War in America. That war and three other great conflicts in the preceding seventy years had drained Great Britain's treasury and piled up a public debt of £136,000,000. To sustain this burden and to meet heavy current expenses—heavy in part because it had been decided to keep a regular army of about 6,000 men in America after 1763—she felt obliged to find new sources of income outside the kingdom; and the prosperous American colonies seemed to be the best available source. The consequence was a series of British financial measures to which the Americans strongly objected. Additional causes for American discontent lay in new restrictions placed upon their paper currency, upon westward migration, and upon their trade, and in demands that the colonists give quarters and supplies to the regular army upon certain occasions. Indeed, the very presence of the regulars in America caused great dissatisfaction when the army was stationed in the settled areas.

The Sugar Act of 1764, a successor to the Molasses Act, which had lapsed, clearly displayed the intention of the British government to secure substantial revenue from the mainland American colonies. It cut the duty on molasses in half, while raising that on sugar; and it imposed other new, though less important, duties. It did not differ greatly in form from the old act, except for one startling assertion. While the Molasses Act had been regarded as only a regulation of commerce, such small revenue as it provided being merely incidental, this new law baldly stated in its preamble that one of its purposes was to raise a revenue; in other words, it was in great part a taxing measure.[5] The British government proposed to collect threepence upon every gallon of molasses entering the colonies from the foreign West Indian islands, and shook up its collecting agencies to make certain that the colonists would pay. They had rather effectively avoided paying the duties set up in 1733.

No one had objected on principle to the Molasses Act, although the colonial merchants had flouted it. However, to the relatively new principle of the Sugar Act there was immediate and, in the minds of the Americans, well founded objection; and nowhere in the colonies was it stronger or more vocal than in this same town of Boston, where Samuel Adams became the leader of resistance. The Americans were all the more unhappy because Britain was determined not only to pass the act but to enforce it, and also to enforce the long disobeyed Acts of Navigation.

Adams declared that taxes imposed on the colonists, "without their having a legal representative where they are laid," reduced them "from the character of free subjects to the miserable condition of tributary slaves." [6] This was the answer in principle. The practical answer was a development of the technique of smuggling to such a degree that the new measures were partly nullified.

But the mother country had another rod in pickle for her refractory children, guaranteed to be proof against the tricks of the wiliest smuggler. This was the famous Stamp Act of 1765 requiring that revenue stamps be affixed to all papers in lawsuits, all commercial paper, bills of lading, ship charters, probates of wills, surveys and conveyances of land, leases, bills of sale, and a host of other legal documents, as well as newspapers, pamphlets, playing cards, and so on. The cost of the stamps ranged from a halfpenny on a small newspaper to £6 on a grant of franchise. Heavy penalties were imposed on violators of the act, and, worst of all, unstamped documents were declared void in law.[7]

As a taxing measure it was fair enough, the taxes being widely and rather equally distributed and easily collected. Nor was it a novel method of taxation, for such stamps had long been in use in England. But it could not in any sense be regarded as a regulation of commerce; it was a taxing act pure and simple, without disguise, palliation, or apology. Against it the colonists reacted even more strongly than against the Sugar Act.

In Virginia, Patrick Henry is said to have suggested to George III that he should profit by the examples of Tarquin, Caesar, and Charles I, and the House of Burgesses declared against tax laws not emanating from its own legislature. Pennsylvania and the other middle colonies passed similar resolutions. Massachusetts called for a congress of colonial representatives to take steps in the matter. The Stamp Act Congress met in New York in October, 1765, with members from nine of the thirteen colonies present.

The Congress proceeded to declare, in substance, the colonies' loyalty to the Crown and "all due subordination" to the Parliament, but asserted that it was essential to the freedom of a people that no taxes should be imposed without its consent; that the colonists were not and could not be represented in Parliament; that only their own legislatures could tax them. The Congress added the practical argument that the stamp taxes were so heavy as to prevent them from buying English goods and so were inimical to the prosperity of England, as well as of the colonies. An address to the King, a Memorial to the House of Lords, and a Petition to the Commons all expressed the unhappiness of the colonists.

Meanwhile, intense excitement prevailed throughout the colonies. The Virginia resolutions were broadcast. Associations called Sons of Liberty were formed in the northern provinces to resist the execution of the law. They acted with vigor, indeed with violence. In Boston they hanged Oliver, the stamp officer, in effigy and smashed the windows of his house. He resigned his office, but the Sons of Liberty were not appeased. They burned the records of the vice-admiralty courts, newly empowered to enforce the customs laws; they sacked the office of the Comptroller of Customs, and they climaxed their vandalism by wrecking the fine mansion of Governor Hutchinson, destroying his furniture, defacing his paintings, and casting into the street and burning his books, historical documents and manuscripts, the finest collection of the sort in America. Terrified stamp officers almost universally resigned their posts or refused to do their duty. When the stamps arrived there was hardly anyone willing to receive and issue them. And when they arrived the colonists destroyed them or secured promises from officials that they would not be sold.

November 1, 1765, the day the act was to go into effect, was observed throughout the colonies as a day of mourning; muffled bells were tolled, minute guns were fired, and flags were set at half-staff. How could business go on? How could the courts function, newspapers be issued, ships chartered or cleared, land conveyed, goods sold, without stamps? The solution was simple. Unstamped newspapers appeared, and though for a time business was suspended it was soon largely resumed. The law was simply disregarded, and the act nullified.

But it still stood on the statute books, a menace to every American interest. To enforce its repeal, a general boycott of English goods was organized, and a movement to encourage manufactures despite their unlawfulness was inaugurated. The effect of these measures was impressive. Factories in England were closed; thousands were thrown out of work; and manufacturers and merchants faced bankruptcy. When Parliament met in December, it had to reconsider its action. The addresses of the Stamp Act Congress might have been disregarded, but not the flood of petitions for repeal of the act that came from the commercial classes of Englishmen. William Pitt, the idol of the English people, declared that Parliament had no right to levy the stamp tax, and after a long and heated debate the obnoxious act was repealed.

The news of the repeal was received in America "in a transport of mingled surprise, exultation, and gratitude." Fireworks, festivities, resolutions, and addresses of thanks were evidences of the joy of the people. Moreover, there was a great outburst of loyalty to England. Statues of the King were voted in New York and Virginia. Pitt, Barré, and Conway, leaders of the movement for repeal, were honored by effigies or portraits displayed in public places. The Sons of Liberty faded away. John Adams said that the repeal "hushed into silence almost every popular clamor." Yet this was in fact but an armistice, a temporary truce and not a permanent peace between the government of Great Britain and the self-assertive colonists.

In July, 1766, there was a change in the ministry. Pitt, though disabled by physical and perhaps even mental infirmities, accepted the responsibility of leading it and then betook himself to the House of Lords as Earl of Chatham. The Duke of Grafton became prime minister in form, but exercised little influence. Leadership of the Commons was assumed by Charles Townshend, no friend of America. Unfortunately for the empire, no doubt, Pitt was too sick to control affairs, and Townshend had an opportunity to shine.

Townshend was a brash young man, whose "wonderful endowments [were] dashed with follies and indiscretions." [8] Early in 1767 he boasted that he knew the mode by which a revenue could be drawn from America without offense to the Americans.[9] His scheme was based on a distinction which had been suggested or implied by some colonists and by some Englishmen between "external taxes," that is, duties on imports, to which they did not object, and "internal taxes" such as those imposed by the Stamp Act, which they denounced. He brought in a bill to impose duties on colonial importations from Britain of glass, certain painters' materals, and tea. The proceeds were to be used to pay the salaries of the colonial governors and judges, thus freeing crown officers in America from dependence upon colonial legislatures. He coupled with this a bill to legalize writs of assistance—general search warrants to be used by the revenue officers in enforcing the new revenue law; a bill establishing new courts of vice-admiralty; and a bill creating a special Board of Commissioners of the Customs in Boston, responsible directly to the British Treasury and controlling completely a reorganized American customs service.

But, in relying on the external-internal tax distinction to procure the acquiescence of the Americans, he failed to realize that most Americans were actually opposed to external as well as internal taxes for revenue. The colonists had tasted blood in their fight against the Stamp Act. They considered that they themselves had in effect repealed that law before Parliament did. What they had once done, they felt able to do again. Moreover, there was a growing discontent with the older statutes, the Navigation Acts and those forbidding manufactures. Though long accepted without objection and, in practice, to a considerable degree nullified by simple disobedience of their provisions, these were now felt to be oppressive.

In this state of mind, the colonists cheerfully threw overboard whatever distinction between the two kinds of taxes they had formerly offered. All taxes for revenue, of whatever sort, were now equally hateful. Since 1765 they had been objecting to the standing army as an instrument of tyranny. Now they denounced the new Board of Customs, which would inconveniently interfere with the custom of smuggling. Also they wanted to pay their own governors and judges, basing the desire upon the feeling that their hold on the purse strings was a safeguard against oppression by these officers.

On more justifiable grounds, they were opposed to the writs of assistance, which would enable any customs officer to search not only any ship, but also "any House Shop Cellar Warehouse or Room or other place," [10] without showing cause for such intrusion.

With the passage of the Townshend acts, the short-lived era of good feeling among the colonists toward the mother country came to a sudden end. Massachusetts made the first move toward effective opposition to the new laws by sending a Circular Letter to the other colonies urging concerted action. The British ministry ordered the colonial governors to compel the various colonial legislatures to rescind all resolutions directed against those laws, and to dissolve the assemblies if they refused. Such steps were taken in half a dozen of the colonies, but they only poured oil on the flames of discontent.

Practical measures were taken by the Americans. The general boycott of English goods was gradually revived by new Nonimportation Agreements. The Sons of Liberty became active in their enforcement. When John Hancock's sloop *Liberty* was seized by royal officials at a wharf in Boston in June, 1768, on a charge of smuggling, a mob attacked them. The Commissioners of Customs fled in terror to Castle William, a fortress on an island in Boston harbor.

These and other acts of violent resistance could not be overlooked by the British government. General Gage was instructed to move two regiments of foot to Boston for police duty. When these regulars landed at the beginning of October, 1768, Boston declined to furnish free quarters in town and certain supplies for them, as seemingly required by an act of Parliament. Colonel Dalrymple, commander of the troops, had to rent any available lodgings for his men and for two more regiments of infantry that joined them in following months. Instead of being concentrated in barracks under firm control of their officers, the soldiers were scattered throughout the town, with unfortunate results.

Bostonians regarded them as foreign troops and accordingly hated them, ostracized them, insulted them in the streets and called them opprobrious names. They responded by swaggering, insolent, contemptuous conduct. The natural result was frequent brawls and rough encounters between the citizens and the soldiers.

On March 5, 1770, this mutual ill-feeling culminated in a serious affair. A mob of citizens pelted some of the intruders with snowballs and stones and reviled them with scurrilous language. There was a close encounter, so close that some of the mob struck at their opponents' muskets with clubs, daring them to fire, and knocked one of them down. The soldiers fired into the crowd. Eleven of the citizens fell, three of them dead, two mortally wounded. This was the famous "Boston Massacre."

Quite naturally, it caused great excitement throughout the town. Bells were rung to summon the populace. The whole town poured out into the streets. Drums were beaten to call out the militia. Several companies formed around the Town House. It looked as if the war was to begin then and there. But Governor Hutchinson succeeding in quieting the people and in obtaining Dalrymple's promise to withdraw the troops to Castle William in Boston harbor.

Meanwhile the continued boycott of British goods was seriously affecting the English economy. Exports to America shrank to half their former value, and there was nothing that the army could do about it. Confronted with this situation, several members of the ministry urged a policy of conciliation and proposed entire repeal of the Townshend taxes; but the King was firm in his demand that "there must always be one tax to keep up the right" to tax. When the others were abolished, in April, 1770, the tax on tea was retained.

At the time of the "massacre" war, at least a local civil war, had been a very near thing; but after the alteration in the tax law and after the excitement in Boston had subsided, there ensued a long period of quiet throughout the colonies. The Americans were back in the golden age of 1763, except for the tea tax. This fact, coupled with a growing weariness of the prolonged conflict, induced a spirit of nonresistance, which degenerated into apathy. The Nonimportation Agreements were violated with increasing frequency. Complaints of such violations by this colony were made by that. Such charges were met by countercharges of the same sort. Intercolonial enmities arose out of these recriminations. The partly built, ill cemented union of the colonies was falling apart. Another shock was needed to revive the fainting spirit of liberty. It came in June, 1772.

The British armed schooner *Gaspée*, while pursuing a suspected smuggling vessel, ran aground in the waters of Rhode Island. Drums beat in Providence. Eight boats full of volunteers put off, surrounded the schooner, seized it, and burned it. In the fracas the British commander was wounded. America hailed the deed as a blow against oppression; England was outraged. British investigators could not discover the names of the culprits, known to many citizens. Finally, the British authorities, perhaps loath to excite renewed animosity in the presently quiescent colonies, dropped the matter.

Distrust of the colonial courts as impartial tribunals now impelled the ministry to revive the project of paying the judges out of the royal treasury, beginning in Massachusetts. That colony astutely countered the move by offering the judges higher salaries than were to be paid by Britain, and the judges accepted the offer. Samuel Adams, who had been almost in despair over the decline of the spirit of resistance and the relaxation of the bonds of unity, saw his chance. In April, 1773, he proposed the organization of Committees of Correspondence to act as connecting links between the various Massachusetts towns. Within a few months, many such bodies appeared, some of them acting for towns, others for colonies. Soon they formed a network throughout the colonies.

Still quietude prevailed throughout America. Only a general abstention from English tea indicated the underlying spirit of opposition to Parliamentary taxation. With characteristic ineptitude the British government seized on that minor element in the contest and erected it into a major dispute.

The East India Company had been hit by the refusal of the Americans to import its tea. In the port of Philadelphia, for example, only one chest of English tea had been entered in the customhouse in five years, while an ample supply had been smuggled in from other sources. Seventeen million pounds had accumulated in the Company's English warehouses, and it was nearing bankruptcy. Government officials were largely interested in the Company. To relieve its embarrassment, an arrangement was made to reimburse the Company for the import duties it paid in England, and to allow it to export directly to its own agents in America instead of through English merchants to American merchants as theretofore. It could then sell tea in the colonies at prices less than those at which smuggled tea was sold, even though its agents paid the threepence a pound American duty to the English government; and the cantankerous colonials would get their tea, tax and all, cheaper than ever before, and even cheaper than it was being sold in England. So why should they worry about the tax? They would surely buy the Company's tea.

But they did worry. News of the scheme was like a bellows blast to the smoldering embers of resistance to "tyranny." After years of quiescence, "the whole country was in a blaze from Maine to Georgia." [11] It is said that "the transition from apathy to agitation was sudden" [12] and widespread. It was an amazing phenomenon. The duties had been legally in force for six years, and for half of that time they had been either quietly paid or tranquilly disregarded. No one was now to be forced to buy the Company's tea. So why should the colonials excite themselves about it?

It has been said that they were aroused by an attempt, at once injurious and insulting, to bribe them to surrender their rights "not to be taxed, by offering them cheaper tea." [13] A more cynical, probably less truthful, statement is that the blaze was not sudden; that it took two full months to work it up; that it was, in fact, ignited by certain Philadelphia merchants who had profited by dealing in the smuggled tea and now saw their business in peril. Be the truth as to this what it may, Philadelphia did take the lead in arousing enmity to the scheme by a series of resolutions denouncing it as "a violent attack upon the liberties of America." Committees pressed the Company's agents, consignees of the expected tea, to resign. Boston followed suit, and so did New York and Charleston. "The cry of endangered liberty once more excited an alarm from New Hampshire to Georgia." [14] Boston was "as furious as it was in the time of the Stamp Act." [15] Whatever the incitement, the resulting conflagration was genuine enough.

The announced intention of the Americans was to prevent the landing of the tea, and it was carried out. At Charleston, no consignee having appeared to pay the duty, a cargo was seized by the customs officers, stored in damp cellars, and left to rot. The captains of the tea ships bound to Philadelphia and New York saw that they could not land their cargoes and carried them back to England. But it was reserved for Boston to climax the opposition in the most spectacular manner. In December, 1773, it held a "tea party," in which an organized mob tossed overboard tea valued at £15,000.

George III, who for a long time had had Boston "on the brain," now saw red. A message from the cabinet to Parliament resulted in quick and drastic action. Four new measures to punish that hotbed of treason were enacted.

The first, known as the Boston Port Act, closed the port of Boston to all commerce and ordered it blockaded. Marblehead and Salem were to be the only Massachusetts ports. The second annulled several parts of the province's charter. Its Assembly was left to function, but the upper chamber, the Council, was to be appointed by the King. The inferior judges, the sheriffs, and other executive officers were to be appointed by the Governor. Juries were to be chosen by the sheriffs, who owed their appointments to the royal chief executive. Town meetings, the very core of self-government in Massachusetts, were to be held only with the Governor's permission, except one each year to choose assemblymen, selectmen, and constables. The third act provided for the removal to England or to another colony for trial of anyone indicted for a capital offense committed in the course of a riot or of enforcement of the revenue laws. The fourth legalized the quartering of troops on the town.

To enforce these laws, General Gage was appointed governor of the province. Which brings us around, at last, to the point where this introductory chapter began.

CHAPTER 2

Boston Port Closed

Boston's population numbered about 20,000, almost all of English origin, there having been but little immigration from the European continent or even from Ireland. It was, of all the colonial ports, the most active in shipbuilding, codfishery, whaling, and sea-borne commerce in general. It contained important American rum distilleries, which were dependent on a supply of molasses from the West Indies. As elsewhere in the colonies, so in Boston the repressive acts of Parliament had prevented the development of manufactures. The town lived on its ships, its wharves, its shipyards, ropewalks, and sail lofts. To survive, it had to have free passage for its vessels. For its food, in some part, it needed access by water to the grazing grounds on the small islands in its outer harbor, where beef cattle and sheep were pastured.

At the stroke of noon on June 1, the Port Act went into effect. From that moment, Boston harbor was sealed against the rest of the world by a tight blockade. General Gage had been instructed to compel "a full and absolute submission" to the new law. The terms of the act made it unlawful to load or receive at any wharf in the port, at any "island, creek, landing-place, bank or other place" within Massachusetts Bay, any goods whatsoever, in any vessel whatsoever, coming from or going to "any other country, province or place whatsoever." Gage construed his mandate as covering every possible movement of goods, even within the harbor. An adjacent island was a "place"; Charlestown, separated from Boston only by the Charles River, was a "place"; therefore the town was cut off not only from the sea by the blockading ships, but also from such "places." "Did a lighter attempt to land hay from the islands, or a boat to bring in sand from the neighboring hills, or a scow to freight to it lumber or iron, or a float to land sheep, or a farmer to carry marketing over in the ferry-boats, the argus-eyed fleet was ready to see it, and prompt to capture or destroy." [1]

The effect upon the town was immediate, universal, and disastrous. Although church bells had tolled, days of fasting and prayer had been observed, and badges of mourning had been displayed, nothing had availed to avert the coming catastrophe. When it came, the town was stopped dead in its tracks. The great warehouses were closed; the wharves were deserted, and the porters and stevedores were thrown out of work. The shipyards suspended operations, and the carpenters were idle. Ships were tied up at the piers, and the sailors walked the streets. Mercantile houses had no more business, and their clerks no more employment. The town was paralyzed and was like to starve. It might have starved, indeed, but for the alms bestowed upon it by other towns and the other colonies. Connecticut sent it hundreds of sheep. From elsewhere in New England came flour, cattle, fish, and other foods. The Carolinas sent stores of rice and considerable sums of money. Delaware sent money and promised more. Contributions of food and money came from all the other colonies and even from Canada; Quebec sent more than a thousand bushels of wheat. For a full year Boston lived in part on these supplies. And with them came messages of encouragement and adjurations to the Bostonians to stand by their refusal to ransom their town by paying £15,000 for the tea that had been destroyed.[2]

Gage, in accordance with instructions from the King, established the capital of the province in Salem and took up his official residence there, leaving Earl Percy, son and heir of the Duke of Northumberland, in command of several regiments of troops who were brought to Boston to support British authority in the summer of 1774.

At Salem, on June 17, the General Assembly met, under protest against the removal of the capital to that place. Gage sent his secretary with an order dissolving the session. The door was locked against him so that he could only read the order to the crowd on the stairs. The Assembly proposed a continental congress and elected five delegates to represent Massachusetts.

Thirty-six members of the Governor's Council were appointed by Gage a few weeks later. Eleven of them immediately declined to serve. The rest were so insulted, ostracized, and in every way harassed by the people that, finally, no more than sixteen remained in office, and these were forced to seek refuge in Boston under protection of its garrison.

In late August a session of the Supreme Court was to be held in Boston.

Gage came over from Salem to give it his personal support. The judges took their seats; but not a single man in the jury panel would consent to be sworn. The judges told the Governor that it was not possible to hold court even in Boston. Nor was it possible anywhere else in the province. Judges, even justices of the peace, sheriffs, and other executive officers, either voluntarily or through coercion, declined to perform their duties. In Boston the King's law, as far as it was pronounced by Parliament in the obnoxious statutes, was enforced by the military. But not even in Boston was enforcement of any other law possible. "Three hundred thousand people continued their usual avocations without a legislature or executive officers, without sheriffs, judges or justices of the peace." [3] Yet order prevailed generally. The habits of a law-abiding people prevailed, even though the machinery for law enforcement had ceased to exist. "Though the tribunals were void and silent, crime was repressed and private rights were secure, because the people were a law to themselves." [4]

In September, Gage incautiously called the General Court, consisting of the Council and the Assembly, to meet in Salem on October 5. But, realizing that his appointees to the Council would not be allowed to take their seats, he withdrew the summons. The members of the lower house, nevertheless, gathered in Salem. After two days of intentional neglect by the Governor they adjourned to Concord and organized as a Provincial Congress—a body entirely outside the law and unknown to it—which acted thereafter as the only effective government of the province outside Boston.

In the meantime Gage had taken up residence in Boston and was steadily accumulating troops. To provide quarters for them, other than the tents on the Common and such empty warehouses as he had been able to rent, he called for workmen to build barracks. Though thousands in the town were unemployed, no one would or dared work for him. He had to send to New York and to Halifax for the necessary artificers. The people of the town countered this move by widespread sabotage. Barges transporting bricks for the barracks were sunk, wagons loaded with bricks were upset, straw for the soldiers' beds was burned. November had come and nearly gone before the soldiers could be removed from their chilly quarters on the Common to more adequate shelter.

The Continental Congress, which the Bostonians had suggested, met in Philadelphia on September 5. Twelve of the thirteen colonies sent delegates to make up the most substantial, mentally vigorous, politically powerful, and determined body of colonial representatives that had ever assembled in America. An address to the King, couched in respectful words, an address to the People of England, and a Declaration of Rights again stated the grievances of the colonies and recited thirteen Acts of Parliament to which Americans could not submit.

The addresses and the declaration made no demand for independence, nor suggestion of a resort to force to uphold the rights claimed. They were only petitions for relief from oppression, which, however, the delegates had little expectation of receiving without more pressure than such petitions alone would exert. To give them practical force, reliance was placed upon a renewal of such a boycott of English goods as had theretofore been so effective. It was therefore voted that an Association of the colonies be formed, agreeing not to import any goods from Great Britain or Ireland, nor any East India tea, nor any of certain products from the British West Indies. In addition it was agreed that consumption of British goods and exportation of goods to Britain be curtailed.

The American petitions availed nothing; neither the King nor the Parliament gave them the slightest heed. The only substantial results of the Congress were the Association and the bringing together for the first time of the leading men of the colonies to act in unison, which paved the way for the next meeting of Congress in 1775 and for united action.

Across the river from Boston, on Quarry Hill in Charlestown there was a magazine, "the powder-house," in which was kept a store of gunpowder belonging to the province and to several of the near-by towns. The towns, during August, had been removing their stocks and storing them within their own precincts, as if in readiness for use. To Gage these proceedings seemed ominous of coming trouble; he decided to take steps accordingly.

On the first of September, at dawn, a force of 260 soldiers embarked at the Long Wharf, crossed over to Charlestown and carried off 250 half-barrels, the entire remaining stock of the precious explosive. While this was going on, a detachment marched to Cambridge and confiscated two field-pieces lately procured by the militia regiment of that town. These guns and the powder were removed to Castle William. This unexpected little operation was effected peaceably, without opposition and therefore without bloodshed; but its results were far more disastrous than the withdrawal of powder by the towns had been.

News of the seizure spread swiftly throughout the province, and, as it spread, it grew in importance. By afternoon it was widely reported that the people of Charlestown had resisted the seizure, and that the troops had fired on them and killed six. By midnight this was known forty miles away in Shrewsbury. Everywhere, the rumor was received as a call to arms, and the people responded. By the next day 4,000 armed men, from all the country within thirty miles of Boston, had crowded into Cambridge; Worcester

County and Hampshire were on the march. On the 3rd, Israel Putnam, down in Pomfret, Connecticut, heard not only that the King's soldiers had shot down six of the people of Charlestown and wounded many more, but also that the King's men-of-war had bombarded Boston. By that time thousands —twenty, thirty thousand, it was said—were moving on foot toward Cambridge.[5]

On the 4th, the Committee of Correspondence of Connecticut sent the dreadful news to New York. Within a week, the Continental Congress in Philadelphia had heard of that "dreadful catastrophe." "The effect of the news we have," wrote John Adams to his wife, "both upon the Congress and the inhabitants of this city, was very great. Great indeed! Every gentleman seems to regard the bombardment of Boston as the bombardment of the capital of his own province. Our deliberations are grave and serious indeed."[6] It was, of course, an absurd idea that Gage would bombard his own town, the only place he held in the colonies. The effect upon the Congress, in unifying its members and hastening their action, was, nevertheless, decided and effective.

Many of the thousands on the march to Cambridge were turned back by word that the rumor was false; those already there were dispersed, and the excitement died down. The incident had been, however, an impressive demonstration of the inflammatory nature of the situation and of the insufficiency of the British forces in Boston to contend successfully with all New England in arms. Gage recognized his weakness and called on the home government for reinforcements: to reduce New England, a very respectable force must take the field. He recognized, also, the insecurity of his position, even in merely defensive operations, and set about strengthening it.

Boston was almost an island, being connected with the mainland by a very slim isthmus known as the Neck, at its narrowest part no wider than the causeway built across a depression that was submerged at high tide. From old times, there had been a slight fortification at the town end of this causeway. The excitement about the powder had hardly died when, on September 5, Gage ordered the erection of substantial defensive works on the mainland beyond the Neck and thereby again alarmed the people.

The selectmen of Boston protested; they apprehended an intention of shutting the town off from the rest of the province, of reducing it to the condition of a garrisoned stronghold. Gage replied that the works were merely to protect the troops and the people of Boston from attack, and that he had no intention of interrupting ordinary traffic. Although strikes and all forms of sabotage delayed the work, he succeeded in erecting a rather elaborate fortification, mounting two 24-pound cannon and eight 9-

pounders, which did nothing to allay the inflammation in the minds of the people.

The Americans did what they could to redress the balance of arms inside and outside Boston. One night they stripped a battery at Charlestown of its guns and delivered them outside the lines. Another night they brought off four cannon from the gun-house near the Common. Countrymen, returning from selling their products in the town, day after day concealed muskets, ammunition, and military gear in their wagons and carried them past the guard at the Neck. Gun running became a popular avocation. Admiral Graves, in command of the harbor blockade, could think of no way to preserve the guns in the North Battery other than spiking them, which he did.

The Provincial Congress, sitting in Concord and later in Cambridge during the latter part of 1774, appropriated what was to them the huge sums of £15,627 sterling for the purchase of twenty fieldpieces, four mortars, twenty tons of grape and round shot, ten tons of bombshells, five tons of bullets, one thousand barrels of powder, five thousand muskets and bayonets, and seventy-five thousand flints, to which the Committee of Supplies, in charge of such purchases, added three hundred fifty spades and pickaxes, one thousand wooden mess bowls, and a supply of pork, flour, dried peas, and rice. These military stores were to be deposited in Concord and Worcester. Provision was later made for securing tentage and various other kinds of munitions and supplies.

The Congress provided for the organization of regiments of "minutemen" (of whom more hereinafter) by drawing one-fourth of the men in the regular militia for that purpose. It also named Jedediah Preble, Artemas Ward, and Seth Pomeroy as general officers in command of all the forces of the province, divided into three corps: one at Charlestown, one at Roxbury, the third at Cambridge. A Committee of Safety was appointed to take charge of all the colony's affairs after the dissolution of the Congress. On December 10 it dissolved itself, having first appointed committees to notify the neighboring provinces, Connecticut, Rhode Island, and New Hampshire, of its acts and to request them to provide men to make up an army of 20,000 in all.

Gage issued a proclamation declaring the acts of the Provincial Congress to be treasonable, which, indeed, they were, and prohibiting the people from complying with its requisitions or recommendations. It had no effect whatever upon the colonials; they were busy all through the winter collecting and storing munitions of war. On every village green throughout New England, the militia were drilling more often than ever before and with more serious intent. The cannon at Fort Island in Rhode Island, six 24-pounders, eighteen 18-pounders, fourteen 6-pounders, and six 4-pounders, were seized and carried to Providence, "to prevent their falling into the hands of the King, or any of his servants." Four hundred Portsmouth, New Hampshire, men demanded the powder of that province, which was stored in the fort at New Castle. The British commander refused to give it up and fired upon them with three 4-pounders and his musketry. They "stormed" the fort, secured the captain and his garrison of five "invalid" soldiers and carried off ninety-seven barrels of powder, fifteen hundred muskets, and several pieces of artillery.[7]

On February 26, 1775, to counter the activities of the Americans in seizing powder and arms, Gage sent Colonel Leslie with 240 men to Salem to seize a few brass fieldpieces deposited there. He sailed on a transport to Marblehead, whence he had to march five miles to his destination. Salem had timely news of his approach. A large crowd, including the militia colonel, Timothy Pickering, and 40 armed men, assembled in a shipyard where carriages for the guns were being made and hoisted the drawbridge spanning a small stream that the British force would have to cross.

Leslie arrived and demanded that the bridge be replaced. He was informed that this was a private road and that no trespassing would be permitted. He turned his attention to two "gundalows," which lay in the stream. But their owners jumped into them and began to scuttle them. There was a scuffle, in which a few of the Salemites were "pricked with bayonets" but no one was seriously wounded.

Leslie had his orders, which included crossing that bridge, but he was at his wit's end as to how to execute them. At length, a Salem clergyman intervened. He told Leslie that if he crossed the stream in opposition to the Salemites he would certainly be overwhelmed by the population, but if he would pledge his word to advance no farther than thirty rods beyond the bridge to a point where the unfinished gun-carriages were, and then, if he found no guns, to return, the bridge would be let down. Leslie agreed, crossed the stream, marched the agreed distance, found no guns, faced about, and returned to Marblehead and so to Boston. In the telling, the proceeding seems farcical, but if he had not yielded Salem might have won the honors later conferred on Lexington by Major Pitcairn and his men, for the alarm had gone forth, the minutemen were responding to it, and a company from Danvers arrived on the scene just as Leslie's detachment was marching away.[8]

The news of violent opposition by the Americans did not shock the King nor, indeed, particularly displease him. "I am not sorry," he wrote, "that the line of conduct seems now chalked out. . . . The New England Governments are in a state of rebellion. Blows must decide whether they are subject to this country or independent." "He was prepared to fight and was in a hurry to begin." [9]

When the Parliament met, on November 29, the address from the throne began with notice of "a most daring spirit of resistance and disobedience to the law . . . fresh violences of a very criminal nature" in Massachusetts, and of the measures the crown had taken to restore "peace, order and good Government" there. Lords and Commons answered that "a rebellion at this time actually exists within said Province," which was not an overstatement, and besought His Majesty to "take the most effectual measures to enforce due obedience to the laws and authority of the supreme Legislature." They also assured him that it was "our fixed resolution, at the hazard of our lives and properties," to stand by him—a gallant assurance, indeed, which seemed to contemplate that the coming war was to be fought against hordes of invading Yankees in the towns, villages, and fields of old England, with the King himself in the battle-front and the lords and gentlemen of the Commons in the firing line.

To avoid such an untoward event, an addition of 6,000 men to the military and naval forces was provided for, with an increase of the force in Boston to 10,000 soldiers. But this Parliament struck a still shrewder blow against the offending Americans with a statute, commonly called the Fishery Act, which restrained the New England colonies from all trade with Great Britain, Ireland, and the West Indies, and excluded them from the Newfoundland fisheries, under penalty of forfeiture of vessels engaged. The scope of the act was soon enlarged to include the other American colonies, except New York and Georgia, neither of which had yet joined in the Continental Association of the colonies boycotting English goods. During the consideration of these measures the Parliament had been bombarded with petitions from the London merchants and from the mercantile and manufacturing interest of all the other great towns, as well as with remonstrances from the colonies, urging the great importance of the American trade and the vast sums already due from the colonial merchants for goods shipped to them (estimated, for the City of London alone, at £2,000,000), which these restrictions would render impossible of payment, and praying that "healing remedies" be applied to restore the normal commerce between Great Britain and the colonies. But the "King's friends" ignored these petitions and voted for the new oppressive acts by such majorities as 260 to 90 in the Commons.

The restraints on ordinary commerce were felt by all the colonies, but the exclusion from the fisheries dealt a dreadful blow to New England, the prosperity of which had been built up and was still largely dependent on the capture of codfish and whales. Nantucket, for instance, had a whaling fleet of 140 vessels, which was the principal support of its 5,000 inhabitants.

At the same time that the Parliament was in session in St. Stephen's Hall, partly warmed, no doubt by good sea-coal fires, the Provincial Congress of Massachusetts was sitting in Cambridge "in a house without a fire," so cold that it was resolved "That all those Members who incline thereto may sit with their Hats on"[10] which seems in a way to symbolize the contrast in resources between the two countries at that time.

The Massachusetts Congress had met on February 1 to take steps to meet those "most speedy and effectual measures for supporting the just rights of his Crown and the two Houses of Parliament" which the King proposed to take, and for which he had asked from the Commons an augmentation of his forces. The steps taken certainly justified His Majesty's accusation of rebellion. Two additional general officers were appointed by the rebels in the persons of John Thomas and William Heath; provision was made for a commissary to receive all "Stores, Ordnance, Arms and Provisions . . . until the Constitutional Army shall take the field"; there were many other arrangements looking toward armed conflict with the King's troops, including an address to the Stockbridge Indians, welcoming and promising "a Blanket and a Red Ribbon" to each one that "enlisted in the service" of the colony; a code of rules to govern the army—usually called "Articles of War"—was adopted; delegates were chosen to visit the other New England colonies and ask them to add their quotas to the forces of Massachusetts. The Congress finally adjourned on April 15—four days before the fatal day of Lexington and Concord.

CHAPTER 3

The Two Armies

While all these events were occurring, Gage had been adding to his forces. By the beginning of 1775, he had in Boston nine regiments of British infantry and parts of two others, the 4th or King's Own, the 5th, the 10th, the 23rd or Royal Welch Fusiliers, the 38th, the 43rd, the 47th, the 52nd, the 59th, three companies of the 18th or Royal Irish, and six companies of the 65th; also five companies of the Royal Artillery. The 64th was quartered in Castle William.

The strength of each regiment was supposed to be 477 of all ranks; but there was always a considerable actual shortage, and it has been estimated that the average effective number of rank and file was about 292. The total number, including the artillery, may therefore be computed at about 4,000. In the harbor lay four ships of the line, the *Scarborough*, the *Boyne*, the *Somerset*, and the *Asia,* each carrying sixty guns or more, "besides frigates and sloops and a great number of transports," from which Gage had drawn 460 marines.[1]

These soldiers were fair samples of the personnel of the British army that was to fight in the war. Their characteristics as soldiers, their equipment, leadership, and organization, were typical of the military power against which America was to contend.

In the eighteenth century, the British army had been built up by the crown contracting with this or that distinguished soldier or gentleman of position to raise a regiment. To him as its colonel was paid so much for each man enlisted, and thereafter an annual sum sufficient to pay and clothe his men. Sometimes, instead of receiving pay for enlistments, the colonel was permitted to nominate the officers, to whom he sold their commissions. A commission so acquired became the property of the holder and entitled him to receive the pay and allowances appropriate to his rank for the rest of his life, subject, however, to a reduction to half-pay if his regiment were disestablished in time of peace.[2]

As a species of property, such a commission could be sold if the holder desired to withdraw from the service; and it was by this means that promotion in the army was commonly obtained. Otherwise advancement was possible only when a vacancy in a superior rank occurred through death; and even then the hope was faint because as many as ten captains, for example, might be candidates for the commission of a dead major. The system of purchase practically restricted commissions to possessors of means.[3] The officers were almost all "men of family," that is to say, technically gentlemen. There were no military schools, except for the artillery. Raw lads of the officer class generally entered the army at the age of sixteen by favor or by purchase, learning their profession thereafter in actual service.

The common soldiers were far removed from the officers in the social scale. They were obtained by voluntary or by compulsory enlistment. The weekly pay of four shillings and sixpence was so reduced by charges for clothing, medicine, and many other impositions that they often got practically nothing in coin. Their food was "notoriously poor," their hardships severe. As a consequence, voluntary enlistment was largely confined to silly lads befooled by the glamour of the scarlet coat or to men and boys who were either desperate or drunk. Debtors released from imprisonment, criminals pardoned on the condition that they enlist, boys and men made drunk by the recruiting sergeant and persuaded to take "the King's shilling" while hardly aware of what they were doing made up a considerable part of the army.[4] "By lies they lured them, by liquor they tempted them, and when they were dead drunk they forced a shilling into their fists." [5]

Compulsory enlistment was made possible by the "Act against vagabonds," a statute authorizing impressment of "any sturdy beggar, any fortune teller, any idle, unknown or suspected fellow in a parish, that cannot give an account of himself . . . anyone who had been in gaol," or was "known as an incorrigible rogue"; poachers were fair game. But, though the recruiting officers interpreted these provisions broadly, enlistments, voluntary and involuntary taken together, were not enough to keep the ranks of the army up to the standard of strength, a condition that compelled the British government, within a short time after the war began, to employ foreign mercenaries.[6]

It would seem that the British army, so made up, would have been lacking in all the elements that go to building a force reliable in camp and on the march and effective in action; but its record in the war is all to the contrary. In the first place, it must be remembered that in conditions of economic hardship criminals are often made out of men not naturally vicious, and that under the extraordinarily severe code of criminal law then obtaining minor offenders were speedily converted into long-term felons or sentenced to death. It must also be observed that desperate men often make the best soldiers. In the second place, the effects of drill and discipline must not be overlooked. At all events, the British soldier in this war unquestionably displayed qualities of hardihood, courage, persistence, and military effectiveness that did honor to his nation.

Each regiment was composed of eight companies of ordinary foot soldiers, a company of light infantry, and one of grenadiers. These last two groups were the élite, the flower of the army, selected from the ranks for special qualities.

The light infantry were chosen for physical ability, vigor, audacity, alertness, and general fighting qualities outside ordinary service in the line of battle. Their chief duties were reconnaissance, skirmishing, outpost work and surprises, and flanking the army on the march.

The grenadiers were likewise selected troops; but they were chosen for qualities additional to those of the light infantry. They were first organized in the British army in 1678 to use a new weapon, a small iron bomb with an ignited fuse that was thrown by hand. As presumably able to throw such missiles a greater distance, the tallest and strongest men in each regiment were picked to be grenadiers. To permit slinging their muskets on either shoulder while they were engaged in such bombing, they wore brimless caps, instead of the usual broad-brimmed hats. These caps in time developed into the tall miterlike headpieces familiar in pictures of grenadiers, which added to their apparent height and gave them a more formidable appearance. The hand grenade had become practically obsolete in 1774, when the grenadiers were armed like the rest of the infantry. They were, nevertheless, retained in the army as a picked corps.

Both the light infantry and the grenadier companies remained in the regimental organization except when detached for special duty. They were known as "flank companies" because, in line of battle, they held the posts of honor at the flanks of their own regiments; they also led or flanked their regiments when in column of march. However, both the light companies and the grenadiers were frequently assembled in battalions of their own class for special operations or even as fighting units in a general battle. Some military critics deplored this practice because it skimmed the cream of the infantry and deprived the regular regiments of their best fighting men, who would have stiffened the line in defense and given it greater élan in attack. Nevertheless, it continued even to the extent of forming permanent regiments, such as the well known Grenadier Guards.

Gage had no cavalry at the beginning of 1775; but in June he did have a mounted force, a contingent of 400 men of the 17th Light Dragoons. These are to be distinguished from cavalry, whose arms were properly a heavy saber and a pair of horse pistols, and whose principal duties were to scout, to protect the flanks of the line or column, to circumvent the enemy's line, to cut communications, to pursue retreating enemies, and to act as shock troops, striking at the opposing force when it showed signs of weakness or disorder. Unlike the cavalryman, the dragoon, who was properly armed with a short musket or a carbine, a sword, and pistols, traveled on horseback but fought on foot; he was simply a mounted infantryman, and his horse, not being intended for shock tactics, was a light, wiry animal. When not engaged in battle he was usually employed for vedette work (as a mounted sentinel in advance of outposts), for orderly duty, and foraging. The distinction between the two arms (indicated in the phrase "horse, foot, and dragoons"), however, tended to diminish; dragoons were sometimes used as shock troops, as in the Battle of Monmouth in 1778 and at Camden in 1780, and the name came to be applied to pure cavalrymen,[7] as in the case of Tarleton's and William Washington's cavalry, often called dragoons.

The uniforms of the British infantrymen were modeled after those in use in Germany. They were highly ornamental, very fine for parade, but as impractical for active service as could well be imagined. The scarlet coat was lavishly decorated with colored linings, facings, and pipings, lace, and brass buttons; the waistcoat was either scarlet or white. The white breeches and the coat sleeves, also the long buttoned gaiters of some regiments, coming well above the knee, were all as tight as possible. The waist belt was broad and tight; it carried the bayonet scabbard. There was also a belt from the left shoulder to the opposite hip, carrying the cartridge box. The standing coat collars were stiff, and the movements of the head were further hampered by a high, stiff leather stock under the chin. The hats were of various types, some with broad brims cocked in the familiar, triangular form, others tall and pointed grenadier-fashion. These were often made of bearskin. None of them had a visor or brim to shield the eyes from the sun.

The hair was generally worn in a queue or club stiffened with grease and white powder, as were the tight curls in front of the ears.

Keeping all this apparatus in order—shining the brass, pipe-claying the leather, cleaning the cloth, blacking the shoes, braiding and dressing the queue, as well as polishing the arms—took from two to three hours a day. In active service, of course, much of this elaborate toilet was necessarily neglected; but the uniform and equipment were the same, so awkward, cumbersome, stiff, and constricting as greatly to hamper the movements of the soldier and to reduce his efficiency.[8]

The infantry officer was armed either with a spontoon—a sort of pike or spear with an ornamental head, which was both a badge of office and a weapon—or with a fusil, a short musket. He also wore a light dress sword.

The standard weapon of the infantry private was the musket, commonly called the brown Bess, after the first matchlock guns introduced into the British army by Queen Elizabeth, their barrels and metal fittings having been browned. By this time, however, the barrels were steel-bright. Any musket that had been inspected in the Tower of London was especially stamped, and was called a Tower musket.[9]

The brown Bess was a smoothbore gun; rifles were not yet in use in the British army. It weighed about ten pounds, was about four and a half feet long, and carried a twenty-one-inch bayonet. It had no rear sight. Its caliber was three-quarters of an inch. Because its bullet weighed more than an ounce, it had great stopping power, but the range was short: a ball fired with a regulation charge from such a gun, held horizontally at a height of five feet, fell harmlessly to the ground at about 125 yards. It was also very inaccurate, because its bore was usually untrue; but that mattered little, for the British soldier was no marksman. He had not been trained to take aim at a single object, nor even at the mass of the enemy. His instructions were to throw his gun to his shoulder in a horizontal position "point it—not sight it—toward the enemy and, at the word of command, pull the trigger."[10] As an English historian, Trevelyan, puts it: "He was taught to point his weapon horizontally, brace himself for a vicious recoil and pull a ten pound trigger till his gun went off: if, indeed, it did go off when the hammer fell." [11]

Loading involved biting the end off a cylindrical paper cartridge that contained powder and ball, shaking a little powder into the pan, closing its lid, dropping the butt of the gun on the ground, pouring the rest of the powder into the barrel, striking the gun to jar some powder into the touchhole, dropping in the ball, cramming the paper into the muzzle, and ramming it down to act as a wad. The process of firing was almost equally involved: when the trigger was pulled the cock fell, striking its flint against a piece of steel called the frizzen; from this contact, a shower of sparks (perhaps) fell on the powder in the pan; the powder flashed; there was a spurt of flame outward from the touchhole and inward into the charge, by whose explosion the bullet was projected. There was an appreciable interval of time between the pulling of the trigger and the explosion of the charge. Often, indeed, there was no explosion. The flint might be so worn as to fail to spark; the powder in the pan might be damp and so fail to ignite; the touchhole might be stopped up.[12]

In the British army the steps in loading and firing were taken in response to a series of orders by an officer. Up to a few years before the Revolution, the manual required sixteen distinct orders to put the soldier through forty-nine motions. By 1764 this had been simplified so that eight orders sufficed to effect priming and loading (but not presenting and firing) in twelve movements. The Americans reduced this to ten motions in response to a single order, "Prime and load!" It was also a part of their instructions to sight, not merely point, the musket. Two or three shots in a minute were reckoned a good rate of fire.[13]

Such delays and uncertainties and such a lack of precision made the brown Bess less useful as a gun than as a stock for a bayonet. Indeed, the "white weapon" was much the most effective British arm throughout the war. The usual practice was to advance the line to within a hundred yards or so of the enemy before firing one or more hit-or-miss volleys, and then to charge with the bayonet. Such attacks were the most dreaded by the Americans and the most often successful.

To oppose the regularly organized, fully equipped and trained British troops, Massachusetts had only its militia. That term must be understood in its true meaning. The militia included the entire potential fighting strength of the province. Every man between the ages of sixteen and sixty years was required by law to possess a gun and its proper equipment of ammunition and accessories, and to be enrolled in the company of his own township. He was supposed to turn out at certain intervals, perhaps four times a year or oftener, with the rest of his company for training; hence the common appellation, "trainbands."

The primary purpose in instituting this system in the early days of the colony had been to provide for defense against attacks by the Indians; there was no intention of sending the militia out of the province. But when, on the outbreak of the French and Indian War in 1754, it became necessary to furnish a force to operate in French territory, a new arrangement was authorized.

Service in several new regiments raised at that time was made voluntary. The officers were appointed by the governor, and each was authorized "to beat his Drums anywhere within the Province for enlisting Volunteers for His Majesty's Service in a Regiment of Foot to be forthwith raised for the Service and Defence of His Majesty's Colonies in North America." [14] This force served until the conclusion of the war in 1763, when it was disbanded, its members returning to the ranks of the militia. By their experience in the trainbands, but more especially by their service in actual war, many Massachusetts men had become familiar with the duties of a soldier. Not all of them, however, were to be useful in the coming struggle with Great Britain. Many were strong in their allegiance to the crown, in whose support they had fought.

When Gage came to Boston, the colonels of perhaps a full half of the thirty Massachusetts militia regiments were stanch Loyalists, who would in no event call out their men for action against the King's troops. The major general, the head of the entire force of militia, was a Tory. To remedy this condition, the Worcester Convention prevailed upon all the officers of that colony's three regiments to resign. It then provided for the organization of its militia in seven regiments, the towns to elect the company officers, who should choose the field officers. It went beyond this by directing the officers of each company to enlist a third of their men to be ready to act "at a minute's notice," these new companies to be made up into regiments. This was the origin of the famous minutemen.

The Worcester idea spread through the colony. Patriot officers willingly resigned, and Tories were so intimidated that they also gave up their commissions. The Provincial Congress, when assembled at Concord in October, 1774, approved the plan and directed that it be followed throughout the colony. Thus the militia of the province was rid of its Tory officers, and, as the minutemen were chosen with regard to the soundness of their political principles, the patriotism of their regiments was assured.

The minutemen have bulked large in the romance of the Revolution; but they had, in fact, a brief existence and were of little importance in the war. The formation of their regiments proceeded slowly; Woburn, for example, voted the establishment of its regiment as late as April 17, 1775, only two days before the Lexington-Concord engagements. In that same month, the Provincial Congress decided to abandon the scheme, to rely no longer upon the militia and the minutemen and to enlist, for a term of eight months, an army of 13,600 volunteers, thus reverting to the system used in the French and Indian War. It recognized the existence of the minutemen regiments by providing that their officers be given preference for commissions in the new army. Thus the minuteman passed out of existence after a career of no more than six months in the earliest companies and of a few days in the latest.[15]

There was a third class of soldiers in the Massachusetts militia scheme, the "alarm companies." These were not, as might be supposed, to be called out on the first alarm. They were, in fact, a last resort, an ultimate reserve, being composed of boys, old men, magistrates, and clergymen. Naturally, they were of little importance in the conflict.[16]

But few of these Massachusetts troops, of any class, were uniformed. The great majority came to their training days and turned out on alarms in their civilian clothes. Their guns were of any sort: brown Bess muskets surviving the French and Indian War; muskets issued in King George's War thirty years before; even perhaps a few Queen's arms, twice as old, dating from Queen Anne's War; American-made muskets of all dates; fowling pieces, blunderbusses, any kind of gun that would fire bullets or buckshot, except rifles. The rifled gun was unknown in New England, so that John Adams in Philadelphia attending the First Continental Congress wrote to his wife of "a peculiar kind of musket, called a rifle," used by "riflemen . . . from Pennsylvania, Maryland and Virginia . . . the most accurate marksmen in the world." [17]

The accouterments of the American militia were few and simple; a powder horn and a bullet pouch or a cartridge box, a bullet mold, and a bag of extra flints were the essentials. There might be added a haversack and a rolled blanket. Some of them, not many, had bayonets.[18]

CHAPTER 4

Lexington

During all the months from Gage's arrival in May of 1774 through the summer, fall, and winter, the British army lay inactive in Boston. No hostile move into the surrounding country was made, except Leslie's fruitless expedition to Salem. There were, however, a few peaceful excursions to exercise the troops, which were viewed with suspicion by the Provincial Congress. One day in February it interrupted its morning session at Concord to appoint a committee "to observe the motions of the troops said to be on their way to this town." [1] These expeditions, though harmless in themselves, did forebode more purposeful forays; Gage had not forgotten the stores of provincial munitions at Concord and Worcester. Also they put the Americans on the alert.

Late in February, Gage sent Captain Brown and Ensign De Berniere with one private to sketch the roads and test the political situation in Suffolk and Worcester counties. They were disguised, in "brown cloathes and reddish handkerchiefs" around their necks, so carefully that a Negro serving maid in the first tavern they stopped at recognized them at once as British soldiers and told their man that if they went much further "they would meet with very bad usage." At the next tavern the landlord, contrary to Yankee custom, asked them no questions at all, because "he had seen all he wanted without needing to ask." Farther on, they were overtaken by a horseman who looked them over carefully "and then rode off pretty hard." Later certain other equestrians asked them point-blank whether they were British soldiers, and at Marlborough they found the town "alive and buzzing." If they had not precipitately departed in the darkness of night from a certain Loyalist's house there, they would have been seized by the Committee of Correspondence for the town, which a few minutes later searched the house from garret to cellar. They got back to Boston thoroughly convinced that the political situation west of Boston might be very much better indeed without being too good, and that to surprise Concord invisible troops would be needed.[2]

By March, the tension in the people's minds was so great that a simple exercise march aroused the countryside; "expresses were sent to every town near," a couple of cannon were posted on the Watertown bridge, the planks were removed from the bridge at Cambridge, and the Provincial Congress voted that whenever troops of the number of 500 marched out of Boston "the Military Force of the Province ought to be assembled." [3] This nervous apprehension was nowhere more intense than among the patriots in Boston itself.

Thousands of men in that town were out of work, with nothing to do but loaf on street corners, loiter near the fortifications on the Neck, linger about the wharves, watch what was going on, and talk about what they saw. Paul Revere, silversmith, engraver, and ingenious craftsman, as well as express rider when important news was to be carried to New York or Philadelphia, had a group of watchmen "chiefly mechanics." They patrolled the streets, met secretly, exchanged the results of their observations, and reported them to Dr. Joseph Warren, who conveyed them to the Committee of Safety at Concord. Several other secret societies were similarly engaged. There was not much done in Boston that was not observed.[4]

When on April 15 the grenadiers and light infantry were ordered "off all duties 'till further orders" to learn "new evolutions," Lieutenant John Barker of the King's Own was not alone in suspecting this was "by way of a blind" and there was "something for them to do." [5] Revere's patrolmen were equally suspicious. They had an eye on the waterfront, and they had already seen the boats belonging to the transport vessels, which had been hauled up for repairs, "launched and carried under the sterns of the men of War." They too "expected something serious was to be transacted." [6] And, Yankee-fashion, they guessed, and guessed right, that an expedition was being prepared to go by boat across Back Bay to East Cambridge and so by road to Concord. Next morning Warren sent Revere to Lexington to warn John Hancock and Samuel Adams.

Returning to Boston that night, Revere arranged with "a Col. Conant & some other Gentlemen" in Charlestown "that if the British went out by water, we would shew two lanthorns in the North Church Steeple, and if by land [across the Neck] one, as a signal." This arrangement was made, not to inform Revere himself awaiting it in Charlestown booted and spurred and "impatient to mount and ride," as in Longfellow's poem, but to notify Conant and the "other Gentlemen" so that they might send word to Concord and elsewhere, Revere being "apprehensive" it would be difficult for him to cross the Charles River, "or git over Boston neck." [7]

Gage had planned a secret expedition to surprise Concord. To intercept wayfarers and prevent news of the foray from anticipating it, he sent mounted officers on the afternoon of April 18 to patrol the roads. The soldiers to be engaged in the enterprise were not to be notified until just before the time to march, when they were to be awakened "by the sergeants putting their hands on them and whispering gently to them" and "conducted by a back way out of the barracks without the knowledge of their comrades." The strictest silence was to be observed by everyone concerned.[8] But Boston's ears were cocked, and not all the British soldiers were muzzled.

One Jasper, a gunsmith, is said to have heard about the intended move in the afternoon from a British sergeant. John Ballard, a stableman, is reported to have overheard someone in the Province House say that there would be "hell to pay to-morrow." Earl Percy had been taken into Gage's confidence that evening; while crossing the Common immediately afterward, he heard one man say to another, "The British troops have marched, but they will miss their aim." "What aim?" inquired his lordship. "Why, the cannon at Concord." [9] Solomon Brown, a young man of Lexington, met the interception committee on his way home from Boston. He carried the news to William Munroe, sergeant of the Lexington minutemen, who collected eight of his company and posted them as a guard over the house where Hancock and Samuel Adams were lodging, to prevent their being kidnaped, and sent three others back toward Boston to watch the British patrol.[10]

Joseph Warren had the news before the British expedition had more than started from the barracks. He sent for Revere and William Dawes, another experienced express rider. Dawes was the first to come and was immediately dispatched to Lexington, to warn Hancock and Samuel Adams, and then to Concord. Revere arrived at Warren's house soon after Dawes. There were two main roads leading to Concord. One was by way of the Neck towards Roxbury, then around to Cambridge and Menotomy—now Arlington—and on through Lexington; it was much the longer. The other went from Charlestown to Medford and then to Menotomy, where it joined the other. Dawes managed to elude the guard at the Neck by mingling in the darkness with some soldiers passing that way, and took the first road. Revere stayed long enough to get his boots and surtout and to bid Captain John

Pulling, Jr., set the two lanterns in the Old North Church steeple. Two friends then rowed him with muffled oars across the river to Charlestown. Conant and some others, having seen the lights in the steeple, were at the wharf to meet him. A horse was furnished, and about eleven o'clock he was on his way.[11]

For this expedition, Gage had detached the grenadier and light infantry companies from his regiments, under general command of Lieutenant Colonel Francis Smith of the 10th foot. Major John Pitcairn of the marines led the light infantry, which marched in advance.[12] The number of men in the detachment is variously stated, from 600 to 800.[13]

They assembled at the foot of Boston Common at about half past ten in the evening of the 18th of April, embarked in boats on the Back Bay, and crossed to Lechmere Point, opposite the north end of the town. Because the water was too shallow to allow the boats to touch dry land, the men had to wade ashore. Lieutenant John Barker of the 4th (King's Own) regiment has described the subsequent proceedings: "After getting over the Marsh where we were wet up to the knees, we were halted in a dirty road and stood there 'till two o'clock in the morning waiting for provisions to be brought up from the boats and to be divided, and which most of the Men threw away, having carried some with 'em. At 2 oclock we began our March by wading through a very long ford up to our Middles." Thus inauspiciously began the journey to Concord.[14]

In the meantime, Dawes and Revere were speeding on their errands of alarm. Dawes met with no obstacles or interruptions, but Revere encountered a number of difficulties. He had intended to cut across from the road through Medford to Cambridge and so on to Menotomy, but he had hardly entered the crossroad before he saw two horsemen waiting in his path, British officers. "I was near enough to see their Holsters & cockades." One started toward him; but he wheeled about and "rid at full Gallop" back to the main road and so through Medford, alarming the dwellers of roadside houses as he went. At Medford he called on Captain Hull to turn out his company of minutemen. He woke up Menotomy and the houses beyond it and at last came to Lexington about midnight. At Parson Clarke's house he called on the guard to let him in. The sergeant asked him not to make so much noise, the family were asleep. "Noise!" Revere is reported to have said. "You'll have noise enough before long. The regulars are coming out!" That was enough. Hancock and Adams prepared for a hasty escape.[15]

Revere waited at Clarke's house half an hour for Dawes to come up by the longer road, and together they set out again for Concord. They were overtaken by young Dr. Samuel Prescott, who was returning home from a long evening with his sweetheart in Lexington. The three went on, alarming the houses they passed. About halfway between the two towns, they met two British officers, and two more emerged from a field beside the road. Dawes wheeled his horse about and rode hard back to Lexington. Revere and Prescott were ordered, at pistol point, to turn off the road into a pasture lot. Doing this, they immediately put spurs on their horses to escape in different directions. Prescott jumped his over a stone wall and got away. Revere struck out for a wood, but was met and taken by six other officers who had been concealed there. With them appeared three other prisoners, the men who had been sent out by Sergeant Munroe from Lexington to observe the enemy. That was the end of the Ride of Paul Revere.

He was dismounted and questioned. He told his captors that the country had been alarmed and that five hundred men were assembling at Lexington. They heard "a voley of [alarm] Guns, which appeared to alarm them very much." They took Revere's horse for one of their sergeants, gave him the small nag the sergeant had ridden, marched them all back toward Lexington, cut the bridles and girths of their captives' horses, drove them away, and rode off. Revere walked back to Clarke's house, found Hancock and Adams ready to leave, and went with them to Burlington in a chaise driven by the parson's son.[16]

Colonel Smith was so determined to preserve the secrecy of the foray that, on leaving the "dirty road" at Lechmere Point, he avoided the bridge across Willis Creek, for fear that the tramping of his men upon its planks might give the alarm, and led them through the ford mentioned by Barker. So, wet to the waist, they marched on through the cold night. Sometime after two o'clock, they halted in Somerville to let the men drink at a well. Then they went on, picking up prisoners here and there to prevent an alarm. Cambridge was next; then, at three o'clock, Menotomy, where three members of the Provincial Congress heard their tramp-tramp, fled from their beds in their nightgear, and hid in a field of corn stubble. Here six companies of light infantry, under Pitcairn, were detached and sent ahead. Now they were drawing near to Lexington.[17]

All through the night, as they passed through town after town, men awoke, dressed, took to horse, and rode away to call out the thousands who were finally to overwhelm these redcoats.

At Lexington, Revere's alarm at midnight had called out Captain Jonas Parker and his company of minutemen. One hundred and thirty of them gathered on the village green; but no more news came and the night was cold. After they had stood around cheerlessly and, as it seemed, pointlessly for an hour or so, Parker dismissed them with orders to respond again at the beating of the drum. Many went back to their near-by homes; the rest waited in Buckman's tavern close to the green.[18]

At half past four came the expected news. Riding at full gallop, Thaddeus Bowman brought it. The British were coming! They were close at hand, less than half a mile behind him! Alarm guns were fired. The minutemen in the tavern came on the run; others came from their houses. But some had no ammunition. They hurried to the meetinghouse, where the town's supply was kept. Men without guns gathered to look on. There was confusion all about the green. Finally, seventy armed men at the most were drawn up in two lines spaced somewhat apart.[19]

Lexington Green was a triangle bordered by roads. The road from Boston to Concord ran along its base.[20] Parker's men were drawn up not more than a hundred yards from this road, by which the British must march. What Parker expected to do with his three score men against Smith's six or eight hundred no one knows. He would protect the town, someone has suggested. But such an effort was hopeless, and besides Lexington was in no danger from the British. Their object, as everyone knew, was the stores at Concord. None of the towns on the way had been molested. Gallant as Parker's stand may have been, it was in effect nothing more than a challenge to the enemy which, if accepted, could only result, as it did, in futile bloodshed.[21]

It was a cold day for the season of the year, with a strong east wind; but the sky was blue, and the sun shone clear. The polished steel of ordered ranks of gun barrels and bayonets glittered brightly as Pitcairn's column came in sight, and one of the Americans saw the situation in its true proportions. "There are so few of us," he said, "it is folly to stand here." "The first man who offers to run shall be shot down," replied Parker. So there they stood, an offering for a sacrifice.[22]

Pitcairn's six light companies came on in column of march and saw the minutemen in form to oppose them. The Marine Major ordered his men into line of battle. As was customary, the rear ranks came forward at the double to line up with those in front, shouting and huzzaing as they ran. To the militia it appeared that they "rushed furiously," as if with bloody intent; but they only formed a line three deep in two sections or platoons, a little apart from each other.

Parker gave an order to his men: "Stand your ground! Don't fire unless fired upon! But if they want to have a war, let it begin here!" Some of the men, nevertheless, did drift away.

Pitcairn, with two other officers, rode to the front, within a hundred feet of Parker's lines. "Lay down your arms, you damned rebels, and disperse!"

Parker at last saw the hopelessness of the situation and ordered his men to disband and not to fire. They began to melt away, taking their muskets.

"Lay down your arms! Damn you! Why don't you lay down your arms?" shouted Pitcairn.

"Damn them! We will have them!" cried one of the officers, meaning the rebels' muskets.

Then there was a single shot, and from some one of the British officers, not Pitcairn, a command: "Fire, by God! Fire!" A volley from one platoon rang out—"They did not take sight," says a witness; the bullets went high over the Americans' heads. Pitcairn "struck his staff or Sword downward with all Earnestness as a signal to forbear or cease firing," but without avail. "The Soldiery and young Officers wanted to have at the damned Dogs, & in their impetuosity burst out into firing & continued it contrary to the Command of Pitcairn." [23] There was another volley that tore through the already retreating American ranks, answered by the feeble discharge of a scattered few, and then the Redcoats charged. Jonas Parker had fired once and had been wounded by a bullet; yet he stood his ground and was reloading his gun when he was cut down—his is a name worthy of remembrance. The rest fled, the British firing at them as long as they were within range. Eight dead men lay on the ground; ten wounded got away. Of the British, one private was slightly wounded in the leg, and Pitcairn's horse was grazed in a couple of places. The British officers had great difficulty in re-forming their men, who "were so wild they cou'd hear no orders." [24] When they were formed at last and when Smith with the main body came up, they fired a volley, gave a great cheer for their victory, "the musick struck up"—there was no hope of secrecy now—and they started off toward Concord, just as the sun rose.

That was the famous Battle of Lexington, which of course was no battle at all, not even a skirmish, for there was no contest. But who fired the first shot is a question unanswered after 165 years. The older American historians patriotically say Pitcairn. George Bancroft, for example, says so baldly and asserts further that he gave the order to fire; and so does John Fiske. For many years Pitcairn has been held in odium as a murderer of unresisting men, a "bloody butcher." But he denied it; he "insisted upon it to the day of his Death" at Bunker Hill "that the Colonists fired first: & that he commanded not to fire & endeavored to stay & stop the firing after it begun." Ezra Stiles, President of Yale College, recording this denial, believed that he was innocent, that he fired no shot and gave his men no order to fire, but that he was deceived as to the origin of the first shots. Stiles suggested, most reasonably, that these came from some of the British soldiers behind Pitcairn "as he turned to give Orders" not to fire, and regarded him as "a Man of Integrity & Honor" which, indeed, he was.[25] Pitcairn has been characterized truly as "a man whose humanity and tact had won him the love of his command, and the respect of people of all shades of opinion in the town . . . a brave and humane man." [26] His fall in battle two months later so grieved his command that their firing "slackened for some minutes, many of his men echoing these words—'We have lost a father!' " [27] A certificate of character not lightly to be disregarded.

CHAPTER 5

Concord

The alarm had gone forth, not only by Revere and Dawes to Lexington, but far and wide throughout eastern Massachusetts. Conant and his friends at Charlestown took care of the country roundabout; and from town to town, as the news came, riders carried it on posthaste. Lynn, ten miles to the north, was awakened in the early morning. Billerica, seventeen miles northwest, was aroused by two in the morning, and Acton, five miles farther, soon after. So it spread by an interlacing of expresses. Woburn was out before break of day. Reading at sunrise heard the alarm guns. At Danvers bells rang and drums beat at nine o'clock. At Tewksbury, twenty miles from Boston, a hard-riding messenger awoke Captain John Trull about two o'clock, and Trull fired his gun to awaken General Varnum at Dracut across the Merrimack. Andover, twenty-five miles away, heard the alarm at sunrise; Pepperell, thirty-five miles, at nine o'clock. Before noon, a white horse, dripping with sweat and bloody from the spur, galloped into Worcester, its rider crying: "To arms! To arms! the war has begun!" and it reached the church before it fell exhausted. So the news spread. Everywhere in the counties of Middlesex, Essex, Norfolk, and Worcester bells, guns, and drums called out the minutemen. Everywhere they were afoot and on the march.[1]

To Concord young Dr. Prescott, who had escaped when Revere was captured, brought the evil tidings between one and two o'clock in the morning. The alarm bell was rung, and the first to respond, gun in hand, was the Reverend William Emerson, minister of that town. Then came the minutemen, Captain David Brown's company, Captain Charles Miles's, and Captain Nathan Barrett's. Captain George Minot's alarm company of old men and boys gathered with the rest at Wright's tavern on the town square. Uncertain as to the truth of the news, they sent a messenger back to Lexington to confirm it. Meanwhile, they set about removing and hiding the military stores.[2]

The chief depository was at Colonel James Barrett's house. After the first alarm he hurried home, and the work of concealment and removal went on. Much of the stores had been sent away the day before. Now musket balls, flints, and cartridges were put into barrels in the attic and covered with feathers. Powder was hauled into the woods and hidden. A plow was got out, furrows were struck in a near-by field; light cannon and muskets were laid in them, and other furrows covered them up. By this and that means, the movable articles were put away.[3]

The road from Lexington, as it approached Concord, swung in a curve along the base of a long, narrow ridge which rose abruptly from the plain to a height of sixty feet. Near the end of this ridge lay the principal buildings of the village, the meetinghouse, courthouse, two or three taverns, and perhaps twenty-five dwelling houses. Passing these, it swung to the right beside a similar elevation at right angles to the first, turned squarely to the left, crossed the so-called North Bridge over the Concord River, beyond which was a third eminence two hundred feet high, called Punkatasset Hill, and so went on to Colonel Barrett's place, the chief objective of the British expedition.[4]

The first reinforcements of the little Concord companies came from nearby Lincoln, Captain William Smith's company. The force assembled now made up "150 of us or more." It seemed proper to make a reconnaissance. "We thought," wrote Corporal Amos Barrett of Brown's company, "we wood go and meet the Britsch . . . We marched Down to wards L[exington] about a mild or a mild [and a] half and we see them acomming. we halted and stay[d] till they got within about 100 Rods then we was orded to the about face and march[d] before them with our Droms and fifes agoing and also the B[ritish]. we had grand musick." [5] So, with rattle of drum and squeal of fife came the war to Concord.

Captain Minot's alarm company, the Reverend William Emerson wrote in his diary, had taken post on the first ridge above the meetinghouse, where stood the Liberty Pole, as the most advantageous situation—that is to say, at the end of the first ridge overlooking the town. But, with the news that the enemy "were just upon us & that we must retreat, as their N[o] [number] was more than thribble ours," the old men and boys withdrew to the second ridge overlooking the bridge. The able-bodied minutemen, however, held their station on the first ridge.[6] It was now about seven o'clock in the morning.

The British came on, the light infantry in advance, followed by the grenadiers. Seeing the provincials on the height above the road, Colonel Smith threw out the light troops as flankers to clear the ridge, while the grenadiers kept to the road. Pitcairn's men "ascended the height in one line, upon which the Yankees quitted it without firing," [7] and retired to the second ridge already occupied by the alarm company.

"Scarcely had we form'd," says the clergyman's diary, "before we saw ye brittish Troops, at the Distance of a ¼ of a Mile, glittering in Arms, advancing toward [us] with ye greatest celerity. . . . Some were for making a Stand notw[ithstanding] ye Super[iority] of y^r^ [their] N^o^ but others more prudent tho't best to retreat till our Strenth sh'd be equal to ye Enemy's by Recruits from neigh^g^ [neighboring] towns y^t^ were contin[ually] coming into our Assistance." [8] Colonel James Barrett, in general command of the militia of the district, had now returned from his work of concealing the stores. He ordered all the Americans to withdraw across the bridge, take post on Punkatasset Hill, and await reinforcements.[9]

Without hindrance the British came on into the village. Three of the light companies, under Captain Laurie, were stationed to guard the North Bridge: one at its eastern end, the two others on two near-by hills. Three others, led by Captain Parsons, crossed the bridge and marched up the road to Colonel Barrett's place; and the rest, under Captain Pole, were posted about the South Bridge.

While the British superior officers refreshed themselves in the taverns, carefully paying for what they had, the grenadiers began to search the houses.[10]

The search was not very successful, nor was the loss to the Americans very severe. Two 24-pound iron cannon were found in the town and their trunnions broken off—but they were later repaired. A hundred barrels of flour were found, and some were broken open; the others were rolled into the millpond—but the outer flour swelled and waterproofed the rest, so that much of it was salvaged. Five hundred pounds of musket bullets were thrown into the millpond, but most of them were afterwards dredged up.[11] A number of gun carriages were destroyed by fire, together with a lot of trenching tools and some wooden spoons and trenchers; and the British set fire to the courthouse and a blacksmith shop, but soon extinguished the flames themselves. All in all, the rewards of this laborious and, as it proved to be, fatal expedition, were small indeed.[12]

Meanwhile, the men on Punkatasset Hill had moved down to a smaller elevation nearer the bridge. On that little mound clouds had been gathering that were soon to break into a storm. From Acton, minutemen, 38 of them under Captain Isaac Davis, and two companies of militia of unknown numbers, Simon Hunt and Joseph Robin commanding, were the first to arrive. Bedford answered the call with John Moore's and Jonathan Willson's minutemen, 79 strong. William Smith had brought 62 from Lincoln. Unattached volunteers made up a force of three or four hundred. They watched the grenadiers at work in the town, and saw smoke rising from they knew not what fires. Colonel Barrett consulted with his officers. Joseph Hosmer, adjutant, came to them with a question: "Will you let them burn the town down?" They answered with a decision "to march into the middle of the town for its defence or die in the attempt." [13] Barrett gave the order. They were to march, but not to fire until fired upon. So down the hill they marched to do battle with the flower of the King's army.

Major John Buttrick with Lieutenant Colonel John Robinson of Westford at his side led the procession. Isaac Davis's little Acton company in double column, two fifers shrilling the notes of "The White Cockade," two drums beating time to the tune followed. Miles's Concord company fell in next, and then Brown's and Barrett's. Hunt followed with his Acton militia. Bedford and Lincoln and the unattached volunteers closed the column.[14]

Captain Laurie, in command at the bridge, saw them coming and sent to Colonel Smith for reinforcements. Smith ordered two or three companies forward, "but put himself at their head by which means he stopt 'em from being [in] time enough, for being a very fat heavy Man he wou'd not have reached the Bridge in half an hour tho' it was not half a mile to it." [15]

Laurie withdrew his men to the east end of the bridge, leaving a few to take up the planks. Buttrick shouted to the men at work to stop and quickened the pace of his militia. For some unknown reason, the men lifting the planks stopped and went back to their own ranks. Laurie tried to dispose his men to resist the Americans, but "the Rebels got so near him that his people were obliged to form the best way They cou'd . . . the three companies got one behind the other so that only the front one cou'd fire: the Rebels when they got near the bridge halted and fronted, filling the road from top to bottom." [16]

The first fire came from the British, two or three "dropping shots" that splashed harmlessly in the water. But one bullet whistled by the ear of one of the captains. In utter astonishment, "God damn it! They're firing ball!" exclaimed Captain Timothy Brown. Then came a single shot from the British. The bullet struck Luther Blanchard, one of the fifers who had played them down the hill, in the side, making a slight wound. Then a volley rang out. Captain Isaac Davis, at the head of the Acton company, sprang high in the air and fell dead; Abner Hosmer, also of Acton, collapsed on the ground with a bullet through his head. Two others were wounded. Buttrick turned to his men and shouted, "Fire, fellow soldiers! For God's sake, fire!" And they did. Three British privates fell dead; four out of the eight British officers at the bridge, a sergeant and four men were wounded.[17]

The fight at the bridge was all over in two or three minutes. The British retreated in disorder towards the village, leaving their dead and one wounded man, met Smith's reinforcement of grenadiers, re-formed their ranks, and withdrew into the village. The Americans crossed the bridge and pursued the enemy, but only for a few rods. Then, undisciplined as they were, they broke ranks. A number of them went back across the bridge, picked up the bodies of Davis and Hosmer, and carried them off. About two hundred went a little farther, to the near end of the ridge on which they had taken their second position earlier in the day. Strung along behind a stone wall, they waited; but the enemy never came within range. Because of this disruption of the American force, the British light companies under Captain Parsons that had gone to Barrett's place were able to return, cross the bridge, and rejoin their comrades unscathed.[18]

Smith's grenadiers and the light companies from the bridge got back to the village about ten o'clock. An hour later, Parsons's men joined them. Another hour elapsed before they were ready for the return march. At noon they set out, having commandeered two chaises to carry their wounded.[19]

For the first mile, they marched unmolested. But then followed one of the strangest battles of the war, nearly sixteen miles long and a few hundred yards wide. It began at Meriam's Corner on the road to Lexington.

Only three to four hundred men had been in the fight at the bridge; but others had been on the way. Chelmsford sent 60 under Captain Oliver Barron and 43 under Moses Parker. Oliver Crosby, Edward Farmer, and Jonathan Stickney brought a hundred from Billerica. Framingham turned out 147 under Simon Edgett, Jesse Emes, and Micajah Gleason. The roads were black with hurrying men. Reading outnumbered the other towns with 290 men in four companies, Captains John Bacheller, Thomas Eaton, John Flint, and John Walton commanding. Woburn "turned out extraordinary" and rivaled Reading with 256 led by Samuel Belknap, Jonathan Fox, and Joshua Walker; and Sudbury's six companies, numbering 249, under Nathaniel Endworth, Aaron Haynes, Isaac Locker, John Nixon, Joseph Smith, and Moses Stone, were a good third. William Whitcomb led 81 from

Stow, while Westford added 113 under Oliver Bates, Jonathan Minot, and Joshua Parker.[20]

The men who had fought at the bridge had hurried northward across the Great Meadow to Meriam's Corner. The rest had followed or came up with them there. A few companies were gathered about the Meriam house. Smith had thrown out flanking parties parallel to the highway and at some distance from it on either side. As those on the side of the road nearer the house passed by, they wheeled suddenly and fired a harmless volley. The Americans replied, and two of the enemy fell; others were wounded. So this second battle began.[21]

Nearing a small stream, the flankers went down to the road to cross a bridge with the others. Dense groves of trees lined the road at this point; they were full of Americans, who had hurried ahead. Into the crowd pressing across the bridge, they poured a deadly fire. "A grait many Lay dead and the Road was bloddy." [22]

The British column went on. The Americans hurried to get ahead, take cover, and fire again. Parker's company from Lexington, now with full ranks, 120 strong and hot with anger, joined the hunters in Lincoln township. From Cambridge came Captain Thatcher's company, 77 men. Others from the near-by countryside flocked to them. "It seemed as if men came down from the clouds." [23] From houses and barns, from behind walls, rocks, and trees came flashes of flame and puffs of smoke, and redcoats dropped, the dead to lie where they fell, the wounded to keep on as best they could and as long as they could. To some of the British, it was a new sort of warfare, not the kind they had been drilled for, where men faced each other and shot it out, where a bayonet charge might prove decisive. It was dishonorable, this hiding and shooting at men who could not even see you. It was downright savagery. Their anger was fierce, the more bitter because it had so little vent in reprisal. "They were so concealed," said Lieutenant Barker, "there was hardly any seeing them." [24]

But it was not all one-sided. The flanking parties, well back from the road, were sometimes forgotten by the too eager Americans, who were between them and the main column. Many were shot in the back as they were drawing trigger from behind a wall or tree. The flankers took a heavy toll of their adversaries.

The British force was no longer a marching column. It was a disorderly mass of men crowding the road. Soldiers were leaving what had been ordered ranks, ransacking roadside houses and taverns for meat and drink. As they entered Lexington township, Smith halted his men and posted a rear guard to hold back the Americans while he re-formed his ranks. But there was no pursuing force to hold back. Their enemies were all around them on every side. From behind a pile of rails came a blast of fire. Smith was wounded in the leg. Pitcairn's horse plunged, threw its rider, leaped a wall, and ran directly toward the ambuscade. It was captured, and Pitcairn's pistols are now preserved in an American museum.[25]

The attempt to reorganize was not successful. The rearguard was driven in, and the rout continued. Barker reports of this time that the Americans were "increasing from all parts," while the British were "reducing from deaths, wounds and fatigue, and we were totally surrounded with such an incessant fire as it's impossible to conceive, our ammunition was likewise near expended." [26] De Berniere likewise describes the confusion of the British: "When we arrived within a mile of Lexington, our ammunition began to fail, and the light companies were so fatigued with flanking they were scarce able to act, and a great number of wounded scarce able to get forward made a great confusion . . . so that we began to run rather than retreat in order—the whole behaved with amazing bravery, but little order; we attempted to stop the men, but to no purpose, the confusion increased rather than lessened." [27]

So they passed through the village, along the edge of the green, where the conflict had begun that morning. With the least bit of organization among the Americans, Smith's force might have been stopped there, surrounded, and either taken or destroyed. But it was not an American army that so pursued and hemmed them in; it was simply a horde of angry, revengeful, individual men, each on his own, with no coherence, no concert of action. So the invaders were permitted to stumble on, fatigued to the last degree, but still able to go a little farther before they fell utterly exhausted.

There was one more effort to reduce the confusion in the British ranks. Near Lexington village "the officers got to the front and presented their bayonets, and told the men that if they advanced they should die: Upon this they began to form under a very heavy fire." [28] It was the last gasp of British discipline, before those beaten men fell on their faces under the protection of a rescue party.

When Smith had first got to Menotomy, between two and three o'clock in the morning, he had been alarmed by the increasing and seemingly hostile curiosity of the countryside about the movement of his force and had sent an express back to Boston asking for reinforcements. But Gage had already anticipated the need of relief for his Concord expedition and had given orders in the evening of the 18th for the 1st brigade and a battalion of the Royal Marines to parade at four o'clock the next morning—a reasonable precaution which was largely nullified by a series of errors.[29]

First, the brigade major was not at home when the orders were delivered to his servant. He came in late, and his man forgot to tell him about them. There was no parade at four o'clock. At five, Smith's express arrived, and the matter was looked into. At six, part of the brigade was on parade, but no marines. That stirred inquiry again, and it was found that the orders had been addressed to Pitcairn, and left at his quarters, he being then on the way to Concord. It was nine o'clock when the relief started, a delay nearly fatal to Smith's force.[30]

The relief consisted of the 4th or King's Own Regiment, the 23rd, Royal Welch Fusiliers, the 47th, less their flank companies who were with Smith, and the 1st battalion of marines with two 6-pound fieldpieces. The whole force numbered about 1,000, and was under the command of Brigadier General Earl Percy. With all their fifes and drums derisively playing "Yankee Doodle," they marched across the Neck.[31]

Percy was the son and heir of the Duke of Northumberland. There is a legend that as his force passed through Roxbury a schoolboy laughed so heartily at the tune the fifers were playing that Percy asked him the reason. He answered, "To think how you will dance by and by to Chevy Chase," the reference being to the ballad in which appears this verse:

> To drive the deer with hound and horne
> Erle Percy took his way.
> The child may rue that is unborne
> The hunting of that day! [32]

At Cambridge the planks of the bridge across the Charles had been lifted, but piled on the far side. Soldiers crossed on the stringpieces and replaced them; but the supply train of two wagons with its guard of twelve men had to wait until they could be well secured, and then proceeded far in the rear of the column. It soon fell easy prey to a dozen "old men of Menotomy," led by a half-breed Indian, who took both wagons and supplies after two of the guard had been killed and several wounded by a discharge of musketry from behind a stone wall.[33]

Percy was beyond Menotomy village when he first heard the sounds of warfare.[34] "As we advanced," Lieutenant Frederick Mackenzie of the Royal Welch Fusiliers wrote in his diary, "we heard the firing plainer and more frequent, and at half after 2, being near the Church at Lexington, and the fire encreasing, we were ordered to form the Line, which was immediately done by extending on each side of the road. The Grenadiers & Light Infantry were at this time retiring towards Lexington, fired upon by the Rebels, who took every advantage the face of the Country afforded them." But as soon as they "perceived the 1st Brigade drawn up for their support, they shouted repeatedly, and the firing ceased for a short time." [35]

It was high time for a rescue. "We had been flatter'd ever since the morning," says Barker, "with expectations of the Brigade coming out, but at this time had given up all hopes of it." [36] The wasted remnants of Smith's command hurried to the protection of Percy's line, "so much exhausted with fatigue, that they were obliged to lie down for rest on the ground, their tongues hanging out of their mouths, like those of dogs after a chase." [37]

"We could observe a Considerable number of the Rebels, but they were much scattered and not above 50 of them to be seen in a body in any place. Many lay concealed behind the Stone walls and fences. They appeared most numerous in the road near the Church and in a wood in the front and on the left flank of the line." [38] On these Percy trained his guns, harming only the church, through which he sent one ball, while the provincials retired behind a swamp. Some of his men, seeing the Americans retire, broke from their ranks in pursuit, but the swamp stopped them. They then entered the village, looted some houses, and burned one large group of farm buildings and several dwellings.[39]

All this while, the Americans were dodging here and there, creeping around the enemy's flanks, appearing and disappearing as they took cover behind trees, walls, and houses, sniping or firing small volleys, and inflicting much injury upon the massed British troops.

Percy gave the exhausted men an hour's rest. At half past three he resumed the retreat, with Smith's men in front covered by the fresh troops and strong parties on the flanks. The more impressive array of the combined forces and the vigilance of the flankers somewhat daunted the Americans, and, for a time, the British marched in comparative safety. Of necessity they proceeded slowly, and there was a fine chance to loot the roadside houses. Percy exercised no restraint on such depredations. He evidently wished to terrorize the countryside. Many of his men carried heavy burdens of household goods of all sorts. But as he neared Menotomy the aspect of affairs began to change again. The Americans were pressing more closely on his rear guard and against his passing column, and the firing from cover grew stronger and stronger, for his enemies were rapidly increasing in numbers. New companies of minutemen and militia had been hurrying to the battle from the eastern towns and now were arriving.

Brookline brought 95 men into play; Watertown, 134; Medford, 59;

Malden, 76; Roxbury, 140. Needham sent 185; Beverly, 122. Menotomy turned out 52, and Danvers, 331. Dedham was left "almost literally without a male inhabitant before the age of seventy and above that of sixteen"; its 337 topped all the rest.[40] There were 2,000 or more men to resume the attack. General William Heath and Dr. Joseph Warren urged them on against the British rear guard. Percy halted his column and turned his two 6-pounders on them, but with no effect, except to scatter his pursuers temporarily. So they went on again. The flankers kept the Americans back from the roadside or shot down those who were too reckless in making a near approach. They entered the houses, looted them, tried to burn them. At one point a group of minutemen, too few to stand openly against the enemy, had retreated into a house. Twelve were bayoneted, and the house was plundered. "We were now," says Lieutenant Barker, "obliged to force almost every house in the road, for the Rebels had taken possession of them and galled us exceedingly . . . all that were found in the houses were put to death." [41] The fury of the fight was at its height. Forty Americans fell in Menotomy, and forty British. Many of these were killed in close personal encounter, clubbed muskets against bayonets.

In Cambridge there was a mile and a half of continuous battle. The sight of the burning houses and of the British soldiers loaded down with plunder had inspired the Americans with a fierce rage. If it had been possible to organize them into a single body, get ahead of the column, obstruct the road with felled trees, send out detachments to waylay and destroy the flanking troops, which were not numerically too strong, and, from the stone walls beside the road, concentrate their fire on the main column, Percy's troops might have been held up and destroyed. But there was no central control over the various elements of the American forces, these township companies. Heath at Menotomy tried to form them into regiments; but he had no staff to carry his orders, and, if there had been one, it could not have brought together and reduced to order those half-trained men scattered over the country who did not even preserve their companies as units.[42]

At Cambridge, Percy, to avoid the bridge over the Charles, shrewdly and unexpectedly changed his course from that on which he had come from Boston and took the road to Charlestown. It was shorter as well as safer. But in what is now Somerville he was forced to renew the fight. His fieldpieces were again in action, with no more substantial result than before. Fire from a grove of trees cut down a number of his men. The rest hurried on faster. At Prospect Hill there was a considerable gathering of Americans, and many of the invaders fell. Once more Percy halted his column and made play with the guns, and these were unlimbered again a little farther on. In spite of the harassment of the retreating troops, the looting and destruction of property continued.[43]

The weary, almost exhausted soldiers at the head of the column, Smith's men, had expended almost all their ammunition when, after sunset, they at last crossed the little isthmus that connects Charlestown with the mainland and were free from their pursuers. In the twenty hours that they had been afoot they had marched thirty-five miles, had fought continuously for half that distance, had had little to eat, and many of them had been wounded.

The British losses that day were 73 killed, 174 wounded, 26 missing, a total of 273 casualties out of about 1,800. The Americans lost 49 killed, 41 wounded, and 5 missing, a total of 95. It has been computed that 3,763 Americans were engaged in the day's fighting at one time or another, though perhaps not much more than half that number at any one time.[44]

The fact that in so long a battle, subjected to the fire of so numerous a force, the British lost no more than 15 per cent of their men is noteworthy. If each American, in his whole day's work, had hit his mark only once, the British force would have been destroyed twice over. The militia and minutemen were supposed to carry thirty-six cartridges, or the equivalent in loose powder and bullets. If the average man fired only twenty charges (and we hear of many who fired nearly twice that number) no fewer than 75,000 shots must have been discharged at the enemy, with a total of hardly more than 247 hits. Only one bullet out of 300 found its mark. In all his day's work, only one man out of 15 hit anybody.

It is of course true that the flankers kept the roadside walls and other close cover fairly free of the Americans, compelling them to use the second line of walls at more than point-blank distance from the marching column. It is also true that those same roadside walls protected the British, in some places "almost to the height of their shoulders." [45] Nevertheless, there were many times when a heavy fire was poured upon them at short range, and the results of the entire proceeding should prove the fallaciousness of the belief so often expressed that the Yankees were superior marksmen, dead shots in fact. They were not. They could not be when armed only with the musket or fowling piece of the period. Their inaccuracy and short range have been previously noted, and the Yankees had had little practice in shooting, because of the infrequency of training days and the scarcity and expense of gunpowder.

The comments of the English officers engaged are interesting. That of Percy is noteworthy as showing a change in his opinion that the Americans were "cowards" and "timid creatures." He noted that "many of them concealed themselves in houses & advanced within 10 yds. to fire at me and other officers, tho' they were morally certain of being put to death themselves in an instant . . . nor will the insurrection here turn out so despicable as it is perhaps imagined at home. For my part, I never believed, I confess, that they wd have attacked the King's troops, or have had the perseverance I found in them yesterday." [46]

Lieutenant Barker thought the whole affair was "as ill plan'd and ill executed as it was possible to be." Especially, he complained of the "three hours on Cambridge marsh waiting for provisions that were not wanted." That delay, he thought, allowed the country people to get intelligence of the movement and gave them time to assemble. But for it, there would have been "no interruption at Lexington" and a surprise at Concord.[47]

Captain Evelyn, however, still called "the Yankeys . . . the most absolute cowards on the face of the earth," and attributed their conduct to "enthusiasm and madness." [48]

CHAPTER 6

The Siege of Boston

At ten o'clock in the morning of April 19, Israel Bissel, postrider, mounted his horse at Watertown. In his pocket was a letter:

> *To all Friends of AMERICAN Liberty let it be known:* That this morning before break of day, a Brigade consisting of about one thousand or twelve hundred men . . . Marched to *Lexington* where they . . . Killed 6 Men and wounded 4 Others . . . another Brigade are now upon their March from Boston supposed to be about 1000. The bearer Israel Bissel is charged to alarm the Country quite to Connecticutt and all persons are desired to furnish him with fresh Horses as they may be needed. . . .
>
> J. Palmer—one of the Com^y^ of S^y^

At noon Bissel's horse fell dead at Worcester, thirty-six miles away. No fresh horse was immediately forthcoming, so he spent the night there; but by seven the next evening he was at New London, Connecticut, having given the tidings to Israel Putnam at Pomfret on the way. In the night he went on. Lyme had the news at one o'clock in the morning, Saybrook at four, Guildford at seven, Branford at noon, New Haven in the evening. A night there and on again. Fairfield saw him at four in the afternoon. Connecticut had been alarmed, but Israel Bissel did not stop. He was in New York on the 23rd. There the "faction," as the Loyalists called the Rebels, immediately "paraded the town with drums beating and colours flying." A sloop, loaded with provisions for the British in Boston, was unloaded. The arsenal was entered, and a thousand stand of arms were seized. "The whole city became one continued scene of riot, tumult and confusion. Troops enlisted for the service of the rebellion." So New York, hesitating and doubtful before, was aroused and began to swing into line with the other colonies.

But the furore he had excited did not stay Bissel. He was off again southwards, riding night and day through New Jersey, New Brunswick at two in the morning, Princeton at six, Trenton at nine, then Philadelphia. A feat of endurance was that ride of Israel Bissel's.

A second dispatch, with fuller details, came to New York on the 25th and went on by relays of express riders, again riding night and day. Baltimore had it on the 27th at ten in the evening; Annapolis, at half past nine the next morning; Edenton, North Carolina, on May 4th; and finally, having been given out at every town and village the whole way, it reached Charleston, South Carolina, on the 10th.[1]

From every point on the road the "momentous intelligence" spread to the outlying districts and, by letters and word of mouth, reached the farthest corners of the colonies, the towns on the seaboard, the villages and farms, the backwoods settlements. Everywhere the response was a call to arms.

The veteran Colonel Israel Putnam, who was now retired to his Connecticut farm after having seen hard service in the French and Indian War, was "in leathern frock and apron . . . assisting hired men to build a stone wall' when Bissel brought him the news. He instantly answered the call, in his working clothes. Rousing the militia officers as he rode through the towns, "he reached Cambridge at sunrise the next morning," a hundred miles in eighteen hours on the same horse.[2]

Massachusetts men were flocking to Cambridge even before Putnam had the news. By one o'clock of the 20th, New Hampshire was afoot. Sixty men from Nottingham, joined by others on the way, made the distance to Haverhill, twenty-seven miles, by dusk, "having run rather than marched," and were in Cambridge, fifty-five miles, within twenty hours. Colonel John Stark, hardy backwoodsman, was in command of 300 of his fellow colonists at Chelsea by the morning of the 22nd. Two thousand of them were ready to come the next day.[3]

Connecticut's action was swift; thousands were on the way by the 24th. Rhode Island was on the march before Percy got back to Charlestown. Within the shortest possible time Boston was surrounded from Roxbury to Chelsea by an unorganized, undisciplined mass of men.

The minutemen had never been really organized; their officers had not even been commissioned. As separate bodies they soon ceased to exist. The militia was composed of boys and men varying in age from sixteen years to sixty. The responsibilities of many of them would prevent them from entering upon a continuous campaign. It was no army that surrounded Boston, and what force was there was soon melting away. Within four days after Concord the Massachusetts men, many of whom had departed immediately after the fighting was over, were greatly reduced in numbers, and hundreds from New Hampshire had gone home. General Artemas Ward wrote to the Congress that he was in danger of being "left all alone." [4]

The Massachusetts Provincial Congress, sitting on Sunday April 23, voted that an army of 30,000 men be "immediately raised and established," of which 13,600 were to be "raised immediately by this Province." The thousands needed to make up the full number were not provided for; but committees were sent to the other New England colonies to "request their concurrence." [5]

Rhode Island's assembly promptly voted a brigade of three regiments, 1,500 men, and appointed as brigadier general Nathanael Greene, who was "worth a thousand men" and more.[6] New Hampshire fixed 2,000 as its quota, with Nathaniel Folsom as the major general, but Colonel John Stark "the most trusty officer" in command.[7] Connecticut ordered the enlistment of 6,000, with David Wooster as the major general and Joseph Spencer and Israel Putnam as brigadiers. Of the Massachusetts forces, Artemas Ward, John Thomas, William Heath, John Whitcomb, and Joseph Warren were appointed major generals.[8] Not all the promised thousands materialized; Connecticut never sent more than half her quota; both New Hampshire and Rhode Island fell short of theirs. But, by June, there were perhaps 15,000 men encamped before Boston.

They stretched in a half-circle around Boston, from Roxbury to Chelsea. The center, at Cambridge, was held by Ward with fifteen Massachusetts regiments, Major Samuel Gridley's battalion of four companies of artillery, Putnam's own regiment and other Connecticut troops, 9,000 in all. The right wing, at Roxbury, Dorchester, and Jamaica Plains, was commanded by General Thomas. He had 4,000 Massachusetts men, Greene's Rhode Island regiments, and the greater part of General Spencer's Connecticut troops, three or four artillery companies, a total of about 5,000. On the left, there were three companies of Colonel Samuel Gerrish's Massachusetts regiment at Chelsea; Colonel John Stark's New Hampshire regiment, the largest in the army, at Medford; and the much smaller regiment under Colonel James Reed, also from New Hampshire, near Charlestown Neck, about 1,000 in all from that state.[9]

General Artemas Ward was in supreme command of the Massachusetts troops; and the New Hampshire troops had been directed to place themselves under his orders.[10] The other colonies' forces were at this time amenable only to their own commanders, though Connecticut also submitted her men to Ward's orders after Bunker Hill. Yet from the first they all seem to have cooperated in obedience to Ward.

This hastily assembled force was short of supplies of every kind—arms, ammunition, tents, blankets, provisions, and camp utensils. Of ordnance fit for siege operations, it had practically none—no more than a few large iron cannon, two or three mortars and howitzers. Sixteen fieldpieces, of which perhaps only six were fit for service, constituted their mobile artillery. Late in June, New Hampshire offered "some" 24- and 32-pounders, and the Massachusetts Committee of Safety asked for three of the smaller size.[11]

The supply of small arms was better, for generally each man brought his own firelock; yet more than a thousand men were deficient in this respect in the middle of June. Bayonets were conspicuously lacking, and uniforms almost altogether absent. The greatest shortage was in the most essential element, gunpowder. Much of Massachusetts' small stock had been seized by Gage. Late in April there were but 82 half-barrels available; on May 25 the Committee of Safety drafted 68¼ barrels from five of the eastern counties.[12]

Massachusetts had only 1,100 tents, but set about making more out of ships' sails. As many of the troops as possible were crowded into dwellings, which had been vacated by their owners removing from the combat zone. The buildings of Harvard College gave shelter to many.[13]

How to feed such an army was a problem, as it continued to be throughout the war—often, indeed, almost insoluble. In the morning after the battle "all the eatables in the town of Cambridge, which could be spared, were collected for breakfast, and the college kitchen and utensils procured the cooking." Some beef intended for the Boston market was secured, and "a large quantity of ship-bread at Roxbury, said to belong to the British army, was taken." After that the Commissary General was directed to "supply the troops with provisions, in the best manner he can, without spending time on exactness"; and somehow he managed to do it.[14]

All communication between the town and the rest of the province was now cut off. But in the town there were thousands of patriots who wished to leave it, and outside it were many Loyalists who longed for the protection the British troops could afford them. After a complicated negotiation an agreement was made allowing an exchange. Gage stipulated that all the inhabitants should first deposit all their arms in Faneuil Hall, which they did to the extent of 1,778 firelocks, 634 pistols, 973 bayonets, and 38 blunderbusses. Those coming in and going out were allowed to carry their personal effects except arms and ammunition, and the exception was soon extended to include salable merchandise, provisions, and medicines.

Thousands took advantage of this arrangement. It has been estimated that "near half" of the patriots went out. Wagons from outside were allowed to enter the town, to bring in and carry out the effects of those coming and going. Plans were made to distribute an estimated 5,000 poor refugees from Boston in various other towns. But after a while the Tories in Boston protested against the Whigs' being allowed to go out, wishing to hold them as hostages against an attack and, perhaps, a burning of the town. Various obstacles and delays developed, and the system broke down.[15]

The condition of the British army, shut up in the town with no access to the country, unable to procure fresh meat or vegetables, was unenviable. Captain George Harris of the 5th Regiment wrote home about it: "However we block up their port, the rebels certainly block up our town, and have cut off our good beef and mutton. . . . At present we are completely blockaded, and subsisting almost on salt provision." He was cultivating his own little garden of salads and greens. Lieutenant Barker wrote, "We can get no fresh provision, but must live on our allowance of salt meat." [16]

From a military point of view, the situation was a stalemate. Boston was blockaded on the land side, but it was not properly besieged. As long as the fleet kept open communication by water, the Americans could not hope to starve it out. Unless there was some definitely active move on one side or the other, the condition might last until doomsday. But the Americans dared not attempt to take the town. For one thing, they could not concentrate all the available force of the four provinces against it; the seacoast towns, in fear of attacks by the fleet, were holding their own men at home and calling for more. There were no siege guns to batter the defenses, and the men were not sufficiently disciplined and coordinated for storming operations. As for the British, they had had their lesson on April 19; they knew they had not nearly enough to try offensive operations outside the town.

There were, however, some little excursions from both sides. Gage needed hay for his horses and the few beef cattle he had. On May 21 he sent four sloops, with a subaltern and thirty men, to bring off a supply from Grape Island in the harbor. General Thomas sent three companies in a lighter and a sloop to oppose them. There was a harmless exchange of fire before the British were driven off, with only seven or eight tons of hay; the Americans burned all the rest, eighty tons.[17]

The Americans countered, on May 27, with an expedition against two other harbor islands, Hog and Noddle's, on which a considerable number of horses, cattle, and sheep were at pasture. Wading through a narrow

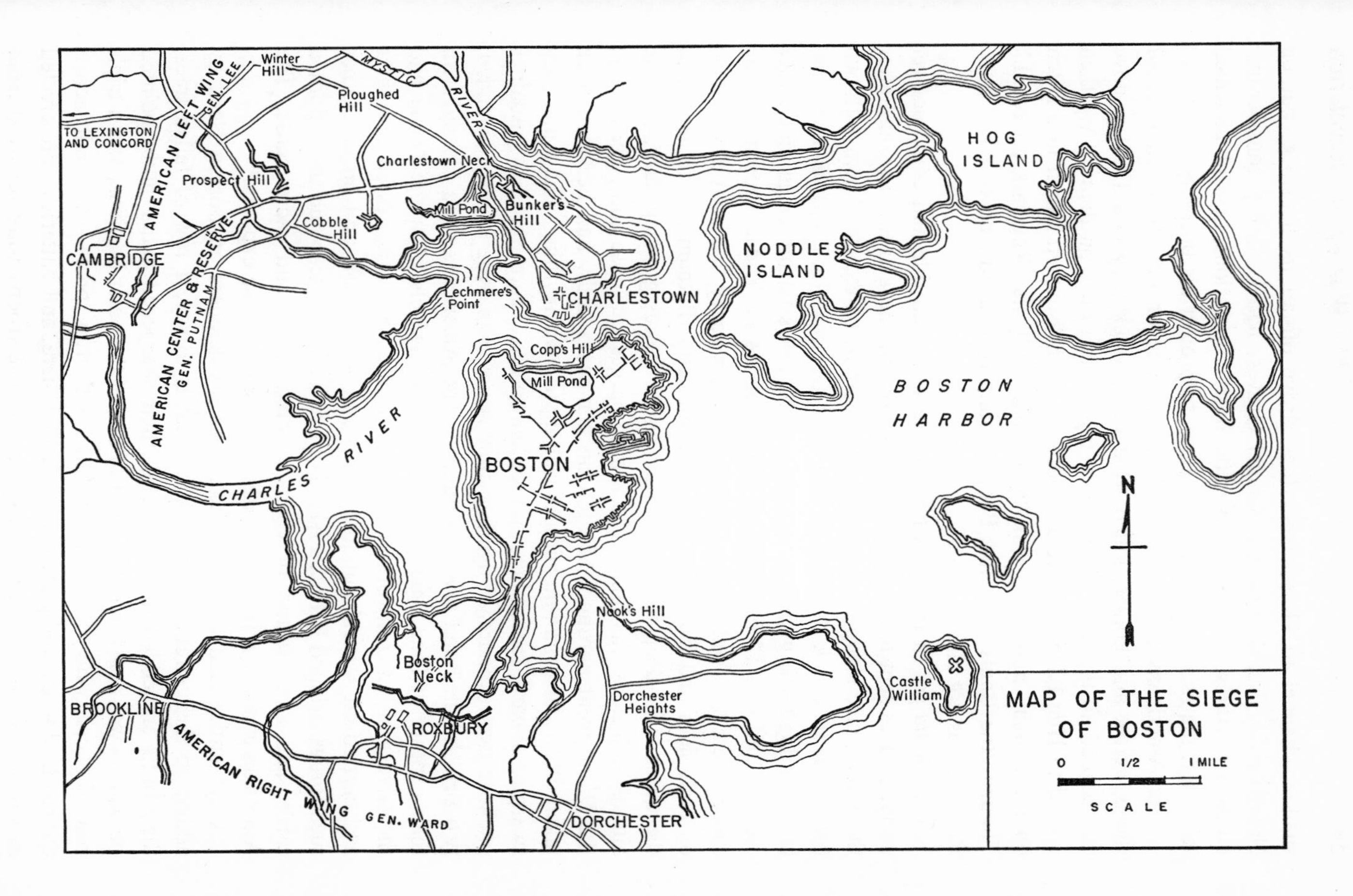
MAP OF THE SIEGE OF BOSTON
0
1/2
1 MILE
SCALE
N
Winter Hill
MYSTIC RIVER
Ploughed Hill
TO LEXINGTON AND CONCORD
AMERICAN LEFT WING
GEN. LEE
Charlestown Neck
Prospect Hill
Mill Pond
Bunker's Hill
Cobble Hill
CAMBRIDGE
AMERICAN CENTER & RESERVE
GEN. PUTNAM
Lechmere's Point
CHARLESTOWN
HOG ISLAND
NODDLES ISLAND
Copp's Hill
Mill Pond
BOSTON
BOSTON HARBOR
CHARLES RIVER
Nook's Hill
Boston Neck
Dorchester Heights
Castle William
BROOKLINE
ROXBURY
AMERICAN RIGHT WING
GEN. WARD
DORCHESTER

shallow channel to Hog Island, they drove off all its livestock, but on Noddle's the British admiral, Samuel Graves, had landed a considerable quantity of stores. Having observed the hostile operations, he sent an armed schooner, the *Diana*, with forty marines, to protect his property.

The Americans had already taken off three or four hundred head of sheep, cattle, and horses, killed what other stock they could not remove and burned all the hay, when the enemy began to fire on them. They then retired to Hog Island, where a handful of them "squated Down in a Ditch on the marsh" and there was "a hot fiar untill the Regulars retreeted." Though "the Bauls Sung like Bees" around their heads, no one was hurt. But that was not all.[18]

The *Diana* got in trouble with adverse wind and tide and could not get away. Graves sent ten or twelve barges from the fleet to tow her, and after them the armed sloop *Britannia*. Putnam marched a thousand men with two fieldpieces to attack this little flotilla from Chelsea Neck. Graves answered by mounting three guns from his ship on Noddle's Island. Gage sent eighty marines and two 12-pounders to assist him. As the *Diana* approached the shore where the Americans stood, there was a heavy fire from all the guns on both sides and from the American musketry. Putnam led his men into the water waist-deep to get in closer range. It was growing dark, and the aim of both sides was blind. The towing barges cut loose and rowed away; the *Diana* went aground. She fell on her beam ends, and her men were taken off by the *Britannia* without waiting to save anything. The Americans swarmed aboard, looted her, and set her on fire. There were few casualties in those twelve hours of fighting; four Americans were slightly wounded, two British killed and several wounded. The Americans were pleased with their capture of four 4-pounders and twelve swivels from the *Diana* and the salvage of her ironwork. They went back to the islands three days later and carried off several hundred sheep and some cattle and horses. Other such forays stripped Pettick's Island of five hundred sheep and thirty horned cattle, and Deer Island of eight hundred sheep and more cattle. The American commissariat was greatly refreshed by these exploits.[19]

Gage anticipated a possible attack on his defenses on Boston Neck by adding to their strength. An abatis—that is to say, a row of felled trees, their butts embedded in the ground, their sharpened major limbs pointed outward—was constructed in front of one of the outer bastions, and a triple row of *chevaux-de-frise*—timbers fitted with iron spikes—was built across the road. Mortars and guns were mounted there, and batteries were erected at various points of vantage in the town. The troops were removed from their barracks to a camp on the Common, and heavy details, as many as a fifth of the whole force, were constantly on guard duty.[20] But all this was defensive, calculated merely to hold the town; there was no sign of any intention to go beyond that. The British government, however, had awakened to the fact that Gage's force was inadequate to achieve more than such a negative success; reinforcements were on the way.

Six regiments, or parts of regiments, the 35th, 49th, 63rd, 64th, 65th, and 67th, had landed in Boston in April, May, or early June, or were on the way across the ocean, also the 17th Light Dragoons, a detachment of 600 marines, and some drafts to recruit the regiments already there. With such additions Gage had, by the middle of June, a force of about 6,500 rank and file.[21]

On May 25 the frigate *Cerberus* arrived. She had on board three very distinguished gentlemen and members of Parliament: Major General William Howe, Major General Henry Clinton, and Major General John Burgoyne. They were entering upon a service from which two of them were to emerge with blasted reputations, the third with but little credit.

William Howe, not yet a knight, was in his forty-fifth year, a tall, soldierly-looking man, although his figure had been overextended and his naturally heavy features coarsened by excessive indulgence in food and drink. He was of a very dark complexion, like his brother the admiral, whose nickname was "Black Dick." He was a man of easy manners and easy morals, an inveterate gambler, a hearty drinker; his intimate relations with Mrs. Joshua Loring during his stay in America were notorious. In politics he was a Whig, and he had been opposed to coercing the Americans. When he stood for Parliament in the Whig interest at Nottingham, he promised his constituents that he would decline any command against the Americans that might be offered to him. When the King, less than a year later, assigned him to such a command, he asked whether he was to consider it as a request or as an order. He was told that it was an order and accepted it, excusing his compliance to his constituents by saying he "could not refuse without incurring the odious name of backwardness to serve my country in distress."

He had started his career as a soldier at the age of seventeen, with a cornet's commission in the Light Dragoons. After considerable military experience on the European continent, he first saw service in America as a major of infantry at the capture of Louisburg in 1758. In the next year he gained distinction for gallantry in leading the advance, a "forlorn hope" of twenty-four men, up the Heights of Abraham in Wolfe's attack on Quebec. He was always foremost in battle and conspicuously cool under fire. He became a major general in 1772.

He was a clever strategist, an able tactician; his plans were excellently conceived and well carried out, but he was too often content with victory in the battle itself, failing to follow up his successes as he might have done. The fault was marked at Long Island, in the succeeding operations on Manhattan Island, and, indeed, in all his campaigns, as will be seen hereafter. These repeated failures have been attributed by some to his Whiggish proclivities, which were favorable to the Americans; by others to his naturally sluggish temperament, which was aggravated by his dissipation; by others again, especially when he found the Americans intrenched against him, to memories of the slaughter of his troops at Bunker Hill. On the whole, though he outmaneuvered Washington repeatedly and won battle after battle, his conduct of the war in America was a failure; and he returned to England to face a Parliamentary inquiry, which might have condemned him had it been pushed to a conclusion.[22]

Henry Clinton, the only son of a British admiral and colonial governor of New York, was but thirty-seven years old when he came to Boston. He was not a man of colorful personality and, in contrast to his companion generals, he seems rather a negative character in the drama of the Revolution. He had obtained a commission as a lieutenant in the 2nd Foot Guards at the age of thirteen years; he was a lieutenant colonel at twenty, a major general at thirty-four. He had seen some service in Germany between 1760 and 1763.

In his American career Clinton showed no indubitable evidence of military ability, certainly none of brilliance in his profession. He commanded the first unsuccessful attack on Charleston, in 1776, and the second, which resulted in its capture in 1780; and in neither did he display unusual talents. His most able exploit was the conduct of his army in its removal from Philadelphia across New Jersey in 1778, when he reached New York without serious losses, in spite of attacks by Washington's pursuing forces. He cannot be blamed for his failure to relieve Burgoyne at Saratoga in the circumstances then existing. His successful attacks on Forts Clinton and Montgomery in 1777 were planned with soldierly skill and carried out with sufficient audacity; but on the whole his career in America was far from brilliant. After his return to England, he was the object of adverse criticism by Lord Cornwallis, with whom he engaged in a bitter controversy.[23]

In John Burgoyne we meet with a character of conspicuous interest, who aspired to renown in such diverse fields as war, statesmanship, and literature. It is ironical that he was defeated in that field in which he showed most ability.

He was a scion of an ancient Lancashire family of repute and substance; at this time he was in his fifty-third year. He was handsome in the full-fed

British style of the period, and was a wit, a playwright, a man of fashion, and a member of Parliament. He was also a good soldier, and in certain military respects was much in advance of his time. His treatise on the duties of officers urged that soldiers be treated like thinking human beings; they should not be subjected to frequent and brutal corporal punishment, and there should be no "training men like spaniels by the stick," as he called it. He insisted that the officers should read books, learn how to write accurately, know something of mathematics, and acquire a practical knowledge of the equipment of their calling; in all these points there was vast room for improvement among the British officers of the day, whose ignorance was generally of "Stygian density." Practicing his own precepts, he was popular with his men, who nicknamed him "Gentleman Johnny." "On every occasion he was the soldiers' friend."

He had entered the army in 1744 at the rather advanced age of twenty-two years, but sold out in 1747 and did not rejoin until 1756, being merely a captain at the age of thirty-four. He served on the European continent as a brigadier with considerable credit for seven years. His capitulation at Saratoga finished his military career.[24]

The arrival of the three generals produced no improvement in the situation of the British army. If any one of them had displaced Gage in supreme command, he would undoubtedly have seen, like Gage, that the pressing need was for still more troops. The army could not take the aggressive until the large forces which Gage had consistently demanded since the fall of 1774 reached America.

Burgoyne, indeed, was of no help to Gage; he was, on the contrary, a menace. He began a voluminous correspondence with some of the home authorities in which he dilated upon Gage's errors and thus injured him in the judgment of the ministry.

In a different and well meant endeavor, he gave his chief a push down the declining path of reputation. Gage, instructed by the cabinet to proclaim martial law in Massachusetts, decided to use the proclamation as a "last effort . . . to spare the effusion of blood." Burgoyne wrote it for him, and "no manifesto was ever worse adapted to the taste of its intended readers." Its flamboyant, inflated, and verbose style widened the eyes of the simple New Englanders in sheer amazement; its accusatory and threatening substance aroused bitter resentment where it did not excite derision.

It called the people an "infatuated multitude . . . conducted by certain well known incendiaries and traitors." It warned that "those who are invested with supreme rule . . . do not bear the sword in vain," and threatened "the fulness of chastisement." It asserted that the leaders of the Americans imposed on the credulity of their followers with "the grossest forgeries, calumnies, and absurdities that ever insulted human understanding," and used "the animated language of ancient and virtuous times . . . to countenance the most abandoned violations . . . of the just rights and interests of mankind." It noted that the rebels "with a preposterous parade of military arrangement have effected to hold the Army besieged."

Proceeding to a generous offer of pardon to all persons who would lay down their arms and return to the ways of peace, except "Samuel Adams and John Hancock, whose offences are of too flagitious a nature to admit of any other consideration than that of condign punishment," it announced, of course, martial law throughout the province.[25] That from a general who dared not set his foot outside the town of Boston and could no more enforce martial law throughout the province of Massachusetts than he could throughout the empire of the Khan of Tartary.

Even in London the preposterous character of this manifesto was appreciated; its style was recognized as Burgoyne's, and much fun was made of it: "They *affect* to hold the army besieged . . . the next time you write to your friends, say in plain English that the Americans have *effected* the siege." [26]

That proclamation was issued on the 12th of June. Five days later much was to happen, but previous events in another part of the colonies must be given attention before the story of the siege of Boston is continued.

CHAPTER 7

Ticonderoga

Fort Ticonderoga was called "the Key to the gateway to the continent," by which was meant the way from Canada to the English colonies. In a wilderness the best route is by water; from Canada southward this was furnished by the St. Lawrence River, the Richelieu, Lake Champlain, and the Hudson. At the point where Lake George discharges its waters into Champlain, the larger lake narrows to a width of half a mile, and at one point two opposite headlands leave a passage between them of less than a quarter of a mile. There on the western side, on an eminence rising a hundred feet above the water, stood the fort.[1]

The French first occupied this position in 1755. After plans by Vauban, the great military engineer, they built a fort with stone bastions surrounded by a star-shaped outer wall, the whole complete with glacis, counterscarps, covered ways, and demilunes. They called it Fort Carillon. In 1758 with a garrison of 4,000, under Montcalm, they held it against 6,000 British regulars and 10,000 provincial troops under Lieutenant General James Abercromby. In the next year, Sir Jeffrey Amherst invested it with 11,000 men; the French commander, Bourlamaque, had but 3,500. He blew up the works and retreated. The British rebuilt it in less substantial fashion and named it Ticonderoga. After the Peace of Paris in 1763, ending the French and Indian War, there was no frontier between Canada and the colonies to be guarded; the fort was manned by a skeleton garrison, used only as a supply post on the route, and allowed to fall into decay.[2]

When the relations between Britain and her American colonies became strained to the point of breaking, the New Englanders had cause to fear that

Guy Carleton, in command at Montreal, might enlarge his small force of regulars with French Canadians and Indians and attack them in the rear. To discover the inclinations of the Canadians in the contest with Britain, the Massachusetts Provincial Congress in February, 1775, sent John Brown of Pittsfield to Montreal and Quebec. His report was discouraging, and to it he added: "One thing I must mention to be kept as a profound Secret, the Fort at Tyconderogo must be seised as soon as possible should hostilities be committed by the King's Troops. The people on N. Hampshire Grants have ingaged to do this business and in my opinion they are the most proper Persons for the Jobb." Brown's information as to the New Hampshire Grants people taking on the job had been derived from one Ethan Allen whom he had met in Pittsfield.[3]

Ethan Allen was a true son of the backwoods, born in a log cabin in Litchfield, Connecticut, the eldest son of a substantial farmer. He had begun his schooling under a clergyman with a view to entering Yale College; but on his father's death he had to care for a family of a widow and seven other orphans. After a short tour of duty with a Connecticut regiment in the French and Indian War, he set up an iron furnace, tried lead mining, and, in 1768, removed to the New Hampshire Grants, now Vermont.

In the conflict between the settlers there and the government of New York, which claimed ownership of the Grants, Allen was a colonel of the Green Mountain Boys, defenders of their rights to land under grant of the Governor of New Hampshire. The contest was violent and tumultuous, just the sort of fight to suit such a man as he.

In 1775 he was thirty-seven years old. He was tall (he is often described as "gigantic"), broad-shouldered, lean, and straight; his bodily strength was enormous. He has been credited with "boldness, adroitness, toughness, pride, fortitude, cheerfulness and a terrific volubility in invective . . . an amplitude and appalling humor of profane swearing," also with "rough and ready humor, boundless self-confidence and a shrewdness in thought and action equal to almost any emergency." Although his schooling was brief and scanty, he was a great reader and was later to produce several pamphlets on the rights of the Green Mountain Boys, as well as a narrative of his captivity by the British, composed of "staunch, blunt, boastful, blundering, fearless words," and, rather surprisingly, a tract entitled *Reason the Only Oracle of Man,* a very cogent deistic argument.[4]

Another man had thought about Ticonderoga. When the news of Lexington and Concord came to New Haven on the 20th of April, Captain Benedict Arnold summoned his company of militia to march to Cambridge and applied to the authorities of the town for ammunition; he was thought too hasty, and his request was refused. His answer to that was that he would break in the magazine and take what he wanted. "None but Almighty God shall prevent my marching," said he. They gave him the ammunition.[5]

Arnold was familiar with the Lake Champlain and St. Lawrence country. Happening to meet Colonel Samuel Holden Parsons on the way to Cambridge and hearing him lament the lack of cannon in Ward's army, he told him that a plentiful supply could be had at Ticonderoga. Parsons went on to Hartford with this suggestion in mind.[6]

At Cambridge, Arnold broached the matter to the Committee of Safety, giving it "certain information" that there were eighty pieces of heavy cannon, twenty brass pieces, and a dozen large mortars, besides small arms and stores, at Ticonderoga, three or four more brass guns at Skenesboro near by, and that the fort was "in a ruinous condition and has not more than fifty men at the most." [7] The committeemen were interested indeed. On May 3 they gave him a colonel's commission and authorized him to enlist "not exceeding 400" men, to march to Ticonderoga and "reduce the same," taking possession of "the cannon, mortars, stores &ca." This was to be a special commission for a "secret service," and the committee reserved the right to dismiss the force to be raised "whenever they shall think proper." [8]

Benedict Arnold was at this time thirty-four years old. Though only of middle height, his appearance was commanding. He was well formed, muscular, capable of great endurance, active, graceful in his movements, and exceptionally adept in athletic exercises, such as running, fencing, boxing and skating; he was also an expert marksman with gun and pistol, and an accomplished horseman. His salient facial features were clear cut and handsome; his hair was black, his skin swarthy, his clear, bright eyes light in color.

He came of a substantial family; a collateral ancestor of the same name had been governor of Rhode Island. He had a fair common-school education, which included some Latin. As an apprenticeship to a druggist he ran away at the age of seventeen to fight in the French and Indian War. He was advertised in the newspapers in 1759 as a deserter. In any case, he returned to finish out his term. At twenty-one he set up his own drugstore and bookshop in New Haven. His business flourished, and he branched out into the West Indies, sometimes sailing his own ships. He is also said to have shipped horses between Canada and the West Indies, which gave the British a chance to belittle him as a mere "horse-jockey." By the year 1775 he was a well-to-do merchant, the "possessor of an elegant house, storehouses, wharves, and vessels."

In the Revolutionary War he had an adventurous and, as was inevitable with his disposition, a stormy career, but proved himself to be a soldier of outstanding merit. He was original in his ideas, audacious in action, quick to form his plans, and swift to execute them. Though imperious of will, arrogant, restive under orders, and possessed of a passionate belief in his own judgment and in his own superior ability as a soldier, he was a most capable commander of men. He did not merely order his troops forward, he led them; he was a fighting man, and he had, as he deserved to have, the devotion of his troops. An old soldier of his command at Saratoga said of him: "He was our fighting general, and a bloody fellow he was. He didn't care for nothing, he'd ride right on. It was 'Come on boys!' 'twarn't 'Go, boys!' He was as brave a man as ever lived."

His treason has become almost the only popularly known element of his career, overshadowing and blotting out the memory of his expedition against Quebec, his exploits on Lake Champlain, his relief of Fort Stanwix, and his services in the fighting which led to Saratoga. But for his betrayal of his charge at West Point, he would have stood out in American history as one of the great soldiers in the Revolution.[9]

Parsons, arriving at Hartford after his roadside conversation with Arnold, "undertook and projected" with four or five others the taking of Ticonderoga. They sent an express to Ethan Allen at Bennington, asking him to gather a force of Green Mountain Boys and hold them in readiness for the proposed adventure; they appointed Major Halsted, Captain Edward Mott, Captain Noah Phelps, and Bernard Romans as a committee to conduct their part of the affair, and provided them with a war chest of £300. Phelps and Romans went on in advance on the 28th, and were followed by Epaphras Bull, Captain Mott and sixteen associates the next day. At Pittsfield, Massachusetts, they met James Easton and John Brown. Easton raised between forty and fifty men, and the whole party set out for Bennington, where they met Allen with about a hundred of his Boys.[10]

A Committee of War was chosen, consisting of Easton, Phelps, and Bull, with Mott as chairman; Allen was given command by a "universal" vote, with Easton and Seth Warner as his first and second lieutenants. It was decided to send Samuel Herrick with thirty men to surprise and capture Major Philip Skene at his settlement, Skenesboro—now Whitehall—and take his boats.[11] Captain Asa Douglass was sent to Panton, also to procure boats. Other small parties were directed to secure the roads to the north, to prevent warning of the attack from reaching the fort. Gershom Beach, a backwoods blacksmith, was detailed to rouse more Green Mountain Boys; he is said to have covered sixty miles of wilderness in twenty-four hours.[12]

These proceedings in the evening of May 9 were hardly over when a very impressive gentleman in a brave uniform with a scarlet coat arrived and informed the gathering that he had come to take command of them by virtue of a commission and orders from the Massachusetts Committee of Safety. It was Benedict Arnold, who, having heard of the expedition from Pittsfield, had left recruiting officers at Stockbridge and, with one manservant, had hurried on to Castleton.[13]

The men of the little army were "extremely rejoiced" to learn that the Committee of Safety endorsed the project, but "shockingly surprised when Colonel Arnold presumed to contend for the command of those forces that we had raised, who we had assured should go under the command of their own officers." Although the leaders "generously told him our whole plan, he strenuously contended and insisted that he had a right to command them and all their officers."

But Arnold had met more than his match. His demand had "bred such a mutiny among the soldiers which had nearly frustrated our whole design, as our men were for clubbing their fire-locks and marching home."[14]

Allen was not present at this discussion; he had gone forward to Shoreham—now Orwell—two miles below the fort, where, in Hand's Cove, the forces were to assemble. The next morning, all those at Castleton followed him. Arnold renewed his contention as to the command and finally got, as he says, joint command with Allen, until he could "raise a sufficient number of men to relieve his [Allen's] people." It is doubtful, however, that he got more than the right to march beside Allen at the head of the men in the attack on the fort.[15]

Early in the morning of May 10, about two hundred men had assembled at Hand's Cove—Easton's and Allen's forces, augmented by others from the country roundabout. Between them and the fort stretched two miles of water. The moon had set, the sun not yet risen; it was dark, and squalls of wind and rain were blowing up to make the crossing more hazardous. There were no boats; those expected from Skenesboro had not come. It was near dawn when a scow appeared; it had been commandeered by two boys who had heard of the proposed attack. Soon after, Asa Douglass brought another, with a few recruits.[16]

Allen and Arnold, with eighty-three men, crowded into the two boats and landed about half a mile below the fort at daybreak. The boats were sent back for the rest, but there was no time to wait if there was to be a surprise. Allen drew the men up in three ranks and addressed them. He reminded them that, for a long time past, they had been "a scourge and a terror to arbitrary power," and that their "valor has been famed abroad." He now proposed to lead them upon "a desperate attempt, which none but the bravest of men dare undertake. . . . You that will undertake voluntarily, poise your firelocks!" Every firelock was poised.[17]

Allen and Arnold, side by side, led the advance, Arnold in his fine uniform, Allen in one of his own devising—a green coat, with large gold epaulets, and yellow breeches. Behind them went a straggling column of men in every sort of garb—buckskin, linsey-woolsey, or what not, beaver hats, felt hats, coonskin caps, buckled shoes or moccasins—armed with firelocks, pistols, swords, knives, or simple clubs, not a bayonet among them all.[18]

The main entrance in the south wall of the fort was in a ruinous condition. The leaders and their men swarmed through and over the ruins and came upon a single sentry, guarding a wicket in the curtain of the main fort. He pointed his musket at the intruders and pulled the trigger; it flashed in the pan. He turned and fled through a covered way into the middle of the fort, shouting an alarm, the attackers close behind him, yelling like Indians. Another sentry slightly wounded one of the officers with a bayonet. Allen hit him on the head with the flat of his sword and ordered him to show the way to the officers' quarters. Leaving their men drawn up in two lines, back to back, Allen and Arnold followed the sentry to a staircase in the west barracks.[19]

A door at the head of the stairs opened and disclosed an officer, Lieutenant Jocelyn Feltham, wearing coat and waistcoat, but carrying his breeches in his hand. Allen shouted at him, "Come out of there, you damned old rat," (or "skunk," or "bastard," according to different accounts), and dashed up the stairs along with Arnold and followed by others. The astonished officer asked by what authority they intruded. Allen, according to his own later account, rose to the occasion with a deathless utterance:

"In the name of the Great Jehovah and the Continental Congress!" he shouted.

It has been remarked that the officer had about as much respect for the Continental Congress as Allen had for the Great Jehovah.[20] But this astounding speech and the demands that followed for immediate surrender of "the Fort and all the effects of George the Third," with the alternative of a massacre of every man, woman, and child in the place, brought the commander, Captain William Delaplace, to terms; he handed his sword to Allen and ordered the garrison paraded without arms.

The entire force consisted of the two officers, two artillerymen, a couple of sergeants, and forty-four privates, many of them invalids; but there were also twenty-four women and children. In fact Ticonderoga, with its ruined walls, its meager garrison, its flock of women and children, was more like a backwoods village than a fort. Allen's report to the Continental Congress characteristically tells of the taking of "the Fortress of Ticonderoga by storm" and of "the resistless fury . . . of the Soldiery [who] behaved with uncommon ranker when they Leaped Into the fourt." [21]

They certainly did behave with "uncommon ranker" after the surrender. "There is here at present," Arnold reported the next day, "near one hundred men, who are in the greatest confusion and anarchy, destroying and plundering private property, committing every enormity and paying no attention to publick service." He had forbidden them to behave so riotously, but Allen had "positively insisted" that he should have no command, and he was powerless to control them.[22]

It was necessary now to dispose of the prisoners. Allen wrote to Governor Jonathan Trumbull of Connecticut of the 12th, "I make you a present of a Major, a Captain and two Lieutenants of the regular Establishment of George the Third." The major was Skene, whom, with his daughter and various dependents, Herrick had captured at Skenesboro. These prisoners were dispatched to Hartford. Lieutenant Colonel Seth Warner took a party to Crown Point, another disabled British post, and, without resistance, captured the garrison, one sergeant, eight privates, and ten women and children, also a number of cannon.[23]

Arnold's discontent with his anomalous position in the fort, where he had no recognized command and very little good-fellowship, was relieved on the 13th, when Captain John Brown and Captain Eleazer Oswald arrived in a small schooner and several bateaux, captured at Skenesboro, with fifty recruits "enlisted on the road." Arnold was a sailor; Allen was not. So there was no objection to Arnold's having command of a naval expedition against St. Johns, a frontier Canadian post on the Richelieu River, some miles beyond Lake Champlain. When he had yet thirty miles to go, the schooner was becalmed. Arnold and thirty-five men in two bateaux rowed all night and, early in the morning of the 17th, surprised the unresisting garrison, a sergeant and fourteen men, and took the post, along with a 70-ton sloop, armed with two brass 6-pounders, and its crew of seven. There were others of the King's forces at Chambly, twelve miles away, and reinforcements for St. Johns, to the number of two hundred, were hourly expected. Arnold's men took all the more valuable stores, destroyed five bateaux, and set sail with four others, the sloop, and the schooner, for Crown Point.[24]

But Allen had his ambitions for further conquest, too. He had embarked with ninety men in four bateaux and followed Arnold. The two expeditions, Allen's going, Arnold's returning, met about six miles south of St. Johns and saluted each other with three volleys apiece. Allen boarded Arnold's sloop and learned that he was too late, that St. Johns had been taken, and that its garrison was now in irons in the hold. But, though it had been taken, it had been abandoned. That did not suit Allen; he would occupy it and hold it. However, at the moment, he was in straits, "his men being in a starving condition," as Arnold put it. In fact, Allen, in his enthusiasm for conquest, had neglected the purely incidental matter of feeding his men *en route*. Arnold supplied him, and he went on in spite of warnings as to the impracticability of his venture. At St. Johns, Allen learned that the expected reinforcements were near at hand. He first decided to ambush them, placed his men accordingly, and sent out scouts. But cooler thoughts supervened; his men were tired after three days and nights with little sleep and little food. When the new forces were within two miles of him, he withdrew across the river, where his wornout men lay down to sleep. They were surprised by a volley of grapeshot from six fieldpieces ranged on the other side; the relief for the garrison had come up. They swarmed into their boats with such celerity as to leave three of their number behind, and rowed lustily away, exchanging harmless shots with the enemy as they pulled out of range.[25]

Arnold, now at Crown Point, reported to the Massachusetts Committee of Safety that he had one hundred fifty men of his own—"Colonel Allen's men are in general gone home"—and that he had determined to hold the fort at the Point until the arrival of wheels and of draught animals should enable him to remove the cannon.[26] He had armed his sloop and his schooner with "carriage guns" and swivels in anticipation of an attempt by the British to recapture the place. But the ambitions of the two leaders were not yet satisfied. They decided to send a force to Pointe au Fer and fortify it. Allen's designs went far beyond that; he was going to conquer all Canada. "I will lay my life on it," he wrote to the New York Congress, "that, with 1500 men and a proper train of artillery, I will take Montreal . . . it would be no insuperable difficulty to take Quebeck." [27] But they were stopped in their tracks by word from the Continental Congress.

The Congress had news of the taking of Ticonderoga on May 18. It at once resolved that the fort should be abandoned and all the guns and stores removed to the south end of Lake George, with a provision that an exact inventory of them be taken, "in order that they may be safely returned when the restoration of the former harmony between Great Britain and these colonies so ardently wished for by the latter shall render it prudent." [28]

But Arnold, even if he could not go any farther, had no intention of giving up the ground he had gained. On May 29 he wrote to the Continental Congress and to the Massachusetts Provincial Congress stating his surprise and alarm at the proposal, which would leave "our very extensive frontiers open to the ravages of the enemy." The same day he wrote to the Provincial Congress of New York, giving full details as to the number of men and the amount of supplies needed to hold the posts on the lake. Allen was equally averse to giving them up and even more eloquent in expressing his views to the New York Congress.[29]

These two were not alone; New England wanted the forts held; so did northern New York. Alarmed by reports that an expedition to retake the Champlain posts was contemplated in Canada, and that Guy Carleton was soliciting the Six Nations of Indians to join in such an effort, the northern colonies protested against the abandonment of Ticonderoga, the strongest position on the lake, and persuaded the Continental Congress to change its mind. On May 31 it resolved that Connecticut be requested to send strong reinforcements to Crown Point and "Ticonderogo" and that New York be requested to furnish supplies. Connecticut had already ordered four hundred men to march to the forts, with 500 pounds of its "pittance of powder," followed by a thousand more men under Colonel Benjamin Hinman. The forts were to be retained, but not with Colonel Benedict Arnold in command.[30]

A committee from Massachusetts, sent up to ascertain the needs of the forts, brought Arnold the news that he was to be second in command under Hinman. To the colonel, who had been signing his name as "Commander-in-Chief," and had just sent a long letter to the Continental Congress outlining an elaborate plan for the conquest of Canada which he was willing to undertake, and in which Hinman's regiment was to play a subordinate part, this demotion was displeasing. It was more than that, it was humiliating and altogether disgusting; "he would not be second in command to any person whomsoever." He immediately left the service under a double impulsion, his discharge by the committee and his own resignation.[31]

No exercise of military genius was involved in the taking of the Champlain posts, nor was there needed any display of valor. They fell like ripe apples from a shaken limb. Nevertheless, their capture was of vast importance to the colonies. Leaving out of consideration their subsequent value in the operations in that territory, the guns which they yielded were of inestimable value to the Americans. Many of them were found to be in such bad condition as to be useless, but no fewer than seventy-eight were serviceable, ranging from 4-pounders to 24-pounders. There were also six mortars, three howitzers, thousands of cannon balls of various sizes, nine tons of musket bullets, thirty thousand flints, and a large quantity of miscellaneous apparatus. The guns were what the army besieging Boston most needed. They were not at once removed, for lack of transport, but in the coming winter a way was found to carry them to the army.[32]

CHAPTER 8

Bunker Hill

When the frigate *Cerberus* with the three major generals was entering Boston harbor, General Burgoyne was told that "10,000 country people" surrounding the town were holding its garrison in check. "What?" he is said to have exclaimed. "Ten thousand peasants keep five thousand of the King's troops shut up? Well, let us get in, and we'll soon find elbow-room." [1] It may have been at his suggestion that Gage and his three colleagues, not long after their arrival, decided to seize and fortify Dorchester Heights on the Charles River, which, though a commanding position overlooking the town of Boston, had been neglected by both sides. This operation was to have been effected on June 18.[2]

Five days before that date, news of the intended movement was conveyed to the American command; and on June 15 the Committee of Safety decided on countermovements: that "Bunker's Hill in Charlestown be securely kept and defended, and also some one hill or hills on Dorchester Neck be likewise secured." Bunker's Hill was to be cared for at once, Dorchester being left to further consideration.[3]

Charlestown was a peninsula, roughly triangular in shape, opposite the north side of Boston. Its base was separated from Boston by the half-mile width of the Charles River. Its peak terminated in a narrow isthmus, the Neck, so low as to be often overflowed at high tide. The Mystic River washed its northeasterly side; the Charles widened into a large bay on the northwest. Its length was about a mile from north to south; its greatest width was about half a mile.

It had a rolling surface culminating at three points in low hills. The first,

Bunker's Hill, began at the Neck and rose gradually for 300 yards to a rounded top 110 feet high, sloping on its east and west sides to the water. This was connected by a low ridge with Breed's Hill, the second eminence, the top of which was about 600 yards distant; its height was 75 feet. The easterly and westerly slopes of this hill were steep. At the water side on the west was the village of Charlestown. Near the base of Breed's Hill, on its easterly side, the approach was broken by brick kilns, clay pits, and an area of swampy land. The third and smallest hill, Moulton's, only 35 feet high, lay at the southeast corner of the peninsula near the meeting of the Mystic and the Charles. Outside the little town the whole surface of the peninsula was divided into different holdings, separated by rail fences or stone walls and used chiefly for hay and pasture, with orchards and gardens here and there. In the middle of June, 1775, some parts had been mowed, the hay left on the ground to cure; in other places, and particularly on the sloping approach to Breed's Hill from the southeast, the grass, fully knee-high, was still standing. A narrow road ran from the Neck, passed Bunker's Hill, and encircled Breed's.[4]

At the recommendation of the Committee of Safety and on the day that it was made, General Artemas Ward assembled a council of war. The names of all the officers attending have not been ascertained; but it appears that General Putnam, Joseph Warren, lately appointed a major general but not yet commissioned, Brigadier General Seth Pomeroy, and Colonel William Prescott were there. The matter was discussed. Ward and Warren had been opposed to fortifying Bunker's Hill when it had been proposed at earlier meetings, and seem to have been reluctant now. The lack of powder—there were only eleven barrels in the whole camp—rendered rather more than doubtful the ability of the Americans to hold it, even if it should be successfully fortified. But Putnam was strong for the adventure. "The Americans," he is supposed to have said, "are not at all afraid of their heads, though very much afraid of their legs; if you cover these, they will fight forever." Pomeroy seconded him, and Prescott agreed, whereupon the others consented and the order was made, without deciding how the defenders were going to "fight forever" after their ammunition gave out.[5]

Artemas Ward, on whom the major responsibilities of American leadership were descending, was a descendant of William Ward, one of the early Puritan settlers of New England. His father was a well-to-do farmer of Worcester County. His education was that of the average country boy of the period in the short terms that "school kept" in Shrewsbury, supplemented by some home study under the supervision of the local preacher.

which led to his entry into Harvard and his graduation there, followed by a later degree of A.M.

In 1755, at the age of twenty-eight, he was a major of militia, and three years later he marched with Abercromby's army against Ticonderoga. In the course of a year's service he attained a lieutenant colonelcy; but had little experience in that grade. He came home with his health impaired, and never again was a robust man. He was politically active in the civil disturbances following the Stamp Act, and was a delegate to the First and Second Provincial Congresses.

Ward was a man of medium height, "too stout for his forty-seven years," and at this time was afflicted with bladder stone, but not physically incapacitated thereby. He was precise, even elegent, in his dress. His long, sharp nose, pointed chin, and bright, knowing eyes indicated intelligence, but did not reveal his really dominant mental characteristics—slowness of thought, extreme caution, taciturnity, and inflexibility of opinion. These elements of his character were displayed in his measured speech and his habit of using biblical terms and phrases in conversation. As undistinguished as his appearance was his character, except for honesty, firm patriotism, and devotion to the American cause.

Ward was, in fact, better fitted for the council chamber or the judicial bench than for military leadership, especially in enterprises demanding forthright boldness of plan and unhesitating speed in execution.[6]

General Israel Putnam is a colorful character about whom legends have clustered so thickly as to conceal the man within. His name is still universally known, while much greater men have faded from memory since the Revolution, showing how effectively romantic adventures create reputations and embalm them.

He was a farmer, fifty-seven years of age, widely known throughout New England by the affectionate title of "Old Put." He had led the first Connecticut company sent out in 1755 in the French and Indian War, in which he saw long and hard service and was engaged in many sensational exploits. He was captured by Indians, tied to the stake to be burned, and rescued at the very last moment by a French officer. He was a prisoner at Montreal for a long time until exchanged. He led a regiment to attack Havana and was shipwrecked on the coast of Cuba. He fought the Indians again in 1764. This record, strengthened by the tradition of his victorious battle with a veritable werewolf, and by the later story of his escape from capture by the British, by riding his horse at a headlong gallop down a flight of rocky steps, has made his name a household word throughout New England. In

1775 he was believed to be not only a good soldier, but a great soldier, fit to be a major general, which he was not.

He was a rather short, broad-shouldered, burly man, with a big round head crowned by an unruly shock of gray hair. His round, open face gave evidence of the frank, generous, outspoken, jovial disposition that made him universally popular. He was courageous, enterprising, energetic, active, and persevering. As colonel of a fighting regiment, he would have been admirably placed; he would have led his men against the enemy, and they would have followed him with a cheer. Of the conduct and care of an army, of strategy in major operations, of shrewd planning of a campaign or even of a single battle, of careful preparation for the execution of plans, of the management of large bodies of men in the field, of resourcefulness in taking advantage of unexpected opportunities in battle on a large scale, or making unexpectedly necessary changes in plan, he knew nothing and should not have been expected to know anything. *Colonel* Israel Putnam he should have remained throughout the war.[7]

Colonel William Prescott, who was to lead the detachment to Bunker's Hill, was born in 1726 to a Massachusetts family of wealth and position. His early education was limited in scope, but he made up for that by his devotion to books. In person he was tall, over six feet, well set up and muscular; his features were strong and clear-cut. His disposition was kindly, his manners simple but courteous; yet he had the habit of command and the power to exact obedience from his men, whose respect he deservedly enjoyed. His customary movements were unhurried, and his coolness and self-possession in moments of danger were notable.[8]

Another important participant in the enterprise was Joseph Warren, who was but thirty-four years of age. His family dated from 1659 in Massachusetts. He was well educated with the degree of A.M. from Harvard. He had studied medicine and had acquired a large practice in Boston; his wife was Mercy Otis, the brilliant sister of James Otis. After the passage of the Stamp Act he undertook "a serious examination of the right of Parliament to tax the colonies" and, as a result, allied himself with those who resisted British measures.

His natural enthusiasm and strong impulses led him to take an active part in politics, in which he became an associate of Hancock, the Adamses, and the rest of the patriot malcontents; he was in especially close relationship with Samuel Adams. He soon became one of the leaders of the movement, to which he lent his abilities as a writer and an orator. He was the author of the Suffolk Resolves, one of the earliest and boldest declarations of refusal of obedience to the oppressive acts of Parliament. He frequently acted as presiding officer of the Provincial Congress, and was chairman of the Committee of Safety.

Though Warren had had no military experience, he was chosen to be major general, and is said to have intended to pursue a career in arms.

He was of middle height, well built, graceful in figure, active in movement, scrupulously neat in attire, and elegant in address. His fine, open countenance was indicative of his integrity, his modesty, and his gentle, friendly, and courteous disposition; yet he was courageous morally and physically, swift of thought and action, high-spirited, enthusiastic, capable of quick resentments and fiery impulses, and hot of speech in support of the cause which he had adopted. To that cause he unreservedly devoted his fine talents; indeed it had become the ruling passion of his short life. His too early death in the coming battle was universally and most feelingly lamented as an irreparable loss to his friends and to his country.[9]

Ward ordered the Massachusetts regiments of Prescott, Colonel James Frye, and Colonel Ebenezer Bridge, with a fatigue party of two hundred men drafted from Putnam's Connecticut regiment and commanded by Captain Thomas Knowlton, as well as Captain Samuel Gridley's Massachusetts artillery company, forty-nine men and two fieldpieces, to parade in the camp at Cambridge at six o'clock in the evening of June 16. They were to be equipped with packs, blankets, a day's rations, and the necessary entrenching tools. They would have made up a party of about fourteen hundred all told; but Prescott's regiment turned out only two-thirds of its paper strength, and the other two were short of their full number, so that there were between a thousand and twelve hundred actually assembled. Frye being ill with the gout, his men were led by Lieutenant Colonel James Brickett.[10]

When they were properly drawn up on the Cambridge Common, the Reverend Samuel Langdon, President of Harvard College, offered a prayer for the success of their undertaking. At about nine o'clock a column was formed, and they set out for a destination of which they were ignorant, not even the company officers having been informed of the purpose of the expedition. Colonel Prescott, preceded by two sergeants carrying dark lanterns "open in the rear," led the way; by his side marched Colonel Richard Gridley, a veteran who had seen service at Louisburg thirty years before and in many other campaigns. He was now chief engineer of the American army. Prescott wore military costume, a blue coat, "lapped and faced," and a three-cornered hat. Some of the other officers may have worn uniforms, but not the common soldiers. They were "mostly husbandmen," and they wore their ordinary clothes.[11] An eyewitness of their assemblage has left an engaging description of them:

> To a man, they wore small-clothes, coming down and fastening just below the knee, and long stockings with cowhide shoes ornamented by large buckles, while not a pair of boots graced the company. The coats and waistcoats were loose and of huge dimensions, with colors as various as the barks of oak, sumach and other trees of our hills and swamps, could make them and their shirts were all made of flax, and like every other part of the dress, were home-spun. On their heads was worn a large round top and broad brimmed hat. Their arms were as various as their costume; here an old soldier carried a heavy Queen's arm, with which he had done service at the Conquest of Canada twenty years previous, while by his side walked a stripling boy with a Spanish fusee not half its weight or calibre, which his grandfather may have taken at the Havana, while not a few had old French pieces, that dated back to the reduction of Louisburg. Instead of the cartridge box, a large powder horn was slung under the arm, and occasionally a bayonet might be seen bristling in the ranks. Some of the swords of the officers had been made by our Province blacksmiths, perhaps from some farming utensil; they looked serviceable, but heavy and uncouth.[12]

At Charlestown Neck they were met by General Putnam, Major John Brooks, and some wagons loaded with fascines, gabions, empty hogsheads, and entrenching tools. Here Captain John Nutting of Prescott's regiment was detached, with his company and ten of Knowlton's men, and sent into Charlestown to watch for movements of the enemy, while the main body marched on over Bunker's Hill and to the foot of Breed's. Prescott then called the officers together, told them for the first time the purpose of the expedition, and consulted with them as to the position of the proposed entrenchment.[13]

His orders were explicit, to fortify Bunker's Hill, but there seemed to be reasons for choosing Breed's instead. It was nearer Boston. On the other hand, Bunker's was higher and nearer the Neck, their only avenue of escape if driven from their works. The matter was debated. Putnam and another general officer, whose name does not appear, were for Breed's but Putnam urged that they should first fortify Bunker's to cover a retreat, if that became necessary. The debate was prolonged; Gridley became impatient at the delay, urging a quick decision, as much valuable time was being wasted. At last it was decided first to erect the main works on Breed's, and then the auxiliary defenses on the other hill.[14]

Gridley marked out the lines of a redoubt about eight rods square. The south side, facing Charlestown, was the strongest, having near its middle a redan, or angular projection. The north side, towards Bunker's Hill, had an open entrance. There was a sally port at the southeast corner, protected by a blind.[15]

It was about midnight when the pick-and-shovel work was begun. Thoroughly used to those tools, the farmers worked steadily and swiftly to make up for the delay. They had but four hours before dawn would discover them to the enemy and expose them to attack.

Prescott detached Captain Hugh Maxwell's company of his own regiment and sent it down to patrol the shore on the Boston side of the peninsula. More than once he and Major Brooks also went down to see that there was no alarm in the enemy's camp. It was a warm, still night, dimly lit by the stars in a cloudless sky. They could see the dark outlines of the ships lying at anchor in the narrow channel of the Charles and, very near to the shore on which they stood, the *Lively* with her twenty guns, the *Falcon* sloop with sixteen, the *Symmetry,* armed transport with eighteen, the *Glasgow* with twenty-four, and the great sixty-eight-gun *Somerset.* They could hear their bells marking the half-hour and the reassuring cry of "All's well" from the British sentries. Finding everything quiet, Prescott recalled Maxwell's men a little before dawn.[16]

Soon the faint light of the coming day discovered to the watch on the *Lively* the walls of the redoubt, now six feet high. Without delay, her captain put a spring on her cable, swung her about so as to bring her guns to bear, and opened fire. The sound of her cannon aroused the British camp and the whole town of Boston. Admiral Graves signaled the *Lively* to cease firing; but about nine o'clock it was resumed by his order, and began from the other ships and the battery on Copp's Hill as well.[17]

When Prescott looked about him in the light of day, he saw his little redoubt, perched all alone on that hilltop, with no outworks, no support whatever, except the houses in Charlestown, the fences and walls on that side, and a swamp at some distance on the other. There was really nothing to prevent its being outflanked by troops marching out of musket range on either side. He prepared at once to extend his defenses on the east by running a straight line of breastworks about twenty rods long from near the southeast corner of the redoubt and parallel with its eastern face, down the slope of the hill to the swamp. The Charlestown houses, walls, and fences would have to be relied on for protection of his other flank.[18]

The ships, chiefly the *Lively, Falcon,* and *Spitfire,* and the Copp's Hill battery kept up their bombardment of the redoubt. The fire from the vessels was ineffective; their guns were too light, and they could not be elevated sufficiently to bear on their target. The battery was too far away to do much damage. The roar of the guns was terrifying to the inexperienced American soldiers; but the round shot bounced about without doing any harm, and the work on the defenses went on without interruption. At last one of the men, working on the outside of the redoubt, was hit and killed. That was a shock to them all. One of the subalterns announced the casualty to Prescott, and asked what should be done. "Bury him," said the colonel. The brusqueness of the reply shocked the questioner. "What?" said he. "Without prayers?" A clergyman present volunteered to perform a burial service. Many of the men laid down their tools and gathered about the body. Prescott ordered them back to their work, "but religious enthusiasm prevailing, the chaplain again collected his congregation," and the corpse was interred in due form.[19]

This incident worked upon the fears of some of the men. A number of them left the ground and never returned. To reassure the rest, Prescott mounted the parapet, and, thus exposed to the fire of the enemy, walked along it, encouraging his men and directing their labors. But more than fear of the big guns was working on the minds of the weary men, more than mere fatigue was exhausting their bodies.

As the sun rose in a cloudless sky, the temperature also rose; the day became one of the hottest of that summer. There was little movement of the air outside the redoubt; inside, there was none. Dust from the disturbed, dry earth hung about them in clouds; they breathed it; their lips were caked with it; their faces were grimy with sweat and dirt. Inexperienced in warfare and inefficiently organized, many of them had neglected the order to bring a day's food; now they were faint with hunger. A cannon ball smashed the two hogsheads that had held their supply of water; no more could be had except when carried in buckets from the wells in the village. "We began to be almost beat out," Peter Brown wrote to his mother after the battle, "being tired by our Labour and having no sleep the night before, but little victuals, no Drink but Rum," which though undeniably stimulating does not, when taken straight, quench thirst.[20]

All that was bad enough, but there had begun to creep into their minds doubts as to the capacity and good faith of their leaders, a suspicion that they were deserted by their comrades in Cambridge. They had been promised relief in the morning; none had come, no new men, nor any food. "The Danger we were in," wrote Brown, "made us think there was Treachery & that we were brot there to be all slain, and I must & will say that there was Treachery, Oversight & Presumption in the Conduct of our Officers."[21] It is a wonder that there was not a wholesale desertion, that the whole enterprise did not break down before any British soldier appeared in the field.

That would have been the outcome, one is forced to think, but for one man, Colonel William Prescott.

He never swerved from obedience to his orders, never faltered in the prosecution of his task. When some of his officers urged him to send to headquarters to ask for relief, for his tired men to be replaced by others, he refused. "The men who have raised these works are the best able to defend them," said he. "They have learned to despise the fire of the enemy; they have the merit of the labor, and shall have the honor of the victory." He did, however, send for supplies and reinforcements.[22]

Because of the heat he had discarded his uniform coat and put on a banian, a light linen coat. His hat and wig were laid aside; his bald head glistened with sweat, as he went about inside and outside the redoubt, encouraging his men or driving them to their labor with sharp commands, keeping them at it by the sheer power of his will, until by eleven o'clock they had finished the works, made the banquettes (or fire steps), and could rest. One veteran of the day said long afterward, "I tell ye that if it had not been for Colonel Prescott, there would have been no fight." [23]

The Neck was so raked by shot from the armed transport *Symmetry* and two gunboats that Captain Samuel Gridley refused to risk one of his artillery horses across it when Major Brooks, bearing Prescott's request to Ward for reinforcements, asked for a mount; Brooks had to go on foot. He reached headquarters in Cambridge at ten o'clock. Ward had already refused an earlier request from Putnam; he still hesitated. At the very time when courage and resolution to take risks and to dare possible dangers were most needed at headquarters, they were wanting. Ward doubted that the British would attack Prescott; he feared they would rather take this opportunity to seize his own stores of munitions and supplies at Cambridge and Watertown; and he did not wish to weaken his forces there. He referred Prescott's request to the Committee of Safety, then in session in his house. Richard Devens of Charlestown, one of its members, was so "impassioned and vehement" in urging that troops be sent that the Committee recommended their dispatch, and Ward yielded. The New Hampshire regiments of Colonel John Stark and Colonel James Reed, then at Medford, were ordered to go.[24]

All this while Putnam was not idle. His particular post was on Bunker's Hill, where he had planned to erect defenses to cover a possibly necessary retreat from Breed's. But while waiting for the completion of the redoubt, so as to get the intrenching tools, he was never idle; "burning with zeal and intrepidity," he was riding about here, there, and everywhere. He was a general and a whole general's staff at once. Twice he had ridden to Cambridge, crossing the Neck through the ships' fire there, fearless and unhurt, to demand reinforcements, which Ward refused. He was now at Breed's, now at Bunker's, now at the Neck or at any other place on the peninsula; he was seen "in so many places that he would appear to have been ubiquitous." When the works on Breed's were complete, he called on Prescott to send the tools to him at Bunker's. Prescott had only about three hundred of his Massachusetts men and Knowlton's fatigue detachment in the redoubt; he feared that any that were sent with the tools would not come back. "They shall every man return," said Putnam. Prescott yielded. "An order was never obeyed with more readiness. From every part of the line within hearing volunteers ran, and some picked up one, some two shovels, mattocks &c., and hurried over the hill." Not one of them came back.[25]

Gage had called a council of war as soon as possible after the first alarm. It was plain to all its members that the American position was bad, since it was nearly surrounded by water that was completely dominated by the King's ships. Its only communication with the other American forces for supplies and reinforcements was by way of the narrow Neck, which was exposed to the fire of the guns of some of the British ships. The only question discussed was how best to capture or destroy the provincials. Clinton, it is said, favored an immediate landing, with a force of five hundred men, on the peninsula south of the Neck and in the rear of the redoubt. Some of the ships or gondolas could then blast the Neck itself with such a concentration of fire that no aid could reach the redoubt. Cut off from either supports or retreat, the Americans must starve in their fort or come out and fight in the open between two fires, for another force could be landed at the other end of the peninsula to cooperate with the first.[26]

Gage and the majority of the council objected to this plan. It was argued that it was not good military practice to interpose a force between two bodies of the enemy—in this case, the men on the peninsula and the rest of the American army. However sound the maxim, it was not so sound as to overrule all other considerations in a particular case. A different plan was proposed and adopted. As matters then stood, it was not a bad plan. The British would land a strong force below Moulton's Point on the southeast corner of the peninsula, march it up the east side along the Mystic, out of musket shot of the redoubt, flank it, and attack it in the rear. It must be remembered that at that early hour, when the extended breastwork had not even been begun and the redoubt stood all alone, there was ample clear space for this maneuver; it might easily have succeeded, had it been promptly executed. But it was fatally delayed.[27]

"As the shore where it was judged most proper to land was very flat, the

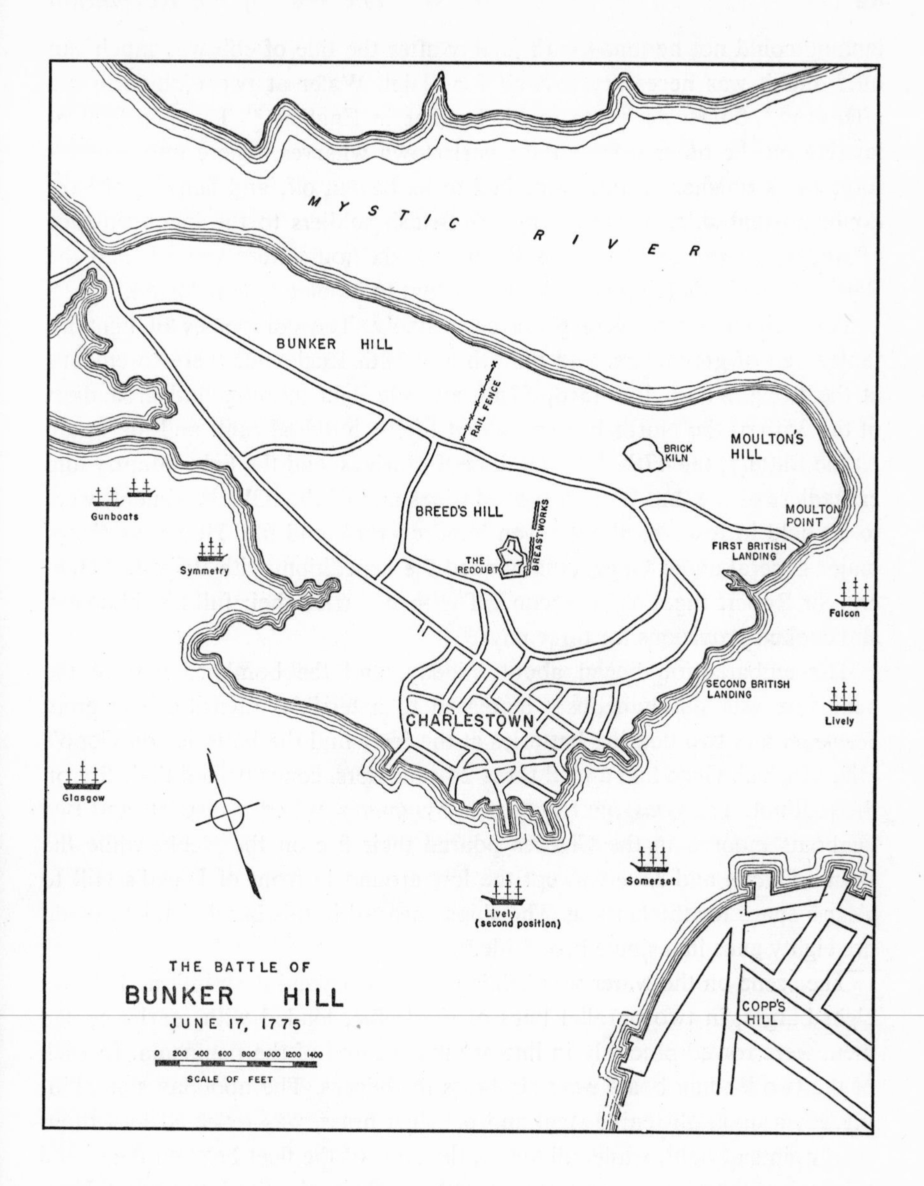
MYSTIC RIVER
BUNKER HILL
RAIL FENCE
BRICK KILN
MOULTON'S HILL
Gunboats
BREED'S HILL
BREASTWORKS
MOULTON POINT
THE REDOUBT
FIRST BRITISH LANDING
Symmetry
Falcon
SECOND BRITISH LANDING
CHARLESTOWN
Lively
Glasgow
Somerset
Lively (second position)
THE BATTLE OF
BUNKER HILL
JUNE 17, 1775
0 200 400 600 800 1000 1200 1400
SCALE OF FEET
COPP'S HILL

landing could not be made with facility after the tide of ebb was much run off," and it was necessary to wait for "High Water at two o'clock in the afternoon." So Howe wrote to his brother in England.[28] Thus, instead of landing on the other side at the Charlestown wharves, where only a weak force of skirmishers would have had to be beaten off, and flanking the redoubt on that side, or subjecting the British soldiers to the inconvenience of wading ashore at Moulton's Point, full six hours were wasted, and the Battle of Bunker's Hill had to be fought out to its bloody conclusion.

The British orders were given accordingly. Ten companies of light infantry, ten of grenadiers, and the 5th and 38th Regiments were to embark at the Long Wharf, the 43rd, 52nd, and the light infantry and grenadiers of the 35th at the North Battery, about fifteen hundred rank and file in all. At the Battery, the 47th, 1st Battalion of Marines, and the light infantry and grenadiers of the 2nd Battalion of Marines and of the 63rd Regiment, were to be held in reserve, about seven hundred rank and file. Howe, as senior major general under Gage, commanded the expedition, with Brigadier General Sir Robert Pigot as his second. The men carried their full kit, blankets, and cooked provisions for three days.[29]

The embarkation began about midday, and the bombardment of the peninsula was simultaneously increased to a terrible intensity. The great *Somerset* and two floating batteries at the ferry and the batteries on Copp's Hill, to which Gage had added three 24-pounders, concentrated their fire on the redoubt. The *Glasgow* frigate, the *Symmetry* armed transport, and two gunboats moored in the Charles poured their fire on the Neck, while the sloops *Falcon* and *Lively* swept the low ground in front of Breed's Hill to clear a space for the landing. The ships engaged in this bombardment could fire eighty guns in a single broadside.[30]

The scene on the water was brilliant almost beyond description. Twenty-eight barges, in two parallel lines of single file, loaded with scarlet-coated men, were rowed precisely in line around the end of the peninsula. In each of the two leading boats were six brass fieldpieces. The noonday sun, shining down upon glistening steel and polished brass, was reflected in a thousand points of light, while, all about, the guns of the fleet belched flame and smoke in a thunderous roar. It was such a sight as the tired, hungry, thirsty, dirty, shirt-sleeved farmers, peering over the walls of their little fort, had never before seen, war in all its pride and glory, before it dissolved into blood and horror.[31]

The landing was made about one o'clock without resistance, and the troops were at once formed in three lines on Moulton's Hill, while Howe was examining the American works. He saw at once that the situation had changed since the early morning. Whereas then the redoubt had stood alone, with no supporting defenses, leaving a broad way around it on the east, now the breastwork extended eastward and dangerously narrowed that way. Yet it was not entirely cut off; there was still room for a flanking movement. There was, however, another matter to be considered. On Bunker's Hill there was a considerable crowd of men who had left the redoubt at various times, or who had crossed the Neck and stopped there. Putnam held them to erect his proposed covering works. But to Howe they doubtless looked like a reserve force. There was a danger that his flanking movement might land him between two American forces. Also he saw a column emerge from that formless mass of men and march toward the redoubt. The Americans there were being reinforced. He was going to need more men than he had brought. He ordered his men to break ranks and refresh themselves with the food they had brought, while he obtained his reserves and part of his main force for which there had not been room in the first embarkation.[32]

The reinforcements that Howe saw marching to the redoubt from Bunker's Hill were the New Hampshire troops under John Stark and James Reed. When they received their orders to march from Cambridge, there were no cartridges on hand. To each man were issued two flints, a gill of powder, and about a pound of lead, cut from the organ pipes of a Cambridge church. They were directed to march to their quarters and make up fifteen cartridges each. Those that had bullet molds used them; the others pounded bits of lead into slugs to fit their muskets. Few of them had cartridge boxes; the rest carried loose powder in their horns and the bullets in bags. They then started on a four-mile march to Charlestown. Stark's regiment, consisting of thirteen companies, was the largest in the army. Reed's was small.[33]

Meanwhile, the news of the landing of the British had thrown Cambridge into confusion. Bells were rung, drums were beaten, and officers ran hither and thither calling out their men to do they knew not what. Orders arrived from Putnam for the Connecticut troops to come on. Ward, with the stubbornness of his natural disposition, would not be convinced that this was the real attack; he still feared that it was a feint, and that his stores were in danger. Exactly what orders he gave is not known. It appears that some provisions, including barrels of beer, were to be sent to the peninsula; but the supply that reached the troops was tantalizingly scanty. It also appears that he reserved his own regiment, John Paterson's, Thomas Gardner's, and a part of Ebenezer Bridge's, and ordered the rest of the Massachusetts troops to Charlestown. But no one knew clearly what he was to do. Jonathan

Brewer's regiment, John Nixon's, Moses Little's, James Scammon's and Samuel Gerrish's, all Massachusetts troops, were under arms and marching about, with vague notions of what was expected of them. When Colonel Stark, leading his regiment and Reed's, approached the Neck, he found two regiments halted in the road, fearing to cross through the barrage thrown by the *Symmetry* and her attendant gunboats. Stark asked them, if they did not intend to cross, to let his men through, which they gladly did. He marched his men across the Neck at a very deliberate pace. Captain Henry Dearborn of the front company suggested "quickening the march of the regiment," that it might sooner be relieved of the cross fire. "With a look peculiar to himself," says Dearborn, "he fixed his eyes on me and observed with great composure—'Dearborn, one fresh man in action is worth ten fatigued men.' " At the top of Bunker's Hill, Stark halted to survey the scene.[34]

When Prescott saw the British forces landed at Moulton's Point and deployed as if for immediate action, against his left, he realized that the gap between the far end of the breastwork and the edge of the peninsula offered an avenue for flanking and even encircling his main position. He at once ordered Knowlton to move his Connecticut troops from the entrenchments and, with two guns, to oppose the enemy's right wing in its approach on that side.

Near the base of Bunker's Hill and about six hundred feet behind the line of the breastwork, there was a fence "half of stone and two rayles of wood." It was about two hundred yards long, running parallel with the breastwork to the river bank, and, if held, it would prevent Howe's flanking movement. Knowlton took post there. To strengthen this frail barrier, his men tore down a near-by rail fence, set it up in front of the other, with a little distance between, and stuffed this space with newly cut grass which lay all about. It seems to have been, as one of his men said, "a slight defence against musquet-ball," but it had a sufficient appearance of strength to deceive the enemy.[35]

From his place on Bunker's Hill, Stark saw that this fence was thinly held by Knowlton's men, fewer than two hundred on a two-hundred-yard length. He "harangued his regiment in a short but animated address," to which they responded with three cheers, and then led them at the double down the slope of Bunker's Hill to the fence to reinforce Knowlton. It was fortunate for the Americans that Stark came to that point, for he saw at once that, while the fence extended to the river bank, there was still a way around it. The edge of the hard ground was a bluff eight or nine feet high. Below it was a strip of beach, narrow at the near high tide then prevailing, but wide enough to permit a column to pass along it. With stones from adjacent walls, he built a breastwork across the beach clear to the water's edge. He lined this with a triple row of his best men, posting the rest and Reed's men along the fence with Knowlton.[36] One other minor element of the American defenses has been generally overlooked by historians of the battle. To cover the ground between the east end of the breastwork and the west end of the rail fence, three small flèches, V-shaped entrenchments, had been built.[37]

There were, then, four distinct elements in the fortifications: the redoubt, the breastwork, the rail fence, and the wall on the beach. When the battle began they were manned as follows: the redoubt and the breastwork by Prescott's and parts of Brewer's, Nixon's, Woodbridge's, Little's, and Ephraim Doolittle's Massachusetts regiments, the last named under Major Willard Moore; the fence by Knowlton's Connecticut troops, Reed's New Hampshire, and part of Stark's; the wall on the beach by Stark himself and part of his men.[38]

Two other unfortified positions were held by the Americans to guard Prescott's right flank on the side of the redoubt toward Charlestown. In a cartway along a fence, near the right of the redoubt a company of Little's regiment and a few other troops, including Nutting's company, which had been guarding the shore in the village, were posted. Three companies—Wheeler's of Doolittle's regiment, Crosby's of Reed's, and one from Woodbridge's—were stationed in the main street of Charlestown at the foot of Breed's Hill; these constituted the extreme American right.[39]

Before the battle began two notable volunteers appeared on the field and were greeted with cheers. One was Joseph Warren. As he had been appointed a major general, Putnam offered him command at the rail fence; he declined it. He asked only where he could be of most service as a volunteer. Putnam indicated the redoubt, where he would be under cover. Warren said he did not seek a place of safety. "Where will the attack be the hottest?" he asked. Putnam still pointed to the redoubt. "That is the enemy's object. If that can be maintained, the day is ours." At the redoubt Prescott offered to yield his command. Warren again declined, and fought in the battle as a simple soldier.[40]

The other newcomer was General Seth Pomeroy—old Seth Pomeroy, carrying his nearly seventy years as lightly as he bore the musket which he himself had made and had carried at the siege of Louisburg thirty years before. He had ridden to the Neck on a borrowed horse. As it was not his own, he would not submit it to the raking fire there, but dismounted, crossed on foot, and trudged all the way to the rail fence, where he took his place with the others amid an enthusiastic welcome.[41]

Soon after his first landing Howe had pushed forward two outposts: one of four companies of light infantry in front of his main body in a depression which sheltered it from the fire of the redoubt; the other, two battalions under Pigot, to a position farther west and just below the southern foot of Breed's Hill. This detachment became the nucleus of Pigot's wing in the attack.[42]

Pigot, in his position on the British left, was annoyed by the fire of the Americans from Charlestown on his left. Admiral Samuel Graves had come ashore to see what help the fleet could give. Pigot spoke to him about "the mischief his left wing sustained by the fire from Charlestown." Graves sent orders to burn the place. Under a shower of red-hot cannon balls and of carcasses (hollow iron balls pierced with holes and containing lighted combustibles) from the ships and the batteries on Copp's Hill, it was "instantly set on fire in many places." It had been practically deserted, except for the few American troops, who were soon driven out by this bombardment. No effort was made to extinguish the fires, and soon the entire town was in flames.[43]

The reserve ordered up by Howe landed between one and two o'clock west of Moulton's Hill below the western foot of Breed's, and near Pigot's outpost. Howe then disposed his troops for the attack. His own right wing was drawn up in three lines, the classic British battle order, the light infantry in front, the grenadiers in the second line, the 5th and 52nd Regiments in the third. Pigot had three companies of light infantry, three of grenadiers, the 38th, 43rd, and 57th Regiments, and the 1st Battalion of marines. The two divisions were about equal in number, thirty-seven companies in Pigot's, thirty-eight in Howe's; but Howe's was stronger, because he had the greater number of flank companies, picked men.[44]

Howe is said to have addressed his troops in the usual eighteenth century manner. He was happy to have the honor of commanding so fine a body of men, who, he was sure, would "behave like Englishmen, and as becometh good soldiers." He would not desire one of them "to go a step further than where I go myself at your head"—a promise he kept, for, in the good old fashion, he fought in the front ranks.[45]

Before advancing his infantry, he sent his artillery forward and opened fire on the redoubt, the breastwork, and the rail fence. Three ships, three floating batteries, and the battery on Copp's Hill, from six different directions, centered their fire on the works. Howe's fieldpieces were, however, soon silenced, not by the feeble fire from the American artillery posted in the gap between the breastwork and the rail fence, but by the discovery that their side boxes contained twelve-pound balls, instead of six-pound. Howe sent off for the proper balls, ordering the substitution of grape in the meanwhile; but the distance was too great for grape to be effective. There was a further difficulty when the guns, supported by the grenadiers of the 35th, were pushed forward to support the attack. They got into boggy ground and could not be moved. Altogether, Howe's fieldpieces were of little avail at that time, except to scare the Americans, who had an exaggerated idea of the deadliness of artillery.[46]

From the formation of Howe's line, it would have seemed that he intended to advance in the conventional three-line formation directly upon the American works, with no other plan than to make a dogged frontal attack. This, indeed, has been the story of the battle in most of the histories and pictures of the combat; but such was not the case. Howe was too able a strategist to employ such a wasteful method if a flanking movement were possible, as was to be proven more than once in this war. He still had in mind his original plan flanking and encircling the American left. Although the defenses had been so greatly extended since that plan was formed, it still seemed possible to carry it out by smashing the extreme left while appearing to lead his men to a direct attack on the works, and this he proceeded to attempt.[47]

He drew off his front line of light infantry to the right and formed them, eleven companies, in column on the beach. This left his battle line in two ranks, grenadiers in front. With these his advance began. In heavy marching order, carrying knapsacks, blankets, and all their accouterments—with their ammunition, food, and firelocks, an estimated weight of a hundred pounds for each man—the main body of redcoats marched down from Moulton's Hill, across the lowland, and up the lower slopes of Breed's toward the breastwork and rail fence. At the same time Pigot's division breasted Breed's Hill against the redoubt, which he intended to envelop.[48]

The day was hot. The unmown grass, through which they had to march, was thick and long, reaching to their knees. There were walls and fences, which they had to throw down or climb over. The brick kiln and its adjacent ponds in the hard ground between two swamps broke their ranks, which had to be re-formed. They stopped from time to time to let the artillery come up and resume its fire. Altogether, the march against the American works was as painful as it was slow. As seen from Boston, across the Charles, it was, however, a brilliant and awe-inspiring spectacle. The people thronged the river shore; they crowded the hills; they perched on rooftops and gazed at "one of the greatest scenes of war that can be conceived," as General Burgoyne wrote to a friend in England.[49]

There were those two scarlet-clad lines of men pushing forward slowly, so slowly that the suspense was heavy to bear, their gun barrels and bayonets flashing back the rays of the sun. There were the guns, the fieldpieces, the great guns on the ships and on Copp's Hill, flashing with flame, emitting clouds of white smoke in a continuous rolling of thunder. In the foreground was Charlestown, scores of houses in one great blaze, its tall church steeples flaming high in the air, ships upon the stocks burning, the crash of buildings, whole streets of buildings, falling together. From it vast, billowing clouds of smoke arose, drifted toward the central scene, now obscuring this or that element, now lifting and disclosing it again. And, in the midst of it all, that little redoubt anxiously yet grimly silent, as it awaited the shock of battle. It was, said John Burgoyne, "a picture and a complication of horror and importance beyond anything that ever came to my lot to be witness to." [50]

The plan for the attack seems to have consisted of three parts. Pigot's division was to march against the redoubt and the breastwork, not to attack them, but to engage the attention of their defenders and hold them in check. The light infantry were to storm the little position on the beach, break through, and come onto the field behind the rail fence. Then Howe's grenadiers and regulars would fall on the rail fence, which would be under the fire of the light infantry in their rear. Thus the whole American left would be shattered, and the redoubt and breastwork isolated and surrounded.

As soon, therefore, as the whole line started its slow advance, "frequently halting to give time for the artillery to fire," [51] the 11 light infantry companies formed in column of fours on the narrow beach, those from the 23rd Regiment, the famous Royal Welch Fusiliers, in the lead, followed by those from the 4th, the King's Own Regiment. They were ordered not to fire, but to take their objective with the bayonet. The beach was level and unobstructed by grass, walls, or fences. Their advance could therefore be more rapid than that of the main forces, and, as theirs was to be the first attack, they doubtless made good time.

The familiar story has it that the Americans were told not to fire until they could see the whites of the enemies' eyes, nor until the order was given, and then to aim low. Stark's men from behind their roughly piled stone wall on the beach could see the scarlet-clad column advancing steadily and swiftly upon them, coming nearer and nearer until it was almost close enough to deploy and charge. It was only 150 feet away when the order came. A blast of fire struck the Fusiliers and tore the leading ranks apart.

The column halted, recoiled, but came on again, the King's Own pushing through the broken Fusiliers. Again the Yankee muskets spoke, again men fell in heaps. The officers shouted at the men, urged them forward. Though they did re-form and try once more, it was like pushing a wax candle against a red-hot plate—the head of the column simply melted away. Ninety-six lay dead on the beach; they "lay as thick as sheep in a fold." The rest turned and ran. That part of Howe's plan had failed.[52]

But with his grenadiers and his regulars Howe had to go on. His pretty plan was wrecked. There would be no turning movement of his enemy's extreme left, no confusion and dismay behind the rail fence caused by fire on its flank and rear. He had to make a direct, frontal attack on the fence, whether he would or no. He did go on. His men marched steadily forward. They were checked and obstructed by fences and walls at the point where their bayonet charge should have begun, and there the fire from the fence broke upon them in a withering blast that shattered their lines. Every man in Howe's personal staff was either killed or wounded.

The grenadiers in front stopped, began to fire instead of charging; but they aimed too high, most of their bullets passing over the heads of the Americans, while the renewed fire from the fence still fell heavily upon them. The second line came up and "mixt with them" in disorder, and at last the whole force fell back in confusion, out of range. Meanwhile Pigot had made his attempt against the redoubt, hardly more than a feint, and had also fallen back. So ended the first attack.[53]

In the American lines there was joy and exultation. These farmers had met the famous British regulars and beaten them. At but little cost, they had strewn the ground with their enemy's dead. But Prescott knew that the battle was not yet won. The British would not give over their attack after one repulse. He mingled with his men, praising their valor, reminding them that there was yet work to be done, and encouraging them to stand to it. There were pitifully few in the redoubt now, no more than one hundred and fifty. Putnam, who had been at the fence, rode back over Bunker's Hill, where there were hundreds of men, calling on them to reinforce Prescott. He rode down to the Neck. Ward had sent men from Cambridge; but they had halted, fearing to penetrate the feeble barrage still being laid down upon that isthmus. Putnam rode through it, called on them to follow him, and rode back again, entreating them to come on. A few did, but only a few. Nor did he get many more from Bunker's Hill.[54]

Howe soon re-formed his shattered ranks. Within a quarter of an hour the second attack began, but not on the same plan. The American left, the rail fence, had proved to be too strong. His light infantry, rallied from their defeat on the beach, had rejoined his force. They were now to march against the fence to engage American attention, while Howe and Pigot threw their whole force against the redoubt and the breastwork. The artillery left behind, columns were formed and marched forward until they were within a hundred yards, where they deployed in line of battle and opened fire. The American lines were silent, until the enemy were within a hundred feet. Then came from them a blast of fire, more devastating than before. It was not merely a single volley. The Americans loaded and fired again and again, not only from the redoubt, breastwork, and fence, but also from the three little flèches, "from whence the Grenadiers received a very heavy fire," and from some buildings on Pigot's left.

Though mown down like grass under the scythe, the British struggled to advance. A bayonet charge was intended, but, against that fire, it was sheerly impossible. "An incessant stream of fire poured from the rebel lines; it seemed a continued sheet of fire for nearly thirty minutes. Our Light-infantry were served up in Companies against the grass fence, without being able to penetrate—indeed, how could we penetrate? Most of our Grenadiers and Light-infantry, the moment of presenting themselves, lost three-fourths, and many nine-tenths of their men. Some had only eight or nine men a company left; some only three, four and five. On the left Pigot was staggered and actually retreated. Observe, our men were not driven back; they actually retreated by orders." [55] Whether they retreated by order or by the instinct of self-preservation, they did retreat, down the slope of the hill, far out of range of the American muskets, and there was a long cessation in the fighting, so long that the Americans began to think they saw a victory.[56]

Putnam had been incessant and indefatigable in his efforts to reinforce the lines from the crowd on Bunker's Hill, but with little success. Captain John Chester, who with his company had been called by Putnam from Cambridge to the scene of action about noon, describes what he found on his arrival. He had marched at the same time as three regiments. When he got to the hill "there was not a company with us in any kind of order. They were scattered, some behind rocks and hay-cocks, and thirty men, perhaps, behind an apple-tree." British bullets, flying high over the American lines, had landed among the men on the hill, and the guns on the ships had been pouring their fire on it. Some of the men there were wounded. Their solicitous comrades carried them to safety, "frequently twenty men round a wounded man, retreating, when not more than three or four could touch him with advantage. Others were retreating, seemingly without any excuse, and some said they had left the fort with leave of their officers, because they had been all night and day on fatigue, without sleep, victuals, or drink." [57]

Putnam found one of these reinforcing regiments scattered about on the safe side of Bunker's Hill. Its colonel, Samuel Gerrish, who was "unwieldy from excessive corpulence . . . prostrate on the ground," declaring that he was "completely exhausted . . . Putnam ordered them on to the lines; he entreated them, threatened them, and some of the most cowardly he knocked down with his sword, but all in vain." The adjutant, Christian Febiger, who was to distinguish himself by more than one act of valor, did rally a detachment and led it to the lines.[58] Gerrish was afterward cashiered. Two other Connecticut companies, under James Clark and William Coit, arrived in time to have some part in the battle. Colonel James Scammons marched his regiment to Lechmere Point. He was ordered to "march to the hill." He marched to Cobble Hill, about a mile from Bunker's. After a while, he went on to Bunker's, "where the shot flew very thick." "Before we got to the top of the hill, Colonel Scammons ordered a retreat," and retreat they did. Scammons was later tried by court-martial; but, on his plea that he had misunderstood his orders, was acquitted.[59]

Four hundred fresh men, the 63rd Regiment and the 2nd Battalion of marines, sent for after the first attack, had now joined Howe, and he began his preparations for another assault, in spite, it is said, of the remonstrances of some of his officers, who urged that it would be downright butchery of his men to send them again into that deadly fire. He ordered all knapsacks and other superfluous equipment laid aside. The troops were to advance in columns, without firing a shot, and take the works with the bayonet. The artillery was to be pushed forward into the gap between the east end of the breastwork and the west end of the rail fence, so as to enfilade the breastwork and drive out its defenders. Preparations were made accordingly.

Clinton, watching the scene from Copp's Hill, was not restrained by lack of orders from Gage. He crossed and, when he landed, "collected all the guards and such wounded men as could follow, which to their honour were many, and advanced in column with as much parade as possible to impress the enemy," a heroic picture. He joined Pigot's division in the attack.[60]

Within the American lines there had been little loss of men, but there was a depressing scarcity of powder; not much was left in the powder horns. The few remaining cannon cartridges were broken open, and their contents distributed. The defenses were manned with as much resolution as before, but with little hope.[61]

The British guns were brought up. Their columns were on the march again. There was to be only a slight demonstration against the rail fence, while Howe threw his division upon the breastwork, and Pigot and Clinton concentrated on the redoubt. The artillery secured its desired position and opened a raking fire on the breastwork's defenders. They were swept away, either off the field or into the redoubt. The infantry plunged forward with their bayonets advanced, and once more met a deadly fire. The Americans "rose up," wrote young Lord Rawdon, "and poured in so heavy a fire upon us that the oldest officers say they never saw a sharper action. They kept up this fire until we were within ten yards of them, nay, they even knocked down my captain . . . after we had got into the ditch of the entrenchment. . . . There are few instances of regular troops defending a redoubt till the enemy were in the very ditch of it." [62]

On Pigot's extreme left, which had curved around to the west side of the redoubt, the marines had a hard time. They were checked by that desperate fusillade, fell into confusion, and began to shoot instead of charging. Major Pitcairn, their commander, was killed, along with many others. The 47th came up and formed beside them. Under the urgent commands of their adjutant, they ceased firing, "rushed on, leaped the ditch and climbed the parapet, under a most sore and deadly fire." [63]

But that was the end. Those last volleys faded out into a sputtering finish, "like an old candle," for there was no more powder. Nor were there bayonets to meet bayonets. The British swarmed over the parapet, leaped down into the redoubt. Its defenders met them with clubbed muskets and stones. The bayonet work of the British, said Adjutant Waller of the marines, was shocking. Yet there were only thirty of the Americans killed in the redoubt. Prescott ordered a retreat. Some of his men clambered over the parapet and got away. The rest crowded toward the gateway in the rear wall, where there might have been a ghastly massacre; but the dust hung so thick in the air that the British could hardly tell friend from foe, and did not fire into the mass at the gateway. Prescott had to fight his way to it, his sword against a British bayonet.[64]

When the beaten men emerged from their fort, they found themselves between the two bodies of their enemy, which had come around opposite sides of the work. Each was afraid to fire for fear of hitting the other. But when the retreating men were clear of those two forces they were heavily fired upon. Joseph Warren, one of the last to leave the redoubt, was shot through the head; and many others fell.[65]

The defenders of the rail fence had suffered little in this last attack, which on their part of the works was but a feint. They withdrew with some degree of regularity, taking their only fieldpiece with them. Old Seth Pomeroy, grasping his veteran musket, its stock shattered by a bullet, walked away backward, still facing the foe. Chester's company, lately arrived with some others, hurried down from Bunker's Hill, posted themselves behind a stone wall, and, "by a brisk fire from our small-arms," covered the retreat as best they could.[66]

But there were others who might have helped and did not. The men behind the rail fence, Knowlton's and Stark's, might have attacked the British right wing in its rear, while it was busy with the redoubt. Unfortunately, there was no concert of effort between them and Prescott; the two wings of the Americans fought as if they had been engaged in different battles. There were many hundred, perhaps a thousand, fresh men with Putnam on Bunker's Hill no more than six hundred yards away—enough, with Stark's and Knowlton's men, to turn the tide of battle if they had come up and attacked the disorganized enemy; but they themselves were a mere mass of men without organization or unified command and they did not even fire a shot to cover the retreat. Prescott, going off the field, came upon Putnam, and asked him why he had given the fighting men no support. "I could not *drive* the dogs," Putnam answered. To which Prescott is said to have replied, "If you could not *drive* them up, you might have *led* them up." [67] The Americans had two things yet to learn, how to organize a real army, and how to stand up and fight in the open.

But the retreat was not a rout. The American rear guard kept up "a running fight from one fence or wall to another, till we entirely drove them off the peninsula." So Rawdon wrote. And Burgoyne testified that "the retreat was no flight; it was even covered with bravery and military skill." Yet it was in the retreat that the Americans suffered the heaviest losses. While the greater part of them were passing over the slopes and the top of Bunker's Hill and across the Neck, they were under continuous fire from the ships and batteries as well as from the muskets of their pursuers. More men were struck down then than in the battle itself.[68]

The defeated men withdrew to Winter Hill and Prospect Hill on the road to Cambridge, and immediately began to fortify. They worked all night under the indefatigable Putnam, and by morning had built an entrenchment on Prospect Hill a hundred feet square. Putnam's son came to him the next morning and found him "dashing about among the workmen. . . . He wore the same clothes he had on when I left him on the 16th, and said he had neither put them off, nor washed himself since, and we might well believe him." [69]

The "almost exhausted" British did not cross the Neck. With the aid of fresh troops from Boston, they threw up a line of breastworks on the northern side of Bunker's Hill, content to hold the ground they had so hardly won. This line was afterward elaborated until it became a strong fortress, well ditched, palisaded, fraised, and protected by outlying entrenchments, making such a strong post that no attack upon it was ever seriously proposed by the Americans.[70]

The losses of the British in this battle were exceedingly heavy. Out of about 2,400 engaged, including the late arrived 400, who had taken part in only the last attack, 1,054, including 92 officers, had been shot; 226 of them were killed. Howe had twelve officers in his staff on the field; every one of them was shot down. Among the light infantry and the grenadiers, who bore the brunt of the battle, the losses were staggering. Every man but four of the grenadiers of the 4th, the King's Own Regiment, was killed or wounded. Of the grenadiers of the 23rd, the Royal Welch Fusiliers, only three remained unhurt. Lord Percy wrote to his father: "My Reg^{t}, being one of the first that entered the redoubt, is almost entirely cut to pieces: there are but 9 men left in my co, & not above 5 in one of the others."[71]

The losses of the Americans have never been accurately ascertained. Besides the original 1,200, there may have been 2,000 more on the peninsula, but it is doubtful that more than 1,500 were actually engaged in the battle at any one time. Of these, perhaps 140 were killed, 271 wounded, and 30 captured, though the figures from various sources vary somewhat. The greatest loss was in Joseph Warren's death. His devotion to the cause, his energy, ability, and personal charm were not equaled by any of the other New England leaders at that time.[72]

To the courage, energy, and unbending will of Colonel Prescott it was undoubtedly due that the redoubt and the breastwork were held after the first assault. He inspired his men in the redoubt with his own tenacity and, by force of personal example and unalterable purpose, held them to their task. Their persistence made it possible for the defenders of the rail fence to hold out.

The stories of the part played by the American artillery are as confused (even on the number of guns in action) as its service was ineffective. There were three companies led by Major Scarborough Gridley and Captains Samuel Trevett and John Callender, having two guns each. Two of them were in disgrace after the battle. Gridley led his men a short way on the road from Cambridge, halted on Cobble Hill, and opened a futile fire against the *Glasgow*. Being urged to go forward, he took his guns to the redoubt and fired a few ineffectual shots at the British batteries on Copp's Hill. Burgoyne reported that two of these cannon balls "went one hundred yards over our heads." Gridley "swang his Hat round three Times to the

Enemy and then ceased to fire." He moved to the space between the breastwork and the rail fence, where he was joined by Callender. They seem to have been with Knowlton at the fence for a time, where "Gridley's guns were soon disabled and he drew them to the rear." Callender said his cartridges were too large for his pieces, and withdrew them to Bunker's Hill. Putnam ordered him back; he went, but "soon left his post and was soon deserted by his men." Captain Ford of Bridge's regiment took the guns back to the rail fence. Trevett, against the orders of his superior, Gridley, who was then firing on the *Glasgow*, took his two guns to Bunker's Hill, where one of them was disabled. He took the other to the fence. After the battle, his one gun was the only one carried safely off. Callender and Gridley were tried by court-martial, and both were dismissed from the service. Callender, however, remained with the army as a volunteer in the ranks and at the Battle of Long Island fought "with such signal bravery" that Washington erased his sentence from the orderly book and restored his commission.[73]

The effect of this battle on the minds of the British leaders appears in a letter from Gage to Dartmouth. It was shown that the Americans were "not the despicable rabble too many have supposed them to be." He recognized in them "a military spirit . . . joined with uncommon zeal and enthusiasm. . . . The conquest of this country is not easy." [74] It has often been held by American historians, probably without good cause, that the memory of his enormous loss in this battle intimidated Howe and deterred him from future frontal attacks on fortified positions, particularly on the day after the Battle of Long Island.

By the American people in general, the battle was at first regarded as a defeat, which, of course, it technically was. The whole enterprise was denounced as rash in its conception and discreditable in its execution. "No one, for years, came forward to claim the honor of having directed it; no notice was taken of its returning anniversary." [75] With the passage of time, emphasis began to be laid on the fact that the defenders of the redoubt gave in only when their ammunition was exhausted; their bravery and their effectiveness as long as their powder held out was recognized. At last, it was held to be a virtual victory, and was so celebrated. Its final effect was, in the minds of Americans, to exalt the American raw recruit to a degree of efficiency equal to that of trained and disciplined regular soldiers—a most unfortunate result.

From a military point of view, this conflict was unnecessary, inadvisable, and without justification. There was no good reason for the Americans attempting to hold the Charlestown peninsula against the British. It could give them no advantage in the siege of Boston, unless they were able to mount there such big guns as would dominate the water route to the town and prevent ships from reaching it. They had no such guns. Again, to hold it they would have had to divide their forces, with no means of communication between them and no means of supplying the force on the peninsula except by the Neck, which would always be under fire from the ships. Success in the Americans' effort was impossible by the very nature of the situation.

As for the British attack, enough has already been said in describing their divided counsels to show that the dreadful wastage of their men was probably unnecessary. Seizure of the Neck was feasible, and the consequent surrender of the garrison would have been inevitable.

CHAPTER 9

Washington Takes Command

The Continental Congress sitting in Philadelphia did not formally, by recorded vote, accept responsibility for the army besieging Boston, or, in the phrase commonly current at the time, "adopt it," until July 25, 1775; but it had ordered powder to be bought for it as early as June 3, and practically committed itself to some degree of responsibility early in that month by other resolutions touching on "the Continental Army." The Congress had even gone so far, on the 15th, as to appoint a general "to command all the continental forces, raised or to be raised, for the defense of American liberty," George Washington.[1]

The selection of a Virginian to command an army composed exclusively of Yankees may seem strange, yet there were cogent reasons for it. The most obvious was the fact of his experience in warfare. That experience did not include large and important commands; nevertheless, his reputation as a military man was more widespread throughout the colonies than that of any other colonial. He was a rich man, an aristocrat, and therefore influential among men of his own class, too few of whom were in sympathy with the American cause. He was a southerner, and the support of the southern colonies was needed in a contest hitherto waged by New England alone. He was a moderate man, still hoping for reconciliation with England; putting him at the head of the army would be notice to other moderate men that the radicals were not to have full sway. He was a sound man in his judgments and his decisions, as everyone who came in contact with him quickly realized. He had taken little part in the debates, and so had not aroused ill feeling in the minds of any of his colleagues. Tall, of commanding appearance, reserved in manner, yet plainly capable of energetic action, he looked like a leader. He was the only one of the delegates in the Congress who wore military garb, the blue and buff uniform of a Virginia militia colonel.

Perhaps as accurate a description of Washington's appearance as may be had is that given in 1760 by Captain George Mercer, his aide-de-camp in the Braddock campaign:

> He may be described as being as straight as an Indian, measuring six feet two inches in his stockings and weighing 175 pounds. . . . His frame is well padded with well-developed muscles, indicating his great strength. His bones and joints are large, as are his feet and hands.
>
> He is wide-shouldered, but has not a deep or round chest; is neat waisted, but is broad across the hips, and has rather long legs and arms. His head is well shaped though not large, but is gracefully poised on a superb neck. A large and straight rather than prominent nose; blue-gray penetrating eyes, which are widely separated and overhung by a heavy brow. His face is long rather than broad, with high round cheek bones, and terminates in a good firm chin. He has a clear though rather a colorless pale skin, which burns with the sun. A pleasing, benevolent, though a commanding countenance, dark brown hair, which he wears in a cue.
>
> His mouth is large and generally firmly closed, but which from time to time discloses some defective teeth. His features are regular and placid, with all the muscles of his face under perfect control, though flexible and expressive of deep feeling when moved by emotions. In conversation he looks you full in the face, is deliberate, deferential and engaging. His voice is agreeable rather than strong. His demeanor at all times composed and dignified. His movements and gestures are graceful, his walk majestic, and he is a splendid horseman.

Captain Mercer neglected to mention that his "colorless pale skin" was pitted with the scars of smallpox, as were the skins of so many of his contemporaries.

John Adams and Samuel Adams were astute enough to recognize the reasons in favor of selecting Washington to be the commanding general. John made the motion. He noted that "Mr. Washington, who happened to sit near the door, as soon as he heard me allude to him, from his usual modesty, darted into the library room." Hancock, who wanted the job, or at least the refusal of it, showed "a sudden and striking change of countenance. Mortification and resentment were expressed as forcibly as his face could exhibit them." The motion was unanimously approved, and thus, as John Adams wrote to his wife, "the modest and virtuous, the amiable, generous and brave George Washington Esquire" was made "General of the American Army." [2]

Washington's acceptance of the appointment was admirably modest and sincere. He was distressed by a consciousness that his abilities and military experience might not be equal to the task, but he yielded to the desires of the Congress and promised to exert every power he possessed in the cause. He declined payment for his services, asking only for reimbursement of his expenses.[3]

Artemas Ward, Charles Lee, Philip Schuyler, and Israel Putnam were chosen by the Congress as major generals, ranking in that order. Eight brigadier generals were elected: Seth Pomeroy, Richard Montgomery, David Wooster, William Heath, Joseph Spencer, John Thomas, John Sullivan, and Nathanael Greene. Horatio Gates was appointed adjutant, with the rank of brigadier general. Pomeroy, presumably because of his age, did not accept the offered commission. Washington appointed Thomas Mifflin his first aide-de-camp, and Joseph Reed his secretary.[4]

The commander in chief received his orders on June 20. They were in general terms suitable to the occasion, but contained one parenthetical clause which had a far-reaching and seldom salutary effect. He was authorized in all unforeseen contingencies, "or any occasions that may happen, to use your best circumspection and (advising with your council of war) to order and dispose of the said Army as may be most advantageous." [5] It soon became evident and for a long time remained evident that he took that to mean that he must not merely listen to the advice of his generals, but have their express authority before acting in any particular case. The result was that the activities of the army were sometimes dictated and directed by a majority vote of the subordinate generals rather than by the judgment of the commander in chief. This interpretation of his instructions was a consequence of his faithful adherence to the idea that he was merely an instrument of the Congress and not an independent executive. His native modesty and his distrust of his own abilities as a soldier also conduced to this subordination of himself.

Washington left Philadelphia on June 23 in a cavalcade which included Philip Schuyler, Charles Lee, and Thomas Mifflin. They were escorted with much ceremony by a number of the congressional delegates in carriages, accompanied by mounted servants, "a large troop of light horse in their uniforms; many officers of militia besides, in theirs; music playing, etc. etc.," as John Adams wrote to his wife.[6] Little John, plump as a partridge, unquestionably an indoor man, a desk man, envied the gallant soldiers, as all little men envy tall men, all civilians envy the man in uniform, all riders of ambling pads envy the man on a tall horse. "Such is the pride and pomp of war," Adams moralized. "I, poor creature, worn out with scribbling for my bread and my liberty, low in spirits and weak in health, must leave others to wear the laurels which I have sown." No doubt there recurred to his mind what he had lately written: "Oh, that I were a soldier! I will be. I am reading military books." But he never was.

New York, divided in counsel about the conflict, hesitating to take its stand definitely in one camp or the other, was embarrassed when it had to receive the rebel generals on the same day that it must welcome back from a visit to England its royal governor, William Tryon. Fortunately, they landed there several hours apart, so that "the volunteer companies raised for the express purpose of rebellion," as the loyalist judge, Thomas Jones, put it, "the members of the Provincial Congress . . . the parsons of the dissenting meetinghouses, with all the leaders and partisans of faction and rebellion," could meet the generals at four in the afternoon, and conduct them to Leonard Lispenard's house, "amidst repeated shouts and huzzas," and, at nine o'clock, "the members of his Majesty's Council, the Judges of the Supreme Court, the Attorney General . . . the Clergymen of the Church of England," and so on, all the dignified, respectable, and highly placed officials, "with a numerous train of his Majesty's loyal and well affected subjects," could meet the Governor and conduct him, "with universal shouts of applause," to the residence of Hugh Wallace, Esq. "But strange to relate . . . those very people who attended the rebel Generals in the morning . . . now, one and all, joined in the Governor's train and with the loudest acclamations . . . welcomed him back to the colony. . . . What a farce! What cursed hypocrisy!" exclaims the loyal judge.[7]

In New York, Washington detached Major General Philip Schuyler, who was to take command of all the troops in New York colony, and to occupy the posts on Lake George and Lake Champlain. Incidentally, he was to "keep a watchful eye upon Governour Tryon" and, if he attempted "directly or indirectly, any measures inimical to the common cause, [to] use every means in your power to frustrate his designs . . . if forcible measures are judged necessary." While the Continental Congress was not in session, Washington would order such measures; if it were sitting, Schuyler must get his orders from it, because "the seizing of a Governour [was] quite a new thing, and of exceeding great importance." [8]

The rest of the party went on to Cambridge, delayed somewhat on the way "by necessary attentions to the successive Civilities which accompanied me in my whole route," as Washington wrote to the Congress,[9] yet reaching their destination on July 2, only ten days from Philadelphia. He immediately assumed command of the army. Tradition has it that this was done while he stood under a tree on Cambridge Common, known thereafter as the Washington Elm, the troops being paraded before him. But there seems to be no historical basis for the legend. The army was spread over ten miles of defenses, and all trustworthy indications point to his having immediately inspected them piecemeal, without any central ceremony.[10]

At Watertown, on his way, Washington had been received by the Massachusetts Provincial Congress. Its address of welcome apologized for the character of the army he was to command: "The greatest part of them have not before seen service; and although naturally brave and of good understanding, yet, for want of experience in military life have but little knowledge of divers things most essential to the preservation of health, and even life. The youth of America are not possessed of the absolute necessity of cleanliness in their dress and lodging, continual exercise and strict temperance to preserve them from diseases frequently prevailing in camps," [11] all of which Washington soon learned was true enough. "I found," he says, "a mixed multitude of People here, under very little discipline, order, or Government. . . . Confusion and Disorder reigned in every Department." But he did not despair. Within three weeks of his arrival he was able to say, "We mend every day and I flatter myself that in a little Time, we shall work up these raw Materials into good Stuff." [12]

The army lay sprawling about Boston in a great crescent of installations. The Reverend William Emerson, who had been so active in the Concord fight, wrote at this time:

> 'Tis also very diverting to walk among ye camps. They are as different in their form as ye owners are in their dress; and every tent is a portraiture of ye temper and taste of ye persons that incamp in it. Some are made of boards, some of sailcloth, and some partly of one and partly of ye other. Others are made of stone and turf, and others again of Birch and other brush. Some are thrown up in a hurry and look as if they could not help it—mere necessity—others are curiously wrought with doors and windows done with wreaths and withes in ye manner of a basket. Some are your proper tents and marquees and look like ye regular camp of ye enemy. These are ye Rhode-islanders, who are furnished with tent equipage from among ourselves and every thing in ye most exact English taste. However, I think that ye great variety of ye American camp is upon ye whole rather a beauty than a blemish to ye army.[13]

One particular phase of the reformation of the army, the enforcement of proper distinction between officer and private, was fundamental in Washington's idea of an army. The "leveling spirit," the opinion that every man was just as good as any other man and a little better, was rife in New England, and was utterly subversive of discipline in the army. The officers could not maintain proper dignity and superiority to their men, could not give an order and exact obedience. Instead, they must truckle to them, conduct themselves with humility, and persuade their men to do their duty. This spirit of equality and lack of dignity was prevalent among the officers themselves.

Joseph Reed saw one of them "shaving one of his men on the parade." [14] Another officer, a colonel and the army's chief engineer, was seen carrying a large piece of beef, his rations, to his tent. He cheerfully explained that he did it "to set the officers a good example." [15]

In an army without uniforms, there was no apparent distinction between officer and private. The first step toward curing the evils of the leveling spirit would naturally be the introduction of distinctive dress. It was not possible to supply uniforms, but it was possible to distinguish the different grades by simpler methods. In one of the earliest of Washington's general orders provision was made to effect this purpose. The Commander in Chief was to wear "a light blue Ribband . . . across his breast, between his Coat and Waistcoat." Washington entered, in his expense account, an item of three shillings and fourpence, the cost of this decoration. Major generals were to wear purple; brigadiers, pink; aides-de-camp, green. The field officers were to have red or pink cockades in their hats; the captains, yellow or buff; the subalterns, green. The sergeants were to wear a shoulder knot of red cloth on the right shoulder; the corporals, a green knot.[16] These arrangements, coupled with the close attention given even to details, soon produced the desired effect. An observer noted "a great overturning in the camp as to order and regularity. New lords, new laws. The Generals Washington and Lee are upon ye lines every day. . . . The strictest government is taking place, and great distinction is made between officers and soldiers. Everyone is made to know his place and keep in it." [17]

Washington felt the need of uniformity of dress among all his men. "I know of nothing," he wrote, "in a speculative view more trivial, yet which . . . would have a happier tendency to unite the men, and abolish those provincial distinctions, that lead to jealousy and dissatisfaction." He proposed to the Congress the procurement of 10,000 hunting-shirts. These were long, loose shirts, of tow cloth, either of its natural color or tanned to "the shade of a dry or fading leaf," belted at the waist and having double shoulder capes. They were worn outside the breeches like a frock. Being in common use among the American backwoodsmen, they came to be regarded, especially by the British, as the distinctive garb of the riflemen. But, though the Congress approved, and Washington canvassed several of the colonies for the necessary material, he had to give up the project, because of the scarcity of tow cloth. Except in the case of a few militia companies, such as Benedict Arnold's and Joseph Chester's, which wore blue coats faced with red, the army continued to display its motley dress.[18]

One of the first things that Washington did was to call on the adjutant of each regiment for an exact return of its men, equipment, and supplies. These, which should have been completed in half a day, owing to "the imperfect obedience which had been paid to . . . [orders] of a like nature from General Ward," were not forthcoming until after a week had elapsed. They showed a total of 16,770 men on the rolls, of which number 1,598 were on the sick list, 1,429 were absent for one reason or another, leaving 13,743 present and fit for duty.[19]

There was a prompt reorganization of the army into six brigades of six regiments each, and three divisions of two brigades each. Ward was given command of one division to constitute the right wing of the army, posted at Roxbury. Lee commanded another at Prospect Hill, the left wing; Putnam the third, in and about Cambridge, the center.[20] The need for improvement in the fortifications was apparent, and the men were put to work all along the lines. "Thousands are at work every day from four to eleven o'clock in the morning. It is surprising how much work has been done," wrote William Emerson as early as July 17.[21]

The problem of feeding thousands of men, in such a hastily assembled and completely unorganized mass as had swarmed around Boston after the day of Lexington and Concord, had been solved in a haphazard fashion during the two months before Washington took command. The first summons to arms had been sudden and unexpected. The men who hurried from their farms and homes, having no expectation of entering into a protracted service, had brought along pocketfuls of food, those from a distance relying on the inns and taverns to supply them on their march. Each Massachusetts town was, by custom, responsible for supplying its own militia in active service until the province could take over the job. Massachusetts had made provision for the collection of food, and considerable stores had been collected, which were sufficient to feed its men. Each of the other colonies had to care for its own.

Connecticut, having a patriot governor, Jonathan Trumbull, was prompt. An embargo was laid on the export of food. Joseph Trumbull was appointed commissary to collect provisions and supply them to the Connecticut forces; he did the work efficiently. Rhode Island was handicapped at first by its Loyalist governor, Joseph Wanton. But he was soon displaced, and a member of the Committee of Safety was made Chief Commissary with good results. The New Hampshire towns carried the burden for a while, each for its own men, until the province relieved them in May. Being, however, the poorest of them all in the production of foodstuffs, it was obliged to buy from the others, especially from more fertile Connecticut. On the whole, these hastily contrived measures were effective in furnishing the men a sufficient, indeed a comfortable, sustenance.[22]

When the army was adopted by the Congress, Washington was ordered "to victual at the continental expense all such volunteers as have joined or shall join the united army." [23] He appointed Joseph Trumbull commissary general. The daily ration comprised fresh beef or pork or salt fish, bread, peas, beans, or other vegetables, and milk, with a weekly addition of rice or Indian meal. Spruce beer was to be a daily drink, with molasses as a substitute. Candles and soap were also to be provided.[24]

In spite of many difficulties, particularly in the procurement of sufficient wheat flour and in recurring shortages of funds, Trumbull succeeded in his arduous tack of feeding the army during its stay before Boston. In June, 1776, Washington wrote to the Congress, "Few Armies, if any, have been better and more plentifully supplied than the Troops under Mr. Trumbull's care." [25]

In July and August there were brought into the army the first soldiers drawn from outside New England, and remarkable men they were. The Congress on June 14 had voted "That six companies of expert rifflemen, be immediately raised in Pennsylvania, two in Maryland and two in Virginia," each to consist of sixty-eight privates and the usual officers. Recruiting was promptly effected. In Pennsylvania there were so many candidates that three additional companies were authorized, and the whole nine were organized as a battalion, with William Thompson as colonel and Edward Hand second in command. Virginia turned out its share, Daniel Morgan raising his company, ninety-six men, within ten days. Maryland's first company was commanded by Michael Cresap, a veteran Indian fighter; its second, by Thomas Price.[26]

These men were drawn chiefly from the wilder, western parts of their respective colonies—Scotch-Irish many of them. They were backwoodsmen, "remarkably stout and hardy men; many of them exceeding six feet in height." Their garb was simple: round wool hats, hunting shirts, breeches, stockings, and shoes or leather leggings and moccasins, Indian style. "On the breast [of their shirts] in capital letters, is their motto 'Liberty or Death.' " They had to march from four hundred to seven hundred miles to reach the camp, bivouacking in their blankets at night. Morgan mounted his men and rode with them six hundred miles in twenty-one days. So fit were they, and so inured to exposure and physical exertion, that not a man was lost by sickness on the way. All these added 1,430 men to the army.[27]

They also added a new weapon, before that practically unknown in New England. Rifling the barrel of a gun, that is to say cutting spiral grooves inside the barrel so as to make the bullet rotate in its flight and thus increase its accuracy, was not an American invention. It was practiced in Central

Europe as early as 1500. But the so-called Kentucky rifle was evolved in the American colonies and differed greatly from the European rifled guns, which were short, heavy, clumsy, perhaps an inch in bore, and terrific in recoil. The necessities of American frontier life demanded economy in powder and lead, and therefore a small-calibered weapon of great accuracy. By immigrant expert gunsmiths, chiefly German or Swiss settled in Pennsylvania, such a gun was produced.

The rifle was slender and graceful in appearance and as much as five feet long, sometimes more, the greater length of the barrel being supposed to increase its precision. It carried a ball weighing only a half-ounce. Its range and its accuracy in the hands of an expert were extraordinary. While a musket ball dropped harmlessly to the ground at 125 yards and had little certainty of hitting a target less than man-size at half that distance, expert riflemen put ball after ball into a mark seven inches in diameter at 250 yards. Exhibitions of marksmanship and trick shooting by these men amazed and delighted the Yankees around Boston.[28]

The rifle had, however, its disadvantages. The loading was slower than with the musket. In order that the ball might have close contact with the grooves in the barrel, getting its twist and at the same time the full propulsive effect of the powder, a small disk of greased linen or buckskin was placed on the muzzle, the ball laid upon it and the whole rammed home. This took twice the time necessary to load a musket, and, besides, with its small bore and the grooves in the barrel, the rifle soon fouled and had to be swabbed out. Then, too, the lighter bullet had less stopping power against a charge. For sharpshooting and bush fighting it was a superior weapon; but in such a battle as that on Breed's Hill the musket was more useful.

These backswoodsmen proved to be difficult to deal with in the camp. They were accustomed to acting entirely on their own, and their stubborn individualism was slow to yield to army discipline and routine. The inactivity of the siege chafed them. For a while they found satisfaction in sniping sentries or other exposed men in the British lines, where their reputation for deadly accuracy was great and universal. "They are grown so terrible to the regulars," wrote Joseph Reed, "that nothing is to be seen over the breastwork but a hat." But such practices were regarded by Washington as merely a waste of the scanty supply of powder, and had to be stopped. Washington's orders irked the freeborn riflemen, and, although they were at first pampered by exemption from entrenching and general camp duties, they became unruly and troublesome.[29]

If a rifleman was confined in the guardhouse for some disdemeanor, his comrades broke open his prison and released him. On one occasion such a culprit was removed to the main guardhouse in Cambridge for safer keeping, whereupon some of Captain James Ross's Pennsylvania company, armed with loaded rifles, swore by God they would release him or lose their lives, and "set off as hard as they could run." Washington strengthened the guard to the number of five hundred men, and ordered several regiments under arms. He, with Lee and Greene, pursued the mutineers and overtook them. When he ordered them to ground their arms, they, "beginning to be frighted at their proceedings," obeyed. They were then surrounded by another Pennsylvania company and marched back to camp, where they were tried, convicted of mutiny, and fined 20 shillings each.[30]

On the whole, the riflemen were of little use in the siege. "Gen. Washington said he wished they had never come; Gen. Lee has damned them and wished them all in Boston." General Thomas wrote that the generality of them were "as Indifferent men as ever I served with, their Privates mutinous and often Deserting to the Enemy, unwilling for Duty of any kind, exceedingly vitious and I think the army here would be as well without them as with them." The whole trouble was that they were, by nature and by experience, totally unfitted for inactive life in camp. Many of them served excellently in the expedition against Quebec, and later in the war when they were in active service.[31]

Washington thought he had not enough men in his army; but, from the first, he knew he had not enough ammunition, either powder or lead. On August 4 he had but 9,940 pounds of powder, "not more than 9 Cartridges a Man." He repeatedly called on the Congress for more, on all the New England colonies, and on New York. By the 24th, with help from Philadelphia, he had built up his store to 184 barrels, equal to twenty-five rounds, and in September he got 7,000 pounds from Rhode Island. But he never had enough to allow his men to have more than twelve or fifteen rounds at a time while the British kept their soldiers always supplied with sixty cartridges apiece.[32]

To supplement their weapons during the shortage of ammunition, and particularly to make up for the lack of bayonets, several thousand iron-pointed pikes with twelve-foot shafts were procured. As missile weapons, Benjamin Franklin suggested the use of bows and arrows, supporting his recommendation with excellent philosophic reasons, which, however, did not sufficiently commend themselves to the military mind; none was employed.[33]

The shortage of ammunition alone would have prevented any major hostile movement by the Americans; but there were also other dissuasive reasons. The British losses on Breed's Hill had been more than made up by the arrival in June and July of reinforcements, so that their number of effectives was over 6,000, with 1,400 sick or wounded in hospitals.[34] Their defenses at Boston Neck had been built up and greatly strengthened, and on Bunker's Hill they had built an elaborate fortress, with a thick parapet, well ditched, fraised, and abatised, of which Washington said "Twenty thousand men could not have carried it against one thousand had that work been well defended." A large part of their army was in barracks in that fort or encamped about it. Except for the dragoons and a few of the infantry, the rest was in the defenses on Boston Neck.[35] An attempt to storm either of these two main positions, especially with an undisciplined amateur army, would have been suicidal.

On the other hand, the Bunker's Hill battle had convinced the British command of the folly of a major attempt against the fortified positions of the Americans, which stretched from Roxbury on the southeast around to Winter Hill and Prospect Hill on the northwest, and which were constantly being strengthened. The British generals knew that even a successful attack would bring no worth-while results. The two forces were therefore in an equilibrium which neither cared to disturb, and a long cessation of major hostile operations on both sides followed Bunker's Hill. There were, however, minor clashes.

In the early morning of July 8 a party of volunteers under Major Benjamin Tupper and Captain John Crane, with two fieldpieces, attacked a British advance post on Boston Neck, drove off the guard, and burnt its house. A similar attack on another post was made three days later and brought forth a harmless cannonade from the works on the Neck. Other little flurries of the same sort helped to enliven the month of July, in one of which the restless riflemen were given a chance against a post on Charlestown Neck. They crept, in true Indian style, on their hands and knees around the post, but, just as they were about to surround it, a relief for the guard arrived. There was an exchange of fire, five of the guard were killed, and two captured. There were no casualties among the Americans, except the loss of one man taken prisoner. The British retaliated by cannonading the American works on Sewall's Point, at the same time attacking and burning a tavern near Roxbury, held as an American outpost, and driving in an American advance guard of sixty men near Boston Neck. The guard was reinforced, and there was a little fight in which several of the British fell, but no Americans. Each of these affairs was noisy, and greatly alarmed the civilians in Boston, who thought a general battle was on.[36]

On the 21st an American party under Major Joseph Vose set off in whaleboats for Nantasket Point. There they drove back a British guard and destroyed the lighthouse on Great Brewster Island, a mile or so offshore. Ten days later, while the British were rebuilding it, Major Benjamin Tupper landed with three hundred Americans and killed or captured all the work party, demolishing their work. Boats from the warships were driven off after a hot little fight. In all, the British lost fifty-three men; the Americans, one killed and two or three wounded.[37]

For nearly a month after that there was little activity on either side. Then came a more important affair. Ploughed Hill was a low eminence on the road connecting Charlestown Neck with Medford, to the west of Winter Hill and Prospect Hill, the two strong points on the American left. It was of value because it was close to and commanded the Mystic River, and because it was within point-blank shot of Bunker's Hill. Washington decided to seize and fortify it.

In the night of August 26 General John Sullivan led out a fatigue party of 1,200 and a guard of 2,400, including 400 of the Pennsylvania riflemen. Work went on all night, and by daylight there was "an Intrenchment in such forwardness as to bid defiance to their Cannon."[38] Bunker's Hill, a ship, and two floating batteries bombarded it all that day. Sullivan had one nine-pounder in place, which he used so skillfully that he sank one floating battery, injured the other, and put a sloop out of commission. The next morning, a column was seen to be forming on Bunker's Hill. It seemed that a battle was imminent. A general alarm was sounded along the American lines, and 5,000 men were marched to the new post. But the enemy did not advance. For several days they continued to fire on the works. Four Americans were killed, two of them by their own folly in attempting to catch cannon balls bouncing along on the ground.[39]

Two other minor incidents occurred before the year ended. A party of 300 British light infantry raided Lechmere Point on November 9 and carried off a dozen head of cattle, despite the efforts of Thompson's Pennsylvania riflemen and parts of two other regiments to stop them. Both sides claimed a victory: the British because they got the beeves; the Americans because the raiding party left hurriedly under fire. Two weeks later a detachment under Putnam, working at night, fortified Cobble Hill, a mound south of the works on Prospect Hill, without physical objection.[40]

These little affairs accomplished nothing toward a final decision in the contest between the two armies. It was desirable for the Americans that a decisive action should be brought on under favorable conditions; but Gage showed no disposition to enter into a general engagement, nor was the condition of the American army such as to promise it a victory. There was still a deficiency in ammunition, and the army was still too uncertain a force to rely upon in an all-out attack on strongly entrenched regulars. Yet it seemed that something must be done; the existing stalemate could not last much longer.

Inactivity was demoralizing the besieging force; desertions, always a major problem among the Americans throughout the war, were much too frequent now to be ignored. The army was further weakened in September by the detachment of 1,000 men, including Morgan's riflemen, to go on the expedition against Quebec under command of Benedict Arnold. There was also to be considered the approaching dissolution of the whole army by expiration of its terms of enlistment; the Connecticut troops were engaged only to December 10, the rest to January 1. There was, also, in the army and among the people generally a growing feeling of dissatisfaction with a merely defensive policy. It was vocal "in Congress, in the newspapers and above all in the taverns." [41] "Murmurs began to be audible that the army was inactive; and that a superiority of numbers might justify an attempt against the town." [42]

Washington was harassed by the conflict among these various considerations. He could not answer the critics of his defensive policy by disclosing the condition of his powder magazines, which was known to few, and thus expose his weakness to his enemies. In this state of mind, he took refuge in the admonition of the Congress to advise with his officers. On September 8 he addressed a circular letter to the general officers, proposing the question "whether in your judgment, we cannot make a successful attack upon the Troops in Boston, by means of Boats, cooperated by an attempt upon their Lines at Roxbury." He pointed out that the coming winter would require better quarters for the men, supplies of clothing, fuel, and blankets, which could not be had. The daily wasting of the stock of powder, the coming dissolution of the army, and, "to sum up the whole . . . the expence of supporting the army will so far exceed any Idea that was form'd in Congress of it, that I do not know what will be the consequence." Yet "to avoid these evils we are not to loose sight of the difficulties, the hazard, and the loss that may accompany the attempt, nor what will be the consequences of a failure." [43]

It can hardly be said that these reasons for an attack were either cogent or compelling, nor that they indicated a conviction in the mind of the commander in chief that the suggested action should be taken. The council of war evidently did not think so; they voted, on September 11, "unanimously that it was not expedient to make the attempt at present, at least."

This result was communicated to the Congress.[44] That august body entertained the idea that it was perfectly competent to direct the operations of the army in the field. On October 3 it voted that "General Washington may, if he thinks proper, for the encouragement of an attack on Boston, promise, in case of success, a month's pay to the army and to the representatives of such of our brave countrymen as may chance to fall, and in case success should not attend the attempt, a month's pay to the representatives of the deceased." [45]—a half-hearted nudge to action, backed by the inducement of a niggling, cheese-paring promise of reward. Another council met and again disapproved the attempt.[46]

Washington had written a very long letter to the Congress on September 21, describing the condition of the army, indicating its needs for the coming winter and especially calling attention to its approching dissolution.[47] The Congress appointed a committee, consisting of Benjamin Franklin, Thomas Lynch, Sr., and Benjamin Harrison, to confer with the commander in chief and with representatives of the New England colonies "touching the most effectual method of continuing, supporting, and regulating a continental army." [48] They were in conference in the camp for five days. Their report resulted in congressional resolutions calling for an army of "30,732 men, officers included," divided into twenty-six regiments (exclusive of riflemen and artillery) of 728 men each, of all ranks. It fixed their pay and rations and the color of their uniforms, brown with distinctive facings for the different colonies.[49]

Although this narrative concerns itself with the fortunes and misfortunes of the American land forces only, and will not attempt to tell the story of the naval operations, some notice must be taken of the exploits of American seamen at this time, and the beginnings of the navy of the United States, because these early maritime exploits were but an extension of the emerging military power of the colonies.

They began in an effort to protect the coasts and ports of the colonies against attacks by British vessels carried on chiefly for the purpose of foraging and seizing supplies. Rhode Island was the first of the colonies to take steps, by chartering, in June, two armed vessels to oppose the British frigate *Rose,* which had been annoying its coast. Massachusetts was next, taking over a schooner and a sloop which the town of Machias in the district of Maine had armed to protect itself against attack. Connecticut followed by arming two similar vessels against a threatened British raid on Gardiner's and Fisher's Islands. So far the Congress had not assumed any responsibility for the protection of the coasts against naval aggression. On July 18 it resolved that each colony, at its own expense, should provide for the protection of its harbors and coastal towns.[50]

All such preparations contemplated merely defensive measures; but offensive operations might greatly profit the American cause. The British army, cooped up in Boston, had to draw all its supplies from sources outside that town: fresh meats and vegetables, for instance, from the West Indies or the more southern American posts; and its other provisions, its munitions of war, clothing, and every such necessary from England. Confident of no interruption of this traffic, because there was no American naval force, the British had armed their coasting vessels lightly, with no more than small arms, while the transocean merchantmen carried no armament at all and sailed without naval convoy. It seemed to be possible, as Governor Nicholas Cooke of Rhode Island pointed out to the Massachusetts Provincial Congress on June 27, for a swift American vessel, even a small one, carrying a suitable armament, to intercept any of these ships and take her, cargo and all. Although the Massachusetts Congress took no action Washington saw the point, and after some hesitation decided to make the experiment with one vessel.[51]

His commission was in the military line only; no authority had been given him in naval matters. However, he found a way. He appointed the shipmaster Nicholson Broughton a captain in the army and ordered him to take command of a detachment of soldiers "and proceed on Board the Schooner *Hannah* . . . lately fitted out & equipp'd with Arms, Ammunition and Provisions at the Continental Expence." His orders were to cruise "against such Vessels as may be found on the High Seas or elsewhere . . . in the Service of the ministerial Army, and to take and seize all such Vessels, laden with Soldiers, Arms, Ammunition, or Provisions for or from Sd. Army." [52]

Broughton soon captured the *Unity*, a vessel laden with provisions and naval stores. Encouraged by this success, Washington sent out other ships, and the Congress took notice. Having information of the sailing from England of two unarmed brigs, "loaded with arms, powder and other stores," it authorized the General on October 5 to apply to Massachusetts for two armed vessels to go after the unprotected brigs and any other such transports. Also, it asked Connecticut and Rhode Island to send out their vessels, all to be "on the continental risque and pay." [53]

By the end of October six schooners were ready for sea, the *Lynch* commanded by Broughton, the *Franklin* by John Selman, the *Lee* by John Manley, the *Warren* by Daniel Adams, the *Washington* by Sion Martindale, and the *Harrison* by William Coit. This was the first continental fleet. It sailed under the pine-tree flag. The *Washington* was captured by the British warship *Fowey* in November, but the others had better luck; many prizes variously laden were brought in. Manley in the *Lee* was conspicuously successful. His capital prize was the ordnance brig *Nancy*, in the entrance to Boston harbor. Her cargo of 2,000 muskets, 100,000 flints, 30,000 round shot, and 30 tons of musket bullets was of immense value to the army. That was something to crow over. "Such universal joy ran through the whole camp as if each grasped victory in his hand." What chiefly excited them was a 13-inch brass mortar. "Old Put mounted on the large mortar . . . with a bottle of rum in his hand, standing parson to christen" it *Congress*. Manley made other captures: an armed ship loaded with provisions, another vessel full of military stores. "His praise was in every mouth." The little navy gave the army sorely needed supplies and equipment.[54]

During that winter "it was a miserable life inside Boston for troops who had sailed from England in the belief that they were to take part in a triumphant and leisurely progress through a series of rich and repentant provinces." [55] It was indeed, and for more reasons than one.

Everything that the British army ate, wore, or used in any way, except small supplies obtained from the West Indies and the other parts of America, had to be brought from England in slow-sailing ships, exposed to the perils of the sea and to the danger of capture by the small but active American fleet. In the cargoes of food there was a heavy loss by mildew and rot on the way. Of eighteen hundred barrels of flour in one cargo, more than eight hundred were spoiled; of six hundred in another ship, only five were edible.[56]

There was generally enough salt meat and dried peas to eat, and occasionally fish. Flour was always scarce; of potatoes, fresh vegetables, and fruits there were practically none. Most of the available milch cows had been slaughtered for beef, and milk was an extreme rarity. There were no longer any cattle or sheep on the islands in the harbor, and but a handful in any of the fields on the near-by coasts. The rejoicing over the dozen head that were taken by three hundred soldiers in the raid on Lechmere Point is an indication of the extreme need of fresh meat. Even when raids on Fisher's and Gardiner's Island in Connecticut yielded two thousand sheep and some oxen, most of them had to be devoted to their "poor sick and wounded people with whom their hospitals were crowded." [57] Scurvy, induced by the lack of vegetable food, appeared among the troops already infected with smallpox, which "raged in the streets and cantonments." [58]

Even fuel was lacking. When cold weather set in, this became serious.

The main force in the works on the Charlestown peninsula suffered severely from the cold, accentuated by the cutting winds and driving snows of an unusually severe winter. On December 12 all except a guard of six hundred were drawn in to winter quarters in Boston. Fire for warmth and for cooking was needed, but there was no store of fuel. Coal and wood were shipped from England, but many vessels with such cargoes were taken by the American cruisers. To meet this want, the unconsumed wooden buildings in Charlestown were torn down. The Old North Church, the steeple of the West Church, wharves, old ships, trees, and a hundred old houses were condemned to be broken up. The Liberty Tree, a great elm under whose shade many patriotic meetings had been held, yielded fourteen cords of wood. Still there was not enough. The soldiers demolished houses and fences indiscriminately. So frequent were such offenses that the provost was ordered to go his rounds, "attended by an executioner," and "to hang up on the spot the first man he should detect" in such depredations.[59]

To the officers, accustomed to various amusements, their stay in Boston was excessively dull and boring. There were no diversions of any sort beyond those they themselves could contrive; they did their best. To make a riding school, the pulpit and pews of the Old South Church were ripped out, and the floor was covered with tanbark. The gallery became a refreshment room, and the church library was fed into the stoves. Faneuil Hall was turned into a playhouse. An original burlesque, "The Blockade of Boston," was presented, in which Mr. Washington, an uncouth figure wearing a huge wig and a long, rusty sword, was attended by a rustic orderly armed with an absurdly long musket. Mr. Washington with an army of rustics was actually and efficiently blockading Boston at the time, so that the jest had a strong tincture of bitter irony.[60]

For the enlisted men there were no such amusements; nor was there any military activity to engage their interest and keep their spirits up except digging for new fortifications, which was not very enlivening. Idleness and boredom bred indiscipline and slovenliness, and the British regulars lost their characteristic smart appearance. Unpowdered hair, dirty linen, unbuttoned gaiters, unpolished arms were surface indications of the deterioration of the rank and file. They were even so degraded "as to borrow from the enemy that habit which was the least worthy of imitation, and chewed tobacco." [61]

And it was all so useless and so hopeless. Gage and his thousands of troops had been in possession of Boston for a year and a half, yet all he had accomplished was to ruin the business of the town and capture one hill with the loss of nearly half of his best troops, while the rest of the province and the rest of America remained in the hands of his enemies. All he could hope to do from Boston was to take more hills, without any more valuable results. There were plenty of hills: Cobble Hill and Ploughed Hill and Winter and Prospect, any one or all of which the Americans would have been glad to sell him at the price of Breed's. The occupation of Boston was entirely barren of advantage at the time, and gave no promise whatever of advantage in the future.

Gage's three colleagues, the major generals, had realized this and had "presumed . . . to offer their advice" to their chief to remove to New York. Clinton elaborated on the advantages of that town and the disadvantages of their present situation. Let victory here be "ever so compleat, it leads to nothing." [62] Burgoyne wrote home about it shortly after Bunker's Hill: "Look, my Lord, upon the country near Boston—it is all fortification. Driven from one hill, you will see the enemy continually retrenched upon the next; and every step we move must be the slow step of a siege." [63] Gage himself had long been of the same opinion. On October 1 he wrote to Dartmouth that "no offensive operations can be carried on to advantage from Boston." Even if he did drive the rebels from their entrenchments, "no advantage would be gained but reputation." It would be "more advisable to make Hudson's River the seat of war," taking New York and leaving only a defensive garrison in Boston.[64]

On August 2 Dartmouth wrote to Gage, communicating the King's order that he return to England "in order to give His Majesty exact information of everything necessary to prepare . . . for the operations of the next year," a polite way of recalling an officer in whom the British government had lost faith. Simultaneously, Howe was given command of the army in the Thirteen Colonies.[65] A month later, Dartmouth wrote to Howe that it seemed "not only advisable, but necessary, to abandon Boston before the winter, to dismantle Castle William and . . . to remove with the Troops either to New York or some other place to the Southward," affording means to "the well-disposed" Bostonians of "getting safely away with their families and effects." [66] Howe assumed the command on October 10.

Howe received Dartmouth's letter on November 9. So, by that time, all the commanding officers in Boston and the authorities at home were in agreement as to the uselessness of holding on to Boston, and orders had been issued and received directing the move to New York. But there were not enough ships. To carry away the army with its equipment and stores and the fugitives with their effects, Howe calculated, 35,172 tons of shipping would be necessary; and he had, of every sort of craft, only 23,570 tons. The army had to stay where it was until spring.[67]

To cheer up the besieged troops, great quantities of supplies were dispatched from England: 5,000 oxen, 14,000 sheep, vast numbers of hogs, 10,000 butts of strong beer, 180,000 bushels of coal, quantities of faggots, oats, beans, and hay for the horses, dried vegetables, "cured by a new process," and near half a million pounds "in Spanish and Portuguese coinage." But the transports sailed too late in the fall. Contrary winds held them back. The preserved vegetables rotted. More than half of the animals died, "and the tides carried their carcasses in thousands up and down the Channel." Nearing America, the supply ships met adverse winds. Some were driven to the West Indies. Others went ashore on the American coasts and were boarded and plundered. Not a few were picked up by the American cruisers. It was a sorry remnant that reached Boston; but what did arrive, supplemented by supplies from the more southern colonies, Nova Scotia, and the West Indies, much improved the condition of the British army.[68]

In the American camp, in November, all was going well on the surface. The 17,000 men were well fed, well housed; "the army in great order and very healthy."[69] True, there was a shortage of blankets and of fuel, but on the whole the appearance of things was promising. That it was deceitfully promising was soon to be made evident.

Underlying difficulties that were to threaten the very existence of the whole army arose out of the impending termination of its period of enlistment. By December 31 the engagement of every man in the camp would expire; the whole army would fade away. Unless the province of Massachusetts and the whole of New England were to be given over to the enemy, a new army had to be enlisted and organized before the new year.

A plan for the organization of the new army had been laid down by the Congress, as described in detail later in this book. In certain respects it differed from the system in vogue in the New England colonies. For instance, in some of them the generals were colonels as well, the colonels also captains. This was not permitted by the congressional plan; and the proposed new order, in this respect, bred dissatisfaction.[70]

The old army was composed of thirty-eight regiments varying in size, those of Massachusetts, New Hampshire, and Rhode Island numbering 590 enlisted men each, while some of Connecticut numbered 1,000, others 600. The plan of the Congress called for only twenty-eight regiments of 728 men each, including officers. To rebuild the army according to the new plan, not only would ten regiments be eliminated, with a corresponding reduction of their officers in number or in rank, but the companies in them must be either increased or diminished in size. All sorts of jealousies and objections were generated by this proposal. The custom in New England was to pay the soldiers by the lunar month, four weeks. The pay was now to be by the calendar month, thus cutting out one month's pay in a year. This was naturally displeasing to the men.[71]

Also, Washington had to contend with the ingrained localism of the New Englanders. A national spirit had not yet developed; these men were citizens of their own respective colonies, of their own respective counties and townships, not of the United Colonies as a whole. Washington wrote to Joseph Reed: "Connecticut wants no Massachusetts man in her corps; Massachusetts thinks there is no necessity for a Rhode-Islander to be introduced into hers; and New Hampshire says, it is very hard, that her valuable and experienced officers . . . should be discarded, because her own regiments, under the new establishment, cannot provide for them." John Adams upheld this contention of the colonies: "Can it be supposed that the private men will be easy to be commanded by strangers, to the exclusion of gentlemen whom they know, being their neighbors? It is, moreover, a reflection, and would be a disgrace upon that Province [Massachusetts] to send abroad [to another colony] for commanders of their own men. It would suppose that it had not men fit for officers." It was absurd, of course, but nothing could change this spirit; Washington strove against it, but had to yield to it.[72]

New Englanders had been accustomed to receiving bounties from their own provinces on enlistment. The Congress had been asked to provide for such payments, and had refused to do so. There was discontent on that account. Another thing that displeased the troops was the increase in pay of the company officers; the captains were to receive $26⅔ a month instead of $20 as before, the lieutenants $18 instead of $13⅓, and the ensigns $13⅓ instead of 10, while the privates' pay remained at $6⅔. That emphasized the distinction between officer and man, violated the new England principle of equality, and "chilled the spirits of the commonalty." [73]

Then, too, as the winter drew on, there was increasing hardship. The men's clothing, fit for summer, was now too thin and worn to keep them warm. Blankets were lacking; fuel was worse than scarce. Nathanael Greene, on the last day of the year, wrote: "We have suffered prodigiously for want of wood. Many regiments have been obliged to eat their provision raw, for want of fuel to cook it; and notwithstanding we have burnt up all the fences; and cut down all the trees for a mile round the camp, our sufferings have been inconceivable." [74] Washington told the Massachusetts Assembly that "different Regiments were upon the Point of cutting each others throats for a few Standing Locusts . . . to dress their food with." Ten thousand cords of wood were needed, he said.[75]

Underneath all these causes of discontent was plain and simple homesickness. The men were not professional soldiers, detached from civilian life. They were farmers for the most part. They had homes and families from which they had now been separated for many months. They were tired of the dreary routine of camp life, the endless round of uninteresting duties as well as the hardships. They had agreed to serve for a certain period. They had a very clear notion of the meaning of the terms of a contract. They would meet those terms, but would not go beyond them. " 'Tis the cast of the New Englanders to enlist for a certain time and, when the time is expired, to quit the service and return home, let the call for their continuance be ever so urgent." As John Adams remarked, on another aspect of the situation: "We cannot suddenly alter the temper, principles, opinions or prejudices of men." [76]

In spite of all these difficulties and discontents, it was Washington's task to disband his old army and create a new one, as far as possible out of those experienced though reluctant men, and at the same time to hold the British army where it was. "It is not in the pages of History perhaps to furnish a case like ours," he wrote to the Congress on January 4, 1776. "To maintain a post within musket shot of the Enemy for six months together, without powder, and at the same time to disband one Army and recruit another within that distance of twenty odd British regiments is more than probably ever was attempted." [77]

He could look for little assistance from his major generals. Schuyler was at Albany, in command of the troops in northern New York. Artemas Ward was ineffectual. Putnam was hopeless in matters of administration, and the eccentric Charles Lee, English by birth, could not handle such a situation. The job had to be done by Washington alone.

On November 12 the enlistment papers for an army to serve until December 31, 1776, were issued. The first week after that would test the willingness of the men to renew their engagements. It did. Out of 6,000 to 7,000 men who made up the eleven old regiments, 966 enlisted. The general officers issued an address to the troops. The struggle was not hopeless, they said. Victory was assured. The southern colonies would help. New England must not fail. And, as to the more immediate, personal considerations, they urged that never had soldiers' "pay and provision . . . been so abundant and ample." [78]

Another week passed, and the returns showed that no more than 3,500 had agreed to stay. The Connecticut troops brought the trouble to a head. Their enlistment was to end on December 10, and, in the confusion of the records, many of them believed, as Washington at one time also did, that it ended on December 1. Their officers had fancied they could be persuaded to stay at the end of the month, and had so assured Washington. Now it appeared that most of them would refuse even so short an extension of their term of service; they were going home when their time was up. Such a defection in the face of the enemy might prove fatal. The vacancies caused by their departure must be filled, temporarily at any rate. Washington called on Massachusetts for 5,000 militia and on New Hampshire for 2,000 to fill the gap until January 15, and besought the Connecticut men to stay until these should arrive. But most of them decided to leave the camp on December 1, and many did go. Charles Lee undertook to stop their premature departure.[79]

They were paraded on December 1. The men that were disinclined to stay even for four days after their enlistments expired were formed in a hollow square, and Lee addressed them. "Men," said he, "I do not know what to call you. You are the worst of all creatures." Then he "flung and curst and swore at us and said if we would not stay he would order us to go to Bunker Hill [i.e., to attack the British stronghold] and if we would not go he would order the riflemen to fire at us." They agreed to stay the four days. They got a drink of rum, and were promised another on the morrow.[80]

But they would not remain any longer than that. Washington was disgusted with them. "Such a dirty, mercenary spirit pervades the whole, that I should not be at all surprised at any disaster that may happen," he wrote to Joseph Reed. Indeed, he was almost disheartened. "I have often thought," he wrote on January 14, "how much happier I should have been, if instead of accepting a command under such circumstances, I had taken my musket on my shoulder and entered the ranks, or, if I could have justified the measure to posterity and my own conscience, had retired to the back country, and lived in a wigwam." [81]

General Sullivan wrote to the New Hampshire Committee of Safety denouncing the Connecticut troops, who "to their Eternal Infamy Demand a Bounty to Induce them to Tarry only the three weeks. This is Such an Insult to Every American that we are Determined to Release them at the Expiration of their Term at all hazards." He asked New Hampshire for 2,000 militia to serve only until January 15, 1776.[82]

New Hampshire responded nobly, as did Massachusetts. On December 11 Washington could write: "The Militia are coming fast, I am much pleased with the Alacrity which the good People of this province, as well as those of New Hampshire, have shewn upon this occasion: I expect the whole will be in this day and to Morrow, when what remains of the Connecticut Gentry, who have not inlisted, will have liberty to go to their Firesides." They left amid the jeers and hoots of their more steadfast companions; "they were horribly hissed, groaned at and pelted." [83]

On December 31, when the terms of enlistment of the rest of the army expired, "the same desire of retiring into a chimney-corner seized the troops of New Hampshire, Rhode Island and Massachusetts . . . as had worked upon those of Connecticut." Though many of them offered to stay until the new enlistments had sufficiently made up the strength of the army, they left "by hundreds and by thousands." [84]

General Orders of January 1 began thus: "This day giving commencement to the new army, which, in every point of View, is Continental, The General flatters himself, that a laudable Spirit of emulation will now take place and pervade the whole of it." [85] Then was first "hoisted the union flag in compliment to the United Colonies." There are various accounts of this flag. One describes it as the ensign of Great Britain, but with thirteen stripes, alternately red and white, instead of the superimposed crosses of St. George and St. Andrew, in the canton where are now the stars.[86] Another says that "the combined crosses of England and Scotland, which cover the British flag, on the new ensign shrank to occupy but one corner, while the larger field was crossed by thirteen alternate stripes of red and white." [87]

So the army was now the Continental Army; but a strange army it was, a medley of those old soldiers who had reenlisted, of raw recruits, and of Massachusetts and New Hampshire short-term militia. With such an uncoordinated mass of men as his only force, Washington regarded the situation as "truly Alarming and of this General Howe is well apprized . . . no doubt when he is reinforced he will avail himself of the Information." [88]

There was not only a shortage and a confusion of men; there was also a lack of arms. Few of the new men had brought muskets. Washington had tried to retain the guns of those who departed, valuing and paying for them. But so many of them were in bad condition, and so many were carried off by stealth, that, by the middle of January, he had no more than a hundred muskets with which to arm incoming recruits.[89]

Enlistments continued to lag during January. In the first two weeks no more than a thousand new men were added to the rolls. Washington wrote that the "discontented officers," displaced by the reduction of the number of regiments, "have thrown such difficulties and stumbling blocks in the way of recruiting that I no longer entertain a hope of completing the army by voluntary enlistments, and I see no move or likelihood of one, to do it by other means. . . . Our total number upon paper amounts to about ten thousand five hundred." But many of those on the lists had not come to the camp in spite of orders to do so, and there was little hope of their early coming.[90] They did, however, finally arrive in almost the full number.

January, 1776, was a quiet month. Although Howe's army had been somewhat reinforced and more men were expected, he wrote Dartmouth, "I am under the necessity of repeating to your Lordship, that the apparent strength of this army for the Spring does not flatter me with Hopes of bringing the Rebels to a decisive action." [91] It was, in fact, well settled in his mind that he would evacuate Boston as soon as sufficient transport could be gathered. Meanwhile, he had but to hold on.

The Americans were also inactive. Obviously they were in no condition to attempt the capture of the town. Their energies were sufficiently engaged in re-forming and increasing their army. One little diversion occurred on the 8th, when Major Knowlton with two hundred men crossed at night on the mill-dam to Charlestown, killed one resisting guard, captured the rest, five men, and burned eight out of fourteen still standing houses, which the enemy were daily pulling down for fuel. The flames alarmed the British, and there was much cannonading, with no harmful result to anyone, except to the audience in the Faneuil Hall playhouse, who were then enjoying the burlesque of Washington previously mentioned. They dispersed, "everyone endeavouring to get out as fast as possible, amidst fainting and shrieking among the females." [92]

Continued successes of the American attacks on British shipping cheered the army. Colonel Lord Stirling, soon to rise to the rank of brigadier general, having heard of a transport in distress off Sandy Hook, seized a pilot boat at Amboy, embarked forty men, and, with the assistance of three smaller vessels, took the prize without opposition. She was laden with coal and provisions.[93] Of greater importance, indeed of very great importance to the American cause, was a service rendered by General Knox.

Henry Knox was destined to play so great a part in the war that some special notice of him at this point is desirable. He was born in 1750, the son of a shipmaster who, meeting with financial reverses, was obliged to retire to the West Indies. Henry therefore had to leave school and go to work in a bookshop. Being a studious lad, he took the opportunity the shop provided to continue his education by reading. He became familiar with the classics in English translations and especially with Plutarch's Lives, which turned his taste toward military studies.

At the age of twenty-one he set up his own "London Book-Store" in

Cornhill, Boston, stocked with a miscellaneous shipment from London. It became "a fashionable morning lounge" and prospered. His military studies continued, and he became a member of the Ancient and Honourable Artillery Company, which gave his interest in military science a special character and determined his role in the war.

He had gained some acquaintance with engineering and his services were employed at the outbreak of the war in planning the American fortifications around Boston. After Washington took command he recommended Knox's appointment as colonel of artillery, and he was so commissioned. His subsequent services are a part of the history of the war.

Knox was a young man of large proportions, tall, broad, and thick. In spite of the hardships of the military service during the war, at its end he had attained a weight of 280 pounds. His face was large, full-cheeked, and florid; his gray eyes, rather small but brilliant. His expression was frank and kindly; he was fond of society, gayety, and laughter. His voice was noted for strength, volume, and resonance. His ability as an artillerist has not been questioned, and his integrity as a man, in addition to his technical achievements as a soldier, lent strength to the Revolutionary cause.[94]

Short as the army was of small arms, the lack of artillery was even greater. No offensive operation against Boston could be undertaken without heavy cannon. There were plenty of them at Ticonderoga and Crown Point. Because of bad roads or no roads, and no means of transport, they had lain entirely useless for six months when Washington in mid-November decided to try for them. On the 16th he ordered Knox to go after them: "The want of them is so great that no Trouble or Expence must be spared to obtain them." [95]

Knox reached Ticonderoga on December 5. There he selected for removal eight brass and six iron mortars, thirty iron and thirteen brass guns, and a howitzer. Only one of the cannon was a 24-pounder, the rest ranging from 12 to 18 pounds. Three of the iron mortars were great 13-inchers, weighing a ton each. To these he added a quantity of lead and a barrel of flints. No available wheeled vehicle being strong enough to carry such prodigious weights, they had to be transported on sledges; and Knox constructed forty-three of these. Eighty yoke of oxen to haul them were secured. He drew them to Lake George, loaded them on gondolas, flat-bottomed scows, floated them down to the head of the lake. Snow had fallen but lightly, and a thaw held him up. At last he brought them on sledges to Albany, having crossed the Hudson four times.

At Albany, one of his largest guns broke through the ice at a ferry and sank. He fished it up and went on, down to Claverack and up over the Berkshires. There the snow lay thick, and the grades were heavy; his oxen and horses had hard work. At Framingham the heavier pieces were temporarily deposited; the smaller, he brought on to the camp, where he had the pleasure of presenting to his chief what he justly called "a noble train of artillery." It soon permitted Washington to make a move that hurried the British out of Boston.[96]

CHAPTER 10

Dorchester and Falmouth

As time drew on, and inactivity continued to prevail in both camps, Washington became restive. He felt that throughout the colonies there was a growing demand that his army, now much larger than that of his opponent, should force matters to a conclusion. "To have the Eyes of the whole Continent fixed, with anxious expectation of hearing of some great event, and to be restrain'd in Every Military Operation for want of the necessary means of carrying it on is not very pleasing," he wrote.[1] The lack of necessary means included both small arms and powder. Among his nearly 9,000 men 2,000 were without muskets, and powder was as always dangerously scarce. On February 8 there were no more than nine musket cartridges per man in the camp, and fewer than one hundred fifty barrels of powder in the magazines.[2] Powder from abroad, however, began to come in at New York and Philadelphia, and the promise of a supply encouraged Washington to plan an attack.[3]

On February 16 he called a council of war. The harbor was frozen over, "affording a more expanded and consequently less dangerous Approach to the Town." About half of the 7,200 militia who had been called for had come in. With the 8,797 fit for duty already in camp and 1,405 absent "on command," who might be recalled, the army would number over 13,500. There were believed to be no more than 5,000 British in Boston, which was an error. Therefore, although not much help could be expected from heavy artillery because of shortage of powder, and the principal reliance must be on small arms, yet, he thought, "a stroke, well aimed, at this critical juncture" before the British received expected reinforcements "might put a final end to the war." [4]

But the council, very wisely, demurred. They thought the King's forces in the town were much more numerous than 5,000, as indeed they were: there were about twice that many. Even if not so many, the officers said, they were well furnished with artillery and were backed by their fleet; and an assault should be preceded by a heavy and continued bombardment, which could not be had. There was, however, a practical move to be made, the seizure and fortification of Dorchester Heights "with a view of drawing out the enemy" to an attack.[5] This verdict did not please Washington. "Behold!" he wrote to Reed, "though we had been waiting all the year for this favorite event, the enterprise was thought too dangerous!" But, magnanimously he admitted, "perhaps, the irksomeness of my situation led me to undertake more than could be warranted by prudence . . . it is now at an end, and I am preparing to take post on Dorchester, to try if the enemy will be so kind as to come out to us." [6]

The extreme right of the curving American lines was somewhat beyond Roxbury, near the village of Dorchester. Beyond that a peninsula, about a mile long and half a mile wide, stretched toward the southeast, its extreme end being three-quarters of a mile from the island on which was Castle William. Dorchester Heights were two small hills in the middle of the peninsula and within 250 yards of the water. In front of them, close to the water, was another little hill. From the northern shoulder of the peninsula a sharp spur of land pointed directly at the town, with a space of water not much more than a quarter-mile wide between it and the Neck. At its extremity was another elevation, Nook's Hill.[7] It will be seen that possession of the Heights would threaten the town, the shipping, and Castle William, while heavy guns on Nook's Hill could blast the defenses on Boston Neck with a plunging fire and devastate the greater part of the town.

The fortification of Lechmere Point, close to the water at the left of the American lines, which had been under way for some time, was now complete, and some of the heavy ordnance from Ticonderoga had been mounted there. Several mortars were emplaced at Roxbury, and active preparations for the attempt on the Heights were begun.

The plan was to duplicate the surprise at Breed's Hill by completing the proposed entrenchments in a single night. But the ground was now frozen hard to a depth of eighteen inches, so that quick pick-and-shovel work as at Breed's was not possible. It had taken more than two months to complete the Lechmere's Point works. Therefore, some different method had to be adopted at Dorchester. Colonel Rufus Putnam suggested building the breastwork on the ground, instead of digging it out of the ground. His plan was to use chandeliers, heavy timber frames in which gabions, fascines, and bales of hay could be fitted, thus creating quickly a breastwork which could afterward be strengthened with earth. It was to be faced with an abatis made out of neighboring orchard trees. In front of all, there were to be placed barrels full of earth—a novel form of offensive defense, for they were to add an appearance of strength to the works but, if the British assaulted, could be rolled down the hill to break their ranks and their bones as well.[8]

This novel plan was accepted. The camp was busy in the last days of February and the first of March making chandeliers, gabions, and fascines, and baling hay. It was also busy in other preparations. Washington planned, in case the British should embark for an attack on the Heights, to send 4,000 picked men in two divisions—one under Sullivan, the other under Greene—with General Israel Putnam in general command, across the Back Bay against the undefended west side of Boston, to attack the British works on the Neck in the rear and open a way into the town for other troops. For this purpose, two floating batteries and forty-five bateaux, each to hold eighty men, were secretly collected in the Charles River. All the militia of the neighboring towns were ordered to be in readiness to join the army before the day of the attempt.[9]

To divert the enemy's attention from the real purpose, a heavy bombardment from Lechmere Point, Cobble Hill, and Roxbury was begun on the night of March 2. With a prodigal disregard of the consumption of powder, the artillery "continued in throwing in Shot and Shells 'till daylight." [10] The British replied with a heavy fire. Little harm was done to either army, except by the bursting of three 10-inch and two 13-inch mortars of the Americans, one of which was that big brass 13-incher captured by Manley on the *Nancy* and christened "Congress" with such gusto by Old Put. The cannonade was resumed on the next night and the next after that. As soon as the firing began on the third night, March 4, General Thomas, with a fatigue party of 1,200 men, led by a covering party of 800 under arms and followed by 360 oxcarts loaded with entrenching materials, marched to Dorchester Heights. To conceal from the enemy the necessary passage back and forth during the night, a screen of hay bales was placed along Dorchester Neck.[11]

The covering party was divided, one half going to Nook's Hill, the other to the extreme point toward Castle William. On the two Dorchester hills the chandeliers were placed on the lines of two small redoubts already marked out, and the fascines and bales of hay put in place. Picks and shovels were soon at work on the frozen ground, first to fill the gabions and the barrels and then to strengthen the breastwork, while axmen felled the orchard trees and made the abatis. The carts went back again and again for more materials. At three o'clock in the morning the fatigue party was relieved by a fresh force. So the work went on all through the mild night, lighted by a bright moon, but concealed from the enemy by a haze that hung over the lowland in front. The noise of the big guns drowned the sound of pick and shovel. When the Americans got below the frost line and the digging became easier, the parapets were thickened with earth piled against them. More men, including five companies of riflemen, came over to man the works. By daylight, the two little forts were ready. "Perhaps," said General Heath, "never was so much work done in so short a space of time." [12]

In the British camp the activity did not go unnoticed. At ten o'clock the night before, Lieutenant Colonel Campbell had somehow discovered and reported to Brigadier General Francis Smith "that the Rebels were at work on Dorchester heights." But this was the same General Smith that had led the march against Lexington and Concord, that "very fat and heavy man" who was so slow in coming up to the fight at the Bridge. This time he did nothing at all. The first positive news the British army had of the works was the sight of them at daybreak. It was a complete and astounding surprise. Howe viewed them through his glass, and is said to have remarked, "The rebels have done more in one night, than my whole army could do in months." [13] In a dispatch to Dartmouth he wrote that it "must have been the employment of at least twelve thousand men." [14] Lieutenant General Archibald Robertson of the Royal Engineers wrote in his diary, "A most astonishing night's work [it] must have Employ'd from 15 to 20,000 men." [15] Another officer said the works were "raised with an expedition equal to that of the Genii belonging to Aladdin's Wonderful Lamp." [16]

Surprise speedily gave place to serious consideration of a new problem. Rear Admiral Molyneux Shuldham, commanding the fleet since the recall of Graves in December, told Howe that he could not keep his ships in the harbor under the guns on the Heights, and the army in Boston was in equal danger. Either the British must evacuate the town, or they must drive the Americans from their new stronghold. Although Howe fully intended to evacuate very soon, he could not stomach an expulsion by the colonists. He tried first a bombardment, but the guns could not be elevated enough to throw their shot to the hilltops. Then he decided to attack, and immediately made his preparations.[17]

Brigadier General Jones, with 2,200 men, was to make the attempt. Five regiments were ordered to embark at the Long Wharf and proceed to Castle William. From Castle William they were to land on the extreme point of Dorchester peninsula and attack the nearer redoubt, being sheltered by it from the guns in the other. Two more regiments, with the light infantry and grenadiers, were to embark in flatboats, land on the north side of the peninsula, and join in the assault on that side. In case of success at Dorchester, these troops and certain reinforcements were to attack the lines at Roxbury. The men were to carry their blankets, a day's supply of food, and canteens filled with rum and water. No musket was to be loaded. The bayonet was to be the only weapon.[18] It is said, perhaps untruly, that the men, drawn up before embarking, looked "in general, pale and dejected" and told each other, "It will be another Bunker's-hill affair or worse." [19] So thought the inhabitants of Boston. Again they crowded the hilltops and other high places to watch the show, while the American troops continued all day long to labor at strengthening their works, and Putnam's division, ready for the attack on the town, was paraded on Cambridge common.[20]

The British attack on the Heights was to be delivered that night; but a storm arose, "A Hurrycane or terrible sudden storm," as Timothy Newell wrote in his diary.[21] Heath described it: "About midnight the wind blew almost a hurricane from the south; many windows were forced in, sheds and fences blown down and some vessels drove on shore." [22] The surf was so high on Dorchester beach that no flatboat could land. There was no attack that night, nor on the next day, for the wind continued to blow, and there was a torrential downpour of rain.[23]

That storm has been credited with preventing the planned attack. Howe, in his general orders the next morning, March 5, wrote, "The General desires the Troops may know that the intended Expedition last night was unavoidably put off by the badness of the Weather." But that was not exactly the truth. In fact, the decision to withhold the attack and to evacuate the town had been made five hours before the storm arose. There was a council of war in which some of the officers "advised the going off altogether . . . the General said it was his own Sentiments from the first, but thought the honour of the Troops Concerned." It was "agreed immediately to Embark everything." Howe's statement in the general orders was merely a face-saving device.[24]

While preparations for the evacuation of the town were afoot, the inhabitants who were to remain there became fearful that it might be destroyed, either by bombardment from the American works or by the incendiary torch of the departing army. A delegation of citizens obtained from Howe a promise that he would not burn the town unless the Americans molested his troops during their embarkation. A paper stating this promise, signed by four of the selectmen of the town, was brought to the

American lines. As it was "an unauthenticated paper . . . not obligatory upon General Howe," Washington refused to take any official notice of it. He made no agreement with Howe, but the town was nevertheless tacitly spared by both sides.[25]

While the British in Boston were hurrying their preparations to leave, the Americans went on with their Dorchester works. A party was sent in the night of the 9th to fortify Nook's Hill, the place most dangerous to Boston. Discovering it, the British bombarded the hill, and the American batteries in all the posts from Cobble Hill around to Roxbury responded. The continued thunder of the cannonade terrified all the good folk within hearing distance but, as usual, although more than eight hundred shot were fired, this long-range cannonading had little effect on either side; only five Americans were killed. But Nook's Hill was abandoned by them.[26]

In August, 1775, Dartmouth had written to Gage that if he were driven out of Boston "care must be taken that the officers and friends of the government be not left exposed to the rage and insult of the rebels, who set no bounds to their barbarity." [27] The preparations for the evacuation therefore included their transshipment to whatever destination was chosen for the army. They were to be rescued from "rage and insult," but they were forced to pay a fearful price for that rescue.

The Tories in Boston, both those whose proper residence was in that town and those who had come seeking the protection of the British troops, included many of the personally or politically outstanding people of the province, the wealthiest people, the greater landholders, the more substantial men of business, the best educated, in short the aristocrats. These had looked down on the Adamses, Warren, Otis, and the other agitators for their resistance to the crown, accusing them of various base or petty personal motives. To John Hancock, the only one of the rebel leaders who had a claim to rank in wealth and fashion with themselves, they ascribed wounded vanity as the cause of his recalcitrancy. As a class these Tory leaders were hearty free livers, free spenders, fine dressers, arrogant in their regard for social distinction, scornful of the mob. "Caste-feeling, intense, aggressive and almost universal, beyond any doubt, prevailed in the Tory society of America." [28]

The Tories very generally ridiculed the provincial military leaders raised suddenly from obscurity in the lower walks of life—Knox from his bookshop, Greene from his blacksmithing, Putnam from his tavern and his plow, Pomeroy from his gunsmith shop—to become officers pretending to rank with the gentlemen of His Majesty's army. And now, suddenly, these superior people were to be driven from their offices, their countinghouses, their houses and lands, and their churches (eighteen of them were clergymen). They must abandon their homes, their own country. They who were as firmly wedded to their native land as any other Americans, who loved it as dearly as any of those upstart rebels, they whose patriotism was indeed as strong and as pure, according to their lights, as that of any of the so-called patriots, were now to be forced to flee to the foul, ill-smelling transports and to be carried God knew where, to an exile wherever it would be, with no certainty of ever returning. It is not strange that, in Washington's words, "No Electric Shock, no sudden Clap of thunder, in a word the last trump could not have struck them with greater consternation" [29] than did Howe's order to abandon the town.

The last days of the British army in Boston were days of confusion and distress, of haste and waste, of crooked dealing and actual plundering. The first move was to bring the transports to the wharves and load them with all the ordnance, arms, and stores that could be stowed in them. The lines were stripped of their brass cannon and mortars; iron pieces replaced them. But three great brass mortars broke their lifting tackle and sank in the water; a fourth, the British tried unsuccessfully to burst and had to leave behind. There was no room for the dragoon and artillery horses. There was "a vast deal of Confusion in every Department and no settled plan of operations." [30] Great quantities of stores had to be abandoned, much of them being as nearly destroyed as was possible in the hurry of departure.[31] The soldiers misbehaved, "acting Licentiously and breaking up some stores." It was suggested by one of the officers that "it would be prudent to seize All Cloth, linnen, Shoes, Stockings, etc. in the Different stores in Town . . . which the Rebel Army were very much in need of." [32] Howe directed one Crean Brush, a New York Irish adventurer, to do this. He broke open stores and storehouses and looted their contents indiscriminately to the value of many thousands of pounds, giving worthless receipts. Dwelling houses were not exempt from this thievery. His loot made a full cargo for the brigantine *Elizabeth*. Brush's labors were in vain, however, for he and his vessel, with all the stolen goods, were soon after captured by the Americans.[33]

The poor Tories had pretty much to shift for themselves. They had received vessels, but had been told they must find the sailors to man them.[34] By a liberal use of money they managed to get such portable goods as they most valued aboard and to hire enough seamen to navigate their craft; but they embarked in sad condition. One of them, Benjamin Hallowell, former Commissioner of Customs, had to take into his cabin thirty-six others, "men, women and children; parents, masters and mistresses, obliged to pig together on the floor, there being no berths." [35]

Meanwhile, Washington was becoming impatient. He had no desire to bombard the town, but he wished to hurry the evacuation; and to that end he made more threatening approaches. He threw up a redoubt on the point of the Dorchester peninsula nearest to Castle William. As a final move, "a notice to quit," he again seized Nook's Hill and in spite of a bombardment, ineffectual because only "a few old Iron Guns were left" [36] to be brought to bear on it, he fortified it. With his guns in that position, he could fire on the ships at the wharves at close range and cannonade the rear of the works on Boston Neck.

But it was now the last day of the lingering evacuation, the 17th of March. At nine o'clock in the morning all were on board, except two engineer officers and a few men, left "to fire some houses if there had appeared any Enemy in our rear, but none appeared and we went all off in the greatest order." [37] Yet there were a few minor hostilities. Castle William had not been abandoned; the 64th Regiment posted there was engaged in mining it for its destruction. Some Americans, working on fortifications on Dorchester Point, were fired upon from the Castle, and there were a few shots in reply. At nine in the evening, the fuses of the mines were lighted, and the remaining British boarded their transports, the last ever to set hostile foot on the soil of present-day Massachusetts.[38]

But Charlestown seemed yet to be held. Sentinels could be seen at their posts on Bunker Hill. Two men went over to investigate, and "found the Centinels to be Images dressed in the Soldiers Habit with Laced Hats and for a Gorget an Horse Shoe with Paper Ruffles, their Pieces Shouldered [with] fixed Bayonets, with this Inscription wrote on their Breast (viz.) Welcome Brother Jonathan." [39]

The American troops at Cambridge and Roxbury had been paraded. When the last of the enemy had left, General Ward with five hundred men crossed the Neck and entered the town. Others occupied Charlestown peninsula. On the 20th the main force was in full possession of Boston.

Still there was some apprehension as to the intentions of the enemy. The fleet had anchored in Nantasket Roads about five miles below the town—for what purpose, no one in Boston knew. Washington wrote to Trumbull on the 21st, "I cannot but suspect they are waiting for some opportunity to give us a Stroke, at a moment when they conceive us to be off guard." Three days later, he said, "It surpasses my comprehension and awakens all my suspicions." He complained that "the enemy have the best knack at puzzling people I ever met with in my life." [40] His apprehensions were groundless.

The British were only preparing for their voyage in the leisurely eighteenth century fashion, adjusting their cargoes, which had been so hurriedly shipped, taking in water, and so on. On the 27th they put out to sea, bound not for New York, as Washington thought, but for Halifax.[41]

Howe carried off 11,000 soldiers and sailors and nearly a thousand refugees, among whom were a hundred civil officials. Many of these settled in Nova Scotia, suffering the privations and hardships of pioneers. Others went to England. Few ever returned to their old homes.[42]

Although during the fall and winter of 1775–1776 the British army had lain inactive in Boston, there had been one hostile enterprise on the part of its fleet of which notice should be taken.

Vice Admiral Samuel Graves had been appointed in March, 1774, to command the British naval forces in America; he arrived in Boston harbor on July 1 to undertake the thankless job of enforcing the blockade. He had in his charge from twenty-five to thirty war vessels, ranging from the great ships of fifty to seventy guns down to sloops and cutters. The *Asia,* sixty-four guns, was stationed at New York, the *Rose,* twenty guns, and the *Scarborough,* twenty guns, were part of the time at Newport and Portsmouth respectively. Another ship was held at Halifax. Some of the smaller vessels were engaged in cruising off the coast, or from time to time stationed here and there. The rest lay in Boston harbor.[43]

Although the whole British navy at that time was in a scandalously rundown condition, Graves's fleet was of overwhelming strength as compared with the puny vessels of the Americans. But Graves himself was utterly inefficient. The Americans raided the islands in the harbor almost at will, and he could not prevent them. They gathered a fleet of three hundred whaleboats, hid them by day, and by night went about their nefarious business of burning lighthouses, foraging or whatever they would, in spite of the Admiral. He actually stood in fear that they might, by concerted action, take from him one of his capital ships.[44] Burgoyne wrote to Lord George Germain in August, 1775: "It may be asked in England, 'What is the Admiral doing?' . . . I can only say what he is *not* doing." And he went on to catalogue Graves's inactivities; he was not supplying the camp with fresh meat, not protecting the flocks and herds on the islands, not doing anything that he should do.[45]

Graves was probably nettled by the criticism in the camp and angered by his inability to find and capture, on the high seas, the American cruisers that were intercepting the supply ships. He decided to go after them in the ports and harbors where they hived. On October 6 the *Canceaux* with eight guns and forty-five men, and the schooner *Halifax* with six guns and thirty men, to which were added one hundred soldiers, sailed under command of Captain Henry Mowat. His orders were to "burn, destroy and lay waste" the seaport towns all along the northeast coast as far as Machias, and to destroy all their shipping.[46]

Mowat viewed Gloucester, and decided that the houses were so widely scattered that it would be difficult to burn the town. On the 16th he anchored at Falmouth, now Portland. He warned the people to remove "the human species within two hours, when the punishment would begin"; but, at the supplication of a committee of the townsfolk, he agreed to give them until the next day. Indeed, if they would deliver to him four cannon supposed to be there, all other arms and ammunition, and certain hostages, he would ask further instructions from headquarters. The next morning they refused to deal with him. Mowat then opened fire on the town with cannon balls and incendiary carcasses, and a landing party set additional fires among the buildings. By evening the whole town was ablaze. Two hundred houses, the church, the courthouse, the town house, the public library, the wharves and warehouses, and eleven vessels were "all laid into ashes." Four other vessels were taken. There were no casualties among the British, except two men wounded by the feeble resistance offered them. Graves was satisfied by this one outrage, and sent out no more such expeditions.[47]

CHAPTER 11

The Question of Canada

Canada had long been a word of ill omen to the American colonists, particularly to those of Massachusetts, New Hampshire, and northern New York. Time and again, the Canadian French and their Indian allies had ravaged and devastated the settlements of those colonies. Deerfield and Northampton, Saratoga and Schenectady, Keene, Exeter, Brunswick, and many another village, and countless isolated settlers' homes had succumbed to the bullet, the tomahawk, the scalping knife, and the incendiary torch. In one year alone, 1746, thirty-five bands of these marauders had ravaged the borders of the northern American provinces. When Montreal capitulated in 1760, and Canada fell into the hands of the English by the treaty of 1763, the dread of their northern neighbors departed from the minds of the colonists, only to be revived in a different form fourteen years later, when Parliament passed the Quebec Act.

To an understanding of that act in its effects upon Canada and upon the American colonies, a brief review of the character and conditions of the Canadian people may be helpful.

The inhabitants of Canada fell into four well defined classes. The habitants, who formed the first class, were the basic population. They were descendants of the first settlers, and were French in origin, Roman Catholic in religion, tenant-farmers in occupation, numbering perhaps 60,000 or more. These tractable, hard-working agriculturists held their farms under a sort of feudal tenure from the great landholders, who constituted another class, the aristocrats, seigneurs, and had been well-to-do, largely through the emoluments of office, civil or military, until the English conquest deprived them of official employment and ended the various feudal obligations due from the habitants except the payment of rents, which were of small value. Most of them, including practically all the civil and military officers, had gone back to France after the conquest; no more than 130 heads of families remained. Reduced in wealth even to comparative poverty, their political and social influence lost, these few seigneurs were of little importance in the affairs of the province.

Few in numbers, not more than 2,000, but having, as they thought, great potential political importance, were the people of British origin, many of them immigrants from the American colonies. They were commonly called "Old Subjects" to distinguish them from the lately acquired French subjects. The majority of them were in Montreal, engaged in the fur trade. They were a troublesome lot. They quarreled with the military, were at odds with the seigneurs, and contemned the habitants. As the only true-born British subjects, they claimed privileges above the other classes, even to the extent of demanding self-government by elective bodies of which only they would be electors and members. They would even deny the right of the Catholic French to sit on grand juries, an exclusion based on the then prevailing English law, which excluded Catholics from the elective franchise and from all political offices. James Murray, the first British governor of the province, described them as "chiefly adventurers of mean education," all having "their Fortunes to make and little Sollicitous ab^{t} the means." [1] Guy Carleton, his successor, had much the same opinion of them.

The fourth class was composed of the Catholic priests. Formerly of great importance in the government, wielding an almost unlimited and almost unrestrained power, even over the French governors and their councils, the English conquest had brought them so low that they asked only for tolerance in their priestly offices. They had been used to requiring the habitants to pay legal dues to the Church. But there was no longer any basis of legality for such requirement, and the habitants paid or did not pay, as they pleased. The clergy, therefore, existed on sufferance only.

Thus Canada was split into incompatible parties: the seigneurs despised both the habitants and the Old Subjects; the habitants disliked the British, no longer respected the seigneurs, and refused to be subservient to the clergy; the Old Subjects held the seigneurs in contempt, scorned the habitants, and were at odds with the government; the poor priests were in good repute with none of the others. Besides all that, the historic ill feeling between Catholics and Protestants was in full force and vigor.

In 1763 a royal proclamation had made Canada a crown colony without an elective assembly, promising one "as soon as the state and circumstances of the said Colonies will admit thereof." Political power had been placed in the hands of a governor and a royally appointed council. It was the promise of an assembly in the future that gave the Old Subjects their hope of political domination, for surely, as in England, the Catholics would be excluded from voting and from sitting in the assembly.

But they were disappointed. Guy Carleton, who succeeded Murray in 1766, was an English aristocrat, a military man with all the qualities of the professional soldier of high rank. He was reserved, stern, remote from civilians, fearless, and inflexible; but he was also high-minded, incorruptible, and, at bottom, magnanimous. He looked upon the humble habitants as the real Canadian people, the solid foundation of the province, and he was emancipated from the English dread of Catholic "Popery." Partly as a result of his efforts the Parliament passed the Quebec Act in 1774.

That act put an end for the time being to any hope of an elective assembly, definitely annulling the vague promise of the proclamation of 1763. It provided for a governor and a council as lawmakers appointed by the crown. It recognized the Catholic Church, with a proper bishop, and restored its right to collect tithes and other dues. It abolished the religious "test oaths," which had disqualified all non-Protestants from holding civil office. It retained the English criminal law, but restored the French law in civil matters. It extended the boundaries of the province to include Labrador on the east and, on the west, all the land north of the Ohio River between the Allegheny Mountains and the Mississippi.

In many of its provisions the Quebec Act was an excellent law and was in advance of the philosophy of its time; but it was not well received by the Old Subjects. They wanted that promised assembly. They also wanted exclusive right to the offices of honor and emolument, and they objected strongly to the "establishment" of the Catholic Church. The Catholic priests objected to the provision requiring them to be licensed by the King only, and the Catholic laity were incensed by the compulsion to pay tithes. The French did not like the retention of English criminal law. The English disliked the restoration of the French civil law. So the cleavages in Canada's population were deepened.[2]

To the Americans the Quebec Act was anathema for several reasons, the first and most objectionable being the extension of the boundaries of Canada. Some of the colonies, notably Connecticut, Massachusetts, and Virginia, had pretensions to some parts of the western lands now given to their northern neighbor. They had seen them taken from the French by the Treaty of Paris in 1763 and, as they thought, reserved for their own settlement. Citizens of the Old Thirteen Colonies had been peering over the crest of the Alleghenies at the new lands beyond. They had even passed over the mountains and had made new settlements in the Ohio valley. They looked forward to unimpeded occupation quite to the Mississippi. This sudden reversal of conditions, by which the conquered territory was restored to Quebec, and perhaps to their old enemies, the French Canadians, was a shock to all the American colonists. Moreover, they saw themselves surrounded on the north and west by an undemocratic government whose legislature was appointed by the crown, not elected by the people, a despotic government whose power might be exerted against them at the will of the King. Also, the American colonists were Protestants in an overwhelming majority and, especially in New England, fiercely jealous of the prevalence of their religion. They had inherited fear and hatred of Catholicism from old England. Now they saw dreaded Popery practically established in all that great territory enclosing them.

There was, too, for those thinking in terms of a war of rebellion, the fact that the St. Lawrence River was a broad waterway by which troops could be carried to Montreal, where they would have access to that other waterway, Lake Champlain, Lake George, and the Hudson, which would, if held by the British, separate the New England colonies from those to the southward.

All these considerations made it desirable that Canada should be joined with the American colonies in the common cause against Britain. The Second Continental Congress in May had, rather ineptly, tried to induce the Canadians to unite "with us in the defence of our common liberty." [3]

In a letter dated May 29, 1775, and addressed "To the oppressed Inhabitants of Canada," the Congress declared that "the fate of the catholic and protestant colonies [was] strongly linked together." It was urged that "the enjoyment of your very religion . . . depends on a legislature in which you have no share and over which you have no control." [4] "The decent manner in which the religious matters were touched" [5] was received with pleasure by the Canadians. But on October 21, 1774, the First Continental Congress had addressed an appeal to the people of Great Britain, setting forth the grievances of the colonies, among which were the Quebec Act establishing in Canada "a religion fraught with sanguinary and impious tenets . . . a religion that has deluged your island in blood and dispersed impiety, bigotry, persecution, murder and rebellion through every part of the world." [6]

Unfortunately the Canadians read that appeal after they had digested the later one addressed to them, and they were not pleased with it. "They could not contain their resentment, nor express it but in broken curses." "Oh! the perfidious, double-faced Congress!" they cried. "Let us bless and obey our benevolent Prince, whose humanity is consistent, and extends to all Religions; let us abhor all who would seduce us from our loyalty, by acts that would dishonour a Jesuit; and whose Addresses, like their Resolves, are destructive of their own objects." [7]

Well then, if Canada would not willingly join, what about compulsion? What about conquest? The Second Continental Congress was at first unwilling to go so far as that. On the 1st day of June, 1775, it resolved "that no expedition or incursion ought to be undertaken or made, by any colony, or body of colonists, against or into Canada." [8]

But that vigorous and ambitious warrior Benedict Arnold was of a different opinion. On June 13 he reported to the Congress that the Indians would not assist the King's troops against the Americans; that Carleton had been unable to raise more than twenty Canadians to help him; that there were only 550 British regulars in all Canada, scattered among five posts. He proposed an attack on Montreal with 1,700 men, through St. John's and Chambly, Quebec being ripe to fall when those places had been taken. He added that "if no person appears who will undertake to carry the plan into execution . . . I will undertake it and . . . answer for the success of it." [9]

And that other vigorous and restless soul Ethan Allen was of the same opinion. When he heard of the resolution of the Congress, adopted on May 18, recommending the removal of the cannon and military stores taken at Ticonderoga to the south end of Lake George and the abandonment of the captured fort,[10] he wrote to the Congress on May 29 a letter of protest, in which he also urged an expedition against Canada: "The more vigorous the Colonies push the war against the King's Troops in Canada, the more friends we shall find in that country. . . . Should the Colonies forthwith send an army of two or three thousand men, and attack Montreal, we . . . would easily make a conquest of that place." [11] On June 2 he even more eloquently adjured the New York Provincial Congress to favor such an attack. "I wish to God," he fervently wrote, "America would, at this critical juncture, exert herself. . . . She might rise on eagles' wings and mount up to glory, freedom and immortal honour, if she did but know and exert her strength. Fame is now hovering over her head. A vast continent must now sink to slavery, poverty, horrour and bondage, or rise to unconquerable freedom, immense wealth, inexpressible felicity and immortal fame." [12]

Allen wanted his Green Mountain Boys enrolled in the Continental service. To that end, he and his lieutenant colonel, Seth Warner, presented themselves on June 23 at the door of the Congress in Philadelphia, and were admitted to the floor of the house. What he said to the Congress, whether he repeated his advice as to Canada, does not appear in the records. He did attain his chief object; his Boys were to be enlisted in a regiment of their own, under officers of their own choice.[13] It may well be that what he told the Congress then influenced it, within the next four days, to reverse its policy as to Canada, and to direct General Schuyler to proceed to Ticonderoga and Crown Point, and "if [he] finds it practicable and that it will not be disagreeable to the Canadians, he do immediately take possession of St. Johns, Montreal and any other parts of the country." [14] At all events, Ethan Allen may be credited with some of the impetus behind that resolution.

Major General Philip Schuyler was a representative of the best Dutch blood in New York, and one of its wealthiest landed proprietors. He was at this time in his forty-third year, slender yet well muscled, erect and commanding in figure, quick and energetic in movement. His face was noticeably florid and unusually expressive of his emotions, its features rather large, but not distinguished. His hair was dark brown, as were his keen, piercing eyes. His voice was clear, inclining to sharpness. His dress was always in accord with the prevailing mode. The manner of life in his mansion in Albany and his country seat at Saratoga was generous and hospitable, elegant indeed, with numerous servants, an ample stable, and a full cellar to care for his guests.

He was not lacking in intelligence, nor in kindliness, nor in courtesy to his equals, though to those of pronounced inferiority of station or of doubtful integrity he was apt to show his sense of his own superiority. In depth and breadth of mind, in stability of intention, in firm decisiveness to plan and to execute, in the ability to meet a confused situation, discern its essentials, and expend his energies upon them only, Schuyler was somewhat deficient. Thus he lacked the executive power needed to make him an effective and successful general officer; nor had his slight martial experience as a captain in the French and Indian War been sufficient to induce a habit of command. Moreover, he had not the physical vigor nor the ruggedness needed to cope with the hardships and deprivations of a wilderness campaign. This want showed itself in the outbursts of temper and exasperation which often succeeded an exhibition of uncomplaining patience on his part. He was a high-minded, public-spirited gentleman and above all a patriot, wholly devoted—rather singularly among the men of his own class in New York—to the American cause. He was wrongly placed as a chief military officer; his proper place was at the council table.[15]

Brigadier General Richard Montgomery was Schuyler's second in command. Born in northern Ireland, the son of a baronet and member of

Parliament, he was well educated, and from his seventeenth year had been a soldier in the British army. He had fought under Amherst at Ticonderoga and Crown Point in 1759. At the age of twenty-six he was a captain. For ten years, he held that rank. In 1772 he resigned from the army and returned to America. In the next year he married one of the Livingstons, a family of wealth and high social position. Two years later he was commissioned a brigadier general in the Continental army. Although of studious habit, preferring the library and domestic life to the camp and the field, he was ardent for the cause of the colonies and responded to the call to arms.

He was tall, slender, of graceful address, yet strong, active, and capable of long endurance of fatigue and hardship. Forceful in command, aggressive in action, patient in adversity, cool in judgment, never negligent of duty, never avoiding danger, he was the complete soldier.[16]

With those two as aide-de-camp was Captain John Macpherson, Jr., the twenty-one-year-old son of a well-to-do Philadelphian. His portrait shows a notably handsome and refined face, and his character was in keeping with it. Bancroft has described him as a "pure-minded, youthful enthusiast for liberty . . . full of promise for war, lovely in temper, dear to the army, honored by the affection and confidence of his chief." [17]

Schuyler's instructions, when he was detached by Washington at New York City on June 25, gave him command of the New York Department. He was to occupy the several posts in the Champlain region, put them "in a fit posture to answer the End designed," and, besides keeping an eye on Governor Tryon, "watch the Movements of the Indian Agent," Colonel Guy Johnson "and prevent, as far as you can, the Effect of his Influence to our Prejudice with the Indians." "The Temper and Disposition" of the Canadians were to be investigated "that a proper line may be mark'd out to conciliate their good Opinion, or facilitate any future Operation." [18]

It will be noted that this was a cautious approach to the possible invasion of Canada, there being no definite orders or directions on the point. The Congress, however, as has been related, gave orders on June 27 for an aggressive movement if Schuyler should find it practicable and not disagreeable to the Canadians.

The Colonel Guy Johnson whom Schuyler was to watch was son-in-law and successor in office to Sir William Johnson, who had been appointed Superintendent of Indian Affairs in the northern department in 1755 and, with a rare talent for dealing with red men reinforced by his "marriage" with the sister of the Mohawk chief, had exercised a strong and generally prevailing influence over the Iroquois League, of Mohawks, Oneidas,

Onondagas, Cayugas, Senecas, and Tuscaroras, or Six Nations.[19] Besides these, there were in Canada the Seven Nations, allies of the League, not so numerous nor in general so warlike, yet including the Abenakis on the St. Francis River—formerly most savage of all and most dreaded by the colonists—and the Caughnawagas, whose chiefs were all "of English extraction Captivated in their infancy." Their superior intelligence made the Caughnawagas important, although the tribe could not muster two hundred braves. Beyond these to the north and west were unnumbered other, unrelated tribes, a great reservoir of potential savagery.[20] Guy Johnson as Superintendent of Indian Affairs since 1774 could cause infinite trouble to the Americans.

There was another influence which prevailed in Canada. Louis St. Luc de La Corne, a Frenchman, had been Superintendent of the Canadian Indians under the French régime, and his son-in-law, Major Campbell, now held a similar office. La Corne was hated and dreaded by the colonists as a "fiend incarnate" and was believed to have been responsible for the massacre of the prisoners taken at the capture of Fort William Henry in 1757.[21] He was now on the side of the British. It was evident to the colonists that the Indian question was one of the most important with which they had to deal in the contemplated invasion of Canada.

Johnson, La Corne and Campbell, Joseph Brant, otherwise called Thayendanegea, a Mohawk chief, and Colonel John Butler, Johnson's assistant, worked assiduously to enlist the Indians under the British standard in 1775. La Corne was especially busy, giving them powder and brandy. At a price of two johannes (about $16) a piece, he got some of the young Caughnawagas to engage; but the older men took the money from them and returned it to him.[22] To help Carleton break down the sales resistance of the Indians, the home government sent a cargo of inducements, "hundreds of proved fowling-pieces, with blue barrels, walnut stocks, trimmings of wrought brass and silver sights . . . neat, bright Indian hatchets," brass kettles, gold laced hats, ruffled shirts, pipes, greatcoats, barrels and barrels of gunpowder and of bullets, pots of paint for facial adornment, blue, rose, yellow, vermilion, all to the value of £2,500.[23] Johnson had the effrontery to deny that he was inciting the red men to fight the Americans. The charge, he said, was manifestly absurd. It was true that he had fortified his house in the Mohawk valley, and that it was guarded by Mohawks; but that was only because he had heard that the New Englanders or the people from Albany were coming in "a considerable number to seize and imprison me." [24] But there were witnesses against him. Samuel Kirkland, missionary among the Iroquois, testified to the contrary. Thirty Indian chiefs, on a mission to the Congress, corroborated Kirkland's testimony. By the middle of July, it was said that Johnson was ready, with 800 or more Indians, to invade Tryon County in the province of New York.[25]

Reports as to the ultimate intentions of the Indians varied. In March, John Brown said he had word from reliable sources that the Caughnawagas, although "repeatedly applied to and requested to join the King's troops," had "peremptorily refused and still intend to refuse." [26] In June, Ethan Allen thought the Indians as a whole were attached "to our interest." He was cynical enough to believe that they acted "upon political principles and consequently are inclined to fall in with the strongest side. At present ours has the appearance of it." [27] This was immediately after Ticonderoga had been taken. But a man who had been in Montreal in the same month reported that the Caughnawagas had actually "taken up the hatchet." [28] In July another, similarly experienced, said they had refused to join Carleton though threatened with dispossession of their lands, and that the Indians were "pretty generally determined to take no part in the quarrel." [29] This was confirmed, also in July, by Captain Remember Baker, a Green Mountain Boy who had been scouting on his own hook. He said the "Seven Nations had agreed not to fight the Yankees." [30] But in August "two persons who have lately come from St. Johns" stated that Johnson had 500 Indians at Montreal "just going to join the English." [31] It was all very confusing and very disconcerting to the Americans, and it was clearly time that something was done about it.

The Continental Congress, in July, had formulated "A Speech to the Six Confederate Nations" telling them at great length about the King's oppression of the colonies and the contest to relieve it. It was couched in the language of parables. "This is a family quarrel between us and Old England," the speech said. "You Indians are not concerned in it. We don't wish you to take up the hatchet against the King's Troops. We desire you to remain at home and not join on either side, but keep the hatchet buried deep." [32]

A "council fire" was held at Albany, commencing August 23 and carried on, with great deliberation, by 700 Indians for more than a week. When they were "weary from having sat long in council," they thought it was "time for a little drink." General Schuyler, Colonel Turbott Francis, and Volkert P. Douw represented the Congress. Samuel Kirkland and James Dean, missionaries among the Indians, were also there to exert their influence. The peace pipe was passed around, which must have been a slow proceeding among 700, and then the Speech was delivered. It was a long speech, and the simple savages took three days to digest it. On the third day Little Abraham, a sachem of the Mohawks, made an elaborate reply. The essential paragraph was heralded by an injunction, "Now, therefore attend and apply your ears closely." It went on to say: "We have fully considered this matter. . . . This, then, is the determination of the Six Nations: Not to take any part, but, as it is a family affair, to sit still and see you fight it out." [33] It should be noted, however, that the Indians at the council fire were chiefly Oneidas and Mohawks of a certain canton of that nation. Most of the Mohawks, with the chief men of the Onondagas, the Cayugas, and the Senecas had gone to Montreal with Brant and Johnson. Therefore this compact was not so reassuring as it seemed on its face to be.[34] In October, however, the Caughnawagas undertook to promise for all the Seven Nations of Canadian Indians that they would not "in the least molest" the colonists.[35]

It must not be supposed that the colonists were averse to having the Indians in the war at all. Massachusetts enlisted the Stockbridge Indians in its forces immediately after the outbreak of the war. There was some excuse for that; they were at least semicivilized.[36] But its Provincial Congress sent a commissioner to the Maine Indians to enlist them and lent a willing ear to a proposal of the Abenakis to take up the hatchet for the colonists, "for which we have no immediate occasion," the Congress said.[37] Ethan Allen had had no compunctions about soliciting four tribes of the Canadian Indians "to help me fight the King's troops," offering them "money, blankets, tomahawks, knives, paint and anything there is in the army, just like brothers." [38] Some seventy or eighty of the red men joined Arnold in Canada; but otherwise very few were, in fact, employed by the colonists early in the war except as scouts, messengers, or guides.[39]

Schuyler and his companions left New York on July 4. After certain necessary delays at Albany and Saratoga, they arrived at Ticonderoga on the 18th and found a sad state of affairs.[40] At the landing place, held by a captain and a hundred men, a sentinel "quitted his post to go and awake the guard, consisting of three men, in which he had no success. I walked up and came to another, a sergeant's guard. Here the sentinel challenged, but suffered me to come up to him, the whole guard, like the first, in profoundest sleep. With a pen-knife only I could have cut off both guards and then have set fire to the block-house, destroyed the stores and starved the people there." So Schuyler reported to Washington on the night of his arrival.

This was his introduction to a post, which he soon found was "in a perfectly defenceless state," not only because "not one earthly thing has been done for offence or defence," but also because the garrison was in a wretched physical and mental condition.[41]

There were about 1,300 men in the posts on the lakes, 600 at Ticonderoga, 400 at Crown Point, 300 at Fort George. They were composed of Colonel Benjamin Hillman's Connecticut regiment, 1,000 men, part of a Massachusetts regiment under Colonel James Easton, numbering a little more than 100, 200 New Yorkers, and a few Green Mountain Boys.[42] At Ti, as the principal post was currently called, the men were "crowded in very bad barracks," insanitary to a degree; many were ill. They were largely without discipline. Those from Connecticut, especially, feeling themselves in Yankee fashion quite the equals of their officers, were insubordinate. Food was scarce: "sometimes we have no flour." The "constant cry for rum" went unappeased.[43] Schuyler found that there had been "a very considerable waste or embezzlement" of the stores.[44] Ammunition was wanting, and when it came to building boats, as the Congress had directed him to do, for an attack on St. John's, he had "not a nail, no pitch, no oakum," and no boards until he could set up a sawmill.[45]

The helpless, defenseless condition of these posts was largely due to the inefficiency of Colonel Hinman. He had come to Ti, as he said, merely to reinforce its garrison and, although he had accepted the chief command of a wilderness post far removed from any superior officer, his idea of his duty was "to wait for orders" and to do nothing until he got them.[46] He had welcomed the news that a superior was on the way to direct him. "I wait, Sir, with impatience for your arrival, as I find myself very unable to steer in this stormy situation," he plaintively wrote to Schuyler, on July 7.[47] He did not last long in the Continental army, not longer than December 20, 1775. After that, he returned to the militia.[48]

Schuyler had recognized the difficulties of his task before he came to Ticonderoga. There were under his command in the whole New York Department, present and fit for duty, no more than 2,500 men.[49] The Congress expected him to add to these the regiment of Green Mountain Boys, 500 in number, which Ethan Allen had been authorized to raise. But Allen had lost favor with the Boys. When some of "the old farmers on the New Hampshire Grants" met at Cephas Kent's tavern in Dorset, on July 27, to nominate the officers of the proposed regiment, they ignored him and elected Seth Warner lieutenant colonel, leaving the colonelcy vacant.[50] Allen came to Ticonderoga alone and solicited a place in Schuyler's force. Schuyler was "apprehensive of disagreeable consequences arising from Mr. Allen's imprudence . . . his impatience of subordination." But after he had made "a solemn promise . . . that he would demean himself properly," he was admitted as a volunteer.[51] The other 499 Boys failed to arrive.

If and when Schuyler attacked Canada with the force then in hand, he would have to use at least 200 of his men to guard the posts he already held, marching with not much more than 1,000 to take Carleton's fortified positions. The British had at least 700 regular troops, to which they might perhaps add as many Indians and a number of whites which he could not even guess at, because Hinman had obtained no information as to the probable attitude of the Canadians toward the proposed invasion.[52] Even without regard for the lack of matériel of every kind, the lack of man power was discouraging. So "with a strange and almost fatal patience," inherent in his Dutch blood perhaps, or resulting from "his patrician habit to order and not to do" or his lack of physical stamina, he lingered at Ti for more than two months, waiting for reinforcements.[53]

Not that he was idle; he got out planks for bateaux and built them, enough finally to carry 1,300 men with twenty days' provisions; he even had, on July 31, "a boat on the stocks (and nearly finished) sixty feet in length," large enough to carry "between two and three hundred men," and had started another. Also he called and called again on New York for more troops, for tents, and for equipment of all sorts from field artillery to bullet molds.[54]

In June, New York had voted to raise four regiments. On July 21 Schuyler asked for them. A week later he did "most earnestly entreat" that they should be sent up to Albany.[55] On August 14 Hinman caustically observed, "The Province of New York abounds with officers, but I have not had my curiosity gratified by the sight of one private." [56] But New York had its reasons for the delay. Its Committee of Safety had written on July 15, "Our troops can be of no service to you; they have no arms, clothes, blankets, or ammunition, the officers no commissions, our treasury no money, ourselves in debt. It is in vain to complain; we will send you soldiers, whenever the men we have raised are entitled to that name." [57]

They started at last. Colonel James Clinton arrived in Albany near the end of August with six companies. Three of these had serviceable muskets, two had guns needing repairs, the sixth had none. Lieutenant Colonel Philip Van Cortlandt got there about the same time, with four companies, "many of the men wanting shirts, shoes, stockings, underclothes," having, that is to say, no uniforms at all except coats and breeches. Three-fourths of them had no blankets, and they had no tents; but thirty men did have muskets. No barracks being available, they were kept penned up in their boats, to their great disgust. "Give us guns, blankets, tents . . . and we will fight the devil himself," they cried. "But don't keep us here in market-boats, as though we were a parcel of sheep or calves." The first of them, four companies under Lieutenant Colonel Rudolphus Ritzema, reached Ticonderoga on August 22.[58]

In his search for more men, Schuyler cast his eyes on Brigadier General Wooster's Connecticut troops sent down to help out in the defense of New York City. On July 17 the Continental Congress directed Wooster to send 1,000 men to Schuyler.[59] Colonel David Waterbury brought his full regiment. New Hampshire offered Schuyler three companies of Rangers, not part of the Continental army, under command of Colonel Timothy Bedel. They were to join him on his march to St. Johns. So, in one way and another, Schuyler gathered a little army.[60]

But, although Schuyler labored to improve the discipline of his men, they were for a long time "much inclined to a seditious and mutinous temper," partly because of their lack of good food, supplies, and equipment, and partly because of intercolonial jealousies. Major John Brown of Massachusetts thought "New York have acted a droll part, and are determined to defeat us, if in their power." [61] A Connecticut man wrote to Governor Trumbull complaining that "all the places of profit" were "filled up with men of the York Government," while Connecticut men were "obliged to do all the drudgery. . . . Commissaries' places are profitable. . . . Why should they have all the places of profit? . . . The advantage of their situation is such that it will make them rich. Are we to be wholly ruled by the Committee of New York?" [62] General Wooster, commanding the Connecticut men sent down to New York, thought it was dishonorable to his province to be subjected to the direction of a body of men—to wit, the New York Congress—when he could have "no faith in their honesty in the cause." "You know not, Sir, half their tricks," he wrote to Trumbull.[63] This distrust of New York permeated the New Englanders, and affected their relationship with their commander, Schuyler, a New Yorker himself.

In July, Schuyler had sent John Brown north to secure information about Carleton's post at St. Johns, the magazines of arms and ammunition in Montreal, and the inclinations of the Indians and Canadians in the contest. This man Brown was one of those remarkable characters that one finds hidden in the crannies of history, almost unknown even to historians. He was an educated man, a graduate of Yale and a lawyer, who had held the office of King's attorney in New York province, whence he had removed to Pittsfield, Massachusetts, to practice his profession. But he was not satisfied with such a sedentary life. He was "a strong, bold, active, fearless man . . . of noble personal appearance, genial air and chivalric manner," the best type of the gentleman adventurer.[64]

We have had a glimpse of him in February, 1775, when the Massachusetts Provincial Congress sent him on a mission to Canada, and have seen that his report recommended the seizure of Ticonderoga, in which he had afterward had a part. That journey was a severe test of his ability as a woodsman, his physical strength, and his pertinacity. It was made in the dead of winter, through deep snows, in intense cold, and over a most difficult country. On Lake Champlain amid broken ice he and his two companions, an old hunter and one who had been an Indian's captive for years, had been frozen in for two days. Thence they had gone on foot through a flooded country. It was a fortnight's journey of "almost inconceivable hardships," he said. At Montreal he talked with all sorts of people while his companions discussed matters of interest with the Caughnawagas. His report did not encourage the hope that the Canadians in general would join the colonists, but he did succeed in establishing friendly relations with some of the Old Subjects, notably one Thomas Waller, and in providing "a channel of correspondence" with them.[65]

He left Crown Point on this second errand, under Schuyler's orders, on July 24, with four companions, a Canadian and three soldiers. The journey could not be made openly as the first had been, for since the taking of Ticonderoga Canada was enemy country. Danger of captivity was now added to the difficulties of travel. After arriving in Canadian territory by boat, they "had a tedious and fatiguing march" of three days "through a vast tract of swamp." In one house where they lodged for the night, they were "surrounded by a large party of the enemy . . . escaping out of a back window,"and on their return trip they were "pursued two days." Nevertheless, they remained in Canada four days, protected by friendly inhabitants, and brought back a full and convincing report, dated August 14.

The French, he said, would not fight against the colonists. The Indians were minded to be neutral, except that they might scout for the British. St. Johns was being fortified. It was supported by two bateaux mounting nine guns each; and two sixty-foot vessels to mount twelve guns each were on the stocks. There were 700 of the King's troops in Canada, 300 of whom were at St. Johns, only 50 at Quebec, and the rest at Montreal, Chambly, and elsewhere. "Now, Sir, is the time to carry Canada. It may be done with great ease and little cost, and I have no doubt but the Canadians will join us. There is a great defection amongst them." [66] By Canadians he meant the Old Subjects.

Information from another source, coming on August 3, confirmed Brown's report except in the disposition of the King's troops, of which there were said to be 470 at St. Johns, 110 at Chambly, 80 at Quebec, and about

20 at Montreal. Samuel Mott, who got this news, urged that "we go forward now with 1500 men [rather] than with 3000 one month hence." [67]

But Schuyler lingered. There were reasons why he did, sufficient in his mind at least. He had no tents, no carriages for his fieldpieces. Many of his men were sickly—194 of them on August 14—and his expected reinforcements had not come. He was fully determined to go on, "unless your Excellency or Congress should direct otherwise," he advised Washington on August 6. As late as August 27 he wrote again to Washington, "To do it has been my determination, unless prevented by my superiours." [68] It may be unfair to Schuyler to suggest it, but that recurrent conditional clause seems to suggest a hope that he might be prevented.

On August 17 he went to Albany to attend the council fire with the Indians, leaving Montgomery in command on the lakes. That active soldier had, it seems, been tugging at the leash. On the 19th he wrote that "every intelligence from Canada evinces the necessity of a vigorous and speedy effort to crush their naval armament before it gets abroad." Now, in Schuyler's absence, he slipped the leash.

Montgomery had received a letter from John Brown, whom he had sent north on another scouting expedition, telling him of the near completion of Carleton's two vessels: "Their hulls seem to be finished . . . their masts are preparing . . . they appear of large size." He apologized for "writing in a dictatorial style," and would not have done so if it were not certain that the two vessels and their attendant bateaux "can easily sweep the lake. . . . I therefore humbly beseech that some effectual measures may be immediately entered into to keep the command of this lake." That was enough for Montgomery.[69]

He at once wrote to Schuyler that he was so much of Brown's opinion that he thought it "absolutely necessary to move down the lake with the utmost dispatch." He had therefore, without waiting for Schuyler's approval, given orders for an advance to Ile aux Noix in the Richelieu River beyond the foot of the lake, which, with the aid of two 12-pounders and a log boom, he intended to hold and so prevent Carleton's vessels from entering Champlain. He hoped Schuyler would follow him in a whaleboat, "leaving somebody to bring on the troops and artillery." He apologized for taking this step without orders, but felt that to hold back the enemy was of the utmost importance. "If I must err, let it be on the right side." [70] Schuyler was usually very touchy about his superiority in command, but he now learned "with pleasure" that Montgomery had acted in such an important matter without even consulting him. He seemed, indeed, to be glad that he had been relieved of responsibility for the venture.[71]

CHAPTER 12

Montreal

Montgomery was now about to begin the attempt against Montreal so long considered. From Ticonderoga his course lay north by way of Lake Champlain to Crown Point. Beyond that the lake widened between shores of almost unbroken wilderness, narrowed again, and emptied at the 45th parallel of latitude into a river, indifferently called the Richelieu or the Sorel, flowing nearly due north. At that point it was almost blocked by an island, the Ile aux Noix. Twenty miles farther north was St. Johns, a small settlement. Ten miles beyond that was Chambly, still smaller. At the mouth of the river, where it emptied into the St. Lawrence, was another little village, Sorel. But, at Chambly, a road led northwest to La Prairie and Longueuil, directly opposite Montreal, the main objective.[1]

In the evening of Monday August 28 the greater part of Waterbury's Connecticut Regiment, four companies of Ritzema's 4th New York, and Mott's small section of artillery, about twelve hundred men in all, embarked in the schooner *Liberty,* the sloop *Enterprise,* and a fleet of gondolas, bateaux, row-galleys, piraguas, and canoes. In the bow of each sailing vessel a 12-pounder was mounted. With a fair wind and a sufficiency of fresh and lusty oarsmen, the excursion began auspiciously, the men evincing "great cheerfulness." [2]

But at ten o'clock it began to rain heavily. They went ashore and bivouacked damply under the trees. On Tuesday they worked their way up to Crown Point. "A barbarous north wind" held them there one day, but the next morning a fair southerly breeze set in. So day by day they went on, going ashore at night to sleep, until, just beyond Isle La Motte, on a "fine, sandy beach" they disembarked to wait for Schuyler.[3]

Returning from the Albany council fire, Schuyler reached Ticonderoga on August 30, "very much indisposed . . . with a bilious fever and violent rheumatick pains"; but the next morning, after ordering forward five hundred of Hinman's regiment, three hundred of Colonel Goose Van Schaick's, and some artillery, he set out in a whaleboat to catch up with his ambitious lieutenant. In the morning of Monday September 4 he found Montgomery awaiting him and at once gave orders to move on. That evening they pitched their tents on Ile aux Noix. Hopefully, they fired three cannon shots, the signal agreed upon with their Canadian friends, who were to gather and join them. There was no response.[4]

The next day found Schuyler in rather worse condition, but he drafted an address to the Canadians telling them that "the Grand Congress" had ordered him to expel the British troops, who wished "to enslave their countrymen." The Congress, he said, "could not conceive that anything but the force of necessity could induce you tamely to bear the insult and ignominy that is daily imposed on you, or that you could calmly sit by and see those chains forging which are intended to bind you, your posterity, and ours, in one common and eternal slavery." Therefore it had ordered him "to cherish every Canadian . . . and sacredly to guard their property." [5] This document he directed Ethan Allen and John Brown to take to James Livingston, a merchant at Chambly who was well affected toward the colonists, and with whom he had been in correspondence.

On September 5 the troops embarked again, with three days' cooked provisions and their arms "in good firing Order"; their tents, baggage, and supplies were left behind under a guard. They were sailing now, all stripped for action, down the broad Richelieu between its heavily wooded shores. At three in the afternoon, they were in sight of the fort at St. Johns, two miles away. As they gazed at it, they saw white puffs of smoke break from its walls, heard the boom of its guns, and realized that they were being "kindly saluted" with round shots and bombs, though none of the missiles reached them.[6]

Half a mile farther on they went ashore "in a close, deep swamp" and started "in grounds marshy and covered with woods" towards the fort. Major Thomas Hobby and Captain Matthew Mead of the 5th Connecticut led a flanking party on the left and a little ahead of the others. They were crossing Bernier's Brook, a deep, muddy, winding stream, when they were met by a surprising blast of close fire. A hundred Indians led by Captain Tice, a New York Tory, had ambushed them. Several of the Americans fell, but the rest fired on the unseen enemy, then wheeled smartly to the left into dense thickets and for half an hour or so there was irregular bush fighting before the Indians retreated. Eight of Schuyler's men were killed or fatally wounded, and eight, including Hobby and Mead, injured less severely.[7]

They advanced no farther. As night fell, they dug "a small intrenchment" where they stood. But the enemy "kept continually throwing their bomb-shells" at this place, so, without tarrying long, they retreated a mile and entrenched again out of reach of the British guns.

That night there came to Schuyler "a gentleman, Mr. ———," whose name he disclosed only to Washington, begging him to erase it from his letter. This person had more effect upon the expedition than all the bombs and Indians. He told the general that the fortification at St. Johns was "complete and strong and plentifully furnished with cannon"; that the vessel there would be ready to sail in three or four days and was to carry sixteen guns; that no Canadians would join the Americans; that they had better not attack St. Johns, but rather return to Ile aux Noix.[8] Such resolution as Schuyler had was not proof against this kind of advice. He told a council of war the next morning that he considered it "absolutely necessary" to retire. The rest of its members agreed "to take measures for preventing her [the ship's] entrance into the lake," measures which, because of "the weak state of our artillery" could be effected only at Ile aux Noix, where an already prepared boom could be thrown across the channel. There they would await "intelligence touching the intentions of the Canadians" and, when reinforced, march by land against Montreal, "should the Canadians favour such a design." [9] So, instead of "expelling" the King's troops from all Canada, or even from the little fort at St. Johns, they all withdrew "without noise." If Major Preston's force at St. Johns had not been so weak that he feared to venture out of his fort, there might have been noise enough at this retirement.[10]

The news was spread abroad in Canada of their fight and flight, in which, so the tale went, 60 Indians had defeated 1,500 Americans in entrenchments, killing 40, wounding 30 more, and sending them back to their refuge at Ile aux Noix; and the victory was celebrated in Montreal by "a grand mass with a *Te Deum*." If anything were needed to ensure the abstention of the Canadians from joining Schuyler, this retreat provided it.[11]

The river was boomed, the island fortified. Now the colonials were in an excellent defensive position, very satisfactory if defense was all that was wanted. And there they received reinforcements, 300 of Hinman's Connecticut troops, 400 of the 2nd New York under Colonel Goose Van Schaick, with three pieces of cannon. Counting certain detachments sent out before that, Schuyler had altogether 1,700 men, more than twice the British regulars in all Canada. And he had five guns and three mortars.[12]

At this juncture (September 9) Schuyler received a reply to the letter he had sent by Ethan Allen and John Brown to James Livingston, the well affected merchant living at Chambly. Livingston urged him to interpose a force between St. Johns and Chambly so as to prevent Preston and his vessel from escaping to the St. Lawrence. If Schuyler would do that, Livingston promised to help him with "a considerable party of Canadians." They might even capture the vessel, loaded with "provisions and warlike supplies" and "slenderly manned." [13]

Schuyler fell in with this suggestion. He made elaborate plans. Two row-galleys, each carrying a 12-pounder, the sloop, the schooner, and ten bateaux "with 350 picked men" were to lie in the river to prevent Preston's vessel, the *Royal Savage*, from going south to the lake; and 700 men were to go again to a point near St. Johns, 200 of them to act as a covering party, protecting the boats, while 500 circumvented the fort and invested it on the north.[14]

On the 10th of September 800 men set out and landed at about ten o'clock in the evening near the first breastwork erected in the former attempt. The covering party of 300, under Montgomery, held that position, while Colonel Ritzema with 500 New Yorkers started along the shore to march around the fort. Flankers were thrown out in the woods on their left. It was dark in that forest, and the flankers, remembering the ambush on the former expedition, were nervous and apprehensive. There might be an Indian behind every tree. They drew toward the right, toward the open beach and, suddenly in the darkness, collided with the head of the main column. An instant and overpowering panic set in. They were ambushed again! They were certain of it, though only one chance shot from one of their own men had been heard. The covering party heard a noise as of many men coming in a hurry. Back they came, the whole 500, scrambling through the woods, through swamps as hard as they could go, for the boats. Ritzema was the last to come, all by himself.[15]

Montgomery took them in hand, rallied them, exhorted them "to act like men," formed them, and started them off again. They had gone a quarter of a mile, when some small shells and grapeshot from one of Preston's bateaux crashed and rattled through the trees. Half of them turned tail and ran again for the boats. But Ritzema, with the rest in a straggling band, went on to the second entrenchment of the previous excursion. A few of the enemy were holding a small house there. Ritzema had only 50 men with him. A few shots were exchanged, and two of the enemy were killed. Though 200 more of his men came up, he decided to retire. It was then three o'clock in the morning. The whole expedition spent the night at the landing place, their only satisfaction being that one of their 12-pounders had gone through that bateau of Preston's from stem to stern, torn it apart, and perhaps destroyed its crew of 35 men, or, at least had given them a ducking.[16]

In the morning another council of war decided to try again. But the officers were uncertain of the obedience of the men. They felt it necessary to call a sort of town meeting and let the privates vote on the question. The men agreed to go on. But just then Lieutenant Samuel Lockwood, who had been scouting down the river, returned and told them that the *Royal Savage* lay a little below "completely equipped." Part of Waterbury's New Yorkers at once ran to the boats, intending to get away as quickly as possible. Faced by such demoralization, fearing, too, that the schooner might come up and destroy their bateaux, the officers gave up the attempt. They embarked again for Ile aux Noix.[17]

Montgomery was not satisfied to retreat so ignominiously. After they had gone a few miles he stopped the fleet, went ashore with his officers, and called on the men to follow him on a march against St. Johns. But one of them called out that the schooner was coming. That finished it. "The Troops were hardly restrained from pushing off without their officers." So back to their haven of safety they all went, an expedition defeated by imagination.[18]

At the main camp the returning heroes were received with such jeers and upbraidings by those who had stayed safe at home, that they were "unable to bear the reproach of their late unbecoming behaviour." Schuyler, who was so ill that he could not leave his tent, concerted with Montgomery to take advantage of this state of mind. On September 13 they ordered the artillery into the boats, with the intention of carrying the whole force down the river again. The main party was to land as before, against St. Johns. The schooner and the row-galleys, manned by "determined volunteer crews and good rowers," were boldly to attack and board the *Royal Savage*. But the next day it rained, and on the next after that Ethan Allen came in to report his findings as to the disposition of the Canadians, which necessitated further consideration. That night Schuyler's "disorder reattacked . . . [him] with double violence." The 15th was again rainy, and Schuyler was so ill that "every prospect of a speedy recovery vanished." On September 16 he "was put into a covered boat and left Isle aux Noix."[19] Montgomery, of course, assumed command.

It would have been useless to call for volunteers in any event. Six hundred of the men were on the sick list, including half of Waterbury's contingent of Connecticut paladins. Sulkiness was prevalent throughout the camp, and mutiny was in the offing. One man cocked his gun and threatened to shoot an officer. Unauthorized parties wandered about the island, plundering its few inhabitants. Frequent false alarms of enemy approaches kept the camp in a turmoil. Courts-martial were of no avail, for no witnesses could be found to testify against the culprits. The officers were about ready to give up the whole expedition as a hopeless job when things took a turn for the better.[20]

Allen had helped by reporting that all the Caughnawagas had deserted Preston at St. Johns, and on the 16th the expected reinforcements began to arrive: Seth Warner and 170 of his Green Mountain Boys, "able bodied, stout, active fellows, used to the woods"; Colonel Timothy Bedel and 100 New Hampshire Rangers; and an Independent Company of Volunteers, including some Dartmouth students. These were soon followed by Captain John Lamb's Independent Company of New York Artillery—in all, something more than 400 men. Montgomery had now about 2,000 in his camp. Besides these, Easton's 200 men and the 1st New York Battalion, 125 strong, were coming from Ti.[21]

At the time Schuyler took over the command of Ticonderoga, the post at St. Johns was but a barracks, some brick buildings, and a stone house; but plans had been made to strengthen it. Two redoubts about a hundred feet square and six hundred feet apart were built of earth. One surrounded the brick buildings; the other, the stone house. A strong stockade, defended by a seven-foot ditch and fraised with pointed pickets in part and in part abatised, was drawn around the redoubts on three sides; and a moat was dug on the fourth, the river side. Cannon were mounted on the redoubts. Altogether, it was a sturdy little fort, offering a chance for a stubborn defense.[22]

Carleton's whole force of regulars was composed of 376 of the 7th Regiment, the Royal Fusiliers, and 263 of the 26th, the Cameronians.[23] Fewer than 200 men drawn from these regiments, with a few artillerymen and Indians, had garrisoned St. Johns fort at the time of Schuyler's first abortive attempt upon it. Carleton might have abandoned it and the whole Richelieu River and concentrated his forces for the defense of Montreal; but the Canadians and the Indians would have interpreted that as evidence of weakness and of fear, and would have been moved to withhold the help he so sorely needed. He had therefore decided to make a strong stand at St. Johns. To its garrison were added enough regulars to make up 500. His dire need for more men and the curiously amphibious character of the river operation appear in his withdrawing, in August, a midshipman and 12 sailors from the newly arrived armed brigantine, *Gaspé,* and sending them to the fort.

Earlier in the year, he had helped Lieutenant Colonel Allan Maclean, an old campaigner, to raise troops among the veteran Scottish soldiers who had emigrated to Canada. Maclean enlisted 70 in a company called the Royal Highland Emigrants. These went to St. Johns, and 100 Canadian volunteers with 40 artillerists and a few artificers increased the garrison to about 725 men all told. But Carleton felt he must have more.[24]

He tried the Canadians. Among the Old Subjects "damn'd rascals of Merchants, [he] met with little or no success." [25] They mostly favored the Americans. The seigneurs and the clergy used their influence among the French Canadians, but the sturdy habitants answered with armed opposition to enlistment, and with oaths on the Cross never to fight the Americans. The Indians had failed him. He had to do with what he had.[26]

On September 16 Montgomery organized his naval force, his schooner and sloop, ten bateaux, and two row-galleys (each with a 12-pounder), and 350 men, and sent them to lie in the river to prevent the *Royal Savage* from running upstream and cutting his communications with his base, Ticonderoga. He then embarked the rest of his troops and landed them at St. Johns.

He had already sent Major John Brown with 100 Americans and 30 or 40 Canadians to Chambly. Brown heard that a British supply train was on the way to the fort. He waylaid it in the night of the 17th about two miles north of its destination and captured the supplies. Expecting prompt aid from Montgomery, he entrenched. But before any help came, 100 British regulars and as many of the volunteers with two fieldpieces sallied out of the fort to attack him. Brown withdrew into the woods with his booty. There was a considerable exchange of fire until Colonel Bedel came up with 500 men and drove the enemy back to their stronghold. This new force was then posted in an entrenched camp about a mile north of St. Johns, while Brown went on with his foraging, which was quite successful. He gathered in twenty wagons laden with clothing, "rum, pork, wine &c." Montgomery sent other parties to take posts at Longueuil and La Prairie and hold those two approaches to Montreal. The rest were encamped about the fort. On the south side entrenchments were erected, and batteries of two guns and some small mortars were put in place. The siege of St. Johns was properly begun.[27]

Montgomery had promptly sent Ethan Allen on to Chambly to gather and take command of a body of Canadian volunteers. John Brown had gone to La Prairie on a similar errand. The very next day after he was dispatched, the energetic Allen wrote to his chief that he was at St. Ours, within twelve miles of Sorel, that he had 250 Canadians under arms, that, "as I march, they gather fast," and that he might be expected at St. Johns with 500 men in about three days. In a week's time, he could raise one or two thousand, he said. "I swear by the Lord I can raise three times the number of our army in Canada, provided you continue the siege; all depends on that. . . . God grant you wisdom, fortitude and every accomplishment of a victorious General . . . to fail of victory will be an eternal disgrace, but to obtain it will elevate us on the wings of fame." So wrote optimistic and eloquent Ethan to the general upon whom he was never to lay eyes again.[28]

At Longueuil, looking across the river at the twinkling lights of Montreal, Allen had a vision. He had told Trumbull in July that, if he had been given command of the Green Mountain Boys regiment, he would have advanced into Canada and invested Montreal. He was in Canada now, and there, just across the river, lay Montreal, practically defenseless. He could see victory before him and hear the rustle of the "wings of fame." Opportunity was knocking at his door.

But his Canadian recruits proved unstable; all but 80 of them drifted away. So he forgot his dream and turned back for St. Johns with his diminished force. He had gone but a little way on the road, when he met Brown, who had about 200 men. These two ambitious and daring souls agreed upon a scheme not merely to invest, but to take Montreal. Allen was to cross below the town, Brown above. Each would, as silently as possible, approach the town gate at his end. Brown's party was to give three huzzas as a signal of his arrival on the Montreal side and his readiness to attack.

Allen, having added 30 "English Americans" to his force, attempted a crossing in the night of October 24. There were so few canoes available that only one-third of his men could go at a time. They were all across before daylight, approached the town, and waited for Brown's signal. It never came. It was too late to retreat and make those three crossings again. At daybreak he would be discovered. Two-thirds of his men, left on the Montreal shore, while the first contingent crossed, would be too weak even to defend themselves. He took a good position two or three miles from the town, and waited for an attack.

News that "Ethan Allen, the Notorious New Hampshire Incendiary," was at hand threw the town "into the utmost Confusion." Carleton ordered the drums beaten. "The better sort of Citizens English & Canadian turned out under Arms." Thirty or forty soldiers, followed by about two hundred volunteers and a few Indians, issued from the Quebec Gate and advanced upon the intruders. Allen had posted his men behind trees and buildings and behind a small stream, and a smart little fight ensued. But two parties of

English and Canadians, constituting Allen's flanks, soon fled into the woods. Allen saw that he was to be surrounded. He retreated, keeping up a running fight, but was so hard pressed that he had to surrender himself and his forty remaining men.[29]

Allen's impetuosity was definitely harmful to the American cause. The complete failure of his attack heartened the loyal Canadians and disheartened those who might have joined Montgomery. The Indians now favored the winning side. "Thank God, that day's Action turned the minds of the Canadians," wrote one of them. Seth Warner wrote, "His defeat hath put the french people in to grate Constarnation." Schuyler, at Ticonderoga, reported to the President of Congress that he was "very apprehensive of disagreeable consequences arising from Mr. *Allen's* imprudence," and recalled for Hancock's benefit that he had "always dreaded" Allen's "impatience of subordination"—which was of course quite true. Carleton seized upon this turn of affairs and sent word through the province that 15 out of every 100 men must take up arms. Though the habitants in general refused to obey, Carleton did gather 900 new men to add to his force, but they began to desert "thirty or forty of a night"; he was approaching "as forlorn a State as before." [30]

The siege of St. Johns was continued, but under great difficulties. It was growing colder, and heavy rains set in. "Whenever we attempt to raise batteries, the water follows in the ditch when only two feet deep." [31] The camp was in low, swampy ground, and nothing could be kept dry. "Our men Sometimes have been Wet near Twenty Days together," said Jonathan Trumbull. "We have been like half-drowned rats crawling through a swamp," wrote Montgomery.[32] There was a vast amount of illness among the troops. Supplies of all kinds were short. Late in September the men were on a half-allowance of pork, and the flour was giving out. Powder, as always, was scanty.[33]

All this sowed seeds of dissatisfaction among the men, and they had favorable ground to grow upon. The Yorkers disliked the Yankees, and the Yankees distrusted the Yorkers. Besides, there was that ineradicable "leveling spirit" among the New Englanders, "such an equality among them, that the officers have no authority. . . . The privates are all generals," said Montgomery. He disliked, too, some of the men from his own province: "The first reg^{t} of Yorkers is the sweeping of the York streets." [34] The whole army was unruly, frequently near to mutiny. The men had to be coddled, their permission obtained before this or that could be done. At one time, when Montgomery wanted to erect a battery in a certain position, his field officers absolutely refused to do so. "I cannot help observing to how little purpose I am here," he wrote. "Were I not afraid the example would be too generally followed, and that the publick service might suffer, I would not stay an hour at the head of troops whose operations I cannot direct." He complained to Schuyler that it was impossible to command men "who carry the spirit of freedom into the field, and think for themselves." [35]

Schuyler, down at Ticonderoga, had found a similar condition, "a scandalous want of subordination and inattention to my orders," which had been chiefly responsible for the lack of supplies at St. Johns. He took hold, however, and in six days sent as much in the way of provisions as had before been shipped in three weeks. Conditions at the siege were immediately bettered. But he met with that same intercolonial jealousy, that disinclination of the troops from the various provinces to merge their identities so as to make a united army.[36]

It prevailed even among some of the higher officers. General David Wooster's distaste for submission to commands emanating from New York has been already mentioned. When the Continental mustermaster wanted to enroll Wooster's troops in the Continental army, he demurred "not thinking himself a Continental officer," and his men refused to sign.[37] They were sent up to Ticonderoga. Two hundred and fifty arrived in October, in advance, and Schuyler ordered them on to St. Johns. They answered that they did not "choose to move" until Wooster arrived. "Do not Choose to move! Strange language for an Army," the disgusted major general wrote to the Continental Congress. "But the irresistible force of necessity obliges me to put up with it." One of their lieutenant colonels demurred when he was directed to send a small detachment with powder and rum up to St. Johns, fearing he would be blamed by Wooster for obeying Schuyler's order. But Schuyler believed that ultimately they would "condescend to go." [38] When Wooster came, however, Schuyler found him tractable. He agreed not to dispute Montgomery's superior command at St. Johns.[39] So a regiment of the Connecticut men, 335 all told, sailed on October 22 for St. Johns, though "with the greatest reluctance," [40] and arrived on October 26. With them were 225 men of the 4th New York under Major Barnabas Tuthill.

Meanwhile, the siege had continued; and the fact that so many of the King's troops were bottled up had made some impression on the Canadians. St. Luc de La Corne found that the Indians were inclining to the Americans. He sent some Caughnawagas to Montgomery "with a string of wampum" and indefinite "proposals of an accommodation." Montgomery distrusted him but would not overlook any chance for aid. "He is a great villain and as cunning as the devil, but I have sent a *New Englander* to negotiate with him"—a left-handed compliment to the Yankee whom he sent, the ubiquitous Major John Brown. The conference came to nothing.[41]

At Chambly, down the river from St. Johns, there was a fort, an impressive, castlelike stone structure, with walls sixteen feet high and higher bastions at its corners. However, the walls were very thin and were pierced only for muskets. It was held by Major Stopford with a garrison of 88 officers and men. In the nighttime, two American bateaux carrying a few 9-pounders slipped past the guns of St. Johns and of the *Royal Savage* and landed at Chambly. James Livingston brought up 300 Canadians; Brown and Bedel brought down 50 Americans. They established batteries, and opened fire. The guns shot a couple of holes in the thin masonry and knocked down a chimney. Stopford surrendered the fort, with 10 officers, 78 privates of the Royal Fusiliers, 30 women, 51 children, 6 tons of gunpowder, 3 mortars, 150 muskets, 6,500 musket cartridges, 500 hand grenades, 300 swivel-shot, and 138 barrels of edible provisions.[42]

The investment of St. Johns was now tight above and below, but there was one thing left to bother the Americans, that armed schooner of Preston's anchored close to the fort. At last they concentrated their fire on her and on her mate, the floating battery. The *Royal Savage* and her companion both went down.[43]

Carleton had long considered a rescue. Allan Maclean had gathered a force of his countrymen. These, with 60 of the Royal Fusiliers from Montreal and a large number of Caughnawaga Indians, nearly 800 in all, assembled on an island in the St. Lawrence. On October 30, Carleton and La Corne leading part of them, they started across to Longueuil. But Seth Warner with his Green Mountain Boys and the 2nd New York was on the opposite bank. They opened fire with grapeshot from a little 4-pounder and with musketry. The boats were thrown into confusion, and the expedition turned back. Another party, led by Maclean, tried for a landing farther up the river. At the sight of a detachment of Americans posted there, they also retreated.[44]

There was by this time a strong battery on the west side of the Richelieu, with only the river and the moat, no walls, between it and the interior of St. Johns fort. Its bombardment was effective. The stone house was wrecked, the brick houses were shot through and through. There was no safe refuge anywhere in the enclosure, but still the garrison held on. It seemed evident that nothing less than an assault through a breach in its walls would take the fort.

To effect that, the position that Montgomery had before been prevented from taking by "the general dissatisfaction" of his troops, was occupied on the 25th. It was a hill on the northwest side of the fort. A battery of 12-pounders, some lighter guns, and several mortars was erected there. For about six hours all the artillery played on Preston's hold, but even this concentrated fire made no breach in the fort's earthen walls.

Then Montgomery tried other tactics. He sent one of the prisoners taken from Carleton's rescue force to tell Preston his case was hopeless, and Preston saw the point. On November 2, after holding out for fifty-five days, and with only three days' provision left in his magazines, he capitulated.[45]

The next day Montgomery drew up his troops before the fort. A motley array they were. The Yorkers were in uniform, as were Lamb's artillerymen, theirs being blue with buff facings. The Green Mountain Boys wore great-coats of green turned up with red. But the Connecticut men, though admired for "Strength, Stature, Youth & Agility," wore any sort of clothes they happened to have. There marched out of the fort first the Royal Fusiliers in red coats faced with pale yellow, then the handful of the Royal Artillery in dark blue coats, red facings and sashes, white waistcoats and breeches, gold-laced cocked hats, and jack boots. The marines from the *Gaspé* in their short petticoats followed, with the Royal Highland Emigrants in kilts and the assorted mob of Canadians, artificers and workmen bringing up the rear. They were paraded, and Captain Lamb's artillerymen with a detachment from every regiment of the Americans marched past them and into the fort. Then Preston's men laid down their arms. One of the officers taken that day was the unfortunate John André.[46]

Montgomery treated his captives well. The officers were allowed to retain their side arms and private effects. The men were given the reserve store of clothing.[47] When this became known, "the officers of the First Regiment of Yorkers and [of Lamb's] Artillery Company were very near a mutiny . . . there was no driving it into their noddles, that the clothing was really the property of the soldier, that he had paid for it," wrote Montgomery. "I wish some method could be fallen upon of engaging *gentlemen* to serve." [48] The Canadians were allowed to go home. The regulars were to proceed to some port where they could embark for Great Britain.

Now it was necessary to proceed promptly to Montreal and to possess it. The Connecticut men were unwilling to go farther. Montgomery had "to coax them" by promising their dismissal as soon as Montreal was occupied.[49]

The march was begun on November 5, and it was most difficult. The old corduroy road had disintegrated into a succession of rotten logs and half-frozen mudholes. It snowed and rained. In places the mire was knee-deep.

The men were badly clothed and ill shod, but they pulled through to La Prairie. On the 11th, the first of them crossed to an island in the river and, on the next day, in a gale of wind, landed above Montreal.

Carleton, with something like 150 regulars and a few militia, remained in the town until the 11th; but its walls were so thin that they "could only turn Musketry," and in part had fallen down. The place was not defensible against even light artillery. He therefore put on shipboard the most valuable military stores and destroyed the rest as soon as he heard that the Americans were at La Prairie. He sailed on the 11th under fire from the American shore batteries. Montgomery spoke fairly to a deputation of Montreal citizens, and they surrendered on the 13th. At Sorel another battery threatened Carleton's little fleet. The wind was adverse. The ships turned back a few miles. Then Major Brown boarded one, under a flag, and told its commander that he had two 32-pounders in his "grand battery" at Sorel—a gross exaggeration. The *Gaspé*, two other armed vessels, and eight smaller craft were surrendered, with not only their cargoes and their crews, but also the soldiers formerly garrisoning Montreal.[50]

Carleton himself remained in the *Gaspé* until shortly before its capture. Then, "dressed like a man of the people" and accompanied by one or two of his officers, he was rowed with muffled oars down the river and by an obscure channel through the islands opposite Sorel, escaping finally to Quebec.[51]

CHAPTER 13

Arnold's March to Quebec

If one's antagonist can be forced to fight on two fronts at once, he is always at a disadvantage. While Schuyler's forces were still lingering at Ticonderoga, preparing for the advance toward Montreal, Washington in Cambridge had been pondering this strategic axiom. There was another front which might be developed: Quebec, 150 miles down the St. Lawrence from Montreal. If those two towns were attacked at the same time Carleton would be at a serious disadvantage and would be easy to overcome at one or the other, probably at both. Quebec, then, should be the object of an expedition simultaneous with that against Montreal.

The road seemed to be open—a waterway. The best, often the only possible route through a wilderness was a waterway, which permitted men to travel in boats with their provisions and supplies, escaping the hardship of a struggle through dense forests. This route had been considered in reverse by the French more than once as affording a means of attacking Boston. It had been repeatedly mapped and described, with varying degrees of correctness. It had been discussed during the French and Indian War "as a Rout by which an Army might pass, the best and shortest way, to attack Canada and Quebec." [1] In the spring of 1775 Colonel Jonathan Brewer of Massachusetts had offered to lead 500 volunteers against Quebec by this route, a project which he believed "he Could Execute With all the feility [felicity] Imaginable." [2] It is possible that Washington was made aware of this proposal.

The way led up the Kennebec River to the Great Carrying Place, where the Indians bound to Canada from New England used to leave the Kennebec and take their canoes across a twelve-mile stretch of land to the Dead River. The stretch was broken into four portages by three ponds, across which boats could float, so that they had to be carried only about eight miles. After paddling about thirty miles up the Dead River, the Indians would proceed across the Height of Land about four miles to a stream emptying into Lake Megantic, from which the Chaudière River flows into the St. Lawrence within four miles of Quebec. Various portages were to be expected wherever falls or rapids on the rivers interfered with passage by water. The map of Captain John Montresor, a British army engineer, and his description made this rout seem to be quite feasible. Montresor had not told the whole tale of its difficulties and dangers; Washington, however, accepted at more than its face value the scanty information concerning it which had been conveyed to him.

On August 20, 1775, he wrote to Schuyler: "The Design of this Express is to communicate to you a Plan of an Expedition which has engaged my Thoughts for several Days. It is to penetrate into Canada by Way of Kennebeck River, and so to Quebeck. . . . I can very well spare a Detachment for this Purpose of one Thousand or twelve Hundred men, and the Land Carriage of the Rout proposed is too inconsiderable to make an objection." [3] That last sentence clearly shows how little he knew of the proposed "Rout." His thoughts about such an expedition soon crystallized into a decision to send it, and he looked about for someone to lead it. His choice of a commander could hardly have been bettered.

After resigning on June 24 his command at Ticonderoga, Arnold went to Cambridge to settle his accounts with the Provincial Congress and secure from it the sums of money due him. He was at loose ends while this business dragged to a long deferred conclusion, because he had no office in the Continental army nor any connection with it. When Washington offered him command, as colonel, of an expedition against Quebec, he offered it to a man who still cherished the desire to invade Canada—a desire which had been frustrated at Ticonderoga. Arnold accepted with avidity.

It appears, indeed, that matters were far advanced before Washington wrote that letter to Schuyler, for on August 21 Arnold was writing to Reuben Colburn, a Kennebec boatbuilder who happened to be in Cambridge, making certain inquiries on behalf of the commander in chief. How soon could 200 light "Battoos" be procured or built at Kennebec, capable of carrying six or seven men each with their provisions, "say 100 wt. to each man," each boat to be furnished with four oars, two paddles, and two setting-poles? What would they cost? Could a quantity of fresh beef be procured at Kennebec? He also wanted information as to "the Difficulty attending an Expedition that way, in particular the Number, & length, of the Carrying Places, wheather Low, Dry land, Hills or Swamp, Also the Depth of Water in the River at this Season, wheather an easy Stream or Rapid." [4] This inquiry discloses Washington's ignorance, and Arnold's, of the nature and condition of the river they proposed to use as a road to Canada.

Colburn's reply was satisfactory as to the boats and their cost—40 shillings each with their equipment—for on September 3 Washington gave him an order for them. He also directed him to engage a company of twenty men, "Artificers, Carpenters and Guides," to go along under Colburn's command, "to bespeak all The Pork and Flour you can from the Inhabitants upon the River Kennebeck," and to notify the public there that the commissary would be in the market for sixty barrels of salted beef.[5] To get the desired information as to the route, Colburn sent Dennis Getchell and Samuel Berry to examine it and report to him.

On September 5 notice of the expedition appeared in General Orders. The detachment was to consist of two battalions of five companies each, comprising in all, with the usual battalion and company officers and musicians, 742 men; also Captain Daniel Morgan's company of Virginia riflemen and two companies of Colonel William Thompson's rifle regiment from Pennsylvania, under Captains Matthew Smith and William Hendricks, about 250 in all. To these should be added the surgeon, his mate and two assistants, two adjutants, two quartermasters, the chaplain, and six unattached volunteers, a total of 1,051. Service in the expedition was to be voluntary, and it was desired that none but "active Woodsmen" "well acquainted with batteaus" should present themselves. They were all to parade on Cambridge Common in the morning of September 6. The desire for woodsmen acquainted with bateaux was, unfortunately, not met in fact; nor does it appear that any effort was made to comply with that suggestion in the order. The men other than the riflemen were drawn chiefly from Massachusetts, Connecticut, Rhode Island, and New Hampshire Regiments, and were mostly farmers, few of them having had any experience in the wild woods or in the management of bateaux.[6]

The unattached volunteers were an interesting lot. Matthias Ogden of New Jersey, Eleazer Oswald of Connecticut, Charles Porterfield and John McGuire of Virginia, and Matthew Duncan of Pennsylvania were five, all of whom afterward became officers in the Continental army. But the sixth deserves more particular notice, because of his subsequent career.

Aaron Burr was a youth of distinguished lineage, the grandson of the great Jonathan Edwards, the son of the Reverend Aaron Burr, second president of the College of New Jersey at Princeton. Young Aaron had been ready to enter the college at the age of eleven, "a strikingly pretty boy, very fair, with beautiful black eyes and such graceful engaging ways as to render him a favorite." For want of age his admission was postponed for two years, and then he entered as a sophomore. After his graduation in 1772 at the age of sixteen he continued his residence in the college and for a while read theology. Skepticism soon undermined his hereditary beliefs, and he turned to the law. Lexington and Concord inflamed his naturally aggressive spirit. After Bunker's Hill, he called a college mate, Matthias Ogden, to the colors, and together they joined the army as independent volunteers immediately after Washington took command. Idleness fretted Burr's restless soul, actually worried him into an intermittent fever. When he heard of the proposed expedition to Quebec he got up from a bed of sickness and, despite the remonstrances of his friends, insisted on being allowed to go along.

He was nineteen years old, no more than five feet six inches tall, of slight figure and boyish countenance, but with a surprising capacity for enduring fatigue and privation. It was his indomitable will rather than his physical strength that sustained him. His intelligence was abnormally keen, his spirit unbreakable, his ambition unbounded. His subsequent career in the army was brilliant. He was in command of a regiment at the age of twenty-one, and in command of a brigade in the Battle of Monmouth at twenty-two.

He had the defects of his qualities. His overleaping ambition, his keen perception of the readiest means of bringing to pass what he desired, and his habit of ignoring conscientious scruples, resulted in the errors of conduct in civil affairs that ruined his life and blotted out the fame he won as a soldier.[7]

In the list of officers one name stands out above all the rest—Daniel Morgan of Morgan's Rifles. Although born in New Jersey to a Welsh immigrant family, Morgan was a true son of the backwoods. He ran away from home at the age of seventeen and went on foot through Pennsylvania into the wilder parts of Virginia, now West Virginia. There his character was formed and he acquired his fame as a backwoodsman.

He was first employed to run a sawmill and then became a teamster. Within two years he had set up in business with his own wagon and horse, hauling supplies to the remoter settlements. In this capacity he was employed in Braddock's expedition against Fort Duquesne. He served with distinction first as a private and then as an officer of the Virginia militia throughout the French and Indian War, in the war against Pontiac, and in "Lord Dunmore's War" with the Indians. That he was commissioned to raise a company of Virginia riflemen to join Washington's army at Cambridge has already been told.

He was a tall man, well over six feet, broad-shouldered, deep-chested, and stout of limb, weighing over two hundred pounds, all bone and muscle, yet active, even graceful, in movement. His physical and mental hardihood in endurance of fatigue under the most severe conditions matched his powerful frame. Although his usual manner of speaking was abrupt and severe and he was prone to swift angers and stern judgments, his open countenance indicated the good-humored, kindly character that lay beneath the surface and was displayed to his friends and to his men when they merited his approval. His schooling had been of the scantiest; he read with difficulty, wrote almost illegibly, and was puzzled by the simplest problems in arithmetic. But his natural genius and acquired knowledge of men and affairs, his keen intelligence, and his sound reasoning served him well in all his enterprises. His courage, daring, and resourcefulness in military affairs, added to his other characteristics, made him a great leader of men in the war upon which he was now entering.[8]

Washington's orders to Arnold were full and comprehensive, impressing upon him the necessity of discovering "the real Sentiments of the Canadians towards our Cause." If they were "averse to it and will not co-operate or at least willingly acquiesce . . . you are by no Means to prosecute the Attempt." Arnold was to restrain his men from the "Imprudence and Folly" of showing "Contempt of the Religion" of the Canadians "by ridiculing any of its Ceremonies or affronting its Ministers or Votaries . . . and to punish every Instance of it." There was to be no plundering of either friend or foe; all provisions and supplies were to be purchased and paid for. Although the expedition was to be pushed with vigor, yet, "if unforeseen Difficulties should arise or if the Weather shou'd become so severe as to render it hazardous to proceed in your own Judgment and that of your principal Officers (whom you are to consult) In that case you are to return." To the last injunction, it would seem Arnold paid little attention.[9]

In the expeditionary force the riflemen made up one corps. The musketmen were in two battalions, the first under Lieutenant Colonel Roger Enos and Major Return Jonathan Meigs, both from Connecticut, with five companies commanded by Captains Thomas Williams of Massachusetts, Henry Dearborn of New Hampshire, Oliver Hanchet of Connecticut, William Goodrich of Massachusetts, and Scott, whose first name and province of origin are unknown. The second battalion was led by Lieutenant Colonel Christopher Greene of Rhode Island and Major Timothy Bigelow of Massachusetts, with five companies under Captains Samuel Ward, Jr., of Rhode Island, Simeon Thayer, John Topham, Jonas Hubbard, and Samuel McCobb, all of Massachusetts. Isaac Senter of Rhode Island was the surgeon, Samuel Spring the chaplain. Christian Febiger was brigade major.

On September 11 the riflemen set out for Newburyport; but the musketmen, when paraded on Cambridge Common, "refused to march till we had a month's pay," says the journal of Ephraim Squier, a private. Whether it was back pay or pay in advance does not appear; but the matter seems to have been promptly adjusted, for by the 13th all had marched.[10]

By the 16th the expeditionary force had arrived in Newbury or the adjacent Newburyport, where a fleet of eleven sloops and schooners had been assembled. Three scouting vessels had been sent out to see if there were any British ships in the way. No news of such dangers having been received by the 19th, the fleet sailed, "drums beating, fifes playing and colours flying," [11] Arnold's topsail schooner in the lead. With no untoward incident on the way, except the extreme seasickness of most of these landsmen—"such a sickness, making me feel so lifeless, so indifferent whether I lived or died!" wrote Simon Fobes in his diary—the fleet made the voyage of a hundred miles to the mouth of the Kennebec in eleven hours. Sailing up the river, it reached Gardinerstown by the 22nd. There Arnold went ashore, a spruce figure in a scarlet coat, with collar, lapels, and cuffs of buff, silver-plated buttons, ruffled shirt, white linen waistcoat, breeches and stockings and black half-garters, the whole topped by a plumed cocked hat.

He inspected the bateaux provided for the expedition and found that there were 200 of them as ordered, but many were "smaller than the directions given and very badly built." [12] It was hardly Colburn's fault that they were not first-class. He had had only eighteen days to go home from Cambridge, assemble the workmen, and put through such a building program as he had never before been called upon to undertake, even with a sufficient time allowance. There was not nearly enough seasoned timber available, and so he had, perforce, used green stuff. It was unfortunate but unavoidable. Arnold could not reject them; he had to content himself with ordering twenty more.

These bateaux were of a type in common use on the Kennebec, with narrow, flat bottoms, widely flaring sides and long, pointed stems and sterns, capable of carrying heavy loads and not easily capsized. They were to be propelled by oars or paddles in still or flowing water and to be poled up rapids. They answered well on the lower Kennebec, but no one had ever tried to take them all the way up, past waterfalls, through the most difficult portages, across high, rough country, all the way to the St. Lawrence. Canoes, yes, but such heavy boats, especially when so ill built, emphatically no.

Besides the bateaux Colburn had to furnish information as to the route. The two men, Getchell and Berry, whom he had sent out had returned. Their report was not reassuring. They had gone as far as the Dead River, had met an Indian, Natanis by name, who told them he was employed by Carleton "to Watch the Motions of an Army or Spies that was daily expected from New England," and that a British officer with six men was posted on the Chaudière to look out for the Americans. Natanis declared that if the two scouts were any farther he would inform Carleton. By another Indian they had been told that a great number of Mohawks in Johnson's pay were at Sartigan, the uppermost settlement on the Chaudière. Otherwise, they said, the way was fair and was marked by blazed trees, the portages "pretty passible," the water shoal. Arnold read this report, but paid little attention to the threats of Natanis: "a noted villain," he called him in a letter to Washington, "and very little credit, I am told, is to be given his information." [13]

More helpful were a map of the route and a description of "the quick water and carrying places to and from Quebeck," furnished him by Samuel Goodwin.

By the 24th Arnold's force had reached Fort Western—now Augusta—thirty miles up the river, some in the sailing vessels, the rest in the bateaux. This "fort" was a couple of blockhouses and a magazine surrounded by a palisade, useful in the French and Indian War but no longer held as a military post. It was the real starting point for the expedition. Here Arnold detached and sent off two advance parties.

Lieutenant Archibald Steele of Smith's company of riflemen, "a man of an active, courageous, sprightly and hardy disposition," with seven men selected from the rifle companies, was ordered to reconnoiter the way to Lake Megantic, the source of the Chaudière. Steele had orders to capture or kill that "noted villain" Natanis.[14] Lieutenant Church, with a similar party and a surveyor, was to note "the exact courses and distances to the Dead River." These parties set out in canoes with guides.

The main force was then split into four divisions. The first was composed of the riflemen under command of Morgan,[15] who were to go forward as quickly as they could to clear the road, especially over the Great Carrying Place between the Kennebec and the Dead River. They departed four or five men in each bateau, the rest marching beside the river and taking turns in the boats.

The second division of three companies of musketmen left the next day, led by Lieutenant Colonel Greene and Major Bigelow. Major Meigs led the third division of four companies on the following day, and Lieutenant Colonel Enos with the fourth, three companies and Colburn's artificers, got away two days later. Arnold then started in a canoe to get to the head of the column. The bateaux of each division carried provisions estimated to be sufficient for forty-five days, although Arnold expected "to perform the march," which he figured at 180 miles, in twenty days.[16]

As the river for half a mile beyond Fort Western came against them in impassable rapids, the boats and supplies were presumably hauled by the neighboring inhabitants in wagons or on sleds to a point whence they could go by water. But even then the water was so swift that it was hard to propel the boats by oar and pole. It took them two days to make the eighteen miles to Fort Halifax, another abandoned military post. Above that, they came to Ticonic Falls, which no boat could ascend; here was their first real portage. The bulk of the cargoes was unloaded and carried to the next point of embarkation, each barrel of flour, pork, and so on being slung on two ropes, through which two poles were thrust, so that four men could take the ends on their shoulders. The bateaux were similarly carried by four men on two poles. The boats weighed 400 pounds each, and there were about 65 tons of provisions, ammunition, and general supplies, say in all 100 tons weight of the most unhandy material, to be carried in this instance a half-mile. It was a case of going back and forth until all was got over.

Not far above they came to Five Mile Falls, a series of tumultuous rapids, "very dangerous and difficult to pass." [17] They had "a scene of trouble to go through." The boatmen had often to leap overboard and struggle with their clumsy craft to keep them straight or drag them over shoals. They would be in the icy cold water to their waists, to their chins, even over their heads when they plunged into an unexpected "deep bason." "After much fatigue and a Bondance of difficulty," [18] they got through, but not without damage.

The rocky river bottom, sunken logs, tree roots had scraped and torn the bottoms of the boats and opened their seams. They "began to leak profusely." Indeed, at least one of them, Dr. Senter's, was "in such a shattered condition" that he had to buy another from a near-by settler [19] the day before they came to Skowhegan Falls.

Even the approach to Skowhegan was difficult. The river made a sharp turn between two ledges no more than twenty-five feet apart, forming a

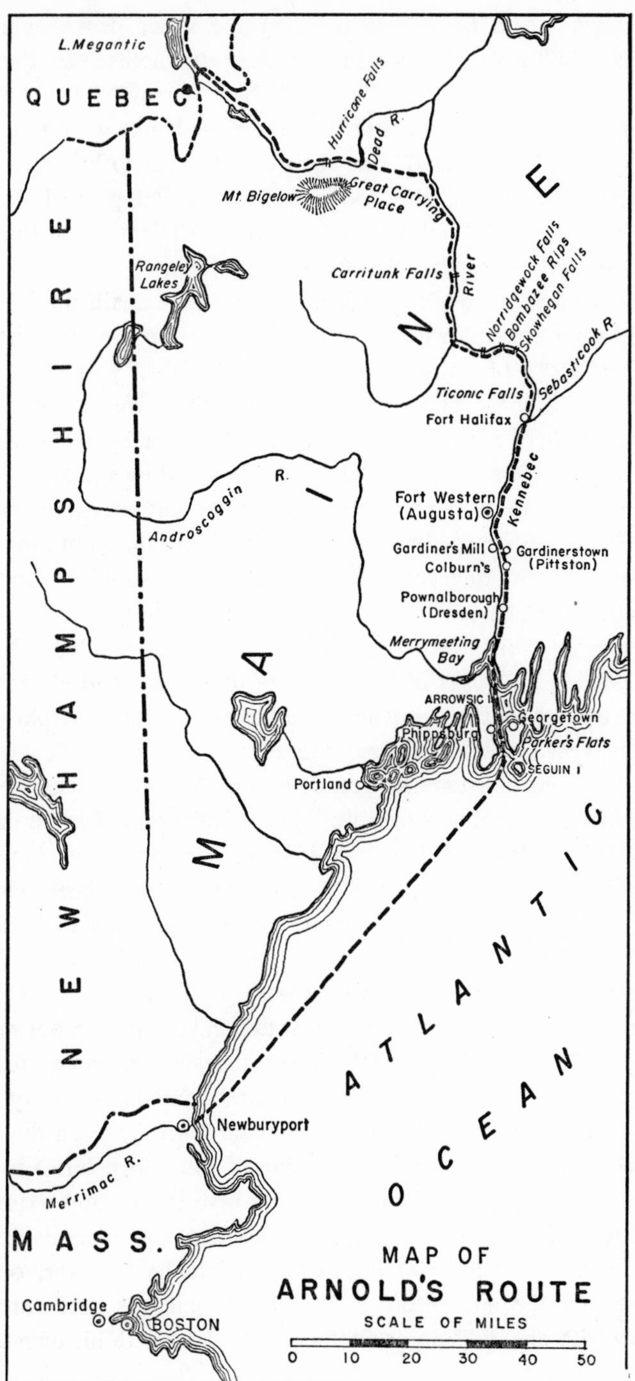

MAP OF
ARNOLD'S ROUTE

chute through which the whole force of the water drove against them. There was a half-mile of this and then the falls themselves, divided by a towering mass of rock split in the middle by a narrow cleft. There was no going ashore for a carry on either side; the river banks were not banks but vertical rock walls. The boats and their cargoes had to be carried through that cleft, narrow, steep, and rough underfoot, and pushed through five miles of "small falls and quick water" above it.[20] The men lay that night, as often they did, in wet clothes that froze upon them.

So they went on, through Bombazee Rips, where again the banks closed in and the water came down in a torrent, until they came "face to face with the roar and foam of the great Norridgewock Falls." [21] These were three falls, a half-mile apart, and the carry around them was a mile and a half long. Some settlers appeared with two sleds drawn by oxen, and helped with the supplies, but the bateaux had to be carried by the men.

Those boats were in bad shape now, "nothing but wrecks, some stove to pieces." [22] Colburn's carpenters set to work to repair their bottoms and caulk their seams. But nothing could be done regarding supplies spoiled in the leaky boats. Quantities of dry salted codfish had been loaded loose in them. The water had washed away the salt, and the fish had spoiled. The salt beef had also gone bad. Casks of bread and of dried peas had absorbed water, swelled, and burst. All this provender had to be thrown away. Arnold's men had nothing now but salt pork and flour.

Three days were consumed in getting around Norridgewock and in repairing the boats. On October 9 they were again under way. Eleven of Arnold's estimated twenty days for the whole journey were past, and they had gone but one-third of the distance. Up to this time they had been within reach of civilization of a sort, occasional settlements and isolated farms from which they had sometimes been able to buy beef cattle. Now all that was left behind. The rest was sheer wilderness.

They made fourteen miles in the next two days with one portage around Curritunk Falls. The river was shallower and swifter, harder to work the boats through. The weather grew colder, and continuous, heavy rains fell. On the 11th they came to the Great Carrying Place between the Kennebec and the Dead River. That is, Arnold himself came to it on October 11. It must be understood that the itinerary given here is only approximately correct. The four divisions of the troops had not kept the intervals first allotted to them. This one would get ahead faster than its follower, or that one would overtake the one before it. Arnold himself was backward and forward, now with one division or another, now alone with his own canoemen.

When he reached the Great Carrying Place, Morgan's men and the second division under Greene were already there.

The first portage of the Great Carrying Place was a mere Indian trail, Morgan's men had had little time to do anything with it; the rest of the army was close upon them. It had rained so hard on the 8th that no work could be done. The ground was soaked; there was no dry place to sleep. The army had to sit up all night close to their fires.

The bateau men had to carry their unwieldy burdens, and the rest their cargoes "through a most terrible piece of woods conceivable," [23] through bogs where they sank "half-leg deep," and over rocky ledges, three and a quarter miles to the first pond. Though the pork had been removed from the barrels and strung on poles for easier carriage, seven or eight trips were necessary to get everything across. The weather was exceedingly bad, with heavy winds and snow squalls. "A prodigious number of trout" caught in the pond made a welcome addition to their narrow diet. A moose someone killed also helped out. They were three days on this carry and in crossing the pond, a distance of five miles.

The first pond having been crossed in the crazy boats, the second carry was found to be little more than half a mile, and the footing was fair. But the second pond was disappointing. "The water was quite yellow," and it was all they had to drink. They were greatly worn down by fatigue and hardship. Many of them—"a very formidable number" [24]—were ill, some of them desperately ill. This bad water sickened them so much more that a log blockhouse was built for a hospital. It was "no sooner finished than filled."

The way to the third pond was longer, about a mile and a half. It was "extremely bad, being choaked with roots which we could not clear away." [25] But there were more trout in that pond.

The fourth portage was three miles long, and it was difficult. A mile up and a mile down brought them to what looked like "a beautiful plat of firm ground, covered by an elegant green moss," interspersed with groves of spruce and cedar. In fact, it was a treacherous bog. At nearly every step they sank halfway to their knees and found at the bottom sharp snags and roots that tore their shoes and bruised their feet. There was a mile and a half of this. So, stumbling along, falling now and again, dropping their burdens and recovering them again, they at last emerged, "plastered with mud from neck to heel," [26] at Bog Brook, which led into the Dead River.

While the main body was crossing the Great Carrying Place, it was met by Lieutenant Church's party of pioneers returning to report to Arnold.

Lieutenant Steele also, with two of his men but not the other five, came back to report. Steele's party had reached the Chaudière River without unusual difficulty, but their return march was another matter.

It had started in "a most severe storm of rain," which lasted a day and a night. Their provisions had run out. On the first day of the return trip on the Dead River, John Henry, one of the party, had only "a solitary biscuit and an inch of pork." He ate half his store that day. They shot a duck and divided it. His portion was one leg, another man got the head and feet. The next day Henry ate the other half of his biscuit and pork, and they made fifty miles. The day after that one of the two canoes struck a submerged snag and was ripped through its whole length, its ribs torn from its gunwales. They sewed them in place with cedar roots and patched the skin with birch bark and pitch made out of turpentine and the grease in their pork bag. They had gone five hundred yards when another snag broke the canoe in two pieces held together only by the gunwales. They mended it as before. They shot a moose, smoked its flesh, and ate it raw. They were so weak that they could not carry their canoes across the Great Carrying Place, so they abandoned them and set out on foot. Steele and two others pushed ahead to get help.

The five remaining lived wretchedly on the moose meat for four days. Half cured and without salt or bread, it sickened them. They "staggered along . . . falling every now and then, if our toes but touched a twig or tuft of grass." [27] On October 17 Morgan's pioneers sighted five scarecrows, gaunt, haggard, ghastly creatures, so weak they could scarcely stumble along. The rest of Steele's party had returned.

After Steele had reported the results of his exploration Arnold sent him and Church forward again, with twenty axmen and a surveyor, "to clear the portages and take a survey of the country." [28] He also wrote a letter to a friend in Quebec, John Mercier, telling of his approach with 2,000 men "to frustrate the arbitrary and unjust measures of the ministry and restore liberty to our brethren of Canada," [29] and dispatched it by two Indians, Eneas and Sabatis, and one John Hall, who could speak French. That letter in some way got into Carleton's hands and resulted in the arrest and imprisonment of Mercier.

Now began the trip up the Dead River, a deceptive stream that belied its name. Its black waters were deep, and so smooth that they seemed to be standing still. "A most gentle and leisurely stream" [30] it was, to all appearances. But, though it flowed like oil, its current was swift beyond all expectations. The few oars and paddles were not enough to make headway against it. The boatmen had to grasp the bushes on its precipitous banks and pull themselves along. And it meandered in such great bends and windings that, after two hours' hard work, they "seemed to have gained nothing in our course." [31] But they made thirteen miles before they camped that night. They also made a most discouraging discovery. Their food was on the point of giving out.

Although Arnold had written only a day or two before to Enos, commander of the fourth division, that the first three had provender enough for more than three weeks, Greene's division, which had got ahead, now found itself out of bread and almost out of flour. While it had been passing Morgan's riflemen they had helped themselves to Greene's supply of food without his knowledge.[32] Arnold sent Major Bigelow with three lieutenants and 100 men in twelve bateaux back to get flour from Enos, in whose division there was supposed to be a surplus. Morgan's and Meigs's divisions, somewhat better supplied, pushed ahead; but Greene had to lie in his camp for five days, awaiting Bigelow's return.

Bigelow came back with two barrels of flour, all Enos would let him have. It was a desperate situation for Greene's men. There was nothing to do but send back the least able men; the rest had to tighten belts and push on after the other divisions.

Rain began to fall gently on the 19th. It increased in volume on the next day, and by the 21st it developed into a raging tempest, driven by winds of hurricane force. Trees crashed into the river, "tumbling on all quarters" [33] and blocking the way. Floods of water drenched the men and their few supplies. Tents were few. In camp most of the men had no protection except such as could be had from hemlock boughs. The river rose and flooded the country. It overflowed its eight- or ten-foot-high banks and poured into the camp of Morgan's men during the night of the 21st. Where a campfire had burned at evening, the morning saw a lake four feet deep. Barrels of pork were swept away, and bateaux filled and sank.

About midnight the rain had ceased and stars had come out; but the wind still blew, and it grew very cold. Wet through, chilled to the bone, and hungry, the men looked out upon a strange scene that morning. The whole country was under water. The river, which had been but sixty yards wide, was now two hundred, and it was a torrent of "terrifying rapidity" and overwhelming force. "None but the most strong and active boatmen" tried to breast it. The rest started on foot, "making large circuits" to avoid the drowned land. "This was one of the most fatiguing marches we had as yet performed . . . having no path and being necessitated to climb the steepest hills and that without food." [34] But they had to go on or starve to death.

Those who took to the boats had an almost impossible task. The swift current tossed the clumsy bateaux here and there, upset them, and threw the boatmen and the precious provisions into the ungovernable flood. At last it seemed that the expedition must break down completely. A council of war was held. Arnold's unwavering determination so inspired officers and men that the council voted to go on. The men responded with more than courage. When any of them, exhausted by fatigue and hunger, were told by their comrades that they "would not be able to advance much further, they would raise up their half-bent bodies and force an animated look into their ghastly countenances, observing at the same time that they would soon be well enough." [35] But twenty-six hopeless cases were sent back to the hospital; forty-eight more soon followed them. Captain Hanchet of Meigs's division, with fifty men, undertook to hasten forward to get food in the Chaudière valley. Arnold went ahead of him with a small party. The supply in Greene's division was so low that the men were reduced to boiling some tallow candles in a gruel made of water and a little flour.

The rear division had now, October 25, come up with the second, Meigs having gone on. Arnold had ordered Greene and Enos to send back "as many of the Poorest men of their Detachment as would leave 15 days provision for the remainder." [36] Greene, Enos, and the officers of their respective companies met for a conference. Although not covered by Arnold's orders, the question was put whether the two whole divisions should go on or go back. Greene, his major, Bigelow, his three captains, and Enos voted to go on. Enos's captains, Williams, McCobb, and Scott, his adjutant, Hide, and Lieutenant Peters voted to abandon the expedition. It was six to five in favor of going on. Enos, "though [he] voted for proceeding, yet had undoubtedly pre-engaged" with his officers "to the contrary, as every action demonstrated." [37] He decided to abandon the enterprise. Greene's party then asked for a division of the food. Their "expostulations and entreaties" were in vain. Being "the weakest party," they could not compel the others "to a just division." Enos said that "his men were out of his power" and he could not enforce an order to divide. At last two and a half barrels of flour were given up, and Greene's men went back to the foremost divisions, "with a determined resolution to go through or die." Enos led his party down to Fort Western in eleven days of comparatively easy travel.

So the remains of the little army, now fewer than seven hundred men, struggled on. The boatmen in the few surviving bateaux fought the swift current through rapid after rapid. Those on shore found the country rougher than ever, full of hills and hollows, rocky ledges and bogs, ravines and dense forests. At last the expedition came to a point where it could leave the river and enter on a chain of ponds that extended to the edge of the Height of Land.

Their provisions were now virtually at an end. In all, there were only four or five pounds of flour for each man. "The riflemen were wholly destitute of meat before this for eight days." They took rawhide intended for mending their moccasins, chopped it into bits, and tried to make soup of it; but it remained only rawhide. Some of the officers, on the night of the 27th, had nothing but "the jawbone of a swine destitute of any covering." [38] They boiled it, with a little thickening of flour, and that constituted their "sumptuous eating." On such fare, after so long a period of starvation, they had to try the longest portage yet encountered, four miles and a quarter over the Height of Land, the watershed between the streams flowing north to the St. Lawrence and those flowing south to the Kennebec.

It was not, however, a portage for most of them; they had nothing to carry. The bateaux had been wrecked and lost until few were left. Morgan kept seven, the other companies only one each. The rest were abandoned. There was a trail of sorts, but it was interrupted by blowdowns, tangled heaps of fallen trees acres in extent which no man could penetrate. Several inches of snow had fallen, covering whatever trail should have been visible. There were mountains, ravines, bogs, and trackless woods to be got over or through. A broken leg, even a sprained ankle, meant death, for no man was strong enough to carry another. Perishing for want of food, worn down almost to the breaking point, they stumbled on and at last got over the divide and down into a beautiful meadow by the side of a brook known as Seven Mile Stream, that being its length from the meadow to Lake Megantic. But Seven Mile Stream was more than a hundred miles from Quebec, and it afforded no relief from marching, except to the few in the remaining bateaux. They had divided the rest of the provisions, five pints of flour and two ounces or less of pork to each man.

On they went, following the stream. The land fell away into a swamp, and the stream divided and divided again into false mouths, as the Mississippi divides and redivides in its water-logged delta. The marching men, struggling through the swamp in different companies, strayed from the stream at its first false mouth. They strayed again at its second. They were now deep in the swamps, far off the right track, hopelessly lost, but still floundering onward, desperately trying to reach Lake Megantic. "We went astray over mountains and through swamps, which could scarcely be passed by wild beasts," says one account, "waded a small river up to our waists, then marched on until night in our wet clothes. At night found ourselves within five miles of the place we started from. We marched fifteen miles in vain."

That night each man made himself a thin gruel of a gill of flour in water, or baked a little cake in the ashes, and nibbled a tiny scrap of pork. The country was the same as before, bogs and thickets and forests. At last the rest came on the tracks of the one company that had found Seven Mile Stream, and not long after they saw Lake Megantic, at which sight they gave "three huzzas." [39]

The Chaudière, a swift running stream, drops 1,100 feet in 75 miles and is broken by dangerous rapids and falls. Arnold and Morgan tried it in their bateaux. In one rapid six of them crashed against rocks. The baggage, arms, and food in them were lost, and one man was drowned. There was a piece of good fortune in this disaster, however, for just below that rapid there was a waterfall unknown to them. "Had we been carried over [it, we] must inevitably have been dashed to pieces & all lost." [40] The two boats of Smith's and Goodrich's companies were wrecked and everything in them was lost.

"November the first dawned upon a famishing army," [41] lying in camps stretching over a distance of twenty-one miles. A few had a little food; many, having eaten their shares without care for the morrow, "set out weak and faint having nothing at all to eat; the ground covered with snow." They ate soap and hair grease. They boiled and roasted moccasins, shot pouches and old leather breeches, and chewed on them. "No one," says Morison, "can imagine, who has not experienced it, the sweetness of a roasted shot-pouch to the famished appetite." Goodrich's men "had been out of provisions for two days," without "a mouthful." They killed the captain's Newfoundland dog and ate all but the bones, which they kept for soup.

The next day many were so weak they could hardly get up from their beds. Some of them could not, and lay there waiting for death. The strongest "stumbled on . . . mile after mile," staggering "like drunken men," their heads hanging, eyes half closed, their brains in a stupor, dully wondering whether they could go one step farther. Men were dropping out of the straggling ranks and falling down, unable to get on their feet again.

"Never perhaps was there a more forlorn set of human beings collected together in one place," wrote Morison, "every one of us shivering from head to foot, as hungry as wolves and nothing to eat save the little flour we had left. . . . It was a dispiriting, heart-rending sight to see these men whose weakness was reduced to the lowest degree, struggling among rocks and in swamps and falling over the logs . . . falling down upon one another in the act of mutually assisting each other. . . . We had all along aided our weaker brethren. . . . These friendly offices could no longer be performed. Many of the men began to fall behind. . . . It was impossible to bring them along. . . . It was therefore given out . . . by our officers for every man to shift for himself and save his own life if possible." The "haggard looks" of those left behind, "their ghastly countenances, their emaciated bodies and their struggles to proceed with us . . . we saw with the bitterest anguish."

And then, at the very verge of their endurance, at the very last moment, the foremost party saw what they could not believe they really saw, horned cattle, driven by men on horses, coming to meet them. The glad cry "Provisions ahead!" was passed back from one group to another and so to those that had been left behind in the camps. "Echoes of gladness resounded from front to rear." [42] Two canoeloads of mutton and flour followed the beasts.

There was little ceremony about the slaughter of the first animal, or its division. The men grabbed the first bits they could lay their hands on, the entrails, and tore at them "as a hungry dog would tear a haunch of meat." [43] The rescue party took joints of the beef and rode on to those in the rear, the last stragglers being many miles behind. At the place of slaughter, two hundred of them, "an assembly of spectres rather than of men," [44] built fires, "laid our meat on the embers and for the first time for more than three weeks past were regaled with the incense of a sumptuous banquet." [45] "We sat down, eat up our rations, blessed our stars, and thought it luxury," says Dr. Senter.

On a pound of meat a day and a little oatmeal they pushed on with renewed spirits, although in sad physical condition. On moccasins worn through and broken shoes—Ogden had tied up his bursted shoes in a flour bag—they had yet sixty or seventy miles to march to the St. Lawrence.

But the wilderness was behind them. They were approaching civilization, or at least, Indian settlements, Sartigan the first. Arnold was there and had laid in a stock of provisions. "The men were furious, voracious and insatiable." In spite of the advice of the officers "to insure moderation, the men were outrageous upon the subject. . . . Boiled beef . . . potatoes, boiled and roasted, were gormandized without stint." Many of them fell ill; three of them died "by their imprudence." [46]

At this place they met that "noted villain," Natanis, whom Arnold had directed Steele to capture or kill, and found him to be a rather agreeable person. It appeared that he had hovered about the army all the way from the

Great Carrying Place, afraid to join it for fear he would be killed. Now, after Arnold had made a pacific address to a large group of Indians, Natanis and about fifty others joined the expedition and started with it down the Chaudière in their canoes.

The straggling force was brought together at the village of St. Mary, about halfway between Sartigan and the St. Lawrence. At this point they left the Chaudière and marched through snow, mud, and water knee-deep due north across the plains of Canada toward the great river.

On the 9th of November the habitants on the bank of the St. Lawrence saw, emerging from the woods, a band of scarecrows, their clothing "torn in pieces . . . hung in strings—few had any shoes but moggasons made of raw skins—many without hats, beards long and visages thin and meager. . . . So at last came to Point Levi 600, much resembling the animals which inhabit New Spain called the Ourang-Outang,"—600 out of 1,100 men who had started. Their journey had taken forty-five days, instead of twenty, as Arnold had predicted. They had traveled 350 miles, instead of 180, from Fort Western.[47]

Arnold's journey to Quebec is one of the most famous military marches recorded in history. If it had resulted in the capture of that stronghold it would have been celebrated as a great triumph. That it failed, by so little as it did, should not obscure its fame as a magnificent exploit. For sustained courage, undaunted resolution, and uncomplaining endurance of almost incredible hardships, those men who grimly persisted to the end deserved high honor and unstinted praise.[48]

CHAPTER 14

Quebec

The city of Quebec stands on a bold promontory between the St. Lawrence, which bends around it, and an affluent, the St. Charles. The blunt nose of the promontory points northeast, and its highest point, on the southeastern or St. Lawrence side, is Cape Diamond, a precipitous, rocky cliff that rises more than three hundred feet above the water. Toward the northwest, the St. Charles side, and toward the southwest the ground declines to somewhat lower levels. Along the base of the great cliff and around the point of the promontory a narrow band or fringe of lowland slopes gently to the water's edge and widens on the St. Charles side. Part of this, around the promontory's nose, was built up and was known as the Lower Town. It was defended in 1775 at its southern end by a blockhouse behind a double row of palisades just below the height of Cape Diamond. There were also timber barriers through which one might penetrate to Sault au Matelot, a narrow, crooked street, slanting upward from the base of the cliffs to an equally narrow, ladderlike passage into the Upper Town, the real city.

This Upper Town occupied the whole end of the higher level of the promontory and contained all the important buildings, including the citadel situated on the height of Cape Diamond. It was defended on the landward side by a strong wall thirty feet high and three-quarters of a mile long drawn across from one river to the other, from which six bold bastions projected, whereon were mounted heavy cannon. It was pierced by three gates, St. Louis Gate in the center, St. Johns near the northern part, and Palace Gate at the northerly approach to the Lower Town. Outside the main wall were certain built-up suburbs, the Palais toward the St. Charles River, St.

Roche in front of the north end of the wall, and St. Johns opposite its middle section. Beyond St. Roche and St. Johns to the west stretched the Plains of Abraham, where Wolfe had fought the great fight by which he took Quebec from the French in 1759.

Such was the fortress at which that little band of gaunt, ragged, starved Americans, shivering in the cold autumn wind, gazed with hope born of determination on the morning of November 9, 1775.[1]

They had come a long way and a hard way. They had reached the end of their march; yet a mile of water rolled between them and their grand objective. It was not an unguarded river that they had to cross. The frigate *Lizard* with twenty-six guns, the sloop-of-war *Hunter* with sixteen guns, four smaller armed vessels, and two transports lay at anchor, and small boats were constantly on patrol.

The shore on which Arnold's army stood had been cleared of every sort of craft by which a crossing might be made. It is not surprising that Matthias Ogden thought the "situation now seem'd somewhat ticklish. . . . We determined, however," he wrote in his journal, to "make a bold push for Quebec at all events." [2]

The first necessity was boats. They scoured the country for them. One party found twenty birch-bark canoes and carried them on their shoulders twenty-five miles to the camp. The Indian Natanis and his friends offered others. A dozen dugouts were discovered elsewhere and brought by night to the mouth of the Chaudière, where the little fleet was hid. Iron heads for pikes were forged in a near-by smithy and scaling ladders prepared. A supply of flour was procured from a neighboring mill. By Friday November 10 they were ready to attempt the crossing.[3]

But that night a storm arose, rain and a gale of wind which whipped the river into waves that would have swamped their canoes. In the evening of the 13th it blew itself out; and at nine o'clock, in black darkness, Arnold with as many of his men as could crowd into the boats started across. Midway in the river one of the canoes collapsed. Its crew was picked up by another, except Lieutenant Steele, who could find no room in the rescue boat. He clung to its stern and was towed the rest of the way, arriving nearly dead from the cold. They landed in a cove, the one in which Wolfe had landed to capture the city sixteen years before. In a deserted house a fire was kindled, and Steele was "restored . . . to his usual animation." The boats went back and brought another detachment, but when it had landed, at three in the morning, the tide was running so strong, and the moon was shining so brightly that it was deemed unsafe for the remaining 150 men to cross. They stayed on the opposite shore until the next night.[4]

The journal of one of the participants in the expedition asserts that Arnold, even with so few men, might have taken the city by attacking at once, as he had originally planned to do, because the keys of St. Johns Gate had been lost and it was unfastened. Others have denied that the gate was open. At all events, Arnold could not have known of this defect in the defenses that night. With only a part of his force at hand and no scaling ladders (there had not been room for them in the boats), he wisely did not attempt an assault.[5]

When all the men had been brought over they assembled and climbed to the level above, not by the goat-path that Wolfe had found, but by a slanting road since cut. They were now on the Plains of Abraham within a mile and a half of the city, near a large house that belonged to Major Caldwell, commandant of the Quebec militia. At the approach of Arnold's men, its occupants fled. The Americans crowded in and slept there.

The coming of the Americans was neither unexpected nor unobserved. A patrol boat had sighted the fire in the house in Wolfe's Cove and had been fired upon at Arnold's order. News of their actual arrival on the Quebec side of the river had been conveyed into the town, where there was considerable perturbation, with good reason. Carleton's command had originally consisted of two regiments of British regulars, the 7th and 26th. But at Ticonderoga, Crown Point, St. Johns, Chambly, and Sorel nearly all of them had been killed or captured. Remaining to him in Quebec were about seventy men of the 7th and a few artillerists.

During the storm that had delayed Arnold at the river side, the active and energetic Allan Maclean had slipped into the city with a force of Royal Highland Emigrants he had raised—Scottish veterans of former wars, brave in scarlet jackets faced with blue and laced with white, tartan kilts and hose, and blue bonnets edged with checkered white, red, and green; but they were few, not more than 80. Hector Cramahé, the governor of the city, had raised 200 British and 300 French Canadian militia. There were also 37 marines from the warships, 271 sailors from the armed ships in the harbor, and 74 from the transports. Maclean figured the total to be about 1,200.[6] But there were long walls to defend, and some of the militia were thought to be unreliable, inclined to desert. On the whole, Quebec, though well provided with munitions and food, was not strongly held. Cramahé felt that way about it. He wrote to General Howe, "There is too much Reason to apprehend the Affair will be soon over." [7]

But in Arnold's opinion 2,000 men would be needed "to carry the Town," [8] and he had not much more than a quarter of that number; nor had he cannon to breach the walls. Moreover, he was short of ammunition and even of small arms. So many cartridges had been spoiled by water that there were only five rounds for each man. Over a hundred muskets were found to be unserviceable. He had no artillery and no bayonets. All he could do at the time was to blockade the town on the land side, and that at the respectful distance of a mile and a half from its walls, where his men were quartered in houses.

There were occasional diversions. A small party of the garrison sallied out and captured an incautious rifleman on sentry duty. Arnold immediately paraded his troops and marched them "bravado-like" [9] "within 80 rods of the wall . . . in such a manner that they could not discover of what number we consisted of," [10] which must have been a difficult job of deception. Cannon were fired upon them, with no hurt. They "gave 3 huzzas" and returned to their lodgings.

In the afternoon following their arrival, Arnold had sent Matthias Ogden, with a white flag and a drum, to deliver to Cramahé a demand for surrender. Ogden was within a hundred feet of St. Johns Gate when a gun thundered and an 18-pound shot hit the ground near him. He "retreated in quick time." [11] Assuming a misunderstanding of his intentions, Arnold sent another letter the next day, with a similar result. The only course was to continue the blockade.

It was no hardship. For the first time since they set out from Newburyport, two months before, the troops had clean, warm, comfortable lodgings and plenty of good food. They would doubtless have been glad to fight it out on that line—in that manner—if it took all winter. That was also quite evidently the intention of Maclean, who had taken over the command of the city from Cramahé. He burned a part of the suburb of St. Johns and certain other houses near the walls, to prevent the Americans from using them as cover, and settled down to hold out against the siege.

But the Americans were soon routed out of their comfortable quarters. On the 18th they had news that Maclean was about to make a sortie and to attack them with 800 men. Also it was reported that a ship with 200 men was coming up the river, and that the *Lizard* had taken a station above the camp to cut off their retreat. A council of war decided to withdraw. So, at four o'clock in the morning of the 19th, "a severely dark and cold night," [12] the entire force started on a march to Pointe aux Trembles—now Neuville—twenty miles up the river. "Most of the soldiers were in constant misery during this march, as they were bare footed, and the ground was frozen and very uneven." [13] In a village at the point they were again quartered in houses. There they remained for nearly two weeks, recuperating their wasted bodies and availing themselves of an opportunity to make shoes out of the hides of the beeves they had killed for food.

It was a gloomy time. For all the effort they had made, all the hardships they had endured to get to Quebec, this period of inactivity was their only reward. The coveted city seemed as far away as when they left Fort Western. They were not even blockading it. Provisions and fuel were being smuggled into it without hindrance. On their march up the river, they had seen an armed schooner go past them, and a little later the sound of a salvo of artillery was heard. Carleton had come to take command, as they soon learned. That was bad news.

But at last good news did come. On December 2 a topsail schooner and several other craft were sighted coming down the river. In the evening a boat put off from the schooner, and, in the light of lanterns and flaring torches, there stepped ashore into a foot of snow "a gentle, polite Man, tall and slender . . . resolute, mild and of a fine Temper," [14] "well limbed, tall and handsome, though his face was much pock-marked," with "an air and manner that designated the real soldier." [15] Richard Montgomery had come from Montreal.

He had brought 300 men and, what was even more important, artillery and "a good supply of ammunition, clothing and provisions." [16] To the troops paraded in front of the little church he made an "energetic and elegant speech, the burden of which was an applause for our spirit in passing the wilderness, a hope for perseverance . . . and a promise of warm clothing. . . . A few huzzas from our freezing bodies were returned to this address of the gallant hero. Now new life was infused into the whole of the corps." [17]

The men liked Montgomery, and he liked them. He wrote to Schuyler: "I find Colonel Arnold's corps an exceeding fine one, inured to fatigue. . . . There is a style of discipline among them much superior to what I have been used to see in this campaign. He himself is active, intelligent and enterprising. . . . I must say he has brought with him many pretty young men." [18]

Montgomery had captured a year's supply of clothing of the 7th and 26th British regiments. Their winter uniforms were Canadian capotes, long, white, full-skirted overcoats of a heavy blanket material, trimmed and bound with blue, and with cape-hoods. The underjackets were of similar material, with corduroy sleeves. Leggings of heavy blue cloth, really overalls, were strapped over sealskin moccasins and reached to the waist. The caps were of red cloth, with a band of brown fur around the base, and were ornamented at the back with a fur tail.[19] These garments were now distributed in part.

Supplementary distributions were made later to the whole force. On the 5th, they marched back to Quebec, the artillery and stores following in bateaux.

The two American forces took up positions before the town: Arnold on the left, the northern side, in half-burned St. Roche, taking over the General Hospital in that suburb; Montgomery on the Plains midway between St. Roche and Cape Diamond. Now again Quebec was blockaded, but it was not Montgomery's intention to rely upon siege tactics. He well knew that they would not suffice to fulfill the desires of his superiors and of the American colonies in general. They wanted the town taken, and they expected him to take it. Schuyler wrote on November 18 that "in all probability the entire possession of Canada . . . will be [ours] soon." [20] Knox had "very little doubt" of Montgomery's success.[21] Washington on December 5 wrote to Schuyler, "I flatter myself that it will be effected when General Montgomery joins him [Arnold] and our Conquest of Canada be compleat." [22] Indeed, the commander in chief was relying on the spoils of Canada for his own troops, as he wrote to Montgomery: "I must beg . . . your attention to the Wants of the Army here, which are not few, and if they cannot in some Parts be supplied by you, I do not Know where else I can apply." Powder he wanted and arms, blankets, and clothing, of all which he understood there was "an Abundance in Canada." [23] The Congress was urgent for the possession of the town and vocal in its urgency. Clearly, Quebec must be taken by one means or another.

But a siege, without great battering guns to breach the wall, must needs be a slow, long drawn-out affair, and of time Montgomery had little to spare. He could not dig trenches to approach the town in the classic manner. He had no engineer to plan them, and they could not be dug in frozen soil. The term of enlistment of all Arnold's New England troops would expire with the year, and Montgomery had no hope of retaining them after that. It would be most difficult, if not impossible, to obtain fresh supplies of ammunition, and even of food, for Montgomery had no money except Continental paper, which would not pass in Canada. And by April, when the ice in the river broke up, British reinforcements could certainly come. A siege would not do.

Montgomery had been fully aware of all that even before he came, and had no intention of relying on a siege. He had written to Robert Livingston from Montreal giving his reasons why "to storming the place . . . we must come at last." [24] He wrote to Schuyler on the day of his arrival before Quebec that he meant "to assault the works, I believe towards the lower town, which is the weakest part." Meanwhile, he proposed "amusing Mr.

Carleton with a formal attack, erecting batteries, &c." He was sorry to have to assault, because he knew "the melancholy consequences," but saw no escape from it.[25]

First, however, he must go through the customary formality of summoning the garrison. He wrote a letter to Carleton in the usual terms. Being mindful of the manner in which Arnold's similar letters had been treated, he had recourse to a ruse. A woman carried the summons to the Palace Gate and said to the guard she had an important communication for the General. Being admitted, she told him she had a letter for him from the American General. Carleton called a drummer boy and bade him take the paper with the tongs and thrust it into the fire. He sent her back to tell Montgomery that he would receive no communication from a rebel.

Ten days later Montgomery tried again. He wrote a fierce letter, calling Carleton's attention to the weakness of his situation in the town, the great extent of his works manned only by "a motley crew of sailors, most of them our friends . . . citizens, who wish to see us within the walls, a few of the worst troops, that call themselves soldiers." He boasted of his own men "accustomed to success, confident of the righteousness of the cause they are engaged in, inured to danger and fatigue, and so highly incensed at your inhumanity . . . that it is with difficulty I restrain them, until my batteries are ready, from assaulting your works, which would give them a fair opportunity of ample vengeance and just retaliation." If Carleton persisted "in an unwarrantable defence," the consequences were to be on his head.[26] In a word, he tried to scare Carleton. But Carleton refused to take fright. When another woman smuggled this demand into the city, she was first imprisoned and then drummed out of town. As a last resort and in an effort to alarm the citizens, a flight of arrows, each bearing a copy of the letter, was shot over the walls with as little result.

Meanwhile, Montgomery was at work on those threatened batteries. Arnold's force advanced to within 150 yards of the wall, and planted five small mortars. On the heights, 700 yards from the town, in the fiercely cold night of December 10, in a heavy snowstorm driven by a northeast gale, a more formidable American battery was begun. Night by night after that gabions were set up there, filled with snow, and then drenched with water, which froze them into solid blocks of ice. In this battery five 6- and 12-pounders and a howitzer were emplaced. From these two positions a heavy fire was poured upon the walls and into the town, "with very little effect," as Montgomery admitted.[27] But Carleton's response with 13-inch shells and 32-pound balls was too much of an answer. Several men were killed, the ice-battery was shattered, and the guns were dismounted.

One more effort was made to induce Carleton to surrender. Arnold and Macpherson, with flag and drum, approached the walls. To a messenger sent to meet them they announced a desire to speak with Carleton. The reply was decisive. He would not see them. Would he receive a letter, then? He would not. They could make the best of their way off, for he would receive nothing from Mr. Montgomery.

Within the town Carleton had organized his men. The fusiliers of the 7th, the marines and Royal Scottish, 425 in all, were commanded by Maclean. Major Caldwell commanded 330 British militia. Colonel Voyer led 543 French Canadian militiamen, and Captain Hamilton the sailors and artificers from the ships, 570 of them. Thus there were over 1,800 to defend the town against Montgomery's force, no more than 800 in all. But *Audaces fortuna juvat* was Montgomery's motto.[28]

He was preparing for the attack, but he met with obstacles. The town-meeting spirit became prevalent, especially among Arnold's New Englanders —so much so that it was recognized as necessary "to have the approbation of all the officers and soldiers." That was hard to get. Everybody wanted the town taken, but not everybody wanted to take it. Many of them "appeared unwilling to attempt so daring an enterprise." [29]

The trouble seems to have originated in three of Arnold's officers, Captain Oliver Hanchet of Connecticut and Captains William Goodrich and Jonas Hubbard of Massachusetts. Hanchet, who had "incurred Colonel Arnold's displeasure by some misconduct and thereby given room for harsh language, is at the bottom of it," [30] wrote Montgomery to Schuyler on December 26. These three proposed to organize a separate corps under command of Major John Brown, who had disliked and distrusted Arnold from the time of their first meeting. Montgomery would not allow this. The three companies then appeared to be "very averse from" the proposed assault. "This dangerous party threatens the ruin of our officers," said Montgomery. But he met Arnold's officers "to compose some matters, which were happily settled." [31] He then paraded Arnold's troops, and addressed them "in a very sensible Spirited manner, which greatly animated" them.[32] "The fire of patriotism kindled in our breasts," wrote one of the Connecticut recalcitrants, "and we resolved to follow wherever he should lead." [33]

The attack was to be made in a dark and stormy night, "in the first northwester." [34] The Lower Town, the weakest in its defenses, was to be the primary objective. While a third of the troops, with ladders, feinted an escalade of the Cape Diamond bastion, another third was to attack the

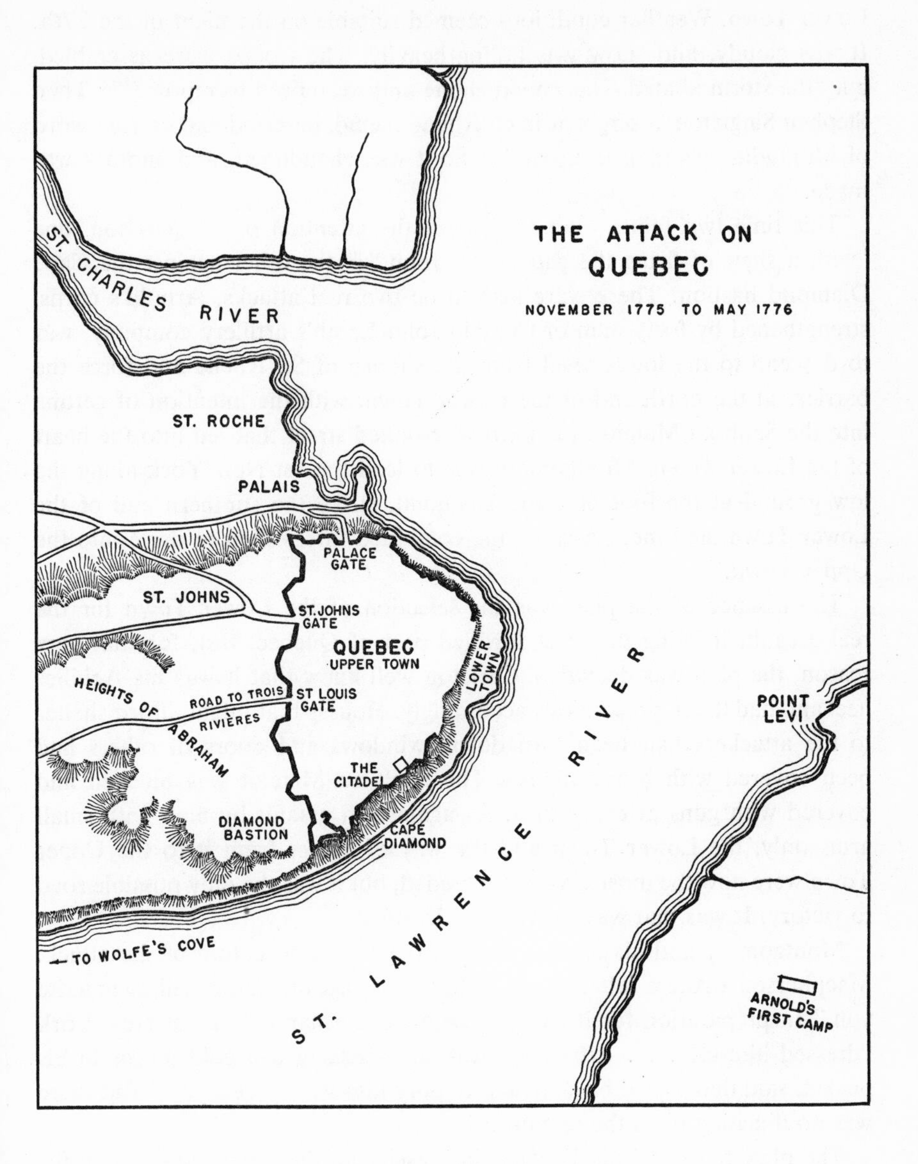
THE ATTACK ON
QUEBEC
NOVEMBER 1775 TO MAY 1776
ST. CHARLES RIVER
ST. ROCHE
PALAIS
PALACE GATE
ST. JOHNS
ST. JOHNS GATE
QUEBEC
UPPER TOWN
LOWER TOWN
HEIGHTS OF ABRAHAM
ROAD TO TROIS RIVIÈRES
ST LOUIS GATE
THE CITADEL
DIAMOND BASTION
CAPE DIAMOND
POINT LEVI
ST. LAWRENCE RIVER
TO WOLFE'S COVE
ARNOLD'S FIRST CAMP

Lower Town. Weather conditions seemed suitable on the night of the 27th. It was cloudy, and snow was falling heavily. The troops were assembled, but "the storm abated—the moon shone and we retired to repose." [35] Then Stephen Singleton, a sergeant from Rhode Island, deserted and carried word of Montgomery's plan to Carleton. So it was abandoned, and another was made.

This time two feints were to distract the attention of the garrison, one "with a shew of firing the gate of St. John," [36] the other against the Cape Diamond bastion. There were also to be two real attacks. Arnold's corps, strengthened by forty men of Captain John Lamb's artillery company, was to descend to the lower level from the suburb of St. Roche and force the barriers at the north end of the Lower Town, with the intention of getting into the Sault au Matelot, the narrow, crooked street that led into the heart of the Lower Town. Montgomery was to lead the 1st New York along the low ground at the foot of Cape Diamond, strike the southern end of the Lower Town, and meet Arnold, the combined forces then to drive into the Upper Town.

The essence of the plan was the selection of the Lower Town for the real assault, it being the least fortified part of Quebec. But, for that very reason, the plan was defective. Carleton well knew that it was his Achilles heel and had taken precautions accordingly. Houses that might afford shelter to the attackers had been torn down; windows and doors of others had been covered with heavy planks. The Sault au Matelot was blocked and covered with guns at every turn. As against an assault by men with small arms only, the Lower Town and the way of access from it to the Upper Town were now the most strongly defended; but it was the only possible road to victory. It was that way, or not at all.

Montgomery and his officers realized the desperate nature of the attack. Macpherson wrote a letter to his father, "the last this hand will ever write you." In preparation for it Captain Jacob Cheesman of the 1st New York "dressed himself . . . extremely neat, and, putting five gold pieces in his pocket, said that would be sufficient to bury him with decency." [37] But there was no flinching from the attempt.

The plan made and all the parts in it assigned, the Americans waited for a dark and stormy night. But the weather on Thursday the 29th and on Friday was "clear and mild." Saturday morning was fair; but in the afternoon the sky was clouded, the wind rose and brought a spit of snow. Heavy darkness came at sunset. As the night wore on the snow fell more and more heavily, "a thick small Snow" driven by an "outrageous" [38] wind into great drifts heaped and piled upon that which had fallen before, and which had already covered the earth to a depth of two to three feet. The time had come.

At two o'clock in the morning the men were assembled at their respective stations. Soon after four o'clock signal rockets were fired, and the advance began. The storm, a terrific blizzard, was at its height. The wind from the northwest drove snow mixed with hail into the faces of the men as they stumbled through six-foot drifts in the blackest darkness.

The rockets were a signal to the Americans, but they were also a signal to the town. Drums beat to arms. The great bell of the cathedral, the lesser bells of the Jesuit College, of the Recollet monastery, and of the Hôtel Dieu clanged the alarm. Officers ran through the streets shouting, "Turn out! Turn out!" The city's troops rushed to their posts. Lanterns on poles were thrust out over the top of the walls. Flaming fire balls were thrown from the ramparts to light up the ground outside. The little American mortar battery at St. Roche went into action, throwing shells into the town to divert the enemy's attention from the real points of attack. The guns on the walls roared in reply.

Amid this tumult the two feinting parties made their way toward the walls. Livingston's corps of Canadians was near St. Johns Gate, when they broke and ran. The other party, a hundred Massachusetts men led by Captain Jacob Brown, John's brother, kept up a rattling fire against the Cape Diamond bastion. Some militia were sent to reinforce the defenders there, but otherwise little attention was paid to Brown's efforts. Carleton's mind was not distracted from the Lower Town.

Meanwhile, Montgomery and Arnold had marched. Montgomery at the head of the 1st New York, about 300 men in single file, set out on the long circuit around the Diamond bastion, down the slanting road to the fringe of lowland along the river. The way down to Wolfe's Cove was a mile long, steep, narrow, and heaped with drifted snow; and the storm still raged. That part was bad almost beyond bearing. The rest was worse. On the narrow strip of land below the heights the high tides had piled "enormous and rugged masses of ice," [39] creating such obstacles that the men had to clamber up the steep slope of the cliff to get around them. They slipped, slid, and fell. Those that carried the unwieldy scaling ladders, which had been brought across the river, could hardly make way at all. There were two miles of this before they reached the first defenses of the Lower Town.

Arnold had formed his own corps of 600 men, with a forlorn hope of twenty-five men in advance led by himself and Eleazer Oswald, a volunteer. A hundred yards behind these Captain John Lamb and his forty artillerists dragged a 6-pounder on a sled. Behind them again came the riflemen, Morgan's company, followed by Smith's under command of Lieutenant Steele, and Hendricks's company. The New Englanders (except Dearborn's men, who had been late in assembling) with about forty Canadians and Indians, brought up the rear. They set out from St. Roche in Indian file and passed a two-gun battery without discovery. Hurrying on through deep snow, "deeper than in the fields" above, the van got by the Palace Gate unassailed. The main body, "covering the locks of our guns with the lappets of our coats, holding down our heads" against the driving storm, had also safely passed the Gate, when it "received a tremendous fire of musketry from the ramparts above." For a third of a mile, men falling here and there, they ran that gantlet without a possibility of a reply. "We could see nothing but the blaze from the muzzles of their muskets." [40]

At the waterside ships were moored with cables stretched to the houses. In the darkness some of the men ran into these and were thrown down violently. At last they came into a narrow street blocked by a barricade, mounting two guns.

Arnold's plan was to separate his force, right and left, and let Lamb's gun batter the barrier, while Morgan went around its end on the river ice and took it in the rear. But the 6-pounder had been abandoned in a snowdrift sometime before this. One of the guns of the barrier was fired at them with little effect. The other failed to go off. Arnold called on his men to rush the barricade. They responded, ran to it, and fired through the portholes. A bullet from one of the near-by houses hit a rock, ricocheted and hit Arnold in the leg below the knee. He still shouted encouragement to his men; but his wound was bleeding freely, and he had to be supported by two men to the rear and so to the hospital.

By general acclaim Morgan was called upon to take command instead of Lieutenant Colonel Greene. A ladder was set against the barrier, and Morgan mounted it, calling on his men to follow. As his head topped the barricade, a blaze of fire met him. Stunned, he fell backward and lay in the snow, with one bullet through his cap, another through his beard, and grains of burnt powder embedded in his face. In a moment he was on his feet. Up the ladder again he went, and over the top of the fence. His knee hit one of the cannon, and he rolled beneath it. Before any of the defenders could get at him, Charles Porterfield was over, and then the rest. The enemy, followed by the riflemen's bullets, fled into a house and out the back way. But Morgan had run around it, and he shouted to them to surrender if they wanted quarter. They all surrendered. The way into the Lower Town was open.

The Sault au Matelot lay ahead. They entered it. Two or three hundred yards up that street there was another barrier. Behind it was a platform with cannon. The gate in the barrier was open. Now was the time to break through, for the garrison was offering no resistance. Some of them, Canadians, seemed ready to welcome the Americans, shouted, *"Vive la liberté!"* and held out welcoming hands. The whole town appeared to be panic-stricken. Morgan urged his officers to push on through the gate. But there were few men with him. The rest of that long straggling line had not yet come up. He actually had more prisoners than he had of his own men. It was pitch-dark. The storm was still raging. None of the men knew the way through the crooked street and its alleyways, and they had no guide. This was the place appointed to meet Montgomery. The officers decided to stay there until their whole force came up and Montgomery joined them.

After a time the rest of the troops began to arrive, Hendricks and his riflemen, Greene, Meigs, and Bigelow with the Yankees. It was about daybreak when the major part of the American force was again assembled and formed for another attack. But the town had recovered its senses. Troops had been sent to meet the Americans. A party of them sallied out through the gate in the barrier. Lieutenant Anderson, leading them, called on Morgan to surrender. Morgan shot him through the head. Anderson's men retreated, and for a while there was a pause. The spirit of fraternization again prevailed. Men from either side called to the others by name. But that was soon over, and the Americans went at the high barrier.

Mounds of snow were heaped up, ladders set on them. Morgan climbed one, Porterfield another. Humphreys, Lamb, Greene, Meigs, and yet more went up, but the houses in the street beyond were filled with fighting men. Muskets blazed from the windows. A little way up the street a double line of fusiliers presented their bayonets. No one could dare that defense. And upon the Americans and among them fell a shower of bullets. Humphreys fell, and Hendricks, and many another. Lamb and Steele, and more and more, were wounded, while their assailants were safe in the houses.

Yet, though their pieces were wet and most of them failed to fire, the Americans fought on. They tried to outflank the barricade, but it stretched from the bluff to the river. They dared the ladders again and again, even thrust one over the fence to climb down on; but to go over the top would have been sheer suicide. There was a stone house at the end of the barricade, whose gable-end windows looked down beyond the barrier. Riflemen there could shoot down on the defenders, perhaps drive them back. The Americans broke in, but the enemy had perceived the threat of the house. The ladder the Americans had left inside the barrier was set against the house, and a party of the defenders climbed it, entered through a window, came down the stairs, bayonets fixed. There was a fierce fight, in the house, but the Americans were driven out.

In the street again they were under fire of a 9-pounder hastily brought up, and of musketry as before. They retreated for a space, and the officers consulted. Some of them still looked for Montgomery and wanted to hold their position until night. The majority saw the hopelessness of the situation. It was decided to give up the attempt and withdraw.

But Carleton had moved to prevent that. He had sent Captain Laws out of the Palace Gate, with 200 men and two fieldpieces to follow the Americans' tracks down to the lower level and take them in the rear. Laws came running up the Sault au Matelot, and shouted to the Americans to surrender. They jeered at him, cried out that he was their prisoner. He looked around and saw that he was quite alone. His men had not followed as fast as he had run. Expecting them to come on at once, the Americans threw themselves into the houses along the street.

Laws's delayed party arrived, and for a while a desultory fire was maintained. But the Americans' situation was desperate. Hemmed in, front and back, the officers hastily consulted again. Morgan proposed cutting through the force in their rear. Others were for holding on until Montgomery came. But their plight was beyond hope. They were, in Carleton's words, "compleatly ruined . . . caught, as it were, in a Trap." They began to throw down their arms.

Morgan had disdained the shelter offered by the houses. He stood in the street facing his enemies. When he saw that surrender was inevitable, he set his back against a wall, and, with tears of rage and disappointment streaming down his face, defied the enemy to take his sword. They threatened to shoot him. His men implored him not to sacrifice his life. He saw a man in clerical dress in the crowd confronting him and called to him, "Are you a priest?" He was. "Then I give my sword to you. But not a scoundrel of these cowards shall take it out of my hands." [41] So ended that fight, three hours long, in the Sault au Matelot.

But where was Montgomery? His tale of disaster is soon told.

He and some of his men, having overcome the obstacles in their way, came to a barricade. Saws went to work on it. Montgomery himself took a hand, tearing down the half-sawed posts. With Macpherson and Captain Cheesman at his side, he led the forlorn hope through and was confronted by a blockhouse. No more than fifty or sixty of his men followed him. The rest were still struggling with the difficulties of their road. Montgomery and his little band advanced against the blockhouse. No shot was fired from it. They passed it, went on for a hundred yards, came to another barrier, cut through it, rounded Point Diamond, entered on a narrow road, and saw another building before them, a dwelling house. It was loopholed, armed with four small guns, 3-pounders, and held by a corporal with eight British militiamen, a captain and thirty French Canadians, a ship captain, Adam Barnsfair, and nine sailors. John Coffin, a Boston Tory, was with them. Montgomery "called to his men to Come on; they did not advance as quick as he thought they might, he Spoke to them again in the following moving Terms, saying Come on my good soldiers, your General calls you to Come on." [42]

Coffin encouraged the men in the house to withhold their fire until the Americans, indistinctly seen in the darkness and snow, should come closer. Barnsfair and his men stood by their guns with lighted matches ready. Montgomery, Macpherson, and Cheesman, with Aaron Burr, Edward Antil, a sergeant, and a dozen men pushed forward. They were within a few paces of the house, when there came from it a burst of gunfire, grapeshot and bullets. Another burst and another raked the narrow street, until not one of that forlorn hope was left standing. In the snow lay a dozen men. Montgomery was dead, shot through the head. Macpherson and Cheesman lay beside him. Burr, Antil, and one or two others got away unhurt.

That was the end of the attack on the Cape Diamond end of the Lower Town. Colonel Donald Campbell took command and ordered a retreat. What was left of Montgomery's corps struggled back through the storm. Dearborn's belated company, trying to come up with Arnold's division, was caught on the road between two fires and surrendered. Carleton sent out a small force which seized the little battery at St. Roche, picking up Lamb's 6-pounder on the way.

Carleton captured 426 men, sound or wounded, including 30 officers and 5 gentlemen volunteers. The number killed or wounded and not captured may have been 60. The British loss was 5 killed and 13 wounded.[43] There were left to Arnold perhaps 600 men, including such Canadians and Indians as had joined him. Of these, more than 100 time-expired men soon left him, and there were other defections.

Arnold withdrew his little force about a mile, erected defences of frozen snow, and sent Edward Antil to Montreal for reinforcements. But General Wooster, in command there, had only five or six hundred men with whom to hold that town, as well as Chambly and St. Johns. No help could be had from him. Antil went on to Schuyler at Albany. But everything there was in confusion and alarm, because of Tory uprisings along the Mohawk and in Tryon County. There were no reinforcements available for Arnold. Antil went on to Philadelphia, to the Congress, bearing a letter from Schuyler. The Congress, on January 19, voted to reinforce the army in Canada "with all possible despatch," called on New Hampshire, Connecticut, New York, Pennsylvania, and New Jersey for troops for that purpose, and asked Washington to detach one battalion and send it north. It also authorized Moses Hazen to raise a regiment in Canada, Antil to be lieutenant colonel.[44]

From Montreal, Wooster sent 120 men near the end of January, and himself followed later with 60 more. In February, 25 came from Massachusetts. Hard money, some $28,000, was sent to encourage Arnold, now a brigadier general by grace of the Congress. Troops were coming from here and there, but slowly. In the middle of March, Arnold had 617 rank and file, besides Livingston's not very trustworthy Canadians. But smallpox had put 400 of Arnold's men in hospital, and every sort of supplies, food as well as military equipment, was lacking in Montreal and in Arnold's camp. Yet, all this while, Carleton made no move to attack those few hundreds who were still, with some success, blockading his town. He may have had in mind the fate of Montcalm's army, when it sallied out to meet Wolfe on those same Plains of Abraham. At all events he made no hostile move, but busied himself with strengthening his defensive works.

At last, on April 2, Wooster came to the camp with troops that made up the American force to 2,000 men. He took command. Arnold, injured by a fall from his horse, withdrew to Montreal. Wooster mounted batteries on the Heights and on Pointe Lévis and bombarded the town, to which it replied vigorously and with heavier metal. He also made an unsuccessful attempt to burn the vessels in the harbor by means of a fireship.

Early in May, Wooster was superseded by General John Thomas, a more capable, more energetic officer. He found the army, which had been built up to 2,500 men, now reduced by discharges, death, and desertions to 1,900, of whom no more than 1,000, including officers, were fit for duty. The time of 300 had already expired, and 200 more were under inoculation. No more than 500 could be relied upon. A mere ghost of an army was besieging a strongly fortified town of 5,000 inhabitants, mounting 148 cannon, with a garrison of 1,600 fit to fight, besides a frigate, a sloop of war, and several smaller armed vessels as auxiliaries. It was an absurd situation, yet Carleton remained within the walls.

More men were on their way to Thomas, the 2nd New Jersey Regiment and six companies of the 2nd Pennsylvania. Some of them had already arrived when, on May 2, there came bad news from the opposite quarter. A

British fleet, fifteen ships, had entered the mouth of the St. Lawrence. On the 7th, their masts and spars could be descried. General John Burgoyne was coming, with seven Irish regiments, one English, and 2,000 hired German mercenaries. That was the end of the siege of Quebec.

A force of 900 of the garrison, with four fieldpieces, issued from the town. Thomas, with difficulty, gathered a force of 250 to oppose it; his stand was but momentary. His whole army began to retreat, and in no orderly fashion. In a panic the gunners abandoned their pieces. The men under inoculation threw away their muskets and fled. The invalids in the hospital left their beds and stumbled and staggered toward the woods. The Canadian teamsters employed in the service of the army threw up their jobs and left. Clothing, provisions, and stores, even the orderly books and records in headquarters, had to be abandoned. Bateaux loaded with invalids and such stores as could be hastily gathered pushed up the St. Lawrence. Two tons of precious gunpowder, a hundred barrels of flour, and all the hospital stores were seized by the enemy, as they were about to be loaded into boats. One of the American regiments, across the river at Pointe Lévis, was intercepted and had to scatter into the woods. The main body marching on the road by the river, deep with mud, was divided for lack of food. Parties went here and there to levy on the inhabitants, took food by force. It was a mob of muddy, hungry, tired men, wounded men, men sick with smallpox, rather than an army, that streamed westward, leaving the dead and dying in its wake. Enemy ships passed them. Marines landed to cut them off, were driven back, and the struggle westward went on.

At Deschambault, forty miles up the river, Thomas halted his shattered forces and held a council of war. A stand at that point was voted down, and the retreat was resumed, to end at last on the 17th at Sorel, at the mouth of the Richelieu, where certain troops on their way to Quebec were met. Colonel William Maxwell's 2nd New Jersey, which had been left at Trois Rivières as a rear guard, was called in. The regiment which had fled from Pointe Lévis had made its way to the main force. So now all that was left of Thomas's army was gathered together in a disorganized mass, with hardly a trace of military system, "without order or regularity, eating up provisions as fast as they were brought in," [45] a mere mob.

Thomas described it: "A retreating army, disheartened by unavoidable misfortunes, destitute of almost every necessary to render their lives comfortable or even tolerable, sick and (as they think) wholly neglected and [with] no prospect of speedy relief." He himself was ill with the smallpox. There was nothing to do except to continue to retreat. On the 2nd of June, while his men were on the march up the Richelieu to Chambly, he died.

Moses Hazen, temporarily in command at Montreal in the absence of Arnold (who had gone down to Sorel and up the Richelieu with Thomas's force) directed Colonel Timothy Bedel, with 400 men, to hold a small, fortified post at the Cedars, about thirty miles above Montreal. With 150 English and Canadians and 500 Indians, Captain Forster marched against it. Bedel, suffering with the smallpox, went back to Montreal, leaving Major Isaac Butterfield in charge. On the arrival of Forster's troops, Butterfield surrendered without any real contest. A reinforcing American regiment under Major Henry Sherburne was waylaid and, after a gallant fight, overpowered and captured. Arnold, indignant at Butterfield's cowardice, took the field, met Forster, demanded and obtained the return of the captives by promising an exchange, and returned to Montreal.

But reinforcements for Thomas's sadly battered troops were on the way. Brigadier General William Thompson, formerly colonel of one of the Pennsylvania rifle regiments at Cambridge, was coming with a brigade of four regiments dispatched by Washington, comprising 2,000 musketmen, a company of riflemen, and one of artificers. Brigadier John Sullivan led a brigade of 3,300 from New York. He had been directed to take over Thomas's command. On June 1 he arrived at St. Johns, where Thompson's troops had been lying for two weeks. With the fresh and full supplies of food, ammunition, small arms, and cannon brought by these new troops, the prospects for a reinstatement of American fortunes in Canada seemed bright. Everybody was on tiptoe for a second march against Quebec.

The primary objective was to be Trois Rivières, about halfway between Montreal and Quebec, and the coveted stronghold. It was supposed to be held by no more than 800 regulars and Canadians under Maclean. Sullivan ordered Thompson to take it with 2,000 of the best of the Americans. On June 6 they embarked in bateaux and dropped down the river to a point ten miles above Trois Rivières. In the evening of the next day they embarked again for a night attack. William Maxwell, Anthony Wayne, Arthur St. Clair, William Irvine, all men of mettle, led their respective regiments. Thompson himself was a notable fighting man.

At three in the morning of June 8 they landed about three miles above the town. Leaving 250 men to guard the boats, they marched in silence, intending to attack at four points with St. Clair, Maxwell, Irvine, and Wayne leading the several detachments. They had for a guide a habitant, one Antoine Gautier. Whether intentionally or not, he misled them. They tried to recover the right road by going across country, got into a great swamp, and were completely mired. They floundered about in the slimy mud. Shoes and even boots were sucked off their feet. It was near daybreak when they got out and found the road along the shore and close to the river.

Two or three armed vessels fired on them as they came up. For three-quarters of a mile they were under a fire that, having no artillery, they could not return. They swung away into the woods, intending to make a circuit and to return to the road. But they got into "the most Horrid swamp that ever man set foot in," [46] sank in it up to their middles.

Warning of their approach had been brought to the town. A surprise was no longer possible. But they had been told by the Congress that it was "of the highest importance that a post be taken at De Chambeaux." [47] Washington had said to Thomas, "The lower down [the river] you can maintain a stand the more advantageous it will be." He had said, too, that the Quebec "misfortune must be repaired," [48] and Trois Rivières was the first step to that end. They kept on.

For two or three hours they fought their way through the swamp and the tangled forest. At eight o'clock they saw a clearing a quarter of a mile ahead, firm ground. They had been divided, even scattered, in the swampy jungle. Wayne, with 200 men, got out first and saw a body of regulars bearing down upon him.

He threw forward a company of light infantry and one of riflemen, formed the rest, and opened fire. The enemy, twice as many as they, gave back, broke, and fled. Thompson and the rest of his force came out and saw the village lying between them and the river. But between it and themselves they also saw a line of entrenchments. Burgoyne with more than 8,000 men was on his way up the St. Lawrence, and perhaps three-quarters of them had arrived at Trois Rivières.

The Americans attacked, probably not aware of the odds they faced. A heavy fire from the ships and from the trenches converged upon them. It was impossible to advance against it. They fell back into the woods. Thompson tried to rally them for another effort, but they were scattered and disorganized. An irregular fire was kept up for a time. Then the inevitable retreat began.

A British force was landed from the ships above them to cut them off. They could not escape by the road, and another column was coming against their rear. Broken up into larger or smaller parties, each acting for itself, now making a stand and now retreating, they left the road, took to the woods. They were stalked by Indians, ambushed by Canadian irregulars. Through endless swamps and a wilderness of forest, they fled northward for two days. Major Grant held against them their only gateway of escape, the bridge across the Rivière du Loup. Carleton might have captured them all, but he did not want them. What would he do with them? He had no provisions to spare, nor were there any in Quebec. Let them go and tell of his mercy to the people at home. He recalled Grant from the bridge, and on the third day after the battle, the remains of that proud little army, 1,100 men "almost worn out with fatigue, Hunger & Difficulties scarcely to be paralleled," [49] their faces and hands swollen by the stings of "Musketoes of a Monstrous size and innumerable numbers" reached Sorel.

Their losses are not ascertainable. In spite of his prudent leniency Carleton found that he had 236 prisoners on his hands, men who had given themselves up rather than attempt a seemingly impossible escape. The guards of the Americans' bateaux had escaped in their boats. About 400 in all were killed, captured, or lost in the woods and swamps. The British lost in killed and wounded about a dozen.

There were supposed to be 8,000 American troops in all the Champlain and St. Lawrence regions; but, because of the inroads of the smallpox and the results of fatigue and deprivation, not 5,000 could have been counted as effectives, even by straining that term to the limit, before the affair at Trois Rivières. After it, nearly half of that number, six of the freshest regiments, had been routed, cut to pieces, and completely demoralized. Supplies of every kind, including food, were lacking, as usual. To get them up from New York would take weeks at best. There was no money to buy provisions in Canada. And over 8,000 hearty, well furnished British regulars were gathering at Trois Rivières. They might march around Sorel to Chambly and bottle up Sullivan's army on the Richelieu below, then cut off Arnold's force at Chambly. They were, in fact, on June 13, on their way up the river by land and in transports.

A letter from Sullivan to Schuyler describes the plight of his army. He wanted to hold Sorel, he said, but he had only 2,500 men there and 1,000 at other posts, "most of the latter being under inoculation, and those regiments, which had not the small-pox, expecting every day to be taken down with it." The enemy's force was reported to be "exceedingly superior to ours," which was certainly true. "I found myself at the head of a dispirited Army, filled with horror at the thought of seeing their enemy. . . . Small-pox, famine and disorder had rendered them almost lifeless. . . . I found a great panick . . . among both officers and soldiers . . . no less than 40 officers begged leave to resign. . . . However strongly I might fortify Sorel, my men would in general leave me." [50]

Even the aggressive Arnold thought there was "more honour in making a safe retreat than in hazarding a battle against such superiority." "The junction of the Canadas is now at an end," he wrote to Schuyler. "Let us quit them and secure our own country before it is too late." [51] There was no doubt in anyone's mind that the game was up.

It was by a close margin that the Americans got away at all. The British fleet was at Sorel within an hour after the last of Sullivan's bateaux pulled away up the Richelieu. Arnold, back at Montreal, held on to that town to the last moment. Then, with the remains of its garrison, no more than 300 men, he crossed the river to Longueuil and set out for St. Johns, with the enemy close at his heels.[52]

The two forces having been joined, the whole army, if that mob of hungry, ragged, beaten men, discouraged, disorganized, and rotten with smallpox, could still be called an "army," crowded into boats sent up by Schuyler and pushed off for Ile aux Noix. They were hardly out of musket shot when the van of their pursuers arrived on the shore.[53]

Ile aux Noix is a low, flat island, about a mile long and a quarter-mile wide. A single farm occupied a slight elevation in the middle of it. The rest was a brush-covered waste, with swamps here and there. On this unwholesome desert the 8,000 wretched fugitives disembarked. Two thousand of them were hospital cases already, smallpox cases. Within two days after they landed, a quarter of the rest were stricken with malarial fever or dysentery.

There were not tents enough to shelter even the desperately sick men. Frequent thunderstorms drenched those that lay under rude shelters thatched with brush and grass. Mosquitoes and black flies swarmed in millions, tormenting and torturing sick and well alike. There was no food except salt pork and flour, and not enough wood for fires to cook even that. Medicines gave out. The few surgeons were exhausted. The moans and groans of the sick, of the dying men tortured by the itching and burning of that most loathsome disease, smallpox, could be heard everywhere. And they died like flies. Common grave pits were opened and filled day after day with corpses wrapped in their filthy blankets.

The sights and sounds of that pest-ridden camp were unbearable. Officers, unable longer to stand them, gathered in groups and deliberately drank themselves into insensibility. To stay there was to invite complete destruction. The helplessly sick were bundled into the boats. The half-sick took to the oars. Humiliated by defeat, enfeebled by fatigue, hunger, hardship, and disease, utterly demoralized in every respect, the wreck of a once proud little army rowed away from that island of death.

In the first days of July, Crown Point saw them again, what was left of them. So they came back to that place whence Montgomery had set out, just ten months before, to conquer Canada.

CHAPTER 15

Washington in New York

Washington's uncertainty as to the destination of the British fleet and army at the evacuation of Boston on March 17, 1776, did not deter him from promptly moving to defend New York, which he thought might be next attacked by the enemy. On the 18th he dispatched to that city a Pennsylvania rifle regiment, three companies of Virginia riflemen, and General Heath's brigade. Sullivan's brigade followed on the 29th, then Greene's and Spencer's, and Knox's artillery, in quick succession. Putnam was sent down to take general command. Five regiments were left in Boston under General Artemas Ward. On April 13 Washington himself was in New York.[1]

On June 20, 1775, when Washington had been directed by the Continental Congress to take command of "the Army of the united Colonies," it was in fact an army of the four New England colonies only. Except the few hundred riflemen from Pennsylvania, Maryland, and Virginia who joined him in July and August, 1775, no troops from the other colonies came to reinforce him. When the movement against Canada was begun it was evident that additional troops would be needed. On July 25, the Congress resolved that "a body of forces not exceeding five thousand be kept up in the New York department,"[2] but no specific plan for raising them was provided. That was left to the New York Provincial Congress. Not before October did the Continental Congress begin to plan for and provide a real Continental army. On the 2nd of that month it authorized a committee to go to Cambridge and consult with Washington on the subject.[3] On November 4 the report of that committee was considered, and it was resolved that "the new army intended to lie before Boston" should consist of 20,372 men, officers included, enlisted "to the last day of December, 1776."[4]

It appears that Washington had agreed to a one-year term of enlistment on the advice of a council of his general officers, who thought it would be "impossible to get the men to enlist for the continuance of the War," [5] but it also appears that the one-year term was contrary to his own judgment. In a letter to Joseph Reed dated February 1, 1776, he enlarged upon "the evils arising from short, or even any limited enlistment." It took, he said, two or three months to acquaint new men with their duty, and even a longer time to bring them into "such a subordinate way of thinking as is necessary for a soldier." By that time the end of the enlistment period is in sight, and "you are obliged to relax in your discipline, in order as it were to curry favour with them" so as to induce them to reenlist. And "with every new set you have the same trouble to encounter." The disadvantages of the one-year period were so great that it would be better "to give a bounty of 20, 30 or even 40 Dollars to every man who will Inlist for the whole time." [6]

He rehearsed this argument in a letter to the Congress dated February 9, 1776, pointing out that the apprehension of his troops leaving him on December 31 had driven Montgomery to his fatal attack on Quebec "under disadvantageous circumstances." He also referred to his own experience in having to dissolve his army at the end of 1775, the evils of which he forcefully particularized. Under such a system, he said, "you never can have a well Disciplined army." [7]

Washington's arguments were and are cogent and convincing to one with an open and unprejudiced mind, but the collective mind of the Americans of that period was not unprejudiced. In an overwhelming majority they were of British extraction. Their ancestors had, to a large extent, left England at the time when the Stuart kings were seeking to create a standing army to oppress the people and deprive them of civil and religious liberty. Cromwell had defeated the Stuarts, only to use his own troops as instruments of tyranny. By both sides of the civil conflict in England, the idea of a standing army was hated and dreaded, and that dread and hatred was an inheritance of their descendants in America. An army for the duration of the war was at this time impossible of acceptance by the general run of the colonists.

But the Congress had not awaited the report of its committee before going ahead. On October 9, 1775, it had "recommended to the Convention of New Jersey, that it immediately raise, at the expense of the Continent two Battalions, consisting of eight companies each, and each company of 68 privates." [8] Three days later a similar "recommendation" for one battalion was made to Pennsylvania, and calls were soon after made on North Carolina for six battalions, on Pennsylvania for four more, on Delaware for one, on Virginia for nine, on Rhode Island for two, on Massachusetts for six, on New Hampshire for two, on South Carolina for five, including one regiment of artillery and one of rangers, on Maryland for two, and on Georgia for one regiment of rangers. It also requested a "German battalion" of eight companies, four to be raised in Pennsylvania and four in Maryland.[9]

Slowly and gradually building up the Continental army, the Congress sought in addition to provide temporary additional reinforcements for "the army at New York." On June 3, 1776, Massachusetts, Connecticut, New York, and New Jersey were called upon for 13,800 militiamen. As a defense for "the middle colonies" a Flying Camp was to be established. Ten thousand militia were called for, 6,000 from Pennsylvania, 3,400 from Maryland, and 600 from Delaware. Perth Amboy in New Jersey was chosen as the site of the camp. Without going fully into the history of this attempt, it may be said that it was a failure. There was an insufficient response to the appeal, and the militia that did respond made but a short stay. Two Continental regiments—one from Maryland, the other from Delaware—were called upon to strengthen this force, but they remained only a few days before they were sent on to New York. By the end of the year, the Flying Camp passed out of existence.[10]

The regiments of the Continental army were to consist of eight companies of 76 privates each, with the usual officers, noncommissioned officers, drum, and fife. The pay and provisions were sufficiently generous according to the standards of the time. The pay for the officers ranged from $50 a month for a colonel to $13⅓ for an ensign. Privates were to receive $6⅔; but out of this sum there were stoppages for clothing furnished them at the rate of $1⅔ per month. Their uniforms were "as much as possible" to be brown, with different regimental facings. They were to receive "good firelocks with bayonets," each musket having a ¾ inch bore, the barrel 3 feet, 8 inches long, the bayonet 18 inches. Their rations were prescribed in detail: "1 lb. of beef, or ¾ lb. pork, or 1 lb. of salt fish . . . 1 lb. of bread or flour" daily, also a pint of milk and a quart of spruce beer or cider per day, with a weekly allowance of peas, beans, or other vegetables, rice or Indian meal, candles, and soap.[11] It needed hardly be said that these provisions for uniforms, arms, and rations, made in a hopeful spirit were seldom realized in fact.

In uniforms, there was little uniformity. Many of the regiments were supplied at the time of enlistment according to their own fancy. The soldiers of Delaware's regiment, for instance, were handsomely turned out in blue coats, faced and lined with red, white waistcoats, buckskin breeches, white woolen stockings, and black spatterdashes or gaiters. They wore small, round, blackjacked leather hats without a visor, but with a peaked front, somewhat after the fashion of the taller hats of the British grenadiers. They were armed with fine English muskets "lately imported," complete with bayonets.[12] But that regiment was said to be "the best uniformed and equipped in the army of 1776." [13] Smallwood's Maryland regiment is frequently described as arrayed in scarlet coats faced with buff; but, although that was its dress uniform at home, only the officers wore it in the Long Island battle, the privates appearing in brown hunting shirts. In the rest of the army military uniforms were rather the exception than the rule. The riflemen usually wore the conventional hunting shirt of gray or brown tow cloth, though Miles's men wore black.[14] The standards for muskets fixed by the Congress were not achieved at this time, nor were they ever in the whole course of the war. They differed in caliber, greatly to the disadvantage of the troops, since no standard size of bullets or cartridges could be maintained. Also bayonets were scarce, and continued to be so to the war's end.

Washington was impressed with the importance of holding New York against the British army. "It is the Place that we must use every Endeavour to keep from them," he wrote to Brigadier General Lord Stirling, who had been left in command there on General Charles Lee's departure for the South early in 1776. "For should they get that Town, and the Command of the North River, they can stop the Intercourse between the northern and southern Colonies, upon which depends the Safety of America." It would also give them "an easy pass into Canada." Its retention by the Americans was of "vast importance," of "infinite importance." [15] So, in spite of the great difficulty of fortifying it against "a powerful sea armament," as Lee had pointed out on his first arrival in New York, Washington concentrated most of his forces there, and busied himself exceedingly with its defensive works.

The town was small in extent, occupying about a square mile at the southern tip of Manhattan Island. Lee, who had been sent down to supervise its defenses, had planned to erect in and about it an elaborate system of forts, redoubts, batteries, entrenchments, and barricades. As they played no part in the actual battle for its possession, they need not be described here, except to note that numerous batteries were to be erected on both sides of the North and East rivers to prevent, or at least to hinder, the passage of enemy vessels to the northward of the town. Lee's opinion early in 1776 was that New York could not be indefinitely defended against the British, but that the British could be made to pay for possession of it.

He had had at first only 1,700 men to work on these extensive defenses. But before he left in March others had come in from Connecticut, New

Jersey, and the outlying districts of New York, and Stirling carried on with them. All the men of the town, white and black, were called out, and a prodigious amount of pick-and-shovel work was done by them and by the troops from Boston when they arrived. But, to defend the town, it was necessary to go beyond its limits and the limits of Manhattan Island.

Directly across the East River lay Long Island, and particularly the little village of Brooklyn and its environs. Brooklyn Heights rose a hundred feet above the water. A recollection of the domination of Boston by Dorchester Heights and of the effect of their occupation by the Americans in making that town untenable was not needed to convince Lee of the importance of these others in the scheme of defense. He had proposed to secure them by "a post or retrenched encampment" [16] for 3,000 men. This work was immediately begun.

The ground chosen was a broad, irregularly shaped peninsula facing the East River and lying between Wallabout Bay on the northeast and Gowanus Cove on the southwest. Those two bodies of water indented the sides of the peninsula, making a neck of land about a mile and a half wide. An irregularly curved zigzag line of entrenchments was drawn from the bay to Gowanus Creek. At the upper end Fort Putnam, a redoubt with five guns, was erected. From a point near the fort, the entrenchments turned at a right angle to the main line and ran to the bay. From the fort, at intervals along the main line to Gowanus Creek, there were built redoubts called, in order, Fort Greene, the Oblong Redoubt, and Fort Box. Each of these works was armed with a few guns.

Within the lines and nearer the river was Fort Stirling, armed with eight guns. On Red Hook, the extreme westerly corner of the fortified peninsula, was Fort Defiance, mounting four 18-pounders and intended to prevent the passage of ships between that point and Governor's Island. There were also two other small works of minor importance. In all they mounted twenty-nine guns, most of them of iron, old and honeycombed with rust.

These forts and the main line of earthworks were ditched and fraised with sharpened stakes set into their embankments, crossing each other and projecting outward at an angle, their points breast-high. The main line was also defended by a broad area of abatis, felled trees, their butts embedded in the ground, their pointed limbs thrust outward. The work of constructing all these defenses, in the town as well as on Long Island, was performed under the supervision of Brigadier General Lord Stirling, a vigorous and energetic officer.

William Alexander, "Earl of Stirling," was not an earl, nor was he a nobleman of any degree. His father, James Stirling, had fled to America in

1716 to escape the consequences of his activities in the cause of the Old Pretender in the year before, and had attained some eminence in his new home as a lawyer, politician, and scientist. William, his only son, was born in 1726. He had engaged in business profitably, and had served as a major of colonial forces in the French and Indian War. His father claimed to be heir to the lapsed title of James Alexander, 1st Earl of Stirling, through some degree of cousinship, but had taken no steps to assert his right on the death of that nobleman in 1737.

When his father died, in 1756, William laid legal claim to the earldom. When his case was first tried in Edinburgh, a jury found in his favor, and he was proclaimed earl at the Market Cross. The decision was reversed in the House of Lords, but he continued to assert his right to the title, and was so addressed in America throughout his life.

In person Stirling "showed a burly figure, and a fresh-coloured visage." [17] He was fond of sociability, and his detractors accused him of undue fondness for the bottle; but it does not appear that this ever lessened his efficiency in his military duties, at least not until evening. He was conspicuous for personal bravery in action. The officers on Long Island gave him "the character of as brave a man as ever lived." [18] He prided himself on his acquaintance with the technical side of his profession. Early in the war he was noted for maintaining a harsh and captious discipline. However, he "shook off the martinet, and became a practical soldier of considerable value in the field. . . . there was sure to be plenty of tough and steady fighting in the quarter towards which Stirling and his division had been ordered." [19]

At the time of Washington's arrival in New York, his army there consisted of twenty-five regiments, numbering about 9,000 rank and file. These he divided into five brigades, under Heath, Spencer, Sullivan, Greene, and Stirling. But, before the end of April, Sullivan was ordered to Canada with six regiments as has been mentioned. The rest were rearranged in four brigades, three of them posted on Manhattan Island, one on Long Island. With such of the militia as had responded to the call of the Congress on June 3, with the return of what was left of Sullivan's detachment, and with the arrival of other Continental regiments from the Flying Camp, the army had been increased to a paper strength of about 28,500 of all ranks by the late summer of 1776. Of these, about 19,000 were present and fit for duty, but the larger part of them were raw recruits, undisciplined and inexperienced in warfare, and militia, never to be assuredly relied upon.[20]

A new arrangement divided this force again into five divisions before the Battle of Long Island. James Clinton's brigade of four Massachusetts regiments, John Morin Scott's four regiments from New York, and John

Fellows's four regiments from Massachusetts made up Israel Putnam's division. The second division, under William Heath, contained Thomas Mifflin's brigade of two Pennsylvania regiments, two regiments from Massachusetts, and one from Rhode Island, also George Clinton's brigade of five New York regiments. Joseph Spencer's division included the brigade of Samuel Holden Parsons—four regiments from Connecticut and one from Massachusetts—and James Wadsworth's seven Connecticut regiments. John Sullivan, who had returned from Canada, commanded a division composed of Lord Stirling's brigade—one Maryland regiment, one from Delaware, a Pennsylvania rifle regiment, a Pennsylvania musketry battalion, and three corps of Pennsylvania militia—and Alexander McDougall's brigade, two regiments from New York, one from Connecticut, and one of artificers. Nathanael Greene had in his division John Nixon's brigade of three Massachusetts regiments, two from Rhode Island, and one from Pennsylvania, Nathaniel Heard's brigade of five New Jersey regiments, Oliver Wolcott's brigade of twelve regiments of Connecticut militia, and Nathaniel Woodhull's two regiments of Long Island militia. Colonel Henry Knox commanded the artillery.

Up to a short time before the battle, Putnam's, Spencer's, and Sullivan's divisions, with the Connecticut militiamen, say 20,000 in all, were posted in and about the city. Heath's division was separated into several parts; Mifflin's brigade of 2,400 men was on Manhattan Island at Fort Washington, and George Clinton's 1,800 were at Kingsbridge. Two regiments of Greene's division were on Governor's Island. Greene himself, with the rest, fewer than 4,000, was on Long Island.[21]

Long before Howe evacuated Boston, it became apparent even to the British government that the plans for subduing the American colonies had been conceived on too small a scale; Howe's 7,000 men were not enough to do the job. By October, 1775, the plans had been enlarged to call for a total British army of 55,000 men, and an addition of 12,000 men to the navy. Recruiting was begun in all parts of the British Isles; but, as an English historian says, there was in Britain "hardly any enthusiasm for the war among the classes from which soldiers were drawn." Ireland was combed, but the Irish were enjoying a year of unprecedented agricultural prosperity. Food was plentiful; hunger, the usual incentive to enlistment, was unknown. Scotland showed better results. There were many land-hungry Highlanders who hoped to appease their desires in the vast acres of a conquered America. But on the whole the enlistments were not enough. It was necessary to look elsewhere.[22]

The petty princes of Germany had soldiers for rent. From the Duke of Brunswick, the Landgrave of Hesse-Kassel, and the Prince of Waldeck, England hired at this time 17,775 men to be shipped to America, where they were all called by one hated name, Hessians. Others were added in the course of the war to a total number of 29,875.[23]

On June 25 three warships arrived in lower New York Bay, bringing General Howe from Halifax to the scene of his next conflict—for him, more fortunate. He hoped to use New York as a base for the conquest of the colonies. He had only a small force, but it was the forerunner of a greater soon to come. Four days later its real magnitude began to develop. Forty-five more ships hove in sight, and in another day eighty-two appeared. One hundred and thirty ships of war and transports disembarked 9,300 soldiers on Staten Island. But this was not all. Admiral Lord Howe, brother of the general, followed with a fleet of one hundred fifty sail, full of fighting men fresh from England. On July 12 they joined the others. A little later Admiral Sir Peter Parker, with nine warships and thirty transports bearing 2,500 men under General Henry Clinton and General Lord Cornwallis, came limping northward from their defeat at Charleston. Commodore Hotham brought six men-of-war and twenty-eight transports on August 12, and disembarked 2,600 of the Guards and 8,000 Hessians.[24]

In the British camp on Staten Island, across the Narrows from Long Island, there were twenty-seven regiments of the line, four battalions of light infantry, four of grenadiers, two of the Guards, three brigades of artillery, one regiment of light dragoons, and 8,000 Hessians, with Major General Howe and Generals Clinton, Lord Percy, Lord Cornwallis, and von Heister, all of them skilled in the science of war and the art of command. It was an army of 32,000 trained, disciplined, professional soldiers, completely armed, fully equipped, abundantly supplied—the greatest expeditionary force Great Britain had ever sent out from its shores. It was supported by a fleet of ten ships of the line, twenty frigates armed with 1,200 guns, and hundreds of transports, manned by more than 10,000 seamen. Britain had drawn from her war chest the staggering sum of £850,000.

To oppose this mighty force the Americans had 19,000 largely untrained, undisciplined, untried amateur soldiers, poorly armed, meagerly equipped and supplied, led by an amateur commander in chief, who was supported by amateur officers. They were backed by not a single warship nor a single transport, and their war chest was in large part a printing press in Philadelphia emitting issues of paper dollars, worth whatever one could induce another to give for them and diminishing in value day by day. To be sure they now had something very specific for which to fight, because independence had been declared early in July.

To make matters worse for the Americans, their inadequate force was divided between New York and Long Island with the broad expanse of the East River separating them, and with no means whatever of keeping open a line of communication if British warships were interposed.

In their camp the British soldiers were unseen by the Americans; but their fleet was only too visible. "Onlookers gazed with awe on a pageant such as America had never seen before—five hundred dark hulls, forests of masts, a network of spars and ropes and a gay display of flying pennants. There were ships of the line with frowning sides, three tiers of guns and high forecastles; there were graceful frigates, alert and speedy . . . tenders and galleys to land the thousands of men from the unwieldy transports." [25] It is no wonder that panic fear was in the hearts of half of New York's people, and gleams of joy were in the eyes of the other half, who were opposed to independence and who supported the British.

The first definitely threatening move was made by two warships, the *Phoenix* of forty-four guns and the *Rose* of twenty-eight. On July 12, with two tenders, they stood in toward the town. In the American camp the alarm was sounded; the troops took their posts. As the ships swept by the town on their way up the North River, the batteries there and those on Paulus Hook—now Jersey City—opened fire. The ships replied with broadsides.[26] Throughout the town there was a mad panic. Washington described its effect on the women: "When the men-of-war passed up the river, the shrieks and cries of the poor creatures, running every way with their children, were truly distressing, and I fear they will have an unhappy effect on the ears and minds of our young and inexperienced soldiery." [27]

Past battery after battery, batteries that were supposed to prevent their passage, the ships held their course to Tappan Bay, forty miles above the town. Fireships were sent against them, with no success. Six days later, they came back, running the same gantlet and anchored again in the Narrows, practically unharmed.[28]

It seems that the whole fleet, or any part of it, might have landed troops at any time on the north end of Manhattan Island and cut off the whole American army from any possible retreat, to bag it at leisure. Nothing of the sort was done, however, and, from the time of the first arrival of the British, what form the attack would take, whether against New York or against Long Island, remained an open question, puzzling and harassing to the American command. It was at last answered.

C H A P T E R 1 6

Long Island: The Preliminaries

At dawn on the 22nd of August three British frigates, *Phoenix, Rose* and *Greyhound,* and two bomb ketches, *Carcass* and *Thunder*, took station in Gravesend Bay, Long Island, about a mile east of the Narrows. Another frigate, *Rainbow,* anchored in the Narrows off Denyse Point, the part of Long Island nearest to Staten Island. Seventy-five flatboats, eleven bateaux, and two row-galleys, built for the occasion and manned by sailors from the fleet, were assembled at Staten Island, and 15,000 soldiers, fully equipped for active service, and forty fieldpieces were drawn up before the British camp.[1]

At eight o'clock in the morning a British advance corps, consisting of four battalions of light infantry and Preston's 17th Light Dragoons, and a reserve, four battalions of grenadiers, the 33rd and the 42nd, or Black Watch Regiment, and Colonel Carl von Donop's corps of Hessian grenadiers and jägers, 4,000 men in all under the command of Clinton and Cornwallis, embarked. In ten well ordered divisions they were rowed across to Denyse Point. Under cover of the guns of the *Rainbow* they went ashore and were drawn up in military formation. The next trip of the boats brought 5,000 more men to a point below the others, which was under the guns of the three frigates and the two bomb ketches. By noon 15,000 men had been landed without opposition, mishap, or delay.[2] Three days later, on the 25th, they were joined by two brigades of Hessian grenadiers under General Philip von Heister, "a tough old soldier of the Seven Years War." [3] These were ferried over standing in the boats, "with muskets sloped and in column of march, preserving the well-considered pomp of German discipline." [4]

"The Soldiers & Sailors seemed as merry as in a Holiday, and regaled themselves with the fine apples, which hung everywhere upon the Trees in great abundance." [5]

There was no American opposition whatever to any of these landings. Colonel Edward Hand and 200 men of the 1st Pennsylvania Continental Regiment had been in camp in an outpost near Denyse Point. On the first alarm they marched toward New Utrecht, "to watch the movements of the enemy," who were soon discovered approaching them on the way to Flatbush. Hand turned, and marched parallel with the enemy advance guard, but at a respectful distance from it, "in the edge of the woods." Finding "it impracticable for so small a force to attack them," [6] he sent a detachment ahead to burn all the standing grain and slaughter as many cattle as possible, while his main body returned to its camp, gathered up its baggage, and after some light skirmishing, took up a position on Prospect Hill.

Cornwallis, with the reserve, ten battalions of light infantry and von Donop's Hessians, possessed the village of Flatbush and camped there.[7] The main body encamped nearer the shore, along the road running from near the bay in the vicinity of Gravesend to New Utrecht. Its camp extended from that village on the west to Flatlands village on the east.[8]

The British now occupied a broad, low plain extending from the shore northward from four to six miles and eastward a greater distance. In it lay the four villages named. Looking north from their camp, the invaders faced the most prominent feature of the terrain, which was to be their battleground.

Stretching northeast from near the waterside at Gowanus Cove nearly all the way across the island and forming a barrier between the British army and the Brooklyn defenses, ran a ridge or range of hills, varying in height from one hundred to one hundred fifty feet. It was called the Heights of Guan, or Guian. On the southerly side, fronting the British, the rugged face of the heights rose abruptly forty to eighty feet from the plain, then ascended less precipitously to the full height of the ridge. On the northerly side the ground sloped more gradually to the lower land beyond. The entire surface of the ridge was covered by dense woods and thickets penetrable only with difficulty by men on foot, entirely impassable by horse-drawn artillery or by troops in formation except at four points where roads led through natural depressions or "passes." One of the roads circumvented the westerly end of the main ridge; the others went through at different points toward the east.[9]

The first road, to the left of the British, starting at Gravesend ran westerly through New Utrecht to a point near the shore of the Narrows, then turned north parallel with the shore, finally quite close to the edge of Gowanus Cove, and so around the westerly end of the ridge on its way to Brooklyn. It was called the Gowanus Road. The second ran from Flatbush almost due north, through Flatbush Pass, then split in two, both branches coming finally to Brooklyn. The third road took off from the second just before Flatbush Pass, swung to the east, then to the north, and ran through Bedford Pass to the village of Bedford, whence a straight road ran to Brooklyn. These three roads accounted for more than three miles of the length of the ridge between the westerly and easterly passes. The fourth ran northeast from Flatlands to Jamaica Pass, nearly three miles east of Bedford Pass.[10] These four passes, with their respective roads, were obviously to be defended in force if any attempt was made to hold the ridge against an advance from the south.

After the arrival of the British on Staten Island there were changes in the command of the American troops on Long Island. Major General Nathanael Greene fell ill of a fever and took to his bed in New York. On August 20 Washington turned the command of the troops about Brooklyn over to Major General John Sullivan. This change was unfortunate, because Greene, a much abler general officer, had a thorough knowledge of the Long Island terrain, while Sullivan knew little of the lay of the land. Still more unfortunate was another change, made on the 24th, by which Major General Israel Putnam superseded Sullivan in general command on Long Island, Sullivan being retained there as a subordinate.[11] Putnam, who knew practically nothing of the topography of the island, was for other reasons totally unfit for the controlling position into which he had been put.[12]

There were changes in the forces defending the Brooklyn position as well. Immediately on receiving news in New York of the landing of the British on the 22nd, Washington sent over Miles's Pennsylvania riflemen, Atlee's Pennsylvania musketry battalion, Chester's and Silliman's newly raised Connecticut regiments, Lasher's New York Independent companies, and Drake's New York minutemen, about 1,800 men in all.[13] There were consequently about 5,800 men in and about the Brooklyn lines; but more than two-thirds of these were militia, not dependable even behind entrenchments and totally unreliable in a stand-up fight in an open field. Even the loyalty of the New York and Long Island contingents was seriously suspected.[14]

Although Washington knew of the landing of some of the enemy on Long Island, he was led to think, even as late as the 24th, that they amounted to no more than eight or nine thousand, a minor part of the whole force. Therefore, expecting an attack on "our works on the Island and this city at the same time,"[15] he retained three-quarters of his whole army on the New York side, including many of the better regiments. Any respectable intelligence service, of which he had at this time almost none, could have told him that the major part of the British army and all its best general officers were on Long Island, and that without doubt the grand attack, the only immediate attack, was to be made on Brooklyn. Nevertheless he did send over other reinforcements, Parsons's Connecticut Continentals, Lutz's Berks County (Pennsylvania) militia, Hay's militia from Lancaster County, and Kachlein's Berks riflemen, perhaps fewer than 2,000 in all. These Pennsylvania militiamen were about half of Stirling's brigade, and Stirling crossed with them, leaving his best two, his only thoroughly dependable regiments, Smallwood's Maryland and Haslet's Delaware Continentals, in camp on the Manhattan side.[16]

Washington expected an immediate attack after the British had settled themselves on Long Island; but Howe was in no hurry. There was brisk skirmishing in front of Flatbush Pass on the 23rd. At the same time von Donop's Hessians made a move against Bedford Pass, evidently to try it out; but they met a sharp fire from Hand's corps, which advanced to meet the enemy, drove them back, and burned some houses they had held. They returned in force and regained their former position, the Americans retiring to their post on the ridge. From the ridge on the following day the Americans harassed the Flatbush camp with round shot and grape from their fieldpieces. But the heavier artillery of the Hessians soon silenced them. There were few casualties on either side.[17]

In the afternoon of the 26th Cornwallis, leaving the Black Watch and the Hessians in the Flatbush camp, moved the rest of his troops to Flatlands village, where the British headquarters had been established. The Hessian General von Heister, who had landed the day before with two brigades, took over the command at Flatbush.[18] This movement to Flatlands might have indicated to an intelligent observer that neither the Flatbush nor the Bedford Pass was to be the scene of the main attack, because it shifted the weight of the British force away from them; but none of the Americans on the ridge seems to have understood its meaning.

By this time, however, Washington had come over from New York. At last he realized that the strength of the British was on Long Island, and that "the grand push" was to be against Brooklyn.[19] He ordered more men over, Lieutenant Colonel Thomas Knowlton with 100 Connecticut Continentals, two or three independent companies from Maryland, and, most important, Smallwood's Maryland and Haslet's Delaware Continental regiments, the best equipped and (the Delawares) the largest in the army. By a singular coincidence the Smallwood and Haslet regiments arrived under command of their majors, Mordecai Gist for Maryland and Thomas McDonough for Delaware; their colonels and lieutenant colonels had been detailed to sit in a court-martial in New York on that day. Now Stirling's brigade was complete in its camp outside the Brooklyn lines. By these additions, Putnam's command on Long Island was built up to about 7,000 men fit for duty.[20] On the evening of the 26th the coast, or Gowanus, road was guarded by Hand's 200 of the 1st Pennsylvania Regiment, half of Atlee's Pennsylvania musketry battalion, some part of Lutz's Pennsylvanians, and certain detachments of New York troops, perhaps 550 in all. On their left, more than a mile and a half distant at the Flatbush Pass, the center of the line, were Daniel Hitchcock's Rhode Island and Moses Little's Massachusetts Continental regiments, commanded, respectively, by their lieutenant colonels, Elias Cornell and William Henshaw, and Knowlton's detachment of Connecticut Continentals, perhaps fewer than 1,000 in all. They held a rude fortification of felled trees, mounting three guns and one howitzer.

At the Bedford Pass about a mile to the east were stationed Colonel Samuel Wyllys and his Connecticut Continentals and Colonel John Chester's Connecticut State Regiment, under command of Lieutenant Colonel Solomon Wills, about 800 men, with three guns and a fortification like that at Flatbush Pass; also Colonel Samuel Miles with about 400 Pennsylvania riflemen. Thus there were probably fewer than 2,800 men in all posted along more than three miles of the densely wooded ridge in separate detachments, with no communication between them except by sentinels stationed at intervals. It was a long line and a thin line; pierced at any point, it must give way. Facing them on the plain below were seven times their number; in military efficiency, man for man, one might say fifteen times their number.

But what about Jamaica Pass, three miles to the east of the Bedford road? It was guarded, too—by a mounted patrol of five young militia officers. While the right of this long line rested on Gowanus Cove, its left was in the air.[21]

CHAPTER 17

Long Island: The Battle

At about midnight on the 26th of August, Hand's Pennsylvanians, who had been on constant duty for four days picketing the American right, were relieved by a detail of Kachlein's and Hay's troops under Major Edward Burd. Hand's men, "not having lain down the whole time and almost dead with fatigue," [1] retired to the fortified lines to rest. Now all was quiet along the American front; but on the British side something was happening.

At the far left of the British positions, near the Narrows, lay Major General James Grant with his two brigades, 5,000 strong.[2] In the center von Heister's Hessians and the Scottish Black Watch still occupied Flatbush. But the main body of the British army had been massed at Flatlands. All these were astir that night.

At nine o'clock in the evening a column of march was formed at the principal post at Flatlands. General Henry Clinton led the van, made up of the 17th Light Dragoons and a brigade of light infantry. General Lord Cornwallis came next with the reserve—that is to say, the 1st Brigade of four battalions of grenadiers, two regiments of foot, and the 71st (Fraser's Highlanders), with fourteen pieces of field artillery. After them fell in General William Howe and General Lord Percy with the main body—the Guards and three brigades of infantry comprising twelve regiments, with ten guns. Bringing up the rear were one regiment and the baggage train with its guard and four guns. In this column were 10,000 soldiers and twenty-eight pieces of artillery.[3]

Led by three Tories from Flatbush, this formidable array set out on the road to the Jamaica Pass. Proceeding with the utmost caution, it left the

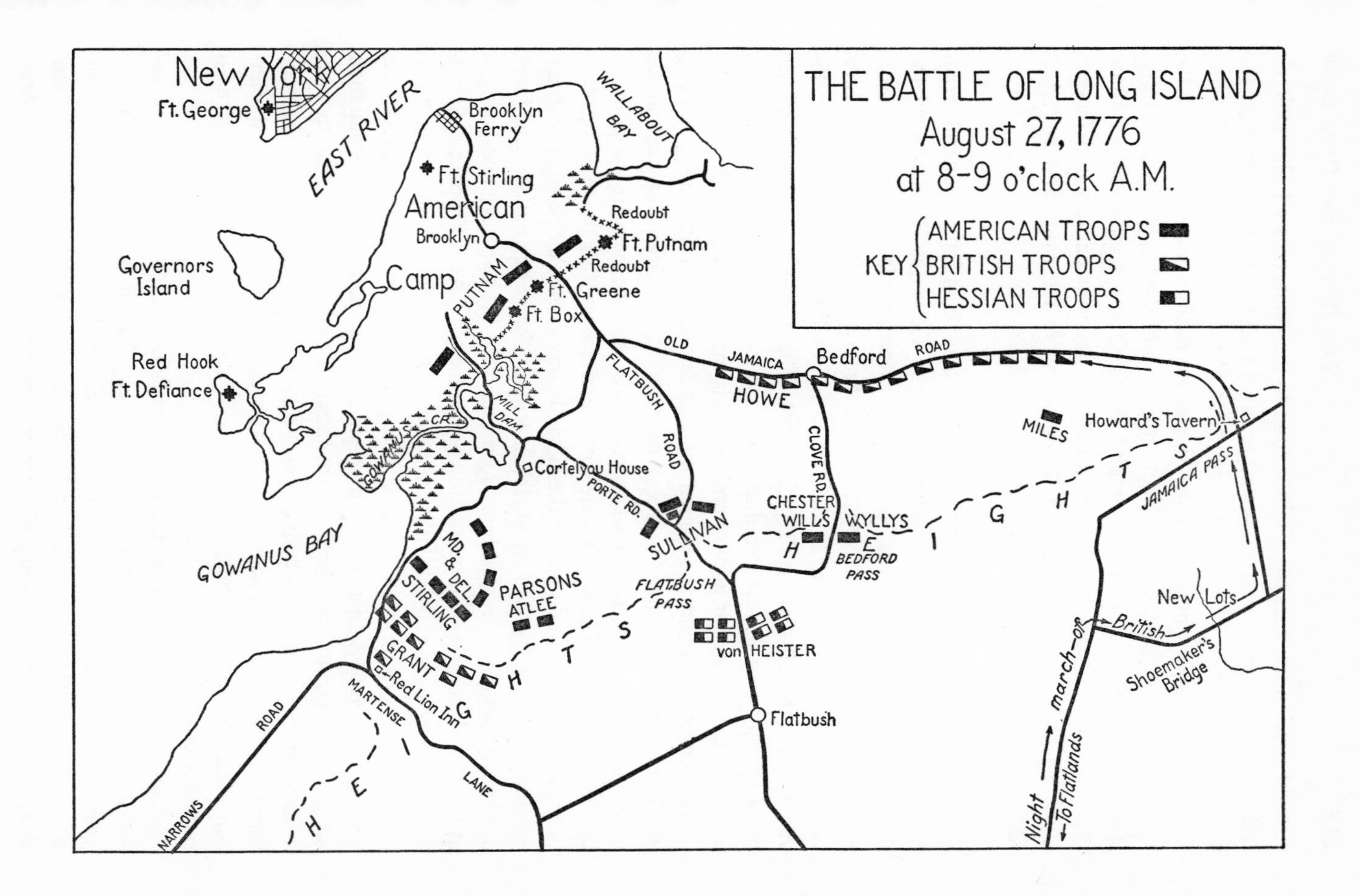
THE BATTLE OF LONG ISLAND
August 27, 1776
at 8-9 o'clock A.M.
KEY
AMERICAN TROOPS
BRITISH TROOPS
HESSIAN TROOPS
New York
Ft. George
East River
Brooklyn Ferry
Wallabout Bay
Ft. Stirling
American Camp
Brooklyn
Redoubt
Ft. Putnam
Redoubt
Ft. Greene
Ft. Box
Putnam
Governors Island
Red Hook
Ft. Defiance
Gowanus Cr.
Mill Dam
Old Jamaica Road
Bedford
Howe
Flatbush Road
Cortelyou House
Porte Rd.
Sullivan
Clove Rd.
Chester
Wills
Wyllys
Bedford Pass
Miles
Howard's Tavern
Jamaica Pass
Gowanus Bay
Md. & Del.
Stirling
Parsons
Atlee
Flatbush Pass
von Heister
Grant
Red Lion Inn
Flatbush
Martense Lane
Narrows Road
New Lots
British
Shoemaker's Bridge
Night march of
To Flatlands
HEIGHTS
HEIGHTS
HEIGHTS

straight road to the pass for a minor road to the right, crossed Shoemaker's Bridge along a narrow causeway, and reached Halfway House, very near the entrance to the pass, between two and three o'clock in the morning. Having made this circuitous approach, the van came around into the rear of the patrol of five men posted there. Captain Evelyn of the King's Own infantry, leading the advance, surrounded and captured the hapless five without resistance. From them it was learned that the pass was entirely undefended. Clinton's army marched through this gateway in the ridge and halted at dawn for rest and refreshment.[4]

Some time after the departure of the British flanking force, General Grant and his 5,000 men began an advance up the Gowanus Road toward the American right. Grant's task was largely to occupy the Americans while the main British attack developed on the American left. At the Red Lion Inn, where the road swung to the left to follow the shore line closely, his van came upon Major Burd's picket post. There was an exchange of fire before Burd's men started to fall back toward the ridge; but in the confusion and darkness the major and a number of his men were captured.[5]

The sound of the firing alarmed the detachment guarding that pass, and word was sent to Putnam in the American camp. Grant, in accordance with the general plan, had not continued his advance beyond the point of the first encounter. There was time for a reinforcement of the main position of the Americans on that end of the ridge. It was three o'clock when Putnam got the news. He hurried to Stirling's tent in the camp outside the lines, awakened him, and directed him "to march with the two regiments nearest at hand" to meet the enemy and "to repulse them." [6] As it happened, Smallwood's Marylands and Haslet's Delawares lay nearest. Responding "with alacrity" [7] to Stirling's call, these untried young soldiers less than two weeks with the army, less than a day in their new camp, and fresh from their homes, their farms, and their shops, marched out in the darkness to meet 5,000 British veterans. Three-o'clock-in-the-morning courage is proverbially the rarest kind. Dawn came while they were on their way. It was noted afterward that the sun that morning "rose with a red and angry glare," [8] as if portending coming evils.

About half a mile short of the Red Lion Inn, Stirling came upon Colonel Atlee with 120 of his Pennsylvania Musketry battalion, who had been on guard at that point,[9] and Lieutenant Colonel Joel Clark leading Huntington's regiment of Connecticut Continentals. Grant's van, again in motion, was in sight, marching directly toward them. Stirling ordered Atlee forward to hold the enemy until he could form his troops on the ridge.[10]

Atlee took a position in an orchard beside the road at the foot of the west end of the ridge. Although his men had never before faced an enemy in battle, they held their ground and exchanged fire with Grant's advance until Stirling had selected his ground and drawn up his troops. Then they retired to join him.

The ground chosen was on a slope running up from the Gowanus Road to a wood at the top of that end of the ridge. Because of the lay of the land and the position of the road, Stirling's line was most peculiarly shaped like a V. On the right branch, as viewed from behind, the Marylanders were drawn up; on the left, Haslet's Delaware regiment.[11]

The right wing of the line rested on a marsh at the foot of the hill; the left had no support. The two parts of Atlee's regiment—the men originally on guard there and those now newly arrived—having been joined together, Stirling posted them and Huntington's regiment in the woods on his unprotected left. Kachlein's Pennsylvania riflemen had now come up, and he divided them, placing half behind a hedge in front of his right and the rest in front of the woods near Atlee.[12] This extreme left, somewhat separated from Stirling's own troops, was put under command of Brigadier General Samuel Holden Parsons of Connecticut, who was early on the scene.

The shape of Stirling's line created a singular condition, in that his extreme left was nearer his extreme right than either was to his center. Because of this anomaly, a part of the Delaware battalion, held in reserve on the end of one wing, was called upon in the course of the fighting to meet and repulse the advance of the 2nd British Grenadiers attacking the end of the other wing.

Another remarkable thing about Stirling's formation was that, instead of letting his men break ranks and take cover, he drew them up in the open in formal order, and, in the words of one of them, offered the British "battle in the true English taste." [13] So in line they stood, to quote Haslet, "upwards of four hours, with a firm, determined countenance, in close array, their colors flying, the enemy's artillery playing on them all the time." [14]

Their position was precarious. In their rear was a marsh bordering Gowanus Creek. They had no connecting support on the left except Parson's command at some distance, and beyond that none at all. On their far right was the bay commanded by the British fleet, and in front was Grant's division outnumbering them four to one, for Grant soon brought up the 42nd Highlanders, drawn from von Heister's corps at Flatbush, and two companies of American Loyalists. He had then about 7,000 men facing not more than 1,600 Americans. In reply to the American challenge, he drew up his troops as if for immediate attack. One brigade was extended in a double line in front of the Americans' right, the rest in a single line against their left. The extent of this latter line threatened to overlap the Americans. Stirling accordingly desired Parsons to move Atlee's and Huntington's regiments to a point in the woods farther to the left, leaving Kachlein's riflemen nearer at hand. This shift, though necessary to meet Grant's tactics, separated the two bodies by a considerable distance, and left Stirling, with not much more than a thousand men, to oppose Grant.[15]

Parsons's troops, filing off to the left, saw before them "a hill of clear ground," which seemed to be a desirable position from which to watch the enemy's movements. As they were approaching within forty yards of its top, they were surprised by a volley of musketry from the 23rd and 44th British regiments and a part of the 17th Light Dragoons, who had penetrated the woods. They wavered and fell back in some confusion; but most of them were soon rallied, and they advanced again with somewhat surprising coolness. Their fire was so effective that the enemy retired, leaving twelve dead and five wounded. The American loss in this preliminary encounter included Atlee's lieutenant colonel, Caleb Parry, and a few minor casualties. Parsons's contingent held the hill.[16]

Within half an hour this detachment was again attacked by the same British regiments; but, partly under cover of trees and fences, partly in the open, it delivered such a heavy fire that again the enemy were repulsed. In the engagement the British Lieutenant Colonel Grant was killed. Parsons's men exhausted their ammunition, and would have been obliged to retreat but for the timely arrival of a new supply.[17] A third attack was threatened, but the enemy did not carry it out, contenting themselves with holding the Americans' attention at a safe distance. As a matter of fact the strategy of the whole battle did not call for a full-scale assault upon the American right at this time. These several little engagements, though hot, were intended merely to hold the Americans' attention while the larger plan for the battle was being worked out.

Returning now to Stirling, and going back somewhat in time, we find his men in ordered line of battle as first drawn up, and Stirling addressing them. Recalling that he had chanced to be in the gallery of the House of Commons when General Grant, then a member, had made his famous boast that, with 5,000 men, he could march from one end of the American continent to the other, Stirling told his men: "He may have 5,000 with him now. We are not so many. But I think we are enough to prevent his advancing further on his march over the continent than that mill-pond." [18]

It is noteworthy that this was the first time that American and British forces ever met in formal array in the open field. It may also be remarked that Stirling's formation was the only one on the American side that was preserved throughout the battle.

Grant's next move was to advance a small body of light infantry within 150 yards of Stirling's right. Protected by the trees and hedges of an orchard, they opened fire, to which the Americans briskly replied. This exchange continued about two hours, after which the light infantry withdrew to the main line. A two-gun battery under Captain Benajah Carpenter of Rhode Island had come from the American lines and was posted to command the road. It opened upon the enemy. To answer it, Grant posted one howitzer about 300 yards from Stirling's right, and another 600 yards from his left.[19] There followed sustained and vigorous cannonading from both sides. Except for the body of light infantry while they were in the orchard, it does not appear that any part of the two forces was within musket shot of the enemy. The few American accounts of this stage of the battle dwell on the "heavy fire from their cannon and mortars." "The balls and shells flew very fast," yet did little damage.

The plain fact again was that Grant did not intend to drive Stirling from his position until the proper time according to the plan of the high command. But Stirling's men did not know this. At every moment of the four hours of the cannonading they seemed to face the possibility of attack by the overwhelming number of their opponents. That they, raw recruits as they were, stood firmly in line under the fire of heavy guns—always formidable to untried soldiers—while awaiting that assault, redounds greatly to their credit, especially so since all the time their ears were assailed by the guns of the warship *Roebuck* bombarding the fort at Red Hook, and the fort's batteries replying.

Admiral Lord Howe had tried to bring five other warships up the East River within supporting distance of the land forces. But a strong north wind and a swiftly ebbing tide kept back all save the *Roebuck,* which itself could not sail above Red Hook. Had the attempt succeeded, he could have poured terrible broadsides on Stirling's troops and on the Brooklyn fortifications. Thus bombarded, and at the same time cut off from retreat to New York, the Americans must have been overwhelmed; Washington, Putnam, Stirling, Sullivan, and all the Long Island army would have been killed or captured, and the Revolution might have ended then and there.[20]

At nine o'clock in the morning, after four hours of all this cannon fire, Stirling heard two heavy guns far in his rear—sounds more ominous than the thunder of Grant's guns or the roar of the *Roebuck*'s broadsides. But no interpretation came to him from headquarters or elsewhere, no orders to withdraw. He could only surmise some danger behind him, wonder what it was, and continue to hold his ground.

Up to this time General von Heister's Hessians had contented themselves with cannonading the American center in the Flatbush Pass, varying it with a sufficient show of advancing to keep the defenders in constant apprehension of an assault. About nine o'clock, General Sullivan rode out from the Brooklyn lines and took command of the posts at the two middle passes, Flatbush and Bedford. He remained at the Flatbush post, with the troops of Hitchcock, Little, and Knowlton. The post at the Bedford road was about a mile distant, separated by rugged, broken country.[21]

It may seem impossible that anyone could further stretch and weaken the already attenuated and feeble American line; but Colonel Miles did just that. At about seven o'clock, he says, he became convinced that "the main body of the enemy would take the Jamaica Road." Accordingly he thought best to get into that position first.[22] It was a good guess, except that it was made about four hours too late. However, he marched his Pennsylvania riflemen through the woods toward the Jamaica Pass and away from Wyllys and Wills, nearly two miles. He was still proceeding at eight o'clock when he disconcertingly came into contact with the enemy's army—not with its van, but actually with its baggage and rear guard.

The British, after breakfasting just beyond the Jamaica Pass, had taken a straight road toward Bedford. Their column of 10,000 men, almost two miles long, with horse, artillery, and wagons, had been marching five or six hours over that road in the rear of the American lines, parallel with Miles's line of march but in an opposite direction and within half a mile of him without his having observed them.

Their entire movement was a masterpiece of secrecy and silence. Where it was necessary to cut down young trees to clear the way for the artillery and wagons, these were sawed instead of chopped for fear that the Americans might hear ax strokes and be alarmed. They had marched nine miles.[23] Their van had by this time almost reached the village of Bedford, without any of the Americans even suspecting its presence in the rear of the ridge.

Miles was completely cut off from a retreat to the lines. His 400 men could do little against the foe. After two or three slight encounters he and half of his men surrendered. The rest scattered in the woods, found their way to the American camp, and gave Putnam the first news of the encircling march of the British.[24] There was still time to send word to Stirling and to the Flatbush, if not the Bedford, post to withdraw from a position that had become untenable and concentrate in the fortification. Putnam sent no such word, nor did anyone else. Nothing whatever was done to avert coming disaster.

At nine o'clock, in the village of Bedford, the British fired two heavy guns, the signal for action. Wyllys and Wills at the Bedford Pass heard them. Already alarmed by the firing on their left, between the enemy and Miles's men, they realized their danger and immediately started for the fortified lines.[25] Sullivan, at the Flatbush post, heard the guns, too, and knew the enemy was behind him. Leaving pickets and outposts to delay an attack by the Hessians in front, he fell back, only to meet the British light infantry and dragoons pouring down upon him from Bedford. His men turned their three fieldpieces on these unexpected foemen. But four companies of the Guards overwhelmed the gunners. The Americans recoiled, turned about, and met von Donop's Hessian jägers coming up over the ridge.[26]

In anticipation of the signal von Heister had formed his troops on the plain below the pass, dressing their lines as if on parade, with von Donop's jägers on the right and left flanks, his artillery meanwhile playing on the American position. At the expected sound of the guns he had given von Donop the word. The jägers had dashed forward, reached the top of the wooded ridge, taken cover as they had been trained to do, and advanced from one protected point to another, driving back the American outposts.[27] After them came the Hessian grenadiers. Muskets at shoulder, bayonets gleaming, halting at intervals to re-dress their lines, they advanced "with colors flying, to the music of drums and hautboys, as if they were marching across Friedrich's Platz at Cassel on the Landgrave's birthday. They did not fire a shot, but pressed steadily forward until they could employ their bayonets." [28]

At the top of the ridge the Hessians deployed and fell upon Sullivan's men thrown back by the British. The rifles in the hands of the Americans were good for only a few shots before bayonets were at the breasts of the riflemen, and a clubbed rifle is a weak weapon against half a dozen bayonets. Driven back and forth between the British and the Hessians, the Americans fought as long as they could, and then, along with what was left of Miles's men and Wyllys's and Wills's and the rest, they fled. Through the woods, down the slopes, across the fields, singly, in groups, in companies, they fled. Meeting here and there light infantry, dragoons, and grenadiers who fired at them, they ran for the fortified camp. Many of them reached it, but many were killed and many captured, among them Sullivan. It was in these ragged encounters that most of the American casualties occurred.

The wave of attacks swept westward. Detachments of von Heister's grenadiers, swinging to their left, struck at Parsons's command, Atlee's regiment, Huntington's contingent, and Kachlein's riflemen. There was no possibility of successful resistance; they retreated in broken groups, only to meet the British grenadiers in their rear. Atlee's journal says: "We kept up a close fire until the grenadiers retired. Then not being able, through the weakness of my party, already greatly fatigued and . . . destitute of ammunition, to break through the enemy . . . I filed off to the right [towards the camp] to endeavor, if possible, to escape." He soon fell in with Parsons "and a small number by him." They decided to try to break through the enemy. "I then pushed off," he continues, "with such of the officers and men that were willing to run the hazard."

Almost immediately they came upon a party of Highlanders, from whom they retreated, receiving in their flight "the fire of this party and sundry others, through which we were obliged to run for near two miles." With a handful of men Atlee tried to find a way to the north, toward Hell Gate, but at last had to surrender to a Scottish battalion.[29]

By eleven o'clock the British, as a result of their skillfully planned and perfectly executed strategy, had established themselves within two miles of the American camp, and had swept the ridge clear of their enemy—of all but Stirling's two regiments. These were still holding their ground, "ranks full, their uniforms smart, their weapons the best that money could purchase, their courage high." [30]

Up to this time Grant had made no move against Stirling's position. He had heard the signal guns, but, possibly because he had run short of ammunition, he had not acted as quickly as the other British and Hessian commanders. He had sent to the fleet for more powder and shot. Admiral Howe had sent him not only the desired supply, but also 2,000 marines, a scarcely needed reinforcement of his 7,000 men against Stirling's men. When they arrived, the real attack on Stirling began.

Grant's full force struck at Stirling's center. Unable to withstand the blow, the American line recoiled. The 33rd foot and a detachment of grenadiers swept down from the rear to join Grant. With a party of von Heister's Hessians they attacked the American left. Stirling called up some of Haslet's men, held in reserve, to strengthen his line. They came up and opened fire. The colonel of the 2nd British Grenadiers, whose men were under fire, saw that his assailants, the Delawares, wore uniforms of blue faced with red—the Hessians' colors. They were Hessians, of course, firing on their British comrades in arms by mistake! He sent Lieutenant Wragg of the marines forward with a sergeant, a corporal, and twenty men, to tell them to stop. The unfortunate Wragg was so close to the Delawares when he discovered the mistake that he could not withdraw. He and his entire party were taken by Haslet's men and sent across the Gowanus marsh and creek to the lines.[31]

But this was merely a momentary diversion. Grant's 7,000 and those others that had come to help him would not be denied by Stirling's 950. It was clear that the American position could not be held much longer. Nor was the direct way of retreat to the rear open. Cornwallis was there with the 71st Regiment. The 2nd Grenadiers also overlapped Stirling's left and rear.

Cut off from their natural line of retreat, Stirling's men had only one possible avenue of escape; and that was but barely possible. On their right rear was Gowanus Creek at its widest, and not only that stream, but also the broad marshes lining both its shores. The creek and its swamps were usually considered impassable, but the detachment with the prisoners had crossed them, and there was no other way.

To attempt such a crossing with his whole force in retreat, under the fire of the musketry and cannon of the British before and behind him, was to court and probably to suffer complete disaster. But Stirling met the emergency with characteristic resolution and courage. He detached Major Gist and about 250 men of Smallwood's Maryland regiment. He then ordered Major McDonough with the Delawares and the rest of the Marylands to retreat across the creek. They faced about and, "in perfect order," their shot-torn colors flying, marched away.[32]

Gist's 250 Marylanders. Stirling leading, set out up the Gowanus Road to meet the enemy. If possible, Stirling meant to cut his way through the British. If not, he might be able to engage them and hold them off until the remainder of his command crossed to safety. His plan was born of desperation, a forlorn hope.

Cornwallis in person commanded the British right wing pressing against what had been Stirling's rear. He had established himself in and about the Cortelyou House on the Gowanus Road. Against this position Stirling led his men. When within gunshot, he opened fire and received the enemy's reply which came not only from their musketry, but also from two field-pieces. The British artillery added grape and canister to the rain of bullets.

The little American column halted and fell back, only to advance once more. Again and again and again, five times, the Americans were driven back, and five times returned to the fight. Stirling "encouraged and animated our young soldiers," wrote Major Gist, "with almost invincible resolution."

"General Lord Stirling fought like a wolf," wrote another participant.[33] It seemed at last that they would force Cornwallis to retire and let them through. A sixth time they advanced, but Cornwallis had now been reinforced. For the last time the brave young Marylanders were thrown back, this time "with much precipitation and confusion." They had done all they could, but they could not win through. They broke up, and in small, scattered parties tried to find a way to the American entrenchments; but only Major Gist and nine others succeeded. The rest, all that had not fallen in the fight, were captured, and 256 were either killed or taken prisoner. Stirling alone tried to find a way out, but the enemy, before and behind and on both sides, kept up a "constant firing" on him. He made his way around "the point of a hill" that covered him from their fire, then sought out General von Heister and surrendered his sword.[34]

It was reported at the time that Washington was on a hill within the lines, whence, with a glass, he watched Stirling's fight, and that he displayed great emotion, exclaiming: "Good God! What brave fellows I must this day lose!" [35]

Meanwhile, still in good order, in column of march (so the historians say, though it may be doubted that there was no confusion), McDonough's Delawares and Marylands were retreating. They had made no more than a quarter of a mile when they met a party of the enemy and were fired upon. The artillery in their rear also still played upon them. Apparently with no thought of surrender, they replied to the enemy in front and forced him to give way. Through an opening thus created they got down to the edge of the marsh, and started across the creek.[36]

At that point, Gowanus Creek was eighty yards wide, deep and swift with the inflowing tide. The retreating Americans waded in knee-deep, waist-deep, neck-deep, here and there over their depth; some of them had to swim. Four fieldpieces were firing upon them, and an unknown number of muskets. Fortunately, Smallwood had come over from New York early that morning, too late to join his regiment in the battle. He had foreseen that the retreat must be made at that point if at all. He had secured from Washington "a New England regiment and Captain Thomas's company," and had posted them with two guns to cover the crossing. Their fire dislodged the enemy guns that were firing on the fugitives. Except for half a dozen men either shot down or drowned, the fleeing Americans came safely "out of the water and mud, looking like water-rats." [37]

Howe claimed that the Americans lost 3,200 men in this battle, but the American returns on October 8 showed 1,012 casualties of whom probably

200 were killed, the rest captured. The British casualties were 392 killed, wounded, and taken prisoner.[38]

The Battle of Long Island, as the first in which the American and British forces met in the open field in formal battle array, was of very great importance as an indication of what was to be expected in such encounters thereafter. The disastrous defeat of the Americans boded ill for their future. Consequently, it was extremely desirable to ascertain wherein their army was at fault, and whether the blame for their discomfiture should rest upon the rank and file or upon the leaders. There was much discussion of the question at the time, and it has continued among historians ever since.

Sullivan has been blamed because, being in command of the troops outside the lines, he failed properly to guard the Jamaica Pass; but he denied that he held that command, asserting that it belonged to Stirling and his own function was to command within the lines as subordinate to Putnam.[39] He is credited with having posted the captured patrol at the Jamaica Pass; but, if that be true, it boomerangs upon him because it shows that, in spite of his disclaimer of authority outside the lines, he did in fact exercise such authority. In which case, the pitiful weakness of the post he thus established reflects discredit upon him.

Putnam has been blamed because, having reconnoitered the enemy's positions on the 26th, he should have concluded from the concentration of their forces that they intended to launch their main attack against the Jamaica Pass, and should have arranged for an adequate defense.[40] The fact that Washington, Sullivan, "and others" were with him on that reconnaissance cannot exculpate him, though it may prove them equally blind.

Putnam has been censured also because, having received news, "early in the morning," of the British advance along the road to Bedford, he failed to inform Washington or to order Stirling and the others on the ridge to withdraw while there was yet time.[41] It is true that the news was brought to him first only by one or more fugitives in the rout of Miles's battalion; and doubtless it was long delayed by the distance it had to be brought through the woods. Nevertheless, it does seem that he received it in time to recall Stirling and the others.

George Bancroft blames "the incapacity of Israel Putnam" for "the extent of the disasters of the day," specifically because, "having sent Stirling and the flower of the American army into the most dangerous position," he "neglected to countermand his orders." [42] "The Militia are most indifferent troops." They "will do for the interior Works, whilst your best Men should at all hazards prevent the Enemy's passing the Wood, and approaching your Works." [43] Clearly, if there was error in disposing the American forces, it cannot be ascribed to Putnam alone.

The most all-inclusive charge is made by General Francis V. Greene, who says: "No one exercised general command," although it had been conferred on Putnam. "Putnam did practically nothing as a commanding general." [44] And it is certainly true that, having sent his "best men" out to defend the ridge, he did none of the things proper and necessary to save them from disaster. Even Washington's orders were no warrant to him for leaving them to be surrounded and captured by the British turning movement, which Washington certainly did not expect when he gave the orders.

Washington has been blamed for the defeat, because, though he was familiar with the ground and had arrived within the lines on the 26th, thus certainly putting himself in command superior to Putnam, he did not alter Putnam's dispositions and allowed a manifestly inadequate force, strung out along six miles of the ridge, to attempt to defend it, instead of "keeping his men in the redoubts and repeating the performance of Bunker Hill." [45] He has been censured, too, for not having any cavalry to patrol between the various passes, so that word of the flanking movement could be brought to the camp in time to withdraw the troops from the ridge before they were hopelessly enveloped. Washington Irving says the flanking of the Americans "might have been thwarted had the army been provided with a few troops of light-horse to serve as videttes." [46]

There was no cavalry in the American army. None had been provided by the Congress. Washington had not called for any, nor made a move to organize any on his own. Charles Francis Adams says he "apparently had no conception of the use to be made of cavalry, or mounted men, in warfare," [47] and develops that thesis at length. Yet, strange to say, there was available to him at the time a mounted force which could have provided the patrols so needed. He refused to use it.

There had come over from Connecticut, on the 8th of July, a regiment of four or five hundred volunteers called rather absurdly "Light Dragoons"—mostly farmers mounted on "rough, country horses" and armed with muskets, fowling pieces, or whatever sort of guns they owned. They were not a stylish lot. Dapper, or at least dapper-minded, Captain Alexander Graydon of Philadelphia made great fun of them in his memoirs.[48] Washington received these cavaliers rather cavalierly. He said they could not remain in New York because forage for their horses could not be furnished, "and, if it could be, it would only be at great expense, without a single advantage arising from it." [49] They were discharged, and went home.

Sir George Trevelyan comments that Washington "surveyed that quaint procession too much in the spirit of a country gentleman who rode to hounds. There was plenty of capability and some youth" among them. Two hundred of the best might have been chosen and trained in the next six weeks. "Captain Henry Lee or Captain William Washington would have got a small body of cavalry into shape soon enough. . . . On the 27th of August, 1776, a couple of troops of yeomanry posted and handled by two such officers would have saved many hundred Americans from capture." [50]

One of these horsemen, lingering on the scene, was picked up by the British. Captain Graydon reports, "On being asked what had been his duty in the rebel army, he answered that it was '*to flank a little and carry tidings.*' " No one could have put in fewer or more apt words just what Washington needed on Long Island—someone "to flank a little and carry tidings."

On the whole, it seems impossible to avoid placing the bulk of the responsibility for the mismanagement of affairs on Long Island upon the shoulders of the commander in chief, George Washington. Such has been the verdict of the later and more judicious historians of the war. "There was no excuse for the local dispositions of the defense," says Thomas G. Frothingham.[51] And those dispositions had been made in accordance with Washington's specific orders. Claude H. Van Tyne refers to Washington's "almost fatal errors in both strategy and tactics." [52]

Most of these criticisms of the conduct of the affair on Long Island are directed at the tactics employed there. The fundamental fault lay deeper, in the strategy of the campaign, the attempt to hold New York. That city could not be held without holding Brooklyn Heights. Those Heights could not be held without dividing an army far too weak, even as a whole, successfully to oppose the British. To divide it was to expose the two parts to the danger of being held apart by the British fleet and of being separately and successively overcome by the British army.

Even if Brooklyn Heights had not been there to bring about this unfortunate result, the Americans could not have held New York, for the British armada commanded the waters environing the town. Indeed, New York could easily have been a fatal trap for the American army, since it had only one readily available exit to the mainland: Kingsbridge.

It has been said that the attempt to hold it was based upon political instead of military considerations, that the Congress wanted it held, that the attempt to hold it was necessary to fortify the American spirit of resistance.[53] But if a commanding general sees that a task is impossible of accomplishment, though he may risk and sacrifice an expendable detachment in the attempt, how far is he justified in risking his whole army, the whole army of his country, and with it his country's cause? If on the other hand he fails to perceive the obvious impossibility of the task, how can he be allowed merit as a military leader? And Washington did not perceive the impossibility of holding New York before he attempted it, not even after the defeat on Long Island. As late as September 2 he wrote to the Congress, "Till of late I had no doubt in my mind of defending the place [New York], nor should I have yet, if the men would do their duty." [54]

The truth is, in Van Tyne's words, that Washington had "little genius and not much natural aptitude for war." [55] Or, as the English military historian Sir John Fortescue, a most generous critic of the American commander in chief, puts it, "Though every Englishman must admire him as a very great man and a brave and skilful soldier, it is, I think, doubtful whether he has any claim to be regarded as a really great commander in the field." [56] As Van Tyne says: "It was courage, noble character, the gift of inspiring confidence, and the ability to learn by experience" rather than military genius that were "to place him in the forefront among the leaders of men, safe and competent as a commander-in-chief. Even in the midst of his worst errors, his greatness and his magnanimity surmounts everything." [57] And Fortescue, after commenting on the "very grave flaws in the campaign of 1776 about New York" and in the campaign against Howe about Philadelphia, in 1777, culminating in the Brandywine disaster, recognizes "his constancy, his courage and his inexhaustible patience" as his "finest qualities." [58]

CHAPTER 18

Long Island: The Retreat

By noon of August 27 all the Americans that had escaped death or capture were within the fortified lines on Long Island, expecting with anxiety a concentrated attack. But it did not come. The British grenadiers and the 33rd Regiment had pursued the fugitives to within musket shot of the lines. Hot with the ardor of battle, they were eager to storm the entrenchments, so eager that, in Howe's own words, "it required repeated orders to prevail on them to desist from this attempt." He "would not risk the loss that might have been sustained in the assault," it being, as he is reported to have said, "apparent that the lines must have been ours at a very cheap rate by regular approaches." He therefore withdrew his men to a safe distance.[1]

Astonishingly enough, not recognizing the peril of his position, Washington called for reinforcements from New York; and early the next morning Colonel John Shee's 3rd Pennsylvania Regiment and Colonel Robert Magaw's 5th, also Colonel John Glover's Massachusetts Continentals, came over. There were then within the works perhaps 9,500 men.[2]

For two days following the battle the Americans held their lines, while within a mile or so and in plain sight lay the British camp. There was skirmishing throughout the 28th, "pretty smart" skirmishing, Washington called it.[3] To present a bold face to the enemy, he encouraged the riflemen to keep up their fire, thus not only maintaining a show of resistance, but also sustaining the morale of his men.[4]

Pickets and riflemen were thrown out by the Americans about a hundred rods in front of the lines. About sunset of the 28th the enemy made a push to drive them in. "The fire was very hot," Colonel Moses Little of Massachusetts wrote. "The enemy gave way & our people recovered the ground. The firing ceased, our people retired to the fort." By the next morning the British not only possessed the disputed ground, but had dug trenches and built a breastwork within 150 rods of Fort Putnam. Howe's "approaches" had begun. This first breastwork was a menace of disaster nearing the Americans.[5]

On that same day a northeasterly storm blew up, and a downpour of rain began. It had one immense advantage for the Americans: it prevented Admiral Howe from sending ships up the East River to lie between Brooklyn and New York and thus to cut off their only line of retreat. Otherwise it was exceedingly distressing to them. "We had no tents to screen us from its pitiless pelting," wrote Captain Alexander Graydon of Shee's regiment in his memoirs; "nor, if we had had them, would it have comported with the incessant vigilance required to have availed ourselves of them, as, in fact, it might be said, that we lay upon our arms during our whole stay on the island." [6] In food also they were badly off. They had only hard biscuits and pickled pork, which must be eaten raw, for cook fires were impossible in that downpour.

The rain continued all the next day and the day after that. The camp became a morass and worse. Water lay "ankle deep in the fort"; and in some parts of the trenches the men stood waist-deep in water. Not only was the clothing of the troops soaked, the ammunition of nearly all of them was saturated. But even those who managed to keep a few dry cartridges could not use them, for their muskets were practically valueless, as are all flintlock guns when the flints, the priming pans, and the touchholes become wet.

Howe's reluctance to storm the works immediately after the retreat of the Americans has been attributed to the memory of Bunker's Hill, to the lesson he there learned of the steadfastness and the deadly fire of the Americans, even the militia when behind breastworks. Trevelyan says that the minutemen who defended the redoubt on Breed's Hill saved the American lines on Long Island. But that lesson should have been no deterrent to an assault on the second day or the third day after this battle. No overwhelming fire such as had met him in that former battle could have been delivered against him now. British bayonets would have been met by few American bayonets—the Americans had but few. It is difficult to believe that a determined assault upon those entrenchments would have failed against their tired and hungry defenders, discouraged by defeat and disorganized by the loss of so many officers.[7] Howe may have assumed that his brother's fleet could prevent an American retreat, and that an expensive frontal assault was unnecessary. A veritable Caesar on the battlefield, Howe was commonly sluggish before and after the fighting.

It was an extraordinary situation. "Nine thousand disheartened soldiers, the last hope of their country," says Trevelyan, "were penned up, with the sea behind them and a triumphant enemy in front, shelterless and famished on a square mile of open ground swept by a fierce and cold northeasterly gale. . . . If Howe's infantry had been led to the assault, they would have walked over the intrenchments behind which the beaten army was now gathered." [8] It would have been more than a victory in a battle. Washington was there, with three or four of his ablest generals and the best of his whole army. By their capture the British might have won the war then and there. But Washington *was* there, and he finally saved the day.

On the morning of the 29th he sent orders to General William Heath at Kingsbridge and to Hugh Hughes, Assistant Quartermaster General in New York, to gather every boat of every sort fit for transporting troops and to assemble them on the New York side by dark. Was he planning a retreat? He did not say so. On the contrary his orders to Heath intimated a reinforcement of his lines.[9] But late in that day a council of his general officers agreed that it was "eligible to remove the Army to New York" for eight severally stated reasons, any one of which seemed to be sufficient in itself.[10]

So there was to be a retreat—if it could be accomplished. But the troops were not informed until the last moment. If the truth had been known among the militia and volunteers a panic desire to get out in the first boats might have resulted in riotous confusion. Accordingly general orders were issued in the following terms: "As the sick are an encumbrance to the Army & Troops are expected from the flying camp in New Jersey, under General Mercer, who is himself arrived & cover is wanted for the [new] troops, the commanding Officers of Regt's are immediately to have such sick men removed. . . . As the above Forces under Gen'l Mercer are expected this afternoon, the General [Washington] proposes to relieve a proportionate Number of Regiments & make a change in the situation of them. The Commanding Officers of Regiments are therefore to parade their men with their Arms, Accoutrements and Knapsacks, at 7 o'Clock at the Head of their Encampments & there wait for Orders." [11] Washington could tell a lie when it was needed. He told half a dozen in that one order.

It was obviously necessary that the lines should be manned while the removal of the great body of the troops was in progress, so as to prevent the enemy from discovering the movement and assaulting while the camp was in disorder. To this honorable and dangerous duty Haslet's Delaware regiment was assigned, along with Shee's and Magaw's Pennsylvanians, Chester's

Connecticut battalion, and the remains of Smallwood's Marylanders. This detachment, the pick of the army, was commanded by General Thomas Mifflin.[12] The post of greatest danger, at Fort Putnam, within 250 yards of the enemy's approaches, was taken by Smallwood's and Haslet's men. When Glover's Marbleheaders were withdrawn from their left to help man the boats, the Delaware and Maryland men were exposed to a flank attack which would have been impossible to stem.

At dusk the boats began to arrive. The two amphibious regiments, Glover's from Marblehead and Hutchinson's from Salem, all fishermen or sailors, took them in charge. Between nine and ten o'clock the regiments on parade were drawn off one by one, the volunteers and militia first. With their baggage and equipment on their backs they marched to the ferry landing to embark. Other regiments were marched into their places or extended to right or left to fill the gaps and keep up an appearance of completeness in the line. The utmost quiet and orderliness were preserved; no unusual lights were shown. In fact, the embarkation was begun in almost complete darkness.

The first detachments were ready to embark and the next were on their way to the landing when the elements, which had so far befriended the Americans by preventing Admiral Howe's ships from coming up the river, made trouble. The northeasterly wind so increased in force and the ebb tide began to run so strongly that even the practiced sailors manning the sloops and other sailboats could not make the crossing. There were not enough rowboats to take all the men across in one night. It seemed that the attempt to withdraw must end in disaster. But the wind lessened about eleven o'clock and shifted to the southwest, favoring the sailing craft.

The work went on. Stores of ammunition, supplies, and provisions were brought to the landing. All the artillery was assembled there except five heavy cannon, old and worn and of little value. They were spiked and abandoned.

At two o'clock in the morning, when everything seemed to be going well, an error occurred that might have been fatal. Major Alexander Scammell, acting aide-de-camp to Washington, came to General Mifflin and told him that the boats for the covering party were waiting and he was to march his men to the landing at once. In spite of a protest that there must be some mistake, Scammell insisted that there was none. Accordingly the sentinels and advanced posts were called in. The entire detachment abandoned the lines and marched toward the landing. They were well on their way when they met Washington. He was aghast at this seeming desertion of their duty.

"Good God!" he exclaimed. "General Mifflin, I am afraid you have ruined us by unseasonably withdrawing the troops from the lines." "I did it by your order," Mifflin answered hotly. Washington said that could not be so. "By God, I did!" said Mifflin. Washington replied that it was a dreadful mistake, that there was confusion at the ferry, and that unless the covering party could resume their posts before the enemy discovered their abandonment "the most disagreeable consequences would follow"—surely a masterpiece of understatement. The troops were faced about and their posts, unguarded for nearly an hour, were again occupied.[13] Major General Heath characterizes the immediate return of these men to their posts as "an instance of discipline and true fortitude." "Whoever," he says, "has seen troops in a similar situation, or duly contemplated the human heart in such trials, will know how to appreciate the conduct of these brave men on this occasion." [14]

To the troops holding the lines within sound of the thudding pickaxes and the scraping shovels of the British working on a new and nearer approach, that night must have seemed interminable. Would the hour of their relief come before daylight and certain discovery of the retreat by the enemy? Would they, a few hundreds, be compelled to face an attack by thousands? It was daylight when the order to embark came, and those steadfast battalions marched away.

It was full time they did, for British reconnoitering parties, suspicious of the unnatural silence within the American lines, were already creeping up to spy on the camp. Before daybreak a corporal's guard pushed cautiously through the abatis. At four o'clock the British were peering over the breastworks. Thirty minutes later the British pickets were inside. There was still time to catch the rear guard at the landing, but freakish Nature again favored the Americans. A dense fog settled down. Even at a little distance nothing could be seen. Under its cover the last boats with the last regiments and Washington himself pushed off.

Through six hours of that night, "the hardy, adroit, weather-proof" [15] Marblehead fishermen of Glover's regiment and Hutchinson's skilled Salem fishermen had rowed and sailed from shore to shore. By seven o'clock in the morning 9,500 men and all their baggage, field guns, and horses, equipment, stores, and provisions, "even the biscuits which had not been and the raw pork which could not be eaten," [16] were safe in New York. Howe captured three stragglers, who had stayed behind to plunder.

Both the contemporary and the later historians have praised this successful retreat. Charles Stedman, an officer in the British army at that time, called it "particularly glorious." Alexander Botta wrote, "No military operation was ever conducted by a great captain with more ability and prudence." Irving calls it "one of the most signal achievements of the war." Trevelyan says it was "a master stroke of energy, dexterity and caution, by which Washington saved his army and his country." Frothingham describes it as "a feat that seemed impossible." General Francis Vinton Greene, a military critic of distinction, says, "A more skilful operation of this kind was never conducted." Any number of others might be quoted in similar terms.[17]

The credit for the achievement must unhesitatingly be accorded to Washington, who not only conceived and planned it but personally supervised its effective accomplishment throughout the night. Although, as he wrote to the Congress, he had hardly been off his horse and never had closed his eyes in the forty-eight hours preceding the retreat, all night long he rode his gray charger to and fro watching the movements of his men, or stood by the landing to superintend the embarkation. He seemed to be everywhere at once; and everywhere he cheered, calmed, and encouraged his troops through one of the most difficult trials a soldier has to endure. He was the last man to step into the last boat that left the island.

Both Howe's attack and Washington's retreat were masterpieces of planning and execution, and each was successful because of the mistakes of the other principal. Washington exposed an inadequate force on the ridge and neglected the Jamaica Pass, thus permitting Howe to encircle his army and defeat it; Howe failed to follow up his first success by assaulting the American lines, thus giving Washington a chance to withdraw to New York. Both of them were destined to repeat the same errors in a future battle with similar results, which throws light upon their respective abilities as military leaders.

The results of this battle created a great sensation on both sides of the Atlantic. The surrender of Boston had depressed England, and news of succeeding events in America was anxiously awaited. Howe's report of the battle, greatly exaggerating both the number of American troops engaged and their losses, reached London on October 10. Immediately the court was "filled with an extravagance of joy." The King conferred the Order of the Bath on the victorious general. In various towns throughout the kingdom bells were rung, windows were lighted, cannon were fired, and bonfires blazed. The English Tories thought the war practically finished. British stocks rose in Amsterdam. The American agent Silas Deane wrote from Paris, "The last check on Long Island has sunk our credit to nothing." [18]

In America disappointment and gloom were widespread. General Greene wrote to Washington, "The country is struck with a panic." [19] Washington wrote to the Congress that the defeat had "dispirited too great a proportion of our troops and filled their minds with apprehension and dispair. The militia . . . are dismayed, intractable and impatient to return" to their homes. "Great numbers of them have gone off; in some instances, almost by whole regiments . . . their example has infected another part of the army. I am obliged to confess my want of confidence in the generality of the troops." He urged the Congress to put no dependence "in a militia or other troops than those enlisted and embodied" for longer periods than were then in vogue, and declared his conviction that "our liberties" might be lost "if their defence is left to any but a permanent standing army; I mean, one to exist during the war." [20] The Congress overcame its dread of "standing armies" and resolved on September 16 that eighty-eight battalions be enlisted "as soon as possible to serve during the present war." [21]

CHAPTER 19

Kip's Bay

"On this 30th of August, 1776, Washington was probably the most astonished man in America. He had snatched a beaten army from the very jaws of a victorious force, and practically under the nose of the greatest armada ever seen in American waters." [1] He may have been astonished at his successful retreat; he was certainly perplexed as to his next move. He had his army in New York, but what to do with either the army or New York was a puzzle whose solution was far from obvious.

The army was in a deplorable condition, mentally and physically. Dispirited by its recent defeat, dejected by its hardships, dismayed at the prospect of the future, the militia was in the condition described by Washington in his letter to the Congress of September 2. The Continentals were similarly affected, though in a lesser degree. Such discipline as had been achieved in that hastily gathered army of practically raw recruits was greatly relaxed. Their commander in chief took notice of the resultant disorder in general orders on September 4. He expressed his "amazement and concern . . . that the men of every regiment are suffer'd to be continually rambling about, and at such distances from their respective quarters and encampments, as not to be able to oppose the enemy in any sudden approach." He therefore not only commanded but earnestly exhorted "the officers to remedy this fault." Two days later he expressed his purpose "to put a stop to plundering . . . either public, or private property" and threatened to break "with Infamy" any officer who connived at it by inaction.[2]

A more fundamental evil was a growing distrust of Washington himself—not of his character as a man, but of his ability as a general, or at least of the plans for the campaign made by him and his associates in the high command. This feeling was not uncommon among the regimental officers. Colonel John Haslet of the Delaware Regiment, an officer of proven sagacity and sound judgment, expressed it in a letter to Caesar Rodney on September 4 in the words: "The Genl I revere, his Character for Disinterestedness, Patience and fortitude will be had in Everlasting Remembrance, but the Vast Burthen appears to be too much his own. Beardless youth and Inexperience Regimentated are too much about him. . . . W'd to Heaven Genl Lee were here is the Language of officers and men." [3]

Physically, too, everything was in sad condition. The men were tired, soaked to the skin, hungry, and in some part leaderless, by reason of the loss of officers. Their disorganization showed itself in the wet clothing, accouterments, and tents spread about in complete confusion to dry in front of the houses and in the streets.[4]

Desertion was consequently rife, especially among the militia. They went off in whole companies, in whole regiments.[5] Within a few days the Connecticut militia dwindled from 8,000 to 2,000 men. "The impulse for going home," wrote Washington, "was so irrisistable, it answered no purpose to oppose it, tho' I could not discharge, I have been obliged to acquiesce." [6]

The prime necessity, if order was to be restored, was obviously a reorganization of the army. Three grand divisions were made up. Major General Putnam commanded one, composed of Parsons's brigade of Connecticut and Massachusetts regiments, James Clinton's and Fellows's brigades from Massachusetts, Scott's from New York, and Silliman's from Connecticut. Spencer was to command another, until Greene should recover from his illness. It included Nixon's brigade, composed of Hand's Pennsylvania riflemen, Varnum's and Hitchcock's brigades from Rhode Island and Prescott's, Little's, and "Late Nixon's" brigades from Massachusetts. The third division, under Heath, consisted of George Clinton's brigade from New York and Mifflin's brigades comprising Magaw's and Shee's Pennsylvanians, Hutchinson's, Sargent's, and Andrew Ward's brigades from Connecticut, Haslet's Delawares, and Smallwood's remnant from Maryland.[7]

Before these divisions could receive their respective posts, the great question had to be answered: Should New York be held or abandoned? And, if abandoned, should it be left intact and unscathed to the enemy? There were differences of opinion.

Greene's answers were given in a letter to Washington. The city could not be held in the face of an enemy that could land on both sides of the island in its middle section and cut in two the American forces to the north and the south. "The City and Island of New-York are no objects for us . . .

in competition of the general interests of America. Part of the army already has met with a defeat; the country is struck with a panick; any capital loss at this time may ruin the cause. . . . A general and speedy retreat is absolutely necessary. . . . I would burn the city and suburbs" because, "if the enemy gets possession of the city, we can never recover the possession without a superiour naval force. . . . It will deprive the enemy of an opportunty of barracking their whole army together, which, if they could do, would be a very great security. . . . Not one benefit can arise to us from its preservation." Anyhow, "two-thirds of the city of New-York and the suburbs belongs to the Tories," so why worry about its loss by burning? [8] Colonel Joseph Reed, the adjutant general of the army, agreed that it should be burned. Colonel Rufus Putnam, the army's chief engineer, and John Jay, one of the largest propertyholders in the town, likewise urged its destruction.[9]

Washington had already put the question up to the Congress on September 2, before Greene's letter was written: "If we should be obliged to abandon the Town, ought it to stand as Winter Quarters for the Enemy?" And the Congress answered on the 3rd that no damage should be done to it, if abandoned.[10] So that settled that. But the question of evacuation was still open.

Washington himself was in two minds about it. He acknowledged the obvious danger to his whole army, if the enemy should "enclose us . . . by taking post in our rear" and "oblige us to fight them on their own Terms, or surrender at discretion." Yet he still debated whether he should not try to hold the town, because giving it up would "dispirit the Troops and enfeeble our Cause." [11] He put the matter up to a council of war on September 7.

It was generally admitted by the members of the council that the town was untenable, but the majority could not face the logical consequences of their own opinions. The decision was a compromise. Putnam's division, 5,000 men, was to remain in New York. Heath with 9,000 was to hold the ground from Harlem up to Kingsbridge. Greene with five brigades, mostly militia, posted along the East River chiefly in the neighborhood of Turtle Bay and Kip's Bay, at the end of what is now Thirty-fourth Street, was to hold the intervening space.[12] As is the case with most compromises, this one served neither purpose; it was not effective to secure the city, nor to save the army. In fact, as one military historian has said, it was, "of course, fatuous." [13] It strung the army out in three divisions widely spaced over a length of sixteen miles, with its weakest element midway between the two ends, and so invited the enemy to cut it in two and defeat the ends separately—a chance which was not overlooked by the British. Nevertheless, the troops were posted in that manner.

In his letter to the Congress, September 8, telling of the decision of the council of war, Washington said that some of the officers had been not "a little influenced in their Opinion" by their belief that Congress wished the defense of the town "to be maintained at every hazard." [14] To this the Congress replied on the 10th that "it was by no means the sense" of their resolution of the 3rd against destroying the town "that the army, or any part of it, should remain in that city a moment longer than he [Washington] shall think it proper." [15]

Greene was much disturbed in mind by the council's decision disposing the troops in that "so critical and dangerous" manner. Before he heard of this last resolution of the Congress he and five other officers asked Washington to call another council to consider the matter.[16] That council was held on the 12th, and ten of its thirteen members voted "to reconsider" the former decision, that is to say, voted to withdraw from the city.[17] In this decision Washington concurred. "We are now," he wrote to the Congress on September 14, "taking every Method in our Power to remove the Stores &ca. in which we find almost insuperable difficulties; They are so great and so numerous, that I fear we shall not effect the whole before we shall meet with some Interruption." [18]

Lack of transport was the difficulty. Although all the horses and wagons found in the town were impressed and cargoes were shipped up the Hudson in boats, both methods of carriage were too little and too late.

It was not Howe's fault that Washington was pressed for time in reassembling his forces and removing his cannon and stores. The British army lay inactive on Long Island in camps stretching from Brooklyn to Flushing for more than two weeks while Washington was tying and untying the apron strings of the Congress and finally making the proper decision.[19]

There had, indeed, been hostile demonstrations by the navy. On September 3 the thirty-two-gun frigate *Rose* sailed up the East River towing thirty flatboats and anchored in Wallabout Bay above the city. She was fired upon by the batteries on the New York side, and after suffering "a good deal of damage" [20] she retired with her tow to a safer position in the mouth of Newtown Creek. On the 13th, four frigates, the *Phoenix* and the *Roebuck* of 44 guns each, the *Orpheus* of 32, and the *Carysfort* of 28, passed up, and "in supreme Contempt of the Rebels and their Works, did not fire a Gun." The next day, another warship and six transports joined them. The *Renown* of 50 guns, the *Repulse* and the *Pearl*, 32 guns each, with an armed schooner, also went up the Hudson, daring the American batteries, which cannonaded them "as furiously as they could," but with little effect. They anchored above the American works, and thus prevented the further removal of stores from the city by water.[21] The stage was now set for the next act. Howe was ready to attack Manhattan.

The sun rose in a clear, blue sky on Sunday September 15, with a fresh breeze blowing. Early in the morning five warships took stations in the East River, in a line from Kip's Bay towards the south at about two hundred yards from the shore and broadside to it. At ten o'clock eighty-four flatboats laden with British soldiers put out in four divisions from the Long Island shore. At a little before eleven, the ships opened fire on the entrenchments along the New York side of the river, "such a fire as nothing could withstand." [22] "About 70 large pieces of Cannon were in Play, together with Swivels & small arms," making "so terrible and so incessant a Roar of Guns few even in the Army & Navy had ever heard before." [23] And all this fire was poured upon a line of entrenchments at Kip's Bay held by Captain William Douglas with a brigade of Connecticut militia. "Entrenchments," they were called; but in fact "they were nothing more than a ditch dug along the bank of the river, with the dirt thrown out towards the water." [24]

The boats came up with the line of ships. The fire ceased, but the boats came on, crowded with redcoats and looking like "a clover field in full bloom." They reached the shore at Kip's Bay. The light infantry leaped from them, clambered up "the steep and just accessible rocks" [25]—and found no one to oppose them. Douglas's troops, their frail defensive works already beaten down by the gunfire, had fled "with the utmost precipitation." [26] Wadsworth's brigade, next below them, followed.[27] Parsons's and Scott's militia, farther south, took notice and retreated up the Bowery Road.[28]

Washington, at Harlem when he heard the sound of the bombardment, took horse and rode at full speed to the scene of action. On the Post Road, now Lexington Avenue, about where Forty-second Street crosses it, he met Douglas's men, still retreating precipitately and in confusion. "The demons of fear and disorder seemed to take full possession of all and everything that day," one of them said.[29] Parsons's brigade, also in complete disarray, hurrying north for safety's sake had come up with them.

Washington tried to halt them, to rally them. "Take the walls!" he cried. "Take the cornfield!" Some of them ran to the walls, some into the cornfield. With Putnam and several other officers he tried to form them behind the walls, but there was no controlling them. Washington's anger was spectacular. "He dashed his hat upon the ground in a transport of rage," crying out, "Are these the men with whom I am to defend America?" He snapped a pistol at them. With his riding cane, "he flogged not only private soldiers, but officers as well," a colonel, even a brigadier general.[30] But nothing would do. At the sight of sixty or seventy Hessians coming at them they broke, flung away muskets, knapsacks, even coats and hats, and ran "as if the Devil was in them." "The ground was literally covered" with such discarded encumbrances.[31] And they left Washington almost alone within eighty yards of the oncoming Hessians. Blinded with rage—or with despair—he sat his horse, taking no heed of his imminent danger. He would have been shot or captured had not an aide-de-camp seized his bridle and "absolutely hurried him away." [32]

Putnam, seeing that no stand could be made there, galloped south through Wadsworth's and Scott's brigades coming up in full retreat, to attempt the rescue of Sullivan's brigade, Knox's artillery, and the others still in the town before the British could stretch across the island and hem them in.[33]

He gathered the troops in the city, abandoned the heavy guns and the remaining military stores, and started north. But he knew as little of the geography of Manhattan as he had known of the terrain on Long Island. The Post Road on the easterly side, the main artery leading north and the only one he knew, was held by the enemy. He would have found himself hopelessly entrapped, had not young Aaron Burr, his aide-de-camp, guided him to an unfrequented road along the west side, close to the Hudson.[34]

The day had become intensely hot. Dust hung in stifling clouds over the troops. The water in their canteens was soon exhausted. With dust in their parched throats, sweat streaming from their faces, they slogged along dejectedly. It was hard to keep them going at a reasonable speed. But Putnam now displayed his best native qualities, courage and energy. He rode up and down the two-mile-long column, heartening his men, hurrying them along. They met a detachment of the enemy, beat it off, and at last after dark ended their twelve-mile exhausting march in the main camp at Harlem, where the rest of the army was now collected.[35]

The first division of the British army was led by Howe, Clinton, Cornwallis, Vaughan, Matthews, Leslie, and von Donop. It comprised three battalions of light infantry, four battalions of British grenadiers, three of Hessian grenadiers, the Hessian jägers, and the brigade of British Guards, about 4,000 in all. Immediately on landing, Leslie and the light infantry swung to the right. Von Donop's Hessian grenadiers turned left, met Wadsworth's retreating New York militia, and after a short engagement captured three or four hundred of them. Howe and the rest advanced to Incleberg, otherwise called Murray Hill—a height of land lying between the present Fourth and Sixth avenues and Thirty-fifth and Fortieth streets. There they halted to await the arrival of the second division for which the boats had been sent back.

Repeated trips of the boats brought this division to land about five o'clock. It comprised five brigades and two regiments of British regulars, one brigade of Hessians, and the artillery, about 9,000 men. One brigade was then sent south, and its men were billeted in houses and barns along the Post Road all the way down to the town.

With the main army Howe marched north to McGowan's Pass and rested there for the night.[36] On the way up the Post Road they marched for a time parallel with Putnam's sweating militiamen, separated from them by no greater distance than the width of the present Central Park; but neither force was aware of the other's proximity.[37]

During the afternoon detachments of the British force had ranged about, picking up prisoners here and there, singly or in groups. The Americans lost 17 officers and 350 men that day, nearly all captives; very few were killed. But fifty or sixty cannon and a very considerable amount of ammunition, stores and baggage had been left behind in the town.[38]

That night the British rested, presumably in comfort, in their billets in New York and in the tents of their camp, which stretched across the island from Bloomingdale on the Hudson to Horn's Hook on the East River. Not so the Americans within the hastily entrenched lines on Harlem Heights. "Our soldiers," wrote Colonel David Humphrey, "excessively fatigued by the sultry march of the day, their clothes wet by a severe shower of rain that succeeded towards the evening, their blood chilled by the cold wind . . . and their hearts sunk within them by the loss of baggage, artillery and works in which they had been taught to put great confidence, lay upon their arms, covered only by the clouds of an uncomfortable sky."

That wild flight from Kip's Bay was a sad exhibition. Washington called it "disgraceful and dastardly," but such strong epithets were hardly merited. Douglas's men were not trained, experienced, disciplined soldiers; they were raw militia. With their slight defenses battered down and in the face of an advancing foe of overwhelming numbers, it was natural, indeed it was proper, that this thin line of men should leave their indefensible positions. After that withdrawal they might have rallied, as Washington called on them to do, and annoyed the oncoming enemy for a while. But to what end? They could not possibly have held those stone walls. They would have been enveloped and swallowed up with little delay. A retreat was the only sensible move, though, of course, it ought to have been made in good order.

That is not to say that they reasoned this out. After that withdrawal from their trenches the simple fact is that they were panic-stricken. Panics are often inexplicable in their origin and usually ungovernable in their course. Crowds of people are infected by them without knowing how or where they started. They grow by what they feed upon, ignorance of the reason for their existence. Yielding to them does not prove a lack of personal courage. Habits of discipline, well drilled into men so that they automatically obey orders without questioning the reasons for them, are the only safeguard against such occurrences as this in any army at any time. The militia at Kip's Bay had never had even a chance to acquire such habits.

CHAPTER 20

Harlem Heights

The position to which the Americans retreated from New York was on the narrow neck of land that lies between the Harlem River and the Hudson and is the upper part of Manhattan Island. A plateau called Harlem Heights, occupying the full width of the neck, was bordered on the south and on the two river sides by rocky heights, making it a good defensive position. On this plateau Washington had planned a series of three fortified lines, each extending its full width.

On the first line, about a mile back from the southerly edge of the plateau, three small redoubts had been built at the time of the retreat. The connecting entrenchments were now pushed to completion. The second line with four redoubts, about three-quarters of a mile behind the first, and the third line perhaps a half mile behind the second, were to be built later. The plan, therefore, provided for a defense in depth from the rugged edge of the plateau north for nearly four miles.[1]

The returns of the American army under Washington, dated September 21, show a paper strength of 27,273 infantry rank and file, 104 horse, and 543 artillery. Of this number, 16,124 are listed as "present, fit for duty." [2] But to man the Heights there were probably not more than 10,000, the rest being posted farther north at and about Kingsbridge, where the Harlem River turned west to join the Hudson.

The various elements of the force on the Heights were disposed in depth as follows: Greene's division, comprising Nixon's, Sargent's, and Beall's brigades, 3,300 strong, along the southern edge of the plateau; Putnam's division of James Clinton's, Heard's, and Douglas's brigades, 2,500 men, about halfway between Greene's division and the first fortified line; Spencer's division of Fellows's, Silliman's, Wadsworth's, and Mifflin's brigades, 4,200 men, within the first lines.[3]

Facing this plateau on the south was another, the northern edge of which ran very irregularly across the much broader part of the island. Its nearest approach was on the westerly side, where it extended in a sort of peninsula or tongue of land of about the same width as the northern plateau. At this point the two elevations were separated by a narrow depression, perhaps three-quarters of a mile at its widest, a quarter at its narrowest, called the Hollow Way. At its easterly end it widened to an extensive plain with Harlem village at its eastern side.[4]

The British army encamped on the evening of the 15th on the southerly plateau in lines extending on a two-mile front from Horn's Hook on the East River to Bloomingdale on the Hudson. Its front line was thus two miles or less from the front line of the Americans. Two brigades, including the Guards, lay more than a mile in the rear of the lowest line of the main camp and so about three miles back from the American front line.[5]

In the heights at the northern edge of the southern plateau was a gap called McGowan's Pass, through which ran the only road connecting Harlem Plains and the southern parts of the island. It was held by the British.

Washington had much confidence in the strength of his position, but not in the steadfastness of his troops. In the early morning of the 16th he wrote to the Congress: "We are now Encamped with the Main body of the Army on the Heights of Harlem, where I should hope the Enemy would meet with a defeat in case of an Attack, if the generality of our Troops would behave with tolerable resolution. But, experience, to my Extreme affliction, has convinced me that this is rather to be wished for than expected." [6] His confidence in the strength of his position was justified provided Howe made a frontal attack. His apprehensions as to the behavior of his men, engendered by the rout of the militia at Kip's Bay, were almost immediately dispelled.

The great question in the minds of the American command the night of the 15th was whether Howe would follow up his success by an immediate attack. From the American lines, because of the dense woods on the heights to the south of the Hollow Way, nothing could be seen of the enemy's camp in that quarter. Hence there could be no knowledge of preparations for attack, nor of its launching, until the van of the attacking force emerged from the woods into the Hollow Way. To obtain such information a reconnaissance was necessary.

There was in the army a corps of Rangers, about 120 volunteers chosen chiefly from the Connecticut regiments for detached duty, scouting, and the like. They were commanded by Captain Thomas Knowlton, a figure of note. "Six feet high, erect and elegant in figure and formed more for activity than strength," cool and courageous in battle, "courteous and affable in manners . . . the favorite of superior officers, the idol of his soldiers," he had already achieved reputation at Bunker Hill and on Long Island. To him and his corps Washington looked for information as to Howe's intentions.[7]

Before dawn on the 16th Knowlton led his men down from the American position, across the Hollow Way, and up through the woods on the opposite heights behind which lay the British left. They came at length upon a stone house considerably in advance of the main body of the enemy, and at the same time upon the pickets of two battalions of British light infantry under General Leslie holding an advanced post.

At the alarm the light infantry, about 400 strong, advanced. The Rangers took a position behind a stone wall and opened fire. A brisk skirmish ensued. The Americans had fired eight rounds when they discovered the 42nd Highlanders, the Black Watch, coming up on their left and threatening to flank them. Ten of Knowlton's men having fallen, he gave the order to retreat. The British light infantry pushed forward after them through the woods, but the Rangers got away in good order.[8]

The sound of the firing put both armies on the alert. In the American camp the advancing light infantry could be seen emerging from the woods on the opposite height. It might prove to be the beginning of an attack.

The Americans were ordered under arms, but the enemy halted at the edge of their plateau. Pleased by the sight of the Rangers in retreat, the British "in the most insulting manner sounded their bugle-horns as is usual after a Fox-chase. I never felt such a sensation before—it seemed to crown our disgrace." So Colonel Joseph Reed wrote to his wife.[9] Washington, that old fox hunter, must have recognized the taunting notes of the horns as the customary signal of a fox gone to earth. On top of yesterday's affair at Kip's Bay it was too much. Something must be done to wipe out that disgrace and arouse the spirits of his men.[10] He planned a frontal feint with a small force to draw the British light infantry down to the open ground of the Hollow Way, so that a stronger detachment could encircle their right flank and cut them off. For the feint he ordered out 150 volunteers from Nixon's brigade, led by Lieutenant Colonel Archibald Crary of Rhode Island. Knowlton's Rangers and three companies of riflemen from Weedon's 3rd Virginia Regiment, under command of Major Andrew Leitch, were to be the flanking party, about 230 in number.

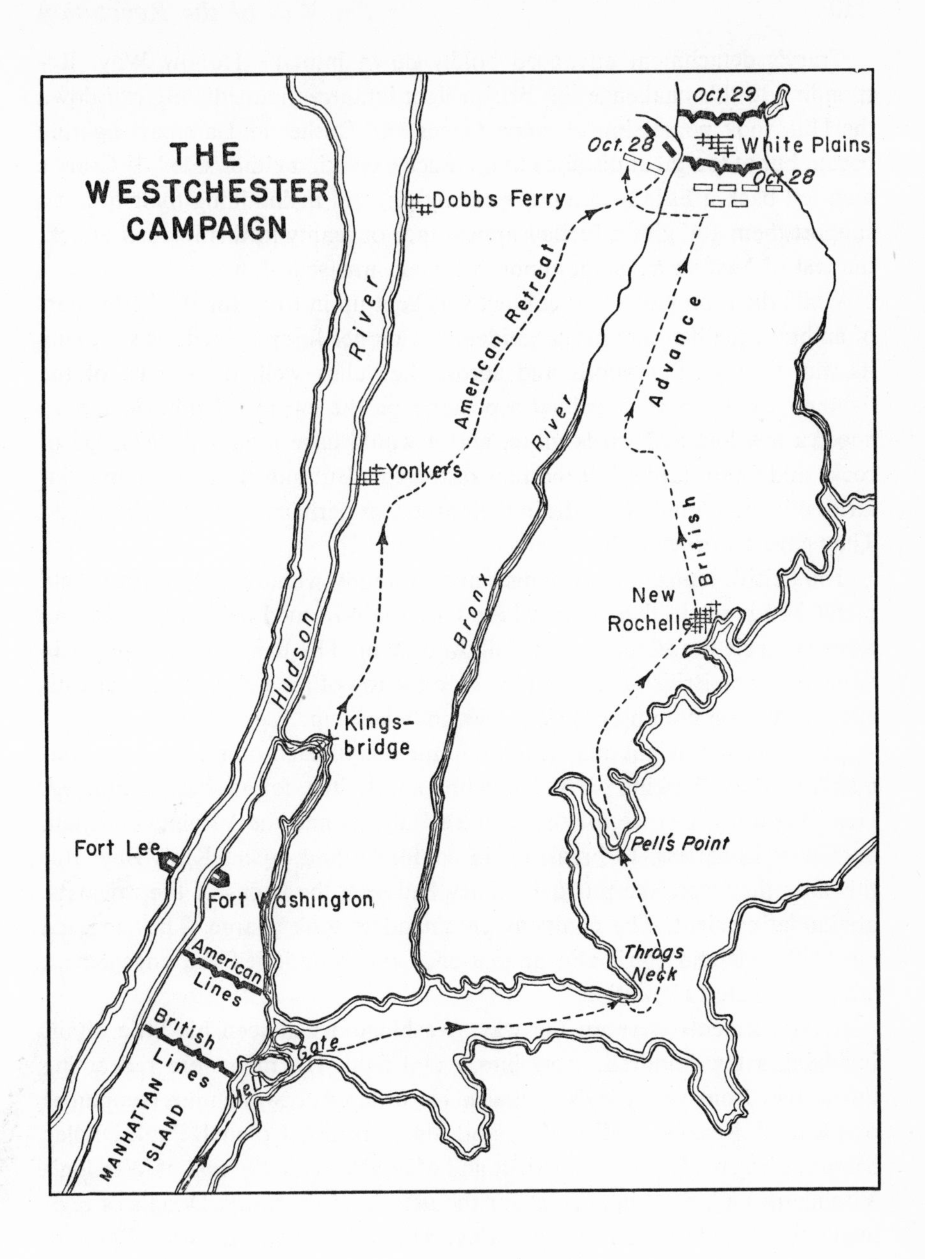
THE
WESTCHESTER
CAMPAIGN
Oct. 29
Oct. 28
White Plains
Oct. 28
Dobbs Ferry
American Retreat
River
Advance
River
Yonkers
British
Bronx
New
Rochelle
Hudson
Kings-
bridge
Pell's Point
Fort Lee
Fort Washington
American
Lines
Throgs
Neck
British
Lines
Gate
MANHATTAN
ISLAND

Crary's detachment advanced boldly down into the Hollow Way. Responding to this challenge the British light infantry "immediately ran down the Hill, took possession of some fences and Bushes and a smart fighting began, but at too great distance to do much execution either side." [11] Crary's men fell back a little to draw the enemy on, still maintaining their fire. To support them and give a further appearance of reality to this feigned attack, the rest of Nixon's brigade, about 800 men, was sent down.

While the semblance of a conflict was kept up in front for the better part of an hour, the flanking party, guided by Colonel Joseph Reed, was making its way through the woods and across the valley well to the east of the fighters. Unobserved, it gained a position on the enemy's flank. So far, so good; a few hundred yards more, and it would have mounted the ledge of rocks and swept around in the rear of the foe. But unfortunately some "inferior officers" could not restrain their ardor, or perhaps control their nerves. They gave an order to fire.

The British realized their danger and promptly withdrew to an open field about 200 yards in their rear, where they again formed behind a fence and resumed their fire. Crary's men followed them. The flankers also joined in the battle. The British again fell back, to the top of the ridge, the Americans after them. The fire on both sides was hotly kept up.

On top of the height and within ten minutes of each other, the two commanders of the flanking party, Knowlton and Leitch, fell mortally wounded. Here was a fine chance for the Yankee Rangers and the Virginia riflemen, both now leaderless, to break up in confusion and repeat Kip's Bay. But this time they were the pursuers. They had seen the backs of the redcoats, a stimulating sight. The company commanders took charge. They pressed on "with splendid spirit and animation," and "continued the engagement with the greatest resolution."

Reinforcements were on the way. Washington had seen his little affair, involving a few hundred, grow into a real fight. His men were redeeming themselves from yesterday's disgrace. He ordered forward nine companies of General Reazin Beall's Maryland state troops, Colonel Paul Dudley Sargent's brigade from Connecticut and Massachusetts, the rest of Weedon's Virginians, and, most important for the morale of the army, Douglas's regiment, the one disgraced at Kip's Bay. That old warhorse, Israel Putnam, hurried to the fray, along with General Nathanael Greene, General George Clinton, and two field guns. Meanwhile, the first British contingents had retired into a buckwheat field, the American light artillery having "put them to flight with two discharges." [12] There they were reinforced by additional light infantry and by the Black Watch.

The fighting grew hotter, the Americans firing steadily and the British stubbornly holding their ground. As the American reinforcements came on, Leslie called on the British reserve in that quarter for more troops. From their post three miles in the rear, on the run, "without a halt to draw breath," [13] came British grenadiers, the 33rd Regiment, a battalion of Hessian grenadiers, and a company of jägers, with two fieldpieces hauled by men. This addition brought the number of British engaged up to 5,000.

The jägers and the Highlanders with the two field guns got there first. For two hours, from noon to two o'clock, the combat was spirited. The British guns fired sixty rounds. Then the Hessians and the Scotsmen, their ammunition running low, retreated. The Americans followed them in hot pursuit, back into an orchard, down a slope, and up another hill. The Hessian grenadiers came up to them. The rest of the British reserve was near at hand, when Washington, seeing that the affair was developing into a general engagement in full force, which he by no means desired, sent an aide, Tench Tilghman, with orders to his troops to withdraw. "The pursuit of a flying enemy was so new a scene that it was with difficulty our men could be brought to retire," but they "gave a Hurra! and left the field in good order." [14]

The losses on both sides were, as usual, variously reported, each side minimizing its own and exaggerating the other's casualties. Howe reported for the British 14 killed and about 78 wounded,[15] but Major Baurmeister, a Hessian, said there were 70 dead and 200 wounded.[16] Washington said his loss was "about sixty"; [17] but more probably there were 30 killed and something less than 100 wounded and missing.[18] In the deaths of Knowlton and Leitch the Americans suffered their severest loss. Knowlton was, in Washington's words, "a valuable and gallant officer." [19] Leitch had arrived in camp with Weedon's Virginians but a few days before the battle. He was a brave soldier of great promise.

Though gallantly fought on both sides, it was a small affair. Yet its effects in both camps were immediate and important. Among the Americans the depression engendered by the recent succession of defeats and retreats was dispelled. Many of the soldiers who had fled from Kip's Bay without firing a shot had now helped to drive the British and Hessian regulars back more than a mile, had fought them in the open field at forty yards range for more than an hour, and had withdrawn in good order to their own lines only when commanded to do so, without being pursued. That was good news for the whole army. Caesar Rodney wrote to his brother about it: "That New England men placed to defend the landing-place [Kip's

Bay], behaved in a most dastardly, cowardly, scandalous manner, is most certain; but that courage is not always to be found the same, even in the same person, is equally true, and verified in the very same men; for some of them the day following were in the other engagement and behaved with great bravery." [20]

Moreover the "Southern" and New England troops had fought side by side with equal courage; neither could criticize the other. To be sure, both claimed the honors of the day. Captain John Gooch of Rhode Island gave "the first Lawrells" to the Yankees, while Lieutenant Tench Tilghman of Maryland wrote, "The Virginia and Maryland Troops bear the palm"; [21] but that was only human. As a whole the army had recovered its self-respect and gained greatly in morale. "You can hardly conceive the change it has made in our army," wrote Colonel Joseph Reed. "The men have recovered their spirits and feel a confidence which before they had quite lost." With some suggestion of doubt he added, "I hope the effects will be lasting." [22]

To the British this affair was an eye-opener. The rebels could stand up and fight bravely against the best of the British and Hessian regulars. The campaign was not going to be an easy succession of Kip's Bays. In the light of this discovery, some thought must be given to the next move. So, for nearly four weeks, Howe contented himself with fortifying his lines, forgoing further offensive movements until what he had gained had been secured.

CHAPTER 21

Throg's Neck and Pelham

While the two armies sat facing each other in their respective fortified positions, there was much speculation in the American camp as to Howe's next move. "The General Officers," says Heath in his memoirs, "were divided in opinion." Some of them expected an effort by Howe to make himself master of the whole island, and thought that the reduction of Fort Washington would be first attempted. That stronghold, upon a height overlooking the Hudson, was a mile or more in the rear of the American lines on Harlem Heights, and it is not clear what plan for its conquest was attributed to Howe that did not involve first a frontal attack on Washington's entrenchments. Others looked for a landing at some point on Long Island Sound in a line with or in the rear of the Americans' more northerly defenses, so that they could be flanked.

With this difference of opinion prevailing, it was "determined in council to guard against both." Ten thousand men were to be held on the Manhattan Island "at or near Fort Washington," that is to say, within the existing lines. Heath, with ten thousand, was to hold the Kingsbridge sector at the upper end of the Harlem River, a floating bridge being thrown across that water so that communication with the first body could be maintained. Greene was to command five thousand on the other side of the Hudson at or near Fort Constitution, which was directly opposite Fort Washington.[1]

Washington had 25,000 troops on paper, but only on paper. As has been said, no more than about 16,000 were present and fit for duty, and of these a large proportion were militia, no more to be depended upon than "a broken staff," as Washington put it.[2] The success of this ambitious plan, therefore, would appear more to be desired than expected.

Washington fully realized his difficulties. "It is not in the power of words," he wrote to his brother on September 22, "to describe the task I have to perform. Fifty thousand pounds would not induce me again to undergo what I have done." And to his cousin: "Such is my situation that if I were to wish the bitterest curse to an enemy on this side of the grave, I should put him in my stead with my feelings." [3]

It was not only that he had too few men to defend all the threatened positions, but also that those he did have were not of the best quality. Although the troops engaged in the recent affair at Harlem Heights had proved themselves good soldiers, the American army was not entirely composed of heroes. The present, too long period of inactivity was undermining the army's morale and sapping its discipline. "A spirit of desertion, cowardice, plunder and shrinking from duty, when attended with fatigue or danger, prevailed too generally throughout the whole army," Colonel Joseph Reed wrote of this period.[4]

Courts-martial sat day after day trying cases of insubordination, mutiny, theft, cowardice in the face of the enemy, desertion, and other offenses. Such crimes and misdemeanors are, of course, common in all armies, but in this they were far too prevalent. Washington wrote to the Congress: "Such a spirit has gone forth . . . that neither publick or private property is secure. Every hour brings the most distressing complaints of the Ravages of our own Troops who are become infinitely more formidable to the poor Farmers and Inhabitants than the common Enemy. . . . The Baggage of Officers and the Hospital Stores, even the Quarters of the General Officers are not exempt from Rapine." [5]

Besides these defects in its personnel, the army as a whole was "in want of almost every necessary; Tents, Camp Kettles, Blankets and Clothes of all Kinds." Reinforcements from New England were coming in "without a single Tent nor a necessary of any kind . . . not a pan or a kettle," [6] and winter was on its way. Even now it was cold at night on Harlem Heights.

All this was bad enough, but the prospect for the near future was worse. The entire army could look forward to its dissolution and complete disappearance within the next two or three months, when its term of enlistment would expire. It was true that the Congress had at last, on September 16, overcome its "jealousy of a standing army," [7] and voted for a new army of eighty-eight battalions "to serve during the present war." [8] But who could foretell when that projected force would be an army in being?

Howe remained inactive for twenty-six days while with characteristic deliberation and with equally characteristic sagacity he made his plans. The

American lines were too strong to invite a frontal attack. Nor was that Howe's favored strategy. Circumvention was less costly and more nearly certain of good results.

There was a small peninsula sticking out into the Sound from the mainland almost due east of the American lines, Throg's Neck—originally Throckmorton's, hence Throck's and Throg's, but also Frog's Neck or Point. And there was a road running northwest from that point to Kingsbridge, well in the rear of the main fortified position of the Americans. Howe finally decided to use that road in the hope that he could sweep the American left flank and possibly pin the American army against the Hudson.

Leaving Lord Percy to hold his lines with three brigades, Howe embarked his main army in the evening of October 12 in eighty vessels of all sorts, passed through Hell Gate under cover of a fog and landed an advance force of 4,000 on Throg's Neck. But it was not a neck, a peninsula; it was, in effect, an island, separated from the mainland by a creek with marshy borders. There were but two approaches from it to the main, a causeway and bridge at the lower end, a ford at the upper, and those approaches were not unguarded. Had Howe landed his men farther to the east, his flanking movement would have had much greater chances of success.

General Heath had posted Colonel Edward Hand with a small detachment of his 1st Pennsylvania rifle regiment at the causeway. The riflemen had removed the planks of the bridge and concealed themselves behind a long pile of cordwood beside its western end. When the van of the enemy approached the gap, it was met by a sudden well aimed fire. The surprised troops were thrown into confusion and fell back to the top of the nearest elevation. No further effort was made to pass that way. Twenty-five American riflemen behind a woodpile had stopped the British army. Another British detachment had headed for the ford, but it too was checked, by a guard posted there. Both of these outposts were promptly reinforced. Colonel William Prescott's Massachusetts Continental regiment and Captain-Lieutenant David Bryant with a 6-pounder and its crew went to Hand's aid. Captain John Graham led a New York regiment of Continentals, together with Captain Daniel Jackson and his fieldpiece, to the post at the ford. The defenders then numbered about 1,800 men. Both sides now began to dig in at their respective positions, the riflemen and the jägers keeping up "a scattered popping at each other across the marsh."

The rest of Howe's force arrived in the afternoon, and the bulk of the British army was at the Neck. But Howe saw that the creek and the marshes were not easily to be crossed against such determined opposition. His men went into camp and lay there for six days while their baggage and supplies were brought up from New York.[9]

Howe had got off to a bad start, but his course was not yet run. Throg's Neck was not the only available landing place. There was Pell's Point, only three miles to the east, which was part of the mainland. It offered the Americans no narrow way to defend.

Howe's flanking move placed the American army in great peril, and a council of war assembled at Washington's headquarters on October 16 to consider the situation. General Charles Lee, who had just rejoined the main army after winning laurels by a successful defense of Charleston in South Carolina, vehemently urged a general retreat to safer positions. However, Congress had resolved on October 11 that Washington be "desired, if it be practicable, by every art and whatever expence, to obstruct effectually the navigation of the North River, between Fort Washington and Mount Constitution." [10] That meant that the line of sunken hulks and the "chevaux-de-frise" stretching across the river from Fort Washington to Fort Constitution, which line had already been found to be easily penetrable by British ships, should be maintained, if "practicable." If the chevaux-de-frise was to be maintained, the two forts had to be defended. Since the barrier had already been proved to be useless, the council of war need not have been concerned about this resolution. Accordingly there was no need to hold Fort Washington. However, the generals decided that, as "the enemy's whole force is in our rear at Frog's Point," it was not possible to hold the present positions on the Heights, and at the same time "that Fort Washington be retained as long as possible." [11]

The proposed withdrawal was to go as far as White Plains, leaving Fort Washington, with its garrison of 2,000, fifteen miles away and completely isolated in a country entirely held by the enemy, with no possibility of succor or supplies except from Fort Constitution across the Hudson. Yet it was to be held. A worse military decision has not often been made. The cost incurred was to be frightful.

Stirling's brigade was hurried northward to seize and hold the desired position at White Plains until the main army should arrive. It made the march in about four hours. The movement of the main army northward was begun on the 18th. Over Kingsbridge, which crossed the Harlem River, and along the west bank of the Bronx River, the American column, 13,000 men with artillery, baggage, and supplies, made its slow and toilsome way—slow and toilsome because of the lack of horses and wagons. After a day's journey, the wagons would dump their loads by the wayside and return for more. The artillery was dragged by hand. Thus, by starts and stops and with infinite labor, a day's journey was accomplished in four.[12]

Meanwhile, entrenched posts were established at intervals along the heights on the west side of the Bronx River to protect the movement of the troops on the road farther west and close to the Hudson. Spencer's division held that line until the main American army had reached White Plains.

Howe finally found that more favorable landing place at Pell's Point. On the same day that the Americans started their northward trek, he embarked his army at Throg's Neck and landed it on the Point.

Colonel John Glover, of the amphibious Marblehead regiment, was then commanding a small brigade made up of four skeleton Massachusetts regiments—his own, Colonel Joseph Read's, Colonel William Shepard's, and Colonel Loammi Baldwin's—in all about seven hundred fifty men with three fieldpieces. He had been but lately posted near the little village of Eastchester to guard the roads from Pell's Point towards the American rear. Early in the morning of the 18th he ascended a near-by hill with his glass and discovered in Eastchester Bay, beside the Point, "upwards of two hundred [boats] . . . all manned and formed in four grand divisions." He turned out his men and marched to meet the landing force.

Glover took a position on the road about a mile from the Point. His own regiment was stationed in the rear as a reserve. The others were strung along behind stone walls lining the road, Read's at the front end or left of the line, Shepard's next, and then Baldwin's. A captain and 40 men were detached and sent forward. They met the enemy's advance guard and, at 50 yards distance, received their fire without loss. Their own reply struck down four men. Five rounds were exchanged in which two Americans were killed and several wounded. When the enemy were "not more than thirty yards distant," Glover ordered his little party to fall back, "which was masterly well done." "The enemy gave a shout and advanced." When they were within a hundred feet, Read's men, lying undiscovered behind their stone wall, "rose up and gave them the whole charge; the enemy broke and retreated for the main body to come up."

For an hour and a half there was no further conflict. Then the whole advance unit of the British, 4,000 men with seven guns, came on. At fifty yards distance Read's men again arose and delivered a volley. The British replied with musketry and fieldpieces. Seven rounds were fired by this regiment before it retreated to take a position behind the wall beyond Shepard's battalion. Again the enemy "shouted and pushed on till they came to Shepard, posted behind a fine, double stone-wall." His men fired by platoons seventeen rounds, "causing them to retreat several times."

Another backward movement of the Americans carried Shepard and Read behind Baldwin. Then Glover ordered his brigade off the field, across a creek, and to a position in his rear on a hill. "The enemy halted and played away their artillery at us and we at them, till night, without any damage on our side and but little on theirs," says Glover. After dark the Americans marched away, about three miles, and encamped, "after fighting all day without victuals or drink, laying as a picket all night, the heavens over us and the earth under us." [13]

Glover lost eight killed and thirteen wounded. Howe reported three killed and twenty wounded; but the chief of the attacking force were Hessians, and their losses were not always included in the British official reports. The Americans thought the Hessian losses were very heavy.[14]

Another interesting little affair occurred on October 22. Major Robert Rogers, noted for audacity and ruthlessness in the French and Indian War, commanded a corps of Tories called "The Queen's American Rangers," about five hundred strong. Looked upon as renegades, he and his men were especially detested by the American troops. Moreover they had been aggressively active, attacking and defeating militia companies and capturing quantities of army stores. They were now in a detached camp at Mamaroneck not far from the right wing of the main body of the British. It was decided to try to cut them off.

"The redoubtable Colonel Haslet" was chosen to conduct this enterprise, with his Delaware regiment,[15] "which since the bravery exhibited on Long Island . . . seems to have been chosen for all feats of peculiar danger." [16] Reinforced by certain Virginia and Maryland companies, his force was made up to seven hundred fifty men.

Late in the night of Tuesday the 22nd, Haslet's force set out on the road from White Plains to Mamaroneck, about five miles. It led them so close to the British right that the most profound silence was necessary to avoid discovery. Having accurate knowledge of the usual disposition of Rogers's men, they approached his camp at a point where but a single sentinel was posted. They seized and silenced him. The way seemed open for a surprise attack on the whole camp, but the astute Rogers had that day concluded his encampment was insufficiently guarded and had posted Captain Eagles and sixty men between the lone sentinel and the main position.

Haslet's vanguard came upon their bivouac, fairly stumbling over the sleepers in the darkness. The rest of his force came up on the run, and there ensued a hurly-burly of a fight. To deceive their assailants, the Rangers echoed the Americans' cry: "Surrender, you Tory dogs! Surrender!" In the darkness friend and foe could not be distinguished. There was a hopeless tangle, Rangers and Haslet's men grappling each other indiscriminately. In the turmoil Eagles and about a third of his men slipped away. The rest were subdued and captured.

Haslet then pushed on toward the main camp. Rogers's troops, thoroughly alarmed, had turned out. There was an exchange of fire, but the advantage of a surprise had been lost. Haslet, contenting himself with a partial success, called off his men and marched back to White Plains with thirty-six prisoners, a pair of colors, sixty muskets, and as many highly prized blankets. He had lost three killed and twelve wounded. The Rangers' loss, besides the prisoners, remains unrecorded. General Heath praised it as "a pretty affair . . . conducted with good address." [17] Like Glover's little fight, this enterprise was chiefly valuable as a stimulus to the fighting spirit of the Americans.

CHAPTER 22

White Plains

Before Howe moved in force against the American position at White Plains the American army was again reorganized. Charles Lee was again with the main army, and also Sullivan and Stirling. Sullivan had been released from captivity in exchange for General Richard Prescott, taken by Montgomery when he captured the British ships at Montreal. Stirling had also been freed, in a trade for Montfort Browne, former royal governor of West Florida. Seven divisions were formed, under the command respectively of Generals Greene, Lee, Heath, Sullivan, Putnam, Spencer, and Benjamin Lincoln. Greene, with about 3,500 men, held the fort across the Hudson from Fort Washington formerly named Constitution but now called Lee in honor of that much respected soldier. About 1,500 men under Colonel Robert Magaw occupied Fort Washington. The main army under Washington numbered about 14,500 present and fit.[1]

Washington had chosen a position on a series of hills overlooking the White Plains. Putnam's division was posted at the right on Purdy Hill, Heath's at the left on Hatfield Hill. Washington himself held the centre at White Plains village. Two lines of defensive works were thrown up, in a shallow curve from the Bronx River on the right to a millpond on the left. The ends of the lines were drawn back so as to defend the flanks.[2]

On October 19, when Howe left his camp at Eastchester, the American retreat from Harlem Heights to White Plains was only well begun. If he had seized his chance then or on the next day and sent his light infantry, grenadiers, and jägers, 4,000 strong, across by the straight road to Kingsbridge, only six miles away, in a swift attack upon the long, straggling line of Washington's army in the confusion of its movement, there could hardly have been any other result than a complete rout of the Americans. Instead he lay at New Rochelle for three days, and then only moved to Mamaroneck, two or three miles. There he encamped for four days. It was not until the 28th that he arrived before Washington's position at White Plains. He had advanced about seventeen miles in ten days.[3] Why Howe executed his flanking movement so slowly is not known.

"The sun had set and risen more than forty times," wrote Trevelyan, the English historian, in acid comment on the progress of the British army, "since General Howe broke up his Summer cantonments on Staten Island. In seven weeks—with an irresistible army and a fleet which there was nothing to resist—he had traversed, from point to point, a distance of exactly thirty-five miles." [4] Trevelyan's judgment of Howe is perhaps too harsh, on this and other occasions.

Meanwhile the British general had received reinforcements, in any event. On the day he landed at Pell's Point there came into New York harbor 120 sail bringing the second grand division of German mercenaries, 3,997 Hessians, 670 Waldeckers, and a company of jägers, all under command of Lieutenant General Wilhelm von Knyphausen, also about 3,400 British recruits. The Germans were at once dispatched by water to New Rochelle to hold that position while Howe proceeded toward White Plains.[5]

The opposing armies clashed again in the morning of the 28th. Spencer, with a half-dozen New England regiments from Lee's division, about 1,500 men, had been sent out to meet the British advance. They took a position behind stone walls about a mile and a half below the American lines and held their fire until the British van was within one hundred feet. Then they delivered a volley that halted it and threw it back. But when Colonel Rall's regiment of Hessians was about to turn their left, the Americans retreated to another wall and after that to another, holding each position until nearly outflanked. At one time a general volley delivered at close range scattered an attacking party of Hessian grenadiers "like leaves in a whirlwind; and they ran off so far that some of the Americans ran out to the ground where they were and brought off their arms and accoutrements and rum that the men who fell had with them, which we had time to drink rounds with before they came on again." So wrote one of the American officers.[6]

But the Hessians did come on again and drove Spencer's troops back across the Bronx River and to Chatterton's Hill, which two militia regiments were engaged in fortifying under the direction of Colonel Rufus Putnam. Rall's regiment, checked by the fire from that elevation, retired to a small hill just south of Chatterton's. The loss of the Americans in this series of encounters was 12 killed, 23 wounded, and 2 missing.[7]

Chatterton's Hill was about half a mile from the right of the main American lines, separated from it by the narrow valley of the Bronx River. It was a ridge three-quarters of a mile long in a north and south direction, rising one hundred eighty feet above the river, which ran along its eastern foot. That side of the hill was steep and heavily wooded. The gently rounded top was divided by stone walls into cultivated fields. Because the hill was a menace to the westerly end of the American lines a belated effort to fortify it was now being made.[8]

After the retreat of Spencer's corps Washington ordered Colonel Haslet with his Delaware regiment to reinforce the men entrenching there. Haslet took post a little below the top of the hill on its eastern side. Later General Alexander McDougall's brigade was also sent there. It was composed of McDougall's own regiment, the 1st New York, Ritzema's 3rd New York, Smallwood's regiment of Marylanders, lately strengthened after its disaster at Long Island, Webb's from Connecticut, and two fieldpieces. These, with Haslet's men, made up a force of about 1,250 rank and file. With the militia already there, the American detachment numbered about 1,600.[9] As senior officer McDougall took command.

Before he arrived several enemy fieldpieces had opened fire on the hill and had hit one of Colonel Putnam's militiamen. "The whole regiment broke and fled immediately and were not rallied without much difficulty." [10] On McDougall's arrival the two militia regiments, Brooks's from Massachusetts and Graham's from New York, were stationed on the right behind a stone wall, at Haslet's suggestion. Smallwood and Haslet held the centre, from which McDougall's, Ritzema's, and Webb's regiments extended to the left.[11]

The whole British army was now coming on in the plain below. It halted, and its general officers gathered in a wheat field for consultation. To the Americans on Chatterton's Hill and in their fortified lines, it presented a brilliant, though formidable, spectacle. "The sun shone bright, their arms glittered, and perhaps troops never were shewn to more advantage than those now appeared," wrote General Heath in his memoirs.[12] An officer in Webb's regiment even more eloquently described the scene: "Its appearance was truly magnificent. A bright autumnal sun shed its lustre on the polished arms; and the rich array of dress and military equipage gave an imposing grandeur to the scene as they advanced in all the pomp and circumstance of war." [13]

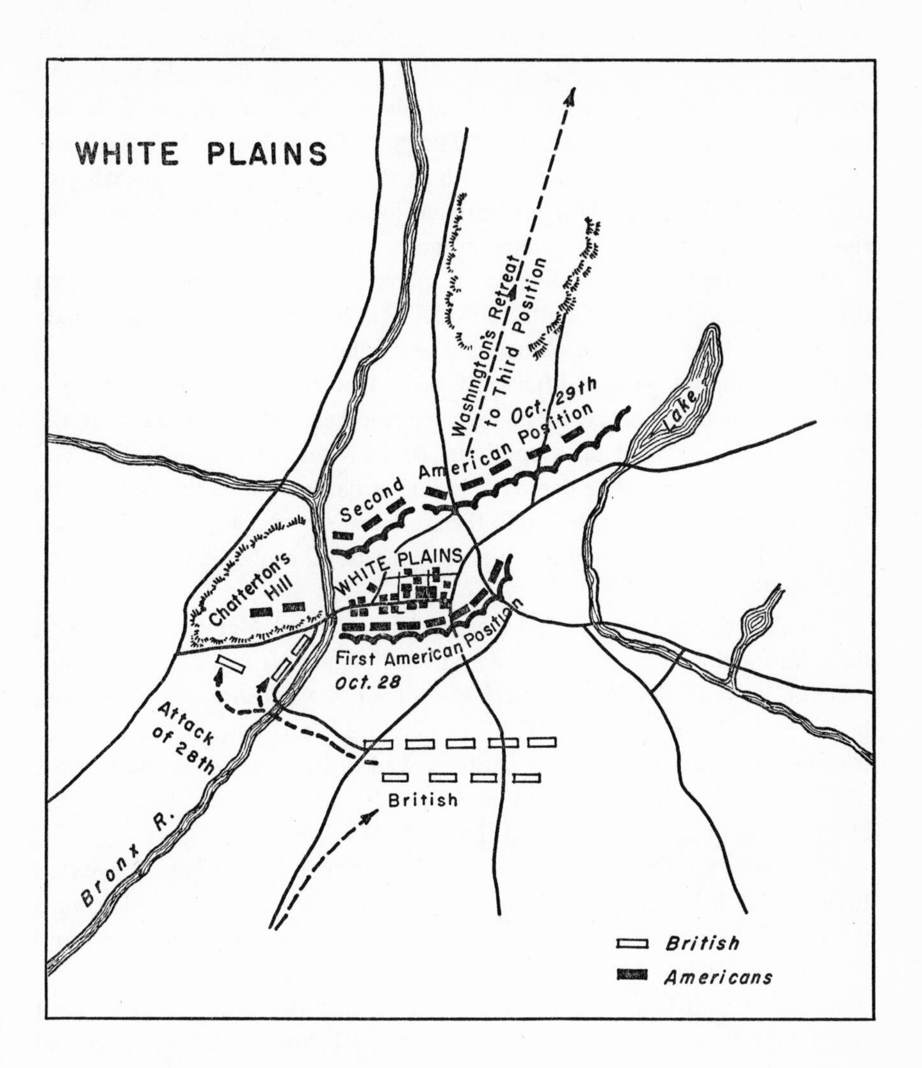
WHITE PLAINS
Washington's Retreat to Third Position
Oct. 29th
Second American Position
Lake
WHITE PLAINS
Chatterton's Hill
First American Position
Oct. 28
Attack of 28th
British
Bronx R.
British
Americans

After the council in the wheat field a British detachment of eight regiments, 4,000 men, and a dozen guns drew away from the main body and marched to a hill facing Chatterton's at about a half-mile distance. It was obvious that they were to attack McDougall's force. The rest of the army "all sat down in the same order in which they stood, no one appearing to move out of his place," [14] a professional audience of 10,000 awaiting the rise of the curtain on an interesting drama.

The overture to the performance was played by the British artillery. From the high ground facing Chatterton's Hill, it began a furious cannonade against the little force of Americans awaiting the attack. General von Heister's adjutant general afterwards said that these guns made such a thunderstorm that one could neither see nor hear. Haslet wrote that the enemy's artillery "kept up a continual peal of reiterated thunder." [15] The attacking force meanwhile deployed in line of battle on the other side of the Bronx River. It was obscured from the Americans by the woods on the slope below and by the smoke of a fire among the trees, probably ignited by the artillery discharges.[16]

The Americans had two fieldpieces. Haslet urged McDougall to bring them into action. The general ordered one forward. It was "so poorly appointed," says Haslet, "that myself was forced to assist in dragging it along in the rear of the regiment. While so employed, a cannon-ball struck the carriage and scattered the shot about, a wad of blazing tow in the middle. The artillerymen fled. The few that returned made not more than two discharges when they retreated with the field-piece." [17]

As soon as the British line was formed a battalion of Hessians, supported by a British brigade and von Donop's Hessian grenadiers, started toward the river. The little Bronx was unusually high because of recent rains, and was much obstructed by an accumulation of old tree trunks and by the remains of ancient beaver-dams. The Hessians declined to try to cross it. It was therefore necessary to construct a rough bridge by felling trees and laying fence rails across them. While the bridge building was in progress, Smallwood's Marylanders and Ritzema's 3rd New York came more than halfway down the hill and opened fire, throwing the Hessians into disorder.

The British General Leslie was then informed of a ford a short distance downstream. He called on the 28th and 35th British regiments to show the Hessians what true British courage could do. Cheering lustily they followed him to the ford and across it. Immediately he ordered a charge with the bayonet; but the hill was steep, the trees thick, and the fire of the Americans heavy. The attackers were thrown back upon the 5th and 49th regiments and the Hessians, who were hurrying to their support.

The whole attacking force had now crossed the stream, either by the bridge or through the ford. It formed in column, marched north along the base of the hill, faced into line parallel with the Americans, and started up the steep slope. Ritzema and Smallwood contested the advance with great gallantry. A detachment of British light infantry tried to turn the Americans' left flank. Webb's Connecticut regiment moved to the left, met the detachment and drove it back.

The British cannonade was now imperiling the attack well advanced up the hill. It was silenced, and orders were sent for attack from another quarter.

Rall's Hessian regiment, unobserved by the defenders since it had betaken itself to the hill on their right after driving back Spencer's force, now went into action. Suddenly, it swept down the slope, across a little intervening valley, and charged up Chatterton's Hill against the New York and Massachusetts militia regiments of Brooks and Graham. They changed front to face the attack, and fired a good volley. But then Birch's British light dragoons came into view, kettledrums beating, trumpets sounding a charge. The galloping horses and the flashing sabers struck terror into the hearts of the green militiamen, who had never seen cavalry in action. They broke and fled in the utmost disorder. The horsemen pursued them, cut off their retreat to the camp, fell upon them in scattered groups, killing and wounding many. For half a mile this rout continued. Then a hundred of the fleeing men rallied and tried to resist, but in vain. Some of them escaped into the woods. The rest surrendered.

The flight of the militia had uncovered the right flank, had left the Delaware regiment unsupported on that side. Haslet drew his men back toward the north, but Rall's Hessians fell upon them in full force. A part of the first three Delaware companies broke and were driven from the field, but Haslet held the rest, lined them up behind a fence, and "twice repulsed the Light Troops and Horse of the enemy." [18]

"During the struggle thus made by the heroic Haslet," [19] the frontal attack had continued. The New York and Maryland troops were driven back. Smallwood's men fought desperately. Smallwood himself was twice wounded, and at last his regiment was thrown into confusion. Ritzema's New Yorkers made an equally gallant effort, but the weight of the onslaught was too heavy. McDougall saw that further resistance was hopeless. He retreated with the New York and Maryland troops to a road leading to the American camp and held them there to protect the withdrawal of the Delawares, standing alone on the field.

Now the dragoons were returning from their chase and forming for a charge on the Delawares, along with all the rest of the attacking force. "Seeing ourselves deserted on all hands," says Haslet, "and the continued column of the enemy advancing, we also retired." [20] "In a great body, neither running nor observing the best of order," they were the last to leave the field, and they brought off the one remaining American gun.[21]

Trevelyan says, "The Delaware regiment, which had learned at Long Island that prisoners are not easily made, unless they make themselves, brought up the rear and fought sullenly and composedly while any of the assailants followed them within shooting range." [22]

The retreating troops were met by a detachment from the main body coming too late to help them in the fight. Haslet then re-formed his men and "marched into camp in the rear of the body sent to reinforce us." "The British ascended the hill very slowly; and, when arrived at its summit, formed and dressed their line without the least attempt to pursue the Americans." [23]

The loss of the Americans is variously reported. Bancroft says fewer than a hundred killed and wounded. Irving says three to four hundred, including prisoners taken. Whitton, citing an English account, says very definitely 313. Hufeland, citing regimental returns, says 175.[24] On the other side, as officially reported, there were 28 killed, including 5 officers, and 126 wounded, also including 5 officers. Among the Hessians there were about 77 casualties.[25]

This battle, measured by the numbers engaged, was a small affair, but it had important results. The check Howe received changed the course of events, as will be seen.

CHAPTER 23

Fort Washington

The British army dug in on Chatterton's Hill, establishing in that position the left wing of a line of entrenchments that extended eastward in a curve threatening both flanks of the American lines. Anticipating further British attacks, Washington prudently had his sick and wounded removed to a safer place in the rear and, even while the battle on the hill was in progress, transferred much of his baggage and equipment to a stronger position on the heights of North Castle.

The results were uncomfortable to the Americans who had been engaged in the fight. When they got back to camp they found that their baggage had been removed. For three or four nights they slept in the woods without even blankets, covered only by the snow that fell upon them.[1] In the night of October 31 the American army slipped away to the North Castle heights, leaving Stirling's brigade to hold the old position temporarily. The garrison at Fort Washington was not moved.

Howe, reinforced by two brigades from Percy's force on Manhattan, now had about 20,000 men. He took possession of the old American lines but made no other hostile move for the next four days except a brief and unimportant artillery engagement with Heath's division on November 1.[2]

Washington busied himself with his entrenchments. Three redoubts, with a line of earthworks in front, were erected with what must have appeared to the enemy to be magical swiftness. Indeed, there was something of magic about them, that is to say of illusion, for that line of earthworks was, in fact, largely made up of cornstalks pulled from near-by fields, with lumps of earth clinging to their roots. They were piled, tops inward, clods outward, and covered with loose earth.[3]

Considering these apparently formidable defenses, Howe altered his plans. During the night of November 4, the sentinels at the American outposts heard sounds like the rumbling of heavy wagons in the British camp. In the morning it was seen that their advanced sentinels had been withdrawn. Some hostile movement of their army was apprehended, and the Americans were ordered under arms. But before long it appeared that the enemy forces were on the march towards the southwest. They were, in fact, on the way to Dobbs Ferry.

A cheering sight to the Americans was this withdrawal. They were again feeling satisfied, in spite of Chatterton's Hill, having "good flour, beef and pork in plenty, with grog to wash it down." They had been retreating and retreating. But now it appeared that they had balked Howe's repeated efforts to get behind them and hem them in. He had given up and was decamping. Contented with the results of the strategy of their generals, war-worn and ragged though they were, soldiers and officers were "in high spirits, loath to give an inch to their enemies." [4]

But where were their enemies going right now? That was, as Washington wrote to the Congress, "a matter of much conjecture and speculation." His own belief was that Howe would "make a descent with a part of his troops into New Jersey, and with another part invest Fort Washington." [5]

A council of war was held on November 6. It was decided that, "supposing the enemy to be retreating towards New-York," it would be "proper to throw a body of troops into New Jersey immediately," and that 3,000 men should take post at Peekskill and the passes of the Highlands.[6] But no serious consideration seems to have been given to abandoning Fort Washington, against which, as soon after appeared, Howe was now actually marching.

The northernmost part of Manhattan Island, extending from Washington's old lines on Harlem Heights to Spuyten Duyvil Creek, a distance of about four miles, is a narrow tongue of high land lying between the Harlem River and the Hudson, its width about three-quarters of a mile. It is bordered on both rivers by precipitous rocky cliffs a hundred feet high. These flank a plateau which rises close to the Hudson, to a narrow hill one mile long and 230 feet high above the water. This hill, called Mount Washington in 1776, is now known as Washington Heights. On the Harlem River side was Laurel Hill, nearly as high. Between the two there was a narrow valley, a gorge through which a road led to Kingsbridge beyond the Harlem. The sides of these two eminences were steep, rocky, and rugged. They and most of the whole tongue of land were densely wooded.[7]

On Mount Washington Colonel Rufus Putnam, the American army's chief engineer, had laid out the lines of a fort which the 3rd and 5th Pennsylvania regiments had erected in July under the command of Colonels John Shee and Robert Magaw.

The fort was a pentagonal earthwork with five bastions. It covered about four acres of ground, but it was a simple, open earthwork with a surrounding abatis and no ditch worth mentioning. It had no casemates, no bombproofs, no barracks, no buildings of any sort except "a wooden magazine and some offices," [8] no fuel, and no water. There was no well, nor any interior water supply whatever. In case of a siege water could be got only from the Hudson, 230 feet below. It had no outworks except "an incipient one at the north, nor any of those exterior, multiplied obstacles and defences, that . . . could entitle it to the name of fortress, in any degree capable of withstanding a siege," wrote Captain Alexander Graydon in his *Memoirs*.[9]

The function of the fort, its only important function at least, was to defend the eastern end of a line of sunken hulks and a chevaux de frise stretching across the Hudson. The purpose of these was to prevent the passage of British ships up the river. The western end of the line was similarly supported by Fort Lee on the New Jersey shore. That anyone should have seriously considered trying to hold such a fort against Howe's whole army of more than 20,000 completely equipped soldiers, operating freely both by land and by water, seems incredible. That such an attempt should have been persisted in after November 7, when the passage of three British ships around those obstructions had proved them to be ineffective and, by the same token, demonstrated the uselessness of both forts, is still more unbelievable. Yet such was the case.

Israel Putnam, with his characteristic exuberant optimism, had "an overweening confidence" [10] in the impregnability of Fort Washington. Colonel Magaw, its commandant, said he could hold it "till the end of December," and that, "should matters grow desperate," [11] he could carry off the garrison and even the stores to the New Jersey side. Strangest of all, Nathanael Greene, one of the most competent general officers in the army, entertained a similar delusion. He could not "conceive the garrison to be in any great danger." He was sure that it could be "brought off at any time." [12] Washington, however, doubted.

On November 8 Washington wrote to Greene, who commanded the troops in both forts: "The late passage of the 3 Vessels up the North River . . . is so plain a Proof of the Inefficacy of all the Obstructions we have thrown into it, that I cannot but think, it will fully Justify a Change in the disposition which has been made. If we cannot prevent Vessels passing up, and the Enemy are possessed of the surrounding Country, what valuable purpose can it answer to attempt to hold a Post of which the expected Benefit cannot be had; I am therefore inclined to think it will not be prudent to hazard the men and Stores at Mount Washington, but as you are on the Spot leave it to you to give such Orders as to evacuating Mount Washington as you Judge best." [13]

Four days later the commander in chief crossed the Hudson and rode down to Greene's camp at Fort Lee. The matter was discussed, "but finally nothing concluded upon." That the failure to give Greene positive orders to evacuate the fort was an instance of the indecision that so often throughout the war beset Washington's mind is proved by his own words. Three years later he wrote to Joseph Reed that Greene's opinion, the wishes of the Congress, and various other conflicting considerations "caused that warfare in my mind, and hesitation which ended in the loss of the garrison." [14] It is somewhat difficult, however, to find fault with Congress in this connection.

Two days after his visit to Greene, Washington made another, and was rowed with Greene, Putnam, and Mercer to Fort Washington early in the morning, "to determine what was best to be done." They were just in time to hear the beginning of Howe's attack on the fort, "a severe cannonade." It was too late to determine anything, except that it was too late. They went back to Fort Lee.

The decision of the council of war to maintain the post having been left standing, the question had arisen whether the Americans should try to hold, in addition to the fort, "all the ground from King's Bridge to the lower lines," that is to say the old American lines on Harlem Heights. On October 31 Greene had asked for Washington's opinion. "If we attempt to hold the ground, the garrison must still be reinforced, but if the garrison is only to draw into Mount Washington and keep that, the number of troops is too large." [15] To this Washington's secretary, replying for him on November 5, wrote that "the holding or not holding the grounds between Kingsbridge and the lower lines depends upon so many circumstances that it is impossible for him to determine the point. He submits it entirely to your discretion." [16]

Magaw's original force in the fort was made up of his own and Shee's regiments, numbering about 700 of all ranks, including those on the sick list.[17] Various additions had been made from time to time. While waiting for Washington's reply Greene had sent Colonel Moses Rawlings from Fort Lee with his regiment of 250 Maryland and Virginia riflemen and Colonel Baxter with 200 Bucks County, Pennsylvania, militiamen. Magaw's troops had thus been raised to 2,800 or 2,900 too many, as Greene himself had said, merely to hold Fort Washington. Greene's intention, therefore, may have been to try to hold all the ground between Harlem Heights and Kingsbridge, although the council of war on September 12 had declared that 8,000 men would be needed for that task.[18]

In pursuance of this hopeless plan Magaw disposed his force. At the northern end of Mount Washington, half a mile from the fort, Rawlings and his riflemen held a small redoubt and a battery of three guns. In a couple of flèches on Laurel Hill near the Harlem River, Colonel Baxter and his militiamen were posted. Two miles to the south, Lieutenant Colonel Lambert Cadwalader had Magaw's and Shee's Pennsylvanians, a part of Miles's, the Rangers, and some others, about 800 men. They occupied the front line of the old entrenchments on Harlem Heights. Minor detachments were posted at other points, leaving Magaw himself, with a small party, in the fort.[19] It was an ambitious plan, an attempt to hold a circuit of four or five miles with such small detachments posted at such distances from each other.

Howe devoted about 8,000 of his men to simultaneous attacks upon these three points. Lord Percy was to go from New York with a brigade of Hessians and nine British battalions[20] against Cadwalader. General Matthews with two battalions of light infantry and two of the Guards, supported by two battalions of grenadiers and the 33rd Regiment under Lord Cornwallis, perhaps 3,000 men, was to cross the Harlem River and take on Baxter's militia. General Wilhelm von Knyphausen had claimed the honor of making the main attack with German troops alone. Rawlings's position was therefore assigned to him, his force to number 3,000 Hessians and Waldeckers. Besides these three real attacks there was to be a feint by the 42nd Highlanders under Colonel Sterling from the Harlem side at a point between Cadwalader's position and the fort, to confuse the Americans.[21]

Operations began on the night of November 14, when thirty British flatboats were sent up the Hudson, through Spuyten Duyvil Creek, and so into the Harlem River, entirely unobserved by the Americans. The next morning, the British Lieutenant Colonel Patterson with flag and drum approached the fort and demanded a surrender, making the usual threat that the entire garrison might be put to the sword if the fort had to be stormed. Magaw declined with the customary assurance of his determination "to defend this post to the last extremity." [22]

At a little after seven the next morning the battle began. Twenty-one guns in British batteries on the eastern side of the Harlem, and those of the frigate *Pearl,* stationed in the Hudson between the fort and Rawlings's position, opened fire on all the American positions and kept up a heavy cannonade for two hours or more. At ten o'clock, Percy advanced against Cadwalader. His field artillery having driven in a small outpost, he crossed the Hollow Way, gained the heights above it, and approached the lines marching in column. At a proper distance, his fieldpieces and a howitzer opened fire. Cadwalader replied with his lone 6-pounder. Thereupon, to the surprise of the Americans, Percy's column inclined to the left and halted behind a piece of woods, where it remained inactive for an hour and a half. The reason for this seemingly peculiar behavior was that the detachments under Matthews and Cornwallis had been delayed in crossing the Harlem by an adverse condition of the tide and by "some neglect not foreseen before," [23] and the plan for simultaneous attacks compelled Percy to wait.

About noon Matthews and his light infantry crossed the Harlem in the thirty flatboats and landed below Baxter's position. While crossing and on landing they were under a galling American fire, but they came on and, with characteristic gallantry and dash, swarmed up the steep, wooded sides of Laurel Hill. Cornwallis, with the Guards, the grenadiers, and the 33rd, crossed without injury and followed the light infantry. Colonel Baxter was shot down. Leaderless, his militia fled to the fort.

Knyphausen had started his troops from their camp on the mainland side of the Harlem early in the morning. By seven o'clock he had crossed Kingsbridge. In two columns, that on the right led by Colonel Johann Rall, the other by Major General Martin Schmidt, his troops came down into the ground below Rawlings's position; but there, because of Cornwallis's delay, they had to halt. About ten o'clock they got word to advance. They pushed forward eight or ten fieldpieces in the ground below Rawlings and opened fire. Rall led his column to the right through a break in the wooded hills along the Hudson and toward the north end of Mount Washington. Knyphausen, with Schmidt's column, kept to the left and "made a Demonstration . . . as if he intended to attack" [24] the easterly side of that elevation. His men had to wade through a swamp and break through a triple abatis of trees felled by the Americans on their retreat from Kingsbridge on November 2.

Rall's men had "an Excessive Thick Wood" to get through and "Steep Rocks to get up." Struggling up the long, steep, rugged height, grasping bushes to pull themselves up the almost precipitous slope, they came under the fire of the American guns. Grape and round shot were hurled upon them; then came a shower of bullets. The riflemen, in the redoubt and from behind rocks and trees outside, poured a well aimed and deadly fire on their foes. But the persistent Hessians pressed on with great gallantry against the unseen defenders of the height.

When Rall had come near to the top, Knyphausen "made a sudden face to the Right" against the side of the hill assigned to his force and met the same difficulties, the same fire. For nearly two hours these courageous assaults and this stubborn defense continued. But the rifles of the Americans became fouled by the frequent and long continued discharges. Man after man found that he could not drive home a bullet in the clogged barrel of his gun. The fire of the defenders waned and at last was too feeble to hold back the enemy, now nearing the top of the ascent. They had no bayonets to repel a charge with that weapon. A retreat was inevitable. Rawlings drew them back toward the fort. They gained it ahead of their pursuers. This was the hottest fight of the day and the longest.

While all this was going on Percy emerged from his cover and with his two brigades—one English, the other Hessian under Major General Johann Stirn—assailed Cadwalader's lines. An outwork fell to him. He extended his front across to the North River, temporarily desisting from further attack.

After his success against Baxter's small force Cornwallis, foreseeing a necessary retreat by Cadwalader's men, also saw that the proposed feint by the men of the 42nd could be turned into an actual participation in the fight. He ordered Sterling, their commander, to join two battalions of the 2nd Brigade with his Highlanders and come over the Harlem River so that he could strike across Manhattan Island and intercept Cadwalader's withdrawal.

Cadwalader had news of Sterling's embarkation and sent Captains David Lennox, George Tudor, and Evan Edwards of the 3rd Pennsylvania with 150 men to oppose the landing. Magaw sent one hundred men from the fort. They acted with spirit. From an 18-pounder and their rifles and muskets they poured a heavy fire on the boats. But the Highlanders and British were not to be denied. In spite of a loss of 90 men, they made their landing, clambered up the high, steep, rocky ascent from the river, and assailed the Americans with such speed and dash that they actually captured 170 of them.

Percy, hearing the fire from that quarter, pressed hard on Cadwalader. Alarmed by the sounds in his rear and fearing to be caught between two fires, Cadwalader precipitately retreated. He was closely pursued. Near the fort he halted his men in a small wood and delivered a heavy fire, which for a moment checked the enemy. But the 42nd had come across. They drove him out of the wood and took some prisoners. The rest of Cadwalader's men reached the fort just before Rall's Hessians arrived within a hundred yards of it and took a position behind a large storehouse.

Rall peremptorily demanded a surrender. Magaw demurred, asking for time to consider. Rall refused. There were more than 2,500 men in the fort, crowded within a space not adequate to receive more than a thousand. Under bombardment it would become a hideous slaughter pen. Magaw's "last extremity" had arrived long before the end of December. To Knyphausen, who came up with Schmidt's column a little after Rall, Magaw yielded his sword. Two Hessian regiments, Rall's and Lossberg's, were drawn up in lines. Between them the Americans, having laid down their arms in the fort, marched out and gave up their colors, "which were yellow, red and light blue." Knyphausen, a grim and silent man, is said to have looked on these banners "with disdain." It was one of the ironies of the war that these Hessian regiments, thus especially honored, were to surrender their flags to Washington within six weeks.

The casualties in the British army were more severe than in the American, except in the matter of prisoners taken. The defenders had 59 killed and 96 wounded. The British had 78 killed and 374 wounded. Of these the Hessian share was 58 dead and 272 wounded. But the American loss in prisoners taken and matériel captured was stupendous. Officers to the number of 230 and 2,607 private soldiers fell into the hands of the British.[25]

The amount of precious matériel lost was staggering. At Fort Washington, Fort Lee which fell a few days later without opposition, and their various small dependencies, the British took 146 iron and brass guns, ranging from the smallest to 32-pounders, 12,000 shot and shell, 2,800 muskets, and 400,000 musket cartridges, besides tents, entrenching tools, and equipment of various sorts.[26]

It was one of the greatest disasters of the war for the Americans, and the blame for it must rest upon the shoulders of Greene and Magaw for their inexplicable infatuation in attempting to hold the fort, and upon those of Washington for his vacillation and indecision when by prompt and decisive action he might have prevented his inferior officers from persisting in their suicidal folly.

CHAPTER 24

The Retreat Through the Jerseys

After the fall of Fort Washington the main American army was still divided into three parts. General Lee was in command of the position at North Castle with three divisions—his own and those of Generals Sullivan and Spencer, each composed of two brigades. His paper strength was about 10,000 rank and file, but 4,000 men were absent, either on command or sick. Of those present 1,200 were on the sick list. His effectives numbered only 5,500.[1] General Heath had four brigades at and about Peekskill. There was a similar discrepancy between his paper strength and those actually present and fit, 5,400 on paper, 3,200 effective. Washington had the rest, 5,400, including Greene's men at Fort Lee.[2]

Thus there would seem to have been 14,000 able-bodied private soldiers to be relied upon for the rest of the campaign, a substantial force. But the number was rapidly dwindling. For a time after the affair at White Plains, while they were idle at North Castle with plenty to eat and drink, the men were cheerful and hopeful. But the catastrophe at Fort Washington had been enough to chill the ardor of a far more experienced, better disciplined, and more comfortably equipped army than this one.

Winter was coming on. The nights were already frosty. November rains were frequent and chilling.[3] Tents were lacking, blankets scarce, and the men's clothing was too meager and too ragged to keep them even passably warm. An English officer noted in his diary on November 5 that "many of the Rebels who were killed in the late affairs, were without shoes or Stockings, & Several were observed to have only linen drawers on, with a Rifle or Hunting shirt, without any proper shirt or Waistcoat. They are also in great want of blankets." The weather before that, he noted, had been mild, "but in less than a month they must suffer extremely." [4]

No one knew that better than the men themselves. Their terms of enlistment were soon to expire. The time of 2,060 of Washington's own force would be up on December 1, and all the rest, not only of his contingent, but of the whole army, would be free by the 1st of January.[5]

Under these conditions it is not surprising that "the contagion of desertion, which had been epidemic in his [Washington's] cantonments, now raged after the manner of a plague." [6] On November 9 Washington wrote that many of the Connecticut militia regiments had been reduced "to little more than a large company." On November 30 he said that the Pennsylvania militia of General Ewing's brigade, though enlisted to January 1, were "deserting in great numbers." [7] The prospect of any success in the rest of the campaign of 1776 was slight.

A few days before the fall of Fort Washington the American commander in chief moved westward with the force mentioned above, leaving General Lee and his detachment to protect New England. Washington detached Stirling's brigade to find a suitable crossing over the Hudson and to act as advance guard. Stirling crossed from Peekskill to Haverstraw on the 9th, found a gap in the Palisades through which passed a road to the west, posted a hundred men to hold it, and sent scouts to spy out the country beyond.[8] Washington followed on the 10th, marched through the gap, called the Clove, and encamped at Hackensack. From that point he rode down to Fort Lee and became a spectator of the disaster at Fort Washington. The surrender completely upset his plans. Instead of detaining the British army for months in a siege, the fort had fallen in a few hours. Howe was free to move any force he pleased into the Jerseys at once.

On the day Fort Washington was surrendered, the commander in chief wrote to the Congress that he hoped to hold Fort Lee. But three days later he had convinced himself that the fort was "only necessary in conjunction with that on the other side of the river" and was now "of no importance." He proposed to evacuate it and remove his stores. He was a day too late in reaching that conclusion, for Howe had taken prompt advantage of his freedom of movement and was preparing that very night for an attack to be launched on the morrow.[9]

At nine o'clock in the "very rainy" evening of the 19th, the 1st and 2nd battalions of British light infantry, two of British and two of Hessian grenadiers, two of the Guards, two companies of Hessian jägers, and the 33rd and 42nd British regiments, about 4,000 in all, struck their tents. By daylight, under the leadership of Cornwallis, they landed on the Jersey side of the Hudson at Closter, five or six miles above Fort Lee, and marched down the river, intending to cut off its garrison from retreat to Washington's army at Hackensack and pen it up between the Hackensack River and the Hudson.[10] Fortunately an American officer on patrol discovered their advance, rode down to the fort, got Greene out of bed, and told him about it. Greene relayed the news to Washington, ordered his men under arms and out of the fort, and hurried them away, in flight rather than in retreat, to the head of a small stream in his rear, thus gaining the road to the bridge over the Hackensack. Here he assembled as many as possible of his confused and disordered men, left them in charge of Washington, and galloped back on the road to the fort to round up three hundred stragglers and bring them off. But the British force was so hot on his heels that one hundred and five Americans were captured and eight or ten were killed.[11]

When the British arrived at the fort there was no one to oppose them. Three hundred precious tents had been left standing, all the blankets were there, and the breakfast camp kettles were boiling over the fires.[12] Besides the cannon already mentioned in the account of Fort Washington, a thousand barrels of flour fell into the enemy's hands. Fortunately the store of gunpowder had been got away a day or two before.[13]

While there was still doubt as to Howe's intentions, Lee's division had been left at North Castle to oppose him if he moved north. Washington in his instructions to Lee had said that, if the enemy moved westward into New Jersey, "I have no doubt of your following with all possible dispatch." [14] There was no longer any doubt that Howe was throwing large forces into New Jersey. He had actually sent over Cornwallis. It seemed to be time for Lee with his 5,000 effectives to come to the aid of Washington "with all possible dispatch." Colonel William Grayson, one of Washington's aides-de-camp, wrote Lee on the day Fort Lee fell, "His Excellency thinks it would be advisable in you to remove the troops under your command on this side of the North River." [15] Washington wrote the next day, "I am of opinion . . . that the publick interest requires your coming over to this side." [16]

These letters were not couched in the terms of a positive order. Lee did not move immediately, suggesting that part of Howe's army might still move against New England. He wrote to Colonel Joseph Reed, Washington's adjutant general: "His Excellency recommends me to move . . . to the other side of the river . . . but we could not be there in time to answer any purpose." [17]

Lee was vain, as he himself admitted, and his vanity had been fed to bursting by the admiration and adulation which had been his from the moment he joined the army. At a time when the Congress was making generals out of blacksmiths and booksellers, farmers and lawyers, whose military knowledge and experience were of the most meager sort, the appointment of Charles Lee as second in command under Washington was hailed with enthusiasm. Here was a professional soldier who from the age of fifteen had worn a military coat and had flashed a gleaming sword on many a battlefield in Europe and America. His homespun colleagues listened with awe and with but little understanding to his talk of redans and redoubts, ravelins and counterscarps. Simple provincials as they were, they looked upon him as the very epitome of the arts of war in the grand manner and valued him accordingly.

Lee, always ambitious, tended from now on, with his own division separated from that of the commander in chief, to use his own judgment rather than follow Washington's recommendations; and at this crucial time in his career Colonel Reed, Washington's adjutant general, encouraged him to act independently.

On November 21 Reed wrote to Lee in most fulsome adulation: "I do not mean to flatter or praise you at the expense of any other, but I confess I do think it is entirely owing to you that this army, and the liberties of America . . . are not entirely cut off. You have decision, a quality often wanted in minds otherwise valuable." Washington's for one, of course. Reed wanted him to join Washington's army, where his judgment and experience were "so likely to be necessary." He assured Lee of the confidence in him of every member of Washington's staff and of the officers and soldiers generally. Of Washington's part in the retention of Fort Washington he exclaimed: "Oh! General, an indecisive mind is one of the greatest misfortunes that can befall an army; how often have I lamented it in this campaign . . . We are in a very awful and alarming situation—one that requires the utmost wisdom and firmness of mind." Lee's and Reed's to be sure.[18]

Lee answered on the 14th that he too lamented "that fatal indecision of mind which in war is a much greater disqualification than stupidity." Acknowledging that Washington had recommended his crossing over to New Jersey "in so pressing a manner as almost to amount to an order," he had various reasons for not coming at once. He would, however, soon come, "for to confess a truth, I really think our Chief will do better with me than without me."[19]

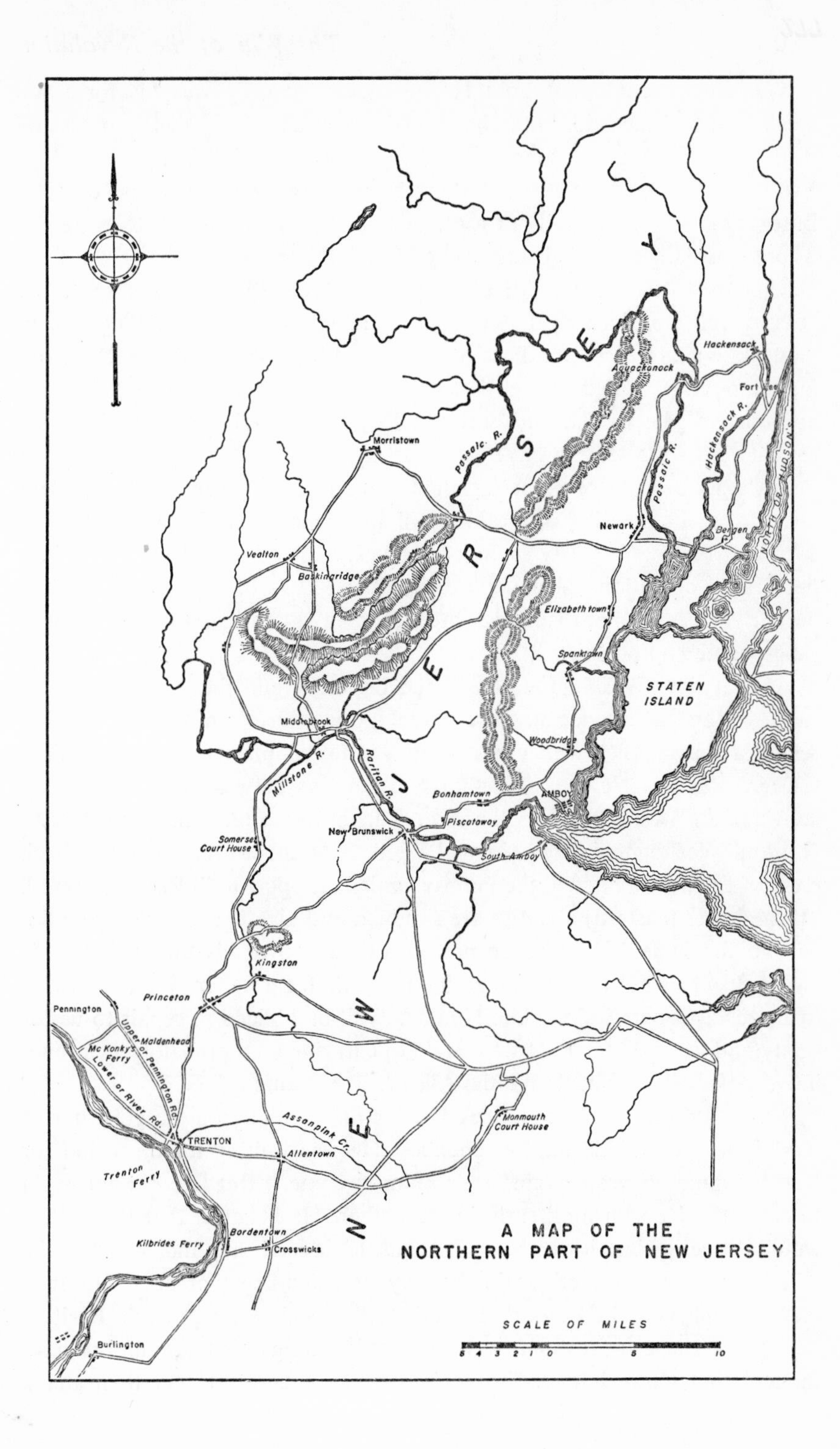

NEW JERSEY
Hackensack
Fort Lee
Aquackanock
Hackensack R.
NORTH OR HUDSON'S
Passaic R.
Morristown
Newark
Bergen
Vealton
Baskingridge
Elizabeth town
Spanktown
STATEN ISLAND
Middlebrook
Woodbridge
Millstone R.
Raritan R.
Bonhamtown
AMBOY
Piscataway
New Brunswick
Somerset Court House
South Amboy
Kingston
Princeton
Pennington
Maidenhead
Upper or Pennington Rd.
Mc Konky's Ferry
Lower or River Rd.
Assanpink Cr.
Monmouth Court House
TRENTON
Allentown
Trenton Ferry
Bordentown
Kilbrides Ferry
Crosswicks
Burlington
A MAP OF THE
NORTHERN PART OF NEW JERSEY
SCALE OF MILES
5 4 3 2 1 0 5 10

Washington could not hold Hackensack. Not only was his force too weak—he had, he said, "not above 3,000 men and they much broken and dispirited" [20]—but the country was, as he expressed it, "almost a dead Flat." Since the fall of Fort Washington and the consequent loss of "500 intrenching tools," he had not a pick nor a shovel with which to entrench. There was danger of his being cooped up in the narrow space between the Hackensack River and the Passaic. He left three regiments to dispute the crossing of the river by the bridge, marched westward on the 21st to Aquackanock, crossed the Passaic there, and hurried on to Newark, arriving the next day. His rear guard at Hackensack destroyed the bridge on the approach of the British and hastened to join the main body.[21] The great retreat across the Jerseys was now well under way.

Stirling's brigade of eight regiments, about 1,200 men, had been sent ahead after its crossing of the Hudson. It reached New Brunswick on the 17th and there awaited Washington. It was, like the rest of the army, in a deplorable condition. Lieutenant Enoch Anderson of Haslet's Delawares wrote: "We arrived at Brunswick broken down and fatigued—some without shoes, some had no shirts."

At that time Washington considered his army and the American cause to be in the gravest danger. The contemporary historian William Gordon relates a conversation which he describes as taking place between Washington and Reed at Newark. Whether Gordon was or was not accurate, the conversation well represents the American army's situation. According to Gordon, Washington asked Colonel Reed, "Should we retreat to the back parts of Pennsylvania, will the Pennsylvanians support us?" Reed answered, "If the lower [eastern] counties are subdued and give up, the back counties will do the same." Washington passed his hand over his throat and said: "My neck does not feel as though it was made for a halter. We must retire to Augusta County in Virginia. Numbers will be obliged to repair to us for safety and we must try what we can do in carrying on a predatory war, and, if overpowered, we must cross the Allegheny Mountains." [22]

Washington lingered at Newark for five days, calling on the governor of New Jersey for militia reinforcements.[23] He was waiting for them and for Lee, to whom he wrote again, urging him to come.[24] But Lee did not begin to cross the Hudson until early in December. He believed that the British would move against lower New England, as indeed they did, and that he might accomplish something in the way of defending that area. His men lacked blankets and shoes, and he hesitated to begin a long march. Besides, he seems to have overestimated the size of Washington's force, and to have thought that Howe intended to go into winter quarters rather than attack

Washington. Lee continued for many days to follow his own judgment rather than the recommendations of the commander in chief. Perhaps Washington did not trust *his* own judgment, since he did not send Lee explicit orders.

Dispirited by a succession of defeats, wearied with marching day after day, lacking tentage, blankets, clothing, and even shoes, Washington's force was indeed, as Reed described it, "the wretched remains of a broken army." [25] It is not surprising that British officers were writing home, "Peace must soon be the consequence of our success." Howe was so confident of his ability to finish off his staggering opponent that he divided his army and sent Clinton, with more than 6,000 men, to possess Rhode Island and winter there. Clinton took Rhode Island without opposition. His troops remained in and about Newport three years. Trevelyan says, "For any effect which they produced upon the general result of the war, they might have been as usefully, and much more agreeably, billeted in the town of the same name in the Isle of Wight." [26]

Washington had called on the Congress and on the governor of New Jersey for more men.[27] The Congress called on the Philadelphia Associators, a volunteer organization, to march. They were coming, but had not yet arrived. The New Jersey militia failed to respond to Washington's call.[28] On the 28th the van of Cornwallis's troops, in their inexorable pursuit of their quarry, marched into Newark as Washington's rear guard was marching out to join Stirling at New Brunswick.[29] November 30 came and went, and with it went the Maryland and New Jersey militia brigades of General Reazin Beall and General Nathaniel Heard, the 2,000 time-expired men: "being applied to they refused to continue longer in service." [30] "But what is still worse," Washington wrote, "Altho' most of the Pennsylvanians are inlisted till the first of January, I am informed that they are deserting in great numbers." [31]

There was a postscript to Washington's letter of December 1, from New Brunswick to the Congress: "½ after 1 o'clock P. M. The Enemy are fast advancing, some of 'em in sight now." At seven o'clock he wrote: "We had a smart cannonade [across the Raritan] whilst we were parading our Men, but without any or but little loss on either side. It being impossible to oppose them with our present force with the least prospect of success we shall retreat to the West side of Delaware [River] and have advanced about Eight miles." [32] At Princeton he did not stop. Pushing on in full flight he came to Trenton the next day. Safety was now his only aim, and the other side of the Delaware offered that.

He had hurriedly ordered the collection or destruction of all the boats on the river for a space of seventy miles above Philadelphia. In such as had arrived at Trenton he immediately began the transportation of his stores and baggage, his sick and wounded men.[33]

At New Brunswick, Stirling's brigade—five Virginia regiments and one from Delaware, about 1,200 men, "the flower of the army, though a faded flower it was" [34]—had joined in the retreat, first burning a hundred of their precious tents, which they had no wagons to carry off. "When we saw them reduced to ashes," wrote Lieutenant Enoch Anderson of Haslet's Delaware Regiment, who was detailed for that purpose, "it was night. We made a double quick-step and came up with the army about eight o'clock. We encamped in the woods, with no victuals, no tents, no blankets. The night was cold and we all suffered much, especially those who had no shoes." [35]

While the rest pushed on to Trenton, Washington left Stirling's brigade at Princeton to hold back the enemy. There it found a welcome though temporary relief from the hardship it had endured. "We had comfortable lodgings in the College," says Anderson.

But Stirling's men were not put to the expected test of holding back Cornwallis, for a most surprising thing had happened. Cornwallis was an energetic, swift-moving soldier. To overtake Washington at New Brunswick he had marched his men twenty miles through a heavy rain, over the most wretched roads deep with mud, in a single day. Washington had destroyed the bridge there, but the Raritan was easily fordable, "in a variety of places, knee deep only." [36] Cornwallis might have crossed it and caught up with the retreating army to its destruction. Instead, he halted his men, and did not move again for four days; meanwhile Washington made good his escape across the river. It was not Cornwallis's fault. He was under orders to remain there until Howe came up with the main army.

Charles, second Earl Cornwallis, was born of an ancient family on December 31, 1738. He began his military career as an ensign of the Grenadier Guards at the age of eighteen. He served in the Seven Years' War on the continent of Europe, was a captain at twenty-one, lieutenant colonel at twenty-three, a colonel of the 33rd Regiment of Foot at twenty-eight. Although he was a Whig and had stood in the House of Lords with Lord Camden and a few others in opposing the taxation of the American colonists, the King made him a major general in 1775 and sent him to America in 1776. Two years later he was made a lieutenant general. Trevelyan has described him as "an English aristocrat of the finest type . . . a man of immense and varied experience; careful and industrious; modest in success and equable in adversity; enlightened, tolerant and humane; contemptuous of money and indifferent to the outward badges of honour . . . he presented . . . a living and most attractive example of antique and single-minded patriotism."

As a soldier, Cornwallis was personally courageous; as a general, he was vigorous, active, and enterprising. Trevelyan contends that "the energy and enterprise, which . . . marked his two campaigns in the Carolinas, revived the dying credit of our natural generalship"; but this is overgenerous praise, for though his notable energy was in strong contrast to the habitual sloth of Howe, and though he is rated by Fortescue as "a good skilful and gallant soldier," it may be doubted that he was a military leader of exceptional genius. Certainly he was outgeneraled in the Carolina campaigns by Greene, who drove him to his final defeat at Yorktown.

In person, Cornwallis was a figure of distinction, thirty-eight years old, tall, erect, and handsome in the full-fed, well fleshed, portly fashion of the period. His features were bold, his nose well shaped, his full lips curved in an agreeable, rather humorous expression, his chin strong and deeply cleft, his face marred by an injured eye, the result of colliding in a hockey game with a future bishop of Durham while they were schoolboys at Eton.

He distinguished himself after the war in America by his services as Governor General of India and commander in chief of the British forces there.

By the 5th of December, Washington was strengthened by the arrival of some of the Pennsylvania Associators and part of Colonel Nicholas Haussegger's regiment of Pennsylvania and Maryland Germans.[37] Having to cross the river and lacking information as to the movements of the enemy at New Brunswick, he decided to "face about with such Troops as are here [Trenton] fit for Service and March back to Princeton and there govern myself by Circumstances and the movements of General Lee." [38] On the 7th he set out with 1,200 men. But when he was within a few miles of the college town he met Stirling in full retreat. Howe had arrived at New Brunswick the day before and had sent Cornwallis forward.[39] While Washington was marching, Cornwallis was on his way to the same destination. Washington turned back.[40]

Haslet's Delawares were the rear guards in that final retreat. Lieutenant Anderson of the regiment has left a lively picture of the commander in chief's personal activities during the withdrawal: "We continued in our retreat—our Regiment in the rear and I, with thirty men in the rear of the Regiment and General Washington in my rear with pioneers—tearing up bridges and cutting down trees to impede the march of the enemy. I was to go no faster than General Washington and his pioneers. It was dusk before we got to Trenton. Here we stayed all night." [41]

Cornwallis had marched slowly and cautiously, with flankers thrown out on both sides to scour the woodlands and look out for ambushes. The broken-down bridges and other obstacles also delayed him. His vanguard reached Trenton about two o'clock the next afternoon, just as the last of the Americans were putting off for the Pennsylvania shore. His light infantry and jägers were greeted by the fire of American batteries across the river and put to flight, with the loss of thirteen men.[42] The British responded, "but," says Anderson, "we were in the woods and bushes and none were wounded that I heard of. . . . That night we lay amongst the leaves without tents or blankets, laying down with our feet to the fire. We had nothing to cook with, but our ramrods, which we run through a piece of meat and roasted it over the fire, and to hungry soldiers it tasted sweet."

The British ranged up and down the river, looking for boats, but found none. Washington had them all on the other side.

The next morning, Washington posted Stirling's brigade in detachments at different landing places up the river to "prevent them from Stealing a March upon us from up above." [43] Howe gave up the idea of crossing and distributed his troops in various posts, at Pennington, New Brunswick, Trenton, and Bordentown. Now, for some little time, all was quiet along the Delaware. Howe seems to have assumed that the campaign of 1776 was ended, and that there would be no further major military activity until spring.

CHAPTER 25

The Crisis

"A thick cloud of darkness and gloom covered the land and despair was seen in almost every countenance," wrote one of the American officers of that period.[1] Said another, "Such is now the gloomy aspect of our affairs that . . . strong apprehensions are entertained that the British will soon have it in their power to vanquish the whole remains of the continental army." [2]

It was indeed the darkest hour of the war. Newport and New York were already held by the enemy. Philadelphia, the largest and finest American city, the seat of such government as the infant republic had, was unfortified, virtually ungarrisoned, open to attack on all sides. Only thirty miles away lay an army of 10,000 British and Hessian soldiers flushed with repeated victories, confident of their strength, and eager for rest and refreshment in such pleasant winter quarters as Philadelphia afforded. There was nothing to hinder a descent upon that apparently doomed town but the Delaware River, Washington's little force "crouching in the bushes" [3] on its western side, and possibly the weather.

The river was no substantial barrier. It could easily be crossed in boats and barges. The material to construct them was at hand in lumber yards in Trenton and, if more was needed, in the wood of its houses. Or the ice might within a few days be thick enough and strong enough to bear the weight of marching men, their horses, wagons, and artillery. The river offered little hope of enduring protection.

Nor did Washington's army seem to offer much more. It numbered no more than 5,000 men "daily decreasing by sickness and other causes," half of them militia or raw recruits, most of them clad like scarecrows in worn and ragged garments, shod like tramps, if shod at all, "many of 'em being entirely naked," said Washington, "and most so thinly clad as to be unfit for service." [4] Shivering in their unprotected posts or in their blanketless, restless sleep, these wretches were trying to cover thirty miles of the western shore of the river against an enemy that might strike at any time, at any place, or at several places at once. Washington was forced to say that he could see no means of preventing the British from passing the Delaware. "Happy should I be," he wrote to the Congress, "if I could see the means of preventing them. At present I confess I do not." [5] He told his nephew that, without reinforcements, "I think the game is pretty near up." [6]

The Howe brothers were ready to take full advantage of America's extremities. They had come to America not only as military commanders, but also as peace negotiators, bearing the King's commission "for restoring peace to his Majesty's Colonies and Plantations in North America." In New York, Admiral Lord Howe issued a proclamation, signed also by Sir William, offering "a free and general pardon" to all who would return to "their just allegiance" and take oath accordingly.[7] The effect of this announcement on the inhabitants of New Jersey was instantaneous. Already disaffected to the American cause by reason of their desire to rank as tranquil and obscure supporters of the winning side, which the American side no longer appeared to be, large numbers of them flocked to the British to take the oath and receive protection papers. Washington was disgusted by this desertion of the cause. "The Conduct of the Jerseys," he wrote, "has been most Infamous. Instead of turning out to defend the Country and affording aid to our Army, they are making their submissions as fast as they can." [8]

Philadelphia took notice. Estimating its chances of continued liberty at their apparent value—not much—its inhabitants in droves sought an asylum in the country. An observer there noted in his diary, "Numbers of families loading wagons with their furniture &c., taking them out of town. . . . Great numbers [of] people moving. . . . All shops ordered to be shut. . . . Our people in confusion, of all ranks, sending their goods out of town." The city was "amazingly depopulated." [9]

The fear of final defeat of the American cause and of the consequent ill fortune of its adherents smoked out many of the more faint-hearted Americans in high places. The wealthy and respected Allens of Philadelphia—John, a former member of the Committee on Observation, Andrew, a member of the Congress, and William, a lieutenant colonel of the 2nd Pennsylvania—went over to the enemy and joined Howe at Trenton. So did Joseph Galloway, a leader of the bar and a talented member of the First Continental Congress.[10]

Even John Dickinson, so prominent in the early efforts for liberty and whose *Letters of a Farmer in Pennsylvania* had done so much to arouse the country, now was said to have "discovered sentiments inimical to the freedom and independence of the American states." When elected a delegate from Delaware to the Congress, in January, 1777, he declined the office on the ground that he was "in a very low state of health . . . forced to attend my wife and child in the country." He retired to his farm in Kent County, whence he wrote urging George Read to exert himself for peace "before we suffer indescribable calamities." [11] Dickinson was discouraged, though hardly disloyal to the patriot cause.

In contrast with Dickinson's conduct was that of another pamphleteer, whose *Common Sense* was also a popular and potent force in the Revolution. Thomas Paine had joined Greene at Fort Lee as a volunteer aide-de-camp. Musket on shoulder, he had tramped day by day, all day long, in the weary retreat. At Newark, however, he began to fight with his proper weapon, the pen, with a drumhead for a desk.

In the middle of December, Paine published in Philadelphia a new pamphlet, *The Crisis*. It began with the eloquent words known ever since to many a schoolboy:

> These are the times that try men's souls: The summer soldier and the sunshine patriot will, in this crisis, shrink from the service of his country; but he that stands it Now, deserves the love and thanks of man and woman. Tyranny, like hell, is not easily conquered; yet we have this consolation with us, that the harder the conflict, the more glorious the triumph.[12]

This little book "flew like wildfire through all the towns and villages." The privates in the army were called together in small groups to hear it read. It animated them to endure their hardships and renewed their determination to prove themselves all-season soldiers and all-weather patriots.

Apprehension of oncoming disaster induced the Congress to order the removal of all the principal military stores from Philadelphia down to Christiana Bridge in Delaware. Then, on December 12, it abandoned completely its control of the operations of the army by conferring on Washington "full power to order and direct all things relative to the [military] department and to the operations of war until otherwise ordered. Having thus prudently shifted to his shoulders additional responsibility for the conduct of a desperate war, it adjourned to Baltimore "amid the jeers of tories and the maledictions of patriots." [13] No doubt Congress was wise to remove to Baltimore and also to vest larger powers temporarily in the commander in chief.

On the very next day after this adjournment, two events occurred which later led the English historian George Trevelyan to remark that the Americans, "a people observant of anniversaries . . . might well have marked the thirteenth of December with a white stone in their calendar," and that these two events "must have presented every appearance of special providences." [14]

The first was Howe's decision, disclosed that day, to suspend military operations until spring and to retire with the greater part of his army into winter quarters in New York, leaving only a chain of military outposts to hold New Jersey. Boats were not to be built to cross the Delaware, and there was to be no crossing on the ice. The pressure on the Americans holding the river was lifted. The patriots in Philadelphia took heart; the Tories were correspondingly downcast.

The second event characterized by Trevelyan as fortunate for the Americans had to do with General Charles Lee. Washington had continued to write to him at every stage of the retreat, from Newark, from New Brunswick, urging him and almost entreating him to come over to the Jerseys. Lee was fertile in excuses for not joining his superior. He wrote Heath that he had "received a recommendation—not a positive order—from the General to move the corps under my command to the other side of the river," and asked Heath instead to send 2,000 of his men to Washington. Heath, being under orders to stay where he was, refused and stuck to his refusal, in spite of efforts to make him comply. Lee then tried to get the 2,000 men from Heath to join his own, Heath's men to be replaced from Lee's forces coming up to the Hudson. "I am going into the Jerseys," he said, "for the salvation of America." Heath again refused, and at last, on December 2, Lee started over the river with part of his original force, the remainder having served out their time, deserted, or fallen ill.[15]

But even then Lee had no intention of joining Washington and giving up his independent command. He thought it would be better for him to act in the rear of the enemy, "beating up and harassing their detached parties." To be sure, he did have an excellent chance to assail the long line of British communications across New Jersey. He was "in hopes . . . to reconquer the Jerseys" on his own hook. New Jersey, he wrote, "was really in the hands of the enemy before my arrival." [16]

Lee's progress southward seems to have been slow beyond any reason or excuse. He marched at an average rate of three miles a day. At Morristown he rested two days. The day after that rest, he made only eight miles, to Vealtown.

In the evening of the 12th he left his army at Vealtown in Sullivan's care, and with a small guard rode off about three miles to a tavern in Basking Ridge to spend the night, indulging in that "folly and imprudence . . . for the sake of a little better lodging," as Washington caustically observed.[17] He breakfasted the next morning and then employed his leisure in writing a letter to his friend General Horatio Gates, in which he characterized Washington as "most damnably deficient." [18] He had not even sent the letter when British cavalrymen surrounded the tavern.

Colonel William Harcourt, with thirty horsemen, had been scouting in the neighborhood under orders from Cornwallis to find Lee's army. He learned of Lee's presence in the tavern. His men surrounded the house and let fly a shower of bullets. Lee's guard, surprised, fled. Within a few minutes Lee was forced to surrender. He was carried off and was locked up in New Brunswick before twenty-four hours had passed. The crowning irony of his capture was that the dragoons, his captors, were of a regiment which he had led in a notable feat of his European military career, a dashing raid across the Tagus against the Spanish in Portugal in 1762.

The news of Lee's capture was a dreadful shock to the Americans; many of them had looked upon him as their most capable leader. To some his capture seemed the last straw. "His loss was almost universally bewailed as one of the greatest calamities which had befallen the American arms." Washington wrote, "Our cause has also received a severe blow in the captivity of Gen. Lee." [19]

Events were soon to prove that the American cause was not dependent upon Lee's services. General John Sullivan, Lee's second in command, promptly marched his troops into Washington's camp on December 20, though there were only 2,000 of them, instead of the 5,000 Lee had led across the Hudson. Gates came from the north with what were called seven regiments, though they numbered only 500 men. A thousand Philadelphia Associators under Colonel John Cadwalader also came in, as did the rest of the German Regiment. There were with Washington by Christmas time about 6,000 men listed as "fit for duty." [20] Something like an American counteroffensive could be undertaken, since Howe's forces were divided and going into winter quarters.

But the condition of these new recruits, except for the Associators and the Germans fresh from home, was no better than that of the men who had retreated across the Jerseys. Sullivan's 2,000 were "in a miserable plight; destitute of almost everything, many of them fit only for the hospital."

Gates's 500 were in no better shape. "Fit for duty" seems to have been a term reeking with optimism. And this army, such as it was, had only about ten days more of life. The enlistments of so many were to expire on December 31 that no more than 1,400 would be left.

To guard "every suspicious part of the river" Washington divided his force into three separate corps. The brigades of Generals Stirling, Mercer, Stephen, and Roche de Fermoy, about 2,000 men, were posted along the stretch from Yardley up to Coryell's Ferry. General Ewing had about 550 along the river from Yardley down to the ferry to Bordentown. Cadwalader, given the temporary rank of a brigadier general, with 1,800 took over the ground south of Ewing down to Dunk's Ferry, with headquarters at Bristol. There were no fewer than nine ferries to be guarded; at each of them a small earthwork was thrown up, and a few guns mounted. There being a great scarcity, almost a total lack, of tents, the men built themselves rude huts. So the army settled down, as it seemed to many, for the winter.[21]

CHAPTER 26

Trenton

"Headquarters, December 14, 1776. The Campaign having closed with the Pursuit of the Enemies Army near ninety Miles by Lieut. Gen. Cornwallis's Corps, much to the honor of his Lordship and the Officers and Soldiers under his Command, the Approach of Winter putting a Stop to any further Progress, the Troops will immediately march into Quarters and hold themselves in readiness to assemble on the shortest Notice." [1] In those words General Howe officially closed the campaign of 1776 in New Jersey —officially, but not effectively.

For "the Protection of Inhabitants and their Property," much of which had already been taken into permanent protective custody by his marauding troops, he established a chain of posts on a line from Staten Island to Princeton. There was one at Amboy, one at New Brunswick, and one at Princeton. Along the Delaware, from Bordentown to Burlington, the Hessian Colonel von Donop was in command of about 3,000 men, Hessian grenadiers, jägers, and the 42nd Highlanders. Half of these were based at Trenton and half at Bordentown, the distance between the two being six miles.

The line was eighty miles long, "rather too extensive" as Howe admitted.[2] The distances between the various posts invited trouble. But who was there to trouble them? Six thousand or so American soldiers,[3] a large part of them untried militia, the rest ragged, war-worn, discouraged Continentals, lay on the other side of the Delaware, whose ice-laden waters seemed impassable. And three-quarters of the whole force would be leaving for home in two weeks or less. Howe had good reason for his trust in "the strength of the corps placed in the advanced posts" and for his belief that "the troops will be in perfect security." [4] For himself there were the comfort and the pleasures of life at headquarters in New York. For Cornwallis there was leave to return to England for the winter. So everything was arranged to the satisfaction of everybody, including the Americans.

On no day, from the time his thin line of posts had been strung along the river, was Washington free from apprehension that an attack on that line was planned, to be carried out in boats especially built for it, or on the solid ice when it should form. He knew well enough that such an attack, properly organized and carried out, could not be effectively resisted, that it would be fatal to his army and perhaps even to his cause. And there was the 31st day of December coming so soon, when his army would practically disappear on one day; he would have left but 1,400 men, sick and well. Before he could be reinforced by newly enlisted troops even a small fraction of his foes, say the three thousand Hessians already on the other shore, might cross and march against Philadelphia.

Here was food for thought. If no adequate defense to an attack launched at some unexpected point were possible, could anything be done to forestall it? Could he possibly, with such a force as he had, reverse the situation, attack instead of being attacked? It was a desperate idea, but his situation was desperate.

Washington had begun to think as early as December 8 that audacious counterattacks upon British detachments might pay. On December 14 he expressed in three letters the same hope, that, if he were reinforced by Lee's troops, he might "under the smiles of Providence, effect an important stroke." [5] The news of the withdrawal of Howe's main force to New York and of the straggling disposition of the troops left to hold the river territory was vastly encouraging; but there was yet the fateful decision to be made, a definite plan to be evolved. One who came with Lee's troops under Sullivan on the 20th observed him in the last stages of his cogitation. "I saw him in that gloomy period," reports the erratic James Wilkinson, "and attentively marked his aspect; always grave and thoughtful, he appeared at that time pensive and solemn in the extreme." [6] And well he might, for it was no ordinary expedition that he was planning, no affair of an American detachment whose defeat would be merely a regrettable incident of the war. His whole army was to be risked. If the attempt failed, it would be cut off from retreat by the river behind it. There could be no hope of another unmolested crossing. It was, indeed, a desperate venture, and Washington knew it to be so; "but necessity, dire necessity, will, nay must, justify my attack," he wrote to Colonel Reed on the 23rd.[7] The next evening, at a meeting with

Generals Greene, Sullivan, Mercer, Stirling, Roche de Fermoy, and St. Clair and several colonels, including John Glover, the plan was discussed and adopted.

The principal objective was to be Trenton. The river was to be crossed at three places by three separate divisions. Lieutenant Colonel John Cadwalader as a temporary brigadier general was to command one, composed of about 900 men from Hitchcock's Rhode Island Continentals, 1,000 Philadelphia Associators, Captain Thomas Rodney's little Delaware militia company from Dover, and two artillery companies, each with one 6-pounder. This division was to cross the river at or near Bristol and engage Donop's forces at Mount Holly so as to divert their attention from the principal attack.

The second division, under Brigadier General James Ewing, was made up chiefly of Pennsylvania militia, with a few from New Jersey, about 700 in all. It was to cross at Trenton Ferry, take up a position south of Assunpink Creek and hold a bridge over that stream so as to close that avenue of escape of the Hessians in Trenton after the attack on the town from the north by the principal division.

The third and principal division was to be commanded by Washington. It was to be made up of about 2,400 men selected from the brigades of Stephen, Mercer, Stirling, St. Clair, Glover, Sargent, and Roche de Fermoy, each of whom was to lead his own men. It was to be divided into two corps under Greene and Sullivan respectively. Colonel Henry Knox was to be in charge of the artillery, 18 fieldpieces in all. Each man was to carry his blanket, cooked rations for three days, and forty rounds of ammunition. This division was to cross at McKonkey's Ferry, about nine miles above Trenton, and take the roads leading down to that town.

When his own and Ewing's division had converged upon and taken Trenton, and after Cadwalader had driven Donop from his cantonments, Washington planned that the three bodies should join and, if circumstances favored, should push on against the British posts at Princeton and New Brunswick.

Provided and equipped as ordered, the various elements of the main division were paraded in the valley behind the hill at McKonkey's Ferry, out of sight of the opposite shore, in the afternoon of Christmas Day. By three o'clock they were on the march toward the river, where the boats had been assembled.

These vessels were for the most part of a kind peculiar to the Delaware. They were called Durham boats from their first builder, Robert Durham, who had been turning them out since 1750. They were from forty to sixty feet long, eight feet wide, and two feet deep, and were provided with keels. Pointed at both ends, they could travel in either direction, the heavy steering sweep fitting either end. Each carried a mast with two sails, useful when the wind served. At other times its crew of four, exclusive of the steersman, used setting poles, two on each side. Thrusting them against the river bottom at the bow, the four walked aft on running boards built along each side, thus pushing the boat forward its full length, and then returned to the bow to repeat the operation. As the larger boats could carry fifteen tons while drawing only twenty inches, they could easily convey artillery, horses, and many men.[8] For this expedition these boats were manned by the amphibious Marbleheaders of Glover's regiment, the same men who had rescued the army after the defeat on Long Island.

At dark the embarkation began. The Virginia Continentals of Stephen's brigade, the advance party, were the first to enter the boats and push off for the opposite shore. The river was full of cakes of ice, so that the crossing was slow and exceedingly difficult even for those hardy and veteran crews. The second section to cross was Mercer's, composed of men from Connecticut, Maryland, and Massachusetts, chiefly Continentals. Stirling followed with his men, drawn from two regiments of Virginia Continentals, Haslet's Delawares, and a Pennsylvania rifle regiment. These three corps constituted the left wing of the expedition, under command of Greene, Stirling's forming the reserve.

Roche de Fermoy followed with men chosen from the German Regiment and from one of Pennsylvania, and then Sullivan's division, drawn from the brigades of St. Clair, Glover, and Sargent—New Hampshire, Massachusetts, Connecticut, and New York troops. This was the right wing, Sullivan commanding, Roche de Fermoy in advance, St. Clair in reserve.

The moon was full, but the sky was so shrouded by dense clouds that darkness covered everything. In this respect the night was most suitable for a secret adventure; but it was a dreadful night indeed for the men engaged. It was bitterly cold, the current was swift, and the floating ice prolonged the passage. About eleven o'clock hail and sleet, driven by a high wind, broke upon them, doubling the difficulties of the boatmen and making the soldiers in the boats or on shore acutely miserable. Captain Thomas Rodney wrote, "It was as severe a night as ever I saw . . . [with this] storm of wind, hail, rain and snow."[9]

It had been expected that the entire division would be over the river by midnight and that it would have five hours before daybreak in which to cover the nine miles to Trenton. But it was past three o'clock when the last man got ashore, and nearly four o'clock when the army formed and began to march.

None of these men were warmly clad; many of them wore threadbare summer clothing. Few were properly shod, and many were not shod at all. Slogging along on the rough, frozen road made slippery by ice and snow, buffeted now by hailstones, now by rain that froze upon their hair and their clothes, they underwent a prolonged and continuous torture. The story of ragged, shoeless men leaving bloody footprints in the snow has been told so often that it has become commonplace, and often fails to impress the reader as it should. But to one of Washington's staff, as to every other man on that march, it was sufficiently real. He made an entry in his diary before the embarkation. "Christmas, 6 p.m. . . . It is fearfully cold and raw and a snow-storm setting in. The wind is northeast and beats in the faces of the men. It will be a terrible night for the soldiers who have no shoes. Some of them have tied old rags around their feet, but I have not heard a man complain." [10]

Added to these physical tortures was the mental stress of the knowledge that they were three or four hours behind time and could not now hope to surprise the enemy at daybreak. It would be broad day before the attack could be launched, and that might make all the difference between victory and defeat, a defeat that might develop into a catastrophe fatal to the American cause.

Such forebodings were, of course, still more depressing to the officers, who were familiar with the details of the plan. Even while crossing the river many of them, well knowing what a touch-and-go affair it was, were despondent.[11] How much more so, then, were they when they realized how sadly the timing of the plan had gone awry. But Washington kept his poise and never faltered. The same officer who wrote about the shoeless soldiers also wrote: "I have never seen Washington so determined as he is now. He stands on the bank of the stream, wrapped in his cloak, superintending the landing of his troops. He is calm and collected, but very determined. The storm is changing to sleet and cuts like a knife." When on the march a man came to Washington with a message from General Sullivan that the storm was wetting the muskets and rendering them unfit for service his answer was: "Tell General Sullivan to use the bayonet. I am resolved to take Trenton." That resolve, that unbending will carried the army to Trenton in spite of everything.

At Birmingham, about four miles from the landing, the column halted for a meal of the prepared rations. When the order to march was given many of the men were found asleep by the roadside and were roused with difficulty.

Two roads led from Birmingham to Trenton. The right-hand road ran roughly parallel to the curve of the river and entered the town at its south or lower end. The other, the Pennington road, swung left in a similar shallow curve and came into Trenton at its upper end. They were about equal in length.

Stephen's advance, followed by Mercer's and Stirling's corps and a small troop of Philadelphia light horse, all under Greene, with four guns, took the Pennington road. Washington rode with this division. Roche de Fermoy followed, with orders to break off to the left and interpose his men between the Trenton garrison and the troops at Princeton. Sullivan, with St. Clair's, Glover's, and Sargent's troops and four guns, set out on the river road.

The garrison in Trenton consisted of three regiments of Hessians, known by the names of Rall, Knyphausen, and Lossberg, 50 Hessian jägers, and 20 light dragoons of the 16th British regiment, about 1,400 in all, with six 3-pounder fieldpieces. Colonel Johann Gottlieb Rall was in command, the officer who had led the flank attack against Chatterton's Hill and had summoned Fort Washington to surrender.

The town had two nearly parallel main streets, King and Queen, running in a north and south direction, but coming together at the north end so as to form a long, narrow wedge. These were crossed near their lower ends by Front, Second, and Third streets. At the south end of Queen Street a bridge crossed Assunpink Creek to the road for Bordentown. The town was largely depleted of its usual residents, whose houses, the jail, the taverns, the churches, and other buildings, mostly along the main streets, now furnished quarters for the soldiers. One company was in an outlying position north of the town, and another south of the creek. Rall had his headquarters in the middle of the town on King Street.

There were no natural defenses against attack from any quarter, except the Delaware River on the west side; the town was approachable over a flat country by many roads from every other direction. Several of Rall's officers had urged him to fortify the approaches, and Colonel von Donop, in command of the district, had actually instructed him to do so. But, although two positions for redoubts were chosen and even approved by Rall, nothing was done. He scoffed at the idea that the miserable rabble on the other side of the river, "nothing but a lot of farmers," were capable of an attack in force sufficient to endanger him. "Let them come!" he said. "We want no trenches. We'll at them with the bayonet!" In this attitude he was supported by General James Grant, who commanded all the British forces in New Jersey. Grant went even further in his contempt of the rebels. When Rall suggested that it would be well to have more troops to keep open his communications with Princton and New Brunswick, Grant is said to have replied to the messenger: "Tell the Colonel he is safe; I will undertake to keep the peace in New Jersey with a corporal's guard." This was the same Grant that had boasted before the war that he could march through all the colonies with 5,000 men.

Christmas Eve and Christmas Day were high holidays in Trenton, celebrated with much feasting and drinking in the hearty German fashion. The merrymaking and revelry were kept up all day and late into the night, interrupted only for a short time in the early evening by an attack on one of the pickets by about thirty Americans, who, without Washington's knowledge, had been scouting in the neighborhood. They had shot up the picket guard as a mere adventure. After an exchange of fire in which six Hessians were wounded the Americans quickly withdrew, carrying off six muskets as trophies. The troops in the town had been called to arms; but the affair was over in a few minutes, and they returned to their quarters.

Rall had then dropped in on a supper party in the house of a wealthy merchant of the town, who seems to have been a political trimmer. The attractions of wine and cards kept the party going all night. Near the middle of the night there came a knock at the door; a visitor wanted to see the colonel. The servant refused to let him in. The caller then wrote a note, which the servant delivered to Rall. It contained the information that the American army was on the march against the town. Rall thrust it into his pocket unread. Perhaps he never read it; it was found in his pocket after his death two days later.

The pickets had been posted as usual. On the Pennington road, by which Greene's column, with Washington, was approaching, there was an outlying post of a lieutenant, a corporal, and twenty-four men at some distance from the town. About halfway between that and the town, Captain von Altenbockum's company of the Lossberg Regiment was posted. On the river road, the route of Sullivan's division, there was a guard of a captain and fifty jägers about half a mile from the town. Other posts were at the Assunpink bridge, on the road to Maidenhead (now Lawrenceville), on the road to the ferry landing, and on the road to Crosswicks, these four being away from the direction of the American attack.

At about quarter to eight in the morning of the 26th, Lieutenant Andreas Wiederhold, in charge of the picket post on the Pennington road, stepped out of the "alarm house," the center of his guard, and saw a small body of men about two hundred yards distant coming toward him from the northwest, the advance guard of Stephen's corps. At the same time his sentinels came running toward him, shouting: "Der Feind! Heraus! Heraus!" (The enemy! Turn out! Turn out!) There was a brief exchange of fire, and the picket turned and fled to Captain von Altenbockum's post in their rear. The company there had turned out on the alarm. It fired one volley, but Stephen's men, backed by Mercer's, charged it with such spirit that the Hessians retreated in haste toward the town, the Americans following and firing as they came. At almost the same moment, the advance guard of Sullivan's division fell upon the picket of jägers on the river road and drove it pellmell back into the town. So far the plan of simultaneous attack at the two ends of the town had been perfectly executed.

Lieutenant Jacob Piel, hearing the musket shots, ran to Rall's house and aroused him by hammering on his door. Rall, in his nightclothes, appeared at an upper window. Piel asked him if he hadn't heard the firing. In a very few minutes Rall was out and on his horse. His own regiment formed in the lower part of King Street. The Lossbergs hurriedly paraded in a cross street with orders to clear Queen. Dechow's battalion of Lossbergs was in the rear at a right angle to the rest, to face Sullivan's men in the lower part of the town. The Knyphausen regiment was held in reserve at Second and King streets.

Meanwhile Stephen's and Fermoy's corps had left Greene's division, swung to the left past the upper part of the town, and drawn a line around it from the Princeton road to Assunpink Creek. Mercer's had turned to the right to the west of the town and down toward the river until it got in touch with Sullivan at the lower end. Stirling, in the rear of the column, had marched straight to the junction of King and Queen streets at the upper end. At that point, from which artillery fire could command the whole length of the town, four fieldpieces under Captain Thomas Forrest were trained down Queen Street and two under Captain Alexander Hamilton pointed down King. Both immediately opened fire.

Rall's regiment and a part of Lossberg's advanced up King Street. Hamilton's shot tore into their ranks. Mercer's corps, coming in on their left, fired upon their flank. The Hessians gave two volleys and then fell back in disorder, throwing the rest of the Lossbergs into confusion. Two Hessian guns that had been brought up opened fire, but the gunners fell under the fire of the Americans. Stirling's troops charged down both streets, Weedon's

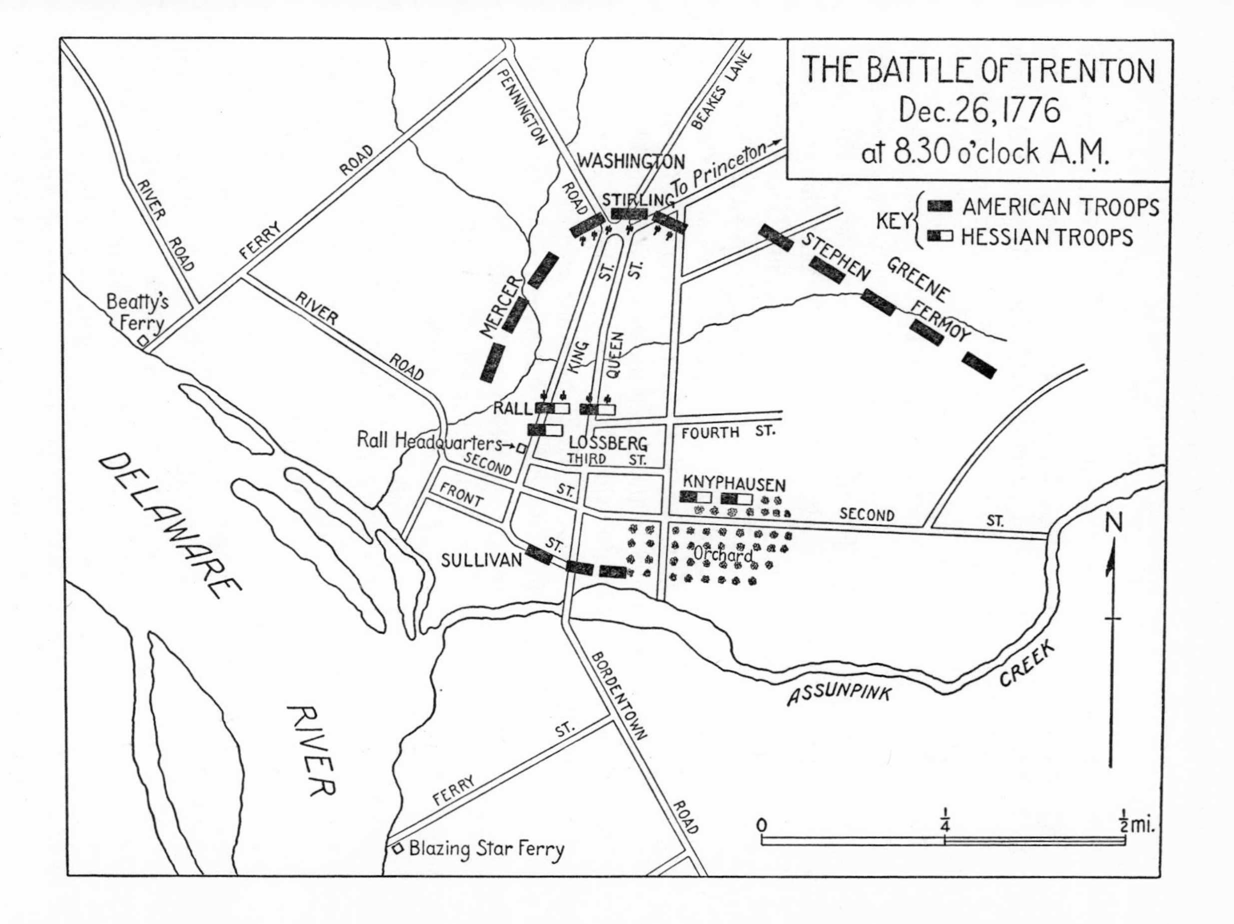
THE BATTLE OF TRENTON
Dec. 26, 1776
at 8.30 o'clock A.M.
KEY
AMERICAN TROOPS
HESSIAN TROOPS
WASHINGTON
STIRLING
To Princeton
STEPHEN
GREENE
FERMOY
MERCER
RALL
LOSSBERG
KNYPHAUSEN
SULLIVAN
Rall Headquarters
PENNINGTON ROAD
BEAKES LANE
RIVER ROAD
FERRY ROAD
KING ST.
QUEEN ST.
FOURTH ST.
THIRD ST.
SECOND ST.
SECOND
FRONT ST.
BORDENTOWN ROAD
FERRY ST.
Orchard
Beatty's Ferry
Blazing Star Ferry
DELAWARE RIVER
ASSUNPINK CREEK
N
0
1/4
1/2 mi.

Virginians ahead on King Street, Captain William Washington and Lieutenant James Monroe leading their men. They fell upon the Hessian battery and captured it. Both Washington and Monroe were wounded.

Forrest's guns were in the meantime clearing Queen Street. A two-gun battery had opposed them there, firing three or four times; but in ten minutes it was silenced. Sullivan's column, which by this time had fought its way into the lower part of the town, met the Knyphausen regiment and drove it back.

Rall, with his own regiment and most of the Lossbergs, had fallen back to the edge of the town. There he re-formed his broken ranks, depleted by the loss of many who had fallen, or who had run away across the bridge toward Bordentown. He started back, intending a bayonet charge to clear the main streets. With a band playing, his men came into Queen Street.

But there were Americans all over the town; the cross streets swarmed with them; the houses were full of them. Their muskets and rifles, being wet, had been ineffective. But they dried their flints and priming pans in the cellars of the houses and in the upper rooms, picked out the touch-holes, and went into action individually and independently. From every window they fired on the returning Hessians. Riflemen picked their men and made sure of them. Forrest's battery still blazed away down Queen Street. The fire from all around was heavy and deadly. With his officers and men falling on every side, Rall ordered a charge. His men faltered, hung back. The Lossbergs tried it, but several officers and thirty men fell before they could get within thrusting distance, and they were stopped.

A retreat was in order, but Sullivan's troops now held the bridge. There was no way out to the south. Rall ordered a withdrawal to an orchard at the southeast corner of the town. He had hardly given the order when he was hit. Two bullets struck him in the side of his body. He fell from his horse and was helped into a house.

Rall's men retreated to the orchard, their only thought being to find a way out. They started north to try for the New Brunswick road; but Stephen's and Fermoy's troops, in their encircling position, met them with artillery and musketry and drove them back. Forrest's guns were trained on them. Regiment after regiment surrounded them at a distance of no more than sixty feet. Their situation was hopeless. They surrendered. Stirling received the swords of their officers.

Meanwhile Sullivan's division was taking care of the Knyphausen regiment and a battalion of the Lossbergs under Major von Dechow at the lower end of the town. Colonel John Stark of New Hampshire, shouting to his men to come on, led them in a charge that drove back the Hessians. Dechow was mortally wounded and gave himself up. His men tried to retreat by the bridge, but it was too strongly held. They tried for a ford above it, but found none. Their two guns were bogged down in a marsh. They left them and made a desperate effort to cross the creek through deep water. Some of them got through, only to meet St. Clair's corps drawn up on the other side ready to mow them down. Amid a shrieking crowd of camp followers, men and women milling about in helpless terror, they lowered their colors and grounded their muskets, while their officers raised their hats on the points of their swords in token of submission. The Americans tossed *their* hats in the air and shouted so loud that they were heard throughout the town. It was nine o'clock, and the battle was over.

That is a description of the Trenton fight in its essentials; in detail it is indescribable. From the beginning to the end, the little town was the scene of a hurly-burly of 4,000 fighting men moving here and there by regiments, by companies, and in smaller groups. Single men fired on their enemies in the streets, from inside the houses, from behind houses and fences. The usual chaos of street fighting was made worse by the fog of gunpowder smoke that hung over the town and by the hail, snow, and sleet that continued to beat upon the fighters. It was a grand mêlée, a great, informal "battle royal."

One outstanding feature of the fight was the comparative lack of musketry fire. The Americans had done the best they could to keep their flints and the pans of their flintlocks dry during that long march through the rain and sleet, by wrapping them in greased rags and covering them with their blankets and the skirts of their coats. The Hessians, emerging from their dry quarters, had their muskets in firing condition. But the rain soon drenched the weapons of both sides. The flints would not strike a spark; the priming charges would not flash; the touchholes were clogged with wet powder. Men on both sides could be seen chipping their flints, pulling their triggers again and again without effect. Those that got into the houses dried their gunlocks and could fire toward the end of the battle. Otherwise, it was mostly an affair of artillery, bayonet, sword, and spontoon.

But there was noise enough. The roar of the fieldpieces, the yells of both sides in their bayonet charges, the vociferous words of command or of encouragement of the officers, the indescribable general tumult filled the little town with a howling pandemonium of sound, even when the musketry fire slackened.

It was a great victory for the Americans, the more important because it was won at such a crucial time. But it was not so complete as Washington had planned and hoped. General Ewing's division was not in its appointed place, south of the Assunpink Bridge to cut off the fugitives. Many escaped that way—the picket of fifty jägers on the river road, the guards at the bridge, the guards at Trenton landing and other outposts, various groups from the regiments engaged and the detachment of twenty British dragoons, who galloped away soon after the first attack. In all about 500 escaped.

Nevertheless, the bag was substantial. Of the Hessians 22 were killed and 92 wounded. Prisoners were taken to the number of 948, including 32 commissioned officers. Of spoils there were six brass fieldpieces; six wagons; 40 horses; 1,000 muskets and rifles with bayonets and accouterments; 15 regimental and company colors; 14 drums; all the trumpets, clarionets, and hautboys of two bands; and 40 hogsheads of rum, which Washington ordered staved in and the liquor spilt on the ground, though perhaps not before his cold and tired men had had at least one drink. The casualties on the American side were two officers and two privates wounded.[12]

The failure of support of Ewing's and Cadwalader's divisions, neither of which had fulfilled its allotted task, made it impossible to proceed with the original plan of pushing on to attack the stations at Princeton and New Brunswick. But it is more than doubtful, considering the hardships and fatigues suffered by Washington's force and the necessity of caring for nearly a thousand prisoners, that that plan could have been carried out even if Ewing and Cadwalader had been at hand. With Donop's troops so near at Bordentown, aroused by the news of the battle brought by the escaped Hessians, it was manifestly inadvisable to linger in Trenton. Safety and rest on the other side of the river were plainly indicated.

Twenty-eight of the badly wounded Hessians were paroled to be left there, including Rall and Dechow, both of whom died of their wounds within two days. The rest of the prisoners were committed to the care of Stirling's corps, and the toilsome march back to the boats was begun soon after noon.

The storm had not abated. The northeast wind still drove the snow and hail against their faces. The road was no better than in the morning. Crossing the river proved even more difficult than before. It is said that three of the American privates were frozen to death in the boats. It was night before they all got across, and it was morning again before all got back to their huts. Some of the most remotely posted did not reach their camps before noon.

These men had marched and fought continuously for thirty-six, forty, and even fifty hours. Some of them had covered more than forty miles, in the bitterest cold and a driving storm, with no more than two or three hours' cessation of the most arduous labor. It is not surprising that more than a thousand were reported the next day as unfit for duty. "This was a long and a severe ordeal, and yet it may be doubted whether so small a number of men ever employed so short a space of time with greater or more lasting results upon the history of the world." [13]

Now it may be asked why Ewing's force was not on hand south of the bridge as ordered, and what Cadwalader's troops were about that night that they did not appear where they were expected. The answer to the first question is short. General Ewing, having seen the condition of the river, thought a crossing impossible. He did not even try it. Concerning the other, there is more to be said.

Cadwalader took a look at the floating ice above Bristol. It seemed to him too great an obstacle. He marched his men from the Neshaminy Ferry a few miles down to Dunk's Ferry. There four companies of Philadelphia militia and Captain Thomas Rodney's Dover company, acting as light infantry, embarked in five large bateaux and three scows about eight o'clock in the evening. They were to land on the Jersey shore and cover the subsequent disembarkation of the rest. They did land, "with great difficulty through the ice," having to walk on it a hundred yards before they got ashore. About two hundred yards from the river's edge, they formed and awaited the others.[14]

About nine o'clock the 1st and 3rd battalions of the Philadelphia Associators, with two fieldpieces, started across. They got no nearer to land than the advance party, but they all scrambled ashore, 600 of them. But Cadwalader did not see how he could land the fieldpieces.[15] The former colonel of the Philadelphia Silk Stocking Regiment therefore gave up and ordered his men back to the Pennsylvania side.[16] Rodney described the scene in a letter to his brother, Caesar: "We had to stand six hours under arms—first, to cover the landing, and till all the rest had retreated again; and by this time, the storm of wind, hail, rain and snow was so bad that some of the Infantry could not get back until the next day." [17] So that part of Washington's plan failed entirely of execution.

Rodney wrote in his diary that the order to retreat "greatly irritated the troops that had crossed the River and they proposed making an attack without both the Generals and the artillery"; but they were dissuaded from the attempt by the argument that, "if Gen. Washington should be unsuccessful and we also, the cause would be lost, but, if our force remained intact, it would still keep up the spirit of America." Washington's plan and his orders involved risking the whole army on the success of the combined attack, so that that reasoning seems to be altogether specious. Rodney expressed the opinion that "if our Generals had been in earnest, we could have taken Burlington with the light troops alone." He concluded that Washington meant these secondary expeditions under Ewing and Cadwalader "only as feints." [18] In this conclusion he was in error. Washington fully intended that those two forces should cooperate with his in reality, the one to hold the Assunpink against Rall's retreat, the other to attack Donop and at best defeat him, but at least to keep him from going to the aid of Rall. Even without those two little fieldpieces, a vigorous and bold commander could have done that much.

That Washington desired such an effort made, under any and all conditions, he had made plain to Cadwalader in a letter written at six o'clock that very evening: "Notwithstanding the discouraging Accounts . . . of what might be expected from the Operations below, I am determined, as the Night is favourable, to cross the River and make the attack upon Trenton in the Morning. If you can do nothing real, at least create as great a diversion as possible." [19]

Cadwalader could have put 1,900 men ashore as easily as 600. Colonel Reed and one other officer got their horses ashore. It would seem that, with the proper amount of courage and dogged determination, even the two 6-pounders could have been landed. Guns have been got over worse terrain than ice which a horse could negotiate. But, with 1,000 well clothed and equipped men, as were these Philadelphia Associators, fresh from home, and even without the guns, Cadwalader could have made "as great a diversion as possible," and held, if not actually defeated, Donop's force. If Washington's victory at Trenton had not been so swift and so complete, he might have had to fight all Donop's troops as well as Rall's to a disastrous finish. One can only conclude that it took a Washington to cross the river that night, and a Ewing and a Cadwalader to funk a crossing.

Washington's prisoners were immediately marched to Newtown in Pennsylvania and thence on December 30 to Philadelphia, where, with the captured colors, they were paraded through the streets. In their handsome uniforms, dark blue for Rall's regiment, scarlet for the Lossbergs, black for the Knyphausens, and dark blue coats with crimson lapels for the artillerymen, they made a fine show. An eyewitness gave an account of this display. "They made a long line—all fine, hearty looking men and well clad, with knapsacks, spatterdashes on legs, their looks were *satisfied*. On each side in single file, were their guards, mostly in light, summer dress and some without shoes, but stepping light and cheerful." [20] They were finally sent, by way of Lancaster, to the western counties of Pennsylvania and into Virginia, where they proved to be the most docile of prisoners.

The effect of the battle on the disposition of the enemy near the Delaware was instantaneous and drastic. Donop immediately withdrew from Mount Holly to Allentown and ordered the Hessians at Bordentown to join him at once. Burlington was evacuated, part of its garrison going to Princeton, the rest to New Brunswick. Within the shortest possible time for the movement of troops, every post in the Delaware River territory was cleared of the enemy.[21]

Howe was staggered by the news. "That three old established regiments of a people, who made war a profession, should lay down their arms to a ragged and undisciplined militia" [22] was simply stupefying. He stopped Cornwallis, who was on the point of embarking for England, and sent him to take command in New Jersey. He himself set out with reinforcements for the scene of trouble.

The effect upon the American people was as instantaneous, but different. From the depth of despair they rose to new confidence. From every direction came news of militiamen on the march to serve for two months, while the new Continental army was being organized.

Washington's reputation as a military leader had been on the wane ever since Long Island. Successive defeats and retreats had cumulatively discredited the commander in chief. But Trenton wiped out all that. "The country awakened to the belief that its general was a genius." [23] The Congress at Baltimore gave him full support. On December 27 it adopted a resolution vesting in Washington "full, ample and complete powers" to raise more battalions, infantry, light horse, artillery, and engineers, to appoint all officers under the rank of brigadier general and to displace them at will, to fix their pay, to commandeer "whatever he may want for the use of the army," and to arrest the disaffected. In short, he was to be something of a military dictator—for a period of six months.[24]

CHAPTER 27

Princeton

In the morning of December 26 Cadwalader, presumably dry and unfatigued in his quarters at Bristol, wrote a letter to Washington, telling him why he did not get his corps across the river. "I imagine the badness of the night must have prevented your passing as you intended." [1] Then he heard the thunder of the guns at Trenton, but could hardly believe his ears. The firing, he thought, must be on the west side of the river. Two or three hours later Ewing disabused his mind with news of the victory. "Such was the exhilaration produced by this intelligence" [2] that he ordered his men to be prepared to cross at sunrise the next day.

About ten o'clock Cadwalader's men began to embark at the ferry above Bristol, the exact point of departure fixed for him in Washington's orders for the night of the 25th, which he had not tried. The condition of the ice in the river could not have changed greatly, but now he was sufficiently "exhilarated" by the news of the victory to try it. He had got nearly all his men and his guns across when he received a reply from Washington to his letter. It politely regretted his failure to cross on the 25th, also Ewing's, which had prevented complete success: "The whole of the Enemy must have fallen into our hands," if Ewing had been at the bridge. Also it announced the return of the army to the west side of the river.[3]

Here was a pretty situation! Cadwalader and his 1,800 men were alone in New Jersey, facing he knew not what force of an aroused and revengeful enemy. There was Donop at Mount Holly, he thought, with perhaps 1,500 Hessians and the 42nd Highlanders, besides 500 of Rall's men who had escaped from Trenton. And Mount Holly was less than ten miles distant. Donop might even have advanced to Bordentown, six or seven miles away. Who could tell and what was one to do? He was "in a dilemma." [4] Among his officers there was "much perplexity and a great variety of opinions." It was urged by some that, as Washington was now back in Pennsylvania, the whole purpose of the expedition had failed. They had no support; Donop was a dangerous menace; if he came up, it would be impossible safely to retreat across the river; they had better go back at once. Cadwalader agreed with this opinion.

Colonel Reed, on the contrary, urged that the militia wanted action without any more fooling. They had crossed that damned river three times, and, if this present movement proved to be a fiasco, they would all go home in disgust. What was needed was enterprise. Follow up Washington's success by attacking a demoralized enemy. "On to glory!" was his watchword. But the majority was against him. At last, as a compromise, it was agreed to march to Burlington, where they were pretty sure no Hessians would be found. The bewildered temporary brigadier general gave orders accordingly.[5]

Cadwalader's men reached Burlington by nine o'clock in the evening and found no enemy there. Reed had been ahead, scouting. He brought word that Bordentown had been cleared of the foe. At four in the morning they marched toward that town through a "scene of devastation. Neither Hay, Straw, Grain, or any live stock or poultry to be seen." The Hessians had swept the area clean. Half a mile from the town they got word that the enemy was only five miles away and "were disposed to return." They lingered for an hour in a cornfield, then heard that "the enemy were flying with all speed." They marched in and "took possession of a large quantity of stores" left by the fleeing Hessians, whom they followed as far as Crosswicks.[6]

Colonel Reed had pursued his scouting activities to Trenton. Finding it entirely devoid of soldiers of either army, he so informed Washington and urged him to come over and follow up his victory. Washington had already planned a return to the Jerseys "for the purpose of attempting a recovery of that country from the enemy." [7] On the 29th his army started to cross the river, but it took two days to get them all across and into Trenton. There he learned that Cornwallis and Grant, with 8,000 men and a powerful train of artillery, were at Princeton, no more than a dozen miles distant, and that their advance troops were already feeling their way toward Trenton. Why Washington ventured to place the river at his back when it was likely that the British would appear in major force is not easy to explain. It would seem that prudence dictated remaining on the west side of the Delaware.

Washington's situation was critical. The hardships suffered by his men in those recent marches to and from Trenton had incapacitated many of them for immediate active service. He had left guards in the camps on the other side of the river. His present force numbered no more than 1,500. Clearly he could not hope to withstand his approaching enemy with so few. He might again retreat to Pennsylvania, but that would dash the hopes raised by his late exploit and depress the morale of his whole army. However, some reinforcements were near. General Mifflin's eloquence had raised 1,600 militia in Philadelphia. They were now at Bordentown. He sent for them and for Cadwalader's troops at Crosswicks, 2,100 men.

But there was still the fact that the enlistment of most of his Continentals would expire on the 31st. Knox and Mifflin addressed them, offering a bounty of ten dollars for six weeks' additional service, which many of the New England men accepted.[8] It was easy enough to promise a bounty, but what about paying it? The military chest was empty. Washington wrote to Robert Morris in Philadelphia: "If it be possible to give us Assistance, do it; borrow Money where it can be done, we are doing it on our private Credit; every man of Interest and every Lover of his Country must strain his Credit upon such an Occasion. No Time, my dear Sir, is to be lost." [9] Morris raised $50,000, paper money, on his own credit and sent it to him.

By the addition of the Pennsylvania militia and Cadwalader's troops, Washington had now 5,000 men and forty pieces of artillery. But many of the men were not merely militia, they were untrained, inexperienced militia, farmers, mechanics, men fresh from offices and shops who knew nothing of war, nothing whatever of the duties of a soldier. Fresh from home, they were doubtless sufficiently clad, properly shod, and in a fairly well fed condition. But the old Continentals, the backbone of the army, on whom alone the General could rely in action, were almost at the ends of their tethers. Ragged, gaunt, footsore, fatigued by their recent exertions, and worn almost to exhaustion by lack of sleep, that "flock of animated scarecrows" [10] was more fit for a hospital than for active service. It seems that they must have carried on rather by force of habit than by their own volition. Against these Cornwallis had 8,000 of the flower of the British army, presumably reasonably fresh.

Cornwallis left three regiments of the 4th Brigade, 1,200 men, under Lieutenant Colonel Charles Mawhood as a rear guard at Princeton, the 2nd Brigade, about as many, under General Leslie at Maidenhead (now Lawrenceville), and with the rest, 5,500 strong, set out for Trenton on January 2 accompanied by twenty-eight guns of various calibers up to 12-pounders.

Washington had sent forward, on January 1, General Roche de Fermoy, with his own brigade, Colonel Hand's Pennsylvania riflemen, Colonel Haussegger's new German battalion, Colonel Charles Scott's Virginia Continentals, and Captain Forrest's two-gun battery. They had taken a position a short distance south of Maidenhead.

It rained heavily that night and, the temperature being high for January, the roads were deep with mud. Cornwallis's troops in three columns had no easy going. His advance came upon the American vedettes about ten o'clock and drove them in. General Fermoy had left his troops and had returned to Trenton "in a very questionable manner." [11] Hand took charge of the detachment and ordered a slow retreat. At every point where they could find a good position, the Americans disputed the advance of the enemy. In the woods beside Shabbakonk Creek they made a stand, and there was a smart skirmish. The Americans' fire was so heavy and so well aimed that the British advance was confused, and two Hessian battalions were drawn up in battle order expecting a general engagement. For full three hours the Americans held this position. Again at the northern end of Trenton, where some little earthworks had been thrown up and four guns placed, they held off the enemy. A British battery was brought up, and an hour was consumed in forcing this point.

Following on the renewed retreat the British advance party, about 1,500 men, entered the town to meet an irregular fire from behind houses and fences and from American batteries posted on the south side of Assunpink Creek, to which the retreating Americans had retired. The main body of the British army, delayed by the condition of the roads, had not yet come up.

Washington had taken a position on a ridge along the south bank of Assunpink Creek, his line extending nearly three miles. Earthworks had been thrown up. Mercer's brigade was in the front line on the extreme left, Cadwalader's in the center, and St. Clair's next. Behind these there was a line of reserves.

It was five o'clock in the afternoon of the 2nd when the British advance neared the creek. They made three attempts to force a bridge. The failing light made the American fire uncertain, but it was heavy enough to hold the bridge. A party of Hessians tried to cross at a ford, but Hitchcock's Rhode Island Continentals dissuaded them from the attempt. For some time there was cannonading from both sides, which gradually died down.

When Cornwallis came up with his main army he consulted with his generals. Sir William Erskine urged an immediate attack in spite of the darkness. "If Washington is the general I take him to be," he is reported to have said, "he will not be found there in the morning." But the others saw the Americans caught with the Delaware River behind them and no way out. Cornwallis decided that he had Washington in a trap, and that he could easily "bag him" in the morning. So the British and Hessians withdrew to the upper part of the town. The Americans lighted their campfires along the ridge, and both armies settled down for the night.

Washington's plans for the "recovery" of the Jerseys seem not to have been disclosed to anyone. Howe's forces in that state, even after the withdrawal from the Delaware River territory, were strung out in a long line of posts from Amboy through New Brunswick to Princeton. The line would include Trenton if and when he recovered it. The main highway from New York to Philadelphia, the main artery of his supply line, ran through those towns. If the Americans cut it at any point, the posts below would be left in desperate straits. It seems probable that Washington intended to do that. Trenton was not of first importance, since it was at the end of the string. New Brunswick was, both because its possession by the Americans would leave Princeton out on a limb, and because it was the principal depot of British military stores in New Jersey. Trenton was merely the first station on the road to New Brunswick.

But Washington had not taken into consideration certain traits absent in Howe, but conspicuously present in Cornwallis's make-up; namely, energy and swiftness of action. Instead of having time to go on to New Brunswick before his foes could be got into the field to oppose him Washington found himself at the very threshold of his adventure face to face with Cornwallis in force. For the moment the British had been held off, or perhaps one should say they had held off. But the morrow was on its way. In a few hours the attack would be renewed in full strength, and Washington had neither the strength of men nor that of position to repel his enemy indefinitely.

His position was only apparently strong. The Assunpink was there, and its only bridge might be held. But it was after all a very small stream, and there were several fords a few miles above the bridge. If Cornwallis threw a body of troops across there, he would be "bagged" indeed, with the Delaware River in his rear, and neither the time nor the means to cross it. It was evident that some plan to extricate the army must be devised.

An American council of war was held. Should they fight it out there, or retreat down the river and try to get across at some lower point? Both attempts would be hazardous in the extreme—a battle because of their obvious weakness, and a retreat because the enemy hot on their heels would make it a disastrous rout and there were no boats below to rescue even a remnant. Then someone made an audacious suggestion. Who made it, no one knows; it has been claimed for several, but it is quite possible that Washington himself proposed it.[12]

The plan was to withdraw in the middle of the night, but not down the river. Instead, the army was to march around the left flank of the enemy, avoid the British post at Maidenhead, strike the British rear guard at Princeton, some twelve miles away, defeat it, and go on to New Brunswick. The very audacity of the plan seized the imagination, and it was adopted.

One obstacle in the way of success was removed while the council was in session. "A providential change of weather" occurred. A cold northwest wind sprang up, the temperature fell, and the roads froze hard.[13]

Preparations for the move began at once. The campfires were heaped high with fence rails. A party of 400 men was detailed to work on entrenchments at certain points whence the sound of pick and spade would be heard in the British camp. They were also to keep the fires going and to make a show of patrolling at the bridge and elsewhere. Finally they were to steal away at daybreak and follow the army as speedily as possible.

The baggage, stores, and three heaviest guns were started for Burlington under a strong guard. The wheels of the other gun carriages were wrapped with rags to deaden their sound on the frozen roads. At one o'clock in the morning of January 3 the march began, no one under the rank of a brigadier general having any knowledge of its destination or purpose.[14]

The Dover light infantry and the Red Feather Company of Philadelphia militia led the van, followed by Mercer's brigade. Beside Mercer's horse Colonel John Haslet, whose Delaware regiment of time-expired men had gone home, trudged along on foot. St. Clair's brigade, with Washington and his staff, came next, and then the rest of the army. Captain Henry, with the other three companies of the Philadelphia light infantry militia, brought up the rear. Orders were given in whispers; the muskets were carefully handled, and every care was taken to maintain silence. So the army passed along the front of the enemy's lines and took the road to Sandtown. That road ran through dense woods and had been lately made. It was rugged and rutted. Stumps had been left standing, which "stopped the movement of some of the guns and caused many a fall and severe bruise to some of the overweary, sleepy soldiers." [15] At Sandtown, they took the road to Quaker Bridge. At some time on this part of the march, "great confusion happened in the rear" among Henry's Philadelphia militia. "There was a cry that they were surrounded by Hessians, and several corps of Militia broke and fled towards Bordentown, but the rest of the column remained firm and pursued their march without disorder." [16]

At Quaker Bridge, the column swung toward the northwest on a road leading directly to Princeton. Two miles from that town it came to Stony Brook. It was then daylight. "The sun rose as we crossed the brook on a clear frosty morning." [17] Here the army was divided. Mercer's brigade of 350 tired, sleepy, hungry men, with Cadwalader's Associators, was split off to the left to secure a stone bridge on the direct road to Trenton, so that, if Cornwallis were pursuing, he could be held or at least delayed there. Sullivan, with three brigades, took a road to the right to enter Princeton on the east.

The British force in Princeton consisted of three regiments, the 17th, 40th, and 55th, with three troops of light dragoons. Lieutenant Colonel Charles Mawhood, the commander, was under orders to march the bulk of these, join General Leslie at Maidenhead, and then push on to Trenton that morning, leaving the 40th as a guard for the stores in Princeton. At about dawn Mawhood set out. He rode a brown pony, and his two favorite spaniels trotted by his side. The 17th, a part of the 55th, and a troop of the 16th light dragoons were with him. The rest of the 55th followed at a short distance. Mawhood had crossed Stony Brook bridge and was at the top of a small hill on the Trenton road when his eye caught the glitter of the sun's level rays reflected from bright metal at some little distance on his left. A searching look disclosed a motley band of armed men just emerging from a wood. It was the vanguard of Mercer's troops on its way to the bridge.

Having no thought of an attack in that vicinity, Mawhood supposed this was some part of the American army fleeing from a defeat by Cornwallis. He sent two mounted officers to reconnoiter the approaching body. As a measure of precaution, in order to intercept the Americans, if indeed they were bound for Princeton, he withdrew his force across the bridge to take up a position in an orchard and some farm buildings on a piece of rising ground on the other side of the stream. He led his men at the double in a dash for the orchard, but the Americans were nearer to it. With equal speed they gained it first and formed behind a hedge facing the British in an open field below.

Mawhood quickly deployed his men in line of battle at a distance of forty yards. Both sides at once opened fire, each having two fieldpieces in play. Mercer's horse was hit in one leg. He dismounted to fight on foot.

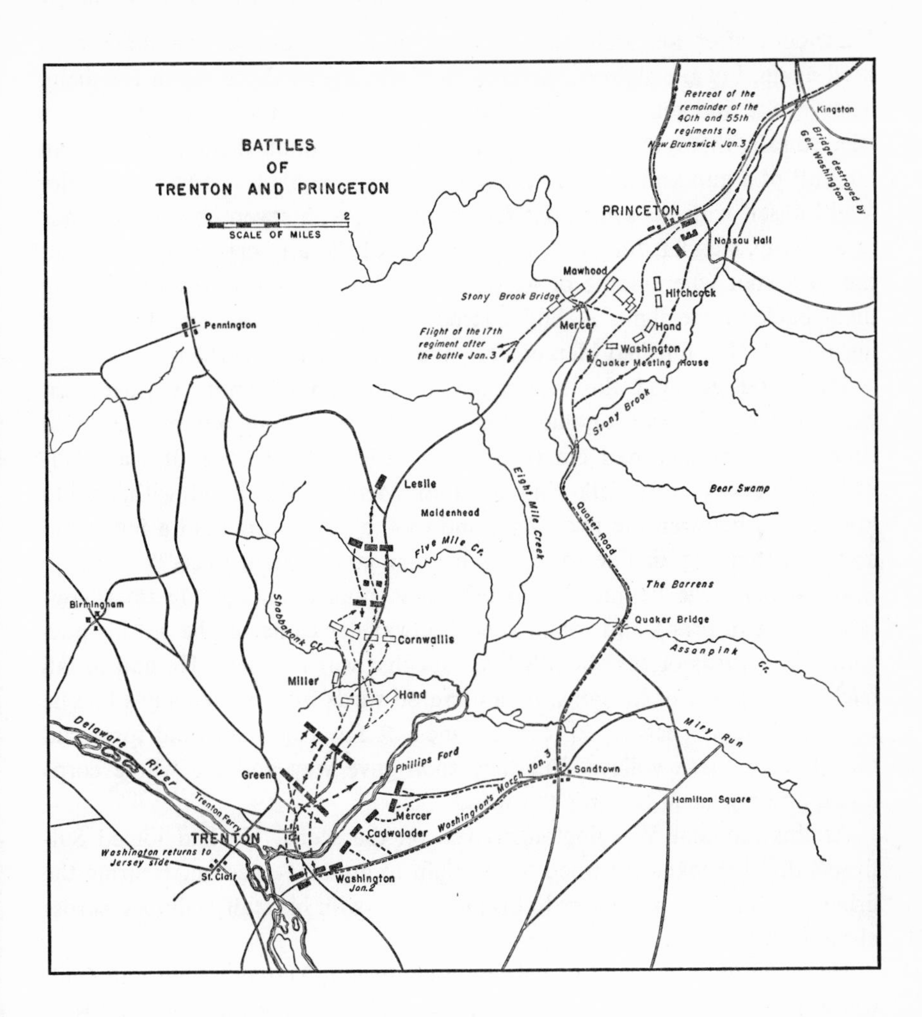
BATTLES
OF
TRENTON AND PRINCETON
0 1 2
SCALE OF MILES
Retreat of the remainder of the 40th and 55th regiments to New Brunswick Jan. 3
Kingston
Bridge destroyed by Gen. Washington
PRINCETON
Nassau Hall
Mawhood
Hitchcock
Stony Brook Bridge
Mercer
Hand
Flight of the 17th regiment after the battle Jan. 3
Washington
Quaker Meeting House
Pennington
Stony Brook
Eight Mile Creek
Bear Swamp
Leslie
Maidenhead
Five Mile Cr.
Quaker Road
The Barrens
Birmingham
Shabbakonk Cr.
Cornwallis
Quaker Bridge
Assanpink Cr.
Miller
Hand
Miry Run
Delaware River
Phillips Ford
Greene
Sandtown
Trenton Ferry
Washington's March Jan. 3
Hamilton Square
Mercer
Cadwalader
TRENTON
Washington returns to Jersey side
St. Clair
Washington
Jan. 2

Mawhood, after his first volley, called on his bayonets. The Americans fired again, but the sight of the cold steel was as usual too much for them. They broke and retreated in confusion.[18] Mercer and some of his officers tried to rally them, but Mawhood's bayonets were upon them. A blow from the butt of a gun knocked Mercer down. He got to his feet and tried to defend himself with his sword but fell again and, with seven bayonet wounds in his body, was left for dead. Captain Neil of the artillery also fell. Haslet ran to a spot where some of Mercer's men had halted and tried to bring them back to the fight. A bullet struck him in the head and killed him instantly.[19] That finished Mercer's brigade. They fled in disorder.

Mawhood pursued the Americans to the top of another ridge, but checked when he saw another American force coming out of the wood from which Mercer had emerged but a little while before. It was Cadwalader's Associators following on after Mercer. Mawhood withdrew to low ground between the two ridges and took a position behind a fence and a ditch, extending his line so that all his men could fire at once.[20]

From the ridge behind the British eight guns were keeping up a continuous fire of grape and round shot. Cadwalader came on; he led his men within fifty yards of Mawhood's line. But that was rashness. He had to fall back, leaving one of his guns. At a hundred yards from the enemy's line he tried, with some success, to form his men. A few companies did form and fired two or three volleys. But they soon gave way and the whole corps broke and ran back towards the woods.

At this moment Washington arrived on the scene. He had joined Sullivan's division when it turned to the right to attack Princeton. Hearing the firing on his left, he put spurs to his horse and, with his staff, galloped across ahead of his troops.

He came upon a scene of desperate confusion, Mercer's men and Cadwalader's in disorganized retreat. Waving his hat to the huddled groups as he passed, and calling on them to stand their ground, he dashed to the front, into the hottest fire and within thirty paces of Mawhood's line, to encourage his troops by the force of his own example.

The British soldiers were amazed at the sight of this big man on a great white horse so recklessly exposing himself. One of his aides thought to see him fall and covered his eyes to shut out the sight. A volley rang out from the enemy's line. The smoke from it shrouded Washington from all eyes. But when it blew away there he was, unhurt and still calling his men to come on.

They did not respond. It seemed that they were completely beaten. Then Hitchcock's Rhode Island Continentals, Hand's Pennsylvania riflemen, and the 7th Virginia came hurrying over from Sullivan's division. The defeated men took heart. Cadwalader's men rallied, and a part of Mercer's.

Meanwhile Captain Joseph Moulder's two-gun battery in the farmyard on the ridge, which had been first occupied by Mercer's men, had held its position and continued to pour grape on the enemy. While the Americans were re-forming for an advance Captain Thomas Rodney brought his handful of men and a few of the Philadelphia Associators to support Moulder. From behind strawstacks and buildings they kept up a good fire, deceiving the enemy as to their numbers by its continuity and rapidity.

At last the retreating troops were re-formed and, led by the Virginians yelling lustily, they came up to the battery's post, firing by platoons as they advanced.[21] Hand's riflemen went against Mawhood's right, and St. Clair's corps attacked the rest of the British 55th, now coming up to support the part of their regiment that had marched with Mawhood. They gave way and retreated across the fields and then along the road to New Brunswick. Mawhood was now almost surrounded, but his men fought on with great bravery. The action increased in intensity. The Americans' fire was hot and was delivered at such close range that they could hear the cries of its victims; they "screamed as if so many devils had got hold of them."

The 40th Regiment, cut off from the fight by St. Clair's brigade, had not come up from Princeton. But gallant Mawhood had no thought of surrender. He ordered a charge with the bayonet, broke through the swarm of Americans on the main road, crossed the bridge, and began a rapid retreat to Trenton, the dragoons covering his rear.

Washington with a troop of Philadelphia light horse led the pursuit, followed by many of his men on foot. The retreating British at first maintained good order, but finally broke and scattered away from the road with the American infantry after them. Many were shot down, 50 were captured. The fields were littered with their muskets and accouterments thrown away in their flight.[22] The pursuit continued until the British dragoons halted and made a determined stand to let such as still followed the road get away. Then it was called off.

Meanwhile the 40th Regiment and the men of the 55th who had not joined Mawhood had been driven back to Princeton. A part of them fled towards New Brunswick, the rest took refuge in Nassau Hall. It was surrounded. Captain Alexander Hamilton fired one ball from his fieldpiece into it, and a party of Jerseymen entered it. A surrender was inevitable; 194 prisoners were taken there.

The actual battle near the bridge had lasted only fifteen minutes; but it had been a very hot combat, fought at close quarters. In that short time 40 Americans were killed or wounded. Among the dead were General Mercer, who succumbed to his wounds, and Colonel Haslet—both of them officers of great merit and promise—Captain Daniel Neil of New Jersey, Captain William Shippen and Ensign Anthony Morris, Jr., of Philadelphia, and Captain John Fleming and Lieutenant Bartholomew Yeates of Virginia.

Washington estimated that the British lost 400, of whom 100 lay dead on the field; [23] but Howe's official report showed 18 killed (to which must be added 10 artillerymen not included in the return), 58 wounded, and 187 missing. As usual, the two claims cannot be reconciled. The Americans took two brass guns, which, for want of horses, could not be carried away, and some blankets and shoes, whose transportation was not difficult.

This victory, like that of Trenton, had an effect on the American cause entirely disproportionate to the number of men engaged. It heartened the people of all the states with hopes of ultimate complete success. Moreover, it strengthened Washington's military reputation at home and abroad, with a corresponding increase of his authority. "From Trenton onwards," says Trevelyan, "Washington was recognized as a far sighted and able general all Europe over—by the great military nobles in the Empress Catherine's court, by the French Marshals and Ministers, in the King's cabinet at Potsdam, at Madrid, at Vienna and in London. He had shown himself (says Horace Walpole) both a Fabius and a Camillus, and his march through the British lines was allowed to be a prodigy of leadership." [24]

A stroke at New Brunswick had been part of Washington's plan; but his men had been under arms for forty continuous hours of bitter winter weather, with no interval to rest or to cook a meal. They had made a most difficult march of sixteen miles over the roughest of roads in the darkness of night, and had then fought a hotly contested battle. They were so spent that there was hardly anything left in them. They were actually falling asleep on the frozen ground, and New Brunswick was eighteen miles away. Moreover, Cornwallis was surely now on the march against them with his much stronger army, and would be deeply interested in his stores at New Brunswick. Also, General Leslie at Maidenhead was only six miles distant.

Halting the pursuit of Mawhood's troops at Kingston after a three-mile chase, Washington held a council of war on horseback and put the question of his next move to his officers. It was agreed that they should give up New Brunswick and push off at once for the hills and the broken, heavily wooded country about Morristown, where a northern base for the army had been already established.

Washington confirmed this inevitable decision with much regret. He wrote to the Congress on January 5 that in his judgment "six or seven hundred fresh troops, upon a forced march, would have destroyed all their stores and magazines" at New Brunswick, "taken (as we have since learned) their military chest, containing seventy thousand pounds, and put an end to the war." [25] If his men had known £70,000 was to be had at New Brunswick, they might have summoned the strength to go and get it, despite their officers' judgment as to their incapability.

The army was on the move none too soon. Cornwallis, when he awoke that morning and overcame his astonishment at the discovery that the American army was not on the ridge across the Assunpink, was informed by the distant sound of guns that it was fighting elsewhere. He broke camp and marched for Princeton with haste and, coming to the bridge over Stony Brook which the Americans had broken down to delay his advance, did not pause, but drove his troops through the breast-deep stream. His speed was so great that his van, when it entered Princeton, was within sight of the American rearguard quitting the town.

Cornwallis was now convinced that Washington was headed for New Brunswick and its treasures. He followed on, but when the Americans took a left-hand road along Millstone River at Rocky Hill he took the right-hand road leading straight to New Brunswick. For how could he tell that the elusive Washington was not making a roundabout march to that valuable objective, in order to deceive his pursuers?

The van of the Americans reached Somerset Courthouse at dusk, but not all were in before eleven o'clock. There they encamped, if sleeping on the frozen ground without blankets, as many of them did, can be called "camping." "Our army was now extremely fatigued," wrote Captain Rodney, "not having any refreshment since yesterday morning." But they were up at daybreak and on the road again. At Pluckemin they halted to "await the coming up of nearly 1,000 men, who were not able through fatigue and hunger to keep up with the main body, for they had not had any refreshment for two days past" and had been "obliged to encamp on the bleak mountains, whose tops were covered with snow, without even blankets to cover them." They rested there for two days and were "pretty well supplied with provision." On the 6th the army went on to Morristown, where it was safe from sudden attack.

Meanwhile American contingents captured Hackensack and Elizabeth-Town, on January 6. Washington had swept the Jerseys clear of the enemy, except at Amboy and New Brunswick, which Howe still held with a force of 5,000 each. They were harmless posts, offering no opportunity for a blow against the Americans. This considerable feat had been accomplished by an army of fewer than 5,000 ragged, shoeless, ill fed, poorly equipped, often defeated amateur soldiers, mostly militia, operating against twice that number of veteran professionals, abundantly supplied with all martial equipment, and within a space of eleven days in the depth of winter.[26]

So ended the New Jersey campaign of 1776, which had ignored the calendar and lapped over a few days into 1777.

CHAPTER 28

Morristown

Morristown was a village of a church, a tavern, and about fifty houses of the better sort, set in an excellent defensive position on a high triangular plateau, with steep declivities on two sides and the bold ridge of Thimble Mountain at its back. It was approachable from the east only through rugged defiles in a chain of hills, while various passes to the west afforded access to a rich country for supplies, as well as ways for retreat, if necessary. For offensive operations it threatened Howe's flank if he should move either towards Philadelphia or up the Hudson.

In Freeman's Tavern on the village green Washington set up his headquarters. The troops were lodged in log huts in and about the village and outlying posts.[1] He had come there, as he said, "to draw the force on this side of the North River together . . . watch the motions of the Enemy and avail Myself of Every favourable Circumstance," [2] expecting to remain a few days. He lay there for nearly five months.

Whatever activities Washington may have had in mind, in the event of favorable circumstances, the condition of his army enforced a winter of inactivity. Depleted by expiration of enlistments and by the usual desertions, worn down by its recent severe service, it was at its lowest ebb in numbers, in physical condition, and in equipment.

On January 29, 1777, Washington wrote to the Congress that, unless speedily reenforced, he would be reduced "to the Situation . . . of scarce having any army at all." [3] By March 14 he had fewer than 3,000 men, of whom two-thirds were militia enlisted only to the end of the month.[4] At times, he was put to it to find men to mount the ordinary guards.[5] Yet with this handful he had to "keep up Appearances" before the enemy. "How I am going to oppose them, God knows," he wrote on April 3, "for except a few hundred from Jersey, Pennsylvania and Virginia I have not yet received a Man of the new Continental levies." [6]

The army was not only small; it was also destitute, "absolutely perishing for want of clothes," many of the men "quite bearfoot," so the General said. An ill organized commissariat failed to supply food. He wrote angrily to one of the commissaries: "The Cry of want of Provisions comes to me from every Quarter. . . . What, sir, is the meaning of this? . . . Consider, I beseech you, the consequences of this neglect and exert yourself to remedy this Evil." [7] He had to use the plenary powers granted him by the Congress in December, 1776, and order that "all the Beef, Pork, Flour, Spirituous Liquors &C &C, not necessary for the Subsistence of the Inhabitants" of lower East Jersey, should be commandeered.[8]

To crown the misfortunes of the army, smallpox ravaged the camp. The commander in chief took vigorous steps to combat it,[9] quartering the troops in small parties in the houses in Morristown and the near-by villages and ordering the inoculation of soldiers and citizens alike. Despite the protests of the dismayed civilians, this was done "with amazing success," [10] although at one time a third of his army was ill from the treatment.[11]

In addition to calling on the states in September, 1776, to raise eighty-eight battalions, Congress had authorized Washington on December 27 to raise sixteen Additional Battalions of infantry, 3,000 light horse, three artillery regiments, and a corps of engineers,[12] a grand total of 75,000 men —on paper, never to be realized in fact.

Recruiting lagged painfully. The soldiers of the old army were loath to reenlist. They had had enough of hardship, enough of cold and hunger, enough of barefoot marching in winter, enough of the dreadful squalor and filth of the "hospitals," where men merely lingered awhile in misery and wretchedness on their way to the grave. They told their tales of woe in the taverns and market places and so discouraged others that might have been ambitious to go a-soldiering.

The bounty system also acted against enlistment in the forces to be raised. The Congress offered $20 to each recruit enlisting for three years or the duration of the war and promised each man who served his full term a hundred acres of land.[13] In their efforts to fill their quotas of the original eighty-eight battalions, some of the New England states began to offer an additional bonus of $33.33. To the men whom Washington tried to enlist in the sixteen Additional Battalions $53.33 in hand looked better than $20 and a hundred acres, if they survived the war. He protested that the colonels appointed to raise the sixteen could not "get Men for 20 dollars when the state allows 53⅓." [14] Massachusetts answered by doubling its offer, making the total bounty $86.66; other states fell in line and went even higher.[15]

Some of the states made difficulties for themselves by raising regiments exclusively for home duty, while their quotas for the eighty-eight Continental battalions were yet unfilled, and paying these home guards £3 a month for "easy and secure duty at, or near their own firesides," against Continental wages of 40 shillings "for hard and dangerous service, far distant from home," as Washington put it in a protest to the executive officials of Massachusetts.[16]

On December 27, 1776, the Congress had called upon the new levies in the states from Pennsylvania down to Virginia "to march by companies or parts of companies, as far as they shall be raised, and join the army under General Washington with the utmost dispatch." [17] A month later Washington wrote, "They are so extremely averse to turning out of comfortable Quarters, that I cannot get a man to come near me." [18] And all through the spring and early summer, he kept repeating his call for more men.

There was a bit of good news in March; a ship from France came in with a useful cargo: nearly 12,000 muskets, 1,000 barrels of powder, 11,000 gun flints, and an assortment of clothes and incidentals, such as "1 case of needles and silk neck-cloths." [19] In its wake came another with 10,000 muskets. Guns and ammunition in plenty, but where were the men to use them?

They came at last. The thin trickle of recruits became a rivulet, then a clear stream, though never a flood. By the middle of May, forty-three of the new Continental regiments had arrived at Morristown, but not in full strength; they averaged 200 each, officers and men. Still, an army of 8,738 soldiers was something to be thankful for, even if only two-thirds of them were actually present and fit for duty. This force was organized in five divisions under Major Generals Greene, Stephen, Sullivan, Lincoln, and Stirling. Optimism returned; Congress moved back to Philadelphia.

Howe had learned the lesson of Trenton and Princeton; outlying posts, even if fairly strong, were not safe from those night-prowling Americans. By January 10 he had withdrawn all his troops to New Brunswick and Amboy. His own winter quarters were in New York, where he diverted himself in "feasting, gaming and banqueting" and in dalliance with his mistress, Mrs. Joshua Loring.[20] His troops were not so well off. Fourteen thousands of them were cantoned at Amboy and New Brunswick and the villages of that district in every sort of makeshift quarters. An entire company was crowded into two rooms; a regiment, in a church. Stables were filled with them. Open sheds were boarded up for them to freeze in. Many lay in the open. And it was not only overcrowding and the cold that made their lot hard. They were hungry, too. Food, as well as fuel and forage, was scarce, for "Amboy and Brunswick were, in a manner, besieged." [21]

The Americans were constantly on the alert to prevent the British from drawing subsistence from the countryside. No British foraging party could venture out of the lines with impunity. Attacks on such parties were frequent, and usually successful. The depredations and ravages committed, by the Hessians especially, but also by the British soldiers, had so angered the populace that they became fervent patriots, spied on the enemy, and kept Washington informed of their every move. The militia turned out in great numbers and aided the Continentals in harassing the foe. General Philemon Dickinson, with 400 militia and 50 Pennsylvania riflemen, fell upon a British foraging party of about the same strength, defeated it, and recaptured 40 wagonloads of plunder, 100 horses, and many cattle and sheep. Even 4,000 men in another party were not safe from attack. Washington kept his own men busy in such affairs and in "incessantly insulting, surprising and cutting off their pickets and advanced guards." [22]

But, except for such sporadic skirmishes, there was no military activity in the Jerseys that winter. Howe was now thinking of Philadelphia as his next major objective, but did nothing to achieve it. There is no doubt that the British army of 27,000 of the best professional soldiers, directed by Howe's military genius, led by the active and vigorous Cornwallis, and opposed only by Washington's meager 4,000, could have attained its object at any time in the first four months of 1777. Washington's position at Morristown could have been circumvented; and if he had seen fit to come down and attack the British on the march Howe would have had his opportunity for a decisive battle in the open field, in which his troops would have had every advantage.

Whether it was Howe's naturally sluggish temperament, or his adherence to the classic tradition that winter was a season for quarters and not for a campaign, or an exaggerated estimate of Washington's total strength, or an imagination of "hordes of Americans" ready to fall on his army if he advanced through the Jerseys, that caused him to waste those winter months and even the whole spring, no one can tell. But waste them he certainly did, while Washington's army grew stronger and stronger and his own job grew more and more difficult.[23]

There was, however, some activity elsewhere. It will be remembered that in November, 1776, when Washington withdrew from North Castle, he left Heath with four brigades, about 3,300 men, at Peekskill to guard the Highlands of the Hudson. Although a very large quantity of military stores had since been accumulated in magazines the troops had been drawn away for one reason or another until few remained. Washington had urged Massachusetts to send eight regiments to hold that post, but without result. In March, 1777, General Alexander McDougall, an inexperienced officer, was there, with but 250 men. The situation invited attention by the British. At midday of March 23 nine or ten British vessels arrived before Peekskill and disembarked 500 men. McDougall attempted to remove some of the stores, with little success. He then retired from the town, having first appealed for aid to Colonel Marinus Willett in Fort Montgomery on the other side of the river. Willett, a capable officer who was to prove his military efficiency a few months later at Fort Stanwix, crossed with 80 men, but the British had already been effectively busy burning the barracks and firing the magazines. He urged McDougall to attack, without avail. However, he obtained permission to try his luck. After firing one or two volleys he charged the British advance guard with the bayonet and drove it back on the main body, which at once took to its boats and withdrew to the ships.

The British had, however, accomplished their purpose, having practically destroyed the town by fire and burned great quantities of provisions, including 400 hogsheads of rum, 150 new wagons, several sloops and boats, and a quantity of entrenching tools. They carried off other stores of food, arms, artillery equipment, and munitions. They boasted that "the destruction was complete and effectual, scarce anything escaping that could be of use," which was no more than the truth. McDougall was relieved of his command and replaced by General Putnam, who held the post seven months before he too proved his incapacity and was removed.[24]

There was a similar British foray against Danbury, Connecticut, in the following month, which will be treated in connection with the northern campaign of 1777.

The Americans had their turn in May. A British foraging party was sent from New York to Sag Harbor near the eastern end of Long Island in twelve vessels protected by an armed schooner carrying 40 men and 12 guns and by a company of 70 men from Lieutenant Colonel Stephen De Lancey's Tory battalion. Colonel Return Jonathan Meigs with one of the Additional Battalions heard of this incursion. He embarked 170 men in whaleboats at Guilford in Connecticut in the evening of May 23, crossed Long Island Sound, which was "full of British cruisers," and landed at Sag Harbor at two o'clock the next morning. Taking De Lancey's troops by surprise, he killed six of them and captured all the rest, burnt all their vessels, except the schooner, also a large quantity of provisions and forage, and was back at Guilford by noon, having covered a distance of nearly 100 miles in eighteen hours. For this feat, the Congress voted him "an elegant sword." [25]

CHAPTER 29

Maneuvers in New Jersey

Winter had gone, spring had come and had nearly gone before the first move was made in the game played by Washington and Howe with Philadelphia and perhaps American independence as the stakes. On May 29 Washington made it.

Fearing that Howe might make a swift march from New Brunswick straight to Princeton and so to Trenton, passing some thirty miles below the American position, Washington marched twenty miles south to Middlebrook, near Bound Brook and about eight miles from New Brunswick. His new position, at which he hoped to intercept Howe, was in the first range of the Watchung Mountains behind certain commanding heights from which the country between Amboy and New Brunswick and the road to Philadelphia could be watched. It was strengthened by entrenchments and artillery posts.[1] At Princeton, he placed Smallwood's Maryland and Delaware brigade and Hazen's "2nd Canadian Regiment," under Sullivan.[2]

It was now Howe's turn. He wanted to get the Americans down on open ground, for a fair stand-up fight in which his trained army might beat them and so open the way to the American capital. To this end he made a series of three maneuvers.[3]

The first began on June 12. The British forces operating in New Jersey had been assembled at Amboy, 18,000 rank and file.[4] They marched to New Brunswick and thence in two columns: one, led by Cornwallis, to Somerset; the other, under von Heister, to Middlebush near Somerset.[5] They hoped not only to entice Washington down from Middlebrook, but also to cut Sullivan off from the main American army. Washington saw Sullivan's danger and ordered him to retire to Rocky Hill, where he could cover the road from that point to Pennington and also have a way of retreat open to the main army. While there he was to "harrass the Enemy by incessant parties when they attempt to march thro the country" but "by no means to risk a General Engagement." [6] A few days later Sullivan was shifted to Flemington on the enemy's right flank. Howe was also foiled in his other purpose. Washington refused to be drawn down from his stronghold.

Washington knew that Howe was "marching light," that is to say, that he had left at New Brunswick all his heavy baggage, his bateaux, and the portable bridge intended for crossing the Delaware. He knew, too, that if Howe really had intended now to march for the Delaware he would have pushed on with speed and would not have halted at Somerset or Middlebush and entrenched there.[7] As Stedman says, the American general "easily penetrated into the designs" of Howe "and eluded them by his cool and prudent conduct." [8] To strengthen his right, his most vulnerable point, Washington called on Sullivan to send him 1,000 Continentals and an equal number of the militia which had joined him and posted them at Steel's Gap in the Sourland Mountain, about two miles from Middlebrook.

Howe was now in an embarrassing position. He could not go on to the Delaware without his baggage, boats, and bridge, and, even if he brought them up, the American army still threatened his flank. Also there was a considerable force of Continentals and militia on the opposite side of the Delaware to oppose his crossing.[9] With Washington in his rear, he would be between two fires. There was, too, an ominously increasing number of Jersey militiamen hovering about his camp like a cloud of mosquitoes, picking up any men that strayed outside and promising more material aid to Washington when it was needed.[10]

But the British general had not yet exhausted his store of artful devices to lure Washington from his position. In the night of the 19th of June, he suddenly and secretly retreated from Middlebush and Somerset towards New Brunswick "with marks of seeming precipitation." [11] This time he was partially successful. Washington was deceived into thinking the movement was a final retreat. He sent Greene with his division of three brigades, reinforced by Wayne's brigade and Daniel Morgan's riflemen, to fall on the rear of the enemy. Orders were sent to Sullivan and Maxwell to cooperate with Greene.

Morgan led the advance along the right bank of the Raritan. At dawn he came upon Howe's Hessian picket guard at the New Brunswick bridge. The picket fled, hotly pursued by Morgan, until it came to the British rear guard. Greene and Wayne came up and charged upon the enemy, driving them through the town and across the bridge to their redoubts on the east side of the river. The Americans pushed them from these works and pursued them as far as Piscataway. But Sullivan had received his orders too late to come up with the pursuit, and Maxwell never got his. So Greene gave over the chase. The main body of the British went on its way towards Amboy, burning houses and barns along the road.[12] An English civilian, who accompanied the army, described this feature of the retreat: "All the Country houses were in flames as far as we could see. The Soldiers are so much enraged" at being called upon to retreat "that they will set them on fire in spite of all the Officers can do to prevent it." [13]

The Americans accomplished little by this affair, but Howe gained a point in the game. Deluded by him Washington came down from the hills to Quibbletown (now New Market) and encamped there, so as to be "nearer the enemy" and "act according to circumstances." [14] He sent Stirling with a strong detachment to the Short Hills in the neighborhood of Metuchen.

Howe's second maneuver having so far succeeded, he grasped at the chance to bring on a general engagement by a third movement. At one o'clock in the morning of the 26th his army moved out of Amboy in two columns. Cornwallis led one towards Woodbridge; Vaughan, the other towards Bonhamton. Howe accompanied Vaughan. Marching on parallel lines, they intended to pinch Stirling between them and to seize the passes back to Middlebrook, thus cutting Washington off from a retreat to the heights and compelling him to fight where he was.

They were long hours on the road. The weather was exceedingly hot. As the sun rose and climbed the sky the heat became increasingly intense. The marching men, especially the more heavily clad and equipped Hessians, suffered almost as much loss from sunstroke as from the bullets of snipers along the way.

The two columns joined before they came to Lord Stirling's camp, "strongly situated and well provided with artillery." [15] They attacked furiously. "His lordship was in no hurry to retreat, but preferred engaging for a while, wherein he made a wrong choice, for he had been nearly cut off by the right column under Lord Cornwallis." [16] He was driven from his position and pursued as far as Westfield where, "on account of the intense heat of the day," Cornwallis halted his men. The losses in this affair are impossible to reckon with certainty. The British claimed 100 Americans killed or wounded and 70 taken captive. They admitted 70 casualties on their side. These figures are all doubtful, but the Americans certainly did lose three small but valuable French brass guns.[17]

Near Woodbridge the British had fallen in with a party of American riflemen. Washington heard their fire, retired at once to the Middlebrook passes, and regained the heights before the enemy cut him off. So there the two armies were again in the same old positions.[18] Howe's third attempt had failed. "Sir William Howe," says Stedman, "being now sensible that every scheme of bringing the Americans to an engagement would be unattended by success, resolved to retire from the Jerseys."[19] He withdrew all his troops to Amboy and thence to Staten Island. By June 30 "the Province of New Jersey was entirely evacuated by the King's Troops."[20]

Now ensued a period of inactivity for both armies. For Washington, however, it was a time of increasing doubt and anxiety as to Howe's next move. General John Burgoyne had arrived in Quebec early in May, intending, as was well known, an expedition southward by way of Lake Champlain and the Hudson to Albany. He had now set out with a force of 8,000 British, Brunswickers, Canadians, and Indians. To Washington it seemed "almost certain" that Howe would go to meet him in Albany. That would mean that the great fleet, which Howe had been assembling for two months in New York waters, would sail up the Hudson.[21]

But there were other possible destinations—Philadelphia, for instance, by way of the Delaware River or Chespeake Bay, or even Charleston in South Carolina. With such a crafty strategist as Howe you never could tell. Then came news of Burgoyne's approach to Ticonderoga. Washington was surer than ever that Albany was Howe's objective.[22] In that case the American forces on the Hudson should be strengthened.

But not too indiscreetly or prematurely. If Washington's army went up there, Howe could make a swift and easy march to Philadelphia, take that city, and still have time for the Hudson River enterprise. Only Varnum's and Poor's brigades were sent to Peekskill, and Sullivan's as far as Pompton "till the intentions of the enemy are more clearly and fully known." In order to be "more conveniently situated for Succouring Peekskill," and yet "near enough to oppose any design upon Philadelphia," Washington transferred his main army to Morristown.[23]

When he received information as to the fitments of Howe's transports for carrying horses and the amount of "Provender taken in"—enough for a month's voyage—he began to doubt that the fleet would go up to Albany and to think of Charleston as its destination.[24] He was puzzled. Nevertheless, he ordered Sullivan farther north, to the Clove in the Ramapo Mountains, a rugged defile through the Highlands on the west side of the river.[25]

Howe began to embark his troops on July 8, but did not immediately sail. For nearly two weeks "both foot and Cavalry remained pent up in the hottest season of the year in the holds of the vessels." [26] The day after the embarkation, Washington learned to his "Chagrine and Surprise" that General Arthur St. Clair, with 3,500 men, had evacuated Ticonderoga, without firing a shot in its defense and that Burgoyne was rapidly advancing towards Albany.[27] He could not believe that Howe would not go up to meet him, and wrote on July 12, "His designs I think are most unquestionably against the Highlands." Washington therefore decided to march "towards the North River and cross or not as shall appear necessary from the circumstances." On his arrival in the Clove he sent Sullivan and after him Stirling across the river to a position behind Peekskill.[28]

On July 23 Howe's fleet of more than 260 warships and transports, laden with fifteen to eighteen thousand soldiers, innumerable horses, field-pieces and small arms, quantities of ammunition, provisions, and military equipment of every sort, set sail from Sandy Hook. It was an impressive armada. A little below, the transports formed in two divisions. The flagship *Eagle*, 64 guns, and the frigate *Liverpool*, 32 guns, led the convoy. After them and on both sides of the transports came the warships *Augusta*, 64 guns, and *Isis*, 50 guns. In the rear were the *Nonsuch*, 64 guns, with its "couriers" the armed schooners *Swift* and *Dispatch*, 16 guns each. Nine frigates "sailed around the fleet at some distance." So they left the Hook bound for—no one on the American side knew where.[29]

Washington, up in the Clove, got the news the next day and perceived that he had guessed wrong. He ordered Sullivan, Stirling, Stephen, and Lincoln, with their divisions, Morgan's riflemen, and the squadrons of horse led by Sheldon, Moylan, and Bland to proceed immediately to Philadelphia. He detached Wayne from his brigade and sent him to Chester in Pennsylvania to command the militia there. With the rest of his army he started southward.[30]

When he gave those orders he was sure Howe was for Philadelphia by way of the Delaware River; but by the time he himself got to that river, on the 29th, he began again to doubt. Howe had then been six days at sea, yet had not appeared at the Delaware capes. Perhaps after all his start southward from New York was merely a ruse to draw the American army away from the Hudson. That fleet might have turned about and be now on its way back to join Burgoyne. He decided to hold his troops on the Jersey side of the Delaware, at Trenton, Coryell's Ferry, and Howell's Ferry. He halted Sullivan at Morristown until further orders.[31]

But the very next day Henry Fisher, a pilot at Lewes, at the mouth of the Delaware Bay, sent an express to Philadelphia telling that the fleet was in sight. Washington got the news at Coryell's Ferry, 150 miles from Lewes, at ten o'clock in the morning of the 31st—in twenty-four hours, a creditable performance for men and horses.[32]

Washington immediately ordered his troops across the Delaware and to Philadelphia, called on Sullivan to come on, and himself took horse for Chester "to look out for a proper place to arrange the army." [33] But on August 2 Fisher wrote that the fleet had left: "A large ship which we took to be the Admiral fired a gun and immediately the whole Fleet backed and stood off . . . to the eastward . . . about four o'clock P.M. they were ought of sight; whether they were bound to New York or Virginia is not in my power to tell." [34]

Nor was it in Washington's power; but he guessed—and guessed wrong again. It seemed to him, he said, that Howe had been "practising a deep feint, merely to draw our attention and whole force to this point." "There is the strongest reason to believe that the North River is their object." "This unexpected event makes it necessary to reverse our disposition." "I shall return again with the utmost expedition to the North River." So he wrote to this and that one of his generals, with orders to hasten back to Peekskill.[35]

But on more sober thought he decided on August 3 to wait until he had sure intelligence that the fleet was back at Sandy Hook before he returned to Peekskill. So he halted Sullivan at Hanover in New Jersey and held his main army at the Falls of Schuylkill near Germantown in Pennsylvania.

Yet again, on the 8th, his fears of Howe's strategy prompted him to move back to Coryell's Ferry; and he was actually on the march when, on the 10th, another flash came from the south. The fleet had been seen off Sinepuxent Inlet in Maryland, thirty miles below the Delaware capes, and was headed south. He halted his army and went into camp beside Neshaminy Creek, thirty miles north of Philadelphia.[36]

Still, he was "puzzled . . . being unable to account upon any plausible Plan . . . why he [Howe] should go to the southward rather than co-operate with Mr. Burgoyne." [37] Even as late as the 21st of August he still thought Howe was making a feint and would return either to the Delaware or to the Hudson, for, "had Chesapeake Bay been his Object, he would have been there long since." A council of war held that day decided unanimously that Charleston in South Carolina was Howe's most probable destination. So sure were the American generals that it was decided to move "to-morrow morning towards Hudson's River," and orders were given accordingly.[38] But on the next day came an express: the fleet was in the Chesapeake, "high up in the North East part of it." [39] The orders were canceled.

Why Admiral Lord Howe, in command of the fleet, and his brother, Sir William, in command of the army, after reaching the Delaware capes, failed to attempt a landing near Philadelphia and instead made the long voyage south, around Cape Charles, and up the Chesapeake, has puzzled many able historians and they still continue to debate the question. Yet the facts seem to give a plain answer.

The fleet had sailed from Sandy Hook on July 23, 1777. Meeting variable weather and winds, it made the Delaware capes on the 29th. After tacking to and fro for a whole day, it was joined by the *Roebuck*, which had long been stationed in Delaware waters under command of Captain Sir Andrew Snape Hamond. Captain Hamond boarded the flagship and gave the Admiral such a report of conditions in the bay and river that it was decided to draw off and make for the Chesapeake.

The first question debated by the historians is whether it was General Howe's intention, when he planned the excursion, to go up the Delaware or the Chesapeake. But that question is certainly easily answered. He planned at first to enter the Chesapeake. However, he wrote to Germain July 6, 1777, "I propose going up the Delaware." The second question is why he changed his mind. That is answered in a letter to Germain dated August 30: "Arrived off the Capes of the Delaware . . . when from information, I thought it most advisable to proceed to Chesapeake Bay." Hamond gave him reasons that quite properly seemed sufficient to make him change his plans.[40] Lieutenant William John Hall of the 45th regiment makes this point clear in a letter dated December 26, 1777: "In our appearance off the capes of Delaware, the *Roebuck* came out and Capt. Hamond going on board the Admiral produced a chimerical draught of fortifications that were never erected and Chevaux de Frise that were never sunk. This intelligence caused us to bear away for the Chesapeake." [41] What was even more important in the situation was that Howe hit upon the idea of using the Delaware because he feared Washington was about to go to the assistance of the American army in northern New York and because he could follow Washington much more readily from the Delaware. When he learned that the American commander in chief was not moving northward, he was able to pursue his original plan.

One may ask two more questions: Was Hamond's advice justified by conditions in the Delaware? Was the decision unfortunate in fact?

The substance of Hamond's objections to going up the Delaware was the condition of the river itself and the condition of its defenses. Of the river itself he said that its navigation was intricate and hazardous; that large ships could pass certain places only at particular times of the tide; that its shores from Henlopen to Reedy Island were marshy and full of creeks; that from Reedy Island to Chester the channel was so narrow as to require four miles of anchorage for the fleet, which must lie within cannon-shot of the shore; that the tidal current ran at three to four miles an hour.[42]

In answer one might urge that the navigation was not too difficult, nor the tidal current too strong to prevent the flagship and twelve other ships from going up in October as far as Chester. As to anchorage, in November there were 100 vessels anchored between Reedy Island and New Castle; although much of the shore was marshy, both New Castle and Chester afforded good landing places, New Castle being a port much used by overseas vessels. On this point Hamond's advice was clearly unjustified.

Of the river's defenses, he said that the Americans had a fleet of one frigate, two xebecs, one brig, and two floating batteries, and that there were numerous channel obstructions.[43] Certainly that little American fleet could offer no substantial opposition to Howe's great warships, and there were no forts and no "channel obstructions" even as far down as Chester. Hamond's advice was bad on all those points, too.

That the decision was unfortunate in fact is equally certain. From the 31st of July, when the fleet left the Delaware capes, to the 14th of August, when it sighted Cape Charles, it fought adverse winds and endured calms. It took eleven more days to reach its landing at the Head of Elk—thirty-two days out from Sandy Hook—having sailed three hundred and fifty miles from Henlopen to land only fifteen miles from New Castle, which it might have reached in less than ninety miles from Henlopen. In all that long voyage men and horses suffered greatly from the rough sea, the heat, the shortage of fresh provisions, fresh water, and forage. Many of the horses, dead or dying, were thrown overboard; those that survived were "mere carrion."

As against Head of Elk, New Castle would have been a much more favorable landing place. From Head of Elk the army had to march fifty miles to Philadelphia. From New Castle, the distance is but thirty-three miles. Better still would have been Chester, only fifteen miles from Philadelphia with no such defensible river to cross as the Brandywine, until they came to the Schuylkill at Philadelphia itself.

As Trevelyan points out, after all that delay and all those hardships, the army at Head of Elk was ten miles farther from Philadelphia than it had been the previous December at Amboy. And it had the same army, but much larger in numbers, to contend with in August as in the previous December.

Altogether the decision to go to the Chesapeake was undeniably unfortunate. But that the fault lay with Howe, because he took advice that sounded convincing from a sea captain who should have been well informed, is probably not true. Howe chose the Chesapeake route in the beginning with a rather vague idea that he could more or less cut off communication between the middle and southern colonies and at the same time possibly force Washington to fight at a disadvantage somewhere east of the Susquehanna River. No doubt he also calculated that he could later open up the Delaware as a safe supply route.

Whatever Howe may have planned, Washington's suspense and anxiety were now at an end. Orders went to Sullivan to join the army "with all convenient speed"; to General Nash to hasten with his brigade and Proctor's artillery to Chester; and for all the troops to march "to-morrow morning very early towards Philadelphia and onwards." [44] News of the American victory at Bennington was given out and greatly cheered the soldiers.

CHAPTER 30

Head of Elk

Washington started southward from his camp on the Neshaminy on August 23, at four o'clock in the morning. That evening he camped near Germantown, and the next morning he formed his troops for the march through Philadelphia in such manner as to impress the strong Tory element there, including the Quakers. His preparations and directions for this display of strength were "pathetically minute." [1]

The army was to march in one column "First—A Sub. and twelve light horse, 200 Yards in their rear a complete troop," then a space of 100 yards, and "a company of pioneers with their axes in &c in proper order." At another hundred yards distance, a regiment of Muhlenberg's brigade, followed by field artillery, then Weedon's, Woodford's, and Scott's brigades, Lincoln's and Stirling's divisions, the artillery, and the cavalry, winding up with a troop of horse 150 yards in the rear of all the rest. The men were to be "made to appear as decent as possible" and to "carry their arms well"; any man who dared "to quit his ranks" was to receive thirty-nine lashes at the next halting place. The drums and fifes were to play "a tune for the quick step . . . but with such moderation that the men may step to it with ease; and without dancing along." To give them some appearance of uniformity in default of uniform dress, they were to wear sprigs of green leaves in their hats.[2]

So, with Washington riding at the head, the Marquis de Lafayette at his side and his mounted staff following, the long column of 16,000 men marched down Front Street and up Chestnut to the awe of the disaffected and the delight of the patriots. John Adams watched the procession. "They marched twelve deep," he wrote to his wife, "and yet took up above two hours in passing by." They were "extremely well armed, pretty well clothed and tolerably disciplined," yet had not "quite the air of soldiers. They don't step exactly in time. They don't hold up their heads quite erect, nor turn out their toes exactly as they ought. They don't all of them cock their hats; and such as do, don't all wear them the same way." [3] Another observer, a military gentleman, Alexander Graydon, who was inclined to be critical, noted that "though indifferently dressed, [they] held well burnished arms and carried them like soldiers, and looked, in short, as if they might have faced an equal number with a reasonable prospect of success." [4]

They marched to Darby that day, and moved on to Naaman's Creek on the next, under orders to "encamp in the first good ground beyond it." The horsemen, however, were to keep on to Wilmington before encamping. Washington himself with his staff also kept on, entered Wilmington, and set up his headquarters in a house on Quaker Hill. Here he learned that the enemy had begun to land that morning "about Six Miles below the Head of Elk opposite to Cecil Court House." He set about gathering in all available troops, called on Armstrong to send on "every Man of the Militia under your command" at Chester and Marcus Hook "that is properly armed, as quick as possible," to march them, indeed, that very night. He called on Baylor to bring "Such Men as you have ready," on Greene's division and Stephen's, also on Sullivan's; but Sullivan was not to press his men "too hard in their march," as they "must no doubt have been greatly harassed" in a futile expedition against Staten Island he had undertaken while at Hanover.[5] Washington had already detached General Smallwood and Colonel Mordecai Gist from their commands in Sullivan's division and sent them to Maryland to take over the militia of that state, called out to the number of 2,000 in accordance with a resolution of the Congress.[6]

On the following morning Washington, accompanied by Greene, Lafayette, his aides, and a strong troop of horse, rode southward on a scouting expedition. From the summits of Iron Hill and Gray's Hill they scanned the country below. Although Gray's Hill was within two miles of the enemy's camp and they could see their tents, they could not form a satisfactory estimate of their numbers. After spending the rest of the day in surveying the surrounding country, they were overtaken by a severe storm. Having taken refuge in a farmhouse Washington showed no inclination to go out into the tempestuous night. His companions urged upon him the danger of capture, perhaps citing the fate of Charles Lee in similar circumstances, but he chose to remain until daybreak. The owner of the house was a Tory; he might have sent word to the British camp of the archrebel's presence and so led to a coup disastrous to the Americans, if Washington's escort had not surrounded the house and guarded against that danger. Washington himself afterwards acknowledged his imprudence at this time.[7]

It was on a Monday morning, August 25, "a distressingly hot, close morning," that the van of the British fleet dropped anchor in the Elk River opposite Cecil County Courthouse and the debarkation began. Two regiments of British light infantry, two of British grenadiers, and the Hessian and Anspach jägers in flat-bottomed boats were the first ashore on the courthouse side and the first to come in contact with the Americans—four companies of militia stationed there, who "fled without firing a shot." The light infantry at once advanced to a post about four miles towards the Head of Elk. The rest of the army landed that day, all except the light dragoons, who came ashore with their horses on the morrow. The troops were ordered to hut themselves with fence rails and cornstalks, which could have afforded little protection from the "heavy storm of Rain, Lightning and Thunder" that broke upon them that night.[8]

Orders were given by Howe to march at three o'clock in the morning, but were countermanded because of another heavy storm that lasted all night and part of the third day. In spite of the rain and the hanging of two soldiers and the severe whipping of five others as a punishment for plundering, the troops indulged in extensive looting of houses and farms. The inhabitants were not to be seen "having deserted their houses and drove off their stock." Not all of it, however, for "the soldiers slaughtered a great deal of cattle clandestinely." [9]

There were other reasons for the British delay than the storm; the troops were not yet sufficiently refreshed from their long confinement in the transports, and the "miserably emaciated" horses—those that had survived—were in no shape to be used. On the 28th, however, the weather being "extremely fine" and the roads somewhat dried, the van of the army marched to Elkton, a town of "about 40 well built brick and stone houses," from which "one thousand men under a Colonel Patterson and the Philadelphia Light Horse" fled to Gray's Hill. They fled again when the British advance guard came up. In Elkton the invaders found "Storehouses full, consisting of molasses, Indian Corn, Tobacco, Pitch, Tar and some Cordage and Flour," which the American troops had failed to remove.[10]

The British army was in two grand divisions. It was the one commanded by Cornwallis that had moved on Elkton; the other, under the Hessian general, Wilhelm von Knyphausen, had crossed the Elk and encamped at Cecil Courthouse. This arrangement was designed to permit an advance up

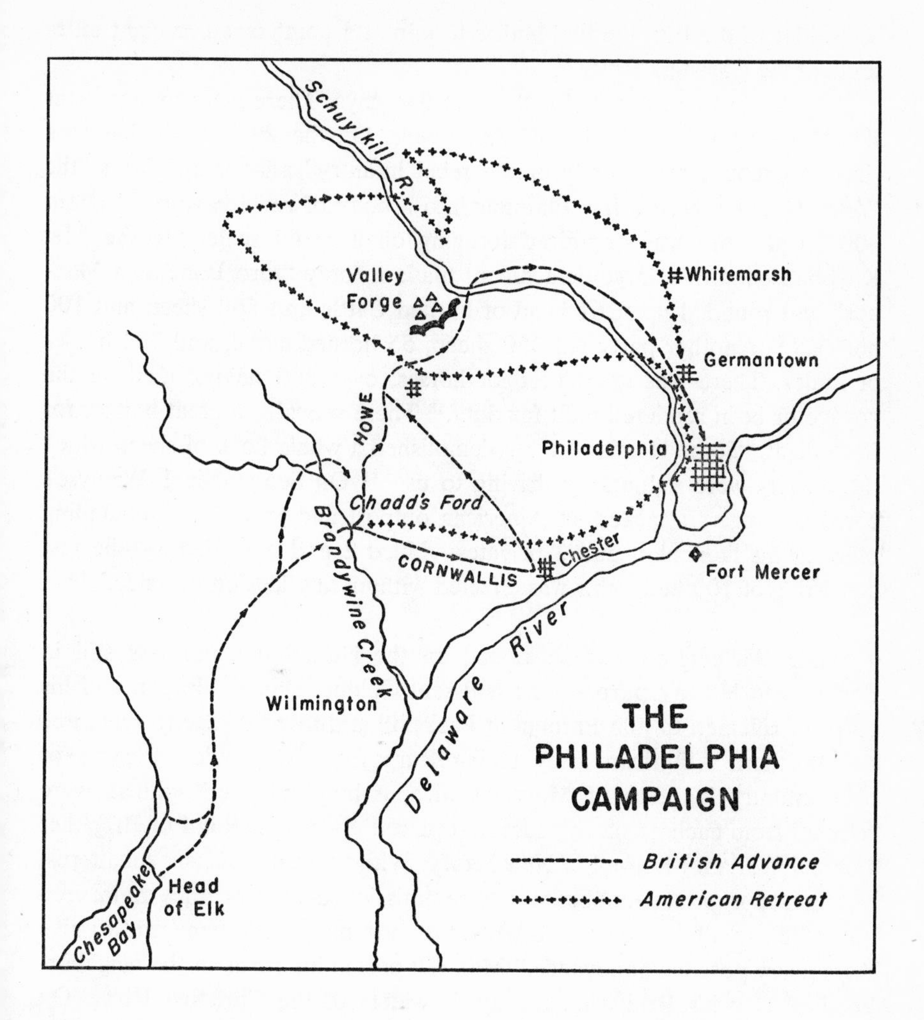
Schuylkill R.
Valley Forge
Whitemarsh
Germantown
HOWE
Philadelphia
Chadd's Ford
Brandywine Creek
CORNWALLIS
Chester
Fort Mercer
Delaware River
Wilmington
THE PHILADELPHIA CAMPAIGN
British Advance
American Retreat
Head of Elk
Chesapeake Bay

both sides of the Elk, the two bodies to join at a point seven or eight miles south of the Christina River.[11]

They lay in those camps for the next five days. There were unimportant skirmishes with small bodies of Americans. On the 29th "the Chasseurs [jägers] encountered a body of the rebel infantry" and on the 30th "the Welch fusileers fired a few Platoons into a body of rebel cavalry of about 200." But there was organized foraging on a grand scale. On the 31st Knyphausen with a large detachment made a foray "thro Bohemiah Mannor" and rounded up "261 head of horned Cattle and 568 sheep and 100 horses." [12] Another party got 350 sheep, 55 horned cattle, and 204 horses or mules. There was great need of horses, over 300 having died on the voyage or been rendered unfit for duty.[13] There was also a great hunger for fresh meat. "Some Hessians . . . demolished a whole flock of sheep which the owners were voluntarily driving to us." [14] On September 1 Wemyss's corps of rangers attacked an American outpost and took the commanding officer, "his lieutenant and 3 privates—killed 2 and wounded 1—the rest consisting of 100 fled—this was effected without any loss on our side." [15]

While Washington was encamped on the Neshaminy and was still in doubt as to Howe's purposes he had sent Colonel Daniel Morgan and his corps of riflemen to join Putnam at Peekskill and to go thence to reenforce the Northern American army facing Burgoyne. To provide a corps of light infantry in place of Morgan's men, a hundred good soldiers were selected from each of six brigades and placed under command of Brigadier General William Maxwell of New Jersey. With two captains, six subalterns, and the appropriate number of noncommissioned officers, they numbered about 720 in all. They were to be "constantly near the Enemy and to give them every possible annoyance." Maxwell posted his corps in the neighborhood of Cooch's Bridge on the upper waters of the Christina River. On September 2 Washington warned him of the intention of the enemy to march next day and begged him "to be prepared to give them as much trouble as you possibly can." [16]

The British army had, indeed, begun its movement that very day. Knyphausen, commanding one of the two grand divisions, marched from his camp at Cecil Courthouse and encamped that night at the Buck Tavern, otherwise called Carson's, just below the present Delaware and Chesapeake Canal.[17] At daybreak on the following morning Cornwallis with the other column, Howe accompanying him, took "the lower road to Christeen by way of Rikin's [Aiken's] Tavern in order to avoid Iron Hill." They had expected to join Knyphausen at the tavern (now the town of Glasgow) "but did not perceive them." They pushed on through a "close" country, "the woods within shot of the road frequently in front and flank and in projecting points towards the Road." [18] Evidently it was the kind of country disliked by the regulars, who preferred combat in the open in regular battle formation.

Along this unpleasant road at about nine o'clock in the morning the van of the column, Hessian and Anspach jägers, under Lieutenant Colonel Ludwig von Wurmb, followed by British light infantry with two small fieldpieces, was making its way—cautiously, no doubt—when it met a sudden fire from Maxwell's men posted among the trees by the roadside. Wurmb formed his men, and there was a hot fire from both sides. The fieldpieces were brought into play; a detachment of Hessians shifted to the woods and attacked Maxwell's right flank; Wurmb charged with the bayonet. The Americans retreated up the road, took a new position under cover, and renewed their fire. Again they were driven back to another stand. The British light infantry entered the engagement; the Americans again retreated, keeping up a running fight. At one point "a body of Riflemen formed a kind of Ambuscade" and gave the British "several close, well-directed Fires." An attempt at getting into the American rear failed because "an unpassable swamp" intervened, "which prevented this spirited, little affair becoming so decisive" as it might have been. But Maxwell's men were now pretty well disorganized. Their retreat became a flight. They were pursued for some distance, but finally made their way to the main army on the White Clay Creek.[19] The casualties were perhaps thirty killed on the American side and about as many killed or wounded on the other.[20]

Knyphausen's column came up to Aiken's Tavern just after this affair, and both columns encamped between Iron Hill and the tavern. They had moved slowly, having to drive a herd of cattle with them and to keep pace with two detachments flanking Knyphausen's column sent out to comb the country for livestock. These brought in "500 Head of Horned Cattle, 1000 Sheep and 100 horses, but not above forty of these Horses were fit for draught." [21]

The next four days the British spent in reconnoitering the country, bringing up provisions from the fleet, and sending back the sick and wounded. Grant, with two brigades left at Elkton, came up on the 6th. All communication with the fleet was then abandoned, and it withdrew down the bay.

On August 28 Greene's and Stephen's divisions, mostly Virginia Continentals, under Brigadiers Muhlenberg, Weedon, Woodford, and Scott, with

Sheldon's horse, were advanced to the White Clay Creek.[22] But an American council of war decided to concentrate the army on the northerly side of the Red Clay Creek near Newport, on the main road to Philadelphia. To that position it was moved on September 6,[23] Maxwell's corps remaining in advance on the White Clay. Washington, having learned that the British had disencumbered themselves of their baggage and tents, indicating "a speedy and rapid movement," ordered his troops similarly relieved. Both officers and men were to retain only their greatcoats, if they had any, and their blankets. Everything else was to be sent north of the Brandywine.[24] Thus stripped for action they awaited the enemy's next move.

It began on the 8th two hours before daybreak when the whole British army advanced by the light of "a remarkable borealis." Washington had expected a movement against his position on the Red Clay and seems to have been desirous of bringing on an engagement there. Howe fostered this delusion by sending a detachment to a point opposite the American position [25] but marched his main army northward. This was construed by Washington as a flanking movement to carry the enemy around his right to his rear and so on to Philadelphia. To prevent this he withdrew his force at two o'clock in the morning of the 9th to Chad's Ford on the Brandywine and on the more northerly Philadelphia road. But Howe was proceeding in good faith to Kennett Square in Pennsylvania. Early in the morning of the 10th the whole British force was collected at that place on the road which Washington held at Chad's Ford.[26]

CHAPTER 31

Brandywine

The Brandywine proper begins at the confluence of two streams, known as the east and west branches, which meet at a place called the Forks about six miles northwest of Chad's Ford. It flows in a valley, now very narrow and again somewhat wider, where meadows border the stream, between hills rising to a height of 200 feet or more three-quarters of a mile from the river edge. In places these hills slope gradually down to the river; in others they drop steeply, 200 feet in a half-mile or even in a quarter-mile. The uplands back of the hilltops were largely cultivated, but the slopes were densely forested. Between the Forks and the Ford the river receives little streams coming down small valleys.

Along the valley ran roads to find shallow crossings. These several roads and fords played an important part in the battle and must be distinguished by name.

The Nottingham Road (now the Baltimore Pike), running eastwards through Kennett Square on its way to Chester and Philadelphia, came to the river at Chad's Ford. Just before it reached the stream, it forked and crossed by two fords, one about 300 feet north of the present bridge, the other about 150 feet below the bridge. At this point the shallow but swift stream was about 150 feet wide.[1]

About a mile upstream, another road crossed at Brinton's Ford. Two miles above that, the Street Road ran to Painter's Ford. A branch of that road used Wistar's Ford, an equal distance farther up. Again there was a two-mile interval to Buffington's Ford, where a road running roughly parallel to the stream on its east side swung to the west to cross the East Branch a little above the Forks. A mile above that Jefferis Ford crossed the East Branch and, opposite it, Trimble's Ford crossed the West Branch. The width of the tongue of land between them was about two miles. About a mile and half below Chad's was Pyle's Ford.[2]

The American army arrived at Chad's Ford in the morning of September 9 and established its center there, Wayne's brigade of Pennsylvania Continentals being posted on the brow of an eminence near Chad's house a little above the Ford, and Weedon's and Muhlenberg's brigades of Virginia Continentals directly east of the Ford. Proctor's Pennsylvania artillery was with Wayne. Greene commanded the center. Light earthworks and a redoubt were erected for Wayne and Proctor as a front line, the Virginians being in reserve.

The right wing was composed of three divisions of two brigades each posted along the east bank of the river, covering Brinton's Ford and running up some distance below Painter's. Stirling held the extreme right; Stephen was next below him; and Sullivan was nearest the center, he being in general command of the wing.

The left wing was posted at Pyle's Ford, where the heights on the east side were steep and rugged and there was little apprehension of a crossing. Its defense was entrusted to a thousand Pennsylvania militia under Armstrong.

To guard the forces above the right wing, Sullivan detached the Delaware Regiment to Painter's Ford, one battalion from Hazen's "Canadian Regiment" to Wistar's and another to Buffington's.[3]

Maxwell's light infantry took a position west of the river on high ground on both sides of the main road. Picket guards were thrown across the upper part of the stream. Colonel Theodorick Bland with the 1st Dragoons, one of Washington's few cavalry corps, which were all commanded by Count Pulaski, was stationed about opposite Painter's Ford. Major James Spear, with a body of Pennsylvania militia, picketed the ground above the Forks near Buffington's Ford. Washington established his headquarters in a house about a mile back of Chad's Ford, and Lafayette set up his a half mile farther back.[4]

September 11, 1777, began with a foggy morning, but ripened to a noon of blazing sunshine and sweltering heat. Before daybreak Maxwell's corps, with three small detachments from the Virginia line, was sent back along the main road towards Kennett Square to feel out the enemy and delay their approach. Maxwell marched as far as Kennett meetinghouse, about three miles from the Ford, and sent a party of mounted vedettes farther forward.

They stopped at Welch's Tavern a mile or so beyond, tied their horses to a rail, and gathered at the bar, waiting for something to turn up. About nine o'clock, one of them espied through a window uniformed men coming down the road and not more than a few rods away. It was Major Patrick Ferguson's Riflemen and the Queen's Rangers, Tory troops, the point of the vanguard of Knyphausen's columns. The vedettes fired a single harmless volley and fled through the back door, leaving their horses.[5]

The Riflemen and Rangers were followed by two British brigades under General Grant, Stirn's brigade of three Hessian regiments, half of the 16th Dragoons, and two brigades of heavy artillery. Behind them the rest of the artillery, the provision train, the baggage and cattle dragged along, followed by the rear guard of one battalion of the 71st Regiment of Highlanders, two others marching beside the train as flankers. There were about 5,000 men in all in this column.[6] They had left Kennett early in the morning and advanced so far without the Americans even knowing that they were on the march.

After dispersing the little band at Welch's Tavern, the column kept on to the Meetinghouse. There it met with a surprise. A sudden burst of fire from Maxwell's corps posted behind the graveyard wall checked the van and threw it into confusion. It rallied and returned the fire. Maxwell fell back slowly down the road, taking cover from time to time and keeping up his fire until he reached the Ford. There he was reinforced. He turned back to high ground above the road and again engaged the enemy. The vanguard was not strong enough to dislodge him, and the British deployed. Ferguson's Riflemen supported by a hundred Hessians were thrown out to the right. But in the meantime Porterfield's and Waggoner's Virginians had crossed the stream to Maxwell's aid. They drove the Riflemen and Hessians back to the shelter of a stone house. The British 49th Regiment, with two heavy guns and two three-pounders, taking a position on an elevation behind Ferguson, backed him up and opened fire on the Americans. The Queen's Rangers, led by Captain Wemyss, and the 23rd Regiment filed off to their left and flanked Maxwell, whose men "had been shouting Hurrah! and firing briskly." The 28th Regiment also went into action, and Maxwell was driven out of the woods and back across the upper branch of the Ford. The Rangers then joined the Riflemen and Hessians at the stone house, swept down on Porterfield and Waggoner and drove them back by the lower ford to the other side.[7]

While all this was going on Porter's artillery was cannonading from its position on the east side; but "though the balls and grapeshot were well aimed and fell right among us," says Captain Baurmeister of the Hessian

Regiment von Mirbach, "the cannonade had but little effect—partly because the battery was placed too low." [8]

Under the covering fire of their guns, mounted hastily in strategic places and on the high ground west of the river, the 28th, 23rd, 55th, and 40th British regiments and the Leib and Mirbach Hessian regiments formed a line on the heights overlooking the Ford; the Combined Battalion and Donop's Hessians held the road; and the 4th, 5th, 27th, and 49th British regiments took position on the slope from the heights down to the lowland along the river. The light troops and outposts were pushed forward close to the stream. The lines were straightened in formal fashion, and one battalion of the 71st, with the 16th (or Queen's Own) Regiment of light dragoons, was posted on the right flank, while two other battalions of the 71st guarded the baggage in the rear. These dispositions were completed by half-past ten. Then things quieted down; the musketry ceased; the artillery fired only occasionally, and was similarly answered by the Americans.[9]

One might suppose that this cessation of activity on the part of the enemy, this desultory firing with no attempt to advance, would have brought to Washington and his officers memories of an exactly similar situation at Long Island a year before, when Grant held Stirling by the same tactics while the main British army was about its business elsewhere; but the same bland confidence that Howe intended a frontal attack seems to have persisted in the minds of all. Washington and Greene spent most of the morning at headquarters, a mile back from the Ford.[10] At the front the hours passed in watchful waiting for the enemy to launch their attack.

This confidence was first disturbed after nine o'clock when word came to headquarters from Colonel Hazen that a body of the enemy had been seen marching up the Great Valley Road, parallel with the river on its western side and leading to Trimble's Ford on the west branch a mile above the Forks. Washington sent a note to Colonel Bland, who was on the west side of the stream opposite Painter's Ford, earnestly entreating "a continuance of your vigilant attention to the movements of the enemy" and calling for reports of such movements, of their numbers "and of the course they are pursuing." "In a particular manner," he wrote, "I wish you to gain satisfactory information of a body confidently reported to have gone up to a ford seven or eight miles above this. You will send an intelligent, sensible officer immediately with a party to find out the truth." [11] Bland reported that he had seen a body of the enemy advancing on "the valley road" towards Trimble's Ford.[12]

On top of this came a dispatch forwarded by Sullivan, from Lieutenant

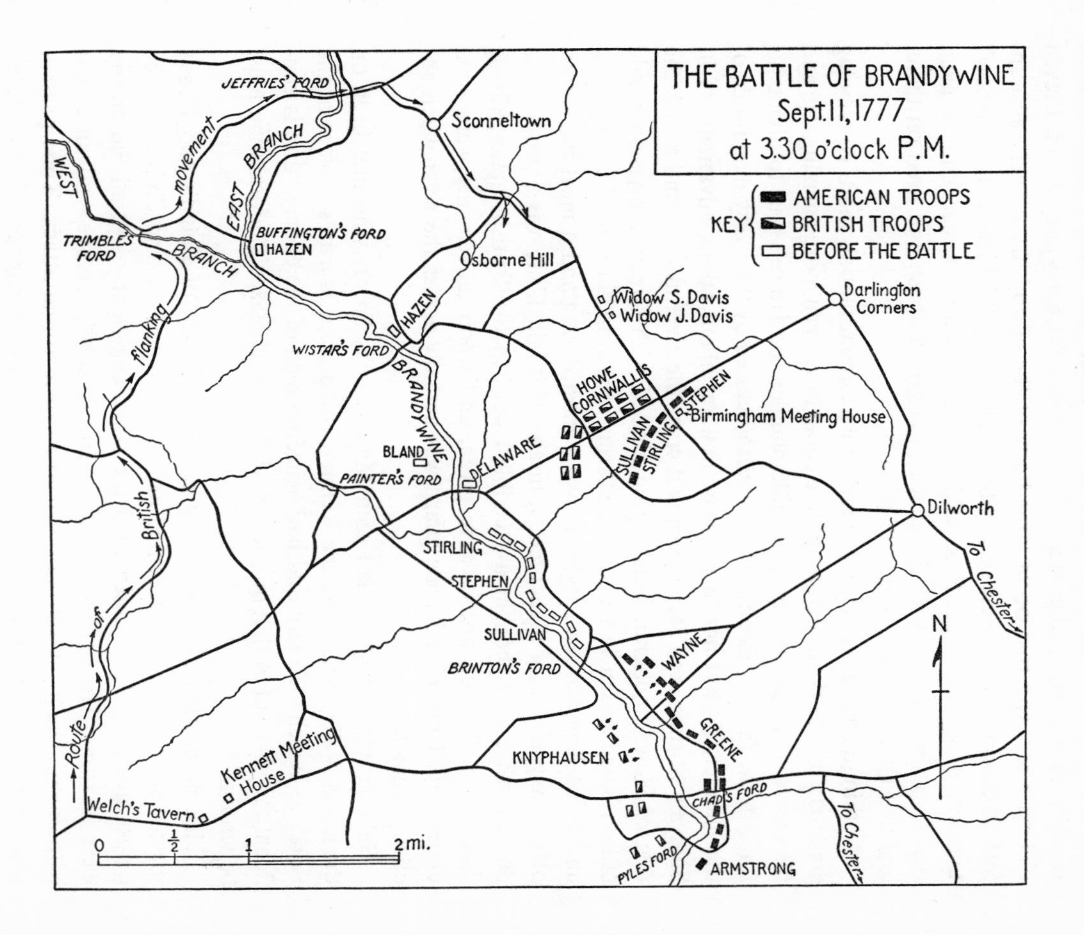
THE BATTLE OF BRANDYWINE
Sept. 11, 1777
at 3.30 o'clock P.M.
KEY
AMERICAN TROOPS
BRITISH TROOPS
BEFORE THE BATTLE
JEFFRIES' FORD
Sconneltown
WEST
movement
EAST BRANCH
TRIMBLES FORD
BRANCH
BUFFINGTON'S FORD
HAZEN
Osborne Hill
Widow S. Davis
Widow J. Davis
Darlington Corners
flanking
HAZEN
WISTAR'S FORD
BRANDYWINE
HOWE
CORNWALLIS
STEPHEN
Birmingham Meeting House
SULLIVAN
STIRLING
BLAND
DELAWARE
PAINTER'S FORD
Dilworth
British
STIRLING
STEPHEN
To Chester
SULLIVAN
N
WAYNE
BRINTON'S FORD
of
GREENE
Route
Kennett Meeting House
KNYPHAUSEN
CHAD'S FORD
To Chester
Welch's Tavern
0
1/2
1
2 mi.
PYLES FORD
ARMSTRONG

Colonel James Ross of the 8th Pennsylvania, who had apparently been scouting in the rear of the enemy. It was dated "Great Valley Road, Eleven o'clock A.M." and told of "a large body of the enemy, from every account five thousand with sixteen or eighteen field-pieces," which had "just now" marched along that road. Ross said that he was on their rear with 70 men, that Captain Simpson with 20 men had lain in ambush and fired on them, and that General Howe was with them.[13]

Nothing could have been clearer, more circumstantial, more convincing than that, and to Washington nothing could have been more amazing. He and his generals thought it was "a terrible blunder" on Howe's part to divide his force in the face of his enemy; they were puzzled by "the very magnitude of the blunder," [14] but not in the least hesitant about taking advantage of it. Sullivan, Stirling, and Stephen should cross the river at once and attack the rear of Howe's column. Washington himself with Greene's division would fall on Knyphausen in front, while Armstrong's militia should cross below and strike Knyphausen's right. It was a most daring and a most dangerous plan, "magnificent, if it succeeded, insane, if it failed." It was a proposal to do just what they thought a "terrible error" in the British tactics, divide their force. But the orders were given, and troop movements were soon under way. Greene's advance guard was actually across the river when another dispatch arrived.[15]

Sullivan wrote that he had seen Major James Spear, who had been on the Great Valley Road and the Kennett Road from Martin's Tavern at the Forks to Welch's Tavern and had heard nothing of the enemy "and is confident they are not in that quarter; so that Colonel Hazen's information must be wrong." [16]

That note, incredible as it may seem in the face of Bland's and Ross's specific statements, was accepted as reliable. There *was* no division of the British army, no force threatened the American right wing; all the enemy were in front. The orders to cross were canceled; Greene's advance was withdrawn. The army settled down to await a frontal attack. Time passed. Knyphausen made no move. Only his intermittent cannonading declared him an enemy. And still no one remembered Long Island. Two o'clock came; no change. Then there was a sudden commotion.

A sweating horseman, a hatless, coatless, barelegged farmer, dashed into Sullivan's lines. He must see the General—Washington—at once. Sullivan couldn't allow that; the General mustn't be disturbed by such an uncouth person. But the man *must* see him; he was Thomas Cheyney, a good patriot, one of the few about there, and he had important news. What was it? He told it. He had been watching the movement of the armies, and had got up that morning early to do a bit of scouting, dressed in a hurry without bothering to put on his stockings. He rode to the top of a hill, and there the British were, not a hundred yards away. He turned his horse and fled. They followed, fired on him, but his horse was fast. He got away, and here he was. They were across the creek and coming down this way. Wasn't that important? It seemed so. He was taken to the commander in chief.

Cheyney told his tale again. Washington was incredulous. He had had that Spear report to the contrary. Probably he thought the man was a Tory, trying to mislead him; they were all Tories, these Chester Countians. The staff smiled and shook their heads. Cheyney turned on them. "I'd have you know I have this day's work as much at heart as e'er a blood of ye!" Then to Washington: "If Anthony Wayne or Perse Frazer was here, they'd know whether I'm to be believed." He dropped on one knee, drew in the dust with his finger a map, the roads, the fords, marked the place where he had seen the enemy. Still Washington disbelieved. "You're mistaken, General," cried the exasperated man. "My life for it you're mistaken. By hell! it's so. Put me under guard till you can find out it's so!" [17]

What to do? It might be so. Those conflicting reports? Then came the thunderclap that cleared the air, banished all doubt, a courier with a dispatch enclosing another:

Dear General;

Col° Bland has this moment Sent me word, that the enemy are in the Rear of my Right about two miles Coming Down, there is, he says about two Brigades of them. 2 of Clock PM he also says he Saw a Dust Rise back in the Country for above an hour.

I am &c JOHN SULLIVAN

The enclosure read:

A quarter past One o'clock.

Sir:

I have discovered a party of the enemy on the heights, just on the right of the two Widow Davis's who live close together on the road called the Fork Road, about half a mile to the right of the [Birmingham] Meeting House. There is a higher hill in front.

THEODORICK BLAND [18]

There at last was the indubitable truth. At four o'clock that morning, a full hour before Knyphausen had started, Howe and Cornwallis had left Kennett Square with the Hessian jägers, the 1st and 2nd battalions of grenadiers, the Guards, two squadrons of light dragoons, one of dismounted dragoons, and the 3rd and 4th brigades of infantry. They had kept to the main road until within a mile and a half of Welch's Tavern. There they had taken a left fork and so had come into the Great Valley Road, which led to Trimble's Ford on the west branch, crossed the two-mile interval to Jefferis's Ford on the east branch, crossed that, turned south past Sconneltown, and come out into the open at Osborne's Hill, a mile and a half east of the Brandywine, in the rear of the American line and within two miles of their extreme outposts on the right.[19]

Hazen picked up his two battalions at Buffington's Ford—the outpost nearest the enemy crossing at Jefferis's Ford—and at Wistar's, and the Delaware Regiment at Painter's Ford, and started south towards the main army.

The van of the British column had halted at Sconneltown, just beyond Jefferis's Ford, to let the rear catch up and then had gone on to Osborne's Hill. It was now half after two. The soldiers had been afoot since four in the morning, marching fifteen miles on a swelteringly hot day. Food and rest were needed; they took both sprawling on the grass, and the countryside turned out to see them.

Joseph Townsend, a Quaker youth of twenty who saw them first when they came out of the woods, wrote afterward: "In a few minutes the fields were literally covered with them. . . . Their arms and bayonets being raised shone as bright as silver, there being a clear sky and the day exceedingly warm." He saw Cornwallis: "He was on horseback, appeared tall and sat very erect. His rich scarlet clothing loaded with gold lace, epaulets &c., occasioned him to make a brilliant and martial appearance." Most of the officers were "rather short, portly men, well dressed and of genteel appearance, and did not look as if they had ever been exposed to any hardship, their skins being as white and delicate as is customary for females who were brought up in large cities and towns." The Hessians interested him: "Many of them wore their beards on their upper lips, which was a novelty in that part of the country." General Howe was "mounted on a large English horse, much reduced in flesh. . . . The general was a large, portly man, of coarse features. He appeared to have lost his teeth, as his mouth had fallen in." [20]

Meanwhile, the Americans had been astir. Washington ordered the whole right wing—Sullivan's, Stephen's, and Stirling's divisions, all under Sullivan—to shift from their position along the river and oppose the approaching enemy. Wayne's brigade of Pennsylvanians, Maxwell's light infantry, and Proctor's artillery were to continue to hold the Chad's Ford position against Knyphausen. Greene's division of two brigades—Weedon's and Muhlenberg's Virginians—was to remain in reserve to help Sullivan or Wayne as needed. Washington remained with Greene.[21]

There was some delay in starting the march of one of Sullivan's own two brigades. Stirling's and Stephen's divisions and even one brigade of Sullivan's, under General Prudhomme de Borré, got away before Sullivan did with the other. When he moved with that other he met Hazen with the "Canadians" and the Delawares on the march down to the main army. Hazen told him that "the Enemy were Close upon his Heels." While these two were talking together, the soldiers still moving on, "the Enemy headed us [Sullivan's men] in the Road about forty Rods from our Advance Guard." This was probably one of two small detachments thrown out to the right of Cornwallis's column to cross at Wistar's Ford or Painter's. To avoid them, Sullivan swung his column to the right and got away without a fight. Soon after that he discovered Stirling's and Stephen's divisions already "Drawn up on an Eminence, both in the Rear & to the Right of the place" where his men were and facing the British force on the opposite hill to the north of them, that is to say on Osborne's Hill. Sullivan had simply overshot his mark by coming up too near the enemy and undershot it by not being near enough to his colleagues. He was separated from them by an undefended space of half a mile.[22]

Sullivan now ordered Hazen's regiment and the Delawares to pass a slight depression between two hills, "File off to the Right & face to Cover the Artillery," thus separating them from his own brigade. With the rest of his troops he fell back and formed them "on an advantageous Height, in a Line with the other divisions," but with that half-mile still open between him and the others. He then rode off to consult with Stirling and Stephen. They told him that the enemy, now advancing down the slope of Osborne's Hill, were aiming to outflank the American position on the right, wherefore his troops should be brought up to join theirs, and "that the whole Should incline further to the Right," to prevent being outflanked. Sullivan went back to his men to bring them up.

The American line was formed on the northern slope of a round hill a hundred rods southeast of Birmingham Meetinghouse and facing Osborne's, with an interval of a mile and a half between their summits. Northeasterly through this valley ran the Street Road from Painter's Ford. The line curved around the face of the hill. De Borré's brigade held the right; Stephen's division was next; and then came Stirling's, these two composing the center. Sullivan was to hold the left. The artillery, four pieces, was "judiciously placed," and several outposts were thrown out in front of the line. "This position," says Captain John Montresor, chief engineer of the British forces in America, "was remarkably strong, having a large body advanced, small bodies still further advanced and their rear covered by a wood wherein their main body was posted, with a natural glacis for ¾ of a mile." The flanks also rested on woods.[23] Cornwallis, watching from the top of Osborne's Hill the arrangement of the Americans, remarked, "The damn rebels form well." [24]

By about half-past three the British army had formed in three divisions on Osborne's Hill. On the right were the Guards; the British grenadiers composed the center; the left was made up of the light infantry and the Hessian and Anspach jägers. The support, from right to left, was the Hessian grenadiers and the 4th Brigade. The 3rd Brigade, under Major General Charles Grey, was held in reserve.[25] A little after four o'clock the advance began in style. The uniforms were gay in their various colors, the muskets and bayonets "shining like silver," the bands playing "The British Grenadiers." So the exactly formed columns marched down the slope of Osborne's Hill and across the vale. There was no irregularity, no hurry. They came on with the arrogant assurance that marked the disciplined troops of that period of formal, dress-parade warfare.

The advance guard almost reached the Street Road. No shot had yet been fired. Then suddenly the jägers, on the left of their line, met a blaze of musketry from an American outpost in an orchard beside the road. They "stepped up" the roadside bank to the orchard fence, rested their muskets on it, and fired a volley. The artillery on both sides opened up, and the battle was on.[26]

The British light infantry and the Hessian and Anspach jägers were the first up the hill. They fell upon the American right, De Borré's brigade of three Maryland regiments, and met little resistance. The brigade broke and fled into the woods behind, exposing Stephen's right flank. The British Guards and grenadiers fired no shot, but advanced up the hill, their bayonets their only weapons.[27] Sullivan's men were on the way to close the gap that separated them from Stirling's left. In a column that straggled irregularly because of excitement and lack of training, they marched right across the front of the oncoming Guards and grenadiers, both British and Hessian. They had hardly formed a ragged line facing the enemy when the bayonets were upon them. Few of the American troops in that war could ever stand against the cold steel of the bayonet. These were unready for battle; Sullivan, their leader, had left them, gone to the center to direct the artillery. They fell back in confusion. Sullivan sent his aides to rally them and re-form them in the rear. He went back himself, "but all in vain," he says; "no Sooner did I form one party than that which I had before formed would Run off." He went back to the artillery, "left them to be Rallied if possible by their own officers and my aid De Camp." It was not possible. The entire left of the American line was swept away. Shorn of its wings, the center of Stirling's and Stephen's divisions with Hazen's "Canadians" and the Delawares now held the field alone.[28]

Miles in the rear with Greene and the reserve, Washington had been awaiting news of the grand attack, either at the Ford or at Birmingham. It came at half past four, in "a sudden burst of cannon from the northwestward," so loud that it was heard in Philadelphia. The grand attack was on up there at Birmingham. It was a signal for Knyphausen; he got ready to cross the Ford. The battle was to be fought on two fronts.

There must have been some hesitation in Washington's mind about the use of the reserve, whether at the Ford or at Birmingham, for about five o'clock his aide, Lieutenant Colonel Robert H. Harrison, was writing to the Congress about the attack at the north: "The Action has been very violent ever since. . . . It still continues." Knyphausen was preparing his attack. "A very severe cannonade has begun here too and I suppose we shall have a very hot evening." [29]

But at last the decision was made. The Ford must be left to Wayne, Maxwell, and Proctor. Greene with the reserve must go north to back up the troops on the hill and hold that road to Philadelphia. Washington himself wanted to be at that scene of action, but he did not know the way to it. Among the country people standing about was an old man, Joseph Brown. Washington asked him to lead the way by the shortest road. Brown demurred; Washington insisted. One of his aides dismounted, threatened the old man with his sword, hoisted him into the saddle. Across country they went; three miles as the crow flies, Washington continually crying, "Push along, old man! Push along!" His staff trailed behind. They came out on the road leading to Philadelphia, half a mile west of Dilworth.[30] Greene was coming along, with Weedon's brigade in advance, Muhlenberg's following. They arrived with speed. Weedon covered nearly four miles in less than 45 minutes.[31]

On the hill there had been hot fighting. Sullivan, Stirling, Stephen, and Thomas Conway the French-Irishman, one of Stirling's aides, encouraged the 3,000 Americans still there to repel the repeated attacks of twice their number of the best soldiers of Britain and Germany. They were seconded by Lafayette, who, ardent for battle, had galloped to the fight ahead of Washington and Greene. On the left Hazen's men and the Delawares with Dayton and Ogden of Stirling's division stood firm, although that flank had been exposed by the flight of Sullivan's brigade.

Cornwallis was edging his troops towards the Americans' extreme right and towards Dilworth, which was the key of the situation because it was on the Philadelphia road. The Americans had to shift and shift again in order to avoid being outflanked.[32]

For an hour and forty minutes, under fire of Cornwallis's artillery, four 12-pounders, the Americans on the hill disputed the way of the enemy. For fifty minutes of that time they fought "almost Muzzle to Muzzle, in such a manner that General Conway, who has Seen much Service, says he never Saw So Close & Severe a fire." A captain of the Delawares describes it: "Cannon balls flew thick and many and small arms roared like the rolling of a drum." Five times the Americans were driven back, and five times they surged forward to their old position. But the odds against them were too great. Stephen's division on the right, upon which the fire had been especially heavy, retreated. Stirling and the rest could no longer resist. The order to withdraw was given.

They were pursued by the British and Hessians, except the British Guards and the British and Hessian Grenadiers, who when they followed Sullivan's retreating brigade had "got entangled in a very thick woods" and "were no further engaged" until near the end of the battle.[33]

The American retreat was developing into a stampede when the fugitives met the head of Greene's column. He opened his ranks, let them through to rally and re-form in his rear, closed again, and stood against the pursuers, turning his artillery upon them. But the pressure was too great. Retreating slowly and in good order, keeping up their fire, Greene's troops at last made another stand in the road from Dilworth about a mile from the Meetinghouse, in a place called Sandy Hollow, "a narrow defile flanked on both sides by woods and commanding the road." [34] Weedon's men were posted in the defile, Muhlenberg's on the side of the road.

The enemy came on and there was hot fighting. The musket fire on the Americans was heavy, and there were repeated bayonet charges. The fighting was so close that some of the Anspach jägers recognized Muhlenberg, who had served in the ranks in Germany in his youth, and greeted him with his old nickname, "Hier kommt Teufel Piet!" (Here comes Devil Pete!) Weedon's brigade, especially the 10th Virginia under Colonel Stephens and Colonel Walter Stewart's Pennsylvania state regiment, which had never before been in action, bore the brunt of the attack. For forty-five minutes, until the sun went down, they held the pass.[35]

At last, again overborne, Weedon's force retired, but in good order. They retreated to the rear of Muhlenberg's brigade, and Greene drew off his whole division. The tired British and Hessians made no attempt to follow.[36]

Meanwhile, there had been desperate fighting at the Ford. The sound of Cornwallis's gunfire was the signal to Knyphausen that his function of "amusing" the Americans, while the flanking march was made, was now fully performed. He first opened fire with all his guns, six 12-pounders, four howitzers, and the light artillery, bombarding the positions held by Wayne, Maxwell's light infantry, and Proctor's batteries, while he formed his troops. After severely blasting the American defenses he launched his attack. A battalion of the 71st Highlanders led the van; the Riflemen and Queen's Rangers with the British 4th Regiment and Knyphausen in person followed. Then came the rest, Stirn's Hessians last. In the face of the American artillery and musketry they advanced to the lower of the two fords, waded in, and gained the opposite bank. Forming again, they attacked "furiously." The American left gave back and lost the battery near the river, three field-pieces and a howitzer.

The British Guards and the grenadiers of Cornwallis's column, who had got lost in the forest while pursuing Sullivan's brigade, now "came blundering through the woods—accidentally, but most opportunely—upon the uncovered flank of the American centre," and the whole American line fell back.

The British followed, "gained one height after another as the enemy withdrew." There was a check, says Baurmeister, when the Americans or some of them made a stand "behind some houses and ditches" and for a time "withstood one more rather severe attack. Finally we saw the entire enemy line and four guns, which fired frequently, drawn up on another height in front of a dense forest, their right wing resting on the Chester road." [37] "Darkness coming on before Lieutenant General Knyphausen's corps could reach the heights, there was no further action." [38]

The battle was over except for one last flare-up. Two battalions of British grenadiers were ordered to occupy a cluster of houses beyond Dilworth. "They marched carelessly, the officers with sheathed swords. At fifty paces from the first houses, they were surprised by a deadly fire from Maxwell's corps, which lay in ambush to cover the American retreat. The British officers sent for help, but were nearly routed before General Agnew could bring relief. The Americans then withdrew, and darkness ended the contest." [39]

It had been a fierce and many-sided fight, but the losses on both sides were less than might have been supposed. Howe reported 90 killed, 480 wounded, and 6 missing. The American casualties were never definitely ascertained. Howe estimated them at 300 killed, 600 wounded, and "near 400" made prisoners.[40] But his figures are properly subject to some discount, because of his customary exaggeration of enemy losses and because the numbers of wounded and captured to a considerable extent duplicated each other. The Americans had to leave many of their wounded on the field, so that they were taken by the enemy; but not many unwounded men were taken prisoner. Among the American wounded was Lafayette, who received a bullet in his leg, but was able to escape capture. One howitzer and ten fieldpieces were lost by the Americans, among them two brass guns captured at Trenton.[41]

The whole American army was in retreat towards Chester. Except for a few regiments and companies that withdrew in good order, its units were completely disorganized. There was no coherence of divisions, of brigades, of regiments, or even of companies. Thousands of beaten men, already dispersed before the final retreat began and now uncontrolled by any sort of military discipline, thronged the road in utter confusion. Darkness added to their bewilderment. All any man knew was that he must hurry forward with the crowd before him and the crowd behind. Twelve miles of this chaos brought them to a bridge across Chester Creek and found at last someone in command of the situation. Lafayette, with an improvised bandage about his wounded leg, had set a guard there to stop the passage of the mob. Washington and Greene (with his division unbroken) soon arrived and aided in restoring order. They all encamped "behind Chester."

And yet, though they had been as badly beaten as any army could be without being entirely destroyed, there had been no panic; there was no suggestion of despair. The American Captain Anderson wrote: "I saw not a despairing look, nor did I hear a despairing word. We had our solacing words already for each other—'Come, boys, we shall do better another time'—sounded throughout our little army." That this was true of the army in general was proven by their ready reorganization the next day and by the spirit in which the campaign was so soon and so courageously resumed.

CHAPTER 32

Philadelphia

Howe's army encamped on the battlefield. But first he sent the 71st Regiment, Fraser's Highlanders, to take possession of Wilmington. They also took possession of John McKinly, President and commander in chief of Delaware, and confined him on the frigate *Solebay,* lying in the river off the town.[1]

At midnight of September 11–12 Washington sent a dispatch to the Congress, informing it of the result of the battle and adding, "Notwithstanding the misfortune of the day, I am happy to find the troops in good spirits." [2] Congress was, as John Adams expressed it, "yet in Philadelphia, that mass of cowardice and Toryism." John Hancock received the dispatch at four o'clock in the morning. The delegates to the Congress were routed out of their beds to meet at six and hear the news. At ten they reassembled, called on Putnam at Peekskill to send down 1,500 Continentals at once, on Philemon Dickinson in New Jersey and on Smallwood and Gist in Maryland to send their militia, and on the Pennsylvania militia generally to join Washington. Aid from Virginia was also solicited. To the soldiers of the army, thirty hogsheads of rum were donated "in compliment . . . for their gallant behaviour," each man to receive "one gill per day, while it lasts." [3]

Washington marched from Chester in the morning of the 12th to the Falls of the Schuylkill and encamped there on the edge of Germantown. Notwithstanding his defeat at the Brandywine, his army was still between Howe and Philadelphia, and his maneuvers were directed toward holding that advantage. He guessed that the British would try to turn his right flank, cut off a retreat to the west, and force him into the pocket beween the

Schuylkill and the Delaware. To prevent that, he broke camp on the morning of the 14th and marched west to the neighborhood of the Warren Tavern and the White Horse Tavern, thus, "with a firm intent of giving the Enemy Battle," [4] interposing his army between the British and Swede's Ford across the Schuylkill, at which point he thought they would try to cross.

On the 16th Howe marched from Chad's Ford in two columns. Cornwallis led one towards the White Horse Tavern, Knyphausen the other towards the Boot Tavern.[5] Early in the morning Washington had news of their approach. Howe heard that the Americans were "advancing upon the Lancaster Road and were within five miles of Goshen Meeting House." He decided to "push forward the two Columns and attack them." [6] Thus, with one intention, the two armies approached each other.

Washington sent Count Casimir Pulaski, newly appointed "commander of the horse" ranking as a brigadier, with the cavalry and 300 infantry to retard the advance of the enemy; but the foot soldiers "shamefully fled at the first fire" and delayed the enemy not at all.[7]

The first real encounter came when Wayne and Maxwell, who had been detached forward to observe the enemy's movements on the Chester-Dilworth road, met Knyphausen's column near the Boot Tavern. Colonel von Donop, with a part of the Hessian jägers, was reconnoitering the road ahead of that column when Wayne and Maxwell suddenly came upon him. He "was almost cut off, but joined the vanguard again with all possible speed, after skilfully executing some manoeuvres to his left." [8] The Hessian jägers and grenadiers immediately formed and advanced in line against Wayne and Maxwell, who had taken a position "on high ground covered with a cornfield and orchards." The jägers delighted in displaying the results of their training and experience in irregular fighting; "ducking behind fences around the fields and woods, [they] had an opportunity to demonstrate to the enemy their superior marksmanship and their skill with the amusettes." There was a considerable exchange of fire before the Americans "retired to a dense forest," leaving behind a number of killed and wounded.[9]

Howe was ahead in the choice of ground; he seized an eminence near the White Horse. Washington started to form his troops in an inferior position, with "a valley of soft wet ground, impassable for artillery" behind his center and left, but was persuaded to withdraw to "high ground on the other side of the valley." [10] A real battle seemed to be in the making when Nature took a hand. The extreme heat of the day at the Brandywine had been dispelled on the 13th by "a hard North West wind," which continued to blow colder and colder. On the 15th it shifted to the northeast and increased in violence; the sky was heavily overcast with clouds. Now the gathering storm broke.

Major Baurmeister had never seen the like of that cloudburst. "I wish I could give you a description of the downpour," he wrote to the "Right Honourable Lord, Gracious and Mighty Colonel von Jungkenn" in Hesse-Kassel. "It came down so hard that in a few minutes we were drenched and sank in mud up to our calves." [11]

That deluge fell upon the two armies in line of battle and about to engage. It soaked their clothes, wet their muskets inside and out, and drenched their ammunition, ruining 400,000 of the Americans' cartridges—"a most terrible stroke to us," said Henry Knox. No flint would flash, no charge ignite.[12] So there the two armies stood, face to face and unable to fire a shot. The British might still have used a favorite weapon that worked wet or dry—the bayonet; but a wind of great force was driving the rain directly into their faces, and the low ground between the armies was a treacherous quagmire. There was simply no fighting to be done by either side.

"At first," Washington wrote to the Congress, "I expected that the loss [of ammunition] was by no means so considerable and intended [only] to file off with the Troops a few Miles to replace it and clean their arms"; but, finding it completely ruined with no other supply at hand, he had to march "as far as Reading Furnace" to refit.[13] So, under the heavy rain driven by the howling northeast wind, the blanketless men, "nearly a thousand of them actually barefooted," slogged along through the mud the rest of that day and much of the night eleven miles to Yellow Springs, and "there Stay'd all night on the Brow of a hill without tents." [14]

At Yellow Springs, Washington discovered the true state of his ammunition supply and realized that he must go at once to a more secure position at Reading (Warwick) Furnace to await a new supply from the magazines. So on the Americans went—it was still raining—nine miles and camped, again without tents. Then up at three in the morning and on, twelve miles more, to the Furnace. Presumably the new ammunition was supplied there, for the third day they were on the march back to Yellow Springs, twelve miles, crossed the Schuylkill at Parker's Ford, through rapid water breast-deep [15]—they were all night at it—marched seven miles towards Swede's Ford and then ten miles to Richardson's Ford, twenty-nine miles in all,[16] and certainly a great feat of endurance in their distressed physical condition. But they were again east of the Schuylkill and between Howe and Philadelphia, their camp being along Perkiomen Creek.

The movement of Howe's army from Goshen was a mere saunter, in comparison. It lay on the field the day after that aborted battle and "suffered much from the weather." On the 18th Knyphausen marched three miles to White Horse, where he joined Cornwallis in going eight miles to camp at Tredyffrin. At Valley Forge they found a store of the rebels' supplies: "3800 Barrels of Flour, Soap and Candles, 25 Barrels of Horse Shoes, several thousand tomahawks and Kettles and Intrenching Tools and 20 Hogsheads of Resin." On the 19th, when the rebels were making that grueling twenty-nine-mile march, the British found halting "very necessary for the men and particularly for our horses," though there was a small shift of Cornwallis's column to another camp at the Bull's Head and Mouth Tavern and a foraging party took 150 horses at New Town Square. On the 20th a post was established at Valley Forge.[17]

Before Washington's army crossed at Parker's Ford on the 19th Anthony Wayne's division, 1,500 men and four fieldpieces, was detached with orders to lie in the neighborhood of the Warren Tavern so as to be in a position to fall on the enemy's rear guard and baggage train. With every effort at secrecy he took post in a wood on a hill about a mile north of that tavern and two miles southwest of Paoli Tavern,[18] confident that his movement and his place of lodgment were unknown to the enemy; but there were too many Tories about, and some of them disclosed his secret to the British.[19] Major General Grey, with the 40th, 42nd, 44th, and 55th regiments of foot, the 2nd battalion of light infantry, and a handful of the 16th Dragoons, was sent to surprise him.[20]

Grey ordered his men to march with unloaded muskets, those that could not draw their loads to remove their flints, and set out at ten o'clock in the evening of the 20th. He advanced by the road leading to the White Horse, picking up every inhabitant as he went along to prevent an alarm. Near the Warren Tavern, he came upon Wayne's outsentries, who fired and ran off; but his van fell upon the pickets with the bayonet and killed most of them.

The reports of the sentries' muskets alarmed the camp. Wayne ordered his men formed for action, himself taking post with the artillery on the right. Unfortunately his men were drawn up in the light of their campfires and thus were clearly in view of the enemy. Grey ordered a charge with the bayonet. The Americans met it with musketry but were overwhelmed by the impetuosity of their opponents and swept into a confused retreat, followed by the stabbing bayonets. Wayne managed to draw off his guns and, at some distance in the rear, re-formed such part of his fleeing men as could be induced to stand. Satisfied with the execution effected, Grey called off his troops and returned to the British camp, taking with him seventy-one prisoners, of whom forty, badly wounded, were left at houses along the road. He also took eight or ten loaded four-horse wagons. The next day a British detachment returned to the deserted field and gathered up and destroyed a thousand muskets abandoned by the fleeing Americans.

General Smallwood and Colonel Gist, with a force of Maryland militia, had been ordered to reenforce Wayne's post; but they were still on the road at the time of the attack. Within a half-mile of the scene they met a part of Grey's troops returning from the fray. At the sight of the enemy the militia fled in a panic.

It is impossible to make a certain estimate of the Americans' loss. The British claimed 300 killed or wounded and 70 to 80 taken prisoner; but their figures are probably exaggerations. The British loss was one officer and one or two privates killed, and four or five wounded.[21]

Wayne's defeat relieved Howe of all fear of attack from the rear; he was now able to move as he would. On the morning of September 21 he set out from Tredyffrin in a northerly direction, marched to Valley Forge, and encamped along the Schuylkill from the Forge to French Creek.[22] To Washington, who had been expecting a southward march towards one of the lower fords, this was a "perplexing manoeuvre." But this northward movement meant that they might turn his right, and it was in the direction of Reading Furnace. That spelled danger for his stores. He believed they had both objects in view.[23] "To frustrate those intentions," he decided to move north, too.

He first ordered Sullivan's division to "a Line between us and the Schuylkill, leaving a small Pickett at each Fording Place as a party of Observation." Then, "two hours before day" on the 22nd, he got his men afoot and marched them ten miles up the Reading road on his side of the Schuylkill. After rest and refreshment they went five miles farther and encamped near Pott's Grove [24] (now Pottstown). They were now well ahead of Howe towards Reading Furnace and well past danger of being outflanked on the right; also they were just where Howe wanted them to be.

He had intended neither the supposed flanking movement, nor yet the capture of the stores at the Furnace. What he did intend was disclosed by what he immediately did. He countermarched swiftly southward in the night to Fatland Ford and Gordon's Ford, blasted away a slimly held American militia post at Fatland with "a few cannon-shot," and sent the Guards, a battalion of light infantry and six guns, with twenty-five dragoons, across the river to hold the opposite end of the ford. Von Donop, with sixty jägers, twenty horse, and a hundred grenadiers cleared the way at Gordon's without difficulty and crossed there. That night "at the rising of the moon" the whole British army began crossing at Fatland. By eight the next morning all except Grant's brigade of British infantry, covering the baggage, artillery, and provision train, were on the east side of the river. The others soon followed, and the road to Philadelphia was clear before them.[25] Thus again Howe, with the greatest of ease, had outwitted the American commander in chief.

Washington got the news, doubtless from some of the expelled militia, while the enemy was still in the act of crossing. Here was an opportunity for an attack while they were in such a disabling condition. But the alertness of the Americans to the danger of being outflanked, and the effort they had made to prevent it, was now their undoing. They were nearly twenty miles from Fatland. With "Troops harrassed as ours had been with constant marching since the Battle of Brandywine" it was "in vain to think" of covering that distance in time to seize the opportunity. As strong a reason "against being able to make a forced March is the want of Shoes," so Washington wrote to the Congress that day. A council of war agreed with him that the best course was to stay where they were until rested and reenforced.[26]

Unopposed and unmolested, the British army continued its march "till three o'clock in the afternoon when it arrived at Norriton" and there encamped, but seventeen miles from Philadelphia, just half the distance of the American army from it.[27]

Washington lay at Pott's Grove for four days, resting his men and awaiting reenforcements. He had called on Putnam in the north for 2,500 Continentals, including McDougall's brigade; on Smallwood and Gist to bring their Maryland militia; on Wayne for his division; on Gates at Saratoga to send back Morgan's riflemen; on Philemon Dickinson for his New Jersey militia.[28] The men he already had were in a sad condition. They had marched 140 miles in the last eleven days. "While in almost continual motion, wading deep rivers and encountering every vicissitude of the season, they were without tents, nearly without shoes or winter clothes and often without food." [29] In the heat of the day and the heat of the battle at the Brandywine thousands of them had shed their blanket rolls and left them on the field. Washington had written to the Congress on the 15th begging for blankets. The Congress had "disguised its impotence" by again making him a "dictator" for a period of sixty days, with special authority "to take wherever he may be, all such provisions and articles as may be necessary for the comfortable subsistence of the army under his command, paying or giving certificates for the same." [30]

Washington accepted the job. He sent Alexander Hamilton to Philadelphia to "procure from the inhabitants, contributions of blankets, and Clothing and materials . . . with as much delicacy and discretion as the nature of the business demands." [31] But "the canny Quakers and the sly Tories 'hid their goods the moment the thing took wind' and the Whigs had already 'parted with all they could spare.' " [32] Washington tried the country districts, ordered Colonel Clement Biddle "to impress all the Blankets, Shoes, Stockings and other Articles of Cloathing . . . that can be spared by the Inhabitants of Bucks, Philadelphia and Northampton," [33] to be paid for with cash or promises, and gave similar orders for Lancaster, with small results from any place.

On the 26th the Americans marched from Pott's Grove to encamp at Pennybacker's Mill (now Schwenksville) on the Perkiomen; and on the same day Cornwallis, with two British and two Hessian grenadier battalions, two squadrons of the 16th Dragoons, and ten guns in his train, took possession of Philadelphia, "amidst the acclamation of some thousands of the inhabitants, mostly women and children," [34] while the major part of the army encamped at Germantown. The Congress had fled to Lancaster eight days before.

CHAPTER 33

Germantown

Reenforcements came to Washington—McDougall, with 900 Continentals from Peekskill, Smallwood with 1,000 Maryland militia, Forman with 600 militiamen from New Jersey, Maxwell's corps of 650 light infantry, and Wayne's division. It is hard to say how large the army then was. Washington informed the Congress on September 28 that he had 8,000 Continentals and 3,000 militia at Pennybacker's Mill,[1] yet Henry Knox declared that the army was "more numerous after the battle of Brandywine than before." [2] There was some thought of an attack on the British camp at Germantown at this time, but a council of war, voting ten to five against that, decided that it would be well to move closer, "within about 12 Miles of the Enemy," and await events.[3] On the 29th the army marched five miles to the Skippack Road, and on October 2, three miles down that road to encamp sixteen miles from Germantown.[4]

There the question of an attack was again considered. Three thousand of Howe's men had been sent down to escort supplies from Elkton, which, because of the obstructions and the forts in the Delaware River, he could not bring up by water. Cornwallis had two British and two Hessian grenadier battalions with him in Philadelphia, and he had just sent one of the British battalions and two regiments of foot across to New Jersey to capture the fort at Billingsport. Probably not more than 9,000 men were left with Howe at Germantown. A council of war decided that conditions were favorable.[5]

Germantown was a village consisting of a string of houses, each in its enclosure of rail fence, stretching for two miles along the Skippack Road, which ran northwest from Philadelphia to Reading. At its center this main street was crossed at a right angle by a road called School House Lane west of the street, Mill Street on the east. At this crossing stood the market house. The village was approachable directly from the northwest by this Skippack (Reading) Road running over Chestnut Hill and Mount Airy and so to its center. There was another avenue of approach from the north by the Limekiln Road, east of the Skippack, which swung into the east end of Mill Street. East of that road the Old York Road came down from the northeast to a crossroad running past Luken's Mill and so into Mill Street. Far to the west, on the other side of the gorge of Wissahickon Creek, the Manatawny or Ridge Road met the west end of School House Lane where the creek empties into the Schuylkill.

The British camp was a little south of the Lane, extending east and west parallel to it and across the main street from the Schuylkill on the left (west) to a point beyond the Old York Road on the right. It had no definite center. Generals Grant and Matthew lay on the right of the main street, with the Guards, six British battalions, and two squadrons of dragoons. Generals Knyphausen, Stirn, Grey, and Agnew lay on the left, with seven British and three Hessian battalions. The mounted and dismounted jägers were on the far left, beside the Schuylkill and below the mouth of the Wissahickon. On the far right and somewhat in advance were the 1st Battalion of British light infantry and the Queen's Rangers. At Mount Airy, on the Skippack Road and about two miles north of the Lane, was an outpost held by Colonel Musgrave's 40th Regiment and the 2nd Light Infantry.[6] Howe's headquarters was in the Logan House at a short distance in the rear of the camp.

The plan of attack called for a division of the American army into four columns, each one operating on one of the four approaching roads above mentioned. Sullivan was to command the first column, composed of his division and Wayne's, flanked by Conway's brigade. Stirling, with Nash's and Maxwell's men, was to follow this column as a reserve. It was to enter the town by the Skippack Road and strike the British left.

Greene was to command the second column, his own and Stephen's divisions, flanked by McDougall's brigade. He was to approach by the Limekiln Road, take care of the light infantry and Rangers advanced on the extreme British right, enter the town by the Mill Street, and attack Grant and Matthews. As this part of the British force was esteemed the strongest, Greene had the strongest column, about two-thirds of the American army.

The third column, Maryland and New Jersey militia under Smallwood and Forman, was to march by the Old York Road, a mile or more east of Greene's route, and fall on the rear of the British right.

Far to the other side, farther still from the main battle, coming down the Manatawny or Ridge Road, Armstrong and his Pennsylvania militia were to cross the mouth of the Wissahickon at Vandeering's Mill and strike the rear of the British left.

All four columns were to arrive "within two miles of the enemy's pickets on their respective routs by two oClock and there halt till four in the morning." They were to make simultaneous attacks "precisely at five oClock with charged bayonets without firing." [7] In that order for a bayonet charge no consideration was given to the fact that the terrain was crossed by many stout rail fences which would repeatedly interrupt the proposed charge and make it practically impossible.

It will be seen that that was a plan for a great pincers movement, in which, while the British main force was to be smashed by Greene and Sullivan, Armstrong and Smallwood were to close in on its right and left wings and crumple the whole line in upon itself. It was to be somewhat like the attack on Trenton, including the element of surprise, but on a grander scale. As the attack was to be made before dawn, each soldier was to have a piece of white paper fixed in his hat to identify him to his comrades.

It was "one of the most carefully elaborated designs" that Washington ever evolved,[8] and it had classical authority. Hannibal had so planned and won the battle of Cannae, nearly two thousand years before. Scipio Africanus had, in like manner, gained a victory at Ilipa in Spain, annihilating 74,000 Carthaginians with 48,000 Romans. There was, however, in both those cases, a difference. Hannibal and Scipio had put their weakest forces in the center, their strongest in the crushing pincer jaws. Washington reversed this arrangement; his two jaws were made up entirely of militia, whom he had so often found to be unreliable.

There were, too, faults inherent in the character of the troops involved and in the terrain, the like of which the Carthaginians and Romans had not confronted. Green troops—even the Continentals were largely new recruits—led by relatively amateur officers, were to march in perfect concert sixteen miles in four columns over roads separated by six or seven miles of rough, broken country, with no means of communication among their several bodies, and arrive at the scene of action at the same moment of time, ready to fall with vigor and determination upon a not much smaller, compact army of professional soldiers led by competent officers. The failure of any one of the four elements of the attack meant the failure of the whole scheme. It was typically the kind of plan easily worked out at headquarters and looking perfect on paper, yet practically impossible of execution in the field. Yet it very nearly did succeed, though not as planned.

The march from Metuchen Hill on the Skippack Road began at seven in the evening of October 3, the several columns taking their respective roads. According to the plan, Sullivan's column, with Conway in advance, followed by Sullivan, Wayne, Stirling, Maxwell, and Nash, in that order, Washington marching with it, was to reach the British outpost at Mount Airy before dawn. But it was a long march on rough roads and a hard march for men so ill equipped, especially so ill shod, and so worn down by their incessant movements to and fro for months past. The column had to stop twice to rest and to bring up its rear. The sun was coming up when it reached Chestnut Hill.

At Mount Airy, Conway's advance brigade came upon the pickets of the first British outpost. Captain Allen McLane of Delaware, with his company of light horse, charged upon this picket, killed two men and, at the loss of one of his own, drove it back, but not before it had fired two fieldpieces as a signal to its support and an alarm for the whole British army.

To the rescue of the retreating pickets came the 2nd Light Infantry, and the real fighting began. They attacked Conway so viciously that he had to throw forward his entire brigade to meet them. The rest of the outpost, Colonel Musgrave and his 40th Regiment, came up. Conway was stopped in his tracks. Sullivan deployed his men in line of battle along a lane to the west of the main road. Musgrave, a courageous man and a fine officer, refused to give way. He led his men against Sullivan's too narrow front. Sullivan called up Wayne's division from the rear to his left and part of Conway's brigade to his right. Then with the bayonet he drove against Musgrave's line. Wayne's division, smarting under the recollection of the Paoli "massacre," fought bitterly. The British fell back, charged, and charged again. The Americans answered in kind and "took Ample Vengeance for that Night's work," striking down "many of the poor wretches who were Crying for Mercy, in spite of their officers' exertions to restrain them." At last a British bugle sounded a retreat.

But the British fell back doggedly, making a stand at every fence, wall, and ditch, firing and falling back again. Sullivan's troops followed, tearing down fences as they came to keep their line. For a full mile they drove Musgrave's regiment and the light infantry before them.

Howe had hurried to the front. He cried shame on the retreating men "Form! Form! I never saw you retreat before! It's only a scouting party.

To the delight of the men he chid, a burst of grape from the American guns rattled in the leaves of a chestnut tree under which he sat on his horse, and showed it was no mere scouting party.

It had been misty at sunrise. The mist thickened into fog; the fog grew more dense, so dense that Musgrave was able to slip aside and throw six weak companies of his regiment into a great, square stone house on the east of the main road, the house of Chief Justice Benjamin Chew. He closed the thick shutters, barricaded the doors, and posted his 120 men at the windows of the second story, whence they delivered a continuous and deadly fire upon Sullivan's and Wayne's men passing on either side of the house.

Now, what to do? The reserve was held up, except Nash's North Carolinians, who pushed on after Sullivan and fought most bravely throughout the battle. Washington and his generals consulted. Some of them were for leaving a regiment to immobilize the garrison in the house and going on. But Henry Knox, deeply imbued with the lessons he had learned while studying the military classics in his bookshop, said "No!" While penetrating an enemy's country, you must not leave an occupied castle in your rear. Washington, always respectful of Knox's larger store of military science, as he was of Greene's military genius, agreed. The "castle" must be summoned in due form. An officer, sent with a flag to demand surrender, was fired upon and killed. So much for classical warfare!

Knox turned his artillery upon the stronghold. His six-pounders blew in the front door and smashed windows, but the balls rebounded from the thick, stone walls; and a barricade of furniture in the hallway, backed by bayonets, denied entry. Burn it, then. The Americans tried, but a would-be incendiary was shot down. In spite of that, two spirited young fellows, Colonel John Laurens of South Carolina and the Chevalier de Mauduit du Plessis from France, volunteered to try again. Laurens got straw from the stables. Mauduit forced the shutters of a window, mounted the sill. A single British officer, pistol in hand, demanded to know what the Frenchman was doing there. "I'm only taking a walk." "Surrender, sir!" Before Mauduit could answer, a British soldier came into the room, took a shot at him, but only hit the British officer. He escaped unharmed. Laurens got a bullet in his shoulder. The artillery resumed its futile bombardment, in which Maxwell's musketry joined uselessly.

But where was Greene, with two-thirds of the American army, all this time? He had four miles longer to march and had also been led astray by his guide, so that his column was an hour late when it drew near. Without orders from Greene, Stephen on hearing the gunfire swung his division off

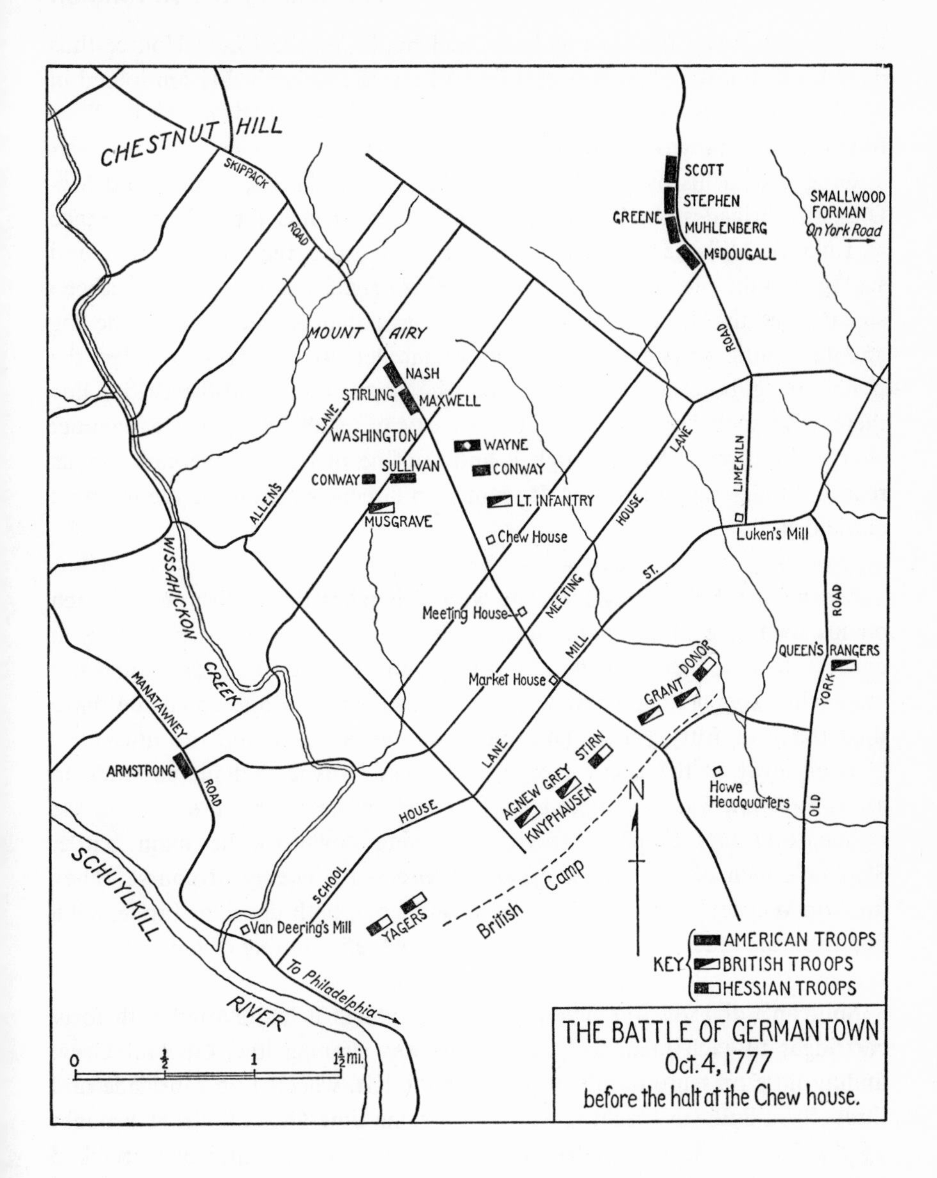

THE BATTLE OF GERMANTOWN
Oct. 4, 1777
before the halt at the Chew house.

to the right away from the column and made for the Chew House, thus departing from the plan. Woodford's artillery of Stephen's division joined in the bombardment with no more success than Knox had achieved. They fought that impregnable "castle" for a full hour.

Greene with his own division, including Muhlenberg's, Scott's, and McDougall's brigades but lacking Stephen's, kept on, met the British advance at Luken's Mill, had a hard time there but drove the enemy back, and swung into the planned attack on the British right. But that wing had been so extended that he was in danger of being outflanked. Shielded by the fog and the battle smoke, Greene countermarched to the right, avoided the British wing, bore down on the market house, and attacked the British line there with such impetuosity that it gave way. Muhlenberg led a bayonet charge that drove clear through it and the line of tents in the camp in its rear and took many prisoners. It seemed to Greene's men to be the moment of victory.

Meanwhile, Sullivan and Wayne were driving at the British center, each on his own side of the main street. They were supposed to be acting in concert, but the fog, thickened by smoke, was so dense that they could not see each other; neither knew where the other was; no one could see more than thirty or forty yards. The uproar of the artillery and the musketry, blasting away at the Chew House, convinced Wayne that his comrade in arms, Sullivan, was in trouble back there. He wheeled about, started to the rescue, and met Stephen's division coming down to the main battle. Stephen's men dimly saw an opposing force—the enemy of course. They fired on Wayne; Wayne fired on them. Suddenly, both divisions broke, each fled from the other, panic-stricken. That was the beginning of the end.

Sullivan's division was fighting on, but, though it had started with forty cartridges to each man, its ammunition was running low. General Grey, finding little pressure on his position on the left, wheeled up a brigade and threw it on Sullivan's right flank. At the same time General Grant brought up the 5th and 45th regiments from the British right center and attacked Sullivan's left, which was without support. Thus engaged on their front and on both flanks and already alarmed by the sound of fighting at the Chew House in their rear, Sullivan's troops fell into a panic on the arrival of a light horseman crying that they were surrounded. A part of them broke, and then the rest. Their officers tried in vain to rally them. "With as much precipitation as they had before advanced," they turned and ran.[9]

Greene had no support, right or left. The British and Hessians who had been fighting Sullivan let his men run without pursuit and swung to the center against Greene. He was caught on both sides. Muhlenberg was far off, more than a thousand yards in the rear of the enemy, far behind their camp. But he turned his bayonets back against the encircling British line, charged through it and joined Greene with all of his regiments but one.

Colonel Matthews, with the 9th Virginia, had been conspicuously daring and successful. He had led Greene's advance, crushed the resistance at Luken's Mill as the division swung in from the Limekiln Road, and fought all the way to the market house, driving the enemy before him and taking a hundred prisoners. He tried to draw them off by Luken's Mill, but a breastwork there had been manned again. The British right wing enveloped him. He lost his captives, and he himself, with his 400 men, was taken. That was the regiment missing from Muhlenberg's brigade.

Now Greene, with Muhlenberg, Scott, and McDougall, faced the divisions of Grey, Grant, and Agnew drawn together to oppose him. The Americans were worn out by their long march and the strain of the battle. There was little fight left in them, but they did fight as they withdrew through the village, using fences, walls, and houses in a delaying rear-guard action. Greene drew off his guns. When the wheels of one were shattered, he got it into a wagon, and it went on. Muhlenberg rode in the rear of his retiring men. His tired horse refused a fence. While his men were pulling it down, the exhausted general fell asleep in his saddle. He was awakened by the whistle of a ball past his ear and by the cries of the oncoming enemy.

Washington tried to check the retreat, to rally the fugitives, "exposing himself to the hottest fire." But his efforts could not avail. Entirely out of hand, the whole army swept on in full retreat, the men holding up their empty cartridge boxes to show him why they ran. Greene and Wayne in the rear did their best to hold back the pursuers, even bringing their artillery, all of which they kept, into play more than once. But it was no orderly withdrawal. It was a confused mass, "past the powers of description; sadness and consternation expressed in every countenance," that swarmed up the Skippack Road. Pulaski's small cavalry contingent, hovering in the rear, was attacked by British dragoons, fled, and, in their flight, rode into and through Greene's men, who thought they were British and scattered in every direction. Greene nearly had to abandon his guns, but got together enough men to save them. The celebrated Thomas Paine, who was on Greene's staff, said: "The retreat was extraordinary. Nobody hurried themselves." With good reason, it was all those tired men could do to tramp wearily onward.

Cornwallis led three fresh battalions, brought up from Philadelphia, after them for eight miles, apparently with as little haste. "The enemy kept a civil distance behind," says Paine, "sending every now and then a shot after us and receiving the same from us," then gave over the pursuit. Some of the American officers would have stopped at that distance, but Washington drove them on, not only to their last camping ground, sixteen miles from Germantown, but clear back to their former camp at Pennybacker's Mill, eight miles farther. All of them had marched that sixteen miles, some of them as much as twenty, the night before. They had fought fully two and a half hours and now they were trudging twenty-four miles more. "Here we old soldiers had marched forty miles," wrote Captain Anderson of the Delaware Regiment. "We eat nothing and drank nothing but water on the tour."

But what of Armstrong and his Pennsylvania militia, Smallwood and the militia from Maryland and New Jersey—the jaws of the pincers, the claws of the crab? Nothing had been heard or seen of them. Well, Armstrong did march his men down the Manatawny Road clear to the point where they were to cross the Wissahickon at Vandeering's Mill. There they found the Hessian jägers, the extreme left of the British line, trained their four guns on them, and drove them back from the bridge. The Hessians retired to a hill and replied with musket fire. Instead of crossing the bridge and charging on the Hessians, Armstrong continued his cannonading until nine o'clock, when the Hessians charged across the bridge and drove him from an opposite height. He and his men retreated three miles, pursued by the same Lieutenant Colonel von Wurmb who had fought Maxwell at Cooch's Bridge. This pursuit relaxing, Armstrong came on a casual detachment of the enemy, was overcome, and made a final, complete evasion. He did not even know what had happened in the main battle. When Smallwood's force, the other pincer jaw, arrived at the scene of action, it was too late for it to do anything but join in the retreat.

Yet, in spite of the failure of the pincers to operate, the battle had been nearly won by the Americans. While Sullivan and Wayne and Greene were still in the fight and Muhlenberg was piercing the enemy's line, victory was within their grasp. It is said that at that time the British were actually appointing Chester as the place of rendezvous after the expected defeat. If Stirling and Maxwell, the reserve, had not been held up at the Chew House, or if Stephen had not disobeyed orders and taken his division away from Greene, or if Wayne had not turned back thinking to help Sullivan and so collided with Stephen, or if Sullivan's ammunition had not been all shot away, or if Armstrong and Smallwood had not failed to attack the British left and right with vigor and determination—if any one or two of these miscarriages had not happened, the Americans might have won. For with all the misadventures it was a near thing, a very near thing. But they all did happen. The whole affair was a tragedy of errors.

The British losses, as officially reported, were 4 officers and 66 men killed, 30 officers and 420 men wounded. The Americans were reported by the Board of War to have lost 152 killed, 521 wounded, and upwards of 400 captured. General Nash of the Americans and General Agnew and Colonel Bird of the British were among the slain. The disastrous siege of the Chew House laid 53 Americans dead on its lawn, 4 on its very doorsteps.

A sad incident of the battle was the discovery of General Stephen, a brave and generally competent officer, helplessly intoxicated, lying in a fence corner. It resulted in his being cashiered. Lafayette, who had been appointed a major general without command, got Stephen's division. In Stephen's defense it might be urged that his condition was the result of overstimulation to combat extreme fatigue; for Conway, a magnificently brave soldier, was found asleep in a barn on the retreat, and Pulaski, whose merit is undeniable, was found asleep in a farmhouse. The exhaustion of those mounted officers casts a revealing light on the wonderful stamina of their foot soldiers, who endured far greater hardship and fatigue in that heartbreaking retreat.

It was unquestionably a defeat for the Americans; but, as has happened more than once in warfare, that fact was of small consequence in comparison with its ulterior effects. In its larger aspects it was of "great and enduring service to the American cause." Trevelyan says: "Eminent generals and statesmen of sagacity, in every European court, were profoundly impressed by learning that a new army, raised within the year, and undaunted by a series of recent disasters, had assailed a victorious enemy in its own quarters and had only been repulsed after a sharp and dubious conflict. . . . The French government, in making up its mind on the question whether the Americans would prove to be efficient allies, was influenced almost as much by the battle of Germantown as by the surrender of Burgoyne." [10] It is doubtful, however, that Germantown had so much effect at the French court.

CHAPTER 34

The Forts on the Delaware

"This morning 36 Sail of the Enemies Ships went past this Town up the Bay and this Evening 47 more were seen from the light House Standing in for the Cape." So, on October 5, 1777, William Peery, captain of the "independent company of 100 men on the Continental establishment" on guard at Cape Henlopen,[1] wrote to Caesar Rodney.

It was a part of Admiral Lord Howe's fleet, which now, more than a month out from the Head of Elk, was about to ascend the Delaware without difficulty, as it might have done two months before, except for the dissuasion of Captain Hamond of the *Roebuck*. The admiral himself, with twelve vessels, had preceded this part of his fleet by three or four days.[2]

The ships went on up the bay and the river, past Bombay Hook on the 9th, past New Castle on the 11th, where General Howe's army might have disembarked on, say, the 9th of August instead of at Head of Elk on the 25th and been nearer Philadelphia than it was on that day. On the 12th, the flagship was off Chester; but that was about as far as it dared try to go, for above that point began the obstructions of the channel and the fortifications of which Captain Hamond had warned the Howes. The main fleet was then anchored in the river from Reedy Island up to New Castle.[3] But it was necessary that the river should be opened to shipping if the British were to continue to hold Philadelphia.

While the enemy army lay in that city Washington's army was active in cutting off its supplies from the back country. The British had to be supported and supplied by the ships. The way from Head of Elk to Philadelphia by land was too difficult, too liable to interruption by the Americans. Therefore water communication was vital to the continuance of the occupation of the rebel capital.

Washington understood that. If the river's defenses, he wrote, "can be maintained General Howe's situation will not be the most agreeable; for if his supplies can be stopped by water, it may easily be done by land . . . the acquisition of Philadelphia may, instead of his good fortune, prove his ruin." [4]

The first obstacle was at Billingsport—a double line of chevaux-de-frise that extended from the Jersey shore across the channel to Billings Island. These were cratelike structures made of heavy timbers, loaded with stones and sunk in the water. They were mounted with wooden beams, shod at the upper end with iron points, slanting upwards to within four feet of the surface of the river at low tides and pointing downstream. They were capable of ripping open the bottom of any ship that tried to pass over them. This line was protected by a small redoubt on the Jersey shore.[5]

That redoubt, however, was a slight affair, unfinished and lightly held. On October 2 Howe sent against it the 42nd Regiment and part of the 71st, under Colonel Sterling. When they landed below the fort and attacked it in the rear, the garrison spiked its guns, set fire to the barracks, and fled. Captain Hamond cut through the chevaux and opened a passage through which six ships passed.[6]

The next obstacle was thirty chevaux strung in a triple line from Mud Island, a little below the mouth of the Schuylkill, across the channel to Red Bank on the Jersey side. This line was guarded by a fort at either end.[7] Above this lay the American fleet, comprising the frigate *Montgomery*, a brig, a schooner, two xebecs, thirteen row-galleys, two floating batteries, fourteen fire ships, and several fire rafts.[8] The best vessel, the frigate *Delaware* of thirty-two guns, had run aground September 7 on the Jersey shore, where it had been set on fire by shots from British batteries and had surrendered.[9]

The first attempt against the forts was made on October 21 by Colonel von Donop with three Hessian grenadier battalions, a regiment of foot, four companies of jägers, and some artillery, about 2,000 men in all.[10] It was directed against Fort Mercer at Red Bank. Washington had garrisoned it with a Rhode Island Continental regiment under Colonel Christopher Greene, and had called on New Jersey for militia to strengthen that force and to cover the rear of the works on the outside, but had met with no response. He had therefore added to the garrison another Rhode Island Continental regiment under Colonel Israel Angell, making a total force of about 400 rank and file. The Chevalier de Mauduit du Plessis, a young

French engineer, had also been sent to assist Greene in strengthening the fort. He found that the Americans, "little practised in the art of fortification," had overbuilt the works to an extent "beyond their strength" to hold. He reduced them by drawing a wall across an extension along the river side "which transformed them into a large redoubt nearly of a pentagonal form." [11] The walls were of earth, guarded without by a ditch and an abatis and mounting fourteen guns.

The attacking troops crossed the Delaware at Philadelphia and marched to Haddonfield, where they encamped for the night. They were again afoot at three o'clock in the morning, but were delayed by having to make a detour where a bridge had been taken up, so that they did not arrive at the fort until noon. Their preparations seem to have been very leisurely; it was half-past four when they made their demand for surrender.

A Hessian officer, with flag and drum, then advanced. "The King of England," said he, "orders his rebellious subjects to lay down their arms and they are warned that if they stand the battle, no quarters whatever will be given." That this summons should be made by one of the hated Hessians added insult to the arrogance of his language. "It only served to irritate the garrison and inspire them with more resolution." [12] Greene replied that he accepted the challenge, and that there would be no quarter on either side.

Von Donop opened fire from a battery he had erected in the rear of the fort. The attack was made in two columns, one against the northern wing of the works, the part that had been cut off and abandoned. The other, led by von Donop, was against the redoubt. Like a torrent the first flowed over the breastworks, the men shouting, "Vittoria!" and waving their hats in air, only to find themselves faced by the new wall forming one side of the redoubt. At the same time, with equal confidence, von Donop's column approached the redoubt. Meeting no fire, they penetrated the abatis, crossed the ditch, and reached the berm, the space between the ditch and the parapet. There they were checked; they had no scaling ladders. Then, and not until then, Greene gave the order to fire—to fire at the broad belts of the Hessians as he had before instructed his men. Such an avalanche of grapeshot and bullets fell upon the Hessians of both columns in front and in flank, from the projecting corner of the redoubt, as had been seldom heard and felt. They went down in rows and heaps. "It may well be doubted," says Trevelyan, "whether so few men in so small a space of time had ever delivered a deadlier fire." [13] The officers, von Donop conspicuous among them, tried to rally their men. Their leader was too conspicuous by his dress, as well as by his efforts. He fell, mortally wounded, and his men

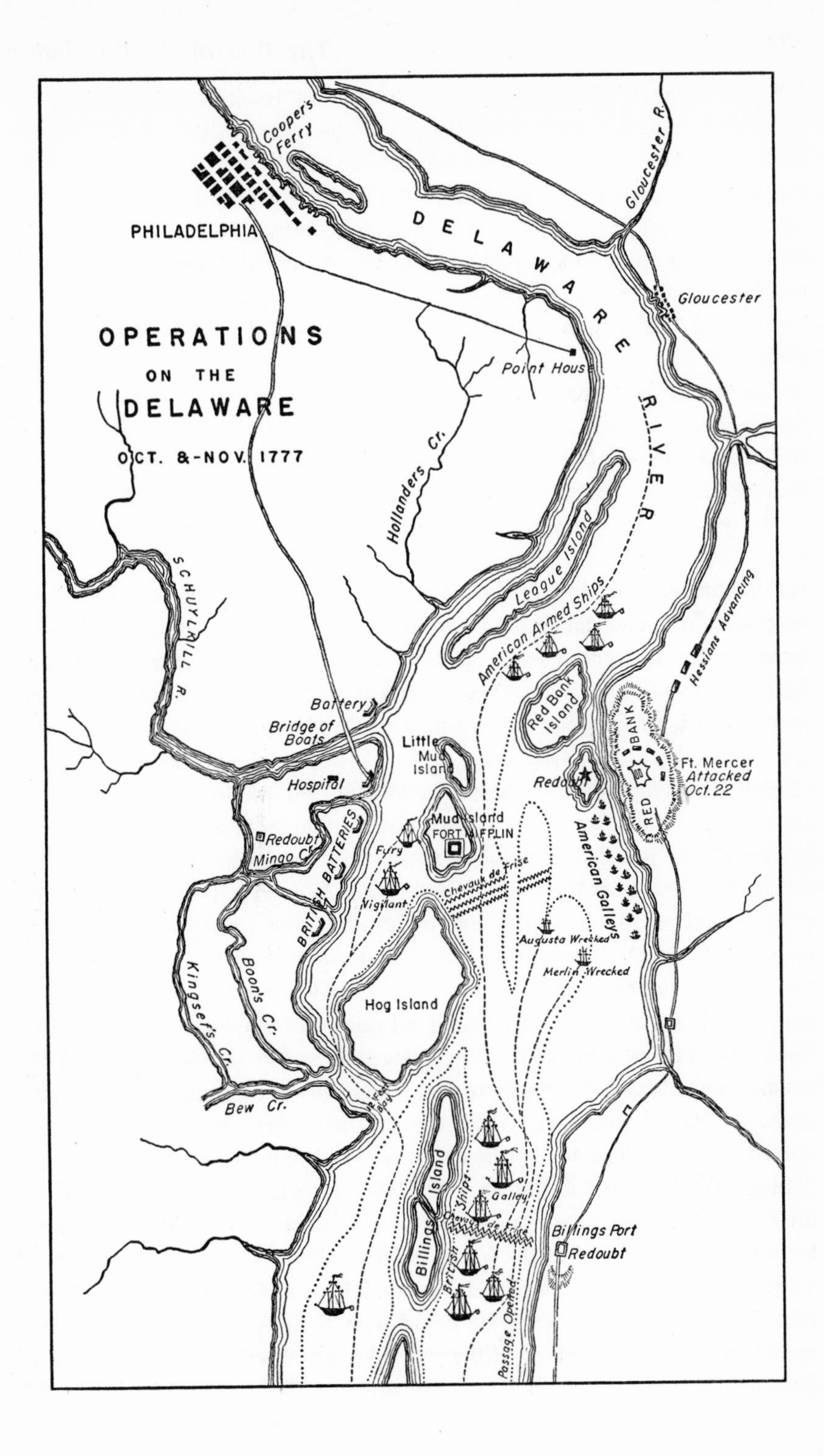
OPERATIONS
ON THE
DELAWARE
OCT. &-NOV. 1777
PHILADELPHIA
Coopers Ferry
DELAWARE RIVER
Gloucester R.
Gloucester
Point House
Hollanders Cr.
League Island
SCHUYLKILL R.
American Armed Ships
Hessians Advancing
Red Bank Island
RED BANK
Ft. Mercer
Attacked
Oct. 22
Battery
Bridge of Boats
Little Mud Island
Hospital
Redoubt
Mud Island
FORT MIFFLIN
Redoubt
Mingo Cr.
BRITISH BATTERIES
Fury
Vigilant
Chevaux de Frise
American Galleys
Augusta Wrecked
Merlin Wrecked
Kingsef's Cr.
Boon's Cr.
Hog Island
Bew Cr.
Billings Island
British Ships
Galley
Chevaux de Frise
Billings Port
Redoubt
Passage Opened

faltered. They tried again against the redoubt on its southern side; but there they were under fire from the row-galleys in the river as well as from the fort, and suffered heavy damage. So they finally withdrew to the shelter of the woods, leaving the ground strewn with dead and disabled. After the fight, twenty of them uninjured were found on the berm, clinging to the parapet so as to be out of danger from the Americans' fire, and were captured. The loss of the Hessians in killed, wounded, and captives was 371, including 22 officers. Within the fort there were 14 dead Americans and 23 wounded.[14]

The British had another setback on the same day. The frigates *Augusta, Roebuck, Liverpool,* and *Pearl* and the sloop *Merlin* ran aground. The Americans opened fire on them from the fort, the row-galleys, and the floating batteries. The *Augusta* caught fire and blew up. The *Merlin* could not be got off; she was abandoned and burned.[15]

Fort Mifflin on Mud Island was "unskillfully constructed." One contemporary observer called it "a Burlesque upon the art of Fortification." [16] Strong in front against vessels on the river, it was weak in the rear and on the north, where only ditches and palisades with four wooden blockhouses, each mounting four guns, offered means of defense. The east or river side and the southern side, also facing the river, were high and thick stone walls pierced with loopholes for musketry. Outside this wall at its northern end were two ravelins, or earthworks forming an angle, towards the river.[17] In the middle of the main enclosure was a small redoubt. The garrison had fallen in numbers to 300 men, to which Washington had added 150 Pennsylvania troops; but it would have required nearer a thousand properly to man the works. North of Mud Island and separated from it by a channel less than 500 yards wide, was Province Island, a mud bank mostly under water at high tide, but having two small humps of dry land. Obviously that weak northern side of Mifflin was dangerously exposed to gunfire, if the enemy erected batteries on Province. They did—five, mounting ten heavy guns, 24- to 32-pounders, two howitzers, and three mortars.[18] The current of the river, deflected by the chevaux-de-frise, had swept a new channel between the Mud Island and the mainland. Into this the enemy brought a floating battery carrying twenty-two 24-pounders and stationed it within forty yards of an angle of the fort. On November 10 all these guns opened a fire on the fort that continued all day long and for five days after, the Americans replying as best they could with their few guns. The barracks were heavily battered, many of the palisades were overthrown, and some of the guns dismounted. A ball knocked down a chimney and its bricks fell on Lieutenant Colonel Samuel Smith, injuring him so severely that he had to be evacuated to Red Bank, Major Simeon Thayer of Rhode Island taking over the command. During those five days many of the garrison were killed or disabled.[19]

On the 15th, the British brought their ships into play. The ship of the line *Somerset*, 64 guns, the *Isis*, 50 guns, the *Roebuck*, 44, the *Pearl*, 32, the *Liverpool* frigate, with 32 guns, moved into position within range of the fort, while the *Vigilant*, 16 guns, and a hulk with 3 reenforced the floating battery in the new channel. The garrison had only two guns that had not been already dismounted by the cannonading of the previous days.

The rain of cannon balls from the ships and the shore batteries was terrific. It was estimated that over a thousand shot were fired every twenty minutes.[20] Within an hour the last two guns were overthrown. The ships were so near that marines in their maintops shot down every man that showed himself in the fort. By night the palisades were gone, the block-houses destroyed, the whole parapet overthrown. Fort Mifflin was only a name. In the darkness Major Thayer and his surviving men crossed the river to Red Bank, after having set fire to whatever was inflammable.[21]

The defense of Fort Mifflin was one of the most gallant and obstinate of any in the war. Two hundred and fifty of the garrison were killed or wounded during the bombardment, their number having been made up by reliefs sent from time to time. They had had no assistance from the American fleet. Its commander, Commodore Hazelwood, having perhaps the safety of his ships too much in mind, had failed to respond to calls for assistance. The loss on the British side was but seven killed and five wounded.[22]

With the fall of Mifflin, Mercer was doomed. Cornwallis took 2,000 men across the river to storm it. Washington had sent General Greene around by Burlington to reenforce it, but Greene found himself so greatly outnumbered by the approaching force that he wisely refrained from attempting to hold it. Colonel Christopher Greene, seeing that his position was hopeless, evacuated it. The idle American fleet was abandoned and burned.[23] The Delaware from the Capes to Philadelphia was now altogether in the hands of the enemy.

For two months after the retreat from Germantown to the campground on the Perkiomen, the Americans engaged in no aggressive military operations. The time was spent in resting the men; combing the countryside for blankets, shoes, and clothing; and drawing troops from the north, from Putnam and Gates,[24] Burgoyne's surrender having permitted such withdrawals. Varnum's Rhode Island brigade, 1,200 men, came, and about a thousand others from Pennsylvania, Maryland, and Virginia. Gates sent down Patterson's and Glover's brigades and Morgan's invaluable rifle corps. By October 29 the army numbered 8,313 Continentals and 2,717 militia rank and file.[25] But the terms of enlistment of many of the Maryland and Virginia troops were about to expire.[26] The army was, as usual, in a state of incipient dissolution. The distress of the men for want of blankets, shoes, and clothing was "amazingly great."

Washington hardened his heart in his search for his army's necessities. "Buy, if you can," was his policy; if not, take, especially from the Tories. He wrote to George Read of Delaware, "You are to take care, that the unfriendly Quakers and others notoriously disaffected to the cause of American Liberty do not escape your Vigilance." "Obtaining these things from the Quakers and disaffected inhabitants is recommended, but at all events get them." [27] The returns from anywhere were never enough. To meet the appalling need for foot covering, Washington offered "a reward of *Ten Dollars*" to the person who should produce the best "substitute for shoes, made of raw hides." [28]

During those two months he was changing his camps restlessly and, except in one instance, with no apparent purpose. On October 8 he marched from the Perkiomen eight miles to a position in Towamencin Township. On the 16th the men "struck tents and marched to the Skippack Road and Encamped on the Same Ground we were at on the 3rd instant." [29] The purpose this time was "to divert the Enemy's attention and force them from the Forts," [30] but the enemy took no notice. On the 20th, the Americans again broke camp and marched to a new one in Whippany Township. On November 2 they made their last shift for the time being; "Cross'd Whissahickon Creek on Skippack Road, march'd to the left & encamped on the brow of an hill on ye North Wales Road White Marsh Township." [31] They remained there nearly six weeks.

The only bright spot in this dull period of marches to and fro was the announcement on October 18, in general orders, of Burgoyne's surrender. Washington expressed his own happiness and adjured his men. "Let every face brighten and every heart expand with grateful Joy and praise to the supreme disposer of all events who has granted us this signal success." A salute by "*Thirteen* pieces of cannon" to be followed by a "*feu-de-joy* with blank cartridges or powder by every brigade and corps of the army" was ordered. To add to the gayety of the celebration, the chaplains were directed to deliver to their several corps or brigades "short discources suited to the joyful occasion." [32]

Other than that, there is little of interest in the records of Washington's army of that period, save such as can be gleaned from the usual, dreary routine of courts-martial for various offenses. Drunkenness was common, desertion frequent. Cowardice was charged against not a few officers; most of them were acquitted, a few cashiered. On conviction of the privates, sentences of reprimand, of lashes on the bare back, of running the gantlet between files of fifty, one hundred, two hundred men, of death for desertion, were imposed. Disobedience usually drew thirty-nine lashes; drunkenness, the same. Sometimes noncommissioned officers were reduced to the ranks.

On October 19 Howe withdrew his troops from Germantown and concentrated his whole force in Philadelphia. He established a chain of fourteen redoubts, connected by a strong stockade and extending from the Upper Ferry on the Schuylkill to the shore of the Delaware above the town.[33]

Washington's army with its recent additions felt its strength. The near-success at Germantown had made it confident of its fighting ability, and Saratoga had aroused a spirit of emulation. On November 25, a council of war discussed the advisability of an attack on Philadelphia. Stirling had a prettily complicated plan for it; [34] Wayne was eager to try it. But eleven of the fifteen officers in attendance, including Greene, Knox, Sullivan, de Kalb, Smallwood, du Portail, and Maxwell, prudently voted against it. An open town, like Germantown, with only a part of the enemy's force to defend it, was one thing; a fortified city, garrisoned by such troops as held Philadelphia, was quite another thing. Disaster would certainly have resulted from such an attempt.

But the mere presence of the American army so near at hand was a continuous menace to the British. Howe decided to try once more to bring on a battle. At midnight of December 4 he set out from Philadelphia, with almost his entire force, to surprise the American camp at Whitemarsh. But that vigilant leader of American partisan troops Captain Allen McLane, who had been constantly scouting between the lines, discovered the enemy's intentions and reported them to Washington. Dispositions to receive the attack were made accordingly, one of them being the dispatch of McLane, with a hundred picked horsemen, to observe the enemy's movements.[35]

The British were advancing in two columns on the Manatawny and Skippack roads. At Three Mile Run on the Skippack Road, McLane, not content with mere observation, attacked the British van with "brilliant cavalry rushes" and with such effect that the front division was obliged "to change its line of march." [36] After that he hovered on the enemy's front and flank, "galling them severely."

At three o'clock in the morning of the 5th the British encamped on Chestnut Hill. When day dawned they "had a fine View of the Rebel Encampment about 3 miles distant on a Ridge of hills lying North of Whitemarsh," the "smoke and huts being plainly in view." [37] Before the British arrived the Americans had "increased their fires lighting many large ones in straight and deep lines, so that it looked as if fifty thousand men were encamped there. By day we could see this was merely a trick to deceive us," [38] says the Hessian Major Baurmeister.

Washington's camp was well defended. "Both wings were fortified by strong abatis; the center approaches were completely covered by several batteries; the whole position was strongly fortified by fifty-two heavy pieces." [39] There was no point in leaving such defenses and attacking the enemy in the open ground. If Howe wanted to bring on a battle, let him assault the American works.

Washington did, however, take the precaution of striking his tents in the early morning and sending his heavy baggage to the rear.[40] At eleven o'clock he sent Brigadier General James Irvine, with 600 Pennsylvania militia, to feel out the enemy. Irvine attacked an advance post held by the 2nd Battalion of British light infantry and supported by British and Hessian grenadiers. There was a heavy fire from both sides, and several men fell in either party. Irvine himself was wounded and captured. His force was driven back, broke, and ran away.[41]

The two armies held their respective positions until one o'clock in the morning of December 7, when the British marched from Chestnut Hill to Edge Hill, within a mile of the American left wing. Their line then was formed in a curve, threatening both the American wings. Washington moved Morgan's riflemen and Webb's Continental regiment, together with Brigadier General James Potter's brigade of Pennsylvania militia, all to the right.[42]

Howe then decided to try again his old Long Island and Brandywine trick. His army moved at ten o'clock that night in one column to Jenkintown. Grey was detached with the Hessian jägers, Simcoe's Tory Queen's Rangers, the light infantry, and the 3rd brigade and sent towards Tyson's Tavern on the Limekiln Road, "where he was to drive in a Post of the Enemy and draw up in view of their camp," says Major André. "While they presumed an attack impending from that quarter, Sir William Howe with the *Elite* and main army was to have made the real attack" on Washington's left.[43]

On the Limekiln Road, Grey's troops were received with a burst of fire from a woody ridge held by Morgan's riflemen and Gist's Maryland militia.

The jägers and Simcoe's Rangers advanced on the right and left, "with great activity and ardor." Outflanked on both wings, the Americans retreated. There were inconsiderable losses on both sides in this engagement, but, as usual, the account of the casualties varies with the side giving it.[44]

On the American left Potter's Pennsylvania militia and Webb's Continentals, with whom were General John Cadwalader and General Joseph Reed as observers, had taken post in a wood in Cheltenham Township. Grey's column attacked them. At the first fire Reed's horse was shot, and he fell to the ground. The British charged; the Americans gave way and fled in confusion. Some of the foe ran to bayonet Reed where he lay, but the ubiquitous McLane was at hand. He and his men charged, drove back the bayoneteers and rescued the injured general.[45] The Americans lost about 50 men.

The main body of the British army now occupied the position which had been held by Potter and Webb. But, says Major André, "the fullest information being procured of the Enemy's position, most people thought an attack upon ground of such difficult access would be a very arduous undertaking; nor was it judged that any decisive advantage could be obtained, as the Enemy had reserved the most easy and obvious retreat. Probably for these reasons the Commander in Chief determined to return to Philadelphia." [46] So both columns started back home.

Grey's column was unlucky in the weight of its artillery and the insufficiency of its horses. A body of American light infantry and some horsemen pursued it, "pressed on the rearmost parties and drove them in." The jägers were drawn up to oppose the attack. The Americans "formed at a fence and delivered a very brisk fire." The Hessians brought their fieldpieces into play and finally drove off their assailants. And so ended the abortive Battle of Whitemarsh.[47]

Washington decided to move his camp again, for what purpose does not appear. Early in the morning of December 11 the Americans left Whitemarsh, intending to cross to the west side of the Schuylkill at Matson's Ford by a bridge "consisting of 36 waggons, with a bridge of Rails between each." [48] Sullivan's division and half of another were across when a body of British soldiery appeared on the opposite hill. It developed as the van of a force of 3,500 led by Cornwallis on a foraging expedition. The Americans were in an awkward position, astride the river with a rickety bridge between the two parts. Washington recalled Sullivan and the others with him and broke the bridge. The two forces were then aligned in battle formation face to face with a river between, which neither dared to cross.

But Potter and his militia, who had been operating on the other side, had not been able to get back before the bridge was broken. Cornwallis scattered them and went on with his foraging. Washington returned to Whitemarsh.[49]

It was getting cold now; snow had already fallen, "though not to lay." It was time to plan for the coming winter. Should the Americans continue their campaign, as they had done throughout the last wintry season, or go into winter quarters in the approved military manner? Washington knew the answer, knew that his worn, half-fed, half-frozen, half-naked men simply could not endure the rigors of a winter campaign. When a committee of the Congress, now a bobtail organization of a score or so of mediocre gentlemen, most of whose names have all but passed into oblivion, came to him to confer on the means of carrying on a "Winter's Campaign with vigor and success," he gave them an earful, plenty of reasons why it could not be done. The committee seemed to be convinced.[50]

Winter quarters, then, but where? Some of the officers proposed a chain of posts from Lancaster to Reading; but such a scattering of a none-too-cohesive army would only result in its disintegration. Wilmington in Delaware was proposed. Greene favored it, and so did Joseph Reed, Lafayette, Armstrong, Smallwood, Wayne, and Scott. Cadwalader urged it. If this step were not taken, he said, the enemy might take over that town and so secure "the lower counties on the Eastern Shore" of the Chesapeake. Besides, gondolas based on that "strong post" could annoy the British shipping.[51] Washington favored the idea, looking for mild weather there and facilities for securing supplies by the river. But Pennsylvania had to be heard from. It raised an outcry.

The Pennsylvania Council and Assembly drew up a hot remonstrance and sent it to the Congress at York. It cried aloud against letting the army go into winter quarters anywhere. Pennsylvania and New Jersey would be ravaged. The inhabitants would be obliged to fly or to submit to such terms as the enemy might prescribe—regardless of the fact that the Philadelphians were already submitting and having rather a better time, on the whole, than Washington's hungry and cold troops.

The Congress submissively sent the document to Washington, and the gentlemen from Pennsylvania got an answer that burned their ears. Who had told them whether he intended to hibernate or to fight all winter? Assuredly, he had not. They were reprobating the idea of winter quarters "as if they thought the Men were made of stocks and stones and equally insensible to frost and Snow," as if they thought the army, in such condition as it was in, could hold "a superior one, in all respects well appointed

. . . within the city of Philadelphia and cover from depredation and waste the States of Pennsylvania and New Jersey." It amazed him still more that these very gentlemen, who, knowing the nakedness of his soldiers, had asked him to postpone his plan of commandeering clothes "under strong assurances that an ample supply would be collected in ten days . . . not one Article of which, by the bye, is yet come to hand"—that these same gentlemen should think "a Winter's Campaign and the covering of these States from the Invasion of an Enemy, so easy and practicable a business. I can assure these Gentlemen, that it is a much easier and less distressing thing to draw remonstrances in a comfortable room by a good fireside, than to occupy a cold, bleak hill and sleep under frost and Snow without Cloaths or Blankets; however, although they seem to have little feeling for the naked and distressed Soldiers, I feel superabundantly for them and, from my Soul, I pity those miseries, which it is neither in my power to relieve or prevent." [52] If the gentlemen of the Pennsylvania Council and Assembly did not curl up under that lash, they certainly had rhinoceros skins.

Washington was already at Valley Forge when he wrote to the state Assembly. That place, selected as a compromise between campaigning and wintering in Wilmington, was suggested by Wayne, a Pennsylvanian, "to cover this Country against the Horrid rapine and Devastation of a Wanton Enemy." [53] Like most compromises, it was not a good solution of the problem—"a most unwise one," indeed. Chester County had been so stripped by both armies that it was "doubtful if any location could have been secured where supplies were more difficult to secure than Valley Forge." [54]

De Kalb expressed himself forcibly against that location for the camp, writing: "The idea of wintering in this desert can only have been put into the head of the commanding general by an interested speculator or a disaffected man." [55] Varnum was even more emphatic: "I have from the beginning viewed this situation with horror! It is unparallelled in the history of mankind to establish winter-quarters in a country wasted and without a single magazine." [56] Nevertheless, the choice was made, and on those bleak and barren hills the army settled down for a winter of torture and heroism.

With this, our narrative will turn back six months to the army on Lake Champlain.

CHAPTER 35

Valcour Island

"Our Army at Crown Point is an object of wretchedness to fill a humane mind with horrour; disgraced, defeated, discontented, diseased, naked, undisciplined, eaten up with vermin; no clothes, beds, blankets, no medicines; no victuals, but salt pork and flour." [1] In those words, which for clearness, force, and accuracy could not be bettered, John Adams described the condition of the American troops who, after the disasters at Quebec and Trois Rivières, retreated from Canada in June, 1776.

Three thousand of them, afflicted with smallpox, dysentery, malarial fevers, and all sorts of camp diseases, were in hospital; that is to say, they were lying in tents and huts with no proper care or treatment. Surgeons were few, medicines almost entirely lacking. For food they had almost rancid salt pork and flour, nothing else.[2] "I can truly say," wrote Colonel Trumbull, "that I did not look into a tent that did not contain a dead or dying man." [3] Five thousand were supposed to be fit for duty, but they seemed mere "walking apparitions." Five thousand men had been lost in the whole Canadian venture.[4]

Schuyler at Albany was in command. Sullivan, his second, was with the troops. But on June 17 the Congress, having news of the disaster at Trois Rivières and of the retreat, had resolved that "an experienced general be immediately sent into Canada" and directed Washington to order Major General Horatio Gates "to take command of the forces in that province." [5]

Washington sent Gates his orders, with the comment, "The Command is important." John Adams wrote him, "We have ordered you to the Post of Honour and made you Dictator in Canada for Six Months or at least until the first of October." [6] To Gates this naturally meant that he was to take over the chief command from Schuyler. But Schuyler thought that only Sullivan was displaced, and that he himself still held the dominant position, pointing out, with some logic, that, while the order gave Gates chief command of the troops in Canada, there were, in fact, no longer any troops whatever in Canada. On July 8 the Congress gave Schuyler support by declaring that its intention was to give Gates "command of the troops whilst in Canada," with no purpose of giving him "a superior command to General Schuyler, whilst the troops should be on this side Canada." It also recommended to both generals that they "carry on the military operations with harmony." [7] So Gates had to accept the inferior position, which, to give him due credit, he did with good grace.

Gates arrived at Crown Point along with Schuyler on July 5. A council of war was held, in which Schuyler, Gates, Sullivan, Arnold, and the Prussian general Baron de Woedtke took part. They unanimously agreed that Crown Point was not tenable, that they should retire to Ticonderoga, sending all the sick to Fort George, and that "a naval armament of gondolas, row-galleys, armed batteaus &c" should be provided.[8]

Some of the field officers were not content with this intention to retreat further. Twenty-one of them signed a remonstrance and delivered it to Schuyler. There was discontent also in higher quarters. Washington was inclined to the view of the malcontents. He wrote to Schuyler that, while he did not wish to encourage inferior officers in setting up their opinions against their superiors' decisions, yet he felt as they did and stated his reasons at length. Indeed, he said, nothing but a belief that, by the time he had news of the intended move, the works had been demolished and the withdrawal already made, plus a fear of encouraging such remonstrances, had prevented him from ordering the retention of the post at Crown Point.[9]

Schuyler defended the decision to withdraw with reasons that were cogent,[10] but not so briefly and briskly stated as were Gates's. "Your Excellency Speaks of Works to be Destroyed at Crown Point," Gates wrote to Washington on July 29. "Time & the Bad Construction of those Works had Compleatly Effected that business before General Schuyler came with me to Crown Point. The Ramparts are Tumbled down, the casements are Fallen in, the Barracks Burnt, and the whole so perfect a Ruin that it would take Five times the Number of Our Army for several Summers to put Those Works in Denfensible [*sic*] Repair." [11]

Under these conditions, no other course was possible, and so the sick were sent on to Fort George, and the rest of the army moved to Ticonderoga. The remnant of their salt pork had become utterly rancid and was thrown away. They had nothing to eat but flour, boiled to a gruel or baked into thin cakes on flat stones. They had no attention except what less than a dozen surgeons could give to 2,000 desperately sick men. Nature and Death took care of them. Some recovered, some did not. By the middle of August, they were down to a thousand.[12]

Three thousand "effectives" were now at Ticonderoga. The 6th Pennsylvania, under Lieutenant Colonel Thomas Hartley, had been left to establish an outpost at Crown Point—one not to be held against the enemy appearing in force.[13] A reenforcement, consisting of the 1st and 2nd Pennsylvania and three companies of the 4th, arrived at Ticonderoga on July 9, without shoes or stockings and almost in rags, "in miserable plight from the fatigue and sickness they had undergone," but, compared with the rest, "robust and healthy." [14]

The army was now divided into four brigades. The 1st, commanded by Arnold, comprised Bond's, Greaton's, and Porter's Massachusetts Continentals, and Burrell's Connecticut. The 2nd, under Colonel James Reed, was composed of his own, Poor's, and Bedel's from New Hampshire and Patterson's from Massachusetts. The 3rd commanded by Colonel John Stark, was made up of his own New Hampshires, Wind's and Maxwell's New Jerseymen, and Wynkoop's New Yorkers. The 4th, General Arthur St. Clair's, had his own, De Haas's, Wayne's, and Hartley's commands, all Pennsylvanians.[15]

The first three brigades were encamped on Mount Independence, on the east side of the lake, to keep them away from St. Clair's Pennsylvanians, encamped on the Ticonderoga side. The intense jealousy and ill feeling between the "southern" troops and those of New England and the consequent disorder had made this separation necessary.[16]

When Ethan Allen and Benedict Arnold took Ticonderoga from the British in May, 1775, it was well supplied with ordnance and ordnance stores; but Knox took most of the heavy cannon to the army at Boston. There were left, however, 120 guns of various sizes from 3-pounders to one 32. But there were not enough carriages to mount more than 43 of them, and there was a great lack of all their equipment, sponges, rammers, and so on. Powder was, as always, deficient, also lead, flints, and cartridge paper, for all which Gates now called on the Congress. He got them at last, on October 6.[17]

More men were needed to man these extensive works. Two emotions, prevalent throughout the northern states, affected the supply of such reenforcements. One was fear of the British invasion, which prompted the militia to come forward. The other was dread of the smallpox in the camp, which deterred them. The first was, however, the stronger. Militiamen from the neighborhood and from the New England states began to come late in July. By August they were coming in considerable numbers, though for the most part they were so ill provided and so worn down by the fatigue and hardships of their march that they were more of a burden to the garrison than a help. But three Continental regiments from Massachusetts really strengthened the army in July.[18]

By August 24 the returns showed twenty regiments in five brigades, a total of 9,157 rank and file, but only 4,899 present and fit for duty, besides 1,500 effectives at Crown Point, Fort George, and Skenesboro.[19]

The Americans had a flotilla on the lake, the schooner *Royal Savage,* captured the year before by Montgomery at St. Johns, the sloop *Enterprise,* which Arnold had taken when Ticonderoga fell, the schooner *Liberty,* taken at Skenesboro by Herrick at the same time, and the schooner *Revenge,* built at Ticonderoga. Arnold, whom Gates adjudged to be "perfectly skilled in naval affairs," had "most nobly undertaken to command" this fleet.[20] But Carleton was building boats at the other end of the lake, and Arnold wanted more than those four. He wanted auxiliary craft, gondolas, row-galleys, gunboats. They had to be built. But how could they be built?

There was plenty of standing timber, but it must first be felled, then hewn into keels and ribs and sawn into planks. Felling axes were scarce. Of broadaxes, adzes, crosscut saws, hammers, grindstones, chisels, augers, and all sorts of necessary hand tools, there were none. There were, to be sure, three sawmills in the neighborhood—one at Ticonderoga, another at Crown Point, a third near Skenesboro. Though disuse and neglect had left them in bad shape, they could be repaired. Planks could be got out in them. But how could those necessary tools be had in that wilderness? Where were bolts and nails, oakum and other naval stores, hawsers and anchors, paint, iron, ropes and blocks for rigging, canvas for sails, and all the hundred and one necessary articles and things for equipment to be procured? [21]

And, if you had all those, who was to use them? Who was to build and rig the vessels? Ship carpenters, sailmakers, and riggers were few in that army. The shipyards and sail lofts along the seacoast were humming with work for shipmasters and privateersmen. Few mechanics were fools enough to join a naked, starved, diseased army, when plenty of work with good pay was to be had at home. Nevertheless, those boats had to be built, and they were built.

Felling axes came first, in quantity, 1,500 from Schuyler at Albany, a thousand more from Governor Trumbull of Connecticut.[22] The soldiers were put to work in the forest. A few ship carpenters, so improvident as to have enlisted, were combed out of the army, a few house carpenters also. These were sent to Skenesboro, where the boatyard was established; Schuyler sent thirty more from Albany.[23] But these were not enough, not nearly enough. The coastal towns were called on.

In four companies of fifty each, bringing their own tools, ship carpenters came on from Massachusetts, Connecticut, Rhode Island, and even from far-off Philadelphia. Not for nothing, however, and not for soldiers' pay. They demanded and they got "prodegious wages," as much as five dollars a day, hard money, it was rumored. Blacksmiths also came and oarmakers and riggers and sailmakers, on similar terms.[24] Brigadier General David Waterbury, Jr., of Connecticut took charge of the work. Arnold came to Skenesboro from time to time, "to give Life & Spirit to Our Dock Yards," as Gates put it.[25] His energy and drive were contagious among the workers, and Waterbury's constant attention kept things going. Hard as it was to get them, spikes and nails being especially scarce, the necessary supplies and equipment came in.

Two types of craft were built—row-galleys and gondolas. The row-galleys were the larger, 70 to 80 feet long and 18 feet beam. They had round bottoms with keels, quarterdecks, and cabins, and were of "Spanish construction" as to their rigging; that is to say, they had two short masts, equipped with lateen sails that gave them an exotic appearance on that lake but made them easy even for landlubbers to handle.[26] Their armament was a 12- and an 18-pounder in the bow, two 9-pounders in the stern, and from four to six 6-pounders in broadside. Their complement was eighty men each.

The gondolas were flat-bottomed, but had keels. They were about forty-five feet long, rigged with one mast and two square sails and carried forty-five men each. They were slower and less handy than the galleys and could sail only before the wind while the galleys could beat to windward. Their armament was one 12-pounder and two 9-pounders.[27]

The schooner and the sloop were not so heavily armed as the galleys. The *Royal Savage* carried four 6-pounders and eight 4-pounders; the *Enterprise*, twelve 4-pounders; the *Revenge*, four 4-pounders and two 2-pounders; the *Liberty*, the same. All the craft also mounted on their bulwarks several light swivel guns. Both galleys and gondolas were equipped with oars, the galley with thirty-six.[28]

While the boats were building, the army was cheered and refreshed by the arrival of beef on the hoof, twenty head a week, and plenty of bread. To those who could afford to pay, sutlers offered vegetables, sugar, butter, cheese, chocolate, rum, and wine. The condition of the troops was much improved.[29] On July 28 General St. Clair read the Declaration of Independence to the troops. They "manifested their joy with three cheers." "It was remarkably pleasing to see the spirits of the soldiers so raised after all their calamities; the language of every man's countenance was, Now we are a people; we have a name among the States of the world." [30]

Carleton had halted his pursuit of Sullivan's retreating army at St. Johns. But he had no intention of remaining there long. He was receiving large reenforcements from Britain, and he intended, if possible, to march to Albany and cooperate with Howe. The plan to isolate New England by occupying the Lake Champlain and Hudson River passageway, attempted in 1777, was to be executed, if feasible. As indicated above, the Americans were alarmed because of the threat of Carleton's army. At St. Johns, Carleton proceeded to assemble and construct a fleet of vessels for the lake, because he could not advance without commanding its waters. There were on the St. Lawrence a three-masted ship, the *Inflexible*, and two schooners, the *Maria* and the *Carleton*; but, because of the ten-mile-long rapids between Chambly and St. Johns, they could not be brought up the Richelieu. He tried to bring them around the falls on rollers, but the ground was too soft to bear their weight; he had to take them apart and carry them up in pieces. From England a frigate had brought him ten gunboats knocked down. These were brought to St. Johns to be reconstructed. A thirty-ton gondola, thirty longboats, and four hundred bateaux were also brought up, either overland or by dragging them through the rapids. The longboats and bateaux were to transport troops and baggage up the lake.[31]

Carleton had little difficulty in securing workmen, materials, tools, and supplies. There were the fleet in the St. Lawrence and the towns along that river to furnish them to his full requirement. The work was swiftly carried on. For instance, the *Inflexible* was rebuilt and equipped within twenty-eight days of the time the keel was laid. With equal dispatch, he rebuilt the others and constructed ten more gunboats and an extraordinary thing called a *radeau*. It was a huge, flat-bottomed affair, with two masts carrying square sails, but it was more like a raft than any other sort of vessel, having very low bulwarks. It was to be manned by three hundred men, and was armed with the heaviest ordnance, six 24-pounders, six 12-pounders, and two howitzers. It was, indeed, a sort of floating fortress. Its name was *Thunderer*.[32]

By October 4 Carleton's fighting fleet was complete and ready to sail. In it were the *Inflexible*, armed with eighteen 12-pounders, the *Maria*, with fourteen 6-pounders, the *Carleton* with twelve of the same, the gondola *Loyal Convert* with seven 9-pounders, the giant *Thunderer*, and twenty gunboats having bow-guns ranging from 9-pounders to 24-pounders.[33]

The British army in Canada had been reenforced by the arrival, in June, of the Regiment Hesse Hanau, 660 in number, and in September by a second installment of Hessians and Brunswickers, making up a total force of 5,000 German mercenaries under command of Major General Baron von Riedesel. Carleton's whole army now numbered about 13,000 rank and file.[34]

On September 10 operations against the Americans on the lake began General William Philips with two regiments, part of a third, and some artillery was posted at St. Johns. Another regiment held Chambly. Lieutenant Colonel Carleton, a younger brother of the general, started up the Richelieu with 400 Indians in canoes, to be strengthened shortly afterwards by the addition of 100 Canadian volunteers under Captain Fraser. And 1,300 German troops embarked in eighty-two boats and moved up the river.[35]

General Simon Fraser with the light infantry, the grenadiers, and the 24th British regiment took post on the river about five miles above the New York State line. Burgoyne with the 9th, 21st, 31st, and 47th British regiments, the Hessian Regiment Riedesel, and the Hanau Regiment, moved up to Ile aux Noix, which had been possessed by the British in August and had been fortified and equipped as a base of supplies with magazines, blockhouses, and barracks.[36]

But it was not until October 14 that Burgoyne and Fraser, having left the 20th and 61st to hold Ile aux Noix, embarked for the final advance against the Americans. All the German troops were left in Canada, except the Hanau artillery, which was with Carleton's fleet on board the *Thunderer*.[37]

Arnold's preparations to meet the enemy had been pushed with such success that, by August 20, the schooners *Royal Savage* and *Revenge*, the sloop *Enterprise* and the gondolas *Boston, New Haven, Providence, New York, Connecticut,* and *Spitfire,* the cutter *Lee,* and the sloop *Liberty* were ready. On the 24th he set sail at Crown Point. At Willsborough, halfway down the lake, a hard storm, with heavy rain, overtook him and nearly foundered the *Spitfire*. The whole fleet had to weigh anchor and run before the wind up to Buttonmould Bay, where, for three days without intermission, it was lashed by the gale. On September 1 the anchors were again

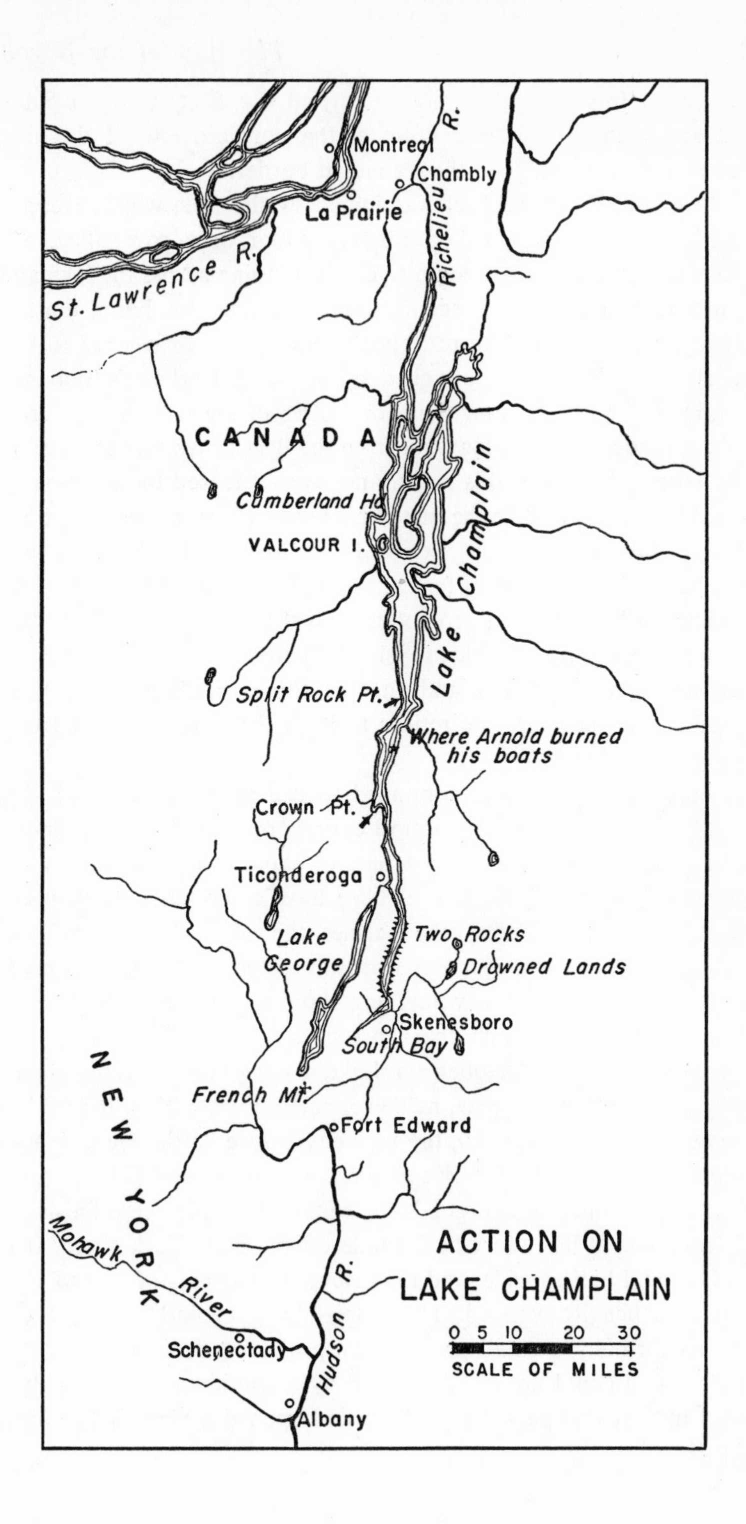
Montreal
Chambly
La Prairie
Richelieu R.
St. Lawrence R.
CANADA
Cumberland Hd
VALCOUR I.
Lake Champlain
Split Rock Pt.
Where Arnold burned his boats
Crown Pt.
Ticonderoga
Lake George
Two Rocks
Drowned Lands
Skenesboro
South Bay
French Mt.
Fort Edward
NEW YORK
Mohawk River
Schenectady
Hudson R.
Albany
ACTION ON LAKE CHAMPLAIN
0 5 10 20 30
SCALE OF MILES

lifted, and a fresh southerly breeze carried the fleet down to Schuyler's Island and then to Windmill Point at the northern end of the lake and within two or three miles of the Canadian border.[38]

At Windmill Point the fleet was joined by the *Lee*, which, sloop-rigged but with oars, might be called either a cutter or a row-galley, and the gondola *Jersey*. Arnold moored his vessels in a line across the lake and sent men ashore to fell spruce trees and make fascines for lining the sides of his galleys and gondolas "to prevent the enemy's boarding and to keep off small shot." [39] They were attacked by some of Carleton's Indians, who were now in the woods along the shore; three of the Americans were killed and six wounded before a few shot from the fleet drove off the assailants.

The lake is narrow at this point, and Arnold feared the erection of batteries on both sides to rake the line of his boats. He therefore retired to good anchorage in a broader part beside Ile la Motte. On the 19th he again shifted his position to a point farther south, Bay St. Amand above Cumberland Head, a long, curved promontory on the New York side of the lake about ten miles north of Valcour Island. While there he took soundings of the channel between that island and the shore. Finding it "an exceeding fine and secure harbour," he retired to it on the 23rd and remained there until the day of battle.[40]

He had been calling and continued to call on Gates to send him 200 sailors. His force was made up almost entirely of landsmen, "very indifferent men in general," he said. "Great part of those who shipped for seamen know very little of the matter." [41] "We have a wretched, motley crew in the fleet," he wrote to Gates, "the marines, the refuse of every regiment and the seamen few of them ever wet with salt water." [42] He also wanted gunners, for few of his men knew anything about laying a gun. And he wanted clothing for his men, watch coats, breeches, blankets, caps, and shoes. It was cold at night in October on Lake Champlain, and the men were scantily clad. But he got none, neither seamen nor clothing. Indeed, his last call was made on October 10, the very day before battle. He did, however, get the rest of his boats: the *Washington, Trumbull,* and *Congress,* galleys, and the *Jersey* and *Success*, gondolas, came on as they were finished.[43]

Valcour Island lies about half a mile off the New York shore. It is two miles long and half as wide, and rises steeply to heights of 120 to 180 feet. It was then heavily wooded. The vessels lying behind it were concealed from the north by a small promontory projecting from the island on its west side, and could not be discovered by a southbound fleet in the main channel until it had passed the island and opened a view of the water behind it.[44]

Arnold moored his fleet—two schooners, one sloop, eight gondolas, and four row-galleys—in a curved line, a "half-moon," between the island and the mainland, keeping the vessels as near together as practicable. He made the galley *Congress* his flagship, taking a position in the middle of the line. General Waterbury on the *Washington* galley commanded the right wing, and Colonel Edward Wigglesworth of Massachusetts on the *Trumbull* galley, the left. The entire force on the fleet was about 800 men.

Carleton sailed from St. Johns on October 4. His fleet consisted of the square-rigged ship *Inflexible*, the schooners *Maria* and *Carleton*, the great radeau *Thunderer*, the gondola *Loyal Convert*, twenty gunboats, four longboats with fieldpieces in their bows, and twenty-four longboats for provisions and stores. The fleet was manned by 670 seamen from the British transports on the St. Lawrence, and each of the four larger vessels carried a company of the 29th Regiment acting as marines. Captain Thomas Pringle was in command.[45]

The fire power which this fleet could bring into action at one time was fifty-three guns, though in the approaching battle it was only forty-two, because neither the *Thunderer* nor the *Loyal Convert* was engaged. On the American side, the number was thirty-two.[46] The weight of metal which the British could throw in one complete discharge was perhaps 500 pounds, not counting the swivels, against the American 265.

The British fleet proceeded up the lake slowly and with apparent caution, yet really, at the last, incautiously. It first came to anchor below Ile la Motte and lay there until the 9th, while scouts went ahead looking for the Americans, without success. On the 10th it went on to an anchorage between Grand and Long islands. Here Carleton got news that the American fleet had been seen in the vicinity.

Getting under way the next morning, it stood up the lake before a strong northerly wind, rounded Cumberland Head, and passed Valcour Island. It was in mid-channel, about two miles beyond the southern end of Valcour, when the American fleet opened to its view.

Then the incaution of its proceeding was made plain. No scout boats had been sent ahead, which might have found the Americans before it had put itself to the disadvantage of having to attack from the leeward, that is to say, against the wind.

The Americans had been on the alert. The *Revenge* had been scouting to the north and had seen the British ships coming around Cumberland Head. On receiving this news Waterbury had urged Arnold "to come to sail and fight them on a retreat in [the] main lake as they were so much superior to us in number and strength and we being in such a disadvantageous harbour." But Arnold persisted in his plan to fight where he was.[47]

When the British discovered the American vessels, they hauled up for them. Arnold ordered the *Royal Savage* and the four galleys to get under way and commence the attack. He himself was on board the *Congress* galley. But when he got out into open water and saw the full strength of the enemy he signaled for a return to the line behind the island. The enemy, who by this time had made some headway in beating against the wind, opened fire at long range on the schooner and the galleys, to which the Americans replied with all the guns they could bring to bear.

The *Royal Savage*, either by misadventure or, as Arnold claimed, by mismanagement, fell to leeward while drawing under the lee of the island. Three shots in quick succession hit her, damaging one of her masts and cutting her rigging. She came up into the wind, but failed to go about on the other tack, hung in the eye of the wind for a long moment, fell off on the same tack as before, and grounded on the island shore. But her crew continued to fire her guns.

Neither the *Inflexible* nor the *Maria* had been able to beat back into close range. They anchored at long gunshot distance, and the *Inflexible* brought her heavy guns to bear on her enemy. Neither the *Thunderer* nor the *Loyal Convert* was engaged.

The schooner *Carleton*, boring into the fight, was caught by a flaw of wind and brought up opposite the middle of the American line. Lieutenant Dacres, her commander, anchored her, with a spring on her cable, broadside to the American fleet. Seventeen of the British gunboats came up into line with her. With no more than 350 yards distance between the two lines, the real battle began about noon.

"A tremendous cannonade was opened on both sides," wrote Baron von Riedesel. To the storm of shot and shell that fell upon the American fleet was added musketry from Captain Fraser's Indians and Canadians, who had landed from their canoes on the island and on the mainland west of the vessels. The crew of the *Royal Savage* was forced to abandon her. She was boarded by a boat's crew from the *Thunderer*, who turned her guns on her former friends. But they were soon driven off by the American fire. Another boat's crew, from the *Maria*, set her afire, and she blew up.

Meanwhile, the Americans' guns converged on the *Carleton*, Arnold himself sighting the guns of the *Congress*. She was hit time and again. Dacres was knocked senseless; another officer lost an arm. Edward Pellew, only a midshipman, a lad of nineteen, assumed command. After hours of fighting, the spring on her cable was shot away. Under the wind, she swung at her anchor, bows on to the enemy and, having no bow guns, hung there silenced, to be raked by every shot. Pringle on the *Maria* signaled her to withdraw, but she could not catch the wind so as to pay off on the right tack. Pellew climbed out on her bowsprit, under heavy musket fire, and tried to throw the jib over to make it draw, but without success. Two boats came to her assistance. Pellew, holding his position on the bowsprit in spite of a rain of musket-bullets, threw them a line, and the *Carleton* was towed away. She had been hulled several times, there was two feet of water in her hold, and half of her crew had been killed or wounded. Pellew further distinguished himself in later years, rising to the rank of admiral, and was honored with the title Viscount Exmouth.

Towards evening the *Inflexible* got within point-blank range and discharged five heavy broadsides against the American line, completely silencing its fire. But about five o'clock she dropped back to a distance of 700 yards from the Americans. The gunboats withdrew, and the whole British fleet anchored in a line across the southern end of the passage between Valcour and the mainland, keeping up a desultory fire until darkness fell.

The Americans took account of their injuries. The *Congress* had been hulled twelve times. She had two holes in her side between wind and water. Her mainmast was hit in two places. The *Washington* had also been severely punished and had one shot through her mainmast. The hull of the *Philadelphia* had been so damaged that she sank about an hour after the battle. All the sails of the fleet had been torn to tatters, and the rigging hung in tangles. The loss among the personnel was grievous; 60 had been either killed or wounded. Their store of ammunition was three-fourths gone. It was not possible to contemplate a renewal of the conflict on the morrow. It seemed that they were trapped and must surrender. But Arnold had another thought—to attempt an escape under the cover of night.

The night was dark. A heavy fog enshrouded the two fleets. A lantern, so hooded as to show a light only directly behind, was fixed in the stern of each vessel. At seven o'clock, the *Trumbull* galley got under way before a light northerly wind. The others fell in line at practicable intervals. The *Congress* and the *Washington* brought up the rear. And so, noiselessly, the whole line crept past the left of the British fleet, the fog so thick that none of the enemy's vessels could be seen. When they were beyond hearing distance the oars were got out, and the crews labored at them and at the pumps all through the night.

By dawn the *Trumbull* galley, with the *Revenge* and *Enterprise,* the *Lee* galley, and the gondolas *Boston, New Haven, Connecticut, Spitfire,* and *Success* had got ahead of the rest. The *Congress* and *Washington* galleys, the gondolas *Providence, New York,* and *Jersey,* which had made only eight miles, put in at Schuyler's Island. There the *New York* and *Providence* were found to be so badly damaged that their equipment was removed and they were sunk. The *Jersey* had run aground and, with the weight of water in her, could not be moved. The other two set out again early in the afternoon.

On discovering the escape of the Americans the next morning, Carleton immediately started after them. But, so upset was he by his surprise and rage, he forgot to give orders to his land forces. When within sight of Schuyler's Island he had to turn back to remedy his oversight.

The wind had shifted to the south, and, although Arnold put his men to the oars again, his battered galleys made little progress. By morning, after sixteen hours rowing, they had covered only six miles, and the pursuing British fleet, favored by a fresh northerly wind, which had not reached the Americans, was in sight in the rear. Also in sight, in front, were four American gondolas, which had been unable to keep up with the *Trumbull* and the others.

The *Inflexible,* the *Carleton,* and the *Maria* came on rapidly, the *Maria* ahead. At eleven o'clock, Arnold opened fire on her from his stern 9- and 12-pounders. But at Split Rock the pursuers caught up, and poured broadsides of grape and round shot upon the fleeing vessels. The *Washington* was overwhelmed by this fire. Waterbury struck her flag. In the course of the retreat, the *Lee,* like the *Jersey,* ran ashore and was abandoned; both were taken by the British.

But the *Congress* and the four gondolas kept on under the favoring wind, which had now caught up with them. For five glasses, two hours and a half, this unequal combat raged. The three British vessels, one on her broadside and two astern of her, concentrated their fire on the *Congress.* Her hull was shattered, her sails and rigging shot to rags, but there was no hint of surrender. Instead, Arnold signaled to the galleys to turn to windward so that the British sailing vessels could not follow, and to run for the east shore.

In Buttonmould Bay he beached his wrecks and set fire to them. He drew his men up on the shore and held them there until he was sure that his boats would blow up with their flags still flying, while the enemy stood off, keeping up a constant cannonade. The remains of his men, 200 in number—46 only of the *Congress* out of a crew of 73—started on a bridle path for Crown Point, ten miles away. They escaped an Indian ambush and reached the Point after dark, finding what was left of their fleet, the *Trumbull,* the *Enterprise,* the *Revenge,* the *Liberty,* and one gondola.

There was no stopping at Crown Point. Lieutenant Colonel Hartley and his garrison of the 6th Pennsylvania Regiment, together with Arnold's survivors, could not attempt to hold it. They burned all the buildings and retreated to Ticonderoga.[48]

A singular occurrence took place immediately upon their reaching that fort. A number of British rowboats came up under a flag of truce and delivered up General Waterbury and the entire crew of the *Washington*, 110 in number. Carleton had paroled them. This generous treatment made such an impression on the captives, and they were so loud in their praise of him, that it was thought dangerous to allow them to mingle with the others. They were immediately sent off on their way home.

Arnold had been utterly defeated, losing eleven of his sixteen vessels and 80 of his men; but his gallantry and theirs was not unrewarded. Indeed, the greatest American victories in the war thereafter were made possible by that desperate fight. The sequence of events is closely connected.

Carleton had been so delayed by the necessity of building a fleet to meet Arnold's, by his subsequent necessarily cautious maneuvering, and by the battle that he reconsidered his decision to attack Ticonderoga and withdrew all his army and his fleet from the lake to St. Johns. He felt that Ticonderoga was too strong to be carried by storm, and the season was too far advanced to allow siege operations. If he should be held up in the attack even for a short time he could not follow through to the Hudson in the winter and of course could not establish communication with Howe. If he could have reached Albany, the effect upon the American cause might have been disastrous. If he could have wintered at Ticonderoga and made it his base of supplies so as to start for the Hudson in the early spring, the British campaign might not have met with disaster in the next year at Saratoga. It was Saratoga that gave the needed encouragement to the French to send land and naval forces to aid the Americans. And those forces ensured the surrender at Yorktown and finished the war. Valcour Island was no defeat, therefore. "It was the American cause that was saved that day." [49]

Captain Alfred Thayer Mahan, the distinguished authority on naval affairs, has endorsed this view: "That the Americans were strong enough to impose the capitulation of Saratoga was due to the invaluable year of delay secured to them in 1776 by their little navy on Lake Champlain, created by the indomitable energy, and handled with the indomitable courage of the traitor, Benedict Arnold." [50]

CHAPTER 36

Burgoyne's Expedition

Canada in the winter of 1776–1777 had no attractions for Major General John Burgoyne. After the retirement of the British army in October, 1776, following the battle with Arnold at Valcour, there would be no more military operations in the North until the spring, which was not to be expected before May. A prospect of six months of idleness in Quebec or Montreal had little appeal to such a restless and ambitious spirit. He could look forward to active service at the end of that period; but the plans for that would not be made in Quebec, nor would commands be allotted there. London was headquarters.

This was his second visit to America. His first had been to Boston in 1775. There he had been subordinate to Gage, Howe, and Clinton and he had not relished that position. He wrote to Lord Rochford after Bunker Hill: "The inferiority of my station as youngest Major-General upon the staff left me almost a useless spectator. . . . My rank only serves to place me in a motionless, drowsy, irksome medium, or rather vacuum, too low for the honour of command, too high for that of execution." So he had gone home in December of that year.[1]

He came back in the spring of 1776, but again as a subordinate, second in command to Carleton. It was Carleton. not he, that had won the victory at Valcour. It might be Carleton that would lead the King's forces in Canada in the coming campaign of 1777. Plainly, something should be done about it. So he went home again.[2]

In London he found conditions favorable to his ambition. Carleton was definitely out of favor. The King had been disappointed and vexed at his failure to press on after Valcour and take Ticonderoga. So had the country in general, including Lord George Germain, colonial secretary, responsible for the conduct of the war in America.

At first Germain was inclined to couple Burgoyne with Carleton as blameworthy for that failure. But there was another element in Germain's feelings toward Carleton, a bitter personal animosity antedating Valcour. He was glad to put all the blame on him, eager, indeed, when he observed the King's attitude towards Burgoyne.[3]

The King had shown a friendly face to the general. "Yesterday morning," announced the *Morning Chronicle* early in January, "his Majesty took an outing on horseback in Hyde Park upwards of an hour, attended by General Burgoyne." [4] Indeed, his Majesty had already indicated to Lord North his pleasure that Burgoyne should command operations from Canada in the spring.

So everything was going smoothly, and Burgoyne did nothing to cause friction. He did not intrigue against Carleton, criticized him not at all—indeed he defended him—and so aroused no opposition among that general's friends. To aid his own cause, he wrote and submitted to the King a paper entitled "Thoughts for Conducting the War from the Side of Canada," which, because of its results, was a very important document of the Revolution.

Burgoyne's plan assumed a strong American force at Ticonderoga, perhaps as many as 12,000 men. It called for a British army of 8,000 regulars, with a sufficient equipment of artillery, supplemented by "a corps of watermen," 2,000 Canadians, and "1000 or more savages." Of this force, he would leave 3,000 to hold Canada. He proposed, after establishing magazines at Crown Point, to embark the rest upon Lake Champlain. Ticonderoga was to be attacked and reduced "early in the summer."

After that, the advance should proceed, preferably by way of Lake George and the Hudson, to Albany. Or, if the enemy should be found on that route in too great force, it should go to Albany by the lower end of Champlain, through Skenesboro and the Hudson. In either case, a chain of posts should be established along the route of the expedition to secure its communications. From Albany, after the end of the campaign, Burgoyne was to establish contact with Howe. He did not expect Howe to send forces northward during the campaign to support him. He would have sufficient strength to reach Albany and to maintain himself there.

Burgoyne also proposed an auxiliary expedition to the same objective, but by way of Lake Ontario, Oswego, and the Mohawk River, which empties into the Hudson near Albany. He did not enlarge upon the advantages of his scheme, nor even specifically suggest its strategic purpose; but an already prevailing idea among the British high command was that holding the Hudson, and thus separating the New England colonies from the rest, was a matter of the first importance to the success of the King's arms in America.

Burgoyne was tactfully silent as to the command of the expedition, except by an indirect reference to it. This business, he said, would depend for its success upon the cooperation of the governor of Canada; to wit, Carleton. His "peremptory powers, warm zeal and consonant opinion" must be had, else "plausible obstructions . . . will be sufficient to crush such exertions as an officer of a sanguine temper, entrusted with the future conduct of the campaign and whose personal interest and fame therefore consequently depend upon a timely out-set, would be led to make." Clearly, Carleton was not suggested for the leadership.[5]

The King liked the plan. Its outlines, he said, seemed to be "on a proper foundation." The Mohawk River diversion, he also approved. Germain issued the necessary orders in a letter to Carleton. He was to remain in Canada and guard that province with 3,770 men of specified British and German regiments, including McLean's Royal Highland Emigrants, and detach Burgoyne with the remainder of the troops, 7,173 in number, "to proceed with all possible expedition to join General Howe and put himself under his command." He was also to furnish Lieutenant Colonel Barry St. Leger with 675 men, "together with a sufficient number of Canadians and Indians," for the Mohawk expedition.[6]

"I shall write to Sir William Howe," Germain went on, "from hence by the first packet." But Carleton, Burgoyne, and St. Leger were also to inform Howe of the plan, so that they might receive instructions from him.[7]

Germain's letter to Carleton was long and insultingly specific in its details. Not only so, but it also charged Carleton with "supineness" in his failure to attack Ticonderoga, and even blamed him for the defeat of the Hessians at Trenton, because that failure had set free American troops to act with Washington against the Jersey outpost.[8]

Such a letter was enough to anger Carleton, and it did. He wrote a spirited reply, defending his actions in forcible language. But, magnanimous man that he was, he added that, in spite of the "Slight, Disregard and Censure" visited upon him, he would give Burgoyne all possible assistance.[9] And he did.

Looking backward, one observes the weaknesses, indeed the stupidity, of Burgoyne's plan. There was little to be gained by a march from Canada to Albany. The cutting of communications between New England and the other colonies, if it had been possible, could have had important results only after the passage of time. And it was necessary that the war be won before Britain's financial resources should be overstrained, and before France should take advantage of the American situation to win revenge for the many defeats Britain had inflicted upon her. The troops set aside for Burgoyne's expedition could have given Howe useful added strength, even strength perhaps sufficient for a final destruction of Washington's army. Further, Burgoyne's army under the plan was to cooperate with Howe's only *after* the end of the campaign. It was to reach Albany unsupported from the south; and Howe was authorized by Lord Germain to move against Philadelphia by sea, leaving only a garrison force in New York. Burgoyne was to travel through the woods to Albany, with an ever lengthening line of communications and with no assurance of help even at Albany, should he need it. Germain finally saw this defect in the plan, perhaps not too clearly, and got off a letter to Howe suggesting that he cooperate with Burgoyne during the campaign. But Howe received Germain's letter in August while he was en route by sea to Chesapeake Bay, and he could hardly act to help Burgoyne at such a late time—at least he could not without completely disrupting his own plan of operation. He did make a gesture toward assisting Burgoyne by asking Clinton, who was in command of the garrison at New York, to do what he could to help his fellow general.[10]

Burgoyne arrived at Quebec on May 6, 1777. Spring had just come; the ice in the river had broken up, "with a most astonishing noise," one week before. He found the troops, after a mild winter, in good condition, except their clothing. New uniforms to replace those worn in last year's campaign had not come from England. To patch the old ones, the tails of the coats of the British regiments had been cut off. They all now wore short jackets, like the regulation coats of the light infantry. Their cocked hats had been cut down into caps. But these alterations were all for the better in forest warfare.[11]

The Brunswickers, too, were far from smart in their appearance. Their duke, in his prudent care for his own purse, had sent them out in worn uniforms and old shoes, and Canada had not afforded complete replacements. But all such matters were merely surface. The substance was sound.

There was one difference in uniforms, however, between the British and German contingents that was important. While the British uniforms had been modeled after those of the army of Germany and were too heavy, too awkward, too tight, and too elaborate for rough campaigning in America, those of these Brunswickers were far worse in all of these respects. Their dragoons, who had come without horses and were to serve dismounted to the end of the campaign, were most preposterously equipped for such service. Their great cocked hats, ornamented with a long plume, their hair worn in a long, stiff queue, their tight, thick coats, their stiff leather breeches, their huge leather gauntlets almost elbow-length, their great jack boots reaching to mid-thigh, weighing twelve pounds a pair without the long brass spurs always worn even on the march, made up as unsuitable an outfit for marching and fighting in a forested wilderness in an American midsummer as could have been devised by the most ingenious. Add to that a long, straight broadsword to trail at the thigh and a short heavy carbine, and one could have no feeling but pity for a Brunswick dragoon.[12]

So much for the main force of British and German regulars; they were fit and ready to go. The same could not be said for the irregular auxiliaries included in the plan. After all, they were French; and, however willing they had been in Montcalm's time to fight for their flag, this war meant little or nothing to them. Instead of the desired 2,000, Burgoyne could round up only 150. The Tories were also backward; only 100 enlisted. With the Indians he had somewhat better luck. He got 400 of the 1,000 he wanted. They were collected and led by La Corne St. Luc and Charles de Langlade.[13]

For his navy, he had the *Inflexible,* the *Maria,* the *Carleton,* the *Loyal Convert,* and the *Thunderer* of last year's fleet. To these were added the *Washington*, the *Jersey*, and the *Lee*, taken from Arnold after Valcour, another ship-rigged vessel, built that winter at St. Johns, the *Royal George,* and twenty-eight of last year's gunboats. Of bateaux for the transport of troops, there was an ample number.[14]

In his artillery section there were 138 guns, ranging from little 4.4-inch mortars and light 3-pounders to heavy 24-pounders. But many of these were mounted in the vessels, others were to be left at St. Johns, others at Ticonderoga and Fort George after they were taken. His field train for the whole expedition was to consist of 42 guns, large and small.[15]

The British advance corps was composed of the 24th regiment, the light infantry, and the grenadiers, including not only those of the expeditionary regiments, but also the flank companies of the 29th, 31st, and 24th, whose "battalion companies" remained in Canada.[16] This corps was under Brigadier General Simon Fraser. The 1st Brigade, the 9th, 47th, and 53rd regiments, was under Brigadier General Powell; the 2nd brigade, the 20th, 21st, and 62nd regiments, under Brigadier General Hamilton. This division constituted the right wing of the army and was under command of Major General William Phillips.

The German advance corps consisted of grenadiers and light infantry, including a company of forty jägers and forty "marksmen" selected from the different British regiments. This whole corps was commanded by Lieutenant Colonel Breymann. The 1st brigade, the Riedesel, Specht, and Rhetz regiments, was under Brigadier Specht; the 2nd brigade, the Prince Frederick and Hesse Hanau regiments, was under Brigadier Gall. This division was the left wing, commanded by Major General von Riedesel.[17]

The British infantry division numbered 3,724 rank and file, the German 3,016. The guns were to be divided between the two and served by 245 regular British artillerymen, 150 men drawn from the infantry, and 78 of the Hesse Hanau artillery company. The Canadian and Tory volunteers were to cover the British right wing, the Indians to cover the German left wing. The Brunswick dismounted dragoons were to act as reserves. In all the army numbered 7,213 rank and file.[18]

It was not a large army, but it was, for its size, a strong fighting force composed of trained, disciplined, and experienced men, under capable officers. Burgoyne, though not a military leader of the first or even second class, was an active, resolute, courageous soldier, well versed in the arts of war and, what is very important in such an extensive expedition as was about to be undertaken, he had the trust and confidence of his men. General Phillips, second in command, had served for twenty years in the British army. He was a distinguished artillerist and an exceptionally able strategist. Fraser was a scion of the noble Scotch house of Lovat. He, too, had had long experience as a soldier, had served with Wolfe at Louisburg and Quebec, and had acquired a high reputation for energy, activity, and good judgment coupled with cool daring. Hamilton had attained his command solely because of his professional merits and accomplishments. Kingston, the adjutant general, had served with distinction under Burgoyne in Portugal. Major the Earl of Balcarres, commanding the light infantry, and Major Acland of the grenadiers were officers of high professional attainments and undoubted courage.[19]

Of the Germans, Baron von Riedesel was the most distinguished. He had been a soldier in the Hessian and Brunswick armies for more than twenty years. At the outbreak of the Seven Years' War he was attached to the staff of the Duke of Brunswick and was employed by him in special duties which called for the use of delicate tact, good judgment, and personal courage. His reputation for intrepidity thus established was later confirmed by his conduct in many dangerous enterprises. He possessed the essential qualities of a good soldier; he was cool and discreet in danger, swift in action. His clear understanding had been studiously applied to the principles of his profession, and now, at the age of thirty-eight, he was at the height of his mental and physical powers. He was of medium height, strongly built, vigorous and hardy. His florid face was full and round, his features regular, his blue eyes notably large and clear. His amiable disposition was displayed in his care for the comfort and well-being of his men.[20] Under his leadership, backed by such experienced professional soldiers as his subordinate officers, the German contingent in Burgoyne's army was bound to give a good account of itself.

Burgoyne's troops were first assembled at St. Johns. There, on June 13, was enacted a bit of pageantry strange to that wilderness. On the *Thunderer,* moored in the river, there was erected the royal standard of Britain, bravely displaying on its embroidered silken fabric the golden lions of England, the red lion of Scotland, the harp of Ireland and, somewhat reminiscently, the fleur-de-lis of France. This symbol of Britain's might was then saluted by a discharge of all the guns of the fleet and in the fort.[21]

Still further to impress the Americans with the majesty of the laws they flouted, Burgoyne a week later issued a proclamation, in language which, according to a contemporary pamphleteer, was characterized by "the tinsel splendor of enlightened absurdity." It was Burgoyne the dramatist at his worst, at his almost unbelievable worst. It is difficult for one reading it now to realize that it is not a parody of some less bombastic manifesto.

Among other emotional appeals, it called upon "the suffering thousands," that is to say, the Tories, in the colonies to declare whether they were not subject to "the completest system of Tyranny that ever God in his displeasure suffer'd for a time to be exercised over a froward and stubborn Generation." It declared that "persecution and torture, unprecedented in the inquisitions of the Romish Church, are among the palpable enormities that verify the affirmative." To consummate this tyranny, it said, "the profanation of Religion is added to the most profligate prostitution of common sense." And so it went on to offer encouragement and protection to all who would take part in "the glorious task of redeeming their Countrymen from dungeons" and reestablishing the rule of the King.

The writer gave warning to those who persisted in this "unnatural Rebellion," that he had but "to give stretch" to his Indian auxiliaries, "and they amount to thousands," to overtake such recalcitrants "wherever they may lurk," for which vengeance upon those persisting in "the phrenzy of hostility" he would "stand acquitted in the Eyes of God and Men." There was a final warning uttered in "Consciousness of Christianity," that "devastation, famine and every concomitant horror that a reluctant but indispensable prosecution of military duty must occasion" awaited the impenitent.[22]

Instead of frightening the rebellious Americans, it first made them angry, then made them laugh. Parodies by the dozen appeared, notably an excellent one by Francis Hopkinson.[23] In England, there was a similar reaction. Horace Walpole called its author "the vaporing Burgoyne," "Pomposo," and "Hurlothrumbo," and remarked upon one who with "consciousness of Christianity" could "reconcile the scalping knife with the Gospel." [24]

A few days after the issuance of that rodomontade, Burgoyne addressed a council of his Indian auxiliaries in equally high-flown language. "Warriors, you are free—go forth in might and valor of your cause—strike at the common enemies of Great Britain and America—disturbers of public order, peace and happiness, destroyers of commerce, parricides of state," and so on at length, an incitement to the usual methods of savage warfare, if ever there was one, it seemed. But no, not that. "I positively forbid bloodshed, when you are not opposed in arms. Aged men, women, children and prisoners must be held sacred from the knife or hatchet, even in actual conflict." After that speech, the savage instincts of the Indians were tamed and subdued, their excitable natures sobered by a distribution of rum and by a "war-dance, in which they threw themselves in various postures, every now and then making most hideous yells." [25]

Again Burgoyne, a good soldier afflicted with a mania for the pen, exposed himself to ridicule. Walpole called it "still more supernatural" than his proclamation. Edmund Burke blasted it in the House of Commons. He supposed a riot on Tower Hill, where the royal menagerie was kept. "What would the Keeper of His Majesty's lions do? Would he not fling open the dens of the wild beasts and then address them thus? 'My gentle lions—my humane bears—my tender-hearted hyenas, go forth! But I exhort you, as you are Christians and members of civilized society, to take care not to hurt any man, woman or child!' " And Lord North, who had sanctioned the employment of the Indians, laughed until the tears ran down his cheeks.[26]

Ticonderoga, familiar name to British and Americans alike by 1777, is a bold, squarish, blunt-nosed promontory a mile long and three-quarters of a mile wide, that juts out from the western side of Lake Champlain, whose waters wash its base on the north, east, and south. At the foot of its southwest shoulder a very narrow gorge extends westward a mile or more, through which the waters of Lake George are poured into Champlain. The highest elevation on the promontory is about seventy feet above the lake.

From the east side of Champlain, another headland, a rocky bluff thirty to fifty feet high called Mount Independence, is thrust out towards the southeast corner of Ticonderoga. The points of the two narrow the lake to a width of about a quarter of a mile. This is the gateway from the upper lake to the lower, also to Lake George. Having passed through it one may go on by water directly south into the narrow, upper end of Champlain, and from its extremity up Wood Creek to within a few miles of the upper reaches of the Hudson. Or one may turn aside at Ticonderoga into Lake George and follow it to a point as near the Hudson.

About two miles to the northwest of the nose of Ticonderoga, Mount Hope commands the road to Lake George. A mile to the southwest, another hill, called Sugar Loaf from its conical appearance as seen from the east—but renamed Mount Defiance by the British after its capture—rises 750 feet above the water. At this time both shores of the lake and all the mentioned heights, except where Ticonderoga had been cleared for its fortification, were densely forested.

As has been hereinbefore stated, the French had built a star-shaped stone fort, with five bastions, on Ticonderoga in 1755. When it was attacked by Jeffrey Amherst in 1759 its retreating garrison blew up a large part of it. The British rebuilt it in less substantial fashion; but after the Peace of Paris, in 1763, it was allowed to fall into decay, though a considerable part of it, facing the lake, was still in serviceable condition in 1777.

While the French held it, they had constructed lines, extending in a curve across the promontory, about three-quarters of a mile behind the fort. These were built of logs heaped upon one another to a height of eight feet, covered with earth and faced with an abatis.

After the evacuation of Crown Point in July, 1776, and the concentration of the American troops at Ticonderoga, vigorous efforts were made to strengthen its defenses. The remains of the old fort were to some extent repaired. Blockhouses were built to protect the flanks and rear of the old French lines, which had been enlarged. Other blockhouses, also breastworks and small redoubts, defended the lower slopes on the north and south and various other points.

On Mount Hope a new barbette battery was built in a position covering the slope down to the outlet of Lake George and the road which ran south along its shore.

Across the lake Mount Independence showed a high, rugged, precipitous face. Its rear was protected naturally by a creek and a wide and deep morass, artificially by batteries and a strong, stone breastwork cleverly designed to take advantage of the irregularities of the ground. On its summit, an eight-pointed star redoubt, enclosing barracks, was the citadel of that position.

To close the water gateway, a boom of heavy logs, strung together on a massive iron chain, was stretched across from the northern point of Independence to the southern corner of Ticonderoga. Behind it, for communication between the two, was a bridge.

The plan of these works was suggested by Colonel John Trumbull; they were designed by the Polish engineer, Colonel Thaddeus Kosciuszko. Trumbull had proposed fortifying Sugar Loaf, but Gates had declared that it was an entirely inaccessible height and could therefore neither be fortified by him, nor be possessed by the enemy. Although Trumbull, Wayne, and game-legged Arnold climbed its steepest face, the eastern side, to the top, and although the northwest side was much less steep and difficult, Gates adhered to his decision not to try to fortify it.

A return of the troops at this post, dated June 28, 1777, showed ten Continental and two militia regiments, but they were slim regiments, ranging in number from 45 rank and file, present and fit, to 265, the average being 160. There were also Benjamin Whitcomb's little corps of 19 scouts, Thomas Lee's Rangers numbering 23, 124 artificers, and 250 in the artillery section. In all, including officers, the garrison might be estimated at 2,500.[27] The outside lines around Mount Independence plus the old French lines behind Ticonderoga were over 2,000 yards long. Even distributed along them in one thin line, with no reserves, no allowance for a force to hold Mount Hope, the blockhouses, and other works, there would have been one man for each yard, a mere skeleton defense. To man the works properly, at least five times the number of that garrison were necessary.

In chief command was Major General Arthur St. Clair. Born in Scotland, he had served in the British army in the French and Indian War, earning distinction at the siege of Louisburg and the capture of Quebec. Having married an American lady of wealth, he left the British service and established a home in Pennsylvania. He took the side of the rebels and was commissioned colonel of the 2nd Pennsylvania battalion in January, 1776. He was creditably concerned in the retreat across the Jerseys and the battles of Trenton and Princeton, as well as in the disaster at Trois Rivières. In February, 1777, the Congress appointed him a major general. He had been selected by Gates to command at Ticonderoga and had arrived at that post on June 12, 1777.

He was now past his fortieth year, tall, well built, and handsome in figure. His features were regular, his blue-gray eyes clear and intelligent, his hair reddish brown.[28] His manners were easy and graceful. Though his service during the war was competent to a degree, it cannot be said that he showed the capacity, the military ability, that would have justified his appointment as major general. A brigadier's rank would have been more suitable to his qualifications.

Serving under St. Clair at that post were three brigadier generals, the Frenchman Matthias Alexis Roche de Fermoy, John Paterson of Massachusetts, and Enoch Poor of New Hampshire, none of whom achieved distinction in the war.

The condition of internal affairs at Ticonderoga was far from satisfactory. There were not only too few men, there was too little of everything—arms, equipment, ammunition, supplies, and even food and clothing.[29] Schuyler came up from Albany and held a council of war with the four Ticonderoga generals on June 20. They agreed that there were too few troops to hold the whole works; that, nevertheless, they should hold on as long as possible and then concentrate all their force on Independence, which they might be able to hold as long as their food lasted; that bateaux should be kept ready for a final retreat.[30]

How they expected to get the troops safely across to Independence in the face of an enemy force that had beaten them out of Ticonderoga, how they expected to preserve that fleet of bateaux and to make that retreat, after the enemy held Ticonderoga and possessed the water gate, seem not to have been considered. But those questions are, after all, merely academic. They never had to be answered.

Two days before that council was held Burgoyne's entire force had assembled at Cumberland Head. It was there that he issued his great manifesto. From that point, the progress of the fleet and army was smooth and deliberate at the rate of eighteen to twenty miles a day.

Twenty or more great canoes, each holding twenty Indians, with another fleet bearing the Canadians and Tories dressed—or undressed—like Indians, formed the vanguard. Then came the gunboats and the bateaux of the British advance, the 24th regiment, the light infantry, and the grenadiers. The fleet was next in line, the tall-masted, square-sailed *Inflexible* and *Royal George*; the two schooners *Carleton* and *Maria*; the gondola *Loyal Convert*; the huge, unwieldy, absurd radeau *Thunderer*, that would "neither row nor sail" [31] but had to be got along somehow; the captives of last year's encounter, the galley *Washington*, the cutter *Lee*, and the gondola *Jersey*; and the gunboats, twenty-four of them.

After the fleet came the bateaux of the 1st British brigade "in the greatest order and regularity," [32] and then Burgoyne and his two major generals, Riedesel and Phillips, each in his own pinnace. The British 2nd brigade was followed by the two German brigades. Ignominiously, the tail of the procession was a motley fleet of boats of all kinds carrying the sutlers, the women, and all the raggle-taggle of camp followers that hung on the rear of the armies of that day.[33]

Against a setting of the blue waters of the lake and the dark green background of its forested shores, the painted faces and bodies of hundreds of Indians and their make-believe savage companions, the masses of British scarlet and of German dark blue, the green of the jägers and the light blue of the dragoons, with their regimental facings of every hue, the shining brass of the tall hats of the Hessian grenadiers, the glinting of the sunlight upon polished musket barrels and bayonets, the flashing of thousands of wet paddles and oars made up a spectacular pageant, brilliant in its color, light, and motion, thrilling in its purpose and intention.

On the 26th General Fraser's advance corps left Crown Point, where the army had by that time been concentrated, and pushed on ahead with the Indians, Canadians, and Tories. On July 1, "the weather being fine," the main army divided, the British taking the west side of the lake, the Germans the east side. The whole expanse of the lake, a mile wide, was "cover'd with Boats or Batteaux's"; as Lieutenant Hadden wrote, "some of the Armed Vessels accompanied us, the Music and Drums of the different Regiments were continually playing and contributed to make the Scene and passage extremely pleasant." [34] Three miles above Ticonderoga, the British landed and encamped on their side, the Germans opposite them. Fraser was a mile in advance. Early the next day the operations against the forts began.[35]

General Phillips, commanding Fraser's advance strengthened by one British brigade, started for Mount Hope. Its garrison set the works on fire, ran down the steep, rear slope and fled to the old French lines, a sensible proceeding proving the folly of the occupation of that outpost so far from the main defenses. A quick movement by the British might have cut off the retreating Americans; but not until one o'clock did they occupy the abandoned position and send Captain Fraser with his Indians and British marksmen on a circuit around the hill for that purpose. Finding no one to cut off, they went on towards the old French lines, drove in a picket of sixty men, approached within less than a hundred yards of the lines, took cover in the woods, and opened fire. St. Clair, thinking that this was a prelude to an assault at that point, ordered its defenders to sit down on the fire steps, keep under cover, and hold their fire. But, when tempted by the very near approach of one of the British marksmen, Lieutenant Colonel James Wilkinson ordered a sergeant to take a shot at him.

At the sound of that single discharge, the entire force within the old

French lines jumped to their feet, mounted the fire steps, and loosed a volley, then another and another. The artillery joined in the fusillade. When at last the officers had succeeded in stopping these unauthorized pyrotechnics and the smoke had cleared away, it was seen that the enemy had retreated to 300 yards' distance, leaving but one man lying on the field, the man Wilkinson had ordered shot. But when a corporal's guard went on to fetch him in and bury him, he was found to be unhurt. He was merely drunk. At least 3,000 musket shots had been fired and eight pieces of artillery had been discharged; yet only one man of 500—all within 80 to 100 yards—had been killed and two wounded.[36]

In the meantime, Riedesel's division had advanced close to the creek behind Independence and had been fired on. But darkness fell before any nearer hostile move could be made. The next day, Mount Hope was occupied in force by the British, and there was a certain amount of cannonading of little avail to either side. But something less noisy, that was to prove immediately decisive of the contest, was on foot.

Burgyone sent Lieutenant Twiss, his chief engineer, to take a look at that neglected Sugar Loaf. Twiss climbed its northwest flank, came back, and reported that it commanded Ticonderoga at 1,400 yards and Independence at 1,500. He could open a road and have guns up there within twenty-four hours. Burgoyne gave the orders. Phillips took charge. "Where a goat can go," said he, "a man can go and where a man can go he can drag a gun." [37] On July 4 the engineers were at work on the road.

St. Clair had been strengthened by the arrival of 900 fresh militiamen. He was looking for an assault on some part of his works, but there seemed to be little enemy activity. Yet there were movements. Burgoyne took Gall's brigade from Riedesel and moved it to the Ticonderoga side, giving him in exchange Fraser's Indians, Canadians, Tories, and British "marksmen." Riedesel was to move to the south around Independence and close the way of retreat by the road on that side of the lake, the guns on Sugar Loaf being expected to prevent any embarkation for retreat by water. But Riedesel had not yet begun his circuitous move.[38]

On the morning of July 5, St. Clair took a good look at something moving on the top of Sugar Loaf. Were there men up there? There were and something else, two guns, 12-pounders, not yet mounted, but on the way to be. He turned to his adjutant, Wilkinson. "We must away from this," said he, "for our situation has become a desperate one." [39] At least, that is the way Wilkinson reports his speech. Doubtless St. Clair was more brief and less stilted.

A council of war, immediately held, promptly and unanimously voted to give up the forts and retreat. But the withdrawal could not be begun by day, in full sight of the enemy. The night promised concealment. There would be a new moon, setting early and leaving comforting darkness.[40]

The relics of Arnold's Valcour fleet, the *Trumbull* and *Gates* galleys, the schooners *Liberty* and *Revenge,* and the sloop *Enterprise,* had been anchored in line across the narrow water behind the bridge. More than two hundred bateaux and other small craft lay beyond these. It was decided to use all these vessels to transport, up the lake to Skenesboro, the invalids and as much of the artillery and stores as could be got away. The main force would march from the east side by a road that ran from behind Independence southeast to Hubbardton, thence around Lake Bomoseen to Castleton and thence west to Skenesboro.

To drown the noise of the preparations for departure and divert the enemy's attention, the heavy guns in the forts and the various batteries opened fire as darkness fell. When it was quite dark, the embarkation of the invalids and stores began. Colonel Pierce Long of New Hampshire, with four or five hundred effectives, was in charge of the boats. The work of loading them was toilsome, and its progress slow, because everything that was got away had to be carried on men's backs from the forts to the spot where the boats were moored.

The cannonade was continuous and thunderous throughout the evening. What the enemy thought of this apparently senseless waste of powder does not appear. One might have supposed that it would lead them to suspect just what was actually in progress. Another signal was a fierce burst of flame from the Independence fort. General Roche de Fermoy had adopted the "scorched earth" policy by setting his headquarters ablaze rather inopportunely. Indeed, some of the enemy were moved to speculate whether the Americans "were meditating an attack or . . . were retreating." [41] But it was not until about daybreak that General Fraser had definite information of the retreat, from three American deserters.

Fraser's headquarters were on the Ticonderoga side, a mile and a half from the bridge. Hurrying to it with his troops, he found that it was partially destroyed, also that several fieldpieces at the farther end were trained down its length. Four men had been left there to fire one blast at the enemy attempting to cross, and then to retire.

But when Fraser's men made a tentative approach nothing happened. They pushed on to find all four gunners lying dead drunk beside a cask of

Madeira. Only one of the guns was fired, by an Indian who picked up a lighted slow match and carelessly dropped a spark upon its priming. Fortunately for those on the bridge, the gun was elevated to such a degree that it fired over their heads.[42]

Burgoyne ordered Fraser's light infantry and grenadiers to pursue the main force of the Americans retreating by land, and directed Riedesel, with his own regiment and Breymann's grenadiers and light troops, to follow in support. The 62nd British regiment was put in charge of Ticonderoga, and Prince Frederick's Brunswickers of Independence. The British fleet was to go on up the lake after the American boats.[43]

It was along but a pretense of a road that St. Clair led his troops towards Hubbardton, a mere wagon track, new, rough, rutted, and spotted with stumps of trees. It ran up hill and down across a broken country, "a continuous succession of steep and woody hills," [44] interspersed with ponds, swamps, and streams. The day, July 6, became hotter and hotter as it wore on. Over that road, shut in on both sides by dense forest walls, there were no cooling breezes, and the men sweltered in the overpowering heat. But there was no stopping until they had gone twenty-four miles and, through a high notch in a line of hills, had come down into Hubbardton, a hamlet of two houses. Even then they did not rest long. Six miles more would bring them to Castleton, where they would be within thirteen or fourteen miles of Skenesboro. St. Clair pushed his men on to that point before night.

Colonel Seth Warner of Vermont was left at Hubbardton with 150 men, under orders to wait until the rear guard came up and then follow closely after the main body. But Colonel Warner, brave and patriotic though he was, lacked discipline. He had been a Green Mountain Boy, accustomed to acting on his own and taking orders from nobody. Instead of bringing on the rear guard, he and Colonel Francis, its commander, agreed to spend the night at Hubbardton. So three regiments, Warner's Vermonters, Francis's 11th Massachusetts, Colonel Hale's 2nd New Hampshires, and a number of stragglers from the main body bivouacked there.[45]

Fraser lost no more time than St. Clair. Starting at four o'clock in the morning, his men marched along the same road until one in the afternoon. Riedesel, behind them, was equally vigorous. When Fraser paused for breath at one o'clock Riedesel himself, with a company of jägers and about 80 grenadiers, came up. He and Fraser decided to go a few miles farther, rest for the night, and go on at three the next morning. They camped within a short distance at Hubbardton.[46]

The careless Americans had thrown out no pickets. They were all together around their campfires cooking breakfast when Fraser and Riedesel, whose Indians had scouted the American camp the night before, marched unobserved through the notch north of the camp. Close to the camp, they deployed their 750 men and charged upon the nearest body, Hale's New Hampshires.

The surprise was complete. Hale and his men fled in disorder, each man for himself. Warner and Francis had but a few minutes to get into fighting order, but they stood their ground and gave the enemy a volley that struck down 21 men. Major Grant of the 24th was killed, the Earl of Balcarres wounded. This was the opening of a bitter fight.[47]

The ground was all forest, covered with standing trees, fallen trees, and underbrush. For the Americans, it was the best of cover. For the British and Germans it was a tangle in which there could be no orderly fighting. Warner's men held the left of an irregular American line, with an extremely steep hill, called Zion, on their left. Francis had the right upon a smaller rise of ground. The whole line extended about half a mile.

Fraser moved to turn the American left, drawing men from his own left to strengthen his right. When he was ready he ordered his grenadiers to go over Zion Hill. It was an almost precipitous ascent. The grenadiers had to sling their muskets, grasp tree branches, bushes, and rocks, and scramble up on all fours. They made it and took a position behind Francis and astride the road to Castleton.[48]

But Francis had adopted Fraser's tactics in reverse. He edged towards the weakened British left. Some of Hale's men were now coming back to fight. The firing was heavy. Major Acland commanding the British grenadiers had been wounded. That movement of the grenadiers around Francis had yielded no good results. The situation for the British was worse than unpromising. In his desperation Fraser was about to order a bayonet charge when there broke on the ears of all the combatants a surprising sound of fifes and hautboys, trumpets and drums playing a German hymn, and of hundreds of lusty German voices singing it. It was the equivalent of the Scottish pipes at Lucknow. The Brunswicks were coming! [49]

Riedesel had heard the firing and had come on with the same advance guard as on the day before. The rest of his troops were following. At Castleton, St. Clair also had heard it. Two of his militia regiments, with their customary freedom from restraint, had dropped away from his marching men the night before and had encamped only two miles from Hubbardton. He sent them orders to go to the aid of Warner and Francis. They refused and hurried on to Castleton.[50]

Without waiting for the rest of his men, Riedesel sent his jägers straight against the American right. The grenadiers, he ordered to try to turn that flank. The jägers, with a band ahead playing as if on parade, marched boldly forward. Francis's troops held their ground for ten minutes, firing as fast as they could in reply to the Brunswickers' volleys. But the turning movement had begun to envelop their right. Francis was shot down, and when Fraser's bayonet charge developed, the Massachusetts men broke and disappeared in the woods. Warner and his Vermonters had been doing well, but when their companions retreated, they could hold out no longer. Warner gave the order, "Scatter and meet me at Manchester." His force at once evaporated. Twelve guns were taken by the enemy.[51]

There had been sharp fighting in that little forty-minute battle. The enemy lost 15 officers and 183 men, killed or wounded.[52] The American casualties, including those captured, were 12 officers and 312 men, out of a force which after Hale's defection did not much exceed 600 fighting men. Hale and about 70 of his men were captured in their retreat. Though of miniature dimensions, that battle was, in proportion to the numbers engaged, as bloody as Waterloo.

In the meantime, the American fleet was pursuing a leisurely course up the lake for Skenesboro. There was no hurry. There was behind them that boom of great logs strung along a massive chain made of inch-and-a-half iron bars. This was backed by a bridge supported by twenty-two piers of timber. Between these piers were floats fifty feet long and thirteen feet wide made of logs "fastened together by rivetted bolts and double chains." It would take some time to cut through that. Colonel Long, in command of the boats, was sure he had a day's start, so he wasted no effort on trying to block the extremely narrow and, in places, tortuous channel.[53]

But he was mistaken in his confidence in the boom. Immediately on the discovery of the retreat from Ticonderoga, British gunboats were brought up, "a few well directed cannon-shots broke in two the collossal chain upon which so many hopes had hung." [54] The bridge piers were cut through. Within a few hours after Long's boats had started, the British fleet was running before a northerly wind up the lake after them. Long's men had landed at Skenesboro at one o'clock. At three o'clock Burgoyne was within three miles of them.

He landed three regiments with orders to get across Wood Creek, a small stream on which Skenesboro was situated and a part of the water road to the south, flowing into the extreme upper end of Champlain just above the mouth of South Bay. They were also to occupy the road to Fort Ann, the only other avenue of retreat to the south. After waiting awhile to give time for this operation, Burgoyne went on with his fleet to attack Skenesboro.

Long, however, had wisely decided that the weak stockaded fort at that place was not tenable against the strong force of the enemy and had sent his invalids and women up the creek, with enough sound men to row the boats. With the rest, he set about destroying the fort. The stockade, the barracks, and other buildings were set on fire. Burgoyne arrived in time to capture the *Trumbull* galley and the schooner *Revenge*, but the *Enterprise*, the *Liberty*, and the *Gates* and everything else combustible that had been brought from Ticonderoga went up in flames. What would not burn was abandoned, and Long, with the remains of his soldiers, about 150, hurried away down the Fort Ann road.[55]

Assuming that the three regiments already sent forward had gained their desired positions to intercept Long's retreat, Burgoyne dispatched Lieutenant Colonel Hill with the 9th Regiment after him early the next morning. But the three regiments were so delayed in getting over a thickly forested ridge that Long got to Fort Ann without interruption. Hill, however, pushed on after him.[56]

The road was in dreadful condition, and its bridges had been broken down. Hill made only ten miles that day. He lay that night within a mile of the fort. Early the next morning an American came to the camp, announced himself as a deserter, and told Hill there was a garrison of a thousand in the fort. Hill had but 190 of all ranks. He sent to Burgoyne for reinforcements.

The "deserter" got away secretly and told Long of Hill's weakness. Long had, indeed, received an addition, 400 New York militiamen under Colonel Henry Van Rensselaer. He now turned on Hill, whose force lay in a narrow, heavily wooded space between Wood Creek and a steep, almost precipitous, rugged ridge.

There was no possibility of regular battle formation on either side. Parties of the Americans crossed the creek and fired on Hill's left, crossed it again, and gained his rear. Although their voices were audible, they were invisible. All he knew was that he seemed to be surrounded. He ordered his men up the steep slope that hemmed them in. With great difficulty they got up, faced about, and held the ridge for about two hours of fairly heavy fire on both sides. Hill's ammunition was running low. Nothing had been heard from Burgoyne. He was about at the end of his tether, when from the woods to the north he heard an Indian war whoop.[57]

The Americans heard it too. It meant to them the arrival of British reinforcements from Skenesboro, and they started for Fort Edward. But they were deceived: there were no Indians behind that war whoop, and only one Englishman, Captain Money. He had been sent ahead with a party of

Indians, who "either stood still or advanced very slow." He had therefore run ahead and tried his luck with that one wild outcry.[58]

When St. Clair, with his main force at Castleton, got word of the disasters at Skenesboro and Hubbardton, there was nothing to do but try to save the remains of his army. He turned to the east and, unmolested, took a straight road to Rutland. Thence, by a circuitous route, he got to Fort Edward on the 12th.[59]

C H A P T E R 3 7

Bennington

While his advance troops under Fraser, Riedesel, and Hill were engaged with the Americans at Hubbardton and near Fort Ann, Burgoyne at Skenesboro was preparing to continue his southward march. He had the choice of two routes. He could return to Ticonderoga, get his boats over into Lake George, and march his army to Fort George at the head of that lake. Thence he could march by a tolerable road ten miles to the Hudson at a point a little above Fort Edward. This way, in his "Thoughts" on the war delivered to the King in February, he had declared to be "the most expeditious and commodious route to Albany."

The other way was up Wood Creek from Skenesboro to Fort Ann, thence by road sixteen miles to Edward. This route he had predicted would offer "considerable difficulties, the narrow parts of the river may be easily choked up and rendered impassable; and, at best, there will be necessity for a great deal of land-carriage for the artillery, provisions &c." [1] Yet he now chose that route.

The principal reason he gave for this choice was his fear of the harmful impression which "a retrograde motion is apt to make upon the minds both of enemies and friends." [2] But it is thought that his decision may have been the result of the advice of Philip Skene.

Skene, formerly an officer in the British army, had obtained grants of 34,000 acres of land at the head of Lake Champlain, had founded a colony there, Skenesboro, and engaged in divers industries, operating limekilns, forges, sawmills, and a shipyard, with much success. In 1775, when Ticonderoga was taken by Allen and Arnold and he was dispossessed, he managed to get to Canada. Now with Burgoyne, he acted as a general adviser on the state of the country, with which he was so well acquainted. Under such conditions, coupled with his personal characteristics—he was "a large, fine-looking person, with a pleasant countenance and affable deportment" [3] —he had much influence with the general. His reason for using his influence in favor of the Skenesboro route is believed to have been the fact that it would require the cutting of a road from his colony to the Hudson, which would be of very great value in the event of the recovery of his property after the war. At all events, for this reason or another, Burgoyne so decided.

He did, however, also decide to send his gunboats, his artillery, and his heavy stores in boats by way of Lake George to its head.[4] That lake being more than 200 feet higher than Champlain, its waters descended through the narrow gorge that connected the two in a series of falls and rapids against which boats could hardly be propelled. It was necessary to carry his bateaux and barges around by land about three miles, a difficult and slow operation.

From the 9th of July until the 25th, Burgoyne's right wing, his British troops, lay on the heights at Skenesboro; his left, the Germans under Riedesel, about ten miles away at Castleton, with Fraser's corps between.[5] The disposition of the German troops was intended to confuse the Americans as to the next move, whether down the Hudson or east to the Connecticut River country. The long delay at this time was caused by the activities of the Americans on the road to Fort Ann and so to Fort Edward.

Schuyler, in general command of the American northern army, had come up from Albany to Fort Edward; and thence on the 8th, as has been said, he had sent Van Rensselaer and his 400 New York volunteers to reinforce Long at Fort Ann. He had at his own post six or seven hundred Continentals and about 1,400 militia. With this puny force, he could not hope to cope with Burgoyne's army, more than three times as large and many more times as strong in fighting quality, equipment, and supplies.

The fort itself was a miserable affair, a dilapidated relic of the French and Indian War.[6] Schuyler wrote to Washington that he had often jumped his horse over the remains of its ramparts. It had some guns, but they lay about on the ground; there were no carriages to mount them. Its garrison, 100 men, was in a sad condition. Not only small, but discouraged by defeat, it was out of hand that its members committed "the most scandalous depredations" [7] on the countryside. It was so short of ammunition that there were but five musket cartridges for each man. If Burgoyne had sent

Fraser's light troops forward, without the encumbrance of artillery or wagon trains, he could easily have taken that pretense of a fort. The Americans had only one circumstance in their favor, the character of the country through which Burgoyne had to march, between Skenesboro and Fort Edward, and through which the British supplies and stores had to be carried, between Fort George, at the head of Lake George, and Fort Edward.

The roads connecting those points were mere traces cut through a primeval forest of enormous pines and hemlocks. They seldom ran straight for any considerable distance. Innumerable huge, fallen trees, "as plenty as lamp-posts upon a highway about London," [8] interrupted their course, and the roads swung around them in a succession of zigzags. The way from Skenesboro to Fort Edward ran in the valley of Wood Creek and, for the most part, close beside the stream. It crossed no fewer than forty deep ravines over which high and long bridges had been built. There were also numerous bogs and swamps. The spring had been unusually wet, and the rains still fell, so that the soil was saturated and the morasses were deep and wide. At one place, if the artillery and wagons were to be got through, it would be necessary to build a causeway or corduroy road two miles long. Such a country afforded opportunity for the creation of almost insurmountable impediments, and Schuyler started to create them.

He put a thousand axmen to work. They destroyed every bridge and dug ditches to carry water from the bogs so as to create new swamps. They felled trees along the Skenesboro road and the creek so that the trunks crossed them both from each side, the tops coming together in a stiff entanglement. The creek itself was choked by great rocks rolled down from its bordering hillsides.[9] He sent out other men to warn the few inhabitants to drive their cattle out of reach of the invaders, to remove or conceal their foodstuffs. They were even induced to burn their unharvested grain. The whole country within reach of the roads was reduced to desolation.

Even without this extraordinary destruction, the passage of the British army, its guns, and its wagons over the roads would have been most difficult. It was sadly short of draught cattle. Of the 1,500 horses Burgoyne had asked for in Canada, no more than 500 had been furnished. On his way, he had managed to commandeer 50 teams of oxen, an insufficient supplement.[10] And the Canadian country carts which he had were ramshackle affairs built of green wood and likely to fall apart under any heavy strain. Under these conditions, the roads in their usual state, and the frail bridges, would have been bad enough to daunt an invader. Now, and until all Schuyler's work had been undone, progress was impossible. But Burgoyne was not stopped.

Into that jungle of obstructions he sent hundreds of his men, expert Canadian axmen among them. Working under the most difficult conditions, tormented by millions of "moschetoes" and gnats—"punkies," the natives call them—in the stifling, sultry heat of the close woods, they hacked away at the trees, drained the bogs, rebuilt the bridges, and made that two-mile causeway. By July 25 he was able to leave Skenesboro and advance to Fort Ann. Four days he lay there while his men worked on the road ahead of him. At last on the 29th, three weeks from the day he landed at Skenesboro twenty-three miles away, he came to Fort Edward.[11]

In the meantime, Schuyler had been reinforced. The remains of St. Clair's force had come in on July 12, as has been stated. Long's detachment, from Ticonderoga, had arrived. Brigadier General John Nixon with 600 Continentals had come on from Peekskill. There were now nearly 2,900 Continental rank and file and more than 1,600 militia, present and fit, in and about the fort.[12] To support the general, who was disliked and distrusted by the New England troops, Washington had sent two Yankee major generals, Benedict Arnold of Connecticut and Benjamin Lincoln of Massachusetts. But even with these acquisitions Schuyler and his generals knew they could not hold that dilapidated fort. Leaving a small rear guard to take care of it until the enemy came, he fell back down the Hudson, first about five miles to Moses Creek, then to Saratoga; at last, on August 3, he reached Stillwater, twelve miles farther. Here Kosciuszko laid out the works of a defensive position, and entrenchment was begun. But within a few days Schuyler again withdrew twelve miles down the river to the mouth of the Mohawk.

The morale of the Connecticut troops was now at its lowest ebb. Continued retreats in the face of a continually advancing enemy, and their sad physical condition, were enough to undermine their confidence in themselves as well as in their leaders; but more active causes of discouragement were working among them. There was a growing belief, now really a full-grown belief, that both Schuyler and St. Clair were not merely incompetent, but actually traitorous.

The most ridiculous of the stories bandied about in the camp was that Burgoyne had bought both generals by firing into Ticonderoga "silver balls," which had been gathered up by St. Clair and sent down to Schuyler: that explained the surrender of Ticonderoga and the subsequent evacuations and retreats. Absurd as the story was, the New Englanders, in their dislike of Schuyler as a New York aristocrat, seem to have believed it, or at least affected to do so. The plague of desertion, to which the American troops, especially the militia, were so subject throughout the war, became an epidemic. Two hundred men were missing between the 20th and 24th of July. By the 4th of August as many more had gone. Of the remaining 4,000, fully a third were Negroes, boys, or old men. And at that time Burgoyne was only a long day's march, twenty-four miles, from Stillwater.

After their slow and enormously difficult march from Skenesboro, the British troops were in high spirits. That terrible wilderness was behind them. Before them the Hudson, a sweetly flowing river, led to their grand objective, Albany. "They considered their toils to be nearly at an end; Albany to be within their grasp, and the adjacent provinces certainly reduced." [13] That they had to wait at Fort Edward for the big guns, the munitions and supplies, and the boats to be brought down from the head of Lake George meant nothing. For the rank and file the delay was a welcome vacation. For Burgoyne, however, this was a period of some anxiety. He was not so certain that his troubles were over. And he knew by August 3 that he could expect no help from Howe, unless Washington attempted to help Schuyler. Howe had written to him on July 17: "My intention is for Pennsylvania, where I expect to meet Washington, but if he goes to the northward contrary to my expectations, and you can keep him at bay, be assured I shall soon be after him to relieve you. . . . Success be ever with you." [14] The day that letter was written, Howe's troops were already aboard their transports bound for the Chesapeake. By the time Burgoyne received it, the fleet was south of the Delaware capes.

Burgoyne did not know that, of course; but one thing he did know—that Howe was carrying out the original plan and that Howe was not coming up the Hudson. There would be no meeting of the two forces at Albany during the campaign. In view of the obstacles still to be faced, might it not be wise to abandon the advance, turn about, and march back to Ticonderoga? It might be done safely enough, no doubt. But no. His orders were to march to Albany, and march he would. He put Howe's letter away, told no one about it, not even Riedesel.[15]

Major General Baron von Riedesel had for a long time been worrying about his horseless dragoons.[16] They were not proper foot soldiers. Their costume was sufficient evidence of that. Yet here they were in their stiff leather breeches,[17] their enormous cocked hats, clumping along day after day in their great, clumsy boots over the miscalled roads of this God-forsaken wilderness in a hell of heat, their spurs catching in the underbrush, the ends of their long broadswords clattering over the stones, their heavy carbines, that might have been slung on their saddles, borne on their shoulders. Something had to be done about it.

All along he had been urging Burgoyne to find mounts for them. He was sure horses were to be had over in the Connecticut River valley. At Skenesboro he had proposed an expedition into that country by the dragoons and the Tories of the army. Burgoyne had approved the plan, but had been too busy with his arrangements for pushing on southward to do anything about it. Now, at Fort Edward, the matter came up again, and Burgoyne and Riedesel drew up the orders for the expedition. These were very specific and very elaborate.

Lieutenant Colonel Baum, who could not "utter one word of English," was to lead the foray—a most unsuitable leader of an enterprise that was to penetrate enemy country and enlist the services of English-speaking people. Its objects and purposes were manifold. Baum was "to try the affections of the people, to disconcert the councils of the enemy, to mount Riedesel's dragoons, to compleat Peters's corps [of Tories] and to obtain large supplies of cattle, horses and carriages," specifically 1,300 horses, besides those for the dragoons. They were to be "tied together by strings of ten each, in order that one man may lead ten horses." To get this loot, he was to impose taxes in kind upon the several districts and to hold "the most respectable people" as hostages for their delivery. He was also to make prisoners of "all persons acting in committees, or any officers acting under the directions of Congress, whether civil or military." [18]

The country to be subjected to this drastic treatment extended from Manchester in the north through Arlington to Bennington in the south, and as far east as the Connecticut River. The whole process was to be effected by a force of 650 rank and file, made up of 170 dismounted Brunswick dragoons, 100 German grenadiers and light infantry, 300 Tories, Canadians, and Indians, 50 of Fraser's British "marksmen," and a few artillerymen with two small fieldpieces.[19] In the orders, it was called "a secret expedition." To help to preserve its secrecy, a German band of musicians was included in the outfit. It seems not to have occurred to Burgoyne that sending such a force upon such an expedition was likely to result in another retreat from Concord.

To assist Baum with advice and to help him "distinguish the good subjects from the bad," [20] Burgoyne added Colonel Philip Skene to the party. His advice, given at a crucial moment, had much to do with the outcome of the excursion.

Burgoyne knew that the remains of Colonel Seth Warner's regiment had gathered at Manchester in obedience to their commander's last order at Hubbardton; but he thought it "highly probable" that they would retreat before Baum. If they did not, he left it to Baum's discretion whether he should fight them or not, "always bearing in mind that your corps is too valuable to let any considerable loss be hazarded." But, besides Warner's men, there were others of whom the British and German generals were ignorant.

The country lying west of New Hampshire had long been claimed by that colony and by New York. It had been settled under grants of land made by the governor of New Hampshire and was therefore called the New Hampshire Grants. Its settlers, the Green Mountain Boys, had long defended their land titles against New York's pretensions. Now, in 1777, it had declared itself the independent State of Vermont and organized a Council of Safety as a preliminary to establishing a regular government. Threatened with invasion by Burgoyne, its council called on New Hampshire and Massachusetts for help.[21]

New Hampshire had already taken notice of the impending danger to itself and had proposed to raise troops for its own defense; but it was thinly settled and poor, so that the problem of the expense of an armed force seemed difficult of solution. It was solved by John Langdon, the speaker of the General Court. "I have," said he, "three thousand dollars in hard money. I will pledge my plate for three thousand more. I have seventy hogsheads of Tobago rum, which shall be sold for the most it will bring. These are at the service of the State. If we succeed in defending our homes, I may be remunerated; if we do not, the property will be of no value to me. Our old friend Stark, who so nobly sustained the honour of our State at Bunker's Hill, may be safely entrusted with the conduct of the enterprise, and we will check the progress of Burgoyne." [22] So goes an old, if not true, story.

John Stark had served in the French and Indian War as a captain in the famous Rogers' Rangers. He had instantly responded to the Lexington alarm, raising a regiment with which he gallantly and successfully defended the American left wing at Bunker's Hill. He had led a regiment to Canada in May, 1776, as a part of the force sent by Washington to succor the defeated American army. In the battles of Trenton and Princeton, he had fought courageously and effectively. He was a brave, a gallant soldier, experienced in warfare, and a great leader of men, with a colonel's commission dated January 1, 1776. Yet, when the politicians in the Congress, in April, 1777, appointed new brigadier generals, they jumped certain junior colonels over his head, as over Arnold's. A proud man, tenacious of his rights and jealous of his honor as a soldier, Stark then resigned his commission and retired to his farm in New Hampshire. But now, at the call of his state, he came forward.

Tall, straight, and sinewy as an Indian, his figure was that of a fighting man. His strong nose, high cheekbones, weathered countenance lit up by steady and piercing light blue eyes, the straight, set line of his thin lips all indicated a character in keeping with his figure. They indicated also that unyielding spirit which in his New England is sometimes characterized as "cantankerous." [23]

Yes, he would take command of the proposed new brigade, but on one condition; it was to be a New Hampshire brigade pure and simple, independent of the Congress and of the Continental army, accountable only to the General Court of the state. The Congress he heartily disliked. Schuyler, he both disliked and distrusted. He would have nothing to do with either. Those were his terms. It was a case of take him or leave him. They took him, commissioned him a brigadier general, and gave him power to direct his operations according to his own judgment.

The response of his fellow citizens to his call was immediate and beyond expectation. On July 18, the day after his commission was signed, 221 men enlisted; the next day, although it was Sunday, the rolls bore the names of 419. Within less than a week, the brigade numbered 1,492 officers and men, 10 per cent of all the enrolled voters in the state, old and young. They had no uniforms and brought their own muskets or fowling pieces.[24]

By July 30, Stark had his command sufficiently organized and equipped to march it to Charleston on the east side of the Connecticut River. In the first week of August, he crossed the river and took post at Manchester, Vermont, where Seth Warner's scattered Vermonters had come together again. Here he had his first and his decisive clash with Schuyler, that disliked and distrusted New York general.

Schuyler was willing that Warner's regiment should remain in Vermont while it was uncertain whether Burgoyne would go south by the Hudson or turn east into the Connecticut valley. He even reinforced Warner with some New England militia and sent Major General Lincoln over there to command them, but he wanted this new brigade of Stark's to strengthen his own weak army. Through Lincoln, he directed Stark to join him.[25]

Stark's reply was prompt and definite. He was, he said, a New Hampshire brigadier, responsible only to its General Court, and by it he had been given a free hand in the conduct of his brigade. No, he would not go to the Hudson on order of Schuyler or anyone else except the General Court of New Hampshire.[26] Lincoln reported this insubordination to the Congress, and it resolved to inform New Hampshire that its orders to Stark were "destructive of military subordination" and to request it to instruct Stark "to conform himself to the same rules which other general officers of the militia are subject to, whenever they are called out at the expence of the United States." [27] But, before that resolution reached New Hampshire, certain events had occurred that caused the Congress to pass other resolutions of a different tone.

On August 8, Stark marched his men twenty miles south to Bennington, where an important depot of American military supplies was situated, leaving Warner at Manchester with the remains of his regiment and 200 rangers whom he had gathered in since Hubbardton.

Three days later Baum's expedition started from Fort Miller, seven miles down the Hudson from Fort Edward.[28] Just as he was leaving, Burgoyne changed his orders. Instead of Manchester, his first objective was to be Bennington, of whose treasures in the way of supplies, cattle, and horses, Burgoyne had just received an exaggerated report.[29] He had also heard that the place was held only by three or four hundred militia. All this was very promising for the success of the enterprise.

After a march of four miles Baum camped on the Batten Kill, a little tributary of the Hudson. There 50 Brunswick jägers came up to be added to his force. On the 13th he marched through a notch in the ridge between Batten Kill and the Hoosic River and down to the village of Cambridge on the Owl Kill.

He had much trouble with his Indians. Preceding the main body, they ran wild, looting and destroying property, killing cows for the sake of their bells and so alarming the country that the inhabitants drove off their horses and cattle instead of leaving them where Baum might have picked them up. There were several light skirmishes with small parties of the local militia, but at Sancoick's—or Van Schaick's—mill on Owl Kill he had his first contact with the American organized troops.

Stark, hearing of the Indian depredations, had sent Colonel Gregg, with 200 men, against them. Gregg was now in posession of the mill.[30] At Baum's approach, the Americans fired one volley and retreated. Baum pursued them. They broke down a bridge, delaying the Germans and ensuring their own escape. Baum had learned that a force stronger than a few militia was at Bennington. He sent a letter back to Burgoyne, announcing the capture of flour, wheat, and potash at the mill, and telling him that fifteen to eighteen hundred rebels were in Bennington, but were "supposed to leave at our approach." He would "fall on the enemy to-morrow early." [31]

Stark, in the meantime, had heard that a strong enemy force was following the Indians, and had set out to rescue Gregg, having first called on Warner at Manchester to join him. About four miles west of Bennington, the opposing forces sighted each other and halted. Between them were the Walloomsac River and a bridge.[32] Baum did not seem disposed to attack, and so Stark withdrew two or three miles towards Bennington. Baum took a position on a height above the river.[33] Both forces bivouacked on the night of the 14th.

The 15th was rainy, and no move was made by either side, except that Baum disposed his troops to meet an expected attack. Stark, however, was reinforced by 400 Vermont militia, also a party from Berkshire County, Massachusetts, and some Stockbridge Indians. He had then about 2,000 men. Baum was strengthened by the arrival of 90 Tories under "Colonel" Pfister, a retired British lieutenant.[34] His force then numbered about 800.

The German dragoons and half of Fraser's contingent were posted on the steep hill where they had encamped, which looked down from a height of 300 feet upon the bridge half a mile away. Trees were felled to make breastworks and one of the two 3-pounders was mounted there. In some log cabins on both sides of the bridge the Canadians were stationed. On the hither side of the bridge the other half of Fraser's force and about 50 German infantrymen, with the other gun, took their stand. In a field southwest of the principal position 50 German foot soldiers and some Tories were supposed to guard the rear of that group. About 250 yards to the south and beyond the bridge 150 Tories were posted and threw up a breastwork. Southeast of the hilltop the 50 jägers were placed. The Indians were grouped on a plateau behind the main position. Having thus scattered his men as effectively as possible all over the landscape—some of the little detachments more than a half-mile from the others—Baum awaited Stark's move.

That move was concerted between Stark and Warner, who had come from Manchester in advance of his regiment. They made a rather elaborate plan. It involved complete encirclement of Baum's main position and simultaneous attacks on his front, rear, and flanks. It was carried out without a flaw.

About noon on the 16th, the rain having ceased, Colonel Moses Nichols with 200 New Hampshire men started on a long circuit to get around Baum's left. Colonel Samuel Herrick led 300 men, Vermont Rangers and Bennington militia, similarly to turn the German right. Colonel David Hobart and Colonel Thomas Stickney, with 200 men, were to go against the Tory position south of the bridge. A hundred more were to demonstrate against the front of the main position to divert Baum's attention. Stark was to hold the remaining twelve or thirteen hundred for the principal frontal attack, the signal for which was to be the first fire by Nichols and Herrick.[35]

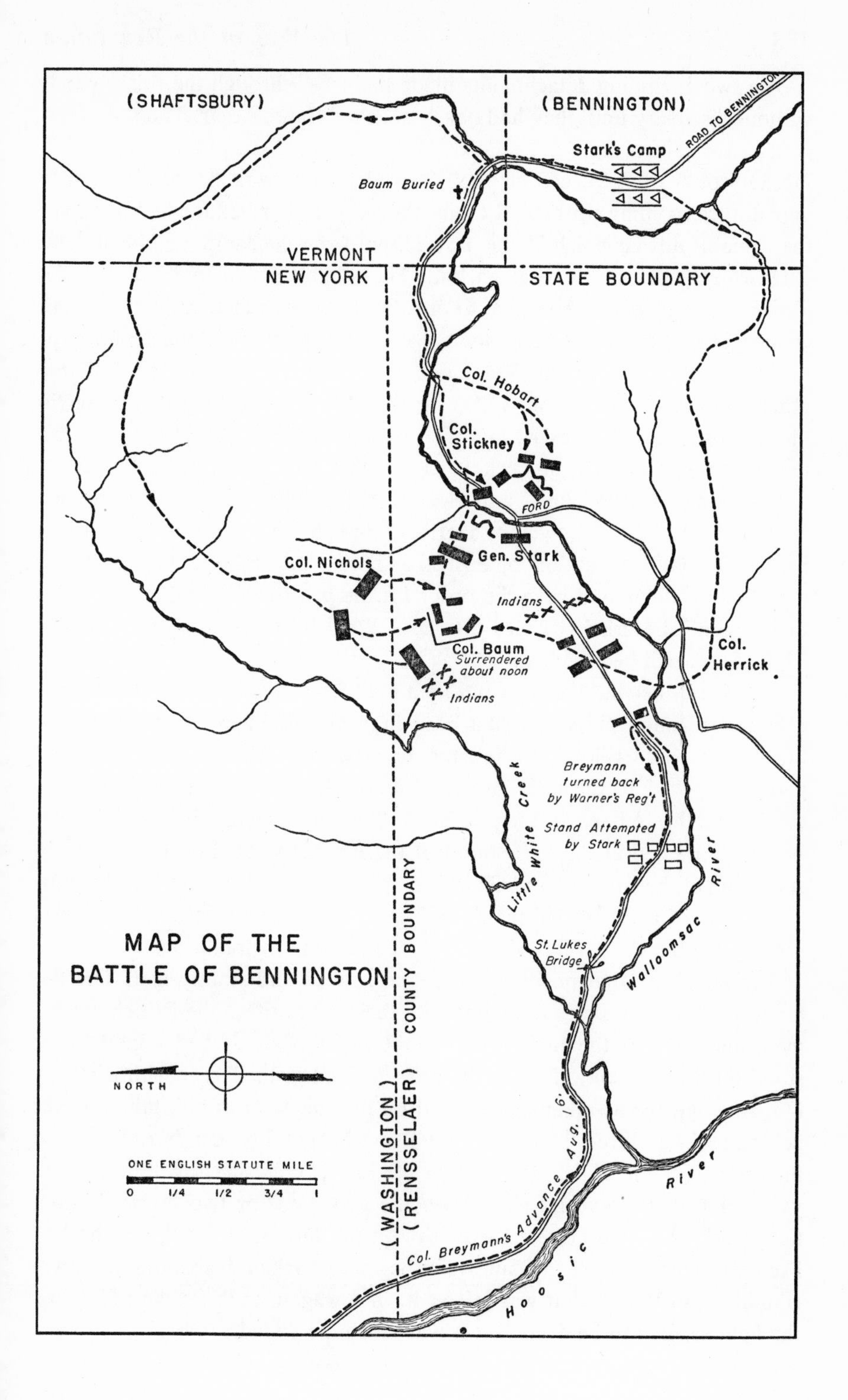

(SHAFTSBURY)
(BENNINGTON)
ROAD TO BENNINGTON
Stark's Camp
Baum Buried
VERMONT
NEW YORK
STATE BOUNDARY
Col. Hobart
Col.
Stickney
FORD
Gen. Stark
Col. Nichols
Indians
Col. Baum
Surrendered
about noon
Indians
Col.
Herrick
Breymann
turned back
by Warner's Reg't
Stand Attempted
by Stark
Little White Creek
Walloomsac River
St. Lukes
Bridge
MAP OF THE
BATTLE OF BENNINGTON
NORTH
ONE ENGLISH STATUTE MILE
0 1/4 1/2 3/4 1
(WASHINGTON) COUNTY BOUNDARY
(RENSSELAER)
Col. Breymann's Advance Aug. 16
Hoosic River

The two encircling detachments made their way through the thick woods without discovery until they had nearly reached Baum's rear. Then the Germans saw several small, irregular bodies of shirt-sleeved farmers, with muskets or fowling pieces on their shoulders, but with no other military appearance, coming up behind them. At once, Baum bethought himself of the valuable advice which Skene, now absent from the camp, had been delegated to give him and had given him. The inhabitants of that countryside, Skene had said, were Tories five to one. On the march to Bennington, small groups dressed like these newcomers, had sifted in among Baum's men, protesting their loyalty to the King, and had been kindly received.[36] These others now approaching must also be friends, either seeking protection in his rear or prepared to assist him. He made no effort to keep them off. On the contrary he drew in his pickets so that they should not be molested.

By three o'clock Nichols and Herrick had gained satisfactory positions. Nichols opened fire, followed by Herrick. On hearing this signal Hobart and Stickney went into action against the Tories beyond the bridge. Stark mounted his horse and gave the order for the principal frontal attack. "See there, men!" he cried. "There they are! We'll beat them before night, or Molly Stark will be a widow." [37]

The Tories beyond the river put up a fight for a few minutes. The Americans waited until one volley had been fired against them and then, before the Tories could reload, rushed the breastworks. Its defenders retreated pellmell down into the little river and across it. The Canadians in the log cabins and the Indians on the plateau, yelling and jangling their stolen cowbells, simply fled at the first sound of the musketry. St. Luc La Corne, in command of the Indians, and Charles de Lanaudière, his son-in-law, in command of the Canadians led their contingents in headlong retreat. There was nothing left but the main position on that steep and high hill.

The attack on that position was fiercely made and stoutly met. The defenders, those Brunswick dragoons with their heavy rifles, the British marksmen, and such of the fugitives from the other posts as had joined them, stood off the encircling foes in the open ground in their rear with a steady fire. In front, the assailants scrambled up that high, steep hill, taking cover behind rocks and trees and firing at will so fast that their gun barrels burned their hands. Some of the New Hampshire militia crept up to within a dozen yards of the artillery and shot down the gunners. For two hours this hot fight went on—"the hottest I ever saw in my life" said Stark, and he had been through many. Then Baum's fire began to slacken; his ammunition was running low. When what was left of it, in a wagon, took fire and blew up, the fight seemed to be over. But it was not quite ended.

Though the rest of his command broke and fled, Baum's dragoons still stood by him. He called for their swords. They drew those fearful weapons to cut their way through their enemies. The Americans had no bayonets to oppose them. The dragoons made a steady, if lumbering, progress through the swarming Americans, the shirt-sleeved farmers who circled around, closed in, fell back, and closed in again; but when Baum fell, fatally wounded, his men gave up the fight.[38]

Now it seemed that nothing remained but to comb the woods for more prisoners and loot the German camp. But there was yet other work to be done. Baum had sent Burgoyne a second note on the evening of the 14th asking for reinforcements,[39] and Burgoyne had ordered Lieutenant Colonel Breymann, with 642 men and two fieldpieces, to march to Baum's support. They set out at eight o'clock in the morning of the 15th. The roads were deep with mud, and a hard rain was falling. The heavily uniformed and equipped Germans were notoriously slow in movement. They had twenty-five miles to go. In rigid, regular formation, halting frequently to re-dress their ranks, they progressed at the rate of half a mile an hour,[40] making only eight miles that day. A courier was sent forward to tell Baum that they were coming, and they bivouacked for the night.

The next day, the day of the battle, they crawled on at the same rate, to reach Sancoick's mill at half-past four, with six miles yet to go. There Breymann received vague and confused reports of the fight. A little later, Stark had word of Breymann's coming.

He had promised his men the spoils of victory, and they were scattered widely among the various enemy positions gathering up their plunder. He rallied as many as he could and sent them back along the road to delay Breymann.

Breymann, pushing on from Sancoick's mill, met the first party of Americans within a mile. It was merely a disorganized body of shirt-sleeved men carrying guns. Skene, who had gone back to meet Breymann, assured him that they were friendly Tories. But when they took a position behind a rail fence on a height by the road and fired a ragged volley, killing Breymann's horse, he had his doubts. He sent a detachment to dislodge them.[41]

From that time on, there was a series of such skirmishes. Three times the Americans took positions on the high ground north of the road, fired into the solid German column, and retreated when hard-pushed. But the Germans moved steadily, if slowly, forward.

Stark was in a bad way. His men were still scattered, still busy looting, and he could assemble only a small part of them. It seemed that he would have to give way and leave the field to the enemy. But Warner encouraged him to hold on.[42] Help was coming from Manchester. Before sunset it arrived.

The rest of Warner's regiment, 130 men led by Lieutenant Colonel Samuel Safford, and 200 rangers, had made a long day's march until midnight. They came on the next day, but slowly, halting to dry their muskets when the rain stopped, again to draw ammunition at Bennington, again to put aside their coats and knapsacks, again to receive a ration of rum, again to quench their thirst with water. But they came to the battlefield at last and went on to meet Breymann a mile or so beyond it.

By this time Stark had collected a good number of his men. He joined Warner. At first they took an unfortunate position in low, swampy ground devoid of cover; but after a few shots they withdrew to a wooded hill north of the road. Breymann attacked. He tried a flanking movement to turn the American right and began to gain ground. But half of Warner's men outflanked and checked the flankers. Meanwhile the rest of Warner's men, with Stark's troops, stretched out to threaten the Germans' right. The fight then went on face to face.

Breymann's two 6-pounders were active. The musketry was continuous and heavy. About sunset his men, who had carried forty rounds,[43] had almost exhausted their ammunition; but the American fire was still sustained. Breymann gave up, ordered a retreat. Many of the artillery horses had been shot. The rest were exhausted. The Germans abandoned their guns, and started west along the road in good order. Those that still had cartridges answered the shots of pursuing Americans. But their pace was slow. The enemy was on their flanks and at their heels, still relentlessly firing. The ordered ranks became confused in the haste to get away, broke up into a pushing, shoving disorder. In the gathering dusk, the retreat became a rout.

Some of the Germans threw down their muskets and ran. Others held them out, as if to surrender them. They dropped out, kneeled down, and cried for mercy. Breymann's drums beat a parley, a call to a conference for a surrender. But the untutored Americans did not know its meaning. To them it was just drums beating. They kept on shooting.

Breymann had been hit in a leg, and there were five bullet holes in his coat, but he held together a small rear guard, himself the last man, and so kept his men going in the increasing darkness. When it was quite dark, Stark called off the pursuit. Breymann, with less than two-thirds of his men, got away. "Had day lasted an hour longer," said Stark, "we should have taken the whole body of them." [44]

It was a notable little battle in that a body of farmers, for the most part entirely inexperienced in warfare, had so decisively beaten two forces of trained, professional soldiers. It is true that in the first fight Stark outnumbered Baum more than two to one; but that was not an overwhelming advantage when the experience and training of the Germans is considered. In the second the preponderance of the Americans in number was much less. Their lack of organization and their fatigue after hours of fighting reduced their advantage practically to zero.

Of the Germans, 207 were left dead on the field; about 700, including 30 officers, were captured. The spoils were rich: four brass fieldpieces, twelve drums, two hundred fifty broadswords, four ammunition wagons, and several hundred muskets and rifles. The Americans lost about 30 killed and 40 wounded.[45]

On October 4 the Congress unanimously voted its thanks to Stark and his men, and appointed him a brigadier general in the Continental army.[46]

Notes

CHAPTER 1

The best general accounts of the Anglo-American crises, 1763–1775, are to be found in Channing, III, Van Tyne, *C,* and Miller, *O*. Miller, *T,* is the most recent account of the period of the Revolutionary War.

1. Belcher, I, 134.
2. Frothingham, *S,* 6.
3. *Massachusetts Spy,* May 19, 1774. Frothingham, *S,* 6. A Boston Tory wrote to a friend in London: "You nor your friends must not imagine there was any honesty in those marks of joy these Bostonians showed the General on this occasion—no sir, it was hypocrisy all" (Force, 4, I, 299 n.).
4. For Gage's personality and career see Alden, *passim.*
5. For a brief discussion of the Sugar Act see Lecky, 55–58.
6. Bancroft, III, 77.
7. For the Stamp Act see MacDonald, 122–131.
8. Bancroft, III, 245.
9. Bancroft, III, 238.
10. MacDonald, 107.
11. Fiske, I, 82.
12. Frothingham, 299.
13. Grahame, IV, 328.
14. Ramsay, I, 129.
15. Frothingham, 305.

CHAPTER 2

1. Frothingham, *S,* 37; Bancroft, IV, 19; Force, 4, I, 669.
2. Gage was astonished at the support given the Bostonians indicating the solidarity of the colonies. "I find," he wrote in September, "they have some warm friends in New York and Philadelphia . . . that the people of Charleston are as mad as they are. . . . This province is supported and abetted by others beyond the conception of most people, and foreseen by none."
3. Bancroft, IV, 95.
4. Force, 4, I, 768. Cf. Trevelyan, I, 317.

5. Frothingham, *S*, 113; Stiles, I, 510–511.
6. Adams, *J*, 31.
7. Percy, 46; Barker, 12; Stiles, I, 503; Force, 4, I, 1041–1043, 1054; Gordon, I, 422.
8. Frothingham, *S*, 48; Stiles, I, 523; Gordon, I, 470.
9. Trevelyan, I, 258.
10. Force, 4, III, 1330.

CHAPTER 3

Fortescue and Curtis are very useful upon the make-up of the British army; French, *C*, and French, *F*, upon that of the American forces.

1. Stiles, I, 515; Barker, 13; Force, 4, II, 441; Frothingham, *S*, 46, 55; Murdock, *B*, 5; French, *F*, 89. Belcher, I, 151, mentions two other regiments, the 29th and 40th, but indicates in a table of the services of the various regiments that the 29th had its first service with Burgoyne in 1777, and the 40th at Long Island in 1776.
2. The regiments so raised bore the name of the colonel up to 1751, when George II gave them numbers. In 1782 they received the names of counties. Thus one such regiment was originally Greville's, then the 10th, then the Lincolnshire Regiment.
3. Smollett in *Humphry Clinker* pictures an officer who, having purchased an ensigncy, had risen in thirty years' service only to the rank of lieutenant, because he had no money to buy promotions.
4. Frothingham, *F*, 99, 102–103; Belcher, I, 249–252, 259. Belcher states that three British regiments were made up entirely of men who had been in prison.
5. Sydney, 346.
6. Belcher, I, 251–252.
7. Belcher, I, 281–282.
8. Belcher, I, 322–325; Lefferts, 148–168. Lefferts's plates show crossbelts, but Fortescue, III, 542, says that it was not until after the return of the army from America that the waist belt was transferred to the right shoulder, thus originating the crossbelt, and Belcher, I, facing 323, shows the infantryman before 1783 with one shoulder belt and after that date the crossbelts.
9. Fortescue, III, 543; Sawyer, 93.
10. Sawyer, 100.
11. Trevelyan, I, 211.
12. Sawyer, 98–100; French, *C*, 28 n.
13. French, *C*, 32–35, citing Bland's *Treatise on Military Discipline* (London, 1753), the British manual of 1764, and Timothy Pickering's *Easy Plan of Discipline for a Militia* (Salem, 1775).
14. French, *F*, 34.
15. For the history of Massachusetts militia and the minutemen see French, *F*, 32–46, and the numerous citations; also *D.A.H.*, III, 413, and French, *C*, 17. The term "minutemen" goes back at least to 1756, when a company of Massachusetts soldiers called themselves "Minnit men." French, *F*, 33.
16. French, *F*, 41 and note, telling of the participation of the alarm companies in the fight at Concord.
17. Adams, *J*, 65–66. A recent apologist (Anderson, 76) for General Howe's conduct of the war attributes the lack of success of his frontal attack at Bunker Hill to the fact that "the men who lined the parapet . . . carried rifles, for the most part, instead of muskets . . . the rifle was vastly superior to the musket in precision. The men who used it on this occasion had acquired their proficiency in the hunting field." Which, he says, "the British command apparently failed to realize." The "fact" was not realized, because it was not a fact. There were no riflemen in the American troops in Massachusetts at that time, nor were there any until July–August, 1775, when 1,400 of them from Pennsylvania, Maryland, and Virginia, under Thompson, Cresap, and Morgan, joined Washington at Cambridge. Before that time, it is quite possible that there was not one rifle in

all Massachusetts (French, *C*, 28). The lack of rifles in New England could be deduced from the fact that, although between 1600 and 1800 many gunsmiths were making muskets in that territory, a single rifle maker is known to have been north of Pennsylvania prior to 1783 (Sawyer, 153–157, 216–219).

18. Sawyer, 132–136.

CHAPTER 4

This account of the affair at Lexington has been drawn from the many sources individually cited below. A complete reconciliation of discrepancies has been impossible—for instance, between the blindly patriotic Coburn and the more broad-minded French and Murdock, and between the monographs of Elias Phinney and Ezra Ripley, champions respectively of Lexington and Concord in the great dispute between the two towns in 1825 for the honor of having been the scene of the first "battle" of the war. In that contest the affidavits of many survivors of April 19, 1775, taken at a later time were marshaled, their recollections differing in many respects from the statements of the ninety-eight survivors of the day whose affidavits were taken by the Provincial Congress within the week following the 19th. These may be found in Force, 4, I, 486–501. The truth is often not easily found.

1. French, *C*, 39.
2. Trevelyan, I, 331–333.
3. Barker, 27–28; French, *C*, 41.
4. French, *C*, 51–52; Coburn, 15.
5. Barker, 29.
6. French, *C*, 65.
7. French, *C*, 66.
8. French, *C*, 75.
9. Coburn, 17; Stedman, I, 119; Frothingham, *S*, 59.
10. Phinney, 15; Ripley, 11; Coburn, 18.
11. Coburn, 22–24; French, *C*, 77–80. The lanterns were seen by British soldiers in Boston. They found the sexton of the church and arrested him, but let him go when he denied all knowledge as to who had displayed them. Pulling, disguised as a sailor, escaped from Boston in a fishing boat to Nantucket and was careful not to return until the British had left (Coburn).
12. French, *C*, 69–70; Murdock, 22. Why a major of marines was detailed to lead a detachment of infantry is a mystery. It is said, without definite authority, that it was because he was familiar with the roads to Concord and had studied the town in disguise. (French, *C*, 70.)
13. Stiles, I, 575, says 600 officers and men; Barker, 31, says "about 600"; Evelyn, 53, says "near 700"; Gordon, I, 477, says 800, "the flower of the army." According to French, *C*, 73, the last is generally accepted by American historians; but Murdock, 48 n., thinks 600 the proper number.
14. French, *C*, 100–101; Coburn, 19; Barker, 31–32; Force, 4, I, 360–364. It seems probable that the march from Lechmere began at one o'clock, to give time to reach Lexington at sunrise (Murdock, 50).
15. Coburn, 30–31; French, *C*, 90–91; Phinney, 16.
16. Coburn, 24–29; French, *C*, 91–94.
17. Coburn, 47–57; French, *C*, 102.
18. Coburn, 60; French, *C*, 95–96.
19. Coburn, 61; French, *C*, 97.
20. French, *C*, 107.
21. French, *C*, 95–99. Heath, 6, says: "This company standing so near to the road, after they had certain notice of the advancing of the British in force, was but a too much braving of danger; for they were sure to meet with insult, or injury which they could not repel. Bravery, when called to action, should always take the strong ground on the basis of reason."
22. Coburn, 63. As to the weather see Murdock, 55, quoting a contemporary diary,

23. Stiles, I, 604–650. Lieut. Barker, who was with Pitcairn, says (p. 32) the Americans "fired one or two shots, upon which our Men without any orders rushed in upon them, fired and put 'em to flight."
24. Barker, 32; Murdock, 24, 39.
25. Stiles, I, 604–605.
26. Murdock, 22.
27. Murdock, 37.

CHAPTER 5

In the main, the story of Lexington and Concord follows two excellently documented accounts. Coburn's *The Battle of April 19, 1775,* is an exhaustive study of both original and secondary materials. It is full of detail and is copiously annotated. French's *The Day of Concord and Lexington* is more discursive, less intimately factual, but is very valuable for its more impartial and less chauvinistic viewpoint. Besides these, the journals and letters of Stiles, Barker, Evelyn, Mackenzie, and Percy, the accounts of Ripley, Phinney, and Reynolds, Frothingham's *History of the Siege of Boston,* and the affidavits and letters, especially the letter of Rev. William Gordon, published in Force, 4, II, have been carefully studied. Murdock's *The Nineteenth of April, 1775,* is an illuminating discussion of the day's events, viewed with detachment and a healthy incredulity as to many generally accepted beliefs concerning certain aspects of the conflict, although his arguments seem at times to be rather casuistic.

1. Coburn, 32–46.
2. French, *C*, 149–151, 156. Rev. William Emerson was the grandfather of Ralph Waldo Emerson and the builder of Hawthorne's Old Manse.
3. Ripley, 21; Frothingham, *C*, 179.
4. French, *C*, 152, map.
5. French, *C*, 156–158.
6. French, *C*, 161.
7. Barker, 32; Stedman, I, 117.
8. French, *C*, 163. Emerson's diary is owned by the Emerson family. French obtained a copy of it; the quotations herein are drawn from his book.
9. French, *C*, 164; Reynolds, 17; Coburn, 75; Ripley, 16.
10. French, *C*, 164–165; Ripley, 17.
11. French, *C*, 177; Coburn, 77; Ripley, 19.
12. French, *C*, 167–182; Coburn, 77; Ripley, 19–20.
13. French, *C*, 186–187; Coburn, 81; Ripley, 18.
14. Coburn, 82–83; French, 187–190.
15. Barker, 34.
16. Barker, 34.
17. French, *C*, 191, 201 n.; Coburn, 84–85; Barker, 35.
18. French, *C*, 207–209; Coburn, 85, 88; Ripley, 28.
19. Coburn, 93; French, *C*, 217. At the bridge, after the fight, occurred one of the most lamentable incidents of the day. A half-grown boy, armed only with a hatchet, hastening after the Americans, found a severely wounded British soldier struggling to his knees. Conceiving it to be his duty to kill the enemy, the boy sank the hatchet in the skull of the wounded man. When Parsons's men came that way from Barrett's place, they found the dead man, his head covered with blood, and reported that he had been scalped and his ears cut off. The story spread; Gage published it; it got to England; and, though the true story was soon made known, the false one persisted. Stedman in his history (I, 119), published in 1794, wrote: 'Several of Smith's party were scalped by the Americans." In 1841, Adolphus in his history wrote that "several were scalped or had their ears cut off by the Americans" (French, *C*, 211–214). And even as late as 1911 Fortescue (III, 153) wrote that "a few of the dead and wounded had been scalped by some rough Americans at the bridge."

20. Coburn, 96–97, Supplement, 14–38.
21. Coburn, 98; French, *C*, 219.
22. French, *C*, 219.
23. Force, 4, II, 359.
24. Barker, 35. A British soldier wrote to his family, "They did not fight us like a regular army, only like savages" (Force, 4, I, 440).
25. French, *C*, 222; Coburn, 107. The pistols are preserved by the Lexington Historical Society.
26. Barker, 35.
27. French, *C*, 224.
28. French, *C*, 224.
29. Coburn, 114.
30. French, *C*, 226–227.
31. Percy, 49; Mackenzie, I, 19. Murdock, 47 n., thinks they were not more than 900.
32. French, *C*, 229 n. Percy had a low opinion of the colonials. He wrote home (Percy, 31, 35, 52): "The people here are a set of sly, artful, hypocritical rascalls, cruel & cowards. . . . I cannot but despise them completely. . . . Such a set of timid creatures I never did see." A similar opinion was general among the British officers in America before Bunker Hill. Captain Glanville Evelyn about this time wrote to his father that he believed "there does not exist so great a set of rascals and poltroons" (Evelyn, 27).
33. Coburn, 116–120; French, *C*, 230.
34. Percy, 50.
35. Mackenzie, I, 19.
36. Barker, 35.
37. Stedman, I, 118.
38. Mackenzie, I, 20.
39. Percy, 50.
40. Coburn, 133–134; Trevelyan, I, 335.
41. Barker, 36. On p. 39 Barker states that the British soldiers on the 19th, "tho' they shew'd no want of courage, yet were so wild and irregular, that there was no keeping 'em in order . . . the plundering was shamefull; many hardly thought of anything else; what was worse they were encouraged by some Officers." Mackenzie, I, 21–22, confirms the forcing of houses, killing, and plundering, but says the officers tried to stop the looting.
42. Heath, 7–8, says he did form one regiment in Lexington, "which had been broken by the shot from the British field-pieces"; but there seems to be little or no evidence that they continued to operate as a unit.
43. Coburn, 150–154; Mackenzie, I, 21. Lieutenant Barker, 36, says of the change in route that it threw the colonials off the scent.
44. Percy, 50; French, *C*, 255 n.; Coburn, 157–160.
45. Heath, 11.
46. Percy, 53.
47. Barker, 37.
48. Evelyn, 53.

CHAPTER 6

1. Force, 4, II, 363–370; French, *F*, 23–24; Jones, I, 39–40. Gage sent a ship to England with the news of Lexington and Concord. Within a week after the battle the Committee of Safety gathered the depositions of ninety-two Americans, one British officer, and two privates, prisoners, all of whom had taken part in the hostilities. The gist of the affidavits was that the British had fired first at both places (the officer could not say who had begun it at Lexington, but admitted the charge as to Concord). A letter was written to "The Inhabitants of Great Britain," giving the story of the day, briefly describing "the ravages of the Troops," protesting against the measures pursued by the British government, but declaring that "thev have not yet detached us from our Royal Sovereign." This,

with the depositions, was dispatched in a light, fast vessel belonging to Richard Derby of Salem and commanded by his son John. Although it sailed four days after Gage's ship, it carried only ballast and it reached England twelve days sooner.

The news flew about London. The King refused to believe "an American newspaper," the *Essex Gazette*, which went along with the other papers. The ministry announced that there was no such official news. Nevertheless, the American report obtained wide credence, and though Gage's dispatches, when they arrived, minimized the affair as much as possible all England knew that a war was on, and that it would take more than Gage's little army to fight it. (Force, 4, III, 437–438; 489–501, 945; French, *F*, 131, 313–316.)

2. Bancroft, IV, 170; French, *F*, 83. Romantic though this story about Putnam be, it is generally accepted by other historians, of cooler blood than Bancroft. For the disturbance in New York, see Jones, I, 39–41.
3. Bancroft, IV, 170.
4. French, *F*, 31, 50, 52, 62; Bancroft, IV, 170; Force, 4, II, 378–379, 384, 446–447.
5. Force, 4, II, 765; Heath, 11.
6. Force, 4, II, 1145; French, *F*, 77–78.
7. Force, 4, II, 655; Bancroft, IV, 174.
8. Force, 4, II, 411; Bancroft, IV, 174–175; French, *F*, 85.
9. French, *F*, 66, 72.
10. Frothingham, *S*, 99; French, *F*, 86.
11. Gordon, I, 492; Force, 4, II, 1122, 1142.
12. Gordon, I, 492; Force, 4, II, 820; French, *F*, 179–182.
13. French, *F*, 184; Barker, 50–52.
14. Heath, 10; French, *F*, 183; Barker, 50–52.
15. Force, 4, II, 370–814. French, *F*, 123–124; Frothingham, *S*, 93–96; Barker, 38, 44; Stiles, I, 541.
16. Lushington, 50, 52; Barker, 38. Burgoyne wrote that the fresh provisions smuggled into the town "were of great consequence to the health and spirits both of army and inhabitants; the former live entirely on salt meat, and I hardly dare to guess how some of the latter live at all" (Fonblanque, 151).
17. French, *F*, 188–189; Barker, 48–49; Frothingham, *S*, 108; Barker, 49.
18. French, *F*, 190–191; Frothingham, *S*, 109.
19. Force, 4, II, 719; French, *F*, 191–193; Frothingham, *S*, 109–110; Barker, 50–53.
20. Barker, 38–41; French, *F*, 163–166; Harris, 51.
21. This enumeration of regiments may not be exactly correct. There has not been found a complete list of an official character. This one has been made up by comparing statements in Fortescue, Belcher, Murdock, *B*, Drake, Swett, Clarke, and others. Swett includes the 14th Regiment, but without support elsewhere except that Drake mentions "One officer of that regt a volunteer" as having been killed at Bunker Hill and one wounded who may have been on detached service. There were but three companies of the 18th and six companies of the 65th. These were combined into an Incorporated Corps. Careful calculations in Murdock, *B*, 7, and French, *F*, 737–739, seem to fix the number correctly between 6,340 and 6,716, not including officers.
22. Partridge, *passim*; Wilkin, 6–24; French, *F*, 195–198; Trevelyan, I, 308. Anderson, T, *passim*, gives a more favorable estimate of Howe's military ability.
23. Wilkin, 46–73; French, *F*, 198–199.
24. Hudleston, *passim*; French, *F*, 199–200; Fonblanque, 136–159.
25. Force, 4, II, 968–970.
26. French, *F*, 204, quoting London *Evening Post*, July 18, 1775.

CHAPTER 7

The material for a story of the capture of Ticonderoga and Crown Point is to be found mainly in original documents printed in Force's *American Archives*, 4th Series, Vol. II, and in *Conn. Hist. Soc. Colls.*, Vol. I. Allen French's *The First Year of the Revolution* and *The Taking of Ticonderoga in 1775* give well supported accounts of the expedition and its results. Arnold's *Life of Benedict Arnold* and Pell's *Ethan Allen* are valuable secondary sources.

1. Greene, FV, 101; French, *F*, 143.
2. *D.A.H.*, V, 268; Pell, 74.
3. Force, 4, II, 243–244; French, *F*, 145–146; Pell, 72. Carleton had in Canada only two regiments of infantry and two companies of artillery; these were widely scattered. French, *F*, 147 n.
4. Pell, *passim; D.A.B.*, I, 185; Lossing, I, 180; Tyler, II, 229; French, *F*, 148–149; Irving, 1, 442–443.
5. Arnold, 36.
6. French, *F*, 149–150.
7. Force, 4, II, 450.
8. Force, 4, II, 485, 750.
9. Van Doren, 145–150; Arnold, 17–29.
10. *Conn. Hist. Soc. Colls.* I, 165–169, 181; Chittenden, 100; Force, 4, II, 556, 557; Dawson, I, 32. The committee says they had 70 men from Massachusetts and 140 from the New Hampshire Grants. Other reports make the force 40–50 and 100; but Mott's letter to the Massachusetts Provincial Congress indicates that there were 170 in all.
11. Philip Skene, an officer in Amherst's army of 1759, had obtained a grant of 30,000 acres at the head of navigation of Lake Champlain and had established there a considerable settlement, with a great stone house, mills, docks, and stores (Pell, 90–91).
12. Pell, 79–80; Force, 4, II, 558; *Conn. Hist. Soc. Colls.*, I, 119, 179.
13. Dawson, I, 23; Lossing, I, 124; *Conn. Hist. Soc. Colls.*, I, 171–172.
14. Force, 4, II, 558; *Conn. Hist. Soc. Colls.*, I, 172.
15. Force, 4, II, 557, 734; *Conn. Hist. Soc. Colls.*, I, 165 ff.; Pell, 81; Gordon, II, 12. Allen French (French, I, 28), who has made a special study of this expedition, is inclined to believe that Arnold did secure joint command with Allen.
16. Pell, 82; Force, 4, II, 1086. French, *T*, 151, says there were nearly 300 men at the cove.
17. Pell, 83; Dawson, I, 34. A different report as to what happened after they landed on the beach may be found in two letters to newspapers that are reprinted in Force, 4, II, 1086–1087. James Easton in the first letter described the affair without even mentioning Arnold's name. "Veritas" wrote to another paper that, instead of two boats, there was but one, in which "Colonel Arnold with much difficulty persuaded 40 men to embark with him"; then he sent it back for "near 50" others. When they landed "some gentleman" proposed "to wait open day. This Colonel Arnold strenuously opposed and urged to storm the fort immediately, declaring he would enter it alone, if no man had courage to follow him. This had the desired effect. . . . Colonel Arnold was the first that entered the fort." Pell (p. 104) thinks "Veritas" was Benedict Arnold himself.
18. Pell, 83–84.
19. Pell, 84–85; Force, 4, II, 623, 624–625.
20. Lossing, I, 125. It is interesting to note that Allen's words have been taken as evidence of his orthodox theological beliefs, whereas, in fact, he was a confirmed deist. Did he use them?
21. Force, 4, II, 556. Pell, 90, preserves the original spelling.
22. Force, 4, II, 557.
23. Pell, 92–93; Force, 4, II, 584.
24. Force, 4, II, 584, 645, 686, 734; Pell, 95–96; French, *F*, 153.
25. Force, 4, II, 645, 693, 734, 839, 840; Pell, 96–99.
26. Force, 4, II, 693, 714–715.
27. Force, 4, II, 892.
28. *Journals*, II, 55–56.
29. Force, 4, II, 732–735. 847. 892. 1066; French, *F*. 154.

30. Force, 4, II, 605–606, 623–624, 705, 706, 711, 713, 715, 719, 720, 721, 730, 735–737, 808, 869, 944, 1382; *Journals*, II, 74.
31. Force, 4, II, 1539, 1593, 1596, 1598, 1649.
32. Force, 4, II, 646.

CHAPTER 8

1. Frothingham, *S*, 114 n. "Elbow-Room" clung to him as a nickname. When he came to Boston as a prisoner after Saratoga, it is said, an old woman in the crowd cried out: "Make way! Make way! The General's coming! Give him elbow-room!"
2. Dawson, I, 66–68.
3. Force, 4, II, 1354; Frothingham, *S*, 116.
4. Frothingham, *C*, 14–15; Frothingham, *S*, 119–120; Ellis, 12; Swett, 16.
5. Ellis, 17; Frothingham, *C*, 10; Martyn, 117–119. Swett (p. 15) gives a graphic picture of this council, which he describes as "Gen. Putnam's statement to his son." He represents Ward and Warren as objecting because "the enterprize would lead to a general engagement." To which Putnam answered that they would risk only 2,000 men and "defend ourselves as long as possible, and, if driven to retreat, . . . every stone wall shall be lined with their dead, and at the worst, suppose us surrounded and no retreat, we will set our country an example of which it shall not be ashamed." Warren, it seems, "walked the floor, leaned on his chair, 'Almost thou persuadest me, Gen. Putnam,' said he, 'but I still think the project rash.' " Pomeroy, to the objection as to the lack of powder, answered that he "would fight the enemy with but five cartridges apiece." Putnam said of him that he was used to going out with three charges of powder and bringing home "two and sometimes three deer." Putnam and Pomeroy were much alike in their disregard of all the basic rules of warfare.
6. Martyn, 91; French, *F*, 49, 83.
7. Tarbox, 320–322; Field, 221–222; *D.A.B.*, XI, 281; Humphreys, *passim*; French, *F*, 214.
8. Swett, 19; Frothingham, *S*, 167; Martyn, 119.
9. Frothingham, *W*, *passim*; Bancroft, IV, 230; French, *F*, 120.
10. Frothingham, *S*, 121–122; Frothingham, *C*, 16–17; Swett, 15–16; Dawson, I, 71.
11. Swett, 16; Ellis, 22; Frothingham, *S*, 122; Dawson, I, 51, 71.
12. Frederic Kidder, *The History of New Ipswich* (1852), 95.
13. Dawson, I, 52; Frothingham, *S*, 122–123; Coffin, 31.
14. Frothingham, *S*, 123, 393–395; Ellis, 23; Swett, 20. The Committee of Safety afterwards stated that Breed's Hill was fortified "by some mistake," which was certainly not the case. It was the deliberate choice of the officers.
15. Frothingham, *S*, 135; Swett, 20.
16. Swett, 21; Ellis, 26; Frothingham, *S*, 124–125.
17. Frothingham, *S*, 125; Ellis, 27–28; Heath, 12; Force, 4, II, 1093.
18. French, *F*, 216; Coffin, 9.
19. Swett, 22; Murdock, *B*, 3, 12–14.
20. Stiles, I, 595; Frothingham, *S*, 126; Ellis, 28.
21. French, *F*, 217.
22. Frothingham, *S*, 127; Swett, 23.
23. Trevelyan, I, 353; French, *F*, 219; Ellis, 23; Swett, 22.
24. Frothingham, *S*, 128; Swett, 24–25; Ellis, 31.
25. Swett, 28; French, *F*, 217–218; Ellis, 31; Heath, 11; Frothingham, *S*, 130 n.
26. Murdock, *B*, 10–11; French, *F*, 220–221; Swett, 23; Ellis, 29–30; Fortescue, III, 158; Trevelyan, I, 353.
27. Murdock, *B*, 11–12; French, *F*, 222.
28. French, *F*, 222.
29. Murdock, *B*, 15–17; French, *F*, 740. Stedman, I, 128, says they carried three days' provisions.

30. Frothingham, *S*, 131; Force, 4, II, 1093; Trevelyan, I, 352.
31. Ellis, 33; Frothingham, *S*, 131.
32. French, *F*, 225; Ellis, 34.
33. Coffin, 16; Swett, 26; Ellis, 31; Dearborn, 16.
34. French, *F*, 225–226; Frothingham, *S*, 132; Dearborn, 17; Frothingham, *C*, 33.
35. Frothingham, *S*, 134, 390; French, *F*, 219; Drake, 17; Coffin, 17; Swett, 26–27; Force, 4, II, 1094.
36. Frothingham, *S*, 134–135; Coffin, 11, 17; French, *F*, 227.
37. French, *F*, 227–228, 741–742.
38. This disposition of the forces in the various parts of the defense is made by Frothingham, *S*, 135–136. He admits that there is no certainty as to its correctness. Some of the troops mentioned may have arrived on the field after the action began. Some regiments were dispersed in companies or smaller parties in all parts of the defenses. The disposition here shown can be only a more or less close approximation of the facts.
39. Frothingham, *S*, 136.
40. Irving, I, 475; Ellis, 38; French, *F*, 225; Frothingham, *S*, 133.
41. Ellis, 37; French, *F*, 229; Frothingham, *S*, 133.
42. Murdock, *B*, 21; French, *F*, 231.
43. Murdock, *B*, 22–23; Force, 4, II, 1089; French, *F*, 231. Landing parties also set fire to some of the houses. Force, 4, II, 1376.
44. French, *F*, 234.
45. Frothingham, *S*, 137.
46. Frothingham, *S*, 138–140; French, *F*, 234; Swett, 290.
47. French, *F*, 233–234; Murdock, *B*, 24–26; Belcher, I, 196.
48. French, *F*, 234–235; Murdock, 27. Stedman, I, 128, says the British carried 125 pounds per man.
49. Murdock, *B*, 27.
50. Dawson, I, 66–67, quoting Burgoyne's letter of June 25, 1775, to Lord Stanley. Fonblanque, 155, contains a letter to Stanley much the same in substance but strikingly different throughout.
51. Force, 4, II, 1098; Belcher, I, 196–197.
52. French, *F*, 237; Coffin, 12; Drake, 32.
53. French, *F*, 238; Belcher, I, 174; Frothingham, *S*, 141.
54. Frothingham, *S*, 142–143.
55. French, *F*, 239.
56. Frothingham, *S*, 146.
57. Frothingham, *S*, 389–391.
58. Frothingham, *S*, 147; French, *F*, 244.
59. Force, 4, II, 1662.
60. French, *F*, 243.
61. French, *F*, 243.
62. French, *F*, 247.
63. Drake, 28.
64. Frothingham, *S*, 150; French, *F*, 249; Drake, 28.
65. Frothingham, *S*, 150–151.
66. French, *F*, 250.
67. Coffin, 13, 14, 19, 30.
68. French, *F*, 252; Frothingham, *S*, 152.
69. Frothingham, *S*, 153, 210; French, *F*, 255.
70. Clarke, 5 n.; Frothingham, *S*, 152; French, *F*, 261.
71. Clarke, 13; Percy, 56; Trevelyan, I, 359; Force, 4, II, 1098.
72. Frothingham, *S*, 193; French, *F*, 263.
73. Fonblanque, 157; French, *F*, 218, 240; Frothingham, *S*, 138, 146, 152, 185; Swett, 36. Reports as to the number of guns vary between two small brass and six iron fieldpieces; five cannon and six swivel guns; six fieldpieces. The last is probably correct.

74. Force, 4, II, 1097.
75. Frothingham, *S*, 154.

CHAPTER 9

1. *Journals*, II, 79, 84, 85, 89, 91.
2. Adams, *L*, 65; Adams, *J*, II, 415.
3. Fitzpatrick, III, 292–293.
4. *Journals*, II, 97, 103.
5. *Journals*, II, 100–101.
6. Adams, *L*, 59, 70.
7. Jones, I, 55–57; Force, 4, II, 1318.
8. Force, 4, II, 1084–1085; Fitzpatrick, III, 302–304.
9. Fitzpatrick, III, 320.
10. See notes of contemporaneous references to assumption of command in French, *F*, 299.
11. Force, 4, II, 1472–1473.
12. Fitzpatrick, III, 371, 374.
13. French, *F*, 300.
14. Reed, I, 243.
15. Graydon, 147–148.
16. Fitzpatrick, III, 339, 357, 362.
17. French, *F*, 300.
18. Fitzpatrick, III, 325, 387, 389, 404, 415, 422, 445, 511; Frothingham, *S*, 891; *Conn. Hist. Soc. Colls.*, II, 254.
19. Fitzpatrick, III, 308; Force, 4, II, 1625, 1629.
20. Fitzpatrick, III, 355–356.
21. French, *F*, 301.
22. This survey of the early commissariat has been derived from the study of it by Victor L. Johnson.
23. *Journals*, II, 100.
24. Fitzpatrick, III, 324, 409.
25. Fitzpatrick, V, 192.
26. *Journals*, II, 89, 104, 173; Bancroft, IV, 247–248; *Pennsylvania*, I, 3–5.
27. Thacher, 31; Gordon, II, 68; Frothingham, *S*, 228 n. Their shirts are variously described as white, ash-colored, and brown.
28. Sawyer, 34–37, 80, 144–153.
29. Fitzpatrick, III, 367; Reed, I, 117.
30. *Pennsylvania*, I, 9–10.
31. French, *F*, 472.
32. See letters to Congress and the colonies in Fitzpatrick, III and IV, especially IV, 288; Reed, I, 118, 119.
33. French, *F*, 272 n.; Trevelyan, I, 406.
34. French, *F*, 321.
35. Frothingham, *S*, 316, 331.
36. Frothingham, *S*, 224–230; *Pennsylvania*, I, 21.
37. Frothingham, *S*, 226–227, 230–231.
38. Fitzpatrick, III, 453.
39. Frothingham, *S*, 234; French, *F*, 481; *Pennsylvania*, I, 6.
40. French, *F*, 482–483; Frothingham, *S*, 265, 267; Fitzpatrick, IV, 118; Barker, 66; Evelyn, 74–75; Moore, I, 166–167.
41. Trevelyan, I, 408.
42. Sparks, *L*, I, 156.
43. Fitzpatrick, III, 483–484.
44. Fitzpatrick, III, 511; Force, 4, III, 767–768.
45. *Journals*, III, 273–274.
46. Force, 4, III, 1153; Frothingham, *S*, 257.
47. Fitzpatrick, III, 505–513.

48. *Journals*, III, 265–266.
49. *Journals*, III, 321–323.
50. French, *F*, 365–366; Force, 4, III, 263–266, 354; *Journals*, II, 189.
51. French, *F*, 364, 370; Force, 4, II, 1118.
52. Force, 4, III, 1416; Fitzpatrick, III, 467.
53. French, *F*, 371–375; *Journals*, III, 278–279, 486.
54. Frothingham, *S*, 261, 269, 272, 289, 308; French, *F*, 370–372, 497; Evelyn, 72–73. For particulars of many captures, see the index to Fitzpatrick, IV, under the names of captains.
55. Trevelyan, I, 385.
56. French, *F*, 533–534.
57. Evelyn, 67.
58. Trevelyan, I, 386.
59. Frothingham, *S*, 281–282; French, *F*, 534–535.
60. French, *F*, 533, 536; Frothingham, *S*, 280, 287.
61. Trevelyan, I, 386; Frothingham, *S*, 294.
62. French, *F*, 332.
63. Fonblanque, 148.
64. Force, 4, III, 927.
65. Force, 4, III, 7.
66. Force, 4, III, 642.
67. Force, 4, III, 642, 1671.
68. Trevelyan, I, 396–397; Frothingham, *S*, 293.
69. Frothingham, *S*, 275.
70. *Journals*, III, 321–324; Fitzpatrick, III, 390.
71. Fitzpatrick, III, 391.
72. Fitzpatrick, IV, 77; French, *F*, 510.
73. *Journals*, II, 220, III, 322, 393; Force, 4, IV, 1245.
74. Frothingham, *S*, 276.
75. Fitzpatrick, IV, 60.
76. French, *F*, 520.
77. Fitzpatrick, IV, 208.
78. Force, 4, III, 1666–1667.
79. Fitzpatrick, IV, 137, 142, 146; Sullivan, I, 29–30; Frothingham, *S*, 273.
80. *Conn. Hist. Soc. Colls.*, VII, 128.
81. Fitzpatrick, IV, 124, 240.
82. Sullivan, I, 130.
83. Fitzpatrick, IV, 156–157, 138 n.
84. Fitzpatrick, IV, 211; Heath, 28.
85. Fitzpatrick, IV, 202, 210.
86. Stephenson, I, 339.
87. French, *F*, 630.
88. Fitzpatrick, IV, 122.
89. Fitzpatrick, IV, 238, 242.
90. Fitzpatrick, IV, 241–242.
91. Force, 4, IV, 699.
92. Fitzpatrick, IV, 319, 243–244; Frothingham, *S*, 287–288 and n.
93. Duer, 124–125.
94. Brooks, *passim*; Fitzpatrick, IV, 74.
95. Fitzpatrick, IV, 93.
96. Sparks, *C*, I, 94–95; French, *F*, 525–526, 655–656; Brooks, 38–44; Heath, 30; Greene, *GW*, III, 94.

CHAPTER 10

1. Fitzpatrick, IV, 336.
2. Fitzpatrick, IV, 314; Dawson, I, 87 n.
3. Force, 4, IV, 1539, 1636.

4. Fitzpatrick, IV, 335; Frothingham, *S*, 290; Dawson, I, 86.
5. Dawson, I, 85–87.
6. Fitzpatrick, IV, 348.
7. See map in Sparks, *W*, III, facing p. 26.
8. French, *F*, 656; Heath, 32–33.
9. Fitzpatrick, IV, 373; Frothingham, *S*, 297; Greene, FV, 19; Gordon, II, 190.
10. Barker, 69.
11. Fitzpatrick, IV, 370; Gordon, II, 191–192; Frothingham, *S*, 297.
12. Gordon, II, 193; French, *F*, 660; Frothingham, *S*, 298; Heath, 32.
13. Gordon, II, 193.
14. Dawson, I, 94.
15. Robertson, 74.
16. Frothingham, *S*, 298.
17. Fitzpatrick, IV, 375; Frothingham, *S*, 298–299.
18. *Orderly Book at Charlestown, Boston, and Halifax, June 17, 1775 to 1776, 26 May* (London, 1890), 71, 313.
19. Gordon, II, 195.
20. Frothingham, *S*, 299; Heath, 33.
21. *Mass. Hist. Soc. Colls.*, 4, I, 261.
22. Heath, 33.
23. Gordon, II, 196; Fitzpatrick, IV, 380.
24. *Orderly Book at Charlestown, Boston, and Halifax, June 17, 1775 to 1776, 26 May* (London, 1890), 313; Robertson, 74.
25. Fitzpatrick, IV, 371–377; Frothingham, *S*, 303–304.
26. Frothingham, *S*, 305; Heath, 34.
27. Frothingham, *S*, 302 n.
28. Trevelyan, I, 435.
29. Fitzpatrick, IV, 444; Frothingham, *S*, 302.
30. Robertson, 79.
31. Fitzpatrick, IV, 448.
32. Robertson, 75.
33. Gordon, II, 197; Frothingham, *S*, 307 n.; French, *F*, 666–667.
34. Fitzpatrick, IV, 449.
35. French, *F*, 665.
36. Barker, 72.
37. Robertson, 79.
38. Robertson, 81; Fitzpatrick, IV, 403.
39. *Mass. Hist. Soc. Proc.*, XIV, 284.
40. Fitzpatrick, IV, 415, 430.
41. Fitzpatrick, IV, 401, 407, 410.
42. Frothingham, *S*, 311.
43. French, *F*, 345.
44. French, *F*, 356.
45. Fonblanque, 196–197.
46. French, *F*, 540. Howe wrote to Lord George Germain, secretary of state for the colonies, that the expedition "was concerted by the General and Admiral for the destruction of Cape Ann [Gloucester] and Falmouth, two seaport towns, that were distinguished for their opposition to government." But, in reply to Germain's inquiry as to the reasons for destroying Falmouth, Howe wrote some time later that Gage's orders to the soldiers were only to assist Mowat "in annoying and destroying all ships belonging to rebels on the coast and in the harbours to the eastward of Boston." Sparks, *W*, III, 520–521. It would seem that the orders of Graves to the sailors and of Gage to the soldiers differed from each other, and that Mowat acted according to the admiral's directions as to what was to be destroyed.
47. French, *F*, 539–544.

CHAPTER 11

1. Smith, JH, I, 37.
2. This description of the inhabitants of Canada and the effects upon them of the Quebec Act is derived chiefly from French, *F*, 395–399, and Metzger, *passim*. While French estimates the number of Old Subjects at "more than 600," Smith, JH, I, 48, apparently on good authority, says "some 2,000."
3. *Journals*, II, 68–70.
4. *Journals*, II, 68–70.
5. Force, 4, II, 230.
6. *Journals*, I, 82–90.
7. Force, 4, II, 231.
8. *Journals*, II, 75.
9. Force, 4, II, 734.
10. *Journals*, II, 55–56.
11. Force, 4, II, 732.
12. Force, 4, II, 892.
13. *Journals*, II, 105, 123.
14. *Journals*, II, 109–110.
15. This description of Schuyler is derived chiefly from Smith, JH, I, 244–265, and Lossing, *S*, *passim*. It is possibly too favorable to Schuyler. For interesting materials on Schuyler's patriotism, see Van Doren, 45–47, 51–58, 231, 239–240, 391, 394–395.
16. Smith, JH, I, 320–321, 367–370, 610; Lossing *S*, 393–394; Bancroft, IV, 292, 308. The first news Montgomery's young wife had of his commission and his acceptance of it was conveyed to her when he asked her to make a cockade for his hat. Observing that she wept while she worked on it, he tried to turn her thoughts from danger to glory by saying, "You shall never blush for your Montgomery"—a remark so exactly in accord with the manner of speech of the period that it might have appeared in the pages of Richardson's *Sir Charles Grandison* or *Pamela*. Stilted though it sounds to modern ears, it was a sincere and touching expression of his pride in himself and his affection for her. She never did have to blush for him.
17. Smith, JH, II, 112; Bancroft, IV, 308. Heitman's *Historical Register* accredits Macpherson to Delaware. He had, in fact, been appointed major in Haslet's Delaware Continental regiment in Jan., 1776, before the fact of his death on Dec. 31, 1775, was made known in the colony.
18. Fitzpatrick, III, 302–303.
19. *D.A.H.*, III, 1–4, II, 280; Bancroft, IV, 448–449.
20. *D.A.H.*, I, 1; Reed, I, 119; Smith, JH, I, 275.
21. Smith, JH, I, 177.
22. Force, 4, II, 914, 1670, III, 301.
23. Smith, JH, I, 356.
24. Force, 4, II, 661, 665, 842–843.
25. Force, 4, II, 1140, 669, 1666; Lossing, *S*, 349, 353–356.
26. Force, 4, II, 244.
27. Force, 4, II, 939.
28. Force, 4, II, 1319.
29. Force, 4, II, 1594–1595.
30. Force, 4, II, 1735.
31. Force, 4, III, 26.
32. *Journals*, II, 178–183. The Speech likened the King to a father, the ministry to his servants, and the colonies to his son, carrying a little pack. The "proud and ill-natured servants [become] displeased to see the boy so alert and walk so nimbly with his pack." They advise the father to "enlarge the child's pack." This being done, "the child takes it up again . . . speaks but few words—those very small—for he was loth to offend his father . . . but the proud and wicked

servants . . . laughed to see the boy sweat and stagger under his increased load." They prevail on the father to double the load, saying, "He is a cross child —correct him, if he complains any more." The load is doubled amid "the tears and entreaties of the child," who staggers under the weight, "ready to fall at any moment. . . . He entreats the father once more, though so faint he could only lisp out his last humble supplication—waits a while—no voice returns . . . He gives one more struggle and throws off the pack. . . . The servants are very wroth. . . . They bring a great cudgel to the father, asking him to take it in his hand and strike the child." Thus persuasively were the great issues of the American Revolution described for the Indians.

33. Force, 4, III, 473–496. At a preliminary meeting an Oneida sachem had, toward the end of the day, blandly suggested that "as this day is far spent . . . [and] we are weary from having sat long in council, we think it time for a little drink."
34. Lossing, *S*, 387.
35. Force, 4, III, 1275–1276.
36. Force 4, II, 611; French, *F*, 758.
37. Force, 4, III, 339.
38. Force, 4, II, 714.
39. Smith, JH, I, 603. Later in the war, in 1777, Captain Allen McLane had a number of Oneida Indians in his partisan corps operating between Valley Forge and Philadelphia.
40. Lossing, *S*, 345–346, 352, 358.
41. Force, 4, II, 1685–1686, 1702.
42. Lossing, *S*, 343, 358.
43. Force, 4, II, 1606.
44. Force, 4, II, 1646.
45. Force, 4, II, 1702.
46. Smith, JH, I, 190; Force, 4, II, 1685.
47. Force, 4, II, 1605–1606.
48. Heitman, 291.
49. Force, 4, II, 1667.
50. Force, 4, II, 760, III, 17–18; Pell, 112.
51. Force, 4, III, 95.
52. Force, 4, II, 1535, 1606.
53. French, *F*, 386–387
54. Force, 4, II, 1729, 1734, 1735, 1759, III, 141, 242, 243. Facing a lack of gunsmiths in New York, the Provincial Congress appointed a committee "to write to Great Britain for four complete sets of Lock-Smiths to make Gun-Locks and . . . to pay the passage of Smiths from Britain to America."
55. Force, 4, II, 1704, 1735; Smith, JH, I, 255.
56. Force, 4, III, 135.
57. Force, 4, II, 1730.
58. Force, 4, III, 447, 452; Smith, JH, I, 256.
59. *Journals*, I, 186.
60. Lossing, *S*, 332, 381, 392.
61. Force, 4, III, 18, 126.
62. Force, 4, III, 47.
63. Force, 4, III, 263.
64. Smith, JH, I, 94–103.
65. Force, 4, II, 243, 1729; Smith, JH, I, 93–96, 99–103.
66. Force, 4, III, 135–136.
67. Force, 4, III, 18–19.
68. Force, 4, III, 50, 135, 442.
69. Force, 4, III, 468.
70. Lossing, *S*, 393.
71. Force, 4, III, 442; Smith, JH, I, 317.

CHAPTER 12

1. French, *F*, 381.
2. Force, 4, III, 467; Smith, JH, I, 321.
3. Smith, JH, I, 397, 323.
4. Force, 4, III, 669, 738; Smith, JH, I, 323–324.
5. Force, 4, III, 671, 669; Smith, JH, I, 324.
6. Force, 4, III, 669; Smith, JH, I, 328.
7. Force, 4, III, 669–670, 757; Smith, JH, I, 328–329, 331.
8. Force, 4, III, 752.
9. Force, 4, III, 672.
10. Smith, JH, I, 330.
11. Force, 4, III, 767; Smith, JH, I, 332.
12. Smith, JH, I, 332; French, *F*, 418; Burnett, *L*, I, 143.
13. Force, 4, III, 738–740.
14. Force, 4, III, 738.
15. Force, 4, III, 741–742, 923–924.
16. Force, 4, III, 723–724, 741–742, 923–924; Smith, JH, I, 333–334; French, *F*, 418–419.
17. Smith, JH, I, 334.
18. Force, 4, III, 723–724, 741–742, 923–924.
19. Force, 4, III, 738, 742.
20. Smith, JH, I, 335.
21. Force, 4, III, 697, 739, 753.
22. Smith, JH, I, 345–346.
23. Fortescue, III, 155.
24. Force, 4, III, 925–926; Smith, JH, I, 343–344.
25. Force, 4, III, 726.
26. Force, 4, III, 926; Smith, JH, I, 347–352.
27. Force, 4, III, 779, 797, 923, 980; Lossing, I, 412–414.
28. Force, 4, III, 754; Lossing, I, 415.
29. Force, 4, III, 952, 799, 953; Smith, JH, I, 380–390; French, *F*, 422–424; Allen, 14.
30. Force, 4, III, 951, 963; Smith, JH, I, 410.
31. Force, 4, III, 1124.
32. Smith, JH, I, 445.
33. Force, 4, III, 954, 839, 951.
34. Smith, JH, I, 418.
35. Force, 4, III, 1097–1098.
36. Force, 4, III, 796.
37. Force, 4, III, 459.
38. Force, 4, III, 1093–1094.
39. Force, 4, III, 1107–1108.
40. Force, 4, III, 1131.
41. Force, 4, III, 1095, 1096, 1098.
42. Force, 4, III, 1133–1134.
43. Force, 4, III, 1132.
44. Force, 4, III, 1342, 1392, 1185, 1395.
45. Force, 4, III, 1344, 1391–1394.
46. Force, 4, III, 1343–1344; Smith, JH, I, 464–465; Lamb, 116.
47. Force, 4, III, 1394, for terms of capitulation.
48. Force, 4, III, 1603.
49. Force, 4, III, 1603.
50. Force, 4, III, 1597, IV, 290, V, 1234; Smith, JH, I, 475–477, 483.
51. Smith, JH, I, 490.

CHAPTER 13

The basic material for a narrative of Arnold's march is to be found in the many journals, diaries, and letters written by those who took part in it. Probably no other expedition of similar length made by so few men has produced so many contemporary records. Arnold's journal tells the tale to October 30, where it breaks off abruptly. There may have been more, but no more has been discovered. He also wrote many letters. No fewer than nineteen other accounts by participants are to be found, written by Dearborn, Senter, Meigs, Thayer, Topham, Humphrey, Wild, Ware, Henry, Stocking, Morison, Melvin, Pierce, Tolman, Kimball, Haskell, Fobes, Squier, and one anonymous person. They are of uneven value, as some were compiled from others, and some were written long after the expedition. Many of them are individually printed, but the most convenient access to them may be had in *March to Quebec*, in which Kenneth Roberts has annotated Arnold's journal and letters and twelve of the other more important accounts, as well as Montresor's journal and Enos's defense. In his novel *Arundel*, Roberts follows closely the actual events of the march and illuminates it with his remarkably vivid imagination, re-creating as truly as the novelist can its scenes and characters.

Among the strictly historical accounts, *Arnold's March from Cambridge to Quebec* and *Our Struggle for the Fourteenth Colony* both by Justin H. Smith, are complete, discriminating, and scholarly. *Arnold's Expedition to Quebec*, by John Codman, is more readable but not so accurate in detail. Allen French's account in *The First Year of the American Revolution* is not so full as Smith's, but is equally reliable. Graham's *Life of General Daniel Morgan,* Parton's *Life and Times of Aaron Burr,* Arnold's *Life of Benedict Arnold,* and Gordon's *History of the Rise, Progress and Establishment of the Independence of America* contain valuable material.

To limit the following notes to a reasonable compass, many references to Smith's and Codman's and French's books and to the journals and letters have been omitted.

1. Smith, J, 10.
2. Smith, JH, I, 498.
3. Fitzpatrick, III, 436. Montresor's journey, on which his map was based, had been made in a canoe, not in a bateau, in June and in the opposite direction from the one now proposed. Moreover, much of the most difficult part had been made at night, when he could not see difficulties which he fortunately escaped.
4. Smith, J, 75–76.
5. Fitzpatrick, III, 471.
6. Fitzpatrick, III, 472–473.
7. Parton, *passim.* French, *F*, 433, says of Burr: "Romance and tradition connect his name with that of an Indian girl, Jacataqua, who is said to have followed the expedition, but the historical foundation of the tale is so slight that the girl is not even mentioned by the best modern student of the march."
8. Greene, GW, III, 94–101; Bancroft, IV, 287–288; Henry, 12.
9. Fitzpatrick, III, 491–496.
10. Morison, 13. Humphrey, 8, says the delay was for the purpose of filling up the ranks of the companies.
11. Stocking, 10. Fobes, 10, says the vessels were "dirty schooners and fishing-boats."
12. Force, 4, III, 960.
13. Force, 4, III, 960–961. Whether Natanis was actually in Carleton's pay and inimical to the Americans, or whether he was merely trying to prevent the expedition from intruding on his hunting grounds, is uncertain. His subsequent conduct indicated no unfriendliness to the expedition. On the other hand, he may simply have inclined toward whichever party was, at the moment, the more useful to him.
14. Henry, 23.

15. Arnold had appointed Greene to lead the riflemen; but Morgan, Smith, and Hendricks, especially Morgan, refused to take orders from anyone but himself, nor would the other two willingly subordinate themselves to Morgan. Arnold yielded and gave Morgan a sort of leadership of the others, rather than official command of them. While he did lead them, Smith and Hendricks showed much independence at various times. Washington gently reproved Morgan for taking such an attitude. Fitzpatrick, IV, 2.
16. Force, 4, III, 960.
17. Smith, J, 468.
18. Dearborn, 6.
19. Senter, 8.
20. Smith, J, 469.
21. Smith, JH, I, 537.
22. Dearborn, 9.
23. Senter, 11.
24. Senter, 11–12; Force, 4, III, 1061.
25. Smith, J, 125.
26. Smith, JH, I, 547.
27. Henry, 46.
28. Smith, J, 472.
29. Smith, J, 131.
30. Smith, JH, I, 554.
31. Smith, J, 474.
32. Melvin (Roberts, 439) says that Morgan's men let Greene's division pass them so that they might have a chance to steal some of the provisions, which they succeeded in doing. Hence Greene's unexpected shortage.
33. Senter, 15. It has been said that this was a West Indian hurricane, following the the same course as that of September 22, 1938, and with similar devastating results.
34. Henry, 52.
35. Morison, 25.
36. Smith, J, 478; Force, 4, III, 1610, 1634.
37. Senter, 16–17. On his return to Cambridge, Enos was court-martialed "for quitting his commanding officer without leave." The only witnesses were his own officers, who had retreated with him. They testified that the return was necessary because of lack of provisions, and Enos was acquitted. But within a month he left the army; and he "never survived the stigma of having done a disreputable act." (Henry, 59–63; Force, 4, III, 1701–1721.)

    Yet there is something to be said for Enos. Though to the rest of the expedition, who went on in spite of hardship and starvation, his departure seemed a base and cowardly act, he had a case. One of his descendants, Rev. Horace E. Hayden, has defended him in a rather convincing manner, for which see Roberts, 631–648.
38. Senter, 18.
39. Smith, JH, I, 586. There were two women in the expedition. One was the wife of Sergeant Grier, "a large virtuous and respectable woman." The other, "beautiful though coarse in manner, was the wife of James Warner, a rifleman, young, handsome in appearance . . . athletic and . . . [such as] seemed to surpass in bodily strength." These two "appeared to be much interested in each other's welfare and unwilling to be separated." In the march up Dead River, Warner gave out, seated himself at the foot of a tree, and "said he was determined to die." His wife "attended him for several days, urging him to march forward," but he could not. Stocking says she "tarryed with him until he died, while the rest of the company proceeded on their way." Being unable to bury him, "she covered him with leaves and then took his gun and other implements and left him with a heavy heart. After traveling twenty miles she came up with us." Henry says she stayed until she found her ministrations unable to save him,

then placed her own share of food and a canteen of water at his feet and left him. In either event, she survived the journey and arrived at the St. Lawrence with the others. (Henry, 61, 64–65; Stocking, 21.)

40. Smith, J, 482.
41. Smith, JH, I, 591; Morison, 28.
42. Senter, 23.
43. Henry, 73.
44. Stocking, 34.
45. Morison, 34.
46. Henry, 73–74.
47. The quotation is from Stocking, 23–24. Exactly how many men had survived that march is uncertain. With the volunteers and Colburn's artificers added to the original draft, about 1,100 started. The defection of Enos subtracted possibly 300. A considerable number of invalids were sent back, and with them went sound men to take care of them. Morison, one of the diarists, figures the total loss on this account at 200, which seems excessive. He says that 510 reached the St. Lawrence; hence he concludes that 70 or 80 had been lost on the way. His estimate has been questioned by Justin H. Smith (Smith, J, 233), who reckons the survivors at 675, that being the number of men for whom Arnold drew clothing from Montgomery on December 5. If that be correct and Enos's men are added, making a total of 975, it would appear that no more than 125 all told were lost by death, sickness, desertion, and as able-bodied caretakers of the invalids. As we know that about 70 invalids were sent back from the Dead River alone, in two parties, it seems incredible that no more than 55 were lost otherwise. It seems probable that the arrivals were not much more in number than half of the original party.
48. Joseph Warren wrote to Samuel Adams: "Arnold has made a march that may be compared to Hannibal's or Xenophon's." Thomas Jefferson also thought it equaled Xenophon's retreat. Murray, the English historian, wrote: "The march of Col. Arnold and his troops is one of the greatest exploits recorded in the annals of nations." A letter from Quebec dated November 9 states: "There are about 500 Provincials arrived at Point Levi . . . by way of Chaudiere, across the woods. Surely a miracle must have been wrought in their favour. It is an undertaking above the common race of men." (Force, 4, III, 1420.)

CHAPTER 14

1. Force, 4, III, 1633–1636.
2. Ogden, 24.
3. Morison, 26; Humphrey, 19.
4. Force, 4, III, 1635–1636; Morison, 36; Henry, 81; Senter, 27; Humphrey, 20.
5. Morison, 36; Henry, 82; Force, 4, III, 1724.
6. The estimates of Carleton's force vary slightly. See Force, 4, III, 1697, 1724–1725, IV, 175. But 1,200 seems to be a proper figure.
7. Smith, JH, II, 16 n.
8. Force, 4, III, 1697.
9. Fobes, 17.
10. Dearborn, 13.
11. Ogden, 29.
12. Fobes, 18.
13. Stocking, 26.
14. Humphrey, 24.
15. Henry, 94.
16. Stocking, 26.
17. Henry, 94.
18. Force, 4, IV, 188–193. The archaic sense of "pretty" as defined by *The Concise Oxford Dictionary of Current English*: "fine, stout, as *a pretty fellow*."

19. Justin H. Smith (Smith, JH, II, 90) seems to have supposed that the clothes brought by Montgomery were the conventional uniforms of the British army, scarlet coats and white breeches, for he describes the troops marching back to Quebec as "drawing a long red mark across the snow." Pierce in his journal (Roberts, 689) tells of drawing "red Coats." These may have been undercoats or waistcoats (Smith, JH, II, 90). However, the journal of Captain Pausch of the Brunswickers, who came with Burgoyne (Pausch, 93–94), describes in detail, as given in the text, the uniforms issued to Burgoyne's army for winter service in Canada. Lefferts, p. 160, pl. XXXIII, also describes and pictures them. Henry in his *Account of Arnold's Campaign*, p. 103, mentions his "fine white blanket coat" and his "cap or *bonnet rough*," which exactly accords with the descriptions of Pausch and Lefferts. Pausch tells of these uniforms being made in Montreal, not brought from England. So they were no new thing for Canada; indeed, they were of proper Canadian fashion. As Montgomery had captured a full year's supply of uniforms of the 7th and 26th regiments, they must have included these winter garments. The sealskin moccasins are also described by Henry. They were made "large, and according to the usage of the country, stuffed with hay or leaves to keep the feet dry and warm." These were, doubtless, also a part of the British equipment, for Burgoyne's entire army was taught how to use snowshoes" (Lefferts, 160). It would not have been possible with ordinary shoes or boots. The Americans were not all equipped with these new warm garments until Dec. 29, when final distribution—delayed perhaps by difficulties of transporting all Montgomery's supplies—was made (Humphrey, 24, 26).
20. Force, 4, III, 1595.
21. Sparks, *C*, I, 95.
22. Fitzpatrick, IV, 147.
23. Fitzpatrick, IV, 231.
24. Force, 4, III, 1638.
25. Force, 4, IV, 288.
26. Force, 4, IV, 289; Stocking, 26–27.
27. Force, 4, IV, 289.
28. Force, 4, III, 1638–1639.
29. Stocking, 27.
30. Force, 4, IV, 464.
31. Force, 4, IV, 464; Smith, JH, II, 117.
32. Dearborn, 18.
33. Stocking, 27.
34. Force, 4, IV, 289.
35. Henry, 105.
36. Leake, 127.
37. Force, 4, IV, 706.
38. Senter, 107.
39. Stocking, 29.
40. Henry, 108.
41. Graham, 102.
42. Dearborn, 21.
43. Dearborn, 23; Lossing, I, 200; Force, 4, IV, 656.
44. *Journals*, IV, 70, 78.
45. Smith, JH, II, 352.
46. Smith, JH, II, 406.
47. *Journals*, IV, 394.
48. Fitzpatrick, V, 78–79.
49. Stillé, 31.
50. Force, 4, VI, 1103–1104.
51. Arnold, 94.
52. Smith, JH, II, 434.
53. Smith, JH, II, 441.

CHAPTER 15

1. Fitzpatrick, IV, 407–408, 440, 442, 444, 462, 467; Heath, 32.
2. *Journals*, II, 207, 225.
3. *Journals*, III, 270.
4. *Journals*, III, 321–325.
5. Fitzpatrick, IV, 121.
6. Fitzpatrick, IV, 299–301.
7. Fitzpatrick, IV, 316.
8. *Journals*, III, 285.
9. *Journals*, II, 107, III, 291, 337, 418, IV, 59. These calls on the various colonies are to be found in *Journals*, III, 285, 291, 387, 418, IV, 59, 235, 237, 331, 347, 355, 357, V, 461, 466, 487, 607, 666. The call on Maryland mentions only two regiments, but four regiments and seven independent companies were actually raised. New York raised thirteen, New Jersey three, Pennsylvania twelve including the riflemen, Massachusetts eleven, Connecticut thirteen. Those mentioned in the text include only such as were specifically called for by resolutions of the Congress passed between October 9, 1775, and July 24, 1776. The absence of a call on Connecticut, except for one more regiment (*Journals*, IV, 360), is probably accounted for by the fact that the troops of that colony at Boston were taken into the army at its adoption in 1775. The text, therefore, is not to be taken as enumerating the whole number of regiments included in the army at the time of the Battle of Long Island, but rather the slow steps by which it was built up to become a real Continental army.
10. *Journals*, IV, 412; Lundin, 122–134.
11. *Journals*, III, 322.
12. *Journals*, V, 631.
13. Lefferts, 26. A Hessian officer who saw the regiment on Long Island remarked on their "most beautiful English muskets and bayonets" (Field, 438, Lowell, 67–68).
14. Johnston, *C*, Pt. I, 123.
15. Fitzpatrick, IV, 395, 397, 399, 414.
16. Sparks, *C*, I, 152.
17. Trevelyan, Pt. II, Vol. I, 179.
18. Field, 525.
19. Trevelyan, Pt. II, Vol. I, 179; Duer, *passim*
20. Johnston, *C*, Pt. I, 63; Irving, II, 300.
21. Johnston, *C*, Pt. I, 126–132.
22. Trevelyan, Pt. II, Vol. I, 32–34.
23. Lowell, 299–300. Lecky, 244, says the hiring of the German mercenaries "made reconciliation hopeless and the Declaration of Independence inevitable. It was idle for the Americans to have any further scruples about calling in foreigners [the French] to assist them when England had herself set the example."

    Before the Germans were hired the British government had tried to get Russians; but the other European governments, "which feared, or hated, or envied Britain," besieged Empress Catherine with "warnings and expostulations" and wrecked the negotiations. The smaller German states were next solicited, successfully (Trevelyan, Pt. II, Vol. I, 42–45). They were willing to furnish thousands of men, at a price. The Duke of Brunswick, for example, agreed to furnish 4,300 men. He was to receive an annual payment of £11,517 17s. 1½d., while his troops were in the British service, and twice as much each year for two years thereafter. He was also to get "head money" at the rate of £7 4s. 4½d. for each man furnished, and, for each one killed, the same sum additional. "According to custom three wounded men shall be reckoned as one killed": so ran the treaty. All this was to go into the Duke's own pocket, the wounded men and the dead men's families not receiving even the extra halfpenny (Lowell, 17–18). In all, during the war six German states sent out to America 29,875 men, of whom 12,562 never returned to Germany, about 5,000 deserting and remaining in America. (Lowell, 20, 300.)

24. Ambrose Serle, who was aboard Lord Howe's flagship as secretary to his lordship, described their arrival in his journal (Serle, 28): "We were saluted by all the Ships of War in the Harbour, by the Cheers of the Sailors all along the Ships and by those of the Sailors on the Shore. A finer Scene could not be exhibited, both of Country, Ships and men, all heightened by one of the brightest Days that can be imagined."
25. Van Tyne, 243.
26. Stedman, I, 198; Kemble, 80; Serle, 28.
27. Fitzpatrick, V, 444.
28. Johnston, *C*, Pt. I, 99–100; Greene, FV, 34; Serle, 67.

CHAPTER 16

The most fully detailed story of the Battle of Long Island and the subsequent retreat is to be found in Henry P. Johnston's *The Campaign of 1776*. Although he fails to cite authority for most of the statements in his narrative, his sources are not hard to trace, especially as he reprints the greater part of the contemporary source material in Part II of his book. Another full account is in *The Battle of Long Island,* by T. W. Field. This also lacks specific citation in the text but has a supplement in which much of the source matter is printed. Field's text, however, is less reliable than Johnston's. His fervor, excitability, and one-sidedness, apparently due to excessive patriotism, and his superabundance of adjectives disqualify him as a reliable historian. In substance and style his account is very much like the Fourth of July orations of eighty or ninety years ago.

Force, Fitzpatrick, Kemble, Serle, Read, Reed, Robertson, Gordon, Ramsay, and the original documents printed in Johnston, Field, and Dawson form the major part of the contemporary or near contemporary authorities. They are supplemented by Carrington, Dawson, Johnston, Bancroft, Trevelyan, Anderson, and other writers.

1. Kemble, I, 84–85; Johnston, *C*, Pt. I, 139–140.
2. Kemble, I, 84–85; Serle, 71; Carrington, 200; Johnston, *C*, Pt. I, 140–141; Dawson, I, 154. A Hessian officer made the following comment in his diary (Lowell, 60): "Not a soul opposed our landing. This was the second blunder of the rebels. . . . Their first mistake was when we disembarked on Staten Island, for they might have destroyed a good many of our people with two six-pounders, and now they might have made it very nasty for us." The officer, however, seems to have forgotten the much heavier guns on the frigates covering the landing, which would have made it even more "nasty" for the Americans attempting opposition.

   Ambrose Serle in his journal (Serle, 73–74) describes the scene of the landing: "The Disembarkation of about 15,000 Troops upon a fine Beach, their forming upon the adjacent Plain, a Fleet of above 300 Ships & Vessels with their Sails spread open to dry, the Sun shining clear upon them, the green Hills and Meadows after the Rain, and the calm Surface of the Water upon the contiguous Sea and up the Sound, exhibited one of the finest & most picturesque Scenes that the Imagination can fancy or the Eye behold."
3. Lowell, 58.
4. Trevelyan, Pt. II, Vol. I, 271.
5. Serle, 71.
6. *Pennsylvania*, I, 306.
7. Lowell, 80; Dawson, I, 154; Kemble, I, 85; Johnston, *C*, Pt. I, 141.
8. Carrington, 201.
9. Johnston, *C*, Pt. I, 142–143.
10. Johnston, *C*, Pt. I, 142.

11. Johnston, *C*, Pt. I, 148–150.
12. Graydon, 179, describes "the celebrated General Putnam, riding with a hanger belted across his brawny shoulders, over a waistcoat without sleeves (his summer costume) . . . much fitter to head a band of sickle-men or ditchers, than musketeers."

    Trevelyan, Pt. II, Vol. I, 275, describes him as "a shrewd, genial, New England uncle . . . well fitted for infusing an extra dose of hopefulness and enthusiasm into soldiers, who, just then, would have been better for a little self-distrust, but he did not possess either the training or the temperament indispensable for the leader of a regular army."
13. Johnston, *C*, Pt. I, 143.
14. Field, 146.
15. Fitzpatrick, V, 485.
16. Johnston, *C*, Pt. I, 148. The lack of intelligence service at this time is in strong contrast with the espionage which Washington organized after his retreat across the Jerseys, and which made possible his subsequent success at Trenton.
17. Lowell, 60–61; Johnston, *C*, Pt. I, 202; Field, 429–430.
18. Carrington, 202; Dawson, I, 153; Force, 5, I, 1255; Stedman, I, 193–194.
19. Fitzpatrick, V, 491.
20. Read, 17; Johnston, *C*, Pt. I, 154; Dawson, I, 152.
21. Johnston, *C*, Pt. I, 155–157.

CHAPTER 17

1. *Pennsylvania*, I, 307.
2. Greene, FV, 37.
3. Johnston, *C*, Pt. I, 175–176; Force, 5, I, 1256; Carrington, 202; Dawson, I, 154; Kemble, I, 85.
4. Serle, 77; Johnston, *C*, Pt. I, 176–177.
5. *Pennsylvania*, I, 310; Johnston, *C*, Pt. I, 160–161, Pt. II, 48.
6. Dawson, I, 151, 152.
7. Irving, II, 319.
8. Bancroft, V, 31.
9. Dawson, I, 151.
10. Field, 353; Johnston, *C*, Pt. II, 33.
11. Johnston, *C*, Pt. I, 164–166; Dawson, I, 151.
12. Field, 354; Johnston, *C*, Pt. I, 166.
13. Field, 488.
14. Dawson, I, 152.
15. Field, 354; Dawson, I, 151.
16. Field, 355.
17. Field, 356.
18. Duer, 162 n.
19. Dawson, I, 151; Serle, 78; Johnston, *C*, Pt. I, 167.
20. Field, 450.
21. Johnston, *C*, Pt. I, 173.
22. Johnston, *C*, Pt. II, 62.
23. Field, 159–160.
24. Read, 172; Johnston, *C*, Pt. I, 182–185; Dawson, I, 155.
25. Johnston, *C*, Pt. I, 183–184.
26. Dawson, I, 155. The Hessian jägers, also commonly called "chasseurs," were an element in the German forces in America, few in number—perhaps about 600—but active and efficient in combat. Their functions were like those of the British light infantry. Most of them had been foresters or gamekeepers in civil life and were therefore used to acting individually and thoroughly accustomed to the conditions of bush fighting. They were armed with short, heavy rifles of large bore, which carried no bayonets. These German rifles were the model from which

the early Pennsylvania gunsmiths, most of them German immigrants, had developed the American long-barreled, small-bore weapon.

27. Lowell, 62–63; Kemble, I, 85.
28. Trevelyan, Pt. II, Vol. I, 279. A Hessian officer in his diary (Lowell, 64) wrote: "Our Hessians marched like Hessians; they marched incorrigibly."
29. Field, 352.
30. Trevelyan, Pt. II, Vol. I, 280.
31. Onderdonk, 152. From a letter of Lieut. Col. Bedford (Read, 173) it appears that three Hessians had been picked up somewhere and were taken to the camp along with these British prisoners. It is amusing to note that the Delawares were accused of unmilitary duplicity in counterfeiting Hessian uniforms to deceive their foe, although, at the time the Delaware uniform was adopted, probably few of them had even heard of Hessians and certainly none had ever seen one in uniform.
32. Bancroft, V, 32.
33. *Pennsylvania*, I, 307.
34. Dawson, I, 147, 151; Johnston, *C*, Pt. I, 137–139; Greene, FV, 38–40.
35. Field, 489.
36. Moore, I, 296.
37. Field, 389, 511; Read, 175; *Archives*, III, 1341.
38. Field, 378. Kemble, I, 86, reports 349 casualties.
39. Dawson, I, 156.
40. Johnston, *C*, Pt. II, 64.
41. Johnston, *C*, Pt. I, 193.
42. Bancroft, V, 33.
43. Fitzpatrick, V, 489.
44. Greene, FV, 40.
45. Greene, FV, 41.
46. Irving, II, 327.
47. Adams, CF, 60.
48. Graydon, 156–157.
49. Fitzpatrick, V, 240.
50. Trevelyan, Pt. II, Vol. I, 203–204.
51. Frothingham, 134.
52. Van Tyne, 25.
53. Fisher, I, 493; Marshall, I, 109.
54. Fitzpatrick, VI, 4–7.
55. Van Tyne, 251.
56. Fortescue, III, 409.
57. Van Tyne, 251.
58. Fortescue, III, 409.

CHAPTER 18

1. Field, 452; Stedman, I, 193.
2. Johnston, *C*, Pt. I, 208.
3. Fitzpatrick, V, 497. Serle, 80, says that on the 28th "the Firing was very con tinual & very hot and lasted till dark night."
4. Trevelyan, Pt. II, Vol. I, 287.
5. Johnston, *C*, Pt. II, 43.
6. Graydon, 165, speaking for Shee's regiment. There were some tents, but not more than half enough for all.
7. Goldwin Smith, 85–94, has written, "Howe . . . though brave, was torpid; probably he was not only torpid but half-hearted. Had he followed up his victory [on Long Island] there probably would have been an end of the Continental army, whatever local resistance might have survived. . . . His subsequent conduct seems to have been marked with a sluggishness and irresolution which the

energy of his lieutenant, Cornwallis, could not redeem. Washington was allowed to pluck victory and reputation out of the jaws of defeat."

8. Trevelyan, Pt. II, Vol. I, 286.
9. Johnston, *C*, Pt. I, 218.
10. Force, 5, I, 1230, 1246.
11. Johnston, *C*, Pt. II, 30.
12. Dawson, I, 152.
13. Reed, I, 227; Johnston, *C*, Pt. I, 223. Of this premature withdrawal Graydon (167–168) wrote as follows: "We received orders to retire. We were formed without delay and had marched near halfway to the river, when it was announced that the British light horse were at our heels. Improbable as was the circumstance, it was yet so strenuously insisted upon that we halted and formed, the front rank kneeling with presented pikes . . . to receive the charge of the supposed assailants." None appearing, "we again took up the line of march and had proceeded but a short distance . . . when we were informed that we had come off too soon and were compelled to return to our post. This was a trying business for young soldiers; it was nevertheless strictly complied with."
14. Heath, 49.
15. Irving, II, 329.
16. Trevelyan, Pt. II, Vol. I, 290. Kemble (I, 86) says, "In the Morning, to our Astonishment found they had Evacuated all their Works . . . without a shot being fired at them."
17. Stedman, I, 193; Irving, II, 335; Trevelyan, Pt. II, Vol. I, 292; Frothingham, 137; Greene, FV, 44.
18. Johnston, *C*, Pt. I, 199–201.
19. Greene, GW, I, 212.
20. Fitzpatrick, VI, 4–7.
21. *Journals*, V, 762.

CHAPTER 19

1. Whitton, 143.
2. Fitzpatrick, VI, 16, 25.
3. Rodney, C, 112.
4. Johnston, *C*, Pt. I, 227 n.
5. Fitzpatrick, VI, 5.
6. Fitzpatrick, VI, 32.
7. Fitzpatrick, VI, 4; Johnston, *C*, Pt. I, 126–131.
8. Force, 5, II, 182–183.
9. Reed, I, 213, 235 n.; Force, 5, II, 120–121; Trevelyan, Pt. II, Vol. I, 294.
10. Fitzpatrick, VI, 6; *Journals*, V, 733.
11. Fitzpatrick, VI, 28–29.
12. Greene, FV, 45.
13. Fortescue, III, 189.
14. Fitzpatrick, VI, 30.
15. *Journals*, V, 749.
16. Force, 5, I, 326–327.
17. Force, 5, I, 329–330.
18. Fitzpatrick, VI, 53.
19. Mackenzie, I, 39.
20. Mackenzie, I, 37–38.
21. Heath, 50; Serle, 90–91, 99–100, 103; Mackenzie, I, 45; Robertson, 97; Force, 5, I, 443.
22. Evelyn, 84.
23. Serle, 103.
24. Johnston, *C*, Pt. II, 81.
25. Evelyn, 85. Trevelyan (Pt. II, Vol. I, 297) says: "It was an imposing spectacle.

The amazing fire from the shipping, the soldiers in scarlet clambering up the steep rocks, and the river covered with boats full of armed men . . . forming one of the grandest and most sublime stage-effects that had ever been exhibited."

26. Fitzpatrick, VI, 58.
27. Johnston, *H*, 34.
28. Johnston, *H*, 35.
29. Johnston, *C*, Pt. II, 83, Martin's narrative.
30. Heath, 52; Gordon, II, 327; Graydon, 174; Irving, II, 353; Rodney, C, 122; Force, 5, II, 1013; Johnston, *C*, Pt. II, 86.
31. Johnston, *C*, Pt. II, 83.
32. Irving, II, 343.
33. Johnston, *C*, Pt. I, 237. Trevelyan (Pt. II, Vol. I, 298) says: "Not one of the retreating battalions would ever have reached the American lines in military order, and with half its full numbers, if Howe had promptly pushed his troops athwart the peninsula [island] which here was less than 3000 yards wide."
34. Stephenson, I, 365. "The Rebels left a great quantity of Cannon, Ammunition, Stores, provisions, tents &c.&c. behind them" (Mackenzie, I, 50).
35. Johnston, *C*, Pt. I, 238–239. Colonel Humphrey (quoted in *ibid.*, 89) tells of Putnam, "for the purpose of issuing orders and encouraging the troops, flying, on his horse, covered with foam, wherever his presence was most necessary. Without his extraordinary exertions . . . it is probable the entire corps would have been cut to pieces."
36. Trevelyan, Pt. II, Vol. I, 298.
37. Van Tyne, 255 n.
38. Johnston, *C*, Pt. II, 90.

CHAPTER 20

The best account of this affair is Henry P. Johnston's *The Battle of Harlem Heights*. It is especially valuable for the considerable collection of contemporary letters, reports, and other documents to be found on pp. 125–234. E. C. Benedict's monograph of the same name is of very little value, being chiefly controversial on unimportant details and apparently generally erroneous in its conclusions. Carrington and Dawson add hardly at all to Johnston's account; nor is there much additional to be found elsewhere.

1. Johnston, *H*, 49–50, map.
2. Force, 5, II, 450–451; Johnston, *H*, 65.
3. Johnston, *H*, 65.
4. Johnston, *H*, maps facing 50, 70.
5. Johnston, *H*, 44–47; map facing 50.
6. Fitzpatrick, VI, 59.
7. Johnston, *H*, 52–55. One of the Ranger captains was Nathan Hale, but he was at this time on duty as a spy within the British lines in New York, a duty in which he risked and forfeited his life.
8. Johnston, *H*, 61–62.
9. Reed, I, 237. Johnston, *H*, 67, quotes from a favorite song of the British light infantry the following stanza:

   Hark! Hark! The bugle's lofty sound
   Which makes the woods and rocks around
      Repeat the martial strain,
   Proclaims the British light-armed troops
   Advance. Behold! Rebellion droops.
      She hears the sound with pain.

10. Johnston, *C*, Pt. I, 251–252; Irving, II, 359.
11. Fitzpatrick, VI, 68.

12. Johnston, *H*, 82–83, 143.
13. Lushington, 79.
14. Reed, I, 238; Johnston, *H*, 177.
15. Johnston, *H*, 204. Lieut. Col. Kemble of Howe's army said that 14 were killed, and that 11 officers, 5 sergeants, 3 drummers, and 138 privates were wounded. (Kemble, I, 89.)
16. Johnston, *H*, 226.
17. Fitzpatrick, VI, 96.
18. Johnston, *H*, 87.
19. Fitzpatrick, VI, 96.
20. Rodney, C, 129.
21. Johnston, *H*, 154, 177.
22. Reed, I, 238. Howe claimed a victory for his side in this affair. As the British held the ground and the Americans retreated, it was technically their success. But Gen. Sir Henry Clinton admitted that the British had been "in a scrape," and Col. von Donop reported that, but for the arrival of his jägers, "two regiments of Highlanders and the British infantry would have all, perhaps, been captured." The improvement in the behavior of the Americans engaged has caused some American historians to regard this little battle "as a turning point in the uphill progress of their national military efficiency." (Trevelyan, Pt. II, Vol. I, 304.)

CHAPTER 21

1. Heath, 53.
2. Fitzpatrick, VI, 96.
3. Fitzpatrick, VI, 96, 138.
4. Reed, I, 240.
5. Fitzpatrick, VI, 91. One ensign was caught leading 20 men "all loaded with plunder, such as house-furniture, tableware, linen and kitchen utensils, china and delf ware," as well as some women's clothing.
6. Fitzpatrick, VI, 117–118.
7. Fitzpatrick, VI, 112.
8. *Journals*, V, 762.
9. Heath, 62–63; Hufeland, 111–112; Force, 5, III, 471, 921–922; Rodney, C, 139; Irving, II, 377–378; Trevelyan, Pt. II, Vol. I, 312; Bancroft, V, 69.
10. *Journals*, VI, 866.
11. Sparks, *W*, IV, 155 n.; Hufeland, 114–115; Heath, 63.
12. Hufeland, 116.
13. Force, 5, II, 1188–1189; Hufeland, 118–122; Heath, 65.
14. Hufeland, 124. The Americans claimed to have shot down "140 or 150" (Stiles, II, 91). Other estimates ran as high as 800 to 1,000, absurd exaggerations, of course. The Americans lost Col. Shephard; the British lost Capt. W. G. Evelyn, a young soldier of great promise (Evelyn, 11).
15. McDonald, Part I, 21.
16. Reed, I, 245.
17. Heath, 66. The principal facts in this account of the affair at Mamaroneck have been derived from McDonald's narrative. See also *Archives*, II, 1030, for an account by Haslet.

CHAPTER 22

1. Force, 5, II, 607.
2. Hufeland, 135–136, map on 130.
3. Kemble, I, 94–95.
4. Trevelyan, Pt. II, Vol. I, 312.
5. Mackenzie, I, 82; Serle, 26; Force, 5, II, 1158; Lowell, 75.
6. Force, 5, III, 473, 725–726.

7. Force, 5, III, 725–726; Hufeland, 134–137; Johnston, *C*, Pt. II, 56; Tallmadge, 17.
8. Hufeland, 136–137.
9. Hufeland, 137.
10. Rodney, C, 142.
11. Hufeland, 137–138.
12. Heath, 70.
13. Hufeland, 140.
14. Rodney, C, 142.
15. Lowell, 77; Rodney, C, 142; Irving, II, 392.
16. Lowell, 75; Hufeland, 141–142.
17. Rodney, C, 143.
18. McDonald, I, 50.
19. McDonald, I, 53.
20. Rodney, C, 143.
21. Heath, 70.
22. Trevelyan, Pt. II, Vol. I, 314–315.
23. Heath, 7. Hufeland comments (p. 143) on the discipline the British and Hessian troops displayed at this point: "All of these men had waded through the cold waters of the Bronx and had fought a bloody battle in their wet clothing on a day late in October, in which hundreds of their comrades were left on the field and yet they formed and dressed their lines before being permitted to build fires to dry their clothing." He compares this "perfect military machine" with Washington's "poorly armed, ill-supplied and inexperienced army."
24. Bancroft, V, 74; Irving, II, 393; Whitton, 149; Hufeland, 144.
25. Greene, FV, 53.

CHAPTER 23

The most complete account of the battle at Fort Washington is to be found in Edward F. De Lancey's monograph *The Capture of Mount Washington*, a pamphlet published in a very small edition in 1877 after first appearing in the *Magazine of American History* for Feb. of that year. The author fortifies his statements by numerous references to original sources, and his story may be relied upon, in general. The best contemporary account by a witness is in the *Diary* of Lieut. Frederick Mackenzie, of the Welch Fusileers, I, 104–110. The *Memoirs* of Captain Graydon give interesting details, as also does the diary of Archibald Robertson. Vols. II and III of Force's *American Archives,* 5th Series, contain much valuable material, notably Howe's dispatches and his full return of casualties, prisoners taken, etc. Heath's *Memoirs* yield some material. From these and the other sources, such as Kemble, George W. Greene, Hufeland, Carrington, and Dawson, the account herein has been compiled. The individual references below are confined chiefly to the sources of quotations.

1. Anderson, 25; Read, 210–211.
2. Hufeland, 148; Greene, FV, 53; Heath, 72–73.
3. Heath, 75.
4. Force, 5, III, 521.
5. Fitzpatrick, VI, 248–249.
6. Force, 5, III, 543–544.
7. De Lancey, 6–7.
8. De Lancey, 9.
9. Graydon, 186.
10. Bancroft, V, 74.
11. Force, 5, III, 619. Graydon says (p. 186) of Magaw: "He had heard of sieges being protracted for months and even years . . . as the place he had to defend was called a Fort and had cannon in it, he thought the deuce was in it, if he could not hold out for a few weeks."

12. Force, 5, III, 619.
13. Fitzpatrick, VI, 257–258.
14. Fitzpatrick, XVI, 150–152.
15. Force, 5, III, 1294.
16. Force, 5, III, 519.
17. *Pennsylvania*, I, 106.
18. Force, 5, II, 330.
19. Graydon, 94–95; Dawson, I, 89; Johnston, *C*, Pt. I, 277.
20. Fortescue, III, 194 n
21. Force, 5, III, 921–925.
22. Sparks, *W*, IV, 179 n.
23. Kemble, I, 99.
24. Robertson, 111.
25. Force, 5, III, 1058.
26. Force, 5, III, 1059.

CHAPTER 24

1. Force, 5, III, 831.
2. Force, 5, III, 822, 833.
3. Mackenzie, I, 114.
4. Mackenzie, I, 97–98.
5. Force, 5, III, 822.
6. Trevelyan, Pt. II, Vol. II, 18–19.
7. Fitzpatrick, VI, 265.
8. Force, 5, III, 634, 639.
9. Force, 5, III, 708, 764; Fitzpatrick, VI, 287, 293.
10. Mackenzie, I, 112; Gordon, II, 352; Greene, GW, I, 276.
11. Force, 5, III, 861, 1058; Greene, GW, I, 276–278; Serle, 144.
12. Kemble, I, 101.
13. Force, 5, III, 828; Greene, GW, I, 277.
14. Fitzpatrick, VI, 266.
15. Force, 5, III, 779; Fitzpatrick, VI, 295 n.
16. Fitzpatrick, VI, 298.
17. Force, 5, III, 792.
18. Reed, I, 255–257.
19. Reed, I, 257–258
20. Fitzpatrick, VI, 298.
21. Force, 5, III, 790.
22. Gordon, II, 354.
23. Fitzpatrick, VI, 303.
24. Fitzpatrick, VI, 305–306.
25. Bancroft, V, 82.
26. Force, 5, III, 926; Trevelyan, Pt. II, Vol. II, 20.
27. Fitzpatrick, VI, 303.
28. Force, 5, III, 1082.
29. Fitzpatrick, VI, 314.
30. Fitzpatrick, VI, 320.
31. Fitzpatrick, VI, 313.
32. Fitzpatrick, VI, 320–322.
33. Fitzpatrick, VI, 325, 397.
34. Trevelyan, Pt. II, Vol. II, 20.
35. Anderson, 27.
36. Fitzpatrick, VI, 33; Stryker, *TP*, 20.
37. Fitzpatrick, VI, 333.
38. Fitpatrick, VI, 331.
39. Force, 5, III, 1316.

40. Fitzpatrick, VI, 336.
41. Anderson, 28.
42. Lundin, 147.
43. Fitzpatrick, VI, 339.

CHAPTER 25

1. *Archives,* III, 1358.
2. Thacher, 67
3. Anderson, 28.
4. Fitzpatrick, VI, 346, 355, 381.
5. Fitzpatrick, VI, 355.
6. Fitzpatrick, VI, 398.
7. Force, 5, III, 927–928.
8. Fitzpatrick, VI, 397–398.
9. Force, 5, III, 1199, 1434; Marshall, C, 105–107.
10. Force, 5, III, 1434.
11. Read, 253–254.
12. Force, 5, III, 1290.
13. Force, 5, III, 1180; *Journals,* VI, 1027; Bancroft, V, 89.
14. Trevelyan, Pt. II, Vol. II, 63, 67–69.
15. Force, 5, III, 794, 795, 834; Heath, 79–86.
16. Force, 5, III, 1121, 1138.
17. Fitzpatrick, VI, 398.
18. Force, 5, III, 1201.
19. Fitzpatrick, VI, 347.
20. Stryker, *TP,* 59–60.
21. Force, 5, III, 1201.

CHAPTER 26

William S. Stryker's book, *The Battles of Trenton and Princeton,* contains the fullest account of the campaign in the Jerseys from Dec. 26, 1776, to Jan. 5, 1777. It is supported by the inclusion, in Part II, of more than a hundred contemporaneous letters and other documents, many of them otherwise not readily accessible. It has not been thought necessary to refer to this material in the footnotes, except in a few instances. Capt. Thomas Rodney's diary is of great value in its full details and in the sidelights it throws on the activities of the army. Force, 5, III, contains much relevant material, as also does Fitzpatrick. Lundin's *Cockpit of the Revolution* covers all the operations of the war in New Jersey in a comprehensive manner. Carrington's and Dawson's accounts are helpful.

1. Stryker, *TP*, 48 n.
2. Force, 5, III, 1317.
3. Force, 5, III, 1401–1402.
4. Force, 5, III, 1317.
5. Fitzpatrick, VI, 366, 372, 373.
6. Irving, II, 469.
7. Force, 5, III, 1376. Fitzpatrick, VII, 427 n., doubts the authenticity of this letter and does not include it in his collection. Whether authentic or not, it well describes the situation.
8. Dunbar, I, 282.
9. Rodney, C, 150–151.
10. Stryker, *TP*, 362.
11. Stryker, *TP*, 137.
12. Force, 5, III, 1443, 1445–1446.
13. Trevelyan, Pt. II, Vol. II, 113.

14. Rodney, T, 23.
15. Force, 5, III, 1441.
16. Force, 5, III, 1429.
17. Rodney, C, 150.
18. Rodney, T, 24.
19. Fitzpatrick, VI, 440.
20. Stryker, *TP*, 213.
21. Force, 5, III, 1462.
22. Irving, II, 500.
23. Stephenson, I, 383.
24. *Journals,* VI, 1045.

CHAPTER 27

The most recent account of events before and after the battle of Princeton is to be found in Alfred H. Bill, *The Campaign of Princeton, 1776–1777* (Princeton, N. J., 1948).

1. Force, 5, III, 1429.
2. Reed, I, 278.
3. Fitzpatrick, VI, 445–446.
4. Irving, II, 494.
5. Reed, I, 278–280.
6. Rodney, T, 25.
7. Reed, I, 281; Fitzpatrick, VI, 447–450.
8. It is usually stated that the extension of time was for six weeks, though Washington wrote to the Congress that it was a month (Fitzpatrick, VI, 45).
9. Fitzpatrick, VI, 457–458. Besides this call for bounty money, Washington asked Morris for more the next day. "We have the greatest occasion at present for hard money to pay a certain set of people, who are of particular use to us. If you could possibly collect a sum, if it were but one hundred or one hundred and fifty pounds, it would be of great service." These people were his spies in New Jersey. His intelligence service was very good at this time, in strong contrast to the lack of it at Long Island and in the Pennsylvania campaign of 1777. Paper money might do for the bounty to the troops, but these gentlemen required real money.
   No more revealing light could be thrown on the financial condition of the time than that of the list of hard moneys collected by Morris by scraping Philadelphia: "410 Spanish milled dollars @ 7s. 6d., 2 English crowns, 72 French crowns, 1072 English shillings" (Force, 5, III, 1486).
10. Stephenson, I, 386.
11. Stryker, *TP*, 259.
12. Stryker, *TP*, 271–272; Fischer, I, 566; Bancroft, V, 105; Irving, II, 504; Frothingham, 173; Lundin, 206; Carrington, 286. G. W. Greene, in *The Life of Nathanael Greene*, says: "Each course had its advocates, when a voice was heard, saying, "Better than either of these, let us take the new road through the woods, and get in the enemy's rear by a march upon Princetown, and, if possible, on Brunswick even.' From whom did this bold suggestion come? St. Clair claimed it as his, and why should the positive assertion of an honorable man be lightly called in question?" But it has been questioned, by Bancroft elaborately, as a tale "written in extreme old age . . . self-laudatory." He gives the credit to Washington, as do Irving, Frothingham, Lundin, Carrington, and Trevelyan. Stryker thinks it more probably originated with General Philemon Dickinson of the New Jersey militia or Reed, because thev knew the country.
13. Reed, I, 288.
14. Rodney, T, 32–33.
15. Stryker, *TP*, 276.
16. Rodney, T, 32.

17. Rodney, T, 33.
18. Rodney, T, 34.
19. Trevelyan, Pt. II, Vol. II, 135: "Colonel Haslet dropped with a bullet through his brain. In his pocket was an order directing him to go home on recruiting service, which he had divulged to no one and had silently disobeyed."
20. Rodney, T, 34.
21. Rodney, T, 36.
22. Rodney, T, 36.
23. Fitzpatrick, VI, 469.
24. Fortescue, III, 205, says, "The whole cause of the rebellion in America was saved by Washington's very bold and skilful action." Nicholas Cresswell, a young Englishman adrift in America, wrote in his *Journal* (pp. 179–180) that the news of Trenton and Princeton "is confirmed. The minds of the people are much altered. A few days ago they had given up the cause for lost. Their late successes have turned the scale and now they are all liberty mad again. Their Recruiting Parties could not get a man (except he bought him from his master) no longer since than last week, and now the men are coming in by companies. . . . They have recovered their panic and it will not be an easy matter to throw them into confusion again."
25. Fitzpatrick, VI, 470.
26. The details of the operations after Princeton have been derived chiefly from Thomas Rodney's *Diary*.

CHAPTER 28

1. Irving, III, 4–5; Lundin, 20; Stephenson, I, 394; Stedman, I, 239; Greene, GW, I, 309; Greene, FV, 75.
2. Fitzpatrick, VI, 472; Irving, II, 4.
3. Fitzpatrick, VII, 29.
4. Fitzpatrick, VII, 288.
5. Gordon, II, 422.
6. Fitzpatrick, VII, 350. Alexander Graydon, a visitor at the camp, wrote in his *Memoirs* (p. 277): "I had been extremely anxious to see the army. Here it was, but I could see nothing which deserved the name . . . the motley, shabby covering of the men."
7. Fitzpatrick, VII, 189.
8. Fitzpatrick, VI, 496–497.
9. Fitzpatrick, VII, 38.
10. Fitzpatrick, VI, 473, and VII, 128, 129, 230; Lundin, 234–235; Trevelyan, III, 56–57.
11. Fitzpatrick, VII, 288. Inoculation, at that time "rarely practised" in America, was the forerunner of vaccination. The patient was infected in such a way that a mild form of the disease was induced. Trevelyan, III, 80–82, gives a full account of the process.
12. *Journals,* VI, 1045. The Additional Battalions were not allotted among the states as the original eighty-eight battalions had been. They could be recruited anywhere, and officers could be appointed without regard to state lines.
13. *Journals,* V, 763.
14. Fitzpatrick, VII, 86.
15. Fitzpatrick, VII, 139 n.
16. *Journals,* VI, 1093.
17. Fitzpatrick, VII, 89; also 91, 120, 133, 138, and especially 349.
18. Fitzpatrick, VII, 66. Washington repeated his call for "companies or half Companies" on Feb. 23 and again on Mar. 6 (*ibid.,* 194, 254).
19. *Journals,* VII, 211. Washington (see Fitzpatrick, VII, 208) had written on Feb. 28, "Nothing distresses me more than the Universal Call . . . from all Quarters for fire Arms. which I am totally unable to supply." Trevelyan (III, 39) says

that the manufacturing capabilities of America were so limited that contracts could seldom be made for more than 100 muskets at a time.

20. Jones, I, 71; Trevelyan, Pt. II, Vol. II, 153; Lundin, 221; Kemble, I, 107.
21. Lundin, 222; Sullivan, I, 310; Stedman, I, 240.
22. Stedman, I, 240.
23. Frothingham, 189. Thomas Jones, a judge of the Supreme Court of New York and an ardent Loyalist, in his *History of New York During the Revolutionary War* caustically comments on a New York incident of March, 1777: "This month was remarkable for the investiture of General Howe with the Order of the Bath; a reward for *Evacuating* Boston, for *lying indolent* upon Staten Island for near two months, for *suffering* the whole rebel army to escape him upon Long Island, and *again* at the White Plains, *for not putting an end to rebellion* in 1776, when so often in his power, for making such *injudicious cantonments* of his troops in Jersey as he did, for *suffering* 10,000 veterans under experienced generals to be cooped up in Brunswick and Amboy by about 6,000 militia under the command of an inexperienced general." Of Howe's "cooped up" condition in Amboy and New Brunswick he says, "Not a stick of wood, a spear of grass or a kernel of corn could the troops in New Jersey procure without fighting for it." (Jones, I, 177, 171.)
24. Hufeland, 209–213; Fitzpatrick, VII, 328 n.; Stedman, I, 278; Jones, I, 177.
25. Jones, I, 180–181; Gordon, II, 468; *Journals*, VII, 579.

CHAPTER 29

The most useful account of Howe's maneuvers described in this chapter is to be found in Troyer S. Anderson, *The Command of the Howe Brothers During the American Revolution.* Anderson is always helpful on the plans and thought of the Howes. He is perhaps too gentle in his treatment of them.

1. Marshall, I, 170; Stedman, I, 283; Irving, III, 73; Lundin, 313; Greene, FV, 80.
2. Sullivan, I, 354.
3. Greene, FV, 81.
4. Montresor, 421; Frothingham, 193.
5. Montresor, 421–422; Marshall, I, 173.
6. Sullivan, I, 383.
7. Trevelyan, III, 61, writes: "To the surprise and amusement of the American officers . . . [Howe] placidly and deliberately began to entrench his camp, as if he had come into their neighborhood to spend a quiet Summer."
8. Stedman, I, 284; Lundin, 317; Sullivan, I, 393; Gordon, II, 470; Fitzpatrick, VIII, 261.
9. Fitzpatrick, VIII, 353; Lundin, 317–318.
10. Lundin, 319.
11. Stedman, I, 284; Montresor, 123; Kemble, I, 121; Fitzpatrick, VIII, 270, 276; Irving, III, 81.
12. Greene, GW, I, 394; Fitzpatrick, VIII, 281–282; Gordon, II, 471.
13. Cresswell, 242.
14. Fitzpatrick, VIII, 298.
15. Stedman, I, 285.
16. Gordon, II, 474.
17. Kemble, I, 123; Lundin, 323–324; André, 34. Trevelyan, III, 63, writes: "Stirling, who was still something of a military pedant, neglected the rare advantages which the locality presented, and drew up his command in parade-ground order; while Cornwallis made no mistakes and gave full play to the indignant valour of his followers."
18. Fitzpatrick, VIII, 307; Montresor, 429; Lundin, 323; Marshall, I, 175–176; Gordon, II, 473–474; André, 33.
19. Stedman, I, 286.

20. Montresor, 426.
21. Irving, III, 74, 85; Lundin, 312; Marshall, I, 176.
22. Fitzpatrick, VIII, 355; Whitton, 179–180.
23. Fitzpatrick, VIII, 336.
24. Fitzpatrick, VIII, 364, 365, 366.
25. Irving, III, 104; Fitzpatrick, VIII, 365; Kirkwood, 104.
26. Stedman, I, 289; André, 34; Serle, 239.
27. Fitzpatrick, VIII, 376, 407.
28. Fitzpatrick, VIII, 386, 414, 454.
29. Montresor, 429; Serle, 241; Baurmeister, 2.
30. Fitzpatrick, VIII, 460–468.
31. Fitzpatrick, VIII, 496, 497, 499. On July 30 Washington wrote to Gates: "Gen'l. Howe's in a manner abandoning Genl. Burgoyne is so unaccountable a matter, that till I am fully assured it is so, I cannot help casting my Eyes continually behind me."
32. *Pennsylvania Archives,* V, 415.
33. Fitzpatrick, VIII, 503, 505, and IX, 5.
34. *Archives,* III, 1380–1381.
35. Fitzpatrick, VIII, 1–5.
36. Fitzpatrick, IX, 37, 45; Kirkwood, 130.
37. Fitzpatrick, IX, 57.
38. Fitzpatrick, IX, 107, 110 n., 113, 114.
39. Fitzpatrick, IX, 115–116.
40. Stedman, I, 290; Fortescue, III, 214.
41. Wilkin, 238.
42. Carrington, 364.
43. Carrington, 364.
44. Fitzpatrick, IX, 119.

CHAPTER 30

There is a wealth of information concerning the movements of the British army on the way to the Brandywine in the journals of Captain John Montresor, Archibald Robertson (an engineer), Ambrose Serle (secretary to Admiral Howe), Major John André, and the letters of the Hessian Major Baurmeister. On the American side, Washington's letters and orders are the chief sources. Edward W. Cooch's *Battle of Cooch's Bridge* is very helpful.

1. Hughes, III, 149.
2. Fitzpatrick, IX, 125–127.
3. Adams, J, 298. The number of men in Washington's army is in doubt. A committee of the Congress, which visited the camp about August 1, reported 17,949 privates, exclusive of certain contingents; including officers, 16,920 were fit for duty, of whom 14,089 were privates. The number of men in September is more generally reckoned at 11,000. See Greene, GW, I, 443; Irving, III, 148, writes: "The disaffected, who had been taught to believe the American forces much less than they were in reality, were astonished as they gazed on the lengthening procession of a host, which to their unpractised eyes, appeared innumerable; while the Whigs, gaining fresh hope and animation from the sight, cheered the patriot squadrons as they passed." See also Fitzpatrick, IX, 127–128.
4. Graydon, 291.
5. Fitzpatrick, IX, 129, 130–135.
6. Fitzpatrick, IX, 128, 147; *Journals,* VIII, 667.
7. Irving, III, 194; Fitzpatrick, IX, 451–452; Stephenson, II, 20; Greene, GW, I, 444; Hughes, II, 150.
8. Montresor, 442; André, 36; Serle, 245; Robertson, 142.
9. André, 37; Serle, 245; Montresor, 442; Baurmeister, 3–4; Robertson. 143.

10. Montresor, 443; André, 38; Robertson, 143; Baurmeister, 4. Lieut. William J. Hale of the 45th British regiment wrote: "We found a great part of the stores remaining in the Town, though they had employed several of the preceding days in removing them to Wilmington. 100 butts of Porter were left in one cellar, Madeira, Rum, Melasses, Tobacco, Yams, Flower etc; a number of Sloops loaded with shoes, stockings and rum . . . fell into our hands."
11. Marshall, I, 182; Irving, III, 198; Montresor, 444; Baurmeister, 7; André, 38.
12. Montresor, 444; Baurmeister, 8; André, 41.
13. Baurmeister, 6; André, 41; Robertson, 144.
14. André, 41–42.
15. Montresor, 443.
16. Fitzpatrick, IX, 146–147, 148.
17. Baurmeister, 8–9, notes that the army's wagon train "consisted of 276 waggons loaded with rum, flour and salt-meat."
18. Montresor, 445.
19. This account of the affair at Cooch's Bridge is based on the accounts of Montresor, 445–446; André, 42–43; Baurmeister, 9; Robertson, 144–145; Irving, III, 198–199; and Cooch, *passim.*
20. Montresor says the Americans left 20 dead on the field. Baurmeister says 30, including five officers. Marshall reckons 40 killed and wounded in Maxwell's corps. On the other side Montresor admits only 3 killed and 20 wounded. Robertson says 30 killed and wounded. Washington wrote to the Congress that a woman said she had seen nine wagonloads of British wounded.

    Montresor says that Maxwell's force consisted of 720 Continentals, "together with 1,000 militia and Philadelphia Light Horse." No other account mentions any horsemen. Marshall says that there were 900 cavalry with Washington's army, who were "employed principally on the lines in watching the enemy, gaining intelligence and picking up stragglers." It is pretty safe to say that there were none at Cooch's Bridge. It is also very improbable that there were any militia in important numbers with Maxwell. They were concentrated elsewhere. Sergeant Thomas Sullivan of the British 49th regiment in an account of the fight (*Pa. Mag. of Hist.*, XXXI, 410) calls Maxwell's men "a chosen corps of 1000 men." He says the British had "3 men killed; 2 officers and 19 men wounded," and claims Maxwell's loss was "the commanding officer . . . and other officers killed and wounded, besides 50 men killed and many more wounded." Maxwell was certainly not killed.
21. Montresor, 446; Robertson, 145.
22. André, 43; Montresor, 446–448.
23. Fitzpatrick, IX, 140.
24. Fitzpatrick, IX, 179.
25. Montresor, 448.
26. Fitzpatrick, IX, 197. Montresor, 449, says: "The Army moved . . . through an amazingly strong country, being a succession of large hills, rather sudden with narrow vales . . . not a shot fired. . . . Rebel Light Horse about, but fled."

CHAPTER 31

1. MacElree, 132–133.
2. Bowen, 7–8; MacElree, 131–133; Lossing, II, 171 n. Some confusion as to these fords has arisen from the fact that change of ownership of the adjacent farms resulted in change of name of some of the fords. Painter's was also known as Jones's, Wistar's as Shunk's, Buffington's as Brinton's, confusing it with the truce Brinton's next above Chad's. To make matters worse some of the actors in the drama miscalled certain fords. Washington called Jefferis's Ford Jones's; and, as if that common name stuck in everybody's mind, Sullivan gave it to Wistar's Ford. In this narrative "Jones's" has been voided, the distinctive alternative name being used in each case.

3. Carrington, 368; Bowen, 10; Fitzpatrick, IX, 425 n.
4. Carrington, 368; Bowen, 7; MacElree, 134.
5. Bowen, 8; Hughes, III, 157–158; MacElree, 136; Lee, 89.
6. Baurmeister, 12. One of the many anecdotes clustering about this battle tells of an English Quakeress, who ran out of her house and implored Knyphausen not to go on to the Ford. "Dear man," she cried, "George Washington is on the other side and he has all the men in this world with him. To which the General replied: "Never mind, madam. I have all the men in the other world with me."
7. Baurmeister, 13; Carrington, 369–370; Bowen, 9.
8. Baurmeister, 13.
9. Baurmeister, 13.
10. Greene, GW, I, 447.
11. Fitzpatrick, IX, 205.
12. Bowen, 10; Carrington, 370; Lossing, II, 174.
13. Sparks, *W*, V, 459.
14. Muhlenberg, 492. It seems strange that Washington should have regarded Howe's division of the British army as "a terrible blunder" after his own action at the Battle of Trenton.
15. Hughes, III, 159; Lossing, II, 174; Bowen, 10, 30. Fortescue (III, 216) regards it as fortunate for Washington that he did not persist in his plan to cross and attack Knyphausen. "For Knyphausen was an able commander, his troops were far superior to Washington's in training and discipline, and, by Howe's forethought, he had been supplied with plenty of guns, so that he would certainly have held his own until Cornwallis came up in the enemy's rear and destroyed the Americans utterly."
16. Sparks, *W*, V, 459.
17. Hughes, III, 161–162; Bowen, 10.
18. Carrington, 342; MacElree, 141. It is impossible to be certain as to the order in which the conflicting messages were sent and received, and the authorities differ. Marshall mentions only Ross's dispatch received at eleven o'clock. Irving speaks only of "an express from Sullivan," giving no time, but states that Washington immediately sent Bland to reconnoiter and then resolved to cross and attack Knyphausen. Bowen sends Bland out first and states that he reported the enemy on the Valley Road and the dust arising there, which was afterwards confirmed by Ross, yet it appears that Bland's dispatch about the dust was dated 2 P.M., while Ross reported at 11 A.M. Carrington puts Bland's message at "between nine and ten o'clock," states that similar news came from Hazen, fixes Ross's dispatch at 11 A.M. and omits reference to Washington's order to Bland. Lossing puts Bland's message first and has it confirmed by Ross and by Hazen. Greene, GW, mentions only a message from Sullivan that the enemy was marching to the upper fords, follows this by Washington's order to cross, then Sullivan's contradicting message and finally Cheyney's arrival. Hughes gives Ross first place, with news of the enemy on the road, makes Washington then order the attack, but send Bland out to scout; after that he brings in the Ross message and then Spear's contradiction. Unfortunately, Washington's order to Bland was dated "11 September, 1777, 20 minutes after o'clock," so that it cannot be placed in time.

    In the text an effort has been made to sort out the times of the messages and arrange them in their proper order. The result may not be in accord with the facts, but it certainly seems to fit in with the known circumstances and the apparently proper relations between the several messages. The questions raised may not be of the first importance, but it is annoying not to be able to be sure of their answers.
19. Montresor, 449; Dawson, I, 281. There is some uncertainty as to the strength of Cornwallis's column. In the American histories it is usually reckoned at 10,000 men. Montresor puts it at "about 7,000." Howe had reported 13,799 privates on embarkation. He had lost some through sickness, a few by capture, but pretty

certainly still had twelve to thirteen thousand. Of these there were about 5,000 with Knyphausen. That would leave Cornwallis perhaps 8,000 rank and file, which is the way an army's strength is usually computed.

20. Townsend, 21–25.
21. Carrington, 376; Marshall, I, 185; Irving, III, 204; Sullivan, I, 463, 472; Greene, GW, I, 418.
22. Sullivan, I, 463, 472–473.
23. Montresor, 449; Lossing, II, 175; MacElree, 144; Irving, III, 185.
24. Bowen, 11.
25. Montresor, 450; André, 46; Dawson, I, 282.
26. Bowen, 11; MacElree, 144; Townsend, 24; Lossing, II, 175; Dawson, I, 276.
27. Montresor, 450.
28. Sullivan, I, 463–464, 476, 555.
29. Fitzpatrick, IX, 206–207.
30. Hughes, III, 164; Greene, GW, I, 449.
31. Greene, GW, I, 449; Gordon, II, 511; Hughes, III, 163–164.
32. Anderson, 36–37.
33. Dawson, I, 282.
34. Bowen, 12.
35. Greene, GW, I, 451–453; Irving, III, 207–208; Montresor, 450.
36. Dawson, I, 282.
37. Baurmeister, 14–15.
38. Dawson, I, 282. Most histories dismiss the fight at the Ford in a paragraph or two, as if there were only a brief resistance by the troops under Wayne, Maxwell, and Proctor, followed by a quick retreat. The account sent by Major Baurmeister of the Regiment von Mirbach, a participant in the action, to his superior officer in Hesse-Kassel, on which the description in the text is based, shows clearly that the Americans put up a stiff and prolonged defense. This may be accepted, if for no other reason, because it began at half past four o'clock and lasted until dark.
39. Bancroft, V, 179.
40. Dawson, I, 282.
41. Montresor, 451; Bancroft, V, 179.

CHAPTER 32

1. Stedman, I, 293; Gordon, II, 513.
2. Fitzpatrick, IX, 207–208.
3. *Journals*, VIII, 735–738; Fitzpatrick, IX, 212.
4. Fitzpatrick, IX, 229, 215, 258.
5. Montresor, 452–453; Baurmeister, 18.
6. Marshall, I, 188.
7. Hughes, III, 181.
8. Baurmeister, 18.
9. Baurmeister, 18; Montresor, 453.
10. Greene, GW, I, 462, gives Pickering credit, on his own statement, for suggesting this move.
11. Baurmeister, 18–19; Montresor, 451–453.
12. Marshall, I, 188; Greene, GW, I, 462; Irving, III, 212; Belcher, II, 269; Brooks, 105.
13. Fitzpatrick, IX, 238–239.
14. Kirkwood, 175; Greene, GW, I, 462; Irving, III, 214.
15. Fitzpatrick, IX, 238.
16. Kirkwood, 175.
17. Montresor, 454–456.
18. Lossing, II, 163.
19. Marshall, I, 189.

20. Montresor, 455; André, 49; Baurmeister, 19.
21. Gordon, II, 516–517; Montresor, 455; Marshall, I, 89; Irving, III, 215; Stedman, I, 294; Lossing, II, 163; Baurmeister, 19; André, 49. This was the celebrated "Paoli Massacre," commonly described as a butchery of defenseless men, fleeing from the dreaded bayonet and stabbed to death while crying for mercy. The commander of the British troops was dubbed "No-Flint Grey" and execrated as a brutal murderer. Lossing says that he "marched stealthily" (an infamous practice in surprise attacks, of course), that he gave "his usual order to rush upon the patriots with fixed bayonets without firing a shot" (another indefensible proceeding), and that his men were *"to give no quarters"*—a statement for which there seems to be no basis in fact. Trevelyan (III, 234) attributes the infamy heaped upon Grey to the dread of the bayonet, which was undoubtedly prevalent among the Americans: "Men always attach the idea of cruelty to modes of warfare in which they are not proficient; and Americans liked the bayonet as little as Englishmen approved of taking deliberate aim at individual officers," against which American practice there was frequent outcry from the British, especially the officers. The dread of unaccustomed weapons and the horror of them as brutal appears also in the white man's objections to the Indian tomahawk, which is certainly, in itself, no more cruel or barbarous than the sword or the bayonet.

    Against the charge that "quarter had been refused and that the wounded were stabbed to death where they lay," Trevelyan urges the fact that only 53 dead were found on the ground the next day—a statement supported by Lossing, II, 164. It should be noted, also, that many wounded, including 40 badly injured, were actually carried away by the British.

    The fact seems to be that the ascription of brutal slaughter to the British was based upon a published letter, said to have been written by a Hessian participant, in which the Americans were described as "running about barefoot and half clothed," while "we killed three hundred" of them with the bayonet. "I struck them myself like so many pigs, one after another, until the blood ran out of the touch-hole of my musket." A sufficient answer to this sanguinary narration is the fact that there were no Hessians in Grey's force. That letter was probably American propaganda.

    Wayne was ordered before a court-martial on a charge of having had notice of the enemy's intention to attack and failing to make "a Disposition till it was too late." He was acquitted "with the highest honor."
22. Montresor, 356; André, 51; Baurmeister, 20–21; Robertson, 149–150; Gordon, II, 517.
23. Fitzpatrick, IX, 257, 259.
24. Kirkwood, 177.
25. Montresor, 456–457; André, 31–32; Baurmeister, 20–21; Robertson, 149–151; Gordon, II, 517.
26. Fitzpatrick, IX, 257–259, 262.
27. Baurmeister, 21; Montresor, 457; André, 52; Robertson, 149–150; Gordon, II, 517.
28. Fitzpatrick, IX, 232–253.
29. Marshall, I, 191.
30. *Journals*, VIII, 752; Bancroft, V, 181.
31. Fitzpatrick, IX, 248–249.
32. Stephenson, II, 31; Fitzpatrick, IX, 275.
33. Fitzpatrick, IX, 269, 270.
34. Montresor, 458; André, 26; Baurmeister, 21.

CHAPTER 33

This account of the Battle of Germantown has been drawn from so many sources that it would unduly laden the notes to assign particular authority to each of its several elements. General reference is made to Fitzpatrick, IX, *passim*; Gordon, II, 522;

Stedman, I, 291; Ramsay, II, 15; Kemble, I, 137; Baurmeister, 24–25; Greene, GW, I, 474–481; Marshall, I, 197; Lossing, II, 110–111; Hughes, III, 187–206; Bancroft, V, 193–195; Greene, FV, 91–92; Sullivan, I, 542–547; Anderson, 44–46; Carrington, 382–391; Dawson, 318–331; André, 54–57; Irving, III, 280–287; Lee, 95; Lowell, 201–203; Trevelyan, III, 237–251.

1. Fitzpatrick, IX, 278.
2. Hughes, III, 185.
3. Fitzpatrick, IX, 279.
4. Kirkwood, 188.
5. Fitzpatrick, IX, 308.
6. Carrington, 384; Greene, FV, 92, map; Dawson, I, 330.
7. Fitzpatrick, IX, 309; Greene, FV, 90; Greene, GW, I, 473; Sullivan, I, 542–543.
8. Dawson, I, 324. Fortescue, III, 223, justly criticizes the plan as "too intricate for inexperienced officers and imperfectly disciplined troops." Chastellux, 106, calls it "absolutely chimerical" and criticizes it in detail.
9. Trevelyan, III, 245, has this to say about the break-up of Sullivan's division: "They had travelled through the night. They had been fighting for nearly three hours. They had fired away all their ammunition. Their flank was unprotected. Their reserves stopped behind to help, or to hinder, the attack upon Musgrave's garrison. . . . The roar of the American batteries around the Chew mansion told upon the nerves of Sullivan's exhausted soldiers. A rumor arose and spread that they were being assailed in the rear by a hostile force; and, to the surprise of the officers who commanded them, they broke their ranks and retired from the field in hurry and confusion."
10. Trevelyan, III, 249.

CHAPTER 34

1. Rodney, C, 240.
2. Serle, 253–256.
3. Gordon, II, 519; Stedman, I, 297.
4. Fitzpatrick, IX, 259.
5. Stedman, I, 296; Ramsay, II, 17; Lossing, II, 86.
6. Robertson, 151.
7. Stedman, I, 296.
8. Lossing, II, 293.
9. Montresor, 459.
10. Eelking, 117; Dawson, I, 356.
11. Chastellux, 124.
12. Chastellux, 125.
13. Trevelyan, III, 258.
14. Dawson, I, 355; Stedman, I, 302; Lossing, II, 87–88, 208.
15. Stedman, I, 303–304; Trevelyan, III, 256–260.
16. Waldo, 301.
17. Lossing, II, 90.
18. Lossing, II, 91.
19. Montresor, 474–476.
20. Fisher, II, 50.
21. Montresor, 474–476.
22. Dawson, I, 336.
23. Lossing, II, 93.
24. Fitzpatrick, IX, 266–268.
25. Carrington, 296; Frothingham, 330–331.
26. Fitzpatrick, IX, 462.
27. Fitzpatrick, IX, 318, and X, 19, 20.
28. Fitzpatrick, IX, 318, 319, 351, 358, 375, and X, 19, 24.

29. Kirkwood, 211.
30. Fitzpatrick, IX, 382.
31. Kirkwood, 226.
32. Fitzpatrick, IX, 390–391.
33. Stedman, I, 302; Trevelyan, III, 266.
34. Sparks, *W*, V, 168 n.
35. Marshall, I, 215; Irving, III, 328.
36. Marshall, I, 215.
37. Robertson, 159; André, 57.
38. Baurmeister, 36.
39. Baurmeister, 36.
40. Kirkwood, 265.
41. André, 67; Robertson, 159–160.
42. André, 68.
43. André, 68.
44. André, 69; Robertson, 160; Simcoe, 31; Marshall, I, 215–216. André says one of Simcoe's men was killed and 9 chasseurs killed or wounded, while 20 to 30 Americans fell and 15 were taken. Robertson says a single British officer was killed, 2 were wounded, and about 40 rank and file were killed or wounded. Simcoe, a rather boastful person, claims "near a hundred" American casualties, " little or none" among the King's troops. Marshall admits one officer of Morgan's corps killed and 27 of his men killed or wounded, besides "a small loss" among the militia.
45. Reed, I, 351 n.
46. André, 70.
47. Marshall, I, 217–218; Reed, I, 354; Fitzpatrick, X, 156; Baurmeister, 39; Robertson, 161.
48. Waldo, 305.
49. Marshall, I, 217–218; Reed, I, 354; Fitzpatrick, X, 156; Baurmeister, 39; Robertson, 161.
50. *Journals,* IX, 1029–1030.
51. Fitzpatrick, X, 133 n., 134 n.; Reed, I, 348 n.
52. Fitzpatrick, X, 195–196.
53. Stillé, 112.
54. Hughes, III, 231.
55. Kapp, 137.
56. Sparks, *W*, V, 241 n.

CHAPTER 35

Original sources of information as to Arnold's Champlain battle are to be found in Force's *American Archives,* 4th Series, Vol. IV, and 5th Series, where many letters from and to Arnold, Schuyler, Gates, Hartley, and others appear. Other contemporary sources are Riedesel's and Wilkinson's memoirs, the journals of Wells, Hadden, and Pausch. Secondary sources of much value are Mahan's *Major Operations,* Jones's *Conquest of Canada,* Allen's *Naval History,* Lowell's *Hessians,* and Patterson's *Horatio Gates.* Kenneth Roberts has told the story, in great detail and with historical accuracy, in his novel *Rabble in Arms.*

1. Force, 5, I, 103.
2. Force, 5, I, 232, 238.
3. Jones, CH, 97.
4. Force, 5, I, 339, 376.
5. *Journals,* V, 448; Force, 5, II, 637.
6. Patterson, 69.
7. *Journals,* V, 526.
8. Force, 5, I, 233, 238.

9. Force, 5, I, 390, 445, 450, 650.
10. Force, 5, I, 559, 794.
11. Patterson, 85.
12. Jones, CH, 105–106.
13. Force, 5, I, 474, and II, 204. Hartley commanded the 6th Pennsylvania after Col. Irvine's capture at Trois Rivières.
14. Jones, CH, 107.
15. Jones, CH, 111–112.
16. Force, 5, I, 390; Jones, CH, 112.
17. Jones, CH, 125.
18. Force, 5, I, 125, 512, 582, 797, 826, 872, 987.
19. Force, 5, I, 1199.
20. Force, 5, I, 649.
21. Force, 5, I, 745–746.
22. Force, 5, I, 350, 399, 400, 620, 623, 624, 932.
23. Force, 5, I, 209.
24. Force, 5, I, 145, 163, 194, 303, 474, 549, 563, 630, 649, 682.
25. Force, 5, I, 340, 512, 649.
26. This description was supplied by Kenneth Roberts, who secured from the British Admiralty drawings of the *Washington* galley made by a British naval officer after her capture. Before this discovery, no description of the galleys had been obtainable, except the meager account in "a letter from Skenesborough, dated August 16, 1776," printed in Force, 5, I, 988, which merely noted that they were "from sixty to seventy feet in keel and eighteen feet in beam" and gave no description of their shape or their rigging.
27. Force, 5, I, 1123, 1201, and II, 1039.
28. Force, 5, I, 988, and II, 1039.
29. Force, 5, I, 969; Jones, CH, 116.
30. Force, 5, I, 630.
31. Force, 5, II, 1179.
32. Force, 5, II, 1178–1179; Pausch, 75 n.
33. Force, 5, II, 1178. The gondola had been taken from the Americans the day the siege of Quebec was raised. Hence its new name, *Loyal Convert.*
34. Lowell, 109.
35. Riedesel, I, 65.
36. Force, 5, I, 626, 799.
37. Pausch, 74–76; Riedesel, I, 59; Jones, CH, 144, 157–159.
38. Force, 5, I, 1266, and II, 969, 1166, 1201, 1266; Jones, CH, 143–144.
39. Force, 5, II, 223. Kenneth Roberts states that these fascines were made by tying small hemlock trees, each into a bundle, and that they were fixed, butts upward, along the bulwarks of the gondolas and galleys.
40. Force, 5, II, 251, 265, 440, 933.
41. Force, 5, II, 224.
42. Force, 5, II, 481.
43. Force, 5, II, 982. The usual lists of Arnold's fleet in the battle total 15, omitting the *Success;* but Wells notes its arrival on September 11, making 16. It may be noted that Riedesel (I, 73) lists 16 vessels in the American fleet, but does not name them all. The *Liberty* galley was away from the fleet, on command, on the day of the battle. The *Gates* galley had not been finished.
44. Force, 5, II, 591.
45. Force, 5, II, 1179. The description there of the longboats puts one gun in each bow. Riedesel, I, 70, gives them "three cannons each," but Hadden, 23, says one.
46. Mahan, 17–18.
47. Force, 5, II, 224. Mahan, 19, emphasized Arnold's "sounder judgment": "A retreat before square-rigged sailing vessels having a fair wind, by a heterogeneous force like his own, of unequal speeds and batteries, could result only in disaster. . . . Better trust to a steady, well-ordered position, developing the utmost

fire . . . The correctness of Arnold's decision not to chance a retreat was shown in the [results of his] retreat of two days later."

48. Force, 5, II, 1040.
49. Van Tyne, 373–374. Riedesel, I, 83, wrote, "If we could have begun our last expedition four weeks earlier, I am satisfied that everything would have ended this year." Four weeks was exactly the time consumed in building the *Inflexible.* That it was the intention of the British command, if feasible, to join Howe on the Hudson that year is indicated by an extract from a contemporary English paper (Almon, IV, 291) of Sept. 6, 1776: "The design was that the two armies commanded by Generals Howe and Burgoyne should cooperate; that they should both be on the Hudson River at the same time; that they should join about Albany, and thereby cut off all communication between the northern and southern Colonies."
50. Mahan, 25.

CHAPTER 36

1. Hudleston, 69.
2. Fonblanque, 226.
3. Fonblanque, 227; Hudleston, 110; Nickerson, 8.
4. Nickerson, 81.
5. Burgoyne, Appendix, iii; Fonblanque, Appendix C; Nickerson, 83–89. Trevelyan III, 71, attributed the conception of this plan to Germain, but every indication seems to point to Burgoyne's authorship of it. He certainly wrote the paper that the King read and approved.
6. Nickerson, 89–90.
7. Nickerson, 91–94.
8. Nickerson, 94.
9. Hudleston, 114.
10. The best analysis of the plan, and of all others in which Howe was concerned, is in Anderson, *passim.*
11. Hadden, 43; Burgoyne, 9; Anburey, I, 121.
12. Nickerson, 110.
13. Burgoyne, 10. Luc de Chapt de la Corne Saint-Luc, commonly called La Corne St. Luc or even La Corne or St. Luc, was a Frenchman who had seen much service as a leader of Indian bands in King George's War and the French and Indian War. He had entered into the spirit and adopted the methods of Indian warfare with so little compunction and with such great success as to evidence an identity of taste and temperament with his savage followers. He had, consequently, great influence among them. Though past sixty-five at the expulsion of the Americans from Canada, he had been active in raising Indian recruits for Burgoyne and, with physical stamina and hardihood unimpaired, had undertaken their leadership in active service. The Americans feared him even more than they hated him. One described him as "that arch devil incarnate, who has butchered hundreds, men, women and children of our colonies . . . in the most inhuman manner." There seems to be no doubt that he was of a brutal, bloody and pitiless nature, cruel and remorseless in his methods of warfare. Charles de Langlade, a French officer associated with him in command of the Indians, had seen service in the French and Indian War. He is sometimes said to have planned and executed the ambush which resulted in Braddock's defeat.
14. Hadden, 34, 44, 53.
15. Burgoyne, 13.
16. Hadden, 49.
17. Hadden, 44–45; Riedesel, 105–107.
18. Burgoyne, 10–17. Fonblanque, 488, gives the total force as 7,902, presumably including officers.
19. Fonblanque, 240–241; Jones, CH, 158, 181; Nickerson, 116.

20. Riedesel, I, 2–17; Nickerson, 117–118.
21. Hadden, 52; Nickerson, 104–105.
22. Nickerson, 120–122; Anburey, I, 184.
23. Hudleston, 148–151.
24. Walpole, X, 188.
25. Burgoyne, Appendix, xxi; Anburey, I, 168, 174.
26. Walpole, X, 188.
27. Wilkinson, I, 155 ff.
28. Nickerson, 182–183.
29. Wilkinson, I, 169 n.
30. Wilkinson, I, 174–176.
31. Hadden, 54.
32. Lamb, 135.
33. Anburey, I, 182.
34. Hadden, 82.
35. Wilkinson, I, 181.
36. Hadden, 82; Wilkinson, I, 180; Nickerson, 41–42.
37. Burgoyne, Appendix, xxviii, xxxix; Anburey, I, 190.
38. Hadden, 84.
39. Wilkinson, I, 184.
40. Wilkinson, I, 184–185 n.; *The Royal Kalendar* for 1777.
41. Anburey, I, 192.
42. Anburey, I, 193.
43. Burgoyne, Appendix, xxi; Riedesel, I, 113–114.
44. Anburey, I, 194.
45. Wilkinson, I, 186–187.
46. Hadden, 92; Wilkinson, I, 186.
47. Wilkinson, I, 188.
48. Anburey, I, 195.
49. Anburey, I, 196.
50. Wilkinson, I, 187.
51. Riedesel, I, 115–116; Hadden, 85–86; Burgoyne, Appendix, xxxii.
52. Wilkinson, I, 187–188 n.; Hadden, Appendix 15. Hadden, 88, gives the enemy losses as 17 officers and 109 men killed or wounded.
53. Burgoyne, Appendix, xxv; Lamb, 146. Hadden, 89, says the lake was "so narrow that the Ships Yards almost touched the Precipes which overhung them."
54. Riedesel, I, 117.
55. Wilkinson, I, 186, 190.
56. Burgoyne, Appendix, xxxi.
57. Burgoyne, Appendix, xxxiv.
58. Lamb, 142.
59. Wilkinson, I, 189.

CHAPTER 37

Among the original sources of information for this chapter and the next following are Burgoyne's *State of the Expedition,* Hadden's *Journal,* Anburey's *Travels,* Wilkinson's *Memoirs,* Riedesel's *Memoirs,* Lamb's *Memoirs,* Digby's journal, and the letters of Schuyler. Secondary sources of value are Coburn's *Centennial History,* Hall's *Battle of Bennington,* Dawson's *Battles,* Lowell's *Hessians,* Lossing's *Pictorial Field Book,* Fonblanque's *Political and Military Episodes,* Hudleston's *Gentleman Johnny Burgoyne,* Patterson's *Horatio Gates,* Neilson's *Original Account of Burgoyne's Campaign,* Stone's *Campaign of Lieut. Gen. John Burgoyne,* Gordon's *History* and Stedman's. Nickerson's *Turning Point of the Revolution,* a large book devoted entirely to Burgoyne's campaign, is the fullest account. Its value to succeeding historians is definitely and considerably less than it might be, because the author has not provided a single footnote or specific reference by which the verity of any statement in it or the validity of any of his conclusions or opinions may be tested.

1. Burgoyne, Appendix, vi.
2. Burgoyne, 17.
3. Hadden, Appendix I.
4. Hadden, 100; Burgoyne, Appendix, xxxvi.
5. Hadden, 91–96; Burgoyne, Appendix, xxxv.
6. Hadden, 109.
7. Nickerson, 186; Wilkinson, I, 192, 200; Sparks, *C*, I, 397–399.
8. Trevelyan, III, 120.
9. Stedman, I, 327; Hadden, 94.
10. Burgoyne, Appendix, xi, xxxvi.
11. Hadden, 95, 97.
12. Wilkinson, Appendix B.
13. Nickerson, 18, gives this quotation with no indication of its source.
14. Burgoyne, Appendix, xii, xlvi, xlix.
15. Riedesel, I, 125–126; Burgoyne, 51.
16. Burgoyne, 137, Appendix, xiv.
17. Riedesel, I, 101, states that, before the southward march of Burgoyne's force began, in June, 1777, he had ordered for the dragoons "long linen trousers, striped with white and blue, and similar to those worn by the inhabitants during summer." That these were actually provided and displaced the leather breeches does not appear.
18. Burgoyne, Appendix, lxiii; Hadden, 111–117.
19. Burgoyne, Appendix, xii; Lamb, 151.
20. Burgoyne, Appendix, lxiii.
21. Coburn, B, 22–23.
22. Lossing, I, 393.
23. Stryker, *TP*, 350.
24. Coburn, B, 31.
25. Lossing, I, 394; Sparks, *C*, I, 397, 423.
26. Lossing, I, 394.
27. *Journals*, VIII, 656–657.
28. Riedesel, I, 128.
29. Burgoyne, Appendix, xi.
30. Dawson, I, 260.
31. Burgoyne, Appendix, lxx.
32. Lossing, I, 395, says there was no bridge there at that time, but only a ford. He calls the river Walloomscoick.
33. Dawson, I, 260.
34. Coburn, B, 40.
35. Dawson, I, 260.
36. Riedesel, I, 130; Lamb, I, 153. Burgoyne, Appendix, xiii, says many of these Americans took the oath of allegiance and were afterwards the first to fire on Baum.
37. Lossing, I, 397 n. This historic order is reported by the historians generally, with slight differences in verbiage.
38. Riedesel, I, 131.
39. Hadden, 118; Riedesel, I, 129–130.
40. Dawson, I, 264; Anburey, I, 233. Burgoyne (Appendix, xiv) wrote to Germain on August 20: "Could Mr. Breyman have marched at the rate of two miles an hour, any given twelve hours out of the two and thirty, success would probably have ensued."
41. Dawson, I, 264; Riedesel, I, 131.
42. Coburn, B, 55.
43. Dawson, I, 264.
44. Dawson, I, 260.
45. The various estimates of losses on both sides differ, as usual. The statement in the text seems to be approximately correct.
46. *Journals*, IX, 770.

THE AMERICAN COLONIES

IN THE

EIGHTEENTH CENTURY

THE AMERICAN COLONIES

IN THE

EIGHTEENTH CENTURY

BY

HERBERT L. OSGOOD, PH.D., LL.D.
PROFESSOR OF HISTORY IN COLUMBIA UNIVERSITY

VOLUME II

NEW YORK
COLUMBIA UNIVERSITY PRESS

Published January, 1924
Reprinted September, 1930

CONTENTS

VOLUME II

PART ONE (Continued)

CHAPTER XVII

PAGE

The Early Extension of the Church of England in the Colonies

CHAPTER XVIII

Culmination of the Leislerian Conflict. Misgovernment of Lord Cornbury in New York and New Jersey

CHAPTER XIX

Harmony Partially Restored in New York and New Jersey under Robert Hunter, 1708–1716

CHAPTER XX

Massachusetts and New England during the Administration of Joseph Dudley, 1702–1715

CHAPTER XXI

Virginia during the Second Intercolonial War

CHAPTER XXII

Maryland during the Second Intercolonial War
Close of the Period of Royal Government, 1699–1713

CHAPTER XXIII

Virginia during the Administration of Alexander Spotswood, 1710–1722

CHAPTER XXIV

Pennsylvania from the Issue of the Charter of Liberties to the Governorship of William Keith, 1701–1717

PART II

THE COLONIES DURING THE INTERVAL OF PEACE BETWEEN THE SECOND AND THIRD INTERCOLONIAL WARS, 1714–1740

CHAPTER I

Attitude of the Cabinet, Parliament and the Board of Trade toward Questions of Commerce and Colonization under the Early Hanoverians

CHAPTER II

The Overthrow of Proprietary Government in South Carolina

CHAPTER III

TRANSITION TO ROYAL GOVERNMENT IN NORTH CAROLINA

CHAPTER IV

New York and New Jersey between 1716 and 1730

PAGE

CHAPTER V

Controversies during the Administration of Cosby and Clarke. The Zenger Episode, 1730–1740

CHAPTER VI

Immigration into the American Colonies during the First Half of the Eighteenth Century

CHAPTER VII

PENNSYLVANIA DURING THE ADMINISTRATIONS OF KEITH AND GORDON, 1717–1736

PART ONE
(Continued)

THE COLONIES DURING THE FIRST TWO INTERCOLONIAL WARS, 1690–1714

CHAPTER XVII

THE EARLY EXTENSION OF THE CHURCH OF ENGLAND IN THE COLONIES

An institution like the Church of England, especially the characteristics which it had come to possess by the early eighteenth century, cannot be adequately described in a few paragraphs. But it may be possible even within a limited space, to indicate some of its salient qualities. Like so much in English history, it is a compromise, a condition nicely poised between Catholicism and the more radical Protestant sects. Its origin was due to balanced relations in both secular and ecclesiastical politics in the sixteenth century, which could scarcely have resulted otherwise than in an institution of that character. The creed of the church embodied the doctrines which were common to the Protestantism of the Continent, but important mediaeval and Catholic elements were retained in its spirit, ritual and government. Under the stress of conflict these elements, centering about the episcopate, its succession and powers, have from time to time been emphasized, making the church one of the most conservative elements in English life. Its leaders have fostered ancient tradition, seeking to antedate even the papacy and to connect in a peculiar sense their communion with the church of the early centuries and of the Roman empire. They have dreamed that in them the churches of the Patriarchates would come to their own again and the legitimate claims both of Catholics and Reformed be harmonized and satisfied.

When, in the reigns of Henry VIII and Elizabeth, the connection with Rome was severed, the union between church and state in England became even closer than it was during the middle age. For this reason the revolt from Rome was always represented to be an important and necessary step toward the perfecting of national unity. The Church, as the result of this step, became more completely subordinated to the crown. The necessity of this was recognized as a means of defence not only against enemies from abroad, but against schism when it began to show itself as a result of the growth of radical Protestantism at home. The union of altar and throne then became one of the watchwords of politics and the throne occupied the leading place in the partnership. Though the Church of itself exercised great social influence, it was used to buttress the civil power in its struggles with enemies foreign and domestic. The duty of loyalty to established institutions has always been one of the chief burdens of its message. A certain section of the Church, which was in close connection with public affairs, even went so far as to teach that resistance to government was a sin. This doctrine and that of the divine origin of the kingship sprang from a common root. The orthodox Church upheld the state and the state extended its protection and support around and beneath the Church. Under the stress of conflict both became acutely sensitive toward dissent as implying possible sedition or even treason. In idea, and so far as possible in practice, they appeared as the two sides of one whole. The Church was thus in the full sense of the word an "Establishment," a most important function of which was to uphold in the domain of morals and religion the mixed monarchical and aristocratic régime which England had inherited from the middle age.

For its hold on the nation the Church relied very largely on its historical antecedents, its hierarchy, the ornate ceremonial of its worship, as well as on the learning and piety of many of its clergy. It sought to worship God in the beauty of holiness and to a large extent it succeeded, though, like all ritualistic religions, with a stupefying monotony and routine. It appealed to the sense of the artistic, the ancient, the formal and institutional, more than to the doctrinal or emotional, as the source of its influence. It did not look exclusively to the Bible, but to the Bible as interpreted by the Church and human reason, as its rule of faith and order; least of all did it find such a rule in the so-called inner light or consciousness of the untrained mind. It set a high value upon learning, but that learning was of a traditional type, and it was limited to the higher clergy and to a favored class among the laity who, as a rule, were closely connected with the nobility. Any schools which it might found were naturally imbued with that spirit. The Church was orthodox, and in its eyes schism or separation was an offence comparable with sedition or treason in the state. In certain ways it was intolerant, as were all religious bodies, but its system of inquisition was by no means as searching into life and morals as was that of the Puritan, or even that of the Quaker after he had stiffened into regularity. The emphasis which the church laid upon ritual betokened a degree of moral and intellectual indifference which the radical Protestant sects deprecated or scorned. Its learning and aristocratic pride kept it from ever descending to the depths of fanaticism and bigotry which have too often found expression in the sects which sprang directly from the people.

After the Restoration much was heard of the policy of comprehension, the object of which was to so modify certain forms and requirements as to open the way for the return of Presbyterians and Independents. But, instead, the reactionary legislation of the early years of Charles II drove a large Puritan element out of the Church, while the schism of the nonjurors which followed the Revolution removed from it a valued conservative group. The former event made nonconformity permanent in England, while the Revolution which gave rise to the nonjurors emphasized anew and in the most decisive way the fact that the English Church was Protestant and that its return to the Catholic fold was impossible. At the same time its separateness from the Protestant bodies on the Continent was fully recognized.

On the other hand, for a long time sympathy with Jacobitism continued to be felt by many more Anglicans than were included in the group of nonjurors, while in quick succession a Calvinist and a Lutheran were brought to the English throne, though under the condition that they should become communicants of the English Church. The Toleration Act was passed in England, and by the Act of Union a few years later the integrity of the Scotch Church as an establishment was recognized. These are indications of the variety of opinions which it was necessary for the church to recognize. With the approach of the eighteenth century a latitudinarian spirit, or readiness to acknowledge that, as the essential truths of

Christianity are few, other sects than one's own may share in their possession, spread among the higher clergy. The spirit of indifference and of rationalism which was growing in the country also had a marked effect on the Church. The aversion to mysticism and enthusiasm, which was always one of its characteristics, was strengthened by these tendencies. The Church felt the effects of the low moral tone which had existed in society since the Restoration, the growth of secular interests, the sense of security which followed the Revolution and the failure of the policy of Louis XIV and the Stuarts, with the result that it fell into a condition of spiritual lethargy from which with difficulty it was awakened by the Wesleyan revival. And yet, in the midst of this period of spiritual decline, by means of various agencies from the archbishop down, and under the lead of missionary societies which were founded at the close of the reign of William, the Church undertook to spread its influence far and wide throughout the colonies. This was regarded as its share in the general task of checking the tendency there toward independence and of substituting ecclesiastical conditions which should be more in agreement with those of England.

In this account of the colonies we have advanced to the closing years of the seventeenth century with only a few scattered references to the English Church. We have seen some Catholics and a great variety of Protestant sects appear and take their place among the composite of faiths which colonial society on its religious side exhibited. From the beginning the English Church had been predominant in Virginia and had occupied a minor position in a few of the other colonies. But the time has now been reached when it began in earnest to seek a place of some prominence in their religious history considered as a whole. In religion even more than in government or industry the colonies had wandered far, and on this side of their development the contrast between England and themselves appears most marked. In England the process of religious development had begun with unity and had tended toward diversity; in the colonies the original condition was one of the widest diversity possible within Protestantism. In America the parent church must content itself with the place of a sect among sects or to an extent overcome the conditions which had naturally grown up in the colonies. To the former alternative she could not at that period bring herself to submit, while the latter object it would never do to proclaim, though her conduct always betrayed her desires and thus provoked jealous suspicion on the part of her opponents. It was characteristic both of the Anglican reaction which followed the Revolution in England, and of the transition to the system of royal provinces which was in progress in the colonies that the church should now seek a larger place in colonial life, and that in undertaking this she would lean heavily upon the support of the state.

That some one English bishop should have jurisdiction over the rising colonial Church followed necessarily from the constitution of the Church itself. But until after the Restoration it was wholly undecided upon whose shoulders this should rest. The archbishop of Canterbury might naturally have occupied the position, but with the exception of the activity of Laud while he held that office, and of one occasion during the reign of James II, he seems scarcely to have been thought of in this connection. London was the centre of trade and the capital where was located the company which founded Virginia. From it also proceeded many other colonizing enterprises. Bishops of London had a certain connection with these, and while he held that office, Laud's tireless activity in the interest of religious conformity extended to regions beyond the seas. But affairs drifted on until after the Restoration before any decision upon this matter was reached. Then it came gradually to be understood that the bishop of London was the metropolitan of the colonies. The fact that this result was definitely reached was due to the activity of Henry Compton, who became bishop of that see in 1675. As the need of episcopal guidance was beginning to be more widely recognized in the colonies, Compton tried to find out what his authority was. The lords of trade were consulted, but no adequate precedents were found. Compton procured the insertion in instructions which after that time were issued to royal governors of the statements that worship should be celebrated according to the rites of the Church of England and that no minister should be presented to any benefice in their colonies without a certificate from the bishop of London that he was in conformity with its doctrines and practices.[1]

The interest of Compton in the colonies and his activities on behalf of the Church within them steadily continued and grew. He was, of course, impressed with the weakness of its hold in the continental colonies, as well as with the imperfect means at his command for exercising control over them and procuring more and better clergy. But he obtained the grant of a bounty of £20 for each minister and schoolmaster who went to the colonies, and an instruction that no one should be permitted to serve in either of these capacities without a license from the bishop of London. Beginning with 1685, clauses were inserted in the instructions to royal governors that they should give all encouragement to the exercise of the jurisdiction of the bishop of London, except in collating to benefices, granting marriage licenses and probate of wills, which remained with the secular authority. Whether this provision was confirmed by an order in council or not, it was acted upon by Compton and his successors, and that without interruption, after the Revolution of 1689.

In the consideration of this subject some reference should be made to the act of toleration which was passed in England in 1690. Though in this no mention was made of the dominions, the dissenters in the colonies often spoke as if they considered it, along with the bill of rights and earlier legislation of the same character, as one of the guaranties of their liberty, and the legislatures of a few of the colonies declared it to be in force within their limits. We hear vaguely of certain utterances of British attorneys general which were in harmony with that view.[2] Of course these statements could only mean that the principle of the act of toleration was recognized as in harmony with ecclesiastical relations in the

[1] A. L. Cross, The Anglican Episcopate and the American Colonies (Harvard Hist. Studies) chapters I and II. Bishop Sherlock's Report (1795) N. Y. Col. Docs. VII, 360. See also the Histories of the American Episcopal Church by Anderson and Perry.

[2] Hawks, Contributions to Ecclesiastical History, Virginia, 109. Maryland declared it in force in 1702 and 1706. Kilty, Statutes, p. 179; Bacon, Laws of Maryland. In New York the declaration was made in an act of 1704 incorporating Trinity Church.

colonies, and that too while apparently they forgot the fact that no reference to the dominions was made in the act of uniformity which was passed after the Restoration. The toleration act provided for the exemption of Protestant dissenters from the penalties of the persecuting acts of Elizabeth, James I and Charles II on their taking the new oath of allegiance and subscribing a declaration against certain leading Catholic practices. But even then their meetings could be held only under a system of registration and license, they were subject to the payment of tithes and their clergy were forced to subscribe to certain of the articles of religion. They were exempted from the penalties of the Sunday laws only on condition of attending their own chapels. On comparing these provisions with conditions as they were in the colonies, it will at once be seen that the act could not be literally enforced there, even in provinces which had made it a part of their own legislation.

It was of course the original intention of the British government, under the Tudors and Stuarts, that the English Church should be planted in all the colonies. It was naturally expected to go along with civil government, as the two were organically connected. Several of the acts of Elizabeth and of James I gave ample legal authority also for the establishment of the Church in the colonies, even to the exclusion of dissent. Had it not been for the Puritan Revolt that policy, toward which Laud and the government of Charles I were headed, would doubtless have been carried into execution. Like the Huguenots of France, the Puritans would have been suppressed at home or driven as exiles into foreign countries and religious conditions would probably have existed in the English colonies analogous to those of Canada, accompanied with an equally blighting effect on their growth. To the fact that the trend of historical development was quite the opposite of this is due, to a very large extent, the character both of modern England and of the United States today.

Such form as was taken by church establishments in the colonies was the result of their own legislation, controlled and limited to a certain extent by instructions to the governors and other executive action by England. Virginia was the only continental colony in which the English Church may be regarded as established from the first and where for a long time there was practically no opposition from dissenters.[1] In 1624, when Virginia became a royal province, it was enacted, "that there be an uniformity in our Church as near as may be to the canons of England, both in substance and circumstance, and that all persons yield readie obedience unto them under paine of censure." Absence from divine service on Sunday without excuse was made punishable by fine. In every settlement a house or room should be procured for church services and ground sequestered for the burial of the dead. By this and later enactments provision was made for the levy of a church or parish rate, payable in tobacco and corn — later in tobacco only — for such purposes as the support of the minister, the building of churches and purchase of glebes. In 1632 the office of church warden was regulated. In the legislation of ten years later vestries came out into full view, with the power of the parishioners to choose their ministers, who should be presented to the governor and by him inducted into office. Clergymen might be suspended by the governor and council but removed only by the general assembly.

In 1662,[2] in harmony with Governor Berkeley's instructions, provision for the Church as established was somewhat extended. It was enacted that there should be a glebe in every parish and that a convenient house for the minister should be built thereon. It was also provided that candidates for appointment should produce testimonials from some bishop in England and subscribe to the laws and constitutions of the Church of England before being presented and inducted. By this and earlier enactments and practice it was made clear that dissent would not be tolerated in Virginia. When, on the appointment of Lord Culpeper in 1679, instructions to the governors assumed substantially their final form, they were empowered to collate to benefices, grant licenses for marriage

[1] Hening, I, 68, 122, 180, 183, 240–242. Anderson, History of the Colonial Church, I, 470, very suggestively criticises Laud for having allowed a system of appointment so different from that of England to get a foothold in Virginia. It was too similar to that existing between the clergy and their parishioners in New England, and, he implies, would have been prevented if he had sent a bishop at once to Virginia.

[2] Hening, II, 29, 44.

and probate of wills, have a care for the orthodoxy of schoolmasters and uphold good morals. The jurisdiction of the bishop of London was by that time clearly recognized, but a considerable part of the functions he exercised in England had been transferred to the governor.

After the Revolution the policy of extending favors to the Anglican communion, going in some cases to the extent of establishment, was not abandoned. The experience of the two Carolinas in this regard, they being at that time proprietary provinces, has been related in a previous volume. But it was more natural that such a result should follow in a royal province, and it did follow in Maryland soon after its government was assumed by the crown and in a part of New York soon after the accession of Fletcher to its governorship.

In Virginia the Anglicans had everything their own way, and it was not until the eighteenth century was well advanced that an opposition of any importance was to develop. In Maryland, Catholics, Puritans and Quakers formed a majority against which the English Church very slowly made headway. There a famous experiment in government under a system of balanced confessions had been made, and Anglicans had held the inferior place. In 1676 John Yeo wrote in his well known letter to the archbishop of Canterbury, that there were but three Protestant ministers of the Church of England in the province.[1] Lord Baltimore, when called before the committee of trade, was able to show that this statement was somewhat exaggerated, but even according to his representation Catholics and Anglicans together constituted only one fourth of the population. Under these conditions the establishment of the Church would seem to have been an impossibility.

But in no colony did the pro-Anglican aspect of the English Revolution reveal itself so clearly as in Maryland. The reason for this has already been explained.[2] By that crisis the Catholics were thrown politically into a position of hopeless inferiority in this province. With the overthrow of the Calverts they lost their natural leaders, and when the

[1] Cal. St. P. Col., 1675–6, p. 435; 1677–1680, p. 117–122. Chalmers, Annals, 365, 375. Hawks, Maryland, 49. Mereness, Md. as a Proprietary Prov., 437 *et seq.*

[2] Osgood, American Colonies in the 17th Century, III, 477 *et seq.*

proprietary family returned to power it was as Protestants. Meantime, into the place of the Catholic executive stepped one which was made up of Anglicans and which had behind it the support of the British government. Though Catholics were not disfranchised till a quarter of a century later, by test oaths they were at once excluded from the assembly and from office.[1] The commission and instructions of Governor Copley concerning religious affairs were the same as those given to all royal governors and steps were soon taken to put them into execution. Presently appeared the Rev. Thomas Bray, an Anglican clergyman of high character, great zeal and organizing power, who was not only very influential in directing the attention of Englishmen to the needs of the establishment in the colonies at large, but who in a very special way forwarded its interests in Maryland.[2] Along with him, after Copley's death, worked Governor Nicholson, whose ample purse was always at the service of the Church, and whose influence in its support was more widely felt than that of any other man who ever held office in the colonies. By these two men, aided by many who were less prominent, and by the natural trend of the times, the establishment of the Church in Maryland was brought about. But it was the church of the minority of the people, and always had to contend against a powerful, though divided, opposition.

The condition of the Church before establishment is indicated by a statement made at the time of Nicholson's appointment. This was to the effect that in Kent county there were two parishes, one church built and another planned, but no minister; Anne Arundel county had four parishes, but no churches or ministers; Calvert county had five parishes, three of which had churches but no ministers; Charles county had four parishes laid out, but no ministers; Somerset county was in similar condition; Cecil county had three parishes, one having neither church nor ministers; of Baltimore, Talbot and Dorchester counties there was no certain information.

The second act, which was passed after the arrival of Governor Copley in 1692, was one confirming to the Church of England in the province all her rights, liberties and fran-

[1] McKinley, The Suffrage Franchise in the English Colonies, 70 *et seq.*
[2] Hawks, 75, 83.

chises, providing that parishes should be organized in the counties, that vestrymen should be chosen and taxes levied for the support of the Church. Four years later this, and an act supplementary thereto, were disallowed in England, the original act because it contained a clause giving to the province the privilege of Magna Charta.[1] In this same year (1696) another act for the establishment of the Church was passed, which contained a clause declaring that the inhabitants of Maryland should enjoy all their rights according to the laws of England in cases where the laws of the province were silent. The Catholics and Quakers were the sects who chiefly opposed the measure, and in London the latter procured its repeal on the ground that it declared all the laws of England in force in Maryland, which was a clause of another nature than that set forth in the title of the act.[2]

In 1700, through the influence of Dr. Thomas Bray, another somewhat rigid act was passed which contained a clause providing that the service books of the English Church should be read in every place of worship within the province. This was objected to by Attorney General Northey on the ground that it might extend to the meeting places of the dissenters. He also criticized its provision for select vestries because it was contrary to the law and practice of England, where the whole body of the parishioners was admitted to a vote and a share in parish business. In England also the vestrymen did not choose the church wardens, but the minister chose one and the parishioners the other. To the power of fining vestrymen for not taking the oath Northey also objected because it would exclude Quakers from the benefit of the solemn affirmation, which they were allowed by the law of England.[3] The Quakers also attacked the measure on the general ground that it provided for an establishment, to which they were opposed. The bill was sent back to Maryland with amend-

[1] Bacon, Laws of Maryland. Acts of P. C. Col. II, 837. Cal. St. P. Col., 1693–1696, p. 636. Hist. Colls. of Am. Col. Church (Maryland), 35.

[2] Md. Arch. XXV, 93. C. O. 5/715, Council to Board, July 1700, Acts of P. C. Col. II, 837. Cal. St. P. Col., 1699, p. 561. Hist. Colls. of Am. Col. Church (Maryland,) 29. Hawks, 89.

[3] Md. Arch. XXIV, 91, 207, 265. C. O. 5/715. Report of attorney general, recd. Jan. 14, 1700/1. Observations of Quakers, same date. Hist. Colls. (Maryland) 41. Hawks, *op. cit.* 97, 107.

ments which made it satisfactory to the lords of trade and was passed by the assembly in 1702 and approved by the crown. Churches which came under the definition of the act were those for the maintenance of whose clergy a definite revenue should be required to be raised by the laws of the province. In a clause at the end of the statute it was expressly declared that Protestant dissenters should have the benefit of the act of toleration and Quakers the benefit of the act 7 and 8 William III concerning the solemn affirmation. In 1704 the system was completed by a law fully guaranteeing the titles of land given to the parishes for glebes.

In New York the predominance of dissenters, and possibly of the irreligious, was greater than it was in Maryland, though it lacked a Catholic element of any importance. The proportion of dissenters to churchmen was estimated as forty to one, and the only church where service according to Anglican forms was regularly held was in the fort at New York. There the governor's chaplain officiated. The Anglicans were also confined to a few sections in the southern part of the province, and in New York City, Westchester, and Queens counties, where they were strongest, they were far outnumbered by dissenters. Among the mixed population were certain French and Germans who might naturally affiliate with the Anglicans, but among the large Dutch population, especially of the north, they could hope to make little progress. The assembly reflected the condition of the province, and all except a few of its members were unfriendly to the Church, especially if its plans appeared to be at all ambitious.[1] Owing to the lack of stated services, so disorderly had the people in Westchester become, that Colonel Heathcote ordered the militia companies to train on Sundays so that public order might be better maintained.[2]

As soon as Governor Fletcher arrived, steps were taken to change this condition. In October, 1692, he recommended the passage of a bill to provide for a ministry in the province,

[1] S. P. G. Mss. Letter of Col. Heathcote to Bishop of Bristol, Feb. 25, 1716; Heathcote to S. P. G., June 13, 1714. Abundant proof of these statements may be found in all the histories of New York City, in Bolton's History of the Church in Westchester County and in the Papers relating to the Churches of Queens County in Doc. Hist. of New York, III.

[2] Bolton, *op. cit.*, p. 24.

but no action was taken. Before a new assembly, about a year later, the same subject was more forcibly presented. A bill was then passed which, because of its loose and obscure wording, was returned by the governor with the request that it be amended.[1] To this the assembly refused to accede, and, though Fletcher prorogued it in the hope of securing a better measure, he failed and had finally to accept the bill as it stood. In due time it was approved by the home government.

The act itself afforded the strongest testimony that New York was not and could not be an ecclesiastical unit.[2] It provided that in the City and County of New York, in Richmond, Westchester and Queens counties a levy should be made on all taxables, the revenue from which should go for the support of "good and sufficient Protestant ministers" there to be settled. Of these two were to be resident in Westchester, two in Queens, one in Richmond and one in New York City. The amount of their support was specified, and in order to the raising of it vestrymen and church wardens were to be chosen, and the vestrymen in cooperation with the county justices should lay the tax. The church wardens should keep and expend this revenue, rendering account thereof before the justices and vestrymen.

Could there have been any doubt as to the intention of the framers of this act to establish the Church of England and no other in the four counties named, it should have been removed by the fact that it provided for vestrymen and church wardens, officials not known in the polity of the dissenting sects. But an ambiguity was introduced into the act by the reference to the settlement of "good and sufficient Protestant ministers." By this, in accordance with Anglican usage of the time, was meant the clergy of the Established Church.[3] But in New York the dissenters, using the term in the broad and non-technical sense, claimed that they and their clergy might

[1] Ass. J. I, 30–34. C. J. I, 39. Dix, History of Trinity Church, I, 78 *et seq.* Bolton, History of the Church in Westchester County, Introduction. The act is said to have been drafted by James Graham, then speaker, and for its execution much depended on the support of Heathcote.

[2] N. Y. Col. Laws, I, 328 *et seq.* This law came up for discussion in 1755, when King's College was founded, and in the "Watch Tower" articles then published in the "New York Mercury" many pertinent observations concerning it may be found.

[3] Dix, History of Trinity Church, I, 86.

share in the benefits of the act, that they might put dissenting ministers into the livings created by the act. The assembly supported this claim, and it furnished an opportunity for any amount of sharp political tactics between the sects, which added not a little to the variety, as well as the futility, of New York politics. Support also was given to the contention of the dissenters by the wording of the Duke's Laws, in which provision was made for boards of vestries and church wardens, to seats in which dissenters were freely admitted.

In New York City, as the majority of those who were entitled to vote for vestrymen and churchwardens were dissenters, they were able for some time to control, or at least greatly to influence, church affairs. The board which was thus elected in the city was the town vestry, and being made up in 1694 chiefly of dissenters who were elected by the freeholders, they insisted that a dissenting clergyman should be called. The governor proposed his chaplain as entitled to appointment. No appointment was made that year. The next year, under a threat of prosecution by the governor, the board chose the Rev. William Vesey, but he was not even notified of this action. The vestry then appealed to the assembly and it resolved that the board had the right to call a dissenting Protestant minister. Fletcher told them it was not their province to explain an act they did not make, and the laws were to be interpreted by the judges. The next board obeyed the law according to its intent and selected Vesey, who was duly inducted as the first rector.[1]

In 1697 this situation was remedied in New York City by the granting of a charter of incorporation to a body calling itself "The Members in Communion of the Church of England Established by Law."[2] In 1704 this same body, with a slight change in its title so as to include the rector, received incorporation by an act of the legislature. The support of its rector was also in part assured by rents from the "Queen's Farm," the title to which was confirmed to it by Queen Anne. This, enhanced by the growth of the city, laid the foundation of the wealth of the parish. By these measures Trinity parish was fully established, with its own vestry and church

[1] Dix, I, 82 *et seq.*

[2] *Ibid.*, Appendix, p. 455.

wardens and its power to act independently of the city vestry. The latter, however, continued to exist for many years, but it could no longer hinder the development of Trinity parish along the lines intended by the framers of the act of 1693. It was later contended with reason that this parish was the only body of Anglicans in New York which was really established.

Under this act, taken in connection with the governor's instructions, the relations between the Church and civil power in New York were illustrated by two well known events. One was the arrest by Cornbury, in 1706, of Mackemie and Hampton, two well known Presbyterian clergymen, because on a passing visit they preached in the province without a license from the governor.[1] The other was the prolonged struggle between the Presbyterians and Anglicans for control over the parish of Jamaica on Long Island. Cornbury, as well as Fletcher, was an active patron of the English Church, though, as with everything else, his interest was measured by the extent to which he could use it for the promotion of his own power and schemes. It was in harmony with the condition of New York polities in the eighteenth century that the Church had to rely so much for its early progress upon such brilliant exponents of godliness as were these two governors.

In the case of Mackemie and Hampton, Cornbury, in utter disregard of usage both in language and government, claimed that his instruction to allow no clergyman to be appointed to a living in New York unless he had a certificate from the bishop of London gave him the right to license every one, whether dissenter or not, who should preach in the province.[2] This interpretation would have been wholly unwarrantable even if it had been applied only to dissenting ministers who were proposing to settle in the province; but the two accused clergymen were only brief visitors and had no intention of remaining in New York. They also brought with them certificates stating that they had taken the oaths and in other ways conformed to the conditions prescribed in the toleration

[1] Mackemie's Tryal, in Force, Tracts, IV. N. Y. Col. Docs., IV, 1186 *et seq.* Briggs, American Presbyterianism, 116, 152, App., IX.

[2] Mackemie's Tryal, p. 34. The Case of Mackemie and Hampton is also reviewed at length in Foote's Sketches of Va., First Series.

act, and Mackemie declared that he was ready to sign before the governor the articles of religion, with the exceptions mentioned in the act. To apply to a man like him the rule improvised by Cornbury and his advisers, was to make the arbitrary will of the governor the sole rule of action. The accused were imprisoned for six months, and only then was Hampton, the less important of the two, released under a writ of habeas corpus issued by Mompesson. Mackemie was brought up for trial under an indictment by a grand jury. He was defended by three lawyers, two of whom were the ablest in the province — William Nicoll and David Jameson. Bickley, the attorney general, represented the government. His argument in the case was to the effect that the penal statutes of Elizabeth, enforcing supremacy and uniformity, were in force in the colonies and that the accused had violated them. This was a notable change of position on the part of the government, and it too was met by a denial that either those acts or the act of toleration were in force in the colonies, and by the assertion that the New York act of 1693 provided for the toleration of Protestant dissenters, as did the instruction to the governor to allow liberty of conscience to all except papists. The jury brought in a verdict of not guilty and the prisoner was released, though he had to pay costs to the amount of more than £83.

The case of the church in Jamaica illustrates the difficulty which the Anglicans found in securing possession of the church edifice and settling a clergyman in a parish where the great majority of the inhabitants were dissenters who had long supported their own ministers. It was a case similar to that which arose in New York City, though it differed in that Jamaica was a country parish and was distant from the seat of government. A church edifice had been built there under the acts of 1693 and 1699. In 1704 Cornbury inducted Mr. Urquhart into the living.[1] But he found Mr. Hubbard, a Presbyterian, in possession and living in the parsonage, he having been called there two years before by the local vestry and church wardens, all or a majority of whom were dissenters. Cornbury issued a warrant ejecting Hubbard, though this

[1] See S. P. G. Correspondence for letters from Urquhart and Heathcote in 1705 and 1707.

naturally caused much dissatisfaction among his parishioners. Urquhart, however, remained in undisturbed possession until his death in 1709.[1] Then, with the approval of the local justices, the Presbyterians again came into possession of the church and parsonage, and a clergyman of their own faith was settled among them. Hunter was now governor, and he inducted Thomas Poyer into this living, Poyer, like Urquhart, having been sent over as a missionary by the Society for the Propagation of the Gospel. Hunter, under advice from Chief Justice Mompesson, decided that a resort to ejectment was illegal, and so Poyer found himself unable to get possession of the parsonage or to collect his salary. When he appealed to the governor for help, he was advised to sue for his rights and the governor offered to pay the costs.

Bellomont, who in so many things was the opponent and critic of Fletcher, was not prominent as a patron of the Church. Hunter stood in a similar relation toward Cornbury and his policies. He was a keen observer and possessed to a degree Swift's powers of sarcasm and denunciation. He clearly saw the hypocritical pretense and sham which were involved in much of the patronage which Fletcher and Cornbury lavished on the Church, and the element of oppression which inhered in it. In some of its features it surpassed anything which the High Church and Tory party attempted in England under Anne. The patronage of the Church by Nicholson involved also a large element of absurdity to those who really knew his character. About Talbot and perhaps others hung the suspicion of Jacobitism and of the nonjuror schism, and of this Hunter was not slow to avail himself in his letters home. Vesey, a man of New England origin and a recent convert, at this period of his career seemed to be a priest of the political type, under whose management it is to be believed that the material more than the spiritual interests of his parish flourished. His name was closely involved with those of men of the Cornbury régime who were engaged in crooked politics, and the least that can be said of him is that his zeal led him into bad company.

[1] S. P. G. Correspondence, Letter from members of Church at Jamaica Feb. 6, 1716. Doc. Hist. of N. Y. III, 198 *et seq.* N. Y. Col. Docs. V, 313, 326, 328, 334, 943, 972. Briggs. *op. cit.* 150 *et seq.*

Proof is afforded as well of the intense passions of the time as of the almost incredible baseness of which some in the colonial communities were capable by acts of desecration which were committed in Trinity Church on a night of February, 1713.[1] This inflamed the resentment of all Anglicans and, so far as the particular outrage was concerned, won for them the sympathy of right-minded Christians of every name. The feelings of jealousy on the part of Vesey toward Hunter were increased by the fact that the latter had the chapel in the fort repaired and services conducted by the chaplain of the garrison resumed there. As the governor attended at the chapel in person and also those who disliked the rector, a permanent reduction in the size of the congregation at Trinity Church was threatened. It was claimed that this step involved the opening of a chapel within the parish without the consent of the Trinity corporation, a proceeding which was calculated to divide the church. A murder committed by blacks on Long Island occasioned the terrorizing of the community by rumors of a negro insurrection — the first instance of this kind in New York — and nineteen presumably innocent human beings suffered death in its most horrible forms as a consequence. The school for negroes which Elias Neau, the catechist, with tireless devotion had conducted for years became the object of undeserved attack and for a time was broken up. These disturbed conditions led not unnaturally to an appeal by the Anglicans to their superior authorities in England. In 1714 Vesey visited England for this purpose, returning late the following year. His salary was withheld during his absence by the city vestry, but assistance toward his support while abroad was granted by the Venerable Society. In abundant letters Hunter, supported by Morris, defended his own conduct and attributed sinister motives to his opponents.[2] Ecclesiastical issues were involved with the politics both of New Jersey and New York, and Talbot and Henderson, along with Vesey, came in for ample denunciation from the pen of the governor. So far as the rector of Trinity was concerned, these

[1] Ms. Correspondence of S. P. G.; Doc. Hist. of N. Y., III, 444–458, reprinted in Eccl. Recs. of N. Y., III; Dix, Hist. of Trinity Church, I, 180.

[2] Doc. Hist. of N. Y. III, 435; N. Y. Col. Docs. V, 310–329: N. J. Arch. IV, 155–226.

charges did not avail. They were disregarded and Vesey returned with the appointment as commissary for New York and New Jersey, and a futile order from the bishop of London to the church wardens of the city to pay his salary. The accession of the Hanoverians to the English throne had meantime relieved Hunter's mind of the pressing fear of removal, while by his astute management a *modus vivendi* had been reached between him and the assembly. Therefore, with the return of quiet in affairs of government, church squabbles in the city tended also to abate, and the commissary and governor were able to maintain tolerable relations until the close of the latter's term.

But this quarrel reacted upon the question at issue in Jamaica. While it was at its height and under the advice of Vesey, Talbot and other ardent Anglicans,[1] Poyer declined to prosecute his opponents without the knowledge of his superiors in England. Vesey and his friends then sent, through the Society for the Propagation of the Gospel, a request to the queen that the governor's instructions be changed so that cases relating to the Church might be admitted to appeal though sums less than £300 were involved.[2] This request was granted by an order in council early in 1713. Under advice given in accordance with this, Poyer finally brought suit before the supreme court of New York, for the recovery of his salary.[3] A favorable judgment was obtained.

But accompanying and following this trial the collection of the rate in the parish was resisted or avoided by dissenters, riots occurred, a long and bitter struggle went on among the county justices and local vestrymen and church wardens, accompanied by summary removals of officers and no end of recrimination.[4] From this the clergymen concerned,—especially McNish, the Presbyterian,—did not keep themselves free. Independents in New England and in Great Britain interested themselves in the struggle,[5] as they had in the case

[1] N. Y. Col. Docs. V, 310–329.

[2] Doc. Hist. of N. Y. III, 265, 268. From entries in the Journal of S. P. G., April and May, 1715, it appears that it saw that the clause was continued in the instructions which were newly issued to Hunter after the accession of George I.

[3] Doc. Hist. of N. Y., III, 275, 280, 304, 309.

[4] *Ibid.*, III, 283–303.

[5] Briggs, American Presbyterianism, 154, 157.

of Mackemie. In 1731, a few months before the close of his life, Poyer wrote to the Society which he had long served,[1] of "the great and almost continual contentions that I have struggled withal among the Independents in this parish, having had several lawsuits with them before I could have the salary which the Country has settled upon the Minister of the Church of England, several other suits for some Glebe lands which we have lost, and at last even the Church itself of which we had the possession 25 years is taken from us by a trial at law." [2] In this last trial Morris presided as chief justice, and though a decision was reached which was evidently in the interest of peace and in agreement with the popular will, his alleged partiality in the case was made by Governor Cosby one of the reasons for the suspension of Morris from his office. The Anglicans, however, by this time and with the aid of Cosby had been able to build themselves a church and so left their rivals in possession of the original edifice. Such struggles as this, though less prolonged, between Anglicans and dissenting majorities occurred in other places in New York under the act of 1693, so that Morris, though an Episcopalian, wrote that he believed the Church would have been in much better position if there had been no act in her favor. In all the towns of Westchester county the Anglicans had to struggle for a foothold against opposing majorities among the people and in the vestries, led in some cases by ministers from New England.[3]

We have seen how that part of the bishop's functions which were mainly secular — the probate of wills, the issue of marriage licenses and the presentation to benefices — had passed by custom in the colonies to the governors. This left to the bishop of London in connection with the colonies the purely ecclesiastical functions of confirming, of consecrating churches, of ordaining, or issuing certificates of orthodoxy to candidates, suspending and degrading ministers, and the other duties which were involved in the oversight and discipline of the Church and clergy.[4] All of these it was very difficult, if

[1] Doc. Hist. of N. Y., III, 307, 310.

[2] *Ibid.*, 312; N. Y. Col. Doc. V, 943.

[3] N. Y. Col. Docs. V, 323. Bolton *op. cit.*

[4] Cross, *op. cit.*, 2–3.

not impossible, for him to exercise from a point so remote as London. Ministers could not be admitted to orders without going to England in person. The rite of confirmation could not be properly administered unless the bishop was present in the colonies. Without a resident bishop, therefore, or a suffragan, the constitution of the colonial church was rightly regarded by its communicants as almost fatally defective. Hence arose the demand for one or more colonial bishops. But for the time the only device which seemed possible was the appointment of commissaries. Their jurisdiction did not extend to the laity at all, but only over the clergy. They were empowered to hold visitations, to call conventions of the clergy and to exercise general supervision over their conduct.[1] The commissaries, acting under the constant direction of the bishop, were to correspond with him and keep him fully informed as to all matters affecting the Church. The only penalty which they could impose was that of suspension, subject to appeal to the archbishop or a great officer of state. The powers of the commissaries were slight, but they well reflected the undefined state of the episcopal jurisdiction in the early eighteenth century. Their weak position might, however, be to a degree overcome by the strong personality of an incumbent.

The royal provinces, and particularly those where the Church was established, were directly under the administration of the bishop, and to these commissaries were sent. Prominent among the clergymen who held this position were James Blair in Virginia, Thomas Bray, Christopher Wilkinson and Jacob Henderson in Maryland, Gordon, Johnson and Alexander Garden in South Carolina, William Vesey in New York. Roger Price held the office for a time in New England. In the person of Blair, the first appointee, who served from 1689 to his death in 1743, the office reached in some respects its highest point of strength and efficiency.[2] Notwithstanding the prejudice against which he had to contend as a Scotchman, Blair maintained himself as one of the leading personalities in Virginia for half a century. His position as councillor,

[1] Cross, p. 295 *et seq.*

[2] Hist. Colls. of Am. Col. Church, (Virginia); Hawks, Contributions to Ecc. History, (Virginia); Motley, Life of Blair, in J. H. U. Studies.

as president of the college and as rector of Bruton parish, the two former offices being such as no other commissary ever dreamed of attaining, not only furnished him an ample support but gave him an influence in Virginia which far exceeded that of a mere representative of the bishop of London. As commissary Blair received £100 a year out of the quit rents, to which was added £200 annually for his services as councillor and £150, later increased to £200, as president of the college. Governors came and went, and the going of three of the most prominent among them — Andros, Nicholson and Spotswood — he hastened, but he remained. For a time Spotswood overtopped him, but his leadership was brief when compared with the life-long activity of Blair in Virginia. His activity as a preacher was continuous and for a time of a rather high order. As a leader of the clergy and in all his secular relations he was able and aggressive, choosing wisely his positions and defending them with vigor. He elevated the office of commissary to a degree of influence which it never reached in the hands of others, though he was never beset by the perplexities which arose from having to contend with a population the majority of whom were dissenters.

The first notable achievement of Blair, in connection with his office, was the founding of William and Mary College, of which he was president for forty-nine years. He was the leader in raising a fund for it in Virginia and in persuading the legislature there to give it support. In England, as agent, he won for the plan the support of the leading bishops. In a memorial which was submitted to the treasury in England it was stated that over £2000 had been subscribed in Virginia, and it was hoped that any deficiency in the income from this source and from expected subscriptions in England would be made up from the impost duty on liquors. As sources from which grants to the college might be made in Virginia, the quit rents and escheats were referred to. In harmony with suggestions made in the memorial the following revenues and sources of revenue in Virginia were transferred to the account of the college: £2,000 from the quit rents of Virginia, a penny in the pound on all tobacco exported from Virginia, a duty on the export of skins and furs, the office of surveyor general with its fees and profits, and 20,000 acres of land, one-half of which lay on the south side of Blackwater swamp and near the North Carolina line, and the other half in Pamunkey Neck near the forks of the York river.[1] The right of special representation in the house of burgesses was also given to the college. The establishment of this institution was the crowning work of the English Church in Virginia and put the seal on that province as the leader in all that Anglicanism as such was contributing to American civilization, For half a century this was the only church college in the colonies, too remote, however, to be in any close sense a rival of the two Puritan colleges of New England. Wherever Anglicanism extended church schools of a lower grade were opened, like the college imitations on a small scale of the stagnant educational system which then existed in England, but all upholding a type of religious conformity which was less severe and inclusive than that of New England.

While Blair was commissary something like a conflict between the Church and the civil power may be said to have gone on in Virginia. It began with Andros, and as the governor maintained his usual reticence concerning these, like other charges, we have only Blair's side of the case.[2] He claimed that Andros in everything adopted a course of action toward the Church which was the opposite of that of Nicholson. Blair accused him of unfriendliness toward the college, of indifference or actual opposition to the increase of ministers' salaries, of diverting the quit rents from the clergy — on whom the privy council had ordered that they should be temporarily bestowed — to other uses, of neglecting to induct, of fomenting jealousy against ecclesiastical discipline, of putting affronts on the clergy. In December, 1697, a long hearing occurred on these charges before the archbishop of Canterbury and the bishop of London, Blair being present both as assailant of the governor and defender of himself, and Andros being defended chiefly by Colonel Byrd of Westover. Blair easily disproved the charges that he had unduly promoted or

[1] Hist. Colls. of Am. Col. Church (Virginia), 3 *et seq.* Hartwell, Chilton and Blair, Present State of Virginia, Cal. St. P. Col., 1689–92, pp. 452, 575, 671; *ibid.*, 1693–96, p. 154; *ibid.*, 1696–97, p. 457. Hening, Stats. of Va., III, 123, 357.

[2] Hist. Colls. of Col. Church (Virginia), 10–65, 75.

favored Scotchmen and that he had wrongfully taken the salary as president of the college while it was in process of construction. He then turned upon Andros, charging him with delaying subscriptions to the college, granting away the land set apart for it, failing duly to promote the collection of the export duty on tobacco which had been assigned to it, and so mismanaging the revenue that less than half of it went to its proper destination. He told how, just before the accounts were to be passed, because he was Scotch-born, the council of Virginia, under the lead of the governor, voted that he could not sit as a member, because the act 7 and 8 William III c. 22 required that all places of trust and those relating to the treasury in the dominions must be in the hands of native-born subjects.[1] The commissary had well worked up his case with the bishops. Their sympathies were clearly on his side. Early the next year Andros, now an old man, resigned his office, Blair claiming that his action had furthered this, as did his advocacy of the appointment of Nicholson as the successor of Andros.

With Nicholson also, notwithstanding the latter's great services to the Church, Blair, along with other members of the council, presently became involved in a most violent quarrel. This had no special connection with ecclesiastical affairs, but was part and parcel of the intolerable relations into which Virginia was thrown by the half insane passion of Nicholson, of which a general account has been given elsewhere. Whatever were the merits of this affair, Blair shared with the leading members in the governor's abuse and helped in bringing about his recall,[2] but his influence with the clergy suffered seriously as the result of the quarrel.

The question of the induction of clergymen into their livings was raised in the controversies of Blair with all three of the governors whom he opposed. The commissary complained that, owing to the failure of Andros to act, ministers were hired by their vestries from year to year and so kept in a subservient position and excluded from the use of the glebes.[3] Nicholson he charged with persistent neglect in this

[1] Blair was later restored to the council; *ibid.*, 81.

[2] *Ibid.*, 69–112, 131–138. On p. 82 *et seq.* is a criticism of Blair by Robert Quary.

[3] *Ibid.*, 15.

matter, and the best explanation of this which Quary was able to give was, that he was waiting for an opinion from the attorney general in England under which the governor would be able to act effectively against vestries which should refuse point blank to receive a candidate whom it was proposed to induct.[1] The opinion rendered by Sir Edward Northey,[2] in 1703, was to the effect that in cases where the parishes presented the candidate and the governor inducted, the incumbent was then in for life and could not be displaced by the parishioners. But if the parishioners did not present within six months after a vacancy occurred, their right should be held to have lapsed and the governor should collate to the benefice and the incumbent should likewise hold for life. The spirited controversy which arose between the governor and the commissary upon this subject is reserved for later treatment.

Dr. Bray, though he was appointed commissary of Maryland in 1696, did not arrive there until the spring of 1700 and returned to England in the summer of the same year. Thus he was in actual service in his province only a few months. While there he held one visitation, the clergy to the number of seventeen being called together at Annapolis.[3] Under his lead they reached resolutions on catechetical instruction, preaching, private labors and the prevention of ministers of scandalous lives obtaining a settlement in the province. Preliminary steps were also taken for disciplining one such clergyman. Save in its lack of answers to queries sent over by the bishop of London, this may be taken as a typical example of work done at a visitation. The great and invaluable services which Dr. Bray performed for the colonial church were rendered in England, where, as the result chiefly of his personal efforts, the Society for the Promotion of Christian Knowledge and the Society for the Propagation of the Gospel were founded in aid of missionary work in the colonies. Both have continued their activities until the present day, enlarging them on a scale commensurate with the

[1] *Ibid.*, 86.

[2] *Ibid.*, 127.

[3] Hawks, Maryland, App. See Hawks' account of Bray, beginning on p. 83 Perry, Hist. of Am. Epis. Church, I, 138 *et seq.*

growth of the British empire. In connection with the former Bray brought together upward of fifty parochial libraries in the colonies and other countries abroad — some containing more than two hundred volumes each — and caused them to be distributed through the various colonies where Anglican ministers were regularly officiating.[1] Then he devoted himself to the task of procuring missionaries, a work the result of which will soon demand our attention. As we have seen, he was also chiefly instrumental in securing the passage and acceptance of the act for the establishment of the Church in Maryland.

Another object to which Bray gave much attention, both in his own interest and on behalf of those who were to follow him, was the effort to provide a maintenance for the commissary.[2] He had a twofold plan, the purchase of an estate for his use at a cost of about £500, and the attachment to the office of the trial of testamentary causes. It was with the understanding that he was to have the proceeds from the last named source — about £300 per year — that he accepted the office. A clause providing for this seems to have been introduced into one of the acts for the establishment of the church, but was lost with the act. The estate also was never secured, and therefore no regular provision was made for the support of the office in Maryland. In Virginia, as we have seen, Blair received his support from his living at Williamsburg and his salary as president of the college.

On Dr. Bray's return to England, he deputed three of the best of the Maryland clergy to exercise his powers, but they never acted. Irregularities resulting, Bray at once applied to the bishop to appoint a commissary, for he had then abandoned hope of returning to Maryland. The Rev. W. Huetson, of the English Church in Ireland, was appointed, but because of Governor Seymour's violent opposition to the residence of a commissary in the province, he never came

[1] A. B. Keep, The Library in Colonial New York, p. 27. In 1697 Bray published in London "An Essay Towards Promoting all Necessary and Useful knowledge both Divine and Human in all Parts of His Majesty's Dominions." In this he set forth his plan for libraries and appended a list of suitable books.

[2] Hist. Colls. of Am. Col. Church (Maryland), 51, 57.

over.[1] The legislature then passed a bill, similar to that which occasioned so much excitement in South Carolina, for the establishment of a lay commission to administer discipline among the clergy, but this was vetoed by the governor. Governor Hart, who succeeded in 1714, cared more for ecclesiastical interests, and soon after his arrival he called the clergy together and propounded queries to them to ascertain whether worship according to the Book of Common Prayer was regularly celebrated, also the sacrament administered, and whether there were sufficient churches and if they were kept in repair, whether ministers had glebes and a competent maintenance, whether they were in orders and members of vestries.[2] Their answers to these queries were mostly in the affirmative, though it is pretty clear that they should not have been so. Notwithstanding the fact that under Seymour severe acts against Catholics had been passed, the clergy also complained of the growth of popery as well as of the immorality of the people. But a letter which Governor Hart wrote later to the bishop of London throws light on the character of the clergy themselves who were making these statements. He said that some of them were in education and morals " a scandal to their profession," and he wondered how such illiterate men could secure admission to orders.[3] It was already the belief of some that the clergy of Maryland suffered from the fact that the Church there was established, and it seemed evident that their character compared unfavorably with the missionaries who were sent over to the colonies where the Church was not in alliance with the state. However that may have been, the need of a commissary was evident, and in 1716 two such were appointed — Jacob Henderson for the Western Shore and Christopher Wilkinson for the Eastern Shore

The organization through which the Church made its growing influence most widely felt in the colonies was the Society for the Propagation of the Gospel in Foreign Parts.[4] This

[1] Hist. Colls. (Maryland), 57 *et seq.* The violence of Seymour's opposition may be accounted for by the fear that the jurisdiction of a surrogate, above referred to, might be transferred from the governor to him.

[2] Hawks, 138. Hist Colls. (Maryland) 74 *et seq.* [3] Hawks, 149.

[4] Humphreys, Historical Account of the S. P. G. Pascoe, Digest of the Records of the S. P. G. Perry, *op. cit.*, I. Overton, Life in the English Church, 1660–1714, Chap. 5.

was one of the leading instrumentalities through which the devotion of Compton, Tenison, Bray and others among the clergy of the age of Anne found expression. The society which at the middle of the century had been formed among the Independents as a result of the work of John Eliot in New England served now as a precedent for action, but the body of which it was a direct offshoot was the Society for the Promotion of Christian Knowledge, which was founded in 1699. A legacy of Sir Leoline Jenkins for the establishment of two fellowships at Oxford, the holders of which should serve as chaplains in the fleet or settle as missionaries in the foreign plantations, indicated the kind of service that was needed and a way in which funds might be procured. After his return from Maryland in 1700 Dr. Bray published "A Memorial representing the present State of Religion on the Continent of North America." This he dedicated to the archbishop and presented to the bishops and other patrons of religion. In this pamphlet the state of religion in the different colonies was briefly reviewed for the purpose of showing the weakness of the Church and the need of missionaries to spread its truths. The conclusion was that forty such were needed in the continental colonies, together with Newfoundland and the Bermudas. Starting from the impressions of George Keith, who had recently come over from the Quakers, the inference was drawn that many of them were ready to embrace Anglicanism and therefore that the conditions were favorable for a general effort. Those who should go out — men of sterling worth — must be supported for the first three years from funds raised in England, and after that period from glebes and other forms of support in the colonies. Therefore Bray urged that the clergy and laity of each diocese in England subscribe enough for the support of at least one missionary.

In the spring of 1701 a committee of the lower house of convocation was appointed to inquire into ways and means for promoting religion in the foreign plantations. The king was made acquainted with the spiritual destitution in the colonies, and therefore, as soon as the necessary legal steps could be taken, a royal charter was issued constituting the Society for the Propagation of the Gospel in Foreign Parts.

Under this name the archbishop of Canterbury and ninety others were incorporated and empowered to receive and hold lands and other forms of property and use the same for the purposes of the society. For the execution of their trust they were to hold yearly meetings for the election of officers, though the charter itself provided that the archbishop of Canterbury should be the first president. After the society had been organized business meetings should be held monthly or oftener, as need should require, and at these meetings members might be added to the corporation. For the proper transaction of business a quorum of seven, together with the president or one of the vice presidents, must be present. At these meetings by-laws could be passed and leases executed, and fit persons appointed to take subscriptions and receive contributions. Yearly the society should account in writing to the lord chancellor, the lord keeper or the justices of king's bench and common pleas for the money received and expended[1] Under these simple forms, the work of this important missionary society was carried on.

Meetings of the Society began June 27, 1701.[2] The archbishop of Canterbury was usually chosen president, and might be regarded as its natural, if not almost its *ex officio*, head. A board of vice presidents was annually chosen. In the absence of the archbishop — which was frequent — the bishop of London or some other bishop presided. Certain others of the clergy — bishops, archdeacons or deans — together with a varying number of lay members, made up the list of those who usually attended the meetings of the Society. The usual places of meeting were at the Cockpit or at the archbishop's library at St. Martin's in the Fields. The Society had from early in its history a standing committee which met weekly at St. Paul's Chapter House and, with a quorum of five — later of three — read and considered all the letters from the missionaries, officials and others in the colonies and also the replies which should be made to them. The secretary, like the holder of the same office for the board

[1] The charter is printed in Humphreys' volume.

[2] Ms. Journal and Correspondence of the Society; Pascoe, Two Hundred Years of the S. P. G.; Hawkins, Historical Notices of Missions of the Church of England in the North American Colonies; Humphreys, *op. cit.;* Dalcho, History of the Church in South Carolina; Perry *op. cit., etc.*

of trade, was the routine executive officer of the committee and of the Society and became one of its chief experts. At first letters were not infrequently read in full before the Society, but later, as correspondence became more voluminous, only those which were of exceptional importance were read, while abstracts were made and submitted of the rest.

There was a considerable lay element in the Society. New members were from time to time admitted, some being men who were prominent in colonial affairs — as Nicholson, Dudley, Lewis Morris, Heathcote, Hunter, Nicholas Trott and others. It was proposed to make the lord mayor and aldermen of London members, but that does not seem to have been done. A number of merchants were members, among them being Micajah Perry. Benefactions were specially sought from merchants, and by preference from those who were engaged in the plantation trade. At the close of 1704, in recognition of the value of his services as a missionary, George Keith was made a member of the Society.

Dr. Bray was often present at early meetings of the Society and was then its agent in soliciting contributions in England. Governors were requested to solicit aid in their colonies. The crown allowed £20 each to ministers on going to the plantations. They also received £15 from the Society for the purchase of books from a list prescribed by it, and an annual salary of £50 from the same source. The audit of the Society's accounts, in February, 1707/8, showed that its yearly income was £763 and its regular expenses £1285; since the previous June £617 had been expended from its capital stock. This shows not only how small were its resources when compared with sums similarly expended in our own day, but how continuous was the need of subscriptions. In 1715 it was stated that expenses had exceeded income. For the year 1709–10 the income of the Society was £1251. Soon after that they had to resort to retrenchment and to agree not to send more missionaries, increase salaries or give gratuities until the debts of the Society were paid. This, when taken into connection with the parsimony of the colonists, furnishes the explanation of the oft-repeated complaints of the missionaries concerning the meagreness of their support.

One would naturally infer that the policy of the Society

was determined in the main by its clerical members. The impression which one gets from reading its journal is that in really important matters the will of the primate and of the bishop of London was decisive, receiving as it did of course the assent of the other clergymen and bishops. This impression is strengthened by the regulation that all orders and minutes of the Society must be laid before the archbishop and the bishop of London. But the Society, of course, had to wait humbly and patiently on the will of the government and of the monarch. With a reserve and submissiveness which can almost be felt it waited on the archbishop and he on the king or queen and government for indications of their purposes or light on what they thought possible or impossible. This appears clearly in the history of the question of the colonial episcopate. Letters were occasionally interchanged with the board of trade or secretary of state. Written representations were occasionally sent to the monarch or to the ministry, for example, to stop the sale of liquor to the Indians, that missionaries among the Iroquois and the Palatines should be supported by the king, that the garrison at Albany should be supplied with a resident minister, that oppressive legislation should be disallowed. Colonial governors were similarly applied to for encouragement and support.

The first important measure of the Society was the dispatch of Keith and Gordon as special missionaries on a preaching tour through the colonies.[1] They crossed the ocean in 1702, on the same vessel which brought Joseph Dudley to his governorship in Massachusetts and Lewis Morris back from his negotiations concerning the surrender of government by the New Jersey proprietors. John Talbot was chaplain of the ship. Keith gave a very favorable account of the voyage, of the civilities of Dudley and Morris, of the daily celebration of divine worship, and of good conversation, "like a college," in the cabin. Gordon died soon after they reached America, and Talbot, as the result of the acquaintance made on ship board, became Keith's companion. In most respects this was a fortunate choice, for Talbot was a man of energy

[1] See Keith's Journal, in Colls. of Prot. Episcopal Hist. Soc.; Hawkins, *op. cit.;* Hills, History of the Church in Burlington, New Jersey.

and ability, an enthusiast in the cause of the Church. He became also an ardent admirer and supporter of Keith.[1] In the course of two years Keith travelled twice through the colonies from New Hampshire to North Carolina, preaching to dissenters, and especially to Quakers, wherever he found an opportunity. For controversy with them he was especially qualified, not only by his general ability as a speaker, but by his knowledge of their tenets, as he had only recently separated from their fellowship. The journeyings of Keith and Talbot suggest in a superficial way the later and more profound Wesleyan movement and the great preaching tours of Whitefield. The preaching of Keith and Talbot was an appropriate introduction to the work of the new missionary society and the information which was given in their letters and reports furnished a basis on which to begin operations.

Prominent Anglican laymen resident in the colonies, like Caleb Heathcote and Lewis Morris, and particularly Governor Francis Nicholson, gave much information orally or in writing. The information also which came from the governors to the board of trade might be at the service of the society. But, like the board of trade, it was continuously in correspondence with its missionaries abroad and it was chiefly their letters which kept it informed and furnished the staple of its business. In the appointment of missionaries — who held their positions during pleasure — the usual precautions were taken to secure good men, inquiries of course being confined within Anglican circles and regard being always had to orthodoxy, as well as to morals and general ability. Candidates were required to preach before members of the Society before they received appointment. Appointees were assigned by the Society to their special fields of work and were not to remove or return home without its consent. The rule of the Society was not to send a missionary to a place unless the communicants there had shown their ability and inclination to contribute toward his support.

As to the scope of the work, the Society in 1702 stated its purpose to be, "to settle the State of Religion as well as may be among our own people there, . . . and then to proceed in the best methods they can towards the Conversion

[1] Many of Talbot's letters are printed in the volumes just referred to.

of the natives."[1] In addition to the Indians, work among the negroes was undertaken by some of the missionaries in the south, where the opposition of the planters was not so strong as to prevent it, and by schoolmasters, notably Elias Neau, in New York. In 1710 it was resolved by the Society that the branch of its design which related to the conversion of the heathen and infidels ought to be prosecuted preferably to all others. In 1715 more than one half of its income was expended for missionary work among the Indians of New York.[2] A missionary was also maintained among the Palatines while they were on the Hudson and later at Schoharie. Among the whites, the field of its operations was in those colonies where the Church was not established or where dissenters were largely in the majority, and its purpose was really two-fold. It was to provide spiritual instruction for the scattered people who were already Anglicans and give them a church organization, and in connection therewith to add to their numbers as many as possible from non-religionists and dissenters. This was properly and inevitably the character of such work. It was frankly sectarian, as such enterprises have almost always been, though its purpose was generally benevolent, as this word was understood at the time. The dissenters, opponents of the movement, of course viewed it from the other angle and spoke of it with a different emphasis. To them it bore the aspect of interference and offensive partisanship. In his correspondence Penn condemned much of the activity of Anglicans in his province as "impertinent and provoking." "They came here poor and are so still, yet have got their bread and some of them estates, and cannot be satisfied to do so; but must in the pulpit inveigh against our principles, . . . as if . . . they would stir up their people against those whose tenderness admits them into shares in the administration to turn them out." After stating that this activity was due in large measure to the incitement of Nicholson and a few about him, Penn continued: "We cannot yet be so self-denying as to let those that had no part of the heat of the day, not one third of the number, and not one fourth of the estate, and not one tenth of the trouble and labour, should give laws

[1] Humphreys, 23; Pascoe, 7-8. [2] Mss. of the Society.

to us and make us dissenters and worse than that in our own country."[1]

In nearly all of the colonies dissenters were already in possession of the ground and regarded the appearance of Anglican missionaries as an intrusion. Being themselves ardent partisans, they usually put upon this the worst possible interpretation and affirmed that the chief purpose of the Society was propagandism, the winning of proselytes from other faiths. The connection between the Society and the British government, and its support by the royal officials in the colonies gave to its policy a political coloring and made it easy to designate it as one phase of the general movement of the time toward stronger imperial influence and control over the colonies. When, as we shall see, the Society began and continued an aggressive campaign far and wide in dissenting communities and made inroads, and especially when this occurred in New England, the development of controversies was unavoidable, with charges of sinister motives on both sides. Under such stress purposes somewhat changed and stiffened and objects were tacitly, if not expressly, pursued, which would never have been acknowledged at the inception of the movement. There was therefore truth in both conceptions, of the purpose of the Society, though both were exaggerated and policies doubtless underwent development.

Naturally it was in New England that the strongest opposition to Anglican propaganda appeared. As usual, this was led by the Mathers, while Sewall entered mournful comments in his diary. The fact that Keith and Talbot appeared in company with Dudley gave added point to their criticisms. Keith officiated as the clergyman at Dudley's inauguration. While the new governor retained his membership in the church at Roxbury, which he had joined in his youth, he was enrolled among the vestrymen of "Queen's Chapel," as it was now called, and with Povey, the lieutenant governor, frequently if not regularly attended service there, thus giving a sort of official recognition to this body as the favorite of the administration.[2] The fact that Dudley had prepared

[1] Penn to Harley, 14 Rep. of Historical Mss. Com., app. 4, p. 32.
[2] Foote, Annals of King's Chapel, I, 151.

for the use of the Society a statement of the population of the different colonies and an estimate of the prospects of the Church for growth in them indicates his interest in its fortunes generally. Keith was kindly received by Myles and Bridge, the two clergymen of the chapel and preached there on the Sunday following Dudley's inauguration. The object of this sermon — which was afterwards printed — was to "heal up the breach if possible" between the Church and the various dissenting sects and to apologize for the censures which he had passed upon her while he was still a Quaker. Conformity, obedience to superiors and the duty of using set forms in prayer were among the six "good rules in Divinity" which Keith recommended as means to the end he had in view. "Whoever denies or disowns her (the Church of England)," he declared, "as too many do of various sorts, do show themselves to be undutiful Children, unless they can prove her to be degenerate, which I am well persuaded they can never do."

In 1688 Keith, in his earlier capacity as a Quaker preacher, had visited Boston and denounced the clergy there in the severe prophetic style,[1] which still survived among the disciples of George Fox. James Allen, Joshua Moody, Samuel Willard and Cotton Mather had been expressly named among those "called preachers in Boston" whom Keith attacked. Their reply was: "Having received a blasphemous and heretical paper, subscribed by one George Keith, our answer to it and him is; if he desires conference to instruct *us*, let him give us his arguments in writing as well as his assertions; if to inform *himself*, let him write his doubts; if to cavil and disturb the peace of our churches (which we have cause to suspect) we have neither list nor lisence to attend his motions. If he would have a public audience, let him print; if a private discourse, though he may know where we dwell, yet we forget not what the Apostle John saith, Epis. 2, 10th verse."[2] The spirit in which Keith replied may be inferred from the title of the next publication: "A brief answer to some gross abuses, lies and slanders, published some years ago by

[1] Perry, Hist. of Am. Episcopal Church, I, 208.

[2] "If there come any unto you and bring not this doctrine, receive him not into your house, neither bid him God speed."

Increase Mather, late teacher of a church in Boston, in New England, in his book called 'An Essay for the recording of Illustrious Providences,' etc., and by Nath. Morton, in his book called 'New England's Memorial.'"

In 1689 Increase Mather had published a pamphlet entitled, "A Brief Discourse Concerning the unlawfulness of the Common Prayer Worship, and of Laying the Hand on and Kissing the Booke in Swearing." This was the first blast from the trumpet of the leading divine of New England against the episcopal innovations which had been set up there by Randolph, Andros and their associates. He pronounced the ceremonies and worship prescribed in the Book of Common Prayer to be popish and heathenish, declaring that they could not be practiced without sin. "In this Age of Light!" he said, "it would in me, (and all others so educated and instructed as I have been) appear to be a great Apostacy should I in the least countenance or comply with the Common Prayer worship." The following year, in an election sermon before the general court, Cotton Mather had again coupled the English Church with the Roman and in the spirit, not of Francis Higginson when he came to Salem, but of the later Puritans when they had become firmly established in New England. He warned his hearers against the "mystical Babylon" which was "just entering into the vintage" and would cause "horrible and fiery plagues to impend over the Heads of those that shall have the Superstitions of Popery polluting them." "Could I speak with a voice as loud as the Last Trumpet, I should not fear to tell you, the God of your Fathers will blast the Worldly Wisdom which counts it a conveniency for us to Dissemble our Non Conformity to what ever vain Worship has nothing but the Tradition of men to Warrant it." [1]

These utterances, both with reference to Keith as a Quaker and also to the English Church, made it certain that his reappearance as a convert to the Church and as an aggressive defender of its claims would arouse the Mathers. This it did, and the elder Mather at once replied to Keith's sermons in a pamphlet in which, though using a form of speech more dignified and restrained than was customary with his son,

[1] Pubs. of Prince Soc.; Slafter, John Checkley, I, 22 *et seq.*

he declared that the adherents of the English Church were dissenters in New England and reminded Keith that a penitent acknowledgment of the blasphemies he had uttered as a Quaker would have furnished better evidence of the sincerity of his conversion. "For him who has been as great a Schismatic as any Donatist in the world now to insinuate that all the holy churches of Nonconformists are Schismatics, . . . deserves severe reproof." So sure was Mather that the churches of New England were built on the true biblical foundation that it was to be hoped that, though an hundred Keiths should come to seduce them, they would not forsake the pure religion which had been left to them by their fathers. There could be no doubt that these were the sentiments of the vast majority of Puritan New Englanders and that the Mathers correctly voiced their opinions upon the subject of episcopacy. In reply to Keith they sounded the first note in a controversy which was to last as long as the connection with England continued. The entire past of New England made it certain that the Church would there meet its strongest opposition. Elsewhere in the colonies it had secured a foothold or even a leading position with little or no difficulty. In New England it must build from the smallest and weakest beginnings and, outside of Rhode Island, must count on the opposition of the colony governments and of the mass of the population. In Massachusetts it had the support of a group of royal officials, small in numbers, but considerable in influence, and of tendencies which were manifest in the practice of the half-way covenant and in the so-called spirit of Arminianism that was abroad told in its favor.

Of the fact that zealots like Keith and Talbot, backed by politicians of the not too exalted type represented by Nicholson and Cornbury, found their chief reward from the work of propagandism not in the moral improvement of their hearers, but in such assaults as they could make upon rival sects, their writings and conduct leave no room for doubt.[1] We may not admire the dogmatism and intolerance of the Mathers and of the New England clergy generally, but in

[1] See Keith's Journal and letters, together with those of Talbot, which are printed in Colls. of Prot. Episcopal Hist. Soc., I; Reed, Church and State in Mass., 152 *et seq.*, University of Ill. Studies, III.

dignity and power of utterance, their superiority is evident, when compared with nearly all the early defenders of Anglicanism in the colonies. In the presence of such men as Keith and Talbot, the New England churches would have been blind had they not seen that they were the chief object of attack and that the healing of the schism in the English Church which now had lasted more than a century, rather than the preaching of the gospel to the destitute, was the object of these so called missionary journeys.

The Quakers also, even more than the Independents, were objects of Keith's attention. Wherever he found their meetings in session, from New Hampshire to the Carolinas, Keith made it a point, if possible, to attend, to interrupt their services, to argue against their doctrines and engage in noisy altercations with Quaker preachers and others who were present. In Rhode Island conspicuous instances of this form of procedure occurred. The ultra-controversial spirit raged there even more fiercely than it had done in the same places when Roger Williams held his famous arguments with the Quakers. According to Talbot, none of the Quakers were able to answer Keith, for he, better than all others, knew "the Depths of Satan within them and all the Doublings and Windings of the *Snake in the Grass.*" On the suggestion of Bray special attention was paid to Rhode Island and to the nearby towns where Quakers were numerous. Because of the strength of Quaker opposition and also of the system of religious freedom which existed there, Rhode Island was considered a favorable field in which to station Anglican missionaries. In Pennsylvania also the battle raged, though in the other colonies the attitude of the dissenters seemed more conciliatory. The Keithian Quakers everywhere were naturally more inclined to listen to their former leader, though he was sometimes called upon to explain the inconsistencies in his past conduct. Upon the name of William Penn himself, Talbot in particular poured out the vials of his wrath, denouncing him as a greater Antichrist than Julian the Apostate and inquiring who was defender of the faith when this "head-Heretick" was made governor and proprietor of a province. So the aggressive campaign went on during the reign of Anne, and whatever comfortable and assuring words might be spoken about it at the meetings of the Society or in other clerical circles in England, in many parts of the colonies it was simply plunging communities more deeply than ever into the slough of sectarian polemics.

It was on the submission of letters by Bray and consultation with Keith that it was decided to send a missionary to Rhode Island. In response to a letter from Vesey it was resolved to send six missionaries to New York, and a letter from Pennsylvania occasioned the designation of three to service in that province. One was to be sent to North Carolina. The securing by purchase or gift of an estate of land either in Maryland or Virginia was discussed before the end of 1702. Letters from Keith, while he was on his missionary journeys, probably led to the formation of a plan for founding a mission among the Iroquois, to offset the influence of the Jesuits. In April, 1703, an order in council to that effect was issued, and the board of trade was to be informed of this action. It was in this connection that Rev. Godfrey Dellius comes into view again after his expulsion by Bellomont from New York for complicity in land frauds. He was now living in the Netherlands. Dudley had made a motion in the Society concerning him and Dellius had repeatedly written to it seeking a new appointment for work among the Indians and setting forth his knowledge of the Mohawk tongue and his acquaintance with their affairs. In the spring of 1704 Robert Livingston, then in London, gave encouragement to the work of Lydius among the Indians and the Society presently dropped its correspondence with Dellius.

In 1705 an inquiry was made into the status and work of the Society for the Propagation of the Gospel in New England,[1] its charter was examined and Sir William Ashurst, its president, wrote them about its revenue and funds. A letter was then ordered prepared by Dudley, the governor of Massachusetts, to the Episcopal clergy in New England, to encourage sending over young students who were inclined to be ordained and become missionaries.[2]

In the winter of 1705/6 Rev. Samuel Thomas, from South

[1] Osgood, American Colonies in the 17th Century, III, 151.

[2] This was a work in which Dr. Samuel Johnson a quarter of a century later became very deeply concerned in Connecticut.

Carolina, was in London and repeatedly appeared before the Society. He presented a valuable memorial on the state of the Church in his province and told how poorly he had been supported by the governor, Sir Nathaniel Johnson, and the people. It was apparently from Thomas that the Society first learned of the clause in the South Carolina act which provided that ministers should be removed by lay commissioners on complaint of the inhabitants. During the discussion which arose over this subject Thomas was called on for information. Complaints against him were later presented by Rev. Edward Marston and Colonel Smith, but Marston's reputation was soon so wrecked that nothing came of this.

The starting of the mission at Stratford, Connecticut, appears in this form in the journal of the Society. In September, 1707, two letters from Heathcote were read and also a clause from the laws of Connecticut.[1] Evans, the missionary at Philadelphia, had been questioned about the matter, and when the subject was taken up again, the bishop of London said he had received an address from some inhabitants of Connecticut asking that Anglican worship be set up among them. But it was voted to send out no more missionaries while the finances of the Society continued in their present state. The following March the question of retaining Honeyman in Rhode Island, against whom charges had been made, came up and Colonel Nicholson, then in London, offered £30 for his support for a year, until his case could be fully investigated. This was accepted. Later, while stating to the committee the great need of sending a missionary to Connecticut, Nicholson said that, if the Society would send one to that colony, he would increase his former gift to fifty guineas. At a later meeting, when Nicholson was present, the committee reported in favor of accepting this offer. A paper entitled "The State of the Church in Connecticut," was read; Evans gave a further account of the subject, and the question was referred back to the committee. At the same time Lord Lovelace, who was soon to go out as governor to New York, was admitted to membership in the Society. The committee reported that a missionary was greatly needed in Connecticut and that the order in council which had vetoed its law concerning Quakers

[1] Hawks and Perry, Church of Connecticut, I, 19, 26.

did not include its law entitled "ecclesiastical," which was made use of against the Church. It also recommended that Rev. George Muirson, of Rye, be the appointee, if any one was sent. The treasurer was appealed to and he said there was too much reason to think that Moore and Brooke had been lost on their voyage to England — which proved true — and, if so, that £200 in salaries would be set free. Thereupon it was voted to transfer Muirson from Rye to Stratford, and the mission was established from which were finally to proceed more important results than from any other similar act of the Church in the colonies.

It was through the influence of Heathcote, Cornbury and Vesey, that Muirson was selected for this work, and it marks the beginning of a reaction on the part of New York upon western Connecticut which was destined to be permanent and far reaching. Muirson had been a schoolmaster at Albany and in New York and by his devotion, tact and ability had recommended himself to his superiors and, after being admitted to orders, was soon instructed with responsible missionary work. From his parish at Rye he and Heathcote had tested the spirit and needs of nearby towns in Connecticut by repeated visits before it was resolved, if possible, to secure the establishment of a mission there. The number of acknowledged Anglicans was few and they were scattered, though with the presence of a clergyman and stated services, accompanied with the baptism of children and the dissemination of literature, the number of communicants was increased. But the opposition which these early efforts met with was determined and led to much genuine persecution. A single quotation from Muirson's letters will indicate its nature.[1] "Though every Churchman in that Colony pays his rate for the building and repairing their meeting-houses, yet they are so maliciously set against us, that they deny us the use of them, though on week days. They tell our people that they will not suffer the house of God to be defiled with idolatrous worship and superstitious ceremonies. . . . They say the sign of the cross is the mark of the beast and the sign of the devil, and that those who receive it are given to the devil. And when our people complain to their magistrates of

[1] Conn. Church Docs. I, 30.

the persons who thus speak, they will not so much as sign a warrant to apprehend them, nor reprove them for their offence." Muirson and Heathcote had already been warned of the provisions of Connecticut law for securing uniformity of worship and of the intention of the local magistrates to enforce them.[1] It was not, however, until the close of 1709, after Muirson's premature death, that refusal to pay the taxes levied for the support of congregational or presbyterian worship, had become so evident as to lead to the fining and imprisonment of offenders. This began at Stratford and extended to other towns, becoming the accepted policy of the Connecticut government, regularly enforced wherever Anglicans appeared in sufficient strength to begin or demand services of their own and to separate themselves fully from the established churches. In some cases, estates were to a large extent confiscated and people were forced by their sufferings to leave the colony. In this way the progress of the Church was checked and its supporters found themselves facing a long and bitter conflict.

The demand for missionaries soon became greater than the supply, but during the first fifteen years of its existence the Society established missions at Newbury, Marblehead and Braintree in Massachusetts; Newport and Narragansett (Kingston) in Rhode Island; Rye, New Rochelle, Westchester, Jamaica, Hempstead, Richmond and Albany in New York; Burlington, Amboy and Elizabethtown in New Jersey; Chester, Oxford and Radnor in Pennsylvania; Newcastle and Dover in the counties on the Delaware; Charlestown, Goose Creek, St. John's, St. Bartholomew's, St. Paul's, St. Andrew's, and St. Thomas' parishes in South Carolina. Assistants were also provided for King's Chapel in Boston, for Trinity Church in New York and for Christ Church in Philadelphia. Elias Neau was appointed a catechist and schoolmaster for the negroes in New York City. A mission was established at Fort Hunter among the Mohawks, and a minister was stationed among the Palatines. In South Carolina some of the most efficient work was done, so that a commissary was sent there after the Church was established; though the Society continued to send ministers there throughout the colonial period.

[1] *Ibid.*, 23, 42.

From time to time the need of one or more bishops for the colonies was impressed upon the Society.[1] The demand came from the Anglican clergy in the colonies and was urged by the Society, partly as a reflection of these demands. Its efforts to secure colonial bishops were especially prominent for some fifteen years after its founding. Then they ceased for a generation, because of the unsympathetic attitude of the government. So strong was the interest of Archbishop Tenison in a colonial episcopate, that on his death he left £1000 for the endowment of such an office. The sympathies of Queen Anne were strong in favor of the same policy. In the same direction tended also the strong High Church and Tory reaction of the later years of her reign. There was great justice in this demand, as has been made clear by what was said concerning the commissaries. Ordination, confirmation, consecration of churches, settlement of disputes between clergymen, churches and factions, the enforcement of discipline, general supervision and leadership in affairs of the Church at large — for all these and more the presence of a bishop was absolutely necessary or very advantageous for the Church. The office was necessary to its complete constitution. At the close of 1704 the standing committee reported to the Society that it had prepared a statement of the case in favor of suffragan bishops in the colonies, and it had been delivered to the two archbishops and the bishop of London, to be laid before the queen. More than six months later this matter was mentioned again, but no action was taken.

Meantime, in letters from the colonies the missionaries and laymen, like Heathcote, Morris, Nicholson and, later, Hunter, expressed in no uncertain terms the need of a bishop and their desire that one should be sent.[2] Moore wrote that the clergy were unanimous in their desire for a suffragan, and of the substantial truth of this there is no reason to doubt. Heathcote expressed the opinion that, if one were sent, many graduates of Harvard College would conform and become Anglican ministers, while his statements of the need of the

[1] Cross, *op. cit.*, 88 *et seq.;* also all the other standard works on the history of the American Episcopal Church.

[2] Ms. Journal and Correspondence of the S. P. G.

churches for prompt action in this matter were many and urgent. The zealous Talbot exceeded all others in the number and force of his appeals. In 1703, after his second missionary journey with Keith, he enlarged on the characteristics of the dissenting sects and on the completeness — from their own point of view — of their polity. "But," he continued, "the poor Church has nobody upon the spot to comfort or confirm her children." Several who were willing to become ministers fell back into "the herd of dissenters" rather than go so far as to England for orders. "Is it not strange," he exclaimed in 1709, "that so many islands should be inhabited with Protestants, so many provinces planted by them. . . . But of all the kings, princes and governors, all the bishops and archbishops that have been since the Reformation, they never sent anybody here to propagate the Gospel — I say to propagate it by imparting some spiritual gift by ordination or confirmation?"[1] The Pennsylvania clergy and a convention of missionaries who were brought together at Burlington, New Jersey, in 1705 as a result of the activity of Nicholson, petitioned the Society for bishops. In 1706 Talbot visited England to support the cause in person.[2]

In 1707 Archbishop Tenison laid the matter before the queen,[3] and she directed him to submit a plan. But when the question was brought up in the Society, it was voted to postpone it till more bishops were present. It was realized that the plan would be received with alarm and opposition in the colonies, not alone by the dissenters, but by the laity of the Church, because a bishop would restrict the control they had over their pastors and also might reprove them for their low morals.[4] The opinion was expressed that, when a bishop should be sent, it should be a suffragan, as being less offensive and easier to change than one of full rank. In June,

[1] Hawkins, 144, 376 *et seq.*

[2] Colls. of Prot. Epis. Hist. Soc. I, 58 *et seq.*

[3] Ms. Journal of S. P. G.

[4] See an unsigned set of observations, probably by the bishop of London, under date of 1707, N. Y. Col. Docs. V, 29. Evans, of Philadelphia, in a memorial on the state of the Church in Pennsylvania, had enlarged on the low morals among the colonists and on the need of a bishop to restrain this, as well as for administrative reasons; Mss. of S. P. G.; Hazard, Pa. Register, III, 337; Cross, *op. cit.*, 95.

1709, the subject was again brought up by the bishop of London, who stated to the Society the great inconveniences that arose from the lack of a bishop in the plantations. But it was moved that, until further steps could be taken, a commissary be sent. So important was the question considered that it was postponed until the archbishop could be present. On July 15 he was present, and he thought the matter had better be put off until the bishops had returned from the country, the entry being made in such form as to show that the subject was a delicate one, to be spoken of very softly.

In April, 1710, after considering conflicts and irregularities in the colonies, and having the needs of the Indians brought forcibly before it by the presence of Schuyler and his Iroquois, the committee reported resolutions reached at a meeting which the archbishop had desired to be held at Lambeth, that the Society could not well carry on the various branches of its work without a bishop, that the early establishment of a French bishop at Quebec appeared to have been a great cause of the successful extension of Catholicism among the Indians, and that this and the other needs of the work be embodied in a representation to the queen, to be drawn by the bishop of Salisbury, Gilbert Burnet, and the bishop of Norwich. The latter then produced a draft of a representation, which was approved and was delivered to the archbishop to be presented to the queen.[1] Though these steps were taken and rumors had already been circulated that Dean Swift was to be sent as a bishop to Virginia, nothing came of it.

In January, 1711, the archbishop of York desired that the proposal to send bishops to the colonies be submitted to Convocation, but in the absence of the bishop of London the motion was dropped. So encouraging, however, seemed at this time the prospect of a colonial episcopate that negotiations were begun for the purchase of a house at Burlington, New Jersey, which was intended for an Episcopal residence. In the fall of 1712 Governor Hunter, on behalf of the Society, closed the bargain for the house, its price being £602.[2] In this same year a bill was drafted, to be offered in parliament,

[1] The four Indians were then called in and the resolutions were read to them.

[2] Hills, *op. cit.*, 106; Ms. Correspondence of the S. P. G.

for the establishment of bishops and bishoprics in America. Renewed representations to the queen were so successful that, had it not been for her sudden death, the object might have been at once attained. But with the accession of the Hanoverians, as events proved, the cause received such a set-back that, in the view of the government, it never afterwards reached the stage of a practical issue.

CHAPTER XVIII

CULMINATION OF THE LEISLERIAN CONFLICT. MISGOVERNMENT OF LORD CORNBURY IN NEW YORK AND NEW JERSEY

THE earl of Bellomont died March 5, 1700/1. The four Leislerian councillors, Weaver, De Peyster, Staats and Walters, were in town and in an hour after the death of the governor they met in council.[1] Lieutenant Governor Nanfan was then in Barbadoes or on his way home from the West Indies. William Smith, acting chief justice[2] and the senior councillor and also one of the aristocrats whose large estates and imperfect knowledge of the law had exposed him to Bellomont's criticism, was on Long Island, seventy miles away. Schuyler and Livingston were in Albany. The peace of the province and the continuance of government, including of course the ascendancy of the Leislerians must be at once provided for. The four councillors issued a proclamation which was ordered to be published in the counties, confirming all officers, civil and military in their places. Expresses were sent to the absent councillors announcing Bellomont's death and desiring their attendance in council. De Peyster, being the eldest councillor present, should act as president till the arrival of Nanfan or Smith. Letters were written to the lords of trade and to Secretary Vernon, stating what had occurred, and asking that Champante might be continued in his position as agent for the province and that, if a chief justice and attorney general should be appointed, owing to the financial straits of New York, they might be paid out of the royal revenues. Champante was asked to use his influence to have good Leislerians put into the council.[3]

[1] Ex. C. Min. The record was surrounded by mourning lines. It was among the volumes destroyed in the Albany fire. N. Y. Col. Docs. IV, 850. Cal. St. P. Col. 1701, p. 108 *et seq.*, 119.

[2] Bellomont had suspended Smith from this office on Dec. 25, 1700, but had not informed him of it. So Smith continued to serve without knowing this, until after Bellomont's death and the arrival of Atwood. Ex. C. Min. June 12, 1702.

[3] Cal. St. P. Col., 1701, p. 121.

On March 11 Smith arrived. Two days later a meeting of the council was held, over which he presided.[1] There was no earlier precedent, unless the practice of other colonies was inquired into, for the situation in which New York now found herself.[2] As the Leislerian councillors would not at first commit themselves, Smith told them that he thought he was entitled to convene, prorogue and dissolve the assemblies and to use the power of veto, and that without him the council could not do business; and finally that outside of the council he should be at the head of the executive. The first meeting with Smith occurred on the 13th and then the Leislerian members came forward with a resolution that the majority should call a council meeting and determine the policy of the government in all things, and if Smith did not choose to act with them on that basis, they would go on without him. Smith presented his view which proved to be the correct one;— but as it was seen by him and his supporters outside, that a refusal to serve was precisely what the Leislerians desired, he added that he would acquiesce and preside under the conditions they specified with a protest for the saving of his rights.

In 1707,[3] because of disputes which had arisen in several colonies over this question, the crown issued a special instruction to the effect that, on the death or absence of the governor, the eldest councillor then in the province should undertake the administration of the government and execute the powers conveyed by the commission and instructions of the governor as the governor would do if he were present. The effect of this was to concentrate authority more definitely in the hands of the president and to remove the indefiniteness in the wording of the previous instruction. It was in line with the claim which had been set up by Smith and made for efficient government, though the New York council correctly interpreted its rights under Bellomont's commission.

[1] Docs. 857; Ex. C. Min.; Cal. St. P. Col., 1701, pp. 125, 186 *et seq.*

[2] Bellomont's commission provided that, in the event which had happened, the council should take charge of the government, and the eldest councillor should act as president with such powers as had been held by presidents in New York, or other provinces. N. Y. Col. Docs. IV, 272. The board of trade seems to have agreed with Weaver and his associates in their interpretation of this clause. Cal. St. P. Col., 1701, p. 429.

[3] N. Y. Col. Docs. V, pp. 3, 5; C. O. 5/210, May 3, 1707.

The next question was, whether the assembly should meet on April 2, the date to which it had been prorogued and it was decided that it should do so, Smith alone dissenting.[1] His reason, which was submitted in writing, was that it was possible that the assembly had legally been dissolved by Lord Bellomont's death, especially as there would be no commander-in-chief to meet it, as was required by the writ and if it should sit, the negative voice would be lost, since the council as a whole could not make use of it. He also called their attention to the order which had been sent to the governors the previous year, that when they were under presidents and councils only such laws should be passed as were immediately necessary for the peace and welfare of the provinces. But in a heated argument the Leislerians maintained that a session was necessary and finally carried it by a majority of one. After protesting at length, Smith, along with the rest, signed the call for the assembly. Smith then returned to his home for a few days on private business.

While he was away Schuyler and Livingston arrived in town, but, though repeatedly notified of its meetings, they declined to attend the council until Smith's return.[2] The members were also pledging their private credit for the support of the forces, and the two Albany councillors declined to be drawn further into such entanglements. Weaver and De Peyster advanced money for this purpose.

Eleven members of the assembly met on the 2nd of April. Two days later a quorum was present, though the entire membership from two counties was absent till several days later. On the 8th Smith presented a statement concerning the assembly as well as the existing administration of the government, but the majority refused to allow it entered on the minutes.[3] The next day they charged Smith with delaying the business of the assembly and claiming larger powers than he was entitled to. They said that his position was merely that of presiding officer of the upper house and the council had charge of the government. To this Smith replied.[4]

[1] Cal. St. P. Col., 1701, pp. 127, 187, 193, 194, 196.

[2] *Ibid.*, 193.

[3] Ex. C. Min.

[4] These papers are in inclosures. Cal. St. P. Col., 1701, p. 194 *et seq.*

After a brief adjournment, the assembly came together again on the 14th. Then the four councillors gave reasons in elaborate form why the assembly should proceed to business with the council as it was then organized.[1] The fort at Onondaga must be built, they said, preparations must be made for an Indian conference and provision for the payment of the troops. The forts at Albany and Schenectady greatly needed repair or rebuilding and the mast timber must be sent to England. Smith, they declared, was hindering them from doing so by claiming exorbitant powers. This paper was sent to the assembly and copies of it also to the absent members of the council. It was equivalent to a program of business and was so accepted by the assembly and they then proceeded with the session in agreement with the majority of the council,[2] though Smith states that it was only by a bare majority vote. The assembly declared that the administration of government was in the council, over which the eldest councillor should preside, and not in any single councillor. Five members of the house, all of whom but one were from Queens and Suffolk counties and were friends of Smith, presented a paper in opposition to this. A committee reported that this was a disloyal act and Matthew Howell, one of its signers, was expelled.

In the statement of their side of the case, which Smith, Schuyler and Livingston sent to England, they charged Weaver with being chiefly responsible for what had occurred.[3] They deplored the fact that, some little time before Bellomont's death, he had been appointed a member of the council. They described him as a stranger, a person of turbulent and violent spirit, a partisan who had been the sole manager of the debates in the council, and that with heat and clamor; that during the short time he had been collector he had imposed requirements on the merchants which were not known in other colonies and, when they complained, had told them that the more he made them protest the better the commissioners of the customs would like him. The writers begged that some steps might be taken in England to abate the heats and animosities by which New York was distressed.

[1] *Ibid.*, 197.

[2] Ass. J. I, 110.

[3] Docs. p. 861, *et seq.* Cal. St. P. Col., 1701, p. 190.

Bayard had already written to Philip Meadows that party spirit was hot, the assembly packed, that men of the meanest origin, most of them Dutch, were in all the offices, that appropriations to pay Leisler's debts and other extravagant measures might be expected.[1] To Bellomont a petition had been presented for an allowance of £2700 to the Leisler family. According to Bayard's view, the removal of Smith from the office of chief justice and the appointment of De Peyster to that position shortly before Bellomont's death, was an early preliminary to measures like the above.[2] He also states that it was planned that Smith, Schuyler and Livingston should be suspended from the council, but that was prevented by the sudden death of the earl. Bayard inclosed in his letter a considerable list of persons on the other side who were suitable to receive appointment.

The assembly resolved that the building of the fort at Onondaga be suspended until Nanfan's return. Stephen Van Cortlandt, who since the removal of Brooke had been collector and receiver general, had recently died. His widow now refused to surrender his books of accounts to the Leislerians who were in control of the government,[3] and so nothing but confused and fragmentary accounts could be found. A report on the subject was submitted to the house, but no decisive action was taken at this time. On April 19, when Smith retired to his country estate and Livingston declared that he would not cooperate with the council until Smith's return, that body resolved that it could not act without Smith, and so the two houses adjourned till June.

On May 19 Nanfan made his first appearance at council.[4] This brought the unusual situation in that body to an end. It meant the complete ascendancy to the Leislerians, at least in the executive and upper house, for the lieutenant governor identified himself fully with them. Because of the activity of the French, Indian affairs occupied much of Nanfan's

[1] Docs. p. 848 (Mar. 8); Cal. St. P. Col., 1701, p. 115.

[2] De Peyster declined to act as justice till some lawyer came from England to preside. Case of Atwood, p. 250. It was known or supposed at that time that a chief justice and attorney general were soon to be sent from England.

[3] This trouble with the "lady mayoress" had begun before Bellomont's death. Cal. St. P. Col., 1701, 213.

[4] Ex. C. Min. Cal. St. P. Col., 1701, p. 254.

attention and it was necessary for him to visit Albany early in July for a conference. But, on June 1, the council voted that, for the peace and welfare of the province, it was necessary to dissolve the existing assembly and that a new one should be elected to meet on the first Tuesday in August.[1] Nanfan also wrote that from the journal he had found the disputes in the house over the legality of their session to have been so heated that it was impossible to think of bringing them again to cooperate in that body. After the dissolution a warning was issued against undue practices and unfair returns in the coming elections.

In the hotly contested election which followed the Leislerians again triumphed, and on August 19 Nanfan met the new house.[2] Shortly before the return of the lieutenant governor from Barbadoes, William Atwood and Sampson Shelton Broughton had arrived from England. They both came with commissions from the king, the former to be chief justice and the latter attorney general.[3] They were trained lawyers and had been sent in response to the urgent request of Bellomont. Atwood was promoted to Smith's place on the bench of the supreme court and De Peyster and Walters were made his assistants. Under direction from the board of trade an order was issued by the governor and council for opening a court of chancery, though it is doubtful if the court ever sat.[4] Atwood was made a member of the council, and placed his legal knowledge and experience wholly at the service of the dominant faction, of which Weaver was the leading spirit. But Broughton held back and soon identified himself with the opposing group.[5]

At the opening of the assembly Nanfan, who had just come down the river, was able to inform them not only that the king had granted £2500 for the improvement of the defences

[1] *Ibid.*, 272, 287, 436.

[2] Ass. J. I, 115.

[3] Out of the royal revenue they were to receive salaries of £300 and £150 respectively. Attorney General Northey stated later that he had known Broughton for many years and that he was a barrister of long standing in the Middle Temple. Broughton died in office in New York. N. Y. Docs. V, 49, 51.

[4] Smith, History of New York, I, 137.

[5] Colls. of N. Y. Hist. Soc. Fund Series, 1880. (The case of William Atwood, Esq.) This was sent as a pamphlet from England to New York in 1703. Ass. J. I, 163; C. J. I, 193; N. Y. Col. Docs., IV, 882, 914, 929.

of Albany and Schenectady and the building of the fort at Onondaga, but of the remarkable treaty which the Five Nations had just concluded with him in which they had apparently made submission to the English and ceded so much territory to them. This, with the peace which shortly before they had concluded with the French, was to insure tranquillity to New York during most of the next war. No more important events than these had ever been laid before a New York assembly, but they passed without notice and the province was again plunged into the agonies of partisan conflict.

Nicoll and Governeur were candidates for the speakership and the latter of course won. An attack was then made on Nicoll and Dirck Wessells in the form of a motion that they were not qualified to sit under the election law which had been passed in 1699,[1] because they were not residents of the counties from which they were returned. Nicoll sought to parry this blow by reviving the old charge that the speaker was by birth an alien and therefore not qualified to occupy the chair and until further satisfaction was given on that point they could not act with him. The house had resolved that it would proceed to no other business until the right of Nicoll and Wessells to their seats was settled, and Governeur refused to answer the charge against him until this resolution had been obeyed.[2] Thereupon Nicoll, Wessells and eight other members withdrew. Among these were four who had signed the protest against the former assembly for which Howell had been expelled. The charge against Nicoll and Wessells was then proven to be true, and also the complaint that the latter had bribed the sheriff who returned him. Their seats were declared vacant and the members who sided with them, continuing to absent themselves, they were expelled and the issue of new writs to fill their seats was ordered. During the interval the house continued with only eleven members, but the new elections raised its number to sixteen.

The next move of the faction was to attack Robert Livingston who, in addition to having been an opponent of Leisler,

[1] Col. Laws I, 405; Journal of Leg. Coun. I, 169; N. Y. Col. Docs. IV, 950. Nicoll had been returned for Suffolk but was a resident of Queens. Wessels had been returned for Albany, but was a resident of Dutchess.

[2] Ass. J. I, 115 *et seq.*

had recently given offence by his support of Smith. From the consideration of the accounts of Van Cortlandt, concerning which there had been some trouble since the last days of Bellomont, the commissioners passed to Livingston, whose accounts were large and of long standing.[1] They said he had declined to report except for the excise of Albany and that he kept no books of his dealings with the government, though he had received over £20,000. A joint committee then reported that, unless he would forthwith account, an act ought to pass confiscating his estate. An order in accordance with this was issued by the house; Livingston appeared and complained of the hardship to which they were subjecting him, but they would allow him no more time. Early in September a bill was introduced into the house to confiscate enough of Livingston's property to meet his indebtedness to the province, which, on account of the excise at Albany alone, was estimated to amount to over £17,000. Other bills extending back to Dongan's time and amounting to £690 had not been settled. His estate was to be sequestered until he should account. The friends of Livingston now attempted to save him by procuring from the Indians an expression of desire that he might be sent to England as their agent. To this the house would not assent and, on the theory that the Indians had probably been imposed upon, it asked Nanfan to suspend him from his secretaryship of Indian affairs and procure his removal by the king.

While the bill against Livingston was under consideration, three of the members from Queens county presented a paper in which the legality of the assembly was questioned because its speaker had not yet cleared himself from the charge of being an alien.[2] The expulsion of Nicoll and his friends and the seating of two others who were said not to have been elected by the people were unfavorably commented on and the charge was made that a bill was in preparation for disfranchising many of the English in the province. The paper closed with the declaration that until the speaker cleared himself from the charge they could not sit with the assembly.

[1] *Ibid.*, 119 *et seq.*; C. J. I, 120 *et seq.*

[2] Ass. J. I, 128; C. J. I, 168. They were Thomas Willett, John Talmon and William Willett.

The signers were at once called to account and were summoned from their homes for the purpose. They refused to attend, whereupon they were expelled and an order was issued for their prosecution, though it appears never to have been executed.

While these attacks on the anti-Leislerians were in progress a petition from Jacob Leisler to the crown for the restoration to his family of £2700, which was alleged to be part of the sum that the elder Leisler had expended for the defence of the province, was laid before the assembly.[1] It was considered in committee of the whole and a resolution was reached that the entire sum should be paid, but measures to that end were not perfected this session. It can well be imagined that when the assembly adjourned the feeling between the two factions had become very bitter. It was reflected in the regular fall election of the City of New York, where a scrutiny had to be taken in three of the wards and a long dispute occurred between the two factions over the swearing in of aldermen and assistants.[2] This was brought out before the supreme court.

The appointment of a governor was expected and it was already reported that Lord Cornbury would be the man. In December, 1701, in order to secure aid and protection against the assembly and its arbitrary acts, three numerously signed addresses were prepared by anti-Leislerians, one to the king, another to parliament, a third of congratulation to Lord Cornbury.[3] Nicholas Bayard and his son were leaders in the drafting of these and in procuring the signatures. The signers came from all classes of the people and from all nationalities and the petitions were circulated in most of the counties. Naturally, however, the majority of the signatures came from New York City and its neighborhood and it was charged, with probable truth, that many soldiers and others signed under influence and without knowing the contents of

[1] Ass. J. I, 133 *et seq.*

[2] Min. of Com. Coun. II, 151, 159 *et seq.*, 179, 181; Atwood's defence, as above, 258 *et seq.*

[3] N. Y. Col. Docs. IV, 933 *et seq.*; Min. of Common Council, 1674–1776, II, 150–198. Thomas Noell was the new mayor who held to his position and claims as obstinately against the assaults of Isaac de Riemer, the Leislerian, and his supporters. Smith, I, 142; Ex. C. Min., p. 264, *et seq.*

the papers. Many signatures were affixed in the tavern kept by Alderman John Hutchins, in New York City, and he was charged by the Leislerians with resorting to various illegal measures in procuring these. In the petitions the whole course of the Leislerian faction was arraigned in the strongest terms. They were charged with designs and practices, with disregard for the interests of the crown, with oppression of their opponents and the promotion of the scum of the people to office. The policy of Bellomont came in for sweeping condemnation and the present assembly was charged with using unwarrantable means to secure the support of Nanfan and Atwood for their illegal measures. The appeal to Cornbury over the head of Nanfan might conveniently be interpreted as a treasonable disregard of the existing government.

It was quite impossible to keep the substance of these petitions from becoming known to the Leislerians, and the council demanded that copies of them should be submitted to it. This demand was refused, and Attorney General Broughton gave it as his opinion that there was nothing criminal or illegal in the petitions themselves, or in the steps taken to procure signatures. But in the midst of the unscrupulous party warfare which was then being carried on, the chance to crush their opponents by prosecutions for treason, as the leaders of the Leislerian party had been crushed in 1691, was too good to be lost. Some boasts uttered, it is said by the rector of Trinity Church, among others, increased the temptation. The act which the anti-Leislerians had passed in 1691 [1] for quieting disorders in the province could be used for the purpose. Bayard had been a leader in the passage of that measure and now he was to be its conspicuous victim. Three justices were on the bench who could be trusted to serve the interests of the faction to the full extent that was possible. Broughton, for giving the above opinion, was pushed one side, and a new office of solicitor general was created to which Weaver was appointed. The other departments of the government were also controlled by Leislerians.

Hutchins was first committed to prison without bail by the council on the charge of treason, because he would not produce copies of the petitions.[2] As a matter of fact, they were

[1] Col. Laws, I, 223. [2] N. Y. Col. Docs. IV, 947, 950.

not then in his possession and he could not produce them. Bayard and his son were bound over under heavy bonds to appear at the April term of the supreme court. Later, on the strength of a statement in a petition of French, Wenham and Rip Van Dam — associates of Bayard — that the petitions were in their custody, Bayard was committed for high treason, and the three petitioners were given six days in which to produce the papers. Later they were threatened with prosecution, but news that Lord Cornbury, the new governor, was about to sail from England put a stop to this, and Bayard and Hutchins were the only ones to feel the full weight of Leislerian vengeance.[1]

The political conflict was now transferred to the court room, Weaver and Nicoll, two of the leading contestants, appearing as counsel. Nicoll had the assistance of James Emott, whose knowledge of the law apparently far exceeded his own,[2] but Weaver had much more effective support from the bench, where Atwood steadily decided every point in favor of the prosecution and his associates feebly echoed his opinions. Though the forms of courteous speech were usually observed the partisanship of Chief Justice Jeffreys was never more pronounced than was that of Atwood in these trials. The somewhat technical objection by the defence, that the indictment was found by eleven and not twelve jurors, was overruled by the court. So also was the argument of fundamental importance, that the New York act under which the charge was brought defined as treason something which was not such by English law. But the justice made a telling point when he argued that the act in question had been confirmed by the king and therefore must stand as law in New

[1] The record of the trial, though imperfect and prepared by Bayard or his supporters, is in Howell's State Trials, XIV. It is known that Bayard took some notes during the trial and they were probably expanded into this version, which was published. An account of the trial written from the opposite standpoint was published in New York soon after the arrival of Cornbury. Atwood says Bayard and Jameson put it out. See an answer to some of its statements in Atwood's Defence, as above, p. 298 *et seq.* Atwood's account is in his defence, already referred to. Cornbury's characterization of it is in N. Y. Docs. IV, 974. An account by Bayard is in *ibid.*, 952 *et seq.* See also Smith, I, 143.

[2] Emott had been connected with the arrest of Kidd. See documents relating to that affair printed in Journal of H. of Commons XIII. References to him in connection with Fletcher's time are in the Colonial Calendar.

York. It was contended by Bayard's counsel that the drawing and signing of the addresses were only the exercise of the right of petition guaranteed in the bill of rights, and that the accused had not been guilty of unreasonable or offensive activity in connection with these. But in his charge to the jury Atwood insisted that the addresses were libels on the government, a disowning of its authority, and were intended to cause its overthrow. The inducing of soldiers in particular to sign them was sedition and an encouragement to mutiny, and in connection with it all Bayard had been previously active. But to a modern mind a fatal defect in the case for the prosecution appears in the fact that the addresses in question were never produced in court or seen by either petty or grand jury.[1] When a jury which the defence alleged had been packed with their opponents, with men whose acquaintance with English was very slight and some of them not even naturalized, had returned a verdict of guilty, all arguments which could be urged in support of a claim for arrest of judgment were set aside and sentence of death, also involving attainder, was pronounced. The trial of Hutchins followed with a similar foregone conclusion. In the trial of one Baker for making alleged scandalous statements about the king, the jury was said to have been forced by threats from the bench to bring in a verdict of guilty.

The anti-Leislerians now seemed humbled and were facing a tragedy comparable with that which ended in the execution of Leisler and Milbourne. The accused appealed to the lieutenant governor for a reprieve until the pleasure of the king could be known. But this was refused,[2] in the case of Bayard, unless he would acknowledge himself guilty of the crime. This for a time he declined to do, but finally signed a statement that he was sorrowful for the offence which by the sentence he found he had committed and begged pardon for it. The reprieve was then granted, though it was interpreted by the Leislerians as an acknowledgment by Bayard that he was guilty of high treason. Hutchins, under the influence of fear, is said to have secured his reprieve by a much more direct confession.[3]

[1] N. Y. Docs. IV, 974.

[2] N. Y. Docs. IV, 953.

[3] Case of Atwood, as above, p. 280.

The Leislerian legislature, which met again in April, 1702, about a month after the close of the trials, passed some measures which were of importance in confirming the position of the party. It outlawed Wenham and French, two prominent opponents, and provided for the payment of a part of the sum of £2700 demanded by the younger Leisler as compensation for what his father was alleged to have spent for the defence of the province. Special commissioners were designated in this act and very stringent provisions were included for its execution. In the law for the continuance of the revenue for two years longer provision was made that the salary of Justice Atwood should be continued and for a special payment in case he should be removed before the end of two years, and both in "consideration of his great services for the good of the province." Another act, also of a decidedly political character, was the one augmenting the number of representatives in the assembly by five from New York City and county and from the region about Albany, those sections where the Leislerian feeling was supposed to be strongest.[1] By still another act, regulating the election of magistrates in the City of New York, the purpose of which was to undo, so far as possible, the counting in of anti-Leislerian officials the previous autumn and to render such proceeding by that party impossible in the future.

While the above acts were being passed Lord Cornbury had arrived in the lower bay, and was attended there by Wenham,[2] French, Vesey and Jameson, who shortly before had retired for safety into New Jersey. Daniel Honan, of unsavory reputation as private secretary of Fletcher, returned with

[1] Col. Laws, I, 476, 478, 479, 487, 490; Ass. J. I, 141, N. Y. Docs. IV, 958.

[2] N. Y. Col. Docs. IV, 955, 1034, 1090. For Cornbury's views of the condition of the province as he found it, see *Ibid.*, 971 *et seq.* For a view unfavorable to Cornbury and containing many vivid touches and useful details, see Atwood's "Case" etc., as above, p. 285 *et seq.* The board of trade remonstrated with Cornbury for taking Honan as secretary and he told the board that he had dismissed him. N. Y. Col. Docs. IV, 925, 927. For other references to Cornbury's arrival and efforts to arrest Weaver, see the Winthrop Papers, 6, Mass. Hist. Colls. III, 91 *et seq.* The opinion which the board of trade had of Honan appears in its letter to Cornbury under date of Jan. 26, 1702/3. Cal. St. P. Col. Honan acted for a brief time as secretary of the province, but he was superseded on the arrival in August, 1703, of George Clarke from England, with a commission as secretary as well as deputy auditor. Ex. C. Min. Aug. 5, 1703.

Cornbury. John Bridges and Peter Fauconier accompanied the new governor. Bridges, an insignificant man, was soon to succeed to the office of chief justice. Fauconier, whom Cornbury called an " expert accountant " and who in England had been a contractor for army clothing, and is said to have been a bankrupt, was appointed naval officer and also one of the commissioners for executing the office of collector, a board which Cornbury established after the suspension of Weaver. He was to be closely concerned with the shady transactions of the administration which was now beginning.

If ever an appointment was due to favoritism in England, it was that of Lord Cornbury. While not without ability, he was the needy scion of a noble house, whose spendthrift habits had left his fortune sadly in need of improvement. He was the nephew of the queen, the heir of the great title of Clarendon and, in due time was to receive it, but not until he had been in a debtor's prison in New York and had done probably more than any other royal governor to bring British administration in America into disrepute. Years before he had recommended himself to William by early espousing his cause, and for this, in the summer of 1701, he had received his appointment to New York with command over the militia of New Jersey and Connecticut.[1] Being a man of military experience, during the long interval between his appointment and his departure for America Cornbury devoted some attention to securing money and supplies for the royal troops in New York. He repeatedly appeared with their agent, Mr. Champante, on errands of this sort before the board of trade, and we know that he had dealings with the other boards as well. He had also been a member of the house of commons. He and Joseph Dudley set sail for their governments about the same time, and we can be sure that by that time Lord Cornbury was reasonably well informed as to the condition of his province.

Cornbury in his instructions was warned to avoid partisan alliances and to use his influence for calming the passions which had been aroused. But what he really did was to assume the leadership of the anti-Leislerians and drive their

[1] See references in Cal. St. P. Col., 1701, and corresponding entries in N. Y. Col. Docs. IV, 912 *et seq.*

opponents from power and office. Weaver, Atwood and their associates had gone to such extremes in partisanship that some reprisals could hardly be avoided. But a mere repetition of the unfortunate tactics of Bellomont did not imply statesmanship, especially if it was not accompanied with efforts toward reform. From Honan and others Cornbury must have learned of the methods of plunder which had been used under Fletcher and of their success. It is possible that he had sought an appointment in New York because he realized that they could best be applied in that province. In Massachusetts they certainly could not have been used to any great extent. Virginia, too, would not have offered a favorable field. The other provinces were too small or were out of his reach. In faction-ridden New York, with its group of merchants and officials who were not above dealings with pirates, and its speculators in wild lands, profitable investments could always be found. With the aid of the same unscrupulous faction which had supported Fletcher, the policy of that worthy could be imitated and extended to robberies of indefinite amount from the public revenue itself. This constituted the chief feature of the Cornbury régime in New York. But before its results are described, an account must be given of the downfall of the Leislerians.

On June 9, 1702, before the executive council, charges were preferred against the five Leislerian councillors.[1] Those against Atwood were based on the extreme partiality with which he had conducted the case against Bayard and Hutchins; those against Weaver proceeded from the alleged irregularity in his accounts. These charges were drawn by Wenham, Nicoll, Jameson and other anti-Leislerian leaders. Cornbury in his letters declared that the accused had planned the removal of the English from all positions of influence in New York and their replacement by the Dutch, whom he called the "black party." This is a much too simple explanation of the Leislerian movement and is not in accordance with the facts. Much nearer the truth was the statement, made by Bayard and others, that its object was to

[1] For Cornbury's opinions on these, see N. Y. Docs. IV, 971, 974, 1010, 1012. Atwood's side of the case is in *ibid.*, 1022, and in his "Case," 285 *et seq.*, 294; Ex. C. Min. June 9, 1702, and later dates.

drive the leading families, both Dutch and English, from power and install the opposing faction, which perhaps stood a little nearer the common people, in their places. Personal jealousy, mere lust for the spoils of office and purely factional zeal were too much combined in the spirit of the Leislerians to admit of their movement being defined as clearly democratic. There was not enough common consciousness then existing among the people of New York to make a democratic movement possible.

The presentation of the charges was soon followed by the suspension of the accused from office and the flight of Weaver and Atwood to New Jersey and thence to Virginia, from which colony they sailed for England. There they were removed from office by order of council [1] and the sentences against Bayard and Hutchins were reversed. The assembly which Cornbury found in existence was dissolved and the acts that had been rushed through during its last session were disallowed.[2] Colonel Smith was restored for a brief time to the chief justiceship, to be soon replaced by Bridges. Prolonged inquiries were made into the accounts of the province while Weaver was collector and receiver general, and they were declared to be in great confusion. He was charged with partiality in his payments to creditors of the province. He had apparently not kept regular accounts of receipts and payments. It was said that for more than a year he had not sent his acounts to England. If half of the charges made against Weaver were true, they show that, like so many of his contemporaries in England and so many who have succeeded him in this country, he was too much absorbed in politics to make an honest official.[3] Atwood, too, was a good example of the political judge.

Apart from the downfall of Atwood and Weaver, the reprisals which accompanied the reaction under Cornbury were

[1] Jan. 21, 1702/3. Acts of Privy C. Col. II, 242 *et seq.*, 820–1.

[2] N. Y. Docs. IV, 961, 999, 1023–4, 1066; Cal. St. P. Col., 1702–3, p. 97, Acts of P. C. Col. II, 414, 849.

[3] On the other hand, there is preserved in one of the Libers of the Surrogate's Office of New York County a detailed and beautifully written statement of the trade of this port, inwards and outwards, for about two years while Weaver was collector. This is a good business document and is valuable, as it is about the only original statement of that kind which has survived.

not many. Bayard and Hutchins began ineffective suits against the associate justices and members of the grand jury who had been concerned in their prosecution, but later they were dropped.[1] In June, 1703, the New York legislature passed an act declaring illegal the proceedings against Bayard and Hutchins and reversing all judgments against them. This was duly approved by the crown.[2] Nanfan, however, who had been an instrument of the chief intriguers rather than a leader, was pursued by Cornbury and his satellites until he was nearly or quite ruined.[3] In the first charge, which had to do with payment for supplies for the four independent companies in excess of what had been sent for the purpose from England, Champante, the agent, was to an extent involved. The second charge was brought by two private parties and was for false imprisonment, which was prolonged for many months, the case as a whole taking the form of malicious persecution. Nanfan repeatedly applied to the board of trade for relief and it warned Cornbury that, if the allegations were true, the ex-lieutenant governor was suffering great hardships. It is evident that Fauconier had a hand in this business. In August, 1704, Champante wrote to the board of trade[4] that Nanfan had been seventeen months in jail for his alleged failure to pay in England certain bills which had been drawn for the subsistence of the troops. But it had been fully shown to the board and admitted by Cornbury's agents that Nanfan had subsisted the troops for four and one-half months longer than the time for which their subsistence had been issued. The board of trade had repeatedly directed Cornbury to state Nanfan's accounts at once, but the governor had delayed or opposed this on the pretence

[1] N. Y. Docs. IV, 1032. Atwood, "Case," 296.

[2] Col. Laws, I, 531. N. Y. Col. Docs. IV, 1123. Acts of P. C. Col., II, 850.

[3] N. Y. Col. Docs. IV, 929, 1018, 1027, 1033, 1073, 1080, 1100, 1114.

[4] C. O. 5/1048, 90, Aug. 28, 1704. There is a mass of papers in this volume which purport to be Nanfan's accounts and they may be the "intricately contrived" statement which Fauconier sent over. The case of Nanfan can be followed through the letters which he sent to the board of trade and the statements of Champante. Cal. St. Papers, Col., 1702–1703, pp. 50, 75, 95, 178, 196, 197, 201, 226, 254, 262, 270, 281, 314–315, 455, 581, 595, 609, 674, 720. The complaint of false imprisonment brought against him by Graves and Prideaux raised an interesting side issue suggesting the possibility, had the charge been valid, of Nanfan's being prosecuted in England under the act for the punishment of governors.

that a large balance would appear as due from Nanfan. At last, writes Champante, Fauconier had "framed an imaginary account, which he has so intricately contrived that it is beyond the understanding of Nanfan or of his friends, and Cornbury has sent this over as a stated account against Nanfan. Besides several other errors in it, he is charged with sums he never received and with off-reckonings he never had anything to do with. This is all Cornbury has done in the matter in about 2½ years." Sometime before this Lord Treasurer Godolphin had ordered £1500 set aside for the payment of the merchants to whom Cornbury claimed that Nanfan was indebted, when the latter's accounts were settled. As there was no prospect of their being settled in New York, Champante now urged that the merchants be paid the above sum and Nanfan released before his ruin was complete. It may well be that this was the way in which the affair was settled.

Lady Bellomont also, who was Nanfan's sister, found it impossible to get the accounts of her late husband settled in New York, and the matter dragged on many months to her great loss, until she returned to England in the hope of obtaining some relief there. Questions growing out of subsistence for the troops were also involved in this case. In 1704 Cornbury wrote to Godolphin at great length on these accounts, stating that referees had been appointed by himself and Lady Bellomont, Fauconier appearing among those selected by the governor. They claimed that no payments by the late governor should be allowed for which vouchers could not be produced and made out that his estate owed the crown more than £24,000.[1] This, of course, her ladyship's referees, who were two New York merchants, would not accept, and so it devolved on the treasury in England to straighten out this tangle which had been caused by careless bookkeeping and partisan colonial politics.

The election of 1702 resulted in a triumph for the anti-Leislerians. Governeur was dropped and Nicoll, with others, who had been so roughly treated by the last assembly, were returned. The majority, after sundry reflections on the loose and partisan government which had preceded, addressed it-

[1] Cal. of Treasury Papers.

self more and more to the financial questions which were the outgrowth of the war and of the dishonest manipulation of expenditures by the provincial executive. Though New York for several years was not directly involved in the second colonial war, yet questions of defence and supply, due to alarms and the necessity of maintaining and strengthening garrisons on the frontier, were prominent subjects of discussion. At the request of Cornbury a new militia act was passed and also a law to prevent the eluding of detachments or drafts by making it lawful for the officers of any company to seize such offenders and have them tried by justices of the peace instead of waiting for trial before the courts of common pleas, which occasioned great delays. By another act [1] it was provided that more stringent measures be taken to collect the arrears of the tax which had been imposed in Bellomont's time toward building the fort at Onondaga. Three special appropriation acts were passed,[2] carrying specific sums — £1800, £1500 and £1300 — to be used respectively for paying 150 fusileers and scouts on the frontier, for the construction of two batteries at the Narrows and for the employment of 100 additional men for the defence of the frontier. The collectors and receiver general were required to keep a particular account of receipts and payments. By two other acts also provision had been made for a committee, whose members were named in the laws, to examine and state accounts.[3] In order to raise the money for the fortification of the Narrows a graduated poll tax was resorted to, bearing rather heavily on councillors, attorneys, well-to-do bachelors and wearers of wigs. After consideration in committee of a report of the commissioners of accounts on the state of the finances, an address was presented to the governor.[4] In this not only was the old complaint about the reduction of the strength of the province by the lopping off of New Jersey and western Connecticut repeated, but the Bellomont régime, was condemned by the statement that a large part of the £2200 which had been granted since the peace of Ryswick

[1] Col. Laws of N. Y. I, 500, 546, 557, 571.
[2] *Ibid.*, 493, 550, 562; Ass. J. I, 164, 165; N. Y. Docs. IV, 1064.
[3] *Ibid.*, 518, 548.
[4] Ass. J. I, 166.

had been profusely used and misapplied, contrary both to the objects for which it was given and to the commission and instructions of the late governor. The fact that duties and fees were fixed without limit by the executive and the union in the same hands — meaning those of Atwood — of the offices of chief justice and judge of admiralty, in the opinion of the legislature were destroying the trade of New York. "It cannot but be obvious," they continued, "what encouragement it is for a man that has something he may call his own to expose it by coming to trade where he has no other assurance of his property but the self denial of a judge awarding against his own profit and interest." The address probably voiced the protest of the merchants against the favor shown by Bellomont and the Leislerians toward import duties as a means of raising revenues as truly as it did a disbelief in the honesty of the New York judiciary.

But a question of more immediate importance was raised by the commissioners of accounts. The assembly addressed the council,[1] enlarging on the misapplication of the revenue and other moneys heretofore granted by the people, as shown by the report of the commissioners, and asked that some proper person be appointed treasurer to receive and pay out the revenue about to be appropriated "as a means to obstruct the like misapplication for the future." They informed the governor how unnecessary and burdensome were the fees, particularly those at the custom house, and how greatly they obstructed trade. They had hoped for relief by law, but had been informed that the governor was prevented from granting it by his instructions. Therefore they asked that he would lay these complaints before the queen, that a treasurer might be appointed who would give good security for the due execution of his office and that instructions might be issued which would relieve them from undue fees and exactions. In his letter home Cornbury briefly commented on the laws which had been passed during the session,[2] but made no reference to

[1] Ass. J. I, 170. It should be borne in mind, as we enter on this period of financial controversy, that by royal instructions to all the governors all moneys had to be granted to the monarch, they had to be accounted for at the office of the auditor general of the plantations, and no money should be issued except by warrant under the governor's hand and with the consent of the council.

[2] N. Y. Col. Docs. IV, 1064.

the subject of the address. The reader can understand why this was so when he learns that, on his first journey to Albany for a conference with the Indians, the governor had spent nearly £2200, a sum far beyond what other conferences had cost. Also no stint was put upon the expenditures for firewood and candles for the fort at New York.[1]

In the brief fall session of 1703[2] a general order was received from the queen, which had its origin more from conditions in Massachusetts than from those which existed in New York, forbidding governors henceforth to receive gifts from their assemblies, meaning by that annual salaries or grants for short terms. The salary of the governor of New York was increased from £600 to £1200, which, in accordance with his instructions, was to be a stated burden upon the royal revenue of the province. It restricted by so much the control over expenditures which the assembly had now begun to desire should be made complete.

In his opening speech before the spring session of 1704 the governor stated that the revenue of New York was small and suggested the revival of an act of 1699 for raising an additional duty.[3] Such measures had occasionally been resorted to in the past as a means of checking the too rapid growth of the provincial debt. In its reply the assembly asked to be informed if the reduction of the revenue — which ordinarily was about £4000 per annum — was to be attributed to a decline in the amount collected or to an increase of expenditures, so that proper remedies might be applied.[4] Under a promise from the governor, Kiliaen Van Rensselaer was at once ordered by the council to carry to the lower house a list of the salaries of the officers of the province, with a statement of the revenue as it was at the close of the previous July.[5] Later the salary list for 1694 was also submitted.[6] The house went into committee of the whole on the revenue. The collectors of Kings county were ordered to attend and

[1] N. Y. Col. Docs. V, 111, 407.

[2] Ass. J. I, 173 *et seq.*; C. J. I, 205 *et seq.*; N. Y. Docs. IV, 1040.

[3] Ass. J. I, 175 *et seq.*; C. J. I, 209; Col. Laws I, 403; Spencer, Phases of New York Government, 111.

[4] Ass. J. I, 176.

[5] C, J. I, 209.

[6] Ass. J. I, 177.

answer a complaint of certain inhabitants arising in connection with the payment of arrears due under the act for the levy of £1000 toward the building of the fort at Onondaga. They appeared and were examined. Mr. Fauconier presented an account of the £1800 which had been appropriated in 1702,[1] for the support of fusileers. During several sessions the house sat in committee of the whole, considering salaries, revenue and the condition of the frontiers. This discussion was carried on in close connection with that on the repeal of the last section of the act of 1691 for quieting disorders, on which had been based the reprisals of previous years.[2]

The committee of accounts reported to the house that, owing to defective collection but chiefly to expenditures which were in violation of the directions expressed in the acts for the levy of £1800 and £1300, the sum of £913 15s. was due to the colony. In the bill which was then introduced for a further appropriation toward the defence of the frontiers provision was made that the amount actually to be raised should be diminished by £913 15s., the "balance due the colony." The council proposed an amendment to this, but the house refused to admit its right to amend a money bill. The council stood firm and the bill, as thus drawn, failed to become law.

On examining Fauconier's accounts the house found in them evidence of overcharges and misapplications of revenue, by Colonel Abraham Schuyler and others, amounting to more than £485.[3] This led them, in formulating the bill for the ensuing grant, to specify not only the number of men who were to be raised, but the number of their officers and where they

[1] Col. Laws, I, 493.

[2] Ass J. I, 176–179, 180–189. C. J. I, 208, 210, 212–218. A controversy also arose between the two houses over the wording of the enacting clause of this bill. The council thought that the words "advice and consent" should be used, but the house insisted that "advice" should be omitted, as not a proper description of the function performed in legislation. The house also insisted that it should be called the "general assembly." The council argued that this expression included governor, council and assembly, that the house was claiming too much and was violating common usage. Conferences were held over the question, and the governor charged the house with innovation, with encroachment on the prerogative, and with claiming the sole power to interpret the meaning of the crown. The house denied these charges. But it was wrong in the claim it made concerning its title, and that designation was not used in the statutes of the period.

[3] Ass. J. I, 183, 188; C. J. I, 218.

should be posted.[1] Men from Albany also were to be employed, if at all, only as scouts. This Cornbury denounced as an encroachment on his powers. He declared that the house had no right to meddle with the expenditure of money, that it was not implied in the power which the queen by instruction had granted the assembly to examine accounts. To this the assembly replied in moderate terms, but yet with a firm insistence on its responsibility for the liberty and property of the people, so often confirmed by English laws, to which they conceived every free Englishman to be entitled. "Whatsoever else may admit of controversy, the people of this colony think they have an undoubted . . . property in their goods and estates, of which they ought not to be divested but by their free consent, in such manner, to such ends and purposes, as they shall think fit, and not otherwise. If the contrary should be admitted, all notion of property would cease; every man is the most proper judge of his own capacity in giving, and the present extreme poverty of this country is both visible and too apparent." Behind these words, following the lines of English precedent, lay the demand of the assembly for responsible government, and in its absence the colonial assemblies generally found their excuse for assuming functions which in any well ordered government belong properly to the executive. This was now to be done in New York.

When the council tried to amend the new revenue bill, the assembly again sent up a resolve that it was inconvenient to admit of any amendment by the council to a money bill.[2] At the request of the council a general conference was held, but the house adhered to its position. At the same time, conferences were held over amendments to a bill from the council for the more effectual collection of quit rents. The result was that both bills failed and the session closed without provision for revenue or defence. But the New York assembly had shown that, during the decade of its existence, it had gained some experience and was now able to enter upon a contest with the executive for supremacy in the province.

The legislature met again in October. The governor stated that in July last he had called out 100 men and sent them to

[1] Ass J. I, 186–188; C. J. I, 215 *et seq.*; Smith I, 154–156.

[2] Ass. J. I, 190, *et seq.*; C. J. I, 218, *et seq.*

the frontier and he thought provision should be made for keeping them there till the close of the following March. He therefore recommended a revival of the additional duty — a bill of the same nature as the one which he had proposed in the previous session. A bill was sent up by the lower house. The council proposed amendments. To these the house objected. The deadlock was renewed, and after a session of about three weeks, of the debates during which the journals give very slight hints, the assembly was dissolved.[1]

Not until June, 1705, did the newly elected assembly meet. Although during these years New York was not involved in the war, yet she was frequently disturbed by alarms. These arose from rumors of French invasion both by land and sea, and necessitated continuous attention to the frontier and to the defence of New York City. A detachment had been sent to Albany in the fall of 1704. For these reasons Cornbury asked the new assembly — nearly all of whose members had been reelected — not only to provide for 100 fusileers and 50 scouts, but for the payment of the debt of the province as well. While the house was discussing provision for the troops asked for, the next forward step was taken, which proceeded naturally from what had already occurred. A motion was made and unanimously carried that the house should appoint a treasurer for receiving and paying out the public moneys to be raised. A bill for raising £1700 for the defence of the frontiers, and carrying with it the designation of Richard Willet as treasurer was then passed by the house. Together with several other bills, it was sent to the council.[2] There it was amended, but the amendments were rejected by the house. The governor then called the assembly before him and told them that he had received a letter from the board of trade, in which it said it saw no reason why the council should not amend money bills. He hoped this would end the controversy. But the house, led as Cornbury thought by French and Coddington of New York county and Garton of Ulster, remained obdurate, and the money bill failed.

In the adjourned September session the struggle was renewed, the bill which was sent up by the house being amended

[1] Ass. J. I, 192, *et seq.*; C. J. I, 221, *et seq.*

[2] N. Y. Docs. IV, 1154; Ass. J. I, 197, 199; C. J. I, 226, 227, 229.

in council so as to bring it into conformity with the royal instructions.[1] The assembly defended the provisions on which it had insisted, claiming that the right given to it to examine accounts was intended as a restriction on the governor, and that it was the real intent of the crown that the house should be thoroughly informed and satisfied that the money granted was applied to the uses for which it was appointed. But, it continued, hitherto it had been quite impossible for the assembly to examine the accounts of the receivers, because they had usually left the province under suspension, because of quarrels with the governors, and their accounts had been found in confusion. The assembly, therefore, had been left in the dark as to the disposition of moneys and the increase and decrease of the several branches of the revenue. Several hundred pounds, voted for the defence of Albany, had not been applied to that use. Sums reported to have been paid were yet unpaid, and parties had received payments for services never rendered. After a further conference and still another attempt of the council to amend the bill,[2] the assembly was prorogued and did not meet again until May, 1706. At the beginning of that session Lord Cornbury presented to them the need of fortifying New York City, of reviving the militia act which had expired in 1704 and of providing revenue for the frontier. In committee of the whole during some twelve sessions the house considered ways and means for fortifying New York City. It conferred with managers of fortifications and got an estimate that the work would cost £4000. It inquired as to the population of the city. It examined reports from Wenham, Fauconier and Byerly as to the expenditure of earlier grants. It finally resolved to raise £3000, one-half of which should be paid by the city and county of New York. At the same time bills for the militia and the frontier were considered and passed. Near the close of these debates nine inhabitants of Albany were taken into custody on the charge of circulating a paper in which false reproaches were made against the justice and integrity of the house.[3] The committee of the

[1] N. Y. Docs. IV, 1165, 1169; Ass. J. I, 205, 206.
[2] Ass. J. I., 207, 208; C. J. I, 236.
[3] Ass. J. I, 211.

council to which were referred the two revenue bills, and of which Justice Mompesson was chairman,[1] favored passing them without amendment; but the bills were held up by the governor until the next session, when he expected further instructions from home.

At the opening of the next session, which began near the close of September, 1706, Cornbury was able to inform the house that he had received authority to permit the assembly to designate a treasurer when it appropriated supplies which were not a part of the standing revenue, but a treasurer so nominated must be accountable to the governor, council and assembly.[2] Warrants might be issued by military officers or others, as the acts should direct, but the governor must always be informed of the need for such, and the persons acting must be accountable to the entire legislature. Though this important concession was made on the chief point contended for by the assembly, in reference to the right of the council to amend money bills the crown adhered to its opinion that they had that right. Before the session closed two important acts were passed which illustrated the principle of the reform just achieved. One carried an appropriation for fortifying New York City and also designated Abraham De Peyster as treasurer and a board of commissioners to see that the sum was properly expended.[3] The other provided under similar conditions for the expenditure of a sum for the defence of the northern frontier. These sums were to be used for the purposes expressed in the acts and no others, and the appropriation for the frontier was made detailed and specific. De Peyster, the treasurer, was required to give security to Nicoll, the speaker of the house, for the proper expenditure of the money and must cooperate with the commissioners named in the act. This shows that the house was to an extent aware of the frauds of which Cornbury and his clique were guilty, though the evidence which we now possess of them did not appear until after Robert Hunter became governor.

Under Cornbury the efficacy of the British system of con-

[1] C. J. I, 239 *et seq.*
[2] N. Y. Docs. IV, 1172; Ass. J. I, 213; C. J. I, 241 *et seq.*
[3] Col. Laws, I, 593, 598.

trol over expenditures in the provinces was put to its severest test. The royal instructions provided that claims should be paid exclusively by warrants issued by the governors on advice of their councils. The administrative check upon dishonesty and extravagance under this system must come from the deputy auditor or possibly from the collector and receiver general. These were appointees of the treasury in England, the former being the representative of the auditor general. Over the appointment of the latter the governor might and usually did have an influence, and in the province he was also *ex officio* a member of the council. In cases where the council was subservient to the governor, he would be under strong temptation to yield to the general current. The men who came to New York during the first year of Cornbury's administration as the incumbents of these offices were George Clarke and Thomas Byerly. Clarke [1] was a nephew of William Blathwayt, his superior in office, and was now to begin a long official career in New York. At this time he held the two offices of secretary and deputy auditor. Of Byerly before his arrival in New York we know nothing. In so far as they might come to an issue with the governor and his confidants, they must present their complaints before the treasury in England, a distant centre, and await its action.[2] The letters of Blathwayt to Clarke, as well as his correspondence with officials in other provinces show that the duties of the auditor general were at this time being faithfully performed.[3] He received detailed reports regularly from both Clarke and Byerly, but observed that Byerly should have made oath as to the truth of his accounts before the governor and council or the chief justice. The

[1] Clarke's jurisdiction as deputy auditor extended also over New Jersey. In New Jersey Fauconier was receiver general.

[2] The spirit in which Byerly went to work is indicated by a letter of his to the lord high treasurer, Nov. 30, 1703. He said that he had begun to frame a rent roll and found that, of the few whom he had registered, most had paid no rents since the patents were granted. Some were 16 or 18 years in arrears. Grantees also were very backward in registering and he designed to give in a list of some in every county to be prosecuted for neglect. Theoretically this was admirable, but it would surely have caused trouble for Byerly if other issues had not diverted his attention. Cal. Treas. Papers.

[3] See Blathwayt's Journal, May 23, 1704, and later correspondence concerning New York's finances; especially Blathwayt's report to the lord treasurer, Jan. 31, 1704/5.

governor, it was expected, would already have made a return of Weaver's accounts in due form and was warned to do so without delay. Clarke was also directed to ask for the accounts for the four months between Weaver's departure and the arrival of Byerly. Ample security was also required from all receivers general, but the remoteness of the colonies from Westminster and official negligence and routine made the enforcement of a system of audit slow and ineffective at best.

During the first year of this administration the commissioners for executing the office of collector, with Fauconier at their head, transacted the fiscal business of the province under the direction of the governor. The council did not know what was going on or calmly acquiesced in what was submitted for its approval. The system of prerogative control over expenditure came into full swing. It was essentially the same system which had always existed in New York, and in the provinces generally, but in the hands of Cornbury what was dwelt upon for a generation or more as the "misapplication" of revenue was carried on more shamelessly than ever, till his name became a synonym for extravagance and dishonesty.

The first instance of this kind was the submission of bills to the amount of £2194 to meet the expenditures on the governor's first visit to Albany, in August, 1702, to confer with the Five Nations. This was clearly an exorbitant sum, far exceeding earlier charges for similar conferences. The charges for firewood and candles for the garrisons were also high. The council supinely consented to the cost of a journey of the governor to New Jersey being defrayed out of the revenue of New York. Under the orders of the governor and without even waiting for the issue of warrants, large sums were paid out by Fauconier, and when he came to make up his accounts extraordinary measures were required. To meet this situation and also to insure the payment of several warrants which had been drawn in favor of Fauconier himself, Cornbury obtained from the council, June 19, 1704,[1] direction for the issue of an order to the deputy auditor to allow all such warrants as the commissioners should present to him, "not-

[1] Ex. C. Min.; N. Y. Col. MSS., pp. 49, 127.

withstanding the said warrants have been issued by me in Council since the supersession of the Commissioners by Byerly and are directed to be paid by them." The petition of the commissioners at this time set forth "the disinterested reasons that made them advance these considerable sums for the credit of the government," and their urgent need of relief. Preferential warrants had been known in New York before, but now they were being used on a larger scale and with a system not before known. Under any conditions the practice was a poor one, and now it was evidently being carried on with dishonest intent.

Byerly was now in the province as collector and receiver general, and the council, under the lead of the governor, ordered him at his peril to make these warrants preferable in payment to all others, except those for the salaries of civil officers. Byerly informed both the council and the former commissioners that the revenue was not sufficient for the discharge of all these claims; if he paid salaries first and allowed the warrants of firewood contractors to be received for customs, he could not pay the demands of the commissioners, even though they had preferable warrants. He desired the council to inform him what order he should follow.

To complicate the situation still further, Cornbury in the summer of 1704 ordered a detachment from the militia sent to Albany after the assembly had failed to pass an act for this purpose.[1] The expenditures for this made the prospect of the payment of Fauconier's demand less probable and he became correspondingly more insistent. Cornbury had already written to the board of trade that he had many causes of complaint against Byerly and had understood that Byerly was making representations against him. The immediate result was the suspension of Byerly by the governor, in April, 1705, upon an alleged technical violation of an act of trade.[2] Fauconier was now made sole commissioner for executing the duties of the office thus made vacant, while he was also collector and receiver general of New Jersey. Warrants for a large part of the sums of which he stood in such dire need were at once issued to him. Blathwayt had already condemned

[1] Ex. C. Min., July 18, 1704.

[2] Cal. of Treas. Papers, June 13, 1705.

various of the early expenditures of Cornbury as excessive and had declared that they ought not to be allowed. Clarke had stated to Blathwayt that he was reduced to a position of impotence, for he could only allow or disallow warrants after they were paid,[1] and urged that some method be found by which accounts might be submitted to him before the issue of the governor's warrant and expenditures other than those approved by the auditor general's office prohibited. As things were, he was subjected to the frowns of the governor and must disobey that official or betray the trust reposed in him. The lord treasurer also wrote to Cornbury that, as Byerly was a revenue officer, he should not have been suspended until the treasury had first been informed of the cause thereof.[2]

Upon his suspension Byerly went to England, where he made up his accounts. The treasury was already considering the New York accounts for the years immediately before Byerly's arrival there, and Clarke was ordered to send an answer on each head, "such as may be satisfactory to the Treasurer, that the accounts may be stated and passed." He was told to be "particularly Satisfied of every Disbursement," and to send the necessary information in all extraordinary matters, that the Lord Treasurer might give directions intelligently wherever he saw cause for retrenching any expense. It was also made clear in the case of Robert Livingston that warrants would not be accepted in payment of customs. The relative position of the parties to an accounting was set forth in the direction, that each account should be stated and sworn to by the collector before the governor or chief justice, then examined, audited and signed by the deputy auditor, and finally viewed by the governor in council and signed by them.

Byerly was absent from New York for two years, when he was sent back with an order to the governor to restore him to his office. During the interval Cornbury, Fauconier and their friends in the council had managed affairs as they wished. During an absence of Clarke in Virginia the council had audited the accounts of Fauconier which were in dispute. In spite of objections from the auditor general, the council ordered Fauconier to continue paying a salary to the second

[1] N. Y. Col. MSS.
[2] Blathwayt's Journal, Jan. 15, 1705/6.

judge of the supreme court till positive commands to the contrary came from England. Sums were "borrowed" from the revenue on the credit of acts of assembly and were made payable to persons to whom preferential warrants were granted. Throughout this time there was no available check on the extravagance and favoritism which prevailed.

When Byerly returned with the approval of the home government and secured a proclamation from the council that he was fully restored, this system could no longer be worked.[1] A violent conflict at once began which lasted until 1708, when the question was taken up in both houses of the legislature. When the custom house was transferred to Byerly, Fauconier retained the book which contained the transactions of his own time, giving as his reason that his accounts were not settled. Byerly refused to receive any of the books without this one, and thereupon Fauconier locked them all up in the desk of the naval office. He also detained certain recognizances or bonds for the payment of excise from innkeepers in several counties. Though these were yet unpaid, Fauconier alleged that he had advanced the money on them out of his own pocket. He offered to deliver them to Byerly if the latter would secure to him the balance he alleged was due him from the queen. Byerly considered that Fauconier was repeating his former tactics of advancing money and charging the queen therefor in his accounts and depending on the council to get his accounts passed. Byerly therefore refused to have anything to do with these recognizances. He also refused to receive warrants for customs and countermanded arrangements for payments which had been made by Fauconier in the matter of the excise. This brought him into conflict with Peter Schuyler and Rip Van Dam. The governor and council of course were hostile, Cornbury finding him quite "unaccountable." On November 20, 1707, on an information that he intended to leave the province and carry with him what money he had of the revenue, he was arrested.

[1] On acknowledging that Byerly was restored to his office Cornbury wrote to the lord high treasurer that, in suspending him, he did not think he was encroaching on his lordship's authority. In the future he would follow the method prescribed, but he begged directions as to what he should do if the collector would not pay warrants issued to him by the governor and council. Cal. Treas. Papers.

On this and other occasions he was compelled to give security to the amount of over £4000.[1]

As the revenue was near expiring, all who had claims against the government were striving to secure payment, and prominent among these was Fauconier, who claimed to have nearly £2000 due him. Pressure was brought to bear by the governor on Byerly to present his accounts to the deputy auditor, but the collector protested that he could not do this until he was in possession of all the books and papers which had been detained by Fauconier. Cornbury seems also to have persuaded Quary to interfere in the affair by ordering Byerly to allow Fauconier the balance he claimed. This Byerly refused to do and maintained himself stoutly against his prosecutors. Such of Fauconier's accounts as were presented to the deputy auditor were objected to for many reasons, while a difficulty arose as to the fees which were charged in auditing. This led to a prolonged dispute concerning the amount of salary which was due to Blathwayt from New York, whether it was 5% on the sum audited or a flat sum the amount of which is variously stated at from £100 to £200 per annum.

Byerly also brought charges in England against Fauconier of so serious a nature as to cause the treasury to issue an order to the governor for his prosecution. This aroused Cornbury to inspect Byerly's accounts, with the result that he claimed to find evidence of frauds to the amount of £52! This was the heaviest stroke which he could deliver against the collector, while he wrote to the lord treasurer that "nothing should be wanting to see his Lordship's commands fully obeyed" in reference to Fauconier.[2] The collector must have been confirmed in his unyielding attitude by knowledge of the opposition which was gathering against Cornbury, not only in official circles but throughout the province. An

[1] N. Y. Docs. V, 28. Cornbury then wrote to the lord high treasurer that Byerly refused to pay anyone, that both the governor and the chief justice were unable to get their salaries. He would not produce his books or accounts as formerly. Cornbury to Lord High Treasurer, Nov. 24, Dec. 29, 1707; Byerly to B. T., Dec. 13, 1707. Cal. Treas. Papers. In C. O. 5/1048, Z9 and 10, are Cornbury's warrant for Byerly's arrest and the order removing his suspension. His suspension from the duties of his office continued from November to February, during which time Fauconier again officiated.

[2] Cal. Treas. Papers, July 4, 1708.

occasion for this was forcibly stated in the summer of 1707 by Robert Livingston in a letter which, for prudential reasons, he dispatched from Connecticut to Lowndes, the secretary of the treasury.[1] He described the absurd and unaccountable conduct of the governor, as well as his wasteful expenditure of the revenue, telling how he was wholly addicted to pleasure, enriching himself by strange and unheard of methods, keeping some few creatures about him whose counsel he followed to the grief of the principal inhabitants. They wished he was not so closely related to the queen. One result which Livingston foretold was that, when the revenue expired the following May, the assembly would not revive it. In the following October Champante wrote that the ministry was well apprised of Cornbury's maladministration in New York, and that "the push we lately made here hath given a shock to his lordship's interest." He was of opinion that, if the gentlemen of New York would make regular and public complaint, they would rid themselves of Cornbury. The chief difficulty felt by persons in power in England was, that "they knew not what to do with Her Majesty's cousin when they had him here."[2]

On August, 1708, this controversy was brought before both houses of the legislature. The council was the first to act,[3] apparently on the initiation of Cornbury and his friends, for the purpose of bringing Byerly to account. Some fifteen questions were put to the council and the answers of each councillor and of the governor were entered in the minutes. These related chiefly to the conduct of Fauconier, Byerly and Clarke, but also to granting Fauconier the power to receive what was due on the recognizances which he held, and to a possible successor to Byerly. Wenham, Schuyler, Beekman and Van Dam voted regularly with the governor, and on some of the questions Barbarie was with them. Mompesson and Phillips, and in some cases Barbarie, were on the other side. Wenham was the spokesman for the majority, the governor also frequently expressing his views, which in every

[1] Cal. of Treas. Papers, June 2, 1707. It was in this letter that the account was given of Cornbury's public appearances in women's clothes and of the extent to which he was running personally in debt.

[2] Rawlinson MSS.; Champante to Mompesson.

[3] Journal of Leg. C. I, 251 *et seq.*

case were more extreme than those of the councillors. The majority upheld the view that warrants issued by the governor, with the approval of the council, were binding in all cases and should be paid unless the crown ordered to the contrary. They therefore condemned Byerly's course, approved the conduct of Fauconier and all his claims, and advised that Byerly should be again suspended. On the question of Fauconier's claims, however, it required the casting vote of the governor to decide the case. The decision went that specific directions from the treasury in England to one of its representatives in the colonies must yield before general discretion reposed in the governor and his advisers. The minority insisted that these matters did not properly come before them, but must be referred to the crown; when, as in this case, there was conflict of jurisdiction, the crown must decide. No one advised that the receipt of revenue should be placed in the hands of Fauconier, but instead De Peyster, the province treasurer, who was responsible to the assembly, was preferred.

The attitude of the assembly toward these matters in some respects resembled that of the council, but yet differed from it in very characteristic fashion.[1] The conduct of Byerly respecting the payment of warrants on the ordinary revenue was brought before it by petitions from several inhabitants, especially those of Schuyler, Van Dam, Ebenezer Willson and Lancaster Symes.[2] Of course this also brought up the attitude of Fauconier toward these payments and the expenditures made by the executive from the revenue raised for extraordinary purposes. Prolonged hearings were held on the case of Byerly and by him and Clarke the statements bearing on the question, which had come from Blathwayt and the British government, were laid before the assembly. It finally agreed with the council in condemning Byerly's refusal to allow warrants for customs, but as to the rest of his conduct they did not find him guilty of any crime, though he had been guilty of many omissions and erroneous acts and by his

[1] Ass. J. I, 221, 225 *et seq.*, 229, 231–233, 236.

[2] Willson was Cornbury's appointee — in the year 1707 — to the office of mayor of New York, and Symes was a lieutenant of one of the independent companies.

partiality had defeated the efforts of the complainants to obtain the moneys which had been allowed them by the governor and council. That this resolution was intended to be an approval of Byerly's attitude in the main, while to satisfy the friends of Cornbury it condemned him in particulars, is shown by the action of the house on the subject of the "misapplication" of the extraordinary revenue.

On the credit of the £1800 act of 1702 Rip Van Dam and Colonel William Peartree advanced sums to the colony at 10% interest. In 1708 the committee of the house found that, including Peartree's loan, the commissioners of the revenue had received under this act £2182.19.7, and under the governor's orders had paid several persons £1471.9.7 for which they had no warrants. The difference between the two sums is £711.10.5, which is the sum ordered to be refunded by an act of 1708,[1] on the ground that it had been borrowed on the credit of the tax of 1702 and had been expended or "misapplied" and now stood as a debt on the revenue. A bill was also introduced to oblige all the collectors and receivers general and commissioners for executing that office to refund the money by them received and not applied to the uses for which the taxes were raised;[2] but this got no further than a second reading. At the instance of Willson and Symes, who desired to obtain payment of firewood warrants for the garrison and who alleged before the council that Byerly was wrongfully detaining over £1000 as his salary for the time before his arrival in the province and during his suspension, a bill was introduced into the assembly to compel him to refund all such sums, but it was not passed.[3] The same bill had passed the council on the casting vote of the governor.

But the house endorsed the dispatch in 1704, on the sole authority of the governor, of a detachment of militia to Albany when the assembly had failed to provide for the

[1] Col. Laws, I, 627.

[2] Ass. J. I, 237.

[3] *Ibid.*, 238. C. J. I, 271–273. In England, on this question, Blathwayt stood pat and in a report to the lord high treasurer implied that the salary should be divided between Byerly and Fauconier. But Northey held that the entire salary belonged to Byerly and that Fauconier's claim should be disallowed. A warrant agreeable to Northey's report was made out. Cal. of Treas. Papers, Jan. 28, 1709/10, March 22, 1710/11.

defence of the frontier. Hendrick Hansen had presented a bill for something over £250 for the subsistence of this detachment, and in the session of 1708 an act was passed for raising this amount by special tax and appropriating it for the payment of Hansen's bill.

The Byerly episode and the session of 1708 revealed in a clearer light than any earlier events the laxity of financial administration under Cornbury. It had much in common with the earlier administrations, but the governor, supported by a majority of interested parties in the council, carried the system to greater lengths than earlier executives. Imperial audit proved inadequate to check the confusion and extravagance which prevailed under the system of executive warrants and preferred payments. As suspicion and opposition arose, the assembly was looked to as offering the only prospect of relief. The reaction first expressed itself in the creation of the office of treasurer and the rejection of the claim — now again repeated — that the council had the right to amend money bills. But the jurisdiction of the treasurer, and through him of the assembly, was at first confined to extraordinary grants, while the ordinary revenue was left to the old methods of control, such as we have seen operating in Cornbury's time. The irregularities which followed were so great that they gave rise to the demand for control through the treasurer and assembly over all the revenue, ordinary as well as extraordinary. It was generally reported that £1500 raised for the batteries at the Narrows was spent by Cornbury in the erection of a pleasure house on Nutten island. Such a house was built, but the source from which came the moderate sum that seems to have been expended on it is not known. "Misapplication" became the cry,[1] and it was repeated in succeeding administrations till it became a tradition and as such an abiding element in the constitutional growth of New York. This strengthened antagonism toward the council and promoted a belief in the omnipotence of the assembly. The tradition of English liberties, of the right of private property and of the freeholders to a control through their representatives over the expenditure of revenue, fell in naturally with this tendency.

[1] Colls. of N. Y. Hist. Soc., Fund Series, 1868, p. 204; Clarendon MSS. 102, ff. 54, 88b; Ass. J. I, 208, 213.

These combined ideas were fully expressed in a report of the committee of grievances which was unanimously adopted as resolutions of the house, September 11, 1708.[1] They condemned the appointment of coroners rather than their election, the erection of a court of equity without consent in general assembly, the collection of extravagant and unlimited fees which were not established by law, the imposing and levying of money under any pretence or color without the consent of the assembly. The protest of a mercantile community against imposts and heavy port charges on trade as an important source of revenue was also voiced in these resolutions, as a source of impoverishment to the colony and sure to prove its destruction.[2]

But in order fully to appreciate policy and methods of government as they were under Cornbury, one must also know what occurred in New Jersey, a province inhabited mostly by dissenters of British stock, where proprietary interests were strong and where the governor and his supporters ventured upon acts which they did not dare to perform in New York. In New Jersey there were a large number of proprietors. In West Jersey they comprised the landholders as a body and these were organized under leaders. In East New Jersey they had become numerous, part residing in Great Britain and part in the province. For this reason they continued to exercise what was practically a controlling influence over, not only the land, but the politics of the province after it had passed under the direct authority of the crown. The contrast between this situation and that in Maryland, with its single proprietor and its royal government, is sufficiently striking. It furnishes the chief explanation of the fortunes of Cornbury and his successors there, for about proprietary interests centered the leading conflicts of the entire royal period.

The group relations in the politics of New Jersey were

[1] Ass. J. I, 223, 224.

[2] Fauconier seems to have remained many years in New York and to have turned his attention to land speculation. According to a memorial of Colden in 1721, Fauconier was then a sharer in extravagant grants to the extent of 400,000 acres or more. The Waywanda and other very large patents lying between the middle Hudson and the Delaware, were the scene of his speculations. C. O. 5/1053. Cc. 84.

very complicated.[1] This arose in part from the fact that it had consisted of two provinces which were now united, and in part from the variety of religious sects in the province. Many Scotch, as well as English, were also concerned, and in those days this involved much national and personal jealousy. The proprietors in both the original provinces were broken up into rival groups and so were the people, and the grouping was different on the two sides of the old dividing line. In East Jersey there were among the proprietors the Morris and Willocks group and the Dockwra and Sonmans group, the latter being small and its members residing mostly in Great Britain. The great body of the British proprietors stood behind Morris and his friends. On the other side of the line was the West Jersey Society with Basse and Coxe as its leaders, and the council of proprietors led by Jennings. Jennings was a leading Quaker, while Basse and Coxe — now identified with the Anglicans — were strongly opposed to that sect. The Morris party in East Jersey was made up chiefly of Presbyterians and Anglicans, but they cooperated politically with Jennings. Hence they were known among their opponents as "the Scotch and Quaker faction." The alignment on the other side was between Dockwra, Sonmans and their following and the Coxe and Basse faction in West Jersey. Basse, as we have seen, had been the leader of the anti-proprietary forces before the establishment of royal government, while Andrew Hamilton had been the proprietary governor and leader. Hence they were sometimes called the Basse and Hamilton parties, though as early as the administration of which we are now to speak Morris and Coxe became the actual leaders.

In character these two men were not unlike. The immediate Welsh ancestors of Morris had been Cromwellians in England and later had become wealthy West Indian planters. Morris himself fell heir to the manor of Morrisania in New York, and to large estates, containing iron mines, in Monmouth county, New Jersey.[2] This, together with his energy,

[1] This is most clearly set forth by Dr. Tanner in his Province of New Jersey, C. U. Studies, XXX, Chaps. 5, 7, 15, 19, 22. See also N. J. Arch. III, 275.

[2] See a memoir of him in Colls. of N. J. Hist. Soc., IV.

his wide acquaintance with business and his good practical knowledge of the law, explains his prominent connection with the politics of both the provinces where he had a residence. Coxe was the son of Dr. Daniel Coxe, who had been physician to the Princess Anne and who had purchased the rights of Edward Byllinge in New Jersey and sold his chief interests there to the West Jersey Society. The son, who had inherited his claims, had settled at Burlington and was a leader among the Anglicans and against the Quakers at that centre.

It was into this complex of groups and sects that Cornbury was introduced in 1703. He held all Quakers in contempt and considered that they were not fit to share in government, but he was bound by his instructions to admit them to office on their making the solemn declaration instead of taking the oaths. Toward dissenters in general he had no kindly feeling, though in New Jersey close cooperation with them was necessary, if anything was to be accomplished. On the other hand, Jerseymen naturally looked askance on any governor who came from New York, and were particularly restive if he did New Jersey business elsewhere than on its own soil. The governor, as the agent of imperialism, looked down on it as one of the "proprieties" and still partaking largely of that character, which it was his duty and privilege to train into regular ways and active loyalty. Also there was the personality of Cornbury himself, the lower depths of which were even more clearly revealed in New Jersey than in New York. In the effort to make headway among the factions of New Jersey an opportunity was presented for profit, as well as for oppression, which New York in some respects could not equal. In England the proprietary factions had contended over seats in the council, with the result that six of the twelve who were named in Cornbury's commission were prominent proprietors, and six were more or less out of sympathy with them. Among the former Morris and Jennings had places and among the latter were Bowne, of East Jersey, and Revell and Leeds of West Jersey, all anti-proprietary men. Robert Quary, who was also a member, sided with the governor and strongly supported the anti-proprietary interest in his letters home, but by virtue of his office to an extent stood apart from the parties of the province.

The point upon which Cornbury first centered his attention was that of procuring a permanent and adequate revenue. His own salary, of course, bulked large in this program. But a salary system had never existed as a part of the very rudimentary finances of the Jerseys. In view of this, the assembly thought itself doing very well when it voted £1000 for the support of the government in general and £300 for the payment of representatives and for incidental charges, the grant to continue for one year only.[1] The next year it voted £1500 and £1000 for each of the two following years. With none of these votes was Cornbury satisfied.

In the election for this assembly the proprietary and anti-proprietary feeling, inherited from the previous struggle, ran high. A clique among the proprietors gave Cornbury a bribe of 200 pounds of plate in the hope that he would "nicely observe his instructions." The members of both divisions were chosen, not by counties or districts, but at large.[2] This enabled Thomas Gordon, sheriff of East Jersey, to fix the polls at a place in that division so inconvenient as to disfranchise many of the voters for that election. In West Jersey also the proprietary interest won, the result being everywhere facilitated by a high property qualification.[3] Such tactics as those of Gordon certainly furnished a strong provocation for the opposing faction and they tried, though in vain, to unseat five of the proprietary members.

The first measure introduced into the assembly was the so-called "long bill,"[4] the object of which was to confirm the claim of the proprietors to the land of the province and to quit rents, and put an end to the grants of Nicolls to the Elizabethtown and Monmouth patentees. The effect of this, of course, would be to reopen the struggle with the Nicolls patentees and that over a question which ought to have been

[1] Tanner, 320, 378, 502, with references.

[2] N. J. Arch. III, 14, 29, 195, 207–209, 276; Tanner, 321, 352 *et seq.*, 378, 605.

[3] This was 100 acres of land for electors and 1000 acres for the elected. Cornbury complained because there was not an alternative money qualification, so as to admit merchants.

[4] N. J. Arch. III, 28 *et seq.* — Cornbury's criticism of this bill. The text of it is not now accessible; see Tanner, 606 *et seq.*

judicially settled. The object of the next bill was to prohibit the unlicensed purchase of land from the Indians. Other measures provided for enforcing the payment of a tax laid in 1700 for the support of government in West Jersey, the collection of which had been a failure, and for the payment of wages and fees to the members of the assembly. It was only after these that the meagre revenue for the year, to which reference has been made, was voted. This course of proceeding indicated that the proprietary element intended, if possible, to dominate the affairs of the province, even though a surrender of government had been made to the crown. It was certainly an exceptional situation, especially in the eyes of so pronounced an enemy of chartered colonies as was Cornbury. He therefore approved only the bill concerning purchases from the Indians and closed the session. Through Quary he then negotiated with the anti-proprietary party and obtained from them an assurance that at the next election they would choose men who would vote the government an adequate support and otherwise effectually answer its ends.

The assembly did not meet again until September, 1704.[1] In his opening speech Cornbury asked for an adequate revenue and said that he did not think the rights of the proprietors should be confirmed in the way provided by the bill of the last session. Legislation concerning the militia and highways was also called for. These matters the house took up, but also introduced bills concerning the rights of the proprietors, with much the same provisions as those of the last session. The support offered was but slightly increased. Thoroughly disgusted and offering as an excuse that he must at once return to New York, he dissolved the assembly and ordered a new election.

As was proved by evidence collected three years later,[2] the so-called "blind tax" had already been levied, that is, a corruption fund of several hundred pounds had been raised by the anti-proprietary party — chiefly by Richard Slater and John Bowne — for the purpose of securing the dissolution of the assembly and the election of another which should be opposed to the proprietors. Cornbury denied that he had

[1] N. J. Arch. III, 66.
[2] N. J. Arch. III, 179, 198–219; Tanner, 609.

received any of this money,[1] but in view of his character, of the circumstances of the case and of what occurred afterwards, his statement was generally disbelieved. But notwithstanding their efforts, and the haste with which it was held, Cornbury and his friends were not wholly successful in the election.[2] Therefore objection was made to the seating of three Quakers from West Jersey, in the session of November, 1704, on the plea that they did not possess the requisite amount of land. Upon this suggestion from two of his supporters, Cornbury refused to receive the affirmations of the three Quakers. Thereupon their accusers desired fourteen days in which to prove their charge; and this was granted, though the day following the accused members produced the surveys which proved that they were qualified. Their temporary exclusion, however, gave a majority of one to the anti-proprietary party and enabled it to pass a bill extending the suffrage to freeholders without further qualification. Acts were also passed for the taxation of all land in the province, including the unimproved land of the proprietors, and for raising £2000 per annum for two years for the support of the government.[3] The session was then brought to an end without the excluded members being allowed to qualify. Though proprietary exclusiveness had been dealt a merited blow, it had been done by such high-handed methods as to discredit the men who were concerned in it. The acts of this session went for a time into force, but finally they were all disallowed, while Cornbury was instructed to restore the former restrictions on the suffrage,[4] with alternative qualifications expressed in terms of money.

The assembly did not meet again till the close of 1705.[5] By that time it had become convinced that the claim of the three excluded members to their seats was valid and they were restored in spite of all the dishonest efforts of Cornbury to prevent it. By this means the proprietary majority was reestablished.

[1] N. J. Arch. III, 194. Morris stated that Chief Justice Bridges, of New York, encouraged the raising of this fund; *ibid.*, 277.

[2] *Ibid.*, 87 *et seq.*; Tanner, 382 *et seq.*

[3] N. J. Arch. III, 69.

[4] N. J. Arch. III, 98; Tanner, 386.

[5] Tanner, 383 *et seq.*

In his first letter home concerning the doings of this assembly, Cornbury made no reference to the exclusion of the three members.[1] But he did describe, from his standpoint, the quarrel in which he had already become involved with Lewis Morris and the suspension of him from the council. Morris was doubtless stirred to action by knowledge of the underhanded proceedings of Cornbury, and he began his assault with the claim that the surrender by the proprietors had been made on conditions and that these had been incorporated in the governor's instructions. These he asserted that Cornbury was violating. The instructions in question related not so much to the territorial rights of the proprietors, which of course would be conceded by all, as to the political requirements embodied in the former property qualification for suffrage and the right of Quakers to vote and hold office. The very prominent place held by Morris in the negotiations for the surrender entitled him to speak with weight upon the intentions of the proprietors at that time, and he now asserted that they intended to make these and the articles concerning territorial rights conditions of the surrender. They were certainly presented at the time and were included in Cornbury's instructions.[2] But they were not in the document embodying the surrender itself and the board of trade asserted that the surrender " was absolute and without Terms." " We did indeed consent, at the Proprietors' desire, to add some Clauses to Your Lordship's Instructions, but that was no condition of the Surrender." This statement of the board was undoubtedly correct. It was in harmony with all the possibilities and probabilities of its action. It never could have pledged itself to perpetuate the very control over the government of New Jersey which the proprietors were resigning. And furthermore, the instructions themselves provided that the restrictions on suffrage might be changed by law. The fact that Cornbury had procured the passage of such a law is not to be condemned, though the way in which he did it was open to the severest censure. But the proprietors, as well as the anti-proprietary party, had their share in bribing him. As to the Quakers, he never really

[1] N. J. Arch. III, 69 *et seq.*; Tanner, 263, 383.
[2] N. J. Arch. II, 406, 452, 510; III, 74, 117, 125; Tanner, 603 *et seq.*

attempted to disfranchise them, though doubtless he gladly would have done so. These were the two important conditions which Morris insisted upon, and they both lay within the sphere of government, where the hands of the crown could not be tied by any mere understanding.

The home government,[1] when it learned how Cornbury had excluded the three members, advised him not to interfere with the privileges of the house, but it supported him and the anti-proprietary party by appointing three Anglicans — Townley, Coxe and Chief Justice Mompesson — to the council. Cornbury was ordered by the board of trade to restore Morris on his making due submission, but it was not made and he did not attend until the next administration.[2] Jennings resigned and joined Morris in the leadership of the proprietary forces. Peter Sonmans was the anti-proprietary candidate for Jennings' place, was also recommended by Cornbury and was ultimately appointed. He was a man of ability, but of low moral character. He became one of the most notorious of the Cornbury clique, and later found the greatest difficulty in keeping himself out of the clutches of the law.[3]

When the assembly met for the fall session of 1705, it soon became evident that the affair of the three members had destroyed all chance of the governor obtaining from it any of the legislation which he desired. It began at once the preparation of bills to confirm the rights of the proprietors and would not consider appropriations till they were passed. The consequence was a prorogation till the next spring, and this assembly never again met for business. In October, 1706, an effort was made to bring a quorum together, but it failed and a dissolution followed. Cornbury's third assembly, which was now elected, contained a strong proprietary majority. Morris, who was under suspension from the council, was returned as a member, and Jennings was elected speaker. These two were the leaders of the house. The proposals of Cornbury's opening speech, that they should appropriate a revenue for 21 years and pass other beneficial laws,[4] were brushed one

[1] N. J. Arch, III, 85, 112, 127, 137.

[2] *Ibid.*, 124.

[3] Tanner, 266 and references. On the struggle which went on in England between Dockwra, Sonmans and the Coxe interests among the proprietors over these appointments, see Tanner, 613 *et seq.* and references.

[4] Tanner, 387 *et seq.*; N. J. Arch. III, 197.

side and they went into committee of the whole on grievances. The committee appointed its own clerk and thus, after a struggle with Cornbury, got rid of his clerk, the clerk of the house, who declared that he was sworn to report debates which were dangerous to the government. The committee then settled down to the taking of evidence concerning the "blind tax" and the exclusion of the three members. John Bowne, one of the collectors of it, was expelled from the house and other vigorous measures were resorted to. An address to the queen was prepared asking for the removal of the governor,[1] and a remonstrance, prepared mostly by Morris, was read to Cornbury himself by the speaker in the presence of the house. In this remarkable document his lordship was charged with a number of offences, such as the arbitrary collection of fees, granting a monopoly of trade on the road from Amboy to Burlington and interfering with the business and records of the proprietors, but the indictment reached its climax in the charge that in return for a large bribe he had excluded the three members from the assembly.

Very rarely was a governor assailed to his face in this fashion, and it must have required much self control on Cornbury's part to have mastered his anger sufficiently to state that he would need time in which to prepare his reply. In due time he read it before the house,[2] though who had the largest share in preparing it is not known. It was skilfully drawn and abounded in denunciation of his leading opponents, criticism of the assembly and justification of his own conduct. He pleaded his instructions and sought to justify his claim to judge of the qualifications of assemblymen. As to the "blind tax," he absolutely denied all knowledge of it or share in it.

A controversy next developed over the submission to the assembly of the accounts of Fauconier, the receiver general. On its refusal to consider appropriations until his accounts were laid before the house, they were produced. The house then called on Fauconier for his vouchers, but he refused to give them without Cornbury's consent. He was appealed to, but replied that the receiver general was accountable alone to the auditor general.[3] The house then, without voting any

[1] N. J. Arch., III, 171 *et seq.*
[2] N. J. Arch., III, 180 *et seq.*
[3] Tanner, 393.

appropriations, turned to the preparation of bills confirming the estates of the proprietors, ascertaining fees and the qualifications of jurymen. Cornbury thereupon prorogued them. An equally profitless session was held in the autumn, the deadlock continuing over the redress of grievances.

Both parties now turned to the home government, Morris writing to the secretary of state a comprehensive account of the administration from his standpoint, and the governor sending an address to the queen [1] from the lieutenant governor and council. While the latter representation was filled with complaints of the turbulence of Morris and Jennings and the factions and confusion in both the Jerseys and Pennsylvania, Morris laid the blame on the governors. Their imprudent conduct, sordid and mercenary measures, "the trash of mankind" who had been their favorites and tools, these had checked the growth of the provinces and filled the chartered governments with people who had emigrated from them; Cornbury's administration he compared to that of Gessius Florus in Judea and asked that he be recalled.

In May, 1708, another brief session of the assembly was held at Burlington,[2] in which the demands of the governor and the protest and statement of grievances of the house were simply repeated and no business was done. With this the experience of Cornbury with assemblies in New Jersey came to an end, for before the house met again he had been called back to England.

[1] N. J. Arch., III, 274–290.
[2] N J. Arch., III, 291–298.

CHAPTER XIX

HARMONY PARTIALLY RESTORED IN NEW YORK AND NEW JERSEY UNDER ROBERT HUNTER, 1708–1716

During the brief administrations of Lord Lovelace and Richard Ingoldsby, which intervened between the retirement of Cornbury and the arrival of Hunter — December, 1708, to June, 1710 — attention was chiefly occupied with preparations for the expedition of Vetch and Nicholson against Canada. This was welcomed as offering a fair prospect of conquest and thus of removing the burden of war or at least the agitation which resulted from frequent alarms. But it imposed a heavy financial burden on the province, and that at a time when its debt was large and its credit was low. Naturally, therefore, the assembly, by taking advantage of the need for revenue, was able to strengthen still further its control over the finances. The new governor expressed the hope that the revenue would be continued for a six year period, as in Lord Bellomont's time, and that the debt might be paid off.[1] During many sessions the house considered the question of supply in committee of the whole[2] and finally it was resolved to appropriate £2500 and that £1600 of this, since he had brought over a large quantity of military supplies, should go to the governor, while the salaries of a number of minor officials were specified. The balance (£750) was set apart for firewood, candles and other incidentals for the garrisons at Albany. Having determined the uses to which the supply should be put, the house resolved itself into committee of the whole on the ways and means of procuring the supply. At this point occurred the death of Lord Lovelace and the assumption of the government by Richard Ingoldsby.[3]

[1] Ass. J. I, 240; C. J. I, 276; Col. Laws, I, 420.

[2] Ass. J. I, 246.

[3] Ingoldsby's commission, as is stated below, had been revoked in 1706, but notice of the fact seems not to have been sent to him. As soon as the board of trade learned of this act of his the queen ordered him to lay down the office; N. Y. Docs. V, 89–91.

The next step taken by the assembly was the passage of a very elaborate act regulating and establishing fees, which was intended to reduce the extortionate sums collected in this form, of which there had been such general complaint under Cornbury. It was approved by the acting governor and council without amendment.[1] But already Colonels Vetch and Nicholson had arrived. Ingoldsby threw himself into their plans and the estimates had to be changed. A bill was now passed appropriating £6000 for the expedition, to be paid out by the treasurer or upon warrants under the hands of commissioners named in the act.[2] They were to procure provisions and other necessaries for victualling the forces, to build storehouses near Lake Champlain and attend to transporting the troops. The warrants were to state to whom, for what service and for what materials they were issued. A committee of three at Albany was also named in the act to receive the supplies and dispose of them there and to the northward. The treasurer was to keep accounts and submit them to the governor, council and assembly when called for.[3] Not the least significant departure from former usage in this session and under the pressure of war was the passage of the first act in New York for the issue of bills of credit.[4]

In the autumn session, when the expedition had been abandoned and the troops had returned, all officials who had been concerned with the expenditure of money were called on to account.[5] Carpenters petitioned for pay. The house addressed the lieutenant governor to take effective measures for the return to Albany of the stores of war sent to Wood Creek and that exact accounts for them should be rendered. In a strong and detailed address to the queen the house set forth what New York had done and the condition of need in which she found herself, now that the enterprise had been abandoned.[6] Additional taxes were then laid — a tonnage duty, a chimney and hearth tax and a tax on slaves, and more bills

[1] Col. Laws, I, 638 *et seq.*

[2] *Ibid.*, 654; Ass. J. I, 268.

[3] Later in the session an act for levying £4,000 additional was passed, with provisions substantially the same as this act; Col. Laws, I, 669.

[4] *Ibid.*, 666.

[5] Ass. J. I, 261 *et seq.*

[6] *Ibid.*, 268.

of credit were issued.[1] To this point had the war brought the fiscal system of the province when Governor Robert Hunter appeared.

Hunter was a Scotchman of good family and training, honest, tactful and possessed of a considerable degree of culture. Cadwallader Colden wrote, many years after,[2] "When I knew Mr. Hunter he was an exceedingly well shaped and well proportioned man, tho' then advanced in years. He understood the Belles lettres well and had an intimacy with the distinguished men of wit at that time in England. Among them Dr. Arbuthnot, Queen Anne's favorite physician, was his most intimate and useful friend, tho' he and the doctor differed greatly in their political sentiments, for Mr. Hunter was a staunch Whig. He wrote some pieces in the Tatlers. When he was appointed Governor of New York a very high compliment was made in one of the Tatlers to him under the name of *Eboracensis*.[3] He wrote some elegant little pieces of poetry, which never appeared in his name. He had an exceeding pretty and entertaining manner of telling a Tale and was a most agreeable companion with his intimate friends. He was fond of men of Learning and encouraged them whenever he had an opportunity. In short he was a Gentleman of extraordinary abilities, both natural and acquired, and had every qualification requisite in a Governor."

This passage has merited quotation in full, because the sources for our period rarely yield characterizations so adequate as this of governors and other leaders who were at that time active in the colonies. The young Colden, who had a strong taste for learning, as well as for official life, was himself the son of a Scotch parson, had studied medicine in Edinburgh and had migrated to Philadelphia where, rather unwillingly, he was settling down with the idea of passing his life as a practitioner of the healing art.[4] But in the latter part of Hunter's administration he invited Colden to remove to New York on the promise of being the next surveyor general. Two minor offices were first bestowed upon

[1] Col. Laws, I, 669, 675, 682, 689, 695.

[2] Colden's Letters to his Son on Smith's History of New York, Colls. of N. Y. Hist. Soc. Fund Series, 1868, p. 192 *et seq.*; Dict. of National Biography.

[3] This is in No. 69 of the Tatler.

[4] Keys, Cadwallader Colden as an Eighteenth Century Official.

him and in 1720, after Hunter had returned to England, but at the governor's instance, the coveted appointment was made and Colden was launched upon his long official career. This fact, as well as the social charm of Hunter, helps to explain the enthusiasm with which, as an elderly man, Colden recalled the memory of the governor. He went on in his sketch to tell how Hunter had served in the army during William's reign and later under Marlborough, from Blenheim to Ramillies, and added, evidently from his recollection of the stories as told by Hunter, some incidents showing his relations with the great duke himself. He might also have added that he knew Addison and Swift and was on familiar terms with the earls of Stair. Colden did record his belief that Hunter was the ablest man who had ever governed New York. In 1707 he was appointed full-rank governor of Virginia, but, being captured by the French, did not reach that province.[1] Subsequent to his service in New York he was made governor of Jamaica and served there till his death in 1734. His letters show literary ability and the firmness and success with which he approached a difficult situation in both New York and New Jersey show him to have been a man of unusual capacity. His coming was immediately connected with the settlement in New York of a considerable body of Palatines, but that is best treated in other connections, and it is our task at present to consider Hunter in his relation to the political problems which he had to face in New York and New Jersey.

In September, 1710, Hunter met his first New York assembly.[2] In his opening speech he referred to them a letter from Governor Dudley of Massachusetts describing the barbarities from which the frontiers of New England were suffering and asking that the New York Indians might make a diversion against the French for their relief. Hunter stated that he had consulted the Indian commissioners at Albany and had found that, if the attention of the French was diverted to New York, it would be found much less defensible than New England, "there being neither money in the Treasury nor Forts, or what is worse than none, no Arms or Men for our Defence; so that we are forced to rest contented with a precarious

[1] N. Y. Col. Docs., V, 451–455; Colden, *op. cit.*

[2] Ass. J. I, 271 *et seq.*

Security, under a suspicious Neutrality that hath no firmer Foundation than the Faith of Savages, whilst our Neighbours' Frontiers are on Fire and the Inhabitants inhumanly butchered." In the light of such an utterance as that, the failure of the Fletcher and Cornbury régime stood fully revealed. It is probable that the stolid and narrowly self-interested Dutch and English who heard it failed to catch its true meaning. New England was bearing the brunt of the conflict, and however faulty may have been its system of defence, the money which was appropriated for it was not stolen. It was spent in some form or other for the purposes intended. Both Fletcher and Cornbury could write brave letters home about what ought to be done and filled with complaints of their neighbors because it was not done, while they were in league with a group of corruptionists to divert a large part of the meagre funds which could be obtained to their own pockets. At Albany trade with the French and their Indians was too valuable to be risked by war. In view of this, and of the interests which absorbed the energies of England in Europe, is it any wonder that Canada was not conquered?

As had been done so many times before, Hunter urged the necessity of repairing the forts and building new ones, and that the militia act, which was about to expire, should be renewed. The debt, too, with which Cornbury had left the province burdened, though New York had had very little real share in the war, ought to be paid. Among certain acts the passage of which Hunter had been instructed, if possible, to secure was one whereby the creditors of persons becoming bankrupt in Great Britain and having estates in New York might be able to recover their debts. This touched a very real and widespread evil connected with colonial trade and business relations. Also the home government had again ordered that no law be passed making presents to governors. To these proposals as a whole the assembly made the usual brief answer, showing good intentions in general, but no specific resolve to act out of the ordinary.

The first subject taken up was that of fees. Hunter had brought over an order in council repealing the act of 1709 on that subject.[1] This was an expression of what had always

[1] New York Docs: V, 143; Ass. J. I, 274.

been the policy of the British government, that the rates of fees should be fixed by the colonial executives. It opposed such legislation as this, wherever it appeared, as an encroachment on the sphere of the executive. But fees had recently become too extortionate and the system sheltered too many evils for the colonists to refrain from repeated attacks upon it. In accordance with the suggestion of the board of trade, the council prepared a new table of fees, based on an earlier one of 1693, while the assembly set about another bill on the subject.[1] While it was found that no ordinance had ever been issued authorizing the collection of the fees of 1693, and it was impossible to base a new table on that list, the assembly did not succeed in securing the passage of another act on the subject and the next year a new table of fees was put into force by executive ordinance.

Immediately after this subject was disposed of, that of the governor's salary came up. The assembly resolved that 2500 ounces of plate — that is of silver of the standard weight and fineness of Spanish coin — equivalent to 6s. 10d. per oz. should be raised for the payment of the governor during the coming year.[2] As Hunter, following the specification when Cornbury was appointed, had been instructed to take £1200 sterling out of the revenue for his salary, and this resolve of the house implied a return to the salary of about two-thirds of that sum, he called the houses before him and told the assembly that he thought he had done nothing to deserve such a vote and he hoped no one would dispute the right of the queen to appoint a salary for her governor, as had been done in her instructions. Other serious cuts were also made by the assembly in the sums deemed necessary by the executive for the support of the government. It was at this time that Lewis Morris, who had so bitterly opposed Cornbury in New Jersey and who had now removed to the county of Westchester in New York, struck hands with Hunter and in the assembly criticised so severely those who opposed the governor's demand concerning his salary that he was expelled.[3] The two, however, continued in close connection,

[1] Ass. J. I, 274, 279; N. Y. Docs. V, 170, 186, 216, 238.

[2] Ass. J., I, 280–1; C. J., I, 302; N. Y. Docs., V, 177–180, 183, 191.

[3] N. Y. Docs., V, 178; Ass. J. I, 283. A copy of the speech which Morris delivered on this occasion was sent by Hunter to the board of trade as an en-

in both New York and New Jersey affairs, and it was as the result chiefly of their joint efforts that Hunter was finally able to secure a working agreement with the various political groups in the two provinces.[1]

Closely connected with the question of his own salary was that of the debt due the widow of Lord Lovelace for his salary and expenditures as governor. The day before his death a resolution granting him £1600 had passed the assembly, but later, under Ingoldsby, the same had been cut down by more than two-thirds. An order had now come from the queen that the assembly should be called upon to make good its former resolution.[2] This Hunter laid before that body and, as an encouragement to liberality, referred to the enrichment of the province which might be expected from the settlement of the Palatines within it. Following a recommendation of the board of trade, he urged that a general act for their naturalization be passed,[3] and from that he went on to a further argument in favor of expenditures for defence. Though several revenue acts were passed, in the opinion of Hunter they would not meet the current expenditures, even according to the estimates of the assembly.[4] As a remedy for their jealousy of the executive in the matter of expenditures, he suggested the insertion of a clause in their bill making the receiver general accountable to the assembly as well as to the crown, and also a clause that no warrants

---

closure with his letter of Nov. 14, 1710. In it Morris reflected on the good faith of the assembly and on the unfair tactics which it resorted to in order to prevent a consideration of the salary question. It was doubtless this which occasioned his expulsion. Another tender spot upon which he touched was the cost of sessions of the assembly in the form of the wages of the members and the extent to which this was increased by spinning out sessions. The members from the city also were offended by the freedom with which Morris, a country member, urged a resort to indirect taxes as offering a source of revenue which would be ample for all needs.

[1] See Spencer, Phases of Royal Government in New York, 133; Smith, History of New York, I, 179 *et seq.*

[2] Ass. J. I, 284; N. Y. Docs. V, 89–90.

[3] As a naturalization act was not passed at this time, Hunter thought of letters of denization, but found that in 1700 all the governors had been prohibited granting these, so he awaited further orders; N. Y. Docs. V, 211; Cal. St. P. Col., 1700, pp. 34, 38, 71, 73–74, 430.

[4] *Ibid.*, 185. One of the bills levying a duty on goods sold at auction, and estimated to yield £500, wrote Hunter, would not yield a farthing, and was really intended by its promoters to bring that method of sale to an end as injurious to their trade.

signed by the governor in council should bind the province till accepted by the receiver general; and, in order that no more warrants should be drawn on him than he had money in hand to answer, the receiver general should submit monthly to the governor a true state of the revenue, and that he should give security in New York as he had done in England.[1] The object of this interesting suggestion was to establish a degree of responsibility on the part of the receiver general to the assembly — a reform which was greatly needed — and thus to avoid the further development of the office of treasurer, with the dualism in government which it would necessitate. But it met with no response.

In his letters home, when commenting on the reasons for economy, the one on which Hunter laid the greatest stress was the fact that the members of assembly received salaries and that made politics a business with them and brought in an inferior class of members.[2] This practice, he found, had begun in 1691 and the rate was the high one of ten shillings per day. For ten years that had continued and had been confirmed by an order in council in 1697. In 1701 the act providing for the rate of pay had been repealed and one allowing six shillings per day was passed.[3] This was still in force. As a result, a fairly long session of the assembly cost half of the total appropriation for the support of government. In view of this Hunter would have welcomed, had it been possible,[4] the issue of an order of council which would have repealed the existing law on the subject and have left the assemblymen without wages. He would also gladly have seen the passage of an act of parliament providing for a uniform quit rent on all the land of the province, and if this should compel the holders of large grants which they could never improve to surrender them, it would remove an obstacle to settlement in New York and check the migration of people into the proprietary provinces. He also proposed a levy by

[1] N. Y. Docs. V, 178. This last proposal was in accordance with a rule of the treasury.

[2] *Ibid.*, 179. That, of course, was a characteristic English opinion of the time, and was held by practically all the royal officials concerning members of the assemblies.

[3] Col. Laws, I, 466; Col. Docs. V, 187.

[4] N. Y. Docs. V, 186, 216.

act of parliament throughout all the northern colonies of export and import duties and an excise on liquors. In the light of these proposals, though we may approve of much that Hunter accomplished in New York politics, it is easy to see how little prospect consistent Whiggism offered for colonial liberty.

When the general appropriation bill came to him, which Hunter regarded as totally inadequate,[1] the council amended it so as to provide that money should be issued under the warrant of the governor. This the assembly refused to admit, though in conference the council plead royal instructions and former practice. As the council adhered to its amendments, the bill was lost. No notice was taken of the request of the crown that the claim of Lady Lovelace should be paid. When the board of trade heard of this result, it promptly recommended to the crown[2] that the governor be instructed to urge again the provision of a revenue, and to support it with an assurance that the assembly must expect that a refusal or neglect would occasion the passage of an act of parliament granting a revenue in New York adequate to the support of its government. The privy council approved of this and ordered the board of trade to draft the heads of a bill to be laid before parliament for this purpose. This was done and, after approval by the law officers, it was submitted to the queen. An early adjournment of parliament prevented its introduction.

The deadlock between the houses, over the right of the council to amend money bills, continued until the end of the session, November 25, 1710, when the province was left without a revenue. The following April a short session was held, at the beginning of which the governor put squarely before the assembly the question whether or not it would support the government and pay its debts and provide for the defence of the frontier in the way the queen had directed.[3] He had previously spoken to them of the care with which royal instructions were prepared and of the inadequate grounds on which he thought they opposed them. Now he applied this

[1] N. Y. Docs. V, 184.
[2] *Ibid.*, 190–192, 197, 285.
[3] Ass. J. I, 287–288; Smith, Hist. of N. Y. I, 181.

to the vote of salaries for governors which was prescribed in them and suggested that it was more economical than the bestowment of presents. "It is necessary at this Time that you be told also that giving Money for the Support of Government, and disposing of it at your Pleasure, is the same with giving none at all; her Majesty is the sole Judge of the Merits of her servants . . ." Whig as he was, no one ever exceeded Hunter in the emphasis which he laid on the binding force of instructions, but he was quite wrong in assuring the assembly that the queen's instruction concerning salaries met with "a cheerful and grateful Compliance in all her other Colonies."

When the house began to quibble over the question of its right legally to meet on the strength of a proclamation which had been issued from Burlington, New Jersey,[1] Hunter immediately dissolved it and ordered a new election. This was just on the eve of the arrival of Sir Hovenden Walker's expedition against Canada. Though nearly every member of the previous assembly, including Morris, was reelected,[2] no conflict between the houses occurred during its first session, because all were so occupied with the outfit of the troops. Bills of credit to the amount of £25,000 were issued and a levy on real and personal estates to the estimated amount of £10,000 was voted.[3]

But in connection with appropriations and the adjustment of accounts after the failure of that expedition, the dispute between the two houses was renewed.[4] The usual bill for a levy on real and personal estates became law, as did an appropriation act for the repair of the forts at Albany and Schenectady and the support of garrisons there. Though the former of these gave the usual powers to the treasurer, the council let it pass. But the bills for a tonnage duty and a chimney tax it amended by leaving out the word treasurer and making the money payable to the receiver general. A message came back from the assembly that the council must

[1] See a representation of the board of trade on this subject. N. Y., Docs., V, 287.

[2] Compare the lists, Ass. J. I, 271, 298.

[3] Col. Laws, I, 730, 737.

[4] Ass. J. I, 301 *et seq.*; C. J. I, 324, 328; N. Y. Docs. V, 292–299; Col Laws I, 746, 750.

be well informed of the "undoubted right and constant resolve of this house not to admit of any amendment to money bills." In the messages which were then exchanged between the two houses the council resorted to historical argument and precedents, citing instances as late as 1703 in which its amendments to money bills had been accepted by the assembly. It also expressed the legalist and royalist view of the origin of the two houses — a view to which Cornbury had given utterance — that they were constituted "by the mere grace of the crown signified in the governor's commission." It was amply assured of the support of the board of trade and that the crown would confirm the power claimed by the council if it desired. But in its reply the assembly drew a sharp distinction between its position and that of the council.[1] It is true, it said, that the share of the council in legislation did not flow from the nature of that board — which was to advise, or "from their being another distinct State or Rank of People in the Constitution, which they are not, being all Commons, but only from the mere pleasure of the prince signified in the commission. On the contrary, the inherent Right of the Assembly to dispose of the money of the Freemen of this Colony does not come from any Commission, Letters Patent or other Grant from the Crown, but from the free Choice and Election of the People, who ought not to be divested of their Property (nor justly can) without their Consent." The acceptance of amendments in former times they termed "condescensions," not precedents. The fact that the board of trade could see no reason why the council had not the right to amend money bills was, in the opinion of the assembly, far from proving that there was such a right.

Whether this statement was drawn by William Nicoll or by other members of the assembly, it must stand as a most significant expression of the colonial spirit. It was an appeal as against concessions from the absolute and indefeasible power of government, to the principle of representation as a guaranty of property — and of course of other rights as well — against the executive. It also voiced a protest which was steadily growing in volume against the position of appointed councils as upper houses of the legis-

[1] Ass. J. I, 307.

latures. But they were an essential part of the provincial system, and if they fell it would be impossible long to uphold the province or even the colonial status. It is no wonder that the issue was regarded as one of deep significance on both sides, and that they were resolved to adhere to their respective positions. The language used by Hunter in a number of his letters shows that he fully appreciated the gravity of the issue. In his speech to the assembly in April, 1711, he had said, " however your Resentment has fallen upon the Governors, it is the Government you dislike." To Secretary St. John he wrote, they " have but one short step to make towards what I am unwilling to name."[1] The bills which were involved of course failed to become law, and when a proposal came from Governor Dudley that New York should be represented in a conference of governors to deliberate on the war, both council and assembly advised Hunter not to attend because of the lack of revenue.[2] A bill concerning fees also failed, and this was followed by a resolution of the assembly, that the establishment of fees without its consent was contrary to law.

For some time before the arrival of Hunter, New York had been without a court of chancery.[3] Suits had accumulated and many petitions were now presented for the reestablishment of such a court. Hunter wrote to the board of trade and it referred him to his commission, which authorized him, with the advice of the council, to establish courts. The council then advised him that he was chancellor by virtue of his custody of the seal of the province. He therefore issued a proclamation for the opening of a court of chancery. This, too, offended the assembly, because it was done without its consent.[4] Though the court was doubtless of utility to the people at large, its more immediate usefulness, as developed before many months, was by the issue of chancery writs to facilitate the collection of quit rents and their arrears.[5] By this means revenue from that source, which had almost ceased, was increased to sums

[1] N. Y. Docs. V, 296.

[2] Ass. J. I, 308; C. J. I, 326.

[3] N. Y. Docs. V, 298.

[4] Ass. J. I, 308.

[5] N. Y. Docs. V, 357, 361, 362, 369–370, 561; Spencer, 143.

varying from £300 to £600 per year. It was also planned, if possible, to secure an income from escheats and other regalian rights. But from these sources only slight relief could be expected and that after a considerable period.

The same question came up under another form in connection with the proposed appointment of Colonel Lodwick again as agent. The bill for this originated in the assembly and provided for a levy of money for his support and for a committee of the assembly to sit continuously to instruct and correspond with him, the governor and council to be wholly excluded from his control. Hunter stated that the interference of Lodwick in the affairs of the province had injured the interest of the crown, for letters of his to John de Peyster had been dropped in the streets and copies sent to most of the counties in order to obstruct the settling of a revenue. Naturally the bill for making him an agent under such conditions failed to receive the assent of the council, as did a similar bill the next session.[1] On all these points the governor was sure of the support of the crown.

During the spring session of 1712 the hostile relations continued, though with some lowering of intensity. Hunter was personally so agreeable that the members of the assembly professed the utmost willingness "to make him easy," as their expression was, if he would put his private interest in competition with that of the crown.[2] He considered that he must give up the most important part of executive authority in order to gain any support from the assembly in its existing disposition. "I have not only expended my own money for all the contingencies of the government since I have been here," he wrote, "but the daily complaints and cries of the officers, who have not received a shilling for their support since my coming, render my condition very miserable and would make it insupportable but for the relief I hope for from home." Under the colonial system of finance official salaries and other forms of support were exceedingly precarious. Governments on both sides of the ocean often failed to keep their promises, and had it not been for fees and perquisites — which by far their largest sources of

[1] Ass. J. I, 319 *et seq.*
[2] N. Y. Docs. V, 340.

income — public servants would indeed have been in a sad plight. During the present session 8025 ounces of plate were appropriated for the support of the government since June, 1710, which barely covered the salary due the governor without additional allowances.[1] Provision was also made for the payment of certain British officers and for the temporary defence of the frontier.

At the opening of the session of September, 1712, Hunter submitted an elaboration of the plan he had suggested two years before, by which the responsibility of the receiver general to the governor and council might be assured and expenditures kept within appropriations, with ultimate accounting to the assembly.[2] This, he claimed, would remove the only material objection to what he demanded. More he could not do, if he would, for he was bound by his instructions. This plan provided that every quarter the receiver general should lay before the governor and council a statement of the money he had received, and all employees of the government and those who had rendered it services should at the same time submit their claims, which should be examined and allowed by the governor and council. Warrants should then be issued for the payment of claims, but not in excess of the amount of revenue available at the close of each quarter, claimants being allowed to bring an action of debt against the receiver general on any failure upon his part to conform to the conditions thus provided. This scheme, if honestly executed, would put all creditors of the government on an equality, would have necessitated a speeding up of the collection of revenue and would have corrected much of the looseness so prevalent in administration. For these reasons, doubtless, as well as the fact that its execution rested too much in the hands of the executive, it was not acceptable.

Though considerable legislating was done at this session, no bills were submitted for the support of the government "but such as they well knew could not pass." [3] Failing to obtain an agent to their liking, the assembly addressed the

[1] Ass. J. I, 314; Col. Laws, I, 753, 756–7; N. Y. Docs. V, 339.
[2] Ass. J. I, 321; C. J. I, 343.
[3] N. Y. Docs. V, 350.

queen in their own defence,[1] and asked her to order the governor to assent to an act empowering the assembly to appoint and pay an agent to present their views and answer objections. Of course no result came from this, and after a long prorogation this assembly was dissolved.[2]

The sectional feeling which had long existed between the country districts and the city of New York, and which had shown itself earlier in the bolting act, had long been gaining headway again and came to full expression in the election of 1713.[3] It deeply affected political issues in the time of Hunter and constituted one of the permanent features of New York history. The issue to which it specially gave rise at this time was that of indirect versus direct taxation, or customs revenue and excise on the sale of liquors as opposed to general levies on real and personal estate. The latter, which fell chiefly on land, affected the country, while the former rested upon trade. Between 1691 and 1709 appropriations of "revenue" had been made for periods varying from two to five years and, as wines, liquors and European goods were the chief objects of levy, the claim was made that it fell largely on the rich or well-to-do who were consumers of luxuries. Morris, in the pamphlet referred to, followed this line of argument and, as a leader of the country party, urged that the rich should bear the chief burden of taxation. He did not believe that the duty would be all transferred to the general body of consumers and appear in an equivalent rise of prices, neither did he think that the policy he defended would drive trade from New York.[4] In proof of this last point he cited the example of other colonies, especially Massachusetts, Connecticut and Pennsylvania, which imposed similar duties but at the same time maintained a flourishing trade and industry. In 1709 the appropriation of "revenue" had stopped, as the result of the dispute over salaries, and it was the intense need of its restoration for

[1] Ass. J. I, 328, 329.

[2] N. Y. Docs. V, 356.

[3] Spencer, in Pol. Sci. Quarterly, Nov. 1915. Address to the Inhabitants of Westchester County (1713), printed anonymously, but evidently the work of Lewis Morris. A copy of this is in C. O. 5/1050, Aa, 131.

[4] William Nicoll, as we have seen, had supported the opposite contention in 1699.

purely fiscal reasons which roused the governor's supporters. To their support naturally came the country interest, the farmers and men of small property up the Hudson and on the frontier, the thinly settled and expanding sections of the province, and their vote contributed strongly not only toward restoring the "revenue" but toward adjusting the complicated financial difficulties of the time.

Long Island, and especially its eastern section, stood in a peculiar relation to this issue and to the sectional feeling which was affecting the course of New York politics. We have already seen [1] how distinct, in the make-up of its population and in its affiliations with New England, this section was from the other parts of New York. This was also reflected in its trade relations, which could be much more conveniently maintained with New England than with the City of New York. Hence the demand of Long Island for a port and the amount of illegal trade, combined with the harboring of pirates, which went on there. But the demand for a port was not granted and New York, in the enforcement of its monopoly in reference to entries and clearances, imposed hardships on the Long Islanders. An important industry in that section was the capture of drift whales. Inasmuch as revenue was now cut off and the credit of the governor was being so heavily drawn on to provide for necessary expenses, attention was directed toward the king's right to royal fish as a possible source of revenue. This bore exclusively upon the industry of the Long Islanders, while the increase of pressure which was being brought to bear to promote the collection of quit rents also affected them. This all gave rise to a violent protest from the eastern end of the island, which was voiced by Samuel Mulford, of Easthampton, as will appear in the sequel.

It is probable also that Hunter himself took a hand in the controversy by publishing an anonymous pamphlet,[2] in which he upheld the prerogative in the strongest terms. He accused the assembly of arrogance, equalled only by that

[1] Osgood, Am. Colonies in 17th Century, II, 106, 121 *et seq.*, 133, 159 *et seq.*; Spencer, *op. cit.*

[2] Entitled, "To all whom these Presents May Concern," quarto, 7 pp., in C. O. 5/1050.

of the Long Parliament, and declared that its policy would leave the queen with no more power in the province than that of an Indian sachem. Defending strongly the policy of imposing indirect taxes, he sarcastically described the party cries which were being hurled back and forth during the election, for it was to influence this struggle that the pamphlet was issued.

The warmly contested election of 1713 resulted in about half a dozen changes in the personnel of the assembly, but not enough to indicate a change in its policy.[1] Therefore Hunter met it, in May, 1713, with the expectation that its life would be short, and then would follow, as in Bellomont's time, a wholesale removal of justices of the peace and officers of the militia, "that ill men may no longer use Her Majesty's authority against her."[2] In his opening speech[3] he told them plainly that he could not depart from the constitution of the province as established, though he would assent to any beneficial acts which conformed with its requirements. But he urged frequent conferences between the houses, and that they should do their plain duty. He could hold over them the threat that parliament might cure their delinquency by stringent action, but with the Tories in power in England Hunter must know that he could hardly play a part in such a measure, even if it was adopted.[4] During several of the early sessions in committee of the whole this speech was considered. Finally, resolutions were adopted to impose customs duties again for the support of the government, something which had not been done for a decade; and further, that the control over their collection and of the revenue from them should be in the hands of the receiver general.[5] If these should not yield £2800, the balance should be made good by the treasurer out of excise. A bill for an excise on the retail of liquors for twenty years was proposed, but it was not perfected and assented to by the governor until the next session.[6] With this was passed an

[1] Dutchess County was then separated from Ulster and given one member.
[2] N. Y. Docs., V, 356, 364.
[3] Ass. J. I, 333.
[4] N. Y. Docs. V, 366, 367, 377.
[5] Ass. J. I, 336; Col. Laws I, 779.
[6] N. Y. Docs. V, 366; Col. Laws I, 785, 789.

act laying a tax on goods sold at auction. By both these the treasurer was given control over their execution and the keeping of the revenue from them.

The measures thus far passed, with their many novel features, indicated that a spirit of compromise was active in the assembly. With this the governor and all concerned must have earnestly cooperated. In a brief speech at the opening of the spring session of 1714, the governor said that they had met to complete business left unfinished at adjournment, chiefly the payment of the public debts.[1] A sufficient fund for this had already been appropriated and the claims had been stated, and he could see no reason for deferring their payment. He would leave nothing undone to keep up a perfect understanding. The house now went into committee of the whole on this speech at nearly every session for two months, with Lewis Morris in the chair.[2] From the petitions and certified claims a long list of specific sums was prepared for payment. An incident of the inquiries was the arrest of Peter Fauconier for fraudulently attempting to secure certain payments on warrants which had already been paid. These sums were all embodied in the most important appropriation act up to that time passed by a New York legislature.[3] It provided for paying the debts of the province to the persons named therein, it made void all other claims, and it carried with it a provision for the issue of £27,680 in bills of credit with which to make these payments. A commission was named for issuing the bills, and the revenue arising under the excise act was pledged for their redemption.[4] The administration of the act was intrusted to the treasurer, as was the care of practically all monies raised by future acts of assembly. Thus the receiver general was kept in the inferior position to which he had been assigned by previous legislation. With this the unrestricted power of the governor to issue money under his warrant suffered a corresponding decline. Though the council amended this measure in several particulars, a conflict was avoided by the assembly declaring

[1] Ass. J. I, 345.

[2] *Ibid.*, 346–360.

[3] Chap. 280, Col. Laws I, 815–826.

[4] The farming of the excise was taken out of the hands of local justices and intrusted to commissioners named in the law. Col. Laws I, 835.

that it was not a money bill.[1] In advocating its approval by the home government,[2] however, Hunter was careful to claim it as a money bill, stating that it was for the support of the government, though for its " past support."

Provision was made for the support of government for one year and also a tonnage duty and an import duty on slaves was imposed for two years.[3] The revenue from the last mentioned act was to go into the treasurer's hands and be expended as the governor, council and assembly should direct, while that from the yearly support bill was to be paid to the receiver general — one of the few instances of this — and no directions were given as to its expenditure.

The death of the queen made a new election necessary, as a result of which several new members were chosen from the northern part of the province, but otherwise there was no change. In this assembly the system of compromises, by which a revenue for a period of years was secured and harmony restored, was completed by the passage of a naturalization act and of an act providing a revenue for five years. The former was a favorite measure with the Dutch and French of the province. It declared that all persons of foreign birth who were inhabitants of the province in 1683 and who had since died seized of lands, should hereafter be deemed to have been naturalized. It also declared naturalized all Protestants of foreign birth who were dwelling in the province in 1715. When Hunter found that one of these bills was likely to block the way of the other, he asked what the assembly would do for the government if he would pass the naturalization bill. " I asked nothing for myself, though they well knew that I had offers of several thousands of pounds for my assent." They at last agreed to settle a sufficient revenue for five years as their part of the bargain. " Many rubs I met with, but with difficulty carried it through both parts of the Legislature." " I have been struggling for bread for five years to no effect, . . . I hope I have now laid a foundation for a last settlement on this hitherto unsettled and ungovernable Province." [4] Presently thereafter Lewis

[1] Ass. J. I, 365.

[2] The act was confirmed June 17, 1715. N. Y. Docs. V, 412.

[3] Col. Laws I, 801, 812. [4] N. Y. Docs. V, 416, 419; Col. Laws I, 847, 858.

Morris was appointed chief justice, "he having by his labors and industry in the Assemblies deserved well of the Government, and to that it is in great measure we owe our present settlement." The naturalization act was criticised in England, but was not disallowed.[1] As a minor feature of the settlement, the fact also should be noted that by statute an agency to England was created. John Champante, who had long been agent for the independent companies, was named in the act and money appropriated for his support, this all being the joint action of governor, council and assembly. Ambrose Phillips succeeded to this office the following year.[2] In 1718 William Nicoll, who had steadily opposed Hunter, resigned the speakership, and Robert Livingston, who had long been serviceable to the governor, was chosen to the place and held it into the following administration.[3]

Though the act of 1715 for paying the debts of the province declared that all other claims except those for which provision was made therein should be void, it was later found that many lawful creditors, who had not been able to make the justice of their claims appear at the time, had been passed over. Therefore, at the close of 1716, another act providing for these was passed.[4] This act called for another issue of bills of credit to the amount of 41,517½ ounces of plate, the redemption of the same to be secured by an excise on the retailing and a duty on the importing of liquors, about twenty years being allowed for the completion of this process. Like its predecessors this act also contained a detailed list of the claimants and of the sums which were due them. As all the parts of the legislature were now working harmoniously, this measure was sprung upon the commercial element in the province as a surprise. They had supposed that the debt paying process, with its imposts and issues of bills of credit, had been completed by the bill of 1715. When it was found that this was not true, a chorus of protest was raised on Long Island and in New York City. The grand jury of New York City and County, among whose members were such men as

[1] N. Y. Docs. V, 495.
[2] Col. Laws, I, 881, 897.
[3] N. Y. Docs. V, 495.
[4] Col. Laws, I, 938.

Stephen Van Cortlandt, Robert Lurting, Henry Lane, John Reed, George Emmot, William Smith, William Walton, merchants and lawyers, sent a protest to the governor, while the bill was pending, asking him to veto it.[1] For petitioning the governor in alleged contempt of the two houses the jurors were brought before the assembly by the sergeant at arms. Their answer was that, though their act was not a proper one, it did not amount to a contempt, and with this the action of the grand jury was allowed to drop. But against the bill, when it reached England, various representations were made by merchants engaged in the New York trade, while the governor and assembly defended it in an elaborate statement to the board of trade, and Hunter repeatedly defended it in his letters.[2] Morris, as chief justice and member of the assembly, was very active not only in supporting the bill but in threatening with the law those who showed any signs of sedition in opposing it. Its opponents charged the governor and legislature with bad faith in passing it, in order to secure money for themselves and provide for sham debts, which had once been rejected when the previous bill had been drafted. These charges met with strong denials and did not specially influence the British government in its attitude toward the measure. To it the questionable feature of the bill was its provision for another issue of paper and the effect which this would have on British trade. Richard West, the counsel of the board of trade, reported on it in August, 1718. About a year before the order had been issued to the governors not to assent to any acts affecting the trade of Great Britain without a suspending clause. As to the effect on debts of the issue of the bills of credit, West thought the merchants could allow for that so as to escape loss; and so the only point upon which he questioned the validity of the measure was in connection with the above order. But this was not considered by the privy council to be sufficient to justify its disallowance, and so the act was confirmed,[3] May 19, 1720. But it was ordered that all the governors be instructed not to assent to acts for the issue of bills of credit without the insertion in them of a suspending clause.

[1] Ass. J. I, 411; C. O. 5/1051, Bb, 131.
[2] C. O. 5/1051, Bb, 131, 153, 154, 167; N. Y. Docs, V, 499, 504.
[3] N. Y. Col. Docs. V, 539.

As steps leading to this settlement progressed, to the mind of Samuel Mulford his own grievances and those of the people of eastern Long Island seemed to grow in number and seriousness. In the course of enforcing the acts of trade, customs duties and port at New York, many of Mulford's neighbors lost vessels and cargoes, or parts of their goods, or were put to great expense and inconvenience in other ways. Mulford and his sons were prosecuted for failure to pay the license fees required for permission to carry on their whale fishing. They were also sued for arrears of quit rents, the elder Mulford being prosecuted in the alleged capacity of trustee for the town of Easthampton, though he declared he had not held that office during the last ten years. These suits cost him much time and expense and many long journeys in attending court. He was a member of the assembly and had been so for about ten years. He was now about seventy years of age, a born fighter whose stubborn independence had not been diminished by his years. During the session of 1714 his patience gave way and in a long, repetitious and passionate speech he denounced the government of New York and hurled his defiance at it. The executive, he declared, controlled everything, their past reforms availed nothing, the assembly was forced to follow the lead of the executive and liberty was dead. He later published this speech and its implications, as Hunter interpreted it, were that the dishonesty of previous administrations was being repeated in his own.[1] He therefore submitted the charges to the council and assembly and Mulford was expelled from the house.

Mulford thereupon went to England to lay his grievances before the board of trade and privy council and demand redress.[2] There his charges broadened out into the general claim that in the assembly of New York the remoter country

[1] A copy of this and of other Mulford material is in C. O. 5/1051. Hunter's arguments against Mulford and his sarcastic references to him are in his letters, N. Y. Col. Docs. V, 474, 480, 498, 501, 505, 510. The arguments used before the supreme court in the case involving the royal rights to whales are in C. O. 5/1050, Aa, 136.

[2] "A Memorial of Several Aggrievances and Oppressions, etc.," also "An Information," in which he attacked the courts and explained his claims in connection with the whaling industry. These are printed in Doc. Hist. of N. Y., III, 363.

districts of the north were over represented. Long Island in particular had been discriminated against in the distribution of seats. The salaries which were paid to the Indian commissioners, the land grants which were made to them, and the presents which were annually distributed among the tribesmen were all brought into alignment with this policy and the conclusion was drawn that the colony was being made tributary to the heathen. Upon this subject Mulford talked much while he was in the assembly and was charged with promoting the scheme of a wholesale destruction of the Indians. The peril involved in this led the assembly, in 1717, to send an address of protest to the governor.[1] In reference to Mulford's charge that the sections were unequally represented, to an extent it was of course true in all the provinces, for the system required that the counties should elect a uniform number of representatives, usually two each. These counties which contained cities, boroughs or manors received additional representation for these jurisdictions. In this arrangement, which was a reproduction of the British system, some regard was had to differences of population, and when additions were made to the number of the assembly the new members came from those parts of the province the population of which was increasing. In the case of New York during the first half of the eighteenth century, it was the region of the upper Hudson and Mohawk rivers, while the rate of increase in New York City and Long Island was less than that of the province as a whole.[2] Mulford's claim, moreover, that in making up quotas of direct taxes advantage was taken of the inferior number of representatives from Long Island in order to impose undue burdens on that section could not be substantiated. The council and assembly, in answering this and other charges which he had made in England,[3] declared that in making up quotas taxable wealth as well as population was considered. As a general statement this doubtless was true, though local cabals and the general tendency of rural communities to transfer the burden of taxation to commercial centres, were also in operation.

[1] Ass. J. I, 403.
[2] Spencer, *op. cit.*
[3] C. O. 5/1051, Bb, 148.

That Mulford and his friends had suffered from the crude and arbitrary methods of government then and always in vogue, there can be no doubt. But his voice was like that of one crying in the wilderness and the reputation which he doubtless gained was that of a troublesome, though no unamiable, fanatic. He added one more to the perplexities with which Hunter had to contend. Nicholson, who now bore the added title of general, had been in the colonies for several years, originally under a roving commission from Anne to inquire into their finances *et cetera.* About the results of this errand it is impossible to gain any definite information, except that the churchmen availed themselves of it to boom both Nicholson and their own cause. The churchmen, as we know, were very bitter against Hunter and doubtless looked back with regret to Cornbury and forward with hope to a time when Nicholson should succeed Hunter. This probably would have come about, had it not been for the opportune death of Anne. It was the return of the Whigs to power on the accession of the Hanoverians which prolonged Hunter's administration until he was able to adjust affairs upon a more tolerable basis in his two provinces. Meantime, even while the elements of opposition were so many and his financial condition so hopeless that he said he expected to die in a jail, Hunter, as we have seen, kept up his spirits by composing, with the aid of Morris, his farce called "Androborus, The Man Eater."[1] In this a diverting picture was drawn of the assembly, with its mixed Dutch and English membership, its intrigues and absurdities. The leading political figures of the province, with Nicholson at their head and Vesey in a prominent place, were introduced under fictitious names and by this means the governor was able to pillory his enemies. "The laugh was turned upon them in all companies," says Colden, "and from this laughing humour the people began to be in good humour with their Governor and to despise the idol of the clergy."

In New Jersey the accession of Lovelace, who was a man of integrity, would have ultimately meant the overthrow of the clique which still controlled the council. But his untimely

[1] Colden, *op. cit.*, 202. One printed copy of this is known to exist.

death prevented the consummation of that result. While he was in office, however, a new assembly, with Thomas Gordon as speaker of the lower house, appropriated a very moderate revenue for one year, reduced the severity of the penalties in the militia law, and passed several other important bills. The issues between the warring factions were also again aired. At the request of the lower house, the governor laid before it a copy of the address sent to the queen in 1707 by Ingoldsby, Quary, Coxe and their friends in the council, in which the chief responsibility for the very offensive conduct of the late house was cast on Morris and Jennings.[1] The house asked that the council should appear before the governor to make good its charges, and that the house itself might be present. On the signers of the address desiring more time in which to collect evidence in support of their charges, Chief Justice Mompesson, one of the signers, admitted that he had put his name to the paper without examining its contents, as was often done in such cases,[2] but signed the later and more detailed set of charges which was submitted by the anti-proprietary group.[3] In this, beginning with Gordon's sharp practice in the East Jersey election of 1703, they traced with great bitterness and violence of language the conduct of the proprietary opposition throughout Cornbury's administration. Though Jennings was now dead, he came in for strong criticism as to his conduct while reading the remonstrance before Cornbury and on other occasions; but the arraignment of Morris and Willocks was prolonged and extremely violent. In view of Morris' career as a whole, it is impossible to doubt the truth of much that was here stated about him, and it all throws a sinister light on the political tactics then in vogue in some of the colonies and on the extent to which they were allowed to pervert private relations as well.

The lower house, in addition to sending its answer to the charges of the council to the queen, attacked Peter Sonmans in matters affecting not only his gross violations of private morals, but his oppressive conduct as councillor and justice of the peace on several occasions.[4] To this he presented a long reply to the governor and no prosecution followed at that

[1] N. J. Arch. II, 364 *et seq.*

[2] *Ibid.*, 374.

[3] *Ibid.*, 390–415.

[4] N. J Arch. III, 385, 394, 416–460; Tanner, 399.

time. Fauconier, however, was removed from the office of receiver general, he failing to submit vouchers for his accounts of the last revenue. Miles Forster, a proprietor, was appointed as receiver general and treasurer in his place. In fact, the death of Lovelace saved the anti-proprietors from overthrow at that time, for Ingoldsby, though an order in council for the recall of his commission as lieutenant governor in both provinces had been issued in 1706, the warrant for which had not been signed and sent, now assumed the office in New Jersey and held it until the arrival of Governor Hunter.[1] The order finally revoking his commission was not signed at Windsor until October, 1709. Ingoldsby supported the Coxe faction, as Cornbury had done, and helped to perpetuate its hold on the council.

The important event of Ingoldsby's brief administration was the Nicholson-Vetch expedition against Canada. While this diverted attention to an extent from domestic politics, the two inevitably interacted with a result which further illustrated the situation in New Jersey.[2] The council, of course, was favorable in every way to the orders of the queen and the program of her agents. But the assembly, with its Quaker membership, was opposed to the raising of a quota by a draft, and insisted that only volunteers should be called out. By sharp tactics on both sides a bill, intended to appropriate £3000 for the expedition, was defeated. The house also defeated a bill from the council for preventing persons leaving the province to escape service on the expedition. After some further bickerings Ingoldsby adjourned the assembly for more than a month, and then he and his supporters in the council prepared an address to the queen, in which they charged the Quakers with responsibility for the delinquency of the province and urged that they be excluded from office. But on the solicitation of Nicholson and Vetch, the assembly was called together again after a recess of ten days and promptly passed bills for encouraging volunteers, raising £3000 and issuing £3000 in bills of credit. These were all agreed to by the council, though not without some futile attempts at amendment. After the expedition, a new assem-

[1] N. J. Arch. III, 460, 469, 475.

[2] *Ibid.*, XIII, 329 *et seq.*; Tanner, 401.

bly having been elected, a controversy arose over the accounts of the expenditures and the issues of currency which were occasioned thereby. Some petty irregularities were brought to light, which furnished occasion for nothing except more party recrimination.

At the time of the accession of Hunter to the governorship the council of East Jersey proprietors had been virtually dissolved; their records and the management of their affairs were in the hands of Sonmans. Little revenue from quit rents had been raised and such as there was had come into his hands. The old opposition in Elizabethtown and Monmouth still existed and supported Sonmans and Coxe in order to escape quit rents. From Monmouth came at this time the most active opponents of the proprietors — the Bownes, Salter, the Lawrences and Gershom Mott. Hunter's advice, given in his first speech to the council,[1] was that they should leave disputes about property to the courts and join in efforts for the public welfare. But the dispute had been too long and bitter for this and the courts were not to be trusted. There were bills which by his instructions should be enacted, and harmony was the condition necessary for this.

The assembly proceeded actively with legislation, in part on lines suggested by the governor, until it had perfected nineteen measures. They included a bill regulating elections, which was required by Hunter's instructions, a bill relieving those injured by the militia act, and a bill so regulating the qualifications of jurors that Quakers might serve.[2] When these and the other measures came before the council, they rejected all but five,[3] defeating them in some cases on the second reading and in others so clogging them with amendments as to necessitate their rejection. Only three important bills were saved — the act of support, that amending the act for the currency of bills of credit and the measure, reviving the militia act.

In the course of proceedings over these bills, the house through a committee tried to get access to the council minutes

[1] N. J. Arch. XIII, 427; Tanner, 625.

[2] N. J. Arch. IV, 19 *et seq.*

[3] *Ibid.*, 51 *et seq.*; Arch. XIII, 434 *et seq.*

to see what action had been taken. Being unable to secure a copy from Basse, the secretary, they applied to the governor and he procured the favor which they desired. The house then desired to see the papers which related to the Canada expedition and for a time was thwarted in this by Basse and the council, though finally the request was granted. A special application, however, had to be made to Hunter before the assembly secured proof of the reasons which led Lawrence and Mott to vote against the appropriation for the expedition. They were then censured and Mott was finally expelled. William Sanford was also expelled, because he had signed the address sent by Ingoldsby and the council to the queen in Cornbury's time. They then sent to the governor an answer to these charges and an able arraignment of the abuses of Cornbury's time and later.[1] Charges were then made against Hall and Basse for numerous illegal acts,[2] the one as a judge and the other as secretary. Sonmans and Pinhorne were also involved. The courts and general administration were shown to be corrupt and arbitrary, and the two houses had become as hostile toward one another as ever.

Hunter, however, had by these means learned what the situation was and had naturally made up his mind that the proprietary party represented the true sentiments of the province. As soon as the session closed, he wrote a full account of affairs to the board of trade and insisted that Pinhorne, Sonmans, Coxe and Hall be removed from the council. An understanding was also reached that no further serious attempt at legislation should be made until such action had been taken in England, and the West Jersey Society supported his demands. In August, 1712, the board of trade, under suggestions from Paul Dominique and his party among the proprietors, recommended their removal and the appointment of Anderson, William Morris, John Hamilton and Reading in their places. Elisha Parker and Thomas Byerly were recommended for vacancies.[3] Though opposition was made by Dockwra in England and by the Anglican clergy in the prov-

[1] N. J. Arch. IV, 24.

[2] *Ibid.*, 71, 79 *et seq.*

[3] *Ibid.*, IV, 115, 140, 152, 168–171, 182. William Morris died before his appointment was made.

ince, action in accordance with the desires of Hunter was taken. Jameson and Farmar succeeded Mompesson and Pinhorne as justices of the supreme court.

Being now secure of a proprietary majority in both houses, the governor met the assembly again in December, 1713.[1] Harmony was the keynote, both in the governor's speech and in the reply. The coming of peace in Europe and America was not unfavorable to this feeling. An unusually long session was held, continuing until March seventeenth. More than thirty bills were passed, many being of importance, and in all the business of the session good feeling prevailed. It was shown in many successful conferences. One of the bills most needed was that which should sanction, once for all, the affirmation of the Quakers and thus guarantee to them the exercise of political rights beyond dispute. "Our men of voice," wrote Hunter, "exerted their talent against it, but in vain." Another measure to prevent malicious informations had also been a subject of earlier conflict. Another useful statute was the one regulating the practice of the law and lowering the cost of litigation.[2] An act confirming conveyances of land was passed, but a bill confirming the rights of the proprietors of West Jersey came too late in the session to receive the governor's assent. There was a general inspection of accounts by the assembly and appropriations for the support of government and the payment of claims in arrear were amicably made, £500 a year and £100 for expenses being fixed as the governor's share. Hunter had kept himself in the background throughout the session and no evidence appears in the journal of the assembly that he interfered with its proceedings.

But the death of the queen and the accession of George I, necessitating also the issue of a new commission to Hunter, brought this assembly to an end. In connection with the new election and even with the issue of a new commission Hunter's enemies had another opportunity to attack him and oppose his policy. In England Dr. Daniel Coxe and the earl of Clarendon opposed the reappointment of Hunter, but in vain.[3] In the province the opposition, led by Coxe

[1] N. J. Arch. XIII, 484 *et seq.*; IV, 195 *et seq.*; Tanner, 420.
[2] See Arch. IV, 196.
[3] N. J. Arch, IV, 199, 202, 203.

and Basse and supported by Talbot and other high churchmen, revived, especially in the western division, and a majority against Hunter was returned. The new assembly was called to meet at Amboy [1] and Coxe was chosen speaker. The governor, in his opening speech, referred to the charges made by Dr. Daniel Coxe and his son in England and that they pretended to have been instructed from this side. The governor bade defiance to the most malicious, conscious as he was that he had always acted for the public welfare. He reminded the assembly of the need of support for the government, but apart from that, so much good legislation had been passed at the last session that the present sitting of the assembly might be short.

But a controversy was at once begun by the opposition over the right of the governor to call the assembly at Amboy. It requested to be removed to Burlington, on the plea that by one of the acts of Ingoldsby's administration, which had been confirmed by the crown, all sessions should be held there. But the instructions, in harmony with the arrangement made after the surrender, provided that sessions should be held alternately at Amboy and Burlington, and Hunter took the ground that the power to call sessions was a part of the power of the crown. The action of the late queen in approving the law, he contended, would have to be confirmed by the new king. After some sparring between the house and the governor, he prorogued it for about a month. When the time came for resuming the session, Coxe and several of his friends stayed away, so that a quorum could not be obtained. Warrants were sent to several of the absentees and in this way a majority was obtained. These met and elected John Kinsey speaker, and organized the house under the control of Hunter's supporters. It voted that Coxe's absence was a breach of trust and expelled him. The absentees were specially summoned, and Lawrence was arrested and forced to acknowledge his guilt. Seven others were expelled for ignoring the governor's warrants. To fill these vacancies new elections were ordered and those who had been expelled were declared incapable of sitting. By this strenuous action a house wholly agreeable to Hunter and the proprietary party was secured,

[1] N. J. Arch, XIV, 7 *et seq.*

and it continued in existence during the remaining five years of his term. The course of legislation and government thenceforth proceeded smoothly till the close of Hunter's administration. The Cornbury clique had been effectually defeated.

Ecclesiastical ambitions and jealousies were even more closely interwoven with this struggle in New Jersey than they were in New York. As is shown in another connection, the plans of Coxe, Talbot and their associates for a colonial bishop centered about Burlington. For that reason, and taking advantage of a certain sectional spirit which survived long after East and West Jersey were combined into one province, the Coxe faction tried to make Burlington the sole meeting place of the assembly. Hunter, as a Whig and a secularist, was opposed to these strivings, and the accession of his party to power in England soon proved as well a death blow to Coxe and the Burlington clique in New Jersey. The right of Perth Amboy, as settled after the surrender, to share equally in advantages which came with sessions of the assembly was firmly established and the balance was maintained between the two sections of the province. The way toward more peaceful relations for the Quakers was also opened by the defeat of the extreme Anglican faction in the province. In 1717 the act of 1709 by which the attempt had been made to make Burlington the exclusive meeting place of the assembly was repealed and the repeal was duly confirmed in England. In 1713, as we have seen, an act was passed not only allowing Quakers to affirm but enabling them also to serve as jurors. The board of trade allowed this to lie by probationary for four years when, hearing no complaint, it was confirmed. At this juncture a number of the old opponents of Hunter petitioned the king in council for the repeal of the act, because it was repugnant to an English law of 7 and 8 Wm. III, continued by later acts, which excluded Quakers from jury service. Of this petition no effective notice was taken.[1]

[1] N. J. Arch. IV, 292, 341, 366; Tanner, *op. cit.*, 592.

CHAPTER XX

MASSACHUSETTS AND NEW ENGLAND DURING THE ADMINISTRATION OF JOSEPH DUDLEY, 1702–1715

A DECADE had passed since the issue of the second Massachusetts charter, and yet with the exception of the disallowance of a number of her acts she had been practically self-governing. This result had been effected by the appointment of Massachusetts men as governor and lieutenant governor and by the fact that Lord Bellomont's connection with New England had been little more than nominal. With the appointment of Joseph Dudley, in 1702, another New England man had been selected for the governorship. But he was a man of a different type from Phips and in a more influential position than Stoughton, and with him royal administration in the full sense of the word began. For the first time Massachusetts was brought to feel the extent of the change which had been made in her condition by the issue of the new charter, the effect of having a genuine royal executive in her midst, one who understood and sympathized with the imperial policy of the time and was prepared to test its possibilities.

Since his failure to secure the appointment on the death of Phips, Dudley had been slowly but steadily strengthening his influence and preparing for eventualities. His correspondence with Lord Cutts and other friends in England show that he was a faithful adherent, where his interests were enlisted, and that he was not without social attractiveness. His letters during the same period to his wife and son reveal the fact that the resources upon which he was living were narrow, though he was able to educate two of his children in England, and that he longed to return to his family and to the only country which he could call his home.[1] He was living

[1] 2 Proc. Mass. Hist. Soc. II, 177 *et seq*; 6 Mass. Hist. Soc. Colls. III, 513 *et seq.*

during a period of change both in England and New England and his career thus far, notwithstanding the offices he had held, had been to a large extent that of an adventurer. The same had been true of many of the leading statesmen of England, emphatically so of the man who was now being launched on the career which was to make him Duke of Marlborough. Cutts and Dudley worked for years in support of their mutual interests. In 1701 Dudley was elected to parliament. There his acquaintanceship broadened and men became aware of his wide knowledge of colonial affairs. To the Society for the Propagation of the Gospel he contributed a paper on the state of religion in the English plantations in North America, and later was admitted as one of the lay members of the Society. He identified himself with the English Church, as he did with the men who seemed likely to succeed in politics, though not to an extent which would make it necessary for him to break wholly with Congregationalism, when he should return to New England. Through John Chamberlain and Richard Steele he maintained a certain connection with the literary world in London. Godfrey Dellius, the Dutch minister of Albany whom Bellomont had driven into exile, found a sympathizer in Dudley and gave him ardent support. Constantine Phips was won over to Dudley, though Sir Henry Ashurst, the other agent of Massachusetts, remained his tireless enemy and "spent many days" in efforts to prevent his appointment as governor. Even the Mathers were placated for a time, though by what means is not clear.[1] It was a selfish and scheming age and Dudley played his game well, developing by prolonged experience a natural capacity as a politician which was of no mean order. After Bellomont's death it was the desire of the old-line conservatives in Massachusetts that Wait Winthrop should be appointed lieutenant governor, and with that in view it was arranged that he should go as agent to England. But the news that Dudley was to be appointed reached Ashurst before that plan could be executed. It was a few months after Randolph, supported by Dudley, had tried to

[1] Kimball, *op. cit.* 74. In 6 Mass. Hist. Colls. III, 501, is a letter from Dudley to Cotton Mather in 1689, in which Dudley tries to show that in Andros' council he had always worked for the liberties of New England.

secure the passage of the first bill for the recall of all the proprietary charters. Ashurst had fought this with all his might. On July 10, 1701, Ashurst wrote to the Winthrops, that on the day before he had appeared against Dudley before the lords justices, in whose hands lay the question of his appointment as governor. "I was not allowed to have counsel," he writes, "but I got all the records and papers I could get and the best counsell I could get. I was three hours debating the cause of New England. I produced the records about Leisler's business, when I heard his friends and he denyed hee had anything to doe in that trial, . . . Hee put in a memoriall in which he denyed his share of Leisler. . . . He also produced a leter from yor Speaker that said that I was dismissed from my agency two years agoe, . . . and that the cause of my prosicuting him was because I was turned out of my agency." Lord Cutts appeared for Dudley and an address, signed by "young Pateridge & Mr. Richards" and many others, was produced desiring that Dudley might be speedily sent to Massachusetts. Blathwayt appears dimly in the background, pulling the wires for Dudley, while the recent appointments of Atwood and Byfield to judicial positions in the colonies were rightly regarded as opposed to the traditional interests of New England. "Honest Mr. Mason" was among the few who appeared with Ashurst. "If I stop him now, I hope it will be for ever." But the general court and people of Massachusetts sent no protest, and Ashurst was beaten from the start. Before his plans could be well launched,[1] Dudley secured the appointment. He had developed an interest with so many politicians that the death of William III and the succession of Anne did not affect his appointment. Thomas Povey, captain of the queen's foot guards, received the office of lieutenant governor.

Dudley was assigned solely to the government of Massachusetts and New Hampshire. The ambitious plan of colonial union which had appeared for a brief time above the horizon with the appointment of Bellomont now sank finally out of sight and New York, in its relations with New England, lapsed back into its natural status, which very much re-

[1] Hutchinson, II, 120; Winthrop Papers, 6 Mass. Hist. Colls. V, 88–92; *ibid.*, III, 86.

sembled that of a foreign community. The people of New England might well be thankful that they were not handed over to the tender mercies of Cornbury and his crew, or even submitted to such measures of reform as Hunter advocated. But they knew so little about these that they were unable, even by way of comparison, to make use of them as a source of comfort amid their own more or less fancied tribulations. It would have been a wholesome lesson for the extreme critics of Dudley's administration to have known what was going on in New York at that time, but so narrow and sectional were they and so possessed by the spirit of ancestor worship that they could approve only that which was framed after the meagre pattern of the first generation of New England settlers.

Dudley was appointed when the tide of imperialism, which had begun to flow under the Stuarts, was at the later flood. Apparently it had not begun to recede and it might still reach such a height that it would sweep away all chartered liberties. In the first destructive onslaught under Charles and James, Dudley had shared, though he had claimed that his part had really been that of a mediator. That aspect of the case his contemporaries, outside of the narrow official circle, were unable to perceive and ever after, among them, he incurred the reputation of a time server, an intriguer or even a traitor. Had he not been a New England man, such charges could never have been made, for so far as he was able he lived up to the instructions he received from the crown and was true to the colonial policy which at the time it was trying to carry into execution. He received the elaborate instructions which were given to all governors, and of special importance for Massachusetts were the requirements that a permanent fort should be built at Pemaquid, that a fixed and adequate salary should be granted to the governor, and that all money should be issued from the treasury by warrant under the governor's hand and with the advice of the council. Dudley was as conversant as a man of colonial birth well could be with the spirit and methods of British administration. He knew the law and he was skilled in the art of administration, with its combination of persuasion, influence exerted through patronage, and imperious command. He was the first royal governor who took up in Massachusetts, with seriousness, intelligence and during a prolonged period, the problems of administration in the way in which they were conceived by those who were most responsible for the conduct of the government both in Great Britain and the colonies. That he measured up well to the requirements of such a position, and that in one of the most important colonies and one of the most difficult to govern, his record amply proves. One might personally like or dislike him, as they did Hunter, Spotswood or Lewis Morris, but no one in his time could deny that a man of varied gifts and resources was occupying the governor's chair. The correspondence which he left is not so voluminous as that of some, but it is clear and, though in some respects intensely partisan, there is no mistaking its intent. His speeches to the general court were models of direct and forcible statements. The policy which he advocated was in general statesmanlike and such as commended itself to the best minds who were concerned with the affairs of the imperial executive. The fact, too, that Dudley was a New England man was stamped upon every feature of his administration, relieving him from the necessity of learning the character of his people at the outset and enabling him to combine tact with initiative and efficiency in most that he did. Dudley was still unavoidably a mediator between the old and the new in New England.

The most immediate and pressing need of the time was that of an adequate defence of the frontier. The conduct of the war in Massachusetts has already been described, and in reference to it all are agreed that, with the exception of the fiasco of 1707, Dudley used the means and methods which were available with judgment and vigor. For that failure he was only remotely and indirectly responsible. For the later failures, the responsibility for which rested wholly on the British government, or those whom it put in command, no colonial official was to blame. The policy which he advocated concerning Pemaquid was wise and statesmanlike, and it was not his fault that it was not adopted. The raids which were organized by Dudley contributed to the wearing down process, and that, under the circumstances, was the only effective way of bringing Indian and French outrages on the New England frontier to an end. It was doubtless the general satisfaction with Dudley's conduct of the war and the confidence which his leadership in that inspired that enabled him to avoid serious conflicts with the assembly. His administration, on the whole, was a quiet one, and did not compare in point of factional conflicts with those of many royal governors. This, of itself, affords sufficient proof of the governor's ability and his general success. No one, moreover, can deny the wisdom from the military standpoint of the effort, with which he was concerned, to bring the militia of New England, so far as possible, under a single command. But, as things were, that was impossible and Dudley only shared in a defeat which was common to all who participated in the effort.

It was on the eve of the declaration of war between England and France that Dudley was installed as governor and first met the general court. As when, more than fifteen years before, he had made his notable speech as president of the Dominion of New England, so now he addressed himself directly to imperial interests. They stood on the eve of a war, he said, the object of which was to maintain the balance of Europe and check the "exhorbitant growing power of France."[1] As under Elizabeth England saw the Spanish forced to abandon the hope of universal monarchy, so under Anne might they also see the defeat of the unjust endeavors of the French king. With slight regard for the peculiar pride of New England, but with strict adherence to the truth, as imperialists and mercantilists saw it, he told them that they were not so immediately profitable to the crown as were the southern and island colonies. They were, therefore, expected to promote in all ways the production of naval stores, which were much needed at this crisis, and make these their staple commodity. They must also provide a ready supply of men and money for defence against the French; and it was in this connection that he began to urge the rebuilding of the fort at Pemaquid. He closed with an appeal for a fixed salary for the governor, lieutenant governor, secretary, judges and other officers, reminding Massachusetts with truth and yet with some exaggeration, that she lagged behind the other provinces in this matter.

[1] Journal of the Upper House, June 16, 1702.

It was only in the case of a part of the colonies that the salary of their governors was paid wholly or in part with the help of frequent appropriations by assemblies. In the case of the larger island colonies provision was made for this out of the permanent revenue of the colonies themselves, the 4½ per cent export duty on sugar in Barbadoes and the Leeward Islands, tavern licences and an impost on liquors in Jamaica, export duties on tobacco in Virginia and Maryland with some additional levies on the first mentioned province.[1] The expenditure for the governor's salary was a part of the establishment of the provinces in question, though its political importance was much greater than the salaries of minor officials or expenditures for defence which might be included. In New York, New Jersey, New Hampshire and Massachusetts, a permanent revenue had not been secured and the governors were provided for by annual grants from the legislatures, very moderate in amount. In New York it had been £600 sterling per annum, which was pronounced by the board of trade "no ways sufficient." With the establishment of the board of trade it became the purpose of the British government to secure a permanent and adequate revenue in all the royal provinces. As the New England colonies, prior to 1690, had developed but the rudiments of a salary system and were accustomed only to annual appropriations,[2] it was natural that Massachusetts should be most reluctant to adopt this system and that a prolonged and violent controversy might arise there over the salary question. That proved to be the case, though in New York the struggle developed more rapidly than it did in Massachusetts. It was in those two provinces that the conflict over this question became most bitter.

Toward the close of Phips' administration an act had been passed appropriating £500 "for his service and expense since his arrival."[3] This was in harmony with Massachusetts custom and was to be in vogue in the other New England colonies for a long time to come. It was the equivalent of

[1] Blathwayt's Journal, Jan. 31, 1704/5 and other entries. Beer, Old Colonial System, I, 203–223; Acts P. C. Col. I, 847; II, 427–432.

[2] Osgood, Am. Colonies in the 17th Century, I, 483 *et seq.*

[3] Mass. Acts and Res. I, 109, 787; Palfrey, IV, 141.

the system of presents in the other colonies, against which the crown in its instructions to the governors had set its face. Phips made a faint protest against both the form and the amount of these appropriations, but no notice was taken of it. Annual grants of £500 continued through his administration.[1] In 1699 and again in 1700 the sum of £1000, in Massachusetts currency, was granted to the earl of Bellomont, though without the express statement that this was his annual salary.[2] The earl resolved never to ask them for anything, though he repeatedly complained that he was their yearly pensioner, that no provision was made for a governor's house and that his support was so narrow that he could not live upon it.[3] Thus the situation was brought to the attention of the British authorities and this, in connection with similar complaints from other colonies, led to the framing of the royal instruction and the opening of the long campaign for adequate and fixed salaries. In 1703 the board of trade reported to the queen that a letter should be written to Massachusetts that, in consideration of its great privileges, a suitable allowance should be settled on the governor without limitation of time, or else effective remedies would be sought. It was also advised that similar letters, though without the threat, should be sent to New Hampshire and New Jersey, and that £600 be added to the salary of the governor of New York out of the royal revenue there. Governors should also be forbidden to receive presents from the assemblies. This report was accepted and royal letters enforcing these commands were sent to all the provinces concerned.[4]

Dudley was expressly instructed to urge the establishment of permanent and adequate salaries for the governor, lieutenant governor and judges and the building of a house for the governor. The first response of the assembly to these demands, when presented by Dudley, was a temporary appropriation of £500 to the governor, the sum which had been annually granted to Phips. The assembly also declared that

[1] Acts and Res. I, 174, 188.

[2] *Ibid.*, 395, 437.

[3] Reports of B. T. to earl of Jersey on salaries, June 12 and 22, 1700; Bellomont to B. T., July 15, 1700; Palfrey, IV, 177.

[4] Journal and Entry Book, B. T. Plants. Gen.; Acts P. C. Col. II, 431; N. Y. Col. Docs. IV, 1040.

the settling of salaries upon royal appointees was new to it and that it could not be thought agreeable to the existing constitution of the province. The present was accepted. Proceeding at once to the eastern parts in order to inspect the defences along the coast as far as Pemaquid, Dudley met the assembly of New Hampshire. It passed three acts for the support of the government and the prosecution of the war — one imposing a land tax, another an export duty on lumber, and a third a powder duty to keep up the fort at the entrance of the Piscataqua. Dudley was much impressed with the liberality of so small and poor a province, and from this appropriation hoped to secure £250 as his salary.[1]

When the governor met the general court at Boston in the fall he renewed his demand, reminding them, with a reference to the low salaries of the judges, that if they hoped to have a government they must support it. The house replied through a committee that, considering the circumstances of the province, it was "not convenient to state salaries, but to allow as the Great and General Court shall from time to time see necessary." The council sent this resolve back for reconsideration, and the house thereupon resolved to add £100 to the amount previously granted to the governor. To this the council replied that it was not "a suitable maintenance for his Excellency," but the house refused to reconsider its vote. Then Dudley called the representatives into the council chamber and read them his instructions respecting salaries, but they remained obdurate and the sum that was offered was finally accepted.

In September, 1703, Dudley read to the court the letter from the queen to which reference was made above. The project of rebuilding Pemaquid was now being actively discussed and the representatives had sent an address to the queen in reference to this subject without consulting the council. A dispute thereupon arose between the houses over a claim of the council to inspect the journals of the lower house. It was also thought that the governor was using considerable discretion in the expenditure of the public funds. These circumstances, together with the demands of the governor, led the representatives, in November, to a formal statement of

[1] C. O. 5/910; E. B. N. Eng., Dudley to B. T., Nov. 11, 1702.

policy. "As it is the undoubted privilege of the English nation," said they, "to raise any sum or sums of money when and to dispose of them how they see cause, and so hath been from Henry III and confirmed by Edward I and ever since continued as the unquestioned right of the subject; so we hope and expect ever to enjoy the same under our most gracious Queen Anne and her successors and therefore do account it inconsistent with her Majesty's interest here, and that it may prove prejudicial to her Majesty's subjects in this province, to state perpetual salaries." According to this interpretation English history would be a very simple tale and its existing practice such as would cripple any executive and end in the concentration of all the powers of government in the hands of a legislative assembly and those to whom it chose to intrust the execution of its commands. The binding power of royal instructions upon colonial assemblies and the claim that these orders were to be regarded as law for the colonists were also brought squarely into question by the policy, and it was one to which Massachusetts continued to adhere. The issue was not so sharply drawn in the other provinces, but the attitude of most of them very much resembled that of the Puritan colony. At the close of this session Dudley wrote to the earl of Nottingham, that the people of Massachusetts loved not the crown and government of England and were ready to put slights upon it.[1]

At the election, in May, 1703, Dudley began the vetoing of the choice of councillors. He told the house that some men of "good ability" had been left out and others of "little or mean estate" had been chosen. Therefore he expunged five of the names in the list, among them being those of Elisha Cooke and Thomas Oakes, who were determined supporters of the principles which had obtained under the first charter.[2] Five others were chosen in their places and approved. At the election of the following May two of the rejected ones, Elisha Cooke and Peter Sargent, the latter a kinsman of Ashurst and with Cooke an opponent of Dudley's policy, were again returned and through its speaker the house asked the governor to accept them; but he curtly refused and "dismissed the house to

[1] C. O. 5/898; Palfrey, IV, 290.

[2] Journal of the Upper House, May 27, 1703.

their business." This time there was a delay of two weeks before the vacancies were filled. Still again, in 1706, Elisha Cooke was returned and a third time this choice, as well as that of another candidate, was vetoed.[1] In 1708 also two councillors were rejected and their places were filled by the assembly.[2] In general the council was submissive to the lead of the governor and no further eliminations were needed. The personal dislike which Dudley had toward Cooke and Oakes, in 1705 led to the exercise by the governor of the power granted to him in the charter of vetoing the choice of speaker by the representatives. The house made the weak plea that the exclusive right of choosing their speaker was secured by the law which provided that it should be sole judge of the elections of its members. Both houses also voted that by the charter the governor did not have the power which he claimed, the language of the instrument, however, being most explicit to the contrary. As the war and public business were pressing, Dudley wished to avoid delay and therefore finally accepted Oakes, along with the full list of councillors. The board of trade later assured Dudley of its approval of his assertion of this right and thought that it was not proper that it should be given up.[3]

In the management of the war and of negotiation with the Indians and by virtue of the authority which he had to issue money from the treasury under his warrant, Dudley sometimes exercised discretion in ordering expenditures which had not been fully or expressly authorized by law or order of the general court. In this he had at least the nominal advice of the council. Upon this point the court repeatedly showed its sensitiveness and made various declarations upon the subject. Finally, in November, 1704,[4] £50 was in this way paid to Povey, the lieutenant governor, for his services as commander of the Castle. This the house asserted to be an arbitrary act and a violation of English liberties and insisted that the sum be returned to the treasury. The council in reply called attention to an act in Bellomont's time by which the estab-

[1] Palfrey, IV, 291, 299.

[2] B. T. N. Eng. O. P. C. O. 5/865, Dudley to Board, July 10, 1708.

[3] C. O. 5/912; E. B. N. Eng. Board to Dudley, Feb. 4, 1705/6.

[4] Journal of the Upper House, Nov. 10.

lishment of the Castle was fixed, to the power given the governor by charter to order expenditure by warrant, and to the provision of the act granting a duty on wines and other imposts, that the revenues from it should be used for subsisting and paying the wages of soldiers in service at the Castle and forts within the province. The resolve of the house was therefore pronounced not only an unjust reflection on the governor and council, but in itself a nullity and of no force. In 1708 the representatives again complained of a number of small sums expended by the governor and council which they considered had not been authorized either expressly or under the head of contingent expenses. The council was able to show that they either were expenses contingent to the general duties of defence, or were petty expenditures on ceremonial occasions and so unworthy of notice.[1] With this the parsimonious legislators seem to have been satisfied, and it is safe to say that in the matter of public expenditures the honesty of Dudley's administration was in strongest contrast to the irregularities which were disgracing Cornbury at this time in New York.

During the closing months of 1704 and in 1705 the questions of the rebuilding the fort at Pemaquid and the granting of permanent salaries were most pointedly discussed. With these the claim was also urged, at the instance of New Hampshire, that Massachusetts should contribute toward the maintenance of the fort at the mouth of the Piscataqua. The council now supported Dudley in asking that a just and honorable support be given him. The house, on its part, had offended the governor by quietly sending an address of its own to the queen against the rebuilding of Pemaquid. They were also frequently asking the crown to send over supplies and munitions of war. Dudley now received a letter from the board of trade informing him of these things and declaring it unreasonable that the assembly should expect to be furnished with stores of war at the expense of the crown — which they had already received to the value of £1000 — while they refused to provide salaries for the governor and other officers. Those considerations Dudley laid emphatically before the assembly, with an assertion of his knowledge of the interests

[1] C. O. 5/790; Journal of Upper House, Sess. of May to July, 1708.

of the province and desire to promote them and his assurance that their affairs would be improved if they thought so of their governor and gave a favorable reception to his servants. The board of trade had also written that the neglect of the queen's commands would show the general assembly to be undeserving of her favor and bounty toward them. At the session of February, 1704/5, Dudley told the house that he was very sensible that their neglect of some of the royal commands had interrupted the course of supplies to the province. The cost of the war had become very burdensome, the bills of credit were depreciating and a proposal was sent up from the house, but rejected by the governor and council, for paying the province debt in silver at the current rate of eight shillings per ounce. During the session of the following September these questions were brought to a decisive issue by the rejection on the part of the assembly of all the proposals of the crown. As to salaries it stated that the ability and circumstances of the province differed so from time to time that the settling of fixed salaries might be prejudicial to the colonists. The maintenance of this attitude was made almost inevitable by the suspicion, amounting approximately to knowledge, that Dudley was working for the recall of the charters and would welcome the decay of much that was cherished in the moral and religious, as well as the political, system of the Puritans. This view was confirmed in the minds of many by the publication in Massachusetts of a letter written by Paul Dudley, the son of the governor, in which he spoke of the affairs of government and the college being disposed of in private meetings and said that the country would never be worth living in for lawyers and gentlemen until the charter was taken away.[1] He and his father, he added, sometimes talked of the queen's establishing a court of chancery in the province and he had written to Blathwayt about it.[2] Such reports and suspicions as these made the Mathers and men of their type prefer as governor even a free

[1] Hutchinson, II, 140.

[2] B. T. Journal for Feb. and March, 1703/4, and July 17, 1705, shows that the board of trade was consulting the attorney general on the possibility, consistently with the charter, of the queen establishing such a court and that Ashurst appear against it.

liver like Sir Charles Hobby to the continuance of Dudley in office. But the opposition to the governor did not become formidable, while his services during the war were of great value. He was also a man of some property, and from this and his official sources of income was able to live tolerably, while he doubtless thought that it was better to take £500 or £700 a year than nothing at all. Thus it was that during his administration an acute crisis in the salary controversy was avoided. As to Pemaquid, when it was seen to be impossible to secure a fort there, Dudley made the very reasonable suggestion that a colony of English or Scotch families be planted there to hold the region against the French.[1]

Of the relations which existed between Massachusetts and the other New England colonies during the second intercolonial war — which was the period of Dudley's administration — much has been said in other connections. As the war was the interest of supreme importance, it led to the bestowment on Dudley, as upon his predecessors, of the command of the militia of the two corporate colonies. In the case of Rhode Island he made a serious, but futile effort to enforce his claim under this commission. Not even that was attempted in the case of Connecticut, and such cooperation as existed between it and Massachusetts during the war was attained as the result of negotiation or of such impulse as resulted from England assuming the leadership. Very little aid upon land was secured from Rhode Island, her activity being directed more toward the sea. Her trade relations were becoming extensive and privateering, with its accompaniment of illegal trade, absorbed much of her energies during the war. In accordance with the traditions of the previous century, Governor Cranston claimed vice-admiralty powers and issued commissions to privateers.

Until 1706, or somewhat later, Dudley, as is well known, was actively interested in the plans for the recall of the proprietary and corporate charters. Dudley's own statement of his attitude was that he was not an enemy of charter government, but rather of the men who on pretence of such a government rendered no obedience to the crown.[2] His criti-

[1] B. T. N. Eng., O. P. C. O. 5/864. Dudley to B. T. Feb. 1, 1705/6.
[2] C. O. 5/912, Dudley to B. T., October 2, 1706.

cisms were immediately directed against Rhode Island and Connecticut. The latter, because of her orderly government, he respected and, however hopeless he might be of overcoming her opposition, he never accused her of irregularities. But charges of this kind, in his letters home, he was constantly making against Rhode Island. The simple and primitive methods which there obtained, provoked his contempt, a large element in which was the feeling which nearly all colonial aristocrats entertained toward Quakers. From the beginning of his administration until he became absorbed in the larger military operation after 1706, and had at the same time to defend himself against serious charges, Dudley poured in to the British authorities a continuous series of complaints against these two colonies.

To the earl of Nottingham he wrote that Rhode Island had rejected military control and admiralty jurisdiction and had made the enforcement of the acts of trade in Massachusetts almost impossible. This was due to the issue by Rhode Island of commissions to privateers, for which she had not authority and those who went to sea thus furnished had much the appearance of pirates. Atwood, to whose doings in New York as well as his tribulations as judge of admiralty for the northern district reference has elsewhere been made, had gone to England and Newton, the deputy judge, was only an ordinary attorney and had no estate in New England. He had condemned three prizes which had been brought in under Cranston's commissions, thus recognizing these in derogation of the vice admiralty commission which Dudley had proclaimed at Newport. The figure made by the governor of Rhode Island, continued Dudley, was scarcely more than that of a head borough in England, and yet that colony possessed the best harbor and outlet in North America.[1] Was it any wonder that sailors and others fit for service ran away from the royal provinces to such a place, where was no government? In raising troops for Jamaica and for the war on the frontier Dudley claimed to have had experience of this kind.[2] The elective tenure of members of the council, as well as of assemblymen, made them absolutely dependent on the

[1] C. O. 5/863, B. T. N. E., O. P., Dudley to Nottingham, Oct. to Dec., 1702.
[2] C. O. 5/910, Dudley to B. T., Nov. 10, 1702.

people. To Dudley it was an offence that only common men, and not men of estates, were chosen, and hence her majesty had no manner of service from them.[1] At the close of 1703 he wrote, that Rhode Island had not had a tax of a penny in the pound for this seven years. To statements of this kind, which were leading the board of trade to write letters of warning respecting cooperation in defence and the evils of illegal trade, Brenton added the report that sheep in increasing numbers were kept on the islands in Narragansett bay, on Block island and Nantucket, and that their wool was carried in small boats to the mainland and formed the material used in a flourishing industry.[2]

Dudley's relations with Connecticut involved him in the Mohegan controversy, and also with Palmes, Hallam and the group of malcontents about New London, who were engaged in what proved a hopeless contest with that colony. The partisan attitude which Dudley's commission assumed in reference to the Indians still further prejudiced the colony against him. For a time the imperialists seemed to have the upper hand, for beginning in 1704 and continuing at intervals until 1706, the board of trade and other authorities in England were clearly preparing for another assault in parliament on the proprieties and, in addition to South Carolina, the two corporate colonies of New England were furnishing the chief counts in the indictment. Ashurst vigorously fought it and the course which he championed was not defeated. After the failure of the bill of 1706 the movement against the proprieties ceased for the time to be dangerous, though some years later Ashurst wrote to Connecticut " ye Canaanite is in ye land and watches for Your halting." In reference to Ashurst Dudley wrote at this time that, though his equal in education and services to the crown, Ashurst had pursued him for twenty years and had interfered with his appointment as governor. After that he had hoped to have a rest from him, but it apparently was not to be. The memories of the Andros régime were revived, appeals were made anew to the cherished ideals of the colonies. Suspicion and dis-

[1] *Ibid.*, Dudley to B. T., Dec. 10, 1702; C. O. 5/911, Dudley to B. T., May 10, 1703.

[2] C. O. 5/911, Mar. 30, 1704.

like of Dudley were increased, and Ashurst lost no opportunity to promote it. Under these conditions the leadership in New England, which otherwise might have centred at Boston, was checked and Dudley could do little except with the resources of Massachusetts and New Hampshire. New England, which geographically was a distinct section and should have been, at least for military purposes, administratively united, remained, as in the seventeenth century, separated into a number of jealous colonies. The plan of union under the aegis of the British government proved as truly a failure as did that which had been formed at the beginning of the New England Council. During the later years of the war attention was drawn away to an extent from the distinctive problems of New England to those connected with the war in its wider aspects and the feeling against Dudley abated.

Had it not been for the presence of the war and the success which in general attended its conduct, it is not improbable that Dudley would have found himself involved in more serious conflicts with his province and its assembly than actually occurred. Though a civilian, he possessed the knowledge, originality and initiative which well fitted him for the administrative tasks that the war imposed. With minor exceptions confidence in the management of the war was maintained from the first. The problem of protecting the frontier against the successive attacks of the French and Indians, of scouting and keeping the militia in training was a simple one. Such also was the fitting out of expeditions to the remoter parts. For all these purposes Dudley found no difficulty in securing the requisite appropriations. Still easier was it when England came directly to participate during the later years of the war. Thus it came about that Massachusetts reached the unexampled expenditure of £30,000 a year during the latter half of the war, and Dudley could boast not only of its liberality but of that of Connecticut as well. The pressure of the war, as an incitement to the Puritan spirit, was adequate to produce this result, and by the colonists at least it was regarded as more effective than any mere administrative and judicial measures could have been. Dudley, as the responsible head of the province and as efficient cooperator in this result, reaped the advantages which went with it. Outside of a limited circle he was never popular, but his ability was known and feared and a grudging respect was given him by the province at large. The success of his administration could not be gainsaid, and he had won it in the face of a prejudice deeper and more persistent than that which any other colonial governor had to meet, a prejudice to which all the narrow and intense moral convictions of the Puritan had contributed. He did not flatter his enemies nor flinch from them, but, being reasonably sure of his tenure of office, he quietly and firmly assumed the management of affairs and held it throughout his term. As compared with himself, his individual opponents were of slight importance and, when his administration closed, Massachusetts knew what it was to be governed by one of her own sons who was also a genuine representative of the crown.

Early in 1706 John Nelson wrote to Secretary Popple, of the board of trade, in support of Dudley and his administration against a faction which was opposing him. Nelson was an honest man and a good judge of the needs of the hour. Dudley's " capacity, experience and interest," he wrote, " render him to all intents the most proper for His Majesty's Interest and the good of this place," and they are very solicitous for his continuance. Nelson applied to Popple as the only proper medium for the communication of these " private thoughts," and he hoped that at a suitable time the secretary would lay them before the board.[1]

The revelation in 1706 of the traffic which Vetch, Borland and their associates had carried on with the French in Acadia furnished the best opportunity that had yet presented itself for an attack upon Dudley by his enemies in Massachusetts. It was easy for them to charge him with complicity in this trade and to make the assumption that this charge was true the occasion for marshalling all other complaints, fancied or real, which had been accumulating for years. The vials of wrath which had long been pent up could then be poured out on his head. This was what occurred in 1707 and 1708, and the Mathers assumed the leading rôle among the accusers.

In view of their relations years before toward Andros and

[1] C. O. 5/864. O. P. N. Eng., 50, Aug. 8, 1706.

his government, and of what was more than suspected to be the inclination of Dudley toward episcopacy, it was not reasonable to expect that anything like sincere friendship could exist between the Mathers and the new governor. The venerable ex-president paid his respects to him in an election sermon. Dudley wrote to Cotton Mather on the prospects of his appointment and Mather wrote a letter in support of his candidacy for the governorship. On the arrival of Dudley at Boston he visited Cotton Mather and the latter told him that, in the colony there were various and divided apprehensions concerning the policy which he was likely to follow toward them, and advised him to carry an indifferent hand toward all parties. " By no means," he continued, " lett any People have cause to say that you take all your Measures from the two Mr. Mathers. By the same Rule I may say without offence, by no means lett any People say that you go by no Measures in your Conduct but Mr. Byfield's and Mr. Leveret's."[1] Dudley was unwise enough to report this foolish speech to the individuals concerned and that, wrote Mather, "influenced them into an implacable Rage against me."

Willard was now president of the college and affairs moved on quietly there for some years. The Brattles were restored to the corporation and, with the settlement of the question of the charter in accordance with Dudley's suggestion, all prospect of Increase Mather being sent to England as agent vanished. In 1707 occurred the death of Willard and the election of John Leverett to the presidency. In one respect Leverett's career resembled Dudley's, for in harmony with the spirit of the age both had turned from the ministry to law and thence had passed into politics and official careers. The choice of a man who was essentially a layman to such a position was unprecedented in those times and anything but agreeable to the Mathers. But the election of Leverett also crushed the ardent hopes of Cotton Mather that he might succeed to the presidency. As Leverett and Dudley were on good terms and this appointment was in harmony with the trend of affairs which the governor favored and the Mathers

[1] Curwen MSS. Am. Antiq. Soc.; Hutchinson, Hist. of Mass. II, 115; Diary of Cotton Mather, I, 465.

opposed, it served to make further silence on their part impossible.[1]

Soon after the beginning of 1708 the Mathers, in their assumed position of spiritual advisers, wrote two letters to Dudley taking him to task in the severest terms for alleged corrupt connection with the traffic in Acadia, charging him also with bribery and with plotting to ruin the country.[2] The admonition of mediaeval pope to emperor never exceeded the cogency of this appeal. Dudley's reply might well rank as a classic in the literature of controversies of this kind. He did not deign to answer their specifications but, with a wealth of scripture quotations which even exceeded their own, showed how they had been led by the bitterness of their spirit to substitute reproaches and vilification for true Christian admonition. They should have been sure of their facts and not have raked together the accumulations of years of prejudice, jealousy and evil surmisings. He pronounced them incompetent judges and the spirit with which they had treated him as unjustified by reason, religion or common civility. One who compares this encounter between the governor and the clergy with the attitude of the elder Winthrop toward the admonitions of the same class will appreciate the change which had come over conditions in Massachusetts.

The Mathers did not cease their attack with this interchange of letters. In two pamphlets, both entitled substantially "The Deplorable State of New England," one published in Boston and the other in London, they soon after appealed to the public at large. Though these were anonymous and in the case of the second devices were adopted to make it appear to have been written in England, there is no doubt that they both emanated from the implacable Mathers.[3] In the first the charge was exploited, that the plan for

[1] In 1701 Wait Winthrop wrote to Ashurst about Leverett, then the speaker of the assembly, "who after the example of some others has left the university which he had begun upon and for which those yt were at the charge of his education had desighened him, and is now an attorny." Winthrop Papers, 6 Mass. Hist. Colls. V, 83.

[2] 1 Mass. Hist. Colls., III, 126–137.

[3] Both are reprinted at the beginning of vol. II of Sewall's Diary, 5 Mass. Hist. Soc. VI, together with a defence of Dudley under the title of "A Modest Inquiry into the Grounds and Occasions of a late Pamphlet, etc."

an exchange of prisoners, first at Quebec and afterwards in Acadia, was only intended to furnish an opportunity for illegal trading with the enemy. The alleged proof of this was found in the fact that the governor's son accompanied Vetch to Canada, that they carried a large store of goods suitable for the supply of the Indians and that they brought back only a few captives, and those individuals of minor importance. On the other hand, many and important French prisoners got their discharge. Ammunition, too, was furnished by Dudley to the Indians of Acadia and Maine and thus the means were given them with which to attack the English. Had it not been for the various supplies which they got in this way, the Indians would have perished from want. The presence of arms and ammunition, alleged to have been procured in Boston, on board a French vessel which came under protection of a flag of truce granted in connection with an exchange of prisoners, was hushed up by the Massachusetts government. Had it not been for the illegal trade which Dudley had promoted with the French and Indians, a large part of the many appropriations which it was necessary for Massachusetts to make for the war would have been unnecessary.

Another charge, which was dwelt upon at length in both pamphlets, was the prevalence of bribery in the Massachusetts government under Dudley and the difficulty of getting any favors without influence or the payment of money. Without money, it was said, justice could not be had. Two or three affidavits in support of this charge were given. The encroachments of the admiralty court, especially in the cases of certain drift whales taken on Cape Cod, on a jurisdiction which, if exercised at all, had lain exclusively with the common law courts, was also condemned. In this connection Paul Dudley came in for criticism. The general conclusion was that the governor's goal was mammon and his drift was toward the ruin of the country.

In the second pamphlet much attention was paid to an address, signed by William Partridge, Thomas Newton, Nathaniel Higginson and others, which had been sent to the queen asking for the removal of Dudley, and especially to the steps taken by the governor to secure the adoption by the two houses of an address in opposition to the above.[1] It was charged that the council was browbeaten into its assent to this, so that later Judge Sewall, for reasons which he filed in writing, withdrew his affirmative vote.[2] Sewall's reasons indicate a sound judgment respecting the whole transaction. They were, that the personal interest of the governor was so deeply engaged in securing a favorable address that he did not leave the council sufficient chance to word it according to its own discretion. Sewall could not bring himself to "firmly Believe that the Governor did in no way Allow Mr. Borland and Capt. Vetch their Trading Voyage to Her Majesty's Enemies, the French," but he did not suspect that the governor by this "designed to Hurt the Province, but to Gratify Grateful Merchants." He also fully acknowledged the wisdom of Dudley's measures for defence of the province and rejoiced in their success. His Diary also shows that, though he received "many a Bite, many a hard Word" from Dudley, the men still remained friends. When the council, immediately after the above session, invited the governor to dinner, Sewall drank to his health and presented his duty to him. On the other hand, he stood by his old friend, Nathaniel Higginson, and could not admit that his address against Dudley was "a Scandalous and Wicked Accusation," as Dudley wished to term it. On this occasion, as in his acknowledgment of error in connection with the witchcraft trials in Salem, Sewall's conduct reached a high point of Christian excellence. The rest of the pamphlet was devoted to an account of the influence and coercion which Dudley and his supporters were alleged to have used with the members of the lower house to secure a favorable address, and even with clergymen and others outside in order to get expressions of approval from them. The fact that by Church's last expedition or in other ways, Port Royal had not been captured, was explained by the unwillingness of Dudley and his corrupt favorites to lose it as a centre for illegal trade with the enemy.

"The Modest Enquiry," which was published in England in reply to these attacks, was an attempt to show their triviality,

[1] 5 Mass. Hist. Colls. VI, 130.

[2] *Ibid.*, III, 202.

while it presented, in the form of counter addresses and a recital of Dudley's notable services, evidence that his administration was a success and the continuance of it was desired by the body of the colonists. As this printed material all came before the board of trade and constituted part of a campaign to secure the governor's removal, he also submitted directly to the board a memorial in defence of himself.[1] In this, besides reviewing his past services to the crown and his successes in the war, he sought to discredit the testimony against him by impeaching the character of those who signed the affidavits, and showing that most of those who signed Higginson's memorial either were insignificant persons, or interested against Dudley, or those whose acquaintance with the province or the transactions of which they complained was too slight to give their statements weight. Favorable testimonials had been received from New Hampshire and these the governor included also in his defence. It, however, must be said that this form of evidence, similar to what was produced in so many cases, lacks precision and leaves the question at issue still in doubt.

It was after the return of peace and in the later years of Dudley that the question of the currency became acute in Massachusetts. That issue had long been growing in importance, as the evils of depreciation increased. Though in New England the problem was not fundamentally different from that which presented itself in the other colonies, war and the prominence of trade and industry in that section brought it earlier and with greater emphasis to the front than was common elsewhere on the continent. In the discussion of this subject the intellectuality of the New Englanders was as evident as in the fields of theology and church government. They have always written and published much, and this characteristic appeared as clearly in their discussion of the currency as of the other eighteenth-century subjects. Upon the subject of the currency a considerable pamphlet literature developed in Massachusetts which, when added to the discussion that went on in the newspapers, far exceeded in amount all that emanated from the press upon this subject

[1] C. O. 5/864, R. 66, referred to in Dudley's letter to the board of trade of Nov. 10, 1707.

in the other colonies.[1] Though many of these publications were of slight importance, and the discussion throughout was marked by the crudities inseparable from the times prior to the development of economics as a science, considering the time and place it shows a curiosity and ingenuity of which the authors had no reason to be ashamed.

The New Englanders had had their difficulties with barter, which the Massachusetts mint had been established to relieve. In common also with the other colonies they had suffered from a permanently unfavorable balance of trade. With the recall of the colony charter the mint had to be abandoned and its reestablishment was prohibited by the British government.[2] Soon the wars with the French and Indians began, and in order to meet the cost of Phips' expedition to Quebec Massachusetts had to resort to the issue of bills of credit. At first only £7000 were issued but the following year (1691) this was increased to £40,000 and that for the time was fixed as the limit. But the steady and severe pressure of the wars upon Massachusetts was believed to necessitate the abandonment of this limit and an indefinite succession of issues in the future.

Though the government of Massachusetts began issues of this kind nearly twenty years before the same policy was generally adopted by the colonies, the subject of credit substitutes for coin and barter had been discussed in New England at even a much earlier period. John Winthrop of Connecticut, was a man of curious and inquiring mind in reference to many subjects. By the middle of the seventeenth century he was pondering "proposalls concerning the way to trade and bank without money." He corresponded with Samuel Hartlib, the friend of Milton, on this subject. "The Key of Wealth," published in 1650 by William Potter, of London, certainly influenced Hartlib and through him may

[1] This literature has been fully discussed and most of it reprinted by Andrew McFarland Davis, in his Currency and Banking in Massachusetts Bay, 3 Pubs. of Am. Econ. Assoc. I and II; his Tracts relating to the Currency of Massachusetts Bay; and his Colonial Currency Reprints, Pubs. of Prince Soc. 4 vols. J. Hammond Trumbull has also contributed to the subject in Pubs. of Am. Antiq. Soc., 1884. J. B. Felt, Hist. Account of Mass. Currency.

[2] See the order in council of Oct. 22, 1686. 4 Mass. Hist. Coll. II, 296. Cal. St. P. Col., 1685–1688, p. 66. Davis, Currency and Banking, I, 32.

have become known to Winthrop. During his visit to England, soon after 1660, Winthrop submitted to the newly formed Royal Society, of which he had been made a fellow, some proposals concerning a bank and credit.[1] The discussion of a land bank, or one the security for whose issues should be land, had already been started in England, and of this plan Hartlib was a supporter. Winthrop seems to have differed from this view, but precisely in what way is not known, for no notice was taken of his plan in England and it was never published.

In 1682 a pamphlet appeared in Massachusetts entitled, "Severals relating to the Fund." Its authorship has been attributed with reason to the Rev. John Woodbridge, of Newbury, a man of somewhat varied experience both in England and America and one whose interests were secular more than they were clerical. In 1649 William Potter himself had imparted to the writer his plan for a bank founded upon the personal credit of a considerable number of able men for the security of bills they might issue. This differed from the plan of a land bank, and may have been what Winthrop had in mind. Woodbridge became greatly interested in the plan and imparted it to some of his friends among the merchants, when he returned to New England. There it was discussed with approval. The attention of the council was attracted to it and an unsuccessful attempt seems to have been made, soon after 1670, to put the plan in operation. A decade later the plan was published in the pamphlet referred to, and the group of those who were interested may have circulated bills among themselves, based on a fund of capital which they mutually subscribed. In 1686, during the presidency of Dudley over the Dominion of New England, John Blackwell, then a merchant in Boston but a few years later striving to maintain the authority of the executive in the post of lieutenant governor of Pennsylvania, submitted to the council a plan for the establishment of a private bank. It was to issue bills based on land and movable capital as security, and thus help to supply the need of a medium of exchange caused by the decay of trade and the scarcity of coin that this scheme

[1] Proc. of Mass. Hist. Soc., 1878, p. 219; Davis, Currency and Banking II, 65.

was proposed. It was approved by the council[1] and an elaborate prospectus with a plan for the organization of the bank was issued.[2] Dudley, Stoughton and Wait Winthrop were to act with Blackwell and others as assessors or managers. These same should be partners and investors, depositing money or other property in the capital fund of the bank. As most of those whose names are mentioned were members of the council, it is evident that a close connection with the government was intended. The plan seems to have been progressing toward an actual trial, when, in 1688, it was abandoned. The reason for this is not known, but it has been surmised that Andros was opposed to it and it may well have been that through him was expressed the opposition of the British government. The experience of banks upon the continent of Europe was not well understood at that time in England. Opinion there upon credit and the possible methods of its utilization was in an extremely undeveloped state, and naturally it was much less developed in the colonies. The times also were troubled and this, along with other schemes for corporate or semi-corporate activities in the colonies, failed to reach the experimental stage. With the exception of a single attempt in the general court, in 1700/1, to bring forward the plan again, nothing further appears concerning it until 1714. Notes of individuals were the only form of credit documents, except the colony bills of credit, which had appeared in Massachusetts and the part played by these notes of private parties was very slight and obscure.

Meantime the bills of credit, first of the colony and, after the grant of the charter, of the province, continued to be issued and kept in circulation. The continuance of the war was held to necessitate the early neglect of the limit which was originally set to the amount of these issues. New emissions were made annually, provision being made for the levy of taxes for their redemption at some specified time in the future and also that they should be received in payment

[1] Dudley Records, Proc. Mass. Hist. Soc., 1899, pp. 24, 272.

[2] See "A Model for erecting a Bank of Credit, etc." London, Printed in the year 1688, Reprinted in Boston in New England in 1714. This is printed by Davis in his Tracts Relating to the Currency of Massachusetts. Two other pamphlets, published in 1691 and concerned with the same plan, are contained in Davis's Collection.

of all public dues. The uncertain status of the colony government when the first issues were made, occasioned distrust and depreciation. To check this the merchants came to the rescue. Phips purchased a parcel of them with a quantity of ready money, and the government received them in payment of public dues at a premium of five per cent.[1] Notwithstanding the increased assurance which was afforded by the establishment of the government under the new charter and the fact that the successive acts of emission were not disallowed by the crown, the premium thus conceded had to be continued until 1720, in a vain effort to prevent depreciation. The old bills were successively called in and reissued, the original colony plates even being used until 1702. In this way the need of paper credit during the first two colonial wars was met and Massachusetts established the earliest precedents for its management in the colonies. By issues and reissues, continued until 1702, Massachusetts had put out about £82,000 in bills of credit, and they had passed freely. Under the governors who preceded Dudley no controversy over this subject had developed. The financial pressure which was caused by the second intercolonial war made it impossible to check the succession of annual issues. They continued until 1715, at the rate of from £10,000 to £58,000 yearly, in no year falling below £20,000. A total of £474,000 were thus put into circulation.[2] In the course of the war the period which was usually set for the redemption of these issues was extended from three to seven years. Thus Massachusetts had become deeply committed to a paper money régime by the time (1709 and 1710) when the other three New England colonies were beginning their issues.

When it was decided not to permit the mint at Boston to be reopened, Andros was empowered to regulate by proclamation the rates at which foreign coins should circulate within the Dominion. With the growth of settlement and trade throughout the colonies in general, such regulation became an important matter. Owing to the lack of sterling and the opposition of the British government to the issue of

[1] Mather, Magnalia, Hartford ed. 1720, I, 174. Trumbull attributes to Mather one of the pamphlets of this period on the subject of a bank of credit.
[2] Kimball, Public Life of Joseph Dudley, 161.

coins from colonial mints, the colonists were forced to use the coinage chiefly of Spain and her dominions.[1] A defect in British colonial policy, comparable with her failure to provide permanent support for her governors, was that of neglecting, through colonial mints or otherwise, to furnish the colonists with an adequate coinage. As it was, they were left at first to the intolerable devices of barter, followed by the use of the confused and unstable system of Spanish coins. Standards of weights and fineness were uncertain and methods of coining crude. Clipping, or other forms of illegally reducing the weight of standard metal in coins, were very general and prevailed to an enormous extent in the West Indies. Following the natural currents of trade, it was chiefly from that quarter that the English colonies received the coins which were actually in use. English coins were not to be found there in large quantities and the English system of coinage served chiefly as an ideal standard to which the colonists sought to make the names, weight and fineness of their coins conform. But prior especially to the recoinage of 1696 the British coinage itself was in a very corrupt state, and the colonists do not seem to have actually known the weight of the standard British shilling. Barter currency or " Country pay " in the colonies ever tended to depreciate, as did the worn and clipped coins which were in circulation.

The establishment of the mint at Boston in 1652 was an effort to bring locally some degree of order out of this chaos by furnishing Massachusetts with a coinage of shillings and smaller silver pieces, the metallic contents of which were some twenty-seven per cent less than sterling, so that the coins might be kept exclusively for colonial use. Their exportation from Massachusetts was strictly forbidden, but that proved futile and they were soon to be found widely distributed through the colonies. In 1672, in order to check the export of silver coins and relieve the consequent scarcity of money, the general court legalized the currency of pieces of eight — Spanish pieces of eight reals — the parent of the later American dollar, at six shillings. But this was an incorrect valuation and the situation had not greatly improved

[1] Sumner, The Coin Shilling of Massachusetts Bay, Yale Review, 1898; The Spanish Dollar and the Colonial Shilling, Am. Hist. Rev., 1898.

when, on the recall of the charter, the mint was closed and the pine-tree shilling soon disappeared from circulation.

In 1692 the legislature of Massachusetts at last defined by weight the pieces of eight at seventeen penny weights, which was in accordance with the usage of the market. This act, however, was disallowed by the crown, because of the provisions which it contained in reference to clipping and other matters. In 1697 the above definition was repeated and it was declared that these coins should circulate as before, at six shillings, they being good Seville, pillar or Mexican pieces of eight. This legislation stood, though the rating was not exact, and became for the colonies the point of departure for certain important developments in the future. "It took up and made lawful," says Professor Sumner, "a state of things which had existed in all probability, by the custom of the market, since 1685. This law and this definition of a shilling were the point of departure for the following period, during which the clipping of silver and over issues of paper produced inflation and confusion." It was in an effort to remedy this that the proclamation of 1704, elsewhere referred to, was issued by the British government, and this was followed four years later by an act of parliament, the two together proving inadequate to remove the evil against which they were directed.

With the close of the war in Massachusetts came a rather definite alignment of parties on the subject of currency and banks. The members of the council, together with the more prosperous merchants and townspeople of the east, conservatives in general, insisted upon keeping the control of this matter in the hands of the government and not allowing a further increase of the bills of credit. Within this body a minority favored the retirement of the currency and return to a specie basis. Opposed to this group was a radical party, whose stronghold was in the country towns. It included the large class of debtors and those who, by reason of the war or from other causes, had failed to be prosperous or became financially involved. Their feelings were reflected by the majority of the house of representatives. They attributed their sufferings to the lack of an adequate quantity of money in circulation and favored larger issues and the prolonging of the periods set for their retirement. By this party the earlier proposals respecting a land bank were adopted and made a central plank in their platform. They demanded the establishment of an institution of this kind, which should issue to the people bills of credit secured by mortgages on their land, and this body of currency should be added to the paper which was already issued by the government. Thus the issue was drawn between the supporters of the land bank and the defenders of the so-called public bank or existing method of the restricted issue of bills of credit by the government,[1] and more than a generation was to pass before this question disappeared from Massachusetts politics. Dudley, as we have seen, had been one of the early supporters of the plan of a private bank, though with the idea that its issues should be secured by commodities in general and not wholly by land. Circumstances and the responsibilities of office had now changed his attitude and he appears as the first in the list of royal governors who were leaders in opposition to plans of this kind.

Early in 1701 a committee of the assembly had reported in favor of creating a land bank and giving it a monopoly of the issue of bills of credit. This proposal was rejected by the general court. It was not until February, 1714, that the proposal reappeared. A project was then advertised in the Boston "News Letter" for the establishment of a bank of credit, and subscriptions were opened for the purpose. Shortly after a joint committee was appointed in the general court to consider the best way in which to supply the deficiency of money and to facilitate the payment of public taxes, whether it should be projected upon a public or a private fund. The committee reported in favor of issues by the public. Though the plan of a private bank of issue was thus rejected, the discussion of the project was continued, especially by reprinting in Boston of Blackwell's scheme of 1686 and 1688 for a private bank,[2] with the emphasis now laid upon land as the favorite form of security. In addition to this the promoters issued a pamphlet of their own, entitled, "A Projection for Erecting a Bank of Credit in Boston, New

[1] Davis, Currency and Banking, II, 82 *et seq.*; Kimball, Joseph Dudley, 164; Journal of the Council of Massachusetts.

[2] Referred to and title quoted above.

England, Founded on Land Security."[1] This was a prospectus for the formation of a company of the kind referred to, with a capital of £300,000. In an introductory paragraph the authors stated their point of view, which was to the effect that there was "a sensible decay in Trade," and that it was due to the "want of a Medium of Exchange," "The Running Cash being Exported, and considerable Sums of the Bills of Credit put forth by the Government, which had their Circulation and supported the Trade, being already drawn in, and the remaining lessening yearly by the payment of the Taxes and other Public Dues; so that without a Medium the Trade must necessarily decay, to the unspeakable detriment of the Landed Interest as well as the Trading Party." The only prospect of relief, as viewed by the projectors, lay in the activity of such a bank as they proposed to establish. No one should subscribe more than £4000 and should pledge his real estate to the amount of his subscription as security. Loans of bills could then be obtained and the same currency should be given to those as to the bills of the province. As an encouragement to the project, the offer was held out that, when £150,000 had been issued, out of the profits £400 a year should be paid toward the support of a charitable school in Boston and £200 a year for the establishment of professorships and scholarships in Harvard College. Among the supporters of this project were John Colman, Elisha Cooke Jr., Timothy Thornton, Oliver Noyes and Nathaniel Oliver.

Paul Dudley, attorney general, and son of the governor, at once presented before the council a memorial attacking the scheme.[2] From statements in one of the pamphlets of the time it appears that the promoters began with consulting the governor and secretary, and from the former they understood that he would favor the plan both at home and in England.[3] They petitioned the general court for the necessary powers. It was at this juncture that Paul Dudley came out with his attack, which was directed chiefly against the legality of proceeding in such an enterprise as this without a charter from the crown, especially as its activities were to be so

[1] This is reprinted by Davis in his volume above referred to.

[2] Davis, Tracts relating to Currency of Massachusetts Bay, 153.

[3] *Ibid.*, 151 *et seq.*

closely concerned with the royal prerogative of issuing and preserving the purity of the coin and money of the realm and dominions. It seemed also to the writer to come under the purview of the act respecting proclamation money. Under the influence of Dudley's attack the council ordered the projectors not to print their scheme or put the same on record or emit any of their notes or bills until they had laid their proposals before the general court. It was this order which led to the publication of the above statement concerning the interview with the governor. As Dudley is on record in a series of speeches to the general court, delivered at intervals since the beginning of his term, enforcing the necessity of limiting the issues of bills of credit and scrupulously living up to the provisions of the law in reference to their redemption, therefore, however diplomatic and non-committal he may have been in the interview the only report of which comes from partisans, it cannot be believed that he was in favor of a scheme like the land bank, which was fathered by one of his bitterest opponents and the effect of which would be to seriously inflate the currency.

In his speech at the beginning of the fall session of 1714 Dudley referred to the project of a land bank and its interest and expressed the hope that such action would be taken as would secure the honor of the British government and the security and benefit of the subjects in their trade.[1] A joint committee of the two houses was appointed, which reported in favor of meeting the alleged need for more currency by issuing £50,000, to be vested in trustees and loaned out in mortgages at five per cent interest.[2] This move threatened to shelve the plan for a private bank and was followed by the issue in pamphlet form of Paul Dudley's argument against the scheme. Two pamphlets were published in reply to him, in one of which the charge of bad faith was made against the governor.[3] The controversy became very warm and extended throughout the province, Hutchinson stating that it "divided towns, parishes and particular families." By petition the land bank party carried their case to England, though there was not the slightest chance that the board of trade

[1] Journal of the Upper House, Oct. 20, 1714.

[2] Hutchinson, II, 190.

[3] All of these are reprinted by Davis.

would give it an approval. Dudley also saw to it that Dummer, the agent, was instructed not to approve the application. But this was unnecessary, as the board was so clear on the subject that it did not hear it argued.

Because of his opposition to the land bank, its supporters sought to procure Dudley's removal. With the death of Anne and the accession of the Hanoverians to the throne and the Whigs to power, Dudley had lost his friends at court. The bank party induced one Elizeus Burgess, who had served with Stanhope in Spain, to accept appointment as governor, promising not to interfere with their plans. William Tailer, who was appointed lieutenant governor, was also friendly to the land bank. In the council of Massachusetts also, after the six months following the death of Anne had passed, the period during which, according to the statute of the sixth of that queen, all who were in office at the demise of a monarch should continue to hold their places, and no word had come from England, or movement developed for the supplanting of Dudley, he proclaimed the accession of George I and, along with the other governors, received express authority to conduct the government until the period of six months after the death of the queen had passed. When, at the beginning of February, 1714/15, that period came to an end, several members of the council, among whom Sewall, Wait Winthrop, Hutchinson and Lynch were leaders, undertook to assume charge of the government under the presidency of their senior member. They issued a proclamation for the devolution of the government, certain commissions to officials, and prepared a proclamation for a fast. They were also preparing to write to England in explanation of their assuming charge of the government. But from Dudley they could secure no recognition of what they were doing, and on March 19 he received a royal proclamation continuing governors and other officials in their places till the king's further pleasure should be known. This was at once published and the plan upon which the council was entering with caution and misgiving was abandoned.[1]

[1] Ford in 2 Proc. of Mass. Hist. Soc. XV, 327–362. The letter of Dudley to the board of trade, dated November 18, 1714, and telling how, notwithstanding the loss of a part of the dispatches by the wreck of the Hazard galley, news of the death of Anne was received and George I was duly proclaimed, is in C. O. 5/915. B. T. E. B. N. Eng. p. 155.

CHAPTER XXI

VIRGINIA DURING THE SECOND INTERCOLONIAL WAR

In previous chapters attention has been called to the normal conditions under which Virginia had existed as a royal province from an early time. To this and to the homogeneous character of its population is to be attributed the quiet and uneventful course of its development, especially after Bacon's Rebellion. This is reflected in the sources of its history. As a rule, sessions of the assembly were held semi-annually. With the exception of Nicholson, during his two administrations, and Spotswood, the correspondence of the governors was limited in amount and rather commonplace in character. The same was true of the responses which came from the offices in England. The tobacco industry bulked large in the correspondence and to it the British merchants contributed material of interest. Considerable intervals also occurred during which Virginia was governed by a president and council, a condition which was almost always accompanied by a partial stagnation of public business. And yet the courts of the province, and of course the county justices, continued to perform their functions, and they were of great importance, especially in the field of social history. But they were regular and routine in their character and the events with which they were concerned do not particularly stir the imagination.

The fact that during the two generations which followed 1690 the history of Virginia did not abound in events of striking character should not lead to the conclusion that it was an unimportant colony. Far from that, it was second in importance to none whether on the continent or among the islands. It was made so by three cardinal facts; its typical form and place as a royal province, its economic structure, and its geographical position. The first of these characteristics has already been sufficiently explained. The second has reference to Virginia as the greatest producer of tobacco. As this was a leading semi-tropical staple and Virginia, in consequence of her devotion to it, became a colony of the plantation type, she belonged economically to the group which lay south of her. She, together with Maryland, formed the northern frontier, so to speak, of that great colonial area which produced the staples for the encouragement of which the mercantile policy of Great Britain had been developed. That territory extended indefinitely into the tropics and included on its southern British frontier the island of Barbadoes. North of Virginia and Maryland lay colonies of a different economic type, whose commercial relations with the mother country and whose industrial and social organization differed widely from the plantation type of colony. As New York was a frontier province in war and a strategic centre for all military purposes, Virginia stood in a similar position economically. Each was a pivotal colony in its own special relations.

Geographically also Virginia was central and held a position of leading importance. Some of the chief waterways of the Atlantic slope lay within her territory or adjacent to it. Her claims extended indefinitely westward and the passage across her mountain barrier led directly into the Ohio basin, which was the central avenue of approach to the Mississippi. When the time for this advance should come, Virginia was bound to hold a leading place in the winning of the west.

In any scheme of joint action which might affect the colonies as a whole Virginia, then, must hold a prominent place. As the typical royal province and chief seat of the tobacco industry imperialist policy, so far as it affected the continental colonies, must be determined to a considerable extent by her interests. Her business and social connections with Great Britain were more intimate than those of most colonies. But in general everything relating to her was so steady and harmonious that decade after decade passed without any stirring events. Growth also was not remarkable, because Virginia was fully caught within the restrictive circle thrown around the colonies by the acts of trade and passed this entire period of her history without a diversified industry and under a growing system of slave labor. Prices of the staple product ranged low and, though complaints of poverty and hard times were not quite so numerous as in Maryland, conditions in the two provinces could not have been essentially unlike.

During the period with which we are here concerned two men of more than average ability were at the head of Virginia affairs, Francis Nicholson and Alexander Spotswood. Between the two came the brief administration of Edward Nott, followed by a period of four years, (1706–1710) during which Edward Jennings administered affairs as president of the council. The fact that Virginia, during the war, was left for so long a time without a governor was due to the capture by the French of Robert Hunter, who had been appointed as Nott's successor, and his failure to reach the province. On his release he was sent, as we have seen, to New York and Spotswood became governor of Virginia.

Early in 1699 Nicholson began his second term in Virginia, this time with the full rank of governor. In 1704 began, however, the appointment of titular governors, who resided in England and by assistance given to the agents of the province, in helping to moderate disputes and possibly in other ways, exerted some influence on events. The first of these was the earl of Orkney, who held the position for thirty-three years — 1704–1737. He was succeeded by the earl of Albemarle — 1737–1754 — who was an officer of high rank in the army and later was ambassador to France and one of the lords justices. Upon the death of Albemarle the office was bestowed in succession on the earl of Loudon and Sir Jeffrey Amherst, both of whom, by virtue of the commands which they held over the army then serving in America, were as much absentees from Virginia as their predecessors had been. With the retirement of Amherst from the office in 1768, the line of titular governors came to an end. Those who actually administered the office under these dignitaries ranked only as lieutenant governors, though the commissions and instructions given to the two were practically identical. Out of the salary of £2000, the sum of £1200 was paid to the non-resident, the lieutenant governor keeping £800. The amount of the salary remained fixed, but with the growth of the province the perquisites of the office increased until the total income of the office reached the sum of £4000 toward the time of the Revolution. Until, about 1720, a residence was provided for the governor, a special appropriation was made for his house rent. When a senior councillor served as governor, the sum of £500, taken from the governor's salary, was added to the remuneration which he received as councillor. Gifts were occasionally made by the burgesses to the lieutenant governors, but these simply expressed appreciation of their services, for no controversy over the governor's salary ever arose in Virginia.[1]

Commissary Blair stated that it was chiefly through his own efforts and the support of the bishops in England that the appointment of Nicholson was made, and that this made it unnecessary to expend the money which Nicholson was ready to supply to procure the office. Before he left Maryland signs of growing arbitrariness and passion had appeared in Nicholson's conduct, and these had involved him in some needlessly bitter controversies. Gerard Sly, John Coode and others had complained of this,[2] and Sly had laid charges before Secretary Vernon, but there is no evidence that they produced any effect or that their truth or falsehood were inquired into at the time when Nicholson's new appointment was being considered. In his first letter as governor of Virginia he made light of the charges, as the slanders of malcontents who were plotting evil against the king's government. The reputation of Coode was certainly not such as to add weight to any charges with which his name was concerned.

Relations between Nicholson and Andros as governors of Maryland and Virginia had not been cordial. This had been shown in connection with efforts to procure the arrest of Coode after his flight from Maryland and perhaps in other matters. Andros, therefore, when he left Virginia, gave Nicholson no account of the state of the province as to revenue, defences or other matters.[3] Of this Nicholson complained to the authorities in England and applied to William Byrd, the auditor, and to the gunners at various points for

[1] Flippen, The Royal Government of Virginia, 1624–1775, C. U. Studies.

[2] Cal. St. P. Col., 1697–98, pp. 245, 290; Perry, Hist. Colls. of Am. Col. Church, Virginia, 75.

[3] Cal. St. P. Col., 1699, p. 47 *et seq.*, 170.

a part of the information which he desired. After the manner of new governors, he reported that he found Virginia financially in a worse condition than when he left it seven years before. Byrd reported that there was a deficit of £4200 in the revenue from the export duty on tobacco and that the province was somewhat in debt. But on further inquiry the arrears were found to be smaller than had been anticipated, while the tobacco crop had been good and there were nearly enough ships in Virginia to take it to England.[1] The court house at Jamestown had been burned and, as the College was already settled at Middle Plantation, it was soon resolved that a new government house or capitol should be built there.[2] This occupied considerable attention throughout Nicholson's administration, as did the question of a residence for the governor soon after that time. By these means Williamsburg was founded and the capital of the province was removed thither. This was all in harmony with the governor's instructions from England, and in connection with the building of the capitol Nicholson made many valuable suggestions for the better classification of public business and preservation of the records. Some of these were carried into practice. In part to pay for this building, a duty was laid by the general assembly, in its session of April, 1699, upon the importation of liquors, except those which came from the realm, and also on servants and slaves imported into the province.[3]

Nicholson submitted a number of his instructions, at the session of the assembly the same spring, thus giving them an opportunity again to express their traditional views, which in many respects were not in agreement with the desires of the home government.[4] For example, they did not approve of the proposal to empower the governor and council to raise a general levy to meet emergencies; they were opposed to the maintenance of fortifications along the coast and insisted that Virginia must be protected, if at all, by a naval force; the province could not afford to build public workhouses for the employment of the poor and it would also be very burdensome,

[1] *Ibid.*, 309.
[2] *Ibid.*, 224, 249, 269, 278.
[3] Hening, Statutes, III, 189 *et seq.*
[4] Cal. St. P. Col., 1699, pp. 202, 260 *et seq.*

if not dangerous, to list and arm Christian servants, for as some Irish Catholics and others who had been soldiers had recently been brought into the province, they were as likely to prove enemies as friends; the levy by poll they considered the best and most equal form of tax; free trade with the Indians they favored, and, as to their conversion, they were content to leave that to the college; negroes born in the country were generally baptized, but it was impossible to make any progress toward the conversion of those who had been recently imported. Efforts to assert the claims of the college and of other would-be settlers in the Pamunkey and Blackwater regions imperilled the permanence of Indian treaties and, in the case of the Blackwater region, led to conflicts of jurisdiction which brought to the front the question of the North Carolina boundary.[1] Commissioners came from that province at this time, to arrange, if possible, for running the line, but on the plea that the appointment of Governor Harvey, who sent them, had not been approved by the king, the governor and council of Virginia resolved not to proceed until an instruction for the settlement of the boundary was received from England.

For additional evidence respecting the questions which, at this time, interested the people of Virginia, as they were distributed through the counties, the numerous statements of grievances which were presented to the assembly of 1699 are enlightening.[2] Several of the counties complained about the times and places of the sessions of the courts, both the general court and the county courts; the appointment of a coroner in every county was urged; the sale of liquor near court houses was complained of by one county; the rates at which foreign coins should circulate also received considerable attention and the burgesses issued a series of resolves on the subject; various aspects of parish government and finance were brought forward; the fixing of the boundaries of counties and parishes or changes in them so that, for the sake of church attendance for one thing, no parish should be divided by one of the large rivers of the province, received much attention, especially from the governor; a demand for the

[1] *Ibid.*, 77, 186, 200.
[2] *Ibid.*, 198.

passage of an act to prevent undue elections was acceded to by the assembly; relations with the Indians received some slight attention and in addition a variety of other petty concerns from the unreasonable killing of deer and the stealing of hogs to the exportation of old iron. Several of the cases of evil conduct to which reference was made were guarded against in one of Nicholson's favorite acts against immorality and for the suppression of blasphemy, swearing, drunkenness and Sabbath breaking, which was placed on the statute book at this session.[1] This all shows that society was static, its advance since Bacon's Rebellion being chiefly in bulk, with the colonial aristocracy firmly established in control.

Another subject of considerable importance, which was recommended to the governor by the board of trade, was the revisal of the laws. As there had been no revisal since 1662, the statutes of the province were in great confusion, for the reason that many had expired or become obsolete and others had been repealed. The necessity of action on this subject was clear and is said to have failed at the last session because of pressure of other business. The plan of the board of trade was that the revision should be made by the governor with the advice of the council, that each act be then passed separately by the general assembly and that nothing be included in any act of a nature different from its title. But this method was not followed. During the present session an act was passed by which this work was intrusted to a permanent committee, with an instruction to report the results of its work to the legislature at successive sessions until it should be completed.[2] This was continued until 1706, when thirty-nine bills were submitted for approval. In 1704 Edward Jennings had been sent to England with the bills as they then stood, and they had been examined by the board of trade and such changes as it judged necessary incorporated and then they were taken back to Virginia to be finally passed by the governor and general assembly.[3] But either

[1] Hening, III, 168.

[2] *Ibid.*, 181; Cal. St. P. Col., 1700 pp. 6, 11.

[3] E. B. Va. C. O. 5/1360, ff. 429–434, 459; C. O. 5/1361, ff. 27–28; Journal of Burgesses, 1702–1706, *et seq*; introd. XXVIII, *et seq*. The laws contained in this revisal are printed in Hening III, 229–481, under the session of October, 1705.

by the veto of the governor or as a result of disagreement between the houses three of the most important of the bills failed. These were the acts concerning the church and clergy, the act for regulating county courts and the probate of wills and administration of estates, and the act for securing the liberty of the subject, the object of which was to give Virginians the benefit of *habeas corpus*. Because of the failure to include these laws, the revisal of 1706 was considered so imperfect that it was not printed and the whole matter was shelved until Spotswood's administration, when it was again taken up, though a satisfactory revision was not completed and published until 1733.

In the long letter which Nicholson wrote to the board of trade after the close of this session, and accompanying the transmission of its journals, he explained the condition of the finances and expressed the opinion that the offices of receiver and auditor — both held by William Byrd — should be separated. He had visited Governor Blakiston in Maryland and they both agreed that, if a lieutenant governor of those two provinces was appointed, he would prevent them from falling under the weak rule of a president and council in case the governor of either should be absent or die. Connected with this was Nicholson's first statement, in this administration, as to the difficulty he had in getting a quorum of the council to attend for business.[1] This was a subject on which he had often to discourse. A year later he wrote that John Custis and Robert Carter made constant excuses for not attending.[2] Ralph Wormley, the secretary, who lived fifty miles away, had absented himself for nearly two years, the office being managed by the clerk of the general court and visited occasionally by the deputy secretary. Daniel Parker was said to be in England, but Nicholson had not been informed that he had the king's leave. Richard Lee was excused on petition. So, in August, 1700, there were but nine members at all available. Of these Scarborough, Carter and Custis, especially the two East Shore men, Nicholson did not expect to see at any sessions except those of the general courts

[1] Cal. St. P. Col., 1699, p. 309 *et seq.*

[2] *Ibid.*, 1700, Letter of Aug. 1; C. O. 5/1311, O. P. Va. No. 19, Statement by Nicholson of places of residence of councillors.

or assemblies. Very often the other six councillors were sick, lame or had special business so that they could not attend. The concentration of offices in the hands of councillors Nicholson did not approve, as it led to neglect of the one function or the other.

The office of secretary, with its manifold functions, was an object of much attention from Nicholson.[1] He described its occupant as the "custus rotulorum" of the province, the county clerks holding commissions from him and they and the general court trying cases of all kinds. But Nicholson intended to keep the records of the admiralty court in the control of its register and out of the hands of the secretary. On the death of Wormley, in 1701, Edward Jennings, who had been deputy, succeeded to the secretaryship and affairs in the office were presumably better managed. The statements of the governor about the council and the office of secretary were confirmed by both Ludwell and Quary, the latter adding that it was difficult to get a qualified person for clerk of court or attorney general who would reside at the seat of government. Among other evils, salaries were too small.[2] The board of trade had also ordered that the secretary furnish a detailed account of procedure in all the Virginia courts, and an abstract of all business done in his office. The secretary protested that that would amount nearly to an abstract of the laws and constitution of Virginia and asked for compensation and for access to the records of all the offices concerned. In view of all this, it is not strange that, as the new capitol approached completion, we find Nicholson planning accommodation in all available parts of it for officials and their papers.

In 1700, under encouragement from the British government, a body of about two hundred French Protestant refugees arrived in Virginia. Some additions were made to their number at a later date. At first it was proposed that they should settle in Norfolk county, but as that region was in dispute between Virginia and North Carolina, the council decided that they should be granted some unpatented land at Manakin Town, on the James river about twenty miles

[1] Cal. St. P. Col., 1699, p. 312 *etc.*

[2] C. O. 5/1360, E. B. Va. ff. 84, 102–107.

above the Falls. Auditor Byrd and Benjamin Harrison were designated to take charge of them until they were fully settled,[1] and this required a good deal of attention because, as they arrived in the summer and without means, they had to be supported until their first crop could be harvested the next year. As was usual, the governor and council were more solicitous for their welfare during this interval than were the burgesses. The latter refused to consider the French as objects of charity and appropriated nothing for their support. But the council caused briefs to be circulated through the province and gifts collected for their temporary support. It, however, asked the governor to inform the queen of the poverty of the refugees and the disability of the province and to ask that no more be sent. In the spring of 1702 a cargo of goods sent by the order of the archbishop of Canterbury and the bishop of London arrived, with orders that they should be sold and the money applied to the purchase of cattle and other necessities for the French.

Though Nicholson thought the French would be valuable as a protection to the frontier, he saw the possibility of their injuring the queen's interest by living together, using their own language and customs and engaging in such handicrafts and trade as England had. Orders were issued that the lands which they held must be surveyed and they must hold by English tenures. This was duly executed by the administration of the oaths and the French community continued to exist under the general rules which governed frontier settlements. They were soon organized as King William's parish, while the method of their naturalization was left to the council committee on the revision of the laws. The result was the passage of a law authorizing naturalization by action of the executive, which was incorporated in the revisal of 1705.[2]

By the beginning of 1701 war was regarded as certain and from that time through the earlier years of the struggle many references appear in all the Virginia sources to convoys and

[1] Cal. St. P. Col., 1700, pp. 449, 472, 620, 656, 745, 760, 762; 1701, pp. 408; Perry, Hist. Colls. of Am. Colonial Church, Virginia, 113; Journal of Burgesses, Dec. 19, 1700 *et seq.*

[2] Hening, 111, 434; Nicholson to the board of trade, Aug, 1, 1700; C. O. 5/1410. Minutes of Ex. Council of Va. 1701, 1702. Journal of Burgesses, April 26, 1704 *et seq.*

to the requirement that Virginia and Maryland vessels should go in fleets. Owing to the fact that tobacco was the only staple, this was a subject of importance to only these two among the continental colonies. In May the collectors and naval officers were ordered by the governor and council not to clear any ships after June 6, and that those cleared should meet at the mouth of the James river and organize into a fleet. They were to sail about June 12 and after that time none should depart until further orders. The accounts of naval officers and collectors should be made up in time to be sent by the fleet. Word was sent to Maryland by the sloop "Messenger," and it was to bring in the Maryland contingent.[1] The "Southampton" was coming to relieve the "Shoreham" and the latter was going home with the fleet. But because of the failure of the "Southampton" to arrive in time, it was resolved to continue the embargo until the twentieth of June. Meantime ships from Maryland were daily leaving in spite of the embargo, which caused great dissatisfaction to the Virginia masters. A strong representation was presented to the governor and council by the masters, alleging that the delay was costing them £100 daily, while if they sailed at once they might arrive before the outbreak of war. As the captain of the "Shoreham" declined to sail before he was relieved and there were several other royal ships in Virginia waters, one of these finally agreed to accompany the fleet twenty leagues or so to sea, while three armed merchant vessels were ordered to sail as permanent convoy. This solution of the difficulty was due largely to Nicholson and for his untiring zeal in the matter the masters voted him their thanks. Fifty-five or more vessels sailed under this convoy, and the affair, taken as a whole, well illustrates the conditions under which trade was then carried on in time of war.[2]

[1] In C. O. 5/1313, 14, is a statement on the subject of convoys as it was in 1704. Further on in the volume is an account of Capt. Moodie of H. M. S. "Southampton" and its experience as a convoy. See the papers concerning the advice boat "Eagle," K5; and more relating to convoys in 1704 appears in the same vol. of Original Papers Va., and Va. Entry Book (C. O. 5/1360) under 1702 and 1703. In Va. Council Minutes, C. O. 5/1412, are also various entries on this subject for 1702 and 1703.

[2] In the original Papers, Entry Books and other sources of Virginia and Maryland history during this period is much additional matter relating to fleets and convoys which might be used in a detailed study of trade in time of war.

During the interval between the two wars the peace of Virginia had been once disturbed by a brisk fight between the station ship "Shoreham" and a French pirate vessel.[1] Nicholson was on board the "Shoreham" and took an active part. The pirate was captured and eight of her men were hung and one hundred or more were sent to England by the Essex Prize, which was convoying part of the Virginia fleet. Because of the danger from pirates who were known at that time to be hovering off the coast, the militia of the coast counties was ordered out, lookouts were appointed and steps were taken to secure suspicious persons who might come on shore. A reward was offered for the arrest of pirates and other precautionary measures were taken, but no further disturbance occurred. This minor event illustrates the measures to which Virginia would have to resort, had a French force appeared on her coast during the war, and the possibility that such a descent might occur — though it never actually occurred — furnished her with a permanent excuse for refusal to act in other directions.

With the approach of war the activity of Nicholson in devising precautionary measures was again exhibited and the council cooperated with him. Early in July, 1701, the governor and council ordered a proclamation to be issued to the commissioners of every county to return an account of all arms and ammunition in their counties and of the persons in whose custody they were. None of these should be exported. The militia, horse and foot, should be well equipped and kept in readiness to muster on an hour's warning. Because of a report that a French expedition had been fitted out against the West Indies, the militia was ordered to be mustered and trained. Delinquents should be punished according to law. From the troops every fifth man — young and brisk — should be selected and these formed into troops for special service, under officers of their own choice. Lookouts should be stationed along the coast. The general assembly was called to meet on the sixth of August, when the public levy would be laid, and the clerks of every county court were ordered to send to the assembly a true list of the tithables in their counties. At some convenient time before

[1] Cal. St. P. Col., 1700, p. 307 *et seq.*; Ex. Council Minutes.

the assembly met a court of claims should be held, in order that burgesses might receive all grievances and propositions from their counties to lay before the assembly. A letter which lately had been received from Secretary Vernon was referred to the committee which was already at work on the revision of the laws. This letter contained a number of queries, the purpose of which was to suggest improvements in the militia system: — that the firearms used should be all of them of the same pattern; that the militia should consist wholly of horse and dragoons, as infantry was of little use; that there should be a magazine in every county; that public prizes should be offered for markmanship and other feats; that there should be a muster-master on every neck to keep exact lists of the militia.

After the session had begun the council resolved to submit to the burgesses proposals to the effect that steps be taken to provide the inhabitants with the entire equipment which they needed to meet sudden attacks, that two skilled engineers should be brought from England, that ferries and bridges be kept in good order and care taken for the speedy conveyance of public letters, that seamen be prevented from deserting and vessels from stealing away in spite of embargoes, and that Christian servants should not be mustered. These were ideals to which measures, as actually adopted, made a remote approximation.

At this very time one William Clay, who had been on the Mississippi, reported that the French were making a settlement there. He also told how he had reported the same to the governor of South Carolina and had told him, as he now stated in Virginia, that he was ready to return to the Mississippi and break up the French settlement. This was in confirmation of the report of Dr. Coxe of what was to be expected in the southwest, and it must have suggested to all the southern tier of colonies the possibility that they might yet have to fight for the preservation of their western frontiers.

But for the present their attention was chiefly centred on the condition of the militia in general, with a view to coast defence. In the course of September, 1701, the governor was able to lay before the council an abstract of all the militia of Virginia, a considerable part of whom were neither well equipped or disciplined. He feared that it would take at least two weeks to call out as many as a thousand armed men to meet an invasion, and during that time an enemy, if he landed, could do great damage. The governor would also be hampered by a law of 1684 which provided that no man's arms or ammunition could be impressed from him. Nicholson wanted that law amended in order that the men actually drafted might be better equipped, and that arms should be bought both in Virginia and England. In order properly to meet expenditures, he desired that an additional duty of 6d. per hogshead be laid for one year on exported tobacco, and that the levy per poll be at the rate of fifteen pounds of tobacco, the increased revenue to be used for arms and other military necessities. The bills of exchange for this could be sent by the "Shoreham" and "Lincoln," which were going late in the autumn to convoy the fleet to England. The council agreed that a law ought to be passed giving to the governor, with its approval, the power to impress all arms and ammunition found in Virginia, to be paid for by the public and that after the service was over all which remained should be placed in the public magazine. An act was passed for strengthening the frontiers by encouraging group settlements there — in pursuance of which apparently nothing was ever done — and specifying the steps which should be taken on the spread of alarms from the coast or the interior. No addition was made to appropriations.

After the close of this session of the assembly both Nicholson and Quary sent to the board of trade very similar and very unfavorable accounts of the state of defence in Virginia. As Quary was present at the assembly, he could also write from a pretty definite knowledge of the situation, though it is not improbable that the two officials wrote with a full knowledge and agreement as to the contents of their epistles. The total number who were liable to military service was about 8000, but they were so undisciplined and so poorly equipped that the writers did not believe that one-fourth of them were fit to oppose the enemy. Virginia had known no conflicts except those of Bacon's Rebellion, and there now were very few survivors who had participated even in the petty encounters of that time. Nicholson knew of no man who was fit to command even a body of 300 or 400 men or to attack an enemy or defend a place. He then described in detail the poor condition in which the most exposed coast and frontier counties were and how 700 or 800 French and Indians might ravage the upper parts of the province before a force could be marched to attack them. It was also evident that, so far as the coast was concerned, an English squadron would be the only protection against a French attack. It was the old story, true on the whole, of all the colonies since their settlement and to continue so long as they were colonies and long afterward. Their chief security was to be found in the fact that the French in Canada were even weaker than they. As a result of the letters of Nicholson and Quary a quantity of arms and ammunition was sent to Virginia in 1702 and that led to various orders by the council there as to the distribution of them among the counties and threatening the prosecution of individuals who failed to purchase what were needed for their supply.[1]

Virginia was in a situation of this kind when the requisition of January, 1700/1, came from England, to the effect that £900 sterling and also a quota of men, if the governor should call for them, should be sent from Virginia to the aid of New York. This called forth an address to the king from the house of burgesses, in which they went to the extreme of charging New York with having as its object the monopolizing of trade with the northern Indians in beaver and deer skins.[2] Making use of the report which had been brought by Clay, they laid increased emphasis on the claim that Virginia was as directly exposed to French and Indian attack as was New York, and therefore that Virginia was a barrier to the northern colonies as well as they to it. It took fifty years more of history to make it appear that this was in any sense a fact. They went on to contrast the alleged richer trade and " more plentiful estates " of New York with " our hard labour in making tobacco, the profit whereof is

[1] Ex. Council Minutes, 1701, 1702; C. O. 5/1360, Entry Book 1701; Memorial of Quary, Mar. 17, 1701/2; Letter of Nicholson, Dec. 2; Cal. St. P. Col., under those dates.

[2] Cal. St. P. Col., 1701, p. 540; J. of Burgesses, Sept. 27, 1701.

exhausted by customs and impositions that amount to three or four times the price of the first cost we have for it, the lasting cause of the poverty of this country." This interesting statement throws light on the ease with which the colonists could use what they claimed to be the effect of the imperialistic policy concerning trade as an argument with which to oppose the same imperialistic policy as to defence. The burgesses then dwelt on the sums which they were expending in the revisal of their laws, in buying land and erecting public buildings at Williamsburg and in protecting themselves against pirates. They dwelt on the efforts they were making for the defence of their own frontiers and that their funds were so exhausted and inadequate that they had laid taxes even upon their servants and slaves. They claimed to be as weak in men and arms as they were poor in money, when the extent of the frontier which they must protect was taken into consideration.

As arguments against sending a quota of men to New York, they dwelt on the difficulty and cost of transporting them thither and the probability that they would arrive there too late for assistance. For every man who was taken out of Virginia for three months, and so from the active production of tobacco, they estimated the amount that the king would lose £20 sterling in customs. On the first notice of a draft, single men and the poorer housekeepers would begin to remove into other provinces, and hence the men to be detached must be freeholders of the better class, and while they were absent their servants and slaves would not raise above half the usual crops of tobacco on their plantations. Therefore persistence in the sending of quotas would probably have as its final result the loss of Virginia and Maryland to the crown.

This statement may be regarded as exhausting the arguments which could be used against the proposed requisition. They had not been by any means so fully stated in the previous war, and during the remainder of the present war it was only necessary to refer to this address and repeat some of its statements. In view of all the conditions which existed the decision which was reached as to the sending of troops was the necessary and only possible one; especially was this true in view of the fact that New York was not engaged in the war until 1709. But the arguments which were used were grossly exaggerated and do not prove that the resources which Virginia could have made available, were inadequate to the effort.

The same question was brought up again in the session of March and April, 1702/3 by a repetition of the order from the crown for aid in men and money to New York. Lord Cornbury had also written more than once to Nicholson on the subject. War was now actually in progress and New York could and did lay emphasis on her need of coast defence, as for the time greater than that of additional frontier posts. As a means of bringing influence to bear on the burgesses, the governor first brought the question before the council, both in executive and legislative session. He also offered again to lend the money himself without interest, if it was proven that the province could not advance it, though he thought that after the deduction of all debts charged against Virginia about half of the amount required was already in bank. The council declared that it would gladly use messages, conferences, or other proper means, as occasion suggested, but they could not violate precedents which left to the lower house the initiative in the making of appropriations. Nicholson's futile reply to this frank acknowledgment by the council of its inferiority in the matter of appropriations was, that he could not allow precedents to interfere with the prerogatives of the crown.

In the burgesses a motion for a free conference with the council at the start was voted down. Then a resolution was unanimously passed that Virginia was not able to furnish the £900 to New York. With this the council was asked to concur and, if they did so, then to appoint a committee to confer with a house committee on the best way of making a representation on the subject to the queen. When this decision reached the council, Nicholson told its members that they should now inquire into the public accounts and the state of the country, to see if the claim of inability was true. The council then desired a free conference, but the burgesses refused to enter upon it until the council had either accepted or rejected the above resolution. The council replied that they desired a conference in order to find out whether or not the country was able to bear the expense and also because it was an approved method of clearing up doubts and keeping a good understanding between the houses. After some further discussion along the same line, the burgesses took advantage of the fact that Nicholson had just urged them to undertake the revision of the laws to plead that as an excuse for asking that the session be closed. Other reasons which they gave in support of the same request were these, that the general court was then in session and would occupy much of the time of the councillors, and also that in the new town of Williamsburg, where the assembly was now meeting for the first time, there were few houses and some of the members had to lodge at a distance and with very ordinary entertainment. The council, in executive session, then advised that the assembly be prorogued, and after the burgesses had prepared their address to the queen stating again the reasons against sending aid to New York which had been given in 1701,[1] the session closed.

It was in harmony with the character and policy of Nicholson that he should make much of conferences between governors. Reference has elsewhere been made to an abortive plan of this kind which he tried to execute in 1699. During the summer of 1703, pursuant to the desire of the board of trade, Nicholson visited Cornbury at New York and conferred with him in relation to attacking Canada.[2] At this time he advanced £900 toward the cause, lest it might have a bad effect if the French learned of the refusal of Virginia to contribute it; but his bills at this time were apparently cancelled. When he returned he told the Virginia council what he had heard in New York of the poor state of the defences on that frontier, and expressed the opinion that, if the French made an advance there, it would be necessary to send a strong force from Virginia. With this all effort to enforce the requisition upon Virginia for aid to New York ceased and, as we have seen, when preparations were made for

[1] C. O. 5/1412, Ex. Council Minutes, March, 1702/3 *et seq.*; Journal of Council in Ass. and Journal of Burgesses of same date.

[2] Ex. Council minutes, Va., Apr. 24, 1703; C. O. 5/1313, O. P. Va., K 15; C. O. 5/1360, Entry Book, Va., ff. 174–178, 180–183. Nicholson to board of trade, July 23, 1703; B. T. to Nicholson Feb. 16, 1703/4.

the expeditions of 1709 and 1711 against Canada, no effort was made to procure assistance from colonies south of Pennsylvania.

The general harmony which had existed in Virginia during the previous war and in Nicholson's first administration was not continued at this time. While relations with New York were under discussion the governor was engaged in a violent controversy with some half-dozen prominent members of the council. Among these Commissary Blair was the leader, and with him Beverley, Ludwell and Harrison were very prominently associated. Owing to relations of an intensely personal nature, the family of Lewis Burwell became closely involved, as did two clergymen, Fonace and Wallace. Captain Moodie, of the guardship Southampton, had had some discussion with Nicholson and the council, during the winter of 1702/3, over a conflict between his orders from the admiralty [1] to sail to England by way of Newfoundland and the desire of the Virginia authorities that he should convoy their fleet and that of Maryland directly across. The governor and council insisted that if they sent to the secretary of state a copy of the records of their proceedings it would be a sufficient indemnity for Moodie. Nicholson also furnished the captain with credit for £100 which he desired. But the correspondence revealed the fact that the government of Virginia had been sharply criticised in some respects for its treatment of the king's ships, while Moodie in turn charged Nicholson with using abusive language to him. He therefore joined in the general complaints against the governor.

The case which now developed, like those of Phips in Massachusetts and Fletcher in New York, involved sweeping charges of misconduct against a governor, which were made the reason of a demand for his removal. The charges concerned matters far different from those which were cited in the case of the New York governor, though they were quite as illustrative of colonial government as it then was. It has already been stated that, during his administration in Maryland, Nicholson had been charged with giving way to fits of passion and using opprobrious language. This reputation followed him when he came the second time to Virginia. The

[1] C. O. 5/1313, I, 30, Original Papers, Va.

quarrel between Nicholson and Blair began with the delivery to the governor, soon after his appointment, of letters from the bishop of London and others cautioning him to greater moderation of speech and conduct. These, taken in connection with the advice which Blair himself gave, occasioned another outburst. Finally Nicholson told Blair to attend to his ecclesiastical business and leave government alone. Because of the governor's zeal for the church and his activity in its service, as well as that of the state, some time passed even after this before Blair broke entirely with him. But things had come to such a pass by 1704, that the above mentioned parties made complaint against the governor in England, Blair going thither as the chief agent for the purpose and submitting a long list of charges, supported by affidavits.

So far as affairs of government were concerned, Nicholson was charged with many arbitrary acts and wholesale assumption of power, especially to the exclusion of the council. Justices of the peace, it was said, he had privately appointed and sometimes blank commissions for that purpose were signed and sealed. The same course was followed in removals. One whole county court, they said, was turned out in that way. The same was true of the appointment and removal of sheriffs, county clerks, naval officers, the secretary, colonels and other military officers. Orders, proclamations and warrants were also issued without advice. Accounts of the revenue passed in the same way, Byrd, the deputy auditor, supporting this with a statement that the custom of audit by the council had been discontinued and he thereby had lost the public testimony to his integrity which he formerly had. Surveyors of land had been totally restrained in their work and rules prescribed for them by him alone. A permanent agent had also been appointed by the governor and paid out of the two shilling duty. Many things were put on record or forbidden entry by him alone. Records of courts were sometimes changed. He had mismanaged the affairs of the college. In council, both when in executive and legislative session, he sought to control and dictate affairs. He was impatient of debate, or monopolized it himself, and reproved or threatened members in a most abusive manner. Much also was made of a charge, inferred from Nicholson's plan to draft quotas from the militia for active service, that he intended to establish a standing army and with this destroy the liberties of the province.[1] Many of the things which were charged it was doubtless possible for a governor to do in those days, though that Nicholson did them on so large a scale as to make his government essentially arbitrary and autocratic is quite incredible.

As in the case of earlier governors, these charges, when presented in England, were *ex parte* and Nicholson had no agent effectively to represent him.[2] On the recommendation of the board of trade and under authority of an order in council the petition and the evidence supporting it were sent over to Virginia, that testimony might be taken on both sides without hindrance or coercion. The governor was required to permit this and, if he needed to visit England for his justification, he was to be allowed to do so. This case did not come to a hearing in England. Individuals were heard before the council in Virginia and affidavits were presented there, although in the presence of the governor and when he was presiding. He stated that all papers in support of his own case, as well as against it, should be free and open for the perusal of the council or even of others, but nothing like a hearing occurred either in Virginia or England. The strength of Nicholson's position appeared when the assembly met and he appealed to the house of burgesses.[3] They supported him in a most loyal address, speaking of him personally in high terms and denying that they or their constituents had complaints to offer or suspected that he intended to introduce arbitrary power. In a number of letters to the board of trade Nicholson denied the charges in general,

[1] Perry, Hist. Colls. of Am. Colonial Church, Virginia, pp. 75–140; C. O. 5/314, O. P. Va. 1704; C. O. 5/1360, 1361, Entry Book, Va. 1702–1705; Minutes of Ex. Council, Va.

[2] John Throle was agent at the time, but he died before this affair was well over. Nathaniel Blakiston was then appointed agent.

[3] Journal of Burgesses, Sess. of May, 1705. The exaggerated character of some of the statements of the councillors is illustrated by the charge of Beverley that Quary had written to the board of trade stating that democratic principles prevailed so in Virginia that only the queen's discipline and an armed force could keep its people to their duty. This drew out an address of protest from the assembly to which the board denied that it had received any such letters from Quary. C. O. 5/1316, Entry Book, Jan. 23, 1705/6; C. O. 5/1314, O. P., 1704.

and some of them in particular, and claimed that they were the outgrowth of the exclusiveness of the council and its resolve to be the real governing body in Virginia. As Harrison, Ludwell and Blair were all related by marriage, his view also was that the opposition was chiefly confined to that group. They were able to carry only one half of the council with them. The view expressed by Harrison on the other side was, that the burgesses were so greedy for office and for treating while the sessions continued that the governor, who dispensed patronage, could easily control them and prevent the expression of any opinion hostile to himself.

Though Nicholson retained his hold on the burgesses, his administration in Virginia came to an end in 1705. A month before the lower house presented to him its favorable address the commission of Colonel Edward Nott to be governor had been drafted in England. An order was issued for the recall of Nicholson that he might give an account of the state of Virginia, but he was also informed by the secretary of state that his recall was not due to any information against him or any displeasure on the part of the queen, but to the fact that such a course, it was thought, would be for her service at that time. His many later and responsible appointments show that this statement was true. The fall session of the assembly, in 1705, brought to light, in the form of an election contest and statement of grievances, the fact that in King William county, where the Huguenots had settled, very strong dissatisfaction existed with the recent conduct of the councillors toward Nicholson.[1] Among their resolves were three to the effect that no one should submit grievances of the province to the crown without the consent of the burgesses, that no affidavits or memorials should hereafter be signed against governors, and that no thanks but rather a check should be given to those who had so done against Governor Nicholson. But so extreme did these views now seem to the burgesses that they ordered this statement of grievances publicly burned and compelled those who were chiefly responsible for it to make humble acknowledgement before the house and pay costs.

Not long before the close of Nicholson's administration William Byrd, the elder, died. He had been deputy auditor

[1] Journal of Burgesses, Oct. and Nov. 1705.

and receiver general of Virginia since he succeeded Nathaniel Bacon, Sr., in these offices in 1687.[1] For reasons of economy, in Bacon's time these two offices had been united in a single hand and had so continued during Byrd's incumbency. As receiver or treasurer Byrd had regularly accounted before the governor and council twice a year and his accounts had passed through Blathwayt's office to the treasury. The accounts under the item of quit rents showed a gain which went toward disproving the pleas of poverty with which the burgesses met every demand for expenditures toward general colonial defence. A report of Blathwayt in 1705 showed that the yield from this source in Virginia had been steadily increasing since 1684 and had now reached an annual revenue of more than £1800. The accumulation had been so large that for the first time a balance of some £3000 could be paid into the royal exchequer. So that Lord Treasurer Godolphin wrote to the governor emphasizing these facts and using them as an argument for greater activity with a view to securing a larger increase.[2] In this connection the need of much more complete rent rolls of the counties was enforced, especially in view of the fact that the number of them had now increased to thirty-five and boundaries had very much changed. Sheriffs and other officials were also to be encouraged to discover land from which rent was due but, because of imperfect surveys or none at all, it had not been paid. The death of Byrd, as well as the fact that his more famous son of the same name, applied for appointment to the two offices, helped still further to centre attention on Virginia finances. As the result of the general inquiry, the two offices were divided and the younger Byrd was appointed receiver general.[3] These events accompanied the appointment of Edward Nott to the governorship of Virginia.

Nott's administration lasted only a year, he dying in office in August, 1706. He was a capable official and found no difficulty in securing the harmonious cooperation of all departments of the government. On his death the president and council wrote, " He was a gentleman of a very happy

[1] Blathwayt's Journal, Feb. 11, 1700/1.
[2] *Ibid.*, April 2, 1705, and later entries.
[3] *Ibid.*, June 4, 8, 12, Oct. 29, 1705.

temper to cure our divisions, and managed whatever was proposed for her Majesty's service in Council and Assembly with great satisfaction and success."[1] During the early months of his administration much attention was paid in the executive council to the straightening out of accounts and correcting the irregularities of officials. For a short time after the death of Byrd Nicholson had discharged the duties of the vacant offices in person and the council had some difficulty in effecting a settlement with him. In that connection further evidence appeared of his assuming to transact important financial business without consulting the council.[2] The practice of reading the minutes of the council at every session was now resumed, and when it came to meet in legislative session Nott absented himself most of the time. This indicated the spirit of the new administration. Plans for the better regulation of the granting of land and of quit rents received much attention. The lowering of the prices at which arms and ammunition, recently sent from England, were sold to purchasers was sought, and detailed orders as to their distribution among the counties were issued. As in Maryland, the right to appoint the county clerks was affirmed, objections of the board to a number of the revised laws were received and considered by the council in executive session.[3] Relations were growing more complicated along the North Carolina border, with conflicting titles to land, all this making more imperative the necessity that the boundary should be settled. Questions relating to the Northern Neck also occasionally appeared. The condition of the vestries and the amount of support which was required by the clergy received much attention. The question of forts and towns was a perennial subject of discussion. The evidence concerning them and other questions of purely Virginia interest show that a good amount of executive business was done. The same was true of the two sessions of the assembly which met during the year of Nott's governorship.

During the spring session of 1706 the burgesses sent up a bill for the levy of a duty on the importation of liquors and

[1] C. O. 5/1362, E. B., Pres. and Council to B. T., Aug. 29, 1706.

[2] Minutes of Ex. Council, Sept. 1705.

[3] See Journal of Ex. Council for June 20, 1706.

slaves, in which no exception was made of those which might come from the English realm. This directly violated instructions and furnished the council with an admirable chance to amend a money bill. Of this, though in courteous terms, it was not slow to avail itself, and the burgesses had to accept the amendment. In May, 1706, came the news of the capture of the island of St. Christopher by the French, and this aroused fears that it might be followed by a descent on the Virginia coast and the plundering of the tobacco fleet. At once there was great activity. The governor exhorted, the houses went into conference.[1] An embargo was laid, the coast watch was revived, and provision made for spreading alarms. Collectors and naval officers on the James and York rivers were called in to report what was necessary for their defence. After consultation with all parties, the governor concluded that Jamestown and West Point on York river were most capable of being fortified, while it was the general opinion that the shipping should be taken above these localities for protection. But fortunately the French did not appear and military activity soon abated.

The only other alarms from which Virginia seems to have suffered on account of foreign enemies during the war were occasioned by the appearance of French privateers off the coast in 1708 and 1709.[2] On the former occasion the vessel came from Martinique and captured a Liverpool ship and a sloop from the West Indies. The guardship "Garland" cruised about the capes, but did not meet the privateers. As it was under orders to convoy the fleet home, the "Garland" had to come up the river to prepare for the voyage. The privateer took advantage of this to venture within the capes, but captured nothing there.

In the spring of 1709 a general alarm was spread by the report that one Hendrix, who knew Virginia well, was coming as a privateer from Martinique. President Jennings had ammunition distributed and such cannon as they had planted along the bay to alarm the country. The "Garland" had not yet returned from a voyage to England, and therefore Virginia had to do the best she could to fit out a brigantine to

[1] See Journals of Ex. Council and of Burgesses for May, 1706.

[2] C. O. 5/1362, Jennings to B. T. June 24, 1708, March 21, 1709.

cruise within the capes, communicate with vessels inward bound, and alarm the country. On occasion of every alarm like this, whether it proved real or not, people had to be withdrawn from their labor to defend the coast and slaves conveyed to places of safety until the danger was over. This was done to prevent them from being taken or running away. As this alarm occurred in the spring, it would have paralyzed agriculture during much of the planting season if some provision had not been made for the protection of the coast. But it occasioned expense, and the cost must for the time be met out of the stated revenue of the queen, with the hope that the next assembly would reimburse the charge. The privateer appeared, but was frightened away by the brigantine — which it was planned should carry ten guns and eighty men — and by the fact that it found Virginia on guard. At the Delaware and at Currituck, in North Carolina, considerable damage was done by the same vessel. During the winter of 1709/10 the "Garland" was lost off the Virginia coast and, as her successor did not arrive till some months later, it became necessary to fit out a sloop for temporary purposes of defence. A vessel which had arrived from New York was taken for the purpose. The continued presence of privateers on the coast made this necessary or else, as Jennings wrote, he would not have had the presumption to resort to the measure.[1] It was with an occasional experience of this kind that Virginia passed through all the later years of the war. In reality nothing more serious than that occurred to her during either of the two first colonial wars. Except for their indirect results, the colonies between the Delaware and South Carolina had no experience of these wars. Occasional alarms somewhat disturbed them and their trade relations were affected, but otherwise they were practically at peace. The burden of conflict in America rested on the colonies at the two ends of the arc, the West Indies and those more or less adjacent to the Gulf of St. Lawrence. The vast intermediate territory was not directly involved. This was due to geographical conditions and to the fact that operations at large were controlled by the exigencies of naval warfare.

[1] *Ibid.*, Jennings to B. T., June, 1710.

As the only other military operations in which Virginia was involved prior to 1715 were then connected with the Tuscarora war in North Carolina, and this had no connection with the larger conflict, we can leave Virginia at this point and by this means gain the opportunity to treat the administration of Alexander Spotswood as a unit in itself.

CHAPTER XXII

MARYLAND DURING THE SECOND INTERCOLONIAL WAR. CLOSE OF THE PERIOD OF ROYAL GOVERNMENT

THAT part of Maryland history with which we are concerned in this chapter includes three administrations — those of Nathaniel Blakiston, (1699–1702), John Seymour (1704–1709), Edward Lloyd as president of the council (1709–1713). During the two years also which intervened between the retirement of Blakiston and the arrival of Seymour the affairs of the province were administered by the council and its president, Thomas Tench. When the period ended John Hart had been in office about a year.

During nearly one-half of this time the government of Maryland was in the hands of a president and council, they being natives of the province and not disposed to depart widely from lines of policy which had become established and traditional there. The rule of a president and council, as we have repeatedly seen, was regarded as temporary in its very nature and was expected to pass with as little change as possible. The fact that conditions were generally normal and peaceful in Maryland at that time, that it was nearly free from outside attacks and from internal discontent, caused the administrations of the royal governors as well to pass without serious conflicts or other dramatic events. With the transfer of Nicholson to Virginia, the irritation which had been provoked by the fits of passion and the overweening conceit to which he was now becoming a victim disappeared. Coode, whose real services in the Revolution were recognized, was allowed to return to Maryland, where he ended his days in obscurity.[1] His friends, freed from the danger of prosecution, resumed their places among the peaceful inhabitants of the province. Blakiston assumed an extremely conciliatory attitude, and the two years of his administration, coming

[1] Md. Arch. XXV, 103.

as they did at the close of the brief period of peace between the two colonial wars, left Maryland in a state of almost perfect quiet and harmony.

The new governor was a London merchant of Northumbrian stock, one of whose uncles, Nehemiah Blakiston, we have found prominent in Maryland affairs both before and after the Revolution. He had died there in 1693. The nephew had already served as lieutenant governor of Montserrat and expected that the same harmonious relations would attend him in Maryland as in his island colony.[1] At the time of his appointment piracy was at its height and the Scotch experiment at Darien was in progress. The admiralty courts were in process of establishment and Robert Quary was beginning his career as judge of admiralty at Philadelphia. William Penn was returning for his second visit to his province, which brought Markham's administration to an end and checked in some respects the activities of pirates and illegal traders in that region. The earl of Bellomont was vigorously attacking the same evils in New York. Nicholson, following out his characteristic line of activity, planned a meeting between himself, Blakiston and Bellomont at Philadelphia, where Penn could be present,[2] a plan which was never executed. The settled shores of Maryland, along the upper Chesapeake, were secluded, but they caught glimpses of pirates fresh from Madagascar under the lead of Turner, a companion of Giles Shelley, who had landed off Cape Henlopen. Scotch traders appeared in Maryland as elsewhere.[3] Under the customary orders from England, Maryland officials dealt with these intruders as they were able. A small sixth rate was stationed in the Chesapeake to serve more as an advice boat for communication with Virginia than as a restraint against pirates and illegal traders.[4] Later it was Blakiston's opinion that a sloop which could carry only six or eight men and was small enough to run into the creeks and coves would be more useful for service on the upper Chesapeake than were larger vessels, and it would be much less expensive.[5]

[1] Md. Arch. XXII, 288.

[2] Cal. St. P. Col., 1699, p. 239.

[3] Md. Arch. XXV, 73, 77.

[4] Cal. St. P. Col., 1700, pp. 55, 288.

[5] C. O. 5/715, Memorial from Blakiston to Lord High Admiral, Nov. 19, 1702. Morriss, Colonial Trade of Maryland, 1689–1715. J. H. U. Studies, XXXII.

The tobacco industry was passing through another serious crisis at this time, a crisis which affected Virginia as well as Maryland and the entire belt of colonies which were devoted to the production of this staple. As had been true many times during the previous century, over-production with its accompaniment of low prices was a fundamental difficulty. But, notwithstanding the evidence of the market, the tobacco planters could not be diverted to any serious extent from the industry to which they had so attached themselves at the time Virginia and Maryland were first settled. The production of the weed was large in the West Indies. The Dutch were committing themselves extensively to the industry. The prohibition of the use of tobacco in Russia had been removed and under the lead of Peter the Great its manufacture there was increasing, with possibilities arising from the share which British merchants were taking in this enterprise that caused anxiety to the board of trade and other officials.[1] Still the best quality of tobacco came from Spain, and as between Virginia and Maryland, the older colony had the advantage. The use of the weed was rapidly spreading, but in the race between the smokers and chewers on the one side and the planters on the other the persistence of low prices indicated that there was no likelihood of demand overtaking supply. Though the British government at the start had been opposed to the industry and doubts concerning its utility still lingered, officials and legislators had long since yielded to the temptation offered by large revenue and with them the fiscal motive had supplanted every other. Therefore tobacco, notwithstanding the low form of agriculture to which it gave rise and the unfortunate effects which it had on society in general, had become a favorite colonial product with all the nations, and with the British in particular had long since taken its place among their leading staples, the most valuable which was produced upon the American continent. In the mercantilist's hierarchy Virginia held the highest seat because she was the leading producer of tobacco. Her loyalty rested upon that as a broad and sufficient basis and official pressure cooperated with social inertia to keep her in the straight and narrow path of mercantilist orthodoxy. Like

[1] See material in C. O. 5/1361.

the production of naval stores, the raising of tobacco, in the colonies concerned, was encouraged as a means of diverting the people from manufacturing.

But before 1690 over-production,[1] with the prevailing low prices, had proven a serious drawback, as the tobacco cutting riots and other crude efforts to find a remedy had shown. After the beginning of the colonial wars, exclusion from foreign markets, embargoes, irregularity in the arrivals and sailings of the tobacco fleets added to the difficulties of the situation. These became more serious in the second than in the first war, because Spain was now an enemy of Great Britain. In 1706, and again in 1707, the board of trade, in a memorial to the queen, stated that the tobacco trade of England was under great discouragements in its exports to Muscovy, Sweden, Denmark, France and Spain, those countries being chiefly supplied with tobacco of foreign growth, so that it was found that tobacco of British origin would no longer be used in those countries. Within a decade the output in the provinces along the lower Rhine, where tobacco was chiefly raised, had increased nearly threefold, and had reached an annual production of 27,000,000 pounds. In the cities of the Netherlands the manufacturing and export of tobacco was being carried on upon a large scale, and the board reported that the Dutch by the cheapness of their product had ousted Virginia tobacco from the markets of northern Europe. Certain minor remedies, such as allowing neutral ships to carry British tobacco to France, were suggested to relieve the situation while the war lasted. But John Hinton, a large manufacturer and dealer, urged that a drawback of the entire duty be allowed on the export of manufactured tobacco from England and that perplexing oaths at the custom houses be done away with in order to facilitate exportation.[2] In 1714 the board of trade repeated its statements of seven years before and declared that Virginia and Maryland were in a miserable condition, occasioned by the low price of tobacco, due to the great quantity and

[1] Since the early days of the colonies the average crop per colonist had decreased about one-half, but the increase in population had resulted in a much larger gross production.

[2] C. O. 5/1362, July 1, 1707; Jan. 12, 1709.

cheapness of the European product and to the high rates of duty levied on it in Great Britain.[1] Also, when the tobacco fleets were delayed or for any reason brought inadequate cargoes of manufactured goods, the tobacco colonies suffered from a dearth of these and that tempted them to resort to manufacturing, especially of clothing, and also in some cases to removals into other colonies where the economic system was different. In 1715, because of the decrease of revenue in Virginia due to the decay in the tobacco trade, the board advised that the quit rents be no longer drawn into the exchequer in England, as had been the custom during the past few years, but that they be left in the province and used to meet its expenditures. These statements, supported as they were by frequent wails from the colony and from merchants and leading to the passage of an act by parliament in 1713 to relieve some of the conditions of importation, show that the tobacco industry of that period was not prosperous and that Virginia and Maryland were suffering because of it.

The planters marketed their crop either by sending it to commission merchants in England, or by selling it in the colony to factors or agents of British merchants or to ship captains.[2] Under the former method the planter had to trust the merchant to sell the tobacco at a price which would pay the freight, duties and commission and yield a profit to the planter. The return was usually made in European goods. Under this method the planter bore the risks of transit and also of sale at a loss and of loss through bad debts in England. By the second method these were avoided, but with them the chance of a rise in price in the British market. The merchants generally preferred the former method and those of London followed it; so it was much more difficult for planters to sell their crops outright at their wharves. But in any case, because of the low prices, the profits of the planter were small and they are said to have been generally in debt to the merchants with whom they dealt, sometimes losing their estates as the result of this. With the lapse of time and the growth of demand for a cheaper quality of tobacco,

[1] C. O. 5/1364, p. 33 *et seq.*; C. O. 5/1316, p. 12. The price of tobacco during three years ranged about two pence per pound.

[2] Morriss, Colonial Trade of Maryland, J. H. U. Studies, XXXII.

the character of the crop tended to deteriorate. Stalks were packed with leaves and added their part to the weight on which customs were collected. Much trash was sent and the shipping of tobacco in bulk facilitated this practice. The conditions of marketing also affected the industry as a whole and the social conditions to which it gave rise, but they did not turn any appreciable number to the production of cereals or other commodities for which a favored market did not exist in Great Britain.

What has been said about tobacco in Virginia, is true in general in the case of Maryland. The two colonies had committed themselves equally to this form of industry; but the quality of the Maryland crop was always considered slightly inferior to that of Virginia. The sweet-scented variety raised in Virginia was superior to any which the sister colony produced. The cessation of the war relieved the tobacco trade to an extent in Maryland, as it did elsewhere. But the people in general were poor. When Blakiston was appointed, he was intrusted with suits against a number of Marylanders who had been sureties on forfeited navigation bonds, but the attorney general of the province had certified that not a thousand pounds could be recovered from all of them. The following year the lower house petitioned that further prosecutions be suspended, as the accused must perish in jail through lack of means to pay the judgments against them, and besides in most cases there was no intention of fraud at the beginning.[1] During the war some who continued planting had been compelled to sell part of their land and servants to save the rest,[2] while others resorted more to the manufacture of woolen, cotton, linen, leather and the like for the supply of family and local needs. The debtor class was very numerous and is much in evidence, and out of the general situation arose complaints that not a few were migrating to Pennsylvania and North Carolina.

In replying to a proposal for increased expenditure in 1702 the assembly stated that Maryland had no means of raising

[1] Cal. St. P. Col., 1697–1698, p. 482; Md. Arch. XXII, 428; Morriss, *op. cit.*, 27, 40.

[2] C. O. 5/716. The Present State of the Tobacco Plantations in America (unsigned), recd. Dec. 16, 1708.

money except by imposing duties on exports and imports, about 95% being raised by duties on tobacco. To raise money by a direct tax on the inhabitants was utterly impracticable, for the greater part had not five shillings by them nor any means for raising it, because there was very little money in the province and that in the form of a base coinage which did not circulate in the other colonies. In 1704 Governor Seymour wrote, " Maryland has at present no prospect of increasing its trade and navigation by tillage, the planters being so bent on their crops of tobacco that they scarcely make grain to eat, but are forced to be supplied from Pennsylvania." A law which had just been passed for imposing an export duty on Maryland products,[1] he said, would be of little use, as very few furs or skins were being exported and for seven years past not a barrel of beef or pork had been sent out of the province, but supplies of this nature had been purchased from Pennsylvania and other colonies. Though during the royal period Maryland raised an adequate supply of cattle and hogs and supplied her own demand for corn, she exported no foodstuffs.[2]

After the second war began, the tobacco industry was further depressed by embargoes, added perils of the ocean and consequent irregularity in the supply of shipping for carrying the product to market. Maryland merchants were dependent on the dates set for the sailing of the fleets from Virginia, and sometimes received incorrect notices. On one occasion the commodore sent notice that he would sail in twenty days, but really did not sail for nearly two months. Such delays injured the cargos and were a source of great inconvenience. Though, because of the small returns from tobacco for years past, many of the planters had found their servants and slaves burdensome, yet servants and slaves were being steadily imported at the rate in each case of something like 600 a year.[3] Seymour wrote in 1706 that Charles Carroll, Baltimore's agent, had brought in more than 200 Irish Catholics, to whom assurances of land had been given, when their terms of service should have expired. This the governor regarded

[1] C. O. 5/715. From comments of Seymour on Md. acts, recd. Oct. 1705.

[2] Morriss, 16–21.

[3] Morriss, 77 *et seq.*; C. O. 5/716. Seymour to Board, recd. June, 1706.

as a growing evil.[1] The cry was still raised that, owing to poverty, people were moving away. North Carolina had invited people to settle there under a promise of exemption for five years from the payment of their debts, and Pennsylvania by raising the value of their coin beyond proclamation rates. Seymour proposed to pass a bankruptcy law as a help for people in debt and appealed to the home government for other measures of relief.[2]

During the administration of Lloyd and the council, and at close of the war, the same note was sounded. The tobacco market was poor. What little manufacturing was done in Maryland, was necessitated by the scarcity of imported goods. Trade with the West Indies was small. In April, 1713, the president and council implored the board of trade to have consideration for the "poor province," reduced to most distressed circumstances by the extremely low price of Orinoco tobacco.[3] The inhabitants had been forced to spin the little wool their flocks afforded and some small quantities of flax for necessary clothing. A similar representation was sent by the entire legislature later in the year. Some turned also to the raising of grain and cattle, for the surplus of which a ready market was found in the West Indies.

A minor difficulty connected with the trade arose from the tendency, as freight was estimated by the cask or hogshead, to steadily increase their size. The size which became common in Maryland exceeded that of the Virginia hogsheads — which were the model — by two inches in the diameter, though their lengths were the same. This the Marylanders sought to justify by the argument that the Virginia brand of tobacco was heavier than theirs. But even that difference made packing difficult on board the ships which carried the product to England, and an agitation was kept up by the British merchants until, in 1711, the assembly yielded and passed an act requiring conformity with the size of Virginia casks.[4]

[1] Seymour to Bd., Nov. 18, 1708; *ibid.*, Pres. & C. to Bd., Nov. 4, 1710.

[2] C. O. 5/716, Seymour to Board of Trade, June 23, 1708.

[3] C. O. 5/717, Lloyd to Board, July 15, 1712; *ibid.*, Apr. 16, 1713; *ibid.*, rec'd, Jan. 13, 1713/14; Md. Arch. XXIX, 218, 282.

[4] Md. Arch. XXV, 246; XXVII, 215; XXIX, 74; C. O. 5/716. Memorial from Merchants, etc., rec'd Mar. 16, 1707/8; *ibid.*, Lloyd to Board, Jan. 25, 1711/12.

The ever recurring question of ports and towns, which was so closely connected with the tobacco industry, was also prominent during Seymour's administration. He was strongly in favor of the restriction of the shipping of tobacco and the landing of imported goods to five staple towns, Annapolis, Oxford, Somerset, Patuxent and St. Mary's. To the board of trade he enlarged upon the advantages which would come through this arrangement to all parties concerned, and urged that the plan be put in operation under an act of parliament or by orders from the crown.[1] Seymour was ordered, instead, to recommend that the assembly should pass an act for the purpose desired. Seymour immediately sent to Virginia for information as to its laws and regulations on the subject, which were to be laid before the Maryland assembly. In April, 1706, a long and complicated act was passed by the assembly, modelled apparently on those which had been passed before. It made nearly every important exporter's wharf a port, contained detailed provisions for the settlement of towns which could never exist except upon paper, while the provisions for exclusive trading there related to imports and not to exports. Two supplementary acts followed, and though the governor expressed gratification at what the assembly had done, it is clear that under its enactments the tobacco trade would have remained practically as unregulated as it had previously been.[2]

As soon as these measures reached England, the merchants objected that they required all Great Britain to keep store with their goods in certain places called towns, which at present were without buildings or inhabitants, and allowed the people of Maryland to dispose of their products in any part of the province. Another requirement of this legislation, chiefly directed, it is probable, against the competition of Pennsylvania, was the provision that all British products, being once imported could not be exported out of Maryland; they must be sold there or perish. Because of these objec-

[1] C. O. 5/715, Lowndes and Seymour to Board, Nov. 2, 1705; *ibid.*, rec'd. June 12.

[2] C. O. 5/716, Seymour to the Board, Aug. 21, 1706; Md. Arch. XXVI, p. 636 *et seq.*; XXVII, 159, 346.

tions the three acts were disallowed, late in 1709.[1] In the following August the merchants, in a communication to the board of trade, alleged that they had suffered much from the above-mentioned laws before their repeal, and asked that the governor of Maryland be instructed not to assent to any act concerning navigation and commerce unless a sufficient time was allowed before it went into effect for them to be informed of its provisions. An instruction to this effect was given to Governor Hart and he urged the assembly to take up the matter again because of the advantages to trade which seemed obvious to him in the creation of a number of port towns.[2]

As had been stated by the authors of "The Present State of Virginia," another very inconvenient effect of the too exclusive devotion of the tobacco colonies to their favorite product was this, that they were compelled to use it as a substitute for money. But efforts from time to time were made to escape from this and to secure a supply of coin. In 1694 and again the next year bills were introduced into the lower house, the object of which was to promote the use of money, especially in the payment of duties and officers' fees.[3] In 1701 a bill passed the lower house to encourage the importation of coin and the use of it in paying public levies; but the governor and council thought the change would introduce such complications in adjusting payments as to cause confusion and, for one thing, make it very difficult to execute the provision in the church act for the payment of the clergy. It was also seen to be necessary, if coin was to be used, to equalize its value in exchange with that of neighboring colonies, a thing which could not be done without permission from the crown. For this reason the governor declined to approve the bill until he heard from the board of trade.[4] In his letter to the board Blakiston stated, at the request of the assembly, that coin in Maryland consisted of a few pieces

[1] *Ibid.*, Memorial from merchants, rec'd. Sept. 23, 1709; C. O. 5/717. Order in council, Dec. 15, 1709.

[2] C. O. 5/717. Memorial of merchants, rec'd. Aug. 12, 1710; Md. Arch. XXIX, 394, 469. It is interesting to note that, as early as 1701, a joint committee of the houses was appointed to consider means for the partial substitution of money for tobacco as the medium in which to pay taxes. Md. Arch. XXIV, 172.

[3] Md. Arch. XIX, 47, 252.

[4] Md. Arch. XXIV, 149. C. O. 5/715. Blakiston to Board, May 25, 1701.

of eight and Lyon dollars. The latter passed in Maryland for 4s. 6d. but among their neighbors the pieces of eight passed for 5s. and the Lyon dollars in Pennsylvania at 6s. and in New York at a little less. The result was that coin steadily passed out of Maryland to the colonies where it was more highly valued. The assembly therefore desired permission to rate their dollars at 5s. as in Virginia, since the presence of so little money in Maryland hindered business of all kinds, and public meetings and courts, since persons could not be accommodated without it.

One clause in an act of 1704 for the direction of sheriffs permitted the payment of levies in money in lieu of tobacco rated at 1d. per pound. This was to continue in force for three years. In commenting on this act Seymour expressed the hope that it would not be construed as tending to lessen the planting of tobacco, since without the law money could be used for the purchase of tobacco with which to pay levies, fees and the like. It was also claimed that the act would better enable sheriffs to collect from poor people who raised no tobacco. Another act of the same session for the encouragement of trade with the West Indies had, as one of its objects, the preventing of Pennsylvania drawing off the little coin which was current in Maryland. But no relief came, and in 1706 the governor, council and assembly addressed the queen and suggested as a remedy for the total lack of coin from which they suffered that she grant them a fractional coinage in specie — three-penny and six-penny pieces — to the amount of £700 st. — the same to be repaid and to be current only in Maryland.[1]

In 1704 another and related feature of the economic policy of Maryland appeared in the form of an act,[2] which was periodically revived in later years, prohibiting the importation from Pennsylvania or the Lower Counties of any breadstuffs, beer, malt or horses, these being the staple exports of that province. One motive of this legislation, which was very natural in the colonies as they were then situated, was to encourage the production of grain in Maryland and an export trade in it similar to that which flourished to the northward.

[1] *Ibid.*, XXVI, 551.
[2] Md. Arch. XXVI, 314; XXVII, 574; XXIX, 238, 255.

But the tobacco industry was too strongly intrenched to permit of success in these efforts. Pennsylvanians also, by importing their grain, "picked up the ready money and Bills of Exchange by which and other like Practices they have heretofore sucked the very marrow of the Province," declared the Maryland council on one occasion. These expressions and the adoption of this policy furnished additional proof of the disadvantage under which the tobacco régime placed Maryland.

As has been stated, the attitude assumed by Blakiston toward the province and its assembly was one of the utmost kindliness and conciliation. To his first assembly, after he had been six months in Maryland, he said that his acts should give proof of his resolve to maintain the interest of the province and to secure for its people the fullest measure of justice they could hope or desire. To him it was like "a fair sheet of paper," for he came not with prejudice toward any person. Notwithstanding the evidences of agricultural distress, he affirmed the real identity of interests between the province and Great Britain; and well might this appear to be true in a colony politically so peaceful as Maryland was at that time. At the beginning of the next session of this assembly the governor expressed the greatest satisfaction with the perfect accord which had existed hitherto and left the houses to proceed on their usual course without dictation on his part. Though an election was held toward the close of his administration, it was not owing to any dissatisfaction on either side.[1]

A number of his instructions which Blakiston, as was usual, laid before the assembly, were calmly ignored by it as inapplicable to the conditions of the province, physical and otherwise. Among these was the requirement that a survey should be made of the landing places on the rivers and harbors and forts erected there. The assembly regarded this as futile for the reasons which we have already found to have largely defeated similar efforts at Point Comfort in Virginia.[2] Though the period of peace was to be short, and toward its close came warnings from Bellomont of activity among the Indians

[1] Md. Arch. XXIV, 8.
[2] *Ibid.*, XXII, 287, 295, 380.

on the northern frontier, the assembly remained inactive. A few rangers were sent out on occasion. Blakiston found such arms as remained lodged with the county authorities,[1] which probably meant that they were inaccessible and out of repair. Though an elaborate militia act was passed in 1699, it was framed on the old lines and nothing had been accomplished toward the improvement of the force.[2] In May, 1701, the lower house even voted to disband the few rangers which were out and not to continue a committee on Indian affairs. The total number then liable to military service in Maryland was somewhat in excess of five thousand.[3]

Disputes over the governor's support did not arise, because the additional appropriation of three pence per hogshead on the export of tobacco which had been given to Nicholson was continued. In the making and expenditure of appropriations, too, the houses shared and there were no disputes between them. In May, 1700, and again in 1701, a joint committee of the two houses was intrusted with the power to assess the public levy already voted, to allow a specified additional amount if it seemed necessary,[4] and to apportion and pay out sums which appeared to be due to parties named in the journal of the committee of accounts. The authority to draw and expend money on an emergency during a recess of the assembly had been previously granted to the council with a committee of the lower house, and the treasurer was ordered to honor their drafts.[5] This continued to be the usage after the beginning of the next war.

At the end of two years Blakiston's health broke down and he returned to England. But his connection with Maryland was not wholly severed. There had been complaint that this province had not kept an agent near the court, and at his own suggestion Blakiston was appointed to this office.[6]

[1] *Ibid.*, XIX, 586; XX, 145, 151; C. O. 5/715, Blakiston to Board, May 25, 1701. Account of arms read, Dec. 8, 1701.

[2] *Ibid.*, XXII, 562; XXIV, 12, 14, 190; XXV, 57, 76.

[3] C. O. 5/716, Seymour to Board of Trade, June 23, 1708.

[4] *Ibid.*, XXIX, 107, 204; XXVI, 350. The journal of the committee of accounts is on pp. 111–124 of vol. XXIV.

[5] *Ibid.*, XXII, 452 *et seq.*; XXIV, 322.

[6] *Ibid.*, 260–261, 316, 393, 395. C. O. 5/715, Blakiston to Board of Trade, Sept. 17, 1702; Memorial of Blakiston rec'd. Aug. 23, 1704. These last are instances of Blakiston's activity as agent.

It was while he was serving in this capacity that Seymour was appointed to the governorship and of him Blakiston sent a favorable account.

Seymour, like at least some of his name in England, was an assertive and self-important man. He was also a strong supporter of the Church, and for these reasons certain features of Nicholson's administration were bound to recur. The war had been in progress in the north for some time when he arrived in Maryland. These facts suggest three important characteristics of his administration, in all of which it differed from the one which preceded. Under Seymour there was considerable legislation — some of it relating to the courts — and the laws were revised. The comments which he made when transmitting these to England show that he must have had some knowledge of the law. As we have seen, the claim of Sir Thomas Lawrence was again brought to the front, while the aggressive attitude of the governor toward Catholics gave new life to charges against the proprietary régime and to controversies with Lord Baltimore over land and revenue. It was just after Seymour's arrival that the final change was made in the act for the establishment of the Church, and about its interests and protection against fancied dangers from Catholics centered not a little of Seymour's activity. It was in harmony with the tendencies of Anne's reign, as reflected in many of the colonies, that this should be so.

The case of Sir Thomas Lawrence, of which we have already heard so much, was revived early in this administration and was kept pretty continuously in view until 1712 or later. The occasion of this was the passage in 1704 of an act diverting the profits which arose from the licensing of ordinaries to the province treasury. This set Lawrence petitioning again for the restoration of what he claimed as his rights.[1] In 1707 an opinion was rendered by the attorney general, Sir Simon Harcourt, favorable to the claim of Lawrence. The act in question, he thought, should be disallowed and a permanent act passed, in the place of the temporary ones which had existed since 1693, vesting the fees in ques-

[1] C. O. 5/715; Memorials of Lawrence to Board, rec'd. Nov. 30, 1705, Jan. 18, 1705/6, May 8, 1707.

tion in her majesty's secretary. Incidentally also he called attention to the fact that Sir Thomas' patent had expired with the death of the late king and had not been renewed; he was therefore serving illegally, as probably were many other officials in the colonies, and this defect should be remedied. An order in council was issued in accordance with that part of the opinion which related to the permanent disposal of profits from the licenses.[1]

But, as Seymour wrote, Sir Thomas was the last person whom the assembly seemed willing to oblige. An ordinance was passed by the two houses, so as to avoid the necessity of submitting it to the crown, forbidding ordinaries to be kept or liquor to be sold without license from the county justices. This, of course, provoked the controversy, and in it Bladen, the clerk of the council, and others became involved. The governor was charged by Sir Thomas with grave injustice toward him and with sacrificing the prerogative. The board of trade condemned the ordinance by which the will of the home government in reference to the act of 1704 was thwarted, but the most that the crown would do was to instruct the next governor to use his best efforts to secure the passage of a permanent law vesting the profits of the licenses in question in the secretary and making him a proper grant in lieu of the profits which he had lost since 1704. But this was never done by the assembly, and Sir Thomas Lawrence died with his claims unsatisfied.[2] The proposal of the lower house to appoint an agent was held up by the council because of the disagreement of the houses over these claims.

The claims of Lawrence also brought him into controversy, as we have seen, with the agents of Lord Baltimore over the custody of land patents and other similar records and the fees which were connected therewith.[3] Charles

[1] C. O. 5/716; Opinion of attorney general, rec'd. Aug. 5, 1707; O. in C. Jan. 15, 1707/8; Md. Arch. XXV, 247; Seymour to Board, Jan. 10, 1708/9; Memorial of Lawrence to Board rec'd. Feb. 24, 1709/10; O. in C. Mar. 30, 1710.

[2] Md. Arch. XXIX, 204, 222, 233, 236, 253, 260, 267, 284, 286, 305, 323, 326; C. O. 5/717, Address from House of Delegates, rec'd. by Board, Jan. 29, 1713/14.

[3] Md. Arch. XXV, 130, 137, 138.

Carroll, who gradually rose to the place of proprietary agent held by Darnall, was now involved in these disputes. They were inherited from the previous administrations and never reached a settlement. The relations between the proprietor and the government of the crown in Maryland were still being illustrated by criticisms which were directed by Lord Baltimore, in his communications to the board of trade, against important acts relating to grants and bounds of land, escheats, the qualification of surveyors, arrears of rent, debts and their collection. Upon acts relating to all these matters the proprietor, during the period which we are now considering, expressed opinions which were dictated by his own interests.[1] In provinces which were situated like Maryland such representations bore a part in all that related especially to the confirmation or rejection of laws. In his comments upon an act of 1699 for rectifying the indefinite bounds which at first had been assigned to land grants, Lord Baltimore emphasized the fact in many ways that he or his conditions of plantation or the rights of his tenants and officials were being infringed. He plead in detail earlier precedents and the claims of the proprietor. In the case of another act which declared bonds void unless they were renewed or put in suit within five years of the contraction of the debt, he complained that it would cause many suits and would greatly injure himself, as well as others, because he had been lenient with many of his debtors. Against an act of 1707, which required that Baltimore's surveyors should qualify themselves as did royal officials, he argued that it was as if all the noblemen's stewards in England should be obliged to take the oaths required of magistrates, which would be absurd. The reply of the assembly to this and other arguments was that for many years the proprietor's conditions of plantation had not been published or his rates of fees published, and abuses were complained of. To this charge Baltimore replied with more or less specific denials. The attitude of the law officers toward his claims was generally fair, and the board of trade

[1] C. O. 5/715, Memorials rec'd. Jan. 11, 1712/3, Apr. 19, 1703; C. O. 5/716, Memorial rec'd. Feb. 20, 1707/8; report of solicitor gen. in same, rec'd. June 7, 1708, C. O. 5/717; Baltimore to Popple, July 7, 1710; Md. Arch. XIX, 209; XXII, 481; XXVI, 143, 574; XXVII, 154, 175.

sometimes sent his statements concerning them to the council and assembly of Maryland for consideration and the remedy of any injustice.

Closely involved with the claims of the Calvert family, until near the close of this period, as well as with the policy of the supporters of the established Church, were the activities of the Catholics in Maryland. The strenuous Anglicanism of Seymour made him very sensitive to any stirrings on their part. The largest group of Catholics lived in St. Mary's county, but they were scattered through several other counties and according to a census of 1708 numbered a little less than three thousand.[1] Among them were relatives and agents of the proprietor, many of whom had fine estates. Priests, some of the Jesuit order, were quietly active among them. The importation of Irish Catholic servants, which occurred to some extent, was viewed with great suspicion by the Maryland government.

In August, 1704, the attorney general reported that two priests, apparently Jesuits, had been presented before the county court of St. Mary's, one for consecrating a chapel and the other for saying mass.[2] They were brought before the governor and council during the next session of the assembly. Charles Carroll appeared as their counsel, but it was decided that they should have none. The priests addressed the governor with great politeness and submission, but were abruptly told that, this being their first offence, they should be let off with a severe reprimand, but must on another appearance expect the utmost severity of the law. Seymour administered the reprimand in the most brutal and insulting manner, closing with the statement, "I am an English Protestant and can never equivocate." To the board of trade he wrote that he was uncertain how far the penal statutes of England which did not mention the dominions extended to them; but though he asked for further orders he took his instructions to mean Catholics were expressly excluded from toleration. He regarded Catholics as formidable in Maryland because of their close connection with the proprietor and of the control which

[1] Md. Arch. XXV, 258.

[2] Md. Arch. XXV, 178; XXVI, 44; C. O. 5/715, Seymour to Board, Sept. 29, 1704, Lawrence to Board, Oct. 25, 1703.

they thereby had over land. Votes favorable to them were few in the assembly, because those who cast them were likely to suffer in grants of land. The Quakers Seymour regarded with almost as great aversion as he did the Catholics and often referred to their general uselessness if not their secret Jacobitism.

In September, 1704, an act was passed forbidding Catholic priests, on penalty of fine, to baptize children or celebrate mass, and threatening them with transportation to England for punishment if they should attempt the teaching of youth.[1] But before the end of the year, in response to a memorial from Catholics, this enactment was qualified by a provision that, for the exercising of their function in private Catholic families, priests should not be prosecuted until eighteen months after the publication of the law had passed or until the pleasure of the crown had been declared. In the course of the following year the attorney general declared in an opinion[2] that, though it was doubtful if the persecuting statutes of Elizabeth extended to colonies which had been acquired since her time, there was no doubt but that any bishop or priest, for saying mass or performing other service anywhere in the realm or dominions, could be adjudged to perpetual imprisonment. As to whether priests could be expelled from a colony, he thought that it could be done if they were aliens, but not if they were natural born subjects.

The first of these acts was regarded by the board of trade and the bishop of London as unduly severe, that it might be used to prevent even private Catholic services and so might in part depopulate the colony. Since the object of legislation was simply to restrain exorbitant practices, they advised that, as the second act was sufficiently mild, it be made permanent, and this was done in 1707.[3] Until the close of his administration Governor Seymour was suspicious of Catholic intrigues, and counted the presence of Catholics in the province as among the things which made government

[1] Md. Arch. XXVI, 340, 431.
[2] C. O. 5/715, report rec'd. Oct. 23, 1705.
[3] Acts of P. C. Col. II, 498; Md. Arch. XXVII, 146.

there uneasy.[1] At the time, too, of the accession of the Hanoverians in England there were fears of activity on behalf of the Stuarts. Some rumors were investigated by Governor Hart and his council and a proclamation to warn offenders and quiet the popular mind was issued, but the transition in Maryland was passed without disturbance. The acceptance of the Anglican faith by the proprietor and his family, which was the condition of his restoration to rights of government in Maryland was a blow to the Catholics and put an end to all fears of possible political ascendancy for them.

During Seymour's term of office and some time afterwards the judicial system of the province was the subject of considerable discussion.[2] The jurisdiction of the provincial court. as related to that of the county courts, was one of the subjects involved. In Maryland, as elsewhere, this question was a phase of the conflict, so to speak, between local interests and convenience and the demand for uniform and regular administration from a centre. It had appeared in the development of the judicial system of mediaeval England and was reflected in many, if not all, of the colonies. In December, 1708, the lower house reported it to the governor as a grievance that the county courts could not finally determine any action which involved more than 10,000 pounds of tobacco or £50 sterling. This was the cause of many suits being brought to the provincial court which, for half the cost and in much less time, might be heard and finally adjudged in the county courts. The governor was asked to issue new commissions empowering the county justices to hear and determine all actions, of what nature soever, except titles to land and criminal cases extending to life or member. The upper house, knowing that the desire of the province for an extension of the jurisdiction of the county courts was strong, agreed to the issue of new commissions, but also desired that the burgesses, or delegates, as they were now called, would prepare a bill for reducing the number of sessions of the county courts, as that would bring relief to the county budgets. But nothing further was then done, and the same subject appeared again

[1] Md. Arch. XXV, 327–336.

[2] For a comprehensive account of the courts of Maryland in 1701, see C. O. 5/715. Scheme, etc., rec'd. Apr. 9, 1701.

among the grievances a year later. A conference committee then reported that the broad jurisdiction of the provincial court was a serious grievance, but as they were thus under the government of President Lloyd and the council the best course would be to enlarge the commissions of the county justices and make application to the next governor for a settlement of the question.[1]

In the autumn of 1710 the lower house sent up a bill to prevent a multiplicity of actions in the provincial court. The upper house expressed sympathy with its object, but again they referred to the instruction that no laws should be passed on new subjects during the absence of a governor. The lower house, however, pressed the matter and the council yielded. A temporary act was passed requiring that suits in which the debt or damages involved did not exceed £20 st. or 5000 pounds of tobacco must be tried in the county where the debtor resided. In explaining their action to the board of trade the president and council stated that they were unwilling to concur with the house but, being aware of the deplorable circumstances of very many inhabitants of Maryland who were daily arrested and brought from the remotest parts to the provincial court, they were prevailed on to pass the bill to continue in force for two years. They could never have done it if they had not thought this law of the greatest importance to relieve the hardships of people in Maryland and prevent their removal, for they knew how it would be misrepresented before the board of trade. Creditors, they thought, would find speedy remedy in the county courts, though they would have to take a little more pains in soliciting their suits there, and yet the cost would not be so great. In 1712 the act was continued till the end of the first session after the arrival of the governor. At the first session under Governor Hart it was reenacted for three years longer.[2]

Among the grievances of 1712 a prominent place was held by the charge that fees taken by the provincial court were very heavy as was the cost of attendance on its sessions. A committee of the houses conferred and there was some legisla-

[1] Md. Arch. XXVII, 296, 300, 426, 431.

[2] Md. Arch. XXVII, 544, 551, 555, 559; XXIX, 439; C. O. 5/717. President and Council to Board of Trade, Nov. 4, 1710.

tion.[1] It was said at the time that losses and the decay of trade during the war had led some to skulk in the woods and ride armed to resist the officers of justice, a peril to public order which it was now hoped would abate.

At the same time there was much complaint of the sheriffs, that in issuing certain writs and attachments they sold the properties which came into their hands at much less than their appraised values to the great loss of both debtors and creditors.[2] In 1713 an act was passed forbidding such practices. The following year a bill was also passed further limiting the fees of sheriffs. In July, 1714, in the report of the committee of the lower house on grievances, appeared the charge that, as the result of the sale of the office of sheriff to the highest bidders, incompetent men had come to hold it, to the great loss of the public. It was urged that the county justices should nominate two or three candidates, from whom the governor and council should appoint.

During Seymour's administration in particular another effort was made better to connect central and local justice in the province, and in this the governor was specially interested. As early as 1694, under the advice of attorneys, the governor and council had proposed to the lower house, that a number of itinerant justices of the provincial court be appointed for each shore and that they ride the circuits like justices of assize in England. The matter was put off. In 1701 a bill for the appointment of itinerant justices was prepared and the subject was referred to the committee on laws. A debate was had on the subject, after which a motion to reject was carried. In July, 1705, Seymour wrote to the board of trade complaining of irregularities of the provincial court and stating that four itinerant justices, properly selected, would do the business better and save expense. In March, 1707, the governor informed the assembly that he had received the queen's instructions to appoint four itinerant justices and enlarged upon the advantages which would follow therefrom. An attempt was then made to pass an act constituting the office and defining its duties, but it failed. The governor a few months later, under instructions from the board of trade

[1] Md. Arch. XXIX, 90, 93–100, 101, 102.

[2] *Ibid.*, 111–117, 119, 149, 255, 342, 392, 393, 445.

and with the assent of the council, had reduced the number of judges of the provincial court from twelve or thirteen to four, and these held four terms yearly and went the eastern and western circuits twice yearly.[1]

This, in the opinion of Seymour, met with general satisfaction, except in the case of some of the county justices who thought their dignity lessened thereby. But when it came to asking the assembly to provide support for the itinerant justices, even though the practice of other colonies was cited, the subject was postponed or met with an absolute negative. The reasons given were, that the office was unsuited to Maryland and that it had been created without their consent. As late as November, 1713, the lower house reiterated these arguments and added the charge that the cost of the provincial court had been increased by the change. "What Trouble and Expences those Gentlemen were at on Occasion of riding the Circuits or what Damages they may suffer in their Estates thereby this House were never the Occasion of; and as they never, on Behalf of the Public requested or acquiesced in any Thing relating to those Commissions for the Assizes but always shewed their Aversion thereto, so they think it very unreasonable the Country should be burthened with the Charge, but that those that set them to work ought to pay them for their Charges,[2] Trouble and Expences." In this dogged fashion did the conservatism of the province and its aversion to institutions imposed from without assert itself in this case.

Another interesting episode in the judicial history of the time arose from a complaint of the lower house, in 1711, that the provincial court was making null and void acts which had passed all the stages of legislation in the province, and especially a law of the last session for relieving certain grievances. This it did, not by a declaration that the act was illegal or unconstitutional, but by the court entertaining petty suits against persons contrary to the terms of the act.[3] This the

[1] Md. Arch. XIX, 42, 175; XXIV, 165, 182; XXVII, 63, 68, 88, 113; C. O. 5/715, Scheme of Md. Courts, rec'd. Apr. 9, 1701. Seymour to Board July 3, 1705; C. O. 5/716, Seymour to Board, June 23, 1708.

[2] Md. Arch. XXVII, 199, 285, 457, 521; XXIX, 225, 293; C. O. 5/717, Pres. & Council to Board, Nov. 4, 1710.

[3] Md. Arch. XXIX, 16, 22–28, 52 *et seq.*

house attributed to the pernicious activity of Lawrence who was secretary of the province, counsellor, and a judge of the provincial court. This led to another protest against the accumulation of several offices in the same hand, and a threat that, if the grievance was not redressed, they would not vote the levy for the year. It was also suggested that some had declared laws to be of no force until the crown had acted upon them. But the firmness of the council prevailed, the levy was voted and further debate on the subject was waived by the lower house.

In March, 1701/2, Governor Blakiston had communicated to the assembly a letter from the king asking that, for the safety of Maryland, £600 sterling should be appropriated toward the building of a fort in New York, and also that a quota of men should be sent thither if occasion should require.[1] The burgesses, after debate, informed the governor that they were unable at best to give more than £300, and to do this they would have to leave debts for a state house, school, church and prison unpaid and the province in a weak state of defence against the Indians. In their judgment it would be better to devote the money to measures of local defence. Various emphatic arguments they used in support of this policy and asked the governor to present them to the crown, as they were plain matters of fact and undoubted truths. The result, they hoped, would be that they would be excused from any contribution in aid of New York.

In February, 1702/3, a letter was received from Lord Cornbury giving an account of the poor condition of the New York forts and asking that the quota be ready early in the spring. When, in May, he asked that the £300, which had been voted, be sent to him in the form of bills on some person in London, the council replied that the province had formerly been at great charge in remitting money to New York and the assembly had resolved that the amount now voted should be paid by the treasurers to such persons as should be sent from New York to receive it. About the beginning of August Sir Thomas Lawrence went to New York to meet Cornbury and offered to carry bills for £300 and bring back a discharge

[1] Md. Arch. XXIV, 208, 225, 227, 235, *et seq.*; C. O. 5/715, Memorial of Blakiston to Board of Trade, recd. Aug. 23, 1704.

for them, but the council decided to make the payment in some other way and nothing was done. In October Colonel Quary, who was going to New York, was asked by the council to remove any misapprehensions there as to reasons why the money had not been sent. He promised to do this, though by this time it would evidently have been difficult to persuade anyone that Maryland was not quibbling. In fact neither money nor bills left the province. At the close of July, 1703, Blakiston, then agent, wrote, "I have fully discoursed the Lords of Trade about it and you need not be under any misapprehension of paying any of your quota unless Virginia or the adjacent neighbors of Pennsylvania club theirs, which I am confident the latter will never be reconciled to and I believe Virginia will never assent to." In the following spring, when a letter from the board of trade with a copy of the royal order for the quota was laid before the burgesses, they repeated this statement as the substance of what their agent had written them. Though they wrote to Blakiston to find, if possible, some way to relieve them from this burden, it was probably not necessary, for there is no evidence that the demand was repeated.[1]

In 1704, while the question of the quota was still under discussion, a rumor came from England that New York cherished a design of making the other colonies tributary to it, to have commissions chosen from them to meet at New York instead of in their own assemblies and to have one viceroy and general of all the forces of the continent. The Maryland council, as if alarmed by this, suggested to the lower house that the £300 which had not been sent to New York might be forwarded to England for use by Blakiston in thwarting such evil designs against the constitution of the province. But the lower house refused to concur and insisted that the fund remain where it was. A conference however was held and a joint address was sent to the queen in which they dwelt on the disadvantage and burdens of such a union, the poor could not endure the cost of it and the rich would avoid it by removing to England, it would draw away merchants and artificers and impose intolerable cost in the form of military

[1] Md. Arch. XXV, 137, 159, 160; XXIV, 386; C. O. 5/715, Sir Thomas Lawrence, Oct. 25, 1703.

quotas and the expense of sending delegates thither to attend councils, assemblies and courts. So different also was the economic and social system of Maryland from that of New York that laws made in the latter place could not be "agreeable to the trade and Affaires of this Countrey nor the constitution of the inhabitants [1] of this province." With these illuminating remarks on the obstacles to colonial union, as they were conceived in the early years of the eighteenth century, this episode closed.

In 1704 Governor Seymour wrote that the militia was then ill-regulated and unserviceable, though the existing militia act might seem to answer the purpose of the royal instruction that all planters and Christian servants should be fitly armed and obliged to muster; but experience showed that it was not practicable in Maryland. As generally was the case, this was due to the inability, for various reasons, of many to provide themselves with arms and ammunition. But the Quaker element in the population of this province bulked large in the mind of Seymour, and he never tired of emphasizing the obstacles which they threw in the way of his administration, in military as in other affairs. Later in the same year the militia law of 1699 was reenacted practically without change and to continue in force for three years.[2] Both of these acts contained the usual provisions about levy, training and service, arms and pay, for troopers as well as for foot soldiers. Slaves and free negroes were exempted from service. Provision was made for the wounded and for the widows and children of the slain. Because of his conviction that the poor could not equip themselves, Seymour urged that they be eased by allowing three taxables to unite for the furnishing of one man and horse and two taxables in the same way for one foot soldier.

In April, 1707, the governor and council informed the burgesses of the orders of the crown that the Quakers be compelled to contribute a proportional share toward the charge of militia and defence, but that levies by distress upon them for their defaults should not be inequitable or in excess

[1] Md. Arch. XXVI, 43, 83, 125, 131, 140, 172–178, 213, 263, 446, 487.

[2] Md. Arch. XXVI, 269; C. O. 5/715, Seymour to B. T. May 23, 1704, July 3, 1705.

of those imposed on others. The governor proposed that this should be provided for in a supplementary militia law, and as the provision for levying fines simply on the goods and clothes of the negligent often failed of its purpose because they had no personal estate, he also urged that they be imprisoned.[1] But to this the burgesses would not agree. In December, 1708, the lower house resolved that the militia act "be not revived as it now stands." Their objection appears to have been to a clause which authorized the governor and council, during a recess of assemblies, to levy an assessment upon the inhabitants, not to exceed 50,000 pounds of tobacco, for the payment of small charges.[2] The governor defended the clause and declared that none who had the least respect for their country would consent to leave it defenceless in case of an invasion, or be so mean as to balance its safety against such a sum as was mentioned in the act; as to that provision, he had not made use of it and had no intention of so doing. The act was revived, but only until the end of the next session of assembly. In November, 1709, after Seymour's death, the council again urged the lower house to empower field officers to cause the arrest as well as to levy upon the goods of those who failed to perform their military duties. The burgesses now consented and the former law was revived with the amendment desired by the council.[3] Because of a defect in its form of enactment this law was disallowed by the crown, but because of its great importance it was soon after passed again and that with the approval of the home government.

Throughout the period which we are now considering relations between Maryland and the Indians were quiet. Treaties with those who lived within her borders were renewed without change in 1704 and again early in Hart's administration, ten years later.[4] In the interval the great Tuscarora war had occurred, but it had not disturbed the quiet of Maryland or its frontiers. In 1705 Richard Clarke, of Arundel county, and

[1] Md. Arch. XXVII, 103, 104, 120.

[2] *Ibid.*, 259; *ibid.*, XXVI, 274.

[3] *Ibid.*, XXVII, 397, 404, 483; C. O. 5/717, Order of Council, Nov. 2, 1710. Lloyd to Board, Jan. 25, 1711/12.

[4] Md. Arch. XXIV, 329, 339; C. O. 5/720, Hart to Bolingbroke, July 11, 1714.

certain sympathizers formed a plot against the government, as to the details of which little is known. It was said that they hoped for aid from the Indians. Such peril as there was brought home to the authorities the great need in which they stood of arms and ammunition, and especially of a storehouse for these at the capital, and of a storekeeper under whose charge they could be preserved and the supply renewed when necessary. Clark himself fled to North Carolina, but was ultimately arrested and executed as a traitor. Two of his accomplices were sold as servants.[1]

In April, 1706, the governor informed the assembly of a recent report that a thousand Senecas were coming from the north to destroy or carry off the Indians of the eastern shore, but the lower house replied that they did not fear any immediate danger and refused to further consider the matter.[2] Early in Seymour's administration an act was passed to settle the boundaries of the Nanticoke tribe, but in 1710 some disaffection had arisen from alleged encroachments on their lands. The lower house appointed a committee to adjust the matter and no further difficulty occurred.[3] The Maryland tribes themselves were already insignificant and, as the French were then situated for war, the internal peace of the province could no longer be broken by rumors of Indian raids combined with plots of the discontented.

In the session of March, 1707, perhaps as a result of the alarms which had preceded, there was considerable discussion of the manner in which the province supply of arms should be kept. At that time they were lodged in the magazine at Annapolis, and the lower house proposed that, as had been the custom, they be distributed among the counties. To this the upper house replied that, although it was sometimes necessary for immediate security and defence that a small quantity of arms and ammunition be stored in the counties, to be made use of by such as were not able to procure them at their own cost, yet as strict account of what

[1] Md. Arch. XXV, 37, 117, 218–224, 262; XXVI, 441, 450, 513; XXVII 139; C. O. 5/715, Seymour to Board, July 3, and Aug. 28, 1705, Mar. 6, 1706/7, Aug. 16, 1707.

[2] Md. Arch. XXV, 190; XXVI, 532 *et seq.*

[3] Md. Arch. XXVII, 505, 546; C. O. 5/715, Seymour's remarks on Maryland laws, rec'd. Oct. 1705, No. 48.

was purchased with the three-penny duty was required by the crown, and as in the past arms and ammunition lodged in the counties had been misused, spoiled and lost, they could not advise the governor to distribute them. After some discussion it was agreed to keep the arms and ammunition in the magazine, but under a guard, so that they might be safe, and the governor promised to dismiss the guard when he was convinced that it was no longer necessary.[1] In 1711 and again in 1712 the upper house urged that small magazines be built in the respective counties for the reception of arms and ammunition, but this was voted down by the delegates, either because it was expensive or because of the loose and easy management of them by the county commanders, in whose hands they usually were.[2]

Captain John Hart, nephew of the then archbishop of Tuam, and a soldier who had served several years in Spain and Portugal, was the fourth and last royal appointee to the governorship of Maryland.[3] Hart assumed the duties of his office in 1713. The death of Queen Anne, which soon followed, and the accession of the Hanoverian king were duly proclaimed by him under the elaborate orders which were sent to all the colonies with a view to securing a peaceful transition at a time of great political uncertainty in Europe. Hart had been appointed governor at the request of Benedict Leonard Calvert, the son and heir of Charles, third Lord Baltimore. Charles Calvert, the same whose powers of government had been taken away or suspended in 1690, was now an aged man. He had remained through life a faithful Catholic and in that faith he died, February 20, 1714/15. Toward the close of 1713 Benedict, probably from motives which were largely political, renounced Catholicism and became a communicant of the English Church. His father, because of resentment at this change, at once withdrew the annuity of £450 which had been used for the education of Benedict's children, and thus forced the son to fall back upon his wife's settlement. The children were taken from the Catholic schools on the Continent, where they had been kept, and were placed in Protestant

[1] Md. Arch. XXVII, 6, 27, 28, 30, 33, 48, 58.
[2] Md. Arch. XXIX, 49, 97, 98, 155.
[3] Md. Arch. XXV, 271 *et seq.*

schools near London. A pension of £300 a year was granted Benedict by the queen, to continue during the life of his father. It was also on his suggestion that Hart was appointed governor, and he out of his profits in Maryland agreed to allow Benedict £500 per annum. By these means the loss of the annuity was more than made good, and the chief obstacle to the restoration of proprietary government in Maryland was removed. The death of the aged Charles Calvert and also of the queen, which soon followed, still further facilitated the change.

With the accession of George I began that policy of conciliation and neglect, followed in the interest of peace and of the new dynasty, which was to give character to the attitude of the British government toward the colonies for the next thirty years. One of the first conspicuous instances of this was the ease with which the new government fell in with the desire of the Calvert family for the restoration of their powers of government in Maryland. Viewed from the strict imperialistic standpoint, which had been maintained during the previous generation, this was a step backward. How was it possible to reconcile it with the bills which had been introduced into parliament for the recall of all the charters? A more reasonable and consistent course would have been to correct the apparent arbitrariness of the original suspension of their governmental powers by inducing the Calverts to make a formal surrender of them. Their influence could not have been such as to make concessions in so important a matter necessary, or to enable them long to hold out against the pressure of government. Randolph was now dead and the voices of others with whom he had been associated in the relentless campaign against chartered colonies were stilled. Therefore, in response to a petition from Benedict Calvert, his right to appoint the governor of Maryland was allowed to revive, and he issued a commission to the same John Hart who had been acting for a year and more under a commission from the crown. This appointment, of course, was duly submitted to the king for his approval and the necessary oaths and bonds [1] were taken and given. The other steps which were necessary to the complete restoration of the proprietary régime followed

[1] C. O. 5/717. Docs. rec'd. and read by Board of Trade, May, 1715.

in regular order. Viewed in the light of what was necessary to a consistent and comprehensive administration of the colonies, this event must be classed with these acts of Charles II by which, during the period of the Restoration, so much was done to multiply and extend proprieties and that at a time when the main trend of colonial administration was in exactly the opposite direction. But the course of British colonial administration was far from being consistent, and out of its inconsistencies in part the system of American liberty grew up.

CHAPTER XXIII

VIRGINIA DURING THE ADMINISTRATION OF ALEXANDER SPOTSWOOD, 1710–1722

In the history of Virginia no other governor after Berkeley impressed himself upon the life of the province as did Alexander Spotswood. When one thinks of Virginia in the early eighteenth century the name and the stately figure of this man are at once suggested to the mind. Though he was at the head of the government by no means as long as Berkeley, he was quite as autocratic in his temper, broader and more progressive in policy, and in every relation a leader and dominant personality. His ample correspondence, the most detailed of all Virginia governors before Dinwiddie, gives one a clearer idea of his character and views than in the case of most officials it is possible to obtain. This is due not merely to the number and length of his letters, but also to the vigor with which Spotswood expressed his own views and assailed those of his opponents. His spirit coincided well with the policy of the reign of Anne, for he was a high Tory and defender of the prerogative in matters of church and state, and an aggressive imperialist in his relations with the Indians, the French and with neighboring colonies. His letters make it clear that he had been on rather intimate terms with William Blathwayt, and these he sought to continue, though Blathwayt was now approaching the end of his long career.[1]

During the interval of some four months between the arrival of Spotswood in Virginia and the meeting of his first assembly, in October, 1710, several routine matters, referred to in his instructions or made important by the war which still continued, came up for consideration. One of these related

[1] Spotswood Letters, in Colls. of Va. Hist. Soc. I, 5. Spotswood Letters II, 298. Spotswood says he served nine years under Lord Cadogan as lieutenant-quartermaster-general of the British army in Flanders. This was in part at least in Anne's reign and so under Marlborough. He had the rank of colonel and was wounded at Blenheim.

to the method of selling the right to collect the quit rents. Some years before this had been changed from the old form of auction, or by inch of candle, to direct public sale. This change Spotswood now confirmed.[1] One of his instructions provided that the positions of naval officer and collector of royal customs should not be in the hands of the same person. This regulation he found had generally been obeyed since the beginning of Nicholson's administration, and there is evidence to show that it became permanent. But the receiver of provincial revenue, popularly called " collector," and a district naval officer had sometimes to be the same person, because the revenue was not sufficient for the support of two. This was true in the case of Nathaniel Harrison, whom Spotswood appointed to the two offices for the upper district of the James river.[2] In pursuance of an order of council, Spotswood issued a proclamation announcing the disallowance of the latest Virginia act establishing ports and towns.[3]

The question of guardships for the coast was suggested by the discovery that illegal trade was being carried on with the islands of Curaçoa and St. Thomas. In the temporary absence of a man-of-war in the bay, vessels had taken on large quantities of tobacco and landed it on these foreign islands before visiting the British colonies for which they had cleared. French and Spanish privateers had also visited the coast and had seized vessels and kept the inhabitants about the capes in continued alarms. Of the guardships which had been stationed in Virginia, one had been lost on the North Carolina coast and another had gone to New York to refit and thence to the Bahamas. In addition to urging the customs officers on the lower James to keep boats and hands for use in inspecting vessels engaged in trade, Spotswood also advised that an agent victualler for the men-of-war be stationed in Virginia, as in other colonies, to provide them with supplies. He also called attention to the fact that, at a small charge, a place for careening vessels could be fitted up at Point Comfort and thus save the necessity of their going to New York for

[1] Spotswood Letters, I, 7, 8; C. O. 5/1363, Va. Entry Bk. Feb. 23, 1709/10.

[2] Virginia was districted for this purpose and there were several naval officers and collectors in the province. An instruction that the two offices should be in different hands had been issued both to Nicholson and Nott.

[3] Spotswood Letters, I, 9, 11, 15, 33.

the purpose. As the fort at the Point was in decay, he urged that it be rebuilt as a place of retreat for vessels when pursued by privateers and a place also to which the sick from royal ships could be brought for care and recovery. He suggested that a company of invalids from Chelsea might be sent over to garrison it, the charge for them in excess of what they already cost being supplied from the quit rents. These recommendations he enforced by the statement that at that time there was not a fort nor a piece of cannon mounted in the whole province. In view of this it is not strange that in his opening speech to the legislature Spotswood "whispered" to them of the state of the militia and defence, because it was so poor that it should be concealed from neighbors and slaves. This last reference may have been suggested by recent disturbances among the slaves in three of the counties. The only comfort he got from the board of trade on this subject was the remark that, if the charge of building a fort at Point Comfort was so small and if it was so important to the inhabitants, they would no doubt readily contribute to that work.[1] But the burgesses could be induced to appropriate money for the fort only on the supposition that the crown would furnish the garrison, and as a result nothing was done.

Before the close of October, however, Spotswood reported that two guardships had come in and so Virginia was comfortably off in that particular. But he continued to argue that New York, with its agent victualler and careening place, was much better provided with convoys and guardships than was Virginia, though the annual tobacco crop of the latter colony was so much more valuable to the crown than the trade of New York. He continued his search for the parties who were guilty of illegal trade with the foreign West Indies, but his inability to get information from the books of the collector and naval officer of the Lower James led him again to urge in council the necessity of searching the outgoing vessels, and he found its members unanimously of the same opinion. But at that time nothing was done. The following spring we find Spotswood, after conferring with Quary, proposing to the customs board the appointment of two additional searchers for the bay, with boats and helpers, that they might continu-

[1] C. O. 5/1363, Va. Entry Bk. Oct. 26, 1710.

ously cruise in the inlets and creeks where small vessels were in the habit of loading. Salaries for these might be found by discontinuing two of the three collectors who had been stationed on the York and James rivers. But of action on this proposal there is no evidence.

The instructions to Spotswood contained a clause to the effect that persons set at liberty by *habeas corpus* should not be recommitted for the same offence except by the court where they were to appear. This involved a recognition of the writ of *habeas corpus* as legal in Virginia, and as such it was proclaimed by the governor among his instructions relating to the liberty of the subject and was duly welcomed by the house of burgesses.[1] In connection with this the governor made known his instruction that two courts of oyer and terminer should be held annually, but the council thought that was provided for by the law establishing the general court, in which it was provided that all criminals should be brought to trial on the fourth day of every session of this tribunal.

Among the royal instructions the one which was to have the most important effect was that which required that on penalty of forfeiture, three acres of land in every fifty granted should be settled and cultivated within three years from the date of the grant. It appears that an instruction on this subject had been given to Colonel Nott in 1705 and a similar one to Hunter in 1707, the latter not reaching the province. Difficulties had been raised against executing it in Nott's time, on the ground that it was inconsistent with the charter and laws of Virginia and contrary to express agreements made with purchasers. Its terms were also said to be hard, so that people would remove to North Carolina rather than submit to them.[2] In order not to prejudice the people at the time of the election of his first assembly, Spotswood did not publish this instruction, but instead issued a proclamation to disabuse the popular mind of the idea that it was more severe than in reality was the case.[3] And yet it was understood that the chief grievance

[1] C. O. 5/1363. Instructions to Spotswood; Journal of Burgesses, 1702–1712, pp. 240, 260, 262.

[2] C. O. 5/1316. O. P. Va., Mar. 24, 1710; Acts of P. C. Col., II, 585, 587.

[3] Spotswood Letters, I, 19 *et seq.*

which would be aired in the next session concerned the taking up of land, and Spotswood thought he discerned among the voters a prejudice against large landholders and a tendency to exclude gentlemen from the election as burgesses. But in the large number of petitions which at the beginning of the session came in from the counties, on subjects local and general, no special emphasis seems to have been laid on this question.[1]

The subject of land grants occupied a prominent place in the business not only of the session of 1710 but of several which were to follow, and two rather important acts on this subject were passed during Spotswood's administration.[2] As the result of general looseness in administration and of speculation in head rights,[3] it had been possible for persons to appropriate large tracts which remained unsettled for indefinite periods. With the connivance of surveyors it was possible for so-called grantees to hold such tracts for many years without even having a survey made or taking out a patent. Sometimes it was possible to secure five hundred acres on the account of one immigrant, though the amount legally allowed was only fifty. It was to check this monopoly, in the interest both of the crown and of future settlers, that Spotswood took up the subject. As an incident of the struggle he also labored to secure a complete rent roll of the province, an object which Blathwayt and the royal governors were always seeking but probably never attaining. The last law on the subject had been passed in 1705, and while it required settlement within three years after the grant, it was not precise as to the amount of land to be cultivated and the terms of the forfeiture.[4] Spotswood's instruction on the subject of settling and cultivating grants at once occasioned complaint and a demand that they revert to former free and easy methods. This demand was voiced in a report of the committee of propositions and grievances in the burgesses, which was sent as a message to the governor.[5] In his reply Spotswood defended his instruction and declared that it was

[1] Journal of Burgesses, *loc. cit.*, 248 *et seq.*
[2] Hening, III, 517; IV, 37.
[3] Spotswood Letters, II, 15, 21, 216.
[4] Hening, III, 314.
[5] Journal, *loc. cit.* 265, 293.

more in accordance with the charter of Charles II and with earlier custom in general, than had been the more recent practice. He added that he could not understand how the belief should obtain that in granting lands the sovereign could not limit the grant or consider the qualification of the grantee. A long and important act on the subject was passed this session,[1] which provided that a failure to pay quit rents for three years would effect a forfeiture of land, and that on a failure of the grantee to give a correct account to the sheriff of the amount he held, and to obtain grants for the surplus, after notice anyone could procure a survey of the land and take out a grant for the surplus. This provision was important, if it could be executed, and Spotswood took considerable credit to himself for its passage. But the new law did not repeal that part of the act of 1705 which referred to the seating of land, while it helped to fasten a law of entail on Virginia which in practice could be broken only by act of assembly. An early act of 1666, which contained some very loose provisions concerning the settlement of land was still unrepealed and this, at Spotswood's request, was repealed the following year.[2] In view of this and of the fact that the law of 1710 did not reenact the provisions of that of 1705 concerning the granting of land, Spotswood considered that granting and settling were now wholly in the hands of the crown, where they belonged. He thought that no more laws should be made on that subject, because they led the people to believe that the issue of such regulations belonged to them as a right. Hence, to preempt the subject for the executive, he issued a proclamation making known the terms of his instructions, and in addition prescribing that no grant in excess of four hundred acres would be made until the governor was informed of the capacity of the would-be grantee to cultivate more.[3] In pursuance of this instruction, that regard be had to the differing varieties of land, it was required that grants

[1] Hening, III, 517. Spotswood later explained this to mean that no lands once entered on the roll of the receiver general would be forfeited until, after a formal demand and a reasonable time given, the owner refused to pay. This would secure all lands which were honestly declared and endanger those which were knavishly concealed. C. O. 5/1318, p. 209, O. P. Va.

[2] C. O. 5/1363, Feb. 22 and Mar. 6, 1710–11, E. B. Va.

[3] C. O. 5/1316, O. 76, Proc. of Dec. 8, 1710.

should be laid out so that their breadth might be at least one-third of their length, unless prevented by rivers and impassable swamps. Surveyors were also required to return plans of the tracts along with their surveys. These regulations occasioned much criticism as being *ex post facto* and also more strict than those to which the colonists had been accustomed. For this reason the governor suspended the proclamation in the case of rights whch had been purchased before any report came of the intended change.[1]

But this, of course, was not the end of legislation on this subject. In November, 1713, an act was passed applying especially to barren, marshy and swampy land, unfit for cultivation but often containing quarries and mines.[2] As settlement receded into the interior, more land was of this quality. The act provided that the breadth of such grants should equal at least one third of their length, and that surveyors should return general statements of the quality of the land they laid out. The keeping of a certain number of cattle, sheep or goats on such grants, or the employment of one man per hundred acres digging in a stone quarry or in a coal or other mines, would be sufficient to give possession. But information laid before the executive council in 1717 shows that the old abuses had not disappeared. Land was then being kept for many years on a bare entry of survey without patent.[3] Entries were also made for lands suitable for the production of pitch and tar without the design of taking out patents and the lightwood found there was gathered and burned, the king being thereby defrauded of his quit rents and others who would improve the land were excluded.[4]

Connected with the question of land grants arose a discussion with the general court over a practice into which it had fallen of receiving petitions for lapsed and escheated lands and ordering the issue of patents for such land. Spotswood regarded that at once as a serious encroachment on the prerogative, adjourned the court and called its members into session as the council. He then told them that he had no

[1] Spotswood Letters, I, 61.
[2] Hening, IV, 37 *et seq.*
[3] Spotswood Letters, II, 216, 217.
[4] Min. of Ex. C. Aug. 13, 1717.

objection to their inquiring into the fact of escheat or of the lapsing of grants, but with that their function ended. The power to regrant rested in the executive and, as it was now arranged, applications for lapsed lands must be made to the governor.

Before Spotswood's first assembly, as usual, came complaints of undue elections, some of which were occasioned by oft-recurring factional disputes over the dividing of existing parishes and the erection of new ones.[1] In connection with this subject Spotswood found opportunity to revive the claims of the executive which had played some part in other provinces, but never to any extent in Virginia. In his instructions the authority to erect and divide parishes was still lodged in the executive though ever since Virginia became a royal province these matters, in the case of both counties and parishes, had been regulated by statute.[2] He fondly believed that governors would act in these cases most disinterestedly and would never have it in their power to distress the people. Under such conditions also factional disputes would have no chance to develop.[3] But he wisely waited for further orders from the board of trade before engaging in a dispute with the assembly over the subject. The difficulty, of course, arose from the existence of both counties and parishes which were so large that people had to go thirty or fifty miles to church or to the court houses. Among the many difficulties which arose under such conditions was that of securing persons to serve as justices of the peace. Another arose from the fact that in some parishes the number of tithables was too small adequately to support a church, while in others there were many more than enough for this purpose. When the governor looked to the assembly for the remedy of these evils, he found that the freeholders who had already located the court houses and churches to suit their convenience, together with those who were indifferent in elections, would always outvote the injured and choose burgesses of their own party. But, he wrote, if the board of trade should order him so to do, he would take up this question and, if he succeeded in the

[1] Spotswood Letters, I, 20.
[2] Osgood, Am. Colonies in 17th Century, III, 81, 82.
[3] Spotswood Letters, I, 37, *et seq.*

struggle, would have a complete survey of counties and parishes made. By this route too he hoped to arrive at a true rent roll of the province, but no order to undertake the task came from England.[1]

In considering the land question and that of the great size of the western-most parishes and counties, the attention of Spotswood had been drawn to the facilities which were opened to Virginia, by following up the course of the James river, to cross the mountains and establish settlements beyond. Reports, as we have seen, had already reached Virginia of the activity of the French in the interior, and before the end of his first year there Spotswood had sent horsemen to explore the first ridge to the westward. He also urged the board of trade to exempt settlers on the upper James from the new and more rigid conditions of land grants, so that they might be encouraged to press forward over the mountains, open trade with the remote Indians and by that means establish a barrier against the French. But from a reply which the board made about a year later it was evident that it took no special interest in this subject.[2]

Such was the permanent and customary attitude of the British government toward projects of this kind. But in this instance Spotswood's interest was kept active by what he learned of deposits of iron which were thought to exist near the falls of the James. He asked the assembly to give him some aid toward the working of mines there, but found the tidewater majority indifferent. When the board of trade heard of this project, it was not only indifferent but actually opposed, because of the prospect it opened of the development of the manufacture of iron in Virginia. It forbade the governor to assent to any act for such a purpose, unless it contained a clause deferring its execution until the queen's pleasure was known. Secretary Popple also wrote him that the board did not consider it to be for the advantage of the kingdom that such an undertaking should be encouraged.[3] But, in 1714, Spotswood was able to settle forty Germans on the Rapidan, where they engaged in mining for iron or other

[1] Spotswood Letters, I, 39, 40.

[2] C. O. 5/1363, E. B. Va., B. T. to Spotswood, Nov. 22, 1711.

[3] *Ibid.*, Jan. 29 and June 29, 1711, E. B. Va.

ores. They had originally come under the Baron de Graffenried to North Carolina, but his plans there had been wrecked by the Tuscaroras, who had just withdrawn. Spotswood located his Palatine miners in this place. Such was the origin of the famous, though not very productive, mining settlement of Germanna, where Spotswood gradually secured a tract of some 45,000 acres, to which he retired after the close of his term as governor, thus laying the foundation of what was to be Spotsylvania county.[1]

Another question, which was largely territorial in its character, was that of the North Carolina boundary. Disputed titles to land in the Blackwater region, as we have seen, made this a live issue until the line was finally established to the satisfaction of both parties. Uncertainty in reference to the subject increased the difficulty of maintaining peace among the Indians, and a petition from certain of those that they might receive the land which had been reserved to them by the articles of peace in 1677, and which lay within the disputed area, helped to bring the subject forward again for consideration. Spotswood urged that a decision be reached on the question and in this was supported by the board of trade; but the condition of anarchy in North Carolina was so general during his entire administration that nothing could be accomplished.

As usual in this period, the price of tobacco ranged low and trade was therefore depressed. Large numbers of slaves were imported and they were employed solely in the production of the Virginia staple. Overproduction was the result, its influence being felt first in those sections which produced the poorer qualities of tobacco. In order, therefore, to procure their necessary clothing the inhabitants were forced to plant cotton and sow flax, and by mixing cotton with their wool to make coarse cloth for negroes and the poorer whites. This had now become so general that in one of the best tobacco counties 40,000 yards of woolen, cotton and linen cloth were reported to have been made in one year. Though other counties had, no doubt, increased manufacturing, it was done

[1] See William Byrd's account of his visit to the ex-governor there in 1732. Basset's Edition of Byrd's "Dividing Line," 355, *et seq.* Spotswood Letters, II, 70, 196, *et seq.*

through necessity and by unskilled workmen.[1] But the knowledge that such a tendency existed, encouraged the governor to enlarge upon the advantages of Virginia for the production of naval stores. Pitch and tar were already produced in good quantities, but hemp, he said, should be encouraged. As merchants thought only of tobacco, enterprise and skill were not devoted to new ventures, and Virginia failed to secure the advantages of the bounties offered by parliament on the production of naval stores.[2] Spotswood therefore proposed that the government accept them in payment of duties on tobacco, and that these products be sent to Europe under convoy with the tobacco fleets. As the condition of the tobacco industry closely affected revenue, it frequently came up in that connection. In 1712, in particular, because the tobacco used in payment of quit rents and taxes was often the worst trash, Spotswood secured the passage of an act requiring that all such payments be made at public stores under the view of sworn officials and inspectors called agents. The notes of the agents, bought by purchasers of this tobacco and circulating like bank bills, would enable them to have their product delivered at any convenient time or place. This subject came up later in connection with discussions of the revenue but that will properly follow some consideration of Virginia affairs as they stood related to the war which was then in its latest stage.

About the beginning of July, 1711, Spotswood received advice from Governor Hunter, of New York, that the queen had directed him to buy a large quantity of provisions for the use of the troops which were to go on the expedition of that year against Canada. Provisions being scarce in the neighboring governments, he desired Spotswood to buy all the pork to be had and to pay for it out of the royal revenue, so far as it would go, and to offer for the rest bills, which Hunter said he was empowered to draw on the British treasury. All the available stock of pork in Virginia — 700 barrels or more — was bought by Spotswood for this purpose, he using the entire balance of quit rents in the treasury and pledging his own credit so far as the royal revenue proved

[1] Spotswood Letters, I, 25, 44, 46.
[2] *Ibid.*, I, 73.

insufficient.[1] He congratulated himself that the assembly was not in session at the time, for it might have hindered him by fixing prices, and also that the quit rents had been increased by the recent discovery of 10,000 acres of concealed lands.

While the resources available for the use of the Virginia executive were being exhausted in this service, the Cary rebellion, followed by the Tuscarora war in North Carolina, demanded Spotswood's attention. A French squadron was also known to be operating in the West Indies and might visit the Virginia coast, where they would find favorable conditions for plunder. The coast also was never free from danger of possible visits by privateers. Under these conditions the problem of defence was of the greatest immediate importance. The militia, while potentially more than 12,000 in number, was as usual almost destitute of ammunition, their arms were poor and they were poorly disciplined. The province also had no coast defences. As in the previous session the assembly had revived an earlier law for the defence of the province in the time of danger, Spotswood now took advantage of that law for the purpose, if possible, of building four small forts and some other lines of defence on the James river and mounting cannon upon them. He was obstructed, however, by certain Quakers, who refused to work or to let their servants work or to contribute anything toward defence. The law was enforced against them to the full extent of fines and other penalties, but with what positive result does not appear.[2]

The first occasion which Spotswood had to use the military force of the province was when, in the early summer of 1711, he called out the militia of several counties along the southern frontier and sent a company of marines from the guardships into North Carolina to overawe Cary and his insurgent followers. This contributed to the restoration of internal peace in that distracted province.[3] But immediately it was

[1] Spotswood Letters, I, 99, 103, 151, 152, 155; C. O. 5/1316, O. P. Va. Feb. 4, 1713. The cost of the pork was £2099, of which nearly £1233 was advanced by the governor of Virginia on his own credit, for which Gov. Hunter was to draw bills on the British treasury. This had not been paid him in 1713. About £867 were also advanced out of the Virginia quit rents, making the above total of £2099.

[2] Spotswood Letters, I, 120, 133.

[3] Osgood, Am. Colonies in 17th century, II, 249, 430.

broken by the outbreak of the Indian war. This called again for a military demonstration for the purpose of keeping quiet the Indians along the southern border of Virginia. The militia of three neighboring counties, to the number of six hundred, were called together at Nottaway Town, and there a conference was held with chiefs of that part of the Tuscarora nation which had not joined in the massacres. They expressed sorrow for what had happened, and their promises on the subject greatly strengthened Spotswood's hopes that, by educating sufficient Indian youths at William and Mary College and elsewhere, that race might be civilized and permanent peace secured.[1]

When the assembly met in November, Spotswood enlarged on these events and policies, and urged that the debts which had been incurred should be discharged.[2] He stated that he had been as frugal as possible, and that he heard that years before as much had been spent against a single privateer. The burgesses first went into committee of the whole on this speech and then referred to a special committee the task of finding out what forts had previously existed in the province, how charges for them had been raised, and the forts themselves kept up. The final purpose of this was to bring forward again the opinions of the previous century on the utility of coast and river defences,[3] whether they had not been allowed to decay because they had not been worth the cost. Another question was, whether batteries were a Virginia charge and, if so, whether such charge should be paid by a poll tax or otherwise. Any member of the house could lay proposals before this committee, and it was to bring in an address to the governor on the subject of fortifications. They should also consider what could be done to prevent allowances made this session from becoming precedents. This, and more, indicated a resolve to present a firm front against some, at least, of the proposals of the intelligent and aggressive governor.

About a week after the beginning of the session Spotswood

[1] Spotswood Letters, 124 *et seq.*; N. C. Col. Recs. I, 781 *et seq.*

[2] Journal of Burgesses. Nov., 1711, to Jan., 1711–2. Several interesting subjects were mooted at this session to which I make no reference here.

[3] Osgood, *op. cit.*, III, 256.

sent in a message on a proposal from King William county that rangers be called out in the frontier counties for protection against the Indians. In view of the Tuscarora war, he thought that it was necessary and stated that he had designated ten men and one officer out of each of the frontier counties to range weekly above the settlements, and that these should be increased to twenty if the number of the enemy required it. Various other communications were sent in by the governor on the defects of the militia and the need of a really effective law on that subject. He held up North Carolina as a fearful example of the anarchy into which failure to provide for defence would plunge a colony. This finally drew from the house a resolution that £20,000 be raised for carrying on war, in case it should be declared against the Tuscaroras. But, in order to provide this sum, the burgesses proposed to levy duties on imports from Europe, including British products. This gave Spotswood the chance to make the charge that they were trying to shift the burden from their own shoulders to those of the English merchants. At the same time he was able to conclude a treaty with a part of the Tuscaroras, which materially reduced the scope of the struggle. In view of this, the council insisted that the title of the appropriation bill be changed, so that it would not imply that they were going to war with the whole of the Tuscarora nation. Among other important criticisms of the bill they also proposed that, in the clause which imposed a duty on imports, exception be made of certain classes of goods brought from Great Britain.[1] The burgesses granted a conference committee on this message, but would accept no amendment by the council except to the preamble and title of the bill. As to the contents and the rates of duty therein prescribed, this was all claimed as the exclusive right of the house. To this the council made reply at length, protesting against being subject to precedents which applied only to the house of lords, especially in view of the fact that the two branches of the legislature in Virginia had so long sat as one house and equally shared all functions.

At this juncture came a sharp message from the governor, to the effect that the session had continued nearly two months

[1] Journal of Burgesses, Dec. 13, 1711. Spotswood Letters, I, 131.

without the passage of any important legislation and that at last they had agreed upon an appropriation bill so extraordinary that it could not be passed without a suspending clause. The house, in its reply to this, explained the attitude it had taken on all the subjects proposed in the governor's speech and showed no sign of acceding any more fully to his views. As this attitude was unchanged when they returned after an adjournment of a month, he dissolved the assembly at the end of January, 1711/12.

Owing to this result, various claims failed of allowance by the burgesses, among them being the keep of eighty French prisoners and of the marines who guarded them, a small sum which Spotswood had expended on batteries, another sum for a spy boat which had cruised for the summer between the capes as a protection against surprise, and the pay of the militia whom Spotswood had called out when he met the Indians at Nottoway Town.[1] Upon the attitude of the burgesses toward all these matters Spotswood enlarged with characteristic force, and doubtless some exaggeration, in his letters which accompanied the dispatch of the journals home. The contrast between the spirit of the house in the previous session and in this made its later conduct to him scarcely recognizable. The parsimony of the average representative of a colonial constituency came in for some pointed comment at his hands. He thought that scarcely any other qualification was necessary for success at the polls. After the session closed some of the members had acknowledged that their proceedings had been due to certain rash votes passed without foresight, which later they could not set aside without breaking the rules of the house, and so they would let the province suffer rather than acknowledge themselves in error. But Spotswood was confident that, though he had broken with the burgesses, the province liked his administration, and he believed that the next election would bring him a loyal assembly. Some of the council had, meantime, advanced money to enable him to execute the treaty with the Tuscaroras, and he hoped to protect Virginia from Indian attacks; but North Carolina was in great danger and he could not aid her as he should like to do.[2]

[1] *Ibid.*, 138 *et seq.*

[2] *Ibid.*, 145, 146.

In the following spring Virginia was saved from the expenditure, which would have been occasioned by sending two hundred men to North Carolina, by the treaty which Barnwell suddenly concluded with the Tuscaroras.[1] But even with this saving Virginia was now in financial difficulties, for an order came for the remission to the English exchequer of £3,000 out of the quit rents, though they had been overdrawn for the Canadian expedition. On account of depression in the tobacco trade, the revenue from the 2s. per hogshead was so low, that the whole of the last year's salaries were in arrear.[2] The debt which had been contracted, together with the necessity of continuing the rangers on the frontiers, necessitated the holding of an election for a new assembly. It came together in October, 1712. As most of the old members had been returned, Spotswood expected little, and in his opening speech briefly told them that he had called them together to provide for the payment of the public debts. But instead the house at once became absorbed in the consideration of proposals, grievances and claims. While they were engaged on this task, an address was received from the assembly of North Carolina calling for speedy aid. Within a year that province had suffered three bloody massacres, and all that its inhabitants now desired to save was their lives, not their property. Spotswood urged the assembly to give assistance at once. A committee of conference with the council was appointed, and before it were laid three letters from Carolina containing, among other things, an appeal for clothing and for the protection of its destitute inhabitants in the approaching winter. As a result of discussion the house agreed not to give but to lend that province 900 yards of duffels and in addition to appropriate £1,000 for their relief.[3] The governor was entrusted with the expenditure of this sum and, at the time when it was appropriated, an agreement had not been reached as to the payment of the claims which were presented at the beginning of the session. As a part of his contribution to the debate, Spotswood laid before the burgesses a statement of expenditure for the past twenty-two

[1] *Ibid.*, 147 *et seq.*
[2] *Ibid.*, 151, 161 *et seq.*
[3] Journal of Burgesses, 1712–1726, pp. 27, 31.

years, with the revenue for the same time, making it appear that, since 1689, the funds which had been raised had fallen short of expenditures for salaries and contingences.[1] But in stating this account he charged the province with salaries which were paid out of the quit rents while he excluded all sums which had come from fines and forfeitures, the purchase of rights to land, and sale of queen's arms, which articles had previously been included in the revenue account and applied to the support of government. But, owing to the cost of the rangers, Spotswood was unable to induce the assembly to provide for the payment of all the claims as he desired, and therefore some had to be postponed until the next session or dropped.

After the appropriation for North Carolina was made Spotswood repaired to the border of that province for a conference with President Pollock and members of its council.[2] But Pollock did not come, and only two of the council appeared, they bringing no authority or instructions except to receive the clothing. They said that, if Virginia sent any men to their aid, it must not expect provisions for them, though the North Carolina assembly had promised to permit such when it asked for help. Their men had deserted the province, concealed themselves in it or sheltered themselves under the mask of Quakerism to avoid bearing arms. Now that they had got the clothing which Virginia furnished, they had no men under arms to use it. It was also evident that, if the cost of provisions was taken out of the £1000 which had been appropriated, the remainder would not suffice to pay even the smallest number of men with whom it would be safe to venture into the Tuscarora country. But it seemed likely that, if speedy relief did not come, all North Carolina would soon be abandoned to the Indians. Therefore, with the peculiar thrift of a royal governor, Spotswood offered to pay for the provisions out of the quit rents if the proprietary deputies would agree to cede to the crown all their territory north of the Roanoke river and Albemarle sound. Of course no agreement could be reached on such a basis, and Spotswood returned to Williamsburg without accomplishing any-

[1] Journal of Burgesses, *loc. cit.*, 41; Spotswood Letters, II, 10.

[2] Spotswood Letters, II, 3, 11; Journal of Burgesses, *loc. cit.*, 67, 68.

thing. But what Virginia proved unable to accomplish, the South Carolinians under Colonel Moore achieved during the following winter, by destroying the principal post of the Indians and thus in the end compelling them to disperse. Peace was thus gradually restored in Carolina.

But as the Senecas had been aiding their fellow tribesmen the Tuscaroras, and their raids took them along the western frontier of Virginia, it also felt the effects of the struggle. Virginia traders were attacked and Iroquois were slain by Indians who were tributary to Virginia. Some of the Tuscaroras also settled temporarily about the heads of the Virginia rivers. Amid these disturbed conditions it was impossible to dismiss the rangers, and in the fall of 1713 it was necessary also to send a small expedition into the frontier counties. But, as necessary to a permanent pacification which would make it possible to recall the rangers, Spotswood concluded treaties not only with such of the Tuscaroras as could be brought together in conference at Williamsburg, but with various dependent tribes of Virginia Indians as well.[1] The object of these was to establish them all, together with various settlements of whites, along the Virginia frontier, under peaceful conditions. It was in connection with this that, in 1714, a small Indian reservation was laid out at Christanna, in the southern part of the province, in extent six miles square and provided with a fort and a guard of twelve men and an officer. So far as possible, all trade with Indians south of the James river was confined to this place, a magazine was to be kept up there and the governor hoped to persuade many Indians to remove thither. The establishment of an Indian school there was also a part of his scheme and, when a congregation should be gathered, the settlement of a missionary among them.

Another most interesting feature of this plan was that a company, consisting wholly of prominent Virginians, should be incorporated and given the monopoly of trade with the Indians. This was held to be a necessity, because Indian trade had fallen to a low ebb. The people engaged in it, because of lack of means, had been forced to buy their goods at retail in Virginia and therefore had exasperated the Indians

[1] Spotswood Letters, II, 34, 53, 57; Journal of Burgesses, Nov. 1713.

by the high prices which they had charged. They had also furnished the Tuscaroras with supplies during the war and the Virginia government had not been able to prevent it. The traders from South Carolina were, moreover, said to be drawing to themselves nearly all the traffic with the Indians along the middle and southern frontier. It was to remedy these evils that an act was passed in 1714 for the incorporation of this company, the duty of maintaining the settlement at Christanna being imposed upon it in return for the trading privileges which were conceded.[1] This project did not originate with Spotswood, but with members of the house of burgesses, the governor seeking to keep it in harmony with his instructions. He also gave the measure his support in his letters home. Robert Cary, a London merchant, as agent for the company, was intrusted with the duty of securing the approval of this act in England. But there it was opposed by the British merchants who were engaged in the Virginia trade, on the ground that it provided for a monopoly and would be injurious to their interests. Though downright monopolists themselves, in this connection they sang the praises of freedom as the best in all dealings with barbarous peoples! The British authorities seem also to have been opposed to incorporated companies, as had been already shown in its discouragement of that method of regulating the production of naval stores. The result was that the act was repealed in July, 1717,—a final argument against it being that it did not contain the suspending clause which should find a place in all laws which affected British trade.[2]

Early in 1712 Spotswood, in connection with the Indian troubles, asked for a further supply of powder and arms and also for three hundred tents, from the queen's stores. The application was supported by the board of trade, but in view of the great waste of such supplies which had previously been sent to the colonies, and of the failure to make repayment for them, strong objection was made by the secretary of state to granting this request. He cited the case of military sup-

[1] This act is not printed in Hening.

[2] Spotswood Letters, II, 144, 230 *et seq.*; C. O. 5/1316 and 1318, O. P. Va. May 1716 and June 1717; Acts of P. C. Col. 1680–1720, p. 721; Journal of Burgesses, 1712–1726, pp. 79, 80.

plies sent to Virginia in 1702 to the value of £3388, repayment for which was to come out of the quit rents, but apparently nothing had been received. This subject was under discussion for several months and finally, in 1713, a considerable quantity of the desired supplies was sent.[1]

During the sessions of the assembly in 1713 and 1714 the governor's Indian policy and that of frontier settlement and defence, together with their cost, were prominent subjects of debate. At the close of 1714 he reported to the assembly that the frontiers were peaceful and that he had been able to reduce expenditures there to less than one-third of the amount spent in preceding years. If this policy was kept up in accordance with his plans, he predicted that a strong frontier would be maintained at steadily decreasing cost. In this connection he referred to the settlement at Germanna as an important part of the general plan and expressed the hope that more Protestants, of the new king's nationality, would be brought in as frontier settlers, they being as suitable as French refugees had been. Without any further supply than had been voted he would for two years more keep up four troops of rangers, the establishments at both Christanna and Germanna, would make a road to the last named place and continue trade with the Indians. Under such easy conditions the policy was naturally agreeable to the assembly and relations continued harmonious. But, in the following year, Spotswood developed the next step in his plan, which was for a standing militia of 3000 foot and 1500 horse in place of the general obligation of the whole body to muster and train. His object in this was efficiency, but it of course provoked criticism, to the effect that he was trying " to huff and bully the people " and establish arbitrary government.[2]

The session of the newly elected assembly, in August and September, 1715, was occasioned by the outbreak of the Yamassee war in South Carolina and the necessity of meeting the cost of such levies as were sent thither, as well as of a more careful defence of the Virginia frontier. Spotswood

[1] C. O. 5/1363, Va. E. B., Apr., 1712, and later dates; Journal of Burgesses, 1712–1720, pp. 79, 80.

[2] Journal of Burgesses, 1712–1726, p. 103 *et seq.*; Spotswood Letters, II, 204–212.

made this the subject of his opening message. But the opinion was now abroad in the counties that Virginia was not prosperous, and discontent began to be voiced in many petitions and grievances presented to the assembly. It had also been shown by unmistakable signs during the election. Recent acts, especially that of 1712, which had been intended for the regulation of the tobacco trade, but which had interfered with favorite local customs, were a leading object of attack. The repeal of the offensive tobacco laws was affixed as a rider to the bill for the relief of South Carolina. Certain county justices, for refusing to certify statements of grievances, were arrested by order of the house, and the governor was specially called upon to aid in the seizure of two of these who had escaped.[1] The executive council condemned the presentation of such petitions without certification by the local court as illegal and seditious, though Spotswood admitted that such had often been the practice in the past. The reproaches of the governor and council drew from the burgesses, on September 2, a sharp expression of complaint concerning the burden of taxation and the lack of regard shown to them and to the grievances which were seeking a voice through them. To this both the council and Spotswood replied,[2] the former in an answer to each of the resolves of the lower house, and the latter in one of the most imperious messages ever sent to a colonial assembly. Spotswood possessed the grand manner and style, and they were fully in evidence on this and later occasions. At this point began his controversies, first with the burgesses and later with certain of the councillors, which were henceforth to disturb what had till this time been a peaceful administration.

" 'Tis fit the world should know," wrote Spotswood, " what these people would have and what you prefer to the defence of your country or the relief of your neighbors. They tell you that those laws shall be repealed which prevent frauds in tobacco payments and restrain them from lessening the king's customs by shipping off their trash; that those shall be altered which oblige them to pay dearly the king's quit

[1] J. of Burgesses, 1712–1726, pp. 122, 124, 132–3, 136, 140, through the session; J. of Ex. C., C. O. 5/1412, Oct. and Nov., 1715.

[2] J. of B., *loc. cit.*, 159, 164, 166.

rents, or enable the governor to inform his majesty of the increase and decrease of the colony; that the act for regulating trade and propagating the Christian faith among the Indians shall be abrogated, the school (at Christanna) for teaching their children be demolished, and the gentlemen at whose charge it was erected be banished out of America and their estates confiscated; that officers' fees shall be reduced below what former assemblys have judged reasonable . . . ; that creditors shall be satisfied with such payments as the debtors shall think fitting to make; that in ordering the militia, securing the frontiers, commissionating justices and placing courts, the notions of the people shall be rather followed than the judgment of the king's governor; that the power of the crown shall be clipt by a triennial bill, and by excluding all officers in places of profit or trust from sitting in the assembly. In short, not to mention all the ridiculous propositions and grievances which the seditious or ignorant vulgar have set their marks to, you are by them directed to reverse such laws as the last assembly raised upon the basis of religion, justice or honour and to make those which will square only with the convenience of the meaner people. Many of them are drawn up in the handwriting of your members, and in violation of the laws for the presentation of grievances have been signed at election fields, horse races and other drunken meetings."

Upon this suggestive list of the offences of the freeholders and their representatives, as viewed from the standpoint of that general providence of Virginia which Spotswood aimed to be, he continued to enlarge in many more paragraphs, and concluded with the statement that the people had chosen a set of burgesses whom heaven had not endowed with the ordinary qualifications of legislators; that the chairmen of their two standing committees could not spell English or write common sense. With this parting shot he dissolved the assembly without giving it a chance to reply.[1] The tone of this speech the board of trade criticised as too incisive and feared it might anger the electors to such a degree that some time would elapse before they could be brought to good temper again.

[1] J. of Burgesses, *loc. cit.*, 166–170; Spotswood Letters, II, 128, 130, 133–135.

An interval of three years now passed before another assembly was elected. During that time much attention was devoted to Indian affairs, to the famous journey across the mountains and to the beginning of visitations by pirates from Providence Island, which were soon to call forth decisive action on the part of Virginia.[1]

The journey of exploration across the Blue Ridge was connected with Spotwood's broad policy of defence and Indian relations, which was ever extending itself so as to take in the western frontier as a whole. As this journey was made a decade before the founding of Oswego, it proves Spotswood and his companions beyond doubt to have been the pioneers among the English in the westward movement. That he fully grasped its significance is proven by a letter of his to the board of trade in 1718, in which he urged that the surplus then in the Virginia treasury might in part be used to fit out an expedition which would enable him to reach Lake Erie and thus, from Virginia, cut the French line of communication between Canada and Louisiana.[2] The danger of the approach of the French from the northwest he fully understood, and contended that a Virginia settlement on Lake Erie would prove an effective obstacle in their path.

The various military enterprises and plans for frontier and coast defence, in which Virginia of late had been engaged, necessitated greater attention to revenue. The attention which Spotswood had given to land grants was closely related to the same subject. Now that the price of tobacco ranged so low, the revenue from the export duty of two shillings per hogshead was not large and therefore other sources of income, especially the territorial, must be developed. As a means toward this end, the governor insisted that the keeping of accounts must be systematized, so that collectors, sheriffs and other subordinates could be held under better control and peculation or fraud prevented. The king would thus be better assured of what was really his due. Spotswood, by insisting on reforms of this kind, had been an advocate of efficiency since the beginning of his administration. For he found that, as a rule, in the offices of the deputy

[1] Va. E. B. C. O. 5/1364, B. T. to Spotswood, June 1, 1716.
[2] Spotswood Letters, II, 295–298.

auditor and receiver general no books were kept with detailed and accurate statements of receipts from all sources and expenditures for all purposes, books, for example, which could be conveniently taken before the council and assembly when there was an audit or any inquiry into the state of the revenue. He could find only general accounts of gross sums and these kept on loose papers. Of escheats, fines, forfeitures, income from sales of crown lands, rent rolls or lists of names and estates which might be used by collectors of quit rents, Spotswood could not find satisfactory records, and this was an evil which affected almost every issue that might come up. Under such conditions the crown must suffer, especially at the hands of the lower officials — collectors or sheriffs — whose dependence upon it was remote. Therefore he insisted that books should be kept of receipts and expenditures in every breach of the revenue, and his effort in this direction dated almost from the beginning of his administration. When he learned that Colonel Nicholson had been appointed commissioner for stating the accounts of all the royal revenues on the continent of America, he awaited action from that quarter. But as the death of Anne terminated that commission and left nothing accomplished, Spotswood took up the question personally.

Taking advantage of orders from the board of trade for statements of the revenue and to the effect that accounts should be laid before the assembly, he called upon the deputy auditor and deputy receiver for a report on the revenue of Virginia.[1] Based on this, a summary of the system as it had come to be in the early eighteenth century may well be given. As was the case in all provinces, the territorial revenue, consisting of quit rents and other minor charges, was not subject to grant by the assembly. The quit rents were levied at the rate of 1s. or 12 pounds of tobacco for every fifty acres. The Northern Neck was excepted from this rule, and its patents, at the time of which we are speaking, paid annually to the king the very moderate sum of £6.13.4 for the entire grant. In spite of much opposition and slackness in payment, with the growth of the province the revenue from this source gradually increased, amounting at the time of which we are

[1] C. O. 5/1316, O. P. Va., Spotswood to B. T. with enclosures, May 24, 1716.

speaking to something like £1500 a year. Virginia was the only colony the quit rents of which were sufficient in amount to admit of a part being paid into the British exchequer. The larger part, however, was retained in the province and used as a surplus for furthering the projects of the crown and of the colonial executive. To no slight degree did this oil the wheels of government and make it possible to carry through policies and conserve executive discretion without unduly antagonizing the burgesses. From no other colony except New York were the quit rents even accounted for to the crown, the reasons being lax administration, various obstacles to collection, and general popular opposition to this form of levy. From this source were also paid £100 annually to the commissary of the bishop of London, £60 yearly to the attorney general and £100 for holding every court of oyer and terminer.

Taxes on land and personalty and on trade were subject to appropriation by the assembly. Among the first, place belonged to the levy of 2s. per hogshead on the export of tobacco. Though this originated just before the Restoration in a grant from the assembly, in 1680 it had been made permanent and, like the similar levy in Maryland, was no longer subject to the chances of temporary grants by the assembly. The annual revenue from this source gradually increased from about £3000 in 1680 to about £7000 in 1760. The other taxes were a tonnage duty, a duty of 6d. per poll for passengers imported, a fee of 5s. for every right to take up 50 acres of land, and occasional temporary levies of impost duties on liquors and slaves.[1] From the permanent appropriated revenue the salary list of the province was paid and other stated claims met. Impost duties were resorted to in order to meet special charges, like the building of the capitol or the governor's house. A general property tax, in the form of a poll tax of 15 or 20 pounds of tobacco on every tithable, also continued regularly to be levied by the assembly to meet province, county and parish expenses. In connec-

[1] The rates on liquors varied from 3d. to 6d. per gallon and on slaves was 15s. or 20s. per head and was intended to be paid by the importer or in part by the master of the importing vessel. Prior to 1710 a duty was also imposed on the importation of servants.

tion with this the services of the committee on claims was called fully into requisition, and the revenue thus secured went toward paying the wages of burgesses,[1] paying the militia and a large variety of claims for special services. To an extent drafts also were made on other sources of revenue toward paying many of these claims. County and parish levies also took the form of poll taxes, and when added to the province levy they raised the total to about 100 pounds of tobacco per tithable.

Of the two leading finance officials of the province, the receiver general and the treasurer, the former received the quit rents, the revenue from the export duty on tobacco, the tonnage duty, and all funds which did not come under the care of the treasurer; escheats, forfeitures, fines, payments on taking up rights of land, prize money were accounted for in his office. From it were paid out, on the order of the governor with the advice of the council or orders from the imperial treasury, the salaries of officers of the colony, of the solicitor of Virginia affairs in England, Virginia's share in the salary of the auditor general, and all claims which were not paid from funds in the hands of the treasurer. The treasurer or speaker-treasurer, an appointee of the burgesses, received the revenues arising from the duty on liquors, servants and slaves imported and from public and special levies authorized by vote of the assembly. He accounted to the assembly and paid out funds under order from that body or from the governor. The issue of treasury notes, when occasionally resorted to, was a part of his duties. Both the receiver general and the treasurer were paid in percentages of the revenue which passed through their offices, and the revenues and expenditures of Virginia were audited and with care reported through the auditor general in England.

In the report, above referred to, which was made to Spotswood, it was stated that the 2s. per hogshead, the 6d. per poll on passengers imported and the tonnage duty were collected by the naval officers, also that rent rolls existed by counties, which were made the basis of assessment and collection of

[1] This was 120 pounds of tobacco per day and travelling expenses. As later commuted into a money payment, it was 9s. or 10s. per day, according as the member came by land or water.

quit rents and other levies by sheriffs. Formerly the quit rents had been deposited with the receiver general in Virginia, so that they might be ready when needed, but of late years they had been ordered into the exchequer in England. The revenue was all paid out by warrants of the governor to the receiver general, who half-yearly brought accounts of receipts and expenditures to the auditor with vouchers, and they were passed by him. Three copies of these were made, one being given to the governor, one kept on record in the council office and one sent to the auditor general in England. Contingent charges were also audited and their payment was then ordered.

Spotswood criticised this report in some points, as that the composition for escheats was not 2d. per acre but 2 lbs. of tobacco per acre, which, especially in the counties where sweet-scented tobacco was produced, was worth more than 1d. per pound. By that means and by the rating in coin which the receiver general gave to the payments made by the Virginia planters, Spotswood claimed that he made a gain of 13% or more on all the money which he received for escheats. The cost of the courts of oyer and terminer, he also said, was paid not out of the quit rents but out of the 2s. per hogshead. It was also a false notion that the quit rents were drawn into the exchequer, for they remained in the hands of the receiver general until ordered to be paid out in the king's name, and so it had always been. In the matter of naval offices, accounts, composition for escheats and quit rents, the deputy auditor and receiver general did not act as a check upon one another, and that for the reason either they failed to keep adequate accounts or the one official accepted the accounts of the other as certified without examining them.

When, with the general situation as just described in view, Spotswood began to insist that books with complete statements of receipts and payments be kept in all branches of the revenue, he was opposed, especially by Ludwell, the deputy auditor, who plead the custom of his office and the instructions of his superior in England. Ludwell also participated, in a way which was offensive to the governor, in the political agitation which accompanied the session of the assembly in 1715. Therefore, finding him so obstinate that nothing could be accomplished, Spotswood suspended him from office, in May, 1716, and sent charges against him to England.[1]

Early the following year a series of fifteen queries, reflecting upon Spotswood's conduct, were presented to the board of trade, and it immediately transmitted them to the governor for his answers.[2] These related scarcely at all to questions of finance, but to the policy of the governor in the case of the frontier, especially the building of defences at Christanna and Germanna, the settling of Indians, the expenditures for rangers and the plan for a standing militia. Other minor subjects came in for comment, all for the purpose of showing that the governor was oppressive and arbitrary in policy. In answer to these Spotswood reviewed much of his administration and had no difficulty in showing that they were, in all essential particulars, unfounded. In replying to the resolves of the late house of burgesses, which were also presented against him, Spotswood challenged his opponents to show that he had taken any fees or rewards which were not his by right, while he claimed to have endured more labors and exposed himself to more hazards on the frontier than any man in the province. The result of the controversy, in this aspect of it, was that both Ludwell and Byrd were removed from their offices as auditor and receiver general, but whether any permanent improvement followed in the bookkeeping of that department the sources do not reveal.[3]

Though the relationships of Byrd and Ludwell within the council were extensive, his quarrel with them did not involve the governor in a conflict with that body as such. But another controversy was already developing in which the governor came directly to an issue with the council. That grew out of his efforts to reduce its judicial powers by appointing special commissioners to sit with the council in courts of oyer and terminer. This was not only in harmony with a law of which the governor had secured the passage in 1710,[4] but with the general authority to establish courts which was given to royal governors in their instructions. Spots-

[1] Spotswood Letters, II, 150, 152, 159, 175–187.
[2] *Ibid.*, 190 *et seq.*
[3] *Ibid.*, 174, 248.
[4] Hening, III, 489; Bassett, *op. cit.*, LXVIII.

wood's justification for his measures was that, since the members of the council were so inter-related by descent or marriage, and since the law required that judges should retire from the bench when cases involving members of their family were to be tried, it was desirable that the court should be differently constituted. When, in 1712, a man was to be tried for his life, Spotswood appointed two of the leading men of the colony to assist the court of oyer and terminer which tried him. But the members of that body, considering themselves the only stated court for criminal causes, looked on this as an invasion of their privileges and refused to act as councillors until the grievance was redressed. Without abandoning his claim, Spotswood then withdrew the new appointments until he should receive instructions from England.

The controversy now extended to the burgesses, and they designated Byrd as agent and sent an address to the king in which, among other things, they supported the contention of the council.[1] Thus he was regularly empowered as agent of council and burgesses and diligently presented the case of both in England. The board of trade, from the beginning, was unanimous in the opinion that the governor had the right to establish courts and appoint judges without limiting himself to members of the council. Later, in 1717, the case was referred to the attorney general, and in an elaborate opinion he sustained the contention of the governor. The board then reported these facts to the king and stated in addition that Byrd did not question the power itself but only desired that it should be restrained, as being specially liable to abuse; but as the governor was answerable for his conduct and as the application did not come from the people of Virginia, but from the councillors who seemed to be claiming power for themselves to the prejudice of the prerogative, it thought that the governor's commission should hold good.[2] With this decision, though unwillingly and under continuous

[1] J. of B., May 24 and 30, 1718. One of the arguments which Byrd submitted to the board of trade, setting forth his fear that the governor would secure too much power if he should appoint the judges, is printed in Palmer's Calendar of Va. State Papers, I, 191.

[2] C. O. 5/1365, Va. E. B. Dec. 31, 1717, and Mar. 3, 1717/18; C. O. 5/1318. O. P. Va., 1717–1718; C. O. 5/1412, J. of Ex. C. Va. Oct. 27, 1716, Dec. 9, 1718; Spotswood Letters, II, 25, 221, 224.

pressure from Spotswood, the council in Virginia acquiesced. The feeling between the Byrd-Ludwell-Blair connection and the governor had by this time become intense. The governor had called Blair a " very ill man " and had made a somewhat violent speech at a meeting of the visitors of the college. In his letters home he was also complaining bitterly of the opposition which he was meeting from these eight councillors and their connections throughout Virginia.

In the course of the election of 1718 a paper, called an " Advice to the freeholders of the several Counties of Virginia in the choice of Representatives to serve in the approaching Assembly," was circulated through the province. Spotswood inferred that it was written by a member of the council, and presumably he meant Ludwell. In this paper the freeholders were urged not to choose representatives who were favorable to the governor and to the group connected with the projected Indian company, who desired an appropriation to pay their charges at Fort Christanna and otherwise to cheat the people. The governor and his supporters, it was said, desired the province to take that fort under its care and man it at a cost of 100,000 pounds of tobacco per year. Creatures, favorites and tools of the governor were trampling down liberty, and the last assembly was abused for upholding the interests of the country against such perils; let no favorites be chosen this time, was the advice. Of course it was not followed and the temper of the assembly, which was now elected, was milder than that of its predecessor.[1]

When the assembly met, Spotswood sought to counteract such attacks by dwelling on the peace and prosperity of the province, as compared with the debts with which its southern neighbors were harassed as the result of their Indian wars. He told the assembly that they had met not to appropriate supplies for defence, but to find out the best way to dispose of " the greatest Bank of money that ever was at one time in the Public Treasury of Virginia." [2] During the session efforts were made by certain neutral members of the council to bring about a reconciliation between the governor and their col-

[1] C. O. 5/1318, O. P. Va. Apr. 24, 1717; Spotswood Letters, II, 276.

[2] This amounted to about £15,000 and was due to the impost on an unusually flourishing tobacco trade.

leagues. Byrd in England was also trying to induce the titular governor, the earl of Orkney, to aid in this work. Spotswood professed to be cooperating, and many glasses of punch were consumed by the parties in the effort to come to terms, though without much result. Spotswood remarked at the end that none of the eight councillors would pay him the civility of a visit, but on one occasion, when he was giving a public entertainment, got up a meeting of their own where healths were drunk, though not to the governor, and liquor was passed round to the people outside who were gathered about a bonfire.

No specially important laws were enacted during this session, and on the surface relations between the governor and the burgesses appeared to be reasonably harmonious. But the discontented councillors and their supporters, in and out of the assembly, were active and a number of controversial subjects were mooted, though they were not allowed to assume the first place.[1] As the result of the presentation of grievances from six counties, an act was passed — the only legislation of public importance — specifying the fees of the secretary, sheriffs, coroners, constables, and clerks of the county courts, as well as those of attorneys. A proposal was also introduced to put £4,000 of the public money into the hands of Archibald Blair, a brother of the commissary, to be kept, as Spotswood supposed, for such uses as the clique, of which the Blairs were members, might desire. Spotswood also remarked that Ludwell and the Blairs were partners in one of the largest trading stores in the province. It can be readily understood why no bill on this subject reached the hands of the governor; it illustrated the danger which lurked in a surplus.

One of the measures of this session, which was aimed at the prerogative, was embodied in a clause that the assembly desired to tack to the fee bill, providing that the secretary should no longer appoint clerks of the county courts, but that they should hold during the pleasure of the elected justices of those courts. This received much support, the argument being used that the clerks in question were often elected as bur-

[1] Spotswood Letters, II, 275–295; Journal of Burgesses, 1712–1726, pp. 173–217.

gesses and, if they were removable by an officer of the king's appointment, it gave the governor too much power over them. Spotswood interpreted this as akin to a proposal made in the last assembly, that all office holders should be excluded from the lower house; and as he had declared that if the clause was kept in the bill he would veto the entire measure, it was dropped. Another bill, which was dropped before it reached Spotswood, was intended to exclude the colonial postmaster from meddling with any sea-going letters and to hamper him otherwise in the discharge of his duties. This was the result of an outcry which was now raised in Virginia on the occasion of the first attempt to establish a regular mail route between Williamsburg and Philadelphia, to specify rates of postage, the times and places for the receipt and delivery of letters and other necessary regulations. As this was done under the authority of an act of parliament, it was said that the rates of postage were a tax, which parliament had not the right to impose nor the postmaster to collect. Complaints were presented to the assembly against the post office and a bill passed both houses which, though it acknowledged the act of parliament to be in force in Virginia, by the provisions just alluded to sought to prevent its execution.

The assembly also refused to pay the expense of the Indian school at Christanna and of the guard and fort there. They advised that the Indian hostages who were kept to secure peace be sent back. As they were not informed of any irregularities in the Indian trade, they were indifferent as to keeping up the regulations. The point was also made by the house that, as Spotswood's plan of forming a barrier of tributary Indian tribes had failed to attract any but the Saponies, there was no use in continuing the fort at Christanna or other features of his policy.[1] At the close of this session Spotswood spoke little, but in his letters to the board he poured forth his bitter criticism of the situation into which the opposition councillors through their influence over the burgesses had brought the province. He considered that his cherished plans had been defeated and his only resource for the time was to ask for the removal of Byrd from the council because of his long absence in Europe, and to enlarge upon

[1] J. of Burgesses, *ibid.*, 207, 213. Spotswood Letters, II, 281 *et seq.*

the ambiguous position of councillors, arising from the fact that they acted for the people of the colonies as well as servants of the king. Though it was not openly avowed, in Spotswood's opinion this idea had taken root in the minds of too many councillors and made them unfaithful to the crown.

In the November session of 1718, after another controversy over the right of the governor to collate to benefices in the church had been provoked by Blair and Ludwell, the issue between Spotswood and the burgesses reached its culmination. At the beginning the session was tranquil and it was expected to be short, because there seemed to be nothing of importance to do except to pass the public levy.[1] But on the ninth day, after, according to Spotswood, several of the less trusted members had gone home, an address to the king was adopted, charging that the governor had perverted the laws, especially those relating to land grants; that he had exceeded appropriations in expenditures on his house; that he had tried to prevent the county justices from levying the salaries settled by law upon the burgesses, and that he had abused the burgesses by provoking messages and speeches. Byrd, as agent, was ordered to present this address, and in the first draft of his instructions several other charges were included, but they were dropped. At the outset it was intended by some expressly to demand the governor's removal, but that also was softened into an expression of discontent at being governed by a lieutenant governor.

But even this mild impeachment, when the governor was informed of it, furnished him the occasion for a speech at the close of the session which was framed in his loftiest style.[2] Though he did call the burgesses " a Cataline crew of malcontents," his tone in general was that of a patriot who, while laboring successfully to bring the province to a high state of prosperity, had been wantonly attacked. But this was only the beginning of his defence. A detailed answer to the charges in the address was sent to England, and to show that the province was with him, he secured favorable addresses

[1] Spotswood Letters, II, 306, 308 *et seq.*; J. of B. *ibid.*, 228 *et seq.*; C. O. 5/1318, O. P. Nov. 1718, March 1719.

[2] J. of B., *loc. cit.*, p. 243.

from twenty-one out of twenty-five counties, from a convention of the clergy, from the grand jury of the colony and from a number of the burgesses.[1] As before, Spotswood traced the origin of the charges to his opponents in the council. His regulations as to the payment of quit rent was the source of their irritation. They were the ruling oligarchs, controlled the vestries and counties, obstructed the collection of the revenue when they chose, and insisted that the governor must yield to them and not criticise their doings. It was the same aristocratic clique of Virginia which had caused the failure of the administrations of Andros and Nicholson. To the student of the politics of the time great interest also attaches to Spotswood's idea of the burgesses, as expressed in his defence against the charge that he had discouraged the collection of their salaries. He said that he had been instructed to keep these at a moderate rate, as their last three sessions had cost 800,000 pounds of tobacco and they had passed only one public act which would stand as law. This the governor considered " an unreasonable Burthen." Their large salaries of more than thirty shillings per day were a great incentive to inferior men to seek election. As all freeholders could vote, the inferior class among them were worked upon by ambitious candidates, and low practices were resorted to, so that those who had nothing to lose carried their points. " These upon an approaching election, set themselves to inventing most false and malicious stories and industriously spread them about the country to poison the minds of the people and prejudice them against such candidates as should seem most worthy in the eye of the government, and as they are the familar companions of the common planters, they have continued opportunities to propagate the scandalous reports and absurd notions among the vulgar." Mobbist politicians, who engaged to pursue the wild schemes of the electors and who withstood all demands of the government, pass for patriots with the multitude. They thrust themselves into the legislature in order to make a larger crop of tobacco at the capital than they could on their own plantations. This, like the utterances of Hunter, well expresses the views of an eighteenth-century conservative concerning colonial assem-

[1] Spotswood Letters, II, 311–316, 320; C. O. 5/1318.

blies, and that it contains much truth concerning these bodies, and indeed concerning legislatures in all times, no one can deny. In Spotswood's opinion, all friends of the British constitution must long to see a check put to the growth of these evils. His remedy and that of the board of trade, as expressed, for example, in its letter of April 23, 1713,[1] was the simple one of raising the property qualification for the suffrage. But it was found that neither the council nor the lower house would tolerate this, and Spotswood had to content himself with further complaints of the intractable temper of the Virginia planters.

This was the end of serious controversy during Spotswood's administration. Two years passed before the assembly was again called together. Then he told them that, if vulgar notions did not prevail to the effect that the body should oppose the head, or invidious distinctions arise between the friends of the governor and the friends of the country, assemblies would undoubtedly be most wholesome parts of the constitution. As he had then decided to spend the rest of his life in Virginia, they no longer had reason, he said, to suspect him of designs against its welfare. He looked upon her "as a Rib taken from Britain's Side," but he warned her that "this Eve must thrive so long as her Adam flourishes, and if she allowed any serpent to tempt her to go astray it would but multiply her sorrow and quicken her husband to rule more strictly over her."[2] The use of this figure to express what he regarded as the relation between the colony and the realm makes this utterance of the Virginia governor comparable with John Winthrop's "little speech" at the close of his famous trial in Puritan Massachusetts.[3] But the sentiment and spirit of the two utterances are notable by way of contrast rather than resemblance, for the Virginia governor took credit for most of the good that was done, and sought to make everything centre about himself and the crown of which he was the representative. The conciliatory sentiments of the governor, however, were fully reciprocated by the burgesses. Peace had

[1] C. O. 5/1363, E. B. Va.

[2] J. of B., *loc. cit.*, 250, 254.

[3] Osgood, Am. Colonies in the 17th century, I, 199.

already been made in the council and Byrd was restored to his seat in that body. Its members abandoned their exclusive claim to the place of judges in the courts of oyer and terminer.[1] The question of the governor's right to collate to benefices was referred to the privy council for settlement. Spotswood gave over into the hands of appointees of the burgesses the principal charge of the completion of his house and grounds.[2] Among the laws passed this session were several which authorized the dividing of counties and parishes and thus satisfied a need upon which Spotswood had insisted at the beginning of his administration.

With the reopening, for a brief period, of war between England and Spain privateers began to infest the Virginia coast. These continued after the suspension of arms, and gave an opportunity for Virginia again to assume a rôle in affairs which affected all the southern colonies alike.[3] She sent Captain John Martin, with an armed sloop as a flag of truce, to St. Augustine to protect and obtain restitution, if possible, for the damage which the Spanish had inflicted. Some Spanish prisoners were restored on board this vessel. Martin's sloop was lost on the bar at St. Augustine, and the governor there disclaimed responsibility for the attacks of privateers; but two small English vessels were restored. These conditions gave rise to complaints that the guardships absented themselves too much, pleading stress of weather as an excuse for sailing away to New York or Barbadoes, and a demand from the general assembly that larger vessels be sent to Virginia and that their captains be ordered not to depart without the governor's permission.

On the appointment of an agent in England and the instructions which should be given him the lower house disagreed with both the governor and the council; hence that project fell through.[4] Neither did Spotswood succeed in inducing the assembly to reimburse the members of the late Indian company for its expenditures in the public service.

The question of most wide-reaching importance which in-

[1] C. O. 5/1412, Dec. 9, 1718; Spotswood Letters, II, 335, 341; Cal. of Va. State Papers, I, 195.

[2] J. of B., *loc. cit.*, 284.

[3] *Ibid.*, 303; Spotswood Letters, II, 341, 347.

[4] J. of B., *loc. cit.*, 308–310, 313.

terested the province and especially its governor during the last two years of Spotswood's administration was that of the progress of French influence in the valley of the Mississippi and its bearing upon Indian relations, as well as upon English interests in general. In this connection mention should be made of the push of settlement westward toward the mountains and the erection in 1720 of the two new counties of Spotsylvania and Brunswick.[1] This act followed quickly on the adjustment of the North Carolina boundary and contained in its preamble, as the reason for its passage, the statement that the frontier toward the high mountains was exposed to danger from the Indians and the French. The object of the measure was to secure the two passes through the Blue Ridge, the one near the upper waters of the Rappahannock and the other near those of the Roanoke. The two counties comprised large and loosely bounded areas, the one at the northwest and the other at the southwest extremity of the province. Settlers in these regions, including the foreign born, were encouraged by exemption from public levies for ten years, which provision was made for supplying them at the public expense with arms and ammunition and for the building of a church and court house in Spotsylvania county. Until local government should be fully established in the new jurisdictions, magistrates of the neighboring counties should attend to the maintenance of the peace among the new settlers. An address was sent to the king urging that a fort be built at each of the passes and garrisoned with one hundred men, all to be supported out of the Virginia quit rents or in some other form from the royal exchequer. It was in Spotsylvania that the governor was specially interested, for to mining projects and the production of naval stores in that region he was already committing himself and there he was to spend the years which remained to him after the close of his governorship. Some interesting proofs also of his activity in procuring land grants in the new county, using dummy grantees for the purpose and thereby increasing his possessions by many thousand acres, came to light in the course of the next few years. The stationing of royal troops on that frontier could not at this early date be generally re-

[1] Hening, IV, 77; J. of B., *loc. cit.*, 289 *et seq.*

garded as a necessity, and the only concession which was obtained from the crown was a remission of the payment of quit rents and purchase money by settlers in these counties for seven years after the passage of the act for their establishment. No person should take up more than one thousand acres in either of the two counties and the conditions of seating and cultivating should be the same as elsewhere. Finally, none who held land in other parts of Virginia should take up land in these counties without at least giving security for the payment of quit rent for the land they already held.[1]

The need of a revision and extension of Indian treaties, especially with the Iroquois, was already evident and from 1720 it was frequently before the Virginia assembly. Apart from the general causes for this which have just been alluded to, attention was drawn to the subject by occasional raids across the Virginia frontier, which were occasioned by the feud between the Iroquois and the Catawbas and other tribes to the south. These were the subject of correspondence with New York and of legislation by Virginia early in 1722 to the effect that neither its tributary Indians nor those belonging to the Five Nations should pass to the east of the Blue Ridge or to the south of the Potomac river, without license and passports from the governors of the respective colonies to which they belonged.[2] Supported by this law, Spotswood visited Albany the following summer and joined in a notable Indian conference. It was the last event of his administration and served as a fitting close of what had been a leading phase of its policy. The history of the conference belongs to that of Indian relations in general, and with this brief reference both it and the adminstration of Spotswood in Virginia will be for the present dismissed.

[1] C. O. 5/1319 B. T. O. P. O. in C., Aug. 6, 1723. The able letter of the board of trade to Lord Carteret on this subject shows that it favored the building of forts and even the stationing of troops in these counties at the expense of the crown. C. O. 5/1365, B. T. E. B. July 17, 1721.

[2] Hening, IV, 103. J. of Burgesses, *loc. cit.*, 286, 300, 351, 352.

CHAPTER XXIV

PENNSYLVANIA FROM THE ISSUE OF THE CHARTER OF PRIVILEGES TO THE GOVERNORSHIP OF WILLIAM KEITH, 1701–1717

PENNSYLVANIA, among all the colonies, was the largest recipient of immigrants from the continent of Europe in the eighteenth century. These added a large German component to its inhabitants and, with the later Scotch-Irish immigration, made its population as heterogeneous as that of New York. But this movement and its effects did not become very pronounced until subsequent to the date with which this chapter closes. Therefore, for the present, we are to consider Pennsylvania as inhabited very largely by people of English descent, with a mixture of Welsh and a certain Dutch and Swedish element along Delaware river and bay. It was through the connection with the Lower Counties that the Dutch and Swedes find their place in Pennsylvania history. Considered from the standpoint of religion, the great majority of the English inhabitants of Pennsylvania still were Quakers. But there was a small, though active, Anglican element in Philadelphia and at a few other points, which received support from the Jerseys and especially from Anglicans who lived in the Lower Counties. The province, therefore, was being managed by Quakers and such controversies or other difficulties as there were arose among them, though they were in some cases increased by the presence of Anglicans, by contact with people down the bay and by relations with the home government. War and the extension of imperial control were the occasion of many perplexities for the Quaker, while questions of trade and of the Lower Counties were involved with the Maryland boundary dispute and conflicting claims to territory and proprietary revenue. The provinces about the Delaware and Chesapeake were bound together in a network of relations, at the centre of which stood Pennsylvania.

For a little more than a decade after his return to England in 1701, William Penn retained his accustomed vigor and activity. During that time his influence was felt in all affairs which concerned his province and his sect, whether in America or in Europe. He left James Logan as his efficient agent in Pennsylvania, with whom he was always in correspondence touching the survey or sale of lands, the collection of proprietary revenue, the management of manors or other estates, a settlement for the daughter of his first marriage, the conduct of his eldest son, and all the varied matters of private and family interest. In addition to these, Penn and Logan were continually exchanging views concerning political questions which agitated or in any way affected Pennsylvania. In this correspondence,[1] which fulfilled a purpose similar to that which passed between the governors of a royal province and the board of trade or secretary of state, Logan in particular discussed from the point of view of proprietary interests all public questions. His powerful and logical mind was unsparing in its analysis of political situations and of public characters. Logan also was not sparing of advice to Penn, and it was usually based on thorough knowledge and sound judgment. He was the proprietor's valued minister as well as private agent — a mingling of functions which was characteristic of the proprietary system — and his letters were far more voluminous and important than any which passed between the governors of the time and the proprietor. They contain indeed a body of fact and criticism such as no other proprietary province can show, and one which it would be difficult to match among the archives of the colonial period as a whole. In this correspondence, so far as political questions are concerned, the part borne by Penn was decidedly secondary and inferior, and, in reading it, one wonders why Logan was not appointed governor. As it was, he was only a member of the board of property, secretary and a member of the council.

William Penn was a man with multifarious interests and

[1] A part of this, included between the years 1700 and 1709, was published years ago, in two volumes, by the Hist. Soc. of Pa. But Logan's letter books still exist in manuscript, in the possession of that Society, extending in unbroken series until after 1730.

connections, religious, social, political and of a business nature, which extended not only to America and to all parts of the United Kingdom and Ireland, but to Holland and Germany as well. Though born into the burgher class, his social affiliations had extended among people of all ranks and many nationalities. Not only had he been welcomed and consulted at the court of the Stuarts, but he had repeatedly suffered imprisonment for his faith. As a Quaker preacher he had journeyed with Fox and Keith, and his writings on Quakerism and liberty were widely read in many circles. He was an international character of the first rank in his generation, and the duration of his life was such as to connect him with the Restoration at the one limit and with the accession of the Hanoverians at the other. A man with such a record and character it is manifestly difficult to locate or classify. He was not a lawyer, nor a statesman, nor a systematic business man. And yet he was always immersed in affairs, private and public, and while he was often charged with greed and craft, his usual attitude toward the world was that of a benevolent idealist. He preferred to be regarded as the father of his province rather than its proprietor in the narrow and legal sense of the term. Concessions he made at the outset were inconsistent with safe administrative rules; and a certain carelessness and lack of system appearing in all his public dealings, while they opened the way to greater freedom, led to misunderstandings and disputes. His place among proprietors was unique, as it was in many other relations. Unlike the Calverts, during his life he received no assistance from relatives in the administration of his province, while his selections of men from outside to be governors were conspicuously unwise. While the province was small and he was present in it, his influence was very great. By mutual concessions all went well. But after his final return to England criticism began. He lost his veto forever. His influence over his governors was slight. While for several years he was active before the board of trade and elsewhere in England as a defender of proprietary rights against royal or parliamentary assaults, his connection with the province was kept up through Logan more than through the ordinary official channels. Finally, as the result of certain untoward circumstances, his influence upon government in Pennsylvania was so reduced as to become, years before his death, a memory rather than a reality. For a time Pennsylvania was nearly as free from the control of its proprietor as were the Carolinas at the same period.

The chief cause of this collapse in Penn's fortunes was his reckless dealings, extending over years, with Philip Ford and his wife. His good nature and unbusinesslike habits had made it possible for them to weave a network of fraud about him. Ford, who was a Quaker and a London merchant, had first been appointed by Penn steward of his Irish estates. About the time of Penn's first voyage to America, in 1682, Ford presented to him an account in which it was made to appear that Penn was indebted to him to the amount of £2851. So absorbed was the proprietor in his many schemes, and so trustful, that shortly afterward Ford secured his signature to a deed of lease and release according to which this debt was increased to £3000 and Penn must pay this or grant Ford 300,000 acres of land in Pennsylvania. This was but the beginning of a long series of fraudulent transactions, in which Ford and his wife played upon the credulity and carelessness of the proprietor till they had made it appear that he was indebted to them to the amount of more than £20,000. A variety of mortgages and deeds of conveyance of the province and territories were also secretly drawn and signed as security for the payment of these sums. Exorbitant rates of interest were also charged by the Fords. In 1697, after Penn had granted to them an absolute release of province and territories, giving up to them the royal charter and deeds of enfoeffment, Ford leased them back to Penn for a profitable consideration, the proprietor hoping thereby to escape the payment of a tax levied in England on borrowed money.

By 1702 Penn had become hopelessly involved for an amount far beyond his ability to pay. He had appealed to some of his Quaker friends to help him out, and finally to the London Meeting. But receiving no adequate assistance, he was forced, in 1705, to proceed against the heirs of Ford by a bill in chancery. In this Penn failed because he had

[1] Shepherd, Proprietary Government in Pennsylvania (Columbia University Studies, VI), 185 *et seq.*

signed so many accounts, deeds and settlements, all apparently in good faith, that the chancellor refused to have the accounts inspected, however unreasonable they might be. The Fords then, in 1706, appointed Isaac Norris, David Lloyd and John Moore, who were supposed to be Penn's greatest enemies, to receive all the quit rents and sell all proprietary lands in the province and territories. Norris refused to serve and went to England to help straighten out affairs; but the financial condition of the proprietor now became pretty well known in the province. The Fords also instituted a suit in the common pleas against Penn for arrears of rent due since 1697 and obtained a verdict for nearly £300. It was because of his inability to pay this that he was arrested and imprisoned for debt in the Fleet.

The Fords now appealed directly to the queen to transfer to them the land and government of the province. But Sir Edward Northey showed that the deeds gave no power of government, that no decree had yet issued from the chancery and the property was not alienated. Finding their plans thwarted at this point, the Fords became more inclined to compromise and, after prolonged negotiations, in return for £7,600 they executed a deed of release in October, 1708. A large part of this sum certain merchants, among whom were Henry Gouldney and Joshua Gee, subscribed on Penn's behalf and he in return mortgaged the province to trustees. They then empowered Logan and others to collect debts and quit rents, sell lands and manage Penn's property there. In this way things again fell back within the control of the proprietor and his friends.[1] But his prestige had greatly suffered and the mortgage which now rested upon the province was a perpetual badge of his weakness. How this affected the question of the surrender of the province to the crown will appear later.

While Penn was becoming involved in these difficulties of a private nature, his experiment in Pennsylvania was confronted by numerous perplexing questions. War inevitably brought difficulties to a Quaker government. It was accompanied with increased emphasis upon imperial control and this threatened the permanence of all chartered colonies.

[1] Many references to the Ford business are in the Penn-Logan Correspondence, II, 200 *et seq.*

Reference has already been made to ways in which it menaced Pennsylvania. With this went the growth of Anglicanism in and about the Quaker province and the increase of those, among its own population and in adjacent provinces, who did not sympathize with its ideals. People of this character were especially numerous in the lower counties, and this section of Penn's domain lay in the centre of a network of complex relations, of which the boundary dispute with Maryland formed an important part.[1] The Marylanders were claiming the entire region under the provision of the royal charter of 1632 which specified the fortieth degree of latitude as their northern boundary, but ignoring the qualification that at the time of its grant the territory in question had been temporarily settled by the Dutch, that soon after it was permanently occupied by Swedes and Dutch, that their colonies then passed by conquest to the English, and later by a complicated series of grants the territory had come into the possession of Penn and had been annexed to Pennsylvania. But the government of Maryland was now in the hands of the crown, the English church was in process of establishment there, illegal trade was rife on the lower Delaware, and it was easily conceivable that the British government would not be indifferent to the Baltimore claim. Now that the government of the Jerseys had been surrendered, the surrender of the lower counties to the crown or their transfer to Maryland would give the queen control over both shores of the bay. But if that occurred, Pennsylvania would be isolated and its port, Philadelphia, cut off from free access to the coast.

The possession of the lower counties was therefore of great importance to Pennsylvania, and by an act of union, passed in 1682 and intended to confirm the indenture from the duke of York the same year,[2] they were united with the province, it being provided that the two should have the same assembly and executive, should be governed by the same laws and share equally in all benefits. But Penn's claim to this territory was by no means clear. It was contested by the British government and offered a vulnerable point which Randolph and Quary were not slow to attack.[3] Its population also was

[1] Shepherd, *op. cit.*, 117 *et seq.*

[2] Hazard, Annals of Pa., 611.

[3] Kellogg, Am. Colonial Charter, Report of Am. Hist. Assoc., 1903, I, 244.

largely of foreign origin and largely of faiths alien to his own. It was not strange, then, that soon after the passage of the act of union signs of dissatisfaction began to appear. Though there was danger that the lower counties might be annexed by Maryland, the chance of that was remote and it did not serve to deter the dissatisfied from action against Pennsylvania. To the other causes of divergence commercial rivalry between Newcastle and Philadelphia now developed. The complaint first made by the counties was that Pennsylvania vessels did not enter and clear at the port lower down the bay. Soon the counties began also to complain that they were unequally represented in the provincial council and among the judges. Procedure and decisions of the courts were criticised. Action by the council affecting the counties, unless an adequate number of members from that section was present, was opposed. The lodgment of a large appointing power in the hands of a governor, who was a province man, occasioned dissatisfaction.

The lower counties were more exposed to attack than was the province, and the attitude of the Quakers toward war was not widely shared by their people. Therefore, when alarms spread and the need of ports and a militia was felt, agitation and action on these matters followed similar to what occurred among the colonies at large. The silent refusal of the province to take action in these concerns provoked resentment in the counties and led to disturbances at elections and refusal to choose representatives. Complaints from the counties of the defenceless condition along the Delaware were made to Penn and he was requested to inform the king.

Still another and a very important element in the situation arose from the fact that there was comparatively little room for the expansion of settlement and increase of population within the limits of the counties, while in the province there was space for a very large growth. The province already considered itself the superior of the two, so that it was felt that acts which were passed when the assembly was in session at Newcastle were not to be obeyed without confirmation at Philadelphia. In 1701, shortly before the close of the last visit of the proprietor, he held a conference with the members over this question and expressed his grief at the prospect of a rupture. But when the members from the lower counties expressed the firm conviction that the union was an unequal one, Penn, with the paternal regard which so distinguished him from all other proprietors, told them they were free to go and might act by themselves if they wished, but it must be upon amicable terms and a due settlement of the legal relations between themselves and the province.[1] "Yield in circumstantials to preserve essentials." With this the members who were present from the lower counties expressed themselves as well pleased. A proviso was then added by Penn to the Charter of Privileges[2] that if, within three years, the province and counties should agree to separate, the three counties of the former should be represented in an assembly of their own by eight members each, besides two from Philadelphia, and each of the three counties in the territories by such a number as they chose. This provision, in the state of feeling which had come to exist, as good as assured the separation of the assemblies, and it came very promptly after the return of the proprietor to England.

The counties refused to accept the Charter of Privileges and sent no representatives to the assembly of October, 1702. The members from the province at once requested that they might organize separately.[3] Governor Hamilton submitted several arguments against this course, which showed that the question had bearings much wider than the local interests of the parties concerned. After calling attention to the fact that the tobacco which was exported from the Delaware region was raised chiefly in the lower counties, and if they were separated it would hinder that traffic, he referred them to papers lately come from England which showed that Randolph and Quary were advocating the separation of the territories in the hope that they might come directly under the crown. If that was accomplished, access from the province to the sea might be hindered and proprietary government there be ultimately overthrown. But these arguments produced little or no effect. The Quakers of the province were

[1] Col. Recs., II, 51, 52.

[2] *Ibid.*, 60.

[3] Votes, I, App., XV, *et seq.*; Col. Recs., II, 72 *et seq.* A recent account of these events is in Keith, Chronicles of Pa., 411.

as ready for separation as was the mixed population of the counties. Both were ready to take advantage even of technicalities for the purpose, as that the election had been held under the charter of liberties in the one section and under writs in the other and therefore that they could not sit together. The result was that a joint assembly was not held during Hamilton's brief administration, and in the session which was held after his death the province only was represented and that by eight members from each county as was provided in the charter of liberties to be the number, if separation should occur. Meantime Penn's title to the lower counties had been declared unsatisfactory in England and confirmation of his lieutenant governors could be secured only by his signing an article, stating that the crown reserved the right to resume government over them.

On the arrival of Governor Evans, in 1704, he ordered the election of four representatives from each of the lower counties and brought them into a conference with the council and the representatives of the province. He urged upon them the desirability of continuing the union and his orders to uphold it.[1] But the province stood out, the technical point as to the number of representatives from the counties being urged as sufficient at this stage to decide the question, and it was found impossible to hold a joint assembly.[2] No later effort was made to bring them together, and the province and counties continued to be governed by a common executive but with distinct assemblies. They also continued under the same judicial system until the issue of the ordinance of 1706 for the establishment of courts.

Logan [3] watched the growth of Anglicanism in the counties as contributing to the separation, and Governor Evans, as a result of his quarrel with the Quakers, was believed to favor the handing of them over to the crown. In 1715 the earl of Sutherland petitioned the king for the grant of the counties in payment of a debt due him from the crown. Their inhabitants, fearing that their property rights might be imperilled, then sought complete reunion with Pennsylvania,

[1] B. T. Proprieties.
[2] Col. Recs., II, 125–131; Kellogg, *op. cit.*, 245.
[3] Penn-Logan Correspondence, I, 191, 267, 282, etc.; Shepherd, 347.

but the offer was rejected, and, except for the occasion this gave for some efforts on the part of Governor Keith to discriminate against Quakers in the counties, no change resulted. Inasmuch as by this result the access of Pennsylvania to the sea might be obstructed and the way be left open to efforts on the part of Maryland to absorb the lower counties, the outcome could not be considered advantageous to Penn's province. On the other hand, it was in harmony with the natural inclination of the Quakers toward seclusion and quietude, and their avoidance of questions which might force them to sacrifice their ideals. With this tendency the Germans, who were already settling in the interior of the province, were quite in sympathy.

We have already seen [1] that in the Frames of Government at the outset concessions were granted in Pennsylvania which made its system complicated and obscured the rights of the proprietor and his execution. Clear definition of rights, as well as consistent practice, was needed if that system was to be worked without friction. But clear definition Penn and those associated with him did not furnish.

The Charter of Privileges of 1701 furnishes a good illustration of the crudity of Penn's attempts to draft what was intended to be a sort of written constitution of the province.[2] It contained clauses about a number of minor subjects which should have found their place in ordinary statutes, and wholly failed to mention others which were of prime importance to government and about which, since they were omitted, disputes were bound to arise. One of these was the right of veto. By the royal charter this was guarantied to the crown, an obligation which was not imposed on any other chartered colony of the seventeenth century. Under the first Frame of Government the governor, as distinct from the proprietor, did not possess the right of veto, and in the Frame of 1683 no reference was made to it, though the fact that he was deprived of his three votes in the council may lead to the inference that he then possessed it.[3] During Fletcher's

[1] Osgood, American Colonies in the 17th Century, II, Chap. 11.

[2] Logan's account of its origin is to be found in his "Memorial in behalf of the Proprietor's Family and of himself, Servant of that Family," which was written in 1725 in reply to William Keith; Votes, II, 419.

[3] Shepherd, *op. cit.*, 239, 251; Works of Franklin (Sparks' ed.) III, 173.

administration and under Markham's Frame of Government the right of assent and dissent was fully enjoyed by the governor. In the Charter of Privileges no reference was made to it and the governors thereafter continued to exercise it as a right effectually guarantied by earlier practice.

But as yet nothing had been said about the proprietor's right of veto, and it is impossible to tell whether or not, when out of the province, he had exercised it. When, however, he commissioned Evans, a clause was inserted reserving to himself this right. That would have placed the legislation of Pennsylvania under a threefold veto, a badge of dependence such as was worn by no other colony. In a conference between the council and assembly, in May, 1704, the latter protested against[1] this claim as one which was not contemplated in the royal charter. As the proprietor was now in England, the inconveniences attending its enforcement would be so great as practically to defeat the objects of legislation. After consideration the council agreed with the assembly that, when the governor had affixed the great seal of the province to an act it could not be annulled by the proprietor without the assent of the assembly. They held that this requirement could be dropped from the governor's commission without destroying the validity of that document, while of course the right of veto would still remain in the king as provided in the royal charter. This view was confirmed by an opinion of Attorney General Northey, in October, 1705, to the effect that the proprietor could exercise the right of assent or dissent when he was in the province; action of this kind by his deputy in his absence was complete and final.[2] We may infer that in this way one of the vetoes to which Pennsylvania laws had been exposed was eliminated. The act of the proprietor's agent, his governor, must thereafter suffice.

Another question, which was not expressly answered by the Charter of Privileges, was that of the share of the council in legislation. At the time of its issue an appointive council permanently took the place of the elective one and, as a result of this, the council ceased to be a legislative body. But

[1] Col. Recs., II, 144, 146. David Lloyd's account of the attitude of the assembly toward this is in Penn-Logan Correspondence, II, 405.

[2] Stats. at Large of Pa., II, 475.

no reference whatever appeared to this fact in the document itself, nor in the commission then issued to the council were its powers so defined as clearly to exclude that of legislation.[1] The documents left it to be a matter of inference from the practice which followed. Is it any wonder that disputes arose? The council at once began to advise the governor in reference to his action on bills sent up by the assembly. He considered these bills in sessions of the council. It thus came by this indirect method practically to exercise legislative powers — under the guise of advice to the governor. When, in the August session of 1704, they were amending a bill for the confirmation of the Charter[2] of Privileges, the assembly resolved that it was inconsistent with the said charter that the council should have a share in legislation except when, on the death of a governor, the entire power of government resided in that body. They also questioned whether the governor should approve laws during sessions of the council.

A third question, which also caused much discussion, was that of the right of the assembly to adjourn itself. This had been conceded to it in the Frames of Government, but without the necessary limitations. Respecting these limitations Penn wrote in 1710: "I designed[3] the people should be secured of their annual fixed election and Assembly; and . . . that they should sit on their own adjournments; but to strain this expression to a power to meet at all times during the year without the governor's concurrence would be to distort government, to break the due proportion of the parts of it, to establish confusion in the place of necessary order and to make the legislative the executive part of government." Accordingly, following the practice in other provinces, when Penn appointed Evans governor, in 1703, he ordered him to call, prorogue and dissolve assemblies. The Charter of Privileges, however, contained nothing decisive on this question, and owing to this omission and to the issue of an instruction which seemed to conflict with the earlier Frames

[1] Col. Recs, II, 56, 61.

[2] Votes of Ass. I², 11. For a comprehensive account of the practice in this regard under Governors Evans and Gookin see Votes, II, 421 *et seq.*

[3] Proud, II, 48.

of Government, the conditions were created out of which a dispute was bound to arise. In its bill of August, 1704, the assembly sought to regulate its sessions by amending and confirming the Charter of Privileges. When this came before Evans,[1] he told them he perceived from it that they were trying to assume fully the power of adjournment and to exclude him from the right given in his commission and instructions. The assembly replied that the exercise of these powers would defeat the plan of annual elections provided for in the Charter and would substitute writs issued at the discretion of the executive. Following the advice of the council in which on this question the voice of Judge Mompesson was the weightiest, the governor expressed the opinion that the proprietor had not granted away the power under discussion and he would await further directions from England. Probably no direct response was received, perhaps none was ever requested. The assembly continued to adjourn itself till the practice was well established; but, when necessary, the governor also called and prorogued it, though amid frequent protests and complaints, all of which were the result of a failure to define properly the limits within which governor and assembly should act in this matter.

John Evans and Charles Gookin, the two men whom Penn appointed as governors after the death of Andrew Hamilton, and who stood nominally at the head of the province from 1703 until 1717, were both unfitted for the task that was imposed upon them. It was practically impossible that a Quaker should be appointed, and as Anglicans they were out of sympathy with the great body of the people whose affairs they had to administer. Both were unknown, inexperienced men of inferior personalities. The doings of both were petty and irritating to all parties concerned. Evans was more or less openly immoral.[2] The eldest son of the proprietor, while sharing in the escapades of the governor, and others, was arrested in a tavern brawl, and, in a fit of anger at the public exposure which followed this, renounced Quakerism and re-

[1] Pa. Col. Recs., II, 146–150, 157, 158; Votes I[2], 14. Penn–Logan Correspondence, I, 298, 299.

[2] See characterizations of him in Penn–Logan Correspondence, I, 318, 322; II, 144, 268.

turned to England. Conduct of this character was as fatal to the success of officials among the sober citizens of Philadelphia as it would have been in Boston. Logan said that Gookin was the "poorest animal" he ever saw in the office of governor, though this shows that Logan was not acquainted with all the colonial governors. Gookin quarrelled with the assembly far less than did Evans, because he obstinately kept silence, but apparently before the end of his service he had forfeited the regard of virtually the whole province. There is no evidence that he ever exercised much influence. Both these men were selected by Penn on the recommendations of friends in England or Ireland. Could Logan have been appointed, he probably would have made a most successful governor, and some other equally faithful, but less able, person as agent could have collected the proprietor's rents, sold his lands and attended to his other private business.

Though the Quakers were still largely in the majority among the population of Pennsylvania and were to control its government for a long time to come, they were not a unit in its support, and controversies developed among them, as they did everywhere else in the colonies. There was a narrow rigidity about their individualism which made them quite as stubborn in the support of their opinions as were the Puritans, while in the arts of factional politics they had nothing to learn from any of the colonists. During the period of which we are speaking David Lloyd, as a member from Philadelphia county, was the leader of the opposition in the assembly. Of several of the assemblies he was speaker and their most influential member. He was accounted a good lawyer, was certainly a staunch Quaker and a partisan leader who was not slow to seize opportunities which might yield political advantage. He was much more representative of the average Quakers of Pennsylvania than was either Penn or Logan, both of whom had seen too much of the world to remain wholly in touch with the rank and file of their sect. Lloyd had been a strong opponent of Blackwell and later took the lead against a variety of encroachments by the executive and judiciary. He was suspended from the council because of an alleged insult to the court of admiralty and the royal commission which authorized it. The direct opposition of Lloyd to Penn began during the latter's recent visit to the province, when they were discussing the revision of the laws.[1] Lloyd had then drawn a so-called charter of property, of which, under pressure, Penn had conditionally approved, but later had revoked his assent. The purpose of Lloyd at that time was to make it possible to legislate with freedom concerning territorial as well as governmental relations. The feeling which was then aroused was intensified by difference of opinion about the acceptance of Andrew Hamilton as governor and questions connected with the separation from the Lower Counties. The points left unsettled by the Charter of Liberties were closely involved, and the attitude which the province should hold toward the war was also under discussion. In the assembly of 1704, action was proposed in these various lines and it was at that juncture that Lloyd appeared as the opponent of the proprietor and the political rival of Logan.

A bill confirming rights of property was passed by this assembly, drawn on lines similar to those of the so-called charter which Penn had rejected; also a bill modifying the charter of Philadelphia and granting additional privileges.[2] These were rejected by Evans, who always acted conjointly with the council. At the close of the session, and after replying finally to the governor, the house resolved to incorporate its grievances in an address to the proprietor. This was to deal plainly with him on the extent to which his commission to Evans was inconsistent with the privileges he had promised the people. The heads of this address were read to the house and approved, but the communication which was sent with them was prepared by Lloyd.[3] This was the famous "Remonstrance" of 1704, of which Logan said that it was "a most virulent and unmannerly invective against the proprietor,

[1] Col. Recs., II, 62, 325. Penn-Logan Correspondence, II, 371 *et seq.*, 402 *et seq.*, where the versions of this by Logan and Lloyd can be compared; Shepherd, 58.

[2] Penn-Logan Correspondence, I, 317; Col. Recs., II, 158; Votes I², 15 *et seq.*

[3] It is printed in Sparks' ed. of the Writings of Franklin, III, 166 *et seq.* On the way in which it reached Penn, see Penn-Logan Correspondence, I. 327, 331; II, 64, 374, 407 *et seq.*

dressing whatever had been mentioned in the minutes by the House in rude and most affrontive language and foisting other matters that he had no shadow of pretence for." This statement is borne out by the text, for it so dwelt on the alleged greed of the proprietor in his territorial and property relations as to lead to a protest against his proposed surrender of the province because it would look like "first fleecing and then selling." It was as much an attack on Logan as it was on Penn. The assembly never made itself responsible for it, and Penn considered it an insult so personal that he threatened to prosecute[1] Lloyd for it. Isaac Norris, when in England in 1707, took off a great deal of the edge of the "remonstrance" by assuring Penn and his friends that, though Lloyd had signed it as speaker and by order, it never regularly passed the assembly or was read there. Norris also circulated a signed certificate to that effect.[2]

The assembly which was elected in the fall of 1704 did not differ essentially in sentiments from its predecessor.[3] It chose Lloyd again as speaker. The former issues were revived by the assembly. It attempted again to revise the Charter of Privileges and to draw from the governor further replies to its messages of the last session. Both of these efforts failed, as did the attempt on the part of the governor and council to secure a copy of the "remonstrance." The assembly deplored the long delay in securing the royal approval of laws, and the proprietor complained of the great expense he incurred in paying the fees which were necessary to secure such approval.[4] The grant of £2,000 made to him before his departure from the province had not been sufficient, and the assembly called for an itemized account of his expenditures in this service and would do what it could to meet the cost. Bickerings were exchanged between governor and assembly in several long addresses over the comparative merits and sacrifices of proprietors and people, quit rents and bill of

[1] Penn, through Evans, told the next assembly that he highly resented the heinous indignity and scandalous treatment of that letter, and if he thought it the act of the people it would be sufficient to cancel all obligations of his toward them. Votes I², 34–36; Col. Recs., II, 187.

[2] Penn-Logan Correspondence, II, 244, 248.

[3] Votes I², 17 *et seq.*; Col. Recs., II, 164 *et seq.*

[4] Votes I², 39–42; Col. Recs., II, 193–197.

property coming into the discussion, and all without result. Feelings were intensified by the remarks of an obscure member to the effect that [1] the governor was a mere boy and should be kicked, and the prosecution of the offender raised a question of privilege. Finally the assembly was dismissed by the governor, he actually exercising the right of prorogation.

The house which was elected in the fall of 1705 was of a very different temper. Joseph Growden was chosen speaker, and perfect harmony existed between it and the governor throughout a long and very fruitful session. Conferences were freely held with the council and fifty-one acts were passed [2] during its first session. This was closed by the governor passing the bills which had been prepared, though in the journal of the assembly there is no entry to show that it did otherwise than to adjourn itself.[3] At the end of the next brief session the assembly also adjourned itself.[4] Thereafter the house seems regularly to have adjourned on an understanding, express or tacit, with the governor.

The governor called the assembly together in September, 1706, in order to consider the passage of a number of laws to take the place of those which had recently been disallowed in England. Word had just been received that, of 105 laws submitted by the proprietor to the crown, 52 had been rejected.[5] Of special importance was the passage of one act for the establishment of courts of justice and a law of property to take the place of those disallowed. The province and counties were now left without courts of justice, but, instead of prompt action to supply so serious a lack, a long controversy arose over details of the judicial system and that led into a struggle over the right to establish courts. David Lloyd, though not speaker at the beginning, was the

[1] Votes I[2], 46 *et seq.*; Col. Recs., II, 200 *et seq.*; Penn-Logan Correspondence, II, 33 *et seq.*

[2] Votes I[2], 49 *et seq.*; Col. Recs., II, 206 *et seq.*; Penn-Logan Correspondence, II, 80 *et seq.* The text of the acts passed is in Stats. at Large of Pa. 171–293.

[3] Recs., of C. II, 230; Votes I[2], 81.

[4] Votes, I[2], 85.

[5] Col. Recs., II, 251–252; Stats. at Large of Pa. II, 449–456. The two acts here referred to are in *ibid.*, 148, 191; and the reasons for their disallowance on pp. 471, 495 *et seq.*

active leader of the house in this controversy, as were Logan and Mompesson in the council.[1]

In the judicial system, as hitherto established in Pennsylvania and the territories, the county courts had been thrown into great prominence and when, after delay, a provincial or supreme court was established, the intention clearly was to make it supplementary to the local courts rather than the chief judicial body in the province.[2] The act of 1701,[3] which had just been disallowed and which applied to both province and territories, began with elaborate provisions concerning the county courts, giving them large jurisdiction, both criminal and civil, as courts of quarter sessions and common pleas. The county justices were also made judges in equity and as orphan courts these tribunals were given great powers over the appointment of guardians and the settlement and administration of estates. The judges of the provincial court, who were to go on circuit, were to try high crimes and hear cases on appeal, but only in a restricted way under writs of error. The idea underlying this was that justice should be brought as near as possible to every man's door, it should be made cheap and suitors from the counties should not be compelled unnecessarily to attend court in Philadelphia. Though the reasons assigned for the disallowance of this act, and later ones of the same nature, referred chiefly to loose expressions used, and some approval of the substance of the measures was expressed, it is not difficult to see that the principle of it, as just described, would bring it into such disagreement with the judicial system of England and of other colonies as to lead to serious objections. Evans also told the assembly that it had been found inconvenient and was complained of by all experienced men who practiced before the courts.[4]

In the history of the colonies there were not many instances like this of Pennsylvania, which by an act so simple as the disallowance of a law found itself deprived of a system of courts which had been in existence twenty years. In such

[1] Votes I², 88 *et seq.* Lloyd, however, was again chosen speaker in October, 1706.

[2] Shepherd, 371.

[3] Stats. at Large, II, 148 *et seq.*

[4] Votes I², p. 101.

a case as this the effect of the royal veto reached its maximum. As the result of it, a prolonged controversy followed in Pennsylvania, in which the judicial system proper to it was discussed in many long addresses and series of resolutions passed between the governor and assembly.[1] The occasion of this was the necessity of passing an act which should take the place of the one just disallowed. As incidents of the discussion some other points became involved. One was the old question of the right of the council to participate in legislation, which the assembly again denied, though throughout this entire controversy nothing is clearer than the fact that the council virtually legislated, although its action did not take the formal shape of the three readings of bills and their actual passage. The struggle was for the ideas which Logan and Mompesson supported as against those of Lloyd and his followers, and it is clear that it was the council far more than Evans that formulated the arguments. On one occasion a free conference was held between the assembly and the governor and council. The action of the council, however, was taken under the form of advice.[2]

Another point which made the action of the assembly offensive to the supporters of the proprietor was this, that the house attempted to incorporate in the measure a provision for appropriating judicial fines and forfeitures toward the payment of the salaries of the judges, instead of their going, as hitherto, to the proprietor.[3] Another encroachment on Penn was seen in the claim that the justices should license taverns and ale houses, and that they should appoint the clerks of their courts. It was also insisted that judicial fees should be fixed either in this act or in another law which should specify the rates of all fees. They also sought to make judges removable on charges presented by the assembly. Other features of the plan which had a decidedly modern tendency were those which favored a method of trying cases involving titles to land which should be free from delays and legal fictions; also the feeling which was shown against undue im-

[1] *Ibid.*, 93–115; Col. Recs., II, 253–279.

[2] Votes I², 108, 111, 121. The governor likened the function of the council to that of the attorney general in England.

[3] In Philadelphia all fines went into the public chest. Col. Recs., II, 355.

prisonment for debt, though it was charged with involving discrimination against creditors.

But the radical fault which the council found in all the proposals that came from the assembly was the extent to which they were intended to push the county courts into the foreground, and that in spite of the almost total lack of trained lawyers in the province with whom to fill the many places on the bench. The main features of the act which had just been repealed reappeared in all their proposals. They seem to have conceived of the provincial court as having a sort of distinct existence in every county, with a clerk's office at Philadelphia where writs should be drawn to run throughout the province. This court should issue no original writs in civil cases, but only remedial, and of these the writ of error was the only one of which use was apparently intended to be made.[1] Original writs were to be returnable before justices of common pleas and quarter sessions. Under this system the counties would be to a large extent isolated from one another judicially, and it would be difficult for a litigant who faced prejudice at home to find another and an impartial tribunal.

As opposed to this plan of the Quaker, Lloyd, the council insisted that the governor and council should be the court of equity for the entire province, that the supreme court should have full common-law jurisdiction throughout the province, this being secured by the power to issue all original and remedial writs which were customarily issued by similar courts in other colonies and by the central courts in England, and by the judges going on circuit.[2] The county courts would then occupy the inferior position which they held elsewhere and the province would become judicially a unit. The courts of Philadelphia should have the same rank as other county courts. Suits should be begun in the provincial as well as in the county courts. Process would extend from county to county, or equally over the whole province. It contended that the common man would be adequately served under this

[1] Votes I[2], pp. 95, 102.

[2] Col. Recs., II, 257 *et seq.* It was claimed by Lloyd that part of the ancient Ordinance of Wales was revoked by act of William and Mary because it gave the president and council the power of a court of chancery; the equity power was vested in the counties. This, he said, was the precedent for his bill. Votes I[2], 114, 121, 123.

system, while it insisted that the rights of creditors should be duly guarantied, as well as those of the proprietor, including that of establishing courts by executive action.

The controversy was prolonged, with most tiresome repetition and detail. In its later stages the question of the tenure of judges and the obligation of the governor to remove them on an address from the assembly came more into prominence.[1] The governor declared that he would not part with the power to remove purely on his own discretion, though he should always give great weight to an address from the assembly, especially if accompanied with proofs. While a conference was being held, a dispute arose between Evans and Lloyd over the failure of the latter, as speaker, to stand when he addressed the governor.[2]

Finally, on February 28, 1706/7, Evans issued the ordinance which he had so long threatened, for the establishment of courts.[3] In this he followed some of the main features of the assembly's bill,[4] though the ordinance provided for a better compacted system, referred carefully at all points to English precedents, and was much more clearly drawn than was Lloyd's measure. The assembly presented a long remonstrance against this act,[5] in which they claimed that the ordinance power granted by the royal charter did not extend to this, and that in law the courts could not be revived without the cooperation of the assembly.

But some time before this the personal feelings of Lloyd and his supporters toward Logan had become so strong as to result in an attempt to impeach him before the governor.[6] The charges which they preferred were based on the claim that Logan was attempting to introduce arbitrary government into the province.[7] His interpretation of it was that the real object of their attack was the proprietor and his system of government, but this was probably no more true than the

[1] Col. Recs., II, 302, 311.

[2] *Ibid.*, 314 *et seq.*

[3] Stats. at Large, II, 500; Col. Recs., II, 337; Votes I², 152.

[4] Compare the ordinance with Votes I², 95 *et seq.* The provision for the establishment of the provincial court was taken from Lloyd's bill, but equity jurisdiction was given to the justices of the provincial court.

[5] Votes I², 157–159; Col. Recs., II, 349–353.

[6] Votes I², 113.

[7] Col. Recs., II, 344, *et seq.* 353.

oft-repeated charge of royal officials that the colonists were aiming at independence. The charges, so far as they were specific, had reference to the alleged foisting upon the province of the proprietor's veto and of the governor's right to prorogue and dissolve the assembly, to the fact that Logan held both offices of secretary and surveyor general, and to certain acts of his in the administration of the property rights of the proprietor and in reference to the election of a sheriff in Philadelphia. Of some of these charges Logan disclaimed all knowledge and in regard to the others he showed that he had simply followed the ordinary routine of business. But the case never came to a trial, for the reason that the governor had no authority to sit as judge in an impeachment case, while the assembly refused to acknowledge that the council had any judicial powers.[1] There was no "middle state" in the constitution of an American province, corresponding to the house of lords, which could hear and determine impeachments. Hence the process failed, though Logan plead for a full hearing and exoneration, since the publication by the house of its charges had injured his reputation and business.

Justice continued to be administered under the ordinance until after the close of Evans' administration, early in 1709. But the dissatisfaction also continued, and Gookin, Evans' successor, found included among the grievances laid before him the complaint that the courts of the province did not as yet rest on a sure statutory basis.[2] Penn had ordered that all ordinances and commissions should continue in force till his further pleasure was known, and it was under the authority of this that the courts were held until 1711; then, as the result of further discussion, a detailed judiciary act was passed.[3] In substance this was based upon the ordinance of 1706, but it contained many elaborate provisions concerning appeals, the issue of writs and action thereunder and in regulation of suits for the recovery of debts. Three years later — early in 1714 — this act,[4] along with several other

[1] Col. Recs., II, 365 *et seq.*

[2] Votes, II, 30.

[3] Col. Recs., II, 519, 522–529. Stats. at Large, II, 301 *et seq.* Shepherd, 382.

[4] Stats. at Large, II, 545–549.

Pennsylvania laws, was disallowed, the reasons being that some of its provisions tended unduly to multiply suits, and that among certain English statutes which were adopted by the act it was stated that one of them should be put in execution, "so far as circumstances admitted," which the attorney general regarded as an improper statement.

Because of these faults, which might have been removed by referring the measure back to the assembly for amendment, Pennsylvania was again plunged into judicial chaos. In July, 1714, Gookin reestablished the courts by ordinance,[1] its provisions being similar to those in the ordinance which Evans had issued. This raised again the old question of legality, though without the former violent controversy. In May, 1715, five separate acts were passed — one establishing courts of quarter sessions, another the courts of common pleas, a third the provincial court, a fourth providing for better ascertaining the practice of courts of judicature and a fifth regulating appeals to Great Britain.[2] Provision was now made for a supreme court which should sit in Philadelphia and have original jurisdiction, its powers being as ample as the common law courts at Westminster. In 1719 all of these laws, except the one relating to appeals to Great Britain, were disallowed.[3] The representation of the board of trade against these acts shows that the objections again were so frivolous as almost to raise the suspicion that they were trying so to perplex this proprietary province in its judicial business as to force a surrender of its charter. Against a provincial court organized according to the best model they revived Raymond's objection to it as defined on a different basis in an earlier act, while the board condemned the laws concerning the other courts because they contained the expression "as near as conveniently may be," when referring to the observance of certain details of English judicial procedure, an expression which had been used so often in all sorts of documents which the British government itself had issued in reference to the colonies as to make it a commonplace.

[1] *Ibid.*, 556.

[2] Stats. at Large, III, 32, 33, 65–83; Col. Recs. II, 578–585, 595; Shepherd, 384. Though Lloyd was still speaker, the journals show no evidence of disagreement between the assembly and council.

[3] Stats. at Large, III, 464–468.

The various riders which the assembly for a long time tried to pass with the court bills of course failed in that form. Fines and forfeitures continued to go to the proprietor, as did the revenue from tavern licenses, though by an act of 1711 the county justices had received the right to recommend those who were to be licensed. The governor had shown no opposition to the regulation of fees, and in 1711 and again in 1715 comprehensive acts providing for those were passed. But both of these acts were disallowed in England on the ground that it was the intention to reject the court act and that would remove the reason for specifying the fees of justices who would not be appointed.[1]

With the failure of the first bill for the establishment of courts and also of the proceedings against Logan the anger of the assembly had broken forth against Evans. There was nothing which could longer shield him from the expression of profound dissatisfaction with which he had long been viewed. In order fully to understand the depth of this feeling, it will be necessary to refer to the attitude of Pennsylvania toward the war and the doings of Evans in that connection. In 1704 the first requisition of the crown since the beginning of the second colonial war reached Pennsylvania. It was that £350 st. should be contributed toward the defence of New York.[2] The assembly declined to accede to this proposal, giving as an excuse that they had the back settlements of Indians to secure and protect. In any case, and especially as circumstances then were in Pennsylvania, this was clearly an evasion of the issue. It was intended to divert attention from the real objection to the demand, which was the refusal of the Quakers to be at all concerned with war. Governor Evans was not content with the reply and pressed the subject again, using the argument that their refusal of the aid would probably hinder action by the queen in confirmation of their laws and prejudice the interests of the province in other ways.[3] The assembly was also told that the proprietor expected they would refund to him the salary of the late Governor Hamilton, and it was suggested that a salary should

[1] Stats. at Large, II, 96, 331, 357, 440, 466, 543.

[2] Col. Recs., II, 133, 136, 139; Penn-Logan Corr. I, 329 *et seq.*

[3] Col. Recs., II, 142–3. Shepherd, *op. cit:* 297 *et seq.*

be provided for the present incumbent. Judge Mompesson, Edward Shippen and James Logan carried this message to the house, but reported that "there was some appearance of dissatisfaction upon it."

Evans, however, soon issued a proclamation commanding all persons, whose persuasion in religion would permit them so to do, to provide themselves with arms and enlist in the militia which he now began to organize.[1] Naturally, activity in this line was greatest in the lower counties, though enlistments were encouraged in Philadelphia by exemption from certain civic duties. This experiment, though greatly needed at the time, was frowned upon by the Quakers. No appropriation, of course, could be obtained toward the payment of its cost. Both the resources and the personal character of the governor were too narrow to enable him to meet the situation liberally. As a result, a few companies of volunteers were formed and continued in existence for about two years and then disbanded. During that time, however, the disgust of the Quakers with the governor was raised to the point of culmination,[2] on account of the false alarm which was spread by him and others, in May, 1706, on the pretence that a French naval force was advancing up the bay. This half-insane freak was followed by the passage of a law in the lower counties for the erection of a fort at Newcastle, where a tonnage duty in powder should be collected from every vessel that went up and down the river.[3] This touched the sensibilities of the Pennsylvanians anew, for it interfered with their freedom of trade along the river and bay. But they soon managed to abate the evil by seizing and disciplining the commander of the fort and making a strong protest to the assembly at Newcastle which had caused it to be built. Thus ended in failure and in mutual irritation the efforts of Evans to provide in some measure for the defence of Pennsylvania.

In the summer of 1707 the assembly preferred a long list of the alleged private and public misdeeds of the governor to be sent to their agents for presentation to the proprietor.

[1] Proud, I, 459. Penn-Logan Corr. II, 159.
[2] Proud, I, 468 *et seq.*
[3] *Ibid.*, 471, *et seq.*

To these they added certain charges against Logan. Then, ignoring the command of Evans that they should make known all their addresses to him, they adjourned themselves till fall. But from Logan, through Norris after the latter's arrival in England,[1] and in other ways, Penn had received information of the unfitness of Evans for his post. Norris told him that he thought as good a head was required for the government of Pennsylvania as for that of most of the other plantations. It was already evident that Penn intended to remove Evans, but whether William, the heir-at-law, would be appointed his successor Norris could not make out. As Penn was then a prisoner in the Fleet, to outward appearances the fortunes of the proprietorship could not have been lower.

Finally, in March, 1708,[2] Penn wrote that the three agents of the assembly had visited him and stated how lamentable was the condition of the province under Evans, and had said that, if he were not discharged and an acceptable person put in his place, they would bring the complaint of the assembly before the queen and council. Penn, deploring especially the moral obliquities of Evans, had thus been forced to turn aside from his more personal troubles to find a successor. Charles Gookin was the man whom he found, a man of whose family Penn had had "some knowledge" for forty years, who was highly recommended by Generals Earle and Cadogan, and by others, including some friends in Ireland. Sobriety, good morals and a general spirit of fidelity seemed the chief qualifications of Gookin, as valuable perhaps as those which most of the military men possessed who were sent over by the British government. At the same time also Penn reached a settlement with the Fords and immediately mortgaged the land of the province to Henry Gouldney, Joshua Gee and other friends in England who had aided him in his difficulties. Logan and others were ordered to care for Penn's property, sell lands and collect what was due him in the province. This put a somewhat brighter face on his affairs, but they were in the midst of war, and dangers

[1] Penn-Logan Corr. II, 238.

[2] *Ibid.*, 267 *et seq.* These were Whitehead, Meade and Lower, who were informally selected to act for the assembly because they were known not to be on friendly terms with Penn.

from various quarters still threatened the continuance of proprietary government in Pennsylvania.[1]

During the first two years of Gookin's administration (1708–1710) he was beset by the troubles which were inherited from his predecessor. Lloyd still remained speaker of the assembly and it continued, as heretofore, to voice his animosities. The fact that when they first[2] met the new governor was absent at Newcastle did not improve their temper, but it gave them an opportunity of again asserting the right of adjourning themselves, a practice which, under minor restrictions, was now becoming pretty well established. When the assembly met first for business, in March, 1709, in its address the complaints against Evans were again rehearsed and marshaled as grievances. In his reply Gookin, after giving the members good advice about laying aside the jealousies of the past and applying themselves to the business of the present and future, expressed his approval of the attitude which Evans had taken on the establishment of courts, and deprecated the calling of the advice "evil" which was given by the council.[3] He urged the passage of various measures, among them one for the support of government and for the security of its people. This was immediately followed by a sweeping assertion from the assembly that Logan and others of the council were chiefly responsible for the miseries and confusion of the province. The assembly was also at issue with the provincial treasurer on the ground that he, instead of paying the public debts on orders signed by the speaker, had leaned for advice on the council, of which he — Samuel Carpenter — was a member.[4] With the delivery of a long remonstrance to the governor,[5] filled with minor complaints and insinuating that Gookin had shown lack of zeal in public service, the house adjourned for a short recess.

When the session was resumed the requisition had come from the queen for a quota of men in aid of the expedition under Colonel Vetch which was planning for the conquest

[1] Proud, I, 485. Penn-Logan Corr, II, 306, 352. Shepherd, 198. Keith, Chronicles of Pa., 488 *et seq.*

[2] Votes, II, 17 *et seq.*

[3] *Ibid.*, 19, 20.

[4] See Stats. at Large, II, 290; Votes, II, 5 *et seq.*, 24, 29.

[5] *Ibid.*, 32.

of Canada.[1] To the fate of that demand reference has elsewhere been made. Here it should be stated that it was kept alive for months. The governor repeated the demand, the assembly offered a gift of £500, which was so small that Gookin drew a contrast between the heavy taxation to which England was then submitting and a sum which was so much less than the reasonable proportion of Pennsylvania.[2] The actual appropriating of the £500 went over till the next session, after harvest. The house, however, caught up a hasty remark of the governor about some of its members being turbulent and this made the discussion more personal. About midsummer Lewes, at the mouth of the bay, was plundered by French privateers, while it was felt that some attention should be paid to the Conestoga Indians. These events, combined with growing unrest in the lower counties, owing to their exposure without means of defence, various defects in their government, and the efforts of Lord Baltimore to get possession of them, led to serious reflections upon the possibility of Penn being able to retain his proprietorship. To the mind of Logan and others the ability of Quakers long to manage the government of a province which was exposed to the perils of war was clearly open to question. Robert Quary was now in the later days of his activity and continued to be an object of Penn's keen distrust. But Logan thought him useful as a critic of the attitude of the assembly, and that he was not unfriendly to the governor, council and those who were supporting Penn and trying to carry on the government in conformity with British ideas.[3]

In its session of the late summer of 1709 the assembly began to dicker with the governor over a slightly increased appropriation and a redress of grievances. Among the grievances the lack of a statute for the establishment of courts held a prominent place, and the discussion led to the passage of Gookin's act, to which reference has already been made. It was while the court bill and its accompanying act for the regulation of fees were under debate that the controversy over Logan again blazed up.[4] Robert Ashton, a leading

[1] *Ibid.*, 34 *et seq.*

[2] *Ibid.*, 38–40, 42; Penn-Logan Corr., II, 343, 346, 349–353.

[3] *Ibid.*, 358.

[4] Votes, II, 53 *et seq.*

lawyer of Philadelphia, and the attorney general were at first joint objects of attack with the secretary. Several months before, Logan had complained to the governor that he had not been permitted to clear himself from the former charges. Now, on the last day of the session and just before the fall election of 1709 the assembly, under the name of a remonstrance,[1] launched another savage attack at Logan, charging him with responsibility for all the alleged evils of the province, and with favoring arbitrary government. It was said that he controlled the council and that without its consent the governor could not act. This was used to influence the election in favor of Lloyd, and the old members of the house were returned. Lloyd was again elected speaker and the former hostile attitude was resumed. Logan now in a communication to the governor attacked Lloyd with equal vehemence and demanded an opportunity to clear himself[2] from the charges. He also petitioned the house on the subject, demanding a trial. It resolved that he should at once answer all the charges which had been brought against him at his impeachment. But meantime charges which Logan had made against the speaker came before the house, and the quarrel becoming greatly embittered, it ordered the sheriff of Philadelphia to arrest and imprison Logan. The governor interposed and forbade him to proceed, his reason being that Logan was not a member of the assembly and so was not under its jurisdiction, and also that, as he was about to sail for England, the object of this move was to prevent his going thither on business important to the province and the proprietor. Gookin also claimed, since the assembly had come together after an adjournment for several days earlier in the session without his calling it, that it was no longer a house which he was bound to recognize. Though it was now only the beginning of December, 1709, no further business was done. Several favorite bills of the assembly failed and it soon adjourned never to meet again. Before the next election the futility of Lloyd's opposition seems to have been made clear to the electors and a new set of assemblymen

[1] Penn-Logan Corr., II, 360 *et seq.*; Votes II, 65.
[2] *Ibid.*, 70 *et seq.*; Col. Recs., II, 507; Proud II, 39 *et seq.*

was chosen, in October 1710.[1] Richard Hill was elected speaker and between this assembly and the governor and council thorough harmony prevailed.[2]

In marked contrast to recent assemblies, this body devoted itself strictly to the business of legislation and not to the drafting of controversial addresses. Its first session passed without incident and at its close fourteen laws were accepted [3] by the governor, the product of its activity. These included comprehensive acts for the establishment of courts and regulation of fees, for the support of the government, for the licensing of inns and against riotous sports and games.

Before the house met for its second session the summons had come from the queen for a contribution toward the land expedition of 1711 against Canada.[4] The assembly voted £2000 for the queen's use, by a combination of the general property tax and poll tax. The question arose as to whether the amount so raised should be paid directly to the governor or to the treasurer and be issued by him on the governor's order. On the advice of the council Gookin insisted upon the former method. This led to delay till a later session, but did not change the resolve of the assembly,[5] and the treasurer was made the immediate custodian of the grant; the amount, however, to be used for the expedition was to be paid by him to the governor and to be transferred by him in turn to the officers empowered by royal authority to receive and expend it. The expedition, as we know, was abandoned in its early stages, and as late as 1713 Governor Gookin was complaining to the assembly that this appropriation had not been collected. Persons whose servants had gone on the expedition had not yet been paid.[6]

The manifold difficulties with which Penn and his province were beset had led him as early as 1703 to think of surrendering his rights of government, or of both land and government,

[1] Lloyd's vindication of himself against Logan's attacks is in Penn-Logan Corr., II, 402 *et seq.*

[2] Votes, II, 73.

[3] Col. Recs., II, 529; Stats. at Large, II, 301–399.

[4] Votes, II, 97 *et seq.*, 101; Col. Recs., II, 534, 535 *et seq.* Payments were to be made in money, wheat or flour.

[5] Stats. at Large, II, 396.

[6] Votes, II, 138. The question of compensation for the loss of servants who ran away to New Jersey and enlisted also came up at this time.

to the crown. The attacks made upon him by Randolph, Quary and others, the manifest purpose of the board of trade to overthrow all chartered colonies, the surrender of New Jersey, the fact that so much of his fortune had been spent in the experiment, all conspired to bring him to this resolution.[1] In June, 1703, he submitted a number of proposals on the subject, among which was the confirmation by the crown of the laws and constitutions of the province and the concession to Penn and his heirs of the privilege of nominating two or more persons for governor, one of whom must be appointed. The object of these conditions was the safeguarding of the interests of the Quakers. The land, of both the province and the lower counties, he desired to reserve, under conditions not unlike those which the Calverts enjoyed in Maryland. The offer was not acceptable to the crown and negotiations were suspended until 1705. Then, because of increased pressure by the Anglicans and of the extent to which he had become involved with the Fords, Penn submitted new proposals in which his demand to nominate the governors did not appear. These were rejected and to a query from Penn the board of trade replied that what it demanded was an unconditional surrender of powers of government, with the reservation to Penn and his heirs of rights to the soil and privileges incident thereto. In spite of this, however, Penn again asked that the laws which guarantied to the inhabitants a representative assembly elected annually, with power to make laws, levy taxes and sit on its own adjournments, and that the law granting liberty of conscience should never be abridged, nor the Quakers subjected to any fines or forfeitures by reason of their dress or carriage or be compelled to serve in the militia or contribute to warlike charges. He also asked that the soil of the province and territories be guarantied to him, that he and his family be exempt from provincial taxes and that the county of Bucks be erected into a palatinate. For various reasons, one of which was that the territories could not be considered in the negotiation as they formed no part of the province under the charter, these terms were also rejected. Logan was now advising Penn to make the sur-

[1] B. T. Properties, C. O. 5/1290, June, 1703; Root, Pennsylvania and the British Government, 354 *et seq.*

render, and he strongly urged the board to promote an agreement. But it was now hoped that the result would soon be reached by act of parliament and the negotiations with Penn were dropped.

Early in 1707, however, the board was induced to report to the secretary of state in favor of arranging for an unconditional surrender of the government of both the province and territories, but that a money compensation should be given to Penn. This was intended to be some return for the debt which the crown had originally owed his father and for the large unproductive outlay of the proprietor himself upon a province the trade of which was already large and a growing source of revenue. Inquiries were made as to the cost of administering the government and Penn proposed £20,000 as a satisfactory compensation, but again the matter was dropped. In 1708/9, after Penn had become bankrupt and mortgaged his province, the lower counties began to question his right of government, to complain that no provision was made for their defence and to threaten to appeal to the crown.[1] This feeling was further encouraged by the attitude of the Quakers toward the Canada expeditions and the descent of French privateers on the coast. Proposals of surrender were renewed in 1710, but again no progress was made beyond the point previously reached. Early in 1712 Penn's proposals were passed on by Attorney General Northey and a deed of surrender was drawn up, Penn having established his title to the Delaware region. It was agreed that he should receive £12,000, and £1,000 was actually paid on account before the deed was executed. Before the next step was taken Penn was incapacitated by two strokes of apoplexy, and though two years later the crown tried to perfect the deed by act of parliament, owing to differences between the mortgagees and the Penn heirs this too failed, and Pennsylvania continued a proprietary province. Mrs. Hannah Penn, in conjunction with the mortgagees, and with the advice of Logan, continued to attend, as she was able, to the affairs of the proprietor till

[1] Penn-Logan Corr., II, 303, 311, 324–326, 334, 337, 347. Logan wrote to Penn, Oct. 15, 1713, "I am told that at ye last elections in ye Lower Counties, ye generality of ye people combined not to choose one Quaker, that they might be the better able to inquire what right Penn has to call upon them for Quitrents." Logan Letter Bk. (Ms.) 1712–1715, fol. 155.

his death in 1718,[1] but all the time wishing that the connection of her family with Pennsylvania had been severed before her husband was incapacitated. To this level did the proprietary side of government in Pennsylvania sink during those years.

In the province itself the conduct of Gookin at this time was such as to reduce his influence for any good purposes to zero. In 1713, at a time when, owing to the illness of Penn, the future of the province was uncertain, the break between Gookin and both the council and assembly began. The communications addressed by Gookin to the assembly were always very brief and contained but little, except what he was ordered from England to submit. He apparently left the assembly largely to take its own course — at periods he was decidedly uncommunicative. The salary which was appropriated to him — about £300 a year[2] — was small and was not regularly paid.[3] The dispute which first arose was over the appointment, just before Penn's illness, of a register general and the transfer to the new incumbent of the records of the office.[4] In June, 1712, Peter Evans was appointed by the proprietor and about three weeks later Benjamin Mayne was appointed by the governor. Evans filed the proper bond for the office but Mayne did not, and the latter, having custody of the records, refused to deliver them, the governor stubbornly supporting him in this. The assembly finally took up the case and at last forced the surrender of the papers and the proper installation of Evans into office. Various complaints were also made from Philadelphia, and during this session the assembly was occupied for some time with grievances. At a later session of the same assembly the governor refused to recognize it because two-thirds of its members were not present on the opening day of the session.[5] The house admitted that an attendance of two-thirds was necessary

[1] Penn MSS. Three Lower Cos., 11 *et seq.*; Penn and Baltimore, 1653–1754.

[2] Logan L. B. 1712–1715, fol. 301 *et seq.* (Logan to Hannah Penn, Aug. 17, 1715); Col. Recs., II, 611, 612.

[3] Votes, II, 123, 130, 138.

[4] Votes, II, 140–142, 144–146, 147; L. L. B. (MS.) 1712–1715, fol. 118 *et seq.* Gookin may have been moved by some doubt as to the competency of Penn when he supposed Evan's appointment was made. See letter of Hannah Penn, Feb. 16, 1713–14; Penn MSS. P. F. to L., fol. 62.

[5] Votes, II, 148–149.

for legislation, but a less number could meet and adjourn, and this was all they attempted to do on the occasion referred to. But when a committee was sent to state this view to the governor, he refused to receive their message and bade them be gone about their business or he would order the sheriff and constables to send them going.

Gookin soon broke also with the council, and in October, 1714, Logan wrote, "we have also at present such a Governor and affairs are so oddly managed amongst us that ye like has seldom, I believe, been seen. Matters of ye highest importance are transacted without any advice of council; but all factions against ye proprietor being over, we are generally pretty easie."[1] Soon after, Gookin is said to have been acting as if he was absolute in the Lower Counties, appointing rangers without advice of council.[2] It was in counties that affairs came to the worst pass before his administration ended. As a result of a personal quarrel he turned all the magistrates of Newcastle county out of office and left the people for several weeks without a court of justice.[3] Because of the fact that the connection with the Lower Counties might be completely severed, such conduct as this was viewed with special alarm. The members of the council claimed that they had made all reasonable efforts to conciliate the governor but without success.

Finally Gookin broke completely with both the council and assembly over the question of the oath. Of the bearings of that question on relations with the British government and the repeal of the acts of 1700 and 1706 providing for the affirmation an account has already been given. In 1711 still another act providing for the affirmation without the use of the word God was passed in Pennsylvania and disallowed in England,[4] the impulse thereto being given by a petition from Rev. John Talbot and the leading members of his vestry and church wardens at Burlington, New Jersey. In 1714 an act of parliament[5] was passed making the act 7 and 8

[1] Logan to Mrs. Penn, L. L. B. 1712–15, fol. 184.

[2] *Ibid.*, 202. Corr. of James Logan, I, fol. 75; Wm. Penn, Jr. to Gookin, Sept. 17, 1714.

[3] Letter of Council to Penn, Aug, 11, 1715, in Pa. Reg. II, 69; P. F. to L. II, 83 *et seq.*; Council to Hannah Penn, Oct. 8, 1715.

[4] Pa. Stats. at Large, II, 355, 536 *et seq.*

[5] 1 Geo. I, C. 6.

William III relating to the affirmation by Quakers perpetual in the realm and extending it for five years in the plantations. As the affirmation provided for in the act of William contained the name of God and also provided that no Quaker should give evidence in criminal cases or serve on juries or hold any place of profit, Gookin began to claim that these conditions were now in force in the province and would invalidate the commissions and acts of all judges and other officers who could not administer or take an oath.[1] The issue was thus raised in October, 1716; while more than a year before that Gookin had assented to an act making substantially the same provision for the affirmation as had been included in the laws already disallowed.[2] This last act had not yet been repealed and it was held by the assembly to be the law of the province.[3] In this view the council concurred. The view of the governor was that it would be such, had it not been for the extension of the act of William to the plantations. The legality of the entire official system of Pennsylvania and of its administration of justice was thus challenged, and in the opinion of his opponents it was the desire of Gookin to get even with them that led him to take this course. To make the crisis more acute Gookin also charged Richard Hill and James Logan — the former being both speaker of the house and mayor of Philadelphia — with being Jacobites and disaffected toward the government of Great Britain.[4] This was a charge often brought against Quakers by those who wished maliciously to cause them trouble in England, because they refused the oath. When his reasons for this charge were demanded Gookin denied that he was obliged to give reasons to the house and said that he would state them to the board of trade at home. The assembly was deeply stirred by the charge, of the truth of which it declared that no evidence whatever could be found. Not content with this it appointed a committee, among whose members were Isaac Norris and David Lloyd, to prepare an elaborate representation to the governor on the state of affairs in the province and

[1] Votes II, 194 *et seq.*

[2] Stats. at Large, III, 59.

[3] It was not disallowed until 1719.

[4] Votes II, 196–200.

adjourned for several days until this was ready. Then it was fully discussed and approved.[1] In this they fell back upon the royal charter to Penn, contending that its plain intent was to make possible a Quaker colony, which of course implied that such practices as the affirmation should be provided for by its laws and recognized as valid. The prohibition based on repugnancy must be so interpreted as to permit this or the enterprise would have been made impossible from the first. Quoting Governor Hunter and Chief Justice Jameson, who were fighting the same battle for the Quakers in New Jersey,[2] they declared that the act of William did not bar any laws favorable to them which were made in the colonies, but rather, when extended thither, made such privileges as they enjoyed in England also the permanent possession of the colonists. In the light of the controlling facts of the situation, this interpretation favorable to freedom was the only possible one. To it Gookin, who a few months later was superseded, never made an answer. Finally, after the hopelessness of the situation had repeatedly been made clear to them, the members of the Penn family, amid their perplexities, and with the advice of the mortgagees and other friends, selected Sir Col. William Keith as Gookin's successor.[3]

[1] *Ibid.*, 200–207. Also printed in Proud, II, 74 *et seq.*

[2] Tanner, Province of New Jersey, 490 *et seq.* (C. U. Studies).

[3] For the correspondence leading to this, see Penn Family to J. Logan and Letter Book (MS.). Gookin repeated to Governor Keith his wild charge that Logan was disaffected toward the government, but when called before the council he abjectly failed to substantiate his statements. Col. Recs., III, 15 *et seq.*

PART TWO

THE COLONIES DURING THE INTERVAL OF PEACE BETWEEN THE SECOND AND THIRD INTERCOLONIAL WARS
1714–1740

CHAPTER I

THE ATTITUDE OF THE CABINET, PARLIAMENT AND THE BOARD OF TRADE TOWARD QUESTIONS OF COMMERCE AND COLONIZATION UNDER THE EARLY HANOVERIANS

In July, 1715, news reached England of the imminent peril which the inhabitants of South Carolina were facing in the war with the Yemassee Indians.[1] Governor Craven wrote directly to the secretary of state upon the subject and appealed for aid to preserve the valuable frontier province. Spotswood also wrote from Virginia on the same subject. The board of trade was at once ordered to inquire into the situation and report what should be done. The proprietors were summoned to attend, but even before that they had written the board offering to repay the government for the men, arms and ammunition which they could not provide but which they felt were necessary for the preservation of the province. Not long before this Abel Kettleby, of the Inner Temple and already a landgrave, had been designated by statute as agent of the province to look after its interests in the matter of the bounty on naval stores and other subjects. He now appeared at the board of trade along with Johnson and Shelton and an offer was made to mortgage their charter for military assistance. Several other meetings of the board were held to discuss this subject, at one of which both secretaries of state were present, and later the board was called before the cabinet. The result of this was that a series of questions was put to the proprietors, replies to which brought out their estimate of the help they needed in order to save the province.[2] The last query related to the surrender of the province, and to this the proprietors replied that they were willing to do

[1] B. T. Journal, July 8, 1715, and later entries; N. C. Col. Recs., II, 177, 187 *et seq.;* McCrady, South Carolina under Proprietary Govt., 537 *et seq.;* Kellogg, The Colonial Charter, 308.

[2] N. C. Recs., II, 193.

this only for an equitable consideration. Their ancestors had expended large sums in settling and improving the colony and the revenue from rice and skins made it valuable to the crown. In the past its defence had cost them much. The fact that several of the proprietors were minors and could not act prevented them from making surrender at that time.

The agents of the province had been instructed, in case the proprietors did not offer relief, to apply to king and parliament. The board of trade also suggested to the secretary of state that by legislative action the colony be taken directly under protection. The house of commons referred the subject to a committee, papers were sent for and on August 10 leave was given to introduce a bill for the better regulation of charter and proprietary governments.[1] Popple, the secretary of the board, was busy in presenting the bill and it was advanced as far as the second reading. Protests or appeals against it were presented on behalf of the various proprietors and the agents of Connecticut and Rhode Island also appeared. Lord Carteret, who was now palatine of Carolina and was rising to large influence as a statesman in England, exerted himself to such effect in support of himself and the other petitioners that the bill was smothered in committee.[2] With this came to a close efforts in parliament to recall the charters by legislative act.

But the board of trade continued its attacks upon them, as did royal officials in America, and anxiety on the part of some of the chartered colonies led them to continue precautions for defence of their rights through agents or in other ways.[3] One of the agents who had been concerned in the defence of this cause against the bill of 1715 was Jeremiah Dummer, who represented both Massachusetts and Connecticut in England. The success of the favorite policy of the

[1] C. O. 5/1265, B. T. Properties; J. of H. of Commons, XVIII, August 2, 1715, and succeeding entries, pp. 250, 262, 268, 270, 273, 274. The committee which had the bill in charge included Molesworth, Chetwynd and Docminique of the board of trade, Steele, Bladen, Pitt and all the merchants of the house.

[2] Dummer's statement was that the house thought fit, "upon hearing the Petitions presented to them on that Occasion to drop their Proceedings . . ." Dummer's "Defence of the Charters." This bill was presented to the house by John Chetwynd, a member of the board of trade.

[3] Kellogg, 311.

board of trade in South Carolina, followed in 1721 by a strong repetition of its views in its elaborate report to the crown, caused anxiety, and Massachusetts, through Dummer, presented an address to the king for the continuance of their chartered privileges. This was followed by the publication in England of Dummer's "Defence of the New England Charters," prefaced by a dedication to Lord Carteret.

In this able pamphlet we have a reply, as nearly conclusive as it was possible to make it, to the partisan attacks, in support of which many exaggerated and random statements had been made and repeated on every possible occasion, from the early days of Randolph through the period of Quary's activity to the time of its publication. New England was the classic land of the chartered colony. Dummer was a New England man and he knew its people, their spirit and history as neither Randolph nor any royal official imported from Great Britain could possibly know it. Among the earlier defenders of proprietary rights, since the fall of the first Massachusetts charter, William Penn had held the leading place. But he had passed away, and now a New England writer took up the theme again and so condensed the views both of the past and the present on this subject as to satisfy the feeling, at least of his section, and to furnish them with a justification upon which they could safely fall back in the future.

He voiced the conviction at the outset that, owing to blunders of the agents or in some other unexplained way, Massachusetts failed to secure the restoration of her liberties when her second charter was issued. He contended that by the reservations of that document the dependence of Massachusetts on the crown was effectually secured. As to the charters themselves, in contrast to those granted to corporations in England in return for past services, Dummer claimed that the colonial charters were given as premiums for services to be performed, "Grants upon a valuable Consideration," and therefore carried greater weight and stronger title. The old New England contention that they were of a higher nature than corporations in the realm he also reaffirmed. He then went on to enlarge upon the great cost in money, courage, endurance and suffering which had attended the founding of those colonies. To this he added an account of the profits and other advantages which came to Great Britain from the colonies — the large value of her products which they took and their exports which were sent to her. In that connection a specially strong point was made by Dummer when he showed that, were it not for the supplies of lumber, provisions and horses which were furnished by the northern colonies, the island colonies would not be able to carry on their production of sugar and other staples. The contribution which New England was making — and much more might have been done — to the growth of the British navy and mercantile marine also came in for due attention. To strip New England of its charters after such services had been rendered and while they were still being rendered in increasing measure seemed to Dummer to be "abhorrent from all Reason, Equity and Justice."

Dummer then passed to the reasons which were urged in support of the attacks upon the charters and to one of the palliations that was suggested as an excuse for it. The latter was to the effect that though the charters were taken away the crown would not take away the soil. In answer to this he declared, like Roger Williams, that the Indian title to the soil was the only fair and just one, and that the most which the crown could grant was the right of preemption, that is the right to occupy and to extinguish Indian titles as against the intrusion of other nations. And, he continued, the soil over which it gave this right at the beginning was worth nothing and was almost inaccessible and such value as it now possessed had been given it by the settlers. This, of course, was true and in the light of it the claims of royal officials in London and the colonies shrink to much smaller dimensions than they appeared to have when first uttered.

But the British, even if they acknowledged the justice of Dummer's argument thus far, would say that the colonies were defended by their fleet and if it was not for it they would be lost and with this all the advantages which the colonists had won would be sacrificed. This suggests the subject of defence and the complaints on that score which had occupied so prominent a place in the indictment of New England and of the chartered colonies generally. In answer to this

Dummer reviewed the record thus far of New England, and especially of Massachusetts, in wars with the Indians and the French, in aid to Jamaica in 1703 and Nevis in 1705 and in efforts to extend British territory on the northeast and to conquer Canada itself. In this argument, which was never forgotten, he met the complaint which in this connection was directed against New England as a whole and showed the contrast between its activity and the neutrality under which New York had existed so long.

In another section Dummer returned to the argument which Winthrop had used nearly eighty years before by explaining the system of elections, the jury system and other guaranties of civil rights which existed in New England, though like his predecessor he avoided reference to the position of those who dissented from the established religion in Massachusetts and Connecticut. This was the answer of both Winthrop and Dummer to the charge that the government of their colonies was arbitrary. Dummer could cite the Andros régime — which Winthrop could not — as an example of what a government was which was really autocratic in its relations to the entire people. In answering the charge respecting illegal trade, the author called attention to the magnitude of this evil in Great Britain itself and to the arbitrary conduct of customs officials, for example in Connecticut, which tended to provoke rather than to remedy such offences. He then went on to show how fully organized were the customs service and admiralty courts in New England at that time, supported by acts of parliament and manned by officials of royal appointment, and that this system had been established notwithstanding the charters and would scarcely be affected by their recall. The right, too, of the common law courts to issue writs of prohibition against the admiralty courts, of which so much complaint was heard, was not only necessary and a highly valued protection in England where the admiralty jurisdiction was much narrower than it was in the colonies, but provision for it in Massachusetts was made in laws confirmed by the crown and which the recall of the charter could not change. The question of repugnancy of colonial laws to those of England was discussed largely from the language used respecting it in the act of 7 and 8 William III, c. 22, and the conclusion was drawn that no laws to which that term could properly be applied existed in the colonies. In the writer's opinion not only did the system of English liberty exist in them, but they had improved on the liberty of the subject as it then was in the mother country.

As to prospects that the chartered colonies would grow powerful and throw off dependence on England, Dummer scouted the idea. On the other hand he called attention to the drawbacks which inhered in the temptation of royal governors and their appointees to oppression and corruption. How inconsistent, he exclaimed, was the nourishing of tendencies of this kind with that freedom which commerce demanded, that interest from which came the great advantage that England derived from her colonies. Finally, he protested against the method of recalling charters by act of parliament, without giving the accused a proper chance to be heard, as severe and oppressive beyond measure. And neither agents nor any other device in common use gave the colonists proper representation in or before parliament, while the board of trade was continually armed with complaints which it was ready to marshal against them. Under these circumstances the policy which it advocated could be executed only at the sacrifice of liberty.

Neither the board of trade nor any other organ or representative of the British government ever undertook to answer this argument of Dummer. His pamphlet closed a discussion which had been in active progress for more than a generation. It was not seriously reopened until after another forty years had passed. But during that interval and later his pamphlet remained a valued possession, especially of New Englanders, and in the future they could safely turn to it for a statement of their case which needed only slight expansion and readjustment to meet any exigency which might arise. With the exception of Benjamin Franklin, no colonial agent ever rendered a service to his constituents of a nature so valuable and dignified as this. It was, to be sure, the argument of an advocate and some important points were slurred over or omitted. It minimized some perils, as the future was conclusively to show. The only utterances on the other side with which it can properly be compared are the best among the representations of the board of trade relating to the chartered colonies. But the superiority in almost every respect of Dummer's pamphlet to any of these is evident. Their spirit was that of official routine and their substance consisted of facts and views which had been selected and formulated by officials. Of the earlier conditions under which the colonies had been founded they took no account. Of sympathy with the spirit and aspirations which might naturally have developed in these remote communities there is no indication. Everything was viewed from the standpoint of Great Britain and its interests. The same formulae, largely derived from Randolph and his like, were repeated with tiresome iteration. The difference between that and the spirit and point of view expressed by Dummer was as wide as the Atlantic and there was little prospect in sight of their being harmonized to the mutual satisfaction of the two parties. The course that was now chosen by the British government was to drop the discussion, and to confine action in reference to charters to individual colonies. Until after 1760 no new administrative measures of a general nature which were intended to promote the execution of the acts of trade were adopted. So far as weighty utterances upon the general subject went, the colonists so far had had the last word.

The colonists also, outside New England as well as within it, continued along their accustomed ways. This was evidenced at the very time of which we are speaking by conflicts over jurisdiction between the admiralty courts and common law courts, which arose in several of the colonies but were specially numerous and prolonged in New England. That such conflicts as these were sure to occur we have already seen reason to believe from the experiences of Randolph as collector of the customs in New England before 1689, from the circumstances under which admiralty courts were established in the colonies and their enlarged jurisdiction there and from events in Pennsylvania, Rhode Island and Connecticut a little later.[1] In order to resolve its doubts concerning this jurisdiction, the board of trade in 1702 secured an opinion from Northey, the attorney general, which may be considered as expressing the

[1] Osgood, Am. Colonies in 17th Century, III, 228 *et seq.*

law of the case.[1] His opinion was that under the original navigation and trade act of 1660 the admiralty courts had jurisdiction only when ships were taken at sea as violators of it; that under the acts of 1663 and 1673 they had no jurisdiction in the plantations, but that the provisions of the statute of 1696 were so sweeping that they gave to the admiralty courts "jurisdiction of all penalties and forfeitures for unlawful trading, either in defrauding the king of his customs, or importing into or exporting out of the plantations prohibited goods, and of all frauds in matters of trade and offences against the acts of trade committed in the plantations." The one exception, according to Northey, to this inclusive jurisdiction was that of trading in unqualified ships, — that is, the navigation law proper; offences against this, at the election of the informer, might be either in a common law or an admiralty court.

In the West Indies, from the beginning, the navy had been specially active in the seizure of illegal traders. When such captures were made at sea there was no question that the trials which resulted therefrom should be held in the admiralty courts. But when a capture was made within a port, it was a matter of doubt and controversy whether the case should be tried in an admiralty or a common law court.[2] A conflict of interests in connection with this question existed between officers of the navy and governors. When vessels were condemned in the admiralty courts the officers of the navy received one-half of the proceeds, while under common law procedure the informer or the party who made the seizure was entitled to only one-third. On the other hand, if the forfeiture was decreed by a common law court, the governor was entitled to a third, while he would receive nothing if the same result was reached by an admiralty court. This was the situation before the passage of the act of 1696 and the general establishment of admiralty courts in the continental colonies which soon followed. Though it was the intention of the originators of this policy that the admiralty courts should

[1] Chalmers, Opinions. Sir John Cooke, advocate general of the admiralty, rendered an opinion at the same time. As a student and practitioner of the civil law he went further in his claims for the admiralty than did Northey.

[2] Beer, Old Colonial System, I, 305.

have exclusive jurisdiction over cases involving illegal trade, and from the standpoint of the prosecuting officers the advantage of this course was great, a variety of powerful interests in the colonies were opposed to this and the policy met with bitter and prolonged opposition. So few and scattered were the vessels of the navy which were stationed along the American coast that seizures had chiefly to be made by customs officers, and were usually made within ports. From this fact arose almost the certainty that common law jurisdiction would be asserted and the cherished claim of trial by jury vindicated. In the chartered colonies, and wherever their tradition was strongly inherited, such a course was extremely probable and the private interests, even of royal governors, might incline them quietly to favor it.

During a decade and more following 1714 the chief collisions between the two jurisdictions occurred in Massachusetts and South Carolina.[1] Nathaniel Byfield, who was judge of admiralty in Dudley's administration, complained of the issue of a prohibition against his court in a case involving a dispute over the ownership of a drift whale, which was said to have been harpooned at sea and then floated to the beach. Sir Charles Hedges, judge of the High Court in England, advised that Byfield proceed no further in this case, as it lay properly within the common law jurisdiction. In defending his claim, Byfield tried to maintain that, as the original purpose of the writ of prohibition was to protect the rights of the crown, it should never be used to destroy those rights, as must necessarily be its purpose when used against the admiralty jurisdiction in the colonies.[2] He also complained of the sympathy with the superior court shown by Governor Dudley and his son Paul. The latter, he said, was a practitioner before both courts, giving his services where the fees were highest, and arguing before the common law judges against the claims of the admiralty.

John Menzies succeeded Byfield as judge in the New England district. James Smith and Robert Auchmuty were succes-

[1] See Admiralty In Letters, above referred to, and a letter from Dummer, the agent, to the board of trade, April 28, 1726. O. P. Mass. C. O. 5/869.

[2] In this letter Byfield cited Cowell's Interpreter and the argument as used under the early Stuarts, when writs of prohibition were used to protect the rights of the crown against the church.

sively advocates before his court. These officials, during a decade or more following 1715, complained often and loudly of encroachments of the common law courts on their jurisdiction. Much correspondence on the subject passed between them and solicitors of the admiralty in England, and on occasion the latter had to moderate or deny extreme claims made by the colonial judge. The admiralty officials thought that the general court had no right to fix the amount of their fees, but on this point, too, they had to yield. Shute, even, was accused of irregularities in his treatment of the admiralty court. Appeals to the High Court in England, or a representation to the secretary of state and the privy council, were urged as means of bringing about reform. Several cases were taken on appeal before the High Court from Menzies' decrees in Massachusetts; one of Oulton and Waldo vs. Savage, involving the question of a ship's registry, has a long history.[1] Cases involving the goods of pirates were also prominent, and in this connection doings of Rhode Island officials came up for criticism. In such cases Archibald Cumming, or whoever else might be agent for the rights of the admiralty in the colonies, was likely to be interested and active. The extension of the admiralty jurisdiction, by the act of 1722, over questions involved in the destruction of the forests was the cause of endless irritation in northern New England, and served further to prejudice those who knew about this against all admiralty officials.

In 1726 the controversy in Massachusetts culminated in the issue by the superior court of prohibitions against the proceedings of the admiralty court in the case of three vessels seized by the collector at Salem. The admiralty officials now joined in a memorial to the board of trade, which was supported by Shute and by a letter from Dummer, and the facts were also stated at length to the admiralty board. An authoritative opinion was urgently requested which should settle the points at issue. On the advice of the solicitor the cases were referred to Philip Yorke, the attorney general. In August, 1726,[2] he rendered an opinion in reference to two of the cases. In regard to the first, which concerned the

[1] See Admiralty Court Libels, vol. 132, 1720 *et seq.*

[2] Admiralty In Letters.

seizure of a vessel that had come from Portugal with goods on board without a cocket, Yorke held that the prohibition should not have been issued. The facts in the second case were not clearly stated; but his opinion in general was that over cases arising merely under 15 Chas. II, c. 7, and which did not fall within any provision of 7 & 8 Wm. III, c. 22, admiralty courts would have no jurisdiction. They also could have no jurisdiction on land or within a port,[1] unless given by act of parliament. The same was true of revenue cases. When his majesty's courts in the plantations were referred to in a statute, by construction they meant the common law courts. This appears to have quieted some of the extreme claims of admiralty officials in New England, and not so much is heard later about conflicts between the two jurisdictions.

In South Carolina, about 1723, the issue lay between Smith, the judge of admiralty, and Governor Nicholson and no special legal questions were involved. It was simply an instance of the abuse and finally the imprisonment of an official by a tyrannical governor, growing out of a personal and political quarrel. It was advised that the lords justices be petitioned to protect Smith.

Commercial treaties and the manipulation of tariffs played a prominent part in mercantilist policy and the trade rivalries of the time. The demand of the Whigs, from the beginning of the struggle with France and even much earlier, had been for as strict a prohibition of trade with that country as possible. The growing jealousy of French influence during the reign of Charles II led to the submission to parliament in 1675 of " A Scheme of the Trade, As it is at present Carried on between England and France," the object of which was to show that the balance was heavily adverse to England.[2] This contributed to the passage, three years later, of a law

[1] Related to this aspect of the subject was the opinion of Northey, in 1716, that the trial of cases under the woolens act belonged to the common law courts and that they were right in issuing prohibitions against the admiralty courts in such cases. His particular reason in this instance was, that the woolens act applied also to Ireland and trials under it there were held in the common law courts. O. P. Mass. C. O. 5/886.

[2] Ashley, Tory Origin of Free Trade Policy, in Quart. Jour. of Econ., II, 335, and references.

prohibiting the importation of French wine, brandy, silks, paper and other commodities, on the ground that the "Wealth and Treasure of the Nation had been much exhausted" by their introduction and consumption. The Tories, of course, were opposed to this policy and procured the repeal of the act in the reign of James II. But after the Revolution the prohibition was renewed and continued until the close of the first war. A slight relaxation followed, but the War of the Spanish Succession restored the prohibition.

Meantime, in 1703, the Methuen treaty with Portugal was concluded. This was a famous Whig measure prompted by political motives and intended to bring Portugal into the Grand Alliance and furnish an entry for British trade and arms into the Spanish peninsula. It provided that, in return for the removal by Portugal of its prohibition of the import of English woolens, Great Britain would admit Portuguese wines on the payment of two-thirds the duty imposed on French wines. As early as 1678 it had been suggested that the growing taste for French wines should be checked and that for port substituted, because the former had to be paid for in money while the latter could be purchased with British manufactures.[1] The Methuen treaty stands as a fitting preliminary to the occupation of Gibraltar a few years later, the two appearing together as the great initial steps in the process, then beginning, of establishing British control over the Mediterranean.

In the opinion of Whig mercantilists of this period trade with France was wholly bad.[2] Not only was it trade with the arch-enemy, but it resulted in the introduction of harmful luxuries — especially brandy — and was carried on under conditions which made a heavy adverse balance permanent. The high rates of duty which had been imposed by Colbert, though later reduced, were not soon forgotten. The fact that

[1] Hewins, English Trade and Finance, 132.

[2] John Cary wrote: "The French trade is certainly our loss, France being like a Tavern with whom we spend what we get by other Nations." "The Ballance of That and the East India Trade is always against us, from whom we have in Goods more than we ship them, and therefore must lessen our Bullion. The Ballance of Spain and Portugal is always in our Favour, . . . As for the Dutch, Germany and Hamburgh, their Ballances are not yet agreed on." "Those who cope with us in our Manufactures are chiefly French." Cary, Essay Towards Regulating the Trade, *etc.*

under the Methuen treaty Portugal suffered from the unfavorable balance and had to discharge its payments in the precious metals, effectually proved the wisdom of that measure in the opinion of British merchants. And yet Englishmen would drink French wines and use goods of their manufacture and the smugglers saw that they got them in sufficient abundance. As the wars progressed the volume of writing from Tory sources against the extreme hostility to the French trade increased. With this appeared also in the writings of such Tories as Dudley North, Child and Davenant suggestions of more liberal views concerning trade in general, though their theory was still fundamentally mercantilist.

When the political reaction came in 1709 against Whig domination and the war, and the Tory government of the last four years of Anne was brought into power, opinions less hostile to France came to the front, and under the lead of Bolingbroke became the basis of the commercial treaty which in 1713 was negotiated with that country. As was the case in 1675, when the policy of commercial war with France was initiated, the commissioners of trade were now called upon to draft such provisions as it was desired to incorporate in law. In 1713 Arthur Moore was probably the leading spirit in this work. The result of the negotiation was agreement upon a treaty, to accompany the treaty of Utrecht, the purpose of which was greatly to promote freedom of trade and thus to encourage good feeling between the nations which had so long been hostile. Its two most important articles were those which guarantied to both parties the advantages of the most favored nation, and provided that the duties imposed by Great Britain on French goods should not be higher than its duties on the goods of any other country. All prohibitive laws passed since 1664 should be repealed and by France British goods should be rated according to the moderate tariff of 1664.[1]

As soon as the terms of the projected treaty were known, a storm of protest was raised by the protected interests which for a quarter of a century had received additional nourishment from the war spirit. The merchants and manufacturers who dealt in silk, woolen and linen joined with the sugar-bakers

[1] The high tariff of Colbert was imposed in 1667.

and distillers and all who were interested in the trade with Portugal in a chorus of denunciation.[1] The struggle was carried into the house of commons, and the press was called actively into requisition on both sides. Under the patronage of Bolingbroke and Oxford the "Mercator" was started and ran as a periodical until near the close of July, 1714. Daniel Defoe was its editor and largely its author, and his abilities were conspicuously shown in defence of the treaty. On the other side, under the patronage of the earl of Halifax, the "British Merchant" supported the Whig cause and the Methuen treaty and denounced all free and liberal dealings with France, the traditional enemy. Henry Martin, Charles King and Joshua Gee were its chief literary sponsors.[2] When, some years later, after the Whigs were firmly established in power, it was reedited for publication in a three-volume edition, in the list of its subscribers appeared the names of the leading Whigs, nobility, gentry and merchants, of the early Walpole era. In the list one reads the names of John Chetwynd,[3] Martin Bladen and the other leading members of the reorganized board of trade, and last but not least the name of Colonel Francis Nicholson.

On reading "Mercator" and the other commercial writings of Defoe, one finds that he was a mercantilist, but that he appropriated and was utilizing the more liberal articles of that creed as they had been expounded by the Tory writers to whom reference has just been made.[4] Like them he argued that trade should be divorced from politics and that national prejudice should not be allowed to control it. The French needed and must take large quantities of British manufactures

[1] Hewins, 139.

[2] The leading maxims of the "British Merchant" concerning trade were copied and published also in the "Guardian," no. 170.

[3] It incidentally appears that there were two other Chetwynds, all in office.

[4] See especially his "Plan of the English Commerce," which was published in 1728. In this the confidence which he expressed in the superiority of England in the race for commercial and industrial supremacy was so great that it swept away all tendencies toward a policy of timidity or suspicion. To him merchants and tradesmen were the saviors if not already the rulers of England. France does not come in for exceptional or hostile treatment, and the distinction between the island and northern colonies, of which many tried to make so much, was lost in Defoe's enthusiastic appreciation of them all according to their respective capacities. It is breezy, non-technical, and shows that Defoe might easily have become hospitable to the ideas of Adam Smith.

and it was the undoubted interest of Great Britain to trade largely with them in spite of the national struggle which was going on. On all hands it was accepted as a fundamental principle, that trading nations should never prohibit the export of their own manufactures. Letters from Scotland were printed to show that there was a marked difference between her relation to French trade and that of England. French wines and brandies the Scotch would have and salt they must have for their fishery. At the time of the Union the advantages of French trade to Scotland had been insisted upon as something which the northern kingdom was surrendering in order to throw in its cause with England. As to the Methuen treaty or commercial relations with any of the other minor powers, Great Britain need not fear that, because of the agreements she was trying to reach with France, they would cut off her imports. They could not do without British manufactures, while Great Britain could sell its products even though Portugal, for example, did not exist. This, in fact, was the upshot of his argument — the invincible superiority of British manufactures, especially of wool, over those of other countries. Great Britain, therefore, was already so far in the lead that it was for her interest to be liberal. Let her people trade largely with the French, as they necessarily would do, treaty or no treaty. British manufactures in several lines were already superior to those of France. The progress which she had made had been facilitated by the prohibition of British exports for so long a time. Keep back English raw wool and send over freely the manufactured product, and the inferiority of French wool would insure the speedy triumph of England in the competitive struggle.

This robust type of nationalism the Whigs and their writers in the "British Merchant" did not exhibit, and more than a century was to pass before industrial progress and changes in economic thought made an attitude something like this seem natural. The defeat, by a small majority in the commons, of the proposed treaty of 1713, and the wreck of the Tory party which followed the death of Anne, sealed the fate of such proposals as Defoe was advocating. Though, owing largely to the exhaustion of France, a long period of comparative peace was beginning, Great Britain was now committed to Whig guidance. From the first it had been the war party. Its ideas concerning trade were strictly, dogmatically of the politico-economic type. They had been formulated — to speak of no earlier time — during the period of commercial rivalry with the Dutch and had served well their purpose in that connection. George Downing had been one of their formulators, and their most authoritative expression was in the acts of trade, in the increasingly complicated tariff adjustments, in the multitudinous acts and orders which were intended to secure such a distribution of employments within the empire and such relations with all peoples outside as would best conform to the accepted principles of national growth and strength. The continuous increase of the navy and extension of the sweep of its influence were among the prime objects of this policy. War, especially with any dangerous rival, though not always upon issues which were expressly or mainly commercial, was always regarded as one of the most effective means of enabling the empire to surmount crises and reach its destiny. Chiefly for dynastic reasons, war was now to be suspended for a generation, but the politico-economic theory which had guided and profited Great Britain in the past was not abandoned or in any way changed.

The exposition of this theory, which during the period of Whig ascendency was accepted as authoritative, was contained in the "British Merchant." Following the view which Samuel Fortrey had advanced in 1663 and which had been increasingly accepted as orthodox ever since, they condemned trade with France as freighted with an "overbalance" against England and sure to bring heavy loss without countervailing gain. Standards of wages and living in England were imperilled by the prevailing cheapness in France and by the low standard of living among the masses of its people — the pauper labor argument. During the wars also the necessity of sending large amounts of bullion abroad to pay the expenses of the armies on the continent affected the British balance adversely.[1] Trade with nearly all other countries

[1] Gee, Trade and Navigation of Great Britain Considered, Ed. of 1738, p. 194. After the Bourbons had been seated on the throne of Spain, and events

and quarters of the globe brought in valuable commodities which could not be procured in Great Britain, or yielded a favorable balance in the precious metals either directly or indirectly through roundabout exchanges of commodities. The staple products of France, however, were harmful luxuries or commodities which could better be raised or manufactured at home; if not so, they could be more safely procured elsewhere. Freights also, as between England and France, were sure to be favorable to the latter. The analogy between the attitude of the writers toward France and that of the same body of mercantilists toward the northern colonies on the American continent is striking. The real source of trouble seems to have been that both France and the northern colonies were situated on about the same isothermal lines as Great Britain and therefore they all produced from their extractive industries the same general class of commodities. In the case of France the competition which thus resulted was now intensified by political rivalry and war. The result was a theory of trade which, so far as France was concerned, was so labored and artificial as to be fantastic.

After developing their argument through two volumes, the authors of the "British Merchants" concluded as follows: "I hope by this time my Readers are thoroughly convinced of the destructive Consequences of opening the Trade to

were leading toward the Family Compact, trade with that country in the eyes of Englishmen fell to an extent into the same category. Owing to political considerations trade with Portugal was good and orthodox while the trade of the rest of the Peninsula was falling into the hands of the enemy. At Paris, of course the opposite view prevailed. The lack of a judge conservator to give a certain protection to British merchants in Spain was much dwelt on. Evidences of the growing hostility of the Spanish to English merchants in Spain were abundant and one can see the relations in their early stages which were leading to the outrages by sea and land of a few years later. It was believed that the French were winning away from the English their chief advantages in trade with Spain. "The Complaints of every one are," said the "British Merchant," that we are not so much favoured in Duties as the French; that we are in a worse condition than we were in the reign of Charles II; that more excessive customs are exacted now than when we were in actual war with the Spanish Nation; that none of our Goods are despatched and that all our trade is stopped; that the French in the meantime have a full Trade, by the connivance of the King of Spain, to the West Indies; and that whole Ships are entirely laden with French Effects for those Countries, besides money which the French themselves send directly for the South Seas." On this view both the Asiento and the establishment of the South Sea Company came in for condemnation.

France, upon the Terms of the Treaty, or indeed upon any Terms whatsoever; that none of our Manufactures, Home or Foreign, can ever be sold in France; and that it is better for us never to have any open Trade with them, but to lay a general Prohibition on all Commodities imported from thence, for they have none that we want or what is not our Interest to be without; on the contrary we have several Commodities which they cannot be without, but must have, and will have, either directly or at second hand; and whatever they amount to is so much clear Gain to the Nation. This, in my Opinion, is the best and most advantageous Foot we can fix our Trade to France upon." It would be difficult to excel this as an effort to combine "war after the war" with that other principle, of "business as usual."[1] The writer, moreover, did not appear to see that by his admission concerning the character of the French demand for British goods he was giving away most of his case. Though the members of the board of trade under the early Hanoverians, so far as they attended to their duties, were administrators and therefore were sure to have their theories modified by contact with actual conditions, they cherished the views just set forth and the general trend of their policy was bound to be in harmony with them. Their views, so far as individual members expressed them, confirm this statement. The reports, representations, instructions, letters of the board are all attuned to this key, though they do not reflect all the extreme notions which appear in the controversial writings of individuals. The same is doubtless true of officials throughout the departments and of Whigs generally, in parliament and out. But the board of trade heard these ideas expressed most continuously and to it the inquirer naturally looks as the chief official exponent of the Whig theory and policy.

Concerning the personnel of the board of trade between 1714 and 1748 little need be said. With the accession of the

[1] A glimpse may be obtained of the discriminations from which British merchants had later to suffer in France as a result of this policy, from a letter of Pultney to the board of trade, dated Feb. 20, 1719/20. Pultney was then serving as commissioner for the adjustment of boundaries with France. B. T. Journal, Minutes and Letter Book, 1719. Commercial reprisals, which were essentially a continuation of the war, now began with Spain and continued with increasing ferocity until they produced the next general struggle.

Whigs to power its membership was entirely changed. Thenceforward, until after the fall of Sir Robert Walpole, its members were chiefly noblemen of no particular significance, placemen and, in two or three instances, officials and members of parliament who were recognized as men of ability and usefulness. At the head of these last stood Martin Bladen. He was a member during almost the entire period — from 1717 to 1746. During most of that time he was also a member of parliament at Westminister and sat for several years as a member of the Irish parliament. He also held minor diplomatic positions,[1] and wherever he was the evidence is clear that he was an active and useful official. Large credit may be given to him for whatever the board of trade did or advocated throughout the period we are now considering. In addition to Bladen, Paul Docminique and Daniel Pultney are specially worthy of mention, though the latter served for only four years — from 1717 to 1721. Docminique, however, was a member from 1714 to 1735 and the evidence goes to show that he was more intimately connected with the work of the board than any one except Bladen. As a member of the West Jersey Society, Docminique may have been brought into closer connection with the affairs of certain of the colonies than was common with British officials.

At the beginning of 1715, and therefore early in the history of the reorganized board of trade, Stanhope, as secretary of state for the southern department, sent to it a "Scheme" relating to the plantations in America.[2] The opinion of the board concerning it was requested. Though no record of such opinion appears, the document is interesting as a statement of the views of one who may have been a West India merchant concerning the colonies and certain defects in their government which should be remedied. Basing his opinion on the imports from the individual colonies, the writer declared his agreement with the generally accepted view that the tobacco and sugar colonies were the most valuable. He looked askance on the fact that the northern colonies sup-

[1] In 1719 he was sent with Pultney to France as a commissioner to adjust the boundaries between the possessions of the two crowns in America; but no agreement was reached. B. T. Plants. Gen., Ent. Book. B. T. Journal, vol. 29.

[2] N. C. Col. Recs., II, 154–166.

plied the islands with provisions and some manufactures, receiving their products in return, thus depriving Great Britain of a certain amount of trade which she might utilize to advantage in adjusting her foreign balance. The courts in the plantations came in for extended criticism, as did the conduct of governors on occasion and the liability of the people to suffer from their oppression and the difficulty of securing redress. The cost and delays incident to appeals to Great Britain for redress in such cases, with the frequent references back to the colony for additional evidence and the failure of the board of trade to use the privilege given in its commission to examine witnesses under oath, were well described. The paper closed with certain sweeping criticisms of the board, as it had been, on the ground that none had been appointed to its membership who had perfect and personal knowledge of the plantations, their people and laws. The plantation merchants and those who had served as governors or in other high office in the colonies, in the opinion of the writer, should be represented on the board.

This, it is needless to say, was not followed. Instead of the board becoming more expert in these respects and more hospitable to new ideas it became less so as the years passed. During the years immediately following 1715, in addition to the ordinary routine of business with the colonies separately which was connected with appointments, the drafting of commissions and instructions for governors, and with subjects of every variety which were brought in by letters from the governors, petitions and appeals submitted through agents or in other ways, the board was much occupied with the subject of naval stores. Joshua Gee who, it will be recalled, was a collaborator in the publication of the "British Merchant," after referring to the commercial embarrassments occasioned by the two wars with France, and to measures originating in Russia and Sweden subsequent to the treaty of Utrecht which were intended to prevent Great Britain from being supplied with naval stores from those countries except "at their own Prices and in their own Shipping," states that further consultations were held and the lords of trade were put upon inquiry whether those supplies could not be obtained from the colonies in America. "And accordingly in the Year 1716 they sent for sundry Persons to consult what Methods might be taken to raise and produce them there." [1] The evidence, therefore is clear that the struggle with France determined the direction which for several years the most important activities of the board of trade and other bodies concerned were to take and that the Whig merchants and Whig government were closely cooperating to secure for Great Britain the greatest practicable independence of foreign states in the production of naval stores. The strengthening of the navy to meet future contingencies, and the organization of trade and industry in such a way as to support the navy with effective national strength, were the policies of these militant Whigs. As we know, the consideration of naval stores always suggested that of manufactures in the colonies, the latter to be checked and discouraged in all available ways in the interest of the former, and also, to a very much larger degree, in order to prevent any competition which might be troublesome to British manufacturers. The subject of the navy and naval stores furnished the appeal to patriotism which powerfully aided the cause of the merchants and manufacturers. The account which follows indicates the course of action which was taken by the board of trade and the circle of ideas within which it moved.

At hearings, continued at intervals during several years, Gee presented much evidence and submitted several memorials on the subject of naval stores and British trade in general. In a memorial presented in 1718 he dwelt on the extent to which the importation of tar from the plantations had reduced its price and affected the balance of trade with Sweden and other Baltic countries, and advocated the application of a similar policy in the case of iron and timber in order to affect similarly the eastland countries in reference to these products and also economize the supply of wood in England. In a longer memorial, presented in 1721, Gee enlarged upon the triumph which the British had won over the Dutch by supplanting them in the carrying trade of western Europe. This achievement he used as a preliminary to an exhortation to the British to continue in the same line of policy as

[1] Gee, *op. cit.* 196. For an account of the hearings before the board of trade on this subject and the action which was taken, see the chapter on the production of naval stores.

affecting the world at large, and to this end fully to utilize the vast resources of the American colonies in timber and in the capacity for the production of hemp, flax and tar. His demand was that they should be encouraged by bounties and that restraints on the exportation of the more bulky commodities directly from the colonies to the continent of Europe should be taken off. These arguments he elaborated with abundant detail in his "Trade and Navigation of Great Britain Considered," which was published in 1729 and re-issued in several later editions. In this pamphlet even the plan and arrangement of material of the "British Merchant" was followed, though with a much briefer treatment of the foreign trades and a correspondingly greater emphasis on the plantations and the American aspects of the problem. Because of these features, the work of Gee is to be considered as, after the "British Merchant," the next important exposition of the spirit and policy of the militant Whigs.

Gee did not specially cherish the prejudices of the West Indian. He recognized as well the advantages which came from the continental colonies and strongly favored the increase of facilities for their trade with the south of Europe, as a means of extending further the triumph of the British over the Dutch in the carrying trade of that region. The large attention which he devoted to naval stores and ship building had to do exclusively with the northern colonies, and he clearly saw that, in both war and peace, the island colonies depended for their very existence on the supplies which were brought to them from the continent. But, like all the rest, Gee would check all important developments toward manufacturing in the north, though he did advocate the making there of the cruder products of iron. Another new demand which he voiced was that for the encouragement of the production of raw silk in the colonies south of the Delaware river, a policy which proved futile in the end, but one which was further emphasized in the founding of Georgia.

No one surpassed Gee, if any equaled him, in the thoroughgoing expression which he gave to the degree of industrial and social dependence in which the colonies were kept or wherein it was desirable to keep them.[1] Speaking of the plantation

[1] See his pamphlet, ed. of 1738, p. 149 *et seq.*

provinces, all but one-fourth of their total product, he said, was sent to Great Britain and what they carried back was wholly of its manufacture. Their savings were deposited in England and thither they sent their children to be educated. When planters had accumulated a sufficiency, they came to England to live and only an overseer was left on the plantation, the whole produce then being remitted home. In addition, plantations were often mortgaged to British investors and the high rates of interest were added to the profits of the trading class. In these few statements were sketched the chief characteristics of absenteeism in the West Indies. As to the northern colonies, they were under greater difficulties in making returns to England, and therefore clothing and other goods of "ordinary Sort sells with them, and when they are grown out of Fashion with us, they are new fashioned enough there." Young merchants also went thither as factors and, when they had got a start, returned home and others took their places, a constant interchange, like that of bees in a hive, being kept up. The immense gains which came from the increase of shipping and seamen in the plantation trade were also emphasized, and it was stated that though, in the recent French wars, the capture or destruction of British ships by the enemy had been very great, shipbuilding had kept pace with the losses. But "our own Interest is not [to be] mistaken for that of the Planters; for every Restraint and Difficulty put upon our Trade with them makes them have Recourse to their own Products which they manufacture, a thing of great Consequence to us and ought to be guarded against. For if they are supplied with their own Manufactures, one great Part of the Advantage we should otherwise receive is cut off; and therefore, . . . if Care is taken to find them Employment and turn their Industry another Way, now in their Infancy, it may be done with very little Trouble; and it is hoped the Regulations proposed in this Discourse would entirely effect it."

In order to complete our view of this system of benevolent despotism, the commercial and industrial aspects of which were so aptly described by Gee, we have only to refer to his statement of the policy which he would follow in reference to colonial legislation.[1] He was well aware that by means of pressure on governors, by the passage of temporary laws, and in other analogous ways, all made possible by delays and other failures in the process of disallowance, many advantages were lost by Great Britain. Owing to this and other causes, it had been impossible — and fortunately was ever to remain so — to attain the ideal of mercantilism and put this cut-and-dried scheme into full operation. But Gee was ready to take the decisive step toward this result by applying to the colonies the system of the Poynings act in Ireland, and, except in cases of emergency legislation for defence, to require that no law should be passed there until a copy of the same had been examined and approved by the king in council. The results of this policy in Ireland were well known and Gee, like all mercantilists, was well aware of the likeness between the position of Ireland and the colonies in the British commercial system, and the effect of the measures which he advocated would have been to make their positions virtually identical. To this as an ideal militant Whiggism was committed. The board of trade furnished a sort of clearing house for the expression of ideas and proposing of plans largely in harmony with it. There was much in the relations between Great Britain and the northern colonies which made a more stringent policy seem desirable. Faults, as they existed, seemed most serious to those who were most fully aware of them, whether as merchants or as administrators. Among these were members of the board and Gee, a merchant-theorist, was one of its most trusted advisers in the line of his specialty for a decade after the accession of the Hanoverians. The trend of his thought we have seen.

At about the time when Gee was active, a very comprehensive treatise, entitled "A Survey of Trade," was published.[2] Its authorship has been attributed to the ironmaster, William Wood, the protégé of the government in the contract for coining Irish halfpence and farthings and made famous by Swift in the Drapier Letters. In this book, which was intended to be a standard Whig treatise on British trade in all its aspects, heavy drafts were made on Davenant's writ-

[1] *Ibid*, 157–159.
[2] The date of its publication was 1718.

ings, but the whole was cast in a narrower mould, with a spirit of stolid antagonism toward France and a reassertion of mercantilist orthodoxy in reference to all subjects affecting trade and the colonies in their commercial relations.

The discussion of naval stores, which had proceeded so vigorously, led in 1719 to the introduction of a bill into parliament for their further encouragement.[1] But the British ironmasters procured the insertion of clauses, one in the commons and the other in the lords, which provided that there should be no manufacture in the colonies of iron ware, of any kind, out of pigs or bars, and that no forge for the making or bars or rods should be built in the colonies. So disappointed were the colonial supporters of the bill by the introduction of these provisions, that they were glad to see it dropped altogether. The agitation of the subject, however, was continued, as involving one of the most important issues of the time, and in 1722 the act, referred to elsewhere, was passed which insured the continuance of existing favors to the industry for sixteen years longer.[2]

In 1721 the board of trade, at the command of the king, submitted one of its elaborate reports[3] on the condition of the continental colonies, a document to which reference under the subject of naval stores has already been made. This was signed by Chetwynd, Bladen, Docminique and Ashe. In it were doubtless summed up the chief results, general and specific, of the inquiries and deliberations of the board in reference to this group of colonies since its reorganization in 1714. Every colony, from Nova Scotia to South Carolina, was considered separately, Rhode Island and Connecticut, owing to lack of information, receiving very brief mention. The existing condition of the respective colonies and their characteristics both as to trade and government were sketched. Taking the American colonies as a whole, the board, using the unreliable custom-house returns of the time, estimated that their trade, including their products which were

[1] Macpherson, Annals of Commerce, III, 72.

[2] An interesting pamphlet on this subject appeared in 1720 under the title of "A Letter to a Member of Parliament concerning the Naval Stores Bill of 1719." This was an argument against the policy just mentioned and in favor of the value to England of the crude manufacture of iron in the plantations.

[3] N. Y. Col. Docs., V, 591–630.

reexported, furnished employment to one-third of the shipping which annually cleared from the United Kingdom. Exports to the continental colonies exceeded imports thence by about £200,000 per annum. This debt fell upon the provinces north of Maryland and they were enabled to discharge it by their trade with the island colonies and to Europe in commodities which were not enumerated. This was a good showing, but the board was persuaded that the balance in England's favor might be greatly improved if the production of naval stores of all kinds was sufficiently encouraged and also the production of commodities which Great Britain needed but which she could procure only at a disadvantage in foreign countries. If this course were pursued, the trade of the empire might become still more concentrated by the northern colonies becoming able to pay their balance to England without carrying on a trade with foreign countries which in some respects was detrimental to the mother kingdom. On the minor issue of rice in Carolina, the board was in favor of permitting its export direct to southern Europe.

Turning to questions of territory and government, the board dwelt at length on the dangerous extension of French settlement and claims in the Mississippi Valley and deplored the neglect which had allowed this to go so far.[1] The board now considered it imperatively necessary to meet this by building forts along the frontier and by specially strengthening the colonies on the north and south. The board was fully aware of the weakness of Nova Scotia and urged that steps be taken to settle it and that four regiments of foot be stationed there. The same number of troops should also be stationed in South Carolina, and forts should be built on its principal rivers. Spotswood's suggestion that a fort should be built on Lake Erie was approved, as also the plan which Burnet was forming for occupying Niagara. The board was also in favor of extending settlements beyond the mountains. The strengthening in every way of friendly relations with the Indians — especially the Iroquois — was strongly urged,

[1] They acknowledged special indebtendess to a report by William Keith on this subject. It had also been discussed in a memorial by a Mr. Harris, whom the board had consulted. The negotiations of Bladen and Pultney in France had touched upon the same subject. O. P. Plants. Gen., 1719.

by presents, by missions, even by intermarriages, but above all by trade. As a means of securing all these objects the board again recorded its conviction that, in the interest of trade and political control, all the charters should be recalled. It had fault to find with the laws and administration in all the colonies relating to trade, quit rents, the taking up of land, the preservation of the forests, the discharge of official duties by deputy. To remedy these and other abuses, to strengthen defence and promote efficiency the board urged the appointment of a captain general over colonies, to reside possibly in New York and to be constantly attended by two or more councillors, deputed presumably by the governor and council of each colony. With the help of these, quotas of men or money, it was thought, might be raised. In this purely executive or autocratic form appeared the favorite plan of the British government for securing colonial union, the first which had been put forward since the issue of the commission to Lord Bellomont. Chalmers is authority for the statement that the earl of Stair was requested to accept the office of captain general but declined, and then the plan was laid on the shelf.[1] The final recommendation of the board was that its president should have, under the king, the full charge of plantation business, as was the case with the departments of the treasury and admiralty. In this way the confusion occasioned by the distribution of colonial business between the offices of the secretary of state, the privy council and the board of trade would be avoided.

Though the board in the prosecution of its imperial policy had not committed itself to colonial taxation, its members were familiar with the idea. If they needed further reminders on this subject, Archibald Cummings furnished them by submitting a "Scheme" in 1723 in which he proposed to tax about everything possible.[2] His purpose was to secure means for the support of some six thousand troops on the American continent, and he was moved to make the proposal at this time by Râle's war in northern New England. His "Scheme" provided that the drawbacks on all foreign linens, canvas,

[1] Introd. to the Revolt of Am. Colonies, II, 43; Dickerson, *op. cit.*, 215.

[2] B. T. Journal, Nov. 26, 1723; O. P. Plants. Gen. Recd., Dec., 1722, read Nov., 1723.

calicoes, muslins, tea, coffee, pepper, paper and fruits exported to the plantations be taken off and that the amount thus saved to British revenue — estimated at £40,000 per annum — be used for the purpose indicated. About £30,000 proclamation money Cummings proposed to raise by a stamp duty in America. He was the first to propose import duties on a large scale on the trade between the foreign West India islands and the northern colonies — on rum, molasses, cotton, cocoa, indigo; also on wines from the Canaries, Madeira and the continent of Europe. A tax of 6d. per acre should be collected annually on all unimproved land which had been granted in the colonies, and forty acres from the ungranted land there should be bestowed as a bounty on every soldier who should be brought into service under this plan. Considering the date when this plan was formulated, it shows that the minds of certain officials and merchants at least, with the help, when needed, of precedents drawn from their enemy, the French, could speedily reach very sweeping conclusions when once they were set going along the lines of parliamentary autocracy. Viewed from the practical standpoint, however, Cummings' "Scheme" at the time was simply a curiosity. It was filed away, whether or not for future reference would depend on conditions and the degree of interest on the part of later official minds concerning such matters.

The Whig mercantilists, in their efforts to create a closed and self-sufficient empire, and especially to exclude the traditional enemy, found two special points of leakage, Newfoundland and the West Indies, the two extremes of the colonial area. Owing to the lack of established government in Newfoundland and the presence of so many nationalities among the fishermen who visited those seas, all sorts of European goods were said to be carried thence to the other colonies. In March, 1716, the board of trade prepared a representation on the abuses of this kind which were connected with the fisheries in those seas. This was not the first or the last that was heard of complaints of this nature. Under the circumstances it was also inevitable that the trade which was growing up between the northern colonies, or even the British islands, and the foreign West Indies should be viewed with suspicion in England. Some correspondence about illegal trade at Martinique, and possibly elsewhere, led to the issue of a circular letter to the governors, in August, 1714, requiring them to see that no such trade was carried on.[1] Early in 1717 a letter was received from the governor of Barbadoes mentioning the trade between the English colonies and the French and requesting directions concerning it. The board of trade found that the fifth and sixth articles of the treaty of neutrality of 1686 between England and France prohibited this, and a letter was sent to Secretary Methuen asking whether that treaty was still in force.[2] Again, in 1724, Cummings brought this subject up and some correspondence followed. At the close of 1730[3] it came up once more in decisive form, not only in connection with its illegal aspects but with its economic significance in certain broad relations, and this time it was not permitted to rest until a serious effort at readjustment had been made.

The development of manufacturing in the colonies also continued, as ever, to be a subject of continuous solicitude on the part of the mercantilists in and about the board of trade. In the deliberations of that body and in the correspondence of governors, as has been indicated, it occupied a place nearly as prominent as that of naval stores. As we have repeatedly seen, these two, like the woolen and linen industries in Ireland, were always considered together as mutually conditioning one another. The policy of encouraging the production of naval stores was always urged, not only in the interest of the navy and the mercantile marine, but as a means of diverting the people of the northern colonies from manufacturing. Like sugar, tobacco and rice, naval stores were treated as the products of staple extractive industries, to the pursuit of which it was the desire of the imperialistic mercantilists to limit the economic activities of the colonists. They were to be kept as exclusively as possible an agricultural people, and Great Britain was to do their manufacturing for them, using their products so far as was necessary, as well as her own, in the process. In the transportation of these products, as

[1] See B. T. Journal; Acts P. C. Col., 1680–1720, p. 559.

[2] These provided that English vessels caught trading or fishing in French possessions — stress of weather excepted — should be confiscated, and the same restriction was imposed on the French in their relations with the English.

[3] B. T. Journal.

well as her own, across sea the colonists, according to their ability, were to share. Foreign shipping was not to visit the colonies, but colonial shipping when laden with non-enumerated commodities, or commodities in which trade south of Cape Finisterre was permitted, might visit alien countries. Therefore, so long as all American products were not enumerated, the colonies were not excluded from the opportunity to trade legally with foreign peoples. Illegal trade, whether extensive or not, also contributed to the same end, and therefore the dependencies of the empire were not commercially shut within a closed circle. Until near the close of the colonial period, they both legally and actually enjoyed much freedom.

Analogous conditions existed in the case of American manufactures.[1] Since, irrespective of the navigation act, shipping of a minor and subsidiary sort was absolutely necessary for local and intercolonial traffic, so without manufacturing in some form the colonists who settled along the Atlantic seaboard could not have existed. The preparation of their food, the clothing of their families, the clearing of the forests, the building of their houses and churches, the construction of roads, the building of boats, ships and vehicles, every process of individual, family or community activity demanded tools, machines or even mills for their prosecution. The limited supplies of all kinds which were brought by colonists when they came from Europe were soon worn out or exhausted, and in a large proportion of cases, especially in the northern part of the continent, their places were filled not by imports from Europe but by the products of colonial labor. The colonists came from advanced industrial communities of the time in Europe. Artisans of varied skill always occupied a place among their members and their labor always formed a part of the total activity of the colonies.

Homespun industries, carried on in the households and with a minimum of specialized skill, were an original and always the most important of the forms of manufacturing which went

[1] In the preparation of the sketch which follows I am greatly indebted to the very thorough work of Victor S. Clark, on the History of Manufactures in the United States, published by the Carnegie Institution. The earlier works, like Bishop, have also been abundantly used, together with the Colonial Laws and the references which are scattered through the Colonial Papers.

on in the colonies. The spinning wheel and the hand loom were their most characteristic implements, and, by means of them, were produced the larger part of the textiles which were worn by colonists of lower and medium ranks, north and south, and especially in the remoter inland communities. Wool was the chief material used in these, and to a lesser extent flax, hemp and cotton. "Hardware, tools and implements, furniture, clothing, shoes, caps, and bedding were made in the family. Many southern plantations conducted, with slave labor, household manufactures sufficiently extensive to supply what under a different labor system would have been a community market."[1]

Classifying industries according to the market, when homespun manufactures had developed so far as to enter local or neighborhood exchange, they became domestic-commercial. Other industries, like tanning, saddlery, glass-making, brick-making, the manufacture of hollow ware and bar iron, of soap and candles, were domestic-commercial from the beginning. Hats fall partly in this and partly in the next class. Many other commodities with a similar history might be mentioned. The extent of the domestic market within which they were salable varied with every commodity or with any given commodity at different times and places, from the neighborhood where it was produced to the adjacent section of a colony or to an entire colony or a group of colonies which were subject to similar economic conditions. To the two classes of goods just mentioned doubtless belonged by far the larger part of the manufactures produced in the colonies.

The third class was the foreign-commercial manufactures. They were produced for the foreign market, and this for the most part meant the island colonies and Europe. But under the existing means of communication the remoter southern colonies were so far away from New England that these two sections might well be considered as foreign to one another. Transportation of these products was almost wholly by sea, and in general a scale of production and transportation facilities adequate to reach such distant markets was not developed until the middle or later colonial period. To commodities of this class belonged lumber, pitch, tar, iron, flour, salt,

[1] Clark, *op. cit.*, 92.

provisions, potash and rum. Ships, sent to the European market, might also be included in this class. With the exception of rum, none of these commodities was affected by the Indian trade.

It was not until about the close of our colonial period that the inventions were made which led to the development of the factory system in England. Steam was not yet available as a motor power and, on both sides of the Atlantic, water, mechanical and animal power were all that was available. This fact helped to determine the location of manufacturing enterprises and also to limit the scale on which they were prosecuted. Factories did not exist, and apart from the household the workshop was the typical form of industrial establishment. The managers of these in some cases gave out work to be done or completed in households or elsewhere. Grist mills, saw mills, tanneries, breweries, ropewalks, tar kilns, paper mills, glass works, iron furnaces, slitting mills, potash and pearl ash works, and the like, all fall under the class of workshops. With the incoming of the Scotch-Irish the manufacture of linen by methods to which they had been accustomed at home was established in several localities. The Germans in Pennsylvania developed iron and glass works on a considerable scale.

The scale on which manufacturing developed was affected or determined not only by the availability of raw material and facilities for transportation, but by the cost of labor, the abundance of capital, the condition of the circulating medium, density of population, and by everything which affected the extent of the market and the intensity of demand. Wars and causes affecting general prosperity and credit also had their influence. From time to time local and sectional crises and periods of depression occurred. The amount of available capital was small and, like everything else in the colonies, it was widely dispersed. Labor was affected by analogous conditions and, as land was so abundant and returns therefrom so easy and relatively large, wages averaged high. This was especially true as compared with Europe, while the purchasing power of money, when not affected by depreciated bills of credit, was great. Here lay the secret of the attractiveness of the colonies to the common man.

The largest fortunes were invested in land or in foreign trade, not in manufactures. The corporation as a means of bringing small accumulations together for joint enterprises was only slightly developed or utilized. There was general lack of specialization. Many things were done on a small scale, but nothing on a large one. There was a general diffusion of manufacturing throughout the colonies, especially in the northern and middle sections, and this had grown up chiefly to satisfy local and sectional demand for things which it would not be safe for any community to be left without.

The colonial legislatures were, of course, aware of these conditions and made many efforts, temporary or continuous, to promote or regulate manufactures by statute. In a loose and unsystematic way the protectionist ideas of the time were held by the colonists and were applied in their legislation for the encouragement of domestic industries. The favorite policy, especially for the encouragement of textiles, was to grant bounties for either the raw materials or the finished product. Flax and hemp and linen were the objects of such favors in very many of the colonies. Occasionally woolens were the object of similar treatment; potash and salt also. The introduction of new industries in general or of specified industries was not infrequently encouraged by grants of land, on the part of towns and colonies. The setting up of a grist mill or saw mill was naturally rewarded in this fashion; in the same way the making of salt, brick or glass. Public loans were also made for the same or similar purposes, such action being taken also by localities as well as colonies. Lotteries were sometimes resorted to for raising the money thus loaned. Monopolies and patents were sometimes used as encouragements or rewards, and the compulsory use of a variety of staple products as money had a similar influence. Embargoes on exports, as well as export duties, were frequently used as means of guaranteeing a stock of materials or fostering domestic industry. The low import duties of the time were considered, especially by Great Britain, to have incidentally a protective influence. Frequently such duties were levied on goods coming into a colony from neighboring colonies, and sometimes a petty tariff war would result. Tonnage duties were frequently levied in such a way as to favor the vessels of the colony which imposed them. The colonial legislation for the encouragement of manufactures was large in amount and varied, and, though many of the acts were temporary, its purpose is clear and its total effect was a certain encouragement of colonial industries which were properly deemed necessary to the security and progress of communities, which, like these, were located on a remote continent. As population, especially toward the middle of the eighteenth century, rapidly increased and the open spaces were filled and means of transportation improved, the volume of colonial manufactures grew. The extension of settlement toward the interior also necessitated a more self-sufficient economy for such communities, because they were excluded from easy communication with the coast.

Attention must now be directed to the attitude of the British government and its agents toward these industries and the policy which the colonies were instinctively following for their promotion.[1] Their attitude of suspicious watchfulness has already been indicated, but specific proofs of its nature and growth must now be presented. Wool being the great British staple, anxiety was specially strong concerning the progress of sheep raising and the manufacture of wool in the colonies. This, as we have seen, led to the legislation by parliament in 1699 on the subject. The board of trade in a report to the queen, in October, 1703, on the subject of the woolen industry in general, expressed the opinion that of late years great numbers of people were being enticed over into the plantations and that there they clothed themselves and their children with the woolen manufactures of America. Workmen also were carried over on specious pretences of a more easy livelihood in the colonies and there, in spite of the prohibition of the woolens act and contrary to the proper design of such settlements, they so improved their skill that they were making as good druggets as were manufactured in England.[2] In the following year Brenton, then surveyor of the woods, wrote to the board at length concerning the wool

[1] For this the material in the B. T. Journals and Entry Books and Original Papers of the Series Plantations General, and in the series B. T. Commercial is abundant. The chapter on this subject in Lord's Industrial Experiments is also helpful.

[2] B. T. N. Eng., Oct. 28, 1703, B. T. Journal.

industry in New England. He said that the greatest number of sheep in that section were kept on the islands of Nantucket and Martha's Vineyard and the islands of Narragansett bay and Massachusetts bay. The reason for this was that wolves were numerous on the mainland. In the inland towns, except when serious attempts were made to enforce the wool act, they raised but few sheep, because it could not be done without shepherds, and these because of high wages they could not afford. The inhabitants protested that the wool act was not intended to hinder the transport of wool by water within the same colony and so it had been found impossible to prevent its being carried from the islands to the mainland. Since the passage of the act of 1699 the numbers of sheep in the inland towns had increased and the inhabitants worked up their wool, though they had formerly sold it for money with which they had bought finer English woolens.[1]

Soon after Bridger was appointed surveyor he wrote about the "dangerous growing manufacture of wool in New England" and the large importation of wool-combs and cards for the purpose.[2] The absurd extremes to which some merchants were ready to go was now illustrated by the proposal to force the planters to clothe their servants and slaves in coarse woolen cloths of British make, for which they should barter commodities such as naval stores. To this the board replied that such a policy could not be executed without the consent of the assemblies, and that British goods should be recommended by their goodness and cheapness rather than imposed by a policy which would meet with general opposition.[3] The board, however, prematurely expressed itself as sanguine that labor was being so diverted to naval stores that the woolen industry would be abandoned. But the letters of Partridge, Dudley and Bridger showed that this was a vain hope. Partridge stated, after the war had well begun, that New England no longer had any returns to make for English woolens and must manufacture for herself or go naked. War had also cut off her market for fish in Spain and war with the Indians had

[1] E. B. New Eng. C. O. 5/911. The quality of wool raised in the colonies was always very inferior to that produced in England.

[2] Lord, 130.

[3] E. B. Plants. Gen., Dec. 3, 1706.

deprived her of the fur trade.[1] In 1708 Bridger wrote that the people had returned to the woolen manufacture, "so that not one in 40 but wears his own carding and spinning." They would not believe him when he told them they could make more at tar and pitch than they could at carding and spinning. The next year he wrote that the woolen industry was steadily increasing, while the war was retarding the production of naval stores.[2] It was, of course, natural that all officials who were engaged in stimulating the production of naval stores should lay all the emphasis that was possible on the growth of manufactures. Dudley, in 1709, wrote that, owing to high prices and lack of dealings with England, her woolen trade with New England was falling off and, unless the lumber trade and ship building were encouraged, the woolen trade would grow less every year in spite of the increase of population. Banister, in his "Discourse on the Trade of New England," written in answer to queries from the board of trade, clearly stated the view that high prices and the unfavorable balance of trade with England, together with heavy duties on naval stores there, had forced New England, about nine years before, to a very decided increase in the manufacture of woolens. The lack of coin, with the disorganizing attempt to substitute paper credit, had also contributed to this result.

From New York, about 1708, came reports written by Lord Cornbury and Caleb Heathcote,[3] that the same unfavorable balance of trade had occasioned a considerable development of woolen manufactures on Long Island and in Connecticut. Heathcote stated that three-quarters of the linen and woolen which the people wore was made by themselves and, if it was not stopped, they would carry it much further. Cornbury mentioned at some length the varieties of woolen fabrics which were made in New York. In 1705 Logan wrote to Penn about the trouble into which an inhabitant of Chester had inadvertently fallen because he had brought two packages of wool from Maryland. Penn replied that he would try to have the act amended, though in England they were very jealous

[1] B. T. New Eng.

[2] Quoted by Lord, 131. Down to the close of 1713 or later — see Cal. of Treasury Papers — Bridger continued to write in this strain.

[3] N. Y. Col. Docs., V, 59, 63; Lord, 131.

of encouraging manufactures in the colonies.[1] The low price of tobacco in Virginia and Maryland at this time was having a similar tendency there also. In November, 1708,[2] Perry and other Virginia merchants attended the board of trade, the occasion being the arrival of a letter from Jennings, president of that colony, dwelling on the low price of tobacco and the necessity that supplies of clothing should be sent from England as the only effectual means of keeping the people from manufacturing linen and woolens. The merchants stated that the immediate occasion of the difficulty was a delay of some seven months in the sailing of the Virginia fleet having on board a large quantity of British manufactures. They also took occasion to say that, unless the high duty on the importation of tobacco into England was removed, they did not see how a stop could be put to the growth of manufacturing in Virginia.

And so the discussion continued, its purpose being largely to justify such a limited utilization of the resources of the colonial territory as would best enrich and strengthen Great Britain and prepare her better for the rivalries of Europe and the world, and especially for the struggle, dynastic, military and commercial, in which she was engaged with France. The examples which have just been given are drawn from the years immediately following the passage of the woolen act and relate specially to that commodity. At that time wool was the colonial industry which was chiefly worrying British merchants and officials. As immigration into the colonies increased and population grew, other industries began to attract attention. The discussion was continued with even greater energy after the treaty of Utrecht and far on into the period of peace that followed. During the years 1715 and 1716 the board of trade was much occupied with the causes of an alleged decline in the British woolen industry.[3] During nearly two decades after the accession of the Hanoverians the subject of naval stores, as we have seen, was uppermost, and when that was under discussion the topic of colonial manufactures lay just in the background and might be brought

[1] Penn-Logan Corresp., II, 8, 68. Clark, 23.

[2] B. T. Journal.

[3] Defoe denied the truth of this.

to the front at any time. In 1715 Governor Hunter, with his usual common sense, wrote that the farmers and poorer sort of country people wore no clothing except of their own manufacture, and a law to oblige such as were not able to wear English manufactures to go to the expense of doing so would be a law requiring them to go naked.[1] In 1720 Armstrong, who was sent by Bridger's successor to be deputy surveyor of the woods, wrote very pessimistically about New England, stating that the assemblies were encouraging experts to come and teach them how to manufacture their own products, that they were now well able to manufacture woolen, linen, iron, copper and other commodities and nothing could divert them from it. "I presume," he added, "in a few years they will set up for themselves independent of England."[2] The enterprise of Spotswood in Virginia, with statements from Byrd and others, called attention to iron and its possibilities. In its report of 1721 the board of trade found New Hampshire safely committed to fishery, lumber and naval stores, but in Massachusetts a considerable variety of manufactures had been established, from necessity, it supposed, and not choice.[3] "The most natural method of curing this evil would be to allow them all proper encouragement for the importation of Naval Stores and minerals of all kinds." Respecting no other colony did the board express anxiety on the score of existing manufactures, though it was aware of the large deposits of iron, especially in Pennsylvania, and of the desirability that the yield of these in proper form, as well as their lumber, should be taken off, so that the Pennsylvanians would "be diverted from the thought of setting up any manufactures of their own."[4]

As the impression conveyed by many was that the woolens act was not being satisfactorily obeyed, in November 1728, an order came from the privy council directing the board to lay before it the best information to be obtained of any silk, linen or woolen manufactures erected in any of the plantations.[5] Sir William Keith, Spotswood, Shute, Robert John-

[1] N. Y. Col. Docs., V, 460.
[2] Quoted by Lord, 136.
[3] N. Y. Col. Docs., V, 598.
[4] *Ibid.*, 604. [5] B. T. Journal; N. J. Arch. V, 203–206.

son — all ex-governors — and Gee were summoned. Keith presented a written memorial, in which he stated that the colonists who lived south of Pennsylvania, except in Somerset county, Maryland, were too fully employed in the production of tobacco and rice to manufacture either wool or flax to advantage. The people to the north of that Mason and Dixon's line, which has signified so much in American history, kept some sheep, raised a little flax, and at odd times kept the children, servants and women in their families at work making from these coarse cloth, bags, halters and plough traces for the use of the household and on the farm. The lack of facilities for land carriage from remote inland settlements to the market made it necessary for them to limit their crops of corn and grain and that left them time to spare for the working up of wool and flax for domestic use. Keith also called attention to the high cost of labor as an effective check on large-scale manufacturing in the colonies. His view was a true and liberal one, though he admitted the desirability also of a diversion into the production of naval stores.[1] Spotswood said that in Virginia servants were employed in household manufactures of wool, but never when the returns from tobacco equalled the cost of its cultivation. Shute, who had written in moderate terms on earlier occasions, expressed himself concerning conditions in New England to the same general effect as Keith and Spotswood. Johnson said he did not think there was any danger of the establishment of woolen or linen manufactures in either of the Carolinas if the production of naval stores was encouraged. Gee reported what he had heard about Germans in Pennsylvania raising both hemp and flax and manufacturing some linen for sale. All agreed with the opinions of the ex-governors, and the board prepared a representation to that general effect. In that document,[2] while following chiefly the statement of Keith, they used the suggestion of Gee as the basis for a recommendation that care should be taken to prevent the growth of the manufacture of linen in the colonies. As linen

[1] On similar grounds, in 1729 Keith urged the encouragement of the production of pot and pearl ashes in the colonies, and that industry gradually became the object of some attention. See Keith's reply to an inquiry by Thomas Lowndes, N. J. Arch. V, 246.

[2] N. J. Arch. V, 207.

had been made the sole specialty of Ireland, so apparently naval stores should be the sole specialty of the northern colonies. The board would not prevent the poor settlers from clothing themselves, but yet it thought the wool act should be extended so as to prevent such goods from being exposed for sale.

It was at this juncture, in connection with the naval stores act of 1729 and of the discussion of colonial manufactures, that Spotswood gave the board of trade an able account of his enterprise in Virginia.[1] As he was engaged in the production of iron, as well as in experiments with tar and hemp, his work lay in both the two spheres of manufacturing and the production of naval stores. The peculiarity of iron was that it was or might be a purely manufactured product or a form of naval stores, and it was at this time that iron first appeared prominently on the scene. Spotswood said that when he first went to Virginia, on every man-of-war were two Russians learning the principles of navigation, and this was permitted for the sake of the hemp which England was to buy from Russia. Then he thought of the court which England had to pay to Sweden in order to secure naval supplies. These thoughts, together with a recent speech from the throne, moved him to see if iron, tar and hemp could not be produced in Virginia. He invested largely himself, went into partnership with others and induced all the colonists to embark on the production of these stores. He took up 55,000 acres of crown land, of which 40,000 were devoted to hemp, tar and pitch and the remaining 15,000 acres, because of deposits, were devoted to iron. On the first tract over one hundred Germans were settled, they being provided with houses and all necessities for the support of their families for five years. They were charged no interest on these advances and no rent for three years, but afterwards a pound of hemp or flax per acre. Spotswood also had a large plantation stocked with the best of his negroes and managed by an Englishman, who instructed them in hemp raising. In this he found the best results from wild seed grown in America. His tar burners succeeded well, with the use of knots and decayed limbs, until the new method prescribed by act of

[1] O. P. Plants. Gen., March, 1712/8; B. T. Journal.

parliament compelled them to stop; it destroyed trees too fast and could be made to yield no satisfactory results.

Spotswood claimed to have set up the first furnace in America for making pig iron. The quality of what he produced had been approved in England and partnerships were formed in Bristol and Birmingham to enlarge its production. Some encouragement was also given in Virginia. But, because results came more slowly than was expected, the partners lost interest and Spotswood took over the entire business. The bounty act also expired and bills were passed in Virginia forbidding any one to take up more than 1000 acres of land and laying a duty on the importation of negroes. These various causes, together with the recall of Spotswood in the midst of his plans, discouraged the enterprise. In 1724 he went to England and claimed to have helped convince the board of trade that tar could not be made with the class of labor in the plantations according to the new method, and had urged that tar burners be brought from Finland for the purpose. But he had been so rebuffed that he said he had lost interest in hemp and tar, though he should continue the production of pig iron.

This suggestive statement by Spotswood was followed by the presentation, through Viscount Townshend, of another "Discourse" addressed by Keith to the king. This was much longer than its predecessor and dealt with the subject of colonial settlement as well as that of trade.[1] There is evidence that this essay had been written three years or more before and that Martin Bladen had seen it and had expressed to Townshend the purpose of adding some further hints on the subject.[2] What he may have written is

[1] O. P. Plants. Gen., Dec. 31, 1728. This is printed in N. J. Arch. V, 215–230. The same paper is also printed in N. C. Col. Recs., II, 626.

[2] N. C. Recs., II, 625. In 1740 Keith published his writings under the title of "A Collection of Papers and other Tracts." In this volume the essay in question, under a modified title and with a long addition in defence of the issues of paper currency in the colonies, occupies a prominent place. The fulsome introduction, which appeared in all the versions, might well have provoked the satire of Thackeray. Speaking of George II and the courtiers who surrounded him, Keith declared that the paths of virtue and honor, with a strict adherence to truth, would be the only avenues of access to the sovereign's esteem and the only claims to favor. Patriotism and liberty were the watchwords and inspiration of sovereign, ministers and people.

not known, but that it would have been in substantial agreement with the views of Keith can hardly be doubted.

Upon the benefits which came to the parent state from trade with the colonies he dwelt at length, stating them under several distinct heads. The acts of trade he believed should be strictly executed and all products of the colonies for which the manufactures and trade of Great Britain had a steady demand should be enumerated. The same should be done in the case of every valuable and rare product for which there was a demand in Europe, so that by passing through Great Britain they might assist her in the balance of trade with other countries. The colonies also should be absolutely restrained from laying any manner of duties on shipping or trade from Europe or upon European goods transported from one colony to another. "Every Act of a Dependent Provincial Government," wrote Keith, "ought to Terminate in the Advantage of the Mother State, unto whom it owes its being and by whom it is protected in all its valuable priviledges. Hence it follows that all advantageous Projects or Commercial Gains in any Colony which are truly prejudicial to or inconsistent with the Interest of the Mother State must be understood to be illegal and the practice of them unwarrantable, because they contradict the End for which the Colony had a Being and are incompatable with the Terms on which the People claim both Priviledge and protection."[1] A well regulated province, "like a choice Branch springing from the Main Root, ought to be carefully nourished and its just Interests well guarded." If colonies could not be made to contribute profitably to the "Generall Ballance of the whole State" it would be much better for the state to be without them. To the mind of Keith the principles involved were few and simple, their application clear and the result a mercantilist empire as regular in its structure as a blockhouse and as easily understood. The similarity in tone — though the policies advocated were diametrically opposed — between Keith's dogmatic views of society as con-

[1] Chalmers states that this idea had been expressed by Stephen Godin, a merchant, in a memorial submitted to the board in July, 1716. Godin had specially in mind the levy by the colonies of discriminating duties on British goods. Chalmers, Introd. *etc.*, II, 6.

structed on the mercantilist plan and the writings of extreme Manchester men, like MacCulloch, a century later in support of free trade, is striking.

Coming to the subject of government, Keith drew the natural inference that it should be the faithful servant and protector of the trade system as he had just outlined it. Were the system and the motives underlying it clearly understood, there would be little need of instructions and prohibitions, for all would leap spontaneously to its support. He even considered that it was improper to speak of legislative power in a dependent government. He repeated the worn-out dictum of the Stuart period, one which the Andros régime exemplified, that colonies were to be considered as so many "Corporations at a distance, invested with an ability to make temporary By Laws for themselves agreeable to their respective Situations and Climates, but no ways interfering with the legal Prerogative of the Crown, or the true Legislative Power of the Mother State." In criticising the colonial governments Keith, in accordance with his views and policy as revealed in Pennsylvania, laid great stress on the evils which came from the councils and the obstacles which they frequently put in the way of the exercise of royal, that is autocratic, power through the governors. He thought that they should not have the negative voice and of course scouted any pretension on their part to a place analogous to that of the house of lords in the English constitution. So amateurish were the judges in the colonies and so unqualified were the people, owing to the lack of schools and proper instruction, for jury service that the only security for liberty and property there which Keith could discover lay in the dispatch of judges from England to go on the circuit through the colonies. But the difficulty here lay in the fact that, before this could be done, revenue for the payment of their salaries must be procured in the colonies. As to the colonial militia, Keith rightly considered it of little utility. On the other hand, he questioned how far it would consist with good policy to give the able men of the colonies a really good military training, and concluded that the safest course would be to keep an adequate regular force so distributed through the colonies that it might be used to meet any emergency. By this he did not mean to facilitate colonial union, for he approved of the divided condition of the colonies and of their mutual jealousies, and considered it the part of wisdom to keep them in that condition. Coming to the vital subject of revenue, upon which so much depended, Keith agreed with Cummings in suggesting that the British stamp duties on parchment and paper should be extended to the colonies by act of parliament. And finally, in order to simplify and facilitate colonial administration in England, he urged that all business in that department be centered in the board of trade and that its president be raised to cabinet rank.

With the subject of trade as a feature of colonial policy the privy council had little directly to do. The hearing of appeals and passing on colonial laws were the two chief subjects of its attention. These, together with other less continuous activities, brought a large variety of colonial matters before it, but they did not often relate directly to trade.[1] As to the treasury and the admiralty, they considered questions of colonial policy only so far as they affected the special work of these departments, imperial revenue in the one case and the navy in the other.[2] Action by the treasury was for the most part confined to sanctioning or rejecting items of expenditure already endorsed by some other official or body of officials. As the customs board and the office of auditor general were subordinate to the treasury, there was frequent communication between them and the board of trade, the navy board, the paymaster general of the forces and the ordnance board about expenditures affecting the colonies. But these formed an insignificant part of the grand total and had little to do with the subject now under discussion. The policy to be followed relating to trade was determined by the king and cabinet and the parliament, all making use of the proofs and arguments furnished by the board of trade and by the merchants and officials on whom it drew for facts and opinion. In the cabinet the voices of the secretaries of state and prime minister may be considered in general most

[1] The truth of this can be seen by following through the entries in the Acts P. C. Col.

[2] In the case of the treasury this can be confirmed from the material in the Cals. of Treas. Papers. Matter relating to the admiralty is far less accessible and probably less abundant.

weighty on these subjects. But upon the measures with which we have to do little direct expression of opinion by leading British statesmen is accessible. As these were not government measures, probably little that was definite was expressed by them in public. All statesmen of the time were mercantilists of a more or less decided type. But they were deeply engaged in the game of politics and questions of trade and colonial administration, except in connection with appointments to minor offices, had only a remote interest for them. Even in the case of such a busybody as Newcastle, this fact becomes perfectly clear to a reader of his correspondence. Though in general the king and his cabinet approved of the policy recommended by the board of trade and furthered it, they viewed it from the standpoint of the practical more than the theoretical and favored its execution only in parts and to a limited extent. In their minds mercantilism and projects of colonial autocracy were diluted by mixture with many other plans and were actually applied in much reduced strength. This was especially true so long as Walpole was in power and under his Whig successors until after 1760.[1]

But the cabinets acted in conjunction with parliament. There the condition was somewhat analogous, though of course very different. Several of the more active members of the board of trade held seats in the house of commons and were active there also. One or two peers were always included among the working members of the board. The merchants as a class were also pretty well represented in the commons and, as time passed, their influence increased. In both houses there was, of course, a vigorous and growing interest in the subjects of trade, the navy, the colonies and commercial supremacy. At the time of which we are speaking, this was distinctly shown in the lords as well as in the commons, and it is proven by the frequency with which both houses called upon the board of trade for information and by the many and large committees which were appointed,

[1] The orders, warrants, and fragmentary minutes of the secretaries of state and cabinets yield virtually nothing on the subject of trade and the colonies. The correspondence of some of the statesmen is more valuable on these subjects.

especially in the lower house, to consider the reports and evidence submitted.[1] For about a decade after its creation it was customary for the house of lords to call annually for a report from the board of trade concerning the condition of commerce and the plantations in general. The African trade in particular and the struggle which was then in progress between the Royal African Company, to retain its monopoly, and the interlopers to gain access to its territory or to change from a joint stock to a regulated form, were subjects of frequent discussion in parliament, and of final action. The same was true respecting the East India Company. Any or all of the "trades" and the companies or groups of merchants that controlled them might at any time become subjects of discussion and action in parliament. So far as the "trades" in Africa, the East Indies and many parts of Europe were concerned, the trading companies corresponded institutionally to the colonies and plantations in America.[2] In the case of the former only factories or trading posts had been established among alien peoples, while in the case of the latter British colonies with organized governments had been planted and the native inhabitants were in process of subjugation or extermination. But these communities, under whatever form, with their backers in Great Britain, were equally subject to inquiry and control by the executive and parliament of the realm. The fact itself and abundant illustrations of it, so far as the colonies were concerned, and as existing from the first, have already been cited. The English Revolution had forced the recognition beyond cavil of the sovereignty of parliament in the constitution, and the results of it were now being worked out in practice. In theory, however slight the correspondence to it might be in fact, the realm and dominions were being treated as a unit, with the navy and merchant marine and the administrative officials of every variety as the physical and human ligaments which bound it together. So remote and disjointed were the parts that it required and still requires an unusual

[1] Abundant proof of these statements may be found in the Journals of the Lords and Commons.

[2] See W. R. Scott, The Joint Stock Companies to 1720; also Cunningham, Growth of English Industry and Commerce.

flight of the imagination to realize this fact, but the sources for the time make the fact indubitably clear.

Since the Revolution, moreover, and to an extent before it, imperial control and the formulation of commercial and imperial policy had ceased to be matters alone or chiefly for the British executive. They had now been taken up by political parties and social groups and classes, all of which were more or less fully represented in parliament. The merchant class in particular, which was so enthusiastically described by Defoe, was now rising to control and, after the inventions of the middle of the century, was to broaden into the industrial aristocracy of later times. Questions in which they were specially interested were now coming to furnish more and more of the staple of debate in both houses. In theory at least no subject was exempt from such criticism and action and no section of the earth's surface where British interests were established; and as time passed fact came more and more to correspond with theory. Concerning any or all of these subjects and interests questions were asked, petitions presented, bills introduced, committees appointed for special consideration of subjects and report thereon, debates upon the floor of the houses followed, sometimes in committees of the whole, sometimes in regular session. The consideration of interests, policies or measures was sometimes prolonged at intervals for weeks or months, or perhaps during the entire period were never disposed of or laid wholly to rest. Action under all these forms might be initiated by the government or from the floor, and in all cases prior or concurrent action by the cabinet and its members and by the appropriate administrative boards was required. Final action was taken when statutes were passed. In them were summed up the principles upon which the parliament and executive as a whole had decided for the time to act. Until changed, they were law.

We have seen that the board of trade was a clearing house for opinions and policies respecting trade and colonial government. It was deliberating and acting continuously. The privy council gave to the deliberations of the board on many subjects the necessary executive authority. The treasury and admiralty, in their spheres, acted in more direct connection with the cabinet. The parliament, on the other hand, was by on means continuously in session. But, notwithstanding that, it was the supreme clearing house for all imperial, as well as domestic, questions and to its deliberations and actions the entire British executive was and is contributory. Parliament is the centre of the organism, the ultimate depository of authority. The due recognition of this is necessary to any proper discussion of imperial control over the colonies, over trade and war, and ultimately over international relations in general. Allowance must, of course, be made for large initiative and discretion on the part of the executive in all these activities of government, but ultimately, though possibly after years of delay, as the result of the financial check or the political check exercised through elections, it must submit to the judgment of the nation expressed through parliament. This was a principle of the Whig party, held as time went on with the firmness of a dogma. It is also a commonplace of English history. Therefore, if the treatment of imperial control over the colonies during the period now under review is to be adequate, this fact must be fully recognized. The inquiry will by no means terminate with the board of trade and privy council, but will extend to the abundant material, and proofs and indications of action, to be found in the journals of the two houses. Like the study of the journals of the colonial assemblies, the examinations of the contents of these journals is of prime importance. The close connection which existed between the board of trade and the parliament is made perfectly evident, both through the information furnished to the houses by the board and by the fact that certain of its members were active workers in them. Except in the lines of legal and judicial control, the only way in which the board could make its views effective was through procuring their acceptance by the cabinet and parliament.

The character of the cabinet and its probable influence as a refracting medium upon cut and dried theories of trade and colonial government — or in fact upon any other theories — have already been indicated. The two houses offered another medium, which might even be called refractory, through which many an attractive plan failed wholly to pass or was so modified in its passage as to be scarcely recognizable by its originators. The merchants, all more or less zealous and imbued with mercantilist theories, were influential, especially in the house of commons. Members of the board of trade were there, often serving on committees and reporting bills. Their representations, together with much additional evidence, were presented to the houses. There were probably no members of either house who were not mercantilists, either consciously or half consciously, and they responded favorably to the appeals of that intensified form of nationalism which the empire, the navy and trade supremacy evoked. But only under the pressure of great crises or of thoroughly convinced and impassioned leadership can legislative bodies be brought to act decisively or with unanimity. Under Walpole and his immediate successors the kind of leadership and the crises referred to were lacking. The landed interests, moreover, were still strong especially in the lords, and it did not easily respond to the appeals of the merchants. For these and many other reasons, which this is not the place even to attempt to analyze, the two houses lagged considerably behind the board of trade and its favorite advisers in the thoroughness with which they were prepared to apply schemes which looked toward more rigid imperial control. The legal authority and the power were there in reserve, but only limited provision was made for their exercise and that along traditional lines. In this diluting effect which the cabinet and parliament exercised upon the plans of the board of trade and its so-called experts lay the only real guaranty of colonial liberty. No other was possible under the British system as it then was. It remained operative, as a certain tacit understanding, until after the middle of the century.

In earlier chapters the legislation affecting the colonies, which was passed by parliament before the close of the reign of Anne, has been discussed. The questions which came up, or which reached a decision, during the first fifteen years of Hanoverian rule did not involve any new ideas or policies. For some time the house of commons was more or less occupied with the adjustment of the accounts of expenditures during the last years of the war, and among these the accounts of Hovenden Walker's expedition occupied a rather prominent place. In connection with this Hunter's claims and the fortunes of the Palatines in New York received some attention from a committee of the house. The bill for the recall of the colonial charters, which was a favorite with the board of trade, then failed of passage. Among the yearly estimates for the army appeared always the small sums desired for the payment of the few companies of regulars which were stationed in Nova Scotia, New York and elsewhere, and for ordnance stores intended for the colonies. Piracy and the unsettled conditions in South Carolina were repeatedly noticed and the way was thus prepared for the law of 1729 abolishing the Carolina proprietorship. Early in 1717 a bill continuing the liberty to import Irish linen free of duty to the plantations became law,[1] though petitions against it came from the linen drapers of London and Manchester. The privilege was to be continued as long as British merchants might export to Ireland linen of British manufacture free. In 1718 and 1719 the subject of naval stores was discussed and a clause was added to an act against the clandestine running of uncustomed goods which provided, on account of complaints made by the navy of the poor quality of pitch and tar recently imported from America, that no certificate should be granted for a premium until it was proven that the product was clean, good and merchantable.[2] In 1722 the second important statute, continuing the policy of Anne's reign concerning naval stores, was passed.[3] During the discussion at this time the subject of iron received some attention, petitions and arguments being presented by British officials, merchants and manufacturers on both sides of the question, some advocating the liberal importation of pig iron from America in order to economize the forests of England and to make Great Britain more independent of the Baltic countries, and others prophesying the ruin of the British iron industry if such a policy should be followed. As this was the first time when iron was prominently discussed, naturally no action was taken. Piracy and the transportation of felons to the plantations were also considered, the latter subject repeatedly and

[1] 3 Geo. I, c. 21, continuing 3 & 4 Anne, c. 8.

[2] 5 Geo. I, c. 11.

[3] 8 Geo. I, c. 12. The king's speech at the opening of parliament in October, 1721, dwelt upon the importance of encouraging the production of naval stores in the colonies. So the government as a whole was committed to it.

at length, and respecting it two important statutes were passed.[1] Several later acts providing for the transportation of felons were passed at intervals toward 1750.[2]

In 1721 beaver skins and other furs and copper ore from the plantations were added to the list of enumerated commodities.[3] In 1722 Micajah Perry and others who were importers of tobacco from Virginia complained loudly of the extent to which the Scotch were out — competing them in this trade and were selling tobacco in Holland more cheaply than they could do. It was also declared that extensive frauds in the customs were being committed in Scotland. The subject attracted much attention in the commons, but instead of a separate bill being passed for preventing frauds in the tobacco trade, this was merged in an act enabling the king to put the customs administration of Great Britain under one commission.[4] Early in 1729, as the result of a general effort made by the Virginians and the merchants who were interested in their trade — Perry, who was a member of the commons, again leading — the clause in an earlier act prohibiting the importation of tobacco stripped from the stalk was repealed. This was done out of consideration of the importance of the tobacco industry, and it was claimed that, by allowing the importation of the lower and shattered leaves, the total marketed product would be increased by a fifth.[5] At about the same time, for the encouragement of the fishery and at the instance of Perry and other merchants, acts were passed allowing the importation of salt direct from the continent of Europe into Pennsylvania and New York.[6] In 1729 the act for the further preservation of the woods, about which there was so much contention in New England, was passed.[7]

Rice, which since the close of the previous century had become one of the staple products of South Carolina, along

[1] 4 Geo. I, c. 11 (1717), and 6 Geo. I, c. 23 (1719).

[2] 12 Geo. I, c. 29 (1725); 7 Geo. II, c. 21 (1734); 12 Geo. II, c. 21 (1739); 16 Geo. II, c. 15 & 31 (1743); 20 Geo. II, c. 46 (1747).

[3] By 8 Geo. I, c. 15, and 8 Geo. I, c. 18.

[4] 9 Geo. I, c. 21.

[5] Commons Journal, XXI, 261 *et seq.*; 2 Geo. II, c. 9.

[6] 13 Geo. I, c. 5, and 3 Geo. II, c. 12. In the first of these acts doubt was expressed whether the term "New England," used in 15 Chas. II, extended to Pennsylvania. Commons Jo. XX, 746 *et seq.*; XXI, 461, 485, 531.

[7] 2 Geo. II, c. 22.

with molasses had been placed in the list of enumerated commodities in the reign of Anne.[1] The yield of rice increased rapidly, so that before its enumeration the American product, considered the best in the world, had come to monopolize the Portuguese market and was making headway in Spain. Large quantities also were sold in northern Europe. A suggestion that its direct exportation to the south of Europe was injurious to England easily secured its addition to the enumerated list. But the roundabout voyage by the way of England so increased the cost of freight that the Portuguese market was lost. The result was that while on the average during the years 1712 to 1717, of the 2,800,000 lbs. which were imported from Carolina and the other plantations, more than 2,000,000 lbs. were sold in northern Europe and less than 250,000 lbs. to the countries south of Cape Finisterre. In 1720 Boone,[2] the agent of South Carolina, dwelt on the loss of this trade, and the board of trade in its report of 1721 fully stated the fact and its cause. The board recommended as a remedy that permission for the export of rice direct from South Carolina to parts of Europe south of Cape Finisterre be granted, but that security be required that every vessel which took advantage of this should touch in England on its return voyage. But no action was taken and the South Carolinians continued their arguments and complaints for a decade longer.[3] It was a demand for a larger market, as the capacity of South Carolina to produce rice largely exceeded the demand from northern Europe alone. Finally, in 1730, liberty was granted to carry this product to any part of Europe south of Cape Finisterre in ships legally built and owned. Five years later the same concession was made in favor of rice from Georgia.[4] This was not done by taking rice off the list of enumerated commodities, but by legalizing the system of special licenses with security which had been suggested by the board of trade. The provision was continued by later acts and the Portuguese market was promptly

[1] 3 & 4 Anne, c. 5 sect. 12; N. Y. Col. Docs., V, 612.

[2] B. T. S. Car. O. P.

[3] See Francis Yonge's "View of the Trade of South Carolina," presented to the board in 1723. B. T. S. C. O. P., and many other references.

[4] 3 Geo. II, c. 28; 8 Geo. II, c. 19; Commons J. XX, 62, 443, 500, 535 587, 813; Lords J. XXIII, 566–576.

recovered, the price of rice ranging high during the later colonial period.

About 1730 the manufacture of hats reached such proportions in a few of the colonies as to attract the attention of the organized leaders of that trade in England. Beaver obtained in trade with the Indians and afterwards wool were used in this industry. New York, Massachusetts and South Carolina were the colonies where the making of hats chiefly developed. At first the term feltmakers was used to designate those who followed this trade, and they begin to appear about 1700 on the lists of burghers in New York City. During the next thirty years it is thought that the industry progressed so as largely to supply the demand for the common quality of hats and caps throughout the colonies. Some also were exported to the West Indies. Thomas Coram was one of the most careful observers of such developments, and early in 1732 he supported the petition of the hatters before the board of trade.[1] Under an order from the commons, the board at that time was investigating the laws made and the manufactures set up in the colonies which might affect the interests of Great Britain. Coram was an ultra mercantilist and, in a long memorial which he now presented on the general subject of colonial manufactures, he portrayed the situation in strong colors and recommended a strenuous policy. Wool, hats and shoes came in for special mention, and his conclusion was that manufactures in these lines should be restrained or totally prohibited while they were in their infancy, lest they should grow to such strength that it would be dangerous or even impossible to suppress them. The hatters at the same time petitioned that the colonists might be prevented from wearing or selling any hats except those which were made in Great Britain. The immediate result, so far as the industry of hat making was concerned, was the passage of the act, 5 Geo. II, c. 22, which applied to that industry the kind of treatment which had been prescribed for woolens in 1699. Intercolonial trade in hats and felts was prohibited under heavy penalties, and in addition hat making in the colonies was restricted to those who had served an apprenticeship of seven years and the masters were

[1] B. T. Journal, N. J. Arch. V, 308.

prohibited from keeping more than two apprentices each. No negroes were to be employed in hat making. The effect of this law upon the industry was not appreciably different from that of the legislation of 1699 on the manufactures of wool. Hat making was not suppressed, and since no provision was made in either the law of 1699 or that of 1732 for special officials of royal appointment for their execution, we hear little or nothing of special measures for restricting the manufacture of hats.

It therefore appears, from this review, that up to about 1730, though the cabinet and parliament were much occupied with questions of trade, no new principles were evolved, though the application of those already accepted was slightly extended. Of special importance is the fact that no wholesale changes in the administrative or fiscal policy of Great Britain toward the colonies were considered or probably even mentioned in those bodies which were really responsible for the conduct of the British government.

CHAPTER II

THE OVERTHROW OF PROPRIETARY GOVERNMENT IN SOUTH CAROLINA

In none of the proprietary provinces did government sink to a lower point of efficiency than it did in the Carolinas. In the northern part of the original province it never had more than a nominal existence. In South Carolina, while for a number of decades their administration was reasonably vigorous, before the beginning of the eighteenth century the activity of the proprietors began to relax.[1] At the same time the ecclesiastical policy to which they gave their support was so reactionary as deeply to offend not only the dissenters but many of the Anglicans in the province. During the second intercolonial war also the Spanish in Florida and the French from the west were a menace to this region, and the proprietors were too weak to afford the inhabitants appreciable aid or protection. Fortunately the enemy made no serious attack, but during this war and for years thereafter the danger of leaving a frontier province under such weak control was repeatedly brought home both to its people and to the British government. The proprietors themselves openly confessed their inability to provide for its defence, and yet the peril was not so great nor the plea of military necessity so strong as to lead the government to take over the province and provide directly for its defence.

In 1715, just after the close of the war, a formidable Indian conspiracy was formed against the whites. At the head of this were the Yemassees who not very long before had removed from Spanish territory and settled near Port Royal. They were the most powerful tribe who lived in the immediate vicinity of the white settlements. Apalachis, and others joined in their conspiracy till it was widely extended to the

[1] For the cause of this, see Osgood, Am..Colonies in the 17th Century, II, 201, 202.

northward and westward. The usual causes impelled them to it, namely, encroachment on the lands of the Indians and ill usage on the part of traders. The plan of the natives was to exterminate the settlers, and they did inflict terrible slaughter and destruction of property, extending their ravages to within twenty miles of Charlestown, St. Bartholomew and near Port Royal.[1] The parish of St. James, Goose Creek, the residence of the Moore family, was later attacked. When the report first reached Charlestown that war was to be expected, Nairn, the Indian agent, was sent to allay, if possible, the dissatisfaction of the Indians; but he and those who accompanied him were massacred, and with that the carnage began.

South Carolina could then muster not more than 1200 men fit for service, against a force of Indian allies roughly estimated at 8000. Governor Craven acted with energy and some success. The assembly supported his action with such laws and orders as were possible. But the supply of arms and ammunition was very inadequate and aid from outside seemed absolutely necessary if the colony was to be saved from destruction. With £2500 appropriated by the assembly a messenger was sent to New England to purchase arms. Arthur Middleton was also sent to Virginia to seek its aid. North Carolina, which had recently been helped by its southern neighbor, sent a small body of volunteers, placing no condition on its offer. Without delay Governor Spotswood sent by the royal guardship 160 muskets and some powder and ball from the magazine at Williamsburg. Somewhat later 118 men were sent and preparations were made to send enough men to increase the total to three hundred. Spotswood had some personal interest in this, for he feared that the Indian war might spread to the Virginia frontier. If Carolina were destroyed, there was also danger that the French would seize it and stir up a war along the entire frontier. But in giving the aid Spotswood showed the superciliousness of the royal governor by remarking that, even though the Carolinians lived under proprietors, they were subjects of the king in common with the inhabitants of Virginia. Unusual terms also were imposed, for Virginia insisted that an able-bodied slave

[1] McCrady, South Carolina under Proprietary Government, 531–548 and references; N. C. Col. Recs,, II, 177 *et seq.*; Letters from missionaries in MS. Recs. of S. P. G., 1715 and 1716.

be sent to take the place of every man whom she contributed and that the slaves remain throughout the war. This condition it was found impossible to enforce. The Virginia militia were also poorly armed and thought by the Carolinians to be inefficient. Spotswood was at last forced to accept £4 per month in South Carolina currency as the pay of every man sent and no clothing or slaves. Many of the Virginia soldiers were also said to have been induced or forced to remain permanently in South Carolina, and a long controversy followed between the officials of the two colonies over this affair, echoes of which were heard by the imperial authorities in London.[1] To such extent was this interesting experiment in joint colonial action marred by the usual recriminations. Hunter of New York expressed his interest by trying to induce the Senecas to attack the Yemassees.

The war lasted for nearly a year and many months passed after that before outrages ceased on the frontier. The people of two parishes were either slaughtered or driven in a body from their houses, and great damage was inflicted upon the colony. But under the efficient leadership of Governor Craven, slaves being enrolled to serve with their masters, the inhabitants at last succeeded in destroying their enemy and driving the remnant of them across the border into Florida. Had the Yemassees received aid from the more important tribes of the interior, the chances are that the whites would have been entirely overwhelmed. As it was, the Spanish, though it was a time of peace, were charged with sheltering Yemassees at St. Augustine, furnishing them arms and ammunition and receiving slaves which they brought across the border from South Carolina. It was also said that Spanish privateers were unusually numerous off the coast and were preying on British commerce. These charges were laid by the board of trade before Secretary Methuen,[2] and they were closely connected with that course of Spanish policy which soon led to the renewal of open hostilities.

[1] Colls. of Virginia Hist. Soc., Spotswood Letters, II, iii, 114, 117, 119, 121, 126–129, 131, 141, 144, 164, 207, 238, 242; Va. Ex. C. J., C. O. 5/1416, 1715 and 1716; N. C. Col. Recs., II, 203, 225, 227, 234, 253, 254. Virginia sent, in all, about 150 men to South Carolina, and North Carolina sent about fifty. J. of Va. Burgesses, Session of Aug. and Sept., 1715.

[2] C. O. 5/382, B. T. to Methuen, Dec. 17, 1716; B. T. to Sec. Craggs, Nov. 17, 1720.

When the Indian war was at its height appeals were sent to the proprietors for aid and Governor Craven wrote directly to Lord Townshend, one of the secretaries of state.[1] In an urgent address to the king the commons house asked to be taken directly under royal care and government, as the only course which offered assurance of safety. They hoped the king would command Virginia and the other colonies to aid them. Joseph Boone and Landgrave Kettleby, one the agent of the governor and council and the other of the assembly, backed by a number of merchants, offered a ship to carry what could be at once despatched and called earnestly for troops in addition. The fact that South Carolina was a border province and also a great producer of rice, naval stores and skins added greatly to the force of these appeals. The proprietors, of course, confessed their inability to do more than to contribute their receipts from a small quantity of rice received and to order their receiver in South Carolina to expend what he had in hand for arms and ammunition, and to promise a repayment of these debts thereafter. The board of trade urged them to surrender the government of the province to the crown, but an agreement as to terms could not be reached. Chiefly through Lord Carteret as their mouthpiece they plead the large expenditures of the proprietors in settling the province and its great value to the empire. Therefore it advised the king, in view of the importance of South Carolina as a border province, to assume direct control.[2] The case also came before the house of commons and was inquired into by one of its committees. But as the Hanoverian family had recently come to the throne and was just then threatened by the Jacobite uprising of 1715, the crown found obstacles in the way of its action almost as great as those which were faced by the proprietors. The result was that no troops were sent, but instead only a supply of arms to continue their hold upon the government of the province.

Meantime the colonists themselves repelled the enemy and the crisis was passed, a good example in miniature of the way in which events of this nature usually turned out in the continental colonies. By the defeat of the Indians a con-

[1] *Ibid.*, August and later, 1715.

[2] C. O. 5/383, B. T. to Secy. Stanhope, July 19, 1715; N. C. Col. Recs., II, 177, 191–199, 230; McCrady, *op. cit.* 538 *et seq.*

siderable territory between the Cambahee and Savannah rivers was opened for settlement and the hold of the natives upon the region which was to become Georgia was weakened. The injuries which for years to come they were to continue to inflict came in the form of raids from beyond the Spanish border. This struggle cost South Carolina about £150,000 and some provision had to be made for bearing this burden of debt and restoring prosperity. To this task the assembly addressed itself in the spring of 1716. Governor Craven had then returned to England and Robert Daniel was acting as deputy governor, while the proprietors were preparing to appoint Robert Johnson, son of Sir Nathaniel Johnson, as governor to succeed Craven. He arrived and assumed office in the autmum of the following year. The feeling of hostility in the commons house toward the proprietors was strong. It immediately instructed its agents in England to urge upon the crown the necessity of taking over the government of the province if it was to be protected against its enemies.[1] In obedience to this the agents sent a strongly worded memorial to the board of trade. In this they set forth again the delinquencies of the proprietors and the dangers to which the colony was exposed not only from the Indians but from the French and Spanish. They assumed that the French had stirred up the Indians to the recent attacks, and expected still more disastrous experiences when there should be another rupture with France. The advantage of fortifying the excellent harbor of Port Royal, together with a corresponding post on the Bahama islands, as a means of controlling the Florida Passage did not escape their attention. They also enlarged on the great value to England of the staple products of South Carolina and on the heavy debt which it must now bear as arguments in support of their demand for protection. The board of trade was of course sympathetic with these desires, but the ministers were not yet ready to act.

The assembly at Charlestown meantime passed some very important laws. The expulsion of the Yemassees led the proprietors at once to withdraw the prohibition on the settlement of the lands between the Cambahee and Savannah rivers, which nearly two years before had been reserved for the

[1] N. C. Recs., II, 224, 229 *et seq.*; McCrady, *op. cit.*

exclusive use of the Indians with the idea that they would form a buffer tribe between the whites and the hostile Indians to the south which were under Spanish influence. The assembly repealed the act of 1707 under which that prohibition had been enforced and Protestant colonists from Great Britain, Ireland and the other dominions invited on specified terms as to size of grants, quit rents and time of settlement. Impressed with the rapid increase in the number of negroes as compared with white servants in the colony, the receiver was ordered to pay a bounty for every white servant imported, provided they were not Roman Catholics, native Irish or persons of known scandalous character. The narrowly Protestant and Anglo-Scotch spirit of the colonists at that time is thus clearly indicated.[1] In another act an effort was made directly to check the importation of negroes by imposing a duty of £3 currency per head upon those brought in from Africa and £30 per head on those imported from other colonies. This measure was opposed to the desire of the home government that no obstacle should be put in the way of the traffic of the Royal African Company. Authority was given for additional emissions of currency to the amount of £45,000. A law for the regulating of Indian trade was also passed.[2]

By another very important act the assembly sought to decentralize elections in the province. Hitherto, in spite of one or two experiments to the contrary, they had been held exclusively in Charlestown, where tumults often occurred and undue political influence was always exerted. It had been the policy of the proprietors to support this arrangement and it was a feature of the general tendency to concentrate government in the hands of a few, for which they showed decided sympathy. The act which was now passed provided that elections should be held in all the parishes under the charge of the church wardens, and made a new proportional distribution of members among the parishes. Some changes were also made in the property qualifications of voters and members and provision was made for voting by ballot. In this way it was planned to assimilate the electoral system of South Carolina to that of other provinces and to weaken the control

[1] See Osgood, Am. Colonies in 17th Century, II, 419.

[2] Statutes of S. C. II, 641, 647, 649, 662, 682, 683; McCrady, *op. cit.* 555 *et seq.*; Yonge, in Carroll, Hist. Colls. of S. C., II, 149.

over it of proprietary officials at Charlestown.[1] By an act of the following year the anti-proprietary spirit of the assembly was further shown by a provison excluding from seats in that body all who held offices or perquisites from the proprietors. Electors were also required to have been residents for six months in the parish where they voted and representatives were required to be free-born subjects of Great Britain or naturalized by act of parliament. Boone and Beresford were at the same time laying another address from the assembly before the king asking him to take over the province and charging the proprietors with continued inactivity except in support of a faction of office holders and dependents. In reply to this Lord Carteret, before the board of trade, declared that, as the assembly had been dissolved, the agents had no standing and cast doubts upon the earlier representations concerning the seriousness of the Indian War and the peril of the colony.[2]

When Governor Robert Johnson arrived in South Carolina it was entering upon its dramatic struggle with the pirates under Stede Bonnet and his associates, the last important conflict which was to occur with that gentry on the North American coast. Under the lead of William Rhett, as we have seen, the pirates were conquered, and through the firmness of Nicholas Trott, the chief justice, they were tried, condemned and executed But this affair cost rather heavily and added to the already burdensome debt of the province. It was also an exciting episode and one in which the settlers had again shown their prowess. In view of the commercial interests which were at stake it was an important service to Great Britain and to all merchants who traded in those waters, and the victory must have appreciably increased the self-confidence of the colonists. Governor Johnson, acting very likely under the advice of Lord Carteret, was more outspoken in support of the proprietors than had been any of his predecessors since the days of his father. In his first speech to the assembly he reproved them sharply for their disrespectful behavior in sending remonstrances to the crown without previously consulting the proprietors or seeking their

[1] S. C. Statutes, III, 3.
[2] N. C. Col. Recs., II, 280; Rivers, Hist. Sketches of S. C., 464.

mediation. The lord palatine could personally have better acted on their behalf. In proof of the good will of the proprietors toward the colonists he called attention to "their donation to the public of all the arrears that are due to them, whether from lands sold or for rent, and all growing rents that shall come due to the first of May 1718, the charges of the civil government only deducted." This was a fair proposition on their part and was about the only contribution which it was in their power to make toward relieving the burdens of the colonists. But on the other hand the paper currency in which their rents and dues must hereafter be paid had greatly depreciated, and to protect themselves as creditors they required that the former selling price of £3 per hundred acres for their land should henceforth be increased to £12 to allow for the depreciation in the paper medium in which payments must thereafter be made. The governor also desired that a rent roll should be prepared. Toward these proposals the assembly, without going seriously into their merits, expressed its impatient opposition, rejecting with contempt the idea that the substitution of £12 for £3 constituted a donation.

The governor and the assembly also had a sharp encounter over the appointment of the powder receiver. Under earlier acts the appointment of this official, like that of the receiver general and controller of duties, had been taken over by the assembly [1]; but Johnson now attempted to recover this for the proprietors. Appointments to the office were made by both himself and the assembly, and Johnson ordered that the keys of the magazine should be kept by his appointee, as he was the head of the military and granted commissions. The house refused to proceed with business if this order was executed, but their threats to appeal to the public only induced the governor to consent that both appointments should stand, his appointee keeping the magazine and giving receipts to the other for all the powder which was delivered into his keeping. To this the assembly refused to agree, and immediately posted a public notice commanding all who were liable to the payment of powder duty to discharge their obligation to Colonel Michael Brewton, who, in accordance with an act of 1707, had been appointed powder receiver by the house, and to no

[1] Osgood, *op cit.* II, 230.

one else.[1] To this for the time being the governor had to yield.

These pointed differences, however, did not wholly prevent legislation; but among the laws passed was a revenue act, certain clauses of which were bound to be rejected by the home government. By these it was provided that negroes and all liquors, goods and merchandise which were imported in any vessel which belonged to the inhabitants of the province should come in free, and that those which were imported in vessels built in South Carolina but whose owners lived outside should be liable to only half-duties, and that goods imported in vessels built out of the province but owned by inhabitants of it should be liable to three-quarters duties. These provisions all contained discrimination against British trade and British-owned vessels, which brought from the privy council an order to the proprietors to repeal the act. This they did, but in addition the proprietors repealed the act of 1707 which declared the right of the commons house to name the public receiver, powder receiver and other officials to whom salaries were granted out of the public treasury. The recent election law and the act opening the Yemassee lands for settlement they also repealed; and the Indian trade act of the previous session, the latter on the ground that it granted a monopoly of that trade to a company, it being alleged that a Virginia act had recently been disallowed by the crown because it contained a similar offensive provision.[2] The order for the repeal of these acts was dated in July, 1718. In the following March the assembly met again, this time under the inspiriting influence of the victory over the pirates. Appropriations were made for paying the cost of the expeditions against the pirates and the other debts of the province, for reducing a part of the currency and for the support of the government.[3] Evidence that good feeling between the assembly and the governor was apparently restored was also afforded by the passage of an act empowering the receiver general of the proprietors or his deputies to go into every parish and there procure a sworn statement from all land-

[1] Rivers, Sketches, *etc.* 282, 283; McCrady, *op. cit.* 582.
[2] S. C. Statutes III, 30; Colls. of S. C. Hist. Soc. II, 233, 235.
[3] S. C. Stats. III, 56–84.

holders of the amount of land they had received, the conditions under which they held it and the time when they last paid their quit rent. Provision was also made for the collection of arrears of rent in money or merchandise and for the use of such surplus as should remain after payment of the salaries which were due from the proprietors toward the building of a state house and prison. In the preamble to this act the resolve of the assembly was expressed to see that justice was done the proprietors in the matter of their land and rents. This law was passed just before the arrival of the order from the proprietors for the repeal of the measures above referred to. It was accompanied by an order to the governor to dissolve the assembly and hold the election of a new one in accordance with the regulations of the earlier statutes.[1]

This action on the part of the proprietors had been encouraged by Chief Justice Trott and his brother-in-law, the receiver general. For some time now these two men had run the affairs of the province, constituting with their friends one of the narrowest and most oppressive official cliques which ever existed in any American colony. Trott was a lawyer and official of great shrewdness and experience resulting from a long career in the Bahamas and South Carolina. Though he at first figured among the planter opposition in South Carolina, after the arrival of Sir Nathaniel Johnson as governor, Trott cast in his lot with the Tories and high churchmen. He cooperated in the reactionary measures of the reign of Anne and in conjunction with Lord Carteret maintained that attitude to the last. He was a firm believer in witchcraft and was probably the last American judge to enforce such belief in a charge from the bench. He did a valuable service by revising and ultimately publishing the laws of South Carolina, but in general he was a thoroughly self-seeking and unprincipled man, one of the large class in the colonies who did not scruple to use high office, even in the

[1] Another act of the proprietors, of more importance at this time, but one which found a place among the complaints, was the increase of the members of the council from eight to ten. This was the result of the abandonment of the old system of filling the council by deputies of the proprietors and of a desire to conform to the practice in other colonies. N. C. Col. Recs. II, 307. Carroll, Hist. Colls. II, 158, 169.

judiciary, to further his personal and political ambitions. Having risen from the office of attorney general to that of chief justice, Trott during a visit to England in 1713 and 1714 gained such an ascendency over the proprietors that they made him a member of the council with the special power that without his presence there could be no quorum of that body. At the same time he received several other special rewards and dignities, and thenceforward carried on a regular correspondence with Shelton, the secretary of the board of proprietors. Though at a later time the proprietors withdrew from Trott the veto power which they had given him in the council, he retained his seat there, being by virtue of that a member of the court of chancery and was in addition made judge of admiralty. By this accumulation of offices Trott monopolized the administration of justice in the province and there was no way of escape from his rulings.

Rhett was a man of the military and purely official type. As receiver general, active member of the assembly and at times its speaker, and as commander of the forces of the province against the pirates, he also exercised great influence. Whenever an election was held this was especially evident, he and the chief justice marshalling the voters who came to the polls at Charlestown and returning a large proportion, if not a majority, of the members. They protested by letters to England against the laws which were passed in 1716 and helped to secure their repeal.[1] For years these two men dominated the politics of South Carolina and often threw the governors into the shade. As Shelton, with whom they regularly corresponded, did most of the business of the proprietors and his sole decision often stood for an act of that board, the circuit was effectively completed and proprietary government in that province was reduced to its simplest terms. It was against this machine and its narrow and arbitrary policy that the colonists now revolted and handed South Carolina over to the crown.

Just before the arrival of orders for the repeal of the acts of the previous year, thirty-one articles of complaint against Trott had been submitted to the assembly.[2] They charged

[1] Colls of S. C. Hist. Soc. II, 255.

[2] Yonge in Carroll, II, 151 *et seq.*; Hewatt in Carroll, I, 214 *et seq.*

him with partiality on the bench, with acting as counsel in cases which were pending before him as judge, with taking exorbitant fees, unduly prolonging causes and monopolizing the administration of justice. As Trott refused to recognize the right of the assembly to take action in this matter, it asked the governor and council to join them in a representation to the proprietors that they would remove him from his judicial offices. To this Johnson and a majority of the council agreed. But before the appeal was sent news came of the disallowance of the acts and the order for a new election. The assembly, as was done in other proprietary provinces, now denied the right of the proprietors to veto acts which had been approved by both houses and the governor. At a conference between the houses, Trott in a speech defended the right which the proprietors had just exercised. Their action was, however, ignored by the governor and assembly to the extent that a new election was not ordered, and Francis Yonge, a member of the council, was sent to England as agent to explain the situation fully to the proprietors.

This errand Yonge performed in London in the late spring and summer of 1719, though during the absence of Lord Carteret, who was then on an embassy to Sweden.[1] After long delay he obtained a conference with a part of the proprietary board, but was unable to induce them to depart in any way from their traditional attitude. They approved of Trott and insisted upon their rights in every point. They criticised Yonge, who was a deputy of one of the proprietors, for undertaking the agency. They reproved the governor for not literally obeying their instruction to dissolve the assembly and hold a new election, though by so doing a considerable amount of revenue would have been sacrificed and a revolt threatened. The repeal of the acts they ordered him at once to publish. They also sent over a commission for a new council of twelve members,[2] from whom Skene, Broughton and Kinloch, former members of the council who had sided with the opposition, were dropped. Trott was among the

[1] Yonge in Carroll, II, 153 *et seq.*; McCrady, 635 *et seq.*

[2] The council had previously consisted of eight members, all originally being deputies of the proprietors.

councillors continued in office and the board was filled with men who were understood to be supporters of the proprietors. Orders were also issued that no more land should be granted, but that fifteen baronies should be laid out as near as possible to Port Royal for the use of the proprietors,[1] thus effectually shutting out several hundred immigrants from the north of Ireland who had come to settle on the Yemassee lands. These orders, when they reached Charlestown, Governor Johnson considered that he had no alternative but to obey. The new councillors were sworn in and, sharing the responsibility with them as advisers, he proclaimed the repeal of the acts, dissolved the assembly and ordered a new election to be held at Charlestown. The issue was now squarely drawn.

As the formation of the Quadruple Alliance by Cardinal Alberoni for the purpose of overthrowing the treaty of Utrecht had again brought Great Britain into hostile relations with Spain, an expedition against South Carolina was reported to be preparing at Havana. Some months previously the governor had written to the board of trade on the need of a station ship at Charlestown[2] and arrangements had been made for sending one but it had not been actually despatched. On learning of the danger, Johnson called a conference of such of the council and newly elected members of the assembly as could be gotten together and proposed a voluntary subscription for the repair of the fortifications. But falling into a dispute with Trott over the question whether or not revenue could be collected under one of the acts which had been repealed, but the repeal of which had not been recognized by the assembly, the conference broke up.

Johnson now turned to the military and commanded the field officers to review their regiments and order a rendezvous against the approach of the Spaniards. This afforded the opportunity which was desired. Articles of association were prepared which were signed by the militia almost to a man,[3] Alexander Skene, who had been excluded from the council and who had been secretary of Barbadoes, acting as leader in this movement. It took the form of a resolve to throw off

[1] Yonge in Carroll, II, 159.
[2] S. C. Hist. Colls, II, 258.
[3] Yonge in Carroll, II, 164

entirely the authority of the proprietors and declare South Carolina a royal province, November 28, 1719. As Johnson had not incurred special dislike, he was asked to continue in office, but to " hold the Reins of Government for the King till his Majesty's Pleasure be known." Johnson received this message at his plantation and came at once to town and consulted the council. It was decided to postpone action until the new assembly should meet.

Meantime the leaders of the uprising obtained signatures to their association from nearly all the people of the province. When the session opened, December 10, the governor proceeded as usual with his part in the organization, but through the lips of Arthur Middleton, who had been returned as elected, the assembly informed Johnson that they owned him as governor because he had been approved by the king, but the new council, because of its large membership, they did not recognize as legal and would not act with it. They had also resolved that the acts which had been repealed were still in force and therefore that the recent election was void and they no assembly. The proprietors, they continued, by such proceedings had unhinged the frame of government and forfeited their right to it. They therefore as a convention delegated by the people, to prevent the ruin and loss of the province, offered the governorship to Johnson until the crown could be consulted. After receiving from the council notice that, in view of the general defection, mild measures ending in a possible dissolution were the only ones possible, Johnson made to the assembly or convention a long speech.[1] In this he required an explicit statement from them, whether they renounced the authority of the proprietors *in toto* or only that of the council as at present organized. If they chose the former alternative, he warned them of the seriousness of overthrowing a charter by other than regular judicial process and the danger to their land titles which might be involved therein. In their reply they adhered to the former alternative, but with language so mild and with such expressions of confidence in him that Johnson thought it possible to solve the difficulty by a dissolution. But when he tried that his proclamation was torn from the marshal's hands and the insurgents organ-

[1] Yonge in Carroll, II, 170 *et seq.*

ized themselves as a convention and ordered all officials to obey them. On December 21, in the presence of the militia drawn up in the market place, Colonel James Moore was proclaimed governor in the name of the king. Johnson on that day exerted himself to the utmost to prevent this being done, but he found no support and was obliged to retire to his plantation and allow the revolt to take its course. A council of twelve, after the royal model, was organized and Sir Hovenden Walker, now a Carolinian, was made president.

The next move of the convention was to vote itself an assembly and as such to appoint a secretary, provost marshal and other officers. Trott was removed and a new chief justice appointed. Under an order exempting those officers who had to do with the property and revenue of the proprietors Rhett escaped removal. A declaration of what they had done and the reasons therefor was published and Colonel John Barnwell was sent as agent to England to lay their case before the crown and ask to be taken under its protection.[1] Johnson also sent to the proprietors and the board of trade a careful account of his own course of action and of the reasons why he felt bound to stand by the proprietary cause. As he had not been guilty of maladministration he hoped that the king, if he took control of the province, would continue him in his office. Trott, who was now leaving for England, proposed that if Johnson would contribute to his expenses he would give the proprietors so favorable an account of his conduct that they would continue him in his office. But this offer was curtly declined and Trott from that time was Johnson's enemy. Rhett also accepted from the revolutionary government the office of overseer of repairs and fortifications in Charlestown. He was also receiver general for the proprietors and comptroller of the king's customs. In this latter capacity he rejected the proposal of Johnson to refuse clearance to all vessels until they paid duty to him as public receiver, thus keeping fees out of the hands of the officials of the Convention. By this act Rhett also veered away from the former governor and trimmed his sails for continuance in office under the crown. Under Rhett's superintendence the work of repairing the fortifications at Charlestown was very

[1] McCrady, 656.

carelessly done, though at heavy cost. But fortunately the expedition of the Spaniards ended disastrously at the Bahamas and did not reach the Carolina coast. After it failed the Flamborough, man-of-war, took up its station at Charlestown and the Phoenix halted in the harbor after a cruise. As the commanders of both these vessels declared in favor of Johnson's claims to be the legal governor, he tried once more to regain his authority by a threat to bombard the town. But the people remained unmoved and the threat was never carried into execution.

Though these proceedings were revolutionary and in their general course corresponded rather closely with the Revolution of 1689 in England, they were viewed with decided approval by the British government, and especially by the board of trade, the more active members of which had been working toward such a result since the days of Edward Randolph. The enthusiasm with which the people of South Carolina now welcomed royal government appears as an effective and dramatic close to the long campaign against the proprietors which had begun with the attack on Massachusetts soon after the Restoration. For three decades and more to come policy in this direction ceased to be aggressive, until it was resumed as part of the far broader movement that led to the general colonial revolt. And yet the results which had thus far been achieved at Charlestown were only provisional. They must be ratified in England, and even then, unless further steps were taken, they would only bring the governmental powers of the proprietors to an end in the province. Their right to the land would continue unimpaired. The result, in other words, would be similar to that reached in Maryland and New Jersey. Beyond that point, indeed, for a decade after the uprising the settlement with the Carolina proprietors did not advance.

At the time when matters came to a crisis disputes concerning titles to the original shares of the earl of Clarendon and Sir William Berkeley were unsettled and several years were to pass before they reached a final adjudication in the Chancery or House of Lords.[1] These were purely questions of property, involving purchase, sale or inheritances arising

[1] McCrady, *op. cit.* 673 *et seq.*, 714.

between parties in England and subject to the jurisdiction of its courts the same as if the land involved had been situated in the realm. The questions were of a character similar to those which at the same time were agitating the Penn family. Until they were settled it was impossible to arrange a transfer of title to the land of the province to the crown, and they were not settled until 1725. In the suit over the Clarendon share the English relatives of Chief Justice Trott were closely interested. Occasionally during the interval the proprietors tried to assert powers of government by the appointment of officials for the province, but these were not recognized and no progress in that direction was made.

As the revolt in South Carolina occurred just at the time of the speculative excitement in England known as the South Sea bubble, it was quite natural that some of the proprietors should form the project of a company to which as an investment they hoped to sell the province for a good round price.[1] This, of course, never came to anything except to increase the irritation of the colonists toward proprietors who had so obviously ventured to treat them as an object of sale and speculation. In the winter of 1719/20 Barnwell joined the other two agents in London, bringing with him authentic news of what had happened at Charlestown, and a petition from the convention or assembly there that South Carolina might be made a royal province.[2]

In justification of this they presented a list of ten grievances against the proprietors. These covered the entire record of neglect and misgovernment on the part of the proprietors from the reactionary church legislation of 1704 through the neglect of defence against Indians, Spaniards and pirates during the succeeding years, the misdeeds of Trott, the repeal of the recent acts and the exclusion of settlers from the lands just won from the Indians in order that they might be appropriated to the use of the proprietors.

At the time when this address was presented the king was absent on the continent, and the lords justices expressed the hasty conclusion that the proprietors had forfeited their

[1] N. C. Col. Recs,, II, 384. McCrady, *op. cit.* 669.

[2] C. O. 5/382, Petition of council and assembly to king, Feb. 3, 1719/20.

charter. The attorney general was therefore ordered to procure a writ of *scire facias* against them. But this plan was not pursued, very possibly because of the difficulty, under the very general terms of the charter, of proving such misgovernment as would justify forfeiture by judicial process. Of general neglect the proprietors had long been guilty, and they had neglected the northern part of the province much more than the southern. But the people of North Carolina expressed no dissatisfaction and its council sent to them a loyal address and refused to recognize Moore as their governor.[1] The situation was really one which called for political adjustment, and it was decided to wait until the conflicting claims among the proprietors had been settled and then to negotiate a contract with them for the surrender of their territorial rights, the whole to be confirmed and legalized by an act of parliament.

But the crown proceeded immediately to the organizing of royal government in the province, though from the nature of the case it must remain in some sense provisional until the territorial relations could be adjusted in the way just indicated. The veteran Sir Francis Nicholson was selected as the first royal governor, a choice which illustrated the power of routine rather than an intelligent desire to further the interests of South Carolina. His commission was naturally modelled after that of the late Governor Copley, of Maryland, while his instructions conformed in all general respects with those of other royal governors. He arrived in the province, accompanied by Barnwell, in May 1721. Royal government was then instituted in accordance with the usual forms. Johnson, the ex-governor, ceased all efforts to exercise authority in the name of the proprietors and joined with the people and legislature in a full recognition of the new government.[2] The new council, twelve in number, included Alexander Skene, Ralph Izard, William Bull, Thomas Smith, Joseph Morton and Francis Yonge. All proprietary officials were required to bring in their commissions for perusal, while the councillors were asked to present a list of such as were fit to be further employed. A large number of new appointments were soon made, among these being James Smith as

[1] N. C. Col. Recs., II, 374, 375, 382. [2] C. O. 3/425, Min. of Ex.C.

judge of admiralty, Benjamin Whitaker as attorney general, Charles Hart as secretary. The council voted that Trott ought not to be continued in the position of chief justice and Francis Yonge seems to have been named for that place, though very soon after he was sent with John Lloyd as agent to England. A complete list of militia officers and local magistrates for the counties was also appointed. James Moore was chosen speaker of the assembly, while Moore and Robert Johnson were associated as lieutenant generals in command of the militia. A new receiver and treasurer of the province was appointed in the place of Rhett but he held his office in the customs until his death, early in 1723,[1] though grave charges were made against him of being concerned with Captain Hildersley, of the Flamborough, in trade with the Spaniards in St. Augustine.[2]

Before Nicholson's appointment the attention of the home government had been repeatedly called to the importance of establishing an armed post on the Altamaha river. When, in 1717, Sir Robert Montgomery applied for a grant of the territory between Savannah and Altamaha rivers under the name of the Margravate of Azilia, one of the strong arguments used in support of the project was that it would be a barrier against the Spanish and Indians. Attorney General Northey suggested at that time that the Carolina proprietors surrender their rights of government over this region, so that it might be erected into a royal province.[3] This proposal the proprietors did not accept and the plan was abandoned until Oglethorpe revived it in a permanent form with the founding of Georgia. Boone and Barnwell, in their reports to the board of trade, insisted strongly on this as an important part of a comprehensive plan of defence against the Spaniards and French. As the result of their representations and of its own knowledge of the needs of the southern frontiers, the board made an elaborate report to the king on this subject.[4] It insisted that an independent company should be sent over, with sufficient ordnance supplies, to serve as a garrison and that several hundred acres near by the post should be laid

[1] McCrady, S. C. under Royal Govt., 56.
[2] S. C. Entry Bk. C. O. 15/400.
[3] Colls. of S. C. Hist. Soc. II, 232, 233, 234, 256.
[4] S. C. Entry Bk. C. C. 5/400, Sept. 23, 1720.

out as a town, so that abundant food supplies might be at hand and a permanent establishment insured. Much correspondence on this subject passed between Barnwell, Nicholson and the various offices in London, while the governor's instructions were preparing and afterwards.[1] The advice of the board of trade was followed in all essential particulars. The company was sent and its commander was ordered carefully to examine the adjacent country and report to Nicholson whether in his judgment the post should be located on St. Simon's Island or on the mainland. Nicholson, on his arrival, informed the council of the king's design and they recommended Barnwell as the person best fitted to have charge of it. At the request of the governor and council he presented a memorial on the subject, and it was then ordered that the building of the fort be left to him, and such a commission and instructions as he approved were drawn and duly signed. A sloop was hired for his use and the lieutenant of the independent company was ordered to deliver ordnance stores to him, as also were the powder receiver and commander of the forts at Charlestown. A site near the mouth of the Altamaha was selected for the post and when the works were completed they were named Fort King George. Thus a work of defence was begun on the extreme southern frontier and it was intended to be more of a fort and town and less of a trading post than Oswego, which was founded at about the same time on Lake Ontario. In both instances the forward step was the direct result of the intervention of the crown or of the activity of its appointees.

In connection with the building and maintenance of Fort King George, however, the usual difficulties had to be experienced and in part overcome. The independent company which came over with Nicholson consisted of 94 men and it was kept for a time in barracks at Port Royal. The engineer who, it had been promised, should accompany them, did not arrive until the late fall of 1721.[2] The heat and moisture of

[1] C. O. 5/358.

[2] This was Capt. John Barker; Upper House J. Feb. 9, 1721/2, *et seq.* The journals of the two houses show that this man had dealings with them in reference to the fort, the opening of better communication by water with it and the disposition of the independent company. Much business was done during these years respecting all these matters for the full tracing of which my space is quite inadequate.

the climate was a perpetual menace to health. As funds for the enterprise had to be furnished by the assembly the details of its management were presented to both houses by Barnwell and the governor, and they were considered in connection with the general system of defence of the province. At the close of the proprietary period this consisted of the defences of Charlestown, a fort on the Santee, one at Port Royal, Fort Moore at Savannah Town just below the modern Augusta, Georgia, and Congaree Fort near the site of the present city of Columbia.[1] The assembly made the usual objections to paying the cost of building Fort King George and were inclined to make an appropriation only if the governor would assure them that the king would reimburse the province. Nicholson replied that the extra charge would not be great and he would present their desires in reference to the matter to the crown. The appropriation was made, as requested,[2] but during the discussions the commons house expressed its mind freely as to the location of the fort and the proposed removal of certain people from Port Royal to settle in its neighborhood. Nicholson also had to yield to their demand that the soldiers of the independent company should be put promptly into service at Port Royal and Fort Moore. The lower house took the chief part in designating commissaries for these posts and fixing their salaries and in arrangements for transferring troops from one to another. As the province had long been under only nominal control from England, it was natural that the legislature should practically determine the number of the garrisons, should fix salaries and prescribe or greatly influence all appointments in the militia. The assembly also insisted that the cost of provisioning the independent company should not be in excess of that of the province militia and that a contract should be made for this purpose at accepted rates. Barnwell was voted a liberal allowance for his services previous to the arrival of the engineer. In all these matters the lower house was most active and influential.[3]

[1] Smith, South Carolina as a Royal Prov., 192, 208; C. O. 5/425, U. H. Journal, 1721.

[2] In all about £11000 sterling was expended by the province on Fort King George. U. H. Sess. of May 1722.

[3] Upper and Lower House Journals, 1720–21.

The Spanish authorities at St. Augustine at once complained to their home government of the building of the fort on the Altamaha as a bold encroachment on what, in the absence of settled boundaries, they regarded as their own territory. The Spanish minister in London promptly reported the act to the English government as a grievance.[1] This was also accompanied by complaints of Indian outrages in Florida. The board of trade was called upon for a report on the boundary question thus raised and in reply defended the claim of the English as expressed in the Carolina charters of 1663 and 1665, asserting that this had been adequately supported by trade with the Indians in that region and now by settlement, while the Spaniards had no post north of St. Augustine, one hundred miles to the south. Orders were sent to the two governors, of Florida and South Carolina respectively, to meet and reach an amicable agreement as to the boundary. Two envoys were sent from St. Augustine to Charlestown in 1725. Arthur Middleton was then in charge of the government, and the discussion between him and his council on the one side and the Spaniards on the other resulted in nothing whatever affecting the boundary, most of the time apparently being spent in discussing the treatment of fugitive debtors, felons and slaves. But a few months later, that is, early in 1726, the fort on the Altamaha was burned. Capt. Edward Massey was sent from England to take command there and the fort was carelessly rebuilt at the expense of South Carolina. According to the statement of Nicholson, the garrison was too lazy to cultivate their gardens or even to fetch pure water. But Massey insisted, after he had been there for a time, that the post was too remote, its location too unhealthy and the garrison too weak and too much exposed to diseases which arose from the eating of salt provisions to justify its continuance. He said that the province denied quarters for recruits and the common necessities of camp life; that there was no guard house, no oven for baking bread or fire-place where the men could boil their meat; they had cannon but no ball, rammers or sponge. These representations he made in 1727 in a letter to Henry

[1] C. O. 5/359. S. C. Orig. Papers, Sept., 1721, May, 1723; C. O. 5/400, S. C. Entry Bk. Dec., 1722; McCrady, *op. cit.* 74 *et seq.*

Pelham, and on the strength of these representations and of the unwillingness of the province to do more, the post was abandoned and the garrison withdrawn to Port Royal. The region of the Altamaha then remained unoccupied until the founding of Georgia, a few years later, and till removed to that colony the independent company was kept at Port Royal.

As was always the case, Indian relations were closely involved with plans for defence in South Carolina. By an act of 1716, passed under the influence of the Yemassee war, the board of Indian commissioners of the province had been incorporated [1] and a complete monopoly of the trade conferred upon them, the net profits of which were to go into the public treasury. Because of complaints on the part of the traders and others, the proprietors in 1718 disallowed this act. But in March of the following year another act was passed reestablishing the incorporated board of commissioners, though with its monopolistic powers slightly reduced.[2] Three commissioners were named in this act and, subject to responsibility to the assembly, they were given full authority over the employment of agents, the licensing of traders, sales of furs and skins bought from the natives and of Indian goods procured from England and the keeping of accounts. Trade was to be carried on at three factories only, Fort Moore, Congaree Fort and at Apalachicola Old Town on the Savannah river, the last named place being substituted for Winyaw in the previous act.[3] Private traders might, though with difficulty, procure annual licenses from this board on paying a fee and giving bonds in £500 each to deal justly with the Indians and with their follow traders and obey all the instructions which were given them. All traders who were not licensed might be ordered away by the commissioners, and those who were licensed were taxed ten per cent on their Indian purchases and were forbidden to trade within twenty miles of a garrison.

This system was continued until 1721, when the corporate powers were taken from the commissioners and much less rigid restrictions were imposed upon Indian trade.[4] The new

[1] Statutes, II, 677–680; Smith, S. C. as a Royal Prov., 214 *et seq.*; Osgood, *op. cit.* II, 409, 417–419.

[2] Stats. III, 86–96.

[3] Winyaw was in the north.

[4] Stats. III, 141–146.

appointees were William Bull, George Chicken, who distinguished himself in the Yemassee war, and John Herbert. By this act trade with certain small bodies of Indians who lived adjacent to the white settlements was thrown open, but annual licenses were required for traffic with all remoter and comparatively independent tribes. The conditions under which these were granted were made somewhat easier, though an annual journey to Charlestown on the part of those who desired licenses was required and a considerable license fee was collected.[1] The close connection between Indian policy and defence was also illustrated by the requirement that the commissioners should twice a year visit all the forts and garrisons in the province, including that on the Altamaha, and inspect their condition and that of their soldiers and their supplies; they might order such changes and improvements there as they saw fit and the officers must obey these requirements.

Indian traders from Virginia who had to pass into or across the remoter parts of South Carolina to reach the Creeks and Cherokees, and who, though not expressly mentioned, were included under the terms of this act, complained of the great inconvenience of the annual journeys of hundreds of miles to Charlestown which they would be compelled to make to procure licenses. The difficulties which were involved in this were so great that they might amount to a total prohibition of an old established trade. This, as well as earlier legislation of South Carolina, indicated a purpose to exclude Virginians entirely from Indian trade within her borders, and this policy had long been the occasion of disputes and complaints. The Virginians now presented their grievance to the home government through John Carter, who was then the agent of that province in England. Yonge, the Carolina agent, made no reply to this. The board of trade referred the question to their counsel, Richard West, who submitted a careful report, in October 1722.[2] In harmony

[1] From time to time Indian conferences were also held at Charlestown, and to these there are many references in the journals of the two houses. Cherokees, Creeks and others came thither and met the governor and members of the council. For the south in this relation Charlestown corresponded in a way to Albany for the north, but it was never so important a centre for Indian conferences as was Albany. See, *e. g.*, C. O. 5/359, S. C. Original P., Mar. 2, 1723.

[2] Chalmers, Colonial Opinions, 592.

with an opinion which had been expressed by the board in 1709, he condemned the requirements of the South Carolina law as arbitrary and inconsistent with intercolonial comity. Notwithstanding this favorable report, it does not appear that the act was repealed. In fact, the main features of it were continued for years to come. But it was thought that money might be saved by imposing upon the governor and council the duties, including those of inspecting the forts and garrisons, which had been entrusted to a special board of commissioners, and that change was made by an act of 1722.[1] But it was soon found that this, in addition to their other duties, imposed too heavy a burden on the governor and council, and in 1723 the duties in question were bestowed on a sole commissioner, James Moore being named for that office. Moore died a few days after his appointment and George Chicken was the first appointee really to serve under this law. With the exception of a few months in 1751–2, this system was continued in force by South Carolina until, in 1756, the crown took the administration of Indian affairs out of the hands of the individual colonies and organized them under two commissioners, South Carolina constituting a part of the southern district.[2]

During Nicholson's administration the only subject which aroused serious controversy was that of the issue of bills of credit and this question, when once raised, continued uppermost until after the complete establishment of royal government and the arrival of Robert Johnson as governor. Reference has elsewhere been made to the origin of such issues in South Carolina and to the failure of its government to redeem them as provided in the acts of issue until depreciation had advanced to considerable length. The excuse for this — and it carried considerable weight — was the frightful losses and sufferings caused by the Yemassee war and the need of protecting the colony by means of forts and other defences against the Spanish and French. These certainly imposed a heavy burden upon its small population and limited resources. In common with all the other colonies it also suffered from a lack of specie and also from the difficulty of

[1] Stats. III, 184.
[2] Smith, *op. cit.*, 218.

keeping such supplies of coin as did come in the course of trade. It was the planter element, constituting the great majority of the members of the lower house, which demanded ever increasing issues of paper and the indefinite postponement of the dates of their redemption. On the other side stood the merchants and importers of Charlestown, who filled most of the seats in the council and who, like the British merchants with whom they had continuous dealings, suffered from the fluctuations in exchange caused by excessive issues of paper and its consequent depreciation. As creditors they were ever exposed under such a régime to the danger or even the certainty of loss. The conflict between the two houses over this question was essentially one between the debtors and creditors in the province, and the creditors stood with the crown officials in opposition to the demand for ever increasing issues of paper. Nicholson occupied to such an extent a neutral position between the two that he did not come to an open breach with the lower house.

In 1712 a so-called bank act had been passed which provided for the issue of £52,000 in bills of credit, £16,000 of which were to go toward the redemption of old bills, £4,000 for contingencies and the remaining £32,000 to be loaned at 12½% interest per annum for twelve years.[1] One-twelfth of these loans, together with the interest must be promptly paid every years, and the security for the payments was mortgages on land and negroes to double the amounts borrowed. At the end of the period, if all worked well, the government would have received back the total original issue with a profit. The bills were made compulsory legal tender for all debts. This was one of the typical land bank schemes which were so favored among advocates of paper money in the eighteenth century.

But the plan did not work. The issues of 1712 so depreciated the value of the currency that by 1715 its ratio to sterling was two to one. Then came the Yemassee war which stopped payments on the emission of 1712 and occasioned two other issues aggregating £50,000. Funds intended for the

[1] Smith, *op. cit.*, 232 *et seq.* Bull's Account of the Rise of Credit and Progress of Bills of Credit in S. C. 1740, C. O. 5/365; printed in S. C. Stats. IX, 766–780, and in Sound Currency, V, No. 4; Journal of the two houses.

redemption of these bills were diverted to other purposes, but no more issues were made until 1720, when Moore, the revolutionary governor, approved an emission of £34,000. These were known as rice bills, for they were to be redeemed by taxes payable in rice at 30s. per hundred. Depreciation had now advanced to such an extreme that the rate of exchange between sterling and paper was five to one.

But in 1722 and 1723 Nicholson assented to two acts which were still further to increase inflation.[1] The former of these provided for the levy of a direct tax, but it also contained a clause for the reissue of £15,000 in rice bills which should have been destroyed. The latter was intended in part to further a new and fresh issue to take the place of the old and worn bills which were then in circulation under several previous issues. For the former purpose £40,000 were provided, and for the latter £80,000, the total amount in bills now ordered to be printed being £120,000. The provision made for the redemption of the £40,000 was not to become operative until 1738 and was then to continue at the rate of £5,000 per annum until 1745. The entire issue was made full legal tender.

Over the latter of these measures the issue was finally drawn between the supporters and the opponents of the policy. In an elaborate report the committee of ways and means of the lower house claimed that there was much less proclamation money per head in South Carolina than there was sterling per capita in England,[2] which very likely was true. They referred to the certain destruction of many bills during the Indian war and told how, with the revival of trade after the war, there was a stringency and many actions for debt, usurers exacting 25% and 30% from those who could not procure bills even in exchange for the most valuable commodities. Because of its scarcity, silver could be procured either not at all or only at very high prices, and people were being forced to leave the province. What little silver they had was being carried off by traders from the northern colonies in exchange for their commodities. The prices of clothing and other necessities were so high that the soldiers in the

[1] Stats. III, 149, 188 *et seq.*
[2] L. H. Journal, Nov. and Dec. 1722.

frontier garrisons were forced to pledge all their wages and more long before they were paid, and this furnished them a strong temptation to desert and leave the frontier unprotected in a time of increasing danger. The charges of the government during the ensuing year would amount to over £43,000, while the revenue from duties not expressly appropriated would be only £6800, leaving a balance to be covered by taxes of nearly £37,000. Recent losses from winds and floods had rendered the inhabitants incapable of raising this by taxation, and the issue of more bills of credit was their only resource. It was after a full consideration of this report that the second of the above mentioned acts was passed.

In the previous session one Francis Goddard had been compelled to apologize for a violent attack he had made upon the assembly.[1] At the same time also a committee which had been appointed to consider an Essay on the Nature of the Public Credit, which had been offered to the house, reported that a number of persons ought to be taken into custody for casting reflections on the assembly. In the fall session the attack on the policy of the house was renewed in the form of a memorial from the merchants of Charlestown,[2] reviewing the experience of the province with bills of credit from the beginning. They showed how promises of redemption made in the laws had always been broken and how in the resulting depreciation and rise of the rate of exchange creditors had lost most or all of the sums that were due them. Orders from the proprietors to Governor Johnson and others had proved powerless to check the evil. It was plain that the bills then out had no intrinsic value, and traders had to contract for the produce of the country rather than for money, while London merchants were prevented from trading with the province at all. All who received salaries or fixed incomes were suffering and in general they feared that South Carolina was approaching bankruptcy.

With these arguments a group of creditors, bound by their contracts in Europe, and a community of planters faced each other, the latter unprovided or very poorly furnished with coin, always on the verge of barter, securing temporary credit

[1] Journal for Session of May and June 1722.
[2] L. H. J. Dec. 6, 1722; C. O. 5/358, S. C. Orig. Papers.

at enormous cost, living isolated and exposed from time to time to withering disasters. They were fluctuating between a system of barter and one of money economy and were unable to adapt themselves to either. The British government should have furnished them with an adequate coinage or have encouraged the province to provide them with one, as Massachusetts had done in the previous century. Had this been done, for all the colonies, many a perplexing problem of finance would have been solved and irritation prevented. As it was, the colonists were left in a condition of chaos to flounder about as best they might. As Nicholson evidently felt, and many another governor as well, there was much to be said for the arguments which they urged. The picture which they gave of their difficulties bears the marks of truth, and in the reply which the house made to the memorial of the merchants it denied all design to injure or defraud any one. But injury was inflicted, as the merchants were quite able to show.

The sensitiveness of the house under the charges of bad faith which were made by the merchants was shown by its taking into custody those who had signed the memorial, on the ground that it was false and scandalous, a base reflection on earlier proceedings of the assembly and a high indignity to the present house. The merchants petitioned the governor and council to be heard and the latter resolved that it was a privilege of English subjects that they should be heard, though afterwards they might be returned into custody.[1] This the commons house declared to be a breach of its privileges, it being impossible that they should be released except by the power that committed them. To the governor they insisted upon their right as the sole representative house to consider first all petitions against bills, especially those which concerned money and supplies, and in case the bill in question was passed by the lower house, that then the petitioners might be heard before the governor and council. But further controversy over this episode was prevented by the accused merchants confessing their fault and paying their fees. A conference was then held between the houses, the council claiming that the issue of £30,000 in addition to the amount

[1] U. H. J. Dec. 12, 1722 *et seq.*

which was required to replace the old bills would suffice, but the commons house had its way and the bill became law. The merchants then petitioned in London for repeal of the currency act of 1721 as well as that of 1722. They secured an order to that effect in August, 1723,[1] together with an instruction to Nicholson not to consent to any law for increasing paper credit or altering funds for redeeming bills before royal government was established and to urge the assembly to provide sufficient funds for the speedy redemption of the bills which had since been issued. A sinking fund act[2] was accordingly passed in February, 1723/4, providing for the redemption of the £53,000 which had been issued under the two repealed laws by revenue from customs duties, and as the bills were paid in they should be burned every six months until all had been destroyed.

With the merchants in their attack on bills of credit cooperated Richard Shelton, the secretary of the proprietors. He also at this time opposed before the board of trade an act for the incorporation of Charlestown, stating that it had been secretly passed against the wish of the majority of the inhabitants, was illegal and in various ways undesirable.[3] The agent, Yonge, defended the act against these charges, and Counsellor West in an opinion approved of many of its provisions, though not of the appointment of the mayor and other officers for life. The act, however, was repealed. The complacent attitude of Nicholson toward paper money and his approval of the Charlestown act were now urged by his opponents along with other reasons for his recall. The committee of the privy council heard the complaints of the merchants on this subject, and as Nicholson was advanced in years and now asked for a license to come to England, it was granted, and his activities in the colonies finally terminated in 1725. Until he went, however, and thereafter, the lower house kept up the agitation over the currency, seeking to evade the new sinking fund law and also to secure new issues.[4] In October 1724, the merchants complained to the board of

[1] C. O. 5/259. S. C. Orig. Papers; C. O. 5/400. S. C. Entry Book.

[2] Stats. III, 219.

[3] *Ibid.*, 179. The text of this is not extant.

[4] See the Journals of both houses for the years in question; also C. O. 5/359, Orig. Papers, Aug. 1724 *et seq.*

trade that they were still compelled to take paper and that the duties imposed for the redemption of bills laid a burden on British manufactures. On the other hand, crops were good and trade was on the increase and, therefore, in the opinion of the governor, the grand jury, the petty jury and the council, the merchants in 1725 were not greatly suffering and the amount of paper money was not more than sufficient for the needs of trade.[1]

With the accession of Arthur Middleton, a native of the province, to the lead in affairs as president of the council, the planter element naturally thought that the prospect was good for a continuance of their favorite policy. Their idea was that about £100,000 in currency was needed as a permanent sum in circulation to make exchange and business easy in South Carolina.[2] The event which brought up again the question of more issues was the burning of Fort King George early in 1726. Middleton insisted that the post should not be abandoned and called for an appropriation or rather a loan to the king of £3,000 for rebuilding it.[3] The house replied that the fines and forfeitures would be sufficient till the king's pleasure was known. Middleton replied that these could not be used because the respective rights of the king and proprietors had not yet been determined. After other proposals had failed of approval the assembly urged that the paper money be used which was lying in the treasurer's hands ready to be burned. To this Middleton assented, though, as it was an evasion of the sinking fund, he requested that the grant be made in the form of an ordinance or joint resolution, which was done. But in connection with this act sharp criticisms passed between Middleton and the assembly growing out of the sale of certain offices by the president on which severe comments had been made by Benjamin Whitaker, attorney general and one of its members.[4] These were duly reported to the home government.

[1] C. O. 5/359, Sept., Nov. 1725.

[2] This is stated in a petition of the assembly to the king, May 13, 1625; C. O. 5/383.

[3] Journal of the two houses, Feb., 1725/6, *et seq.*; C. O. 5/428; Smith, *op. cit.*, 244 *et seq.*

[4] Journal of L. H. Feb. 3 and 4, 1725/6; see also Entry Book and Orig. Papers, 1728, C. O. 5/400, C. O. 5/350.

Another plan which was early brought forward by the assembly for the issue of £40,000 additional was rejected by the council on the ground that the existing currency was sufficient, while Middleton excused himself from approving it by citing the instruction which forbade the eldest councillor when administering the government to pass any except the most necessary acts without a special order from the king. Early in 1727 another attempt was made to increase the circulation by an issue of £86,000 in bills, but this the council rejected.[1] Thus affairs drifted on without the planters and farmers being able to attain their object, and after the passage in March, 1727, of the bill for the year the assembly was prorogued until the following October.

Almost immediately meetings began in the country parishes.[2] An association was formed and statements of grievances prepared to be sent to the president and council. In this it was declared that the people were the victims of a clique of lawyers, merchants and rapacious officials at Charlestown who hoarded the money of the province and charged exorbitant prices and fees. The farmers, to get money to pay their debts and taxes; were compelled to sell their estates often at a fourth of their real value. The concentration of courts of justice at Charlestown greatly increased their burdens and the power of the greedy combination against the people. In addition to relief from the steadily contracting currency, a demand was made for the more general trial of cases in county and precinct courts. Thomas Smith, son of Landgrave Smith and a member of the assembly from St. James's, Santee, was one of the leaders, and his arrest by one of the council increased the tumult and finally a body of 200 armed men appeared before the council chamber at Charlestown and delivered their representation to the president. They, however, withdrew without violence and soon a general meeting of the rioters was arranged to be held in July at Dry Savannah, about twenty miles from Charlestown. Landgrave Thomas Smith, a member of the council, now

[1] C. O. 5/429; Journal of L. H. Jan. & Feb., 1726/7.

[2] Smith, *op. cit.*, 246 *et seq.* A representation of the council of S. C. to the king, 1729, C. O. 5/360; also in same vol. letters of Middleton to Eng. in 1727–8. An abstract of this is printed in Colls. and various other material of S. C. Hist. Soc., 300; Journals of the two houses, 1727–1730.

joined the rioters and was evidently planning to seize the presidency, when Middleton had him arrested and called out the militia to prevent the meeting at Dry Savannah and protect the government at Charlestown. The militia of Goose Creek, under Capt. William Dry, now took the lead among the opposition and prepared to seize Alexander Skene by way of reprisal.

As the agitation continued, the assembly was called together on August 1. It at once passed a series of vigorous resolutions to the effect that the right to present grievances jointly or separately and to petition for their redress was at stake, that all commitments and prosecutions for such petitioning were illegal and that whoever asserted the contrary was a betrayer of the rights and liberties of the people. It also denied that it had ever proposed to the council any bills that were disadvantageous to the public or contrary to royal instructions and condemned all statements to the contrary as reflections upon its honor. Petitions and complaints from the various parishes were heard and copies of these resolutions were given to the petitioners to be circulated through the province. Landgrave Smith also presented a memorial praying for a writ of *habeas corpus* to free him from his illegal imprisonment. He stated that some seamen from a man-of-war had aided in his arrest, and complained of the chief justice for refusing to grant him the writ, and asked to be heard before the bar of the house. This request was at once granted. The council was greatly offended that one of their members should thus apply to the house for redress, and Middleton interposed in the name of the "royal prerogative," and commanded that all papers relating to Smith be sent to the council and that the assembly cease its interference in his case. This it did not do, but listened to the argument of his attorney, Nicholas Trott, at their bar to the effect that Smith was rightfully entitled to the writ of *habeas corpus*. Had it not been for threatened hostilities with the Spanish and Indians, the assembly would upon this have been dissolved; but instead the president and council decided to prorogue them for a month.

But attacks of the Yemassees on the southern frontier necessitated the meeting of the house again on August 23.

To equip a body of militia and build necessary forts they proposed to appropriate the duties arising under the sinking fund act and to loan the bills which were in the treasury waiting to be burned. To this the council agreed, though unwillingly, on condition that as soon as possible provision be made by a tax for the repayment of this money and that it be burned. As the Indian troubles occasioned an expedition under Colonel William Palmer which ravaged the scattered Spanish settlements in Florida up to the gates of St. Augustine, the subject of defence occupied for some time much attention in the assembly and outside. The French also were becoming more active among the Creeks and Cherokees, as was evidenced by the building of Fort Alabama some distance up the Mobile river and the presence of their agents among these tribes. This also demanded attention, and Captain Tobias Fitch was sent to counteract French influence among the Creeks and Colonel George Chicken on a similar errand among the Cherokees.

It was the desire of Middleton and the council to keep the attention of the lower house fixed upon these questions of defence, but the crisis offered too favorable a chance for exerting pressure on the subject of the currency, and from this the assembly was not to be diverted. It also appears that planters had been purchasing many negroes, for whom they had run in debt to the merchant inspectors. These debts they were finding it increasingly difficult to pay as the currency began to contract and the rate of exchange to decline under the enforcement of the sinking fund act. Hence the outcry continued. And now Whitaker and the other leaders in the house brought forward the ambitious scheme of fixing by law both the amount of currency which should be in circulation in the province and its rate of exchange with proclamation money. By this means they proposed to check the redemption of outstanding bills and keep the exchange value of the whole body of currency practically where it was at that time, 1728. There was a little more than £100,000 in bills outstanding and that or a little more they conceived to be necessary for the easy transaction of such volume of business as the province then had.[1]

[1] Their best statement of this view is in the long message to the council of March 6, 1727/8, in reply to an equally full statement of the opposing views of the council under date of the 29th of the previous February.

Proclamation money was then about five times as valuable as South Carolina currency; the ratio of exchange between the two was 5 to 1. "It is undeniable," said the committee of the house, "that the value of paper money is not intrinsic as that of silver has become, but depends on the faith of the government that creates it. Now we would support our bills at the rate of £500 of our bills for £100 proclamation money. Since they are thus brought to a standard and their value ascertained, why should it not be declared by a law that invades no man's property but ascertains it, which is indeed easing the people but with the utmost justice by letting every one know what he has to pay?" Certainly this was a able statement in its extreme form of the doctrine that money is the creature of law.

They also contended that the values of the two forms of money in the province were already bound together by law in the provisions under which fees and fines were being paid, an act of 1721 specifying the equivalent rates of these in both currency and proclamation money. What the theorists of the lower house claimed that they were trying to do was to make this universal by extending it to all contracts and payments. They also claimed that such a law would not violate the governor's instruction because it was a subject of very universal importance; and that it would not violate the act of parliament which specified the rates at which proclamation money should circulate, because the object of that was to prevent the overvaluing of money by indirect practices in order to draw it from one colony to another.

But the council held immovably to the opinion that such a law as this would nullify the act relating to proclamation money, that it would violate the governor's instruction and could not be passed without a suspending clause. It reviewed the history of the controversy thus far, dwelling forcibly on the seditious conduct of the opposition throughout the province. They had endeavored by all possible arts to keep the currency afoot despite orders for sinking it. And now, in their frantic attempts to accomplish this, they were proposing by law to settle the course of exchange "which is always governed by trade," "a thing never before attempted in any part of Europe, much less in subordinate governments in America." Carrying further their analysis of the way in which the bill must operate, they showed that the assembly must fix periodically the rate of discount on paper bills and the rates and proportions they should bear to proclamation money, and the courts would be bound to recognize these rates without argument. By this process, if possible, the council held, the rating of coin must be changed as well as that of the bills, and so the act of 6th of Anne would be violated. They enlarged upon the losses and sufferings of creditors which resulted from the depreciation of the currency and dwelt on the purpose of the assembly to keep this condition permanent until debtors could all discharge their obligations in depreciated currency, without regard to the rate of exchange when the debts were incurred.

At intervals during this long controversy the existence of assemblies was terminated by encounters over personal questions. One instance of this kind arose from the revival of the case of Landgrave Smith in May 1728. He had now lain in jail a year, because of the refusal of Allein, the chief justice, to grant the writ of *habeas corpus*. The judge was served by the house with a very strong memorial on his conduct and ordered to attend at the bar. He refused; the house resented this and ordered its messenger to take him into custody. The messenger found Allein at a session of the council and tried to arrest him there, but was turned out of the room by the president. This conduct the house denounced as arbitrary, unprecedented and a violation of its privileges. A dissolution followed, but as nearly all the old members were returned at the next election, it was without result. Early in the following year a dissolution was occasioned by the arrest of the deputy secretary under order of the house because he refused, as an officer of the governor and council, to answer certain of its questions about papers in his custody. Of these later assemblies William Dry, who had previously commanded the insurgent Goose Creek militia, was regularly elected the speaker. At intervals Indian affairs and defence were discussed and some consideration was given to tax bills, but in every case the currency issue blocked legislation, especially that which called for appropriations and expenditures. Middleton held stiffly to his connection with the merchant group at Charlestown and was wholly unable to effect a compromise. By temperament as well as by his close connection with factions in the province he was unfitted for this. His administration was therefore a failure and when Robert Johnson arrived as the first royal governor in the full sense of the term, he found the province in a disturbed and weakened state.

Throughout the decade while these events were occurring the control of the proprietors over the land of the province legally continued. But as they had no distinct land office and no record appears of any resident officials in South Carolina to enforce their rights, Governor Nicholson seems to have freely granted lands. The proprietors complained that he made extravagant grants, but that was denied and decisive proof on the subject is not at hand. Of the fact that the proprietors during these years emphasized the provisional character of royal government in South Carolina there is abundant proof. Nicholson and other officials continued writing to Lord Carteret as palatine, not only about such matters as the building of the fort on the Altamaha, but about strictly local affairs which would not be brought before a minister who was not at the same time a proprietor.[1] Trott and the Rhetts were specially interested, of course, in the restoration of the proprietary régime and used such influence as they still had to bring it about. They repeatedly complained of Nicholson's proceedings as being in utter disregard of proprietary interests. Nicholson had a personal quarrel with the elder Rhett over the appointment of a naval officer and denounced him as a "haughty and insolent fellow" and "cheating scoundrel." Rhett in turn insisted that Nicholson should be turned out and he himself appointed governor. The question of bills of credit also played its part in these complaints, while the dissenters naturally had some criticisms to make of so pronounced an Anglican as Nicholson.

In 1726, after the retirement of Nicholson, the proprietors went so far as to urge the crown to approve of the appointment of Colonel Samuel Horsey, under their commission, as governor of South Carolina. This was opposed by the

[1] S. C. Hist. Colls. I, 230 *et seq.*

council and assembly of the province in a petition to the king that they might remain under royal government. A return to the proprietary régime, they said, would be followed by the loss of the province to England. Francis Yonge, the agent, presented this petition and it was referred to a committee of the council for report. Yonge also kept the authorities in the province informed as to the doings of the proprietors in this connection. They petitioned for the issue of additional instructions to the governor to assist in the collection of their rents and in other ways, and in this they spoke of the governor as "provisional." Shelton, the secretary of the proprietors, also prepared a memorial, containing many arguments to show that the suspension of their authority in 1719 was the work of a minority of the inhabitants, that its consequences were very imperfect and that their power should be restored. This was printed under the title of the "Case of the Lords Proprietors of South Carolina" and circulated among the members of the privy council.[1] These arguments were duly answered by the agent and they were too inconsistent with the interests of the crown, particularly in the case of a border province, to change the natural course of events. In 1729 the question was finally settled in a manner which will be described in the following chapter on the northern part of the original province.

[1] C. O. 5/383, A .W. S. S. C. 1715–1736; papers and letters under date of 1726.

CHAPTER III

TRANSITION TO ROYAL GOVERNMENT IN NORTH CAROLINA

IN earlier volumes of this work the unformed and chaotic conditions which existed in North Carolina have been briefly described. This province in its early days exhibited more of the characteristics of a purely frontier community than did any of the other colonies. Owing to the neglect of the proprietors, its settlers in matters of government were left largely to their own devices. The lack of a port, or of a coast line which offered facilities for direct trade with Europe, confined them to coastwise traffic with colonies to the north and south, and this was carried on mostly by New Englanders. Thrown back on their own meagre resources, the inhabitants made most of the coarse cloth which they wore and lived without the comforts or luxuries of Europe. Their exclusion from the direct trade with Europe proved a serious obstacle to the introduction of negroes and, when taken in connection with the policy which prevailed of restricting the size of land grants, it preserved this colony to a considerable extent from the régime of slavery. European goods were received largely through Virginia and at enhanced prices. Beginning in 1679, Virginia prohibited the importation of tobacco into her territory from Carolina or other localities outside the capes, there to be "laid on shore, sold or shipped."[1] As tobacco was then the chief product which the people of North Carolina raised for export and as they had no port which vessels coming direct from England could enter, this policy gave to the New England skippers the monopoly of their tobacco trade and proved a serious handicap to the province. A prime condition for the advance of North Carolina to social stability and prosperity was the securing of a port through which trade and intercourse could pass to and from Europe, and this she was now to obtain by the settlement of the region about Cape Fear.

[1] Hening, II, 445, III, 243.

The year 1715 may in general be taken as marking a turning point in North Carolina history. The cruel Tuscarora war had then been ended and that involved the destruction or subjugation of all the Indian tribes within the province east of the mountains. Thenceforward, so far as the natives were concerned, conditions were to be similar to what they had long been in the settled parts of Virginia — a few small groups of Indians continued to live submissively on reservations among the whites and the numbers of those steadily declined until the stock disappeared. The soil was thus opened for settlement with little further hindrance from the natives, and population began to extend toward the interior of the province. The northern province also found itself in a position to give some aid to its southern neighbor when she was in the agonies of the great Yemassee war, and by that event the soil was partly cleared for the settlement of Georgia and the middle portions of South Carolina. That also, as we have seen, contributed directly to the revolt which placed South Carolina under royal government and thus severed the last bond of connection which remained between it and the northern half of the original province. This, together with the loss of Georgia on the south and the advance of the settlements on the north, threatened for a time seriously to reduce the territory of South Carolina and made the fixing of her northern boundary a matter of pressing importance. Finally, with the end of Cary's rebellion which occurred at about the date of which we are speaking, formal uprisings in North Carolina ceased. The government was not again openly defied by any appreciable part of the population. Society was still very crude, government was weak, laws were few and poorly executed.

No more striking evidence exists of the primitive conditions of the time than that which shows the extent to which barter was used and the resort to staple products as medium of exchange. By a law of 1715 nineteen commodities were rated and declared to be tender in the payment of public and private dues, and to be operative both in dealings with outsiders and between colonists. In the list were included beef, pork, butter, cheese, pitch, feathers, wheat, leather, a variety of hides and skins, tallow and Indian corn, as well as tobacco.

Though efforts were made to banish this cumbersome device from the domain of taxation and revenue, they were on the whole unsuccessful. Governor Johnston wrote in 1749 that the system had continued to that time with very little change. It occasioned great and continuous loss to the revenue, for as between the different commodities, as well as different qualities of the same commodity, the poorest was always paid.[1] But North Carolina was never again to be so disorganized as it was during Cary's rebellion. More orderly relations were gradually established and with the growth of population, the extension of settlement and the increase of wealth and prosperity which characterized the period that was now beginning the province slowly emerged from its earlier weakness and chaos.

Among the tangible evidences that a period of greater regularity was approaching is the revision of the laws which were issued by the assembly at Little River in 1715.[2] In the spirit of the royal charter the laws of England, so far as they were applicable, including the body of the common law, were declared to be in force in the colony. The colonists also claimed the benefit of certain English statutes which did not mention the dominions, but were of fundamental importance as guaranties of liberty. Special precautions were taken against breaches of the peace and all words and acts in the province which tended in that direction. The parish system with vestries and church wardens was confirmed. The solemn affirmation of the Quaker was recognized as legal in all civil suits, but he was denied the right to give evidence in criminal trials, to serve on juries or to hold office. Following the example of the Fundamental Constitutions, this assembly passed an act for biennial elections and gave the suffrage to freemen of its respective precincts. Sessions were to be held in November of every year. Albemarle was the only region as yet fully organized and its four precincts were empowered to send five members each. The county of Bath, south of Albemarle Sound, was already in existence and the three precincts which were to form part of it, being as yet but sparsely settled, were given a representation of only two

[1] N. C. Recs. IV, 920; XXIII, 54.
[2] *Ibid.*, XXIII, 1-96; Ashe, History of N. C., I, 196, 198.

members each. Thus a distinction was established between the precincts of Albemarle and those further south which was long to continue and later to give rise to an important sectional issue. Bath, however, was created a town by this assembly and an effort was soon made to develop it into a port.

In a number of these laws the granting and settlement of land was regulated. The " great deed " of 1668 was declared to be the basis of the system, though deviations from its provisions were recognized as possible.[1] Every precinct was required to prepare a rent roll, to have a register of deeds and to keep a register of births, deaths and marriages. The fees of most officials were specified, the jurisdiction of the courts was defined and provision made for appeals. Indian relations received some attention and a militia law, which was later pronounced ineffective, was included. Provision was made for the building of fences, roads, mills, and for maintaining a pilot at Roanoke and Ocracoke inlet, for raising £2000 annually until the public debt should be paid and the outstanding bills of credit redeemed. A public treasurer was elected, Edward Moseley, who was speaker of the assembly, being chosen to this office. Christopher Bale and Tobias Knight were among the proprietors' deputies who at this time formed the council and these men, together with Governor Eden, may be considered as the leaders in this work of revision. It comprised, with some additions, what was regarded as of permanent value in the legislation of the proprietary period thus far, and it now became an important object of reference for the time to come.

The proprietors, when the acts were submitted to them, immediately objected to all interference by the assembly in the rents and sale of their lands.[2] They objected to receiving bills of credit and insisted on quit rents being paid in sterling. They also declared that sales of land should no longer occur in the province but only before their board in England. They would examine the entire body of acts and confirm such as they found suitable, but none should

[1] For the colonial view of this deed, its origin and object, as stated by one of Burrington's assemblies and also by himself, see N. C. Recs. III, 569, 601.

[2] N. C. Recs., II, 235, 250.

continue in force longer than two years unless they were confirmed by the proprietors. There is no evidence that they were confirmed and yet, with the exceptions which always obtained in such frontier communities, these laws remained in force, many of them for a long period of time.

Nearly twenty years passed before the process of development to which reference has just been made reached a point where decisive results began to appear. Not until the administration of Gabriel Johnston do the records become sufficiently abundant to enable one to trace clearly such efforts as were made toward the improvement of conditions. In the interval which preceded three governors held office, of whose administrations some account will be attempted in this chapter. They were Charles Eden (1714–1722), Sir Richard Everard (1725–1731), and George Burrington. The last named had two administrations, the first as proprietary governor during the brief interval between Eden and Everard and the second as the first royal governor from 1731 to 1734. Toward the end of the second decade the province, with the exception of the proprietary eighth which was reserved by Carteret, was fully transferred to the crown.

As the flow of immigration into the colonies was now becoming considerable, it would have been expected that Bath county, which comprised the middle and southern parts of the eastern half of North Carolina, would have been settled. People did move slowly into it, especially along the Cape Fear river, and new precincts were formed. But the process was obstructed by the policy of the proprietors, who closed the land office in that county and for years forbade the sale of land there except for prices so high as to place it beyond the reach of most of the settlers. The payments also were required to be made at the office of the proprietors in London.[1] The governors, however, not without the knowledge of the proprietors, connived in some cases at violations of these rigid conditions, as low as 3d. per hundred acres being accepted for some grants. According to accounts which later were officially accepted as true, when the Virginia boundary had been settled, many blank patents for land were issued by the connivance of the governors and council. These

[1] N. C. Recs. IV, 296, 299, 318.

patents were drawn up in form, signed and sealed, but the names of the grantees, the number of acres, the boundaries and sums paid were left blank, to be filled up later as the parties to these transactions saw fit. It was charged that Moseley and the other North Carolina commissioners who ran the Virginia line received their reward in lands granted after this fashion and profited largely in addition. The practice was kept up, chiefly among the governors by Sir Richard Everard, until the purchase by the crown in 1729 and even later. In this way speculative claims arose to several hundred thousand acres, and in many cases by purchase or otherwise many of these claims were transferred to other parties. When, after the establishment of the royal government, it became necessary to regulate titles, collect quit rents and introduce some degree of order into the land system of the province, blank patents became an important political issue and gave rise to much controversy both in the province and in England. It illustrated well the transition from proprietary conditions, where all sorts of irregularities, not to say fraud, were connived at, to the attempts at orderly administration which followed the transfer to the crown.[1]

That relations during and after the assembly of 1715 were not quite harmonious is indicated by the action of the council, after the session closed, on certain resolves which purported to come from the other house. These were directed against the impressing of inhabitants or their property by the executive for alleged public services and without authority from the assembly, against some alleged unfair treatment of the Core Indians, and against those who were increasing the depreciation of the bills of credit by refusing to take them in payment of fees or quit rents. It was insisted that a representation should be made by members of the house to the proprietors on the deplorable condition of the province and on the necessity that they should continue to sell lands in both the Carolinas and receive bills of credit in payment therefor. The council protested against each of these resolves and declared that, as none of them had been communicated to it

[1] In another chapter the passage of South Carolina through this same phase of development is described.

during the session, they had been secretly passed and entered in the journal for the purpose of creating unreasonable jealousies and weakening the authority of government.[1]

The scanty records of the time afford us only a glimpse of these differences between the two houses; and we know even less of the causes which induced Christopher Gale, the chief justice, to go to England in 1717 to complain against the governor.[2] Gale evidently did not succeed in his errand, for Eden was continued in his office and made a landgrave, while Gale remained out of the province for several years. In 1718 Eden's administration was smirched by its connection with the pirate Teach and his crew. Tobias Knight, secretary, member of the council and chief justice appears to have been in closest connection with them, for a part of their plunder was found on his premises. The destruction of Teach and the capture of his vessel, by the expedition which Governor Spotswood sent from Virginia, by its very thoroughness was the more humiliating to such pride as the Carolinians may have had in these matters. Thomas Pollock questioned the right of Spotswood to act as he did, and Spotswood patronizingly explained what he had done to Lord Carteret, the palatine. But however it might imply the inferiority of the backward proprietary province, the good work had been so thoroughly done that no one was inclined to protest.[3] The death of Knight, which followed soon after the scandal had been aired, removed the person about whom contention chiefly gathered and helped to bring quiet.

But while the excitement was at its height, Edward Moseley and Maurice Moore, who were the natural leaders of the opposition in North Carolina, broke into the private house at Sandy Point where the secretary's office was kept and searched the records for criminating evidence against Knight and the governor. For this offence Eden sent a posse and had them arrested. Moseley, as was his wont, spoke out boldly, intimating that the governor was more interested in the arrest of peacable citizens than of pirates. The two accused men were indicted for the great scandal and de-

[1] N. C. Recs. II, 243,244.
[2] *Ibid.*, 284, 297.
[3] *Ibid.*, 319, 322, 325, 329, 333–340, 341–349.

famation against the governor. They were tried before the general court in October 1719. Light fines were imposed for breaking and entering the secretary's office, but Moseley for his seditious utterances concerning the governor was, by special verdict, found guilty and sentenced to a fine of £100 and to be incapable of holding office or place of trust in the colony for three years.[1] Jones, who was chief justice, stated to the council that, as Moseley had the largest practice of any lawyer in the province, many persons would suffer great hardships by being deprived of his services in cases where he had already held retainers. The force of this argument was appreciated by the council and Moseley was allowed to serve his clients in the cases for which he had pledged himself before sentence was passed upon him.

While Moseley, who was probably the ablest man in the province and who certainly spoke and acted more boldly against what was regarded as official usurpation than did any other, was obeying the terms of his sentence, the revolution which brought proprietary government to an end in South Carolina occurred. The North Carolina settlements were so remote and their circumstances so different from those on the Ashley river that no corresponding movement among them occurred. Its effect, however, was to make proprietary control even more shadowy than it had previously been and to invite in England proposals to bring it completely to an end. But events drifted on and nothing was done. In the province itself assemblies met in 1720, 1722 and 1723, but of their proceedings, except a part of the meagre product of their legislation, no record has been preserved.[2] In 1722 Governor Eden died. Thomas Pollock and William Reed succeeded him for brief intervals in the capacity of president of the council.[3] Christopher Gale had returned to North Carolina and was now serving again as chief justice, as well as the collector of the royal customs at Beaufort.

George Burrington arrived and assumed the office of governor as successor of Eden at the beginning of 1724. In some respects his character was like that of Francis Nicholson,

[1] *Ibid.*, 321, 329, 351, 359, 364, 368, 379. Ashe, *op. cit.*, 202, 204.
[2] N. C. Recs. II, 462., XXIII, 97–110.
[3] *Ibid.*, 449, 460.

though his career was much shorter and his activities were more devoted to the interests which were distinctly colonial. Like Nicholson, his activity was constant and in many respects it was directed to the best advantage of his province. He at once became interested in the Cape Fear region, then nominally included in Bath county, explored much of it in person and led in promoting its settlement. This was the most important forward step taken in this period of North Carolina history, for it not only secured a port for the colony but it opened up a large and valuable territory for farms and gave the colony a much needed extension toward the south. It was also an event of more than local importance, for it insured the filling with population of the wide and almost impassable tract which had separated the middle colonies from the settlements which were growing up in the remote south. A serious obstacle to communication between the colonies at large was thus gradually removed. Burrington was interested in the beginning of road building through North Carolina, in the exploration of the coast with a view to the improvement of navigation. In these interests he travelled widely and at much personal risk and discomfort. In all these respects the similarity between him and Nicholson is marked.

As immigrants were seeking admission to North Carolina, the assembly at Edenton, in April 1724, desired the governor and council to issue such orders as would make it possible for settlers to take up lands, paying suitable rents therefor until the proprietors should declare the prices for which they would sell land and how the purchase money should be paid.[1] This they said was necessary in order to prevent immigrants from turning to other colonies. The governor and council accepted the suggestion and ordered that lands might be taken up on the annual payment of three shillings per hundred acres, and that when the proprietors should issue new conditions of settlement the titles thus secured should be accepted as valid. This order applied to Bath county, including the Cape Fear region, as lands in Albemarle county were considered by the colonists to be held under the " grand deed " of 1668. Like the appeal of the council of 1718, the

[1] N. C. Recs. II, 529.

object of these measures was to break through the restrictive policy which the proprietors had been following in reference to land in the interest of more rapid settlement, and Burrington, so far as we know, was heartily in their favor.

But, as in the case of Nicholson, Burrington was often guilty of arbitrary acts and still oftener of the use of most abusive language. Both men were unable to control their tempers and both became involved in violent controversies with some of the leading men in their councils. In little more than six months after his arrival Burrington had quarreled with the naval officer and the collector of the customs at Roanoke, imprisoning one and publicly thrashing the other. He then undertook to discharge the duties of port officers himself. Because Chief Justice Gale had sustained these officers, Burrington assailed him not only with violent language but threatened extreme personal violence, even to the extent of laying him by the heels and burning his house at Edenton or blowing it up with gunpowder.[1] As Burrington had made so direct an attack on imperial officers, Gale went to England and laid his case before the treasury. Burrington's connection with Cape Fear and Maurice Moore, who was one of that prominent South Carolina family who had recently settled in that region, his friendly relations with Moseley and seeming tendency toward independence of the proprietors apparently furnished Gale with the ground for a charge that the governor was planning a revolt against proprietary rule like that which James Moore had just led in the southern province.[2] The result was that Burrington was immediately removed, his administration continuing in all only a year and a half.

Sir James Everard, the new appointee, was in no respect an improvement on Burrington, while there is no evidence that he devoted himself with special effect to the development of the province. Like Burrington, he early quarreled with the members of his council and throughout the last half of his administration their criticisms of him were most extreme.[3] They reported to the home government that if they expressed

[1] N. C. Recs. II, 561, 562, 577.

[2] Ashe, *op. cit.*, 210; N. C. Recs. II, 577.

[3] N. C. Recs. III, 2, 5, 25, 31; Ashe, *op. cit.*, 212, 225.

opposition, though in the politest terms, to his unreasonable proposals in council, he would overwhelm them with threats and abuse and then fling himself out of the council room leaving business unfinished. Attempts of members to reason with him outside proved equally futile. Cooperation became impossible with him and, as was so often the case, paralysis of government set in accompanied by frequent arbitrary and illegal acts on the part of the executive. The councillors charged Everard with taking exorbitant fees in violation of the provisions of the law on the subject and with making the most arbitrary use of the courts of justice for the purpose of punishing his real or fancied enemies. Everard is charged with giving his ear to the petty quarrels of his wife and profligate son, and even of the children in the family, and in connection with these to have instituted a sort of inquisition to ascertain what gossip was floating about the community concerning himself and his relatives. The little town of Edenton was kept in a ferment by these doings and government was reduced to a farce.

At first Gale and his friends, Lovick and Little, the former enemies of Burrington, were Everard's trusted advisers. But he later broke with them and charged them and their misrepresentations of their rivals with responsibility for his own initial mistakes. They therefore became his bitterest enemies, as also did Edmund Porter, another prominent colonist. Burrington, too, remained in the province and actively interested himself in the election of Everard's first assembly. The ex-governor himself was chosen a member and his friends controlled the body, among them being Maurice Moore, Edmund Porter, John B. Ashe and others. By law the stated time for the meeting of this body was in November 1725, but on the advice of the council a proclamation was issued before it met proroguing it until the following April.[1]

The assembly, however, came together on November 1. Maurice Moore was elected speaker.[2] They at once denied the power of the governor and council to prorogue them as they had done. Everard refused to recall his proclamation, acting doubtless chiefly under the advice of Gale. The house

[1] N. C. Recs. II, 571.
[2] *Ibid,*, 575 *et seq.*

unanimously resolved that the prorogation was illegal and an infringement on their liberties and those of the people and that they would not proceed to business until their privileges were confirmed by the governor and council. But as the council did not recognize them as in session, their only resort was to address the proprietors. This address they prepared and sent by three agents, one being Edmund Porter. In it they highly praised Burrington and disowned the criticisms both of him and of the people of the province. They denied that the colonists were turbulent or that they desired to rise and throw off proprietary rule, as had been done in South Carolina. The chief cause of trouble they found in the misconduct of certain officials, the leading place among whom they would doubtless assign to Gale, who now held the office of chief justice and judge of admiralty.[1] The house now adjourned until April.

Immediately Burrington began the most scurrilous attacks upon Everard calling him out of his house and abusing him, and later, in company with Cornelius Harnett, committing an assault upon the house and person of the constable.[2] Everard replied in kind with the result that Edenton was agitated for weeks by these riotous demonstrations. Even the ministers became involved.[3] The records of the court, over which Gale presided and where these cases of riot were prosecuted, contain the only accounts which have come down to us of these occurrences. When the assembly met in April, in reply to a brief conciliatory speech of Everard, they poured forth a denunciation of alleged harsh proceedings of judges and juries against themselves and their friends.[4] Approval of Burrington was again expressed and an address similar to the preceding one was sent to the proprietors. No laws were passed and little serious business was done. But though prosecutions were held over the head of Burrington, no effort was made to arrest or punish him nor could there be under such conditions. The feud gradually abated and in 1728 the cases against Burrington disappeared from

[1] The other leading offenders were John Lovick, the secretary, and William Little, the attorney general. Little was son-in-law of Gale.

[2] N. C. Recs. II, 648–653, 659, 666, 669, 170, 671, 687, 701, 705, 713, 823.

[3] *Ibid.*, 579, 604, 624; Ashe, I, 212.

[4] N. C. Recs. II, 608 *et seq.*

the docket with an entry of *noli prosequi*. After a time he removed to the Cape Fear region, where he lived quietly until 1728.[1] In that year the northern boundary of the province was finally run and a question which had long been at issue with Virginia was settled.[2]

The time, too, had now come when the British government and the proprietors were able to agree upon terms for the surrender of the Carolinas to the crown. Proprietary government had never had more than a nominal existence in the northern province and there were no indications that it was becoming really more effective. For nearly thirty years past important restrictions had been imposed by the home government on the powers of the proprietors. The proprietors of Carolina had already confessed their impotence and the province was not a source of profit. On a moderate estimate quit rents were in arrears to the amount of £9500. For these reasons they were ready to sell and expressed themselves to that effect soon after the accession of George II.[3]

To the crown, even in Hanoverian times, the advantages of taking the Carolinas directly under its control were obvious.[4] They were stated by Thomas Lowndes to the general effect that it would make the southern and western frontier more defencible against the Spanish and French; that the quit rents accruing from large stretches of good land would be made immediately available to the crown and by these, as well as in other ways, the royal revenue would be increased[5]; referring particularly to South Carolina, he also dwelt on the advantages which would come from a naval station at Port Royal. Other reasons might have been added, but it needed little persuasion on either side.

[1] Ashe, *op. cit.*, 215.

[2] See chap. on Virginia in William Byrd, The Dividing Line.

[3] N. C. Recs. II, 721; III, 6.

[4] *Ibid.*, 10.

[5] Lowndes and Samuel Horsey are credited by some with having acted as agents for the proprietors at the time of the surrender. Both were landgraves and held or were candidates for office in South Carolina. Lowndes probably expressed his highest preference when, in a later communication to the board of trade, he suggested that North Carolina should be made a district of Virginia, for then its quit rents would be really collected and from a fund thus gathered a survey and charts might be made of the coast to the great advantage of trade; *ibid.*, 49. On Lowndes see article in the Dict. of National Biography.

An agreement was reached between the crown and the parties who then held each of seven of the original proprietary shares for the sale of their respective holdings at £2800 each, making a total of £17,500. A lump sum of £5000 was to be paid for the surrender of all claims to arrears of quit rents and other public or semi-public dues to which the proprietors might be entitled. These payments should be made and the deed of surrender enrolled in the British Court of Chancery before September 29, 1729. As John Lord Carteret declined to surrender his share, the contract became effective for only seven of the original eight shares, and provision was made for laying off his one-eighth and his enjoyment of revenue and territorial rights over it much as was the case in the Northern Neck of Virginia. It should also be borne in mind that this surrender included the territory of South Carolina as well as of North Carolina, in other words of all which had been granted to the proprietors by the charter of 1665. This, of course, extended to the Florida boundary and included the territory which was soon to become the province of Georgia. The act, in other words, completed and gave full legal sanction to what had begun in South Carolina with the revolt of 1719. To give the contract the highest effect in law, it was embodied in an act of parliament which also was passed in 1729.[1] Until this time the terms barony and landgrave were occasionally used and the council was in part filled by deputies of the lords proprietors. But with the establishment of royal government the last traces even of the nomenclature of the Fundamental Orders disappeared.

Everard had held an assembly in 1727 and another in November 1729.[2] Each of these passed a few statutes, one of the most important being the act of 1729 providing for the issue of £40,000 in bills of credit, £10,000 of which were used in redeeming old bills and the rest was distributed among the precincts for circulation. As a result of the passage of this bill, he received a grant of £500. Notwithstanding the sale of the province the governor issued many grants of land, in some cases leaving the number of acres blank, to be filled in by the grantees, if they chose, in very large figures, and demanding

[1] N. C. Recs. III, 32.

[2] *Ibid.*, 49; XXIII, 111-116.

no purchase money.[1] Lovick, Moseley and Little were said to have been concerned in these transactions. This shows, as was charged, that Everard had broken with Gale and had gone over to the popular leaders. Gale and his friends now exposed the alleged fraudulent grants of land and made such other complaints to the board of trade and secretary of state concerning Everard's conduct and loyalty in general as to make impossible his appointment as first royal governor.[2] Burrington, meantime, had gone to England and presented such a justification of his own career as governor as to make it appear that his previous removal by the proprietors was unjustifiable.[3] The result was that Burrington was selected to be the first royal governor. This was presumably the work of Martin Bladen and Newcastle. Among his instructions an order was introduced that he should investigate the charges against Everard and his associates and, if he found them substantiated, institute prosecutions against them, making a full report of what he did to the authorities at home.[4] Prominent among those whom he selected to be members of his council were Edmund Porter, John B. Ashe, Matthew Rowan and Cornelius Harnett, while Bladen selected for him William Smith, a young London barrister, to be chief justice, and Nathaniel Rice, Bladen's son-in-law, to be secretary. John Montgomery was later appointed attorney general.[5]

Burrington did not arrive in the province until February 1731. During this interval of nearly two years after it was known that the crown had bought the province, government had been to a large extent suspended.[6] The general court had not met, neither had some of the precinct courts or the legislature. The admiralty court, under Edmund Porter as judge, was charged with many arbitrary acts involving undue extension of its jurisdiction within the body

[1] N. C. Recs. III, 219, 222, 246, 273–4. In reply to later charges by Everard, Lovick was able to show to the satisfaction of the council that some of these grants or sales had been made to defray the cost of running the Virginia line and that they involved no fraud.

[2] N. C., Recs. III, 18, 49, 51, 61 *et seq.*, 83, 90, 101.

[3] *Ibid.*, 28.

[4] *Ibid.*, 31, 62–65, 101.

[5] *Ibid.*, 85; Ashe, 226.

[6] N. C. Recs. III, 142, 211 *et seq.*

of the counties and in disregard of prohibitions from the common law courts. Porter was also said to have used it as an instrument for the punishment of his friends, if not for his own enrichment. So indifferent was the home government to North Carolina that no provision was made for an interim government and a full year was allowed to pass between the decision to appoint Burrington and the drafting of his instructions. Naturally, on his arrival Burrington found the province in great disorder. He pronounced Everard utterly incompetent, a weak man who was drawn now in this direction and now in that as he fell in succession under the control of the leaders of the contending factions.[1]

In April an assembly was called, of which Edward Moseley was chosen speaker.[2] Immediately the lower house came to an issue with the governor over his right to appoint their clerk. His appointee they ignored, but appointed the same person by their own authority. Of this conduct the board of trade disapproved and Burrington stated that he would insist on his right in this matter. In 1733 the assembly contended that the appointment of the clerk had always belonged to them and referred the matter to a committee to examine precedents. This committee of course reported in full accord with the sentiments of the house and failed to find that the proprietors or their officials had attempted to appoint the clerk, sergeant, messenger or doorkeeper.[3] Here the matter rested until Johnston's administration, when the practice which came to obtain in the royal provinces generally, that the governor should appoint the clerk, was established in North Carolina.

In his speech at the opening of his first assembly, Burrington called their attention to a number of his instructions which contained some of the cardinal principles that the crown was always attempting to enforce. They were: that a permanent revenue should be granted; that excessive grants of land should not be made — not more than fifty acres for every individual in the family — and that grants which were not settled or on which quit rents were not paid should be

[1] *Ibid.*, 142, 155, 224–232, 333.

[2] *Ibid.*, 257, 285 *et seq.*

[3] *Ibid.*. 288. 289. 354. 483. 576.

declared forfeited; that all grants should be recorded in the office of the deputy auditor and that a copy of this list — which would form the basis of a rent roll — should be sent to England; that quit rents, fees and salaries should be paid in proclamation money, quit rents being not less than 4s. for every hundred acres[1]; that a property qualification should be required for jury service; that the church and morality should be promoted and cruelty to servants, slaves and peaceful Indians restrained or punished. Burrington also urged that steps be taken to check the depreciation of the currency, to promote direct trade with Europe and the West Indies, that an agent be appointed to reside in England, that a town be built on Cape Fear river, that in every precinct wills be proved and licenses be granted, that the chief justice and assistants go on circuit. All these were subjects which the growth of the province and the establishment of royal government made necessary. But they were inconsistent with some of the provisions of the laws of 1715 and with many more practices which had long been in vogue in North Carolina. They proceeded also from a sovereign power outside the province which seemed much more likely to enforce its will than the proprietors had ever been. They were therefore sure to encounter opposition in the assembly which, taken in connection with the violence of speech that Burrington habitually used in defending himself and attacking his enemies, made harmony impossible.

Fees, salaries and quit rents were closely connected as subjects of contention. The former had been fixed, at least for most officials, in one of the laws of 1715. But in Everard's administration even the council charged him with taking what fees he thought proper[2] and he seems to have continued the practice in spite of general protests against it. The requirement that fees should be paid in proclamation money now aroused general protest. Officials who obeyed this instruction were charged with taking fees four times in excess of the amounts to which they were entitled by the laws of 1715. The lower house held that, as English subjects, they should not be taxed or made liable to pay any sums or fees other than such as were by law established. They asked the

[1] *Ibid.*, 95, 102. [2] *Ibid.*, 3.

council to join in a proclamation strictly prohibiting such practices. The council resented this as an assumption on the part of the assembly of the sole power of determining fees and denounced its proposal as an invasion of the prerogative.[1] Burrington proposed that fees be settled in the same manner as in Virginia. This, together with his remarks on the occasion, increased the irritation of the house and it proposed to pass new bills on the payment of rents as well as fees which should be in harmony with Carolina practice and, they believed, with the royal instructions. According to that instruction both the governor and council asserted that they had the right to determine the rates of fees and salaries. Two bills were passed by this house specifying various commodities in which payment could be made, in addition to bills of credit and proclamation money. But both were rejected by the governor on the ground that their effect would be greatly to reduce the amount of payments.[2] Charges and countercharges upon the subject were exchanged between Burrington and the assembly until the close of his administration, the one affirming that fees were ruinously low, much lower than they were in other colonies, and the other affirming the contrary.[3] The truth seems to have been that the officials in the main determined the rates of fees, but that the inferior or fluctuating character of the medium in which they were paid brought down the high nominal rates to low actual ones.

In reference to quit rents and the possibility of having to pay them regularly and in proclamation money, with possible resurveys and disallowance of claims originating under blank patents, such feeling was aroused that the assembly of 1731 at once ordered the "great deed" of 1668 brought in and the original entrusted to the custody of the speaker while a copy was entered in the journal of the house.[4] They declared that there was not enough specie in the province to pay one-twentieth of the quit rents and the salaries of officials. They objected to the payment of any salaries because the miserably

[1] *Ibid.*, 95, 262, 264.

[2] *Ibid.*, 143, 151, 157, 160, 265, 269, 270, 276, 279.

[3] *Ibid.*, 335, 482, 552, 591, 600, 607.

[4] Osgood, Am. Colonies in the 17th century, II, 36. The quit rent prescribed in the "great deed" was about 2s. per hundred acres or one-half that which was required by the royal instruction.

small salary account of the proprietary period had been met from quit rents and sales of land. As to land grants, they asked that conditions of settlement be more easy and objected to the requirement that three acres in every fifty must be settled.[1] In the fee bill of this session the house inserted a provision for registering future grants of land in the auditor's office, but it also provided for the payment of these rents not only in proclamation money but in some eighteen commodities at specified rates. Its attitude toward the "great deed" also showed that they could not be easily brought to pay the rate stated in the governor's instruction. When for these reasons among others Johnston was forced to reject this bill, he repeatedly wrote to the board of trade about the impossibility he found in harmonizing his instruction upon quit rents with what the people firmly believed they were entitled to under the "great deed." This brought from the board the reply that the "great deed" could be understood only as a temporary letter of attorney from the proprietors, revocable at their pleasure and that it had been in effect revoked when they had directed Governor Eden to grant no land without reserving 1d. per acre. Moreover, the payment of 4s. proclamation money per hundred acres, as well as the payment of officer's fees in the same money, and the registering of all grants of land, were the terms upon which the crown had agreed to remit all arrears of quit rents, and if the people would not comply with these terms, orders soon might be expected for the collection of arrears. Burrington searched the records and made inquiries and was not able to find the alleged order to Eden to grant land at a penny per acre; neither could he find that any grants had ever been issued at that rent or at any rate higher than 2s. per hundred acres, the same as in Virginia. He also was impressed by the fact that the "great deed" had always been held to be as firm and valid a grant as the royal charter itself and in agreement with its terms all land in the northern part of the province was held. Therefore Burrington did not venture to make out patents on terms different from these and maintained an attitude toward the "great deed" which was essentially the same as that of the people. He also stated to the board of

[1] N. Car. Recs. III., 144 *et seq.*, 292 *et seq.*

trade more than once how great an obstacle he found his instructions to be to the administration of territorial affairs.[1]

The attempt of Burrington, as royal governor, to enforce his instructions also brought up the question, of interest in so many provinces, of the appointment of the public treasurer or precinct treasurers. These governor's instructions required him to appoint and thereby to retain control over expenditures. The council supported him in his claim, while Burrington's opinion was that the practice of the choice of treasurers was, in idea, of New England origin. Besides the treasurer of the province, there were from time to time in North Carolina precinct treasurers, all of whom the assembly had come into the habit of choosing. Burrington searched the records in the effort to find how the office of treasurer came into existence in North Carolina, but was unable to find any statutory or other positive basis for it. Originally, as in other provinces, the receiver general had been the only finance officer. Then during the confusion of Cary's rebellion and the Indian war, when it first became necessary to issue bills of credit, treasurers, or public treasurers, were designated in the acts, to superintend the issue of the bills and the business of the loan office in general. That was the only power they had at first. Edward Moseley was prominently connected with this policy and the measures to which it gave rise and therefore he came to hold pretty continuously the office of public treasurer. As he was the leader of the popular group in the assembly and outside, it was against him first of all that Burrington and the council had to contend in all these related questions. In view of this record, Burrington of course claimed that a public treasurer, in the sense of receiver general or chief finance officer of the province and appointee of the assembly, did not legally exist in North Carolina. But Moseley was actually in such a position and claiming its powers, and it was very difficult, if not impossible, to oust him.[2] Burrington appointed Smith, the chief justice, to the office, but he withdrew before his commission was made out.

[1] *Ibid.*, III, 150, 331, 337, 354, 479, 600, 608.

[2] *Ibid.*, 151, 263, 265, 266, 335, 354, 483–487. Unfortunately in the new edition of the laws of North Carolina the acts which were disallowed and some others deemed of temporary importance have been omitted. The student is thus deprived, as in this case, of some most important proof material.

The assembly asserted that its claim was based on several statutes, especially one of 1729, which created a number of precinct treasurers, but they could not make out a clear case. Because the acts of 1729 had been passed after the purchase by the crown, Burrington considered them all of doubtful validity and as they contained many provisions which he thought inconsistent with the king's service, he insisted on sending home all the laws which were in force for inspection. It was decided that all acts which were passed before Everard had notice of the sale were valid, including the currency act, though it was probably passed after the news in question had reached Carolina. In 1733 the lower house designated two precinct treasurers and the upper house substituted another man in the place of one of these and this substitution was accepted by the lower house.[1] Thus the question was left at the end of Burrington's administration, no word having come from England.

In order to follow this subject to its conclusion, it should be stated that during the long governorship of Gabriel Johnston the question was settled in favor of the contention of the assembly. Early in 1735 the lower house nominated two persons for each of three vacancies in the office of precinct treasurer, the upper house made one change and the governor appointed one of the nominees to each place.[2] In November 1739 the governor and council appointed the chief justice public treasurer for the northern counties.[3] In the following February an act was passed for appointing a public treasurer for certain counties, it being one of those on which, when the upper house was equally divided, William Smith, the president, who was also chief justice, voted a second time.[4] In 1748 two treasurers were appointed by act of assembly, one for the northern counties and one for the southern counties — corresponding to similar arrangements for the east and west shores of Maryland — and thenceforward vacancies were filled in this manner.[5]

At the time when this controversy was in progress North Carolina had no forms of taxes except the poll or general

[1] *Ibid.*, 546, 547, 580.
[2] N. C. Recs. IV, 106, 155.
[3] *Ibid.*, 354.
[4] *Ibid.*, 480; XXIII, 131.
[5] *Ibid.*, 273, 331 & 349.

property tax, of about five shillings per poll in currency, and the tonnage duty Provision was made for both of these in the laws of 1715, tithables being defined so as to include free males sixteen years of age or over, and slaves of both sexes who were twelve years of age or over. By an act of 1723 free negroes were also made taxable, with the same age limitation as slaves. Lists were taken by the constables. The tonnage duty was one pound of powder, four pounds of swan shot, twelve flints or ten shillings of current money, for every three tons burden of vessels entering the province.[1] In 1723 a part of the revenue from this was appropriated for the improvement of navigation through the inlets and channels of the coast. But in 1731 Burrington wrote that the revenue from this source had ben used chiefly in paying assemblymen and that navigation had been shamefully neglected. Not until 1734 was a small import duty levied on wines and liquors not imported from Great Britain. Objects of expenditure were few, the only permanent object of importance prior to the militia act of 1746 being payment for the services of councillors and assemblymen during sessions of the legislature. For war, erection of forts and public buildings there were almost no appropriations. Early in 1732 Burrington wrote to the board of trade, "It has been a Policy of the Subtle People of North Carolina never to raise any money but what is appropriated, to pretend and insist that no Publick money can, or ought to be paid, but by a Claim given to, and allowed by the House of Burgesses; insomuch that upon the greatest emergency there is no coming at any money to fitt out Vessells against a Pirate, to buy Arms, Purchase Ammunition, or any other urgent occasion. . . . The whole amount of the Publick Levys and Powder Money paid by shipping little exceeds two Hundred Pounds sterling a year."[2] Burrington was considering the establishment of a court of exchequer but had not yet reached the point where this seemed feasible.

Over the group of related questions which have just been discussed the quarrel between Burrington and his first assembly even became so violent that at the end of five weeks the

[1] N. C. Recs. XXIII, 45, 106, 154, 194.
[2] N. C. Recs., III, 336.

session was brought to an end without anything being accomplished. The assembly was never called together again.[1] By favoring the establishment of a second town in the Cape Fear region — the later Wilmington — which would be a rival of Brunswick where the Moores from South Carolina had settled, Burrington alienated that family and its connections. Harnett's presence in the council Burrington pronounced a disgrace to it. He went to great length in denouncing the connection of Moseley and his friends with the alleged illegal granting of land. By members of the council in general the governor was criticised for the manner in which he conducted the inquiry into the charges against Everard. With Smith, the new chief justice, he came into hopeless relations over the position of assistants whom he was appointing to the supreme bench. At first Burrington held that these men had no judicial power whatever, and a few days later he completely reversed his position and declared that their share in determining the judgments of the court was equal to that of the chief justice. Both opinions were extreme and erroneous and they occasioned a violent quarrel, as a result of which Smith returned to England, threatening to procure Burrington's recall. These were some among the personal and political details which Burrington had to report to the board of trade at the close of his first year as royal governor.[2] Though the province was generally prosperous and increasing in wealth and population, it had no forts either inland or on the coast and was destitute of an organized or disciplined militia.

Soon after the close of the first year of Burrington's administration complaints against him began to reach the home government. During the two succeeding years complaints, defences and counter-complaints were drawn and filed before the board of trade in large numbers and dealing with every feature of the dispute. Some phases of the controversy were aired before the council of North Carolina. Smith, Porter, Ashe, Moseley and other councillors whom Burrington had attacked presented many long statements and affidavits showing the violence and arbitrariness of his conduct toward them.[3]

[1] *Ibid.*, 415.

[2] *Ibid.*, 235, 244, 310, 322, 331–339, 415; Ashe, *op. cit.*, 232.

[3] N. C. Recs., III, 375–391, 405–414, 439–535.

On one occasion, when Moseley was defending Porter before the court and because he had not received a license from Burrington to practice as an attorney, though he had a license of a much earlier date, the governor in a great rage ordered his arrest and imprisonment. On a later occasion he had Moseley imprisoned again on an equally frivolous charge, and because his new appointee to the chief justiceship would not yield to his arbitrary will, he was forced out of office and William Little was appointed as his successor. A violent private quarrel over property, which Burrington apparently provoked, led to the arrest of Ashe and the placing him under heavy bonds, intended, it was alleged, to prevent him from going to England to present charges against the governor.

The controversy, as it developed, produced one valuable result. It occasioned the preparing of a number of papers which throw light on obscure points in earlier North Carolina history. By the one side or the other, the nature and binding force of the " great deed " was discussed,[1] the origin of the office of treasurer and its connection with the early issues of bills of credit,[2] and the methods followed in the issue of warrants for the taking up of land, together with the size of grants. The question of the right of the executive alone to erect precints and endow them with the right to send representatives to the assembly was also debated at length.[3] Relying on the Fundamental Constitutions and early practice, Burrington argued that the governor and council had this right and they had erected several precincts in Bath county in this manner. He contended that earlier assemblies by accepting representatives which had been elected in precincts thus created had recognized that form of origin as legal. As to his royal instructions they were silent on this subject, and Burrington declined to be bound by instructions to other provinces or their practice. On the other side it was argued that this practice gave to the upper house control over the whole legislature by enabling it to fix the number of the lower house and to determine the bounds of precincts. They declared the procedure illegal and cited the practice

[1] *Ibid.*, 480.
[2] *Ibid.*, 466, 484–490.
[3] *Ibid.*, 439, 442, 450 *et seq.*

in Virginia and later practice in North Carolina in justification of their claims. They sought also, though wrongly, to bring the instruction which forbade the governor to erect new courts of justice to bear on this question. The truth of the case was that the right claimed by Burrington was an incident of his territorial power and was exercised as such in the early years of the province; but as the legislature and political consciousness behind it became more developed it had to be abandoned and matters of such importance it became necessary to regulate by statute. Among the royal provinces this may be said to have become the universal practice.

Burrington's second assembly met at the beginning of July, 1733 — Moseley being again speaker — and continued in session a little more than two weeks, when the governor dissolved it.[1] The reason for this was that agreement between himself and the lower house on any of the questions which had formerly been in dispute was found to be impossible. Burrington had delayed calling the assembly until he had received a reply to his report to the board of trade on the payment of fees and quit rents. The board had adhered to its former requirements — that they should be paid in proclamation money. The assembly on its part continued to insist that they might be paid in currency or in kind, that is, in the current money of the province, and that there was by no means enough gold or silver in the province to meet this demand. The tenure of land in Albemarle county and the amount of quit rents which was due there were closely connected with this, and again the house refused to admit that the "great deed" was revocable. The council, being small in number and those mostly the governor's beneficiaries for the time being, had nothing significant to say. The questions just referred to were again discussed at length in messages which passed between the governor and the assembly, without anything new being brought forward. The proceedings were marred by ill temper on both sides. Burrington told the house that its reply to his opening speech was drawn by his most inveterate opponent among their number, Edmund Porter, and was pushed through with a noise and violence

[1] N. C. Recs. III, 540–611.

which stifled all opposition.[1] Among other things it contained a charge of perverting justice and taking exorbitant fees, against Little, the chief justice. This drew from Little a defence and plea for a hearing in which his reputation might be cleared from this grave charge. This Burrington ordered to be held before the council after the close of the session. Smith, who was soon to succeed as chief justice, was also involved in these charges, preferred in this case by the governor. The assembly ordered Little's arrest and sent a very severe communication to the governor,[2] in which they charged that parties whom he had injured or opposed had no relief before the courts, that the laws were disregarded, justice in a manner stopped and oppression and arbitrary power had almost overrun the province. When he received this, Burrington called the assembly before him and dissolved it.

For about a year Burrington now nominally governed the province without an assembly or even a council. During the time he suffered a long and dangerous illness and Nathaniel Rice, the senior councillor, was sworn in as president. Some of the councillors had died and with most or all of the others Burrington became involved in bitter quarrels. Smith, Rice and Montgomery finally tried to assassinate Burrington [3] and later, to escape arrest, fled to Virginia, where they remained until after the arrival of Johnston. One other assembly met just before his arrival, but it did nothing of importance.[4]

Notwithstanding Burrington's merits, the accumulation of evidence as to his oppressive and arbitrary conduct, most or all of which was laid before the board of trade,[5] was such as to make his recall a necessity. One thing which made it inevitable was a left-handed reflection in one of his letters on Martin Bladen, implying that he was planning the governor's recall in order to make room for one of his relatives.[6] So thorny did Burrington find his path to be, without salary and involved in endless broils, that finally he begged to be relieved of office and allowed to return to England. He wrote that he had been compelled to sell not only his household

[1] *Ibid.*, 560, 567.

[2] *Ibid.*, 606-609.

[3] *Ibid.*, IV, 165; Ashe, *op. cit.*, 240.

[4] N. C. Recs. III, 612 *et seq.*

[5] *Ibid.*, 631.

[6] *Ibid.*, 344, 370; Ashe, *op. cit.*, 235

goods, but even his linens, plate and books, and to mortgage his land and stock, while his constitution had been impaired by many sicknesses.[1] Burrington had steadfastly and often ably upheld the policy of the home government, but he had not succeeded in moving the assembly or the province from its traditional attitude in any essential particular. By temperament and by his recent experiences he was too deeply involved in the internal feuds of the province successfully to mediate between it and the crown. Another long administration was needed to bring North Carolina even measurably into line with British principles of government.

[1] N. C. Recs. III, 625.

CHAPTER IV

NEW YORK AND NEW JERSEY BETWEEN 1716 AND 1730

THIS was a period of comparative quiet, which intervened between the conflicts that had their origin in the Revolution of 1689 and in the misgovernment which had accompanied the first two intercolonial wars and the disturbances of the Cosby, Clark and Clinton régime. It also coincided with the first half of the period of peace, during which conditions were preparing for the decisive stage of the struggle between England and France for the possession of North America.

So far as the politics of New York itself were concerned, relations during this period continued very much as they had been determined to be in the settlement of 1715 between Hunter and the assembly. Hunter continued to hold the office of governor for four years after harmonious relations between himself and the assembly had been established. In 1716 an assembly was elected, to which an entirely new list of members was returned from New York county. A few changes of no political significance occurred in the representation from other counties. The fact that Mulford was returned from Suffolk showed that the spirit of opposition in extreme form still existed there. Livingston Manor now sent a representative for the first time and Robert Livingston was naturally its first choice. We know from a letter of Hunter that there was a spirited contest in New York city and county, from which the governor was fortunate enough to emerge victorious. The former members who were dropped — Jacobus Van Cortlandt, Stephen DeLancey, Samuel Bayard and John Read — were determined opponents of the settlement which had been reached between the executive and the assembly and would even now have overthrown it if they could.[1] A merchant named Baker was supposed to be laboring in their employ in England to procure the disallowance of the acts. David

[1] N. Y. Docs. V, 514; Ass. J. I, 367, 381.

Provoost, Johannes Jansen, Jacobus Kipp and Garret Van Horne, the newly elected members, Hunter counted on for steady support of his policy.

During the last two years of Hunter's administration some interesting financial discussions were occasioned by objections which were raised on the part of the home government against the revenue act of July, 1715, and the tonnage duty act of September, 1716.[1] The clauses to which objection was made were those which involved the possible taxation of the trade and shipping of the United Kingdom. In the first mentioned act wine was taxed twice as heavily when it came from places other than those of its production as it was when it came direct from the place where it was produced. In the other act a similar difference was made in the rate of duty levied on negroes, when they were brought in New York vessels, as compared with the rate imposed when they came in other vessels directly from Africa. Hunter met the criticism with the statement, in the one case, that no wine had ever been imported from Great Britain, or in all probability ever would be, and in the other case that he had never heard of any negroes being imported directly from Africa in vessels belonging to Great Britain. What the assembly were really aiming at was the encouragement of New York shipping and the discouragement of the importation of "refuse and sickly negroes here from other colonies." The repeal of the revenue act, the governor also said, might ruin the province. The board of trade therefore returned it for amendment and stated that, if it was not amended, it would be disallowed. An additional instruction[2] was sent to the effect that, besides earlier orders prohibiting the acceptance by governors of bills affecting the royal prerogative or property without first submitting a draft of the same to the king, and forbidding the passage of any law of unusual or extraordinary character without the insertion in each case of a clause suspending its execution till the pleasure of the king could be known, it was his majesty's further will that no act should hereafter be passed which affected the trade or shipping of the United Kingdom without a clause stating that it should not go into effect until approved by the monarch.

[1] Col. Laws, I, 847, 898; N. Y. Docs. V, 501, 509. [2] Ass. J. I, 419.

When this action of the crown came before the assembly, an elaborate address was presented by it to the governor, in which its views on the financial condition and policy of New York since the time of Cornbury were set forth.[1] The immediate bearing of this on the question in hand appears in these two points. In the first place, the assembly showed that, owing to the dishonest waste of revenue by former governors, the levy of imposts on trade had been wholly abandoned in New York, and the only source that was left from which to support the government and pay the cost of the two futile expeditions which had been planned against Canada, near the close of the late war, was the inadequate land tax. Prejudice against the impost had become so strong that the attempt to revive it seemed vain, while the opposition which the merchants were now making against its revival clearly revealed their attitude. In the second place, both the assembly and Hunter referred to the fact that by earlier tonnage acts, passed not only in New York but in Virginia and other colonies, this form of duty had been imposed on British shipping, while an incidental purpose of the law under discussion was to encourage shipbuilding in New York. In view of these considerations and of the great advantages which had come from the fiscal acts of 1715 and succeeding years, it seemed clear to the New York authorities that the peril involved to the interests of Great Britain was insignificant when compared with the benefits which would come from these measures. But the crown did not swerve from the principle which it laid down in the additional instruction, and by an explanatory act passed in 1718 language was used which made it clear that, in the duties on liquors and slaves and in tonnage duties, there was no intention of discriminating against the inhabitants of Great Britain.[2]

For some time after Hunter's return to England — in the summer of 1719 — he acted virtually as agent of the province for the purpose of explaining and defending the measures of his administration and checking thereby the efforts of his critics. He repeatedly appeared before the board of trade and gave information and advice concerning the finances of

[1] *Ibid.*, 421 *et seq.*
[2] Col Laws, I. 1010 *et seq.*; N. Y. Docs. V. 519.

New York, quit rents, Indian relations and the condition of the province in general.[1] At this time the treasury board was considering the encroachments of the assembly on the executive in New York in the management of finance.[2] This discussion drew from Horatio Walpole, who was auditor general of the plantations, a memorial on these encroachments as related to the position of the treasurer and the audit of accounts. Soon after Walpole's accession to his office in 1717, he had ordered his deputy in New York to require from De Peyster, the treasurer, an account of the revenue and its disposition. De Peyster replied that he was accountable to the governor, council, and assembly of the province. This reply he made on several occasions, though it directly contradicted the thirtieth instruction to the governor, which required him to see that no clause should be inserted in any appropriation act whereby accountability to the treasury in England was prevented. Finally it was learned that the assembly had passed a resolution prohibiting the treasurer from accounting to any but the governor, council and itself. Hunter, when questioned upon the subject,[3] confirmed what Walpole had stated, but had no remedy to suggest. Only the quit rents, he said, and such slight revenue as might arise under acts of parliament, now came into the hands of the receiver general, and in view of the insignificance of the office in its present condition it is no wonder that Hunter was unable to secure a salary for its incumbent.

During the fourteen months which intervened between the departure of Hunter from New York and the arrival of William Burnet, his successor, the affairs of the province were administered by Schuyler and the council. One of Schuyler's acts which aroused the fears of Hunter and his friends was the appointment of Jacobus Van Cortlandt as mayor of New York and of Myndert Schuyler as mayor of Albany, both of whom had been identified with the opposition to Hunter. Some other significant changes seem also to have been made, and they together gave rise to the suspicion that Schuyler intended to dissolve the existing assembly and institute a

[1] N. Y. Docs. V. 540, 548, 551 *et seq.*
[2] *Ibid.*, 527, 545 *et seq.*
[3] *Ibid.*, 559.

general change both of men and measures.[1] So unusual would this have been in an interim government, and to such an extent did it worry Hunter, that he urged Craggs, the secretary of state, to write to Schuyler to make no changes except what he himself should advise as absolutely necessary. The board of trade supported this recommendation and such a letter was sent and duly received. It was at this time that William Burnet, son of the famous bishop of Salisbury, was appointed governor of New York. Francis Harison and Dr. John Johnstone were also appointed members of the council, and Cadwallader Colden surveyor general, all of whom were friendly to Hunter and his policies. Schuyler, in a letter to the board of trade, denied that he had sought changes but rather had adhered to former lines of policy with unusual care, though he had to admit that he had appointed his son-in-law mayor of Albany.

The relations between Hunter's last assembly and the executive had been so friendly that orders were sent to Schuyler from England not to dissolve it. Hence this body met Burnet on his accession to office and was continued in existence by successive prorogations until 1726. This result, however, was not reached without opposition. Burnet, a man presumably of sanguine temperament and certainly desirous of an active and beneficent administration, came to New York with his mind full of ideas which he had received from Hunter in England. To the assembly he spoke of Hunter as " my incomparable predecessor," and praised it for having been concerned in " those great measures " by which the peace and credit of New York had been established by methods similar to those which had recently been followed in England.[2] He flattered himself that his task would be much easier than Hunter's had been at his first coming. That indeed it was, but he found that Schuyler, and his chief adviser Philipse, together with three or four other members of the council, favored a new assembly.[3] Burnet found that there were precedents in favor of continuing an assembly from one administration to another, and believed that it would be

[1] N. Y. Docs. V. 534, 535, 537; Col. Ex. C. Min. 275.

[2] Ass. J. I, 439.

[3] N. Y. Docs. V, 574, 578 *et seq.*, 583. The long duration of Irish parliaments was cited as a precedent.

considered legal in England. He privately met the members who raised scruples against it and told them to consider well whether, for reasons the validity of which they could not affirm, they would be justified in blocking supplies for at least nine months to come and neglecting an immediate remedy for the disaffection of the Indians, which was due to the encroachment of the French and to the decay of the forts. The new governor's attitude toward them was so determined that Schuyler and four others desired leave to go into the country, "which I granted them." He then recommended to the board of trade the removal of Schuyler and Philipse from the council and the appointment of Colden and James Alexander in their places. For this action he gave various reasons connected with their opposition to Hunter and the making of some questionable grants of land. Burnet desired that the removals should come from England rather than in the form of suspensions by himself, in order to avoid bitter feelings. In June, 1722, in answer to ten letters from Burnet, ranging in dates from November, 1720, to March, 1722, the board of trade informed him that Schuyler and Philipse had been removed and Colden and Alexander appointed.[1] The opposition did not extend beyond the council, and even there it was of slight importance, for its personnel was rapidly changing during these years and the way was preparing for a new adjustment in New York politics.

At the outset relations between the new governor and the assembly were most harmonious. The address in reply to Burnet's cordial greeting was written by Morris and promised ample support for five years to come. They would also provide for any necessary deficiency and would carry out the policy which Burnet recommended, so far as time, the nature of the thing and the circumstances of the province would permit. The address was presented by the whole house, and in view of the special relations which then existed, it was more than ordinarily significant. A few days before it was agreed to, Captain Mulford had virtually charged this assembly wth having plunged the province into debt to the amount of £35,000. When the address was being signed, he objected to the legality of the house. With this the patience

[1] *Ibid.*, 647.

of the assembly toward Mulford became utterly exhausted, and he was a second time expelled. William Nicoll, long a leader of the opposition and speaker, also retired at this time on the plea of ill health.[1] With these retirements discordant voices for the time were silenced and general harmony prevailed. In this its fall session of 1720 a supply for five years was voted and in the form of specific resolutions appropriations were made, the list starting off with the sum of £1560 per year for the governor. An impost, a tonnage duty and a license tax on the distilling and sale of liquors were the sources of revenue provided for in the act, and bills of credit were to be issued to be redeemed by the yield from these taxes.[2]

In the policy of Burnet Indian relations occupied a more prominent place than they had done in any administration since that of Bellomont. This was due to the fact that peace left time and leisure in which to consider the rapid advance which the French were making along the Great Lakes and in the Mississippi valley. To this, from the first, Burnet was fully alive and urged the repair of forts and the building of new ones, and a more strict regulation of trade in Indian goods. This led, in the first place, to the passage of an act imposing a 2% duty on all European goods imported into the province, the revenue from which should be specially expended in the building of forts in the Indian country. To meet the objection of the home government to legislation of this kind, a suspending clause was inserted in the act, and the governor wrote that the assembly could not be brought to adopt any other expedient for the purpose except the one embodied in this law.[3] He also added a brief review of precedents from New York history, between 1691 and 1702, for the imposing of a duty of this kind, and added that he knew of no reason for the discontinuance of such legislation, except the revulsion against imposts of all sorts which had been occasioned by the fiscal irregularities of Cornbury's

[1] Ass. J. I, 440, 442–445; C. J. I, 452.

[2] Ass. J. I, 448; Laws, II, 16 *et seq.* From C. J. I, 454, 460, it appears that Byerly, the receiver general, protested against the extending of control over this revenue to the treasurer and withdrew when the general support bill was passed.

[3] Laws, II, 32; N. Y. Docs. V, 576, 581, 641, 643, 648, 706.

administration. The act, however, was strongly opposed by the merchants in England and though the board of trade, because of the use to which the revenue from it was to be put, recommended that it should be approved, it was finally disallowed in 1724. In the course of his correspondence on the subject, Burnet called attention to the low rate of the duty, a rate which could easily be borne, because the profits on coarse goods imported from Bristol were from 30% to 40% and on fine goods from London from 20% to 30%. The continuance of the beaver trade, he also argued, was dependent on defence and the object of the act was to procure means for building forts, an object which ought to appeal to the merchants. But his arguments did not weigh strongly against the representations of the merchants, and in the order of council for the repeal of the act, the board of trade was required to draft an instruction to all the governors requiring them not to assent in the future to any act laying a duty on European goods imported into the colonies in English vessels.

Another feature of Burnet's policy which he considered of great importance was embodied in an act of this session which strictly prohibited the sale of strouds, duffels and other Indian goods to the French.[1] This law was strengthened by the passage, two years later, of another more detailed act on the same subject, and the two were continued in force till 1726. Merchants of Albany and to an extent throughout the province had become greatly interested in the sale of these goods to the French.[2] They were produced chiefly or wholly in England, and could be delivered to the French at prices lower than those for which they could import them directly from Europe. The French sold the goods to the Indians and this helped them to monopolize the Indian trade and thus to strengthen their influence with the tribes far and wide. The Five Nations themselves called attention to this tendency. Burnet and his advisers, so far as they were not personally interested, clearly saw the danger of this trade to English interests and sought to prevent it. By means of this legisla-

[1] Laws, II, 8, 98, 197, 248.

[2] Cadwallader Colden was a supporter of Burnet's policy in this matter and the government's view of the case was stated in his report on the trade of New York. N. Y. Docs. V, 687.

tion the governor sought to induce the far Indians, as well as the Iroquois, to come to Albany, instead of Montreal and Quebec, for their supplies and for the sale of their furs. It was enacted that no one within New York should directly or indirectly trade with any French subject in such commodities on penalty of forfeiture of the goods and heavy fine. An east and west line drawn through the northern limits of Albany marked the boundary beyond which, if such goods were found, they and their owners should be subject to the penalties of the act. Veritable writs of assistance might be used for their seizure. But the officials upon whom the government must depend for the execution of the law were the sheriffs and the justices who, as usual, fully shared local feeling, or were themselves interested in the trade they were required to suppress. The Indian commissioners at Albany and the Dutch in the northern sections of the province were more or less persistently opposed to the measure. However broad and statesmanlike may have been the view of the governor, the instinct of gain, which so generally manifested itself even in time of war, was too strong for him. In the fall of 1721 Burnet told the council that the act had been evaded and it would be necessary to station an officer and twenty men at Saratoga, that being the place where much of the clandestine trade centered. In the effort to enforce this policy the tendency to establish posts further on in the Indian country was strengthened. Soldiers were now employed in the enforcement of the act, and that gave rise to the special complaint that civil rights were being violated.

British and New York merchants appeared in force against Burnet's policy.[1] They declared that it was proving a blow to British trade and that, in consequence of it, the importation of beaver into England was falling off. It was also not a hindrance to the French, they declared, for they could supply themselves with the commodities in question from other colonies or from Europe. Gross misrepresentations of the geography of the region were made in support of these arguments. In a memorial to the king the board of trade, in July, 1724, suggested that no action be taken on the laws until Burnet had been informed of the objections of the merchants and

[1] N. Y. Docs. V, 708; Ex. C. Min. Sept., 1721, Oct., 1725.

his answers to these had been received. This course was followed, and on the arrival in New York of this notification of the government's action, all available material in support of the laws, including Colden's report and a report of the committee of the council, was printed and circulated in pamphlet form.[1] Peter Leheup, who was then agent of New York in England, was given full information to be used in support of the laws in England. The merchants employed Mr. Sharpe as counsel to present their case. Formal hearings were held by the board of trade in May, 1725.[2] As was usual in such cases, the evidence presented was incomplete and often contradictory. The merchants presented no proof of their statement that the French manufactured all the strouds which were needed for their trade, though upon that question depended much of the strength of their argument. Of still greater importance were statistics of the export of furs from the port of New York and of their importation into Great Britain since the passage of the laws, as compared with years immediately preceding that date.[3] There were indications of a slight and temporary diminution and also of a slight increase of price. But the interval since the passage of the laws was too short to justify any conclusion; in 1722 beaver had been made an enumerated commodity, and the effect of this on the considerable quantities of furs which had been exported to foreign countries could not yet be known. At the close of the series of hearings Hunter, the ex-governor, was called in and gave his voice strongly in support of the acts. But in the absence of conclusive evidence for either side, the board of trade contented itself with criticising the severity of the oaths and penalties imposed by the acts, and recommended that a new act should be passed for the further development of the avenues of trade which were opening with the Indians, and which should be free from the objections to which the present acts were liable.

[1] N. Y. Docs. V, 760. [2] *Ibid.*, 745 *et seq.*, 760–763.

[3] The reports sent from the New York custom house relating to this trade continued to differ from the accounts at the London custom house, suggesting that the New York reports gave only the numbers of casks or other packages, without reference to the number and value of the skins which they contained. This Burnet finally confessed to be the fact, though it invalidated his claim that under the new laws the export of furs from New York had decidedly increased. N. Y. Docs. V, 779–781, 811.

By 1726 Burnet himself had become convinced that, under the provisions of the existing laws, it was impossible to prevent wholesale evasions.[1] Therefore a detailed act was passed in which the oaths and fines and absolute prohibitions of the previous statutes were dropped and for them was substituted a duty on the trade in Indian goods both to the north and to the west, but the rates charged on the trade to the north, *i.e.*, to Canada, were double those imposed on the direct trade with the Indians to the westward. The collection of these duties was farmed out at Albany.

The establishment of the post at Oswego, in which culminated the policy of Burnet towards the Indians and French, furnished an added occasion for continuing the fines and other sources of revenue connected with the restriction of trade with Canada. These were used as a part of the revenue for the support of Oswego. In two elaborate acts, passed in 1727 and 1728, these two lines of policy were combined and made to contribute to one another, a special board of commissioners being created for their execution.[2]

Meantime in England the merchants continued their attacks on the policy of restricting trade with Canada, and it was represented that the fur trade was suffering greatly thereby. In November, 1729, the board of trade submitted a report on the whole series of six acts which had been passed at that time, approving in general the policy of prohibiting trade with Canada and promoting direct trade with the Indians, but taking exception to several of their administrative provisions.[3] It therefore thought they all should be repealed. This advice was acted on by an order in council of December 11, 1729, against which the assembly of New York filed a long protest a year later.[4] But this was futile, and though Oswego stood, Burnet's policy of restricting trade with Canada failed.

While the subject of trade with Canada was in the foreground Abraham De Peyster, the elder, who had so long been treasurer of the province, became incapacitated for business and his son, of the same name, was appointed to succeed him, June 2, 1721.[5] A search through the journal of the house

[1] *Ibid.*, 781; Col. Laws, II, *et seq.*
[2] *Ibid.*, 372, 484.
[3] N. Y. Docs. V, 897 *et seq.*
[4] Ass. J. I. 607, 621.
[5] Ass. J. I. 452.

failed to bring to light any evidence that the late treasurer had given security for the due execution of his office and the custody of the revenue, or that he had been required to do so except by one appropriation act of the fifth of Anne, which provided that he should account to the governor, council and assembly for the money raised under that law in such manner as should be approved by William Nicoll, the speaker.[1] His successor was now required to give security to the amount of £5000 that he would perform his duties to the satisfaction of the assembly.[2] At this time also the question of accounting to the auditor general through his deputy, for the entire revenue of the province, came up again for discussion. George Clarke, who was afterward lieutenant governor, at that time held the office of deputy auditor. An elaborate memorial was presented[3] by the assembly to the governor, in which the claim of the auditor general was discussed from the New York point of view. The emphasis was, of course, laid on its cost to the province and its uselessness. As to its cost, they argued that express provision for Blathwayt's salary had been made in his commission and it was to come from the West Indies and Virginia. The £500, as provided for, they claimed, was deemed a sufficient reward, and nothing whatever was said about an allowance from New York or other provinces. The auditor general therefore had extended his power when, without authority under the great seal, he had exacted a perquisite of 5% of the entire revenue audited by him. As the revenue of New York averaged about £4000 a year, this payment was about £200. It had originated in the corrupt days of Fletcher and Cornbury and the assembly suspected that it had been pocketed in the province and no account of it sent to England. In 1704 Blathwayt, they said, had declined the 5% as too large, and accepted a stated sum of £150 a year for himself and deputy. It was to avoid a payment to the auditor general in any form that the treasurer had ceased to account to him. But he was and had been ready to account with the governor, through whom statements of revenue and expenditure could as readily reach

[1] *Ibid.*, 467, 468.

[2] *Ibid.*, 454, 467, 468.

[3] *Ibid.*, 459 *et seq.* See Chapter I of Part I of the present work.

the British treasury. There was no intent to cast contempt on the authority of the crown or to withhold from his majesty the state of their revenue; but if so much had to be spent for auditing, arrears and salaries would have to go unpaid, and it was hoped that the governor would induce the lord treasurer to forego the demand.

In the summer session of 1722, while the assembly was still at work upon the accounts of the late treasurer, it was informed by his widow that suits against the De Peyster estate had been begun, on behalf of the king, to force an accounting.[1] After consideration of this in committee of the whole, the house resolved that the accounts in question, up to June 1, 1721, had been audited by a joint committee of the council and assembly and satisfactory reports made thereon to the two houses, and that the crown might appoint an official to receive these accounts, but for this he should receive no perquisites, from either the treasurer or the colony. It was also resolved that such accounting as should be made through the deputy auditor must be from the books as they had been kept and in their forms, and the assembly would see that the treasurer's family should incur no excuses thereby or from any suits which might be brought against them. In accordance with a letter from the treasury, in August, 1720, moneys for the regular support of civil government only should be accounted for and, as the assembly inferred, not the many extraordinary levies which were appropriated for specific uses and without allowance for the auditor.

By this time the rights of the auditor general had become an important political question.[2] Clarke, the deputy auditor, was insistent upon his claims and those of his chief, while the newly elected members of the assembly proved to be strong supporters of the late treasurer's interest. The governor refused to concur in their votes to protect the De Peysters and felt that he had lost credit thereby. But he would not dissolve the assembly, as Clarke advised, for then a revenue would have been voted for only two years instead of five and it would have been reduced in amount. But, in 1723 and thereafter, the governor succeeded in obtaining a yearly accounting to the deputy auditor of the current revenue, and

[1] Ass. J. I, 481. [2] N. Y. Docs, V, 765.

also of arrears since 1715, and the payment of the 5% perquisite for this.

With the fall session of 1725 the aged Robert Livingston, the speaker, because of illness failed to appear, and Adolph Philipse was chosen in his place.[1] This was one of several indications that a shifting of sentiment was in progress in the assembly. At about the same time the governor became involved in unpleasant relations with Stephen DeLancey,[2] one of the leading merchants and an opponent of the acts which forbade trade in Indian goods with Canada. Some personal differences also had arisen between the two over a quarrel in the French church. When, in 1725, DeLancey was returned to the assembly, as he had been to nearly every one for twenty years, and appeared to take the oaths, Burnet unwisely asked him how he became a subject of the crown. DeLancey replied that he was denizened in England. Burnet, being doubtful whether that was a sufficient qualification, said he would consider the question before he administered the oaths. DeLancey then produced before the house an act of a notary public certifying that he was made a subject in England and was entitled to all the privileges that went therewith: a letter of denization under the seal of New York and dated in 1686; a certificate that he had taken the oath of allegiance in 1687 as directed by the law of 1683; and a certificate of his having sat regularly in assemblies since 1702. The governor had meantime consulted Chief Justice Morris, who was also a member of the assembly, and he had rendered an opinion that DeLancey must produce a patent of denization in England or proof of its enrollment, and that one could not be naturalized in the province without an act of the legislature. But, owing to the possibility that in 1686–7 ordinances in New York had the force of laws and to the fact that for forty years the naturalization of DeLancey had been accepted as valid, Morris declined to give an opinion to the effect that his claim to a seat in the assembly was not also valid. The governor then referred the case, with Morris' opinion, to the house, and it unanimously

[1] Ass. J. I, 513 *et seq.*; N. Y. Docs. V, 768 *et seq.* George Clarke to Walpole on the political situation in New York.

[2] Ass. J. I. 514–520; Smith, History of New York, I, 230 *et seq.*

decided that DeLancey was duly returned and qualified. Though this procedure led to no sharp resolves, it caused much irratation and increased hostile feelings toward Burnet among the merchants. It inclined many to an unfriendly attitude when the question of voting support for the next five years was before the assembly.

Burnet had enjoyed several years of quiet and prosperity. Now opinion was drifting away from his plans and he showed less skill than Hunter had done in keeping or winning support. When he found that members were opposing his plan of another five-year grant he expostulated with them and threatened to take from them the honors which he had conferred; but by such means they were not to be coerced and personal resentment was aroused. Burnet asked Clarke to assist him, and the latter used such personal appeals as were not inconsistent with his own interests. The members of the assembly were resolved at first to make a grant for only two years and also to reduce salaries somewhat; [1] but Burnet insisted upon the five-year term, and threatened to call the house together in successive sessions until he had gained his point. But this course he had to abandon as futile, and to compromise with the house on a three-year grant and at a somewhat reduced amount.[2]

The assembly, which had been elected under Hunter and had been in existence for eleven years, was now dissolved and a new election held.[3] But it did not result, as the governor had hoped it might, in the return of a majority favorable to a grant of revenue for a five-year period, and the restoration of salaries and other appropriations to the amounts which had previously been given. Adolph Philipse was again chosen speaker. Burnet, who was greatly interested in the repair of the fort of New York and in the building of a trading post in the Indian country south of Lake Ontario, insisted that the appropriation was insufficient and smaller than the prosperous condition of the province justified. Much

[1] Ass. J. I, 536; N. Y. Docs. V, 878 *et seq.*

[2] N. Y. Docs. V, 778; Col. Laws, II, 254 *et seq.*; Ass. J. I, 534–536. For the Governor's optimistic speech at the beginning of the fall session of 1725 and the entries which show the unresponsive temper of the house, see Ass. J. I, 516 *et seq.*, 526, 529, 536.

[3] Ass. J. I, 545 *et seq.*

talk also had been occasioned by a reduction of the salary of Morris, the chief justice, to which his report on the DeLancey case had probably contributed. But a committee of the house reported that, in their opinion, the appropriation was fully adequate, though, if it should prove insufficient, the assembly would make it good.[1] No increase or change was made, though in 1727 £1682 was appropriated for the building of Oswego, on the southern shore of Lake Ontario. This was one of the most cherished objects of Burnet's policy, and its achievement proved a fitting close to his administration. The life of the new assembly was short, as it was brought to a close by the death of George I. The election of a new house in the fall of 1727 then became necessary.[2] This continued in existence only a single session, for on the transfer of Burnet to Massachusetts at the close of 1727 it was dissolved.

Burnet's successor in New York was John Montgomerie, who, like so many other governors, was bred a soldier, but of late had been a groom of the bedchamber. He was a man of good intentions but small ability and was totally without experience in such an office as the one he was now called to fill. He held office from the spring of 1728 until his death in the summer of 1731. As he favored no particular policy and confined himself to the ordinary routine of government, affairs flowed on in a peaceful current. The fact which now, even among students of the period, chiefly rescues his name from oblivion is that it is attached to the revised charter which in his time was issued to the city of New York.

Controversy was avoided at the outset by the election of a new assembly soon after his arrival. During the last year of Burnet a bitter controversy had arisen over the court of chancery and over prosecutions by information on the part of the attorney general, Richard Bradley. The last mentioned complaint had been brought to the attention of the assembly by the justices of Albany county, who had been summoned before the supreme court on an information setting forth the insufficiency of the county jail.[3] The attorney general met their complaint with the statement that his action had been taken on presentments of grand juries, that he had prosecuted no one and that the fees were only one-half what the com-

[1] Ass. J. I, 534, 549. [2] *Ibid.*, 557. [3] Ass. J. I, 569, 570.

plainants had stated they were. Similar informations however, had been filed in other counties and, in response to the general complaint, an act was passed forbidding such prosecutions in the future except upon presentments of grand juries or by order of the governor and council.[1]

But the more important issue was that which related to the court of chancery.[2] The powers of chancellor were exercised by the governor under the terms of his commission, as was common in the provinces, and no steps had been taken in New York to give this court a statutory basis. This furnished the real foundation for the complaints against the court. The occasion of their being urged so vigorously at this time was the fact that the speaker, Adolph Philipse, had recently lost a case involving rights to land before it; and also that the court had been especially active of late in suits for the recovery of quit rents.[3] Near the close of Burnet's last assembly, at the instance of the speaker, the committee of grievances submitted a strong report against the court, alleging that there was a general outcry among the people on account of its violent measures, which were undermining liberty and property. Because of its illegality and of the excessive fees and bail which it fixed, an act, they said, should be passed declaring all its orders null and void, and the passage of a statute for the establishment and regulation of this court should be taken into consideration. It was because of these resolutions, coming as a surprise at the end of the session,

[1] Col. Laws, II, 406.

[2] Ass. J. I. 571 *et seq.*; N. Y. Docs. V, 847, 874, 876, 931, 946–7; J. of Leg. C. I, 563, 568–571; Minutes of Ex. C., Dec. 19, 1727.

[3] As to the need of activity in this direction, a statement of Dixon, the receiver general, in 1718 is enlightening and it furnishes evidence of the continuance of old customs in New York. He stated the well known fact that, without pressure from a court of chancery, the payment of quit rents had always been systematically refused in New York. As to the size of land grants, he stated that tracts of 20,000 to 50,000 acres were granted at inconsiderable rents. Land holding had become a jobbing business, new purchasers holding of the original monopolizers, paying the prices they asked to the discouragement of settlement and the prejudice of the quit rents. The order in council of 1709, which forbade purchases of more than 1000 acres, was not obeyed. Many titles were illegal, and where quit rents were paid, some paid in money, others in grain, deer, beaver, otter, bear and other skins; some paid a peppercorn and some nothing. Cal. Treas. Papers, June 2, 1718. These same conditions continued and helped to give rise to the agitation respecting a court of chancery in Cosby's administration. *Ibid.*, Dec. 10, 1731, and Dec. 15, 1733.

that Burnet dissolved the assembly. The council, in a brief resolve, defended the court and later appointed a committee which prepared an elaborate reply to the charges. Because this committee called Henry Beekman, a member of the house, before it and questioned him, though unsuccessfully, about the charges against the chancery and their origin, Montgomerie's first assembly denounced this act, as a violation of its privileges in that no member should be called to account outside the house for what was said or done therein.[1] The council, in its turn, moralized on the serious encroachments that the assembly was making upon the prerogative, but the matter went no further at this time. Montgomerie, because of the strong feeling which had been aroused and aware of his total lack of qualification for the task, declined to sit as chancellor till further instructed from England.[2] The board of trade wrote to him that he ought to hold the court, but as it was not in the form of a positive instruction he either did not act at all or, if he did, he did not concern himself with quit rents. Because Rip Van Dam, who succeeded Montgomerie as president of the council, also declined this jurisdiction, the board warned him to act and to show special vigor in the matter of quit rents.

Montgomerie's conciliatory attitude brought immediate advantage in the form of an act appropriating supplies for the support of the government for five years. In accordance with previous usage the governor, by means of warrants, proceeded to adjust salaries so as to correspond with the revenue provided and to avoid a deficit.[3] From time to time salaries had been changed by governors for reasons similar to this, and warrants stating the amounts were simply read before the council without its assent being asked. From 1691 to 1715 the salary of the chief justice had been £130 a year. Because of the expansion of settlement in the province, and also in recognition of the services of Lewis Morris in the financial adjustment of that year, his salary as chief justice was fixed at £300. It remained at that sum until

[1] Ass. J. I, 577; J. of Leg. C. I, 568 *et seq.* 578.

[2] N. Y. Docs., V, 874, 876, 931.

[3] *Ibid.*, 879 *et seq*;VI, 10; N. Y. Hist. Colls., 1868, p. 221 *et seq.*; Ass. J. I, 580.

1726, when the assembly reduced it to £250.[1] But Burnet issued a warrant for the amount, as he did in the case of a few other officials whose salaries had been reduced by this assembly. In 1728 the assembly again voted £250 as the salary of the chief justice, and Montgomerie, considering this a fair amount and desiring to keep down expenditures, made the warrant correspond with the resolution. A protest was at once made in the council by the son of the chief justice. The governor turned to the council and it advised him to sign the warrant as it stood. This he did, and, so far as he was able to find, it was the first occasion on which a warrant of that nature was signed on the express advice of the council. The next day — June 13, 1729 — young Morris read a protest in the council which, in the opinion of that board, contained many false reflections upon the governor's conduct in drawing warrants on the revenue.[2] The council resolved that the governor had acted in the matter in accordance with law and precedent and that Morris ought to ask his pardon. On being called in Morris obeyed the command of the council, but on the 26th he presented another equally offensive protest, and because of this he was suspended from his seat in the council. The practice which Morris attacked was undoubtedly a bad one, a survival of the past which offered peculiar personal and political advantages to the governor.

In his second paper Morris, besides criticising the conduct of the governor in drawing warrants, protested against his sitting and voting with the council in the making of laws.[3] This was a part of a broader argument, that the assembly was drawing to itself all the power in the government and that the governor was playing into its hands, not only by obeying all its orders in reference to revenue warrants but by reducing the authority of the council to a shadow by his active presence there when they were considering bills, appointments or other business. As the controlling relation

[1] It also cut off entirely the salary of Walters, the second judge, who, according to Montgomerie, was wholly unfitted by age and lack of ability for a seat on the bench.

[2] Ex. C. Minutes, June 13, 1729 *et seq.*; Cal. of Ex. C. Min. for same dates. Gov. Cosby stated at a later time that these papers were drawn by the elder Morris, the chief justice. N. Y. Docs., V, 946.

[3] N. Y. Docs., V, 886.

was that existing between the governor and the assembly, and as it was determined by the control of the latter over the purse, the council, according to this view, was prevented by the presence of the governor from doing what otherwise it might as an opposition chamber. In all this Morris made no reflection on the personal integrity of Montgomerie, but he set forth his view, and defended it at length in a letter to the board of trade, as a correct account of the condition of the government in New York. The similarity between this and Logan's description of conditions in Pennsylvania under Keith is striking. Attorney General Bradley at this same time asserted that similar conditions were general in the colonies.[1] So impressed was Bradley with the growing strength of the colonies, with their tendency toward independence and the difficulty of subduing them, should this spirit gain the upper hand, that he thought immediate steps should be taken to make all officers of the crown independent of the assemblies and to place a royal commissioner, like the one who formerly officiated in Scotland, at the head of every one of them.

Before proceeding further with the history of New Jersey it is necessary to refer again to the policy of the proprietors in the management of their territorial affairs. Though politically East and West Jersey had been united, territorially they remained distinct and separate. The overthrow of the opponents of Hunter carried with it the defeat and flight of the intriguer, Peter Sonmans, who, as representative of the minority of the East Jersey proprietors, had assumed to act as agent for their whole board. Sonmans carried with him the records of the proprietors and, though they later fell into the hands of Basse, he refused to surrender them.[2] But affairs were soon set going on a new basis by the appointment of James Smith as secretary of the province and register for the proprietors, while the long and close connection of James Alexander with New Jersey began with his appointment as surveyor general. Soon after Alexander received authority as receiver general to collect quit rents. The supporters of the governor among the East Jersey proprietors also included Morris, Dr. John Johnstone, Gordon and Willocks.

[1] *Ibid.*, 901. [2] Tanner, *op. cit.*, 626, 628; N. J. Arch., IV, 172.

During some years prior to this the West Jersey proprietors, dominated by Coxe and his friends, had been engineering large purchases of land from the Indians in the northern part of the province, and the Coxe group was so manipulating the business as to assure the laying off of very liberal shares for themselves.[1] In the midst of this process, however, the Quaker interest was materially strengthened by the appearance of James Logan as claimant on behalf of William Penn, who had originally been associated with Lawrie and Lucas as assignees of Byllinge. Coxe also presented claims which he said were derived from Byllinge, but the Quaker interest was being strengthened in the board and large claims were made on behalf of Penn. The entire tract to be divided exceeded 200,000 acres. But before the process was completed the Coxe faction was worsted in the province at large. By proclamation of Hunter, Smith and Alexander were installed respectively as register and surveyor general of West Jersey, and Morris, who had quietly aided Hunter, returned to activity in the council of proprietors of West Jersey as its president, thus supplanting Coxe. Steps were now taken with a view of locating all records at Burlington and an attempt was made to adjust relations between the council of proprietors and the West Jersey Society.

Now that a greater degree of order was brought into proprietary affairs, the East Jersey proprietors brought a test suit against the Elizabethtown patentees and won, the decision being rendered in 1717. The Elizabethtown people then bought up such proprietary rights as they could within the tract which they claimed, with a view to further contention over the case in the future. The proprietors also strengthened themselves as they could by dividends from their lands. With the improvement of their status and the introduction of more order into their affairs, the two proprietary bodies addressed themselves to the settling of the boundary disputes which had long existed in the province, that over the line of division between East and West Jersey and that over the boundary between New Jersey and New York.[2] In 1687 and later, attempts had been made to agree upon the division line on

[1] Tanner, 669 *et seq.*
[2] Tanner, 633 *et seq.* and references.

the basis of a survey by George Keith, but this was too favorable to West Jersey to meet with acceptance. In 1719, at the instance of Logan and others, Hunter's last assembly passed an act the object of which was to establish a line in harmony with the provisions of the Quintipartite Deed and also to provide for the permanent maintenance of land offices at Burlington and Perth Amboy, where the proprietary records should be kept. The last named provision was put fully into execution and led to the establishment of offices, which are still in existence. The provision concerning the line failed of execution because of the interference of Coxe, who first entered a *caveat* against it in England and, after the accession of Burnet to the governorship, returned to New Jersey and again became president of the council of West Jersey proprietors. During the administrations which followed no progress could be made toward the settlement of this question, and at the close of Burnet's governorship an attempt even was made to secure in England the disallowance of the act of 1719.

By the close of Hunter's administration the laying out of colonies on the upper Delaware and the appearance of settlers both from New York and the Jerseys had begun to result in disturbances of the peace. Since this dispute, as well as the running of the division line, called for the fixing of the most northerly point of New Jersey, which was supposed to be on the northernmost branch of the Delaware river in latitude 41° 40′, the two questions were connected and provision for running the two lines was made at the same time, in 1719. Commissioners were appointed by the two provinces, the actual surveys being conducted by James Alexander for New Jersey and Allen Jarret for New York. But, owing in part to imperfect instruments, they failed to agree and the controversy was continued, accompanied by collisions between the settlers, until 1767, when the line was finally settled by a commission named by the crown. New Jersey had to give up the point 41° 40′ and accept 40° 21′ 19″, as the source of the Delaware, whence the line was run to the west bank of the Hudson at 41°. In general, it was during the decade and more which immediately followed the administration of Hunter that, under proprietary initiative, surveys of lands in the hilly regions of northern New Jersey were made, Indian titles were extinguished and claims were established which in the future were quite as likely to hinder as to facilitate settlement. The spirit of the New Jersey proprietors was similar to that which controlled the territorial policy of New York and showed itself everywhere as that of feudal landed monopoly.

The last four years of Hunter's administration were passed in comparative quiet. Coxe in England kept up an intrigue against the governor in such fashion that, in 1717, he succeeded in procuring the dispatch to the king of a rather numerously signed address of individuals purporting to be traders and inhabitants of New Jersey.[1] This contained a long list of charges, to which Hunter replied in even greater detail in a letter which he sent to Ambrose Philips, agent for New York. Though this showed that Hunter felt uneasy under the attack, it was neeedless, for his administration was approved by the crown. The assembly, which had supported him so well in 1715, was continued in existence until he retired from the governorship. Between this body and the governor no controversies arose. Considerable legislation of purely local interest was passed. The accounts of the treasurers of the two divisions of the province were inquired into with some care, and in the end, at the request of the assembly, they were appointed by the governor. Much attention was given to the bills of credit which were out, and in general these were well managed by New Jersey. Support for the government was voted for three years and salaries were slightly increased. This in substance is the record of the legislature and of its relations with the executive until the close of Hunter's governorship.

In New Jersey Lewis Morris, as president of the council, managed affairs during the interval between the departure of Hunter and the arrival of Burnet. Nothing of special note occurred except in reference to the running of the boundary lines, of which an account has just been given. In 1728, when Burnet was entering upon his short and troubled term as governor of Massachusetts, Hunter wrote to James Alexander concerning him, "He has an honest heart and good head, but over hott, which I was afraid might Some Time hurt

[1] N. J. Arch. IV, 306, 312; XIV, 71.

him."[1] This remark well illustrates the difference between the two men and is justified by what we know of Burnet's career in the three provinces of which he was governor. In neither New York nor New Jersey did he have serious quarrels, but in neither also did he show the tact and diplomatic skill which characterized his predecessor. In New Jersey he followed the same policy as in New York, by continuing Hunter's assembly in existence. There was some opposition to this course in the first named province, but in New Jersey the feeling against it was so strong that it led to a heated conflict; though before this was ended Burnet received from the board of trade a full approval of his course in this matter. The members, when first called together, refused to consider themselves an assembly, but on the following day met and organized for business.[2] The chief cause of the trouble, however, seems to have been a move on the part of the Amboy group of proprietors to secure an act of incorporation so as to place control over proprietary interests in East Jersey in their hands. George Willocks, the Jacobite, was deep in the intrigue and Burnet came to believe that he was at the head of a plot to discredit his administration. Willocks was arrested for certain alleged acts of sedition and put under security for good behavior.

But good feeling was not restored and, to bring the house to terms respecting his demand for a more liberal support and the question of the currency, Burnet adjourned them from day to day for twenty days.[3] This, of course, had quite the opposite effect from what was intended and, as the session continued, it degenerated into a tiresome interchange of exhortations, complaints and protests between the governor and the house, continued for a period of more than three months. One question at issue was the duration of the grant for the support of the government, — should it be for two years or unlimited in time or at least for five years? As the council supported the governor in this and tried to amend a house bill for a shorter term, the latter roundly asserted that the council had no right to amend money bills. The

[1] N. J. Arch. V, 188.
[2] *Ibid.*, 11, 32, 56; XIV, 145, 151, 183.
[3] *Ibid.*, XIV, 177, 180.

result was that no support was voted. Another question in dispute was, whether members should take the oath and qualify before the governor or the house. In connection with this Burnet insisted that the laws of the province regulating qualifications were not in force, because they had not been confirmed by the crown. He also produced an instruction which required that members should posses an estate of £500 current money.[1] That in these claims Burnet was exceeding what common usage demanded, was clearly indicated by the resolve of the assembly that provincial acts were in force until disallowed by the home government. To that safe position they naturally adhered. Burnet also sought to instill into the New Jersey assembly some of his zeal against the French and his fears that, through the labors of Joncaire, they were winning the Iroquois away from the British alliance. His demand was for an improved militia law preparatory for aid on the northern frontier, and also that forts might be built within New Jersey itself. To the first proposal he found the council amenable — though not to the second — but from the assembly no favorable action whatever could be obtained.[2] Because of the general irritation which had resulted from the tactlessness of the governor he was forced to dissolve the assembly in May 1721.

Burnet now urged the board of trade to procure the disallowance of two acts which were prejudicial to the secretary's office, and also to extend representation in the assembly to Hunterdon county. His objects in this were to adminster a rebuke to the assembly and also to offset the undue weight of the town of Salem, whence "the ringleaders of the opposition" came, and to admit members from a newly settled part of the western division, the inhabitants of which he believed to be friendly to his administration.[3] In the time of Lovelace an act had been passed regulating this subject, but it had not been sent to England for action by the crown. Therefore Burnet claimed that the right to fix the representation of localities in the assembly still remained in the crown and, as in Cornbury's time, could be exercised through instructions. An opinion in support of this view was pro-

[1] *Ibid.*, 163.
[2] *Ibid.*, 198.
[3] N. J. Arch., V, 12, 72–74; Tanner, 323, 328.

cured from Redmond, the attorney general, and members from Hunterdon took the place of the two from Salem Town. This change was accepted without protest, and at the close of Burnet's administration was embodied in law.

Early in 1722 Burnet met his second assembly. The election had resulted in several changes of membership, and Johnstone, the proprietor, was chosen speaker. The governor attributed his troubles with the previous assembly largely to the influence from outside of George Willocks, the Jacobite. That same influence was still feared, and in a burst of temper Burnet suspended a member of the council for venturing to defend Willocks. The fears of the governor were doubtless greatly exaggerated, for Willocks was forced to leave the province and we hear no more of the disturbing elements which Burnet's fussy demands had brought into activity in his first assembly. With the present body, and also with another which was later elected and which was in existence when he was called to Massachusetts, harmonious relations were continued without a break. On two successive occasions appropriation acts to continue for five years were passed, thus assuring the regular work of government, though with very moderate salaries for lower officials, till the close of Burnet's term. A tolerably satisfactory militia law was also enacted. Trent,[1] a New Jersey man, was appointed to succeed Jameson as chief justice, and thus the succession of New Yorkers at the head of the provincial judiciary was broken. Progress was made toward an extended and more adequate salary system, but the assembly ignored petitions for claims on behalf of heirs of a number of officials who had served in the time of Cornbury. Deficiences in the accounts of Thomas Gordon, the former treasurer, occasioned discussion between the houses and the question was finally adjusted by a prosecution of Gordon's estate in the name of the governor.

The improvement in salaries, as well as in the general financial condition of New Jersey, is of course to be chiefly attributed to its growth in wealth and population. But it was the firm opinion of Burnet that it was facilitated by the issue of bills of credit, for which additional provision, to the

[1] Trent soon died and was succceeded in 1724 by Robert Lettice Hooper. N. J. Arch., V, 97.

amount of £40,000, was made in 1724.[1] In recommending this measure to the board of trade for approval Burnet took his stand among the governors who defended the policy of such issues and made a notable argument in its support. He called attention to the straits to which people had been reduced for a medium in which to pay taxes before issues were resorted to. There was so little silver of any sort in the country, he said, that people were forced to cut their Spanish gold and even their rings and ear rings into small pieces to supply the lack. New York and Pennsylvania bills circulated in New Jersey, but were not legal tender. It was much better for New Jersey to have her own currency and receive the profit therefrom. In her issues thus far she had followed the conservative policy of her two neighboring provinces, in contrast to the New England colonies and South Carolina, and was keeping her promises as to redemption. In this way the evils of depreciation were being avoided. For these reasons, and owing to the loopholes in the wording of his instructions, Burnet pleaded successfully that this legislation might stand. But to his successor was issued the instruction, now becoming general, that he should not assent to any more such acts without the insertion of a suspending clause, and the further very restrictive order that he should not assent to any increases of salary by legislation without prior consent of the king.[2]

By the last assembly of Burnet's administration, which met at Amboy at the close of 1727, a triennial act was passed,[3] but this was later disallowed by the crown. Among several items of business the one which involved most controversy was connected with the recording of deeds and land titles and through that the control of territorial affairs. In the provinces, and especially in the proprietorships, this question was always in the near background. The lower houses of the assemblies, or the assemblies as a whole, were always seeking to control these affairs, while the provincial executives insisted that they were exclusively their affairs. The council of pro-

[1] N. J. Arch., V, 86–96, 193.

[2] *Ibid.*, 174.

[3] *Ibid.*, 192, 235, 248; XIV, 470. Burnet thought New Jersey was entitled to this act as a consequence of the practice of annual elections under the proprietors and of the instruction to Cornbury that all beneficial laws should be reenacted.

prietors of East Jersey had recently been formed and it controlled the provincial council or upper house. Therefore, when the lower house tried to secure the passage of a law regulating the enrollment of deeds and conveyances of land, the council opposed and finally, by insisting also on the passage of a bill to prevent frauds and mistakes in obtaining warrants of survey, blocked legislation on this subject and nothing was done.[1]

During recent years John Kinsey, son of a former speaker of the assembly, had been growing in influence.[2] He was a chief originator of the triennial bill, of the act continuing in a somewhat freer form the right of Quakers to affirm, and of other popular measures. Toward the close of Burnet's administration he, with others, began actively to support a demand for complete separation from New York and to plan an address to the king for this purpose. But by threatening to dissolve the assembly, if this subject was not dropped, Burnet succeeded in checking its agitation until after the arrival of Montgomerie. Upon the advice of the council, the new governor decided, as Burnet had done, to retain the existing assembly. The session was held at Burlington and almost the first measure brought forward was a request for a conference between the governor and the two houses upon the subject of separation from New York. Kinsey was the leader in this movement, and it was the result of the consciousness that the advance of settlement and increase of wealth had brought New Jersey to a point where she was fitted for separate government. Montgomerie was so offended by what he considered the boldness of the assembly in proposing such a step without previously attempting to ascertain the king's pleasure in reference to it, that he dissolved the house.[3] In reporting this to the board of trade the governor made a pretext for an attack on the Quakers, in which he declared that they did not deserve what they had received, and urged that both the triennial act and the recent act respecting affirmation should be disallowed. The reply of the board was favorable to Montgomerie's narrow views

[1] Ms. Journal of Assembly; N. J. Arch., XIV, 390; Tanner, 447.
[2] N. J. Arch., V, 262.
[3] N. J. Arch., V, 235, 248; XIV, 399; Ms. Assy. Journal, Jan., 1728/9.

only in one point. Its faithful guardianship of the prerogative made it hostile to triennial bills wherever they were passed. But as to the move for a separate governor, the board thought they should not be discouraged from addressing the crown, while the recent act concerning the affirmation differed little from the provision of English law on the subject and could well lie by probationary in the hope that the conduct of the people would never be such as to necessitate its repeal.

The composition of the next house, which did not meet until May 1730, was much the same as that of its predecessor, and that it would be disposed to support the same principles was indicated by the election of Kinsey as speaker. But the failure of the board of trade to support Montgomerie in his obstructionist attitude had removed the only causes of serious conflict. The chief debate of the session occurred in reference to a bill which, as finally drafted, coupled a provision for support of the government for five years with the converting into the treasury of the interest money derived from the outstanding bills of credit. This latter provision had been incorporated in an act of Burnet's administration and to it the board of trade was opposed. It insisted that the interest money should be used not to meet expenditures and so lessen taxation, but for the redemption of the currency and otherwise strengthening its credit.[1] On this subject Montgomerie expressed the same views as Burnet. He defended the policy of New Jersey in reference to its bills of credit and insisted that their credit was so good that the interest money was not needed to support it. All that he attempted to do was to induce the assembly to separate the two bills above referred to, but with the understanding that both should be accepted. Although the board of trade ordered Montgomerie to procure the repeal of the provision concerning the interest money, he was unable to do this without sacrificing the support and so the board had to acquiesce in this characteristic compromise.[2] With a formal address to the crown in favor of separation from New York and the employment by the assembly of Partridge as agent for five years, thus insuring active support of this demand in England, all except the routine work of

[1] N. J. Arch., V, 249; Tanner, 451, 557.
[2] N. J. Arch., V, 266, 269, 285.

this assembly closed.[1] Before it was called again Montgomerie had died and William Cosby had succeeded him in the governorship.

Between these two events, however, lay an interval of more than a year — from July, 1731, to August, 1732. During that time New Jersey was administered by a president and council. Lewis Morris, as eldest councillor and by all means the most experienced man in New Jersey politics, had already served in the presidency, as we have seen, during the interval between the retirement of Hunter and the arrival of Burnet. He now resumed this position and, in a letter to the Duke of Newcastle,[2] added his testimony to that of others concerning the question of a separate government for New Jersey. He stated that the majority of the people favored it, but that a considerable section of them, who lived near New York, were opposed. If the separation occurred, he thought the appointees to the new governorship would find it difficult to make profit out of their office. "The rendering Governors and all other officers intirely dependant on the people is the generall inclination and endeavour of all the plantations in America, and nowhere pursued with more steadiness and less decency than in New Jersie, and were they Indulged with a separate governour before they had made proper provision for his support and that of the officers of the Government, he must be a man of very uncommon abilities who will be capable of working them up to their duty." Such was one of the pregnant statements of Morris on this question. Another had reference to a possibility that, if separation was granted, an attempt might be made to cramp the trade of New York unless the council of New Jersey was amply furnished with members who had interests in New York as well. In this the contrast between the point of view of Morris, whose interests were equally divided between the two provinces, and that of the Quakers appears with great clearness.

The administration of Cosby in New Jersey passed without notable incident. He continued Montgomerie's last assembly but nevertheless met it for only one session, in 1733. Support was continued for three years and, as previously, the inter-

[1] *Ibid.*, 271; Ms. Ass. Journal, June 5, July 4, 1730; Tanner, 376.
[2] N. J. Arch., V, 314.

est money was appropriated toward meeting the charges of government.[1] It is also true that this act received the approval of the crown. As Cosby was already in the midst of his bitter quarrel with Morris and Alexander, he was naturally in a mood to welcome the proposal to name only residents of New Jersey to membership in the council. He was laboring at the same time to secure the removal of Morris and Alexander and, though he did not succeed, they did not attend the sessions of the council while Cosby was governor. In this quiet fashion, undisturbed by the passions which were agitating New York, New Jersey drifted on toward the time when separation from the neighbor province became possible.

[1] Tanner, 453; N. J. Arch., XIV, 531.

CHAPTER V

CONTROVERSIES DURING THE ADMINISTRATIONS OF COSBY AND CLARKE. THE ZENGER EPISODE, 1730–1740

Rip Van Dam, who, as president of the council and its oldest member, on the death of Montgomerie succeeded for a year to the headship of the government, was a Dutch merchant of New York city. He was one of those who, though he spent a long life in business and in office, never acquired an easy command of the English language. In politics he had been from the first an anti-Leislerian, and his special activities on that side in the time of Nanfan had recommended him to Cornbury and brought him immediate promotion to the council. He was a man of average abilities and during his presidency after the death of Montgomerie attempted nothing of note. At that time, however, the French established themselves at Crown Point (Fort St. Frederic), thus securing military control of Lake Champlain and making their most notable encroachment up to that time on the territory of the Six Nations, a region which was regarded by the English as virtually a part of their own possessions. This move, instead of a direct attack on that post, was the reply of the French to the founding of Oswego.[1] Another question of first importance at this time was the one which was involved in the proposed molasses act. New York held a prominent place among northern colonies whose commercial interests were imperilled by the restrictions which the merchants and planters of the British West Indies sought to impose. Its entire legislature therefore joined in a strong representation to the king against the policy, and by a statute six merchants in London were authorized to act as agents against it.[2]

But that Van Dam was more than casually connected with events of such wide importance, it would be absurd to suppose.

[1] Ass. J. I, 632.

[2] Ass. J. I, 628; Col. Laws, II, 729.

For some years now his name became prominent in New York politics, but it was in connection with events of a very different order. At the close of his brief administration New York entered upon another period of factional conflict as intense and prolonged as that which followed the Leisler uprising, and it was in this local struggle that Van Dam's name appeared with prominence. It was a struggle very typical of New York conditions, though some principles of wider significance found expression in it. With the utterance of these, however, Van Dam had no connection. He was engaged throughout in the stubborn assertion of his claims to money and office, and in the case of neither of these were his pretensions other than extreme and of doubtful validity.

The opponents against whom the claims of Van Dam were so persistently urged, both before the courts and by political measures, were the two men who followed Montgomerie in the governorship, William Cosby and George Clarke. At this point in the narrative it is necessary to speak only of Cosby. In England he belonged distinctly to the Newcastle connection, and his appointment was typical of many made by the duke during his long lease of power. Like so many other colonial governors, Cosby belonged to an Irish family which was prominent in the army. He himself had been an officer and had served as governor of Minorca. His wife was a sister of the second earl of Halifax, and during his residence in New York one of his daughters was married to a son of the duke of Grafton — "my Lord Auggustus" — concerning whom and the fine impression he was making in America, the governor wrote in one of his familiar letters to the duke of Newcastle.[1] Cosby's letters show that he was destitute of culture, but, after his fashion, he was clearly a man of rather strong personality, self-willed and resourceful, accustomed to command, with the contempt of men in general which was characteristic of the soldier and of the ambitious courtier. The need of larger means with which to support a wife and several children with aristocratic connection furnished the motive which brought him to America, and among New York governors he occupies a position alongside of Fletcher and Cornbury as types of the greedy proconsul.

[1] N. Y. Docs. V, 930, 932, 937.

It is probable that Cosby did not so fully deserve this reputation as did his two predecessors, but it was his misfortune to live when the newspaper press was beginning to assert its power, and hostile public sentiment found expression concerning him which twenty or thirty years earlier it would have been impossible to embody in permanent form.

While Cosby was in Minorca he had been charged with taking arbitrary measures to secure the effects of a Catalan merchant, which he ordered seized at Port Mahon while Spain was at peace with England.[1] After his appointment, but before he left England, he had interested himself actively against the sugar bill, while it was before parliament and when New York and the other northern colonies were laboring to prevent its passage. For this service, though in the end it proved unsuccessful, he is said to have been exceedingly well paid. In his first letter to Newcastle after his arrival in New York Cosby expressed the hope that, out of his " wonted goodness and indulgent care of us," the duke would confirm " my son Billy " in a clerkship to which his father had named him. This " will give me a little more power," which he much needed, as the " Boston spirit " was spreading among the colonies, and secretaries and deputies thought and acted as if they were independent of governors.[2] " I make the right use of Mr. Clarke, He was my first minister," wrote Cosby; while with Charles Delafaye, under secretary of state, he was also on intimate terms. It is in letters of Newcastle's dependents, like Cosby and Clinton, that one finds frank avowals of the desire for patronage and acknowledgments of the most direct favors received.

The assembly, which was already in existence, Cosby continued and it proved to be not seriously out of harmony with the governor throughout his administration. However, it adopted resolutions in response, it said, to the general cry of the people, that " no fees can or ought to be exacted from the people by any officer or practitioner of the law whatsoever in the colony, but such as are or shall be established by consent in general assembly," and a committee was appointed to prepare a table of fees and a bill for its enactment.[3] Little progress was made with the matter, and it soon dropped

[1] Smith, *op. cit.*, II, 1. [2] N. Y. Docs., V, 937, 942. [3] Ass. J. I, 637.

out of sight. Cosby experienced the favorable result of the good feeling toward the executive which prevailed at the time of his arrival, in the form of a five-years' grant for the support of the government.[1] In the resolutions his salary was fixed at £1560, with the addition of £400 per year for fuel and candles for the fort and £160 for his journey to Albany, besides presents for the Indians. Not content with these grants, Cosby asked for a further sum in reward for his services in support of the sugar bill. At first £750 was voted, and on Cosby expressing his dissatisfaction with this it was raised to £1000.[2] Even with this, Morris said, he expressed himself as dissatisfied, and that in contemptuous language.[3]

But it was with Van Dam, a man as thrifty and persistent as himself, that Cosby almost immediately came into conflict over a question of perquisites. This occasioned the first appearance of the press in New York as an important agent in political affairs, and opened a series of conflicts which were scarcely to cease until they were merged in the struggle for independence. Van Dam, while president, had with the consent of the council received the whole of the governor's salary. This had been voted him after some hesitation by the council, of February 7, 1731/2.[4] But, in accordance with general usage, Cosby brought with him the order of the king that this and all perquisites and emoluments should be divided for the term of the presidency, with the governor.[5] On November 14, 1732, three and one-half months after Cosby had been sworn in as governor, the council, pursuant to the instruction, issued an order to Van Dam to refund. He, having doubtless been in consultation with James Alexander and other counsel and friends, sought excuses for delay. He would agree to the terms of the instruction, if the governor would divide with him the emoluments which he had received while in England, claiming that they amounted to more than

[1] *Ibid.*, 646; Col. Laws, II, 768.

[2] Ass. J. I, 647.

[3] Smith, *op. cit.*, p. 2. It is probable that the reference by Morris in a letter to Colden, dated Jan. 17, 1734, is to the language which Cosby used on this occasion: "So that I flatter myself that in the next Reign polite literature will be introduced instead of God Dam ye." Ms. Colden Letters.

[4] Ex. C. Minutes, Sept. 3, 1731, to close of Nov., 1732.

[5] This was an additional instruction and was entered in Ex. C. Minutes, Nov. 14, 1732. N. Y. Docs. VI, 10. Smith, II, 4.

£6000, while those of Van Dam were less than £2000.[1] To this Cosby would not agree, and Van Dam refused to pay any of his half. Cosby thereupon instituted suit. He could not bring the suit in chancery, for there he would be judge in his own case. He therefore resorted to the court of exchequer, but suspecting that a jury might be prejudiced and bring in a verdict against him, upon advice he brought the suit in equity, that is, before the judges of the supreme court sitting on the equity side of the exchequer. The judges were the chief justice, Lewis Morris, and the first and second assistants, James DeLancey and the younger Frederick Philipse, a brother of the councillor. Of these the last two were and continued to be firm supporters of the governor; between Cosby and Morris friendly relations had never existed. Cosby said that Morris, who was chancellor of New Jersey, had slighted him when he first went there to receive the seals. They now at once became bitter enemies.[2] Bradley, the attorney general, acted as prosecuting officer against Van Dam, while the latter secured as counsel his friends James Alexander and William Smith, two of the ablest practitioners in New York. The constitutional question which this case at once brought to the front was that of the legality of courts which had no statutory basis, a question that also seriously agitated several other provinces.

When the case came up for trial, the counsel for Van Dam at once attacked the legality of the court, using against it the arguments which in the previous administration had been used against the court of chancery.[3] When their plea and demurrer came to be argued, the chief justice instructed the counsel to consider only that part of the plea which struck at the jurisdiction of the exchequer as a court of equity or on its equity side. The counsel for the government replied that they had prepared to argue the whole plea and could not easily change. But the chief justice overruled them. As soon as the counsel had finished, the chief justice read a

[1] See letters of Van Dam to Cosby, and estimates in the New York Public Library.

[2] For Morris' statement on this point see an appendix to his argument on the court of exchequer as a court of equity.

[3] N. Y. Docs. VI, 10 *et seq.* Opinion of Morris C. J. and arguments of counsel are in N. Y. Public Library.

carefully prepared argument in support of the view put forth by Alexander and Smith, the counsel for the defense.

In this argument the case against the legality of courts established by ordinance in the colonies, and especially against courts of equity with fees so established, was presented with greater show of learning than was probably the case in any other colony or at any other time. It was in brief, following Coke, that a court of equity could exist in England by prescription but not by grant or by commission without an act of parliament; and as to fees, that the erection of an office with a fee attached was generally acknowledged to be a tallage and so required an act of parliament. In view of these facts, it was argued, though instructions might have been framed so as to appear to exclude the assembly from its right to erect courts and establish fees, they must not be interpreted in that sense. What the king could not do in England his governor and council could not do in a colony. Turning then to New York and to the court of exchequer, considered as a court of equity, the chief justice argued that the supreme court was one tribunal, a unit, and it was not contemplated that it should separate into distinct tribunals. Judges could not sit and reverse their own judgments; hence there could not be three distinct courts, as in England. The term court of exchequer then, when applied to the supreme court, must mean a court of law and not of equity. He then went on to show, from the legislation of 1683 and later years, that the supreme court of New York was created by statute and had continued to exist under such authority ever since. It had been claimed that by instruction to Bellomont in 1699, and on the expiration of earlier temporary acts, courts had been reestablished, and that since then they had rested upon ordinance. But this, he argued, was repugnant to the law of England, and could not be done by ordinance; and that furthermore, as the act of 1683 was perpetual, it revived as soon as the later temporary acts expired. The counsel for Van Dam added to the above the further claim that the ordinance, which it was claimed had created the court, expired on the death of George I, and no later one had been issued to reestablish it.

Of the justices, DeLancey and Philipse, the latter was not

a trained lawyer, but the former had received in England the legal training which well-to-do colonials were now beginning to give their sons who were intended for the law. They now, after due preparation, delivered opinions in favor of the contention of the government, that is, of the legality of the exchequer as a court of equity, and that without statutory authority. The next day, after the last of these opinions had been rendered, Morris told his colleagues publicly from the bench that their arguments were mean, weak and futile, and that they were only his assistants, implying that when in opposition to him their opinion would not stand. DeLancey and Philipse resented this and insisted on their joint authority. Morris then left the bench and declared that he would sit no more with them when cases in equity came up. Cosby's suit, of course, was blocked, for no decision on his claim against Van Dam had been reached. Though the governor claimed that the opinion of the two assistants should stand as the opinion of the court, it is evident that the court was divided and no clear decision had been reached as to the legality of the jurisdiction claimed. But the opinion of a colonial court could not be final and, should the case be carried before the privy council, there could be no doubt that it would sustain the government. Of the argument which the assistants made at this time we have no record, but in the famous charge which he gave to the grand jury on libels DeLancey summed up his view concerning the court of exchequer.[1] His argument ran substantially as follows: That a court of exchequer had existed time out of mind in England and it had regularly heard suits in equity by English bill. The laws of New York had come in with the English, as into an uninhabited country, and the equity jurisdiction of the exchequer had been brought in with the rest. Laws, however, could not be executed without officers or courts established without judges, and appointment to office was a prerogative which was necessarily exercised in this case by governors. DeLancey also cited cases where the supreme court had expressly acted as a court of exchequer since the accession of George II and with Morris on the bench.[2] "In

[1] See DeLancey's Charge to the Grand Jury, Jan. 15, 1733/4.

[2] Murray, in a later opinion, cited several such cases.

the winter of 1731," he continued, "during Van Dam's administration, there was held a weekly meeting of judges in town and of the most considerable lawyers; at one of these meetings it was proposed by one of them to bring the equity business into this court and a question arising, whether the judges were sufficiently empowered by their commission to determine causes brought by English bill, My commission and My brother Philipses were brought, and considered, and it was agreed by us all, to wit, Messrs Alexander, Horsmanden, Murray, Chambers, Smith, Jameson and Worrell, who were present at that meeting, that the judges were well empowered, and upon that they resolved to bring the business here accordingly." The reasons for this action were the great delays in chancery due to the frequent absences of the governors in Albany and New Jersey, and that it had better be done while there was no governor lest, when a new one came, he might dislike having business taken from his court and none of the lawyers would then take the initiative. By a writer on the other side it was admitted that these meetings were held and that Morris was interested; also that all were ready for the change, if it were possible and legal, and that because the chancery, as managed, was far from being a benefit to the people.[1] Morris, he continued, was in favor of trying it and probably would have continued in that opinion, had there not been a plea to the jurisdiction; this led him to a more strict inquiry, with the result which has been described.

As Morris had used expressions which he considered derogatory to the prerogative, Cosby sent to him for a certified copy of his argument. Instead of complying, Morris printed and circulated it, with a letter to the governor as an introduction.[2] Inasmuch as the chief justice held during the king's pleasure and was virtually an appointee of the governor, this was a bold act, and the method of it showed more of the political than of the judicial temper. It gave Cosby the opportunity to interpret his course as an appeal to the people

[1] See Observations on Charge of DeLancey. This very likely was written by Alexander and Smith.

[2] The Opinion and Argument of the Chief Justice of New York concerning the Jurisdiction of the Supreme Court of the said Province to determine Causes in the Court of Equity. Printed by J. P. Zenger, 1733.

against the other two judges. This, together with the position of Morris in New Jersey, led Cosby to remove him. It was done in the most contemptuous manner possible by simply advancing DeLancey to the chief justiceship, without any notification to Morris, the advancement of Philipse to the place of first assistant and the appointment of Daniel Horsmanden to the place which Philipse had held.[1] Cosby and his friends interpreted Morris's opinion as an attack on all equity courts in New York and hence on the prerogative. They were greatly impressed with the progress of "Boston principles" in New York, which must be checked by a determined stand for the executive and the crown. This course was taken wholly apart from the technical points in the dispute, which the governor did not pretend to follow or understand. The attitude of Morris and his son, with their other supporters, was equally political. Other chief justices had been removed, but rarely, if ever, a man with the political gifts and pugnacity of Lewis Morris. The conditions therefore were ripe for a spirited political conflict.

In the fall of 1733 Morris and his son Lewis ran for assembly in a by-election, one for the county and the other for the borough of Westchester, and both were elected.[2] The candidacy of the ex-chief justice for the county seat brought him directly into conflict with the Philipse and DeLancey families, both of which had large country estates in Westchester. William Forster, who originally had been sent over as a schoolmaster, but now, on appointment by Governor Cosby, held the offices of clerk of the peace and justice of common pleas for the county, was put up by the Philipse-DeLancey party as their candidate. Partisan zeal was roused to the highest pitch. The freeholders of the factions were marshalled at the polling place at Eastchester, as if in hostile feudal array, and physical conflict between the two seemed imminent. It was a conflict between aristocrats, the mass of the people of the county being their tenants and excluded from the suffrage. The closest approach to a fight at the polls came when, by a partisan decision of the sheriff, a

[1] This was a *supersedeas* without a statement of reason. The governor's instructions, however, required that in such cases he should submit good reasons to the king and board of trade.

[2] Zenger's Journal, No. 1, Nov. 5, 1733; Smith, *op. cit.*, II, 7.

stranger in the county and a supporter of Cosby, thirty-seven Quakers who desired to vote for Morris were excluded because they would not take the oath. Nevertheless Morris was returned by a large majority, and his election was hailed with great rejoicing when he returned to the city of New York.

A year later, at the close of September, 1734, occurred the annual charter election in New York City.[1] Feeling between the Cosby and Morris factions had long been at fever heat in the city. The followers of Morris felt that their liberties were at stake and that they were fighting over again the battles of Leisler and his time. The result at the polls was another decisive victory for Morris and the election of a common council in which there was only a single supporter of Cosby.

A formidable array of lawyers, merchants and people of all classes in the city and near-by sections outside were now in revolt against the government clique. Under the lead of Morris, Alexander and Smith, who probably formed the nucleus of a political club, a form of political agitation, new to the colonies outside of Massachusetts, was started. This was an opposition newspaper, the "New York Weekly Journal," under the editorship of John Peter Zenger. He was the son of one of the Palatine immigrants of 1709. His father was one of the ablest men of that company and became, as we have seen, a leader in their struggles for a tolerable place of settlement after the failure of the experiment on the Hudson. The young Zenger had become a printer in the office of William Bradford, who was the publisher of the "New York Gazette" and by whom all the official printing was done. Though Bradford personally tried to hold a neutral position, his "Gazette" became perforce the organ of the governor's party.

With the appearance of Zenger's sheet a new and much more aggressive spirit was infused into New York journalism and after a time, as public feeling demanded it, this found its way into other papers in various colonies. Zenger himself was more truly the publisher than the editor of his "Journal." But he was held legally responsible for what appeared in its

[1] Minutes of Common Council of City of New York, IV, 217, 228.

columns and his title to fame rests less upon what he can fairly be supposed to have written than upon his nerve and resource as a publisher, and upon the success which attended his fortunes in the famous libel suit which was brought against him. No one can carefully read the discussions which appeared in Zenger's " Journal " during this controversy without being convinced that they were mainly written, and all of them inspired, by the group of lawyers who supported the enterprise.[1] Cosby charged Alexander and Morris with being responsible for many of them, and they not infrequently reflect the views of Morris.[2] All reflect the spirit of political discussions which had appeared in the English press during the previous generation or two, though the legal tone which pervades them is so pronounced, and resembles to such an extent the opinions and arguments of which we know these men to have been the authors, that the origin of the articles can hardly be a matter of doubt.

In the early numbers the subject of the liberty of the press, in its political bearings under a limited monarchy, was discussed.[3] These articles, like many on other subjects, were signed " Cato," and were of the moralizing type characteristic of the eighteenth century. Their authors delighted in classical allusions. The philosophy of Locke lay at the foundation of their views of government, and English history, interpreted in the light of Whig principles, furnished the precedents from which many of their lessons were drawn. Coke was their oracle of the law. One of the later articles was a reprint from the " Spectator," [4] and it is not improbable that a critical examination would show a larger indebtedness to that or other publications of the age of Anne. One of the early articles starts with the idea of contract between rulers and subjects.[5] The liberties of true Englishmen was a favorite subject,[6] and it was asserted that, while it was the prerogative of the prince to choose his ministers, it was the privilege

[1] Smith mentions Trenchard and Gordon as among the authors of these papers. Smith, II, 7.

[2] N. Y. Docs. VI, 6, 21.

[3] Numbers 2 and 3.

[4] An article in No. 82 of the "Journal" is No. 287 of the "Spectator." An article in No. 10 was by Richard Steele.

[5] No. 4.

[6] No. 10.

of the people through their representatives to arraign the conduct of those ministers. Government by law was the principle asserted, and under that system popular privilege and executive power were equally sacred. A practical deduction which brought the discussion more closely home to New York politics was this, that the affairs of government should be public and therefore that it was the business of private men to meddle with government.[1] "Every man ought to know what it concerns all to know. Now nothing on earth is of a more universal nature than government and every private man on earth hath a concern in it, because in it is concerned . . . his virtue, his property and the security of his person. . . ." The necessity of criticising public men was strongly enforced. "The only security we can have that men will be honest is to make it their interest to be honest; and the best defense we can have against their being knaves is to make it terrible to them to be knaves." "Frequently men who are directing government find it their interest to plunder and oppress," and while the public voice is pretended to be declared by one or a few, for vile and private ends, the public know nothing of what is done till they feel the terrible effect of it." "The difference between free and enslaved countries lies principally here, that in the former the magistrates must consult the voice and interest of the people, but in the latter the private will, interest and pleasure of the governors are the sole end and motives of their administration."

From sentiments such as these it was only a step to direct attacks on the executive and ruling clique in New York; communications from private persons soon began to appear in the "Journal," and one of these led, in Number 12, January 21, 1733/4, to a slashing attack on governors. It is not unlikely that this came from Zenger's own pen, for it spoke of the halter as a proper reward for many things which governors had done with impunity. Some governors were likened to wolves, robbers, pirates, enemies, the devil. "There have been Nicholsons, Cornburys, Cootes, Burring-

[1] See Numbers 6 and 19. In Number 16 the administration of government was declared to be "nothing else but the attendance of the trustees of the people upon the interest and affairs of the people," and it was the business of the people to see whether public business was well or ill transacted.

tons, Edens. . . . and many more, as very bashaws as ever were sent from Constantinople" and "there have not been wanting under each of such administrations persons, the dregs and scandal of human nature, who have kept in with them and used their endeavors to enslave their fellow subjects and persuaded others so to do. And had there been any spirit left in the wretches who suffered themselves to be enslaved, they would by a bold and legal resistance have made these men either good governors or at least prevented them from doing much mischief and rendered them as contemptible in their governments as most of them were when they were out of them." Among the advertisements in the paper it was said that a list of names was being prepared of those who were known to have flattered governors and been instruments of introducing and continuing arbitrary power. In order to bring articles written in this spirit within reach of prosecution under the law of libel it was only necessary that they should contain references a little more explicit to living men and contemporary events.

During the winter of 1733/4 the opposition started more than one scandalous charge against the governor or men who were prominently supporting him. One of these was occasioned by the visit of two French vessels from Louisburg to secure provisions to prevent a possible famine at that fortress,[1] due to the failure of crops in Canada whence their supplies were usually obtained. Though the French brought properly accredited letters, the report spread that they were taking soundings in the harbor and the enemies of the governor charged him with betraying the port to the hereditary enemy by his neglect to ascertain what their errand really was. Van Dam incorporated this in the long list of charges against Cosby which he sent to England.

On the night of the first of February an anonymous letter, containing a demand for money on the threat of destroying him and his family, was left at the house of James Alexander.[2] Several persons affirmed that the letter was in the handwriting of Francis Harison, who was a leading supporter of the governor in the council and who also held four other offices,

[1] N. Y Docs., V, 958, 959, 970, 978.

[2] Smith, II, 8; N. Y. Docs., VI. 21.

among them being that of recorder of the city and judge of admiralty.

The matter was brought before the grand jury, but it could find no direct evidence. The council appointed a committee to investigate it, but because Harison was a member of it neither Alexander nor Smith would appear before the committee. This body exonerated Harison in a strongly worded report and expressed the opinion that the letter was a forgery, the purpose of its author being to destroy the reputation of an honorable member of the council. To the candid investigator this seems to be the only reasonable explanation of this clumsy affair. But Harison was an unpopular man and other charges against him were being circulated. He issued an address in self-defence, but this rather increased feeling against him. Partly because of public suspicion he soon removed to England, though it was also claimed that he went to oppose the plans of Morris.

The fact that Cosby, about the close of 1733, procured from the Mohawk tribe a grant to the king of a tract of 1200 acres near Fort Hunter, to which land the city of Albany had for some years held a deed, raised a cry that land grants, especially on Long Island, might be in danger.[1] At the same time also Van Dam sent his voluminous charges to the board of trade, and the council filed a labored answer to them.[2]

The comparative futility of these attacks under the system of privilege, with restricted suffrage and almost total lack of means for creating and focusing public opinion, which then existed, is shown by the fact that Cosby felt strong enough to call the assembly together in April, 1734. Adolph Philipse was still speaker. A large part of the members were practically unaffected by the agitation which was in progress. As no salary question was pending, the session passed peacefully. In his address the governor sought to explain the sluggishness of trade by affirming that New Yorkers had allowed Barbadians to become their carriers, had neglected shipbuilding and had not kept up the quality of flour — their staple product — by proper inspection.[3] He recommended a

[1] N. Y. Docs., VI, 6, 15, 25. Cosby wrote that the Mohawks threatened to leave the province unless they were protected against the Albanians; Smith, II, 25. As to the many large grants made to Cosby, see Keys, Cadwallader Colden, 51.

[2] N. Y. Docs. V, 974 *et seq.*

[3] Ass. J. I 654.

stamp duty as a relief to trade, which then bore the heaviest burden of taxation. He also urged the improvement of the defences of New York and of the frontier, and plans for such were submitted. An act providing that the affirmation of Quakers should have the force of an oath was passed, and such injustice as had been committed at the Westchester election was made impossible. The court party also proposed as popular measures a bill for triennial elections and another for the balloting of jurors; petitions were also presented for an act limiting fees.[1] The opposition made an effort to get rid of the court of exchequer, and on the strength of petitions from Queens and Westchester counties that courts might be established only by statute, William Smith and Joseph Murray were called to argue before the house the question of the legality of that court as established by prerogative. Each made an elaborate plea, bristling with legal learning, Smith against Murray for its legality. For this they received the thanks of the house and the arguments were printed.[2]

In style and argument Smith's plea was decidedly the abler of the two. He showed that in England even the most ancient courts had received statutory regulation and later ones had been erected by parliament, until on the abolition of Star Chamber a decisive pronouncement had been made against purely prerogative tribunals. As to the colonies, the argument was still stronger, for not only did the colonists live under the same constitution as modern England, but judges were more dependent upon the executive in America than in the mother country and therefore needed the backing of the legislatures, which were the great guarantors of colonial liberties. There was no more important work of government, he said, than the establishment and regulation of courts, for upon that depended the purity of justice at the fountain head. Murray, as he was defending the existing system, argued more closely along the line of precedent, broadening it by the contention, as DeLancey had done, that courts of equity had come in, not by virtue of royal commissions, but with the body of English laws, as a part of which they existed.

It was in the theory which he advanced of the mode and

[1] *Ibid.*, 660, 661.

[2] Printed copies of these pleas are in the New York Public Library.

effect of the extension of English law to the colonies that Smith made his most original contribution to the discussion. He argued that, not similar laws but the very same laws as those of England were extended to the colonies, as the Hudson was the very same through its entire course. The use which he made of this idea was to insist that, as in England the nation could choose the laws by which it was governed, choose its courts and determine the way in which the law should be administered, so the colonists could do as the result of the extension of laws and rights to them. As the people in England had the right to refuse submission to any court not erected by lawful authority, so had the colonists. With the introduction of English law went also the right of the colonists to consent to that which should be introduced, that depending on the adaptability of such laws to colonial needs and conditions. If, on the other hand, courts and laws were extended by likeness merely, much might be forced upon the colonists against their choice, much that was not intended for them in the first place and which was not adapted to their needs. The cases of tithes and of the ecclesiastical laws and courts of England in general were cited by Smith as examples in point. It was by this closer analysis of the subject that he sought to meet the contention of DeLancey and Murray and their summary and ready-made statements concerning the way in which English law was introduced. But it was an ingenious claim rather than an argument which was expected to change facts or views as they were generally accepted at the time. " Had the governor appointed other barons," says the historian Smith, " all clamor against the legality of the court of Exchequer must have ceased." " Nothing was less the intention of the contending parties than a just and friendly pacification." The fires of faction were lighted and they had to burn until some of the leading parties were removed from the scene.

In the fall of 1734 steps were taken for the punishment of Zenger.[1] At the October session of the supreme court the

[1] Smith, II, 15 *et seq*, DeLancey in his charge to this jury explained the law of libel, quoting from Hawkins, Pleas of the Crown, and called their attention to the dangerous extent to which public criticism of persons of all degrees had gone and to the necessity of resorting to punishment (Ms. in N. Y. Public Library).

chief justice obtained from the grand jury a presentment of certain doggerel rimes which had appeared in his paper and an order that they be burned. The jury asked the governor to offer a reward for the discovery of the author. The council also took up the matter and asked the assembly to concur in an address to the governor for the prosecution of the printer; but the house tabled this proposal.[1] Then the council, acting in its executive capacity, ordered Nos. 7, 47, 48 and 49 of the "Weekly Journal" to be burned by the common hangman or whipper and that the mayor and magistrates of the city should attend the burning. But the court of quarter sessions of New York county would not suffer the order to be entered and the aldermen forbade the whipper to obey the order.[2] It had therefore to be executed by a negro slave belonging to the sheriff, only Recorder Harison and a few dependents of the governor being present. A few days later Zenger, under authority of a proclamation, was arrested and in prison was denied pen, ink and paper. He was brought before Chief Justice DeLancey for release on bail, but it was fixed at £400 for himself and £200 for each of two sureties. This was more than he could furnish and he was remanded to prison.

On the last day of the court term, the grand jury having found nothing against him, he expected to be released; but instead the attorney general proceeded against him by information for parts of Nos. 13 and 23 of his paper, as false, scandalous and seditious libels. The trial came on in the April term of 1735, Smith and Alexander appearing as Zenger's counsel. They at once attacked the validity of the appointment of DeLancey and Philipse as judges, thus demanding a new constitution, not only of this court but of the courts generally in the colonies. The defects in the commissions of the judges against which they directed their assaults were these: that they were granted during pleasure, that the recipients of them were made justices of both king's bench and common pleas, that the form of their commissions was not warranted by any statute of Great Britain or of New York, and that they were not granted with the consent of the council.

[1] Ass. J. I, 671, 672.

[2] No reference to these events occurs in the Minutes of the Common Council of the city. For events from this point on see Smith, *op. cit.*, and A brief Narrative of the Case and Tryal of John Peter Zenger.

On the following day, after counsel had fully affirmed their readiness to argue those points as exceptions, the chief justice told them that the court would neither hear nor allow the exceptions. "You have brought it to that point," he continued, "that either we must go from the bench or you from the bar." He then declared them disbarred and a decree to that effect was entered, though Smith and Alexander protested against the statement in it that they had denied the existence of the court itself. In view of the revolutionary nature of their plea and its evident political intent, their fate hardly seems strange, even though they were leaders of the bar.

By this event the trial of Zenger was delayed until the following August. Then it was held before the supreme court with a struck jury, John Chambers appearing as counsel for the accused, and Bradley, the attorney general, managing the case for the government. But since the trial had first been called, Zenger and his friends had secured the services of the venerable Andrew Hamilton of Philadelphia as special counsel, though his presence in that capacity was not generally known until he rose to address the court. His talent was now to make up for the loss of the services of Smith and Alexander. The sole issue in this trial was that of libel, and the law as it then stood could not have been more clearly stated than it was from the bench and by the attorney general, while Hamilton's plea for the right of the jury in such cases to inquire into the evidence of the truth or falsehood of libels proved to be the greatest oratorical triumph won in the colonies prior to the speech of James Otis against writs of assistance.[1]

The law and usual procedure in such cases only required of the prosecution that it should prove the fact of publication by the accused, and upon this point alone the jury must render its verdict. The decision as to the character and intent of the publication, whether or not it was false, malicious, scandalous or seditious, was left to the judges. As DeLancey stated it in this case, "The jury may find that Zenger printed and published those papers, and leave it to the court to judge whether they are libellous; . . . it is in the nature of a

[1] Chandler, American Criminal Trials, I, 159 *et seq.*

special verdict, where the jury leave the matter of law to the court."[1] The definition of what was libellous was also so broadly drawn as to include all writings which were in the form of insinuations or innuendoes, the intent of which was to bring a person, or especially an official, into contempt. Under the law as thus interpreted, provided the fact of publication was proven, Zenger could never have escaped the penalty. The net was so spread as to catch every critic of the government whom it was worth while to suppress.

Hamilton began by fully admitting the fact of publication. Bradley then insisted that the jury must at once find a verdict of guilty. But Hamilton claimed the right to submit evidence that the statements in the papers were not false and scandalous, as alleged in the information. This the court refused to permit, on the ground that such publications were libels, even though they were true.[2] Finding his course in that direction blocked by a positive and, as the law then stood, a correct ruling of the court, Hamilton turned to the jury for the purpose of convincing them that their liberties were at stake and for that reason they must assert the right of judging the nature of these publications and the truth which they contained. He then enlarged upon the power of a colonial governor and the difficulty of securing redress against him. The perils and encroachments of power he illustrated from the history of the Tudors and Stuarts, as well as from that of Rome. He enlarged upon the use which had been made of the law of libel in this process, and how jury trial had virtually lost its utility in such cases. In a few cases, however, like that of Penn and Mead and of the seven bishops, juries had performed their rightful function, though at great personal peril. His address, of powerful but restrained eloquence, closed with an appeal to the jury to render a verdict which would help to secure to themselves and their posterity the right to oppose arbitrary power by speaking and writing truth. To the seriousness of the issue the jury was quick to respond by a verdict of not guilty. Under the circumstances this was to have been expected from almost any jury of average colonials, after such a presentation of the subject as Hamilton had given them. That the prevailing

[1] *Ibid.*, 175. [2] *Ibid.*, 167–170.

public sentiment was in full accord with the result was evidenced by the repeated outbursts of applause from the people who crowded into the courtroom and by the greetings which Hamilton received outside, it all culminating in the bestowment upon him of the freedom of the city. Trial by jury in libel cases had been shown to be something more than a farce in New York. In its first encounter with a newspaper press the official clique had been beaten, and this early publication in the colonies which, like James Franklin's "New England Courant" in Boston, had ventured upon trenchant and persistent criticism of the government and of established prejudices was not throttled, but permitted to continue its work. A long time, however, passed before circumstances recurred in any colony, or in the colonies in general, which were so favorable to an attack on privilege as those which existed in New York at this juncture.

In the following October Smith and Alexander submitted to the assembly a petition, setting forth complaints at large against the conduct of the justices of the supreme court and asked for a speedy hearing.[1] Impeachment of the judges was undoubtedly their object. The petition was referred to the committee on grievances, and upon its report the house ordered that the petitioners, within twenty days, should deliver to the justices a copy of their complaints and that in forty days thereafter the judges should make answer thereto; this in turn should be submitted to the petitioners. This was at once understood to mean indefinite delay, and though, in December, the two complainants laid before the committee of the assembly, as a plea against their disbarment, the reasons which had moved them to attack the commissions of the judges. As the court must rest upon the law, this was very different they contended from denying the being of the court.[2] They cited cases where similar pleas had been made both in England and the colonies, but the accused had never been visited with disbarment, an extreme penalty indeed. The hearing of the case against the judges was of course prevented by an adjournment of the assembly, but the decree against the two

[1] Ass. J. I, 682, 683.

[2] Complaint of Alexander and Smith to the Committee of the General Assembly.

lawyers, as we shall see, was later set aside by the court and they were readmitted to practice.

The opponents of the government in New York City now petitioned for the dissolution of the assembly and a new election.[1] This body had been in existence since 1728, and the long intermission between elections was declared to be a most serious grievance. The petition was supported by an expression from the assembly itself of a unanimous desire that it might be dissolved, a wish which it had also expressed nearly a year before. But the experiment was far too dangerous for Cosby to try at that time, and when the petition came before him it met with a flat refusal. Again complaints were urged against the court of chancery as organized, and in connection with suits relating to grants of land in various parts of the province in which members of the council, as well as the governor, were eager to share. It was in connection with these doings that Colden came near losing his office of surveyor general. Horsmanden and Alexander, of the council, were closely concerned in these transactions, the latter being eager by land speculations to retrieve his damaged fortunes.[2] When, in the midst of the quarrel with Cosby, some of these questions were being brought by the attorney general before the court of chancery and the governor proposed to sit as judge, Alexander and some of his friends filed exceptions against the legality of the court.[3] This was the first time that private parties had questioned its jurisdiction, and Cosby refused to entertain their plea. In a letter to the board of trade he added this to his many other charges, particularly against Alexander, and the board in its reply, September, 1735, expressed its hearty approval of the governor's action, assuring him that the legality of the court had been confirmed in the commission of every governor since the infancy of the colony and that he would do well to sit as chancellor whenever there was occasion. They now recommended the removal of Van Dam and Alexander from the council. On another

[1] Ass. J. I, 686.

[2] Light is thrown on these doings by unpublished Colden Papers of dates 1734–1736, in the Library of the N. Y. Hist. Soc.

[3] Ms. Colden Papers, Alexander to Colden, April 8, 1735; N. Y. Docs. VI, 30, 35–36. The grant concerning which this suit was to be brought had been made in Montgomerie's time.

complaint, which at the same time was urged against Cosby, the board of trade disapproved of his action and an opinion was obtained from the attorney general and solicitor general that it was illegal.[1] This was his practice, still common in the province, of sitting and voting with the council when it was in legislative session. The board also disapproved of his alleged practice of insisting that bills which had passed the assembly should be presented to him before they were laid before the council. This action was intended to bring such conduct to an end in all provinces where it still continued, and the board urged that the governors should be instructed accordingly.

Ever since the beginning of the factional strife Cosby, in his letters to the board of trade, had been denouncing Morris, Van Dam and their supporters. As time passed, Alexander came in for a full share of the governor's criticism. He demanded the removal of the two councillors and the confirmation of his removal of the chief justice. It was really a quarrel within the council, in which through the press an appeal was sought to the people in general and an attack was made upon the courts. Toward the end of 1734 Morris quietly left New York for England, in order to support his cause there in person. By this process the charges and counter-charges came before the board of trade and were widely discussed in circles which were interested in Cosby's fortunes and New York affairs.[2] Morris submitted an account of his entire political career, with a full defence of his conduct in New York, against the charges of the governor. He also acted virtually as agent for the opponents of Cosby as a whole, a function for which his wide acquaintance and his experience against the proprietors of New Jersey well qualified him. A decision in the case of Morris was not reached until November, 1735, when an order in council was issued disapproving of the method used by Cosby in his removal and also declaring the reasons which, at the command of the king, he had subsequently given for this act to be insufficient.[3] Morris, however, did not return to the office,

[1] N. Y. Docs. VI, 40, 41.

[2] See N. Y. Docs. V, 951, 975, 979, VI, 8, 36. The case of Lewis Morris (Ms. in N. Y. Public Library); Ms. Colden Papers; N. Y. Gazette, Nov., 1734.

[3] N. Y. Docs. VI, 36.

but when, a few years later, the separation of New Jersey from New York was completed he became the first governor of the new province.

The death of Governor Cosby, after a prolonged illness, on March 10, 1735/6, relieved the situation in one way, but only to open fresh complications of a different, though related, sort. On the 24th of the previous November, when in an early stage of his sickness, Cosby, at a meeting of the council held in his bedchamber, had suspended Van Dam from membership and had said that he would lay the reasons for so doing before the king.[1] This does not seem to have been done, though the governor's correspondence in the past had abounded in charges against Van Dam and Alexander and demands for their removal.

On the death of the governor, George Clarke, who was the eldest councillor remaining, at once called that body together.[2] The royal commission and instructions to the governor were read and also the order for the suspension of Van Dam. The clerk also swore that the notice of suspension had been served on Van Dam. All the members who were present, with the exception of Alexander, voted to swear in Clarke as president and head of the government, and it was done. Alexander stated that he was not prepared to give his opinion.

Clarke had long lived in the province. He was a nephew of William Blathwayt and through him had obtained appointment as secretary to succeed Matthew Clarkson in the time of Cornbury. He had also served as deputy auditor. He married Anne Hyde, a distant relative of Queen Anne, and had a country seat at Hempstead, where he lived much until 1738. His long residence and tenure of various offices made him thoroughly acquainted with New York. In its politics he had quietly, though constantly, participated for thirty years. He was, says Smith, " sensible, artful, active, cautious; had a perfect command of his temper, and was in his address spacious and civil." He was therefore fitted to conciliate, to restore political calm, and yet not to depart essentially from official routine and the accepted policy of the British govern-

[1] Ex. C. Minutes, Nov. 24, 1735.

[2] N. Y. Col. Docs. VI, 43, 46, 48; Ex. C. Min. March 10, 1735/6. See accounts also in N. Y. Gazette and N. Y. Journal.

ment. When the troubles of Cosby's administration were at their height he was in complete retirement at his country estate, and had left DeLancey and Harison among the councillors to bear the chief weight of unpopularity. Though a man of lower type than Hunter, he was well fitted to play a part as pacificator analogous to that by which the Leisler controversies had been terminated.

On the day following the installation of Clarke in the presidency, Van Dam came with witnesses to the gate of the Fort and demanded admission to Lady Cosby. On being told that she was not in a condition to see him, he requested that an open letter which he had in his hand might be delivered to her, and finally gave this letter to an officer of the guard to be delivered. It contained a demand for the commission, seal and instructions. Clarke himself now answered the summons in person, and Van Dam delivered to him a copy of the same letter and demanded his reply in writing.[1] This he sent as soon as possible, with the advice of the councillors who were with Clarke, stating that the documents in question belonged in his custody as the sworn head of the government. Van Dam then published a protest against all that Clarke had done. On the 18th Clarke, in reply to this, published a proclamation that he had assumed the government and warned all the officials to continue in the performance of their duties until the further pleasure of the king was known.[2] He also wrote to the board of trade, to Newcastle and to Horatio Walpole, the auditor general, most urgently insisting that Van Dam and Alexander be removed, as the only means of checking faction, and also that Morris be not restored to the chief justiceship. Popular agitation, he said, was again rising, this time against himself, and Van Dam was being used as a tool by much abler men to provoke an outbreak. In the absence of his father, the younger Lewis Morris was active among the opponents of government. Sundry of the officials and inhabitants of New York City also, as well as freeholders of Queens and Ulster counties, had petitioned the king to appoint the elder Morris agent, but this was reproved by an order in council as irregular and unprecedented.[3]

[1] N. Y. Docs., VI, 44, 45.
[2] N. Y. Gazette, Numbers 543, 544.
[3] N. Y. Docs. VI, 51.

Another perplexing and dangerous element in the situation for Clarke was the assembly. An effort was made to hold a session early in April, but a sufficient number followed Morris, in his urgent insistence that they could not act, to prevent the house from sitting.[1] Clarke then continued the assembly in existence by short adjournments until October, when a session was held. Meantime trenchant articles appeared in Zenger's "Journal" enforcing all the arguments which an acute legal mind could suggest against a recognition of Clarke by the assembly, if perchance its legal existence had not been terminated by the death of Cosby.[2] Clarke meantime, who was not a rich man, had to sustain the dignity of the government, with a very uncertain prospect of salary or reward in the future. A new governor might be appointed, but he hoped that until that occurred the entire salary of the office would be allowed him and that he would be continued in charge of the government long enough to make good his losses. The existing revenue act would expire the following year, and Clarke's opponents were extremely anxious to procure a dissolution of the existing assembly before that time. But while acting in his present capacity he could not dissolve it, and of course his opponents had no candidate whom they could support with the slightest probability of his appointment as governor.

In the meantime Clarke continued to write to the board of trade and to Newcastle assurances that faction was subsiding, and would continue to do so if a new election could be avoided and a continuance of the support of government assured.[3] This he was in due time to receive, for on July 13, 1736, a commission was issued in England making him lieutenant governor.[4] But before that arrived and while the assembly was still prorogued, Morris made his appearance in Boston. The twenty-ninth of September was the day when the governor or acting governor regularly appointed the mayor, recorder, sheriff and coroner of New York City and county.[5] In the city and among its officials sympathy with Van Dam was strong, and they urged Clarke to appoint no new magis-

[1] *Ibid.*, 52–56; Ass. J. I, 688.
[2] Nos 144, 149.
[3] N. Y. Col. Docs. VI, 65, 66, 73.
[4] *Ibid.*, 71, 83.
[5] *Ibid.*, 78–80.

trates, but at most to continue the existing ones, lest, if they received new offices from him, their charter might be violated and they lose it. Van Dam was also approached with the inquiry, whether or not he would appoint. When the day came, Clarke issued an order continuing the officials in their places.[1] Van Dam, however, called a meeting of the executive council, which was attended only by Alexander, and proceeded to appoint Cornelius Van Horne mayor and William Smith recorder, and also a sheriff and coroner. The election for aldermen and members of the common council also went in favor of the party of Van Dam.[2] Fearing an uprising, Clarke now withdrew from the city into the fort and an additional supply of gunpowder was ordered. A paper was circulated declaring that Van Dam was entitled to the government, but this was signed in only two out of the five wards. Morris arrived from Boston and was boisterously received by a great gathering of his supporters. Though he soon left for New Jersey, while he remained his unqualified support was given to Van Dam and his statements, if they were not bluff, showed that he believed the cause would triumph in England.[3] Some rather strong expressions were used in Zenger's "Journal," but when the time came for swearing in the city officials, those whom Clarke had continued in office took the oaths without opposition.

On October 13, just as the assembly was meeting and after it had spent a day before organizing in debating the legality of Clarke's position, he received from England an additional instruction prescribing a change in the form of prayer to be used for the royal family. It was opened before the council, and members of the assembly were at once made acquainted with its arrival. On the strength of it the house organized and Clarke made the customary opening speech.[4] He set before them the need of revenue to support the government and make good arrears, for the repair and improvement of Oswego and the other defences on the frontier, the desirability of encouraging ship building and the production of hemp and other commodities which would be valuable as exports

[1] Minutes of Common Council of N. Y., IV, 276, 347.

[2] *Ibid.*, 345–351; Ex. C. Minutes, Sept. 30–Oct. 6, 1736; Smith, II, 28, 30.

[3] N. Y. Docs. VI, 85 *et seq.*

[4] Ass. J. I, 689; N. Y. Docs. VI, 85, 86.

to Great Britain. Ten rather unimportant acts were passed,[1] but none of them of the character which Clarke most desired. Though they contained no provision for a revenue, he signed them all and relied on promises that due provision would be made next session. He wrote to the board that he had drawn no warrants since those which fell due on June 1. Before this session closed Clarke received his commission as lieutenant governor and all doubt as to his position was removed.[2] Though Van Dam continued to utter idle threats, the faction, as such, was at once reduced to silence, and it was due to this news that promises were made concerning appropriations at the next session.

But though the controversy, in the form which it had assumed in Cosby's administration, was now closed, the leaders of the opposition were still active in the assembly and outside. They were also resolved to raise questions which had been at rest since Hunter's time and to use their power to win further concessions from the executive. In May, 1736, Clarke wrote that during the past two sessions one of the great objects of the opponents of the government had been to secure the dissolution of the existing assembly, and then they would pass only annual appropriation bills.[3] If they gained a majority in the next election, they would not even make annual appropriations without further concessions.

Among these would be the establishment of a court of chancery by statute, the passage of an act declaring that judges should hold during good behavior, and the passage of a triennial act. They would also limit and reduce the fees of all officials and, with that and a system of annual salaries, they would make the entire executive subordinate to themselves. During the troubles of Cosby's administration the assembly had been quiescent and the contest had been fought out in the council and the courts. Now the assembly came again to the front, questions of revenue and appropriation assumed chief prominence, and by means of these the settlement which had existed since Hunter's time was overthrown. A new period of conflict over fiscal questions was inaugurated,

[1] N. Y. Docs. VI, 87–88.
[2] Ass. J. I, 692; N. Y. Docs. VI, 84.
[3] N. Y. Docs., VI, 63.

which resulted in important changes of balance between the assembly and the executive. With these Clarke was occupied during nearly all of his administration, and under the changed relations of war they were revived in the time of his successor.

When the assembly met for the spring session of 1737, the sufferings of Clarke from lack of support had become intense. No salary had been appropriated to him and he had been obliged to support the honor and dignity of the government out of his own moderate fortune.[1] In his speech at the beginning of the session he forcibly stated, that the treasurer's account showed a deficit which arose from insufficient funds and that speedy provision for this was expected.[2] Also, he added, the expiration of the time for which revenue had been voted was at hand and its continuance he desired. On April 27 the committee on the governor's speech, through its chairman, Lewis Morris, Jr., reported upon the deficit and the way in which they proposed to meet it until the first of the following September.[3] By examining the treasurer's accounts they found how much was expected to accrue until that date and what debts of the province would fall due by that time. They then selected from the total number of claims those which they chose to pay and ordered a bill prepared for that purpose. By this means they excluded a certain number of claims, among them being those for the wages of the clerk and doorkeeper of the council and for one-half of Clarke's salary. But the point which most offended Clarke in this procedure was this, that it was done wholly without the intervention of warrants signed by the governor with the advice of the council. It involved the appropriation of revenue by bill to the exclusion of the executive and apparently without the possibility of having it accounted for to the crown through the auditor general. This was contrary to instructions and modified the method of appropriating which was recognized in the laws of the province. It was to prevent such complete subjection to the power of the assembly as this procedure implied that the government in Hunter's time had gone for years without support. Clarke, risking like fate, dissolved the assembly.

[1] N. Y. Docs. VI, 89
[2] Ass. J. I, 695.
[3] *Ibid.*, 9; N. Y. Docs. VI, 94.

In the election which immediately followed the country party easily won. Both the Morrises were returned from Westchester and Alexander, though a member of the council, was elected from New York City. The younger Morris was chosen speaker. A first and unimportant session was held in June, which was brought to an early close by the necessity of the governor visiting Albany for a conference with the Indians. The next session began in September and proved to be one of great importance.[1] The governor, in a conciliatory speech, brought before the legislature the customary needs of the province.

"The deficiencies of the revenue, under which the officers of the government and their creditors groan," said the governor, "call for your early attention, and from your justice and honor I hope to see speedy and ample provision made for them." In anticipation of coming encroachments, however, he announced that he should obey instructions and maintain the prerogative, while he protected all subjects in the full enjoyment of their rights and liberties.

The attitude of this assembly on the question now at issue between it and the executive was explained in an elaborate address, which it prepared in reply to the governor's speech, and which was intended also for use in England.[2] The measures which were insisted on in the beginning as necessary to liberty and security were: the need of free and frequent elections, though they acknowledged that the late elections had been totally free from executive interference; the necessity of basing the courts and their spheres of action on statutes, a practice which was believed to be allowable under royal instructions but which later governors had departed from to the dissatisfaction of the people and disturbance of the province; that fees should be strictly limited by law, for if they rested on ordinance it was taking property without consent. Passing to the criticism of governors, they observed that the conduct of some of these, who had been "buoyed up and bloated with the fulsome addresses and servile flatteries of the instruments of their misrule," had not been "very becoming the representatives of a British monarch governing a free

[1] Ass. J. I, 704 *et seq.*

[2] Ass. J. I, 706. Smith's account of Clarke's administration is in Vol. II, 33–67.

people." They supposed that all the requirements of the crown would be fit and reasonable, if set forth with candor, but the practices of such governors as they had in mind were destructive at once of true prerogative and of the liberty of the people. Instructions, they continued, are "prudential directions to regulate the conduct of a governor" in the exercise of his powers, and they should be as laws to him. But governors had violated them with impunity or heeded them only so far as they thought proper or as it suited their particular ends.

The homily on governors served as an introduction to the treatment of revenue and deficits. Had their loyalty met with suitable treatment from the executive, they asked Clarke to believe that they would have been lavish beyond their abilities. But the miserable condition to which the conduct of governors had reduced the province made the raising of large sums difficult, if not impracticable. "You are not to expect that we will either raise sums unfit to be raised, or put what we shall raise into the power of a governor to misapply, if we can prevent it, nor shall we make up any other deficiencies than what we conceive are fit and just to be paid, or continue what support or revenue we shall raise for any longer time than one year; nor do we think it convenient to do even that until such laws are passed as we conceive necessary for the safety of the inhabitants of this colony, who have reposed a trust in us for that only purpose, and which we are sure you think it reasonable we should act agreeable to, and by the grace of God we will endeavor not to deceive them." There is certainly no more forcible declaration in colonial annals of the resolve of an assembly to control the public purse than this. It was followed in the course of this and later sessions by appropriate action.

Clarke received the address amicably, assuring them that he would assent to bills for frequent elections, or regulating elections, or promoting in any way the good of the province, if he could do so consistently with his duty to the crown. To this submissiveness he was brought by absolute need of revenue. The extent to which the opposition might try to go had already been indicated by a motion of James Alexander for leave to bring in a bill to vacate the seats of representatives in the assembly who should accept any office, gift or grant from the governor or commander-in-chief. Leave was given, though the motion applied to Alexander himself, who was a member of the council.[1] Soon the question came up, whether he should be allowed to retain his seat in the assembly. But on his declaring that he had not acted as a councillor since his election as a representative and would not so act during the continuance of the assembly, it was unanimously resolved that he should retain his seat.

Meantime a notable case of disputed election had arisen. Garret Van Horne, a member of the opposition and former representative from New York city, had died and his son, Cornelius, had run for his seat. Adolph Philipse, late speaker, was the government candidate.[2] After a hotly contested election Philipse, who was a non-resident, was returned by sheriff Cosby. But Van Horne petitioned the assembly that the case between him and Philipse might be heard before the latter was admitted to a seat. With this came also a petition, signed by a large number of New Yorkers, complaining of the unjust conduct of sheriffs in the recent election there. The assembly resolved that neither of the contesting candidates should be seated until the alleged partiality of sheriffs had been inquired into. William Smith, who had been forbidden to practice at the bar, appeared for Van Horne, but in opposition to his demands the supporters of Philipse carried a motion for a scrutiny of the votes. It was the vote of Alexander in the negative on this motion that occasioned the inquiry into his right to a seat in the assembly, with the result already stated. Van Horne and Cosby were both heard and then the court party won another victory by the passage of a motion that Cosby had not so misbehaved himself on election day as to invalidate the election. It being found, on examining the lists of electors, that some Jews had voted for Philipse, Smith raised the question whether or not they were qualified. Murray, counsel for Philipse, briefly argued in the affirmative, because the law mentioned all freeholders of competent estates. But Smith, though without special preparation, launched out upon a prolonged argument

[1] Ass. J. I, 705, 711.
[2] Ass. J.I, 710; Smith, II, 37.

against the right of Jews to vote, based upon the policy of England toward them and on their crucifixion of Jesus.[1] This argument produced a deep impression and resulted in the rejection of the vote of Jews and a resolution, "That they ought not to be admitted to vote for representatives in this colony."[2] With this was also associated the question, whether or not non-resident freeholders had a right to vote. This was decided in the affirmative, though Alexander and his friends had advanced the idea, which was ultimately to prevail, that personal residence was as necessary to the exercise of the suffrage as possession of a freehold. The result of scrutiny was the seating of Philipse,[3] while soon after, through the mediation of the governor, Smith and Alexander were restored to the right to practice law and all charges against them were dismissed.

With the accession of Clarke to office the governor ceased to sit in council when it was in legislative session, and it then began to have a speaker of its own.[4] Abraham Van Horne and Cadwallader Colden were the first incumbents of this office. As befitting this change, the chamber of the common council in the city hall was assigned for the use of the council when in its legislative sessions.[5] During this session the council began the practice — of which there were only three such instances before — of sending messages to the assembly by its clerk or deputy clerk; but the assembly absolutely refused to communicate in this way. The innovation was therefore abandoned and the council resumed the former practice of sending communications by one of its members.[6]

The council, under these somewhat more independent conditions, showed considerable activity in opposing or amending favorite measures of the other house. Because of the opposition of the council, a bill for the appointment of an agent by the assembly alone was dropped. Bills for the regulation of election and of fees, and to prevent corruption at elections, met with a similar fate. In conferences between the two

[1] Smith was a diligent student of the Bible and of Puritan theology.

[2] Ass. J. I, 712.

[3] *Ibid.*, 717.

[4] Min. of Leg. C., I, 661 *et seq.*

[5] *Ibid.*, 665, 666; Ass. J. I, 691.

[6] C. J. I, 687 *et seq*; Ass. J. I, 717, 718.

houses the bill for triennial elections was amended by the insertion of a clause permitting the governor, for good reason and on the advice of the council, to call the assembly to meet in some other place than New York City. This act provided for annual sessions and that no assembly should continue in existence for more than three years.[1] The argument which was chiefly used in support of this measure was that neighboring colonies — meaning especially Pennsylvania and Connecticut — where elections and sessions of assemblies were frequent, were rapidly filling up with settlers; people were leaving New York for these colonies, and as a result town and country property and rents were falling in value. This was deemed especially serious, because New York was a frontier province; and inherently there was no reason why it should be so, because the soil of New York was rich and it had better facilities than any other colony for inland trade and ocean navigation. The fact that this act was not aimed at Clarke is shown by the earnest desire of the assembly that he would support it in his letters home.[2] It embodied a cardinal principle of the opposition since the time of Zenger and would have worked a notable change in the political conditions of New York. But it was disapproved by the board of trade and disallowed by the privy council, on the ground that it took away the undoubted right of the executive to continue an assembly as long as it thought necessary.

At this session also a step forward was taken in the regulation of courts, by an act establishing and specifying the jurisdiction of local courts for trying cases involving forty shillings and under. Provision was also made, in an elaborate act, for meeting the contingent charges of the garrison at

[1] C. J. 691, 693, 694, 696, 698; Ass. J. I, 720 *et seq.*; Colonial Laws II, 951; N. Y. Docs. VI, 112, 113, 130, 136. It was naturally the desire of the opposition to tie the assembly to New York City, where its strength was greatest. The same feeling existed in reference to Boston, and one may surmise that the controversy in which Burnet had been engaged a few years before over the same question in Massachusetts was known to the leaders of the New York assembly.

[2] After the bill had been for some time before the home government, Clarke wrote that he was aware there was no great probability of its being accepted. "What I wrote was purely on the pressing instances of the Assembly." N. Y. Docs. VI, 135.

Oswego. The appropriation for this purpose was made for three years, and the revenue for it was to be derived from a duty on cloths and liquors used in the Indian trade. Commissioners for managing and collecting the duties were named in the act, and some of the strict regulations which were imposed were apparently borrowed from the legislation of Burnet against trade with Canada. The Indian trade at Oswego was also carefully regulated, as was the amount which could be expended on the repair of the fort. The requirements for vouchers and audit were also strict, and in every way those who drafted the act labored to eliminate executive discretion.[1]

In accepting these bills the governor was making concessions in order that he might secure adequate appropriations for salaries and current expenses, and to pay the debts of the province. But he was able to secure this only in the form of an act for the issue of bills of credit to the additional amount of £48,350,[2] and also laws making specific appropriations and granting the usual revenue or duties on imports for one year only. The act for the issue of bills of credit he defended, on the ground that it furnished the only means of discharging the public debts; but going further than that, he made a notable argument in favor of bills of credit, thus placing himself in the growing list of governors who were becoming converts to that view of the subject. He said that specie flowed steadily out of New York, that the rate of interest was consequently high, while the paper from neighboring colonies took the place which the occasional issues of New York failed to fill. Under the influence of the new issue the rate of interest was falling, and Clarke hoped that trade and industry would improve. As to the fiscal system of New York in general, the merchants had long complained because land taxes had been discontinued, owing to the influence of the country members, and the chief burden of supporting the government had fallen upon trade.

These bills Clarke was glad to accept as a relief from suffering, though they curtailed his power. But he bore in mind the hope that, in order to redeem the £20,000 in bills

[1] Col. Laws, II, 964, 994.

[2] *Ibid.*, 1015, 1036, 1047; N. Y. Docs. VI, 116.

of credit which had long been outstanding, an excise would have to be reimposed in 1739 or soon after, and that in connection with this levy he would be able to secure appropriations again for a period of years.[1] "I must not too much rely on that expedient," he continued, "but make use of it in conjunction with other things, to win them to like measures that former assemblies have taken. . . ." Time and good management on the part of the governor effectually removed the active spirit of hostility toward the executive which had existed in the time of Cosby. Judicious appointments contributed to this result. Lewis Morris, the elder, was well advanced in years and was now wholly removed from New York and its assembly by his appointment as governor of New Jersey. In the next session of the assembly Alexander was found usually voting on the side of the governor.

But this does not mean that the assembly abandoned the ground it had won or ceased to strive for more; but the process went on without violence. In his speech at the opening of the fall session of 1738 Clarke declared that more than a year had passed since the last grant of support for the government was made. The funds for redeeming the bills of credit which had been issued in 1714 and 1717, he continued, were now about £17,000 in arrears and provision for them would wholly expire next year. He knew that the assembly would deem it important to secure these bills and, as previously stated, he took advantage of this to secure, if possible, a restoration of appropriations for a longer period. He told the house that he would assent to the continuance of the excise, if it would give as ample a revenue and for as long a time as earlier assemblies had done. In the course of the session, in the hope of spurring them on, he laid before them a report that the French intended soon to make settlements near Wood Creek at the head of Lake Champlain and were negotiating with the Indians to secure a post at Irondequoit, on the south shore of Lake Ontario. About 200 Scotch immigrants had just arrived, and the governor urged that steps be taken to settle them near Wood Creek, and that presents be made to the Senecas to induce them to break off negotia-

[1] *Ibid.*, 111, 112. The bills of credit referred to were issued in 1714 and 1717.

tions with the French.[1] But these efforts of his made little or no impression on the house.

Bills were introduced at the beginning of the session to regulate and establish fees and to regulate the election of representatives to the assembly. The house also made it one of its standing rules of order, that the names of all who voted aye or nay on resolutions passed in the grand committees should be entered in the journal, and also the names of those who declined to vote. This made proceedings better defined and sharpened the responsibility of members.[2] When it came to resolutions on supply, they were made, if possible, more specific than ever before, aye and nay votes being taken on the salaries of the governor, justices, and treasurer. The same procedure was followed in fixing the rates of duty in the revenue bill, and it was carefully limited to one year.[3]

It was the plan of the assembly to tack to the bill for the support of the government for one year a clause providing for the continuance of the bills of credit. When the governor heard of this, he summoned the speaker and told him that he could not assent to such a measure, for it was contrary to the 12th instruction, which forbade the combining of different subjects in the same law. After considering this message, the house unanimously resolved not to grant any money for the support of the government without an assurance that the bills issued in 1714 and 1717, and the excise act, should be continued for a sufficient time after November, 1739, to redeem the bills. The governor replied, that he could not assent to such a bill unless the house would grant support for as long a time and in as ample manner as had been given to former governors; neither could he consent to the appropriation of the money. They had, he said, a large sum of paper out, which next year would be without a fund to redeem it. It would no longer pass and hundreds of people must lose by it. He had offered to continue redeeming it if they would grant a revenue for a term of years, as had been customary since 1690. But what they had resolved upon and adhered to was so daring and unprecedented that he at once dissolved them.[4] The board of trade fully approved of

[1] Ass. J. I, 735, 740, 742.
[2] *Ibid.*, 741, 743.
[3] *Ibid.*, 742, 744.
[4] *Ibid.*, 747; N. Y. Docs. VI, 139.

his course. "You certainly have acted as became you, both in communicating your instruction to them and in adhering to it yourself," was their comment.

Though the election which followed, in March 1738/9, gave additional proof that the anti-Cosby faction was virtually extinct, so that Adolph Philipse was chosen speaker in place of Lewis Morris, Jr., yet the assembly which was brought together was as alert as ever against executive demands. Owing to the ravages of the smallpox in New York City, its first session (April, 1739) was held at Greenwich Village and was brief. Of the two acts passed, the one of importance was the extension of the law for the support of the governor for one year longer. They had been deaf to the governor's arguments and he had to accept the bill.[1] In his letter to the board of trade Clarke gave this statement of the meaning which the assembly attached to the word "appropriation": "to assume to themselves the power in the revenue bill to ascertain every officer's salary and to apply and issue the money they give to those very officers and uses and no other; thereby making the governor and every officer in this government dependent on them alone and wresting from the governor the right of issuing the money. . . . as hath hitherto been done with advice of the council, pursuant to the king's instructions. They have for above twenty years, upon their giving a revenue, ascertained every officer's salary in their votes, and the governors have very seldom in issuing the money varied it. But now they would go a step further and in effect assume to themselves all power, that is to designate not only what should go to the support of government but what should be used for other purposes." Clarke had not opposed this, though he supposed the board would think he ought to have done so.

Because the smallpox had not entirely disappeared, the fall session[2] was held at Hermanus Rutgers' house near the Fresh Water (The Collect). Ignoring for the most part the governor's recommendations, the house resumed its usual course, calling for the accounts of the treasurer under the various revenue acts, calling for the amounts which the loan

[1] Ass. J. I, 752, 754; N. Y. Docs., VI, 141.
[2] Ass. J. I, 756 *et seq.*

offices had paid into the treasury under the act for emitting bills of credit, for the accounts of the vendue master and of the various commissioners who had been named by itself to superintend the erection of a battery and other defences at New York, a stone fort at Albany, a fort at Schenectady, and to have charge of the post at Oswego. These accounts were duly rendered. It was at this time that Laughlin Campbell and others petitioned on behalf of the families of Highland Scotch who had landed at New York and desired to settle near Wood Creek, but the land desired was deemed no longer available because of a prior grant to the late Governor Cosby. A report, however, appears to have been circulated that the obstacle in Campbell's way was a demand on the part of Clarke and Colden, the surveyor general, that they should share in the grant and the fees for making it. Clarke also saw that they were trying to cut his own salary in half (to £780) on the plea that he was only a lieutenant governor; also that they were going to issue more bills of credit and make inadequate appropriations for the various works of defence which were in process of construction.[1]

In the hope of bringing the house to a better mind, on October 3d, Clarke gave it a recess for six days and advised its members to copy the example of parliament, which gave a gross sum for the civil list and did not seek to determine its application, that being within the power of the crown. But this produced no effect. The appropriations for forts which had already been decided upon were adhered to, and on October 25 the governor accepted them, as well as an act for the issue of additional bills of credit. Clarke's assent to this last bill, for which he had to excuse himself to the board of trade on the ground that by this means he secured appropriations for defence, also resulted in a grant to him of a salary of £1300 for an additional year.[2] He wrote to the board that he had used all possible means to bring the assembly to the desired appropriation, but in vain. They knew that the country unanimously agreed with them and that the

[1] *Ibid.*, 761, 768, 783; N. Y. Docs. VI, 147, 150; VII, 629; Smith, II, 49, 50; and Colden in Colls. of N. Y. Hist. Soc. Fund Series, 1868, p. 229, in correction of Smith.

[2] Ass. J. I, 768; Col. Laws, III, chaps, 675, 676, 678; N. Y. Docs., VI, 150, 151, 160.

members were assured of reelection. Because also of the prospect of a rupture with Spain and France, they felt sure that Clarke would lay hold on the present session to put the province in a state of defence. They were also confirmed in their views by the fact that in the previous winter Governor Morris, of New Jersey, had assented to a revenue bill with specific appropriations. Clarke consulted the council, and it was unanimously of the opinion that this was not the proper time to dissolve. The members of the council who at that time were the most regular in attendance were Kennedy, DeLancey, Van Cortlandt, Lane and Horsmanden, all of whom lived in town. Van Dam and Alexander had not been removed, but Clarke had not summoned them, inasmuch as the board of trade at the close of Cosby's administration had reported them as unfit to serve. Colden was much of the time in the country and Livingston lived at Albany. Van Horne pleaded ill health as an excuse for continued absence.

With the outbreak of the war against Spain and the expedition of 1740 to the West Indies, attention was diverted largely to military affairs and special appropriations for defence. But at the opening of the spring session of 1741 Clarke, in a long speech, again brought forward the question of legislative encroachment.[1] He reviewed the history of the encroachments of the assembly, the origin of the treasurership and of specific appropriations, and the extension of the control of the treasurer from the revenue for extraordinary purposes to the entire revenue, a change which involved the extinction of the salary of the auditor general from New York. By this departure from the practice of parliament, he claimed that they had aroused suspicion that the colonies had thoughts of throwing off dependence on the crown. In the truth of this he expressed no belief, but preferred to attribute the course of the assembly to wantonness caused by prosperity. Then he passed to the immediate necessity of defence and, to prove his impotence, declared: "At present, if any part of the province should be invaded and money be absolutely necessary for any service, even in such an exigency I cannot, either with or without the advice of the council, draw for a penny; a circumstance well worth your consideration."

[1] Ass. J. I, 792, 797, 799, 810.

In its equally elaborate reply the house disclaimed all the sinister motives which were attributed to it, and explained its own course and that of its predecessors in the matter solely as a reaction against the "misapplication" of revenue, especially in the time of Cornbury They dwelt upon the beneficent results which had followed, in the form of certainty of payments in definitely ascertained sums instead of general favoritism and uncertainty, with large numbers of warrants remaining unpaid for years or in fact never being paid at all. Instead of admitting the distinction between extraordinary grants and stated revenue, to which Clarke had called their attention, they sought to define revenue as including only the quit rents and permanent dues of the crown, all of which passed through the hands of the receiver general, while all moneys granted by assemblies were temporary grants and hence, according to the governor's definition, fell properly under the control of the treasurer. This was a novel view, not in harmony with the distinction drawn in the past, and was evidently contrived to fit the situation as it had actually come to exist. And as to the auditor general, whose dues from New York had long remained unpaid, the house cited evidence that he had never received anything from Massachusetts, and expressed the opinion that the salary he received in England was probably sufficient for his support. The assembly was so completely master of the situation that all Clarke could do, when their last address was presented, was to receive it with a silent bow.[1] The discussion was not resumed during the two remaining years of his administration.

[1] Smith, II, 63.

CHAPTER VI

IMMIGRATION INTO THE AMERICAN COLONIES DURING THE FIRST HALF OF THE EIGHTEENTH CENTURY

Of the two terms, colonization and immigration, the former is the more comprehensive. It includes the entire process which results in the establishment of dependencies, namely, the occupation of the soil, the transfer and natural growth of population, the establishment of trade relations, the development of political supremacy and of all the institutions which accompany this growth. Immigration, or emigration, is only one step, though a very important one, in this process. It refers to the transfer of colonists from the parent state or other, and usually older, communities to the territory which is being colonized. It may result in the removal of masses of population from one country to another without a corresponding transfer of sovereignty, the immigrants changing their nationality by naturalization. During the past half-century this process has been illustrated on a vast scale in the history of the United States. It also assumed considerable dimensions in the eighteenth century. Many other instances of the same kind could be cited and the difference between them and colonization, in the accepted meaning of that term, is evident.

The British-American colonies were settled by a process of immigration. This formed an important part of the colonizing activity of that time. Under the conditions of resources, knowledge and transportation which then existed, the removal of a considerable body of people from their ancient homes to a wilderness across the ocean was no easy task. No single motive or impulse was sufficient, but a variety of conditions which made life hard in the old world and made it appear to be much easier in the new had to combine to produce the result. Among these in England were congested conditions of population in many localities occasioned by laws of settlement, changes in methods of agriculture, disbandment of soldiers who had long been absent in wars on the continent, crime, religious intolerance, wars and general misgovernment. These gave rise to certain phenomena resembling over-population, but not in fact to excessive numbers in the kingdom as a whole. What was needed was a better distribution and far more elastic conditions within the economic organism. As soon as the way for the founding of colonies was opened the push of motives, like the desire for profit and betterment and the love of adventure, made themselves felt. Religious zeal and the desire to escape from restraints of various kinds at home played an important part. Viewed from this standpoint, emigration involved some of the elements of an emancipation. The spirit of the Protestant Revolt found an outlet in this direction, and in its initial stages the movement was closely connected with the struggle against Spain, as well as that against the restraints of ecclesiastical policy at home.

But such motives as these could operate unaided and effectively upon those only who had the means to pay for the passage across the ocean and to secure a comfortable establishment in the colonies. For a large proportion of those who became colonists this was impossible and for them some form of aided emigration was necessary. Advertising and the provision of means of transportation and settlement were likewise needed for all. These were provided by the companies and proprietors who initiated the movement. They were set forth in part in the conditions of plantation. Cheap land and the prospect of gain from the production of colonial staples and trade therein soon became the chief and most persistent attractions for those who were tempted to removal. But the poorer class, who were to form the mass of field laborers and artisans in the colonies, did not possess the six to ten pounds per head which was required for passage money. They had therefore to pledge their labor and that of their families, if they had any, for years in advance in order to secure transportation. These advances were made by well-to-do planters, merchants or ship captains on the security of a bill of indenture. The government, both of the realm and of towns, became interested in this form of traffic as a means of relief from a part of their poor or worthless and criminal population. Kidnapping also, especially of women and children, under the name of "spiriting," was practiced on a considerable scale. Under the barbarous criminal code which then existed the substituting for a death sentence one of transportation beyond the seas often seemed a desirable act of mercy even to judges and other officials. The transportation of many rebels after the suppression of unsuccessful efforts at insurrection was another common practice. By all these methods combined the mass of indentured servants, known in part as "redemptioners" and in part also as "free-willers," were procured and brought into the British-American colonies. They were crowded upon small vessels, without sanitation, with poor and inadequate food, exposed to the sufferings, fears and diseases of a long ocean voyage. Those who survived and reached the American coast, if they were not already bound to a permanent master, were sold into years of servitude. As a result of a variety of offences or mishaps this period might be prolonged and in the course of it the servant might pass under the sway of a succession of masters. The servant had his rights and his standing before the law and the courts; at the close of his service he had the prospect of fifty acres of land and some part of an outfit; freedom was the goal at the end, with the prospect, in multitudes of cases fully realized, of rising to an honorable place in society. And yet, while it lasted, the position of the indentured servant was a hard one and as such was a true expression of the narrow and inhuman conditions which existed in the centuries of which we are speaking.[1]

The system of white servitude existed in all the colonies, but it prevailed to the greatest extent in Pennsylvania and the tobacco-growing regions of the Lower Counties, Maryland and Virginia. It was to this belt that the largest body of immigrants came, and the indentured servant represented the chief form of assisted emigration both from the United

[1] A literature of considerable extent and much interest exists on this subject. Reference need be made here only to two monographs, one by Ballagh and the other by McCormac in the J. H. U. Studies. The former of these is on White Servitude in Virginia and the latter on White Servitude in Maryland. See also the chapters on the System of Labor in Bruce's Econ. History of Va. Diffenderfer's volume on the Redemptioners relates to the Germans in Pennsylvania.

Kingdom and the continent of Europe. To the north of this section the system of free labor prevailed and to the south negro slavery proved to be better adapted to the climate. In much of the region south of the Potomac river, before the eighteenth century was far advanced, slave labor was held to have proved its economic superiority to that of whites in any form, and white servitude, except temporarily in Georgia, had begun to decline.

Since the main purpose of this work is to explain the nature and growth of government in the American colonies, the fact of immigration has hitherto been taken for granted. The land and the people, the two fundamental elements of the state, have been assumed to be in existence without an attempt to discuss their characteristics in detail. But the point has now been reached where some account must be taken of the process of immigration, with special reference to the distribution of national stocks within the colonial areas and to the extension of settlement. This extension of settled territory was due not simply to the increase of population already in the colonies, but to immigration on a considerable scale. English, Dutch and Swedes were the chief components of the people who, prior to 1690, had settled in small and detached communities along the Atlantic seaboard, and the governments which they established all conformed to a few fundamental types. They were in every case the reflection of the feudal-monarchical institutions which existed in all the parent states of Europe, and their varieties served as additional illustrations of that type. Moreover, the Swedes were very soon subdued by the Dutch and the Dutch in turn by the British, and the process of social amalgamation then went on under the general control of the dominant nationality and into a certain conformity with its institutions. New England was almost exclusively English. So was Virginia, and to a less extent Maryland and the Carolinas. This, of course, does not exclude the truth of the claim that individuals and families belonging to other nationalities, especially Scotch and Irish, were to be found in these communities. But after all allowances are made, it still remains true that New England and the Southern colonies in the seventeenth century were overwhelmingly English. This was not true of the colonies along the Delaware and Hudson rivers. Welsh appeared prominently among the early settlers of Pennsylvania, while in the Lower Counties the Swedes and Dutch, and upon both the upper and lower Hudson the Dutch, established a permanent and controlling influence. These stocks left no decided impress on the political institutions, but in matters of dress, education, religion and social customs their characteristics survived until comparatively recent times, or in some cases have become a permanent part of our national inheritance.

Even before 1690 a difference had thus been established between the middle colonies and those which lay to the north and south of them. This was to be further emphasized in the eighteenth century and to go far in the end to determine the character of our national development. England itself is a country whose population is so mixed in origin as to constitute a standing puzzle for ethnologists. With the addition of the Welsh, the Irish and the Scotch-Irish the complexity of social origins and characteristics was greatly increased. In 1707, by the Act of Union, Scotland, too, was brought completely within the fold, and after that date the term British is properly used to indicate that the English had become only a part of a larger complex whole. Emigration from Great Britain and Ireland to the colonies necessarily reflected the mixture of racial stocks which appears in the populations from which it came. The colonies therefore, and afterwards the United States, became in a way a reflex of the population of the parent state.

But, from the first, emigrants from the continent of Europe obtained a foothold within this colonial area. They arrived contemporaneously with the British. Though they were forced to submit to the political sway of Great Britain, they did not and could not wholly surrender their national characteristics. From the first a certain French element appeared among the American colonists. This consisted of Protestants who, under the pressure of hostile edicts, and when the religious wars began, considered it safer to leave their country. Coligny's experiments in Brazil and at Port Royal and the early participation of Huguenots in the colonization of Acadia, Canada and the West Indies are well known instances of an activity which involved possibilities of vast over-sea expansion for France. But the Huguenots in the end were wholly excluded from this, while a policy of repression was adopted which ended in wholesale emigration from France and exclusion from French colonies. They found a refuge in all the neighboring Protestant countries, including England and the Netherlands. With them in the Netherlands were associated Protestants from the Belgic provinces, of Walloon and Flemish origin, who had fled into Holland to escape Spanish persecution at the beginning of the seventeenth century and earlier. These same Dutch provinces were also the asylum to which Puritans fled from England in the reigns of Elizabeth and James I. When New Netherland was settled a not unimportant part of its population were Walloons or Flemish who spoke French and bore French names. This was the origin of the Bayards, DeForests, La Montagnes and Rapelies who were prominent for so long in New York. French Protestants and even some Waldenses shared also in the emigration to this Dutch province, some settling on the middle course of the Hudson as well as about New Amsterdam.

As the policy which led to the Revocation of the Edict of Nantes was developed and after the decree had actually been issued, a general flight occurred from all parts of France where Huguenot worship existed. Brittany and the region of La Rochelle, Normandy, Saintonge, Poitou, Guienne, Languedoc, Picardy and the Ile de France were the districts chiefly affected. As in the previous century England had offered a refuge to Flemish fugitives, it now welcomed the French, some of whom found a permanent home in London, Bristol and elsewhere. But a large part of those who sought an English asylum found it in the American colonies, some obtaining letters of denization before they crossed the Atlantic. It was in this way, during the later years of the seventeenth century that a most valuable, though not numerically large, element was added to the population especially of New York, Massachusetts and South Carolina.[1] In the first mentioned colony New York City and New Rochelle received the larger part

[1] For the history of the Huguenot Emigration to America the standard authority is the work of Dr. Charles W. Baird. See also Weiss, History of the French Protestant Refugees.

of these immigrants; in Massachusetts they settled chiefly in Boston, in Salem and in Oxford in Worcester County; in South Carolina they settled in Charlestown and on the Santee river. Trade and commerce were their chief pursuits and during the three generations which followed their arrival they contributed some of the most distinguished names to the catalogue of American public men. Manigault, Boudoin (Bowdoin), Faneuil, Pintard, Jay, Bernon and Boudinot came from La Rochelle or its vicinity, DeLancey from Normandy, Le Conte from Rouen, Elias Prioleau and Elias Neau from Saintonge, Mascarene from near Toulouse, Minvielle from Guienne. This body of immigrants was not large — numbering only a few thousands — neither did it settle any special areas of territory or form a distinct political element among the population. In both religion and politics the French combined easily with their British neighbors. They settled near the seacoast and thus mingled with the population by which the colonies had originally been planted. But their high average of morality and intelligence, as well as the distinction which was attained by a number of leaders among them, especially during the American Revolution, not only proved their value as an element in the population of the British colonies, but indicates the difference there would have been in the fortunes of America had they and their compatriots been permitted to migrate to Canada and the Mississippi valley.

As the eighteenth century progressed, one of the most important features of our colonial development was not only the natural growth of population on the soil but immigration from Europe which filled up many of the open spaces near the coast and pushed settlement westward to the mountains. It affected colonial life in many ways, political as well as social, and caused the situation of affairs after about 1750 to differ materially from that which preceded. It strengthened the impression, already given in the seventeenth century, that not the United Kingdom but all Europe and even Africa were to be parents of America, and even of that part of it which lies between the St. Lawrence and the Gulf of Mexico. The immigration of the eighteenth century is therefore a subject germane to the purpose of this work.

The influx of Germans, beginning about 1710, first demands attention. Notwithstanding the brilliant achievements of the Hanseatic and Rhenish cities in trade and the full share which Germany bore in the literary and scientific triumphs of the Renaissance, as a people the Germans took no part in the discovery or exploration of the Americas. The connection of Charles V with the Empire might naturally have committed the Germans to later plans of colonization, but these were limited to grants by him, in return for loans to the Welsers and Fuggers, the great merchants and bankers of Augsburg, of large territories and rights of trade in South America. The grant to the Welsers included the modern Venezuela and that to the Fuggers the southern part of the continent, including Paraguay and Chile. This occurred about 1530 and the only settlements made by Germans were in the northern grant.[1] As was the case with England after the voyages of the Cabots, religious disturbances and wars consequent on the Protestant Revolt soon diverted the attention of Germans from American enterprise. But unlike England, the course of later events, combined with political and geographical conditions, prevented Germany from ever resuming the work of discovery and colonization overseas. On the abdication of Charles V, Spain, and with it the Indies, fell to Philip II. The Empire, ever growing weaker, was too loosely organized to promote any concerted national effort. At the beginning of the seventeenth century, when England as well as France and the Dutch began in earnest their careers as trading and colonizing powers, Germany was devastated by the Thirty Years War. This not only completed the ruin of the Empire as a political fabric, but many parts of the country were so devastated by the robber hordes, into which the contending armies degenerated, that generations and even centuries passed before they recovered even to the degree of prosperity which had existed at the close of the sixteenth century. The victorious invasions of the French under Turenne in the later years of the war were especially destructive in southwestern Germany. But the Thirty Years War proved to be the beginning rather than the end of disasters of this kind. With the reign of Louis XIV in France began the territorial and dynastic wars

[1] Sachse, The Fatherland, in Proc. of Pa. German Soc. VII.

of the seventeenth and eighteenth centuries, an important feature of which was the policy of *réunion,* the term used to designate the annexation of Imperial lands to the French monarchy. Beginning with 1673 and continuing at intervals until the peace of Utrecht in 1713, many or all of the territories along the Rhine were repeatedly devastated by French armies, towns destroyed, fields laid waste and masses of the people left to destitution and beggary. The Rhenish Palatinate suffered most from these visitations, the worst of which occurred during the early years of the war of the League of Augsburg (1689–1697). In religion that territory had become first Lutheran and then Reformed, but beginning with 1690 the new Elector, John William, who was a fanatical Catholic, sought to force his subjects to return to the ancient faith. This occasioned conflicts and acts of oppression which added greatly to the sufferings of the people. The unsettled religious conditions continued far into the eighteenth century, while ravages of French armies were repeated during the struggles over the Austrian succession. The neighboring principalities of Würtemburg and Baden suffered in much the same way, while all the territories of southwestern Germany were grossly misgoverned by their petty princes, who were faithful imitators of the French court and of the fiscal and military exactions to which French absolutism gave rise. These were the conditions which prevented Germany as a nation from sharing in the colonization of America.[1]

Not a few Germans, however, had found their way into the colonies from the beginning, and had settled chiefly among the Dutch and Swedes. The careers of Peter Minuit, from Wesel, and Jacob Leisler, from Frankfort, bear witness to this fact. The well known journeys of William Penn to the continent, especially when aided by the efforts of the Rotterdam merchant, Benjamin Furley,[2] spread broadcast in western

[1] These facts find illustration at any length in the standard histories of Germany. They will be found brought into connection with the emigration of Germans to America, in the writings of Sachse and the other members of the Pa. German Society; in Kuhns, German and Swiss Settlements in Pennsylvania; and in F. Kapp, Die Deutschen im Staate, New York. An earlier but still suggestive account is by Löhr, Geschichte und Zustände der Deutschen in America, 1885. The best general treatment of the whole subject is by Faust, The German Element in the United States.

[2] Sachse, German Pietists of Pa., 433 *et seq.*, Pa. Mag. of Hist.

Germany a knowledge of the plan for the colonization of Pennsylvania and the natural advantages, enhanced by religious toleration and a mild government, which it offered. Penn's "Account of the Province of Pennesilvania in America" and his "Letter to the Committee of the Free Society of Traders" were circulated in German and Dutch translations. Certain of Penn's religious writings were also translated, and the English pamphlets of Thomas Budd and Gabriel Thomas were made known. These and other publications, supplemented by the especial efforts of Furley, brought clearly before the minds of Germans who were inclined to opinions allied to Quakerism the advantages of emigration to Pennsylvania and New Jersey. The immediate result of this propaganda, as we know, was the settlement of Germantown under the lead of Pastorius in 1683,[1] followed a few years later by the arrival of the Pietists who accompanied Johann Kelpius to the banks of the Wissahickon.

But it was not until 1709 that the emigration of considerable numbers of Germans to America began. The forerunner of this was the removal to England, in 1708, of a few score of Palatines, under the lead of Joshua Kocherthal, an Evangelical clergyman. At first it was suggested that they should be sent to the West Indies, but because of the climate and also of the plan to produce naval stores in New York, of which province Lord Lovelace had just been appointed governor, it was resolved to send them thither. These people founded Newburg on the Hudson and their varied fortunes may be followed in the history of that town and its neighborhood.[2] Though they did not engage in the production of naval stores, the suggestion was borne in mind when, in the following year, the much larger body of fugitives from Germany began to appear. The settlers of Newburg, also, were supported during their stay in England, were transported to America and received supplies of food and tools for a year thereafter. Before they left England they were granted letters of denization. A precedent was thus established for state aided and controlled emigration, and if Lord Lovelace and Henry

[1] The ship Concord, which brought over this band, has been well called the Mayflower of the Germans.

[2] N. Y. Docs. V, 8, 44, 45, 53, 62; Doc. Hist. of N. Y., III, 541–551; Kapp, *op. cit.*, Ruttenber, Hist. of Newburg.

Boyle — who just then for a short time was secretary of state — suggested the measure, they showed more than the usual originality.

The winter of 1708/9 was unusually cold in Europe and added to the sufferings which war and persecution had already made almost intolerable in parts of Germany. In February of the same winter the British parliament passed its first naturalization law. Though this cannot be considered to have started the movement, its existence, so far as it became known, may have been furnished a temporary encouragement. Of greater effect were doubtless the widely circulated and exaggerated reports of the generous attitude of the British government, and particularly of the queen, added to the vague notions of liberty and comfort in far off America which had their origin nearly a generation before in the publications of Penn and his Quaker associates. We are also told that Louis Michel had been sent by his canton of Bern, Switzerland, to find suitable homes for Swiss colonists in America and had spent some years in exploring the valleys and inland regions of Pennsylvania, Maryland and Virginia.[1] In 1710 Christoph de Graffenried, a member of the Bernese aristocracy, who was looking for a chance to mend his fortunes, in America or elsewhere, met Michel in London and together they negotiated with the Carolina proprietors for grants of land for a settlement. Land companies may have been more active in advertising America than appears on the surface, but the effect of their efforts appears more clearly a few years later.

The result of the operations of these various motives was a mass emigration, mainly from southwestern Germany and Switzerland through Holland to England. During 1709 thirteen thousand of these people, husbandmen, vine dressers, craftsmen with their families, landed in England. Free passage across the North Sea had been provided for them, but on their arrival they had to be publicly supported until they could be settled in the realm, Ireland or the colonies. As they were a less desirable class of immigrants than the Huguenots who had come a generation before, popular outbreaks against them occurred in a few localities. But the queen, the gov-

[1] Deutsche Pionier, X, 189, cited by Faust.

ernment and the church treated them generously. The episode as a whole may be regarded as connected with the war policy to which Marlborough and the Whigs were so fully committed, for this was the time of the negotiations at Gertruydenberg. For months, though it was in war time, shelter and food were provided for the exiles. The board of trade, using information furnished in part by German clergymen resident in London, considered the problem at many sessions. Briefs and letters were issued which resulted in large collections in the churches and elsewhere. These measures operated as a continued encouragement, till in 1710 decisive measures had to be taken in the Netherlands as well as in England to check the movement, because it was assuming proportions which made it unmanageable. All Catholics who refused to accept Protestantism were sent back and notices were circulated along the Rhine that no more emigrants could be received.[1] In 1712, as a result of the Tory reaction, the naturalization law which had been passed three years before was repealed,[2] though naturalizations already granted under it were not invalidated.

Of these immigrants about five thousand were settled in the British Isles — the larger part in southern Ireland — or found employment in the fisheries. The rest, upwards of seven thousand in number, were sent to the colonies of the American continent. Of these about 650 became participants in De Graffenried's and Michel's North Carolina enterprise. They experienced the usual hardships on the voyage and disappointments in making their actual settlement. The Tuscarora war also brought down upon them an Indian massacre. But the survivors succeeded in establishing themselves permanently at Newbern and thus formed a valuable connecting link between the Albemarle settlement and those which grew up on Cape Fear river, the two giving needed form and extension to the province of North Carolina.[3] The largest

[1] This immigration into Great Britain is treated by all the writers above cited but with especial fulness by Diffenderfer, in a monograph entitled, The German Exodus to England in 1709. Proc. of Pa. German Soc., VII. See also Cunningham, Alien Immigrants in England.

[2] 10 Anne, c. 9.

[3] See the two versions of De Graffenried's Narrative, one in English translation, in N. C. Col. Recs. I, and the other, in German, in German American Annals.

body — over three thousand in number — was sent by the British government to New York, as state supported and controlled colonists, for the purpose of producing naval stores. Governor Hunter was entrusted with the management of this enterprise and it involved a notable extension of the experiment which had just been tried with the Newburg colonists.

Though a part of these people remained permanently on the Hudson, this experiment in state aided immigration proved an utter failure, and the record of it has been outlined in the chapter on naval stores. Hunter was ruined financially and his administration, the success of which in other respects was notable, was seriously marred by this affair. In his management of it he struck hands with some of the reactionary elements in the province, to the repression of which in general the successes of his governorship were due. It is not probable that upon the site which was selected, or in fact anywhere in the northern colonies, it could have been very successful. But the decisive cause of its failure was the withdrawal by a Tory government of financial support of an enterprise which had been inaugurated by Whigs. Hunter, as we have seen, was a Whig and prominent for his Whig connections; and the wreck of his fortune and plan was a small incident which, with the repeal of the naturalization act, the Sacheverell trial, the reaction at court and the abandonment of an aggressive war policy in Europe, accompanied the rise of the Tories to power in 1710. Some £32,000 had been expended and bills for only £10,800 had been honored at the treasury, when payments ceased. Hunter was left as creditor of the government on this account to the amount of more than £20,000,[1] and his urgent appeals, along with those of the board of trade, continued until after the accession of the Hanoverians, but they met with no response. They finally ceased, though the debt never was paid.

When, in the fall of 1712, the Palatines were told that they must find employment where they could, but hold themselves subject to recall,[2] they were filled with dismay. Before they

[1] N. Y. Col. Docs. V, 462. In 1710 Cornbury, then earl of Clarendon, was consulted by the Earl of Dartmouth, secretary of state, respecting the selection of the Hudson river site. Clarendon, to show his dislike of Livingston, condemned it and thus probably helped to prejudice the government against the enterprise, *ibid.*, 195.

[2] Doc. Hist. of N. Y., III, 683.

left England and when they first arrived in New York, the advantages of the Schoharie region as a place of settlement had received attention. Livingston had diverted Hunter's attention from this region and, as a result of this stroke, secured a charter for his manor and, soon after its representation in the assembly, got it peopled in part by Palatines and for their support furnished supplies for which he was paid £20,000. Livingston was the only person who made anything out of the Palatine experiment. Throughout the hard period of their servitude, in the minds of leaders among the Palatines, like Weiser, the attraction of Schoharie, as a place of escape from a system of compulsory labor and manorial tenant right, had been growing. It was said that the Indians who were visiting England with Schuyler in 1709 had promised the Palatines a grant there. At any rate, during the autumn of 1712 some of the leaders went to Schoharie to view the country,[1] and secured from the Indians a grant of land and a friendly reception. This was followed by the migration of fifty families and, in March 1713, of the main body of survivors. The beautiful valley on which they now settled lay on the frontier, south of the middle course of the Mohawk river, fifty miles northwest of the Livingston manor. Seven villages were founded by them, named after the leaders of the colonists. The friendship of the Mohawks helped them over the initial privations of settlement and by the close of the first season they were beginning to enjoy a little of the freedom and abundance of the fertile country to which they had come.

But now began a prolonged and bitter conflict with the governor and the Dutch land speculators of Albany. The extravagant grants of Fletcher's time had now been annulled and those tracts were being broken up into smaller grants, for which some of the petitioners were in certain instances heirs of the original patentees.[2] From the governor and council grants were obtained by Vrooman and the "seven partners" — among whom were Myndert Schuyler, Peter Van Brugh, Robert Livingston, Jr., and Lewis Morris, Jr. — for all the land at Schoharie upon which the Palatines had settled and

[1] *Ibid.*, 707 *et seq.*

[2] See entries in Cal. of Land Papers for the years 1710 to 1714.

ample tracts beside. The demand was then made that the Germans should take out leases and become their rent paying tenants. As in so many other cases, the issue lay between the frontier squatter, with only his Indian title, and the proprietor or speculator in wild lands, equipped with his title from the crown. Hunter was offended that the Germans had left the Hudson without his permission, and actively supported the landlords and magistrates of Albany in their efforts to enforce submission. But the Germans, both men and women, were stubborn and hesitated not to defend their claims by force. Weiser proved their most efficient leader, while his son by learning the Indian tongue was fitting himself to become one of the ablest of all interpreters and agents among the natives. One after another the Albany claimants were driven out of the settlements, and Adams, the sheriff, was attacked with such violence that he barely escaped with his life. In 1717 Hunter called representatives of the Palatines before him at Albany and demanded why they had settled at Schoharie without his permission and would not agree with the patentees. He finally ordered all who would not submit to remove, and since they stood together as a unit the further cultivation of their land was prohibited. Palatines who now ventured to Albany were sure to be imprisoned.

In 1718 Weiser and two associates started secretly for England to lay their grievances before the crown. On the way they were captured by pirates and lost the little they possessed. Arriving penniless in London, two of them were cast into a debtor's prison, where they lay nearly a year, till money for their redemption could be secured from Schoharie. Before their petition could be presented, Hunter had returned to England and his appearance against them insured the success of the "seven partners." In the mind of the resolute Weiser the determination was already formed to leave New York, but Sheff, his companion, refused to agree with him in this and, after submitting a petition setting forth his views, returned to America. Weiser remained, though without any result, until 1722.[1] At the beginning of Burnet's administration the desire of such of the Palatines as were

[1] N. Y. Docs., V, 552, 574, 601.

resolved not to yield to the Albany patentees was gratified by permission to purchase land of the Indians on the Mohawk.[1] About three hundred remained at Schoharie and at least an equal number, under the lead of one Gerlach, removed northward and settled along the Mohawk between Fort Hunter on the east and Herkimer on the west. The last name, together with those of Burnetsfield, Palatine, Palatine Bridge and Mannheim, indicated the origin of this group of settlements. They were planted about 1726, at about the time when Oswego was being founded, and together these towns formed the new frontier of New York until past the middle of the century.

But the territorial policy of New York, together with the exposed position of the frontier and the treatment which the Palatines received, turned the tide of German immigration permanently southward. It is not improbable that when, in 1722, Sir William Keith visited Albany for the purpose of joining in the conference with the Iroquois, he learned of the discontent which existed among the Germans at Schoharie. Weiser and a part of the group who were ready to accompany him resolved not to remain within New York territory. They were encouraged to remove to Pennsylvania, not only by what they learned of the favorable reception with which others of their fellow countrymen were meeting there, but by positive encouragement from Governor Keith. In 1723 a small body of Palatines descended the Susquehanna to the mouth of Swatara creek, up which they ascended to the district known as Tulpehocken, where they settled. In 1728 and 1729 others came and on a grant first obtained from Keith, and later confirmed with some opposition by the commissioners of property, they established a settlement in Berks county, on the remotest point toward the northwest which had then been reached by the extension of the Pennsylvania frontier.[2] With this episode German immigration into New York almost entirely ceased. By accident, as it were, the only distinct settlement made by Germans in New Jersey occurred in 1707. A number of Germans of the Reformed Church who had sailed for New York were carried into Delaware Bay and after landing

[1] *Ibid.*, 634.

[2] Cobb, Story of the Palatines; Kuhns, *op. cit.;* Pa. Col. Recs., III, 322.

started overland for their intended destination. On the way they passed through the Muscanetnong and Passaic river country and were so attracted by the beauty of the region that they resolved to settle there. German Valley came to be the name of the district which they occupied, in the later Morris County, and from there they spread into the neighboring Somerset, Bergen and Essex counties. As usual, they developed the agricultural resources of this part of New Jersey to a high degree, and left a decided Teutonic impress upon the population of that part of the province.[1]

But the tide of immigration from Germany into the colonies in general, and especially into Pennsylvania, was just reaching its early flood. The stream soon ceased to flow into Great Britain, but it continued toward Philadelphia and southern ports in the colonies. It flowed somewhat slowly until 1727,[2] when it assumed large proportions and so continued, except in time of war, until after the Revolution. In this movement the Swiss shared, but their contribution came from the Teutonic part of the country, especially from the Cantons of Bern and Zurich. As emigration continued, opposition at times was made by the various German and Swiss governments, but it was not sufficiently persistent to stop the flow. In addition to the general political and social causes, to which reference has already been made in explanation of its origin, special emphasis should be laid on the influence of Pietism among the Protestant sects of Germany and Switzerland, and on the activity of the so-called "Newlanders" or emigration agents who, purely for the profit there was in it, made a business of encouraging the German peasants to ship themselves under contract or indenture for America.

By Pietism is meant the widespread revolt which developed in Germany and the Netherlands in the seventeenth century against the formalism of the Lutheran and Reformed churches. But its remoter origins were far older and deeper, for it consisted in a reassertion of the simpler and more spiritual aspects of religion as they appeared in primitive Christianity

[1] Chambers, The Early Germans in New Jersey.

[2] Faust, *op. cit.;* Kuhns, *op. cit.;* Diffenderfer, The Redemptioners, Proc. of Pa. Germ. Soc., X; Rupp, Collection of Upward of Thirty Thousand Names, etc., reprinted in 2 Pa. Arch. XVII.

and especially at the time of the Reformation.[1] Of the prophets to whose influence and inspiration the movement in large measure was due, prominent mention should be made of Caspar Schwenkfeld and Menno Simons of the early fifteenth century, Jacob Boehme of the early seventeenth, and Philip Jacob Spener, whose activity fell in the latter half of the seventeenth century. Jean de Labadie came into the group through the Reformed Church of France and the Netherlands about the middle of the seventeenth century. The earliest of these reformers were among the radicals against whom Luther contended and who in some cases suffered from the evil reputation of the Anabaptists of Münster. The lives of the latest among them extended even to the time of the founding of Methodism. Both Quakerism and Methodism in Great Britain sprang from the same root as the movement we call Pietism in Germany. The quality which they all had in common was the insistence on the power of the human soul to gain the closest and deepest view of divine things by direct insight and not through learning and logic. Among them all Jacob Boehme had perhaps the strongest psychic powers and hence attained the profoundest views of the invisible and spiritual universe, of which the material frame of things was to his mind only a very partial manifestation. By trade Boehme was a shoemaker and, while thoroughly acquainted with the Bible and widely read in that part of the literature of his time with which he was naturally sympathetic, he was not versed in the learning of the schools. The other leaders who have been mentioned had university training and as clergymen or publicists belonged distinctly to the learned class. But the religious movement which they started was strongly popular and democratic in its character. They all broke with the state-church system, founded small communities, for the toleration of which they strongly contended. Boehme took a rather high view of human nature and of its essentially divine element, but the rest viewed man as hopelessly fallen and capable of restoration only through the atonement of Christ. All of these sectarians, like other

[1] Ritschl, Geschichte des Pietismus; Heffe, Geschichte des Pietismus; Jones, Spiritual Reformers of the 16th and 17th Centuries; Sachse, The German Pietists of Pennsylvania; Johann Arndt, Wahres Christenthum.

Protestants of the time, were Bible-reading Hebraists and, except in the case of all but a few choice spirits, that was the only element of culture which they possessed. They insisted upon conversion and a strict moral and religious life as the condition of fellowship among them. Ritual was discarded and simple forms of worship and ecclesiastical organization instituted. The quiet and meditative life, leading in some instances to monastic seclusion, was the ideal of some. In the case of the Labadists community life, like that of the primitive Christians at Jerusalem, was preferred. Among the Moravians, in the early stage of their settlement at Bethlehem, some features peculiar to religious communities appeared, but they were not permanent. The Dunkers of the seventh-day persuasion at Ephrata developed the most complete monastic organization of all, but the group always remained small and the life which they led is interesting as a curiosity rather than from any wide influence which it ever had.

It was in the latter half of the seventeenth century that Pietism gained sufficient headway to become a national movement in Germany. Its force continued unabated till the middle of the following century. Among its effective organizers and leaders were Spener at Frankfort and Dresden, Francke at Halle and later the Count of Zinzendorf who, at Herrnhut in Saxony, revived the almost ruined Utraquist church of John Hus and developed it into the Moravian communion of later times. Arndt's "True Christianity," Spenser's "Piadesideria," or "Earnest Desires for a Reform of the True Evangelical Church," were the text books of the movement, and Paul Gerhardt was its poet and hymn writer. The appeal which was made to the Bible and to a life of personal righteousness, rather than to the spirit of orthodoxy and state patronage, gave deep offense to the Lutherans and Calvinists. Among the results was a secession of certain young theologians from Leipzig and the founding of the University of Halle. Prominent among the seceders was Hermann Francke, who founded the famous orphanage at Halle, which became a leading centre of educational and religious work connected with the new movement. It was this institution which Whitefield attempted to imitate on a smaller scale by his orphan house in Georgia. But Francke, though a powerful supporter of Pietism, did not break with the Lutheran Church. It was he who sent Henry Melchior Muhlenberg to America, through whose effective labors Lutheranism attained its later organization and success in the colonies. Francke and his orphanage became the centre to which Muhlenberg and the Lutheran pastors throughout the colonies directed their correspondence and from which they received advice and help in return. This correspondence is printed in the famous "Hallesche Nachrichten" and shows that that centre was for the Lutherans what the bishopric of London and the Society for the Propagation of the Gospel were for the English Church in America. And when the Moravians appeared they too, under the influence of the broad but for the time somewhat visionary ideas of Count Zinzendorf, did not wholly break with the Lutherans and especially with the spirit which emanated from Halle. Such in brief were the religious conditions from the midst of which the German immigrants into Pennsylvania and the other colonies came. It has been necessary to exhibit these in the foreground, because the chief contributions which the Germans made to colonial life were social and religious rather than political.

The sects which emanated from the Pietistic movement were the Labadists, Schwenkfelders, Dunkers or German Baptists, Mennonites and Moravians. The fact that they sought a more radical reform than either the Lutherans or Calvinists excluded them from the protection of nearly all European governments. This, added to the sufferings caused by the wars, turned their attention to America and resulted in the settlement in Pennsylvania and adjacent colonies of groups representing all of these sects.[1] The first to arrive were a small number of Mennonites who came with Pastorius to Germantown in 1683. Eleven years later, in 1694, appeared at the same place and under the lead of Johann Kelpius a band of forty religious enthusiasts, not of the noisy but of the quiet and mystical type. They had been influenced by

[1] See the detailed treatment of these sects in Pennsylvania in the writings of Sachse, also Seidensticker in Bilder aus der Deutschpennsylvanischen Geschichte, and Kuhns and Faust, *op. cit.*

the spirit of Jacob Boehme, were theosophists, believed in special revelations and mystical numbers, and had come to seek perfection in the seclusion of the forest. They secured an ideal site on the wooded and rocky banks of the Wissahickon, a branch of the Schuylkill which lies within the confines of the present Fairmount Park, Philadelphia. There they waited for the millenium, while they also abounded in preaching, teaching and other good works. In allusion to the vivid imagery of the twelfth of Revelation, their community was best known by the name of "The Woman in the Wilderness." One of Kelpius' genial delusions was that by means of this community he might bring about a reunion of all the sects of the Pennsylvania Germans.

It was not until about 1710, after Kelpius' death, that what was to prove the continuous inflow of Pietists into Pennsylvania began. At this time, as earlier, bands of Mennonites[1] were the first to arrive, coming chiefly from Switzerland, whence they were allowed to depart on condition that they would never return. At home they had given special offence by their refusal to take an oath or to bear arms. Their insistence upon freedom of conscience and their simplicity of life and conduct were qualities which further allied them with the Quakers. Those who now arrived settled on Pequea creek, Conestoga, in what later became Lancaster County, and, as their numbers were increased, they became one of the most substantial elements in the German population of Pennsylvania. In that rich agricultural region Mennonite exiles, who came not only from Switzerland but from many parts of western Germany and Holland, continued to settle for years to come. They became farmers and mechanics, indifferent both to politics and to town life, and leaving almost no record of their doings. Elsewhere in Pennsylvania, especially in the Perkiomen district, representatives of the sect found homes. In the further emigrations of Germans southward Mennonites shared, references to them appearing especially in Maryland and Virginia. To this branch of German immigrants, and in marked contrast to the character of most of them, belongs Christopher Sauer, the

[1] On this settlement see especially The Mennonites in America, by C. Henry Smith. This is a doctor's dissertation of Chicago University.

printer of Germantown, whose place in the early annals of the Pennsylvania press rivals that of Franklin.

The fact that the Mennonites rejected all except adult baptism allied them in a way with the Dunkers, who were the next body of exiles to arrive in Pennsylvania. Alexander Mack had very recently founded this sect in Westphalia and after they reached America a group under the lead of Conrad Beissel succeeded and organized the famous monastic settlement of the Seventh-Day Baptists at Ephrata, in Lancaster County. Small groups of similar belief concerning the Sabbath were growing up among English settlers in Rhode Island and elsewhere. The Baptists who continued to observe the First Day were distributed among the settlements of Berks and Lancaster Counties and wherever the Germans went in other colonies. Had it not been for the division caused by their nationality and language, they might have affiliated with their English brethren in many of the colonies; but, as it was, another sect was added to the multitude of such bodies which were increasing with every accession to the population, especially of the middle colonies.

Space permits reference to only one other of the German religious bodies which settled in Pennsylvania and extended from that province as a centre into other regions; that is the Moravians.[1] They were somewhat late in coming, the first body landing in Georgia in 1734. The Salzburgers were German Lutherans, and they had recently sailed for the same province with their pastors, Bolzius and Gronau, and were settling at Ebenezer. Zinzendorf who, with his associates, was full of missionary zeal, was already planning for such an enterprise among the Creek and Cherokee Indians. Spangenberg, his leading assistant and the man who, as bishop, was to play the leading rôle in the establishment of the Moravian interests in America, was sent to London and obtained a grant of land from the Georgia Trustees. Two small groups of Moravian colonists were sent thither, accompanied by Spangenberg and Nitschmann. When, in 1737, hostilities began with the Spaniards in Florida and the

[1] See the Transactions of the Moravian Soc., especially the volumes which contain Reichel's and Hamilton's histories of the Moravian Church. Levering's History of Bethlehem, Pa., is also a valuable work.

Moravians refused to bear arms, a check was put upon the enterprise which resulted in the removal of most of the Moravians to Pennsylvania. But one result of large and permanent importance came from this venture, and that was the bringing of John Wesley into intimate relations with Spangenberg and Nitschmann; finally also with Peter Boehler and so with the Pietistic features of the Moravian faith. From that event Wesley dated his real conversion and that divorce of spirit from the English Church which made him the founder of Methodism.

The Moravians who removed to Pennsylvania remained for a time at Germantown and in the Skippack region to the northeast, without deciding upon any definite place of settlement. Their relations were specially intimate with the small group of Schwenckfelders who were in that district, and Spangenberg also became acquainted with the leaders of the other sects of the province. This was indicative of the attitude, emphasized by Zinzendorf when he arrived, which the Moravians vainly tried to realize, namely to secure an alliance with devout men of all persuasions in practical efforts for the common good. Their missionary zeal, combined with low-power ecclesiasticism and dogmatism, seemed to fit them for a career of this kind. But the cultural basis on which all the sects at that time rested was far too narrow for a result of this kind and it failed. It was, however, in line with this tendency that, in 1740, George Whitefield and Boehler met in Georgia and journeyed to Pennsylvania. Whitefield now formed the plan of establishing a school for negroes in that province and purchased for that purpose a tract of land north of the Forks of the Delaware river. This Whitefield named Nazareth, and without even visiting the place engaged the Moravians to build a house and begin the settlement. But before a year had passed his aggressive and fault-finding spirit led him to break with the Moravians and to order them away from Nazareth. This was followed by their selecting a site for a settlement of their own a little farther south and nearer the Forks. This, on the arrival of Zinzendorf, at Christmas, 1741, was named Bethlehem. Whitefield subsequently abandoned his enterprise at Nazareth and that became the property of the Moravians. Other settlements, like Gnadenhütten, were later founded, and that region — Berks county — became the centre of the Moravian influence in the colonies. It was well located for the purpose of missionary work among the Indians, and that was to be one of the most impressive features in the career of the Moravians. Tulpehocken, the region where Weiser and the Palatines had settled, was further to the southwest on the same frontier, and both it and Bethlehem were favorably situated for mediating between the southern colonies and the Six Nations, a work in which the Germans were soon to have an honorable part.

Enough has been said to indicate in a general way the character of German immigration, so far as it was of religious origin. But it was economic as well, an effort on the part of possibly a hundred thousand Germans, during the first three-quarters of the eighteenth century, to better their condition by removing to America. Even the religious enthusiasts had that as one of their objects, and the multitude who accompanied or followed them were moved by the common and more material motives which always lead to such ventures. The first comers were generally able to pay for their passage and therefore came as free men and free women, but a very large proportion of those who arrived after 1727, when the main current, chiefly from the Palatinate, began to pour into Pennsylvania, were unable to do this and came as indentured servants or redemptioners. In the case of the Germans, the disabilities from which this class always suffered were greatly increased by their foreign tongue. They were not able to converse with the agents of ship masters with whom the contracts were made for bringing them over, or in most cases with those to whom they were sold on arrival. The British immigration agents, called "Newlanders" in Germany and Holland, are represented as being even more dishonest and heartless in their robberies than is usual with people in such callings.[1] The conditions on shipboard were at least as bad as those from which similar emigrants from the United Kingdom suffered, though not a few of the voyages passed rather quickly and not unpleasantly.

[1] See the accounts of Mittelberger and Muhlenberg, reproduced by Diffenderfer in his volume on The Redemptioners. Sauer published much on this subject.

But the overcrowding, the death rate, the complaints about poor and inadequate food and drink, the brutalities which must have been incident to such passages across the ocean unavoidably suggest the horrors of the middle passage. Sauer estimated, in 1705, that two thousand of the passengers on fifteen ships that arrived that year died during the voyage. The stories of sales of service which followed the landing and the long delays which were likely to accompany these, the separation of families which usually occurred and the long years of hard and stolid service which must follow, bring home to the reader the discouraging conditions through which so large a part of our colonial population emerged into the comparative comfort which followed. The sufferings of German servants in particular were so great that, toward the end of the colonial period and after the Revolution, vigorous and organized efforts were made by their fellow countrymen for their relief.

German immigration into Pennsylvania resulted in the peopling of that part of the province, roughly speaking, as far west as the Susquehanna river. It is not claimed that the new belt thus added to the peopled part of the colony was entirely inhabited by Germans, for many colonists from the British Isles settled there at the same time; but the population of the region became predominantly German. Another controlling fact, however, is that Pennsylvania was the region from which immigrants were distributed along the frontier of the colonies to the south. The Valley of Virginia and western North Carolina were settled in this way. So also were parts of western Maryland, especially Frederick county and the region of Hagerstown. The slow advance of population from the coast was met or anticipated by a much stronger current coming overland from the north, and in this way the frontier of the later colonial period was formed. Before this time, as we have seen, a few Germans had settled at Germanna and in its neighborhood, and Adam Müller, the first of that

[1] Kercheval, History of the Valley of Virginia; Foote, Sketches of Virginia; Wayland, The German Element in the Shenandoah Valley; Schmidt, History of the German Element in Virginia; Faust's chapter on the Germans in the various colonies; Bernheim, German Settlements and the Lutheran Church in the Carolinas. There is much illustrative material on the subject in the Va. Mag. of Hist. and in the W. and M. College Quarterly.

nationality who settled in the Valley, came from the eastward, following the track of Governor Spotswood across the mountains. But about 1727 German immigrants from Pennsylvania began to establish themselves on the lower course of the Shenandoah river. They advanced southward through the Massanutten region to Rockbridge, the highest point in the Valley. They also spread westward to the Allegheny range and eastward to and through the South Mountain or Blue Ridge into the Piedmont region of Virginia. The result of this tide of immigration was that the northern half of the Valley was peopled by Germans, while they formed many settlements also to the south, where the country opened toward the valleys of the Ohio and the Tennessee.[1]

This wave of immigration penetrated also into the western part of North Carolina. The settlements there were made in the region of the Yadkin river at about the middle of the century. They, too, were a result of the overflow from Pennsylvania through the Valley of Virginia. A section extending from Mecklenburg and Catawba counties on the southwest to Alamance and Stokes counties on the northeast and covering the entire breadth of the province was occupied by a considerable German population, so that in some parts German was spoken until far into the nineteenth century. Several of the German sects were established there, of especial interest being the Moravian colony of Wachovia, established upon a tract of 100,000 acres in Stokes and Forsythe counties and organized upon the model of Bethlehem. The Palatines at Newbern had no share in the planting of later German colonists in North Carolina.

The Germans who settled in South Carolina and Georgia came through the ports of Charlestown and Savannah. In the first mentioned colony the earliest distinct settlement or town which was founded by Germans was Purysburg, in Beaufort county, thirty miles inland and on the east bank of the Savannah river. This was settled in 1731 by Swiss under the lead of John Peter Pury of Neuchatel. As a colonial agent acting under a contract with the government of South Carolina, according to which he was to receive £400 for every able-bodied man he might bring from Switzerland, he pro-

[1] Va. Mag. of Hist. XII, 134 *et seq.*

cured about four hundred colonists. Forty thousand acres were granted for the colony and the plan was that its chief industries should be the production of wine and silk.

In accordance with the natural tendency of immigrants at this time and especially of those who were assisted to gravitate toward the frontier, the other German settlements in South Carolina were in that region. In 1735 settlements of Germans and Swiss began in the Orangeburg district extending along the Edisto and Congaree rivers and westward through Barnwell, Abbeville and other neighboring counties. Accessions continued to arrive from Europe until nearly 1770. The people were mostly farmers and the climate and soil where they settled were fitted for successful colonization. At Purysburg it was not so, and consequently after a time its inhabitants began to renew the process, continuing until after the Revolution, when the town ceased to exist. Meantime in the upper country Saxe Gotha, in Lexington county to the west of Orangeburg, was settled by Germans from the Rhine country and Switzerland and several other colonies were planted by them, so that a German population became a distinct element in the central and southwestern part of the province. A number of Germans also settled in New Windsor.

In Georgia the settlement of Salzburgers at Old and later at New Ebenezer, the latter town being situated near the river a short distance above Savannah, proved an interesting experiment because of the unusually simple and well ordered religious life which was maintained there under the lead of their two pastors, Bolzius and Gronau. The sectaries of the north did not appear to any extent among the Germans of South Carolina and Georgia. The great majority of them were Lutherans, some affiliating with the Anglicans. On the development of a controversy over the pastorate of the Orangeburg settlement, Muhlenberg visited them, settled the trouble and regulated ecclesiastical affairs in his usually effective manner. Because of the activity and good works of the pastor at Ebenezer, in church, at home and school, that place became the centre of Lutheran influence for both these provinces and was in most direct communication with Augsburg, its parent church, and Halle.[1]

[1] Strobel, The Salzburgers and their Descendants.

In order to complete this review of German immigration in the eighteenth century it is necessary to pass from the southernmost to the northernmost colony, and describe what happened on the coast of Maine. Because of its climate, soil and religious exclusiveness, New England could never be an attractive region for immigrants from the continent of Europe. Its population, after the period of settlement, grew by natural expansion within its own bounds and by additions from the British Isles. But there is one exception, and that is found in the settlement of Germans which was founded in 1740 and later under the lead of Samuel Waldo east of the Kennebec river. Waldo's father was of Swedish Pomeranian descent, came to Boston as agent of a Hamburg house and became one of the leading merchants of his adopted town. His son, as we know, was a man of great prominence in the business and military affairs in New England, and was even in the Hanoverian service when its elector became George I of England. After his return to America Waldo became interested in land speculation in Maine, as a member of a body of thirty proprietors who secured the rights which had originally existed under the Muscongus patent. Having obtained for himself one-half of the territory, he sought Scotch, Irish and later German settlers. Waldoborough was founded by Germans whom he induced to come in 1740 and 1742. In order to execute his plan Waldo visited Germany and advertised for colonists, as was done by the "Newlanders." In procuring the second installment he employed one Sebastian Zuberbuhler as agent. Contracts were made which seemed very favorable to the colonists, but Waldo and his agent failed to perform the most important parts of their agreements, both as to the voyage and provision for the settlers after their arrival on the Maine coast. They were left largely to their own resources and, in the case especially of the second and largest party, which arrived in October, they were exposed with such rude shelter as they themselves could provide to the rigors of a Maine winter. Abandoned by those who should have provided for their needs, ignorant of the English language and with scarcely any colonists near who could render assistance, the fate of these people was at best as hard as that of the Palatines in New York or of the most helpless among the thousands who were brought to America in the eighteenth century. So great were their sufferings that, in the spring of 1743, they petitioned Governor Shirley and the general court of Massachusetts for relief. A committee reported that all the parties concerned had violated their contract, but that money should be appropriated to buy provisions and clothing to help them through the winter. Owing to the absence of Waldo, the matter did not come before the house for decision until September, 1743, and then it rejected the report of the committee and left the colonists to shift for themselves. The next year, after the sufferings of the second winter, war broke out. Some of the men of Waldoborough served on the Louisburg expedition of 1745, of which Waldo was one of the commanders. But in May, 1746, the Indians attacked the settlement and entirely destroyed it. After the peace of 1748 a few of the early settlers who had escaped returned and Waldo brought about thirty families from Philadelphia. The town was rebuilt with more evidences of permanence than before.

Joseph Crellius, who had edited a German newspaper for some years in Philadelphia and who was interested in schemes of immigration, now turned his attention to New England. The Massachusetts government was also becoming aware of the advantages which the other colonies, and especially Pennsylvania, were reaping from foreign immigration. Spencer Phips who, during the absence of Shirley in Europe, was administering the government formed the idea, and in 1749 the general court voted to encourage the settlement of four towns by foreign Protestants, two of the towns to be situated in the western and two in the eastern part of the province. The location selected for the first mentioned town was near Fort Massachusetts, and that for the others was near Sebago Lake, in what is now Cumberland county, Maine. Under the influence of Crellius also, Massachusetts, in 1750, passed an act to regulate the importation of German and other passengers by preventing their crowding and other abuses. Crellius went abroad and carried on other propaganda in order to procure German settlers for these towns. But in doing so he declared himself the authorized agent of Massachusetts and implied that the British government also was supporting his plans, neither of which statements was true. This conduct offended many of the agents who were laboring to procure settlers for Pennsylvania and other colonies. In the violent controversy which followed a very prominent part was taken by Hefret Heinrich Luther, of Frankfort-on-the-Main, who tried to remove the great evils which attended German emigration by inducing the governments of the American colonies to assume responsibility for the safety and comfort of the emigrants. For a time he supported Crellius, but finding that he was no better than the average "Newlander," Luther turned against him also. Meantime, under the patronage of the British government, the settlement of Halifax and the neighboring county of Lunenburg, Nova Scotia, had begun. John Dick of Rotterdam and an agent of his named Kebler, at Frankfort, were attracting many Germans in that direction. This also proved a strong obstacle to the success of Crellius. But, in 1753, the British government checked German immigration into Nova Scotia. Crellius, meantime, had secured sufficient colonists for an additional settlement, called Frankfort (now Dresden), near Waldoborough, and some colonists also came into western Massachusetts. After the movement toward Nova Scotia was checked, Waldo himself again visited Germany and left his son at Frankfort as agent. The result was the procuring of additional colonists, some of whom settled in western Massachusetts. In Maine the later comers founded some additional settlements in the vicinity of Broad Bay and Waldoborough which were permanent and fairly prosperous. The war, hard conditions and disputes over Waldo's territorial rights, which began after his death, discouraged some and, attracted by favorable report of the country, a part of the German settlers later removed to the Orangeburg district in South Carolina. With the exception of a few minor settlements elsewhere, the inhabitants of which in time became wholly absorbed into the surrounding British population, this was the only experiment in German colonization within the limits of New England.[1]

[1] The most important source of information concerning the Germans in New England is the series of articles by Rattermann in Der Deutsche Pionier, Vols. XIV, XV and XVI. See also Colls. Me. Hist. Soc., VI, IX; Eaton Annals of Warren; Williamson, Hist. of Maine. The subject is well outlined by Faust.

Attention must now be turned to the immigrants who, in the eighteenth century, came from the British Isles. A certain element of English transported convicts, indented servants and others came in, but so gradually and with such wide dispersion as to make it quite impossible to estimate their numbers. Relatively, however, they were not numerous, it being one of the characteristic peculiarities of the situation that a steadily diminishing part of the population of the colonies came from England, the country which was the seat of the imperial government and which was the leader in trying to impose authority upon them. So far as the United Kingdom was concerned, in the eighteenth century the great mass of immigrants came from Scotland and Ireland.[1] They were of Teutonic origin with a mixture of the Celtic which is characteristic of the people of the Scottish Lowlands and were a notable addition to the complex of races or stocks which made up the population of the colonies. Though their numbers cannot be estimated even with the degree of completeness which is possible in the case of the Germans, their total was large and perhaps exceeded that of any other stock which helped to people the thirteen colonies. Though the term British is properly used to designate the complex of stocks which was thus forming upon our colonial territory even that, as evidenced by the presence of so many Dutch, Swedes, Germans and even French, is far too narrow to correspond with the reality.

The great mass of immigrants of which we are now speaking were Scotch and Scotch Irish.[2] These two were of common origin, the only difference between them arising from the fact that since the beginning of the seventeenth century the Scotch Irish had lived in the province of Ulster in the north of Ireland, and had been collectively subjected to experiences differing in some respects from those of the Scotch who had remained at home. As in the case of the Germans, so in the case of this immigration, it was occasioned by misgovernment in one form or another. The people were driven from their

[1] The rather well established views on Scottish racial origins are given by Hume, Brown and Andrew Lang in their histories of Scotland.

[2] The works which deal most fully and satisfactorily with this movement are Hanna, The Scotch-Irish; Ford, The Scotch-Irish in America; and Bolton, Scotch-Irish Pioneers.

homes across the Atlantic, or the trend in that direction was started, by oppression, religious and economic, which made them intensely uncomfortable in Europe. So far as cause and motive were concerned, this puts them all in the same class with the Puritans who settled New England. In spirit, too, the Scotch Irish so far resembled the New Englanders that they received a certain welcome there and Cotton Mather, for example, interested himself much in their coming.

The Scotch, so far as they directly shared in the movement, were Covenanters of the period of the Restoration and supporters of the two Stuart Pretenders in the revolts of 1715 and 1745. The home of the Covenanters was in the southwest of Scotland, the same region from which the Ulster Scotch had gone forth. The Jacobites, who were exiled for their devotion to the Stuart cause, were Highlanders. The former were victims of the hideous tyranny which accompanied the efforts of the English Church under the last two Stuarts to establish itself and the crown in ecclesiastical control of Scotland; and they found relief and conditions which were at least tolerable after the Revolution and the accession of William and Mary. The latter, after the expulsion of the Stuarts, and especially after the throne was occupied by a German line, were twice driven by a spirit of romantic loyalty toward their exiled royal house into rebellions which resulted in the death of many and the transportation of many more into the colonies, as the only way to escape from death. To these causes were due the emigration of most of the Scotch who reached America.[1]

The Scotch Irish were those who, with a certain admixture of English, were brought together during the first decade of the seventeenth century for the establishment of a Protestant colony or plantation in Ulster. This was only one step, though an important one, in the long process by which the hold of the Irish, with their clan constitution and chieftainship, upon the soil of the island was being broken. Involved as a contributing cause toward this disastrous policy were the bitter religious conflicts of the sixteenth and seventeenth centuries. As the result in part of confiscations following the

[1] See Woodrow, History of the Sufferings of the Church of Scotland, Vols. II and III; also all the standard histories of Scotland. Buckle, History of Civilization; Lecky, England in the Eighteenth Century, II.

final suppression of the uprisings of O'Neill and O'Donnell, lords of Ulster, more than four million acres of land, the territory of eight counties, fell into the hands of the crown or in other ways became available for colonization. Counties Down and Antrim were first settled by direct agreement between the Irish leaders and certain nobles, with their tenants, of southwestern Scotland. But the great plantation of six counties, in 1610, was planned and executed by the governments of England and Scotland. Surveys were made of the forfeited lands and they were divided into estates of moderate size and granted to men of known wealth and substance, who would bring Protestant colonists with them and actually settle the country. Only the poorer and remoter sections were left for the native Irish, though many of them continued to live as tenants among the colonists. Among the grantees were a number of the liveried companies of London, but far the larger part of the territory was granted to Lowland Scotch, with the preference on the whole to those of the southwest, whose homes lay between the English border and the Grampian Hills. They were all Presbyterians, of the type which had already shown its mettle under Mary and was later to withstand all the barbarities of which the Stuart government and its troops under Claverhouse were capable. They were accompanied by their ministers and the entire moral, religious and educational discipline of the followers of Knox was at once established throughout Ulster. So large was the emigration that by 1641 there are said, though probably with some exaggeration, to have been 100,000 Scotch and 20,000 English in Ulster. Maintaining a distinct interest in the face of Wentworth, during the horrors of the Great Rebellion and the perils of the long civil war which followed, and amid the threatened changes of Cromwellian rule, this body attained a cohesion and toughness of fibre which were to appear so conspicuously at Londonderry and Enniskillen in 1689 and throughout all their later history.

Emigration on a small scale from Ulster to America began about the middle of the seventeenth century and continued through the period of the Restoration. This was probably caused by ecclesiastical pressure, especially upon the Presbytery of Laggan, though it by no means equalled the violent persecution suffered in Scotland itself. Several emigrants of this period sought the eastern shore of Maryland, where a few congregations were established. It was at this time and to this region that the Rev. Francis Mackemie came, who was to be one of the leading apostles and organizers of Presbyterianism in the colonies.[1] Before 1690, as we know, Scotch settlers appeared in many of the colonies, as in Barbadoes and other islands of the West Indies, in Virginia and New Jersey, in Lord Cardross' colony at Port Royal in South Carolina, in Massachusetts; but these were not of Ulster origin. The Scotch Irish emigration on a large scale from Ulster was due to conditions in Ireland which followed the Revolution and which persisted through the eighteenth century. These were both religious and economic. In religion the Presbyterians of Ulster were aggressive and dogmatic, as they had been in Scotland, and this helped to provoke the Anglicans, who, though a hopeless minority, were trying to maintain their claims as an establishment in Ireland and to withhold the privileges which Protestant Dissenters were enjoying under the toleration act in England. In 1704, by an act of the English government which was accepted by the parliament of Ireland, a clause providing for a sacramental test was tacked on to a bill for the repression of popery.[2] The effect of this clause was to exclude Presbyterians from all offices, civil and military, under the crown, and by the influence of the English Church in Ireland it was kept on the statute books until the ascendancy of Grattan and the Volunteer movement forced its repeal in 1779. Legal validity was also denied to marriages celebrated by Presbyterian clergymen, and this disability continued until Grattan's parliament of 1782. It is true that, during much of the period when these disabilities existed by law, their effect was mitigated by indemnity acts or failure to execute, but the galling badge of inferiority remained, while the passage of the schism act, near the close of Anne's reign, seemed for a brief time to imperil the very existence of dissent.

Though the lot of the Presbyterians, when compared with the crushing weight of oppression which the Catholics of

[1] Briggs, American Presbyterianism; Ford, *op. cit.*

[2] Lecky, England in the Eighteenth Century, Am. Ed., II, 440.

Ireland suffered under the penal laws, was a favored one, all sects and classes felt proportionately the evil effects of the commercial policy which the British merchants and the two parliaments caused to be enforced in that island throughout the eighteenth century. The prohibition of the importation into England from Ireland of all cattle, sheep and swine, of beef, pork, bacon, mutton, butter and cheese; the exclusion of Ireland from colonial trade and from the right to import from Europe except through England; the suppression of the wool industry — all of these measures being enacted between the Restoration and the close of the seventeenth century — left Ireland with no form of manufacture except a partially tolerated linen industry. This policy, when combined with the vast confiscations of land which had preceded and the almost total annihilation of the social and religious rights of the mass of its inhabitants, broke the spirit of the people and made Ireland, especially in the south and west, a land of blank and hopeless despair. To multitudes who could command the means, removal to England, to the continent of Europe or to America seemed the only way in which to reach tolerable conditions of existence. Such were the antecedents of the Scotch Irish emigration to the American colonies and of the later Irish Catholic emigration to the United States.

So far as Ulster was concerned, an additional cause for emigration which became operative about 1718 arose from the increase of rents, sometimes to double or treble the former amounts, which was demanded by the landlords as the long leases which had been granted just after the Revolution fell in. Also the payment of tithes for the support of the English Church, the services of which the Presbyterians did not attend, was a continuous source of irritation. Now it was that people in considerable numbers began to leave Ulster for the colonies, going in many cases under the lead of the clergy, and this stream of emigration continued to flow steadily in that direction until the Colonial Revolt. It was made up wholly of Presbyterians, whose spirit had been resolute and aggressive from the first and who now went to America under a sense of indignation which boded ill for Great Britain, in case a collision between it and the colonies should ever occur.

The first body of emigrants was attracted toward New

England by reports brought by Captain Robert Homes, the son of a clergyman who had already migrated to that region. The Rev. William Boyd was sent as an agent of the congregations in the valley of the Bann to see what arrangements could be made for the removal of a large body of emigrants from that section to New England. He brought an address to Governor Shute, of Massachusetts, with more than three hundred signatures, among which were those of nine ministers. On receiving a favorable reply five shiploads of emigrants embarked and reached Boston in the latter part of 1718. Cotton Mather, Judge Sewall and others welcomed their arrival. Some of the newcomers remained in Boston, others repaired to the Maine settlements and still others to Worcester. Those who went eastward settled at Falmouth, Brunswick and elsewhere about Merrymeeting Bay. Owing to the opposition of the church people already established there, the attempt to build a Presbyterian church at Worcester failed, and the intending settlers removed westward to Palmer and Pelham and beyond the Connecticut river, to Coleraine. But the most important settlement which resulted from this emigration was Westfield, later called Londonderry, New Hampshire. There some seventy families settled, a church was at once established, with the Rev. James MacGregor as pastor, and in 1719 a town grant was obtained. The settlement was laid out after the model of New England towns and, being settled wholly by Scotch Irish, it became the centre of the linen industry in New England and for that reason attracted much attention both in the colonies and Great Britain.[1] From this town Scotch Irish settlers and their descendants spread through the frontier counties of New Hampshire and across the Connecticut river into the territory known as the New Hampshire Grants, which later became the state of Vermont.

As years passed, additions were steadily made to the numbers of Scotch immigrants and the tendency to push them outward to the frontier was confirmed, though with the beginning of Rale's War some who had settled in Maine were

[1] Parker, History of Londonderry, New Hampshire; Bolton, Scotch Irish Pioneers; Ford, *op. cit.*, 190 *et seq.*: Colls. N. H. Hist. Assoc., Vols. V, VI, VII.

temporarily forced back into the more southern towns. After the close of this war, under the lead of David Dunbar and later of Samuel Waldo, Scotch Irish immigrants were brought over and established east of the Kennebec river. They settled adjacent to the Germans, to whom reference has already been made, and helped to confirm the hold of Great Britain on the territory between the Kennebec and Penobscot rivers.

To an extent New York and New Jersey also felt the effect of Scotch Irish immigration. In the Wallkill region, in Orange and Ulster counties, New York, settlements were made and Presbyterian congregations were established about 1730. During the decade or more which followed, other settlements were formed in that region and the Scotch Irish gradually advanced northward toward the frontier which was to be the scene of conflicts in the later intercolonial wars. In 1738 and later the Scotch Irish pushed westward into the upper Susquehanna valley and the region of Cherry Valley was occupied by them. The Highland Scotch also shared extensively in the settlement of northeastern New York, the vast region which later went by the name of Washington County, lying northeast of the Hudson and extending thence to the Massachusetts line and into what was to be the state of Vermont. Encouraged by a proclamation of Lieutenant Governor Clarke, in 1737 Captain Laughlin Campbell came over and viewed lands in this region. He was promised a grant of 30,000 acres, free from all but the charges of survey and the king's quit rent. He went home, sold his estate on the island of Islay and brought over eighty-three Protestant families, numbering 423 adults and many children.[1] But, owing to causes more fully stated elsewhere, the plan was dropped and Campbell was unable to procure redress either from the New York assembly or through the board of trade. After prolonged hardships some of the settlers left the country, and it was not until 1764 that justice was done to those who remained by grants of land in Washington county. By successive additions, made just before the Revolution, this region, as well as that about Stillwater and Saratoga, became a strong Scottish centre. This fact, as well as the settlement of

[1] Smith, Hist. of New York, I, 247; II, 50; Colden, Letters on Smith's History, 226 *et seq.*, Colls of N. Y., Hist. Soc. Fund Series, 1868.

the Scotch Irish in New Hampshire and the "Grants," should be borne in mind by those who wish to understand the resistance which Burgoyne met when he attempted to penetrate with a hostile force into these regions. It was the combination of German and Scotch settlers which so strengthened the New York frontier as in the end more than to counterbalance the advance of the French at Crown Point.

But Pennsylvania was the Mecca toward which the great mass of the Scotch Irish, as well as of the Germans, directed their course. Causes material and political, as well as religious, of which the actors were only dimly conscious, produced this result. Some who landed at New York found their way across New Jersey to Pennsylvania. Some stopped on the way and added to the Scotch element which had shared in the early settlement of the Jerseys. Nearly all the counties of New Jersey received accessions, but the westernmost, lying along the Delaware, received the larger part of the Scotch Irish. The great majority, however, pressed on or landed at once in Delaware bay, which in the eighteenth century was the chief gateway through which European colonists found access to the continent. Additions also came from the south through the Chesapeake region and up the Susquehanna river. But most of the new settlers landed at Lewes, Newcastle or Philadelphia. As usual, they followed the valleys and streams. The New Munster region, in Cecil county, Maryland, had earlier received Scotch Irish settlers. Those who landed at the ports of the Lower Counties pushed up the creeks which led back from the bay, helping to people what was to be the state of Delaware and also advancing into Chester county, Pennsylvania, and settling the region of Octerara creek, an eastern branch of the lower Susquehanna. Thence they advanced to Conestoga and spread themselves over parts of Lancaster county. In Chester and Lancaster counties they became neighbors of the Mennonites, Dunkers and other German sects who were also settling in that region. Others, passing up the Delaware and landing at Philadelphia, penetrated into Montgomery and Bucks counties and settled in the neighborhood of the Moravians of that region.[1] Wherever they went they

[1] Hanna, *op. cit.*, II, 60 *et seq.* Hanna's map at the beginning of this volume shows the distribution of the Scotch Irish throughout the continental colonies.

made free with property rights, encroaching upon the manors which had been reserved and showing a general opposition to the payment of rents. It was this spirit which caused Logan to deplore their coming, though their value as a defence against possible Indian attacks was clearly realized. The extent to which they settled along the Maryland border, which was in dispute between the Penns and Calverts, also occasioned some concern.

But the Scotch Irish did not stop east of the Susquehanna river. This they soon crossed and, following the Cumberland valley and the trails which led westward from both Maryland and Pennsylvania, about the middle of the century they penetrated to the vicinity of the later Pittsburg and even across the Ohio river and its southern tributaries. A large block of counties between the Susquehanna and the Alleghany mountains was organized as the result of this movement — York, Northumberland, Huntingdon, Mifflin, Cumberland, Bedford and others — while Westmoreland, Washington and Green were later organized west of the mountains. Thus a distinct section, occupied predominantly by Scotch Irish, was formed in western Pennsylvania, which was to have an important effect on the internal politics of that province.

The arrivals of Scotch Irish by way of the Delaware were far too numerous and persistent for the accommodation which was available in Pennsylvania alone. This was especially evident when taken in connection with the large German immigration wh was in progress at the same time. In 1727 Logan wrote to John Penn, "We have from the North of Ireland great numbers yearly. Eight or nine ships this last fall discharged at Newcastle. Both these sets [Germans and Scotch Irish] frequently sit down on any spot of vacant land they can find, without asking a question. The last Palatines say there will be twice the number next year; and the Irish say the same of their people. . . . They say the Proprietor invited people to come and settle his country; they came for that and must live." This condition led to an overflow southward, accompanying the course of German migration which has already been described. Here, as elsewhere, the progress of settlement can be traced by the foundation of Presbyterian churches, and in that connection it will be considered when the religious conditions of the colonies at the middle of the century come under review.

It was in 1732 that the stream of Scotch Irish immigration overflowed the limits of Pennsylvania and began to pour into the Shenandoah valley. The advent of this population, as well as that of the Germans, was welcomed as a protection to the frontier. Governor Gooch, who was a Scotchman, had been reared as a Presbyterian and was favorable to the toleration of that form of worship, though the majority of the council favored a stiff interpretation of the law against dissenters. The general attitude of the government, however, was encouraging and in the course of a generation the southern half of the Valley of Virginia was filled very largely by Scotch Irish, and their settlements also became abundant east of the Blue Ridge in the Piedmont region of the province. A number of able clergymen, especially William Robinson and Samuel Davies — the latter of Welsh descent — were very instrumental in the extension of the Presbyterian faith. Hanover county became the centre of the Presbyterian interest in Virginia, but Albemarle and Augusta and all the counties which later were founded in upper Virginia came to be thickly populated with Scotch Irish, all of whom were dissenters.[1]

This tide of emigration flowed on into both of the Carolinas and to an extent into upper Georgia. In the Carolinas it expanded till it covered the up country with a network of settlements. In the case of North Carolina an important body of Highland Scotch came over after the suppression of the Jacobite uprising of 1745 and settled in the region of Cape Fear river. These were also Presbyterians, though their spirit of loyalty, as shown toward the Stuart Pretender and afterward toward George III, was much stronger than that shown by the Scotch Irish. All the central counties of North Carolina, where later the Regulator movement centered, were settled largely by Ulster Scotch. The same was true of the upper districts of South Carolina, where developed the bitter partisan conflicts of the Revolution. The effects upon the politics of all the southern tier of colonies of the coming of

[1] Foote, Sketches of Virginia, First Series, Second Series; Foote, Sketches of North Carolina; McCrady, South Carolina under Proprietary Govt. Also the sources already referred to.

this population will appear in the sequel. They were eminenty fitted for frontier life, their settlements extended the frontier to the mountains throughout its entire extent, and by the opening of the Revolution they had begun to break through the mountains from Virginia and the Carolinas and to initiate the work of settlement in Kentucky and Tennessee. It was men from among these immigrants who became the most typical frontiersmen, explorers, and Indian fighters of the late eighteenth and early nineteenth centuries.

A minor element among the immigrants from Ireland during the eighteenth century consisted of Quakers, part of English and part of Scottish origin, whom religious and economic pressure drove to America at the same time with the Presbyterians. They came from all sections of Ireland and became absorbed among the Quaker population of eastern Pennsylvania.[1] They shared also in the later migration of Friends southward into Virginia and the Carolinas and westward to and beyond the Ohio river. Many Quaker meetings were formed or strengthened as a result of this movement, corresponding to the founding of churches and presbyteries which followed the migrations of the Scotch and Irish.

The introduction of large numbers of alien immigrants into the colonies necessitated the adoption of some policy concerning their naturalization.[2] Two methods were known to the English law by which the advantages of citizenship could be obtained — denization and naturalization. The former was granted by means of letters patent from the monarch, and they might be withdrawn by the authority which issued them. Naturalization was conferred by act of parliament, the statute being either general and applying to a class, or special and designating the beneficiaries by name. Following feudal traditions, the rights conferred were civil and not political and had to do primarily with the ownership and transfer of property in lands. The right of inheritance bestowed by denization was limited, but that which resulted from naturalization was complete. Unlike naturalization with us in modern times, it had as a rule no connection with the suffrage.

[1] Myers, The Immigration of Irish Quakers into Pennsylvania; Weeks, Southern Quakers and Slavery.

[2] See articles on this subject in Report of Amer. Hist. Assoc., 1893, and in Am. Hist. Rev., IX.

Prior to the reign of James I the law of England upon this subject had undergone little development and it was not foreseen that naturalization, other than that granted in England, would be necessary in the colonies. In his reign, as a result of the religious controversies of the time, the requirement was introduced into the law that no one should be naturalized unless within a month he had received the sacrament of the Lord's Supper according to the Anglican form and should take the oaths of supremacy and allegiance. The object of this was to exclude Catholics. It was not until the Germans flocked in such numbers to England about the middle of the reign of Anne that any precedent of importance was established in England for the admission of aliens to citizenship by statute. Then, as was noted above, a naturalization act was passed for the benefit of the immigrants, the first general law on the subject. This act of 1709 [1] extended the privileges of natural-born subjects to those strangers who should take the oaths of allegiance and abjuration and partake of the sacrament before witnesses. Children of naturalized persons were also considered as natural-born. The policy of naturalizing Protestant aliens was thus adopted and the provisions of the act were extended to Ireland, where many of them settled. But two years later the Tories repealed this law, though with a provision that persons already naturalized under it should not be prejudiced in any of their rights.[2] By a law of 1714, which was passed at the accession of the German line as a precaution against foreign influence, it was provided that no alien, though naturalized, unless he were born of English parents, should be capable of being a privy councillor or member of parliament or enjoy any office or place of trust or receive land from the crown.

Thus far parliament had legislated without reference to the colonies, except so far as the naturalizing of the Palatines in 1709 had this effect. And yet the early charters had empowered their grantees to transport not only subjects to their colonies, but also strangers who would become subject. In not a few instances letters of denization were granted to such aliens before they left the realm. But probably in more cases,

[1] 7, Anne, C.5.

[2] 10, Anne, C.5.

and certainly in the case of all aliens who entered the colonies directly from foreign countries, no action whatever had been taken to give them the advantage of British citizenship. The colonies therefore had to take this matter up, as was the case with so many other things. As compared with England, their social and economic condition caused them to favor the influx of foreigners. Even New England was not wholly an exception to this, though its attitude was very conservative, and almost no legislation on the subject was passed by Massachusetts and Connecticut. During much of the period Rhode Island was able to make admission as freemen a substitute for such legislation. The middle and southern colonies, into which came the great mass of foreign immigrants, had occasion to act most frequently on this subject. Following the example of Great Britain, they all issued letters of denization and passed general and special naturalization acts. The power to do this was assumed, letters of denization being issued by the governors though no express authority for it was granted in their commissions. The proprietors of Carolina and New Jersey, by their Concessions and Agreements, conferred on their assemblies the power to grant naturalization "unto all strangers as to them shall seem meet."[1] Maryland began earliest to legislate on the subject and passed a long series of special acts in which recipients of naturalization were expressly named.[2] As it was expected from the beginning that many foreigners would settle in Pennsylvania, its early laws on the subject of naturalization were extremely liberal. She legalized by statute the titles to property of all aliens who had died naturalized within her limits as fully as if they had been natural-born subjects. By the articles of capitulation the Dutch inhabitants of New Netherland were declared free denizens and their property was secured to them. They were later required to take the oath of allegiance. In 1683 and again in 1715 acts were passed naturalizing all foreign-born inhabitants. In the former act the only conditions were that they should be Christians and should have taken the oath of allegiance. The act of 1715 declared that all foreigners who were inhabitants prior to November, 1683, and

[1] N. C. Col. Recs., I, 83; N. J. Arch., I, 34.
[2] Bacon, Laws of Md.

now deceased, were naturalized and that all conveyances from them should be deemed good, while those who were still living, being Protestants, should possess all the rights of natural-born subjects, provided they had taken or within nine months should take the oaths appointed instead of the oaths of allegiance and supremacy, subscribe the test and take the oath of abjuration in any court of record. At a later date a large amount of special legislation on this subject was passed, for the benefit of persons named in the acts.

Virginia began legislating on this subject in 1671. The law of that year provided that aliens who desired naturalization should apply to the assembly and, after taking the usual oaths, have an act passed granting them the rights of natural-born subjects within that province. During the next few years a number of acts such as were contemplated in this measure were passed. In 1680 a bill brought over by Lord Culpeper and issued under the great seal of England was passed in Virginia. This authorized the governor, by an instrument under the public seal, to declare aliens who had already settled in Virginia, or such as should thereafter come to settle there, and who had taken the oath of allegiance, to be fully naturalized. With apparent reference to the acts of trade, it was provided that no provision of this law should be so construed as to give privileges to alien-born which were inconsistent with the laws made in England concerning the plantations. In 1705 and again in 1738 the method specified in this law for securing naturalization was reaffirmed. For this reason no such acts as appear with such frequency in New York and elsewhere, bestowing the rights of citizenship on parties by name, were passed in Virginia. The governors bestowed these rights under the authority of general laws.

Though North Carolina received not a few aliens, she did not legislate on the subject of naturalization. But South Carolina, early in 1697, by statute granted full rights of citizenship to all aliens who were then residents of the province, their wives and children. Many were named in this act and its benefits could be secured by others only on condition that, within three months, they should petition the governor or one of the proprietors therefor and take the oath of allegiance. In 1704, in recognition of the general prosperity of the foreign-born already in the province and to encourage the settlement of others, another act was passed for the benefit not only of strangers then in South Carolina but of all who should settle there in the future. This act was unique in that it not only contained the usual provisions about the ownership and inheritance of land, but specified the conditions under which the naturalized might vote for members of the assembly, and also stated that no such naturalized alien should be eligible to a seat in the assembly. When, in 1712, South Carolina adopted a large body of English statutes, included among them was an act of parliament of 1700 (11 and 12, Wm. III, c. 6.) which enabled natural-born subjects to inherit the estates of their ancestors, though their father and mother were aliens. In 1749 this same statute, along with many others, was adopted and made law in North Carolina also.[1]

It was under this comparatively liberal action of the colonies, in which they followed British precedents, though with some degree of freedom, that foreigners settling in America obtained their rights of citizenship. Strictly considered, these colonial laws had validity only in the colony which passed them, though one would hardly be justified in asserting that they would not have been given practical recognition, had circumstances demanded, in the other colonies. I am not aware that a test case of this kind ever arose, but the course indicated would have been in harmony with the vague consciousness of a common citizenship which was gradually growing up in the colonies by the middle of the eighteenth century.

Over the subject of naturalization, however, the imperial government exercised a certain control. The act of trade of 1660 prohibited aliens from acting as merchants or factors in the colonies and some further restrictions were introduced by the law of 1696. The judges and law officers in England were strongly inclined to uphold the principle that the grants of naturalization by the colonies were only local in their effect and could not be regarded as bestowing rights of trade or

[1] The legislation to which reference has been made in the preceding paragraphs will be found in the well known collections of statutes of the colonies mentioned. A North Carolina statute of 1715 also declared in force in that province all English statutes — among others — which provided for the privileges of the people and confirmed inheritances and title to land.

other rights outside the colony where the individual had been naturalized. The action of Governor Fletcher, of New York, in granting letters of denization to Arnold Nodine, to enjoy the rights of a natural-born subject, without restraint and without reference to any English statute, was strongly condemned. In 1698 Governor Nicholson, of Maryland, wrote to the board of trade that he always caused a proviso to be inserted in the acts of naturalization, that they should not operate against the act of trade of 1696. Governor Seymour made substantially the same statement in 1704, and acts of Maryland were cited in confirmation of this. In 1700, as a result of the discussion of the case of Nodine, an order in council was issued forbidding governors to issue letters of denization unless they were expressly authorized to do so by their commissions, and that no colonial act of denization or naturalization would qualify a person to be master of a ship under any statute which required masters to be Englishmen.[1] It was considered that aliens in a colony should not be naturalized in a lump, but in small groups or individually and with due reference to the peculiarities of each. In general, the British government was suspicious of this power, as exercised in the colonies, and was inclined to restrict it by means of instructions to governors and disallowance of their laws, but action was not always consistent and the extent to which colonial naturalizations were generally valid was never settled. If the principle set forth in the act of 1660 and the order of 1700 had been strictly enforced, no alien naturalized in the colonies could have engaged in intercolonial or foreign trade.

In 1740 parliament legislated for the first time concerning naturalization in the colonies.[2] After a recognition in the preamble of the advantages of a numerous population and the probability that many foreigners might be induced to settle in America if they were made partakers in the advantages which were enjoyed by natural-born subjects of the realm, the law provided that, after June 1, 1740, all persons born out of ligeance who had resided seven years in any of the

[1] Chalmers, Colonial Opinions, 333; Acts P. C. Cal., II, 348; Col. S. P. Col., 1700, p. 34; Beer, Old Colonial System, I, 70.

[2] 14, Geo. II, C.7.

British colonies in America, without being absent from said colony more than two months at any time during the seven years, upon taking the usual oaths should be deemed natural-born subjects. Within three months of taking the oaths, unless they were Quakers or Jews, they must receive the sacrament in some Protestant or Reformed congregation and entry thereof be made in the office of the secretary of the colony. Jews, on taking the oaths might omit the words "on the true faith of a Christian." Lists of persons thus naturalized must be kept and sent yearly to the board of trade, and in Great Britain none of these persons should be capable of holding lands or any office or being members of parliament. By an explanatory act, passed in 1773, it was declared that the beneficiaries of the law of 1740 might hold lands and office outside of Great Britain and Ireland.[1] An act of 1761 provided for the naturalizing of foreign Protestants who had served as engineers for two years in a royal regiment, they qualifying themselves as required by law.[2]

[1] 13 Geo. III, C.25.
[2] 2 Geo. III, C.25.

CHAPTER VII

PENNSYLVANIA DURING THE ADMINISTRATIONS OF KEITH AND GORDON, 1717–1736

At the close of May, 1717, William Keith was installed as governor of Pennsylvania. Unlike the executives who had preceded, he was a man of agreeable address and one who had had experience in affairs. He had succeeded Robert Quary as surveyor general of the customs in America, but after a short term in office had been removed by the first Hanoverian king. He came with a well known Scottish connection and while in the colonies had made the acquaintance of Logan and other members of the council at Philadelphia.[1] They recommended him to Mrs. Penn and the trustees for appointment to the governorship. At the close of 1716 Mrs. Penn wrote to Logan,[2] " We have all concerned joyned our helping hands to make you easy therein [i.e., in reference to the governorship] and looking over all other difficulties, have at your requests got William Keith commissioned by my husband, and approved by y[e] crown, and with a general consent he now goes Deputy Governor over that province and territorys, and tho he was pretty much a stranger to me, yet his prudent conduct and obliging behaviour, joyned with your observations thereon, give me and those concerned good hope to believe that he will prove y[e] man you recommended him for. He is certainly an understanding man, and a man of temper,

[1] We are told that the second duke of Argyle, the opponent of Marlborough and victor at Sheriffmuir, was his friend, and that Governor Hart of Maryland had urged his appointment as chief executive of that province, Logan to Wm. Penn, Jr., Dec. 3, 1719. In the Penn Mss. P & B, 1725–1729. 3, is a long account by Paris, the agent, of Keith and his policy, in which a rather intimate connection between Spotswood and Keith is shown to have existed. Spotswood defended Keith in England against the Penn family and rather discredited their claim to the Lower Counties.

[2] P. F. to L., V, fol. 74, Narrative of Sir Wm. Keith's Coming to Pennsylvania, etc.; Penn Papers. Pa. Council to H. Penn, per Wm. Keith, 25, 2, 1716.

and seems to have made himself master of ye affairs of ye Province even beyond what one might expect in so little time." Again Mrs. Penn wrote that Keith had "given me such assurance of his care and zeal in our affairs, as gives us room to hope you may safely consult with him for your own ease and our benefit in cases of property."

The earliest official utterances of Keith after his arrival in Pennsylvania were all favorable to the proprietary interests. He so declared himself when his commission was published at Philadelphia and also when, a few weeks later, he met the assembly of the Lower Counties at Newcastle.[1] On the latter occasion both he and the assembly protested against the assumption of government over the Lower Counties by the crown. Penn had always been their proprietor and such they desired him to continue to be. To the assembly of the province, when he first met it in August, Keith enlarged upon the sums which he had expended in procuring the governorship and in presenting an address in behalf of the Quakers to the prince of Wales, who was then acting as regent in the absence of the king.[2] The need of an adequate support for the governor, and also that it should not be regarded as a burden but as the only means by which he would be enabled properly to serve the province, constituted the chief topic of Keith's address. It drew from the assembly a grant to him of £500, and it is said that during his administration he received from all sources about £1800 per year, Pennsylvania money. This was so liberal an income for a Pennsylvania governor that it alone would furnish strong evidence of Keith's ability and also of the fact that he kept on excellent terms with the assembly,

William Penn, the founder, died on July 30, 1718. In his will it was provided that the earl of Oxford and Poulett, then the famous Robert Harley, should be responsible as trustee for the government of the province until it could be disposed of to the crown or to others to the best advantage.[3] The lands and territorial rights were bestowed upon the widow and eleven trustees, part resident in England and part in Penn-

[1] Pa. Mag. of Hist., XXIII, 488 *et seq.*
[2] Votes, II, 210; Col. Recs., III, 25.
[3] Proud, II, 115, 118, 124.

sylvania,[1] with instruction to sell what was necessary to pay the proprietor's debts and also to convey 10,000 acres each to his daughter, Laetitia, and to his three grandchildren, these last being the offspring of William, his son by his first wife. The great bulk of his American estate Penn's will required should pass to his children by his second wife, of whom three sons, John, Thomas and Richard, survived and, as "the young proprietors," became prominently connected with the province. For William, his eldest son and heir-at-law, no provision was made in the will, he "being well provided for by a settlement of his mother's and my father's estate."

The younger William Penn had long been a trial to his father and was to continue such to the family during the few remaining years of his life. As the Whig ministry was not inclined to add another to the list of royal provinces by completing the arrangements for the purchase of Pennsylvania which had been made in Anne's reign, the way was left open for the disposition of the government as well as the land of the province within the Penn family. Despite the express provisions of the first proprietor's will, outlined above, William Penn, the heir-at-law, now claimed the government of Pennsylvania as his by right. This was in accordance with what he had indicated as his purpose for a year or two before his father's death.[2]

By the clause in an act of assembly passed in 1712 provision had been made, in case of the death of the proprietor, for the continuance in office of the deputy governor until further orders from the crown or the heirs of the proprietor.[3] Upon receiving news of the founder's death, Governor Keith laid the matter before the council and later before the assembly and they agreed that his administration should be continued in conformity with the above cited act. In order to quiet rumors to the contrary, the assembly also unanimously resolved that he had as full powers of government as when the proprietor was alive.[4]

[1] See General Title of the Penn Family, by Rowle, Pa. Mag. of Hist., XXIII, 63 *et seq.*

[2] Penn Family to James Logan I, fol. 89–93; Col. Recs., III, 63–68; Votes, II, 247–8, 250; Shepherd, *op. cit.*, 199 *et seq.*

[3] Stats. at Large II, 438.

[4] Col. Recs., III, 58; Votes, II, 247, 248, 250.

In April, 1719, Keith received a new commission and instructions from William Penn, together with the opinion of three counsellors-at-law to the effect that, because his father's will contained no provision respecting the money which was to arise from the sale to the crown, it operated only to the benefit of the heir-at-law. He also stated that the powers of government were not contested with him by anybody. In view of the fact that not a line had come from any who were concerned for the widow or trustees, Logan had to admit it to be a general belief that, unless the new commission was accepted, " we shall have no power of government among us." Logan wrote to Governor Hunter, of New York, for advice, and the council recommended that as soon as possible the assembly should be called, so that all branches of the government might act together.[1]

But a few days later came a letter from Simon Clements, as also an opinion of other counsel and of the board of trade and lords justices, on the relations in which the province now stood to the crown and to all others concerned under the terms of the proprietor's will.[2] These showed how complicated the situation was, now that the will was admitted to probate. Keith would naturally have been inclined to accept the new commission and to act under it, but his obligations to the proprietary family as a whole forbade this. Logan, too, felt how much simpler it would be if the young proprietor could at once be accepted as such, especially if he could have the land as well as the government. But he knew more of young Penn's reckless character and of his abandonment of Quakerism. He also saw that Penn had done nothing to establish the status which, if he was to be proprietor, he must hold with the British government. He and his step-mother, however, had joined in an amicable suit before the exchequer for the settlement of the property questions at issue. In view of these circumstances it was necessary that Keith should again consult the council and assembly. This he did in the session of May, 1719.[3] The reply of the assembly was that for the present the commission ought not

[1] Col. Recs., III, 63 *et seq.;* Logan Letter Book, II, fol. 62–65. Logan to Gouldney, Logan to Hunter, April 1719.

[2] Logan to W. Penn, Feb. 3, 1719. Logan to Clements, Nov 26, 1719.

[3] Col. Recs., III, 68; Votes, II, 258 *et seq.*

to be published and government should continue on its present basis. The reasons which it gave in support of this advice were that the rights of government did not seem to be transferred to the heir by the will, but that the trustees had claims upon it; and that young Penn had not given the security required of a proprietor by the acts of trade or in other ways qualified himself. Seven of the ten members of the council gave similar advice, though the reason on which they based it was that, if it were not followed, the governor would find himself at issue with the assembly.

The governor acted in conformity with this advice and informed the lords justices of the course which he was following.[1] It received their approval, as well as that of the board of trade which, as usual, was desirous of utilizing the situation for the purpose, if possible, of securing the establishment of royal government in Pennsylvania. After the situation had been cleared to this extent, in the autumn of 1719 the governor issued a proclamation for the continuance of government in both the province and the Lower Counties, under the authority of laws passed in each of the two sections, until further orders should come from the crown or the heirs of the late proprietor.[2]

The excesses of William Penn the younger brought his life prematurely to an end in 1720. But, as his claim was kept alive by his son Springett, this event did not bring peace. On the death of Hannah Penn, the widow, her eldest son, John, who developed more business ability than did either of his brothers, was made administrator both of her estate and his father's. By the decree of the court of exchequer, which was not issued until 1727,[3] property relations within the family were settled and it was provided that John Penn should hold one-half of his father's real estate in America and Thomas and Richard Penn the other half, they all being tenants in common. John Penn, meantime, had come forward for the time being as the leader in proprietary affairs, as is shown by his correspondence with Logan.[4] But the situation was

[1] Col. Recs., III, 73.

[2] Pa. Archives, I, 169.

[3] Pa. Mag. of Hist., XXIII, 68, 224.

[4] See the letters which passed between them in the Logan Letter Books and Penn Papers from the spring of 1726.

still complicated by the uncertainty which existed about rights of government. As Logan aged, his mind was disturbed by doubts on this subject, especially in view of the independence which was assumed by the governors, the attacks which were made on proprietary government and the perils which he saw in the large immigration of foreigners. These subjects, together with details about sales of land, manors, rents and the management of property in general, filled Logan's letters during the later years of his life. But one after another the trustees who were resident in England, all of whom had declined to act, died. Springett Penn also died and all claims which were derived from the heir-at-law were abandoned. The few surviving trustees in Pennsylvania had no thought of asserting powers of government. Until 1730 or after there was occasionally some talk of selling out to the crown, but the indifference of the home government and the growing wealth of the province prevented any plans of this kind from being seriously entertained. In course of time the young proprietors either visited Pennsylvania or otherwise informed themselves about it and the full exercise of territorial and governmental powers came into their hands.

But the uncertainty about the continuance of proprietary government in Pennsylvania, while it lasted, facilitated the plans of Keith to assume a very independent rôle, and the interest attaching to the phenomenon is greatly increased by the use which he made of the situation. The affability of Keith and his apparent fidelity to the interests of the proprietor secured for him the favor of the Penn family and of all its friends during the early part of his administration. On many occasions Logan wrote to various members of the Penn family and to others in the most favorable terms concerning Keith. In June 1717 he wrote, "This gentleman's abilities will render the administration easy to all others as well as just and reasonable in itself." "He is capable of any charge in any government." "From the acquaintance we had with our present Governor, when formerly here, we were apt to believe he could not fail of pleasing wherever he had but an opportunity of being known to persons of judgment." "This gentleman appears so well qualified for the highest posts that I apprehend no other misfortune that can befall on this side if he continues to apply his abilities to the Proprietor's and Country's interests but what may arise from the narrow straits of the people on whom he will scarce be able to prevail for such a supply as his education and present family may require."

Logan and his associates were evidently proud of the governor's good appearance and of the favorable impression which he made in other colonies, so great was the contrast between this and what either of his immediate predecessors was able to do. Late in 1718 he wrote to Joshua Gee, "You will see by everything that comes from the Governor's pen that he is scarce to be exceeded that way. These abilities, with his winning deportment, make him become his post extremely well, and among all our neighbours he is reckoned an honour to the country." The same month he wrote to Thomas Story, "It would, for aught I know, give a general satisfaction to the country here to have our present Lieutenant Governour continued. He wants more money, 'tis true, than any before him, but then he spends it to the credit of the place and his abilities give us a representation among our neighbors." [1]

As the months passed, Keith's desire for an ample support and his ability in securing it made a larger and stronger impression upon the supporters of the proprietary interest. This was due not so much to the sums which he received as to the skill he showed in dealing with the assembly which made the grants possible. In this connection appeared the chief feature of Keith's administration. From an early date he assumed a very independent attitude toward the council and the proprietary interests generally. This had been done in a way by earlier governors, but in their case it had not been combined with any skill in the management of the assembly or in the creation of a political opposition. The proprietary interests were now at a lower ebb than they had ever been before, and Keith was not slow to take advantage of this. But in doing so and in striking out upon an independent course he showed some of the qualities of the politician and agitator. In his case a disregard of the wishes of the Quaker leaders which other governors had shown was combined with the ability to carry the lower house with him.

[1] See the letters of Logan during the years 1717 and 1718.

A career was apparently what Keith was bent upon having, without a very definite idea of the point to which it might lead him or the province. Governor Spotswood, of Virginia, was his friend and they had some connection which might possibly have led to an effort to turn Pennsylvania and the Lower Counties over to the crown. Early in 1718 Logan heard rumors that an address favorable to this policy had passed their assembly, though he hoped that the governor had not been concerned in it. A few months later his suspicions were further aroused by the news that a bill had been drafted for remitting the quit rents in the Lower Counties in return for a grant of £200 a year for the support of the government. This was soon followed by the grant of a charter to Newcastle making it a city and thus strengthening its ambition to be a rival of Philadelphia. Later Logan had to confess that Keith never consulted with the council concerning affairs in the Lower Counties and he almost feared that they would become independent of Pennsylvania.[1] Had the proprietors attempted to turn the province over to the crown, we have seen that it would not have surprised or offended men like Logan, but the possibility that a governor should plan or attempt such a thing was suggestive of sedition and highly offensive. That Keith was consciously aiming at such a result as this, his administration is far from showing; but he did pursue a very independent course and treat the authority of the proprietors, as it then was, with something like contempt. It was not often that a governor departed so far from the position of an agent as did he and assume so much of the appearance of a principal. It was because of this that, long before his administration was half over, the tone of Logan's references to him wholly changed.[2] He was denounced as vigorously as he had been praised and in the end his removal was demanded as an imperative necessity. In this opinion the whole proprietary interest came to share. The events which led to this result it is now necessary to review.

The central fact of Keith's policy which was offensive to

[1] P. Mss., Lower Counties. The figures are not easily read; perhaps the grant was £700.

[2] See Logan's letters and those of the Penn family, from and after 1719.

the proprietary interest was his attitude toward the council. So far as possible he ignored that body. Especially was that true in connection with legislation. As his administration progressed, he ceased to ask its advice concerning laws and, so far as possible, in all those matters dealt directly with the assembly.[1] By so doing he reduced the council to a strictly executive body and took from it the large influence over legislation which indirectly it had exercised ever since the issue of the Charter of Liberties. As the council was a stronghold of proprietary influence and from its standpoint the balance wheel of the system, this was very offensive and occasioned alarm. In reference to purely executive matters also Keith acted with considerable independence, except possibly in Indian relations, and the councillors saw their powers cut down on that side also.[2] Logan and his friends became estranged from the governor and a new man was appointed secretary in Logan's place. In April, 1723, Logan wrote that, were it not for the fact that on the decease of the executive government would devolve on the council, most of its members would drop out and appear no more. The governor appointed new members without consulting the others. "I am now superseded in all things relating to the Government except that I still bear, with the rest, the name of a member of the Council." [3]

Closely connected with this attitude was the refusal of the governor to be bound by proprietary instructions, especially when they came from the hand of a woman, Mrs. Penn. The veto, when the proprietor was absent, had already disappeared, and now when the influence of the family was at its lowest point, came a direct thrust at their right to instruct the governor. In 1723, moved by what was considered to be the dangerous situation of affairs, Logan visited England and brought back with him a long and very forcible letter, in

[1] The two opposing views are well stated in "Reasons given Governor Keith by some Members of Council for leaving that Board, the 22d of February, 1717-8," and in Keith's "Observations thereon," Votes, II, 426, 428, *etc.* The members who withdrew were Norris, Logan, Hill and Dickinson, and the occasion of it was the inadequate time which Keith gave them for considering certain bills which came before him from the assembly. Logan's final statement is in Votes, II, 478.

[2] See Col. Recs., III, where the journal of the council is printed.

[3] Logan to Gouldney, Apr. 8, 1723, Official Corresp. I, fol. 123 *et seq.*

the nature of private instructions, from Hannah Penn.[1] Of course it was easy to understand that this was largely Logan's work, the fruit of his many letters as well as of his present visit. It called Keith roundly to account for his irregularities and neglect of the proprietors, and directed him to assist the commissioners of property, to admit no new men to the council without the consent of its members and to keep at least one half of its membership Quakers, to advise fully with the council in all matters of legislation, and to restore Logan to the secretaryship. At the same time the trustees, Gouldney and Gee, wrote Keith that his continuance in office depended upon his strict compliance with the widow's instructions.

To Mrs. Penn Keith replied, asserting in the strongest terms his independence of the council in all legislative matters and that at most its members could only be present "as solemn witnesses of the Governour's Actions."[2] When the assembly met,[3] Keith by an artful speech drew from them a renewed assurance that their relations with him were perfectly satisfactory, and then he laid before them Mrs. Penn's instructions and his reply. Logan also submitted a memorial on behalf of the rights of the proprietary family and of himself as its servant. The assembly, after some delay echoing Keith's sentiments, replied that the instructions were an infringement of the liberties and privileges granted by charter to the people of the province, and they asked the governor to assist them in preserving these rights and to ignore any of the instructions which seemed repugnant to the charter.[4] The discussion was continued further in an academic fashion by

[1] Votes, II, 414, 416.

[2] *Ibid.*, 417.

[3] *Ibid.*, 404 *et seq.*, 414–427, Norris to Gee, Apr. 31, 1725. Official Corresp., I, fol. 187. Logan's account of this was as follows: "At the House's first meeting upon business on ye 5th of last month, the Governor made a Speech to them, standing in open court house, to which all persons that pleased were admitted, wherein having first laid a foundation for an encomium to himself, he loudly sounded an alarm to the people to take care of themselves." L. L. B., II, fol. 11; J. L. to H. Penn., Feb. 1724–5. Also in O. C., I, 181. He characterized the assembly as consisting "mostly of plain, honest countrymen, well enough skilled in husbandry but not much acquainted with affairs of this kind, together with some persons of this town [Philadelphia] subservient to the Governor's pleasure, for his arts have been more successful on the populace here than in the country."

[4] *Ibid.*, 431.

an elaborate statement by Keith, supported by the legal technicalities of David Lloyd.[1] In the council a personal encounter occurred between the governor and Logan over a charge that the latter had falsified the records.[2] In view of events of this kind, Isaac Norris wrote, " It's plain to everybody here (even his own party say it) that the question now arises whether there be any Proprietary who has power in this province or not."

Turning now to the more general lines of Keith's policy which had contributed to bring about this sharp crisis, a minor point or two connected with the administration of justice should first be noted. In the first year of his administration Keith discussed with the council the question, whether or not judicial commissions should be issued in the name of the king. Practice in this matter had varied both in Pennsylvania and in the other proprietary provinces.[3] Keith, in harmony with the trend of events, argued that they should be issued in the name of the king and attested by the proprietor or in his absence by the deputy governor. On the other side, and doubtless chiefly by Logan, it was alleged that the king in reserving to himself the sovereignty over the colonists declared that they were to continue his subjects and he their natural prince, but his royal prerogative as exercised in England could no more be understood to accompany that sovereignty than could all the statutes of England be regarded as in force in the colonies. In support of this admirable statement of the strictly colonial point of view, certain practices in Pennsylvania which were inconsistent with those of England were cited, such as the election of sheriffs and coroners. But after several months had passed, during which news had come of the death of the founder, Keith quietly informed the council that the new commissions which it was now necessary to issue would run in the name of the king. This continued to be the practice during his administration and for some years thereafter.

In the summer of 1719, as we have seen, six laws which had been passed in 1715 for the purpose of putting the judicial

[1] *Ibid.*, 433, 444.

[2] Col. Recs., III, 242 *et seq.*; Votes, II. 417.

[3] Osgood, Am. Colonies in 17th Century, II, 306; Shepherd, *op. cit.*, 386; Pa. Col. Recs., III, 33–37, 62.

system of the province on a statutory basis were disallowed.[1] In deference to the desire of the council, as expressed in a session at which David Lloyd, then chief justice, was specially invited to be present, Governor Keith declined to resort to an ordinance as the means of keeping the courts going, but simply issued new commissions to the justices empowering them to hold court on the days specified in the laws just repealed.[2] By following this course he quieted the scruples of Lloyd and of the great majority who, like him, considered a judicial system which rested expressly on an ordinance as illegal.

In 1722 another statute was passed reviving the judicial system. The loose expressions to which the board of trade and the attorney general had objected were eliminated, but no enlargement was made in the jurisdiction of the supreme court. This time the act escaped veto, perhaps because it was one of a large number of laws which were not delivered to the board until the five-year period specified in the charter had passed.[3] The extent to which Keith sympathized with the tendency to enlarge the jurisdiction of the lower common law courts was shown in 1724 by his ordering the ship *Fame* to be prosecuted before the court of common pleas in the absence of an admiralty court.[4] This was an incident in a dispute between Keith and Moore, the collector of the royal customs at Philadelphia, over the seizure of this vessel for the illegal importation of East Indian and European goods. Moore refused to presecute before an inferior court because it could not hold pleas of the crown. The ship was tried and condemned in the common pleas, but the case was carried to England on appeal. There the collector was advised by the law officers that the proper tribunal for such a trial was the supreme court, before which in 1726 he obtained a final decree of condemnation against the vessel. Before the same court Moore then prosecuted Lawrence and others who were charged with running goods. They petitioned the assembly, raising the objection that the supreme court had no power to issue

[1] Stats. at Large, III, 440, 463–468.

[2] Col. Recs., III, 90.

[3] Stats. at Large, III, 298; Root, *op. cit.*, 168.

[4] Root, *op. cit.*, 169; C. O. 5/ B. T. Proprieties, XI, R, 52, 53, XII. 84, 87; Stats. at Large, IV, 422 *et seq.*

original processes. Moore defended his procedure. The house then resolved that the law of 1722 be amended and that no original process be issued by the supreme court in civil causes.[1] Moore then asked the governor — Gordon being then in office — not to assent to this bill unless it contained a suspending clause. But in 1727 it was passed in accordance with the resolution cited, though with a clause providing that it should not be retroactive. The new law also took from the supreme court all exchequer jurisdiction and required that all revenue cases should in the first instance be brought before the county courts.

Richard Fitzwilliam, the surveyor general of the customs, now strongly protested against the confirmation of this act, enlarging, as Randolph had often done before him, on the unfitness of the county courts for the trial of cases in which the rights of the crown were directly involved, because of the mean capacities of their judges and the almost certain bias of the jurors. The law, he also claimed, was in conflict with the act of parliament of 1696, which gave the informer the privilege of choosing the court in the colony before which to bring his action, and if the assembly could take from one court its jurisdiction it might do the like in the case of all courts and thus defeat the purposes of English law and administration. When, in 1730, the act came regularly before the privy council Moore, the collector, laid before it the history of the case and asked for the disallowance of the law. This petition was referred to the committee on appeals, before which, in response to their order, the proprietors presented a statement, drawn by Paris, their agent, setting forth again the reasons for the passage of the act and the view of the proper function of a supreme court such as existed in Pennsylvania. The act was referred to the board of trade, and to it Francis Fane, the counsel, presented a brief against its confirmation, replying to several additional arguments of its defenders. After some further consideration by both the board of trade and the privy council, the act was disallowed in August, 1731.[2] When the governor informed the assembly at Philadelphia of this result, it expressed regret, but passed

[1] Votes, III, 8, 11.
[2] Stats. at Large, IV, 422 *et seq.*

a law restoring to the supreme court its jurisdiction as a court of exchequer.[1] With this the struggle over the judiciary in Pennsylvania came to an end, the three applications of its veto power by the crown having secured an original jurisdiction in civil cases to the supreme court.

The chief controversy of Gordon's administration related to the authority under which a court of chancery might be held. In 1720 such a court had been opened under authority of a proclamation issued in accordance with a resolution of the assembly.[2] This course Governor Keith had followed in response to complaints, because there was no such court and after he had taken the best legal advice available as to the method of establishing it. The resolution of the house was that, considering the present circumstances of the province, the governor, with the assistance of certain of the council, should open such a court. It was the authority of the governor as keeper of the province seal which, here as elsewhere, was relied on as the primal basis of this power. In 1727 it was resolved in council that, when the governor sat in chancery, all the councillors who were in or near Philadelphia should be summoned to attend him as assistants, and that no decree should be pronounced except by the governor as chancellor, with the consent of two or more of the six eldest of the council.[3]

This court continued in existence without provoking adverse criticism until near the close of Gordon's life. It is true that only a small amount of business was done in it during these years, Gordon himself stating in 1736 that during the nine years and more when he had presided there only two cases had been brought to decree and those by consent, while very few processes had been entered in the court. Therefore he felt surprised when all at once, shortly before the time at which he made this statement, from Bucks and Chester counties and elsewhere came petitions against this court as then organized. The protests which were then uttered were a part of the general movement which had as its object the bringing of the courts fully under statutory regulation. The

[1] Votes, III, 168.

[2] Votes, III, 254 *et seq.*, 270, 271, 273; Col. Recs., III, 266; Shepherd, 391–395.

[3] Col. Recs., IV, 35–37.

critics now called attention to that clause in the Charter of Liberties which provided that no person should be obliged to answer any complaint concerning property before the governor and council. Possibly having in mind the right to regulate ferry rates, which was then under discussion with the proprietary officials,[1] some of the petitioners stated that the provision in the charter might be a great security to the people if they should ever be involved in any disputes with the proprietors; but notwithstanding its clear provision the governor and council, who were appointees of the proprietor, sat as a court of chancery for the purpose of trying cases involving property rights.

On receiving these petitions, the assembly asked the governor to lay before it the record of the establishment of the court, which he did. The house then resolved that the court, as then established, was a violation of the charter of privileges, and that the power of determining suits in equity should be vested in the supreme and inferior courts of common law, as the legislature should determine.[2] Its prejudice in favor of the county courts was again shown by the unpractical resolve that the justices of the peace should be granted a minor equity jurisdiction. Gordon and his council met the attack of the assembly with an able argument as to the many precedents in the colonies for their course of action, and in the origin of the court of chancery in England. In their zeal to defend the court they ventured even to juggle with the word property in the Charter of Liberties by insisting that it referred to the property of the proprietors, which was under the management of the commissioners, but not to property relations between private parties in general. Jurisdiction over the latter they claimed was distinct and for nearly twenty years had properly rested with the court of chancery. During that time there had been much legislation concerning courts of judicature and some forty sessions of the assembly had been held, but by no one had the need of a statutory basis for the court of chancery been brought forward.[3] But this reason-

[1] Shepherd, 81–83.

[2] Votes, III, 258.

[3] *Ibid.*, 269–275. The statement on behalf of the assembly was probably drawn by John Kinsey and Lawrence Growdon, while Logan was of course active in framing the argument on the other side.

ing did not prevail with the assembly. It passed a bill for the regulating of the court of chancery, which was rejected by Gordon. He, however, sent the papers connected with the subject to England with the request that the proprietors would convey to him their thoughts on the subject. But before anything further was done Gordon died, in the summer of 1736. During the following year, when Logan and the council were in charge of the government, there was no legislation. The law officers of the crown, however, delivered an opinion, at the request of the proprietors, which was intended to confirm the position of the court.[1] They declared that the approval given by the assembly to the action of the court was sufficient to legalize it in spite of the clause in the Charter of Liberties, and that that situation could not be changed by a later resolution of the assembly. But prejudice against the court, because of the feeling that it would be used as a means of supporting the fiscal claims of the proprietors, continued as an immovable obstacle against its establishment. The chancery jurisdiction, in consequence, remained in abeyance and at intervals after 1750 the proprietors were referring in their letters to the desirability of establishing such a court and were expressing their willingness that the assembly should regulate it. They even offered to allow persons other than the governor and council to hold the court; but the opposition of the assembly continued and further steps were not taken.

In following the subject of the judiciary to a natural halting place we have passed beyond the limit of Keith's administration. Returning now to other aspects of his policy, reference should be made to an early infringement by him on the extensive territorial rights of the proprietor by his appropriating some land beyond the Susquehanna river, on which it was believed that a copper mine might be worked to advantage.[2] This, says Logan, occasioned "the first important breach" between the governor and those who upheld the proprietary interests. By ordering a survey of this land without consulting the commissioners of property and by attempting to get a return of the survey entered in the council

[1] Shepherd, 394.

[2] Narrative of Sir W. Keith's Coming, *etc.*, *op. cit.*, 36; Letter of Logan to John Penn, Feb. 9, 1722, O. C., I, 117.

books, Keith seriously offended the entire proprietary interest. It led directly to his breach with the council and to his policy of ignoring it, and this was followed by recriminations and charges of evil motives on both sides. As the so-called mine never yielded anything, Keith was not able by means of it to supplement his income from regular sources, and the episode served only to indicate how freely he proposed to deal with proprietary rights and traditions. It was the opening gun in what was to prove a series of sharp encounters.

But the batteries on both sides were brought fully into action when the governor committed himself to the policy of issuing bills of credit. It was largely about this question that the conflicts of the middle and later part of his administration were waged, and it furnished Keith with the fullest opportunity which could be desired for appeals to the assembly and to the people. Soon after 1720, owing probably in large measure to the rapid growth of the province due to immigration, the demand became general for an increase in the circulating medium of the province. Though they were apparently in the midst of plenty, distress was said to be widespread. Exports to the West Indies had fallen off, law suits were on the increase and also the numbers of those who were imprisoned for debt. With the diminution of trade the supply of coin which was coming in from the West Indies was falling off. In the absence of war, which had furnished the chief justification for the paper money policy in the other colonies, these were among the reasons given in Pennsylvania in defence of it. The property tax levied in 1717 was made payable in money, flour or wheat,[1] but no reference was made in the impost laws to an option of payment in commodities. In 1717/8 an act was passed for the encouragement of trade, in which it was alleged that "divers of our neighboring colonies (by their non-compliance with the late act of parliament for ascertaining the rates of foreign coins, and by their laying duties not only upon the product of this country but upon such British commodities as are exported to those colonies) have drawn away a considerable part of our current cash. . . ." To check this a duty of 10% was laid on goods imported from New York or Maryland.[2]

[1] Stats. at Large III, 131. [2] *Ibid.*, 145.

A comparison of the members of the assembly of 1720 with those who were chosen in the fall of 1721 shows a considerable change in the personnel. In 1723 Logan wrote that the two last elections were "very mobbish and carried by a levelling spirit." The governor fell in with this and in his speeches began to draw distinctions "to the disadvantage of those he was pleased to term the great, rich or knowing." [1] The actual utterances of Keith bear out the truth of this statement, for he was continually appealing to the assembly and to the common people behind it as the element in the constitution upon which he chiefly relied and with which he meant to keep on the best of terms.[2] As he proceeded in this direction, the council dropped into the background and his attitude suggested something in the nature of a plebiscite against the proprietary influence. It was under these local conditions that the demand for a paper currency appeared in Pennsylvania and Keith took it up.

In February 1720/1, a petition was presented to the assembly asking for an alteration in the currency of money. About a year later another petition was presented signed by "a great number of Inhabitants," praying that "the Currency of Money may be raised." [3] Efforts to supply the need by making hemp or other commodities current pay were rejected. In May 1722, an attempt was made by the house to raise the valuation of English money and dollars so as to draw them in from other colonies, but on a statement from the council that it would be a violation of the act of parliament for regulating the value of coin in the plantations, it seems to have been dropped.[4]

In February 1722/3, the demand for a paper currency was expressly voiced in several petitions from the counties, they alleging that, owing to the lack of a medium to buy and sell with, the decay of prosperity in the province was evident.[5]

1 Penn Papers Orig. Corresp., I, 123 *et seq.*; Logan to Gouldney, Apr. 8, 1723.

2 Votes, III, 297, 326, 335, and so on through the speeches of the rest of his administration.

3 *Ibid.*, 286, 303, 305; Stats., III, 314.

4 Votes, II, 313, 317, 325; Col. Recs., III, 173.

5 The best account of the situation, as interpreted a few years later, is in an address of the assembly to the board of trade in 1727. Votes III, 22. According to the view there expressed, trade with the West Indies fell off

A petition from Bucks county asked that the country produce be made current pay and that no paper be issued. After a long debate on the subject, the house voted for a paper currency. Two days later Logan and Norris were admitted from the council and presented a paper in which they urged that, if bills of credit were issued, the amount should be small and their duration short, like the exchequer bills in England. Scrupulous care should be taken for their redemption. Keith, at the request of the assembly, now took a hand in the discussion, sending in an argument in favor of a rather liberal issue of bills of credit. This was also supported in a communication from two of the original petitioners. To this a rejoinder was made by "gentlemen, merchants" and others who were interested in trade.[1] This is not the place for the discussion at length of the economic views which were advanced or suggested by the supporters of the one side or the other of this question. The purpose here is to show the bearing which the controversy had on the growth of opposition to proprietary government in Pennsylvania. Neither side was opposed to paper money as such; they differed in their estimate of the capacity of the legislature and people of the province adequately to provide for its redemption and then to live up to these provisions. The need of a more abundant and better medium of exchange nobody could deny. In their low estimate of the capacity of the colonists for self-restraint in this matter and their high estimate of the need of caution, Logan and his friends had the support of English precedents and opinion. They were backed also by the entire proprietary influence. They could appeal to the experiences of the New England colonies and of South Carolina as warnings against the danger of speedy and heavy depreciation. This experiment, moreover, was not to be made under the

---

in 1720 and, owing to the diminution in the supply of coin which resulted therefrom, a temporary decline of trade and shrinkage of values occurred. This occasioned the demand for currency. Logan referred in his letters before and after 1720 to a shrinkage in trade with the West Indies and consequent suffering among the farmers. Other colonies also felt it. It was occasioned by lack of money in the islands. Logan Letter Book IV, 26; *Ibid.*, 1717-1731, fol. 209.

[1] Votes, II, 339, 342, 245, 348; Proud, II, 151 *et seq.*; Shepherd, 406 *et seq.*

provocation of war. Viewed, therefore, from the standpoint of experience, as ordinarily interpreted, the opponents of paper currency had a decided advantage. Keith and the people who demanded it were of necessity innovators. They were also the debtors, the poorer and more numerous class in the province, whom, according to all proprietary and official traditions, it was unsafe to intrust with the management of affairs. By cooperating with these, as he was forced to do, Keith was again treating lightly at least the spirit of his instructions and the preferences of his superiors. It helped greatly to confirm their opinion that he was a demagogue and widened the breach between him and the council.

An act for the issue of £15,000 in bills of credit was passed in March 1722/3, they to be based on land and houses as security. A loan office was established, as was usual in the colonies where the issues took this form.[1] An act for the issue of £5000, the same not to circulate in Pennsylvania, was passed in the Lower Counties, and this was interpreted as tending to their greater independence. In its autumn session of the same year the assembly passed another act for the issue of £30,000 more, the plea being that the former sum was inadequate.[2] By this law the bills were made legal tender in all payments.

It was after the passage of these acts that Logan made his visit to England and procured the instructions from Mrs. Penn which Keith so directly flouted. In this document she said that merchants in England were inveighing very much against them and the method of their passage was oppressive to the proprietary family and might have tempted them to have the acts repealed. But they had resolved to allow them to pass, though with the expectation that he would assent to no more such measures.[3] West, the counsellor of the board of trade, later gave it as his opinion that they should be disallowed, but this was not done. They were allowed to become law by lapse of time, as was provided in the Pennsylvania charter.

The removal of Keith from the office of governor in 1726 was of course chiefly due to his break with the proprietary

[1] Stats. at Large, III, 324, 360, 385.
[2] *Ibid.*, 389–407, 518, 519.
[3] Pa. Arch., I, 187.

family on the subject of instructions and to his ignoring of the council. But his attitude in reference to bills of credit contributed to the same end, and it was so understood by the assembly at the time.[1] Lloyd, who had then become speaker and manager of the country or governor's party in the house, of course shared this opinion. The extent to which these men, by the end of 1725, had come to believe in the efficiency of bills of credit as a cure for the evils from which the province had suffered is shown in the final address which they then presented to the retiring governor. They declared that they did not have cash enough to carry on their domestic affairs and commerce and that the value of land and country produce was brought so low by the scarcity of money and decay of trade that many families were likely to be ruined. No means, they added, were left for the support of government but an excise and an impost on liquors and these fell short of meeting the public needs. Direct taxation, they claimed, had become impossible. But in two years, under the magic influence of the bills, all these inconveniences had been removed, trade revived, government was well supported without burdening traffic, debtors rescued from the oppression of their creditors, the value of farm products advanced. If the governor's removal, they said, was due to his support of this policy, they wished to declare that what he did was with the advice and concurrence of the people's delegates, constituted by royal grant to act with him in legislation. This declaration they clinched by passing an act for the re-emission of such bills as by the former acts were to have been retired.[2] It was in 1729, soon after the passage of this law, that the young Benjamin Franklin published his "Modest Inquiry into the Nature and Necessity of a Paper Currency." [3] For the time and place this was an unusually acute argument in support of the prevalent opinion, that in Pennsylvania at least more money was needed at the time and that the existing legislation provided for the supply of that need in a satisfactory way. It unduly emphasized the quantity theory of money, as did all opinion on that side of the controversy, that being a natural over-emphasis in a new

[1] Votes, II, 483, 485.
[2] Stats., IV, 38.
[3] Sparks, Writings of Franklin, II, 254.

country with rapidly increasing population and expanding settlements, where means of communication were poor and credit facilities almost entirely lacking. In his "Autobiography" Franklin wrote concerning the pamphlet: "It was well received by the common people in general; but the rich men disliked it, for it increased and strengthened the clamor for more money; and, they happening to have no writers among them that were able to answer it, their opposition slackened, and the point was carried by a majority in the House." "My friends there, who considered I had been of some service, thought fit to reward me, by employing me in printing the money; a very profitable job, and a great help to me. This was another advantage gained by my being able to write." Franklin held throughout his life to the fundamental opinions expressed in this pamphlet.

In the face of such a weight of opinion as this, supported as it clearly was by the example of other colonies which had committed themselves to the policy of issuing bills of credit, it was evident that Patrick Gordon, the new governor, would have still to make concessions to this spirit. On his appointment the board of trade had informed him that if any more acts of this nature were passed, they would be obliged to recommend their disallowance. This information he laid before the assembly at its second meeting after his arrival, and suggested that the last act for re-emitting bills might fall under the censure of the board. The extent, however, to which Gordon at once fell in with the main current of opinion is shown by his speech at this time to the assembly and by a subsequent letter to the board of trade.[1] He was "no wise prejudiced" in favor of paper currency when he arrived in Pennsylvania, but on inquiry into its effects he confessed himself fully convinced of its benefits. In consequence of its issue, more British goods had been imported, more ships built and prosperity in general had been promoted; but what was most encouraging, after a temporary depreciation, the currency had recovered its value to a considerable extent. Logan wondered that Gordon should have yielded so completely, but the truth was, he added, that no adverse comment on the bills would then be tolerated. Logan himself

[1] Votes, III, 4, 24; Col. Recs., III, 264.

had to admit that they had been "of very great service to the country."[1] This, of course, was the natural effect of a supply of a needed circulating medium the amount of which had not yet been increased to excess.

Though the agitation for further issues was continued with the usual result that from time to time they were secured, the governor and council exercising such restraining power as was possible, the currency question never again so seriously affected the course of affairs in Pennsylvania as it did in the closing years of Keith's administration. Keith remained for some time in the province and tried hard to control affairs in both the province and Lower Counties. He was returned to the assembly from Philadelphia county, but failed of election in the Lower Counties. Andrew Hamilton, the famous lawyer, however, was elected to the assembly in both sections and held one or two important offices besides. His support was of great value to the proprietary party. The bill for remitting accrued quit rents, which Keith had tried to get passed, was rejected. On complaints of oppressions by its mayor's court, Gordon removed the magistrates, and thus virtually revoked the charter of Newcastle. By these means the anti-proprietary movement in the Lower Counties was checked.

At this juncture Lloyd broke with Keith and joined the supporters of the new governor.[2] Keith entered Philadelphia with a troop of followers and tried to supplant Lloyd in the speakership. But he received only three votes and his efforts to lead an opposition totally failed. Alexander Spotswood had strongly supported Keith's attitude toward proprietary instructions and had even labored with the Penns in England to prevent his removal, and, because it was understood that Spotswood's chief interest was to see Pennsylvania made a royal province, Keith now boasted that he might yet return as a royal governor. In the spring of 1728 he quietly left for England, where he cultivated for a time the friendship of Springett Penn and may have busied himself somewhat with schemes of colonial union. His activity in the sphere of

[1] Logan Letter Book, IV, fol. 27, Logan to Gee, Dec. 14, 1726.

[2] Votes, III, 55, 67–84; Col. Recs., III, 347, 353–360; Stats., IV, 98–116. Many letters of Logan and Gordan during the years 1726 to 1729. Logan's account of a talk with Spotswood is in O. C., I, 167, letter to J. Gee, March 8, 1724.

Indian relations while governor and as an adviser of the board of trade upon the subject of naval stores and other features of imperial policy after his return to England have elsewhere been noted. After his departure, Keith's supporters for a time caused some disturbance in Pennsylvania. Eight of their number withdrew from the assembly because they could not secure the issue of a writ for the election of a member to take his place. Business, though with some difficulty, was carried on without them and they remained away until the life of this assembly was terminated by the fall election of 1728.[1] So menacing did disturbances of the peace at this time become in Philadelphia that the riot act of George I was proclaimed and the assembly asked for permission to meet in one of the other counties to escape the insults of the populace.[2] But on the failure of Keith to return, disorder subsided and proprietary rule was gradually reestablished on normal lines.

Owing to the death of Hannah and Springett Penn, from whom Gordon's original commission had been issued, doubts arose as to its binding force. Hence, in January, 1732/3, the three younger proprietors, John, Thomas and Richard Penn, issued a new commission to the governor.[3] This, as usual, contained the proviso that he should take no action affecting property without the request of the proprietors. A revised set of instructions was also issued which contained some additions to the former list. One of the new instructions was to the effect that he should consult the council in reference to all acts of government,[4] especially in calling assemblies and passing laws. He was not to approve any more acts for the issue of bills of credit unless they contained a suspending clause. John Penn, by application first to the duke of

[1] Votes, III, 45, 47, 49, 51, 52, 53, 59; Col. Recs., III, 298; Pa. Arch., I, 211.

[2] Col. Recs., III, 340, 341; Votes, III, 62, 89; Logan Letter Book, III, fol. 13. Logan to Proprietors, Apr. 30, 1729. Logan tells of 200 men with clubs who had agreed to come to town and join with others there to coerce the governor and assembly into passing another currency bill, and that three or four score actually came, but retired on notice of the measures taken to keep the peace.

[3] Penn L. B. I, 65, 73, 74. The original commission of Gordon was issued by Sprignett Penn, as heir-at-law, with the consent of Hannah Penn. It was therefore strictly in line with the claim of William Penn the younger.

[4] Pa. Arch. I, 189.

Newcastle and then to Sir Charles Wager, the Walpoles and Lord Wilmington, got Gordon approved, with the direction that he should take the oath and otherwise qualify before the governor of Virginia, "as Colonel Ogle did."[1]

But Gordon was already so aged that it was certain that he could not hold the office many years longer. The course which should be pursued after his death or retirement was already worrying the young proprietors. Thomas Penn had gone to Pennsylvania and John had consulted the act 7 & 8 Wm. III, c. 22 and taken the advice of Paris, the agent, and Willes, their legal counsellor.[2] Both of these were clearly of the opinion that, in order to qualify as deputy or governor in chief, the oath must be taken. They could not act under a law of the Pennsylvania assembly, for that would violate the act of parliament and would also be conceding altogether too much to the assembly. As one possible way out of the difficulty John Penn suggested that they wait until the test act was repealed in England, toward which result the dissenters were then making a combined effort which it was hoped would soon be successful. If the Penns kept quiet till then, they might qualify without an oath. Various courses of action were discussed and the death of Gordon found them still in doubt as to the course which should be pursued. Logan and the council then assumed temporary charge of the government till a new governor should be appointed, but with the express understanding that legislation should be suspended, although the assembly met at the usual intervals, the annual election was held and the discussion of public affairs was encouraged.

[1] *Ibid.*, 88; Col. Recs., IV, 509, 525, 529.
[2] *Ibid.*, P. L. B. I, 78.

COLUMBIA UNIVERSITY PRESS
Columbia University
New York

Foreign Agent
OXFORD UNIVERSITY PRESS
HUMPHREY MILFORD
Amen House, London, E.C.